Educational Research

An Introduction

Seventh Edition

Meredith D. Gall
University of Oregon

Joyce P. Gall
University of Oregon

Walter R. Borg

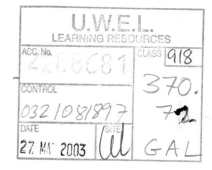

Boston   New York   San Francisco
Mexico City   Montreal   Toronto   London   Madrid   Munich   Paris
Hong Kong   Singapore   Tokyo   Cape Town   Sydney

Series Editor: Arnis E. Burvikovs
Development Editor: Mary Kriener
Production Editor: Christine Tridente
Editorial-Production Service: Colophon
Composition Buyer: Linda Cox
Manufacturing Buyer: JoAnne Sweeney
Cover Administrator: Linda Knowles
Text Designer: DMC & Company
Text Composition: Omegatype Typography, Inc.

For related titles and support materials, visit our online catalog at
www.ablongman.com.

Library of Congress Cataloging-in-Publication Data
Gall, Meredith D.
    Educational research : an introduction / Meredith D. Gall, Joyce P. Gall, Walter R. Borg.
        p.   cm.
    Includes bibliographical references and indexes.
    ISBN 0-321-08189-7 (alk. paper)
        1. Education—Research.   2. Education—Research—United States.   I. Gall,
Joyce, P.   II. Borg, Walter R.   III. Title.

    LB1028 .G342 2002
    370'.7'2—dc21

                                                              2002018689

Printed in the United States of America

10 9 8 7 6 5 4 3 2 1   08 07 06 04 03 02

Dedicated to All Our Students

Brief Contents

CONTENTS

PART III: Research Methods   123

9. Collecting Research Data through Observation and Content Analysis   253

PART IV: Quantitative Research Design   287

10. Nonexperimental Research: Descriptive and Causal-Comparative Designs   288

PART V: Approaches to Qualitative Research   433

PART VI: Applications of Research   540

Educational Research: An Introduction was first published in 1963. Forty years and seven editions later, it still exists as a course textbook and reference work. What accounts for this longevity?

Students tell us that they appreciate the book's clarity, straightforward definitions of technical terms, and examples drawn from published studies. Examples make for a longer book, but students apparently don't mind. The examples bring the field of educational research to life for them. In this edition, as in the past, we searched for examples that illustrate particular research techniques while also highlighting important problems in education currently being studied by researchers and practitioners.

Students tell us, too, that the book is a useful guide when they undertake their own research. The reason is that it gets into the "nuts and bolts" and "do's and don'ts" of the entire research process, from getting ideas for a study to writing up the final report. If students want to learn more about a particular topic, the "Touchstones in Research" margin feature and footnotes in each chapter provide leads for further research. Many students hold on to the book after using it as a course text, turning to it whenever they come across an unfamiliar term or procedure in the research literature.

Instructors tell us that they appreciate the book's comprehensive coverage. It presents an extensive and hopefully balanced collection of quantitative and qualitative methods, and of established methods and methods not yet part of the mainstream. As well, they like the fact that the book assumes no prior knowledge of research. Each chapter covers the basics of the aspect of research methodology under consideration. From there, it moves into a discussion of more sophisticated topics. For example, we explain not only simple descriptive statistics, but also sophisticated statistical methods such as structural equation modeling and item-response theory.

Instructors appreciate, too, the currency of the information in the book. To maintain that distinction, we thoroughly updated this current edition to reflect the most recent developments in research—new methodologies, advances in existing methodology, and conceptual issues that are the subject of current debate in journals and at professional meetings. This edition contains hundreds of new and updated citations referencing the research literature.

It seems, then, that the longevity of *Educational Research: An Introduction* can be attributed to its usefulness in helping students master the art of doing sound, productive research that contributes to knowledge about the field of education. Yet we are under no illusion that the book is sufficient for this purpose. Good research requires intellectual curiosity, tolerance for ambiguity, the inclination to question accepted truths, the ability to secure the cooperation of research participants and one's colleagues, and the willingness to admit mistakes or even failure. These qualities cannot be taught by a textbook alone. Students must be guided by senior researchers who model these qualities in their teaching and their own investigations.

Changes from the Sixth Edition

For the seventh edition of *Educational Research: An Introduction*, every chapter has been revised to incorporate the most current thinking in the field and one new chapter has been added.

The new Chapter 18 takes a look at action research. This approach to inquiry has been in use for many decades, but it is currently reaching new levels of acceptance and use. Action researchers continue to formalize their methods of inquiry, and they are publishing studies that show promise of improving professional practice. We felt that it was time to give action research its proper due by devoting a separate chapter to it.

The coverage of electronic technology and media is more extensive in this edition than in previous ones. Among the topics covered are Internet journals, Web sites pertaining to research methodology, search engines, electronic databases of the education literature, Web-based survey techniques, and software for quantitative and qualitative data analysis.

We updated this edition to include recent thinking about issues that were raised in previous editions. These issues involve such matters as the nature of the relationship between quantitative and qualitative research, the connection between research and educational practice, and the ethical obligations of researchers.

Some aspects of research methodology covered in the previous edition have assumed new significance or have been developed more fully in *Educational Research: An Introduction, Seventh Edition*. Among them are meta-analysis, the use of confidence intervals in statistical analysis, test validity, item-response theory, the performance turn and poststructuralism in qualitative research, life history research, and collaborative evaluation.

Overview of the Book's Content and Organization

Educational Research: An Introduction, Seventh Edition has six parts, each preceded by a brief introduction.

Part I includes one chapter that provides an overview of the field of educational research. We recommend it as a starting point to help students develop an initial understanding of the nature of research before they start learning the specifics of research methodology.

The remaining chapters are ordered to correspond to the order of the research process, for the most part. We recommend that students consider research questions and possible research designs, but not actually undertake a formal investigation until they have read and mastered all the chapters that are relevant to it. Generally, this means reading the chapters in Parts I, II, and III, and then those chapters in Parts IV, V, and VI that correspond to the type of research that the student wishes to undertake.

Part II describes the process of planning a research study: developing a research proposal (Chapter 2); dealing with ethical, legal, and human relations issues (Chapter 3); and reviewing the literature (Chapter 4). Because a good research proposal anticipates the final report, Chapter 2 also describes the last stage of a research study: writing the dissertation, thesis, or other type of final report.

Part III covers general methodological procedures in a research study. These include the various statistical techniques for analyzing research data (Chapter 5) and procedures for selecting the research sample (Chapter 6). Next are three chapters on how to collect research data using tests and self-report measures (Chapter 7), questionnaires and interviews (Chapter 8), and observation and content analysis (Chapter 9).

Part IV covers the major research designs used in quantitative research. Non-experimental designs are discussed first: descriptive and causal-comparative designs in Chapter 10, and correlational designs in Chapter 11. Experimental design are discussed in Chapters 12 and 13.

Part V focuses on various approaches to qualitative research in education. Chapter 14 describes a general approach, the case study method, and Chapter 15 describes a variety of qualitative research traditions that have more specialized purposes. Chapter 16 provides in-depth coverage of one of these traditions, historical research.

Part VI includes two chapters about how research methods can be applied for purposes beyond the generation of scientific knowledge and theory. Chapter 17 describes how research methods are used in program evaluation and R & D projects. Chapter 18 concerns action research, which has the goal of generating knowledge to improve local professional practice.

Learning Aids

The information load in a book of this type is considerable, so each chapter contains learning aids to help the student master its content. These aids include the following:

- A brief *overview* sets the stage for what the student will read.
- *Chapter objectives* that identify major concepts and practices to be covered.
- *Technical terms* boldfaced in the text when they appear for the first time in the chapter, and defined in the Glossary.

A special boxed feature at the end of each chapter that suggests

- *"Recommendations for . . . "* at the end of each chapter which applies the chapter content to one's own research study.
- A *Self-Check Test* at the end of the chapter (answers appear back of book).
- *Touchstones in Research* are marginal citations throughout each chapter that guide students to more information and resources.

Instructor's Manual

The *Instructor's Manual* provides various resources that can facilitate teaching a course on research methods using *Educational Research: An Introduction, Seventh Edition.* The resources include: suggestions pertaining to various course elements, such as content coverage, content sequence, teaching activities, and homework; example of a course syllabus; a form for outlining a research proposal, which can be used as a course project; and a test-item file for each chapter containing closed-form items, short-answer items, and application items based on situations that arise when conducting educational research.

Acknowledgments

Whatever success this book has enjoyed is due in large measure to Walter Borg, who wrote the first edition. He invited one of us (Mark Gall) to become his co-author for the second through fifth editions. Walter died in 1990 after a long, distinguished career as a professor and researcher. Mark's colleague and spouse, Joy Gall, joined him in co-authoring the sixth and seventh editions.

We wish to acknowledge our colleagues at the University of Oregon and elsewhere who continue to stimulate our thinking about educational research and practice. Among them are Juliet Baxter, Russell Gersten, Nancy Golden, Martin Kaufman, Katie Lenn, Marilyn Olson, Richard Rankin, Bruce Thompson, Gerald Tindal, Harry Wolcott, and Paul Yoganoff. We also thank Allyn and Bacon's reviewers for their expert suggestions. They include Shann Ferch, Gonzaga University; Brian R. Hinrichs, Illinois State University; Jay W. Rojewski, University of Georgia; Mark W. Roosa, Arizona State University; David L. Tan, University of Oklahoma; and James M. Webb, Kent State University.

Finally, we thank Mary Kriener and Arnie Burvikovs at Allyn & Bacon, for their expertise and encouragement during the developmental and production phases of this edition. We wish to acknowledge, too, other editors who helped us over the years, including Ed Artinian, Ginny Blanford, Art Pomponio, and Ray O'Connell.

Meredith "Mark" Gall

Joyce P. Gall

Meredith "Mark" Gall is professor of education and head of the Area of Teacher Education in the College of Education at the University of Oregon. He is also the author of *Applying Educational Research: A Practical Guide*, Fourth Edition (with Joyce P. Gall and Walter R. Borg) published by Addison-Wesley and *Clinical Supervision and Teacher Development: Preservice and Inservice Applications*, Fifth Edition (with Keith A. Acheson), published by John Wiley & Sons.

Joyce "Joy" Gall is a courtesy assistant professor and the research and communications specialist for the Administrator Licensure Program in the College of Education at the University of Oregon.

Walter R. Borg, late professor emeritus at Utah State University, was one of the major developers of microteaching, a widely used method of teacher education. He was the senior author of *Educational Research: An Introduction* through its first five editions starting in 1963.

PART I

◆ Introduction

This part of the book provides an overview of educational research as an organized, professional approach to inquiry. You will find that educational research is not a simple matter of discovering facts about education, but rather that it has diverse goals, including the development of theories to explain educational phenomena.

You also will find that educational researchers must deal with important, but still unresolved, philosophical issues having to do with the nature of social reality and how to acquire knowledge about it. Different researchers have taken opposing positions on these issues, and consequently, they have developed quite different approaches to the investigation of education. We introduce you to the two main approaches, commonly known as quantitative and qualitative research. Other parts of the book provide detailed explanations of how to conduct research studies using one or the other approach. You should study this part of the book first, though, so that you understand why these different approaches evolved.

In reading Part I, you will find that research plays an important role in improving educational practice. At the same time, educational research is a very human process and, therefore, is prone to error and bias. Researchers have developed procedures to minimize the influence of error and bias on their findings. In this respect, the approach to educational inquiry that involves the conduct of research is different from other approaches to learning about education and improving it.

CHAPTER 1

✦ The Nature of Educational Research

OVERVIEW

What does it mean to do educational research, and how can it contribute to the improvement of educational practice? These are the questions that we address in this chapter. We explore issues of concern to philosophers of science and show how their insights have opened up new lines of inquiry about educational phenomena. We also respond to recent criticisms of science by showing how educational research and other types of social science inquiry contribute to the search for truth about the human condition.

OBJECTIVES

After studying this chapter, you should be able to

1. Describe the four types of knowledge yielded by educational research.
2. Explain the elements of a theory and the steps that are involved in testing a theory.
3. State several reasons why it is difficult to apply research findings to educational practice.
4. Explain why basic research is worth supporting, even when it does not lead to direct improvements in educational practice.
5. Describe the major epistemological issues in social science research.
6. Explain why postpositivist researchers are careful to distinguish between the perspectives of the researcher, the research participants, and the readers of research reports.
7. Explain how the search for general laws is affected by a researcher's decision to study either cases or populations.
8. Describe several limitations of both quantification and verbal data in social science research.
9. Explain the difference between the mechanical, the interpretive, and the structural views of causation in social reality.
10. State the main differences between quantitative and qualitative researchers in their epistemological assumptions and methodology.
11. Take a position on whether quantitative and qualitative research are complementary or competing approaches to social science inquiry.
12. Describe how postmodernists view social science research.
13. State six features of social science inquiry that characterize its approach to the search for truth.

Contributions of Research to Knowledge about Education

A colleague once speculated that if doctors were to lose their base of medical research knowledge, most of them would have to stop working. They would have no idea how to treat anything except common ailments. Surgeons, for example, could not perform open-heart surgery if they lacked research-based knowledge about heart functions, anesthesia, the meaning of symptoms, and the likely risks of particular surgical procedures. In contrast, if educators suddenly were to lose the body of knowledge that has been gained thus far from educational research, their work would be virtually unaffected. Schools would continue to operate pretty much as they do now. It is difficult to imagine teachers who would refuse to teach students because they did not possess sufficient research-based knowledge about the learning process or the effectiveness of different instructional methods.

✦ Touchstone in Research

Gage, N. L. (1996). Confronting counsels of despair for the behavioral sciences. *Educational Researcher, 25(3)*, 5–15, 22.

The point of this comparison of medicine and education is that, in the opinion of this colleague, research still has relatively little influence on the day-to-day work of educators. Whether true or not, his assessment of educational practice raises an important question: Why should one do educational research?

The usual answer to this question is that educational research develops new knowledge about teaching, learning, and educational administration. This new knowledge is of value because it will lead eventually to the improvement of educational practice. However, if you examine this answer, it raises new questions, especially, What do we mean by *research*? and How does research get translated into practice?

The purpose of this chapter is to explain how various educators and philosophers of science have answered these questions. Hopefully, the ideas that we present will cause you to examine your present notions about educational research. At the least, you should develop a better understanding of why thousands of educational researchers throughout the world believe in the value of their work.

In the next sections, we consider four types of knowledge that research contributes to education: (1) description, (2) prediction, (3) improvement, and (4) explanation.

Description

Many research studies involve the description of natural or social phenomena—their form, structure, activity, change over time, relationship to other phenomena, and so on. Many important scientific discoveries have resulted from researchers making such descriptions. For example, astronomers have used their telescopes to develop descriptions of different parts of the universe. In the process they have discovered new galaxies and have determined the structure of the universe. These discoveries in turn have shed light on questions concerning the origins of the universe and where it is headed.

The descriptive function of research is heavily dependent upon instrumentation for measurement and observation. Researchers sometimes work for many years to perfect such instruments—for example, electron microscopes, galvanometers, and standardized tests of intelligence. Once instruments are developed, they can be used to describe phenomena of interest to the researchers. For this reason, we include several Chapters (7, 8, and 9) that describe the various data-collection instruments used in educational research.

Descriptive studies have greatly increased our knowledge about what happens in schools. Some of the most important books in education, such as *Life in Classrooms* by Philip Jackson, *The Good High School* by Sara Lawrence Lightfoot, and *Amazing Grace* by Jonathan Kozol, have reported studies of this type.[1]

---

1. Jackson, P. W. (1968). *Life in classrooms.* New York: Holt, Rinehart & Winston; Lightfoot, S. W. (1983). *The good high school.* New York: Basic Books; Kozol, J. (1995). *Amazing grace: The lives of children and the conscience of a nation.* New York: Crown.

Some descriptive research is intended to produce statistical information about aspects of education of interest to policy makers and educators. The National Center for Education Statistics specializes in this kind of research. Many of its findings are published in an annual volume called the *Digest of Educational Statistics*. This center also administers the National Assessment of Educational Progress (NAEP), which collects descriptive information about how well the nation's youth are doing in various subject areas.[2] This information sometimes makes its way into newspapers, thereby influencing the way community members and policy makers think about the quality of the educational system.

Prediction

Another type of research knowledge involves prediction, which is the ability to predict a phenomenon that will occur at time *Y* from information available at an earlier time *X*. For example, lunar eclipses can be predicted accurately from knowledge about the relative motion of the Moon, Earth, and Sun. The next stage of an embryo's development can be predicted accurately from knowledge of the embryo's current stage. A student's achievement in school can be predicted fairly accurately by an aptitude test administered a year or two earlier.

Educational researchers have done many prediction studies to acquire knowledge about factors that predict students' success in school and in the world of work. One reason for doing such research is to guide the selection of students who will be successful in particular educational settings. For example, the Scholastic Aptitude Test (SAT) and similar measures are administered to millions of high school students annually. Universities and colleges use the test results, along with other data, to select students who have the best chance of success in the institution's academic programs. Prediction research continues to be needed in order to acquire more knowledge about how well these tests predict, whether they predict equally well for different groups of students (such as ethnic-minority students), and whether new instruments can improve the predictability of success in particular settings.

Another purpose of prediction research is to identify students who are likely to be unsuccessful as their education progresses so that prevention programs can be instituted. For example, there is much concern about the high number of school dropouts nationally.[3] By collecting different types of information about students in the sixth grade, for example, and following those students until they graduate from high school or drop out, researchers can determine which information provides the best predictions. This predictive knowledge can be used to identify sixth graders who are at risk of becoming high school dropouts. With this knowledge, it is possible to develop programs specifically for these students in order to increase their chances of success in school.

Educational research has generated a large body of predictive knowledge about factors that predict various outcomes that have social importance (e.g., academic success, career success, criminal conduct). Procedures for doing research for the purpose of prediction are presented in Chapters 10 and 11.

Improvement

The third type of research knowledge concerns the effectiveness of interventions. Examples of interventions in different professions are drug therapies in medicine, construction materials in engineering, marketing strategies in business, and instructional programs in

2. Jones, L. V. (1996). A history of the National Assessment of Educational Progress and some questions about its future. *Educational Researcher, 25(7),* 15–22.
3. Kaufman, P., Kwon, J. Y., Klein, S., & Chapman, C. D. (2000). Dropout rates in the United States: 1998. *Education Statistics Quarterly, 2,* 43–47.

education. Many educational research studies are done to identify interventions, or factors that can be transformed into interventions, for improving students' academic achievement. Herbert Walberg and his colleagues synthesized the findings of nearly 3,000 such studies that involved interventions, or potential interventions, designed to improve students' performance on various measures of academic achievement.[4] The results of the synthesis are summarized in Table 1.1.

TABLE 1.1

Effects of Instructional Factors on Student Learning Outcomes

Method	Effect Size	Percentile
1. Reinforcement	1.17	88
2. Acceleration	1.00	84
3. Reading training	.97	83
4. Cues and feedback	.97	83
5. Science mastery learning	.81	79
6. Graded homework	.79	79
7. Cooperative learning	.76	78
8. Reading experiments	.60	73
9. Class morale	.60	73
10. Personalized instruction	.57	72
11. Home interventions	.50	69
12. Adaptive instruction	.45	67
13. Tutoring	.40	66
14. Instructional time	.38	65
15. Home environment	.37	64
16. Individualized science	.35	64
17. Higher-order questions	.34	63
18. Diagnostic prescriptive methods	.33	63
19. Individualized instruction	.32	63
20. Individualized mathematics	.32	63
21. New science curricula	.31	62
22. Teacher expectations	.28	61
23. Assigned homework	.28	61
24. Socioeconomic status	.25	60
25. Computer-assisted instruction	.24	59
26. Peer group	.24	59
27. Sequenced lessons	.24	59
28. Advance organizers	.23	59
29. New mathematics curricula	.18	57
30. Inquiry biology	.16	56
31. Homogeneous groups	.10	54
32. Class size	.09	54
33. Programmed instruction	−.03	49
34. Television	−.05	48
35. Mainstreaming	−.12	45

Source: Adapted from Figures 3 and 4 on p. 24 of: Walberg, H. J. (1984). Improving the productivity of America's schools. *Educational Leadership, 41*(8), 19–27.

4. Walberg, H. J. (1984). Improving the productivity of America's schools. *Educational Leadership, 41*(8), 19–27. For a more recent synthesis that includes these and additional intervention variables, see: Wang, M. C., Haertel, G. D., & Walberg, H. J. (1993). Toward a knowledge base for school learning. *Review of Educational Research, 63,* 249–294.

The left side of Table 1.1 lists the interventions that were tested in the studies. Each intervention was the subject of many different studies. The first data column is a statistic called an *effect size,* which is discussed in Chapter 5. This statistic is a quantitative way of describing how well the average student who received the intervention performed relative to the average student who did not receive the intervention (or who received less of it). An effect size of 0 means that on average, a student receiving the intervention did no better or worse than a student who did not receive it. Positive effect sizes mean that the average student receiving the intervention did better than the average student not receiving it. Negative effect sizes mean that the average student receiving the intervention did less well than the average student not receiving it. The larger a positive effect size, the more powerful the intervention. Researchers consider effect sizes larger than .33 to have practical significance, that is, the effect of the intervention is large enough to make a worthwhile improvement in the outcome that was measured.

The second data column in Table 1.1 presents percentile equivalents to further help you interpret the meaning of the effect sizes reported in the table. For example, the percentile for reinforcement (88) means that the average student receiving reinforcement (i.e., the student scoring at the 50th percentile on an achievement measure following an intervention involving reinforcement) had an achievement score equal to that of a nonreinforced student who scored at the 88th percentile. In other words, reinforcing an average student typically moves the student from the 50th percentile to the 88th percentile. To illustrate further, if we look at Table 1.1, we find that providing computer-assisted instruction typically moves an average student from the 50th percentile to the 59th percentile.

Walberg's synthesis of research shows that educational researchers have discovered many effective interventions for improving students' academic achievement. Further research is needed to refine these interventions to make them more effective across different educational settings and for different types of students. Also, research is needed to turn potential interventions into actual interventions. For example, classroom morale is not an intervention per se, but it is potentially manipulable; that is, interventions probably can be developed to increase classroom morale, which in turn should improve student learning. Improvement-oriented research knowledge can be generated using various research approaches, but particularly those described in Chapters 12 and 13 on experimental research, Chapter 17 on evaluation research, and Chapter 18 on action research.

Another approach to improving education through inquiry has become prominent in recent years. Cultural studies, a branch of critical theory, is a type of social science inquiry that investigates the power relationships in a culture in order to help emancipate its members from the many forms of oppression that are perceived to operate in the culture. Researchers who engage in this approach to inquiry would be inclined to state their purpose not as the improvement of education, but as the emancipation of the members of the educational system who are oppressed in some manner. A branch of historical research, called *revisionist history,* also examines power relationships, particularly those that are oppressive, as they occurred in the past. These power relationships reflect large-scale societal and cultural forces that affect students' learning. In contrast, Table 1.1 mostly lists interpersonal interventions at the level of classroom instruction. We discuss critical theory and cultural studies in Chapter 15 and revisionist history in Chapter 16.

Explanation

The fourth type of research knowledge—explanation—is the most important in the long term. In a sense, this type of knowledge subsumes the other three. If researchers are able to explain an educational phenomenon, it means that they can describe it, can predict its consequences, and know how to intervene to change those consequences.

Researchers ideally frame their explanations as theories about the phenomena being investigated. A **theory** is an explanation of a certain set of observed phenomena in terms of a system of constructs and laws that relate these constructs to each other. To illustrate what this definition means, consider Jean Piaget's theory of intellectual development. Piaget's theory is familiar to most educators and has had a substantial influence on American curriculum and instruction.

First, Piaget's theory is a *system,* in that it consists of a set of constructs and their relation to each other. The system is loose in that the constructs were developed and changed in the many treatises that Piaget and his colleagues wrote over a period of decades. Other researchers have attempted to pull the theory together by writing concise descriptions of it. These concise descriptions are representations of the theory-as-system.

The theoretical system is designed to explain a set of phenomena: the behavior of infants and children with respect to their environment. For example, Piaget observed how children of different ages responded to a particular task. The children's responses constituted phenomena to be explained by the theory.

The theory provides an explanation of phenomena by first specifying a set of theoretical constructs. A **theoretical construct** is a concept that is inferred from observed phenomena. It can be defined constitutively or operationally. A **constitutively defined construct** is one that is defined by referring to other constructs. For example, the Piagetian construct of conservation can be defined as the ability to recognize that certain properties of an object remain unchanged when other properties of the object (e.g., substance, length, or volume) undergo a transformation. Note that in this definition *conservation* is defined by referring to other constructs (e.g., *property, transformation,* or *length*).

An **operationally defined construct** is one that is defined by specifying the activities used to measure or manipulate it. For example, the construct *conservation* (defined constitutively above) could be defined operationally by referring to a particular task, for example, pouring a constant amount of liquid into different-sized containers and then asking a child whether the amount of liquid remains the same.

In conducting investigations, some researchers use the term *variable* rather than *construct.* A **variable** is a quantitative expression of a construct. Variables usually are measured in terms of scores on an instrument such as an achievement test or an attitude scale or in terms of categories of a construct (e.g., public vs. private schools).

As we stated above, a theory specifies laws relating constructs to each other. A **law** (also called a *scientific law*) is a generalization about the causal, sequential, or other relationship between two or more constructs. Theorists can posit these generalized relationships and then subject them to empirical verification, or they can take generalized relationships first discovered by researchers and incorporate them in their theory. An example of a theoretical law can be found in Piaget's theory of the stages of intellectual development: sensorimotor, preoperational, concrete operations, and formal operations. Each of these stages is a construct. Piaget proposed the law that these constructs are related to each other as an invariant sequence: The sensorimotor stage always is followed by the preoperational stage; the preoperational stage always is followed by the concrete operations stage; and the concrete operations stage always is followed by the formal operations stage.

Uses of Theory

Theories serve several useful purposes. First, theoretical constructs identify commonalities in otherwise isolated phenomena. Piaget's theory, for example, identifies many isolated infant behaviors as instances of sensorimotor intelligence. In other words, theoretical constructs identify the universals of experience so that we can make sense of experience. Second, the laws of a theory enable us to make predictions and to control phenomena. Because astronomers have a well-developed theory, they can make very accurate predictions about the occurrence of eclipses and other phenomena in the universe. Because professionals in special education work from a well-developed theory of learning (sometimes called *behavioral theory*), they can make instructional interventions that dependably lead to positive changes in student behavior.

Scientists sometimes speak of "small" and "large" theories. A small theory might be developed to account for a limited set of phenomena (e.g., antecedents and consequences of teacher morale). A large theory might account for many phenomena (e.g., behavioral theory and cognitive theory). Also, a theory might grow as it is shown to explain more phenomena or as it incorporates more constructs to explain phenomena. A researcher might start with a small theory of academic achievement. As more determinants of achievement are discovered, the researcher can enlarge the theory to accommodate them.

Approaches to Theory Development

We describe two approaches to theory development in this book. The **grounded theory** approach involves deriving constructs and laws directly from the immediate data that one has collected rather than from prior research and theory. In other words, the constructs and laws are "grounded" in the particular set of data that the researcher has collected. The usefulness of the constructs and laws can be tested in subsequent research. We discuss this approach to theory development in Chapter 14.

The other approach to developing a theory is to start by formulating a theory and then submit it to a test by collecting empirical data. The process of testing has three steps:

1. the formulation of a hypothesis,
2. the deduction of observable consequences of the hypothesis, and
3. the testing of the hypothesis by making observations (that is to say, by collecting research data).

This process is commonly thought of as the scientific method, although some philosophers of science doubt that there is any such thing as *the* scientific method. Paul Feyerabend, for example, states, "The idea of a method that contains firm, unchanging, and absolutely binding principles for conducting the business of science meets considerable difficulty when confronted with the results of historical research [i.e., research on the history of science]."[5]

Example of Theory Testing

The three steps for testing a theory empirically are illustrated in a study of self-attention theory conducted by Brian Mullen.[6] This theory concerns self-regulation processes that occur when an individual becomes the object of his own attention. Self-consciousness and embarrassment are manifestations of self-attention processes at work. One function of self-attention theory is to explain the effect of groups on the individual. The theory states in part that when individuals are in groups of people like themselves, they become more self-attentive as the size of the group decreases. This is because the smaller group becomes more of a focal point for the individual's attention, and as a result, the individual is led to compare himself with the standards represented by the group.

How can we test whether this theory is valid? The first step is to formulate a **hypothesis,** which is a tentative proposition about the relationship between two or more theoreti-

---

5. Feyerabend, P. (1978). *Against method*. London: Verso. Quote appears on p. 23.
6. Mullen, B. (1988). A self-attention perspective on discussion. In J. T. Dillon (Ed.), *Questioning and discussion: A multidisciplinary study* (pp. 74–89). London: Ablex.

cal constructs. In Mullen's study, the hypothesis was that individuals would be more self-attentive in smaller groups than in larger groups. The two theoretical constructs in this hypothesis are *group size* and *self-attention*. They were hypothesized to exist in inverse relation to each other, meaning that as group size decreases, self-attention increases.

The next step in testing a theory is to deduce observable consequences of the hypothesis. To engage in such deduction, the researcher needs to find a real-life or simulated situation. Mullen was able to obtain transcripts of 27 high school discussions in which the size of the discussion group varied. He operationally defined self-attention in this context as the extent of the use of first person singular pronouns (I, me) by students whenever they spoke in the discussion groups. Group size was measured by counting the number of students in each discussion group.[7] Thus, Mullen had a situation in which he could determine observable consequences of the hypothesis. Each construct specified in the hypothesis could be operationally defined and measured using the data available to him.

The third step of testing a theory is to collect empirical data and determine whether they correspond to the hypothesis. Using the transcripts and other data available to him, Mullen counted the number of students and the number of first-person singular pronouns verbalized in each discussion. Mullen then related the two sets of numerical data (group size and number of pronouns) by the statistical method called *correlation,* which is described in Chapter 11. The statistical analysis yielded the hypothesized result: A higher frequency of first-person singular pronouns was found in the smaller discussion groups than in the larger discussion groups.

Mullen's study illustrates the process of testing a theory. Because the hypothesis was supported, that part of the theory to which the hypothesis relates is strengthened, meaning that we can be a bit more confident that the theory provides a good explanation of how individuals act in social situations.

Despite the power of the so-called scientific method to test the validity of hypotheses, it has several weaknesses. One of them is that the researcher may deduce inappropriate observable consequences from the hypothesis, and thus make an inappropriate test of the hypothesis. For example, Mullen assumed that first-person singular pronouns were an appropriate operational measure of self-attention. Such may not be the case. Therefore, other theorists and researchers need to check each study carefully to determine whether appropriate measures and situations were used. It is especially important to make these checks when the empirical results do not support the hypothesis. One would not want to reject a hypothesis, and with it a basically sound theory, simply because it was put to an inappropriate test.

The other weakness of the scientific method is more difficult to overcome: Any observable result potentially can support multiple, sometimes conflicting, theories. For this reason, a researcher can never prove a theory, but can only support it, as we explain later in the chapter. In the case of Mullen's study, he acknowledged several alternative theoretical explanations for his observed results, and he noted that the results of his study did not conclusively eliminate any of them as untenable.

Mullen notes in his report that other researchers have used self-attention theory successfully to predict conformity, prosocial behavior, loafing behavior, antisocial behavior, participation in religious organizations, stuttering in front of audiences of varying sizes, the behavior of lynch mobs, and the discussion behavior of the president of the United States and his aides. Self-attention theory, then, does not stand or fall by Mullen's results alone. The soundness of a theory is judged by the total weight of the evidence.

---

7. Actually, a more complex measure of group size, called the Other-Total Ratio, was computed, but in this study it corresponded closely to the count of the number of students in each group.

Application of Research to Educational Practice

✦ *Touchstone in
  Research*

Robinson, V. M. J.
(1998). Methodology
and the research-
practice gap. *Educa-
tional Researcher,
27(1),* 17–26.

Has research knowledge influenced the practice of education, and if so, how has it influenced practice? What is the proper relationship between research knowledge and educational practice? These are difficult questions to answer. Rather than attempting to do so, we will make several observations that may help you form your own answers. The first is that research knowledge and the practice of education have different goals, as D. C. Phillips observes:

> Research findings take the form, roughly, of "X is Y" or "the probability of an X having the feature Y is p"; in other words, they are statements of the "is" form. On the other hand, implications for practice take the form such as, "person A ought to do Z to person B." In other words, they are statements involving an "ought" or "should" or some other locution involving the passing of a value judgment. But it is a point of logic that from statements only involving the use of "is," a conclusion involving "ought" or one of its locutions cannot validly be deduced.[8]

Questions involving *is* can be answered objectively by well-designed research. Questions involving *ought* are value-laden and can be resolved only through dialogue and a decision-making process that includes various constituencies. Researchers should not expect their findings about *is* to result in educational change immediately, and without critical appraisal. Likewise, practitioners should not look to research for prescriptive advice. It seems much more sensible to use research knowledge about what *is* to inform dialogue about what *ought* to be—a dialogue that should be informed by other considerations as well.

Limitations of Research Knowledge

Although research discovers what *is,* it does so with several important limitations. One is that research findings have limited generalizability. For example, in conducting a study, many researchers select a sample that represents one defined population (e.g., elementary teachers in urban schools). Depending on how well the sampling is done, the results of the study can be generalized to that particular population, but not beyond. Even within the defined population, most likely there will be teachers for whom the generalization does not hold. In other studies, the researcher may study only one or a few cases, albeit intensively. Generalization to other cases can be done, but it must be done on a case-by-case basis. Therefore, it seems that practitioners can look to research knowledge for guidance, but they need to ask themselves, "Are these findings likely to apply to my local situation?"

Another limitation of research knowledge is that while it discovers what is, it always does so within a certain worldview and set of values. As we explain later in the chapter, theories and research are value-laden; there is no such thing as purely objective research. Therefore, putting a research finding into practice also means putting a particular set of values into practice. For example, the interventions shown in Table 1.1 are more or less effective in improving students' academic achievement, usually as measured by performance on standardized achievement tests. Using this research knowledge as evidence for advocating one or more of the interventions, then, means also advocating high test performance as a valued outcome of schooling. There are other valued outcomes of schooling, however, such as curiosity, self-reliance, and humanitarian attitudes, that may not be promoted by these interventions. Also, the investigations that produced this research knowledge imply a certain view of teachers, as Magdalene Lampert observes:

---

8. Phillips, D. C. (1980). What do the researcher and the practitioner have to offer each other? *Educational Researcher,* 9(11), 19.

They . . . assume that *the teacher is a technical-production manager* who has the responsibility for monitoring the efficiency with which learning is being accomplished. In this view, teaching can be improved if practitioners use researchers' knowledge to solve classroom problems. The teacher's work is to find out what researchers and policymakers say should be done with or to students and to do it. How much time should be spent on direct instruction versus seatwork? How many new words should be in stories children are required to read? If the teacher does what she is told, students will learn.[9]

Lampert advances a different view of teachers, namely, teachers as dilemma managers. This view emerged from her own research studies, which revealed that classroom teaching involves many problematic situations involving competing interests that the teacher must resolve.

Lampert's view of teaching is consistent with the views of others who have studied professional practice. One of the most influential of these individuals is Donald Schön.[10] He claims that a flawed model of *technical rationality* dominates thinking about the relationship between research and practice. He describes the model in these terms:

> According to the model of Technical Rationality—the view of professional knowledge which has most powerfully shaped both our thinking about the professions and the institutional relations of research, education, and practice—professional activity consists in instrumental problem solving made rigorous by the application of scientific theory and technique.[11]

According to Schön, this model is flawed because research, especially research in the positivist tradition, assumes a stable, consistent reality about which generalizations can be made and applied, whereas professional practice involves "complexity, uncertainty, instability, uniqueness, and value-conflict."[12]

Schön and many others claim that practitioners need to engage in reflection-in-action, not in the application of research knowledge, in order to deal with the "messiness" of their work. Reflection-in-action has various elements, but chief among them is a kind of experimentation based on practitioners' analysis of each unique situation they confront. (We discuss Schön's views about reflection in more detail in Chapter 18.)

In our view, Schön's model of reflection-in-action does not preclude research knowledge as a basis for professional action. The model only implies that research knowledge cannot be the sole basis for professional action. In fact, researchers have found that the primary venue for professional practice, the classroom, is marked more by sameness of practice than by diversity and uniqueness.[13] One might argue that if practitioners were more aware of research knowledge, they might actually be in a better position to accommodate the great individual and group differences found among their clients and constituencies.

The Importance of Basic Research

Some practitioners believe that educational research is too theoretical and too focused on basic processes of learning (e.g., brain functions underlying memory, or eye movements during reading). They believe that instead of such basic research, priority should be given to applied research that addresses actual problems as perceived by practitioners. This argument raises questions about the relative value of basic and applied research in education.

9. Lampert, M. (1985). How do teachers manage to teach? Perspectives on problems in practice. *Harvard Educational Review, 55,* 178–194.
10. Schön, D. A. (1983). *The reflective practitioner.* New York: Basic Books.
11. Ibid., p. 21.
12. Ibid., p. 39.
13. Sirotnik, K. A. (1983). What you see is what you get—Consistency, persistency, and mediocrity in classrooms. *Harvard Educational Review, 53(1),* 16–31.

While applied research, virtually by definition, seems more likely to contribute to the improvement of educational practice, an important study in the field of medicine gives us reason to reconsider.[14] Julius Comroe and Robert Dripps started their study by identifying the most important clinical advances since the early 1940s in the treatment of cardiovascular and pulmonary diseases, which account for more than half of all deaths in the United States each year.

With the assistance of 140 consultants, Comroe and Dripps identified the bodies of knowledge that needed to be developed through research before the 10 clinical advances could reach their present state of achievement. A total of 137 essential bodies of knowledge were identified, such as the anatomy of cardiac defects, blood typing, the monitoring of blood pressure, and the management of postoperative infection.

The next step in Comroe and Dripps's investigation was to identify key scientific reports that contributed to these bodies of knowledge. Each report was classified into one of six categories:

1. Basic research unrelated to the solution of a clinical problem (36.8%).
2. Basic research related to the solution of a clinical problem (24.9%).
3. Studies not concerned with basic biological, chemical, or physical mechanisms (21.2%).
4. A review and critical analysis of published work and the synthesis of new concepts without new experimental data (1.8%).
5. Developmental work or engineering to create, improve, or perfect apparatus or a technique for research use (3.9%).
6. Developmental work or engineering to create, improve, or perfect apparatus for use in diagnosis or care of patients (11.4%).

The numbers in parentheses above show the percentage of reports assigned to each of the categories.

The remarkable finding is the high percentage of basic research studies (36.8% + 24.9% = 61.7%) that were essential to the development of current treatment of cardiovascular and pulmonary disease. Equally remarkable is the fact that more than one-third (36.8%) of the essential studies were not even related to the practice of cardiovascular-pulmonary medicine. These results suggest that research can influence practice even when this is not its purpose and even if practitioners are unaware of the research.

Funding for Educational Research

Research has demonstrated its ability to improve not only medicine but other fields of professional practice as well. We can think of no reason why education should be an exception. Yet the surprising fact is that there is relatively little financial support for educational research. Of the federal funding for public schools, only 0.1 percent is allocated for research; by contrast, of the federal funding for defense, 15 percent is allocated for research.[15] Why educational research receives so little funding and what might happen to educational practice if funding increased dramatically are questions well worth contemplating.

14. Comroe, J. H., Jr., & Dripps, R. D. (1976). Scientific basis for the support of biomedical science. *Science, 192*, 105–111.
15. Biddle, B. J. (1996). Better ideas: Expanded funding for educational research. *Educational Researcher, 25(9)*, 12–14. See also: Lagemann, E. C. (1997). Contested terrain: A history of education research in the United States, 1980–1990. *Educational Researcher, 26(9)*, 5–17.

Epistemological Issues in Educational Research

As you learn more about educational research, you will find that it is not a unified enterprise. For example, you will find that the approaches to educational research described in Part IV of this book involve the study of samples and populations, and that they rely heavily on numerical data and statistical analysis. In contrast, the approaches described in Part V involve the study of cases; they make little use of numerical data or statistics, relying instead on verbal data and subjective analysis.

♦ **Touchstone in Research**

Cunningham, J. W., & Fitzgerald, J. (1996). Epistemology and reading. *Reading Research Quarterly, 31,* 36–60.

Why does educational research involve such diverse approaches? To answer this question, we need to review the epistemological issues that underlie scientific inquiry. **Epistemology** is the branch of philosophy that studies the nature of knowledge and the process by which knowledge is acquired and validated. Some epistemologists have a particular interest in the nature of inquiry and knowledge in the natural sciences and the social sciences. These philosophers (sometimes called *philosophers of science*) have sought answers to such questions as: Are the objects that researchers study (e.g., neutrons and self-concept) real? How is research knowledge different from other forms of knowledge, and does it have any special authority? What is a theory, and how can it be validated? What does it mean to find "laws" that enable us to predict individual and group behavior? Is inquiry in the social sciences fundamentally different from inquiry in the natural sciences?

As philosophers have investigated these and related questions over a period of many centuries, they have developed different schools of thought. Social science researchers have been influenced by these schools of thought (e.g., positivism, empiricism, phenomenology), and in addition, they have staked out their own epistemological positions about how research in their respective disciplines (e.g., anthropology, psychology, and sociology) should be done. Below we focus on epistemological issues as viewed by educational researchers at the present time. Following this discussion, we show how different researchers take different positions on these issues, and, as a consequence, how they advocate and conduct quite different types of educational research.

To guide the discussion, we will make reference to the simple model shown in Figure 1.1. One of the elements in the figure is the individual person (designated *A*), let's say, a teacher. The teacher interacts with an environment that is both physical (*B*) and social (*C*). For example, most teachers use textbooks. At the level of physical reality, a textbook consists of paper and ink, whose reality is constituted by particular biochemical properties. At the level of social reality, the teacher refers to this object by a label *textbook,* which is used as well by other individuals who are members of a particular group (English-language speakers). The teacher uses the textbook to perform a particular social function (instruction) with a particular type of individual (students). The roles of both teacher and student are dictated in large part by society. Thus, all these aspects of the social environment are socially defined, and in this sense they constitute a social reality.

Educational researchers (*D* in Figure 1.1) or other social scientists (e.g., anthropologists, psychologists, and sociologists) conduct investigations to learn about individual persons (or groups of persons), about aspects of their social environment, or about the interaction between the two (e.g., how teachers use textbooks during instruction). Social scientists generally do not study physical reality, although an increasing number of researchers are investigating the relationship between brain functions (a physical reality) and cognitive processes (e.g., attention and problem solving) that occur while individuals work on intellectual tasks (a social reality).

After conducting a study, the researcher writes a report of her findings (*E* in Figure 1.1), which then is read by other individuals (*F*). The readers might be other researchers,

FIGURE 1.1

The Elements of Social Science Inquiry

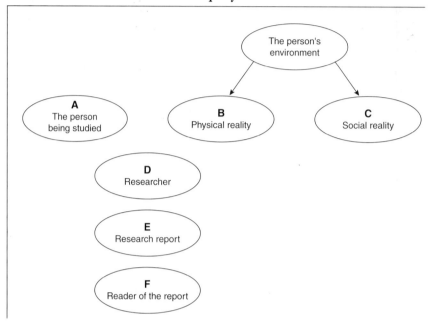

educational practitioners, policy makers, staff members of the agency that funded the study, and members of the general community. Different reports about the same study might be written for different audiences.

Objective Reality and Constructed Reality

Some researchers assume that features of the social environment (*C* in Figure 1.1) have an **objective reality,** which means that these features exist independently of the individuals who created them or who observe them. Suppose, for example, that a teacher pastes a gold star on a student's paper. Under the assumption of an objective reality, this gold star has an existence that is independent of the teacher who assigned it and also independent of the researcher who notices the gold star while studying the teacher's feedback to students. Thus, to the extent that the researcher is free of subjective bias, he can collect data that accurately represents the gold star as it really is.

Researchers who subscribe to a positivist epistemology make this assumption of an objective social reality. Sally Hutchinson, for example, states, "Positivists view the world as being 'out there,' and available for study in a more or less static form."[16] The task of positivist scientific inquiry, then, is to make bias-free observations of the natural and social world "out there." We define **positivism** as the epistemological doctrine that physical and social reality is independent of those who observe it, and that observations of this reality, if unbiased, constitute scientific knowledge.[17]

16. Hutchinson, S. A. (1988). Education and grounded theory. In R. R. Sherman & R. B. Webb (Eds.), *Qualitative research in education: Focus and methods* (pp. 123–140). London: Falmer. Quote appears on p. 124.
17. Several variants of positivist epistemology are described in Chapter 4 of: Phillips, D. C. (1987). *Philosophy, science, and social inquiry.* New York: Pergamon.

Behavioral researchers in education and psychology exemplify an approach to scientific inquiry that is grounded in positivist epistemology. They focus on the study of observable behavior as the basis for building scientific knowledge. Although behavioral researchers use abstract concepts such as *reinforcement* and *punishment,* they define these concepts in terms of the procedures that would be used to observe and measure their behavioral manifestations. Many other researchers besides behaviorists also subscribe to a positivist view of reality and its study. For example, many researchers who study intelligence define this concept as an individual's performance (an observable event) on a particular type of test. The individual's performance is measured as an IQ score, which then can be related to possible antecedents and consequences of intelligence. Much of the research that has been done, and that continues to be done, in education and the social sciences is based on positivist epistemology.

An opposing epistemological position to positivism is based on the assumption that social reality is constructed by the individuals who participate in it. These "constructions" take the form of interpretations, that is, the ascription of meanings to the social environment. Features of the social environment are not considered to have an existence apart from the meanings that individuals construct for them. To return to our example of the gold star on a student's paper, the researcher might consider it as an instance of teacher feedback to students. The teacher might view the gold star as a symbolic message to the student that he has written a good paper relative to other papers he has written. The student might view the gold star as a symbolic message that he has written a better paper than most other papers in the class. Still another student might view the gold star as a sign that the teacher was too busy to provide written feedback and therefore used the gold star as a substitute. Thus, the gold star constitutes different social realities (*C* in Figure 1.1), not a fixed, independent reality.

This view of social reality is consistent with the constructivist movement in cognitive psychology, which posits that individuals gradually build their own understanding of the world through experience and maturation.[18] Formal instruction has some influence, but children do not assimilate it directly. Their minds are not like the philosopher John Locke's *tabula rasa* (meaning "blank slate") upon which knowledge is written. Piaget's theory of intellectual development in children exemplifies the constructivist movement in cognitive psychology.

Educational researchers who subscribe to this constructivist position believe that scientific inquiry must focus on the study of multiple social realities, that is, the different realities created by different individuals as they interact in a social environment. They also believe that these realities cannot be studied by the analytic methods of positivist research. As Yvonna Lincoln and Egon Guba state, "There are multiple constructed realities that can be studied only holistically. . . . "[19] Because this constructivist position was developed in large part subsequent to and as a reaction to the positivist approach to social science inquiry, it sometimes is called *postpositivism.* We define **postpositivism** as the epistemological doctrine that social reality is constructed and that it is constructed differently by different individuals. Thus, if we consider a concept such as intelligence, the postpositivist assumption of multiple constructed realities would lead us to the conclusion that intelligence has no objective reality. Rather, intelligence is a socially constructed label that has different meanings for different individuals and that, if measured, would be measured in different ways by different individuals.

18. Bruner, J. (1986). *Actual minds, possible worlds.* Cambridge, MA: Harvard University Press.
19. Lincoln, Y. S., & Guba, E. G. (1985). *Naturalistic inquiry.* Beverly Hills, CA: Sage. Quote appears on p. 37.

Our above examples involved instances in which individuals (*A* in Figure 1.1) construct the features of their social environment (*B*). An extension of this epistemological doctrine is that individuals also construct themselves. According to this view, we do not have an objectively real self. Each of us constructs a self.[20] In fact, we construct multiple selves, for example, a created self that is totally private to us, and a social self that is created through our style of dress, mannerisms, and other devices displayed to others. This social self forms multiple selves, because we dress and act differently for different groups and on different occasions.

Constructed Realities in Research

There are several methodological consequences of the postpositivist assumption that individuals construct their selves and the features of their social environment. One is that the researcher (*D* in Figure 1.1) must find ways to get individuals to reveal their constructions of social reality. Using the labels of Figure 1.1, we can depict these constructions as A → C (to be read, "A's construction of C"). To determine A → C, researchers typically interview A (generally called a *research participant,* or in the case of ethnographic fieldwork, an *informant*). In talking with the researcher, an informant (A) creates a construction (A → C) that depends upon her view of the researcher and her ability and willingness to communicate with the researcher. In other words, A → C depends upon A → D. Problems can occur as a consequence of this dependency. For example, Paul Stoller and Cheryl Olkes did ethnographic fieldwork among the Songhay people of Niger.[21] Stoller subsequently realized that

> [E]veryone had lied to me and . . . the data I had so painstakingly collected were worthless. I learned a lesson: Informants routinely lie to their anthropologists.[22]

This statement reflects Stoller's appraisal, that is, his construction, of what his informants told him. Thus, just as research participants construct views about the researcher (A → D), so the researcher constructs views about the research participants (D → A).

The situation becomes further complicated when we realize that researchers eventually write reports of their studies and submit them to an audience of readers. The report itself (*E* in Figure 1.1) is a construction by the researcher (D → E). It represents what the researcher chooses to report and how he chooses to report it. Furthermore, no matter what the report states, the reader (*F* in Figure 1.1) will construct her own interpretation of what the findings mean. Norman Denzin describes the process in this manner:

> The researcher creates a field text consisting of field notes and documents from the field. From this text he or she creates a research text, notes and interpretations based on the field text, what David Plath (1990) calls "filed notes." The researcher then re-creates the research text as a working interpretive document. This working document contains the writer's initial attempts to make sense out of what has been learned . . . The writer next produces a quasi-public text, one that is shared with colleagues, whose comments and suggestions the writer seeks. The writer then transforms this statement into a public document, which embodies the writer's self-understandings, which are now inscribed in the experiences of those studied. This statement, in turn, furnishes the context for the understandings the reader brings to the experiences described by the writer.[23]

20. For an example of this view of self, see: Sampson, E. E. (2000). Reinterpreting individualism and collectivism: Their religious roots and monologic versus dialogic person-other relationship. *American Psychologist, 55,* 1425–1432.
21. Stoller, P., & Olkes, C. (1987). *In sorcery's shadow: A memoir of apprenticeship among the Songhay of Niger.* Chicago: University of Chicago Press.
22. Ibid., p. 229.
23. Denzin, N. K. (1994). The art and politics of interpretation. In N. K. Denzin & Y. S. Lincoln (Eds.), *Handbook of qualitative research* (pp. 500–515). Thousand Oaks, CA: Sage. Quote appears on pp. 501–502.

Postpositivist researchers deal with these multiple layers of construction (i.e., interpretation) in various ways. For example, some researchers make explicit their constructivist role in scientific inquiry by writing research reports in which they play a key role alongside their research participants. They describe their personal experiences and reactions in the field, and how their approach to data collection affected the types of findings that resulted. This focus on the researcher's self as an integral constructor of the social reality being studied is called **reflexivity.** In the following statement, David Altheide and John Johnson advocate reflexivity in ethnographic research (we describe this type of research in Chapter 15):

> Good ethnographies show the hand of the ethnographer. The effort may not always be successful, but there should be clear "tracks" indicating the attempt has been made. We are in the midst of a rediscovery that social reality is constructed by human agents—even social scientists!—using cultural categories and language in specific situations or contexts of meaning. This interest is indeed welcome, because it gives us license to do yet another elucidation of the "concept of knowing."[24]

Reflexivity in scientific inquiry has become an important movement not only in ethnography, but also in other social science disciplines. The movement sometimes is called the *reflexive turn* in the social sciences. Positivist researchers in these sciences reject reflexivity, however. Their goal is to keep the self out of the processes of collecting data and reporting their findings as much as possible.

The objective orientation of positivist researchers is reflected in the *Publication Manual of the American Psychological Association,* a guide for reporting psychological research, which for most of its history has been grounded in positivist epistemology.[25] (The *Manual* also is widely used in the reporting of educational research and research in other social science disciplines.) Robert Madigan, Susan Johnson, and Patricia Linton did an analysis of reporting recommendations in the *Manual* (fourth edition). The following are two of their conclusions:

> In APA style, language use is not allowed to call attention to itself. Dillon (1991) described this as the "rhetoric of objectivity" that has evolved to create the impression of neutrality or impersonal detachment and that is generally characteristic of the empirical disciplines. This effect is enhanced by giving the persona of the writer a low profile in the text, keeping the focus on the phenomena under study . . .
>
> APA style [leads] toward practices that make language appear as a transparent medium for conveying objective information about a fixed external reality.[26]

We see, then, that the standard format for writing reports of positivist research is consistent with its epistemology of scientific inquiry, which is objective rather than reflexive in nature.

Cases and Populations

Researchers who subscribe to postpositivist epistemology believe that the study of individuals' interpretations of social reality must occur at the local, immediate level. For example, suppose that a postpositivist researcher is interested in teachers' interpretations of

24. Altheide, D. L., & Johnson, J. M. (1994). Criteria for assessing interpretive validity in qualitative research. In N. K. Denzin & Y. S. Lincoln (Eds.), *Handbook of qualitative research* (pp. 485–499). Thousand Oaks, CA: Sage. Quote appears on pp. 493–494.
25. *Publication Manual of the American Psychological Association* (5th ed.). (2001). Washington, DC: American Psychological Association.
26. Madigan, R., Johnson, S., & Linton, P. (1995). The language of style: APA style as epistemology. *American Psychologist, 50,* 428–436. Quote appears on pp. 433–434.

the act of teaching, that is, the meanings they ascribe to various features of teaching (e.g., lesson planning, student misbehavior in class, and homework assignments). To determine these meanings, the researcher needs to study particular teachers (local) rather than teachers in general (distant). Also, the researcher needs to identify a particular time frame for study. The way that a teacher constructs meanings at one point in time (immediate) may not be the way he constructs meanings at another point in time (past and future). The epistemological assumption about the local, immediate character of meanings implies, then, that the researcher must study particular cases, that is, particular instances of the phenomenon that interests him.

Researchers who subscribe to positivist epistemology believe that features of the social environment retain a high degree of constancy across time and space, just as physicists believe that neutrons and protons have objective features that do not vary from one laboratory setting to another or from one day to the next. For example, in reviewing positivist research on teaching, Frederick Erickson states,

> Positivist research on teaching presumes that history repeats itself; that what can be learned from past events can generalize to future events—in the same setting and in different settings.[27]

This assumption of constancy justifies their search for what is generally true of the social environment. Local variations are considered to be "noise." For example, a positivist researcher might be interested in whether an emphasis on higher-cognitive questions in instruction would improve student learning. In doing a research study, this researcher would not be interested in whether the higher-cognitive questions of a particular teacher make a difference. Instead, she would want to determine general trends for a defined population of teachers. If she found that higher-cognitive questions generally promote student learning, she would claim to have discovered a "law," a "principle," a "rule," or a similar term. The fact that the law does not hold for a particular teacher would be considered "noise," that is, an unexplained variation. We see, then, that positivist researchers study samples and populations, not cases.

The epistemological assumptions that lead to the study of cases or populations also have implications for how findings of a particular research study are generalized. In the study of cases, the critical question for generalizing findings is this: Have we learned something about this case that informs us about another case? Generalization of case study findings must be made on a case-by-case basis.

This approach to generalization is analogous to how we often think in our everyday life. Suppose you are a teacher and you observe another teacher who uses a particular teaching technique successfully. You probably will proceed to study the teacher's work situation (the grade level, the social class of the students, the curriculum, etc.) and decide whether it is similar to your own work situation. If you decide that it is similar, you probably will conclude that the technique has a good chance of being effective in your situation, too. Thus, you generalize from a given case to another case.

The process of generalization is different in positivist research. The researcher starts by defining a population of interest. The population typically includes too many members to study all of them, so the researcher attempts to select a manageable sample, but one that is representative of the population. He then attempts to generalize the findings obtained from studying the sample to the larger population. Statistical techniques are available to determine the likelihood that sample findings (e.g., students in the sample who received

27. Erickson, F. (1986). Qualitative methods in research on teaching. In M. C. Wittrock (Ed.), *Handbook of research on teaching* (3rd ed., pp. 119–161). New York: Macmillan. Quote appears on p. 129.

Method A earned higher test scores than students who received Method B) are likely to apply to the population.

The physical sciences have achieved prominence among the academic disciplines because of their demonstrated ability to discover highly generalizable laws that explain features of physical reality. The social sciences and allied professional disciplines such as education have not achieved the same level of respect and authority because their ability to discover general laws remains in doubt. If one subscribes to the assumption of postpositivist epistemology that meaning is embedded in local, immediate contexts, it follows that generalizations about features of social reality necessarily will be difficult and tentative. The positivist assumption of an objective, relatively constant social reality leads to the more optimistic view that general laws governing social reality can be discovered.

Numerical and Verbal Representations of Social Reality

Alford Crosby claims that the great achievements of Western civilization starting during the Renaissance were the result of a shift away from the qualitative worldview that had dominated society up to then.[28] In the qualitative worldview, symbolism, mythology, and religion were used to explain human events and physical phenomena. For example, time "was envisioned not as a straight line marked off in equal quanta, but as a stage for the enactment of the greatest of all dramas, Salvation versus Damnation."[29]

With the shift toward a quantitative worldview, reality was viewed differently:

> In practical terms, the new approach was simply this: reduce what you are trying to think about to the minimum required by its definition; visualize it on paper, or at least in your mind, be it the fluctuation of wool prices at the Champagne fairs or the course of Mars through the heavens, and divide it, either in fact or in imagination, into equal quanta. Then you can measure it, that is, count the quanta.[30]

Quantitative thinking generated many inventions, including mechanical clocks that break time into ticks of equal length; geometrically precise maps in which gridlines mark off equal units of the earth's surface; double-entry bookkeeping in which goods and services are represented as monetary units; and the use of algebraic notation to indicate known and unknown quantities.

The analysis of reality into quanta is so embedded in contemporary society that we take it for granted. The computer, digital sound, and digital video represent reality in the simplest of quanta—1s and 0s. Western capitalism depends on the capacity to create quantitative representations of property, goods, and services. (Hernando De Soto found that underdeveloped countries have an enormous amount of capital, but cannot access it because they lack this capacity.[31]) Most research advances in the physical and social sciences that we read about in the news involve the quantification of reality and mathematics, especially statistical analysis. In education, too, much of the research that is considered newsworthy involves students' performance on tests, which represent quantification of learning and aptitude.

The use of quantification to represent and analyze features of social reality is consistent with positivist epistemology. Because this epistemology assumes that features of

---

28. Crosby, A. W. (1997). *The measure of reality: Quantification and Western society, 1250–1600.* Cambridge: Cambridge University Press.
29. Ibid., p. 28.
30. Ibid., p. 228.
31. De Soto, H. (2000). *The mystery of capital: Why capitalism triumphs in the West and fails everywhere else.* New York: Basic Books.

social reality have a constancy across time and settings, a particular feature can be isolated and it can be conceptualized as a variable, that is, as an entity that can take on different values. These values can be expressed as numerical scales. For example, a typical achievement test is assumed to yield scores that form an interval scale.

Suppose that we, as positivist researchers, select class size as a feature of the classroom environment to study. We decide to operationally define class size as the average number of students who are enrolled in a teacher's classroom over the course of the school year. We then can observe a sample of teachers' classrooms and make this count. The resulting data consist of numerical scores: Teacher A's classroom has 23 students, Teacher B's classroom has 37 students, and so on. A comparison of the scores would lead us logically to the conclusion that Teacher A's class size is smaller than Teacher B's class size. The scores for all the teachers can be averaged to yield a mean class size for the sample. Also, by collecting additional data, we can determine whether the variable of class size is related to other variables. For example, we can conceptualize a variable called *student off-task behavior*, develop a measure of it, and collect data in the classroom of each teacher in the sample. The two sets of numerical data (class size and student off-task behavior) then can be analyzed to determine whether they are related in some way (e.g., larger class sizes might tend to be associated with higher off-task rates). The great majority of educational research studies have represented and analyzed features of the social environment in just this way.

Some researchers and philosophers of science have questioned this use of quantification in social science research. Marx Wartofsky, for example, raises this issue:

> The question of the limited scope of such techniques as are directly quantitative (in terms of interval or ratio scales) raises the problem of "importance" and "triviality" in social-science research strategy. For it may increasingly become the case that central societal facts which do not lend themselves to such analysis will tend to be overlooked or de-emphasized on such narrowly methodological grounds, by virtue of the easy quantification of other, perhaps marginal facts. Social-science research oriented toward empirical-quantitative studies may very well then take the path of least resistance. But the path of least resistance to quantification may be the path of least significance as well, so that data analysis may proliferate precisely where it is least important.[32]

As applied to our example, Wartofsky's analysis raises the question of whether class size and student off-task behavior are features of the social environment that can be quantified, but that are not particularly significant for understanding how classrooms work and what makes them work well or poorly as arenas for instruction.

Postpositivist epistemology raises another concern about quantification. The operational definition of class size as a count of the average number of students enrolled in a class over the course of a school year assumes that values of this variable have the same meaning across classrooms. Postpositivist researchers, however, would question this assumption. Two teachers both may have 25 enrolled students. In Teacher A's class, though, some of these students may have behavior disorders and may have been assigned to the teacher without her consent. In Teacher B's class, all the students may be able learners, whose presence in class the teacher welcomes. Thus, the number *25* has two different meanings in these situations. For Teacher A, *25* represents an oppressive teaching situation, whereas for Teacher B, *25* represents a comfortable teaching situation. If researchers conduct an investigation to determine whether increases in class size make

32. Wartofsky, M. W. (1968). *Conceptual foundations of scientific thought: An introduction to the philosophy of science.* New York: Macmillan. Quote appears on p. 393.

instruction more difficult, they may be misled because a particular value of the variable *class size* may not have the same meaning for the teachers in all the classes having that value.

Postpositivist researchers attempt to avoid the problems created by quantification of features of the social environment by focusing their investigations on the study of individual cases and by making "thick" verbal descriptions of what they observe. If possible, they also record events on videotape or audiotape, which preserve the events in a fairly authentic manner for subsequent data analysis. The data analysis, too, is primarily verbal rather than statistical. The researcher searches for just the right words to represent the themes and patterns that she discovers in the data.

Analytic induction is involved in this process of discovery. **Analytic induction** means that the researcher searches through the data bit by bit and then infers that certain events or statements are instances of the same underlying theme or pattern. Thus, themes and patterns are induced from the data. In contrast, a deductive approach would involve identifying themes and patterns prior to data collection and then searching through the data for instances of them.

This verbal, visual, inductive approach corresponds to how people in general get to know a person or a situation. In our society, we ask lots of questions (a verbal technique) and get lots of answers (verbal data) in return. We also may take photographs or make a videotape for later reflection. Later, if someone asks what the person or situation we studied is like, we give a verbal description that attempts to be faithful to the original situation. If we are describing a person, we may recount things she said and stories she told about herself. If we have a photograph of the person, we may show it. As you will find in Chapter 14, case study research in education uses similar methods.

Though verbal and visual methods of representation and data analysis appear to avoid the problems with quantification noted above, they have several drawbacks. The words and form of speech that a researcher uses to interview an informant in the field setting being studied may not have the same meaning for the informant as for the researcher. Furthermore, one informant may use the same words as another informant, but with different meanings. In addition, although language is highly versatile, it may not represent all the important features of a social environment. For example, some social science researchers have theorized that certain important features of social life are invisible:

> "What is happening here?" may seem a trivial question at first glance. It is not trivial since everyday life is largely invisible to us (because of its familiarity and because of its contradictions, which people may not want to face). We do not realize the patterns in our actions as we perform them. The anthropologist Clyde Kluckhohn illustrated this point with an aphorism: "The fish would be the last creature to discover water."[33]

If it is true that certain features of the social environment are invisible to those who participate in it, then they, and the researcher as well, may lack the language to make them visible.

Mechanical, Interpretive, and Structural Views of Causation

Explanation is a major goal of scientific inquiry. As researchers, we want to know not only what happened, but why. Also, we want to understand the consequences of alterations in the social environment. That is, we want to understand the causal connections among social phenomena. For example, what factors cause some students to do well in reading or others to do poorly? What are the effects of learning to read well or poorly?

---

33. Erickson, *Qualitative methods,* p. 121.

Different researchers make different epistemological assumptions about the nature of causality, and these assumptions affect their approach to the study of cause-and-effect relationships among educational phenomena. Positivist researchers have what may be described as a "mechanical" view of causation. In Newtonian physics, mechanical causation involves force and matter. For example, when a pool player strikes a ball in a game of pool, this action creates a force that starts the ball rolling toward another ball. The force is transmitted into the second ball, which causes it to start rolling, too.

A similar view of causation permeates positivist research in the social sciences, if only metaphorically. For example, intelligence is thought to cause some students to do well at academic tasks and others to do poorly. Academic success is thought to affect an individual's choice of career and income. In this example, intelligence, academic success, career, and income are viewed somewhat like matter (i.e., real social objects) that can exert force on, or can be affected by the force of, other matter. The research designs that you will study in Chapters 10 through 13 are used by positivist researchers in a search for causal connections of this type. Some designs are more sophisticated than others in enabling a researcher to investigate multiple causes of a particular outcome (e.g., test performance) and the relative "weight" or "force" of each presumed cause.

Postpositivist researchers view causation much differently. They assume that people develop interpretations of the social environment that affect their subsequent actions. For example, postpositivist researchers do not view intelligence as a real entity that causes children to do well or poorly in school. Rather, the child and the people in his life (e.g., parents, teachers, classmates) develop interpretations of the child's intelligence that affect his subsequent school performance. Thus, our interpretations, and especially the intentions we form on the basis of these interpretations, are the true causal agents in the social environment. Therefore, to discover causal patterns in social phenomena, postpositivist researchers investigate individuals' interpretations of social reality.

Some positivist researchers examine individuals' interpretations as causal factors, but these causal factors are conceptualized as personality characteristics rather than as interpretations embedded in transitory, local events. For example, there are quantitative measures of *locus of control,* which refers to whether the individual believes that he personally controls his destiny or whether external forces do. A postpositivist would be more inclined to see these beliefs as situational perceptions: An individual might believe at one time and in one situation that he is in control of what is happening, whereas at another time and in another situation, he might see himself as a "victim" of external forces.

Another epistemological perspective on causation, called *scientific realism,* is beginning to influence research in the physical and social sciences.[34] **Scientific realism** is the philosophical doctrine that the real world consists of layers of causal structures, some of them hidden from view, that interact to produce effects that may or may not be observable. To explain what this means, we will refer again to the example of the pool game. There is more to the story than the first ball causing the second ball to move. To understand the full causal pattern at work, we need to know what the pool player was intending when she hit the first ball (e.g., her intentions about how hard to hit the first ball and in what direction), the idiosyncrasies of the pool table (e.g., perhaps the table has a slant that affects each ball's action), the idiosyncrasies of the cue stick, and so forth. All these factors are causal

---

34. For a more complete explanation of scientific realism, see: House, E. R. (1991). Realism in research. *Educational Researcher, 20*(6), 2–9, 25.

structures that can interact to produce the observed effect. The goal of inquiry, according to scientific realists, is to discover how these causal structures work.

As applied to education and other social science disciplines, scientific realism postulates that the real causes of human behavior are underlying causal structures. Discovering what these structures are is difficult because they may or may not have observable effects in particular situations. For example, suppose a teacher thinks about how to react to a student who is inattentive. He considers various alternatives and, in the end, rejects them all. There is no observable behavior that tells the researcher what causal entities might have been at work. Examples of possible entities might be: the teacher's decision-making process in such situations, the teacher's store of knowledge about consequences of past responses to student inattention, the interpersonal dynamics of this particular classroom, and the teacher's knowledge of the student's home environment and academic performance. Each of these is a potential causal structure that can interact with the other causal structures to produce an effect. Because of the complexity of possible interactions, researchers will not be able to make precise predictions of human behavior. They only will be able to determine trends and probabilities. The various research traditions that have developed in qualitative inquiry seem particularly well suited for discovering what these causal structures might be in educational environments. In fact, research traditions such as structuralism and cognitive psychology (both discussed in Chapter 15) make explicit reference to structures that underlie behavior and influence it.

To summarize, positivist epistemology assumes a mechanistic causality among social "objects." Postpositivist epistemology assumes that individuals' interpretations of situations cause them to take certain actions. Scientific realism assumes that there are multiple layers of causal structures, which are real objects that interact with each other to cause people to take certain actions or, in some cases, to take no action.

Quantitative and Qualitative Research

In the preceding discussion, we demonstrated that different researchers make different epistemological assumptions about the nature of scientific knowledge and how to acquire it. If you favor one set of assumptions, you will conduct one type of educational research. If you favor another set of assumptions, you will conduct a different type.

These two types of research have been given various labels. One set of labels is what we used in the preceding section: *positivist research* and *postpositivist research*.[35] These labels emphasize the epistemological assumptions of each type of research. **Positivist research** is grounded in the assumption that features of the social environment constitute an independent reality and are relatively constant across time and settings. Positivist researchers develop knowledge by collecting numerical data on observable behaviors of samples and then subjecting these data to numerical analysis. **Postpositivist research** is grounded in the assumption that features of the social environment are constructed as interpretations by individuals and that these interpretations tend to be transitory and situational. Postpositivist researchers develop knowledge by collecting primarily verbal

---

35. Egon Guba and Yvonna Lincoln use the term *postpositivism* to refer to a type of research that is grounded in positivist epistemology, but that has been modified in response to criticisms of its assumptions. Their term *constructivist research* corresponds to our use of the term *postpositivist*. See: Guba, E. G., & Lincoln, Y. S. (1994). Competing paradigms in qualitative research. In N. K. Denzin & Y. S. Lincoln (Eds.), *Handbook of qualitative research* (pp. 105–117). Thousand Oaks, CA: Sage.

data through the intensive study of cases and then subjecting these data to analytic induction.

While the terms *positivist research* and *postpositivist research* appear in the literature, it is more common to see the terms *quantitative research* and *qualitative research,* respectively, used to refer to the distinctions we made above. Because these terms are in common use, we employ them throughout the rest of the book, especially in Parts IV and V. These terms emphasize the fact that the two types of research differ in the nature of the data that are collected. **Quantitative research** is virtually synonymous with positivist research. For a definition of **qualitative research,** we refer to the one offered by Norman Denzin and Yvonna Lincoln:

> Qualitative research is multimethod in its focus, involving an interpretive, naturalistic approach to its subject matter. This means that qualitative researchers study things in their natural settings, attempting to make sense of, or interpret, phenomena in terms of the meanings people bring to them.[36]

Table 1.2 provides a further elaboration of the distinguishing characteristics of quantitative and qualitative research.

The label *interpretive research* sometimes is used instead of *qualitative research.* Erickson defines **interpretive research** as the study of the immediate and local meanings of social actions for the actors involved in them.[37] This definition is consistent with the definition of *qualitative research* offered above.

Another term that sometimes is used instead of *qualitative research* is *case study research.* This term emphasizes the fact that qualitative research focuses on the study of cases rather than of populations and samples. As we explain in Chapter 14, much of the methodology used in case studies evolved along lines suggested by postpositivist epistemology and therefore is consistent with the qualitative research traditions described in Chapter 15. However, some case study researchers subscribe to positivist epistemology. In Chapter 14, we note these exceptions to the general qualitative, postpositivist orientation of case study research.

Given that both quantitative research and qualitative research are conducted to investigate education, several questions arise. Is one approach better than the other? Do they complement each other in some way? Do they produce conflicting findings?

Some researchers believe that qualitative research is best used to discover themes and relationships at the case level, while quantitative research is best used to validate those themes and relationships in samples and populations. In this view, qualitative research plays a discovery role, while quantitative research plays a confirmatory role. Bruce Biddle and Donald Anderson endorse this use of the two approaches:

> [I]t is inappropriate to compare the relative efficacy of these two traditions [qualitative and quantitative research] since each has different purposes; broadly these are the generation of insights on the one hand and the testing of hypotheses on the other. Although advocates for discovery [qualitative researchers] decry the arid tautologies of confirmationists [quantitative researchers], and the latter express disdain for the sloppy subjectivism of discovery research, the two perspectives have complementary goals. We need them both.[38]

36. Denzin, N. K., & Lincoln, Y. S. (1994). Introduction: Entering the field of qualitative research. In N. K. Denzin & Y. S. Lincoln (Eds.), *Handbook of qualitative research* (pp. 1–17). Thousand Oaks, CA: Sage. Quote appears on p. 2.
37. Erickson, *Qualitative methods.*
38. Biddle, B. J., & Anderson, D. S. (1986). Theory, methods, knowledge, and research on teaching. In M. C. Wittrock (Ed.), *Handbook of research on teaching* (3rd ed., pp. 230–252). New York: Macmillan. Quote appears on p. 239.

TABLE 1.2

Differences between Quantitative and Qualitative Research

Quantitative Researchers	Qualitative Researchers
Assume an objective social reality.	Assume that social reality is constructed by the participants in it.
Assume that social reality is relatively constant across time and settings.	Assume that social reality is continuously constructed in local situations.
View causal relationships among social phenomena from a mechanistic perspective.	Assign human intentions a major role in explaining causal relationships among social phenomena.
Take an objective, detached stance toward research participants and their setting.	Become personally involved with research participants, to the point of sharing perspectives and assuming a caring attitude.
Study populations or samples that represent populations.	Study cases.
Study behavior and other observable phenomena.	Study the meanings that individuals create and other internal phenomena.
Study human behavior in natural or contrived settings.	Study human actions in natural settings.
Analyze social reality into variables.	Make holistic observations of the total context within which social action occurs.
Use preconceived concepts and theories to determine what data will be collected.	Discover concepts and theories after data have been collected.
Generate numerical data to represent the social environment.	Generate verbal and pictorial data to represent the social environment.
Use statistical methods to analyze data.	Use analytic induction to analyze data.
Use statistical inference procedures to generalize findings from a sample to a defined population.	Generalize case findings by searching for other similar cases.
Prepare impersonal, objective reports of research findings.	Prepare interpretive reports that reflect researchers' constructions of the data and an awareness that readers will form their own constructions from what is reported.

Example of Quantitative/Qualitative Research Complementarity

An example of these complementary goals is suggested by a study of international students conducted by Stephen Stoynoff.[39] English was the second language for the 77 students in his sample, and they had just started their freshman year at a U.S. university. Stoynoff conducted a quantitative research study to determine how well their scores on the

39. Stoynoff, S. J. (1990). English language proficiency and study strategies as determinants of academic success for international students in U.S. universities. *Dissertation Abstracts International*, 52(01), 97A. (UMI No. 9117569)

Test of English as a Foreign Language (TOEFL) and the Learning and Study Strategies Inventory (LASSI) predicted their first-term grade point average (GPA). The results indicated that TOEFL and LASSI scores yielded only modest predictions of GPA. Stoynoff then conducted qualitative case studies of selected members of his sample to determine whether other factors might be more important to the academic success of international students. Stoynoff made the following discovery from the case studies:

> The LASSI does not measure the compensatory methods that students use to help them negotiate the system. Interviews revealed that students sought social assistance from a wide variety of persons. They used tutors and roommates to explain and review homework. They borrowed lecture notes, previous tests, and papers from classmates and friends. They asked teachers for extra help. Students also learned to carefully select their courses based on the recommendations of others. These compensatory methods are not measured by the LASSI . . . [40]

These insights could be used to conceptualize what a "compensatory strategy" means. An instrument (e.g., a self-report inventory) then could be developed to measure the observable manifestations of this conceptualization. The instrument could be administered to a sample in a quantitative research study to test—and hopefully to confirm—Stoynoff's insights. Depending on the results, new qualitative studies might be done, yielding new insights that could be tested in subsequent quantitative studies.

This example illustrates how qualitative and quantitative research can complement each other by playing the respective roles of discovery and confirmation. Several assumptions must be satisfied, however, for this approach to work. One is that the social reality being studied must be stable. Otherwise, the findings of one study are not applicable to succeeding studies in the discovery-confirmation cycle. For example, in the case of Stoynoff's research, if subsequent cohorts of international students enter American universities with stronger language and study skills, compensatory strategies may no longer be a salient feature of their social reality. The second assumption is that it is possible to represent the concepts discovered in a qualitative study by a measure that yields numerical scores. If such a measure is not possible, quantitative research cannot be used for the purpose of confirmation.

Arguments against Quantitative/Qualitative Research Complementarity

Some researchers believe that quantitative and qualitative research are incompatible because they are based on different epistemological assumptions. They argue that it is not possible to believe that social reality exists independently of observers, while also believing that it is constructed by observers. Also, one cannot believe that social reality is constant in the sense of maintaining its identity across time and space, while also believing that it is being continuously created. Perhaps this is true, but it also is possible that neither view of social reality is correct. In other words, both views may rest on faulty epistemological assumptions.

Another possibility is that both views have some measure of truth. For example, you will find in Chapter 15 that researchers in some qualitative traditions, such as ethnomethodology, believe that individuals continuously create the social environment in which they participate, whereas researchers in other traditions, such as structuralism, believe there are stable causal structures that exist independently of individuals. Both views may be valid. Consider the case of language. Individuals constantly create new words, idioms, and styles of speech in the process of using language in speech and writing. More-

---

40. Ibid., p. 112.

over, individuals use language differently in different situations. At the same time, there is a constancy in language structures, such that the language of Shakespeare's plays is still more or less recognizable to us hundreds of years later. Furthermore, there is much evidence from cross-cultural research that language influences how we think and act. Could it have this influence if it were not an objective, independent reality?

At the level of epistemology, then, it is not clear that quantitative and qualitative research are necessarily incompatible or that one type has a greater claim to truth than the other. Both approaches have helped educational researchers make important discoveries. Over time, philosophers of science may have sufficient understanding to resolve the apparent contradictions in the current epistemological assumptions underlying qualitative and quantitative research.

If you are just starting to do research, you might wonder whether to conduct a quantitative or qualitative study. The research question you are posing and the state of research knowledge in your area of inquiry should dictate your decision. However, we have known individuals who chose to do a qualitative study because they feared or disliked the statistical analysis associated with quantitative research, or because they thought that the former is easier. In fact, qualitative research is difficult and time-consuming, and it requires the ability to communicate effectively in writing. Quantitative research studies, especially those that build on previous studies of the same or a similar problem, often are more straightforward and completed more quickly. Some effort might be required to understand the mathematical basis for the statistics you have chosen, but it also requires substantial effort to make sense of qualitative data and analyze them in a rigorous way. In short, we advise you to choose between quantitative or qualitative methodology on the basis of appropriateness for your research problem, not on the basis of supposed ease of use.

Postmodern Criticism of Scientific Inquiry

In the preceding sections, we explained how criticisms of the positivist approach to social science research resulted in a new set of epistemological assumptions, subsumed under the label *postpositivism*. We turn now to a different set of criticisms, which call into question all forms of social science. These criticisms are causing social science researchers to re-examine how they approach inquiry.

To understand the criticisms, we will start with a hypothetical research problem. Suppose a researcher observes informally that some teachers are able to keep their classrooms under better control than other teachers. Proceeding from this observation, the researcher decides to undertake a program of research to document the fact that some teachers are better classroom managers than others, to discover the techniques that the better managers use to keep their classes under control, and eventually to develop a theory of classroom management. (In actuality, many researchers already are involved in this program of research.)

Some critics would claim that the proposed research is biased by the researcher's values. To conduct the studies, the researcher will need to define what she means by the term *classroom control*. The researcher's definition might involve notions about students doing what the teacher expects them to do rather than acting on their own initiative, being quiet rather than unruly, avoiding nonacademic engagement with other students, and not giving the teacher reason to discipline them for misbehavior. If we take the analysis further, we probably will find that the researcher's definition of classroom control is grounded in more fundamental beliefs about what should be taught in the curriculum and what the goals of schooling should be.

✦ **Touchstone in Research**

Constas, M. A. (1998). The changing nature of educational research and a critique of postmodernism. *Educational Researcher, 27(2)*, 26–33.

What the researcher is able to discover about classroom management will be largely determined by her conception of *classroom control* and of other key concepts involved in her formulation of the research problem. If the researcher eventually develops a theory of classroom control, testing the theory will require empirical tests using data-collection measures that correspond to her definitions of *classroom control* and other constructs. Thus, research observations are *theory-laden,* as we explained earlier in the chapter. One really cannot collect data that are independent of the theory, as is required by the tenets of positivism.

Who is to say that the researcher's definition of classroom control is the right one? All we can say is that her definition reflects her particular values and experiences, and perhaps her personal biases as well. Other researchers with different values and experiences might develop other definitions, for example, that classroom control is the teacher's ability to create a situation in which students take responsibility for their own learning, engage in independent learning, and share with the teacher the task of creating reasonable classroom rules. This definition of classroom control will lead these researchers to undertake programs of research that will yield different findings about classroom management.

As critics see it, this situation creates a major problem for scientific inquiry. There is no absolute basis for determining the truth about classroom management. Scientific inquiry, which should be objective (i.e., unbiased), is revealed to be biased by the researcher's values. Thus, critics claim that researchers cannot conclude that one theory about classroom management is more valid than another theory because the research supporting each theory is inherently biased, albeit in different ways. If this is true, then, as the philosopher of science, Denis Phillips observes, we would have to give equal weight to, or at least tolerate, "Nazis, flat-earthers, astrologers, paranoics, Freudians, Skinnerians, and anyone else who ever strongly believed in a theory."[41] The physical and social science of past centuries can be dismissed or cherished, depending on our biases, as the work of "dead white males."

This critique of social science inquiry is prevalent among followers of a movement called *postmodernism.* Just as postpositivism can be seen as a reaction against positivism, so too can postmodernism be seen as a reaction against modernism. Modernism has its roots in the Enlightenment, which promoted the advancement of knowledge through scientific observation and the belief that, "under the seeming surface chaos of the world, of society, there exists a rationality, a basic truth that can be identified and harnessed for human good."[42] Positivist science is a prominent manifestation of the modernist spirit.

Postmodernism, which developed as a reaction against modernism, is a broad social and philosophical movement that questions the rationality of human action, the use of positivist epistemology, and any human endeavor (e.g., science) that claims a privileged position with respect to the search for truth or that claims progress in the search for truth. Laurel Richardson put the matter this way:

> The core of postmodernism is the *doubt* that any method or theory, discourse or genre, tradition or novelty, has a universal and general claim as the "right" or the privileged form of authoritative knowledge. Postmodernism *suspects* all truth claims of masking and serving particular interests in local, cultural, and political struggle.[43]

41. Phillips, *Philosophy, science, and social inquiry,* p. 89.
42. Graham, E., Doherty, J., & Malek, M. (1992). Introduction: The context and language of postmodernism. In Doherty, J., Graham, E., & Malek, M. (Eds.), *Postmodernism and the social sciences* (pp. 1–23). Basingstoke, England: Macmillan. Quote appears on p. 8.
43. Richardson, L. (1994). Writing: A method of inquiry. In N. K. Denzin & Y. S. Lincoln (Eds.), *Handbook of qualitative research* (pp. 516–529). Thousand Oaks, CA: Sage. Quote appears on p. 517.

Thus, postmodernists not only would question the possibility that social scientists could prove that Theory X is valid and Theory Y is not, but they would question whether social science inquiry into Theory X and Theory Y is superior to any other form of inquiry, such as literary studies or astrology. In postmodern thinking, too, all cultures have equal claim to the truth of things. According to postmodernists, the search for truth should be replaced by a "conversation" among "many voices."[44]

Response to Postmodern Criticism

The postmodern critique of scientific inquiry has caused social science researchers, including educational researchers, to rethink their claims to authority, especially in comparison to other forms of inquiry into the human condition, such as art and literature. Their analyses suggest that research in education and other social science disciplines has several characteristics that establish its claim to authority and that distinguish it from other forms of inquiry. The following is a list of those characteristics.

1. *The creation of concepts and procedures that are shared and publicly accessible.* Social science researchers have developed specialized concepts (e.g., validity and reliability) and procedures (e.g., random assignment of individuals to groups in experiments) to help them conduct investigations of high quality. These concepts and procedures are embodied in terminology that allows researchers to communicate with each other and their various constituencies. Ambiguities in existing terms are noted and clarified. New terms come into being to describe new concepts and procedures. This terminology is defined formally in dictionaries, in textbooks such as the one you are reading, and in other publications.[45] The professional community of researchers takes on this responsibility for clarifying, updating, and making public their terminology.

Everyone is free to learn and use this terminology and the concepts and procedures it embodies. There are no secret societies of researchers (at least none that we know of!), and no special initiation is required for access to the research process. Anyone is free to conduct scientific inquiry, as evidenced by the fact that research manuscripts submitted to journals for publication are judged "blind," meaning that reviewers do not have access to the names of the authors or other identifying information about them. In this way, no researcher is privileged over another. Of course, there are power struggles in the arenas of funding and publicity for research findings, but it seems highly unlikely that important theories and findings could be suppressed over the long term.

2. *The replicability of findings.* When researchers publish their findings, they also must make public the procedures by which these findings were obtained. Otherwise, the results will not be published. By making their procedures public, researchers enable other researchers to conduct replication studies to determine whether the use of the same or similar procedures as the original researcher will yield the same results. In fact, some researchers conduct their own replication studies, and only publish the findings if their original findings are replicated. We discuss replication as a research strategy further in Chapter 2.

3. *The refutability of knowledge claims.* Karl Popper proposed a standard for testing knowledge claims that has won general acceptance among social science researchers.[46] Popper, a philosopher of science, argued that science advances by submitting its knowledge claims (theories, predictions, hunches) to empirical tests that allow for their refutation.

44. Doherty, Graham, & Malek, *Postmodernism and the social sciences,* pp. 17–18.
45. Examples of such dictionaries are: Coleman, A. M. (2001). *A dictionary of psychology.* Oxford: Oxford University Press; Vogt, W. P. (1995). *Dictionary of statistics and methodology* (2nd ed.). Thousand Oaks, CA: Sage.
46. Popper, K. (1968). *Conjectures and refutations.* New York: Harper.

As we explained earlier in the chapter, a researcher tests a theory by formulating a hypothesis and then collecting data relating to the hypothesis. If the data are inconsistent with the hypothesis, we can say that the hypothesis is refuted. As a result, the theory from which the hypothesis was derived must be abandoned or modified to accommodate the negative findings. If the data are consistent with the hypothesis, we can conclude that the theory is supported, but not that it is correct. The reason is that another empirical test of the theory may yet refute it. In Popper's view of science, then, we can say that the flat-earth theory has proved to be wrong, but not that the round-earth theory has proved to be correct. We can say only that this theory has thus far withstood all attempts to disprove it.

The refutation test of knowledge claims provides an indirect method for determining whether Theory X is more valid than Theory Y. While the concepts and methods of observation used to test each theory reflect the values implicit in the theory, each theory nonetheless can be falsified by empirical tests of hypotheses derived from the theory. In other words, data-collection instruments are not so value-laden that they are incapable of falsifying the theory from which the instruments were derived. Thus, Theory X or Theory Y can be falsified. If both theories survive efforts to refute them, they can co-exist as alternative explanations of social reality. For example, both behaviorist and cognitive theories of human behavior have a large body of empirical evidence to support them, and so both continue to survive and to influence educational practice. In fact, there has been cross-fertilization between the two theories. Some researchers call themselves *cognitive behaviorists.*

The refutation test of knowledge claims is more rigorous than the way we test everyday knowledge claims. For example, suppose that a university professor decides one term to let his students call him at home or the office for appointments rather than only letting them contact him during posted office hours. The professor notices that the students' evaluations of his course are higher than usual for that term. From this observation, he claims to have proved that allowing students greater access to a professor will cause students to evaluate the professor's instruction more positively. The "proof" rests on shaky grounds, however, because the professor has not demonstrated that all instances of increased access will produce this result. It is possible that we can find other professors, or other occasions when that professor teaches, where the connection between access and improved evaluations does not hold.

Superstitious thinking and fields of knowledge such as astrology are susceptible to this flaw in reasoning. Suppose a person uses her spouse's birthday to select numbers for a lottery ticket, and she wins. From this event she concludes that if she selects numbers from the birthday of her spouse or other family members, she will increase her chances of winning the lottery in the future. Similarly, astrologists may conclude that because certain things have happened to someone born on a certain day, these things are likely to happen to other people born on that day. In other words, they make an observation first and then make a broad knowledge claim. In contrast, researchers who follow Popper's logic make a knowledge claim first and then test it by making observations. The tests are cautious in that contrary data can disprove the knowledge claim, but confirmatory data do not prove it. Instead, if the data are confirmatory, we conclude that the knowledge claim has withstood efforts to refute it.

4. *Control for errors and biases.* Researchers acknowledge the propensity for error and bias in data collection. Thus, they design their studies to minimize the influence of such factors. For example, in making quantitative observations, researchers attempt to use multiple observers and to train them carefully in the system for collecting data on observational variables. Statistical procedures are available for estimating the observers' accuracy.

While observations rarely are completely accurate, they usually are accurate enough for research purposes. With respect to qualitative data, case study researchers typically *triangulate* their data from one method of observation by seeking corroboration from other types of data that they have collected. In this respect, Biddle and Anderson make an important distinction between *case studies* and *case stories:*

> The former [case study] is an inquiry conducted according to rules of evidence. It is rigorous in its observations. Its objective is not to confirm the investigator's commitments but to investigate a problem. The latter [case story] is designed to illustrate conclusions to which the author is already committed.[47]

In the same vein, Thomas Good and Joel Levin criticize the recent emphasis on personal story and personal voice as a self-sufficient type of knowledge for improving education:

> . . . when story is used to supplant research, theory, and empirical evidence, rather than to supplement it, we have serious reservations about its value. . . . Some stories are knowingly distorted and used for self-justification and self-enhancement.[48]

It is important to note that Good and Levin do not reject story and voice entirely. They can provide valuable perspective and insights when considered in relation to relevant research and theory.

The procedures we describe in Chapter 14 are designed to help you do case study research rather than tell case stories. Similarly, the procedures we describe for other research designs and approaches are primarily intended to minimize researcher errors and biases.

5. *Boundedness of knowledge claims.* Researchers have developed procedures to ensure that they do not generalize their knowledge claims beyond what can be supported by their empirical findings. These procedures involve sampling logic, which is explained in Chapter 6. For example, quantitative researchers typically define a population (e.g., fifth-grade teachers in urban school systems) and study a sample that is representative of the population. Findings based on data collected from the sample are generalized only to that population. The amount of possible error in the generalizations is estimated in a manner similar to what we read about in national polls (e.g., "This candidate is viewed positively by 62 percent of American voters, with a ± 6 percent margin of error"). The generalization of knowledge claims beyond the defined population are considered speculative until supported by evidence from new studies involving other populations.

6. *A moral commitment to progressive discourse.* Carl Bereiter observed that, "what makes science special is that scientists have done a better job than most other groups of practicing certain virtues."[49] These virtues involve a commitment to **progressive discourse,** which means that anyone at any time can offer a criticism about a particular research study or research methodology, and if it proves to have merit, that criticism is listened to and accommodated. The process of criticism, debate, and resolution assumes that researchers have made a moral commitment to listen to each other, remain open to new research findings, and change their views when it is appropriate to do so. In this way, the research community progresses in its understanding of the phenomena that are within its scope of inquiry.

---

47. Biddle and Anderson, *Theory, methods, knowledge*, p. 238.
48. Good, T. L., & Levin, J. R. (2001). Educational psychology yesterday, today, and tomorrow: Debate and direction in an evolving field. *Educational Psychologist, 36*, 69–72. Quote appears on pp. 69–70.
49. Bereiter, C. (1994). Implications of postmodernism for science, or, science as progressive discourse. *Educational Psychologist, 29*, 3–12. Quote appears on p. 6.

If you examine issues of *Educational Researcher, American Educational Research Journal,* and *Review of Educational Research,* you will find many examples of critical commentaries on research methodology, research epistemology, and reports of research findings. (These three journals are official publications of the American Educational Research Association.) These commentaries have a cumulative impact on the educational research enterprise, advancing our understanding both of what educational researchers are discovering and how they are discovering it.

The preceding analysis demonstrates that educational research and other social science disciplines make no claims about an absolute, objective standard of truth. (Some researchers may think differently, but they are exceptions.) At the same time, the social sciences do lay claim to a special sort of authority—the authority that derives from its practice of self-criticism, acknowledgement of the refutability of knowledge claims, and the submission of each researcher's findings to replication tests by other researchers. Through the exercise of this authority, educational researchers also make claim to progress of a certain sort. That progress involves successively more comprehensive understandings of educational phenomena, based on the open discussion and resolution of issues and the development of theories that have withstood or have been modified in response to refutability tests.

Postmodernists make a strong case in arguing that other forms of inquiry, such as literature and the arts, also may lay claim to authority. In fact, some educational researchers have made strong cases for literature and art as forms of inquiry.[50] However, they generally do not argue that literature and art are superior to social science inquiry, only different. You can gain some insight into the differences for yourself if you compare literature and art with each of the six characteristics of social science inquiry described above. For example, writers and artists do not subject their "knowledge claims" to the tests of refutability that social scientists subject their knowledge claims to. While postmodernists may claim that "anything goes," all forms of inquiry do not "go" the same way or justify their authority in the same way.

Learning How to Do Educational Research

The purpose of this chapter is to help you understand *why* educational research is worth doing. The following chapters describe *how* to do educational research. However, "book knowledge" of these tools and concepts will not turn you into a competent researcher. To achieve this goal, it is essential that you acquire experience both in reading research reports and in doing your own research. As you read the chapters of this book, we recommend that you also read published research studies in your areas of interest in order to put "flesh and blood" on the ideas that we present. Chapter 4 explains how the research literature is organized and how to access it to identify research studies on particular topics.

As for learning how to do research, the best way—perhaps the only way—is to apprentice yourself to an experienced researcher. You might identify such an individual among the faculty of a university school of education or a research institute. Researchers generally are happy to advise others on their research projects, and they are likely to welcome novices willing to volunteer as assistants on their projects. In addition, you can learn from the larger community of educational researchers by joining their professional association, which is the American Educational Research Association (AERA) and its various di-

50. For example, see: Eisner, E. W. (1979). *The educational imagination: On the design and evaluation of school programs.* New York: Macmillan; Greene, M. (1988). Qualitative research and the uses of literature. In R. R. Sherman & R. B. Webb (Eds.), *Qualitative research in education: Focus and methods* (pp. 175–189). London: Falmer.

visions and special interest groups.[51] Another major association is the American Psychological Association (APA) and its Division 15 (Educational Psychology).[52]

In reading this text, you should reflect on your personal orientation to the various research methods presented in it. You may find that you are more sympathetic to the perspectives and methods of quantitative research, or that your bent is toward qualitative research. It is perfectly acceptable to specialize in a particular approach to research. Most educational researchers do so. At the same time, it is important to become familiar with the full range of research approaches. This is because you will find that when you study a particular problem in education, different researchers are likely to have used different approaches to shed light on it.

✔ SELF-CHECK TEST

Circle the correct answer to each of the following questions.
An answer key is provided at the back of the book.

1. Educational research findings tend not to affect practice directly because
   a. research findings are too neutral.
   b. research findings derive almost entirely from basic research.
   c. policy makers tend to see no value in research findings.
   d. policy makers view research findings as only one basis for decision making.

2. A postpositivist researcher would view the concept of learning disorder as
   a. generalizable across cultures.
   b. theory-free.
   c. value-laden.
   d. value-free.

3. The use of standardized tests, detachment from the persons being studied, and interest in finding general laws are characteristics of
   a. postpositivist research.
   b. positivist research.
   c. interpretive research.
   d. postmodern research.

4. The statement, "Aptitude will be measured by the quantitative scale of the Scholastic Aptitude Test (SAT)," is an example of
   a. a theoretical law.
   b. an operationally defined construct.
   c. a constitutively defined construct.
   d. a hypothesis.

5. A study that tested a hypothesis derived from a theory about how brain chemistry affects short-term memory would be an example of
   a. basic research.
   b. applied research.
   c. postpositivist research.
   d. descriptive research.

6. Case study findings
   a. have no generalizability.
   b. can be generalized to the defined population that they represent.
   c. can be generalized to a population defined by the researcher, but not to a population defined by readers of the research report.
   d. can be generalized to other similar cases.

7. Postpositivist researchers would question the practice of quantification in the social sciences on the grounds that
   a. quantifiable aspects of social phenomena tend to be unimportant.
   b. numerical values of a variable can have different meanings for different individuals.
   c. quantification of social phenomena assumes that these phenomena are constant across time and settings.
   d. all of the above.

51. The Web home page for AERA is www.aera.net
52. The Web home page for APA is www.apa.org

8. Of the following claims, the one that postmodernists most likely would endorse is that
  a. scientific research is a more valid form of inquiry than literature for understanding the human condition.
  b. scientific research is not a more valid form of inquiry than literature for understanding the human condition.
  c. collaboration by scientists and artists will yield genuine progress in understanding the human condition.
  d. non-Western cultures are more likely to advance understanding of the human condition because they are not grounded in positivist assumptions.

9. According to the refutability standard proposed by Karl Popper, knowledge claims
  a. can be disproved, but not proved.
  b. can be proved, but not disproved.
  c. can be proved only by hypothesis-testing.
  d. can be proved or disproved, but only if the knowledge claim is not value-laden.

10. Scientific realists believe that
  a. interpretations are the primary causal agent in social reality.
  b. social reality consists of layers of causal structures.
  c. Newtonian physics provides the best model for understanding causation in social reality.
  d. causation is an unnecessary concept in developing theories of social behavior.

PART II

◆ Planning a Research Study

Reduced to its most essential elements, research is a process of identifying something unknown and then collecting data to make it known. Chapter 2 helps you with the first step of that process: identifying something unknown that, if investigated, would contribute significantly to the knowledge base of education. We show you how to frame the something unknown, called a *research problem,* as an explicit set of research hypotheses, questions, or objectives that you will investigate.

After identifying a research problem, you will need to develop a plan for investigating it. The plan should cover such matters as selection of a sample or case, administration of tests or other measures, and choice of statistics for data analysis. If you are doing the study as a requirement for an advanced degree, the plan must be written as a formal research proposal and submitted to your thesis or dissertation committee for its approval. Chapter 2 shows you how to write the proposal and how to use it as the basis for writing a final report—a thesis, a dissertation, a journal article, or a professional paper—of the completed study.

You have a legal and ethical obligation to use certain procedures to ensure that the persons whom you plan to study are protected from physical and psychological harm. Chapter 3 describes these procedures, which must be planned and approved before you start collecting data. It also describes steps you can take to solicit and maintain the cooperation of research participants and the broader community once the study is underway.

Educational researchers contribute their findings to build a collective knowledge base that informs professional practice and theory development. Chapter 4 shows you how to conduct a comprehensive review of the literature about a research problem in order to determine the existing knowledge base and unresolved issues. The findings of the literature review will constitute a significant part of your research proposal.

CHAPTER 2

✦ Developing a Research Proposal

OVERVIEW

Careful planning is the key to conducting a worthwhile, sound research study. In this chapter, we describe how to identify a research problem that is likely to contribute to knowledge about education, and how to develop the problem into a detailed proposal that will be accepted by your thesis or dissertation committee, a funding agency, or other reviewers. We also illustrate how a well-written proposal serves as the initial draft of several chapters of a thesis or dissertation. Finally, we explain how to report a completed study as a journal article or paper at a professional meeting.

OBJECTIVES

After studying this chapter, you should be able to

1. Distinguish between the desire to contribute to personal knowledge and the desire to contribute to research knowledge in selecting a problem for a research project.
2. Describe the characteristics of a theory-based research project.
3. Describe possible reasons for doing a study that replicates and extends previous research.
4. Explain the advantages of doing a thesis or dissertation study as part of a team project.
5. List the sections of a typical research proposal, and describe the topics included in each section.
6. Distinguish between directional hypotheses, null hypotheses, research questions, research objectives, and statements of purpose in a proposal.
7. Explain why it is advantageous to conduct a pilot study prior to a full-scale, formal study.
8. List the chapters of a typical thesis or dissertation, and describe the topics covered in each chapter.
9. State the factors involved in selecting a journal to which to submit your research study for publication.
10. Explain why and how one might submit a research paper for presentation at a professional meeting.

Introduction

Conducting a research study is a major endeavor. Five stages typically are involved in completing it.

Stage 1: Identifying a significant research problem. Problems to study may come readily to mind, but they may not be ones that contribute significantly to research knowledge or to the improvement of practice. Another possibility is that the problem you identify is significant, but you lack the resources or expertise necessary to study it. In the next section of this chapter, we describe several methods for identifying a research problem that is both significant and feasible to study.

Stage 2: Writing a research proposal. The purpose of a research proposal is to describe the problem you wish to study and how you plan to study it. This process compels you to think through and record on paper your research design (e.g., conducting an experiment or doing a case study) and the procedures that you will use to select a sample, collect data, and analyze the data. It is much easier to find flaws in a written proposal and correct them than it is to discover and correct flaws after you start collecting data. Also, university and college faculty generally require you to write a proposal for thesis or dissertation research. They must approve the proposal before you can start collecting data. If you are seeking financial support from a funding agency, a formal proposal almost certainly will be required. Much of this chapter concerns the proposal-writing process.

Stage 3: Conducting a pilot study. The purpose of a pilot study is to develop and try out data-collection methods and other procedures (e.g., training procedures to be used in an experiment). Problems can be identified and solved now more easily than when the main study is underway. We describe the features of a pilot study later in the chapter.

Stage 4: Conducting the main study. In the main study, you collect and analyze the actual data that you will report in your dissertation or other document. This process is challenging, but you should be able to complete it successfully if you have prepared a good research proposal, conducted a pilot study, and revised the proposal based on what you have learned from this work.

Stage 5: Preparing a report. If you are a graduate student, this report most likely will constitute your master's thesis or doctoral dissertation. (Hereafter, we refer to both types of reports as *dissertations* because they are quite similar.) In addition, you may wish to report your findings in a journal article or in a presentation at a professional meeting. We describe how to prepare these reports at the end of the chapter.

Depending upon the study, the five stages that we delineated above may overlap, or might occur in a different order. For example, many qualitative studies involve an emergent research design: Some data are collected (the fourth stage), and analyses of these data are used to further develop the proposal (the second stage). Another variation is for a pilot study (third stage) to be done prior to writing the research proposal (second stage), or not at all.

Reading this chapter alone will not prepare you to identify your research problem and write a proposal. You first will need to develop an understanding of the research methods and designs covered in this book. Studying this chapter will contribute to this understanding because it provides an overview—an advance organizer, as it were—for the entire educational research enterprise.

Identifying a Research Problem

The imagination and insight that goes into defining the research problem usually determines the ultimate value of a research study more than any other factor. For this reason, you should devote a substantial amount of time to selecting the research problem that you will investigate in your dissertation study. It is entirely reasonable to spend several months or longer thinking about potential problems to study, talking to others about them, and reviewing relevant literature before you reach closure on your research problem and the methods for studying it.

The very process of seeking a research problem to study is an important step in your professional development. At the outset, you may not be able to generate any problems, or you may conclude from your initial exploration of the literature that research has already solved all the problems in education. Your first ideas for research may appear naive after you study the sophisticated formulations of experienced researchers. As you continue reading, though, your own thinking will become more sophisticated, and the problems you frame for study will be better grounded in the existing knowledge base and more likely to advance it.

One reason that students often seize upon a trivial or vague research problem is that they spend too long a time in their graduate program before starting the search for a suitable research problem. They have had years of experience in taking courses; thus the coursework involved in graduate school is familiar, and they are confident that they can complete it successfully. In contrast, the research training component of a graduate program generally is new and often difficult. In fact, every university has a lengthy list of "all-buts," or as they sometimes are called, *Ab.D*s—students who have completed "All but Dissertation." To avoid being an "all-but," you should gain some insight into research and begin your search for a suitable problem as soon as possible after starting graduate work, even if you do not plan to carry out the study until after you finish your coursework and comprehensive examinations.

In looking for a research problem, bear in mind some of the possible benefits of conducting your research study to prepare you for your profession. Because of the extensive reading you must do for your study, you will be building a sizable fund of knowledge. Therefore, it makes sense to develop a research study in an area that is directly related to your professional goals. For example, if you are attracted to staff development as a possible career, you might consider identifying a research problem having to do with this aspect of educational practice. Also, consider the fact that if you conduct a study on a significant problem, you may be able to publish your findings in a refereed journal or present them at a professional meeting. These contributions to the field will enhance your professional status and your qualifications for position openings.

Reading the Research Literature

Some beginning researchers select a problem to study simply because it is of interest to them and they want to learn more about it. They might consider these reasons to be sufficient justification for doing the study. However, there is another criterion to consider: the likely contribution of the proposed study to research knowledge.

Research knowledge is not the same thing as personal knowledge. Both types of knowledge are valuable, but they serve different purposes and must satisfy different standards. Research knowledge is represented in journals, books, and other publications that are judged to be reputable by professional researchers, including the professors who are charged with the responsibility of approving dissertations. Also, research knowledge is cumulative, in the sense that readers of research are interested in determining how a given study relates to and contributes to what is already known about the problem that was studied. Therefore, if a researcher grounds her study only in her personal interests and goals and ignores the research literature, the "gatekeepers" (e.g., professors on dissertation committees and journal editors) will not be able to judge whether and how the study contributes to research knowledge.

It is perfectly acceptable to start the process of identifying a research problem by examining your personal interests and goals. Once you have done so, though, you must make an extensive study of the literature. In the process, you should ask and answer such questions as, Has research on this problem been conducted previously? If so, what has been learned? What more can I contribute to what is already known? Are the methods that I intend to use worse than, as good as, or better than the methods used by other researchers? Is my research problem significant, or are there more compelling research problems that should be addressed?

Prior to studying the literature in a problem area that interests you, you will need to know how the educational literature is organized and how to access it. Chapter 4 provides this information. For example, we list various sources of existing reviews of the literature. If you can locate a published review in your area of interest, it will help you develop an initial understanding of what types of research have been done and how the resulting knowledge is organized. We also list indexes that will help you identify relevant primary sources, that is, reports of research and of theory development by the original investigators.

In reading the literature, keep in mind that researchers often mention problems in need of investigation at the end of their reports. For example, consider these statements in published research articles:

1. From a study to determine whether motivational goals (self-referenced learning goals versus performance goals involving comparison with others) influenced the participation and performance of low-achieving elementary-school students during collaborative problem solving with a high-achieving partner:

    . . . this study took place in an experimental setting outside of the students' regular classrooms over a brief period of time. The students worked on school-like mathematical tasks with partners with whom they were familiar; however, they did this in the presence of a stranger (the researcher) and a video camera. Although the observed results of this study are suggestive, researchers should be cautious about generalizing our findings to the classroom. Follow-up studies are needed to establish whether achievement goals alone would be powerful enough to mediate learning from peers over an extended period of time in naturalistic classroom studies.[1]

2. From a study of the effectiveness of women's studies (WS) classes in developing university students' understanding and acceptance of diverse groups, commitment to working for social justice, and personal confidence:

    One final limitation of this study was that other types of classes (e.g., ethnic studies) that are high in social relevance and have aims similar to those of WS were not assessed. More research is needed to evaluate the pedagogic practices and student impact of such related classes and to consider the extent to which WS may provide unique academic and personal benefits not found elsewhere in the campus curriculum.[2]

3. From a study of the validity and reliability of the Stages of Concerns Questionnaire (SoCQ) that was given to Hong Kong teachers to assess their concerns about implementing a new, large-scale curriculum program in their country:

    The SoC construct might be culture bound and innovation specific. We do not intend to present our five-stage model as *the* model of teacher concerns about innovations. Instead,

1. Gabriele, A. J., & Montecinos, C. (2001). Collaborating with a skilled peer: The influence of achievement goals and perceptions of partners' competence on the participation and learning of low-achieving students. *Journal of Experimental Education, 69,* 152–178. Quote appears on p. 174.
2. Stake, J. E., & Hoffman, F. L. (2001). Changes in student social attitudes, activism, and personal confidence in higher education: The role of women's studies. *American Educational Research Journal, 38,* 411–436. Quote appears on p. 434.

we hope that our findings stimulate researchers to give greater attention to the psycho-metric and conceptual issues when they use SoCQ in future investigations. It is worth-while to replicate the present study in other countries to detect any cultural differences. However, there is a major limitation of our study; that is, the two random halves of teach-ers were not independent because they had come from the same sample and were sub-jected to the same errors and biases. Researchers should try to improve this aspect of the research in future designs.[3]

Any one of these statements can be the stimulus for a research study. Some of our students have identified their idea for a dissertation project by coming across just such a statement in the course of reading the literature in their area of interest. Furthermore, by reading the literature, they have obtained excellent ideas for suitable research designs and procedures to address the problem that they selected for study.

Doing Theory-Based Research

An approach that is likely to produce an outstanding research study is to formulate a re-search problem that will test a theory that you or someone else developed. As we explained in Chapter 1, a theory is an explanation of observed events in terms of constructs and laws that specify how the constructs are related to each other. When a construct is thought of as a characteristic that can vary in quantity or quality, it is called a *variable*.

Theory-based research usually consists of testing a hypothesis (a speculation about the relationship between two or more variables) that is derived from a theory. A **hypothe-sis** is a testable prediction about observable phenomena that is based on a theory's con-structs and their presumed relationships.

Example of Theory-Based Research

Roger Goddard, Scott Sweetland, and Wayne Hoy used theory to guide their research on factors affecting student achievement in urban elementary schools.[4] The primary factor of interest was academic emphasis, which they defined as "the extent to which the school is driven by a quest for academic excellence."[5] The researchers drew upon social cognitive theory to predict how a school's level of academic emphasis would affect students' acade-mic achievement.[6]

Essentially, social cognitive theory seeks to explain how particular factors shape indi-vidual and group perceptions, and how these perceptions, in turn, shape individual and group behavior. An important construct in the theory is *agency*, which refers to the ten-dency of individuals to pursue a course of action to achieve particular goals. For example, a school principal might have a sense of agency that drives her to pursue academic excel-lence. According to social cognitive theory, certain kinds of experiences can influence the principal's perceptions and thereby change her sense of agency and self-efficacy. Goodard, Sweetland, and Hoy use the example of a school staff that perceives another school experi-encing success with a program for at-risk students. The staff can learn vicariously from this experience and can engage in self-regulation by changing their previous practices to those of the successful program. (Vicarious learning and self-regulation are central constructs of

---

3. Cheung, D., Hattie, J., & Ng, D. (2001). Reexamining the Stages of Concern Questionnaire: A test of alternative models. *Journal of Educational Research, 94,* 226–236. Quote appears on p. 236.
4. Goddard, R. D., Sweetland, S. R., & Hoy, W. K. (2000). Academic emphasis of urban elementary schools and stu-dent achievement in reading and mathematics: A multilevel analysis. *Educational Administration Quarterly, 36,* 683–702.
5. Ibid., p. 686.
6. Bandura, A. (1986). *Social foundations of thought and action: A social cognitive theory.* Englewood Cliffs, NJ: Prentice Hall.

social cognitive theory.) These perceptual and behavioral changes, in turn, can produce improvements in students' academic achievement.

Reasoning in this way from social cognitive theory, the researchers hypothesized that teachers' perceptions of school norms and expectations involving academic emphasis will influence their work behavior and, subsequently, student learning. In the researchers' own words: " . . . we hypothesize that the academic emphasis of a school is positively associated with differences between schools in student-level achievement in both reading and mathematics."[7] They tested the hypothesis with a sample of 45 elementary schools. Teachers completed a measure of academic emphasis, and the school district provided data on student achievement in mathematics and reading.

As hypothesized, Goddard, Sweetland, and Hoy found that academic emphasis was a significant predictor of between-school differences in student achievement in both mathematics and reading. The findings also provided support for social cognitive theory:

> The results provide initial support for Bandura's (1986, 1997) suggestion that the concepts and assumptions of social cognitive theory can be extended to organizations and are useful in examining school outcomes. We hasten to add that further testing of social cognitive theory in the schools is needed, but the current results are encouraging because our hypothesis was driven by this theory. We hope that the identification of the theoretical underpinnings of academic emphasis illuminates pathways to future research on school improvement and that school leaders can apply these ideas to make their schools better places for students to learn.[8]

Thus, a hypothesis derived from theory guided the design of a research study, the findings of which both improved educators' understanding of factors that improve student learning and strengthened the theory.

It is worth noting that the researchers stated their findings *supported* social cognitive theory, not *proved* it. Even if a number of studies produce evidence supporting a theory and no disconfirming evidence is found, a theory is never proved. As we explained in Chapter 1, researchers generally accept the argument of Karl Popper (a philosopher of science) that the possibility of disconfirming evidence in the future always exists. On the other hand, one study that produces disconfirming evidence calls for revision or rejection of the theory.[9]

The cognitive dissonance experiment described above was a quantitative research study that tested a previously developed theory. In other words, the theory was developed first, and then a study was designed to test it. The opposite more often is true in qualitative research. Many qualitative studies are done to discover theory. The approach sometimes is called *grounded theory* because the researcher starts by collecting data and then searches for theoretical constructs, themes, and patterns that are "grounded" in the theory. We describe this type of theory-based research in Chapter 14.

Advantages of Theory-Based Research

Theory-based research on educational phenomena has several advantages, irrespective of whether it involves the use of quantitative or qualitative methods. First, theory-based research usually yields important findings. Without a theory as the starting or end point, many studies address trivial questions or contribute nothing to the slow accumulation of knowledge needed for the advancement of a science of education. Second, a theory can provide a rational basis for explaining or interpreting the results of research. Studies

---

7. Goddard et al., p. 690.
8. Ibid., p. 699.
9. For a discussion of how scientific theory is developed and confirmed, see: Krathwohl, D. R. (1985). *Social and behavioral science research.* San Francisco: Jossey-Bass.

without a theoretical foundation often produce results that the investigator is at a loss to explain. Such studies still can help in the development of a theory, but their impact on our understanding of the phenomena being studied is much less clear and immediate than that of research that is firmly based on existing theory or that discovers theory.

Replicating and Extending Previous Research

Another strategy for identifying a research problem is to replicate and extend the study of a problem that was investigated by other researchers. In the physical sciences, important studies always are replicated before their findings are accepted by the scientific community. The need for replication is even more critical in education and other social science disciplines because studies often have weaknesses in methodology or very limited generalizability. Therefore, you might be able to make a valuable contribution by repeating, and improving upon, a research study that other researchers conducted.

We do not advocate a literal replication as a project for your dissertation, however. Dissertation committees generally expect students to carry out a research study that is original in some respect. Therefore, you should extend the study to be replicated in some significant way. The following are types of extensions that are likely to be worthwhile:

1. *To check the findings of a "breakthrough" study.* Occasionally a study is reported that produces new and surprising evidence, that reports findings which conflict with previous research, or that challenges a generally accepted theory. Research involving replication of such studies is useful because it helps support or disconfirm the validity of their findings and interpretations. If supported by replication, such studies often open up a new area of investigation or have a major impact upon educational practice.

An example of a breakthrough study that had a major impact on the educational community is one conducted by David Wiley and Annegret Harnischfeger.[10] They concluded from their data analyses that lengthening the school year by 10 days, increasing the school day to six hours, and raising the average daily attendance to 95 percent would bring about major achievement gains, including a 65 percent gain in reading comprehension and a 34 percent gain in mathematics achievement. Considerable controversy developed over the validity of Wiley and Harnischfeger's findings, thus creating an ideal situation for replication research. One such replication study was conducted by A. Daniels and E. Haller.[11] Daniels and Haller's analysis of data from one high school over a 10-year period suggested that students' mathematics achievement was negatively affected by the school's deliberate reduction in the amount of available classroom time, but that English achievement was not similarly affected.

2. *To check the validity of research findings across different populations.* The typical research study in education is carried out with a small sample of individuals representing a limited population. Without replication, the degree to which the findings from that study apply to other populations cannot be determined. For example, Charles Fisher and his colleagues studied the relationship between specific teacher behaviors and the achievement of second- and fifth-grade students in mathematics and reading.[12] These researchers found that teachers' use of academic monitoring was negatively related to reading achievement but positively related to mathematics achievement. They also found several teaching be-

---

10. Wiley, D. E., & Harnischfeger, A. (1974). Explosion of a myth: Quantity of schooling and exposure to instruction: major educational vehicles. *Educational Researcher, 3*(4), 7–12.

11. Daniels, A. H., & Haller, E. J. (1981). Exposure to instruction, surplus time, and student achievement: A local replication of the Harnischfeger and Wiley research. *Educational Administration Quarterly,* 17, 48–68.

12. Fisher, C. W., Filby, N. N., Marleave, R., Cahen, L. S., Dishaw, M. M., Moore, J. E., & Berliner, D. C. (1978). *Teaching behaviors, academic learning time and student achievement: Final report of Phase III-B, Beginning Teacher Evaluation Study.* San Francisco: Far West Laboratory for Educational Research and Development.

haviors that were positively related to the achievement of fifth-grade students but negatively related to second-grade achievement.

These findings demonstrate the hazards of generalizing research findings across settings. Replication studies are necessary to determine the limits of generalizability. As evidence accumulates about situations where the findings generalize and where they do not, it may be possible to develop a theory to explain the pattern. For example, Fisher found a situation where academic monitoring affected learning and a situation where it did not. With continued replication studies across different situations, a pattern of positive and negative findings might develop that would help us better understand the nature of academic monitoring. This understanding eventually could lead to the development of a formal theory of academic monitoring or to the strengthening of an existing theory.

3. *To check trends or change over time.* Many research results in the social sciences depend on particular historical circumstances. Thus, research findings that were valid 20 years ago may be invalid today. Replication is a useful tool for checking earlier findings and identifying trends. For example, James Baumann, James Hoffman, Ann Duffy-Hester, and Jennifer Ro conducted a modified replication of a major 1963 study of the status of reading instruction in U.S. public elementary schools.[13] They found some similarities. For example, teachers in both the 1960s and today provide explicit instruction in phonic analysis and also report that their greatest challenge is accommodating struggling and underachieving readers. However, they also found some differences. For example, today's teachers have an eclectic perspective about reading instruction in contrast to the strong skills-based emphasis of the 1960s, and school and classroom libraries are more prevalent and better equipped now. According to the researchers, these changes represent a certain amount of progress, but challenges in reading instruction still remain. New replication studies will be needed in the years to come to determine how well these challenges have been met.

4. *To check important findings using different methodology.* In any research study, the soundness of the findings might be compromised by methodological flaws such as the use of measures that yield scores having weak validity or reliability; experimental interventions of too brief duration; or uncontrolled variables. Thus, it is important to replicate studies using better methodology. This was the case in Thomas Goolsby's research study of differences between expert and novice music teachers at the middle- and high-school level.[14] Goolsby had conducted two previous studies of expert and novice music teachers to determine how they rehearsed students to play a band composition. However, he had not controlled for the composition the band rehearsed. Therefore, observed differences between expert and novice teachers could have been a function of the composition the teachers selected for rehearsal rather than a function of their teaching expertise.

In the replication study, all teachers rehearsed the same band composition. Thus, any observed differences between expert and novice teachers could not be attributed to differences in the band composition that was selected for rehearsal. The findings of the replication study generally were similar to the two previous studies, but several interesting disparities were also found.

5. *To develop more effective or efficient interventions.* Educators continually are searching for more effective and efficient versions of instructional programs or procedures. Thus, once researchers have demonstrated that a program or procedure has beneficial outcomes, they or other researchers often do replication-and-extension studies to determine

13. Baumann, J. F., Hoffman, J. V., Duffy-Hester, A. M., & Ro, J. M. (2000). *The First R* yesterday and today: U.S. elementary reading instruction practices reported by teachers and administrators. *Reading Research Quarterly, 35,* 338–377.
14. Goolsby, T. W. (1999). A comparison of expert and novice music teachers' preparing identical band compositions: An operational replication. *Journal of Research in Music Education, 47,* 174–187.

whether it can be further improved. This was the case in a study conducted by David Arnold and his colleagues.[15] The abstract of the published article explains the replication-and-extension process:

> G. J. Whitehurst et al. (1988) taught mothers specific interactive techniques to use when reading picture books with their preschool-age children. This intervention program, called *dialogic reading*, produced substantial effects on preschool children's language development. However, the costs of one-on-one training limit the widespread use of dialogic reading techniques. In this study the authors aimed to replicate and extend the results of the the original study of dialogic reading by developing and evaluating an inexpensive videotape training package for teaching dialogic reading techniques. Mothers were randomly assigned to receive no training, traditional direct training, or videotape training. Results supported the conclusions of Whitehurst et al.: Dialogic reading had powerful effects on children's language skills and indicated that videotape training provided a cost-effective, standardized means of implementing the program.[16]

Many instructional interventions have been developed and tested under similarly artificial laboratory conditions. Replication-and-extension research is needed to further develop and test them to ensure that they are feasible, yet effective in actual work settings.

Working on a Team Project

Some professors and research directors receive financial support to conduct educational research in the form of contracts and grants from federal agencies and private foundations. Their projects may be large enough to require a research team, in which case there might be an opportunity for a graduate student to be a team member. As a rule, the project director provides overall direction, but graduate students can conduct studies that fall within the project's scope of inquiry. For example, one of the authors (M. Gall) codirected a project that investigated the relationship between teachers' instructional practices in algebra classes. Two doctoral students participated in the design of the study and collected data for it. They framed their own research questions within the study, analyzed the database to answer them, and presented their findings as dissertations.[17]

Working on team projects has both advantages and disadvantages. Perhaps the most important advantage is that financial support usually is available for working on the project. This support might only cover paying for test administration or providing needed materials or clerical assistance. However, it might involve receiving a scholarship or research assistantship that is sufficient to meet your major expenses while you complete your graduate work. A team project also offers you an opportunity to participate in a larger, more sophisticated study than would be the case if you were working independently. You also have a chance to learn something about the dynamics of team research. This experience will help you if you have subsequent opportunities to direct, or to be a team member on, other research projects. You also can learn much from other members of the research team because each team member brings a different background of training and experience to the project.

Team research projects involve interdependency, which can be a disadvantage if one or more project members are uncooperative or irresponsible. Also, project members might have incompatible goals. For example, it might be important for you to be finished by a cer-

15. Arnold, D. H., Lonigan, C. J., Whitehurst, G. J., & Epstein, J. N. (1994). Accelerating language development through picture book reading: Replication and extension to a videotape training format. *Journal of Educational Psychology, 86*, 235–243.
16. Ibid., p. 235.
17. Erickson, D. K. (1986). The differential effects of teacher behavior on girls' and boys' achievement, attitudes, and future coursework plans in high school algebra classes. *Dissertation Abstracts International, 47*(11), 3960A. (UMI No. 8629554); Grace, D. P. (1986). Patterns of effective mathematics teaching for low-achieving high school students in beginning algebra classes: An aptitude-treatment interaction study. *Dissertation Abstracts International, 47*(11), 4010A. (UMI No. 8629557)

tain date, but other members might have looser time lines. Disagreements about ownership of data and authorship of reports resulting from the study can arise, too. These and other problems can be avoided if you check the team's level of collegiality beforehand and if you reach agreements at the outset (preferably in writing) about how the project will be conducted and how conflicts will be resolved.

Preparing a Research Proposal

♦ **Touchstone in Research**

Locke, L. F., Spirduso, W. W., & Silverman, S. J. (1999). *Proposals that work: A guide for planning dissertations and grant proposals* (4th ed.). Thousand Oaks, CA: Sage.

If you are ready to do thesis or dissertation research, your faculty committee most likely will require you to write a formal proposal, which they must approve before you can start collecting data. In the case of a quantitative research study, the proposal might need to be a highly detailed plan, in effect, a blueprint for the study. Once the proposal is approved, you can conduct the study, secure in the knowledge that if you execute the specified plan and write a technically sound report, the committee will approve the thesis or dissertation.

If you plan to do a qualitative research study, it is unlikely that you will want or need such a detailed research proposal. In qualitative research, certain aspects of the research design are likely to be emergent, meaning that your initial experiences in the field will affect your plans for subsequent data collection. In our experience, dissertation committees have handled the emergent nature of qualitative studies by asking the student to prepare an initial proposal that is as complete as possible. If the proposal is approved, the student can collect data, but then must meet again with the committee at critical junctures during the fieldwork. In this way, the committee fulfills its supervisory role, and the student is protected from unanticipated criticism when submitting the final dissertation for the committee's approval.

Writing a thorough, carefully reasoned research proposal has several advantages. First, it compels you to state all your ideas in written form so they can be evaluated and improved upon by you and others. Second, the proposal can serve as a guide when you conduct the study. Otherwise, you will need to rely on memory and might forget important procedural details. Finally, a well-written, comprehensive proposal provides a head start on writing the thesis or dissertation. As we explain later in the chapter, a typical thesis or dissertation has much the same organization and content as a research proposal.

A research proposal typically contains the following sections: introduction, review of the literature, research design, research method, data analysis, human subjects protection, and time line. You should check with your faculty advisor or other source to determine whether your university department requires a different format.[18]

Introductory Section

Research proposals usually start with an introductory section that (1) states the research problem, (2) explains how the proposed study is grounded in the research literature, (3) suggests its potential contribution to research knowledge and educational practice, and (4) lists the research hypotheses, questions, or objectives that the study is designed to address. In short, the introductory section of the proposal should *sell* the reader on the idea that the study is worth doing.

Research Hypotheses

As we explained earlier in the chapter, a hypothesis is a theory-based prediction about observed phenomena. If your study will test hypotheses, they should be stated in the

---

18. Various software tools are available to help you in preparing a research proposal, dissertation, or other research report, including: *Methodologist's toolchest* http://www.scolari.com; *Endnote* http://www.endnote.com; and *ProCite* http://www.procite.com

introductory section of the proposal. Each hypothesis should be accompanied by a rationale that explains why it is plausible given the theory from which it was derived. For example, Teena Willoughby, Eileen Wood, and Mustaq Khan conducted several experiments to determine how prior knowledge influences the effectiveness of university students' use of elaboration strategies.[19] One such elaboration strategy is asking oneself, "Why would that fact be true?" when learning a new fact. The researchers described a specific theory—schema theory—and used it to explain why prior knowledge should mediate the effectiveness of this elaboration strategy. Next, they derived a testable hypothesis from schema theory:

> We hypothesized that if students were provided with some type of contextual cue (e.g., pictures) while they were studying facts about unfamiliar materials, activation of an appropriate schema would be facilitated and would be similar to the activation that occurs for familiar materials for which context cues are available.[20]

Thus, the reader is provided an explicit statement of the hypothesis, preceded by a discussion of the theory from which it was derived.

Hypotheses can be stated in two forms, directional and null. The **directional hypothesis** states the researcher's expectations about what the data will show, for example, which of two experimental treatments will yield superior results on an outcome measure. The following are examples of directional hypotheses:

1. There is a *positive* relationship between the number of older siblings and the social maturity scores of six-year-old children.
2. Children who attend preschool will make *greater* gains in first-grade reading achievement than comparable children who do not attend preschool.

In contrast to the directional hypothesis, the **null hypothesis** states that no relationship exists between the variables studied, or no difference will be found between the experimental treatments. For example, in null form the aforementioned hypothesis could be stated thus: There will be no significant difference between children who attend preschool and children who do not attend preschool in their first-grade reading achievement gain scores. The null hypothesis usually does not reflect the researcher's expectations. It is used principally because it fits the logic of inferential statistics (described in Chapter 5).

Readers may be confused by the null hypothesis because it appears senseless to hypothesize the exact opposite of one's expectations. This is a disadvantage of the null form because the researcher's expectations, based as they are upon considerable insight into other research and theory, often make the study clearer to the person reading the research report. Some researchers overcome this problem by stating both a directional hypothesis, which reflects their expectations based on theory or previous research, and a null hypothesis, which is used in performing tests of statistical significance.

Research Questions and Purposes

If a study is not designed to test hypotheses derived from a theory, you instead can state research questions, purposes, or objectives. Depending upon the study, it may be appropriate to use several of these formats. As with hypotheses, each question, purpose, or objective should be supported by a rationale. The reader needs to know why the researcher framed the question or purpose, and how research findings relating to it are likely to advance knowledge and improve educational practice.

---

19. Willoughby, T., Wood, E., & Khan, M. (1994). Isolating variables that impact on or detract from the effectiveness of elaboration strategies. *Journal of Educational Psychology, 86,* 279–289.
20. Ibid., p. 280.

An example of the use of research questions to frame a study is found in an investigation conducted by Cathy Lirgg.[21] The purpose of her study was to determine how boys and girls perceive the "climate" (also called *environment* in the study) of same-sex and coeducational physical education classes. After reviewing the literature and demonstrating the need for the study, Lirgg stated these three research questions:

1. Do boys and girls in same-sex and coeducational classes differ in regard to their perceptions of student behavior, student involvement, affiliation, teacher support, and competitiveness?
2. Do boys and girls in the same coeducational classes view their environment in a similar way?
3. Do perceptions of the environment change from middle school to high school?[22]

Lirgg's data analyses were directed to answering each of these three research questions.

Research questions can be phrased instead as objectives or purposes. Phrasing is more a matter of personal preference than anything else. An example of research purposes is found in a study conducted by Lawrence Picus.[23] He conducted four case studies to determine how four Texas school districts responded to school financing reforms designed to bring greater equity in their funding level. Picus stated that the three purposes of the study were to determine

- whether or not Texas school districts received additional funds under the revised school finance formula, and if so, what types of districts received additional funds.
- if new revenues were received, how the receipt of those funds change school district expenditure patterns, and
- the specific resources school districts purchased with the new funds.[24]

The methodology and data analyses used in the case studies addressed these three purposes.

Literature Review Section

Although you might review many research reports and theoretical writings in developing your research problem, you typically will identify a few as most critical. These publications should be described in the introductory section of the research proposal as part of the rationale for the project. They can be discussed at greater length in the literature review section of the proposal, together with other relevant material, such as

1. The findings of other studies in the line of research that includes each critical study
2. The findings of studies in lines of research that have some degree of relevance to the proposed study
3. A critique of methods used in previous research
4. The conclusions drawn by researchers who previously have reviewed the literature relevant to your proposed study
5. Applications, if any, of previous research findings to professional practice

21. Lirgg, C. D. (1994). Environmental perceptions of students in same-sex and coeducational physical education classes. *Journal of Educational Psychology, 86,* 183–192.
22. Ibid., p. 184.
23. Picus, L. O. (1994). The local impact of school finance reform in four Texas school districts. *Educational Evaluation and Policy Analysis, 16,* 391–404.
24. Ibid., p. 391.

A thorough literature review that includes the topics we listed above could be as long as, or longer than, the combined length of all the other sections of the proposal. This length is justified by the need to ground your research problem and methodology in a deep understanding of the existing knowledge base, as represented in the literature. It would be embarrassing to find after you have completed a study that you had overlooked previous research that, had you known about it beforehand, would have changed the way you framed your research problem or designed your methodology.

The process of conducting the review and writing a report of your findings in the research proposal is time-consuming. Your dissertation must include a substantial literature review, typically in its own chapter. By writing the review at the proposal stage, you will already have completed a significant part of the writing of the dissertation. Detailed procedures for reviewing the literature are described in Chapter 4.

Research Design Section

Part IV covers the major quantitative research designs: descriptive, causal-comparative, correlational, and experimental. Part V describes case study design and designs grounded in various academic disciplines such as anthropology, philosophy, psychology, and sociology. You will need to propose a design for your study and describe how you will implement it in the particular setting that you have chosen to investigate. If you did not explain why you selected that design in the introductory section of the proposal, you should do so in the research design section.

Thomas Scruggs and Margo Mastropieri conducted a study to identify variables that are associated with successful mainstreaming of disabled students into regular science classes.[25] They selected their research design in this manner:

> We identified three classrooms in which exemplary mainstreaming practices were said to be undertaken and gathered evidence that we felt would lead us to some general conclusions about mainstreaming success in science using a design similar to the multiple case study designs described by Yin (1989).[26]

We describe Robert Yin's approach to case study design in Chapter 14. Specification of the research design influences in large part the researcher's choice of methods, which are described in the next section of the proposal.

Research Methods Section

The section on research methods should describe your sampling procedures, data-collection procedures, and any other procedures that are critical to your study.

Sampling procedures are described in Chapter 6. We explain there that it would be a mistake to select a sample (for a quantitative study) or case (for a qualitative study) simply because it is convenient to recruit for participation in the study. You need to use sound sampling logic instead. If you are proposing a quantitative study, you should explain how your sample is representative of a defined population. If you are proposing a qualitative study, you should explain why the case, or cases, that were selected are likely to yield significant insights about the phenomenon of interest.

In describing your data-collection procedures, you should identify each instrument (e.g., a test, a questionnaire, or an interview schedule), the variables it is designed to measure, its validity and reliability, and the steps that you will follow in using it. These matters

---

25. Scruggs, T. E., & Mastropieri, M. A. (1994). Successful mainstreaming in elementary science classes: A qualitative study of three reputational cases. *American Educational Research Journal, 31,* 785–811.
26. Ibid., p. 787.

are discussed in Chapter 7 (tests and self-report instruments), Chapter 8 (questionnaires and interviews), and Chapter 9 (observation and content analysis). A common mistake is to mention a variable in the introductory section of the proposal but not to indicate how it will be measured when describing your data-collection procedures. The converse mistake is to introduce in the research-method section a variable to be measured that was not mentioned in the introductory section.

If you are proposing a qualitative study, other data-collection procedures are relevant and should be described. We explain these procedures in Chapter 14. They include defining the focus of your data-collection efforts and checking your data for credibility, authenticity, and representativeness.

Any special procedures that you intend to use should be described in this section of the proposal. For example, if you plan to do an experiment that tests the effectiveness of an instructional method, you should describe the method in detail, how you propose to train the sample to use it, and how you plan to check whether the sample implemented it as intended. If you plan to do a qualitative study, you might find it necessary to specify your procedures for gaining entry into a field setting and for obtaining the cooperation of informants and other participants.

Data Analysis Section

You should develop a tentative plan for data analysis because it will have a considerable bearing on the sample size you will need, the procedures for scoring tests and other measures, and the procedures for creating computer data files. If you give no thought to analysis until after the data are collected, you may find that it is impossible to analyze them in the way that you wish.

In writing this section of the proposal, you should consider listing all your hypotheses, questions, objectives, or purposes. Then you should indicate the data that will be needed to address each one, and the measures that will yield these data. Finally, describe the method that you will use to analyze the data. This process will serve as a useful check that you actually will be able to test your hypotheses, answer your questions, or accomplish your objectives or purposes when you move from planning to conducting the study.

Protection of Human Subjects Section

As we explain in Chapter 3, any research project involving the participation of human beings must be reviewed by an institutional review board. The purpose of the board's review is to ensure that the rights of research participants to confidentiality and freedom from harm are protected. The board may ask you to complete a separate set of forms on which you provide the requested information. You might find it necessary to append these forms to your research proposal and, in addition, to include a brief summary of your protection procedures in the body of the proposal.

If the research study involves significant risks to participants or involves vulnerable populations (e.g., handicapped children), the board probably will want to review the entire proposal in detail. We know of instances where the researcher needed to revise the proposal significantly because it contained insufficient information for the board to determine whether the potential benefits of the study outweighed its potential risks. (The risk-benefit ratio is an important criterion in reviewing a research proposal for human subjects protection.)

Time Line Section

Your research proposal should include a time line that states each step of the study, the approximate date when it will be completed, and the estimated number of hours or days it will require. Creating this time line will help you think through the entire research process and alert you to possible problems, such as the following:

1. The institutional review board takes longer than expected to evaluate your plan for protecting human subjects or asks you to make time-consuming revisions that you did not anticipate.
2. In order to start your study in October, school officials must be contacted during the summer when they might be unavailable for various reasons.
3. The collection of pretest data for your study needs to occur before the experiment begins, but teachers and students are busy with state-mandated testing during the period of time that works best for you.
4. Several of the key informants that you identified for your study will only be available within certain time windows.
5. If you do not complete the thesis or dissertation by a given date, you might have to wait weeks or months to assemble the faculty committee that will evaluate it.

As you identify such problems and constraints in your time line, you can make appropriate adjustments in your planning. This is far easier than trying to solve these problems after data collection has begun.

A time line that includes only the major steps of the planned study might be adequate. The following is an example (anticipated completion dates in parentheses):

1. Faculty committee reviews proposal. (early September)
2. Institutional review board (IRB) reviews proposal. (late September)
3. Proposal is revised based on feedback from the faculty committee and IRB. (mid-October)
4. Final approval to start data collection is obtained from the faculty committee and IRB. (end of October)
5. Data are collected. (middle of January)
6. Data are analyzed. (late February)
7. First draft of report is completed and submitted to faculty committee for feedback. (end of April)
8. Final draft of report is completed and defended before the faculty committee. (late May)
9. Final revisions are completed, and the dissertation is submitted to the Graduate School. (early June)

Some research procedures are sufficiently complex that it pays to create a time line for them to ensure that you do not omit a step or run out of time. For example, the development of a psychometrically sound test, attitude scale, or other measure involves many steps (see Chapters 7–9). Creating a time line for the development process will help to ensure that you do not omit a step or allot insufficient time to complete it.[27]

Conducting a Pilot Study

Whenever possible, you should include a pilot study as part of your research project. A **pilot study** involves small-scale testing of the procedures that you plan to use in the main study, and revising the procedures based on what the testing reveals. For many quantitative and

---

27. PERT (Program Evaluation and Review Technique) is a sophisticated technique for time planning. An example of its use is presented in: Foster, C., & Lent, J. R. (1986). Application of Program Evaluation and Review Technique (PERT) within a curriculum development project. *Journal of Special Education Technology, 8,* 47–58.

qualitative research studies, two or three participants may be sufficient. An exception would be a pilot study for the purpose of developing an instrument such as an achievement test or attitude scale. Several hundred participants may be necessary in order to develop and refine the instrument to the point that it has satisfactory measurement properties.

In some cases, the pilot study can be carried out after the research proposal has been approved by the dissertation committee. In this case, a brief description of the planned pilot study in the proposal should be sufficient. In other cases, you will want to conduct the pilot study first and describe what you learned from it in your research proposal.

For example, suppose your research problem involves trying out a new procedure for improving students' reading comprehension. You have derived the procedure from a theory of reading comprehension, but there is no precedent for the procedure in the research literature. A dissertation committee might question whether the effort of a full-scale, formal study is necessary as an initial tryout. A pilot study can be done to determine whether the procedure has merit and to correct obvious flaws. If the pilot study indicates that the procedure has merit, this finding and the evidence supporting it can be included in the research proposal as part of the justification for conducting a formal, full-scale study of its effectiveness.

Using the Proposal in Writing the Dissertation

If you have written a detailed research proposal, you will have done much of the work of writing the dissertation. (As we stated above, thesis research generally is similar to dissertation research, so our remarks about writing a dissertation also apply to writing a thesis.) The similarity between the proposal and the dissertation is evident in the dissertation outline shown in Figure 2.1. The first three chapters correspond to the topics and organization of a research proposal.

You should check with your dissertation committee to determine whether they wish you to use a different format or different chapter labels from what is shown in Figure 2.1. Also, keep in mind that the organization of a dissertation reporting a qualitative study may vary somewhat from that shown in Figure 2.1. (We discuss reporting style for qualitative research in Chapter 14.) For example, you may wish to report the findings for each case in a separate chapter, rather than combining all the findings into one chapter, which is the standard format for a quantitative research study.

It is not desirable or necessary to wait until all data have been collected and analyzed before starting to write the dissertation. There are likely to be some periods of time when you are extremely busy collecting or analyzing data, and other periods of time when you must sit and wait. These lulls can be used to revise the research proposal so that they form the first three chapters of the dissertation.

It may seem premature to learn about writing dissertations, journal articles, and papers (discussed below) before you have written your first research proposal. However, this learning process is worthwhile because it gives you a picture of the complete research process—from identifying a problem to reporting your findings. Thus, your initial steps are more likely to be pointed in a direction that will lead to your ultimate goal, that is, making a contribution to research knowledge about education.

We consider general format considerations below and then describe each section of the dissertation. We emphasize issues and problems that, in our experience, commonly arise in dissertation writing.

Format

Some universities prepare a special style manual for graduate students, whereas others refer students to a standard style manual. The most commonly used of the standard manuals is

♦ **Touchstone in Research**

Meloy, J. M. (2001). *Writing the qualitative dissertation: Understanding by doing* (2nd ed.). Mahwah, NJ: Lawrence Erlbaum Associates.

Rudestam, K. E., & Newton, R. R. (2000). *Surviving your dissertation: A comprehensive guide to content and process* (2nd ed.). Thousand Oaks, CA: Sage.

FIGURE 2.1

Organization of a Dissertation Reporting an Educational Research Study

Front Matter

Title page
Preface and Acknowledgments
Table of contents
List of tables
List of figures

Body of the Dissertation

Chapter 1. Introduction
    a. General statement of the problem
    b. Significance of the study
    c. Research hypotheses, questions, objectives, or purposes
Chapter 2. Review of the literature
    a. Review of previous research and opinion
    b. Interpretive summary of the current state of knowledge
Chapter 3. Research method
    a. Research design
    b. Sample selection and procedures for human subject protection
    c. Measures
    d. Other procedures (e.g., description of treatment conditions)
    e. Time line
Chapter 4. Research findings
    a. Overview of statistical procedures
    b. Description of results for each hypothesis, question, objective, or purpose
    c. Supplemental analyses
Chapter 5. Discussion
    a. Interpretation of each result
    b. Limitations of the study
    c. Implications for future research
    d. Implications for practice (if applicable)

Back Matter

Bibliography
Appendixes

✦ Touchstone in Research

Publication Manual of the American Psychological Association (5th ed.). (2001). Washington, DC: American Psychological Association.

APA Style Helper (Version 3.0) [CD-ROM]. (2001). Washington, DC: American Psychological Association.

Publication Manual of the American Psychological Association Web site: <http://www.apastyle.org>.

the *Publication Manual of the American Psychological Association.* You should follow carefully whatever manual you are asked to use. It reflects poorly on your scholarship to make errors in style, especially in your citations. If you hire someone to type your dissertation, you should check that this person knows the style that you are required to use.

It is helpful to ask your dissertation chairperson to identify several outstanding dissertations recently completed at your institution. An examination of these dissertations, together with the prescribed style manual, will give you most of the information needed to satisfy dissertation requirements. Also, study of the dissertations will give you an idea of your chairperson's standards and expectations.

A common problem in writing a dissertation or other research report is figuring the proper tense to use. The general rule is to use the past tense to describe events that occurred at a point in time prior to the writing of the report. For example, you might write: "Sixty students were selected from a local school district . . . "; "Harber (1968) found in her study that . . . "; "The Stanford Achievement Test was developed to measure . . . "; "A *t* test was done . . . " Each of these statements refers to an event or activity that occurred prior to the writing of the report.

The present tense is used to refer to assertions that continue to be true at the time the report is written. For example, you might write: "Research has shown consistently that inserted questions in text facilitate retention of the text content." The research has already occurred; hence, the past tense ("has shown") is used. We can presume that the relationship between inserted questions and retention continues to be true beyond the observations made by the researchers; hence, the present tense ("facilitate") is used. Similarly, you would write, "the Stanford Achievement Test measures various aspects of academic performance" because this feature of the test continues to be true at the time the report is written. Also, you would state that "Table 2 shows that . . . " because the table continues to perform a function. The table did not show a set of results just at one point in time. By the same logic, you would state that "this t value is statistically significant" because the results of a statistical significance test continue to be true beyond the point that the test was performed.

Front Matter

As shown in Figure 2.1, the front matter includes the title page, the preface and acknowledgments, a table of contents, a list of tables, and a list of figures.

The dissertation title should be brief, yet descriptive. It should incorporate words that other researchers are likely to use as descriptors in searching ERIC or other indexes to the literature (see Chapter 4). Suppose, for example, that a researcher has done an experiment comparing the achievement gains of sixth-grade students who used computers while learning American history with the achievement gains of a matched group of students who did not use computers. An appropriate title would be *An Experiment Comparing Conventional and Computer-Augmented Instruction in a Sixth-Grade American History Curriculum.* This title is brief, yet it gives the reader a good sense of the study's purpose. Furthermore, someone who is using such literature-search descriptors as *computer instruction, history instruction, history curriculum, elementary school,* or *experiment* would be likely to come across it.

Introductory Chapter

If the introductory section of the research proposal is well written, it can be elaborated into the first chapter of the dissertation. Both pieces of writing cover essentially the same topics.

Some dissertations start with pages of background information before stating the research problem. This information is meaningless to readers, because they do not know why they are expected to read it. We recommend instead that you state the research problem within the first two paragraphs and then proceed to present relevant background material.

The introductory chapter of some dissertations includes a separate section that presents definitions of technical terms that are central to the study. One problem with this approach is that the terms are defined out of context. Another problem is that if this section comes at the end of the chapter (as it often does), the reader is deprived of these definitions while reading the earlier parts of the chapter. We recommend that you define each term the first time it is used in the dissertation. There is no harm in repeating the definitions again if you wish to present all technical terms in one location, possibly in a glossary that appears as a dissertation appendix.

Literature Review Chapter

If you write a comprehensive review of the literature as part of your research proposal, you can use it as the literature review chapter of the dissertation.

Some dissertations fail to make a connection between the studies that are reviewed and the researcher's study. You do not want the reader wondering how the reviewed studies relate to your study. Therefore, you need to continually show how each set of studies, or each theory, or each methodological flaw in previous research influenced the design of your study. Some researchers make these connections at the very end of the chapter, but that is too late.

Another pitfall to avoid in writing a literature review is that of presenting each study in essentially the same way. For example, some researchers treat each article in a separate paragraph and start each article with the name of the researchers who wrote it. Also, they devote the same amount of space to each study without regard to its importance or relevance. This type of review is tiresome to read and usually does not provide a good understanding of what is known about the research problem.

If you are reviewing many studies on the same problem or topic, it is helpful to organize them into a table. The first step is to decide which features of the studies to abstract, for example: nature of the sample, procedures or treatments, dependent variables, and statistical results for each variable. The next step is to review each study and write a capsule description of each feature. Finally, these descriptions are organized into a table. The advantages of this method are its concise presentation style and the ease with which studies can be compared. Table 2.1 presents a section from a large table of this type that was prepared by Ron Thorkildsen for a literature review in a dissertation study of social skills training for mildly handicapped children. (Thorkildsen's table includes 18 studies, two of which are shown in Table 2.1.) Note that the table concisely presents a great deal of information about each study, and it facilitates comparisons between studies.

Research Methods Chapter

In a good research proposal, the research methods will be described in detail. If so, it will be easy to expand this section of the proposal into a chapter of the dissertation. Of course, if the research design and procedures change once the study is underway, the research methods section needs to be revised to reflect what actually occurred.

In the research methods chapter of dissertations, the main problems we have seen are insufficient detail and vagueness. Your description should be such that the reader has a clear, complete picture of all your procedures during the course of the study. This is a difficult goal to accomplish because, as the researcher, you are close to the study and may not see clearly all that needs to be made explicit. Therefore, it is advisable to give a draft of this chapter to a few colleagues and to ask them to identify anything they find to be confusing or incomplete.

Results Chapter

The results chapter of a dissertation presents the research findings, but does not discuss them; that task is left for the next chapter.

General procedures for processing and analyzing the research data can be described at the beginning of the chapter. For example, you may have decided to remove some of the research participants from the database because they had missing data on too many variables. This decision affects some or all of the data analyses, and so it is appropriate to discuss it at the outset of the chapter. Other matters of general relevance are the computer programs used to analyze the data, transformations of scores to make them amenable to statistical analysis, and the organization of the chapter.

One of the best ways to present the results of statistical or qualitative analyses is to organize them around the study's hypotheses, questions, or objectives. Each hypothesis, for example, would be stated in the same form as it was presented in the introductory chapter

Summary of Research on Social Skills Training Programs for Mildly Handicapped Children

Study Number/ Authors	Social Skills Taught	Subjects/Design	Type of Assessment	Training Techniques	Maintenance Training/ Assessment	Generalization Training/ Assessment	Results
(1) Ballard, Corman, Gottlieb, & Kauman (1977)	Cooperative interaction	$N = 37$ EMR grades 3, 4, & 5 Group design	Sociometric nomination	Cooperative groups formed	No training specified	In natural environment with non-handicapped peers	1. Peer acceptance of experimental group increased and peer rejection decreased more than controls 2. Acceptance of controls decreased and rejection increased 3. Acceptance of experimental subjects was higher and rejection was lower by peers in second activity group than controls 4. Acceptance of experimental subjects by classmates who did not participate with them in group activity was higher after intervention than acceptance of controls by classmates
(2) Berler, Gross, & Drabman (1982)	1. Eye contact 2. Initiating social interactions 3. Praising 4. Responding to criticism 5. Making requests	$N = 3$ LD 8–10 years Single-subject design	1. Sociometric rating 2. Behavior observation 3. Role play tests	1. Coaching 2. Modeling (videotape) 3. Behavioral rehearsal 4. Feedback	No training One-month follow-up	Natural role-playing situations	1. Increased use of appropriate skills during role-playing 2. Performance maintained above baseline levels during follow-up 3. Performance did not generalize to natural school setting 4. Peer acceptance did not change

Source: Adapted from Table 1 on p. 14 in: Thorkildsen, R. J. (1984). An experimental test of a microcomputer/videodisc program to develop the social skills of mildly handicapped elementary students. *Dissertation Abstracts International, 45*(12), 3614A. (UMI No. 8502026)

of the dissertation. Then all findings pertinent to this hypothesis would be presented. If the study tested five hypotheses, there would be five sections of the chapter, each dealing with a separate hypothesis.

A useful approach to preparing the results chapter is to start by putting the results for each hypothesis, question, or objective in a table or figure. These graphic displays present results more clearly and economically than is possible in text presentation. After studying each table or figure, you can write a paragraph or two explaining what it contains and drawing the reader's attention to noteworthy findings.

You should avoid discussing every entry in the table or figure, whether significant or not. This style of presentation is boring, and it defeats the purpose of using tables and figures. The *Publication Manual of the American Psychological Association* explains the distinguishing features of tables and figures, and provides detailed instructions for constructing them.

Often the results of the planned analyses will suggest questions or hypotheses that were not part of the original dissertation proposal. If the available data can be used to address them, it is entirely appropriate to do supplemental analyses and to report them in a separate section of the results chapter. In certain situations, it even is appropriate to report supplemental analyses in the discussion chapter. For example, you may suggest an alternative explanation for one of your results in this chapter, and you may find that you can analyze some of your data to determine whether the explanation is viable.

Similar principles of presentation apply to the analysis of qualitative data. The results of the analyses can be organized according to the study's hypotheses, questions, or objectives. If the study consisted of a set of case studies, the analyses for each case study can be presented separately. If possible, each case study should be organized similarly in order to facilitate comparisons between them.

The results of a statistical analysis can be presented concisely in a table and a few paragraphs of text. In a qualitative research study, however, the analysis of a case may require many pages of text. If you have studied multiple cases, you should consider making each one the subject of a separate chapter. Also, a different reporting style is used for case study findings than for statistical findings. The style relies on literary conventions such as story telling, vivid description, and a subjective point of view. We discuss this type of reporting style in Chapter 14.

Discussion Chapter

The last chapter of a dissertation usually includes a brief summary of the research problem and method, an interpretation of each result, and a discussion of the limitations of the study and the implications of the findings.

A key task in writing the discussion chapter is to identify and interpret the important results. In examining each result, you should ask yourself such questions as: Is this an important result, and if so, why? Is it consistent with the results of previous research? If not, why not? Is there an existing theory that can explain the result? Does the result suggest the need to modify existing theory? Are there alternative explanations of the result? Is one alternative explanation more plausible than others? Does the result merit further investigation to clarify it? If so, what form might such investigation take?

Your answers to these questions will be of great interest to other researchers for several reasons, including the fact that you were an eyewitness to the data-collection process. As an eyewitness, you have a better feeling for what the data mean than do other researchers, who must rely on your report for an understanding of what happened.

In discussing the study's methodological limitations, you should note problems that occurred in sampling procedures, instrumentation, data collection, and data analysis.

Some of the problems may be inherent in the research design, whereas others may have occurred in the execution of the study. If an observed result was contrary to prediction, you should consider whether it was due to methodological flaws.

It is desirable to add a section on the implications of the findings for practice, if there are such implications. You can present speculations here that would be out of place in the results chapter.

Also desirable is a section that suggests questions for further research. The reason for this recommendation is that your experience in doing a study has put you in a good position for identifying the important questions that should be investigated next. Other researchers can combine your judgments with their own in order to design studies with the best likelihood of yielding important new knowledge.

Back Matter

The back matter of a dissertation usually consists of the bibliography and one or more appendixes.

The bibliography must list all the references that were cited in the body of the dissertation. Depending upon your institution, it may be permissible also to include pertinent references that were not cited. Whatever style manual you use, your citations should be accurate down to the last comma.

Appendixes are used to present information that is not critical to the study, but will be of interest to some readers. For example, appendixes are appropriate for statistical results that are not essential to the study (e.g., psychometric data for the research measures) and locally developed research measures (e.g., interview schedules and training materials).

Preparing a Journal Article

You have much to gain by preparing one or more journal articles based on your dissertation as soon as you have completed it. Many employers who have an open position for an educator with an advanced degree are interested in the publications of applicants. If you are able to list one or more publications (especially research publications) on your vita or resume, this will be to your advantage in obtaining a position.

The first step in preparing a research article is to decide what journal is most likely to publish studies on the problem that you investigated. The best candidates can be identified by checking the bibliography of your dissertation. You are likely to find that a few journals published the majority of studies that you cited as pertinent to your research problem. These journals are the ones most likely to accept your article for publication.

Another factor to consider in selecting a journal is its reputation. Some education journals are more widely read and more influential than others. Also, refereed journals generally are regarded more highly than nonrefereed journals. A **refereed journal** is one in which articles are evaluated by a panel of acknowledged experts to determine whether they merit publication. Most refereed journals prominently display their panel of reviewers at the front of each issue.

Once you decide upon the journal in which you wish to publish, you should examine the typical length and format of recently published articles in it. You also should check whether the journal follows the publication guidelines of the American Psychological Association (APA). In fact, most journals that publish educational research do follow these guidelines, which appear in the *Publication Manual of the American Psychological Association*. This publication provides detailed instructions on manuscript organization, content, and reporting style.

♦ *Touchstone in Research*

Cabell, D. W. (1998). *Cabell's directory of publishing opportunities in education* (5th ed.). Beaumont, TX: Cabell Publishing.

A study by Bruce Hall, Ann Ward, and Connie Comer provides insight about criteria that affect a study's publishability in a research journal.[28] They selected a random sample of 128 educational research articles published in 1983 and had them rated by a panel of experienced researchers. The panel judged that 54 of the articles (about 42 percent) should have been rejected or accepted only after major revisions. Hall and his colleagues asked the panel to indicate the specific shortcomings that led them to make these judgments. Table 2.2 shows the most frequently cited shortcomings. Most involved flaws in research methodology (e.g., not establishing the validity and reliability of the measures used) or problems in how it was reported (e.g., not clearly describing the study's limitations). Before submitting an article to a journal, you may find it helpful to check it against this list of shortcomings.

The list shown in Table 2.2 is helpful, but it omits one criterion of research publishability that we believe is particularly important. Ronald Good and James Wandersee allude to this criterion in their statement, "The most challenging and important job that a reviewer or an editor has to perform is deciding whether or not a particular study was worth doing . . ."[29]

As journal editors ourselves, we have rejected research manuscripts because we could not figure out why the study was worth doing, or in other words, why it was important. Conversely, we have accepted research manuscripts for publication because the study was important—despite flaws in methodology. For this reason, we emphasize the need to ground your study first and foremost in the research literature. Your awareness of what is

---

TABLE 2.2

Specific Shortcomings Cited by Judges to Substantiate Decisions to Reject or Require Major Revisions in Educational Research Articles

Specific Shortcoming	Percentage of the 54 Articles Cited
1. Validity and reliability of data-gathering procedures not established	43
2. Research design not free of specific weaknesses	39
3. Limitations of study not stated	31
4. Research design not appropriate to solution of the problem	28
5. Method of sampling inappropriate	28
6. Results of analysis not presented clearly	28
7. Inappropriate methods selected to analyze data	26
8. Report not clearly written	26
9. Assumptions not clearly stated	22
10. Data-gathering methods or procedures not described	22

Source: Adapted from table 8 on p. 188 in: Hall, B. W., Ward, A. W., & Comer, C. B. (1988). Published educational research: An empirical study of its quality. *Journal of Educational Research, 81,* 182–189. Reprinted with permission of the Helen Dwight Reid Educational Foundation. Published by Heldref Publications, 1319 Eighteenth St., NW, Washington, DC 20036-1802. Copyright © 1988.

---

28. Hall, B. W., Ward, A. W., & Comer, C. B. (1988). Published educational research: An empirical study of its quality. *Journal of Educational Research, 81,* 182–189.
29. Good, R. G., & Wandersee, J. H. (1991). No royal road: More on improving the quality of published educational research. *Educational Researcher, 20(8),* 24–25. Quote appears on p. 24.

known and not known about the problem you wish to investigate allows you to create a case for the importance of your study by showing how it contributes to the research literature.

Preparing a Paper for a Professional Meeting

It is a rewarding experience to present a paper based on your dissertation at a professional meeting. You can list it on your vita or resume as a professional accomplishment. Also, it helps you become better known to your colleagues.

Educational associations such as the American Educational Research Association (AERA) and the Association for Supervision and Curriculum Development (ASCD) announce a "call for papers" many months in advance of their annual meeting. The call for papers will appear in one of the association's publications, which are sent to all members. Its purpose is to invite members to submit proposals for papers to be delivered at the meeting. If your proposal is accepted, you usually are obligated to attend the meeting in order to deliver the paper in person. Therefore, it is inadvisable to submit a paper proposal unless you are reasonably certain that you (or a research colleague with whom you have worked) will be able to attend the meeting.

Some associations automatically submit copies of papers presented at their meetings to ERIC (see Chapter 4) in order to widen their distribution. If the association does not do this, you can submit a copy of the paper to the appropriate ERIC clearinghouse (see appendix A) on your own initiative.

Papers presented at professional meetings generally are similar in form to articles published in research journals. You may have occasion, however, to present your study at a meeting of policy makers or practitioners who have limited understanding of research methodology. Patricia Haensly, Ann Lupkowski, and James McNamara developed a method called a **chart essay** that meets this need for a less technical presentation style.[30] The chart essay simplifies the elements of a research study by using charts to focus the audience's attention on aspects of the study that are most relevant to policy making.

Haensly and her colleagues illustrated the method using a study that determined the impact of students' participation in extracurricular activities on their high school grades. A chart essay format was used to present the findings to a conference of educators of gifted children. One of the charts is reproduced in Figure 2.2. The chart's banner states one of the study's research questions. The findings relevant to the question are stated in a form that does not require special expertise in statistics.

The "Trends" stated at the bottom of the chart are concise, nontechnical, and descriptive of the statistical findings. Trends statements are one of the most important elements of the chart essay:

> Taken collectively these trends statements provide the executive summary. At any point in the conference briefing session, they can be easily referenced . . . [We] have found that trends statements are often quoted directly in press releases, administrative reports, and public meetings.[31]

A feature of the chart essay format that helps readers understand complex research results is that each aspect of a study—for example, each research question—is shown on a separate one-page chart.

♦ *Touchstone in Research*

Smith, M. C., & Carney, R. N. (1999). Strategies for writing successful AERA proposals. *Educational Researcher, 28(1)*, 42–45.

---

30. Haensly, P. A., Lupkowski, A. E., & McNamara, J. F. (1987). The chart essay: A strategy for communicating research findings to policymakers and practitioners. *Educational Evaluation and Policy Analysis, 9*, 63–75. See also: Jones, B. K., & Mitchell, N. (1990). Communicating evaluation findings: The use of a chart essay. *Educational Evaluation and Policy Analysis, 12*, 449–462.
31. Ibid., p. 70.

FIGURE 2.2

Sample Chart Essay from a Presentation on a Study of Extracurricular Activities in High School

	High Involvement %	Moderate Involvement %	Some Involvement %	No Involvement %
Research Question Eleven				
Does participation in student government contribute significantly to academic success in high school?				
Very High Grades 'A'	100.00	64.7	38.6	18.0
High Grades 'B'	—	35.3	26.5	39.2
Moderate Grades 'C'	—	—	33.7	39.9
Low Grades 'D'	—	—	1.2	2.9

Trends
- All high school students highly involved in student government (100%) earned very high grades.
- All high school students with moderate involvement in student government (64.7 plus 35.3 or 100%) earned very high or high grades.
- Most high school students with some involvement in student government (38.6 plus 26.5 or 65.1%) earned very high or high grades.
- High school students not involved in student government were least likely to earn high or very high grades.

Source: Figure 4 on p. 71 in: Haensly, P. A., Lupkowski, A. E., & McNamara, J. F. (1987). The chart essay: A strategy for communicating research findings to policymakers and practitioners. *Educational Evaluation and Policy Analysis, 9*, 63–75.

✦ RECOMMENDATIONS FOR *Planning and Reporting Research*

1. Select a research problem early in your graduate program.
2. Ground your research problem in existing literature relating to the problem.
3. Allow sufficient time to plan the study (typically several months or longer) so that it is well designed and likely to contribute to knowledge about education.
4. Conduct a pilot study of the research procedures in order to identify and correct flaws before the main study.
5. Create a realistic time line for completing the various stages of the study.
6. In writing the research proposal and final report, include a sound rationale for each of the study's hypotheses, questions, or objectives.

7. In writing the research proposal and final report, show how the studies included in the literature review relate to the present study.
8. In reporting the results of data analyses, relate them explicitly to the study's hypotheses, questions, or objectives.
9. Consider alternate explanations of the findings in the discussion section of the final report.
10. Study journal style requirements before submitting a research manuscript for publication.

✔ SELF-CHECK TEST

Circle the correct answer to each of the following questions. The answers are provided at the back of the book.

1. "There will be no significant difference between the scores on a measure of achievement of high- and low-anxious students" is a hypothesis written in _____ form.
a. directional
b. interrogative
c. null
d. objective

2. When a construct is thought of as a characteristic that can take on more than one value, it is called a
a. variable.
b. replicable construct.
c. hypothetical construct.
d. theoretical entity.

3. Replication research is particularly useful for
a. identifying new variables that correspond to a construct.
b. determining the social significance of a research finding.
c. testing a hypothesis derived from theory.
d. determining whether a research finding generalizes to other populations.

4. A pilot study generally should be conducted
a. after the research proposal has been approved by the dissertation committee.
b. whenever the research study involves testing the effects of a new instructional procedure.
c. whenever the research study involves replication and extension.
d. after development of the measures to be used in the research study.

5. Limitations of a study's research design and method are discussed in the _____ chapter of a thesis or dissertation.
a. research findings
b. research method
c. discussion
d. introductory

6. A thesis or dissertation
a. is similar to a research proposal except for the research findings and discussion chapters.
b. is similar to a research proposal except for the literature review chapter.
c. is organized very differently from a research proposal.
d. is organized very differently from research articles in journals.

7. A chart essay is
a. a type of research article written for a practitioner journal.
b. a commentary on the direction that research on a particular problem should take.
c. a nontechnical format for presenting research findings.
d. a presentation format specifically intended for reporting qualitative research findings.

CHAPTER 3

✦ Ethical, Legal, and Human Relations Issues in Educational Research

OVERVIEW

If your proposed study involves collecting data from human participants, you will need to describe how you plan to protect them from possible harm, and submit this information to an institutional review board at your university or research agency. In this chapter we suggest strategies for designing a research study that conforms to ethical standards and legal regulations for protecting research participants from various types of harm. We also describe how to build a positive relationship with individuals whose cooperation and involvement you will need throughout your research study.

OBJECTIVES

After studying this chapter, you should be able to

1. Give examples of research situations involving legal, ethical, or human relations issues, and describe how such issues can be handled effectively.
2. Describe codes of ethical standards prepared by the American Educational Research Association and other professional associations.
3. Describe the purpose and procedures of an institutional review board.
4. Describe the procedures that should be included in a proposal for a research study to ensure that participants are protected from harm.

5. Describe several methods that researchers can use to ensure the privacy and confidentiality of research data.
6. Describe two approaches for debriefing participants following research that involves deception.
7. Explain the ethical issues that can arise when publishing reports of a research study.
8. Describe four aspects of field research that require positive human relations.

Introduction

It is commonly assumed that researchers are ethical, because they are motivated by the noble goals of discovering new knowledge and contributing to professional practice. Yet there is evidence that calls this assumption into question. Marcel LaFollette conducted a survey of professional scientists in which they were asked whether they had direct knowledge of research fraud (data falsification, incorrect reporting of findings, and plagiarizing).[1] Nineteen percent of the scientists reported they knew of such fraud. Some cases of fraud or unethical behavior have been widely reported, such as the so-called Tuskegee study which withheld medical treatment for African-American men with syphilis in order to study the progression of the disease.[2]

The fields of cultural studies and critical theory (see Chapter 15) also give us reason to question the ethical basis of research. An essential assumption of these fields of inquiry is that all individuals are enmeshed in relationships of power with other individuals. No one is truly free; rather, we are dominated by other individuals or institutions, often in subtle ways. This is no less true of research. As cultural and critical theorists see it, researchers stand in a position of power over the individuals whom they study. If we accept this assumption, it is important for researchers to become aware of their position of power and to avoid, or minimize, misuse of that power.

One manifestation of this concern is the shift in terminology used to refer to the individuals whom researchers study. The traditional term was *subjects*. Now the preferred term when reporting about individuals who were studied in a research project is *participants* or their customary designation in society (e.g., *students, teachers,* or *administrators*.[3] Use of such terms conveys a sense of individuals' role as active, willing agents in research study. We, too, use this terminology in this chapter. However, some of the literature on protection of research participants, including federal regulations (described below), refers to them as *human subjects,* so we occasionally use this term as well.

Examples of Ethical Problems in Educational Research

Researcher A collects data about the personality characteristics of certain students, and tells the students' teacher about the results. This information influences the teacher to interpret the behavior of certain students in a more negative light than if he did not know the information.

Researcher B presents second graders with a large stack of cards to sort into piles according to shape and color.[4] The task proves overwhelming and unpleasant to some students. One student begins to look around the room and pays less attention to the task, while another becomes tense and begins sorting so fast that her error rate becomes extremely high.

Researcher C identifies some teachers as more effective and others as less effective based on performance criteria (e.g., students' gains on an achievement test). The researcher then observes the teachers' classroom behaviors to determine what makes them effective or ineffective. An administrator learns that one of the teachers was classified as "less effective" by the researcher, and this information influences her to withhold a merit pay raise from the teacher.

✦ Touchstone in Research

Howe, K. R., & Moses, M. S. (1999). Ethics in educational research. In A. Iran-Nejad & P. D. Pearson (Eds.), *Review of research in education* (Vol. 24, pp. 21–59). Washington, DC: American Educational Research Association.

1. LaFollette, M. C. (1994). Research misconduct. *Society, 31*(3), 6–10.
2. Jones, J. H. (1993). *Bad blood: The Tuskegee syphilis experiment.* New York: Free Press.
3. See p. 65 of: *Publication manual of the American Psychological Association* (5th ed.). (2001). Washington, DC: American Psychological Association.
4. This example is taken from page 121 in: Koocher, G. P., & Keith-Spiegel, P. C. (1990). *Children, ethics, & the law.* Lincoln, NE: University of Nebraska Press.

Researcher D does research using a new machine that measures muscle activity during certain sports movements by creating electrical fields around the arms and legs. The machine causes temporary tingling in some individuals' extremities. One of these individuals expresses concern that the machine has caused permanent muscle damage to his arm.

Researcher E sends bilingual research assistants to interview poor Chicano families in Texas about their attitudes toward their children's schools.[5] Her goal is to provide the schools with information to help them meet the needs of children whose families have recently moved to the area. The researcher is not aware that many of the interviewees are illegal aliens, who suspect that the research may involve U.S. Immigration authorities. Some research participants become suspicious of the educators who sponsored the research study and fabricate answers to conceal their citizenship status. Others in the community hide from the researcher, thus ruining the random sample design.

All these problems have arisen in actual research. They harm or create inconvenience for the individuals being studied. Furthermore, they can hamper subsequent studies because legislators, administrators, and other individuals have become concerned about possible complaints, lawsuits, or other negative consequences. Therefore, professional associations and federal agencies have developed policies and procedures to minimize such problems. We describe these policies and procedures in the next sections.

Regulation of Research Ethics through Formal Policy

Ethical behavior in conducting educational research is in large part a personal matter. Your decisions regarding ethical questions and dilemmas that arise in a research study will reflect the depth of your moral reasoning and values. They also will reflect your understanding of ethical policies and procedures that have been put into place by professional associations and the government.

American Educational Research Association

♦ **Touchstone in Research**

American Educational Research Association. (1992). Ethical standards of the American Educational Research Association. *Educational Researcher, 21*(7), 23–26.

Various professional associations concerned with educational research have developed ethical standards to guide the conduct of their members. For example, professional associations have developed specialized ethical standards to guide program evaluation (see Chapter 17) and testing (see Chapter 7). Of more general relevance are the standards developed by the American Educational Research Association. Its publication *Ethical Standards of the American Educational Research Association* contains 45 standards organized under six main topics. Figure 3.1 reproduces the preamble and an illustrative standard for each topic. We recommend that you obtain a copy of the *Ethical Standards* and study it carefully. You will find that some of the standards deal with ethical issues of special concern to beginning researchers.

American Psychological Association

♦ **Touchstone in Research**

American Psychological Association. (1992). Ethical principles of psychologists and code of conduct. *American Psychologist, 47*, 1597–1611. Also available at: http://www.apa.org/ethics/code.html

Many educational researchers belong both to AERA and to the American Psychological Association (APA). APA published a document, *Ethical Principles of Psychologists and Code of Conduct,* to guide its members, state psychology boards, courts, and other agencies.[6] The document contains (1) a general category of ethical standards, followed by standards for (2) evaluation, assessment, or intervention; (3) advertising and other public statements; (4) therapy; (5) privacy and confidentiality; (6) teaching, training,

---

5. This example is taken from page 3 in: Sieber, J. E. (1992). *Planning ethically responsible research.* Thousand Oaks, CA: Sage.
6. APA also has a set of ethical standards for research involving animals: American Psychological Association. (1996). *Guidelines for ethical conduct in the care and use of animals.* Washington, DC: Author.

FIGURE 3.1

Preambles and Illustrative Standards from the *Ethical Standards of the American Educational Research Association*

I. *Responsibilities to the Field*
Preamble. To maintain the integrity of research, educational researchers should warrant their research conclusions adequately in a way consistent with the standards of their own theoretical and methodological perspectives. They should keep themselves well informed in both their own and competing paradigms where those are relevant to their research, and they should continually evaluate the criteria of adequacy by which research is judged.
Illustrative standard. Educational researchers should attempt to report their findings to all relevant stakeholders, and should refrain from keeping secret or selectively communicating their findings.

II. *Research Populations, Educational Institutions, and the Public*
Preamble. Educational researchers conduct research within a broad array of settings and institutions, including schools, colleges, universities, hospitals, and prisons. It is of paramount importance that educational researchers respect the right, privacy, dignity, and sensitivities of their research populations and also the integrity of the institutions within which the research occurs. Educational researchers should be especially careful in working with children and other vulnerable populations. These standards are intended to reinforce and strengthen already existing standards enforced by institutional review boards and other professional associations. Illustrative standard. Educational researchers should be sensitive to the integrity of ongoing institutional activities and alert appropriate institutional representatives of possible disturbances in such activities that may result from the conduct of the research.

III. *Intellectual Ownership*
Preamble. Intellectual ownership is predominantly a function of creative contribution. Intellectual ownership is not predominantly a function of effort expended.
Illustrative standard. All those, regardless of status, who have made substantive creative contribution to the generation of an intellectual product are entitled to be listed as authors of that product.

IV. *Editing, Reviewing, and Appraising Research*
Preamble. Editors and reviewers have a responsibility to recognize a wide variety of theoretical and methodological perspectives and, at the same time, to ensure that manuscripts meet the highest standards as defined in the various perspectives.
Illustrative standard. Editors should insist that even unfavorable reviews be dispassionate and constructive. Authors have the right to know the grounds for rejection of their work.

V. *Sponsors, Policy Makers, and Other Users of Research*
Preamble. Researchers, research institutions, and sponsors of research jointly share responsibility for the ethical integrity of research, and should ensure that this integrity is not violated. While it is recognized that these parties may sometimes have conflicting legitimate aims, all those with responsibility for research should protect against compromising the standards of research, the community of researchers, the subjects of research, and the users of research. They should support the widest possible dissemination and publication of research results. AERA should promote, as nearly as it can, conditions conducive to the preservation of research integrity.
Illustrative standard. Educational researchers should not accept funds from sponsoring agencies that request multiple renderings of reports that would distort the results or mislead readers.

VI. *Students and Student Researchers*
Preamble. Educational researchers have a responsibility to ensure the competence of those inducted into the field and to provide appropriate help and professional advice to novice researchers.
Illustrative standard. Educational researchers should not permit personal animosities or intellectual differences vis-a-vis colleagues to foreclose student and student researcher access to those colleagues, or to place the student or student researcher in an untenable position with those colleagues.

Source: Adapted from: American Educational Research Association. (1992). Ethical standards of the American Educational Research Association. Educational Researcher, *21*, (7), 23–26.

supervision, research, and publishing; (7) forensic activities; and (8) resolution of ethical issues. Several of these standards are relevant to the conduct of research, particularly standards 2, 5, 6, and 8.

The Federal Government

✦ *Touchstone in Research*

Veatch, R. M. (1996). From Nuremberg through the 1990s: The priority of autonomy. In H. Y. Vanderpool (Ed.), *The ethics of research involving human subjects: Facing the 21st Century.* Frederick, MD: University Publishing Group.

Governmental concern for protecting the rights of individuals from unethical research practices grew enormously following the Nazi regime in Germany, which ended after World War II. The Nuremberg Code was adopted as an outcome of the trials of 23 Nazi physicians for crimes against humanity. It provided a statement of the rights of individuals to understand and freely choose whether to participate in research.

The Nuremberg Code greatly influenced the development of medical ethics, which in turn influenced the development of ethics policies by social scientists (see preceding section) and national governments. In the United States in the 1960s and early 1970s, the government established federal definitions and regulations governing research performed with funding from federal agencies.

These definitions and regulations were updated in 1991, when the U.S. Government's Office for Protection from Research Risks (OPRR) published the Code of Federal Regulations for the Protection of Human Subjects.[7] The policy extends legal regulations previously in force and requires any institution that conducts research funded by a U.S. government agency to establish an institutional review board (IRB). Because of the importance of an IRB to the conduct of educational research, we describe it in depth in the next section.

Legal requirements for the protection of research participants in the United States and other countries undoubtedly will change as new issues arise. Therefore, the information we present in this chapter may no longer be current at the time you conduct your research study. Universities and large research agencies typically have a human-subjects compliance office that can inform you of regulations that are in effect for the type of study you plan to do.

Institutional Review Boards

An **institutional review board (IRB)** is a group of individuals who are authorized by an institution to determine whether research studies by colleagues affiliated with the institution comply with institutional regulations, professional standards of conduct and practice, and—most critically—the human-subjects provisions of the Code of Federal Regulations for the Protection of Human Subjects (hereafter, Federal Code). An IRB has at least five members, and their qualifications must satisfy criteria specified in the Federal Code (Paragraph 46.107).

Much of an IRB's work focuses on provisions for human-subjects protection in proposed projects, but it also is authorized to review research in progress. In addition, an IRB might oversee provisions for human-subjects protection in the collection of data in a foreign country by researchers affiliated with the institution, and the use of data that were collected in a previous project (Paragraph 46.101).

The Federal Code specifies that certain types of educational research are exempt from the human-subject provisions specified in the Code, including IRB review. However, it is

---

7. Office for Protection from Research Risks, Protection of Human Subjects. (1991, June 18). Protection of human subjects: Title 45, Code of Federal Regulations, Part 46 (GPO 1992 0-307-551). *OPRR Reports*, pp. 4–17. Also available at www.ohsr.od.nih.gov/mpa/45cfr46.php3; or Appendix B of: Sales, B. D., & Folkman, S. (Eds.). (2000). *Ethics in research with human participants.* Washington, DC: American Psychological Association.

our experience that an institution (typically, a university) will require *all* proposed research projects, including those to be conducted in educational settings, to undergo IRB review. Because the risks to participants in educational research studies typically are minimal, the IRB might expedite the review process.

As with any regulations or regulatory agency, the Federal Code and IRBs are subject to different interpretations and ambiguities. In our experience, one of the main issues involves student-generated research, conducted either out of personal interest or as a course requirement. For example, if a course instructor asks you to develop an interview schedule and test it by using it to collect and analyze data from a small number of individuals, does this constitute a research project that must be proposed and submitted to an IRB for approval?

The Federal Code defines *research* as "a systematic investigation, including research development, testing and evaluation, designed to develop or contribute to generalizable knowledge" (Paragraph 46.102.d). *Generalizable knowledge* has come to mean empirical findings that are reported in a formal manner (e.g., in a conference paper, technical report, or journal article) and that the investigator claims to be a contribution to research knowledge. By this definition, a research project conducted by a student as a course requirement does not constitute research that needs to be submitted, at the proposal stage, to an IRB for approval. Neither would a study conducted by a school district (e.g., a questionnaire survey of teachers' staff development needs or an analysis of student achievement scores across several school years) so long as the study's findings are used internally and not reported as *generalizable knowledge* about school districts in general. However, doctoral dissertation research requires IRB approval because the dissertation constitutes a publication of generalizable knowledge: The dissertation abstract is published in *Dissertation Abstracts International,* and anyone can secure a copy of the dissertation itself.

If you have any doubt about whether your proposed study conforms to the Federal Code's definition of research, you should submit it to an IRB for an opinion. One situation in particular requires special consideration. Suppose you are doing a research study as a course or degree requirement, and the faculty does not require IRB review because there is no expectation that the study will produce generalizable knowledge. However, suppose that you do an excellent study that merits publication in some form. (We have come across undergraduate honor's theses and master's theses of high research quality.) If you have not had prior IRB approval for the study, there are likely to be serious adverse consequences if you try to publish it in a journal or report it at a conference. Therefore, if you have any aspiration to report your research findings, you should discuss the need for advance IRB approval with your faculty advisors or local IRB members.

Criteria for IRB Approval of Research

The Federal Code describes specific criteria that a proposed study must satisfy to provide adequate protection to research participants (Paragraph 46.111). The IRB will use these criteria to assess whether to approve the study. An abbreviated version of the criteria as they appear in the Federal Code is shown in Figure 3.2. In the following sections, we describe procedures and issues that are involved in satisfying these criteria.

Assessment of the Risk-Benefit Ratio

In reviewing the protocol for a planned study, the IRB considers carefully the study's risk-benefit ratio. A **risk-benefit ratio** is the balance between how much risk the participants

FIGURE 3.2

Criteria for IRB Approval of Research

1. Risks to subjects are minimized: (i) by using procedures which are consistent with sound research design and which do not unnecessarily expose subjects to risk, and (ii) whenever appropriate, by using procedures already being performed on the subjects for diagnostic or treatment purposes.
2. Risks to subjects are reasonable in relation to anticipated benefits, if any, to subjects, and the importance of the knowledge that may reasonably be expected to result.
3. Selection of subjects is equitable.
4. Informed consent will be sought from each prospective subject or the subject's legally authorized representative.
5. Informed consent will be appropriately documented.
6. When appropriate, the research plan makes adequate provision for monitoring the data collected to ensure the safety of subjects.
7. When appropriate, there are adequate provisions to protect the privacy of subjects and to maintain the confidentiality of data.
8. When some or all of the subjects are likely to be vulnerable to coercion or undue influence, such as children, prisoners, pregnant women, mentally disabled persons, or economically or educationally disadvantaged persons, additional safeguards have been included in the study to protect the rights and welfare of these subjects.

Source: Adapted from Paragraph 46.111 of: Office for Protection from Research Risks, Protection of Human Subjects. (1991, June 18). Protection of human subjects: Title 45, Code of Federal Regulations, Part 46 (GPO 1992 0-307-551). *OPRR Reports,* pp. 4–17.

will be exposed to and how much good is likely to result from the study. Risk to participants might be physical, psychological, or legal. Benefits can be considered in terms of how helpful the study is to participants, to some other group (e.g., the population to which the results will be generalized), or to the advancement of research knowledge. If risks are more than minimal, an assessment is made of the benefits to be expected from carrying out the study. Then the risks and benefits are subjectively compared to determine whether the latter sufficiently outweigh the former.

To illustrate, consider the example of Researcher D at the beginning of the chapter. (The case is based on an actual study.) The proposed research involved physical risk because of the unknown side effects of the newly developed machine for exciting muscles used by the researcher. To deal with this risk ethically, the researcher first should do an exhaustive review of the literature. The review should seek to determine that no adverse direct effects or side effects have been discovered from use of the type of equipment involved in the proposed research. If any adverse effects are found or suspected, the researcher should note their severity and incidence of occurrence and procedures that can be used to minimize and treat them.

Once the risks are assessed, the benefits of the proposed research should be determined. Is this study really necessary? What new knowledge is it likely to yield? For example, suppose the machine that Researcher D wishes to use proves to be more effective for measuring the speed of muscle recovery after exercise than machines currently in use. This potential benefit, however, still might not outweigh the risk of physical harm to which research participants would be exposed. However, suppose that the machine, if proved accurate, could be used to detect the onset of neuromuscular disease more quickly than existing machines, as well as to measure the effectiveness of different physical education training procedures. In this case, IRB members might judge that the potential benefits of the study outweigh the physical risks to which research participants will be exposed.

Although the risk-benefit ratio appears to be a sound ethical approach, it puts the IRB in the position of "playing god" with other people's lives. One can argue that individuals have absolute rights that an IRB cannot dismiss simply because of a favorable risk-benefit ratio. In fact, these absolute rights are protected through provisions for informed consent, privacy, and confidentiality, which we describe above. Thus, even if an IRB approves a research proposal, it cannot take away the rights of individuals to be informed of the study's purpose and to freely choose to decline participation without penalty.

Selection of Participants

If the researcher's sample includes minors or members of vulnerable populations (e.g., disabled students), he is expected to take special precautions to protect them from risk. In addition, participants must be selected equitably, such that any individual in the available population has a reasonable chance of being in the sample. For example, this guideline would prohibit a researcher from asking a teacher to select a group of students from her classroom to participate in an out-of-classroom experiment. This procedure is unacceptable because the teacher might view participation in the experiment as a special privilege, and therefore choose students whom she wishes to reward for one reason or another. Students who are not selected might feel resentment or a loss of self-esteem. To avoid this potential harm to students, the researcher is expected to take steps to ensure that students are selected equitably. Selecting students by a random drawing would be one way to satisfy this requirement.

Informed Consent

Researchers must inform each individual about what will occur during the research study, the information to be disclosed to the researchers, and the intended use of the research data that are to be collected. If adults are the participants, they must give their consent. In the case of minors, researchers must obtain only their assent, because minors cannot legally give consent. However, in most cases, consent is needed from the child's main caretaker (usually a parent), and also from appropriate school personnel if the research is carried out in the schools.

Each participant should receive an explanation of the tests and experimental procedures to be used. This explanation must satisfy the participant that participation is important and desirable and that it is to his or her advantage to cooperate. Participants also must be informed that they can withdraw from participation at any time, and their requests to do so must be honored. If they are promised payments, rewards, or grade credits for participation, they must be offered these incentives even if they subsequently withdraw from the study. To do otherwise would be to give the impression that there is a penalty associated with leaving the study.

The IRB requires that each prospective research participant receive a letter describing the research and the conditions of their participation. The letter must be written in language that is understandable to them. Individuals who agree to participate in the study need to sign and return a copy of the letter, and keep a copy for themselves. Figure 3.3 shows an informed-consent letter from a qualitative research study carried out by Judy

FIGURE 3.3

Letter to Obtain Informed Consent from Participants in a Research Study of the Composing Process of Patrol Officers

Dear . . . Patrol Officer:

I am a student at the University of Oregon working on my doctoral degree in teacher education. I am particularly interested in teaching writing. There is a large body of research that describes how students write various types of assignments, but very little about how people write once they leave school and enter a profession. I suspect that writing in the professions is, in some ways, quite different from writing in school. This study is my initial effort to discover what differences exist. I have chosen to study the way patrol officers write reports, not only because it is a large part of your job, but also because of the legal importance of those reports. I am seeking volunteers for my study, and I am hoping you will consider being one of those volunteers.

What we know about student writers includes: (a) how they plan/organize, (b) how they get their thoughts on paper (i.e., how many words they write in each burst, how much re-reading they do as they write, etc.), and (c) how much revising, crossing out, or changing they are likely to do. We also know something about how word processors have affected the writing process. These are the things I would like to study among patrol officers, and eventually people in other professions as well.

My study is descriptive, not evaluative. It does not deal with the content of your reports, but merely the process you use to write them. I want to capture realistic scenarios including breaks, interruptions, and any environmental influences on your writing.

If you decide to participate in my study, here is what would happen:

1. I will interview you to find out about your writing style, any writing instruction or assistance you've received, and the writing expected of you as a patrol officer. This interview will likely last 45–60 minutes. I will tape record the interview and transcribe your comments for future reference.
2. I will accompany you in the patrol car during at least 1 shift to learn more about the context in which you write.
3. I will videotape you as you write at least 2 reports. One camera will be focused on the report form you are writing. A second camera will film you at a distance to capture your writing environment.
4. After videotaping the writing of your report, you and I will view the tape together. I will ask you questions about your writing and will tape record your responses. I might ask you how you use your notes, which parts of the report were the easiest or hardest and why, why you chose a particular word, or what you were thinking during pauses. I will obtain a copy of your final report and your notes to use during the analysis phase of my study.
5. After collecting data for my study, I will analyze the results. You will be given the opportunity to read the portion of my dissertation that pertains to you. A copy of the completed dissertation will be given to the . . . Police Department.

Participation in this study is voluntary. Your decision whether or not to participate will not affect your relationship with the . . . Police Department. Furthermore, your captain has guaranteed that the results of the study will not affect your employment or status in the department. If you decide to participate, you are free to withdraw your consent and discontinue participation at any time without penalty. This study will be conducted during your regular working hours. Your Chief and your Captain have agreed to the terms of this study and are willing to be flexible in terms of the time needed to conduct interviews and post-taping interviews.

All data collected for this study become the property of the researcher. Any information that is obtained in connection with this study and that can be identified with you will remain confidential and will be disclosed only with your permission. Data will be handled according to the guidelines specified by the American Psychological Association. Although all possible safeguards will be used to protect your anonymity, the methodology of the study prevents complete anonymity in all situations. The use of pseudonyms will protect your identity from outsiders, but your superiors and perhaps some of your fellow officers will know of your involvement in the study.

By participating in this study, you are contributing to primary research on the nature of police writing. If schools are to adequately prepare students for the demands of writing in various professions, it is essential that researchers document the nature of writing within those professions. This will be the first study to look at the process of patrol officers' report writing and, as such, will offer a realistic description of the writing demands of your job and the various influences upon your writing. It will give each person who reads my final report a clear idea of how patrol officers write and the conditions under which such writing is accomplished.

Ideally, I would like four volunteers for my study. It would be helpful if these volunteers represent different lengths of service as patrol officers. I will include both female and male officers, and officers with varying degrees of expertise in the use of computers.

If you have any questions, please feel free to contact me (Judy Cape, [phone number]) or my university advisor (Lynne Anderson-Inman, [phone number]). If you have questions regarding your rights as a research subject, contact the Research Compliance Office, University of Oregon, Eugene, OR 97403, (phone number). You will be offered a copy of this form to keep.

Your signature indicates that you have read and understand the information provided above, that you willingly agree to participate, that you may withdraw your consent at any time and discontinue participation without penalty, that you will receive a copy of this form, and that you are not waiving any legal claims, rights or remedies. Volunteers will be selected by the researcher from among the applicants submitting this form. You will be notified of your selection by __(date)__.

_____

Signature   Date

Please return this form to Judy Cape before __(date)__ by using the attached self-addressed, stamped envelope. Thank you.

Source: Reprinted with permission of Cape, J. E. (1992). The composing process of patrol officers (Protocol #X26–93). Eugene, OR: University of Oregon, Office of Research Compliance.

Cape at the University of Oregon as part of the requirements for completing her doctoral dissertation.[8] Cape was interested in how adults use writing in their work. She decided to study the writing skills of police officers in a local community. Four patrol officers, selected from a pool of 28 patrol officers employed in the community, served as her primary research participants. Because of the sensitive nature of the study (e.g., police reports are admissible as evidence in courts of law), the informed-consent letter needed to be particularly thorough.

As we noted above, informed consent includes participants' understanding that they have the right to withdraw from the research investigation at any time, and their freedom to exercise that right. The case of Researcher B at the beginning of this chapter involves a potential violation of this aspect of informed consent. According to Gerald Koocher and Patricia Keith-Spiegel, children rarely make clear requests to withdraw from research. However, they can exhibit implicit signs of "wanting out," such as the off-task or inappropriate behavior exhibited by the children studied by Researcher B. Koocher and Keith-Spiegel recommend that investigators assess such cues and assist children in exercising the right to withdraw. For example, they might ask, "Would you like to stop now?" They note

8. Cape, J. E. (1993). *The composing process of police officers:* Writing police reports. *Dissertation Abstracts International 54*(08), 3000A. (UMI No. 9402011)

that it is important to respect a participant's rights for autonomy even if she does not clearly state her apparent wishes, and that results based on data from unhappy, bored, or inattentive children are suspect.[9]

In some types of research, the findings could be invalidated if participants know beforehand the purpose of the study and the specific experiences in which they will be involved during data collection and experimental treatments. For example, some experiments involve deception, such as giving students false information about their performance in order to determine the effects of changes in their motivational level on subsequent task performance. Even in such situations, the researcher should obtain the individual's consent to be in the experiment and should tell subjects that they will be informed of the experiment's purpose *after* the study is completed.

Privacy and Confidentiality

The case of Researcher A at the beginning of the chapter involved a violation of confidentiality. The researcher should not have given the teacher information about the personality characteristics of certain students. When a teacher has such information, students are put at risk because the teacher now has expectations that can influence the teacher's future behavior toward these students. For example, the teacher might relate to a student described as "emotionally disturbed" in a more guarded way during class. Or the teacher might have lowered expectations about a student's ability once the teacher learns that the student has been classified as having an "external locus of control."

The case of Researcher C also involves a violation of confidentiality. In this instance, the confidentiality of teachers is violated when a school administrator obtains data concerning teachers' effectiveness based on research criteria and classroom observations. Teachers identified as ineffective can suffer severe risks in terms of subsequent decisions about them made by the administrator who obtained this information.

Research participants should be told at the outset of the study who will have access to data. Once research data have been collected, the researcher must ensure that no unauthorized persons have access to them, and that the privacy of individuals to whom the data apply is protected.

A good rule to follow is to minimize the number of individuals who know the identity of research participants. In most studies, even assistants who help you collect and analyze research data do not need to know the participants' identity. In fact, it may be possible to collect research data so that no one, including the researcher, can link the data to specific subjects. Otherwise, some sort of linkage system, such as substituting numbers for names, can be used so that only a person who has access to a closely guarded code can identify data for a specific subject.

In some projects, the researcher must retain some means of identifying participants by name. For example, in longitudinal studies the researcher must retain the names and current addresses of the research participants so she can follow them over time. In other research studies, data are gathered from a variety of sources. These data often need to be linked in order to have a clear picture of the phenomenon being studied. Such linkage is difficult unless some means of identifying subjects by name is retained for at least a short period of time.

When a research study deals with controversial or sensitive topics, confidentiality is extremely important. Researchers must take particular care with data that conceivably

---

9. Koocher & Keith-Spiegel, *Children, ethics, & the law.*

could be subpoenaed. In most states educational research data do not have privileged status (as does, for example, communication between husband and wife or between lawyer and client). Confidentiality must be further protected by not using the names of individuals or locations in any publications that result from the research project, unless agreed to by all parties.

While confidentiality always should be protected if research participants have been led to expect it, there are some situations where research ethics may require that their identity be revealed. Judith Shulman carried out collaborative research with beginning teachers who helped develop a casebook on mentoring for use in training new teachers.[10] These teachers told stories about their early experiences in teaching, and they asked that their names be kept on their own case reports. Administrators who reviewed the reports initially insisted on various substantive changes, including that the teacher-authors not be identified by name. Shulman described the careful negotiations between the researchers and school personnel that were necessary to accommodate the school district's major objections, and the argument that was used to convince the district to allow the teachers to be identified:

> The question of identifying teacher informants/collaborators can no longer be automatically answered on the side of anonymity. The ethnographer's traditions of rendering informants invisible were produced in an era when informants were seen as powerless and in need of protection. In our day, research on teaching has become one of the vehicles for the professionalization and empowerment of teachers. The anonymous teacher may no longer be an appropriate focus for all studies of teaching.[11]

If the researcher has determined that confidentiality is essential to protect research participants, it can be provided in various ways, including

1. asking subjects to furnish information anonymously;
2. using a third party (i.e., someone who is neither part of the research team nor affiliated with the institution from whom participants are drawn) to select the sample and collect data;
3. using an identifier (e.g., a detachable section of a questionnaire with a preprinted code) that can be destroyed as soon as the individual's response is received, so that the researcher can tell which participants responded but cannot associate particular responses with the individual who gave them;
4. if data from more than one administration must be matched for each participant, having participants make up an alias or code number (e.g., the birth dates of one's parents or every other digit in one's social security number); and
5. disposing of sensitive data at a designated time after the study is completed.

Vulnerable Populations

The case of Researcher E at the beginning of the chapter involved a violation of ethical principles in conducting research with a vulnerable population, namely Chicano families living in the United States without citizenship. Joan Sieber, who described this case in a book on research ethics, commented that a scientist with an understanding of community-based research would have enlisted community leaders in formulating the research

---

10. Shulman, J. (1990). Now you see them, now you don't: Anonymity versus visibility in case studies of teachers. *Educational Researcher, 19*(6), 11–15.
11. Ibid., p. 14.

procedures, would have trained community representatives to conduct the interviews, and would have closely supervised the entire research process.[12]

In describing the ethics code of the American Psychological Association, Thomas Grisso and his colleagues identified as examples of vulnerable populations individuals in poverty or "vulnerable people in transition" (e.g., people with profound mental retardation or serious mental illness who are moving from large institutional settings to community-based settings).[13] Other vulnerable populations were identified by Frederick Erickson.[14] He noted that any individuals who are the focus of a research study are especially vulnerable in relation to other individuals within their institution or community, and that those who are single occupants of an institutional status (such as the lone kindergarten teacher in a school or the school's principal) are particularly vulnerable. Vulnerability is often accentuated in qualitative research because the methodology typically involves intensive study of one case or a small number of cases over a substantial period of time.

Educational researchers may be very dissimilar in intellectual attainments, lifestyles, or values from the individuals whom they wish to study. This dissimilarity can expose the individuals to risk because of the researcher's lack of knowledge about their particular vulnerabilities. We already have mentioned one strategy that researchers can use to minimize risk, namely consulting with experts who have worked closely with individuals like those the researcher plans to study. Another approach is to involve representatives of the population in designing the research study. For example, Murray Wax reflected on the unique ethics of research in American Indian communities. He claimed that joint planning between the investigator and the tribe

> would encourage researchers to think more deeply about both benefits and potential harms, as viewed by the tribal members. Rather than regarding themselves as the exploited victims of careerist scientists, they might come to define themselves as co-participants with correlative status, responsibilities, and privileges.[15]

This type of joint planning is becoming increasingly common in educational research, especially in qualitative research and in evaluation studies.

Ethical Issues in Conducting Research

✦ *Touchstone in Research*

Christians, C. (2000). Ethics and politics in qualitative research. In N. K. Denzin & Y. Lincoln (Eds.), *The handbook of qualitative research* (2nd ed., pp. 133–135). Thousand Oaks, CA: Sage.

Sales, B. D., & Folkman, S. (Eds.). (2000). *Ethics in research with human participants.* Washington, DC: American Psychological Association.

It is important for you to know the ethical issues that can occur at various points in the research process so that you can anticipate them and employ appropriate strategies to resolve them. Some of these issues were addressed in preceding sections of the chapter, because they are tied to IRB criteria for human-subjects protection (see Figure 3.2). In the following sections, we discuss additional ethical issues that can arise in the course of a research study.

Although these issues apply to both quantitative and qualitative research, some of them take on a different face in the two paradigms. Quantitative studies generally are guided by positivist epistemology (see Chapter 1), which tends to create an impersonal,

---

12. Sieber, *Planning ethically responsible research.*
13. Grisso, T., Baldwin, E., Blanck, P. D., Rotheram-Borus, M. J., Schooler, N. R., & Thompson, T. (1991). Standards in research: APA's mechanism for monitoring the challenge. *American Psychologist, 46,* 758–766.
14. Erickson, F. (1986). Qualitative methods in research on teaching. In M. C. Wittrock (Ed.), *Handbook of research on teaching.* (3rd ed., pp. 119–161). New York: Macmillan.
15. Wax, M. L. (1991). The ethics of research in American Indian communities. *American Indian Quarterly, 15,* 431–456. Quote appears on pp. 453–454.

detached relationship between researchers and participants. Ethical misjudgments are possible in this type of relationship, but they tend not to be of a serious nature. In contrast, qualitative studies require a particular kind of intimacy between researchers and participants in order to discover the meanings and settings that define the participants' lived experiences. These meanings and settings might be secret or highly private in nature, and thus ethical issues concerning deception and obtaining access to data loom large.

In a quantitative research study, most or all of the methodology is determined at the proposal stage. Therefore, the researcher can identify possible risks to participants beforehand and take steps to minimize them. In contrast, the design of qualitative research studies is typically emergent. New questions, new circumstances, and the need for new methods can arise in the course of fieldwork or other naturalistic contexts. These changes, in turn, can create unanticipated ethical risks that are not easily resolved. In such situations, you are advised to discuss the risks and possible courses of action with colleagues and the IRB that is overseeing your study's provisions for human-subjects protection.

Planning and Designing Research

Researcher Qualifications

Because poorly designed research can cause harm to participants, the competence, perspective, and character of the researcher himself is an ethical issue. In discussing the ethics of research involving children, Koocher and Keith-Spiegel argue that researchers should study only those problems with which they are competent to deal.[16] They also recommend that researchers consult with colleagues for feedback on their competence to do the study and on whether their values and biases might compromise the integrity of the research design or the welfare of research participants.

Conflict of Interest

A conflict of interest arises when a researcher's choice of a data-collection instrument or intervention (e.g., use of particular curriculum materials) has financial implications for the researcher. For example, Grisso and his colleagues described cases in which researchers working in the field of biotechnology were in a position to gain financial advantage from research decisions in which they or their colleagues participated. Efforts are currently being made to establish legal guidelines to govern such cases.[17]

Neglecting Important Topics

Experts on research ethics have identified various problems that can arise for research participants or other groups when particular phenomena are studied. However, ethics also are involved in the neglect of certain topics by researchers. Luis Laosa, for example, noted a tendency among some researchers to generalize their findings to populations to which the findings may not apply.[18] Laosa discussed research findings about the use of students' scores on the Home Observation for Measurement of the Environment (HOME) Inventory to predict their intellectual performance. In one study, HOME scores significantly

---

16. Koocher & Keith-Spiegel, *Children, ethics, & the law.*
17. Grisso et al., Standards in research.
18. Laosa, L. M. (1991). The cultural context of construct validity and the ethics of generalizability. *Early Childhood Research Quarterly, 6,* 313–321.

predicted intellectual performance for non-Hispanic white and African-American sam-ples, but the corresponding coefficients for the Mexican-American sample were non-significant and near zero. This finding, among others, demonstrates the potential effects of ethnicity on educational outcomes. Ignoring ethnic differences creates the possible risk of making inappropriate generalizations from one's research findings.

Another example of neglect is found in the field of health. For many years, thousands of school secretaries and teachers—most of them female—used ditto sheets and ditto fluid to run copies of school materials. However, the 1985–86 *Registry of Toxic Effects of Chemical Substances,* published by the U.S. Department of Health and Human Services, included very few studies on the toxicity of methanol, the main chemical in ditto fluid.[19] Five animal studies had been conducted with mice and rats, but none examined possible effects on reproduction. As of that date, there were no studies of the effects of methanol on human beings in general, or on pregnant women in particular.

Research Methodology

Use of Deception

✦ Touchstone in Research

Korn, J. H. (1997). *Illusions of reality: A history of deception in social psychology.* Albany, NY: State University of New York Press.

Deception is the act of creating a false impression in the minds of research participants through such procedures as withholding information, establishing false intimacy, telling lies, or using accomplices. Deception has been used frequently in laboratory studies conducted by social psychologists in order to investigate phenomena that otherwise could not be studied. For example, suppose a researcher is interested in how students respond to another student's cheating. It would be difficult to find sufficient natural occurrences of this situation and to develop an unobtrusive method for collecting data on it. However, the situation could be created frequently and observed reliably by using an *accomplice* (also called a *confederate*), that is, an individual recruited by the researcher to engage in deception. The deception would involve having the accomplice "cheat" in the presence of other students so that the researcher can observe these students' reactions.

Another approach to research on this problem would be to conduct ethnographic fieldwork. The researcher might make explicit his role as a researcher and seek certain students at a school to act as informants. In order to get the informants to reveal secretive information about cheating incidents at the school, the researcher might attempt to seduce them into a buddy relationship, a false intimacy that is a form of deception.[20] Alternatively, the researcher might "go native" by pretending to be a student himself. (In fact, there are cases of adults who have disguised their identity and enrolled as high school students.) The disguise is clearly a deception, but one that is likely to unearth insider data about cheating in school.

Some people are opposed to the use of deception in any research because they believe that it is morally wrong. Others oppose deception for practical reasons as well. For example, Yvonna Lincoln and Egon Guba, two proponents of the constructivist paradigm in qualitative research, argue that "if the inquirer is interested in [respondents'] constructions, then it is pointless to lie to or deceive" them.[21]

---

19. National Institute of Occupational Safety and Health (1985–86). *The registry of toxic effects of chemical substances.* Washington, DC: U.S. Department of Health and Human Services.
20. The use of seduction and related techniques in research is discussed in: Wong, L. M. (1998). The ethics of rapport: Institutional safeguards, resistance, and betrayal. *Qualitative Inquiry, 4,* 178–199.
21. Lincoln, Y. S., & Guba, E. G. (1989). Ethics: The failure of positivist science. *Review of Higher Education, 12,* 221–240. Quote appears on p. 230.

Suppose that the use of deception in a particular study can be justified through analysis of its risk-benefit ratio. In this case, legal regulations require that researchers debrief subjects as soon as possible after the deception. Two different types of debriefing can be used: dehoaxing and desensitization.

In **dehoaxing** participants, the researcher must convince everyone who was deceived during a research study that they were in fact deceived. The purpose is to ensure that the false information will do no future harm to any participant. For example, students participating in a research study might be given fraudulent test scores in order to measure the effect of these scores on their level of aspiration. After data have been collected, the researcher has a responsibility to inform them that the scores were not an accurate measure of their ability. If the students continued to believe that the false scores were correct, this belief might do long-lasting damage to their self-esteem or academic aspirations.

In some situations, simply telling participants that they have been deceived is not sufficient. Instead, it is necessary to engage in **desensitization,** which is a process of convincing participants of the deception and thus removing its undesirable effects. For example, suppose a researcher used deception in an experiment on conformity to college social norms. During the experiment, some students may have exhibited inappropriate behavior more frequently when other people (who are confederates) exhibit the behavior. For example, in the presence of a confederate whom they observed reading a newspaper during a college lecture, some students (unaware that they were being observed as part of an experiment) also might have ignored the professor and done something else unrelated to the class. The knowledge that they were observed engaging in such behavior might cause them to start doubting their commitment to their studies.

Douglas Holmes suggested two approaches for desensitizing research participants in such situations.[22] One approach is to suggest that the participants' behavior resulted from the circumstances of the experiment and was not due to defects in their character or personality. A second approach is to point out that the participants' behavior is not abnormal or unusual. In effect, these approaches provide research participants with rationalizations that make it possible for them to accept the fact that they engaged in behavior that may be in conflict with their own self-perceptions or moral code. Still, others might argue that such a procedure actually promotes unethical behavior on the part of participants, rather than protecting them from such risk.

Control Groups

Participants in experimental research are placed in different treatment conditions, and thus are not treated equally. The treatment group is likely to receive special training or the opportunity to participate in an innovative program, while the control group receives either nothing or a conventional program. An ethical dilemma exists because the control group can be viewed as having been treated unfairly by not receiving the special training or innovative program. For example, Carolyn Evertson described an experiment in which treatment-group teachers attended classroom management workshops at the beginning of the school year.[23] School personnel expressed concern because control-group teachers did not participate in the training program and thus were deprived of its perceived bene-

22. Holmes, D. S. (1976). Debriefing after psychological experiments: I. Effectiveness of postdeception dehoaxing. *American Psychologist, 31,* 868–875.
23. Evertson, C. M. (1989). Improving elementary classroom management: A school-based training program for beginning the year. *Journal of Educational Research, 83,* 82–90.

fits. The researchers dealt with this concern by scheduling the control-group teachers for the same workshops soon after data collection was completed.

Termination of Treatment Conditions

The time frame for terminating an experimental program offered to participants as part of a research study may not coincide with the ideal time to end it in terms of participants' needs. Termination of the experimental treatment may be especially difficult for individuals if they have developed a good relationship with the research team, or if the baseline condition in a single-subject experimental design is re-established. (Single-subject experiments are described in Chapter 13.) To avoid harm to participants in such situations, researchers must weigh the planned schedule of research activities against the needs of participants. They may find it necessary to redesign the activities to minimize potential harm to participants when the treatment condition is terminated.

Use of Tests

The use of tests in research raises many ethical issues. For example, many individuals suffer from anxiety in testing situations. Thus, whenever a researcher administers a test as part of the data-collection process, some or all of the participants may be at risk for test anxiety. If you plan to administer tests in your research study, you will need to figure out how to elicit participants' best performance while minimizing their anxiety.

Personality inventories, attitude scales, and other self-report measures raise a different ethical issue. These measures require self-disclosure, which may be threatening to some individuals. Therefore, you will need to determine how to elicit valid responses to self-report measures while minimizing threats caused by self-disclosure. Assurances of anonymity and data confidentiality are recommended procedures for this purpose.

Recent advances in computer-based test interpretation have added new ethical concerns to those traditionally associated with test taking. For example, some individuals may experience discomfort while taking a computer-administered test and may feel threatened by the knowledge that computer software will interpret their performance or self-report responses. There also is the potential for violation of privacy when test results are stored in computer files. The APA has developed ethical guidelines for testing practices in general and for computer-based testing in particular.[24]

Data Collection and Analysis

The collection and analysis of empirical data is the heart of the research enterprise. Unfortunately, ethical misconduct is known to have occurred in the conduct of these activities. Researchers have fabricated data or statistical analyses. Also, they have misrepresented their findings by "massaging" the data by such methods as deleting data from analyses or failing to report results that do not support their research hypotheses or biases. Highly publicized cases of these types of misconduct have occurred in fields other than educational research, but there is no reason to believe that educational research is immune to this problem.

It is difficult, if not impossible, to monitor researchers' behavior in collecting and analyzing data, or to detect the occurrence of misconduct. Therefore, we must remind our-

24. Fremer, J., Diamond, E. E., & Camara, W. J. (1989). Developing a code of fair testing practices in education. *American Psychologist, 44,* 1062–1067; American Psychological Association (1987). *Guidelines for computer-based tests and interpretations.* (1987). Washington, DC: Author.

selves of the great harm that results to the education profession and its clients if inaccurate knowledge is generated through ethical misconduct. We also must work with other members of the education community to ensure that ethical standards for research exist and are upheld.

Reporting Research

Partial or Dual Publication

Some research practices are ethically unacceptable because they are harmful to one's colleagues or to the profession as a whole. Several of these practices involve the manner in which the findings of research are reported. **Partial publication** involves disseminating research results in the "least publishable unit" rather than as a coherent whole. This situation can arise if a study involves different types of variables. For example, suppose an experiment is done to determine the effects of an instructional method on cognitive and attitudinal learning outcomes, involving students from different ethnic backgrounds. Partial publication would occur if the researcher published the results for the cognitive learning outcomes in one article, the results for the attitudinal outcomes in a second article, and the results for ethnic differences in a third article. An even more serious ethical lapse is **dual publication,** which involves publishing the same research results in more than one publication.

Grisso and his colleagues identified the ethical problems created by these practices.[25] For example, readers of the research literature may not be able to distinguish how several different reports of the same research study differ in focus, scope, or recency, which complicates their ability to grasp the overall pattern of the findings concerning a research problem. An even more serious ethical problem is that professors who engage in partial or dual publication may gain credit for numerous publications from the same study, and thus may receive tenure or promotion more readily than professors who report their findings in the form of fewer, more comprehensive publications. Also, partial and dual publication consume scarce journal space or slots for presentations at professional conferences, and thus may prevent other deserving researchers from reporting their studies.

Another ethical issue involves the submission of research manuscripts for publication. We know of cases in which a researcher has submitted a manuscript to more than one journal without informing the journals that that this was being done. Each journal conducted an editorial review of the manuscript, and both accepted it for publication. Only then were the respective journal editors informed of the dual submission. In this case, the hard work of the editors of the journal rejected by the authors was for naught. For this reason, a researcher should submit a manuscript to one journal and await an editorial decision. If the decision is negative, the researcher then is free to submit it to another journal.

Plagiarism

An editorial in the *Journal of Educational Psychology* identified **plagiarism** (the direct lifting of others' words for use in one's own publications) as an ethical issue of growing concern.[26] Plagiarism, perhaps even more than partial or dual publication, damages an

---

25. Grisso et al., Standards in research.
26. Levin, J. R., & Marshall, H. H. (1993). Publishing in the *Journal of Educational Psychology:* Reflections at midstream. *Journal of Educational Psychology, 85,* 3–6.

author's colleagues and the profession as a whole because it involves taking undeserved credit for something that another professional has written.

The editors, Joel Levin and Hermine Marshall, also argued that paraphragiarism is just as serious an offense as plagiarism. **Paraphragiarism** involves close copying of another writer's words or ideas, for example, extended paraphrases of another's words, one-to-one correspondence in the expression of ideas, and structural similarities in writing. Levin and Marshall make two suggestions to avoid this problem: Cite the author of the original words, ideas, or structures; and do not attempt to paraphrase someone else's thoughts while looking directly at the source, but instead, "close the book and then paraphrase (with appropriate referencing)."[27]

Authorship

Various ethical issues arise in decisions about who is to be the author or co-author of a research report. For example, suppose an individual made significant contributions to a study by designing and conducting the statistical analyses, but did not write the final report. Should this individual be considered a co-author of the report? Suppose the principal researcher includes co-authors in one publication resulting from a research study (e.g., a presentation at a professional meeting), but not in another publication (e.g., a subsequent journal article). Is this ethical? Suppose several researchers do a study and co-author a report. One of these researchers later writes an article for a journal in which he explores implications of the study's findings for improving educational practice. Is it ethical for the researcher not to include his co-investigators as co-authors of this article? If there are several co-authors, how is order of authorship to be determined?

The first step in answering questions such as these is for all co-investigators to read the *Ethical Standards of the American Educational Research Association*, which we described above. We recommend that all co-investigators then meet to discuss their preferences concerning the authorship of any reports resulting from the study. One of us (M. Gall) co-directed a large project in which he put in writing the agreements reached at such a meeting. All those involved in the project were able to express their preferences in the process of reaching consensus, and everyone received a copy of the written statement.

If you are a student who is doing research under the guidance of a university faculty member, you might check to determine whether the university has a policy for handling the various authorship issues that can arise in this situation. These issues can be especially difficult when graduate students are doing research with or under the direction of faculty members, on whom they rely for completion of their degree programs and job placement assistance. Students are vulnerable because of the power differential between them and faculty members.

An informal policy that one of us (M. Gall) has found to work well over a period of many years is this: Be generous about including co-investigators as co-authors.[28] If there is any doubt, give the collaborator the benefit of the doubt, as when a statistician makes a significant professional contribution to your data analysis but does not write any of the final report except for several statistical tables. Regarding order of authorship, his policy—consistent with AERA's *Ethical Standards*—is that the order should be determined strictly

---

27. Ibid., p. 6.
28. The published report of one study that he directed had seven co-authors: Gall, M. D., Ward, B. A., Berliner, D. C., Cahen, L. C., Winne, P. H., Elashoff, J. D., & Stanton, G. C. (1978). Effects of questioning techniques and recitation on student learning. *American Educational Research Journal, 15,* 175–199.

by the amount of work of a professional nature done by each co-investigator, not by the co-investigator's reputation or seniority.

Human Relations in Research

You should have a specific plan to establish and maintain positive human relations with the individuals who participate in your research study. Often these individuals are contacted through a particular institution. Thus, you also need to build a positive relationship with the administrators and other members of the institution from whom you will select your research participants. Below we describe four aspects of field research that require positive human relations: (1) locating a satisfactory research site, (2) securing permission and cooperation for carrying out the research, (3) building a relationship with the institution, and (4) dealing with possible breakdowns.

✦ *Touchstone in Research*

de Laine, M. (2000). *Fieldwork, participation and practice: Ethics and dilemmas in qualitative research.* Thousand Oaks, CA: Sage.

Locating a Research Site

Careful selection of a research site will help to ensure the success of your research study. If you wish to conduct a laboratory study, you may be able to carry it out at your university without much difficulty. For example, the initial research study of one of the authors (J. Gall, working at that time under her maiden name, Joyce Pershing) was conducted in a psychophysiology laboratory at the University of California at Berkeley, where she did her graduate work.[29] She investigated gender differences in grief and sadness, using undergraduate students enrolled in psychology courses as the research subjects. The study involved students individually watching a film about the life and death of President John Kennedy, who was assassinated at the age of 46 while in office. While viewing the film, the student was attached to devices that measured skin conductance and heart rate. After the film, the student filled out a self-report measure of emotions. The use of a laboratory setting allowed her to use experimental controls and data-collection methods that would have been virtually impossible in a field setting.

Field settings—such as schools, homes, and community centers—are more appropriate than laboratory settings for many of the problems that interest educational researchers. It is a major challenge, however, to locate a field setting and enlist the cooperation of the individuals in them whom you wish to study. Geoffrey Maruyama and Stanley Deno suggested several strategies for this purpose.[30] One of them is to contact a state or regional department of education where you might be able to find out about schools with educational facilities or demonstration programs that are consistent with your research interests.

If you currently are employed by an educational institution, you might consider conducting your research study there. In fact, the majority of doctoral dissertations with which we have been associated were conducted at the institution where the student is or was currently employed.

Conducting a research study at your own institution has both advantages and disadvantages. On the positive side, you may find it easier to obtain approval for your study because you have access to the decision makers in your institution. Furthermore, you are familiar with the normal routines of the institution, such as how schedules are arranged,

---

29. Pershing, J. C., & Averill, J. A. (1968). Sex differences in psychophysiological reactions to a sadness-inducing film. Paper presented at the Western Psychological Association convention, San Diego, CA.
30. Maruyama, G., & Deno, S. (1992). *Research in educational settings.* Thousand Oaks, CA: Sage.

or what the best procedure is for setting up a meeting of key staff. On the negative side, your particular position within the institution may cause you to be less aware of some concerns of other members of the institution that might affect your research. Furthermore, you could be hindered in carrying out your study, or vulnerable to certain sanctions, because of your relationship with particular individuals in the institution.

Securing Permission and Cooperation

When conducting research in institutions, you must follow certain procedures in order to obtain permission for your study and to gain cooperation from the individuals who will be affected by it. As a first step, you need a brief, clear, written description of your research design, which you can use to explain your proposed research. The human-subjects protocol that you prepare for your IRB, including letters of informed consent and a description of the measures that you plan to administer, can serve as this description. Having these documents available demonstrates your professionalism, which is essential to obtaining the support of an institution's administrators. Also, they are more likely to give their permission if they know *exactly* what is required of the institution and of individual participants, what problems might arise, and how the problems would be handled.

Some administrators are negative about educational research because of their concern about its possible costs and inconvenience to their institution. For example, a superintendent might worry about staff time taken up by a research study conducted in schools, inconvenience to teachers and students, or possible objections from community members. Thus, before approaching anyone whose permission you will need, you should have prepared convincing answers to questions about such matters.

Of special concern to administrators is whether the research results will reflect unfavorably upon their institution. They may be reluctant to voice this concern, however, so you should bring it up early in the negotiations and discuss it objectively. School administrators, in particular, need reassurance when your study involves assessment of students' or teachers' abilities. You can make the point that you will present your findings in such a way that they do not reflect unfavorably upon the sites used in the study. For example, you can note that research journal articles generally do not identify the sites where data were collected, and that you will follow this practice.

William Eiserman and Diane Behl outlined the types of questions that special education teachers might ask in order to determine whether to become involved in a research study.[31] These questions, which are summarized in Figure 3.4, are a useful guide to the types of questions you should be prepared to answer when communicating with representatives of your prospective research site. We believe that they are relevant not only to special education, but to other situations as well.

When working with any administrative hierarchy, you must take care to follow appropriate channels of authority. For example, if you plan to select research participants from more than one school within a school district, usually you must begin by obtaining approval from the superintendent, or from an authorized representative of this individual. Perhaps you already have spoken with a teacher within a school about your project, and she has expressed support. In this case, that teacher might be willing to be an advocate in suggesting to the superintendent that the research project be approved. After obtaining approval, you should visit each site and present your ideas to the principal, or the individual authorized to represent the principal.

31. Eiserman, W. C., & Behl, D. (1992). Research participation: Benefits and considerations for the special educator. *Teaching Exceptional Children, 24,* 12–15.

FIGURE 3.4

Questions That Educators Should Ask in Determining Whether to Become Involved in a Research Study

A. Conceptual Soundness of the Research
   1. What is the research question, and what type of research (e.g., descriptive, causal-comparative, correlational, experimental, qualitative) does it require?
   2. Is the research question important, that is, (a) does it address issues pointed out in recent literature as needing attention, (b) do policy concerns demand scientific attention to the question, and (c) is this question of particular interest to the teacher whose participation is being requested?
   3. Is the proposed evaluation plan likely to provide an answer to the question being addressed, and in particular, do the proposed duration for the study and the frequency or intensity of the treatment make sense in light of the expected results?

B. Feasibility of the Research
   1. At what point in the day will the research procedures occur, and how will they affect the current schedule?
   2. How disruptive of other activities will the research be?
   3. How will unavoidable changes in the routine such as special school events and holidays affect the research?
   4. If student testing is to be conducted, how much time will be required?
   5. How much additional time will the teacher need to devote to the research?

C. Ethical Concerns
   1. Does the study in any way suggest an unreasonable compromise of any principle or value or place any of the subjects in the study at risk, and what safeguards will be in place to protect the rights of those involved in the study?
   2. Does the proposal clearly specify the obligations and responsibilities of all participating?
   3. How will informed consent be obtained from study participants?

Source: Adapted from: Eiserman, W. D., & Behl, D. (1992). Research participation: Benefits and considerations for the special educator. *Teaching Exceptional Children, 24,* 12–15.

Suppose you have obtained permission from the superintendent, but have run into difficulty with the principal of a specific school. If the principal objects to the study being carried out in her school, the superintendent usually will support the principal, even if he previously gave tentative approval for the project. If the superintendent were inclined to force the principal to cooperate, it would make it very difficult to carry out effective research. The interest and cooperation of *all* persons concerned with the research study is necessary if it is to be carried through to a successful conclusion.

After the principal and superintendent have been briefed as to the purposes of the research and the procedures to be followed, you will need to meet with teachers in each participating school in order to obtain their interest and cooperation. Time usually can be arranged at a regularly scheduled faculty meeting for you to present your proposed study and, hopefully, to obtain the teachers' cooperation.

In most research involving children, parents also must be informed about the study and given an opportunity to express their opinions. Perhaps you can present your plans at a parent-teacher association (PTA) meeting. You also will need to prepare a letter of informed consent explaining the study and send it to parents of all children whose participation is desired. Parents will need to sign the letter to signify approval of their child's participation in the study.

The degree of cooperation you receive from groups in the community that are served by the institution depends on the nature of your research problem. For example, research dealing with academic achievement probably will not require a public relations program, because academics is generally regarded as a central mission of a school. A school-based research study involving personality or social adjustment, in which the role of the school is less clear and some of the measures to be employed might be misunderstood by some community members, is likely to require a public relations effort.

Teachers, administrators, or others who represent the institution sometimes identify potential problems in the research design that you have overlooked. Whenever possible, you should solicit and follow their suggestions, unless doing so compromises ethical or scientific requirements of the study.

Building a Relationship with the Institution

In discussing a proposed research project with school personnel, you need to ensure that all parties understand specifically what their responsibilities are. Try to bring up any questions that could lead to future misunderstandings if not answered clearly at the outset. Keep careful notes during planning meetings. Once you feel that all parties understand their roles in the project, write a letter that spells out the agreement in specific terms, and send this letter to any individuals whose cooperation is critical to your research activities.

You will need to remain accessible to site personnel and interested in their input in order to maintain positive relationships with them while the study is in progress. For example, if problems or questions of teachers whose students are participating in your research study go unanswered, they may refuse to cooperate. Some teachers might even sabotage your work, for example, by complaining to parents that your study is interfering with classwork or scheduling field trips for students on days when you had planned to do testing.

It is wise to keep educators and other individuals in the institution informed of your progress and alerted to upcoming events in the research plan. When doing a small project, you should keep personally in contact with participating teachers and administrators. When doing a large project, you should send periodic reports and newsletters to teachers, parents, and other interested persons.[32] A sample letter, similar to one sent to teachers participating in a project conducted by one of the authors (W. Borg), is shown in Figure 3.5.

Most field research in education depends on warm personal relationships between the researcher and site personnel. Carrying out your research in a setting where you are known as a friend and colleague makes it much easier than if you are regarded as an outsider with unknown motives. If you develop a sincere interest in the problems of practitioners and a respect for their ideas and viewpoints, you will gain insights that improve your research design and contribute to your findings. You probably also will receive a level of cooperation that makes it possible to complete your project when the going gets rough.

An effective method for developing a good relationship with site personnel is to use your expertise to help them with their needs, for example, by locating curriculum materials, conducting a literature search related to a current school problem, design-

---

32. This and other human relations procedures that are applicable to large research projects are described in: Paddock, S. C., & Packard, J. S. (1981). On the conduct of site relations in educational research. *Educational Researcher, 10*(3), 14–17.

FIGURE 3.5

Letter to Maintain Positive Human Relations with Participants in a School-Based Research Project

UTAH STATE UNIVERSITY • LOGAN, UTAH 84322–2810

DEPARTMENT OF PSYCHOLOGY
[phone number]

[date]

Dear Mrs. Oliver:

With your valued assistance we have just finished collecting data for the second year of the Utah ability-grouping study. I realize that this research has caused you inconvenience and has taken time from your classes. I assure you that we are aware of the problems that such a study causes in the cooperating schools and shall continue to try to reduce these problems during the remaining two years of the study. I'm afraid that it is inevitable that progressive school districts, such as your own, that choose to support research and strive to find better ways of educating our youth must pay for their leadership by accepting the problems that major research projects always bring.

I am pleased to tell you that we already have enough important results to indicate that this research is well worth the effort, the problems, and the inconveniences. Our work to date has yielded important new knowledge about ability grouping. The remaining two years of the study will certainly teach us more and will also give us a chance to check the results we have already obtained.

The work under way in the Utah study is one of the first extensive long-term evaluations of ability grouping, and I assure you that through your cooperation you are making a real and important contribution to the teaching profession.

Although I know you have been working closely with Mrs. Johnson from our staff, my deepest regret is that I have had little opportunity to meet personally with the teachers cooperating in this research. I know that many of you have questions about the study that I could answer. I am also sure that you have suggestions and ideas that would help us make this research better. I plan to visit each cooperating school before we start collecting data next year and hope that you will jot down ideas and suggestions so that we may discuss them at that time.

In closing, permit me to thank you again for your patience and cooperation. I am looking forward to meeting with you and exchanging ideas during the coming year.

Sincerely,

Walter Borg

Walter R. Borg

ing a questionnaire to obtain information they need, or helping prepare a research proposal for funding. Researchers who freely give assistance to site personnel create goodwill that eases the problems associated with doing research in institutions such as public schools.

Dealing with Human Relations Problems

In spite of your best efforts to establish good rapport with concerned groups, problems inevitably arise in conducting educational research in real-life institutional settings. Problems can range from accidental omission of a page from one's survey questionnaire to a flu epidemic that decimates one's sample at a critical point in the research design.[33] Each problem, whether your fault or not, can place a strain on your relationship with administrators and research participants. A helpful approach is to build time buffers into the research schedule, so that if problems occur you and the individuals whose cooperation you need can develop solutions that do not burden anyone involved in the study.

Probably the most serious human relations problem that can arise in educational research is a protest by members of the community. For example, some parents might protest over particular items in a self-report measure or complain that participation in the research project is taking away time from their children's schooling. Such protests usually are made by a small, but vocal, group. In many cases, protests can be traced back to the fact that individuals do not understand the procedures, measures, or intended application of the findings of the research.

If your research project is criticized by community members, make an attempt to provide them with your side of the story. You may find it helpful to point out the procedures that you used to obtain the informed consent of your research subjects and the steps that you are taking to protect individual privacy and confidentiality. Also, stress the benefits that research participants will derive from being involved in the study.

33. Maruyama & Deno, *Research in educational settings.*

✦ RECOMMENDATIONS FOR
Ensuring That a Research Study is Ethical, Legal, and Harmonious

1. Follow proper channels in setting up a study in a field setting.
2. Prepare answers for questions likely to be asked by site administrators about the research project.
3. Avoid compromising the integrity of the research design by making changes for the administrative convenience of the institution from which subjects are to be drawn.
4. Follow correct procedures for obtaining informed consent from research participants or their caretakers.
5. Carry out effective debriefing of research participants following deception.
6. Develop adequate safeguards to ensure the confidentiality of research data.
7. Use data-collection procedures and experimental treatments that can be readily defended to possible critics of the research study.
8. Establish good rapport by maintaining ongoing communication with groups that have a stake in the research project.

✔ SELF-CHECK TEST

Circle the correct answer to each of the following questions. The answers are provided at the back of the book.

1. The main purpose of the Code of Federal Regulations for the Protection of Human Subjects is to
   a. protect subjects from unnecessary physical or psychological risk.
   b. inform individuals that they have the right to refuse to participate in research projects.
   c. protect individuals from invasion of privacy by the federal government.
   d. regulate the types of measures that can be used in collecting research data.

2. A graduate student is employed as a research assistant in a psychological experiment involving deception. In studying the research plan, she notices that no debriefing is planned. What is her most reasonable course of action?
   a. Because she is not in charge of the project, she has no ethical responsibility, and therefore she should do nothing.
   b. She should report the investigator to the institutional review board of the university immediately.
   c. She should talk with the investigator and suggest a debriefing procedure in order to protect subjects from harm.
   d. She should resign her assistantship in order to protect her ethical position.

3. If telling subjects the purpose of the research study before data collection might invalidate the results, the researcher's best course of action is to
   a. refer subjects to the institutional review board that is overseeing the study.
   b. inform subjects anyway, because regulations concerning informed consent require full disclosure.
   c. tell subjects that they will be informed of the purpose at the completion of the research.
   d. give reasons other than the true reasons for the research.

4. If a college student agrees to participate in a research project and then drops out partway through the study,
   a. the student should be informed that this is a violation of the ethics code of the American Psychological Association.
   b. the student should be informed that he must contact the institutional review board that is overseeing the project.
   c. nothing should be done because subjects have the right to withdraw at any time.
   d. the student is legally committed to complete the project, and should be informed of this fact.

5. To ensure confidentiality of research data collected from human subjects, it is appropriate for the researcher to
   a. make certain that no unauthorized individuals have access to the data.
   b. inform the subjects about who will have access to the data.
   c. remove the names of the research participants from data-collection instruments and replace them with a code.
   d. all of the above.

6. A risk-benefit ratio legitimately could involve the
   a. cost of doing the study relative to its potential for advancing the researcher's career.
   b. inconvenience to the research participants relative to the study's potential to improve the learning of the population whom they represent.
   c. the probability that the study will yield nonsignificant results relative to the probability that it will significant results.
   d. all of the above.

7. In experiments in which subjects have been deceived, what is the ethical responsibility of the investigator?
   a. Inform subjects before the study that the experiment involves deception, but do not identify what the deception is.
   b. At the end of the study, give subjects a written sheet that states that the study involved deception but does not describe the specific deception.
   c. Inform subjects in writing at the end of the study of the specific nature of the deception.
   d. Personally inform subjects of the deception at the end of the study or carry out demonstrations in order to convince subjects that they were deceived.

8. If a teacher objects to students in the control group not receiving an experimental treatment that is viewed as desirable, the researcher's best course of action in order to maintain positive human relations with the institution is to
   a. explain that the experimental design requires a control group that does not receive treatment.
   b. provide the treatment to control-group students after data have been collected.
   c. provide the treatment to both groups in order to avoid conflict with the teacher.
   d. use a different teacher's students to serve as the control group.

9. A potential disadvantage of conducting research in the educational institution for which you are employed is that
   a. your particular position may interfere with your grasp of key issues or concerns of other members of the institution.
   b. you will probably have more difficulty obtaining permission to conduct the research than would an outsider.
   c. you are unfamiliar with the best procedures for communication among staff of the institution.
   d. all of the above.

10. If a superintendent gives permission for a study to be done in the school district,
   a. it is not necessary to obtain clearance from an institutional review board.
   b. it is not necessary to provide letters of informed consent to the research participants.
   c. it still is necessary to obtain the cooperation of all other individuals and groups that have a stake in the study.
   d. it still is necessary to make any changes in the research design requested by the participants or by others who have a stake in the study.

CHAPTER 4

✦ Reviewing the Literature

OVERVIEW

In order to contribute to research knowledge in your area of interest, you first must review what other researchers have discovered. We show you how to do this type of review in this chapter. Much of our discussion involves the various types of documents that you will come across in a literature review: preliminary sources, which are hard-copy or electronic indexes to the literature; secondary sources, which are published reviews of particular bodies of literature; and primary sources, which are reports of research studies written by those who conducted them. Because your literature search may reveal both quantitative and qualitative research findings, we describe procedures for synthesizing and reporting both types.

OBJECTIVES

After studying this chapter, you should be able to

1. Explain the various ways that a literature review helps a researcher design a study.
2. Describe the four major steps involved in conducting a literature review.
3. Describe the difference between preliminary, secondary, and primary sources, and the role of each type of source in the literature-review process.
4. Locate relevant citations on an educational topic, using either hard-copy or electronic versions of the *Current Index to Journals in Education, Resources in Education,* and the *Thesaurus of ERIC Descriptors.*
5. Describe several types of preliminary sources and their usefulness in doing a literature search.
6. Describe several major secondary sources and their usefulness in doing a literature search.
7. Interpret the results of a meta-analysis of a set of quantitative research studies on a particular problem.
8. Describe methods for obtaining documents that are identified through a search of preliminary and secondary sources.
9. Describe a method for classifying the information contained in primary source documents that are identified through a literature search.
10. State several criteria that are useful in judging the merits of a quantitative or qualitative study.
11. Describe several flaws that weaken the reporting of a literature review.
12. Evaluate the relative advantages of narrative review, vote counting, chi-square, and meta-analysis for synthesizing quantitative research findings.
13. Describe a method for synthesizing a body of literature that consists primarily of qualitative research studies.

Purposes of a Literature Review

Unless your study explicitly builds on the work of other researchers in your area of inquiry, it is unlikely to contribute to research knowledge. Joel Levin and Hermione Marshall emphasized this point in commenting on their experience as editors of the the *Journal of Educational Psychology:*

> For research to make a substantial contribution, it must be based on adequate knowledge of the field, and the study's introduction must reflect this knowledge. . . .Unfortunately, we sometimes receive manuscripts from investigators who base their research on early work that is now dated or from researchers who ignore current work. Reviewers may then be left questioning why the study was conducted, which usually leads to a recommendation of rejection.[1]

Despite the importance of a thorough review of the literature, this phase of the research process is slighted more often than any other phase. In our experience, it requires three to six months or more to do a good review of the literature, especially if you know little about the literature on your research problem at the outset. This time is well spent because a thorough review of the literature serves various important purposes, as we explain below.

1. *Delimiting the research problem.* Studies are doomed to failure if the researcher does not limit sufficiently the scope of the problem. Selecting a limited problem and investigating it in depth is far better than a superficial study of a broad problem. By reviewing the literature, you can find out how other researchers have formulated fruitful lines of focused inquiry within a broad field of interest.

For example, suppose you are doing research on instructional leadership. You might find that researchers have developed separate lines of inquiry about leadership as manifested by individuals in different roles—superintendents, principals, department heads, consultants, and so forth. You might find that some studies focus on describing the behavior of recognized instructional leaders, whereas others focus on the outcomes of effective and ineffective leadership. As you develop insight into how these delimited lines of inquiry arose and progressed, you will become more able to delimit your own problem for investigation.

2. *Seeking new lines of inquiry.* In doing a literature review, you should determine what research already has been done in your area of interest. Just as important, you should be alert to research possibilities that have been overlooked. Your unique experience and background may make it possible for you to see a facet of the problem that other researchers have not seen. These new viewpoints are most likely to occur in areas where little research has been done, but even in well-researched areas someone occasionally thinks of an approach that is unique and creative. For example, one of the authors (M. Gall) advised a doctoral student, Isabella Henderson, on a study of school improvement and change.[2] Henderson discovered that one line of research in this area had sought to understand the work of designated "change agents," that is, persons whose role is to facilitate a change process in an organization. She identified previous research studies of teachers, administrators, staff development specialists, and project coordinators in the role of change agent. However, her particular interest was department chairpersons in high schools who had been given the task of facilitating the implementation of a new social studies curriculum in one province in Canada.

---

1. Levin, J. R., & Marshall, H. H. (1993). Publishing in the *Journal of Educational Psychology:* Reflections at midstream. *Journal of Educational Psychology, 85,* 3–6. Quote appears on p. 3.
2. Henderson, I. M. (1993). The role of high school department heads as change agents in implementing a new social studies curriculum. *Dissertation Abstracts International, 54*(09), 3309A. (UMI No. 9405182)

In reviewing the literature, Henderson found little research on department chairpersons, and none on their possible role as change agents. She realized that conceptualizing this group as change agents and studying them with the methodology that had been developed in change-agent research would open a new line of inquiry. The research that resulted from the insights gained in Henderson's literature review led to new knowledge about department chairpersons. In addition, her findings provided a replication test of findings about change agents that had accumulated from previous research on other types of change agents in education.

3. *Avoiding fruitless approaches.* In reviewing the literature, be on the lookout for lines of inquiry in your area that proved to be fruitless. For example, literature searches sometimes identify several similar studies done over a period of years, all of which employed approximately the same research methodology and all of which failed to produce a significant experimental or correlational result. One or two further tests of an intervention or hypothesized relationship can be justified on the grounds that they confirm the previous finding of no significant effect. Additional studies, however, serve no useful purpose and suggest that the researcher has not done an adequate review of the literature.

4. *Gaining methodological insights.* In reviewing research reports, some individuals give scant attention to anything but the results reported. This is a mistake because other information in the report can help you in the design of your study. For example, a study conducted by one of the authors (W. Borg) tested a procedure for training inservice teachers to use specific classroom management skills.[3] Although the teachers could be taught to use a set of three specific skills in one week of instruction and practice, their use of the skills was awkward and unnatural. Because of this finding, the training program was revised to include four more weeks during which teachers practiced the skills they had learned earlier. This change resulted in much more effective teacher performance. The methodological insights gained in this study might be useful to other researchers who are interested in designing and testing programs to improve teachers' classroom skills.

5. *Identifying recommendations for further research.* Researchers often conclude their reports with a discussion of issues raised by their study and recommendations for other research that might be done. (Examples are provided in Chapter 2.) These issues and recommendations should be considered carefully because they represent insights gained by the researcher after considerable study of a given problem.

6. *Seeking support for grounded theory.* Many research studies are designed to test a theory that has been developed to explain the learning process or other educational phenomena. Barney Glaser, however, proposed that studies also can be designed such that data are collected first, and then a theory is derived from those data.[4] (Glaser's approach is described more fully in Chapters 2 and 14.) The resulting theory is called *grounded theory* because it is "grounded" in a set of real-world data.

Glaser advises researchers who plan to use the grounded theory approach not to conduct a review of the literature beforehand because they are likely to be exposed to other researchers' theories. As a result of this exposure, they might be unable to see their data with a fresh perspective. Glaser instead recommends this approach:

> [W]e collect the data in the field first. Then we start analyzing it and generating theory. When the theory seems sufficiently grounded and developed, *then* we review the literature in the

---

3. Borg, W. R. (1977). Changing teacher and pupil performance with protocols. *Journal of Experimental Education, 45,* 9–18.
4. Glaser, B. G. (1978). *Theoretical sensitivity: Advances in the methodology of grounded theory.* Mill Valley, CA: Sociology Press.

field and relate the theory to it through the integration of ideas. . . . Thus scholarship in the same area starts after the emerging theory is sufficiently developed so the theory will not be preconceived by preempting concepts.[5]

A literature review conducted in this fashion, after researchers have developed grounded theory, might generate support for the theory, might lead them to question their own theory or the theories of others, or might cause them to refine their theory and develop ideas for further investigation.

Glaser qualified his position about the role of literature reviews in research by suggesting that researchers first read the literature on topics that are indirectly related to their area of investigation. The purpose of this reading is to help researchers develop ideas that will inform their fieldwork, without constraining their development of grounded theory.

Major Steps in a Literature Review

◆ Touchstone in Research

Cooper, H. M. (1998). *Synthesizing research: A guide for literature reviews* (3rd ed.). Thousand Oaks, CA: Sage.

Prior to initiating a literature review, you should write a preliminary statement of your research problem. (Chapter 2 discusses this process in detail.) The following is an example of such a statement, one that we will use below to illustrate literature search techniques: "What are effective ways to help parents of at-risk students increase their support of their children's academic efforts?"

Having formulated a problem statement, you are now ready to initiate a literature review. The method that we recommend has four steps.

Step 1: Search preliminary sources. You will need to identify books, articles, professional papers, and other publications that are relevant to the problem statement. **Preliminary sources,** which are indexes to particular bodies of literature, are an essential aid for this task. They are similar to the subject index of a library catalog. By looking in the subject index for a particular topic (e.g., mathematics education), you can find all the books in the library that pertain to this topic. The preliminary sources that we describe below are much more comprehensive than a library index, however, because they index all sorts of publications—not just books—and they include publications wherever they may be located, not just the holdings of a particular library.

Step 2: Use secondary sources. In your examination of preliminary sources, you may find that other researchers already have written reviews of the literature that are relevant to your problem statement. Such reviews are examples of secondary sources. A **secondary source** is a document written by someone who did not actually do the research, develop the theories, or express the opinions that they have synthesized into a literature review. You can use preliminary sources to help determine whether relevant secondary sources are available.

Step 3: Read primary sources. Preliminary and secondary sources index or review research studies, respectively, but not in detail. For this reason, you will need to obtain and study the original reports of at least those studies that are most central to your proposed investigation. These original reports are called primary sources. A **primary source** is a document (e.g., journal article or dissertation) that was written by the individuals who actually conducted the research study or who formulated the theory or opinions that are described in the document.

Step 4: Synthesize the literature. Once you have read all the relevant primary and secondary sources, you will need to synthesize what you have learned in order to write a literature review. The purpose of the review is to inform the reader about what already is

---

5. Ibid., p. 31.

known, and what is not yet known, about the problems or questions that you plan to investigate. Also, you will need to make clear how your proposed study relates to, and builds upon, the existing knowledge base as represented in the literature.

These four steps of the literature review process need not be done strictly in sequence. For example, as you review literature relevant to your problem statement, you may find that you want to reformulate the statement, which may take your literature search in a new direction. Also, you may find that the primary and secondary sources identified by your preliminary sources were only indirectly related to your problem statement. In this case, you will need to go back to the first step and attempt to find a more relevant preliminary source.

To conduct a thorough literature review, you need to know how to use preliminary, secondary, and primary sources. We describe each of them in the next sections.

Searching Preliminary Sources: ERIC

The Educational Resources Information Center (ERIC) is the principal source of information about the literature on educational research and practice. Therefore, we describe it in detail in this section. Once you understand how ERIC works, you will be in a better position to use other preliminary sources.

✦ **Touchstone in Research**

Overview of ERIC at: <www.eric.ed.gov/ about/about.html>.

The structure and services of ERIC are constantly changing, particularly as computers, the Internet, and funding patterns evolve.[6] If you find that ERIC or other preliminary sources are not as we describe them here, we recommend that you talk to a reference librarian to determine their current status or go to the Web site maintained by a service of ERIC called AccessERIC: <www.accesseric.org/index.html>.

ERIC's Structure and Services

The organizational structure of ERIC includes a central office, clearinghouses, adjunct clearinghouses, and support components. To give you a sense of ERIC's comprehensive scope, we list the clearinghouses and other facilities in Figure 4.1. To learn the current status of the clearinghouses and information for contacting them, you can go to this Web site: <www.eric.ed.gov/sites/barak.html>.

ERIC provides various services for education professionals. In the next section, we describe those that are most pertinent to reviewing the research literature.

CIJE and *RIE*

ERIC publishes hard-copy and electronic versions of two preliminary sources: *Current Index to Journals in Education (CIJE)* and *Resources in Education (RIE)*. *CIJE* indexes articles in many hundreds of education-related journals. In contrast, *RIE* indexes various non-journal documents: papers presented at education conferences, progress reports of ongoing research studies, technical reports on studies sponsored by federal research programs, and reports of projects conducted by school districts and other local agencies. These various reports sometimes are called *fugitive literature* or *gray literature* because they are not widely disseminated or easily obtained.

ERIC Clearinghouse staff members known as abstractors have created *CIJE* and *RIE* citations for documents dating back to 1966. *CIJE* and *RIE* now include more than a million citations with each citation referring to a separate document. As we define the term here, a **citation** is all the coded information that ERIC provides about a particular document.

---

6. For a view of where computer access to research literature is headed, see: Willinsky, J. (2001). The strategic education research program and the public value of research. *Educational Researcher, 30*(1), 5–14.

FIGURE 4.1

List of ERIC Clearinghouses and Adjunct Clearinghouses

Clearinghouses	Adjunct Clearinghouses
Adult, Career, and Vocational Education	Child Care
Assessment and Evaluation	Clinical Schools
Community Colleges	Educational Opportunity
Counseling and Student Services	Entrepreneurship Education
Disabilities and Gifted Education	ESL Literacy Education
Educational Management	International Civic Education
Elementary and Early Childhood Education	Service Learning
Higher Education	Test Collection
Information and Technology	United States–Japan Studies
Languages and Linguistics	
Reading, English, and Communication	
Rural Education and Small Schools	
Science, Mathematics, and Environmental Education	
Social Studies/Social Science Education	
Teaching and Teacher Education	
Urban Education	

Coded information includes title, author(s), date of publication, abstract, and so forth. (All of the different types of coded information are described in more detail later in the chapter.) Citations are also called *entries* or *resumes* by ERIC, but to avoid confusion here, we use the term *citation* except when there is a particular need to use a different term.

To clarify terminology further, we use the term **document** to refer to any publication abstracted in *CIJE* or *RIE*. As explained above, these documents are of various types, for example, journal articles, conference papers, and technical reports. When necessary, we use the appropriate term for a particular type of publication. Otherwise, we use the term *document* to refer to a publication without distinction as to its type.

ERIC citations are published in hard-copy and electronic versions. The hard-copy version consists of monthly publications of *CIJE* and *RIE*. (Semi-annual and annual cumulations are also published.) Electronic versions are becoming increasingly prevalent because of their ease of use and incorporation of adjunct services. Therefore, our discussion of *CIJE* and *RIE* emphasizes on the electronic versions. If you understand how they work, it is an easy matter to use the hard-copy versions.

The collection of citations stored in electronic form, sometimes called a **database,** indicates that the citations consist of bits of data that can be retrieved by software designed for that purpose. *CIJE* and *RIE* citations are stored in the same database, so unless necessary, we do not distinguish between these two preliminary sources in the next sections.

The ERIC database is stored in computer files, which, as we explain below, are available on the Internet, CDs, or other electronic format. To search the database for particular citations within the database, you need to use a search engine. A **search engine** is a type of specialized computer software that has a variety of features for helping a user sift through the database to identify citations that satisfy particular criteria. (Google, Yahoo!, and other services have search engines that allow you to find relevant Web sites throughout the Internet.) Electronic versions of *CIJE* and *RIE* vary in how much of the database they include and in their search-engine features.

Coding of Documents in the ERIC Database

All journal articles, reports, and other documents in the ERIC database are coded by ERIC clearinghouse abstractors so that they can be retrieved by users. For example, suppose you wish to find all publications by a particular author, all publications on a particular topic, or all publications that report research findings about this topic. Each document in the ERIC database is coded so that you can find this information as well as other kinds of information. Therefore, you need to know ERIC's coding system to take full advantage of its search options. To explain it, we use the research question introduced earlier: "What are effective ways to help parents of at-risk students increase their support of their children's academic efforts?"

Because all *CIJE* citations are from journals, they tend to have fewer coding features than *RIE* citations, which involve various publication formats (e.g., papers presented at conferences differ in format from reports issues by government agencies). Therefore, we explain the coding of a document using an example from *RIE*. We selected the hard-copy version of *RIE,* because, unlike electronic versions, its citation features are standardized and complete.

To initiate our search for literature concerning parents of high risk students, we turned to the subject index of the December 1992 issue of *RIE.* We found two citations under *Parent role:*

Family Focus: Reading and Learning Together Packet.	ED 347 498
School and Family Partnerships.	ED 347 638

We thought that the second citation might be relevant to our research problem, so we copied down the ED number. Next we turned to the Document Resumes section of the *RIE* issue, where the citations—also called *entries* or *resumes*—are arranged in numerical order. Reading the resume for ED 347 638, we found that it is relevant to our proposed study. The document resume is shown in Figure 4.2. We will use it to explain each feature of an *RIE* entry. Keep in mind that these features, particularly those involving availability and cost, might change over time. (For more information about the features, refer to the most recent edition of the *Thesaurus of ERIC Descriptors,* which is described in the next section.)

1. *ERIC accession number.* ED 347 638 is the identification number for this document. Accession numbers are sequentially assigned to documents as they are processed for indexing in ERIC. The *ED* indicates that this is a nonjournal document rather than a journal article. (Journal articles begin with an *EJ* number instead.) Entries are placed in the Document Resumes section of *RIE* in numerical order by their accession number. If a library maintains a microfiche file of ERIC documents, the microfiches are also stored in accession-number order.

2. *Clearinghouse accession number.* The number *EA 024 079* is an accession number assigned to documents by the specific clearinghouse that processed the document for entry into the ERIC system. EA is the designation for the Clearinghouse on Educational Management, housed at the University of Oregon.

3. *Author(s).* The names in italics below the ERIC accession number are the names of the authors of the document. We find that this document was written by Joyce L. Epstein and Lori J. Connors.

4. *Title.* The title of the document is shown next. In this example it is *School and Family Partnerships.*

5. *Organization where document originated.* If the document was available in print form prior to being placed into the ERIC system, the organization where it originated is

FIGURE 4.2

Document Resume in *Resources in Education (RIE)*

ED 347 638   EA 024 079

Epstein, Joyce L.   Connors, Lori J.

School and Family Partnerships.

National Association of Secondary School Principals, Reston, Va.

Report No.—ISSN–0912–6160

Pub Date—Jun 92

Note—10p.

Available from—National Association of Secondary School Principals, 1904 Research Drive, Reston, VA 22091–1537 ($2; quantity discounts).

Journal Cit—Practitioner; v18 n4 Jun 1992

Pub Type—Collected Works - Serials (022) — Guides — Non-Classroom (055)

EDRS Price — MF01 Plus Postage. PC Not Available from EDRS.

Descriptors—*Educational Cooperation, Family Role, *Family School Relationship, Middle Schools, *Parent Influence, *Parent Role, *Parent School Relationship, School Community Relationship, Secondary Education

Concerns about and characteristics of family/school partnerships are the theme of this issue of a "newsletter for the on-line administrator." Because of the changing natures of students, families, and schools, school administrators must take a leadership role in facilitating parent involvement in education. The six major types of involvement for comprehensive partnership programs are outlined. These include basic obligations of families; basic obligations of the school; involvement at the school; involvement in home learning; involvement in decision making, governance, and advocacy; and community collaboration. Questions to be considered for organization of partnerships are discussed; some of these include the development of a written policy, a leadership and committee structure, a budget, and an evaluation process. Examples of each type of partnership that has been implemented in middle and high schools are provided. A brief program description and contact information are included. (LMI)

Source: Text on p. 61 in: *Resources in Education.* (1992, December). Washington, DC: U.S. Government Printing Office.

specified here. We find that our document originated with the National Association of Secondary School Principals (NASSP) in Reston, Virginia.

6. *Sponsoring agency.* If a different agency from the one in which the document originated was responsible for initiating, funding, and managing the research project described in the document, it is listed after *Spons Agency.* No separate sponsoring agency is shown for our document.

7. *Report number.* If a report number is given, it is the number assigned to the document by the originating organization. In this case, the report number *ISSN-0912-6160* would be used to request the document from NASSP.

8. *Date published (Pub Date).* The Pub Date indicates the month and year in which the document was published.

9. *Contract or grant number.* If a contract or grant number is given, it signifies the number assigned by the funding agency to the project or grant under which the research described in the document was funded. No contract or grant number is given for our document.

10. *Note.* A descriptive note gives additional information about the document, beginning with its page length. We find that this report is 10 pages long.

11. *Availability.* If the document is available from a source other than ERIC, it is listed here. Our sample document is available from the National Association of Secondary School Principals. In 1992, it cost $2 per copy, with quantity discounts available.

12. *Language of document.* If the document is available in a language other than English, this is indicated. This document is written in English only, so no language designation is included in the document resume.

13. *Publication type (Pub Type). Pub Type* is a three-digit code that classifies a document by form of publication. For example, there are separate codes for research/technical reports, dissertations and theses, and instructional materials for learners. Two Pub Types were assigned to our sample document: *Collected Works—Serials (022)* and *Guides—Non-Classroom (055).*

14. *ERIC Document Reproduction Service (EDRS) availability.* This code indicates whether the document can be ordered through ERIC's reproduction service facility (explained in a later section). *MF* means the document can be ordered on microfiche, and *PC* means the document is available in regular paper format. In our example, *MF01* means that the report can be ordered on microfiche. The *01* part of the code refers to a price code schedule contained in the December 1992 issue of *RIE.* (That price code is no longer valid.)

15. *Descriptors.* The descriptors from the ERIC *Thesaurus* that were assigned to this document by an indexer at an ERIC clearinghouse are listed here. These descriptors classify the substantive content of the document. Up to six major descriptors, each preceded by an asterisk, are listed to cover the main content of the document. The document is cited in the subject index of *RIE* only under the major descriptors. Minor descriptors also are listed to indicate less important content of the document or nonsubject features such as methodology or educational level. An educational-level descriptor (e.g., early childhood education, middle schools, higher education) is mandatory for every document and journal article indexed in ERIC, unless it is entirely inappropriate. If the document or article covers a specific age range, an optional age-level descriptor also may be assigned.

16. *Identifiers.* Identifiers are key words or "indexable" concepts intended to add depth to subject indexing that is not possible with the ERIC *Thesaurus* descriptors alone. They generally are either proper names or concepts not yet represented by approved descriptors. They appear in the resume sections of *RIE* and *CIJE* in a separate field just below the descriptors. Major identifiers are marked with an asterisk and appear in the printed subject indexes of *RIE* and *CIJE.* There are no identifiers for this document.

17. *Target audience.* If a document or journal article specifies an intended audience, this information is provided in the entry. Eleven different audiences are identified by ERIC: policy makers; researchers; practitioners, which include the five subtypes—administrators, teachers, counselors, media staff, and support staff; students; parents; and community members. If more than two practitioner groups are identified, only the generic target audience *practitioners* is catalogued. No target audience is specified for the entry shown in Figure 4.2.

18. *Informative abstract.* This is a brief summary of the document's contents, written either by the author or the abstractor at the ERIC clearinghouse.

19. *References.* If references are provided at the end of the document, the number of references is indicated in parentheses. No references are included in our sample document.

20. *Abstractor's initials.* The initials of the person at the ERIC clearinghouse who coded each document is indicated in parentheses at the end of the resume. The abstractor for our sample document is LMI.

Thesaurus of ERIC Descriptors

In the preceding section, we noted that each document in the ERIC database is coded by descriptors. Unless you use appropriate descriptors, you might not retrieve all the documents in the database that are relevant to the research problem you are investigating.

The *Thesaurus of ERIC Descriptors* is a manual that helps you identify appropriate descriptors to use in searching *CIJE* and *RIE* for documents that are relevant to your research

✦ Touchstone in Research

Houston, J. E. (Ed.). (2001). *Thesaurus of ERIC descriptors* (14th ed.). Westport, CT: Oryx.

Electronic version of the *Thesaurus:* <www.ericfacility.net/ extra/pub/thessearch. cfm>.

problem. A **descriptor** is a term that is used to classify all documents that contain information about the topic denoted by the term.

To identify appropriate descriptors for your literature search, you can start by underlining the most important words or phrases in your problem statement. Using our example about parents, we underlined the following words: "What are effective ways to help *parents* of *at-risk students* increase their support of their children's *academic efforts*?"

The next step is to look up each of the three terms in the Alphabetical Descriptor Display of the ERIC *Thesaurus* to determine whether they are ERIC descriptors. We use the 2001 edition of the *Thesaurus* to illustrate this process. When we look up the term *parents,* we find the display shown in Figure 4.3. This display has the following features.

1. *Main-entry designation.* The term **PARENTS** is shown in all capital letters and in boldface in the Alphabetical Descriptor Display. This designation indicates that *Parents* is a main-entry descriptor, meaning that it is used to classify entries in *CIJE* and *RIE.*

2. *Add date.* The notation *Jul. 1966* indicates when this term was entered into the *Thesaurus.*

3. *Postings.* The number 3,438 indicates the number of times, as of October 2000, that this term was used as a major or minor descriptor in *RIE* and *CIJE.*

4. *Descriptor Group Code.* The notation *GC: 510* indicates that the descriptor **PARENTS** is in Descriptor Group Code 510. This three-digit number indicates the broad category to which this descriptor belongs, and is useful for identifying other descriptors that are conceptually related to a descriptor, but do not necessarily appear in the descriptor's display (Figure 4.3). When we look at the categories list on page xxv of the *Thesaurus,* we find that *GC* is the category *Groups related to HUMAN SOCIETY,* and that *GC 510* concerns *THE INDIVIDUAL IN SOCIAL CONTEXT.* The term *group,* as used here, refers not to groups of people, but to groups of conceptually related descriptors in the *Thesaurus.*

5. *Used for (UF) designation.* The *UF* designation preceding the term *Catholic parents* indicates that the descriptor *Parents* should be used instead of the term *Catholic parents* in doing an ERIC search. The information in parentheses after the term *Catholic parents* indicates that this term was a descriptor only during the period 1966 to 1980. The # designation after the term *Catholic parents* refers to a footnote at the bottom of the page of the Alphabetical Descriptor Display where the term appears. The footnote states that two or more descriptors are needed to represent this term. By looking in the *Thesaurus* for *Catholic parents* as a main entry, the reader can learn which descriptors to use instead of this term.

6. *Narrower term (NT) designation.* The *NT* designation identifies narrower descriptors that are included under the main-entry descriptor *Parents.* The ten narrower descriptors shown under *Parents* also can be searched for *CIJE* and *RIE* entries relating to parents.

7. *Broader term (BT) designation.* The *BT* designation identifies broader descriptors that subsume the concept represented by the main-entry descriptor. Thus we see that the broader descriptor *Groups* includes the descriptor *Parents* as a subcategory.

8. *Related term (RT) designation.* The *RT* designation indicates related descriptors that also are main-entry descriptors in the *Thesaurus.* These related descriptors have a close conceptual relationship to the descriptor *Parents,* but do not fit the superordinate/ subordinate relationship described by BT and NT. All the related terms listed under *Parents* appear elsewhere in the *Thesaurus* as main-entry descriptors. Thus, any of these descriptors can be used to search for *CIJE* and *RIE* entries relevant to our research problem.

9. *USE designation.* The information shown in Figure 4.3 does not exhaust the terms relating to the topic of parents in the *Thesaurus.* If we look back through the Alphabetical Descriptor Display, we will find three pages of descriptors that include the word *parent* or *parents,* for example, *PARENTS AS TEACHERS.* Another example is *Parent Absence USE*

FIGURE 4.3

Display for the Descriptor *Parents* in the Alphabetical Descriptor Display of *Thesaurus of ERIC Descriptors*

Parents		*Jul 1966*
	Postings: 3,438	GC: 510
UF	Catholic Parents (1966 1980) #	
NT	Adoptive Parents	
	Biological Parents	
	Employed Parents	
	Fathers	
	Grandparents	
	Lower Class Parents	
	Middle Class Parents	
	Mothers	
	Parents As Teachers	
	Parents with Disabilities	
BT	Groups	
RT	Adults	
	Child Caregivers	
	Daughters	
	Early Parenthood	
	Family (Sociological Unit)	
	Family Environment	
	Family Life	
	Family Problems	
	Heads Of Households	
	Home Schooling	
	Home Visits	
	Kinship	
	One Parent Family	
	Parent Aspiration	
	Parent Associations	
	Parent Attitudes	
	Parent Background	
	Parent Child Relationship	
	Parent Conferences	
	Parent Counseling	
	Parent Education	
	Parent Empowerment	
	Parent Financial Contribution	
	Parent Grievances	
	Parent Influence	
	Parent Materials	
	Parent Participation	
	Parent Responsibility	
	Parent Rights	
	Parent Role	
	Parent School Relationship	
	Parent Student Relationship	
	Parent Teacher Conferences	
	Parent Teacher Cooperation	
	Parent Workshops	
	Parenthood Education	
	Parenting Skills	
	Sons	
	Spouses	

Source: Text on pp. 231–232 in: Houston, J. E. (Ed.) (2001). *Thesaurus of ERIC Descriptors* (14th ed.). Westport, CT: Oryx.

ONE PARENT FAMILY. The *USE* designation tells us that the term *parent absence* is not a main-entry descriptor in the *Thesaurus.* If we are interested in searching for citations relating to parent absence, we will need to use the descriptor *One parent family.*

10. *Scope note.* If we now check the Alphabetical Descriptor Display for our second term, *at-risk students,* we will find the term *AT RISK PERSONS* as a main-entry descriptor, followed by the information shown in Figure 4.4. *SN* is an acronym for *Scope Note,* which is a brief statement of the intended usage of an ERIC descriptor. The scope note clarifies an ambiguous term or restricts the usage of a term, and it may give special indexing information as well. The scope note in this case directs us to a narrower term, *HIGH RISK STUDENTS.* Therefore, we decided to substitute this term in our problem statement.

To determine whether *Academic efforts* is the appropriate descriptor for our search concerning parents of high risk students, we refer to the Rotated Descriptor Display in the *Thesaurus.* A **rotated descriptor display** takes each descriptor in the *Thesaurus* and shows all other descriptors that share any word in common with it. For example, if we key on the word *academic* in *academic efforts,* the Rotated Descriptor Display will show all *Thesaurus* descriptors that also include that word, irrespective of position (e.g., *English for academic purposes* and *academic achievement*). We could do the same kind of search in the Rotated Descriptor Display for the word *efforts.*

We scanned all the phrases beginning with the word *ACADEMIC.* The phrase *ACADEMIC EFFORTS* was not listed, but the phrase *ACADEMIC ACHIEVEMENT* was listed. We decided that the latter phrase better captures the intent of our proposed research, so we rephrase the problem statement to read: "What are effective ways to help parents of high-risk students increase their support of their children's academic achievement?"

Most education topics of any significance are represented by descriptors in the *Thesaurus.* Therefore, if your search does not locate any documents in your area of interest, you should reconsider your descriptors.

FIGURE 4.4

Display for the Main Entry *At Risk Persons* in the Alphabetical Descriptor Display of the *Thesaurus of ERIC Descriptors*

At Risk Persons		*Apr. 1990*
	Postings: 2,514	GC: 120
SN	Individuals or groups identified as possibly having or potentially developing a problem (physical, mental, educational, etc.) requiring further evaluation and/or intervention (Note: If possible, use the more specific term "High Risk Students")	
UF	High Risk Persons (1982 1990)	
NT	High Risk Students	
BT	Groups	
RT	Developmental Delays	
	Disabilities	
	Disability Identification	
	Early Identification	
	Early Intervention	
	Incidence	
	Symptoms (Individual Disorders)	

Source: Text on pp. 24–25 in: Houston, J. E. (Ed.) (2001). *Thesaurus of ERIC Descriptors* (14th ed.). Westport, CT: Oryx.

Searching an Electronic Version of ERIC

You can use the hard-copy version of the ERIC database (i.e., the monthly or cumulated issues of *CIJE* and *RIE*) to do a literature search, but the process is laborious and cumbersome. It is much more efficient to search an electronic version of the database. Different
versions are available on ERIC Web sites and on commercial Web sites and CDs. (See p. xvi
of the 14th edition of the *Thesaurus of ERIC Descriptors* for a list.) The versions differ in how
much of the ERIC database they include and in their search options. (For a comparison of
several widely available versions, see: <www.eric.ed.gov/searchdb/dbchart_s.html>.) You
will need to consult a reference librarian at your institution to determine which version, or
versions, are available for your use.

We chose the Internet database and search engine maintained by the ERIC Clearinghouse on Assessment and Evaluation to illustrate the process of searching an electronic
version the ERIC database. This version has the advantages of being easily accessed and
comprehensive in its coverage of the ERIC database and search options. You can access it
by going to the homepage: <www.searcheric.org>.

Search Strategies

In using ERIC, you will be searching through more than one million documents to find those
that are relevant to your research study. This is a complex problem-solving task that requires
you to experiment to determine which procedures yield the best results. It is essential to
keep a record of your search procedures so you do not repeat procedures you already have
tried, and so you can inform readers about your search procedures in your final report.

As we stated above, our illustrative research question is, "What are effective ways to
help parents of at-risk students increase their support of their children's academic efforts?"
To start our search for relevant literature, we go to <www.searcheric.org>. From there, we
follow a series of steps to take advantage of various search options at this Web site. We describe our steps below, but keep in mind that you can vary the steps and include additional
ones.

Step 1. At the top of the Web page is a "Wizard" feature, which helps us select relevant
descriptors from the ERIC *Thesaurus*. When we type "parents" and click "Look up," we find
approximately the same list as that shown in Figure 4.3. We can check the terms in the list
that we wish to use as descriptors. We decided to check three terms: parents as teachers,
parent child relationship, and parent education.

If we wished, we could sidestep the Wizard and simply enter terms (called *keywords*
in some search engines). The search engine will look for a keyword (or combination of keywords) anywhere in the citation (e.g., title, abstract, descriptors, identifiers) for each document in the selected database. This procedure is quick and appropriate when we are fairly
certain of what we want from the database. For example, in preparing Chapter 3 of this
book, we searched the ERIC database for the keyword combination, "institutional review
boards." We felt confident that any relevant document would use this term in its title or abstract, so we did not feel the need for an ERIC *Thesaurus* descriptor.

Step 2. The search engine allows us to combine our three selected terms into a set,
which is called "Set 1." The set looks like this: PARENTS AS TEACHERS, PARENT CHILD RE-
LATIONSHIP, PARENT EDUCATION. The comma between each term has a special meaning in this context. Each comma represents what is known as a Boolean operator (also
called a *connector*) meaning *or.* In our example, the commas tell the search engine to look
for any document in the ERIC database that is coded with any one of these three descriptors. Thus, we will locate any document coded by "parents as teachers" *or* "parent child relationship" *or* "parent education."

✦ *Touchstone in Research*

Brehm, S. K., & Boyes, A. J. (2000). Using criti-
cal thinking to conduct effective searches of online resources. *Practical Assessment, Re-
search and Evaluation,
7*(7). Available online: www.ericae.net/pare/ getvn.asp?v=7&n=7.

Examples of expert ERIC searches at: www.ericae.net/ scripts/ewiz/expert. htm.

Step 3. We use the Wizard feature again for the term "at risk students" in our research question. As in the hard copy of the *Thesaurus* (see Figure 4.4), we find that "high risk students" is the preferred term. We enter this term as "Set 2." Set 1 and Set 2 are distinguished by the fact that they are related to each other by a connector meaning *and.* An *and* connector here means that the search engine will only select documents in the ERIC database that are coded by at least one of the three descriptors in the first set and the descriptor in the second set.

You will note that an *and* connector typically has the effect of reducing the number of documents that the search engine finds, because each document must be coded by at least two relevant descriptors (one from the first set and the one from the second set). An *or* connector typically increases the number of documents that the search engine finds, because a document will be selected if it is coded by any one of the descriptors in the *or* set.

Step 4. The search engine contains a list of database options. For example, we can include the entire ERIC database in our search, or just documents in the database published from 1990 on. We click on the option that includes only documents published from 1990 on. When experimenting with different descriptors, we might want to limit the database in this way in order to avoid being overwhelmed with too many citations in our search results.

Step 5. The search engine contains a list of "limited to" options. For example, we can request that the search engine limit its search of the ERIC database to documents that have been coded as "research reports." (As we explained above, each document is coded according to publication type; one of the classification codes is "research reports.") You do not need to use the "limited to" option, in which case the default is "not limited." We decide to do two searches—one with "not limited" as the option and the other with "research reports" as the option.

Step 6. The search engine gives us several choices for how the document citation will be displayed: "title", "title & short note", or "title & long note". We choose "title & short note" knowing that we will obtain more citation information, but it will take longer to scroll through the search results on the computer monitor or to download them.

Step 7. We are now ready to ask the search engine to conduct a search of the ERIC database using the search parameters we specified in Steps 1–6. The "not limited" search (see Step 5 above) yielded 176 citations. The search limited to "research reports" yielded 30 citations.

The above are basic steps for using the ERIC database at <searcheric.org>.[7] Similar steps apply to searching other electronic versions of the ERIC database and other literature databases (described later in the chapter). Also, search engines typically contain many features, beyond those described above, that are helpful in designing a literature search. You can learn about these features by accessing the database and experimenting on your own, by working with a reference librarian, or by using the AskERIC service.[8]

Pearl Building

One feature of the search engine at <www.searcheric.org>—pearl building—has special value. **Pearl building** refers to the process of constructing a new literature search using de-

---

7. There is evidence that several of the procedures described in these steps are under-utilized in many ERIC database searches; see:Hertzberg, S., & Rudner, L. (1999). The quality of researchers' searches of the ERIC database. *Educational Policy Analysis Archives, 7*(25). Available online: www.epaa.asu.edu/epaa/v7n25.html
8. If you need help using ERIC from an expert, you can send an e-mail message to AskERIC at www.askeric@ericir.syr.edu

scriptors obtained from document citations in the current literature search. To illustrate the process, we refer to the search described above. As we indicated, the "not limited" search yielded 176 citations. One of these citations is as follows:

> (EJ541644) Kelly, J. F. (1996). Early maternal behaviors during teaching in a high social risk group: A precursor to children's later school behavior. *Child Study Journal, 26,* 333–351.

After reading the abstract of this study (accessible by clicking one of the options adjacent to the citation), we decide that this study is particularly relevant to our proposed research project. Therefore, we wish to know whether other studies similar to it have been done. If we click on the "Find similar" button adjacent to the citation, the search engine will design a new search for us by using the major identifiers, major descriptors, and minor descriptors that the ERIC abstractor selected to code the document. (This information and other information of the type shown in Figure 4.2 is accessed by clicking the "Match info" option.) These identifiers and descriptors might be different, and more relevant, than those we used to construct our own initial search.

We asked the search engine to conduct this new pearl building search (i.e., a new search based on the results of the initial search). The search yielded more than 100 citations that had the same descriptors and identifiers as the research study on early maternal behaviors. If one of these citations looks particularly relevant, we can click on the "Find similar" button and construct a third search to find additional documents beyond those yielded by the second search. We can continue this pearl-building process as long as we wish, stopping when no new relevant citations are found.

Displaying and Downloading ERIC Citations

A complete ERIC citation (an example is shown in Figure 4.2) contains quite a bit of information. Suppose your literature search yields 100 or more citations, this is not uncommon. If the complete citation was shown on your computer monitor, it would take a long time to scroll through all the citations. That is why a search engine typically allows you to view just the title, or the title and short note, for each citation. If a citation seems relevant, you can ask the search engine to give you more information, possibly all the information shown in Figure 4.2.

Once you have identified relevant citations by examining them on the computer monitor, the next task is to save them for subsequent use in designing your study and writing your literature review. Of course, it would be extremely tedious to copy the citations by hand from the screen. Fortunately, search engines give you options for downloading them electronically, for example, saving the citations to a disk; having them sent to you as an e-mail message (either as the message itself or as a file attachment); or creating a hard copy using a printer connected to the computer.

The most desirable option in most instances is to download the citations into a file created by bibliography software such as Endnote (<www.endnote.com>) or ProCite (<www.procite.com>). The software puts each citation into a standard format which includes fields in which you can type notes about the citation and code it using keywords from your own classification system. Furthermore, the software can format your citations into many different standard styles (e.g., APA style). The software also can interact with your word-processing software to import the formatted citations directly into your research report. You likely will need to work with a reference librarian to create the necessary electronic connections between the search engine for a literature database and the bibliography software.

Obtaining ERIC-Indexed Documents

Journal articles indexed by ERIC (indicated by the accession-number prefix *EJ*) are available from various sources:

1. You can obtain the article directly from the journal if your institution's library subscribes to it or if the library can obtain it from you through an interlibrary loan service.
2. You can check for the article's availability at a fee-based article-reproduction service (several are listed at <searcheric.org>).
3. An increasing number of journals are published on the Internet. If you are seeking an article in such a journal, you can access it by going to the journal's Web site. (For example, you can find articles published in *The Qualitative Report* at <www.nova.edu/ssss/QR/index.html>.)

Unpublished documents indexed by ERIC (indicated by the accession-number prefix *ED*) can be obtained by several methods:

1. Almost all the documents are available on microfiche at ERIC Resource Collections located in over 1000 academic libraries and centers worldwide. The locations are listed at <www.ericae.net/derc.htm>.
2. You can order the documents through the ERIC Document Reproduction Service (<www.edrs.com>).
3. You can inquire whether your library has a subscription to *E*Subscribe*. This service gives you access to a high percentage of ERIC-indexed, unpublished documents in Adobe Acrobat PDF format. You can view the document on a computer monitor, save it as a computer file, and make a hard copy on a computer-linked printer. For more information about *E*Subscribe,* go to: <www.edrs.com/products/subscription.cfm>.
4. You can write to the author(s) to request a copy of the document. A directory of educational researchers is available at <www.aera.net.member/directory>.

Searching Other Preliminary Sources

CIJE and *RIE* are the preliminary sources that you are likely to use most often in conducting educational research. Therefore, we explained them in detail above. However, there are many other preliminary sources that can help you in your literature search by identifying relevant documents not indexed in *CIJE* or *RIE*. In particular, professional associations in various academic and professional disciplines—psychology, sociology, anthropology, economics, history, philosophy, medicine, and others—maintain preliminary sources similar to ERIC. Depending on your research problem, one or more of these sources might yield pertinent literature. A reference librarian can give you a list of relevant preliminary sources for the disciplines that interest you.

Appendix A provides a comprehensive list of preliminary sources that index the education literature. The following is a brief overview of the contents of this appendix:

1. Indexes to bibliographies.
2. Indexes to book reviews.
3. Indexes to books in education and related fields.
4. Indexes to curriculum materials.
5. Indexes to directories.

6. Indexes to dissertations and theses.
7. Indexes to journal articles, papers, and reports.
8. Indexes to magazines and newspapers.

In addition to these preliminary sources, there are specialized preliminary sources that index tests and self-report measures. They are described in Chapter 7.

Electronic Bulletin Boards

Educational researchers have formed computer networks on which they can have discussions and inform each other of upcoming events and other newsworthy items. Because these networks make it easy to post or request information of various types, they sometimes are called *bulletin boards* or *listservs*.

Although not a preliminary source in a strict sense, some postings refer to locally created bibliographies and databases. Also, individuals can post messages requesting this type of information. The American Educational Research Association (AERA) maintains a bulletin board for each of its divisions, which are listed below:

A. Administration
B. Curriculum Studies
C. Learning and Instruction
D. Measurement and Research Methodology
E. Counseling and Human Development
F. History and Historiography
G. Social Context of Education
H. School Evaluation and Program Development
I. Education in the Professions
J. Postsecondary Education
K. Teaching and Teacher Education
L. Educational Policy and Politics

AERA has other bulletin boards as well. For information about all the bulletin boards and how to join them, go to: <www.aera.net>. Type *listserv* in the search window.

Using Secondary Sources

Secondary sources in education are publications written by authors who were not direct observers of, or participants in, the events being described. These publications include most textbooks, scholarly books, encyclopedias, handbooks, and review articles in journals. For example, most history textbooks are secondary sources because the authors relied on the reports of others about past events rather than having observed the events themselves.

Some publications combine primary and secondary source information. For example, suppose an author writes an exhaustive review of the research literature on mathematics instruction for a handbook on this subject. If the author reports the results of her own research on mathematics instruction as part of the literature review, that portion of the review would be a primary source. The portion that reports the studies of other researchers, however, is a secondary source.

Secondary sources are useful because they combine knowledge from many primary sources into a single publication. For example, the *Encyclopedia of Educational Research* and the *International Encyclopedia of Education* contain short, readable articles on a wide variety of educational topics of general interest.[9] There is also the yearbook *Review of Research in Education* sponsored by the American Educational Research Association. Among journals, the most comprehensive secondary source is *Review of Educational Research.* The *ERIC Digests* are another source of literature reviews. They provide brief overviews of important current topics and problems in education, and are available online. (For a list of available *Digests,* go to: <www.ed.gov/databases/ERIC_Digests/index/>.) Appendix B lists many other secondary sources that can help you review the literature in your area of interest.

A good secondary source is more than a compilation of research studies on a particular problem or topic. It organizes what is known about the problem or topic into a meaningful structure and shows how various research studies are connected to each other. Frank Murray and James Raths describe these purposes in the following manner:

> The scholarly literature . . . is like a wall that is built one stone at a time, each stone filling a hole previously unfilled, each one mortared and connected to those that came before and after it, each one providing a support for the subsequent ones, and each one being supported by those that came before. The review article attempts to describe the wall itself and to discover its mortar, its architecture and design; the wall's place in the architecture of the larger structure; its relation to the other elements in the structure; its significance, purpose, and meaning in the larger structure.[10]

A good secondary source, then, not only tells you what is known about the problem or topic you are investigating. It also provides a structure for positioning your proposed research so that others can appreciate its significance.

Secondary sources vary in quality. Therefore, you must read them with a critical eye. In a previous section of this chapter we described a literature review as a process consisting of four major steps. The author of a literature review can make errors and misjudgments at any of these steps. For example, you might find that relevant research reports were omitted or that the reviewer's interpretation of a study's findings is inconsistent with the findings as reported in the primary source.

To an extent, secondary sources reflect the biases, values, and agendas of the reviewer. As Patti Lather puts it:

> A review is gatekeeping, policing, and productive rather than merely mirroring. . . . A review is not exhaustive; it is situated, partial, perspectival.[11]

A review of the research literature, the type of secondary source about which Lather writes, is not, then, the "last word" about a research problem or topic. You might think of a literature review as a research study in itself with the studies being reviewed as the data that are analyzed and interpreted. As with any research investigation, the reviewer's findings are subject to refutation, replication efforts, and revision through progressive discourse (see Chapter 1).

Meta-Analysis

Meta-analysis is a statistical procedure that can be used to search for trends in the magnitude of effects observed in a set of quantitative research studies all involving the same

9. American Educational Research Association. (2001). *Encyclopedia of educational research* (7th ed., Vols. 1–4). Farmington Hills, MI: Gale Group; Hustén, T., & Postlethwaite, T. N. (Eds.). (1994). *International encyclopedia of education* (2nd ed.). New York: Elsevier Science.
10. Murray, F., & Raths, J. (1996). Call for manuscripts. *Review of Educational Research, 64,* 197–200. Quote appears on p. 197.
11. Lather, P. (1999). To be of use: The work of revising. *Review of Educational Research, 69,* 2–7. Quote appears on p. 3.

research problem. A secondary source that relies on this statistical procedure usually is called a *meta-analysis.* When using an electronic version of *CIJE* and *RIE,* you can enter the term *meta-analysis,* which is an ERIC descriptor, and connect it to your main topic descriptor with the *and* connector. This procedure will identify relevant meta-analyses if they exist in the *CIJE* and *RIE* database.

To illustrate meta-analysis, we will describe one that was done by Robert Bangert-Drowns, James Kulik, and Chen-Lin Kulik.[12] They reviewed 40 studies of the effects of frequent testing during instruction. The instructional outcome in 35 of the 40 studies was student learning, as indicated on achievement examinations given at the end of instruction.

Table 4.1, which is reproduced from their report, is typical of those found in meta-analyses. Each row of the table summarizes a separate study. The first several columns identify the author(s) of the study, where it occurred, the class levels that were studied, and the content and duration of the course. Then, there are two columns under the heading, *No. of tests.* The *X group* is the experimental group, and the *C group* is the control group. For example, in the study by Palmer, the experimental group took 6 tests during a psychology course, whereas the control group took no tests.

The last column of Table 4.1 shows the effect size for each study. We explain the mathematical basis for an effect size, and its use in different types of research, in the next chapter. Here it is sufficient to note that in this meta-analysis, the effect size is a quantitative expression of the magnitude of the difference between the scores of the experimental and control groups. Effect sizes have the same meaning across studies, even though studies use different measures of student achievement and the measures have different score distributions.

The effect size in Palmer's study was .55. By itself, this number has little meaning. It is necessary to convert this number into a percentile equivalent using the normal curve distribution (explained in Chapter 5). An effect size of .55 means that the average score (i.e., the mean score) earned by the experimental groups would be at the 71st percentile of the distribution of scores earned by the control group. An effect size of .00 means there is no difference between the experimental and control groups: The average score of the experimental group is at the 50th percentile of the score distribution of the control group.

The average effect size for the 35 studies shown in Table 4.2 is .23, meaning that the average final examination score of students who took frequent tests during a course would be at the 59th percentile of the score distribution of students who took infrequent or no tests. Thus, we would conclude that frequent testing has a small positive effect on student learning.

Four of the studies included in this meta-analysis investigated the effect of frequent testing on students' attitudes toward the course. The average effect size for these studies was .59, meaning that students who took frequent tests had a more positive attitude toward the course than students who took infrequent or no tests.

After calculation of an average effect size for all the studies included in the review, reviewers usually examine variations in effect sizes across studies. For example, we find in Table 4.1 that the effect sizes for frequency of testing vary from a high of .96 (meaning that frequent testing had a very positive effect on student achievement) to a low of –.80 (meaning that infrequent testing was much better than frequent testing in this particular study). To understand why these variations occurred, Bangert-Drowns, Kulik, and Kulik coded certain features of each study. They then determined the average effect size for studies that contained each feature, and for studies that did not contain the feature or that contained a contrasting feature.

---

12. Bangert-Drowns, R. L., Kulik, J. A., & Kulik, C. C. (1991). Effects of frequent classroom testing. *Journal of Educational Research, 85,* 89–99.

✦ Touchstone in Research

Hedges, L. V. (1998). *Statistical methods for meta-analysis.* San Diego: Academic Press.

Lipsey, M. W., & Wilson, D. B. (2000). *Practical meta-analysis.* Thousand Oaks, CA: Sage.

TABLE 4.1

Results of a Meta-Analysis of Research on the Effects of Frequent Classroom Testing

Study	Place	Class Level	Course Content	Duration in Weeks	No. of Tests		Effect Size
					X Group	C Group	
Curo (1963)	Indiana	11th	Social Science	6	25	2	0.10
Deputy (1929	State University of New York	College	Philosophy	6	12	0	0.96
Dineen, Taylor, & Stephens (1989)	Nebraska	High School	Mathematics	15	75	15	0.17
Fitch, Drucker, & Norton (1951)	Purdue University	College	Government	15	15	4	0.26
Fulkerson & Martin (1981)	Western Illinois University	College	Psychology	12	8	4	0.07
Gable (1936)	Maryland	High School	Science	7	21	5	−0.80
Keys (1934)	University of California	College	Psychology	15	8	2	−0.01
Kirkpatrick (1934)	Iowa	High School	Science	18	20	2	0.31
Laidlaw (1963)	Fairleigh Dickinson University	College	Psychology	16	16	4	−0.08
Lindenberg (1984)	Illinois Community Colleges	College	Accounting	17	12	2	0.01
Mach (1963)	California State Polytechnic College	College	Mathematics	12	29	1	0.15[a]
Maloney & Ruch (1929)	California	9–11	Reading	10	5	0	0.59
Marso (1970)	University of Nebraska	College	Psychology	15	6	3	0.14
Monk & Stallings (1971)	University of Illinois	College	Geography	15	10	6	0.07
Mudgett (1956)	University of Minnesota	College	Engineering	12	36	2	0.26
Nation, Knight, Lamberth, & Dyck (1974)	University of Oklahoma	College	Psychology	8	8	1	−0.22
Negin (1981)	Marquette University	College	Law	15	3	0	0.70
Noll (1939)	Rhode Island State College	College	Psychology	15	5	1	−0.27

Study	Place	Class Level	Course Content	Duration in Weeks	No. of Tests		Effect Size
					X Group	C Group	
Nystrom (1969)	California Junior College	College	Mathematics	15	50	5	0.31
Olsen, Weber, & Dorner (1968)	University of Illinois	College	Veterinary medicine	15	10	3	0.14
Palmer (1974)	Davison College	College	Psychology	10	6	0	0.55
Pikunas & Mazzota (1965)	Michigan	12th	Science	6	6	0	0.71
Pratt (1970)	Arizona	High School	Social science	9	11	0	0.19
Robinson (1972)	Bringham Young University	College	Psychology	4	3	0	0.10
Rievman (1974)	Florida Atlantic University	College	Psychology	16	10	2	0.34
Ross & Henry (1939)	Iowa State University	College	Psychology	12	10	1	0.06
Selakovich (1962)	West Texas State College	College	Government	15	15	3	0.08
Shapiro (1973)	New York Community College	College	Business	15	10	3	0.26
Standlee & Popham (1960)	Indiana University	College	Psychology	15	14	1	0.26
Stephens (1986)	University of Nebraska	College	Statistics	5	5	0	0.67
Townsend & Wheatley (1975)	California State Polytechnic College	College	Mathematics	12	49	1	0.54[a]
Ward (1984)	Western Illinois University	College	Statistics	15	13	2	−0.15[a]
Wiggins (1968)	University of North Carolina	College	Sociology	5	4	0	0.79
Wilkins (1979)	Louisiana Community College	College	Psychology	12	11	0	0.30
Williams & Lawrence (1974)	Western Michigan University	College	Physiology	4	3	0	0.34

[a]Estimated on the basis of direction and statistical significance of reported values.

Source: Table 1 on p. 93 in: Bangert-Drowns, R. L., Kulik, J. A., & Kulik, C. C. (1991). Effects of frequent classroom testing. *Journal of Educational Research, 85,* 89–99. Reprinted with permission of the Helen Dwight Reid Educational Foundation. Published by Heldref Publications, 1319 Eighteenth St., NW, Washington, DC 20036-1802. Copyright © 1991.

TABLE 4.2

Relationship between Study Features and Achievement Effects in a Meta-Analysis of 35 Studies on Frequent Classroom Testing

Study Feature	N	M	SE
Adjusted number of tests for X Group[a]			
1 to 10	11	0.24	0.09
11 to 20	16	0.23	0.07
21 or more	8	0.21	0.18
Adjusted number of tests for C groups[a]*			
None	11	0.54	0.08
One	5	0.15	0.13
Two or more	19	0.07	0.06
Duration of treatment			
8 weeks or less	9	0.29	0.19
9 to 12 weeks	9	0.30	0.07
13 weeks or more	17	0.15	0.05
Subject assignment			
Random	6	0.36	0.10
Nonrandom	29	0.20	0.07
Control for instructor effect			
Same	29	0.18	0.06
Different	5	0.39	0.17
Control for author bias in criterion examination			
Commercial	7	0.16	0.19
Local and other	28	0.24	0.06
Statistical control in outcome measures			
Postscores only	20	0.28	0.08
Control for covariate	15	0.15	0.08
Class level			
Precollege	7	0.18	0.19
College	28	0.24	0.06
Course content			
Mathematics	6	0.28	0.12
Science	6	0.13	0.21
Social science	17	0.16	0.06
Others	6	0.46	0.14
Year of report			
Up to 1960	10	0.16	0.15
1961 to 1970	10	0.25	0.09
1971 to 1980	9	0.25	0.08
1981 or later	6	0.25	0.15
Source of study			
Unpublished	3	0.41	0.20
Dissertation	10	0.18	0.04
Published	22	0.22	0.09

[a]Number of tests was adjusted for each study to estimate the number of tests that would be given to students over a 15-week interval.

*p < .001.

Source: Table 2 on p. 94 in: Bangert-Drowns, R. L., Kulik, J. A., & Kulik, C. C. (1991). Effects of frequent classroom testing. *Journal of Educational Research, 85,* 89–99. Reprinted with permission of the Helen Dwight Reid Educational Foundation. Published by Heldref Publications, 1319 Eighteenth St., NW, Washington, DC 20036-1802. Copyright © 1991.

The results of this analysis are shown in Table 4.2. The first study feature is the number of tests given to the experimental group during the course. (This number is statistically adjusted to compensate for the fact that course length in some studies was longer than in others.) In 11 of the studies, between 1 and 10 tests were given; in 16 studies, between 11 and 20 tests were given; and in 8 studies, 21 or more tests were given. We see that the effect sizes across the three classifications are very similar (.24, .23, and .21), meaning that the beneficial effects of testing during a course do not depend on how frequently tests are given.

The standard error (SE) for each effect size also is shown in Table 4.2. This statistic indicates, for the studies that contained a particular feature, how much the effect sizes varied around the mean effect size. The larger the standard error, the more the effect sizes varied across studies. For the three comparison groups, SEs are .09 (1 to 10 tests), .07 (11 to 20 tests), and .18 (21 or more tests). These results indicate that there was more variability in effect sizes for research studies that investigated courses with very frequent testing.

Interesting results were obtained for the next study feature in Table 4.2: number of tests given to students in the control group. We find a substantial average effect size of .54 for studies in which the control group took no tests during the course. The effect size is much smaller for studies in which the control group took one or more tests. This finding suggests that it is beneficial to give students at least one test during a course, but it matters little whether more than one test is given. Had the researchers reported only the average effect size for all 35 studies shown in Table 4.1, this potentially important finding would not have been revealed.

You will note that in Table 4.2 some of the features involve instruction (e.g., course content and duration of the instruction), whereas other features involve the research methodology of the studies. The latter features are important because they provide a way of determining whether better-designed studies produce different results than less well-designed studies. For example, random assignment of individuals to experimental and control groups is a good design feature of experiments, as we discuss in Chapter 12. We find in Table 4.2 that the average effect size for studies that employed random assignment is .36, whereas the average effect size for studies that employed nonrandom assignment is .20. This result suggests that the average effect size of .23 for all 35 studies, which include studies varying widely in quality, may underestimate the true effect of frequent testing.

This review of the effects of frequent testing illustrates the power of meta-analysis for analyzing and summarizing the research literature on a particular problem. Therefore, you should pay close attention to a meta-analysis if you come across one in your search of the literature. Later in the chapter, we will discuss procedures for conducting your own meta-analysis as a study in its own right, or as part of a study in which you collect new data.

Reading Primary Sources

A primary source is a direct report of an event by an individual who actually observed or participated in it. In educational research, a primary source generally is a report of a study by one or more of the persons who conducted it, or a report by the authors of their own theory or opinions about educational phenomena.

As we explained above, the research findings and theories reported in primary sources often are reviewed in secondary sources. However, the authors of secondary source reviews may slant their interpretation of primary sources to agree with their own views, or may omit some information that a reader wants to know. Thus, we recommend that for your literature review you not rely entirely on secondary sources, even if they appear comprehensive and are recent. At the least, you should review for yourself the primary sources that are most critical to your proposed study.

If a book, article, or other document is not at your institution's library, a librarian should be able to help you obtain it through an interlibrary loan service or some other service. For example, our university's library has the capacity to have copies of journal articles e-mailed to us as Adobe Acrobat files that we can view on our computer monitor and printed out on a printer. Also, as we indicated in a preceding section, many journals are now available on the Internet.

If a primary source is highly relevant to your study, we recommend that you make a photocopy of the entire document. When you are ready to write your literature review, you will find it much easier to report on each relevant study if you can refer to your own copy of the document rather than relying on incomplete notes or having to return to the library to reread the original copy of the document.

After obtaining copies of primary source documents, we recommend that you read the most recent ones first. The reason is that the most recent studies are likely to be more valuable because they have the earlier research as a foundation.

Classifying Primary Sources

In reading primary sources, you should search for ways to classify them so that they do not remain an undifferentiated mass in your mind. The best method usually is to classify the documents according to the questions or objectives that are guiding your study. For example, one of the authors (M. Gall) served as the dissertation advisor for Douglas Herman, who did case studies of teachers who had been placed on a plan of assistance.[13] A plan of assistance is a remediation process for a teacher who is judged to be deficient in teaching performance or some other job responsibility.

Herman formulated six research questions:

1. What kinds of problems lead to teachers being placed on plans of assistance?
2. How are plans of assistance developed and, as written documents, what do they look like?
3. What kinds of remediation take place during plans of assistance?
4. Are plans of assistance effective?
5. Is the supervision of teachers on plans of assistance consistent with research findings and expert opinion about effective supervisory practice?
6. How can plans of assistance be improved?

He used these research questions to develop the following codes for classifying the documents that he identified in his literature search:

a. Documents containing information about why teachers get into difficulty, including difficulties that precipitate a plan of assistance.
b. Documents containing information about what happens during the various phases of a plan of assistance.
c. Documents containing information about whether plans of assistance are effective.
d. Documents containing information about effective supervisory practice.
e. Documents containing opinions about how teacher remediation and plans of assistance can be improved.

Each document was classified by one or more of these codes. Also, as Herman progressed in his literature review, he refined several of the codes. For example, code (d) was divided

---

13. Herman, D. P. (1994). Teachers on plans of assistance: A descriptive study. *Dissertation Abstracts International, 54*(09), 3279A. (UMI No. 9405183)

into three codes: (d-1) general supervisory practice; (d-2) supervisory practice for preservice teachers, and (d-3) supervisory practice for inservice teachers.

Using such a coding system is helpful in two ways. First, it stimulates you to actively read each document for its relevance to the major topics that underlie your research problem. Secondly, a coding system allows you to identify quickly the documents that concern a specific topic, and thus simplifies the job of writing your literature review.

Critical Evaluation of Research Studies

The first judgment you must make in studying a research report is its relevance to your research problem. If it proves to be relevant, your next judgment should concern the quality of the research described in the report. In making this judgment, keep in mind that the quality of published studies in education and related disciplines is, unfortunately, not high.

This observation is based on our own experience and on a review by Bruce Tuckman of four studies that employed experts in research methodology to judge the quality of educational research published in journals and other sources.[14] On the basis of his review, Tuckman concluded that "much of the work in print ought not to be there."[15] The experts in the four studies concluded that between 40 and 60 percent of the research studies that they judged should have been extensively revised prior to publication or should not have been published at all.

Because both good and poor research is reported in the literature, you need to evaluate carefully the quality of each study that you identify as relevant to your problem. You should give more weight to the better research, and estimate how the results of a given study might have been affected by flaws in the research process.

This evaluation process requires a great deal of skill. Ideally, a researcher should master the entire research process before undertaking a literature review that will be disseminated to a professional audience. At the least, we recommend that you study the rest of this book *before* you conduct a literature review and initiate your own research plan. Most chapters, including this one, end with a section on recommendations for carrying out different types of research or different phases of the research process. These recommendations provide guidelines that can help you evaluate the quality of the research studies you read.

You may find it helpful to refer to Figure 4.5, which lists questions you should ask when evaluating a research report. Some of the questions apply to any research study, and others apply specifically to quantitative research or qualitative research. The questions are further elaborated in two forms contained in the Appendixes. The form in Appendix C is for your use in evaluating quantitative research reports, and the form in Appendix D is for your use in evaluating qualitative research reports. Each form lists the questions appropriate for that type of research, along with a description of the type of information you should look for in the report to answer each question, and a sample answer.

Research reports that appear in journals usually are brief in order to meet the journals' space limitations. Their brevity and standardized format, however, make such reports less interesting to read than popular educational writing. Furthermore, you often must assume or guess about aspects of the study for which insufficient detail is provided. If important details about the study have been omitted, you can note this problem in your literature review. If a missing detail is critical to your planned study, you should consider writing the researcher to ask about it.

---

14. Tuckman, B. W. (1990). A proposal for improving the quality of published educational research. *Educational Researcher, 19*(9), 22–25.
15. Ibid., p. 22.

FIGURE 4.5

Questions to Ask When Evaluating a Report of a Quantitative or Qualitative Research Study

Introduction
1. Are the research problem, procedures, or findings unduly influenced by the researchers' institutional affiliation, beliefs, values, or theoretical orientation?
2. Did the researchers express a positive or negative bias in describing the subject of the study (an instructional method, program, curriculum, person, etc.)?
3. Is the literature review section of the report sufficiently comprehensive? And does it include studies that you know to be relevant to the problem?
4. Are hypotheses, questions, or objectives explicitly stated, and if so, are they clear?
5. Did the researchers make a convincing case that a research hypothesis, question, or objective was important to study?
6. (Quantitative) is each variable in the study clearly defined?
7. (Quantitative) Is the measure of each variable consistent with how the variable was defined?

Research Procedures
8. (Quantitative) Did the sampling procedures produce a sample that is representative of an identifiable population or of your local population?
9. (Quantitative) Did the researchers form subgroups that would increase understanding of the phenomena being studied?
10. (Qualitative) Did the sampling procedure result in a case or cases that were particularly interesting and from whom much could be learned about the phenomena of interest?
11. Is each measure in the study sufficiently valid for its intended purpose?
12. Is each measure in the study sufficiently reliable for its intended purpose?
13. Is each measure appropriate for the sample?
14. Were the research procedures appropriate and clearly described so that others could replicate them if they wished?

Research Results
15. Were appropriate statistical techniques used, and were they used correctly?
16. (Qualitative) Did the report include a "thick" description that brought to life how the individuals responded to interview questions or how they behaved?
17. (Qualitative) Did each variable in the study emerge in a meaningful way from the data?
18. (Qualitative) Did clearly stated hypotheses or questions emerge from the data that were collected?

Discussion of Results
19. Do the results of the data analyses support what the researchers conclude are the findings of the study?
20. Did the researchers provide reasonable explanations of the findings?
21. Did the researchers draw reasonable implications for practice from the findings?

Note: Questions that apply specifically to quantitative research or to qualitative research are so noted. Otherwise questions apply to both types of research.

Source: Adapted from Figure 5.1 on p. 88 in: Borg, W. R., Gall, J. P., & Gall, M. D. (1993). *Applying educational research* (3rd ed.). New York: Longman.

Synthesizing the Findings of Your Literature Review

Suppose you are at the point of having collected a large number of documents related to your research problem. These documents are likely to include literature reviews, opinion articles, theoretical essays, and many research studies. Your task now is to synthesize all this information into a coherent literature review. This is a complex process. It takes many weeks to synthesize a body of literature and write the review. Some parts of the process are creative, and therefore defy precise analysis. The parts that can be made explicit are described below and in the next sections.

We recommend that you start by reading exemplary literature reviews, such as those found in the journal *Review of Educational Research* and in high-quality research articles and dissertations. They will give you a feeling for what a good literature review contains, and a mindset for undertaking the process of synthesizing and reporting the information that your literature search has revealed.

Some literature reviews have flaws that you should strive to avoid. Among them are the following:

1. The literature review stands alone from the other parts of the dissertation or article. In other words, the reader is not shown how the work of other researchers and theorists relates to the study being reported.
2. The review focuses on research findings without considering the soundness of the methodology used to generate the findings. Thus, the reader has no sense of how much confidence to place in your conclusions.
3. The review does not include a description of the search procedures used to identify relevant literature. It is important to mention which preliminary and secondary sources you consulted, the descriptors you used, and the time period covered.
4. The reviewer writes a literature review that consists of a set of isolated findings, opinions, and ideas. This flaw is most often manifested as a disconnected series of paragraphs—one paragraph for each document included in the review. You need to make a concerted effort to fit the findings, opinions, and ideas into a conceptual or theoretical framework developed by you or by other researchers. We think that this is what Richard Elmore had in mind when he stated:

> The most common defect of the literature reviews I have read is that they are pedestrian and mechanical in their judgment, even when they are comprehensive and rigorous in their method. They summarize the evidence, but they contribute nothing to the reader's understanding of it.[16]

To avoid these and other flaws, you should take time to reflect on how the information in the various documents you identified in the literature search relates to a theoretical or conceptual framework and to your proposed study. You also should take note of methodological problems in the studies you reviewed, comment on them in your report, and discuss how your proposed study will deal with them.

In the following sections, we focus on specific strategies for synthesizing research results reported in primary source documents. The strategies differ considerably depending on whether the research results to be synthesized are quantitative or qualitative in nature. Therefore, we describe them separately.

Synthesizing Quantitative Research Findings

The first step is to identify all the documents from your literature search that report statistical results relating to your research problem. Most of these documents will be primary sources. Having identified the relevant documents, you will need to determine how to synthesize the various statistical results reported in them. The following discussion explains several methods for performing this synthesis.

---

16. Elmore, R. (1991). Comment on "Towards rigor in reviews of multivocal literatures: Applying the exploratory case study method." *Review of Educational Research, 61,* 293–297. Quote appears on p. 295.

✦ Touchstone in Research

Dunkin, M. J. (1996). Types of errors in synthesizing research in education. *Review of Educational Research, 66,* 87–97.

✦ Touchstone in Research

Cooper, H., & Hedges, L. V. (Eds.). (1994). *The handbook of research synthesis.* New York: Russell Sage Foundation.

The Narrative Review

Prior to the landmark article by Gene Glass on meta-analysis in 1976, virtually all literature reviews in education were written in a narrative style.[17] These reviews emphasized better-designed studies, and organized their results to form a composite picture of the state of knowledge on the problem or topic being reviewed. The number of statistically significant results, compared with the number of nonsignificant results, may have been noted. Each study may have been described separately in a few sentences or a paragraph.

The major shortcoming of narrative reviews is their subjectivity. Reviewers seldom state their criteria for inclusion of studies in the review and often place too much emphasis on statistical significance in judging the practical or theoretical importance of a finding. (Statistical significance is explained in Chapter 5.) Richard Light and David Pillemer illustrated the subjectivity of narrative reviews by referring to two reviews of research on the effects of the environment on the IQs of adopted children.[18] Although the reviewers synthesized the *same* group of studies, they reached *opposite* conclusions!

Vote Counting

Gregg Jackson recommended a procedure for synthesizing research results that is sometimes called *vote counting*.[19] One version of this method involves classifying each statistical result into four categories: (1) a statistically significant positive result, that is, in the direction hypothesized; (2) a nonsignificant positive result; (3) a nonsignificant negative result, that is, opposite to the direction hypothesized; and (4) a statistically significant negative result.

It is possible that a set of research studies could yield many statistical results, none of which are statistically significant, but with all or most of them in the hypothesized direction. It is possible for no individual result to be statistically significant, but for the trend of of results across studies to be statistically significant. The vote-counting method enables the reviewer to test the statistical significance of this trend of results across studies.

A serious limitation of the vote-counting method is that a large number of statistical results is needed in order to detect reliable trends. Also, vote counting has the weakness that it considers only the direction of the effect, not its magnitude.[20] For example, suppose that one study finds that the experimental group exceeds the control group by 5 points on a criterion achievement test, and another study finds that the experimental group exceeds the control group by 10 points on the same test. If both results are statistically significant, both would be coded as "1" in the above-mentioned category system. The fact that the magnitude of the effect varied substantially from one study to the next would be ignored by the category system. This limitation is overcome by the method of meta-analysis described below.

The Chi-Square Method

An approach advocated by N. L. Gage takes into account the size of the sample and the magnitude of the relationship or difference reported in each study.[21] The method is based on the fact that any p value can be transformed into a chi-square statistic with two degrees of freedom. This method involves first converting whatever inferential statistics are reported in each study (e.g., t, F, r) into exact probability (p) values by checking the appropriate statistical tables or using a computer program for this purpose. The probability values next are converted to chi-square values. Because chi-squares and degrees of free-

17. Glass, G. V (1976). Primary, secondary, and meta-analysis of research. *Educational Researcher, 5*(10), 3–8.
18. Light, R. J., & Pillemer, D. B. (1984). *Summing up: The science of reviewing research.* Cambridge, MA: Harvard University Press.
19. Jackson, G. B. (1980). Methods for integrative reviews. *Review of Educational Research, 50,* 438–460.
20. See Chapter 4 in: Hedges, L. V., & Olkin, I. (1985). *Statistical methods for meta-analysis.* New York: Academic Press.
21. Gage, N. L. (1978). *The scientific basis of the art of teaching.* New York: Teachers College Press.

dom (*df*) are additive, the chi-squares and *df*s for all studies then are summed. To determine the overall level of significance of the studies being combined, it is only necessary to check in a regular chi-square probability table for the summed values of chi-square and degrees of freedom.

The chi-square method has been largely supplanted by the method of meta-analysis, described below. However, meta-analysis generally requires many studies to yield a meaningful synthesis. The chi-square method should be considered when only a few statistical results are to be synthesized and when these results come from studies that are close replications of each other. For example, researchers sometimes do a study, and if they obtain interesting results, they replicate the study to determine whether the results are stable. In this situation, the statistical results of the two studies can be tested for their combined statistical significance using the chi-square method.

Meta-Analysis

Since the late 1970s, meta-analysis has been the most widely used method for synthesizing the statistical results of a group of studies on the same research problem. There are many reports of meta-analyses in the education literature, as we discussed above in the section on secondary sources. Moreover, meta-analyses in other social science disciplines and professions (especially medicine) are common.

Meta-analysis has three major advantages over vote counting and the chi-square method for synthesizing quantitative results:

1. It focuses on the magnitude of the effect observed in each study to be synthesized. For example, meta-analysis informs the reader not only whether the experimental group and control group obtained different scores on a criterion test, but also by how much they differed.

2. Meta-analysis provides a metric, called an *effect size,* that can be applied to any statistic and any measure. This feature of meta-analysis is important because various studies of the same research problem may employ different designs, measures, and statistics. For example, Researcher A might investigate whether the teacher's use of PowerPoint presentations affects the quality of students' note taking. She conducts an experiment in which the experimental group of teachers uses PowerPoint and the control group of teachers does not; students' class notes are rated for quality before and after the experiment on a seven-point scale. The statistical technique known as analysis of covariance is applied to the resulting data. Researcher B, on the other hand, investigates the same problem using a non-experimental research design. He selects a sample of teachers and measures the extent to which they use PowerPoint in their classes. He also rates the quality of their students' class notes on a five-point scale. The statistical technique known as correlation is applied to the resulting data. Even though these two studies used different designs, measures, and statistical techniques, their results can be converted to a common metric, namely, the effect size statistic. This statistic allows the reviewer to determine the magnitude of the relationship between PowerPoint use and quality of students' notes in each study, and whether the magnitudes are similar.

3. Meta-analysis allows the reviewer to determine whether certain features of the studies included in the review affected the results that were obtained. This use of meta-analysis is illustrated in Table 4.2, which shows the effects of different features of studies that have investigated frequency of testing during a course.

A meta-analysis is a time-consuming procedure, because you not only must conduct an exhaustive search for relevant primary source documents, but you must obtain and read them all. You cannot rely on abstracts and secondary source reviews, as you can in conventional literature reviews. You need the primary source documents in order to compute effect sizes and to code relevant features of the studies. For this reason, some students do a meta-analysis as their entire dissertation or thesis project.[22]

Synthesizing Qualitative Research Findings

Qualitative researchers study individual cases, making an effort to understand the unique character and context of each case. How, then, can the findings of case studies be synthesized? The challenge, as George Noblit and R. Dwight Hare explain it, is to "retain the uniqueness and holism of accounts even as we synthesize them."[23]

Rodney Ogawa and Betty Malen suggested a method of synthesizing qualitative studies based on the principles and procedures of the exploratory case study method.[24] Their method applies to what they refer to as *multivocal literature,* which consists primarily of qualitative research but also may include some quantitative research and even nonresearch accounts of a phenomenon.

Because most qualitative research is exploratory, it is appropriate that a review of this research should be exploratory in nature, too. The purpose is to generate insights into the phenomena that were studied, and to develop hypotheses that can guide productive lines of research. In contrast, the method of meta-analysis has the purpose of drawing strong conclusions about whether an effect exists, and if so, how strong it is.

Our analysis of Ogawa and Malen's method suggests that it has eight essential steps.[25] The following description of these steps is not meant to imply that they are discrete, sequential, or applicable to all qualitative research reviews. Rather, our analysis is intended to provide a framework that you can use to develop your own approach to reviewing a body of literature that is primarily qualitative in nature.

Step 1: Create an audit trail. The term *audit trail* is used in qualitative research to refer to documentation about how a case study was conducted.[26] An **audit trail** could be included in a literature review to describe all the procedures and decision rules that were used by the reviewer. If such an account is included in the report of the literature review, readers can understand more fully how the review was done and can replicate the review, if they wish.

You should plan a procedure at the outset of the literature review for maintaining an audit trail of your activities, problems, and decisions. This early planning will ensure that the most important information guiding your decisions and discoveries are recorded. A diary format might work well because it records events in temporal order. In reviewing the diary, you can determine whether and how your thinking and procedures changed as the review progressed.

Step 2: Define the focus of the review. Qualitative research typically deals with complex social phenomena as they occur in a real-life context. For example, Ogawa and Malen described their own review of the literature on site-based school management. It is important that you conceptualize the social phenomenon of interest to you as a construct, and then develop a definition of this construct. For example, Ogawa and Malen developed

22. Two examples of this type of dissertation are: Bennett, B. B. (1988). The effectiveness of staff development training practices: A meta-analysis. *Dissertation Abstracts International, 48*(07), 1739A. (UMI No. 8721226); Rolheiser-Bennett, N. C. (1987). Four models of teaching: A meta-analysis of student outcomes. *Dissertation Abstracts International, 47*(11), 3966A. (UMI No. 8705887)
23. Noblit, G. W., & Hare, R. D. (1988). *Meta-ethnography: Synthesizing qualitative studies.* Thousand Oaks, CA: Sage.
24. Ogawa, R. T., & Malen, B. (1991). Towards rigor in reviews of multivocal literatures: Applying the exploratory case study method. *Review of Educational Research, 61,* 265–286. See also four commentaries on this article in the same issue.
25. Our analysis generally follows the steps described by Ogawa and Malen, but for a few steps we developed our own elaborations and interpretations.
26. Guba, E., & Lincoln, Y. S. (1981). *Effective evaluation.* San Francisco, CA: Jossey-Bass.

this definition of the construct of school-based management: "a form of decentralization that identified the school as the primary unit of improvement and the redistribution of decision-making authority as the primary means through which improvements may be stimulated and sustained."[27]

A definition of constructs is important because it defines the scope of the review. You should include documents about the phenomena that correspond to your definition and exclude documents that do not. To develop the definition, it first may be necessary to study a collection of potentially relevant documents. As you study them, you are likely to get clearer about what you wish to include in, and exclude from, your definition.

Step 3: Search for relevant literature. Many of the social phenomena of interest to qualitative researchers in education also are of interest to other individuals. Ogawa and Malen claim that the writings of these individuals should be included in the literature review because they shed light on the diverse meanings that people attribute to social phenomena and the context in which such phenomena occur. In the words of Glaser and Strauss, the writings of these individuals are "voices begging to be heard."[28]

If you accept Ogawa and Malen's position, your literature review could include not only qualitative research reports, but also nonresearch documents (e.g., newspaper articles, editorials, minutes of meetings, memos, program descriptions) and reports of informal investigations (e.g., internal program evaluations). Reports of quantitative research studies, if available, also could be included if they shed light on the meaning of the phenomena you are studying, but they would not be considered as inherently more valuable than the other documents to be reviewed.

Step 4: Classify the documents. After identifying and obtaining relevant documents, you will need to classify them in order to understand the types of data they represent. For example, Ogawa and Malen classified the documents relevant to school-based management that they examined into four types: project descriptions or status reports, position statements, systematic investigations, and related literature sources. Project descriptions reported efforts to institute or administer a school-based management project, whereas position statements built a case for such projects. Systematic investigations reported empirical data on the operation and outcomes of these projects. Related literature sources reported on topics related to school-based management, for example, the creation of community school boards and participatory decision-making arrangements.

Step 5: Create summary databases. Imagine that you have collected a wide range of documents pertinent to your topic, for example, case studies, program descriptions, minutes of meetings, newspaper accounts, scholarly books, and articles reporting quantitative research results. You cannot simply read all these documents, take casual notes, and then write a literature review. Instead, you will need to develop narrative summaries and coding schemes that take into account all the pertinent information in the documents. This process is iterative, meaning, for example, that you might need to develop a coding scheme, apply it to the documents, revise it based on this experience, and re-apply it. In the words of Ogawa and Malen: "From the reams of raw materials [documents] collected, researchers must develop summations that can be (a) read and reread to be sure they are accurate reductions of the raw materials and (b) examined and reexamined to be sure that all pertinent information is taken into account throughout data analysis and reflected in the final report."[29] This qualitative approach to literature review is very similar to the process of data analysis in case study research (see Chapter 14).

27. Ogawa & Malen, Towards rigor in reviews, p. 277.
28. Ibid., p. 267.
29. Ibid., p. 280.

Step 6. Identify constructs and hypothesized causal linkages. In meta-analysis, the essential information in a quantitative research report is the statistical results, which are expressed as effect sizes. Reviewers of qualitative literature do not have the discovery of something equivalent to an effect size as their goal. As we stated above, their goals are to increase understanding of the phenomena being studied and to guide future research.

What, then, is to be understood in a review of qualitative literature? Ogawa and Malen claim that the reviewer should focus on identifying constructs that represent the major themes represented in the documents. For example, Ogawa and Malen identified *quality planning* as a major construct in their review of the literature on school-based management.

It is not necessary for the constructs to be explicitly labeled, defined, or frequently mentioned in the documents that are reviewed. In fact, different qualitative researchers and nonresearchers may use quite different language to describe a particular type of event or other phenomenon. The task of the reviewer is to search for themes (i.e., commonalities) in these different descriptions. If a theme seems important, the reviewer can generate a construct and accompanying definition that represent the essence of the theme. The reviewer also has a responsibility to explain the relationship between the construct and its various manifestations in the literature being reviewed. An explanation is necessary in order to assure the reader that the construct is valid and emergent. The construct is valid if other individuals can use the reviewer's definition and indicators of the construct to identify or generate instances of the construct. The construct is emergent if it is clear to others that the construct was developed from the literature being reviewed and not just from the reviewer's idiosyncratic perceptions and biases.

In addition to identifying relevant constructs, the reviewer of qualitative literature also needs to develop hypotheses about causal linkages. For example, in their review of the literature on school-based management, Ogawa and Malen identified several hypotheses concerning causal linkages, for example: School-based management leads to renewed organizations, more academically successful schools, and restored confidence in schools. In addition to identifying these linkages, the reviewer needs to identify and evaluate the evidence presented in the documents to substantiate these claims of causal linkage. The reviewer also should judge the value and salience of the hypothesized linkages to the authors of the document and to stakeholders in the phenomena being studied.

Step 7: Search for contrary findings and rival interpretations. In our example of a meta-analysis, we observed that research on the effects of frequent testing has yielded contradictory findings: Many of the findings are positive, but some are negative (see Table 4.1). Rather than ignoring these disparities, the reviewers who did the meta-analysis tried to understand them by analyzing features of the various studies (see Table 4.2).

Similarly, reviewers of qualitative studies need to be alert to the possibility of contrary findings and interpretations different from those that they reach. Ogawa and Malen provided an example of this need to be self-critical. In describing the process they followed in reviewing the literature on school-based management, they noted that their initial claim that this management approach did not improve staff morale was oversimplified:

> We ended, ultimately, by qualifying our assessment. Instead of concluding that site-based management had no effect, we suggested there is some evidence that site-based management may have initial, positive effects on the morale and motivation of some participants but that there is little evidence that site-based management produces sustained improvements in the morale or motivation of a substantial number of participants.[30]

30. Ibid., p. 282.

Step 8: Use colleagues or informants to corroborate findings. Ogawa and Malen recommend that reviewers of qualitative literature give drafts of their report to colleagues for critique. Colleagues may be able to spot weaknesses in definitions, logic, and support for claims; they also can suggest alternative interpretations that should be considered. Authors of documents included in the literature review and participants in the events discussed in the review also can perform these functions.

The preceding discussion demonstrates that reviews of qualitative literature can, and should, be just as rigorous as reviews of quantitative literature. The two types of review differ only in the methods used to achieve that rigor.

✦ RECOMMENDATIONS FOR
Reviewing Research Literature

1. Take sufficient time to identify the best descriptors and best preliminary, secondary, and primary sources in reviewing literature related to the research problem or topic.
2. Obtain and read at least the most important primary sources for your literature review rather than relying on abstracts in preliminary sources or summaries in secondary sources.
3. Examine critically all aspects of a study's research methodology before accepting a researcher's findings and interpretations as valid.
4. When appropriate, synthesize the statistical results of quantitative studies by meta-analytic or chi-square methods.
5. Consider contrary findings and alternative interpretations in synthesizing qualitative and quantitative literature.
6. Maintain a record or audit trail of the search procedures that were used in the literature review, and report them.
7. In writing the literature review, make explicit connections between the findings of your literature review and your research questions, hypotheses, or objectives.

✔ SELF-CHECK TEST

Circle the correct answer to each of the following questions.
The answers are provided at the back of the book.

1. A literature review need not be done prior to data collection when
   a. *CIJE* contains no major descriptors relevant to the research problem.
   b. a relevant secondary source is available.
   c. a relevant meta-analysis is available.
   d. the researcher's goal is to develop grounded theory.

2. If the authors of a textbook report results of their own experiments, that portion of the text would be considered a
   a. secondary source.
   b. primary source.
   c. preliminary source.
   d. literature review.

3. The best preliminary sources for conducting a literature review in education are published by
   a. the American Psychological Association (APA).
   b. the Educational Resources Information Center (ERIC).
   c. the American Educational Research Association (AERA).
   d. University Microfilms International.

4. The best source for identifying relevant papers presented at educational conferences is
   a. *Resources in Education.*
   b. *Current Index to Journals in Education.*
   c. *Readers' Guide to Periodical Literature.*
   d. *Review of Educational Research.*

5. A search engine for the ERIC database
   a. cannot be used for documents published within the most recent two years.
   b. must be used in conjunction with a hard copy of the *Thesaurus of ERIC Descriptors.*
   c. can be used for pearl building.
   d. requires the services of a reference librarian.

6. Connecting two descriptors by *or* when conducting a computer search of the literature usually
   a. increases the number of records retrieved.
   b. reduces the number of records retrieved.
   c. retrieves only those records that include both descriptors.
   d. narrows the focus of your literature search.

7. Meta-analysis is a procedure for
   a. checking the thoroughness of a search for documents coded by ERIC descriptors.
   b. synthesizing the results of documents indexed by *CIJE* or *RIE.*
   c. synthesizing the results of statistical results of different studies about the same research problem.
   d. synthesizing the constructs identified in different qualitative studies about the same research problem.

8. The *Review of Educational Research*
   a. provides bibliographies of research completed in each calendar year.
   b. summarizes the research literature on a variety of educational topics.
   c. produces a current index to preliminary sources in education.
   d. provides brief digests of educational reports originally published in periodicals or newspapers.

9. An effect size is
   a. a limit field in a CD-ROM search of the literature.
   b. a criterion for judging the relevance of a primary source.
   c. a measure of the range of statistical results in a set of research studies.
   d. a measure of the magnitude of one statistical result.

10. The main weakness of narrative reviews is that they tend to:
    a. discuss too many marginally relevant studies.
    b. include too little detail about each study.
    c. be too subjective.
    d. focus more on theory than on actual statistical results.

11. An important purpose of a literature review of qualitative research is to:
    a. develop constructs and hypotheses that can guide further research.
    b. confirm or refute the reviewer's hypotheses.
    c. expose the commonalities in diverse educational phenomena.
    d. all of the above.

12. The rigor of a literature review of qualitative research can be enhanced by
    a. creating an audit trail.
    b. checking emergent constructs against the literature being reviewed.
    c. asking persons who are knowledgeable about the topic to critique the review.
    d. all of the above.

PART III

✦ Research Methods

In designing a study, a researcher must develop a sound plan for selecting a sample, collecting data, and analyzing the data. If the plan is flawed, the results of the study will be difficult or impossible to interpret. In this part of the book, you will learn sampling, data-collection, and data-analysis procedures that are appropriate for different types of research studies.

Chapter 5 provides an overview of the statistical techniques used in educational research. Some statistical techniques are used to check whether tests and other instruments yield valid, reliable measurements. Others are used to analyze the data in order to answer the questions or test the hypotheses that interest the researcher. Statistics play a central role in quantitative research, and they also have applications in qualitative research.

Chapter 6 presents procedures for selecting a sample. A research sample is most likely to consist of persons, but in some studies it is appropriate to sample documents, events, or other phenomena. The researcher's sampling logic depends upon whether a quantitative or qualitative study is being planned. In a quantitative study, the researcher attempts to select a sample that represents a defined population. In a qualitative study, the researcher selects a case, or cases, that likely will yield significant insights about the phenomenon being studied. In either type of study, the researcher's choice of sampling procedure is important, because it affects the extent to which the study's findings can be generalized to other situations.

Chapters 7 through 9 describe various methods for collecting data about the research sample or cases. Researchers can administer standardized tests, personality measures, or questionaires. Other options are to conduct interviews or make observations. We explain the advantages and limitations of each of these methods of data collection.

✦ Statistical Techniques

OVERVIEW

We begin this chapter by describing how statistics typically are used in quantitative and qualitative research. Next, we explain the different types of scores (ranks, percentiles, etc.) that can be generated from measurement data. We then provide an overview of three types of statistical techniques: (1) those used to describe educational phenomena, (2) those used to make inferences from samples to populations, and (3) those used to examine the properties of tests. We conclude with a discussion of three important issues in statistical analysis: the need for exploratory data analysis, the handling of missing data, and multilevel analysis of data.

OBJECTIVES

After studying this chapter, you should be able to

1. Describe the use of statistics in qualitative and quantitative research.
2. Distinguish between the various types of scores that are used in educational research.
3. Describe the purpose of each of the three types of descriptive statistics.
4. Describe situations in which the mean, median, or mode is the most appropriate measure of central tendency.
5. Interpret the meaning of the standard deviation in relation to the normal probability curve.
6. Describe the purpose of a test of statistical significance in educational research.
7. Define statistical power and describe its four main determinants.
8. Explain how confidence limits, replication, and effect size can be used to

supplement tests of statistical significance in interpreting research findings.
9. Describe the use of stem-and-leaf displays and graphs in exploratory data analysis.
10. Explain procedures that can be used to handle missing data when carrying out a data analysis.
11. Explain how different units of statistical analysis (e.g., individual students, classrooms, or schools) can affect one's research findings.
12. Explain how computers can be used to do statistical analyses and what steps can be taken to avoid computing errors and to retrieve data for further analyses at a later point in time.

The Use of Statistics in Educational Research

Statistics are mathematical techniques for analyzing numerical data to accomplish various purposes. For example, the calculation of a statistic known as the *mean* yields a single score that represents many scores, such as the scores of all the students who took a particular test.

Example of Statistical Analysis in a Research Study

Because quantitative research implies the use of numerical data, many people believe that statistics are the exclusive domain of quantitative research. In fact, statistics are used in virtually all quantitative studies, but in many qualitative studies as well. An example is the case study of reading groups in one first-grade classroom conducted by James Collins.[1] The research was part of a large ethnographic study of language differences between working-class black children and middle-class white children in their home and school environments.

After a period of classroom observation, Collins audiotaped and then analyzed 5 lessons from a high-ability reading group and 11 lessons from a low-ability reading group instructed by the teacher and her assistant. Table 5.1, taken from his research report, shows five types of instructional activity in these lessons and the number of minutes that each activity occurred in the high-ability reading group and in the low-ability reading group. Also shown is the percentage of total lesson time spent on each activity.

As Table 5.1 shows, the high-ability reading group spent 70 percent of its time (49 + 21) on passage reading and comprehension questions, whereas the low-ability reading group spent only 37 percent of its time (31 + 6) on these two activities. Conversely, the low-ability

✦ Touchstone in Research

Behrens, J. T., & Smith, M. L. (1996). Data and data analysis. In D. C. Berliner & R. C. Calfee (Eds.), *Handbook of educational psychology* (pp. 945–989). New York: Macmillan.

Bruning, J. L., & Kintz, B. L. (1997). *Computational handbook of statistics* (4th ed.). White Plains, NY: Longman.

Vogt, W. P. (1998). *Dictionary of statistics and methodology: A nontechnical guide for the social sciences* (2nd ed.). Thousand Oaks, CA: Sage.

TABLE 5.1

Time on Task

	High-Ability Group		Low-Ability Group	
	Minutes	**Percentage of Total Time**	**Minutes**	**Percentage of Total Time**
Dictation[a]	0	0	24.5	16
Sound-word identification[b]	10.5	17	48.5	31
Sentence completion[c]	8.0	13	24.5	16
Passage reading[d]	29.5	49	49.0	31
Comprehension questions[e]	13.5	21	9.0	6

[a]Dictation consists of drill in transcribing letters, words or sentences, either copying them from a written sample or in response to an oral sample given by the teacher.

[b]Sound-word drill consists of exercises in identifying letters and words in isolation and in various contexts. 'Sentence completion consists of drill in supplying the appropriate lexical item in order to complete prompt sentences.

[c]Sentence completion consists of drill in supplying the appropriate lexical item in order to complete prompt sentences.

[d]Passage reading (or "reading in the reading books") consists of reading aloud from connected texts, under the guidance of a teacher, and usually in a round-robin style of turn-taking.

[e]Comprehension questions consists of the teachers asking questions of fact and interpretation about the passage being read and evaluating students' answers.

Source: Table 1 on p. 315 in: Collins, J. (1988). Language and class in minority education. *Anthropology & Education Quarterly, 17,* 299–323. Reproduced by permission of the American Anthropological Association from *Anthropology & Educational Quarterly* (19)4. Not for sale or further reproduction.

1. Collins, J. (1988). Language and class in minority education. *Anthropology & Education Quarterly, 17,* 299–323.

group spent 47 percent of its time (16 + 31) on dictation and sound-word drill, whereas the high-ability group spent only 17 percent of its time (0 + 17) on these two activities.

Collins also performed qualitative data analyses, as when he examined the relationship between students' reading-aloud practices and the teacher's correction strategies. Collins found that the children's reading-aloud styles influenced the teacher's conception of their reading abilities, and that the teacher's corrections, in turn, influenced the students' conception of the task. For example, when reading aloud, students in the low- and high-ability reading groups showed systematic differences in how they segmented the text into breath groups and in their use of intonation to signal meaning. Collins noted that

> . . . the staccato quality was more noticeable with low-group readers. They read with pauses between words and frequently placed equivalent stress on all items in a passage. . . . High-group readers, on the other hand, were more likely to have some of the intonational characteristics of fluent, adult reading aloud. . . . [E]ven when they read in a halting, word-by-word fashion, they finished sentences with falling tone.[2]

Collins noted a corresponding tendency for the teacher to focus on correcting pronunciation when low-ability reading group students read aloud, but when the teacher worked with the the high-ability reading group on the same text, "instruction did not concentrate on dialect . . . and instead focused on the meaning of the words and sentences and their place in the passage being read."[3] Collins provided three examples of extended student-teacher communication during the reading-aloud activity to illustrate these qualitative differences.

Collins's study demonstrates that numerical data and statistical analysis are not the exclusive domain of quantitative research. In addition, it illustrates the tendency for qualitative researchers to use statistical analysis as a supplement to interpretive analysis. In this respect, qualitative research differs from quantitative research, in which statistical analysis typically plays the primary role.

The Need for Judgment in Statistical Analysis

Beginning researchers commonly assume that once numerical data have been collected, the application of statistical techniques is mechanical. In other words, they assume that for any set of research data there is a single *correct* statistical technique for analyzing it. In fact, statistical analysis requires a great deal of judgment—not unlike the kind of judgment required in qualitative research.

An illustration of the need for judgment in quantitative research is a dissertation study that one of the authors (M. Gall) advised.[4] The doctoral student, Ron Wolfe, administered a measure of personality and a questionnaire to 52 teachers in three overseas schools. The purpose of the study was to determine how well the teachers' scores on the predictor variables (their scores on the personality scales and responses to questionnaire items such as years of teaching experience) predicted their scores on criterion variables relating to job performance and cultural adjustment.

On the face of it, the correct statistical analysis in Wolfe's research study would be to calculate a correlation coefficient between each predictor variable and each criterion variable for the total sample. (As explained later in the chapter, a correlation coefficient provides a numerical expression of the strength of relationship between two variables.) Many previous research studies on the prediction of overseas teaching effectiveness had used

---

2. Ibid., p. 316.
3. Ibid., p. 319.
4. Wolfe, R. (1993). Experience, gender, marital status, and the 16PF questionnaire as predictors of American teachers' effectiveness in Southeast Asia schools. *Dissertation Abstracts International, 54*(09), 3407A. (UMI No. 9405241)

precisely this method of statistical analysis. However, Wolfe decided to use his evolving understanding of the research setting to guide the statistical analysis.

Wolfe's first step was to re-examine how he had measured the criterion variables of job performance and cultural adjustment. The school principal had rated each teacher on seven items relating to different aspects of cultural adjustment (e.g., "This teacher accomplishes daily living tasks, such as shopping and laundry, with a minimum of difficulty") and five items relating to different aspects of job performance (e.g., "This teacher is able to maintain a classroom atmosphere conducive to student learning").

Wolfe next considered whether the ratings of the seven cultural adjustment items could be summed to yield a single score for cultural adjustment. By using a test statistic known as a reliability coefficient, he determined that five of the seven items were sufficiently consistent that they could be summed. By "consistent," we mean that teachers who get a high rating on one of the items are likely to get high ratings on the other four items; and teachers who get a low rating on one item are likely to get low ratings on the other four items. After examining the two inconsistent items, he decided that these items could be deleted for justifiable reasons, and that the other five items had enough in common that they could be summed to yield a single score that measured the construct of cultural adjustment. He used a similar reasoning procedure to determine that the five items measuring different aspects of job performance could be combined to yield a single score.

Besides obtaining the principal's ratings of each of the 52 teachers in the sample, Wolfe also obtained ratings from the teachers themselves because he wanted to know how teachers viewed their own cultural adjustment and job performance. He needed to perform the same item analysis for the teachers' ratings as he had for the principals' ratings in order to determine which items could be combined to form a total scale.

Wolfe then considered whether the total rating of the teacher's cultural adjustment made by the teacher and the total rating of that teacher made by the principal could be combined to form a single rating for that teacher, which would simplify the statistical analysis. However, he found that although the two sets of ratings correlated with each other, the correlation coefficient was not sufficiently large to warrant combining them. He reached a similar conclusion about the job performance ratings.

Wolfe next considered whether the teachers' self-ratings and the principals' ratings of the teachers should be given the same status as criterion variables. He decided that because principals hire the teachers, it is more important to be able to predict the principals' ratings. Therefore, statistical analyses involving principals' ratings were given precedence in reporting the statistical results.

At this point, Wolfe wondered whether the principals of the three schools actually discriminated in their ratings of different teachers. The reasoning was that, even though they were promised anonymity, the principals might have avoided the issue of evaluating their teachers' cultural adjustment and job performance by giving all or most of the teachers a high rating on each item. To check this possibility, Wolfe computed two statistics called the *mean* and *standard deviation* for each of the two total scores. There was sufficient variability in the scores between teachers to provide some assurance that the principals were making real discriminations between the teachers with respect to their job performance and cultural adjustment.

Having reached this point in the statistical analysis, Wolfe could have decided to correlate each predictor variable with the two criterion variables for the total sample of teachers from all three schools. However, he noted that the three overseas schools had substantially different emotional climates and value systems. For example, two of the schools were secular, but the third was a religious school; also, two of the schools were in the Phillipines, but the other was in Malaysia. Therefore, Wolfe decided to calculate the correlation coefficients separately for the three schools. He found that, in fact, different personality scales correlated with ratings of cultural adjustment and job performance at the three schools. This statistical result means that teachers with one type of personality were more likely to do well in one of the schools, and teachers with another personality type were more likely to do well in another of the schools.

The magnitude of the correlation coefficients for the predictor and criterion variables was substantially greater than found in previous research on predicting the effectiveness of American teachers working overseas. Unlike Wolfe, the researchers who did these earlier studies had not taken into account the types of schools in their samples, and they had not done a detailed statistical analysis of their criterion measures. Wolfe obtained stronger and more interpretable results because his statistical analysis was guided by knowledge of a variety of statistical techniques, careful psychological reasoning, and extensive reflection on the context in which the numerical data were collected.

Acquiring Statistical Expertise

The preceding examples illustrate that you need to know about various statistical techniques whether you are doing quantitative or qualitative research. Also, you should know these techniques in sufficient depth that you can apply them thoughtfully rather than mechanically. In this chapter, we help you move toward this goal by providing an overview of the statistical techniques commonly used in educational research. The techniques are explained once again in Part IV of the book where they are discussed in the context of the research designs for which they are most appropriate.

Types of Scores

Measurements in educational research usually are expressed in one of three forms: continuous scores, ranks, or categories. You need to understand the differences among these score forms, because the form in which the data are expressed usually determines your choice of a statistical analysis procedure. For example, if your research data consist of continuous scores on two groups, you most likely would analyze group differences by calculating mean scores and a statistic known as t. However, if the data are in the form of categories, you would analyze group differences by a chi-square (χ^2) test, which compares category frequencies between two or more groups.

The three types of scores used in educational research are explained below.

Continuous Scores

Continuous scores are values of a variable located on a continuum, ranging from high to low levels of the variable, and along which there are an indefinite number of points at which scores can occur. Intelligence tests, personality inventories, and most other standardized measures yield continuous scores.

In practice, continuous scores usually are limited to whole numbers, but it must be possible, in theory, to compute fractional scores in order for the variable to be considered continuous. For example, IQ scores are considered continuous because an individual theoretically can obtain a score at any IQ point within the broad range of IQs possessed by human beings. Not only should it be possible for one individual to obtain a score of 101 while another obtains a score of 102, but it also should be possible to find an individual who would perform slightly higher than the individual with an IQ of 101 and slightly lower than an individual with an IQ of 102. In practice, however, IQ scores are reported only in whole number units.

Tests typically have multiple items, and the individual's score on each item is summed to yield a total **raw score,** which is a form of continuous score. In the absence of other information, raw scores are difficult to interpret. For example, what does it mean that a student achieved a raw score of 30 items correct on a 50-item test? This raw score can represent good, poor, or average performance depending upon how other students scored or upon our expectations of how a particular student should have scored.

Because raw scores are difficult to interpret, they often are converted to derived scores, also a form of continuous score. **Derived scores** aid interpretation by providing a quantitative measure of each student's performance relative to a comparison group. Age equivalents, grade equivalents, standard scores, and percentiles (described in the next section) are examples of derived scores.

Age and Grade Equivalents

An **age equivalent** is the average score on a particular test earned by students of the same age. Similarly, a **grade equivalent** is the average score on the test earned by students of the same grade level.

Age and grade equivalents usually are determined at the time of test construction. The test developers will administer the new test to a large group of students (sometimes called the *standardization sample*) who represent a wide range of age and grade levels. The developers then determine the mean of the scores obtained by students at each age or grade level. These means are organized into tables of age and grade norms.

For example, suppose a researcher administers a test to a sample of beginning fifth graders (mean age of 11.3 years) and determines that they have a mean score of 56.7 on the test. Referring to the table of norms in the test manual, the researcher might find that in the standardization sample a score of 57 (56.7 would be rounded off to this number) was the average score earned by sixth graders and by students who were 12.7 years of age. On the basis of these norms, the researcher could conclude that the students in her sample were of above-average ability. This conclusion, of course, requires the assumption that the research sample was drawn from the same population as the standardization sample.

Standard Scores

A **standard score** is a form of derived score that uses standard deviation units (described later in the chapter) to express an individual's performance relative to the group's performance. The **z score** is a type of standard score frequently used in educational research. The first step in calculating a z score is to subtract the mean score of the total group from a person's raw score $(X - M)$. The next step is to divide the result by the standard deviation of the group's scores. For any distribution of raw scores, z scores have a mean of zero and a standard deviation of 1.00. Also, z scores are continuous and have equality of units. Thus, a person's relative standing on two or more tests can be compared by converting the raw scores to z scores.

Because z scores can yield negative numbers (e.g., a person who is one standard deviation below the group mean would earn a z score of -1.00), researchers sometimes convert raw scores to standard scores yielding only positive numbers. For example, **T scores** are standard scores that have a mean of 50 and a standard deviation of 10. The **stanine scale,** developed by the U.S. Air Force, is a standard score that has a mean of 5 and standard deviation of 2. The Stanford-Binet test of intelligence yields standard scores having a mean of 100 and a standard deviation of 16.

If you have administered a test for which age, grade, or percentile equivalents are available, it is advisable to report both the raw scores obtained by your research sample *and* the equivalents. The reason for this recommendation is that age and grade equivalents provide useful information about your research sample by showing how their performance compares to a standardization sample. Equivalents, however, should not be used in data analyses involving descriptive or inferential statistics. The reason for this caution is that equivalents have unequal units. Either raw scores or standard scores should be used instead.

Rank Scores

Some types of educational data are available as ranks, for example, a student's high school graduation rank. A **rank score** expresses the position of a person or object on a variable relative to the positions held by other persons or objects. This type of score is useful in situations where it is easier to rank individuals than to assign continuous scores to them.

Rank scores also are useful in situations where individuals might be reluctant to make discriminations. For example, suppose a researcher wants to ask a group of administrators to rate portfolios of twenty teachers completed for the purpose of demonstrating their professional competence. If the administrators used a seven-point rating scale, they might be inclined to give all or most of the teachers a high score on the scale. Consequently, there would be little discrimination between the teachers. To avoid this problem, the researcher could ask each administrator to rank the teachers on their professional competence as demonstrated in their portfolios. If this is done, each teacher would have a different rank, with the scores ranging from 1 to 20.

Percentiles are a commonly used type of rank score. **Percentiles** are obtained by computing the percentage of persons whose score falls below a given raw score. For example, if 50 percent of the sample obtains a raw score of 16 or below, then anyone obtaining a raw score of 16 would be at the 50th percentile. Manuals for published tests sometimes contain percentile equivalents for raw scores based on the standardization sample. Because percentiles are computed from raw scores, they are considered a form of derived score.

Categories

The term **category** refers to values of a variable that can yield two or more discrete, noncontinuous scores. For example, student participation in high school athletics can be recorded in such categories as (1) earned letter in varsity sports, (2) participated but did not earn letter, (3) participated in intramural sports, (4) participated in physical education classes, or (5) did not participate in any athletics.

The term **dichotomy** refers to a categorical variable that has only two values. For example, pass-fail grades are a dichotomous variable because the students can earn only one of two scores: pass or fail. There are two types of dichotomies: artificial and real.

An **artificial dichotomy** results when individuals are placed into two categories on the basis of performance on a continuous variable. The dichotomy of pass-fail grades is artificial because if we carefully tested the students who completed a course, we would find that their test scores form a continuous distribution ranging from those students who learned a lot to those students who learned little or nothing. The point at which we divide this continuous variable into pass-fail groups is based upon an arbitrary cutting point or criterion. If we compared the student who barely passes and the student who barely fails, we would find that they are very similar. Yet they are viewed as very different because their scores happen to lie near the cutoff point.

When individuals are divided into two groups on the basis of a true difference on a variable, the dichotomy is referred to as a **true dichotomy.** A true dichotomy differs from an artificial dichotomy in that it is not necessary to establish an arbitrary cutting point for dividing the cases into two groups. Gender is probably the true dichotomy most frequently studied by educational researchers.

Descriptive Statistics

Descriptive statistics are mathematical techniques for organizing and summarizing a set of numerical data. To illustrate how descriptive statistics are used in educational research, we will refer to a study by Sandra Crosser concerning the relationship between children's age at the time of kindergarten entrance and their later school achievement.[5] Crosser was interested in providing empirical evidence to test the validity of the advice commonly given to parents that they should hold children back an additional year to mature before beginning kindergarten, particularly if the children are male.

Crosser obtained her research participants from seven public school districts in one state. Using school records, she identified all students with summer birthdates, which she defined as dates between June 1 and September 30. The variable of interest was the point at which these children entered kindergarten. The variable was dichotomous: early entrance (the autumn of the year when they were five years old), or late entrance (the autumn of the year when they were six years old). Of the total 253 potential participants, 190 had entered kindergarten at age five and 63 had entered at age six. First each of the students who had enrolled in kindergarten at age six (late entrant) was matched in gender and intelligence with a student who had enrolled in kindergarten at age five (early entrant). The matching process resulted in 45 pairs of students: 29 pairs of boys and 16 pairs of girls. Students for whom no satisfactory match could be found were eliminated from the sample. After completing the matching process, Crosser obtained the reading and mathematics test scores of these children when they were in the fifth or sixth grade.

Measures of Central Tendency

A **measure of central tendency** is a single numerical value that is used to describe the average of an entire set of scores. For example, two groups of 45 children each (total $N = 90$) comprised the sample in Crosser's study of kindergarten entrance. We would have difficulty getting an accurate picture of each group's average performance on the reading and mathematics achievement measures by examining all 180 scores (90 children multiplied by 2 tests) one by one. However, Crosser was able to obtain an easily interpreted description of the typical or average performance of each group by calculating mean scores, which represent one measure of central tendency.

Table 5.2 shows the reading achievement mean scores for early-entry (age five) and late-entry (age six) kindergarten students in Crosser's study, separately by gender. The statistics in the column labeled *M* NCE are the mean scores for a test of students' reading achievement. This test gives each student a score that is a percentile rank, which Crosser converted to a type of standard score known as a **normal curve equivalent (NCE) score.** Like other types of standard scores, NCE scores make it possible to compare students' performance on tests that have different numbers of items and scoring procedures. Normal curve equivalent scores have a mean of 50 and a standard deviation of 21.06. These numbers were selected so that NCE scores would coincide with key percentiles in a score distribution. An NCE score of 1 corresponds to the 1st percentile; an NCE score of 50 corresponds to the 50th percentile; and an NCE score of 99 corresponds to the 99th percentile. Unlike percentiles, however, NCE scores have equal intervals between them.

By examining the descriptive statistics in Table 5.2, we see at a glance that children who enter kindergarten at age six have higher mean reading scores in later grades. We see also that this finding applies both to boys and girls. This difference in achievement would

5. Crosser, S. L. (1991). Summer birth date children: Kindergarten entrance age and academic achievement. *Journal of Educational Research, 84,* 140–146.

TABLE 5.2

Reading Achievement Means at Fifth or Sixth Grade, Compared by Kindergarten Entrance Age

Kindergarten Entrance Age	n	M NCE[a]	SD	Dependent t Ratio	p
Boys	58			2.80	<.01
Age 5	29	49.03	18.49		
Age 6	29	58.17	19.96		
Girls	32			1.88	>.05
Age 5	16	49.43	21.00		but
Age 6	16	57.37	20.07		<.10

[a]NCE = normal curve equivalent scores

Source: Adapted from table 6 on p. 145 in: Crosser, S. L. (1991). Summer birth date children: Kindergarten entrance age and academic achievement. *Journal of Educational Research, 84,* 140–146. Reprinted with permission of the Helen Dwight Reid Educational Foundation. Published by Heldref Publications, 1319 Eighteenth St., NW, Washington, DC 20036-1802. Copyright © 1991.

be much more difficult to detect if we had only the individual reading score of each child in the sample to examine.

Mean, Median, and Mode

The mean, median, and mode are three different measures of central tendency. The **mean** is calculated by dividing the sum of all scores by the number of scores. The **median** is the middle point in a distribution of scores. The **mode** is the most frequently occurring score in a distribution. As noted earlier, the scores reported in the second column in Table 5.2 are mean scores of students' reading achievement. (The *M* in the top row of the table is an abbreviation for *mean.*)

The mean generally is considered the best measure of central tendency. One of its advantages over the median and mode is that it is more stable. Thus, if we study several samples randomly drawn from the same population, the means are likely to be in closer agreement than the medians.

Skewness

When a distribution of scores is symmetrical, the mean and the median are located at the same point in the distribution. When the distribution has more extreme scores at one end than at the other—that is, when it is **skewed**—the mean always will be in the direction of the extreme scores. In this situation, the median will reflect more accurately the average performance of the sample, as can be seen by comparing the two score distributions below.

Distribution A	Distribution B
8	27
6	6
5	5
5	5
4	4
3	3
3	3
3	3
1	1
Mean = 4.2	Mean = 6.3
Median = 4.0	Median = 4.0

The two distributions differ by a single score. In the first distribution, both the mean and the median accurately represent average performance. In the second distribution, however, only the median provides an accurate representation of average performance. Just one person earned a score as high as or higher than the mean (6.3), even though the mean, as a measure of central tendency, is intended to represent average performance. As we shall discuss later in the chapter, this individual (whose score is 27) is called an *outlier*.

When a distribution is highly skewed, as in distribution B, both the mean and the median should be reported. Also, special statistics (presented in most textbooks of statistical methods) can be used to describe the amount of skewness and the shape of the score distribution. However, a visual presentation of the distribution of scores, as in the example in the preceding paragraph, usually is sufficient.

Categorical Data

Measures of central tendency can be calculated for continuous scores and for ranks. Categorical data, including dichotomies, are summarized by creating frequency distributions, as in the following example:

Category	Frequency	Percentage
Students earning letter in varsity sports	21	(11)
Students participating, but not earning letter	37	(19)
Students participating in intramural sports	115	(61)
Students not participating in athletics	16	(8)
	189	99

The most frequently occurring category is easily determined by inspecting the frequency distribution in this example. Also, the frequency of individuals or events in each category as a percentage of the total can be readily determined.

Measures of Variability

Variability is the amount of dispersion of scores about the mean score or other measure of central tendency. The desire to understand variability—also known as individual differences—motivates much of educational research. Thus, the measurement of variability plays a central role in research design and statistical analysis.

Standard Deviation

The **standard deviation** (usually abbreviated SD) is the measure of variability most often reported in research studies. Basically, the standard deviation is a measure of the extent to which scores in a distribution deviate from their mean. Thus, the first step in calculating the standard deviation is to subtract each score from the mean. The resulting deviation scores are then squared and entered into a formula to yield the standard deviation. Referring back to Table 5.2, you will find the standard deviations for students' reading achievement scores in the fourth column.

The standard deviation is the most commonly used measure of variability because it is stable. In other words, repeated samples drawn from the same population are likely to have similar standard deviations. Also, in analyses of research data, the standard deviation is needed in order to compute other statistics. The standard error of measurement, product-moment correlation, and many other statistics are based partly on the standard deviation. The standard deviation also forms the basis for the various types of standard scores described earlier in the chapter—z scores, T scores, stanine scores, and NCE scores.

The mean and standard deviation, taken together, usually provide a good description of how members of a sample scored on a particular measure. For example, if we know that a group of individuals has a mean score of 10 and a standard deviation of 2 on a test, and that the scores are distributed in the form of a normal curve (described in the next paragraph), we can infer that approximately 68 percent of them earned scores between 8 and 12, and that approximately 95 percent of them earned scores between 6 and 14.

Normal Curve

We can use the standard deviation to make these inferences because of the relationship between the standard deviation and the normal curve. The **normal curve** (also known as the *normal probability curve*) is a purely theoretical continuous probability distribution in which the height of the curve for each score point indicates the proportion of individuals who are expected to earn that score.

An example of a normal curve is shown in Figure 5.1. This curve shows that the scores of the majority of individuals tend to cluster close to the mean. As we move farther and farther from the mean, fewer cases occur. If the score distribution is normally distributed, approximately 68 percent of a sample will have scores within the range of plus or minus one standard deviation from the mean. Approximately 95 percent of such samples will have scores within the range of plus or minus two standard deviations from the mean. The curve for many measures of complex human characteristics and behavior has a shape similar to that shown in Figure 5.1.

Suppose that in one set of normally distributed scores, the mean is 3.0 and the standard deviation is 1.5. In another set of normally distributed scores, the mean is 25.0 and the standard deviation is 5.0. Even though the values of the mean and standard deviation of the two sets of scores vary, the properties of the normal curve can be used to infer the dispersion of scores. For example, Figure 5.1 indicates that approximately 16 percent of the scores in any normal score distribution will be one standard deviation or more above the mean (i.e., at the 84th percentile or higher). Thus, we can conclude that in the first set of scores in our example, approximately 16 percent of the scores will be 4.5 (3.0 + 1.5) or larger. In the second set of scores, approximately 16 percent of the scores will be 30 (25.0 + 5.0) or larger.

FIGURE 5.1

The Normal Probability Curve

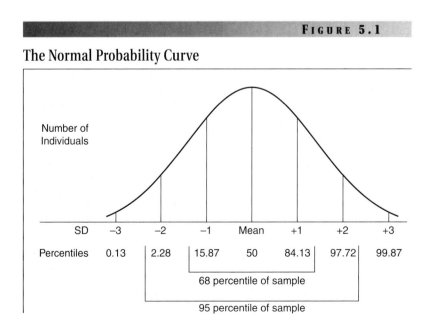

Other Measures of Variability

Occasionally the variance, rather than the standard deviation, is shown in research reports. The **variance** is the square of the standard deviation. For example, if the standard deviation is 4.0, the variance is 16.0. Calculation of the variance is an intermediate step in computing many complex statistics, such as analysis of variance. Another measure of variability that sometimes is reported is the **range.** This measure, as its name implies, is simply the lowest and highest scores in the distribution.

Correlational Statistics

The descriptive statistics presented in the preceding sections involve the description of scores on a single variable. In some types of research, however, we are interested in describing the relationship between two or more variables. Correlational statistics often are used for this purpose.

The **bivariate correlation coefficient** is a statistic that enables us to describe in mathematical terms the strength of the relationship between two variables (e.g., student attentiveness in class and academic achievement). There are many types of correlation coefficients. Selection of the appropriate coefficient depends upon the form of the scores (continuous, ranked, dichotomous, or categorical) that are to be related to each other.

Researchers increasingly are using **multivariate correlational methods.** These methods allow one to describe and explore the relationship between three or more variables at a time. This capability is important because the variables that are of most interest to educational researchers (e.g., academic achievement) usually are not affected by a single factor. Rather, they are affected by a complex of factors (e.g., home environment, personal characteristics, and prior school experience). Multivariate correlational methods enable researchers to study how these factors, both singly and in combination, affect outcome variables such as academic achievement.

The various types of correlational statistics and their use in research are discussed more fully in Chapter 11.

Inferential Statistics

Generalizing from a Sample to a Population

Rarely in educational research can we study every member of a specified population, for example, all sixth-grade students in the United States. Instead, data are collected from a sample of individuals who are randomly drawn from a defined population or who are assumed to be representative of some population. However, the research findings based on a sample are of little value unless they can be used to make *inferences* about the defined population.

Consider the study of kindergarten entrance by Crosser. As shown in Table 5.2, Crosser found that the later reading achievement of boys who started kindergarten at age six ($M = 58.17$) was 9.14 points higher than that of boys who started kindergarten at age five ($M = 49.03$). Crosser was interested not only in this sample of students, however. She wanted to know whether the finding would hold true of the population of students with characteristics similar to her sample.

Crosser's concern can be stated in the form of the following questions: Is this a chance finding? Is it possible that if we studied new samples we would find the same advantage for late entry to kindergarten? If we inferred from this sample that there is a true difference between the entire population of students entering kindergarten early and late, how likely is it that our inference is false?

Statisticians have developed a mathematical procedure, called statistical inference, that enables researchers to answer such questions. **Statistical inference** is a set of mathematical procedures for using probabilities and information about a sample to draw conclusions about the population from which the sample presumably was drawn. To understand these procedures, it is important to distinguish between a statistic and a parameter. A **statistic** is a mathematical expression that describes some aspect of a set of scores for a sample. A **parameter** is similar, but it describes some aspect of a set of scores for a population. For example, the mean of a set of scores for a population would be a parameter, whereas the mean of a set of scores for a sample would be a statistic. In using statistical inference techniques, we are attempting to use statistics computed from a sample to make inferences about population parameters.

The Null Hypothesis

The initial step in testing whether an inference from a sample to the population that it represents is warranted is to establish a null hypothesis (described in Chapter 2). In the case of our example, the null hypothesis states that *no* difference will be found between the descriptive statistics compared in one's research study. For example, the null hypothesis for the boys in Crosser's study can be stated as follows:

Reading achievement indices in fifth or sixth grade for summer-birthdate boys who enter kindergarten at age five will not differ significantly from the reading achievement of summer-birthdate boys who enter kindergarten at age six.

After formulating the null hypothesis, the researcher carries out a test of statistical significance to determine whether the null hypothesis can be rejected (i.e., to determine whether there actually is a difference between the groups). As we shall find in the next section, this test enables us to make statements of the type: "If the null hypothesis is correct, we would find this large a difference between sample means only once in a hundred experiments. Because we have found this large a difference, the null hypothesis quite probably is false. Therefore, we will reject the null hypothesis and conclude that the difference between sample means reflects a *true* difference between population means."

Tests of Statistical Significance

A **test of statistical significance** is done to determine whether the null hypothesis can be rejected. To illustrate the procedure, let us assume that the null hypothesis stated above is correct, meaning that the reading achievement scores of the population of summer-birthdate boys entering kindergarten early and the population of such boys entering kindergarten late are identical. Suppose that we select from these identical populations one sample of summer-birthdate boys entering kindergarten at age five and one sample entering at age six. Furthermore, assume that we repeat this procedure thousands of times. If each time we subtract the mean reading achievement score of the age six sample from the mean score of the age five sample, the difference scores will form a sampling distribution.

Suppose that the standard deviation (SD) of the sampling distribution for the reading achievement test for each population is 5.00. This means that 68 percent of the time the difference scores will have a value between +5 and –5 (one SD above and below the mean). About 95 percent of the time the difference scores will have a value between +10 and –10 (two SDs above and below the mean).

Now consider the fact that Crosser compared just one sample of boys who entered kindergarten early with one sample of boys who entered late. As stated above, a mean difference of 9.14 points was found on the reading achievement measure between the boys who entered early and boys who entered late. To test the null hypothesis, we need to pose and answer the question: How often would a difference score of this magnitude or larger be found between samples drawn from two populations whose means are the same?

Because we do not know the population means and standard deviations that are necessary to answer this question, we must estimate them using the sample means and standard deviations. These sample statistics are combined in such a way as to yield a critical ratio, also called a *t* value (or *z* value if the samples are large). Once a *t* value is obtained, we can determine how often a difference score of a given magnitude between samples of a given size will occur when there is no difference in the population. We make this determination by examining the *p* value associated with the *t* value. Tables of *t* values and their associated *p* values can be found in most statistics textbooks.

In Crosser's study, the *t* value for the reading achievement measure was 2.80 for boys (see the fifth column of Table 5.2). This large a *t* value indicates that if there was no difference in reading achievement between the population of summer-birthdate boys entering kindergarten early and the population of summer-birthdate boys entering kindergarten late, in every hundred samples studied, we would obtain this large or a larger difference less than once. This probability of occurrence is indicated by the *p* in Table 5.2. Next to *p* is "<.01," which means "less than .01" or "less than one time in a hundred." Because the observed difference of 9.14 points is an unlikely event, Crosser rejected the null hypothesis in favor of an alternative hypothesis, namely that there is a true difference in reading achievement between summer-birthdate boys entering kindergarten early and such boys entering kindergarten late.

Levels of Statistical Significance

The *t* **distribution** (or the *z* **distribution** if the sample is large) is used to determine the level of statistical significance of an observed difference between sample means. Generally, educational researchers choose to reject the null hypothesis if the *t* value reaches a significance level of $p < .05$.[6] Occasionally, the lower, that is, more stringent $p < .01$ level is chosen for rejecting the null hypothesis, while in exploratory studies the higher, that is, less stringent $p < .10$ level sometimes is used. You will note in Table 5.2 that Crosser indicated that the *p* value for the *t* test for the difference between early-entering girls and late-entering girls did not meet the usual probability level for rejecting the null hypothesis ($p = .05$ or less), but it did achieve the probability level sometimes used in exploratory studies ($p = .10$ or less).

When interpreting research results, remember that a *higher* level of significance corresponds to a *lower p* value. For example, $p < .05$ is a lower *p* value than $p < .10$, but a difference that is significant at the .05 *p* level is a more highly significant difference than a difference that is significant at the .10 *p* level.

Type I and Type II Errors

You should note that when the .10 level is chosen, there is one chance in 10 that the researcher will reject the null hypothesis when, in fact, it is correct. If the significance level of .01 is chosen, however, there is only one chance in 100 that this will occur. The rejection of the null hypothesis when it is true is called a **Type I error.** Obviously, if we raise the significance level required to reject the null hypothesis (e.g., if we use $p < .01$ instead of $p < .05$), we reduce the likelihood of a Type I error. At the same time, we increase the likelihood of a **Type II error,** that is, the failure to reject the null hypothesis of no difference, when there is in fact a difference.

---

6. For an explanation of the common use of the .05 level, see: Clowles, M., & Davis, C. (1982). On the origins of the .05 level of statistical significance. *American Psychologist, 37,* 553–558.

Interpretation of Significance Tests

Tests of statistical significance frequently are misinterpreted. Because these tests play such a large role in quantitative research design, we will consider common misinterpretations and the proper interpretation.

Alpha and Probability Values

Researchers commonly establish the level of significance (usually .10, .05, or .01) after the statistical analyses have been completed. A z or t value will be computed, and the researcher will refer to a significance table to determine how "significant" this value is. However, the logic of statistical inference dictates that the significance level be established *before* a z or t value is computed. You should make a decision at the outset of your study that if you find a difference between samples that exceeds a given significance level (for example, .05), the null hypothesis will be rejected. You cannot properly wait until after the statistical analysis to reject the null hypothesis at whatever significance level the t or z happens to reach.

The level of significance that is selected prior to data collection for accepting or rejecting a null hypothesis is called **alpha.** The level of significance actually obtained after the data have been collected and analyzed is called the **probability value,** and is indicated by the symbol p. For example, in her study of kindergarten entrance, Crosser properly interprets the p value for female students in Table 5.2: "Six-year-old female entrants scored higher in reading in fifth or sixth grade than did their five-year-old counterparts ($p < .10$), but not at the .05 alpha level set for the study."[7]

You will note in Crosser's statement that she did not indicate the precise probability level associated with the t value. Instead, she indicated that it was less than (<) .10. Until recently, this was common practice, because researchers needed to rely on statistical tables that only reported certain p values (typically $p = .10, .05, .01$, and .001). Statistical packages for computers generally now report exact p values; therefore it is becoming customary to give the exact values in research reports.

Misinterpretation of p Values

1. The p value has been subject to various misinterpretations, which are explained in the following. Some people believe that the p value indicates the probability that the differences found between groups can be attributed to chance. For example, if you found that a mean difference of five IQ points between two groups was significant at the .01 level, it would be a misinterpretation to conclude that there is one chance in 100 that this is a "chance" difference. The proper interpretation of such a finding is that the null hypothesis was rejected (assuming that the .01 level of significance had been established beforehand); this is because the mean difference of five points exceeds the mean difference that we would find once in a hundred samples if the population mean difference was zero.

2. Another common misinterpretation of the level of significance is that it indicates how likely it is that your research hypothesis is correct. (The research hypothesis states that a difference between groups will be found, whereas the null hypothesis states that no difference will be found.) For example, suppose that you hypothesized that constructivist instruction will result in greater student achievement than conventional instruction. If the mean achievement score for students taught by the constructivist method is found to be significantly greater than the mean achievement score for students taught conventionally at the .01 level, you might conclude that the probability is 99 percent ($1.00 - .99 = .01$) that your research hypothesis is correct. However, the level of significance only helps to make a decision about rejecting the null hypothesis; it has only an indirect bearing on confirmation of your research hypothesis. For example, you might find a significant difference

7. Crosser, p. 145.

between two groups but not for the reason that prompted your research hypothesis. Similarly, you might find too small a difference between groups to reject the null hypothesis, but your research hypothesis still might be correct. A Type II error could have occurred, or the measures used to test the research hypothesis could have been inadequate.

3. Still another misinterpretation of p values is to think that they indicate the probability of finding the same research results if a replication study was conducted. For example, you might think that if a difference between the means of two groups is significant at the .05 level, the same difference score will be found 95 times in every 100 replications of the study. However, even if the difference between mean scores that we obtained in our study is a true population difference and is highly significant, we still might find considerable variation in the magnitude of difference scores in a replication of the study. In short, the level of significance cannot be used to predict the results of future studies in which the conditions of the original study are replicated. It only can be used to make a decision about rejecting the null hypothesis.

4. The most common and most serious misinterpretation of the test of significance is to confuse the p value with the practical or theoretical significance of the research results. As we discuss later in the chapter, the level of statistical significance of obtained results is influenced to a considerable degree by the number of individuals included in the research sample. The larger the sample size, the smaller the result needed to reach a given level of statistical significance. For example, with a sample of 1,000 subjects, a correlation coefficient of .08 is significant at the .01 level. In contrast, a correlation coefficient of .42 with a sample of 22 subjects is significant only at the .05 level. However, the latter coefficient may have more significance for improving educational practice, because its magnitude is larger. Also, if the study was done to test a hypothesis derived from a theory, the latter coefficient has different implications for the theory than the former coefficient.

5. As we have already observed, the test of statistical significance is concerned with the inferences that we wish to make from sample statistics to population parameters. Thus, a test of statistical significance is done when we wish to determine how probable it is that the differences we have found between our samples also would be found in the populations from which they were drawn. Therefore, to use a test of statistical significance properly, we should use it only with samples that are randomly drawn from a specified population or, in the case of experiments, with samples that have been randomly assigned to the various treatment and control conditions. However, researchers sometimes do not specify the population or do not use random sampling techniques, and thus the sample may not be representative. In these situations, the use of tests of statistical significance is questionable.

6. A test of statistical significance occasionally is done when the entire population has been studied. For example, suppose that a researcher defines all males and all females at a particular college as two populations. Then suppose the researcher finds, as hypothesized, that the females have a higher grade point average than the males. In this situation it is meaningless to do a test of statistical significance. The difference between grade point averages is a *true* difference because the entire populations have been studied rather than samples drawn from their respective populations.

Criticisms of Significance Tests

The use of statistical significance in educational research has been criticized.[8] One criticism is that educational researchers seldom work with samples randomly drawn from defined populations, even though random sampling is a requirement for using statistical

8. Carver, R. P. (1978). The case against statistical significance testing. *Harvard Educational Review, 48*, 378–399; Oakes, M. (1986). *Statistical inference: A commentary for the social and behavioral sciences.* New York: Wiley. Also see the *Journal of Experimental Education*, 1993, *61*(4), entire issue.

significance tests. Another criticism is that the tests often are misinterpreted, as we indicated above. The *p* value is taken as a measure of the worth of a study rather than for what it really is: a basis for rejecting the null hypothesis. The third criticism is that the *power* of statistical significance tests in educational research tends to be low. (The concept of statistical power is discussed after the next section.)

We believe that each of these criticisms is legitimate, yet they do not justify discontinuation of statistical significance testing. The tests are quite helpful under conditions of random sampling and high statistical power. Conversely, the tests should be used with caution, or not at all, under conditions of nonrandom sampling, nonrandom assignment, or low statistical power.

Our recommendation is for researchers to be wary of accepting an observed difference or relationship as real on the basis of one study, no matter how statistically significant the results are. A significant *p* value in a study is cause for optimism, but replications of the study should be done to get additional assurance that the observed result is real. Jacob Cohen makes this point well:

> The prevailing yes-no decision at the magic .05 level from a single research is a far cry from the use of informed judgment. Science simply doesn't work that way. A successful piece of research doesn't conclusively settle an issue, it just makes some theoretical proposition to some degree more likely. Only successful future replication in the same and different settings (as might be found through meta-analysis) provides an approach to settling the issue.[9]

Also, other indices should be calculated in each study to set *p* values in proper perspective. We discuss these indices—effect size, measures of correlation, and confidence intervals—later in the chapter.

Types of Significance Tests

Thus far in our discussion of inferential statistics, we have been concerned with how to determine whether the difference between two sample means reflects a population difference. A test of statistical significance based on the calculation of a *t* or *z* value is appropriate for this purpose. Other significance tests are available for answering other questions involving inferences from sample statistics to population parameters. They are discussed in Chapters 10 through 13.

Statistical Power Analysis

Researchers rarely want to confirm the null hypothesis. In other words, they do not intend for their research to demonstrate that there is no difference between groups, no correlation between variables, or no effect of an experimental treatment. Instead, researchers usually conduct studies because they want to find differences, relationships, or effects. For example, researchers are more likely to become interested in investigating a method of instruction when they believe it will be superior to conventional practice than when they believe it is no more effective than conventional practice.

Given researchers' interest in discovering differences, relationships, and effects, they want to maximize the likelihood of rejecting the null hypothesis when in fact it is false. To help them, they use **statistical power analysis,** which is a procedure for studying the likelihood that a particular test of statistical significance will be sufficient to reject a false null hypothesis. In this context, the term **statistical power** refers to the probability that a par-

---

9. Cohen, J. (1990). Things I have learned (so far). *American Psychologist, 45,* 1304–1312. Quote appears on page 1311.

ticular test of statistical significance will lead to rejection of a false null hypothesis. The following is an overview of the four factors that are considered in statistical power analysis.

1. *Sample size.* It is a fact that statistical power increases automatically with *sample size,* assuming that the other factors described below are held constant. In other words, the larger the sample, the smaller the difference, relationship, or effect needed to reject the null hypothesis. For example, if you obtained a correlation coefficient of .25 between two variables in a sample of 47 students, you could not reject the null hypothesis at the .05 level of significance. If you obtained the same coefficient (.25) but with a larger sample ($N = 62$), you would be able to reject the null hypothesis at the .05 level of significance.

2. *Level of significance.* The second determinant of statistical power is the *p* value at which the null hypothesis is to be rejected. Statistical power can be increased by lowering the level of significance needed to reject the null hypothesis. Thus, a test of statistical significance with *p* set at .10 is more powerful than the same test with *p* set at .05. ("More powerful" means that it is easier to reject a false null hypothesis.) In practice, *p* usually is set at .05. However, as we explained above, some researchers feel that it is permissible to set *p* at .10 in exploratory studies in order to increase statistical power. A *p* of .10 increases the risk of a Type I error, but it might spotlight a potentially important difference, relationship, or effect that would have been overlooked had a lower *p* value been set.

3. *Directionality.* The third determinant of statistical power is whether *directionality* is specified in the research hypothesis. Directionality refers to the fact that observed differences and relationships can go in two directions. For example, in an experiment, treatment A can be better than treatment B (one direction), or treatment B can be better than treatment A (the other direction). However, we might be able to argue, on the basis of theory or previous research findings, that treatment B cannot possibly be better than treatment A.

If we can determine before doing the experiment that one direction is unlikely, we can increase statistical power by doing a *one-tailed test* of statistical significance. Some researchers, however, disagree with the use of one-tailed tests. They advocate instead the consistent use of two-tailed hypothesis testing, which they view as "more compatible with the growing meta-analytic view of social science as an incremental, cumulative, and shared enterprise."[10]

4. *Effect size.* The fourth determinant of statistical power is **effect size,** which is an estimate of the magnitude of the difference, relationship, or effect in the population being studied. (Effect size is discussed in Chapter 4 and later in this chapter.) To understand how effect size influences statistical power, you need to keep two facts in mind. First, it is a fact that greater observed differences, relationships, or effects will produce lower *p* values. For example, a correlation coefficient (*r*) of .38 in a sample of 20 students is significant at the .10 level. In contrast, an *r* of .44 in the same size sample is significant at the .05 level. Thus, the null hypothesis can be rejected at the conventional significance level (.05) with an *r* of .44, but not with an *r* of .38.

Because the magnitude of an *r* affects the significance level, we need to ask what determines the magnitude of an *r.* This leads us to the second fact: A researcher is more likely to obtain a large effect size in a sample when there is a large effect size in the population. Returning to our example, suppose the value of *r* in the population from which the sample of 20 students was drawn is .65. It is likely, then, that samples drawn from this population will tend to yield similarly large values of *r.* Conversely, if the population value of *r* is

✦ *Touchstone in Research*

Borenstein, M. T., Rothstein, H., Cohen, J., Schoenfeld, D., Berlin, J., & Lakatos, E. (2001). Power and precision: A computer program for statistical power analysis and confidence intervals (Version 2.0) [Computer software]. Mahwah, NJ: Lawrence Erlbaum Associates.

Cohen, J. (1988). *Statistical power analysis for the behavioral sciences.* Mahwah, NJ: Lawrence Erlbaum Associates.

Kraemer, H. C., & Thiemann, S. (1987). *How many subjects? Statistical power analysis in research.* Thousand Oaks, CA: Sage.

10. Pillemer, D. B. (1991). One- versus two-tailed hypothesis tests in contemporary educational research. *Educational Researcher, 20*(9), 13–17. Quote appears on page 13.

small (for example, $r = .30$), samples drawn from this population will tend to yield similarly small values of r. In brief, if the population value of an r is large, it will be easier to reject the null hypothesis than if the population value is small.

The effect size in a population is beyond the researcher's control. For example, suppose one researcher decides to compare instructional method A with instructional method B. Suppose further that in the population, method A actually is much more effective than method B. Another researcher decides to compare method A and method C, which in actuality is just slightly better than method A. Both researchers do an experiment to compare the effectiveness of their two methods in improving student learning. If both researchers use the same sample size and significance level, the first researcher is more likely to reject his null hypothesis (A = B) than the second researcher, even though her null hypothesis (A = C) also is false. The reason is that method A is much better than method B in actuality, whereas method C is only slightly better than method A.

Stephen Olejnik created several tables to show the necessary sample sizes for different values of the various factors involved in statistical power analysis.[11] A condensed version of the tables is shown in Table 5.3. The table shows power analyses for a variety of commonly used tests of statistical significance.

To illustrate how to use this table, suppose that we are doing a research study to determine whether staff development specialists are more knowledgeable about curriculum than school principals. How many individuals do we need in our research sample? To answer this question using Table 5.3, we first need to select an appropriate test of statistical significance. We most likely will select the t test for independent samples, which is the first test shown in the first column. Next we decide that we wish to do a rigorous test of the null hypothesis to minimize the risk of a Type I error (rejecting the null hypothesis when it is true). Therefore, we select from among the sample sizes given for alpha = .05 in Table 5.3.

We see that there are six possible sample sizes for alpha = .05: 620, 386, 100, 64, 40, and 26. Our next step is to decide whether we think that there is a small, medium, or large effect size in the population that the sample is intended to represent. In other words, do we think it likely that the population of staff development specialists has much more (large effect size), somewhat more (medium effect size), or only a little bit more (small effect size) knowledge about curriculum than school principals? In examining Table 5.3, we see that we can get by with a much smaller sample ($N = 40$ or 26) if we are correct in thinking that the difference between the two populations is large. By contrast, we would need a much larger sample size ($N = 620$ or 386) if we thought the difference between the two populations is small.

Suppose we think that the population difference is large, so now we have limited our necessary sample size to 40 or 26. The final step in selecting a sample size is to decide on the statistical power level, which refers to how certain we want to be about rejecting the null hypothesis if in actuality it is false. Table 5.3 shows two levels of certainty: .7 and .5. Because we want to be fairly certain to reject a false null hypothesis, we select the .7 power level. This means that we will need a total of 40 participants in our research sample. Because there are two groups in the research design, we will select 20 staff development specialists and 20 school principals.

Table 5.3 shows a small number of commonly used alpha levels, estimated effect sizes, and levels of statistical power. Tables that contain a wider range of values for these variables are available in other sources.

11. Olejnik, S. F. (1984). Planning educational research: Determining the necessary sample size. *Journal of Experimental Education, 53,* 40–48.

TABLE 5.3

Minimal Total Sample Sizes for Different Hypothesis Tests with Alpha (α) at either the .05 or .10 Level of Significance and with Statistical Power at either the .7 or .5 Level

Hypothesis Test	Small Effect Size[1] Statistical Power		Medium Effect Size[1] Statistical Power		Large Effect Size[1] Statistical Power	
	.7 N	.5 N	.7 N	.5 N	.7 N	.5 N
Independent samples *t* test						
α = .05	620	386	100	64	40	26
α = .10	472	272	76	44	30	18
Related samples *t* test (matching variable r = .7)						
α = .05	188	118	32	22	14	10
α = .10	144	84	24	16	10	8
Related samples *t* test(matching variable r = .5)						
α = .05	310	194	52	32	22	14
α = .10	238	138	40	24	16	10
Analysis of variance, 3 groups						
α = .05	744	498	126	81	51	33
α = .10	600	357	96	60	39	24
Analysis of variance, 4 groups						
α = .05	884	580	144	96	60	40
α = .10	692	420	112	72	44	28
Analysis of covariance, 3 groups (covariate r = .7)						
α = .05	396	255	166	45	27	21
α = .10	309	186	51	33	21	15
Analysis of covariance, 3 groups (covariate r = .5)						
α = .05	579	375	96	63	39	27
α = .10	450	270	75	45	30	21
3 x 4 analysis of variance, 3-group main effect						
α = .05	780	504	132	96	60	36
α = .10	612	372	72	72	48	24
3 x 4 analysis of variance, 4-group main effect						
α = .05	888	588	156	108	72	48
α = .10	696	432	120	84	60	36
3 x 4 analysis of variance, interaction effect						
α = .05	1128	756	192	121	84	60
α = .10	900	564	156	96	72	48
Correlation coefficient (r)						
α = .05	616	384	66	42	23	15
α = .10	470	277	51	30	18	11
Partial correlation ($r_{vx.z}$)						
α = .05	312	195	44	29	21	14
α = .10	238	138	33	21	15	11
Chi-square, 2 x 4						
α = .05	879	576	98	64	35	23
α = .10	688	418	76	46	28	17
Chi-square, 3 x 4						
α = .05	1114	750	124	83	45	30
α = .10	884	553	98	61	35	22

[1]For t tests, small, medium, and large effect sizes refer to .2, .5, and .8 standard deviations, respectively. For analysis of variance, analysis of covariance, and r, small, medium, and large effect sizes refer to 1 percent, 6 percent, and 13 percent explained variance in the dependent variable, respectively. For chi-square, small, medium, and large effect sizes refer to contingency coefficients of .1, .207, and .447, respectively.

Source: Adapted from tables 2 and 3 on pp. 44–45 in: Olejink, S. F. (1984). Planning educational research: Determining the necessary sample size. *Journal of Experimental Education, 53*, 40–48.

Supplements to Significance Tests

♦ *Touchstone in Research*

Thompson, B. (2001). Significance, effect sizes, stepwise methods, and other issues: Strong arguments move the field. *Journal of Experimental Education, 70,* 80–93.

Wilkinson, L., & APA Task Force on Statistical Inference. (1999). Statistical methods in psychology journals: Guidelines and explanations. *American Psychologist, 54,* 594–604. Retrieved October 4, 2001, from www.apa.org /journals/amp/ amp548594.html

Tests of statistical significance should be supplemented by other approaches to explore further the statistical and practical significance of research data. Two of the approaches discussed below—calculation of confidence limits and replication studies—are concerned primarily with clarifying the statistical significance of research results. The other approach—calculation of effect size—is intended to clarify the practical significance of research results.

Confidence Limits

Confidence limits are used to estimate population values (i.e., parameters) based on what is known about sample values (i.e., statistics). More specifically, **confidence limits** define the upper and lower value of a range of values for a sample statistic that is likely to contain a population parameter. (A **confidence interval** is the term used to refer to the all the values within the range defined by the confidence limits.) Confidence limits are a branch of inferential statistics, because they enable researchers to make inferences from a sample statistic to a population parameter.

To illustrate confidence limits and intervals, suppose we know that the mean test score for a sample of research participants is 75. The sample mean and standard deviation can be used to estimate a range of values (the confidence interval) that are likely to include the true population mean. If our calculations reveal that the 95 percent confidence limits for the sample mean are 68 and 83, we can infer that there is a high likelihood that the true population mean lies between 68 and 83. Stated more precisely, we can infer that if we collected data on 100 research samples similar to the one we actually studied, only five of them would contain confidence limits that did not include the true population mean. In practice, we usually study a single research sample, but by calculating 95 percent confidence limits, we can be reasonably certain that ours is not in the 5 percent of sample means whose confidence limits do not contain the true population mean. Sometimes, 99 percent confidence limits are calculated instead.

A typical experiment will yield two posttreatment means—one for the experimental group and one for the control group. If we calculate confidence limits for each mean, we will have an easily interpreted measure of whether the observed difference between two means indicates a true difference between the populations represented by the samples. Suppose the experimental group mean is 24, with 95 percent confidence limits of 20 and 28. The control group mean is 15, with 95 percent confidence limits of 12 and 18. Given these limits, we can conclude that the true mean of the experimental population is unlikely to be lower than 20, and the true mean of the control population is unlikely to be higher than 18. Thus, it appears that the population represented by the experimental group sample actually outperformed the population represented by the control group sample in this hypothetical study.

Now consider what happens under a different set of conditions. Suppose the experimental group mean remains the same (24), but the 95 percent confidence limits are 17 and 31. The control group mean also remains the same (15), but the 95 percent confidence limits are 7 and 23. Thus, the true mean for the experimental population is likely to be as low as 17, and the true mean for the control population is likely to be as high as 23. Thus, we cannot disregard the possibility that the two population means are the same, with a likely value between 17 and 23.

Tests of statistical significance are almost always included in reports of quantitative research studies. Increasingly, researchers are recommending that confidence intervals for key statistics should be reported as well.[12] In fact, the *Publication Manual* of the American Psychological Association strongly recommends them: "Because confidence intervals combine information on location and precision and can often be directly used to infer significance levels, they are, in general, the best reporting strategy."[13] Procedures for calculating confidence intervals for different types of statistics are presented in various publications and software packages.[14]

Replication of Research Results

Tests of statistical significance are used to help researchers draw conclusions about the validity of a knowledge claim on the basis of a single study. In other words, if the null hypothesis is rejected, we conclude that the knowledge claim (i.e., the research hypothesis) is true. If the null hypothesis is accepted, we conclude that the knowledge claim is false. As we explained earlier in the chapter, researchers should not draw such extreme conclusions. This warning applies even if the obtained level of statistical significance is extremely high (e.g., $p < .001$). One reason is that it is difficult to rule out all possible alternative explanations of the result. Another reason is that flaws in research design and execution creep into most studies. Thus, researchers should avoid extravagant claims about the validity of a knowledge claim on the basis of a single test of statistical significance from a single study. The significance test only serves to increase or decrease their confidence in their knowledge claims. They, or other researchers, should repeat the study in order to test further the validity of the knowledge claims.

Replication is the process of repeating a research study with a different group of research participants using the same or similar methods. Results of a study are more "significant"—in the sense of inspiring confidence that they represent true differences, relationships, or effects in the population—if a new study yields similar results, or if the present study repeats the findings of past research. Consider the case of mastery learning, the effectiveness of which has been demonstrated in many experiments.[15] Suppose you decide to conduct a new experiment to determine whether mastery learning is superior to conventional instruction in a situation not previously investigated. As predicted, the experimental group that received instruction based on mastery learning principles earned a higher mean score on the posttest than the comparison group, but the difference was not of sufficient magnitude to be statistically significant. Nonetheless, you are safe in concluding that this most likely is a true difference, because it replicates a consistent set of previous findings.

In fact, statistical significance is multiplicative across studies.[16] Two or more studies using the same methodology each can yield nonsignificant results, but if the results of each study are in the same direction, the p values from the statistical significance tests can be multiplied. For example, if the p value in each of two studies is .20, their combined probability is .04 ($.20 \times .20$). Thus, the null hypothesis (which would be the same in both studies) can be rejected at the .04 level of significance.

✦ Touchstone in Research

Neuliep, J. W. (Ed.). (1991). *Replication research in the social sciences*. Thousand Oaks, CA: Sage.

Schaefer, W. D. (2001). Replication in field research. *Practical Assessment, Research, and Evaluation, 7*(15). Retrieved October 3, 2001 from www. ericae.net/pare/getvn. asp?v=7&n=15

12. Cahan, S. (2000). Statistical significance is not a "kosher certificate" for observed effects: A critical analysis of the two-step approach to the evaluation of empirical results. *Educational Researcher, 29*(1), 31–34; Cohen, J. (1994). The earth is round ($p<.05$). *American Psychologist, 49*, 997–1003.
13. *Publication manual of the American Psychological Association* (5th ed.). (2001). Washington, DC: American Psychological Association. Quote appears on p. 22.
14. See, for example: August 2001 issue of *Educational and Psychological Measurement* (various articles); nQuery Advisor, Release 3 <www.statsol.ie>.
15. Block, J. H., Efthim, H. E., & Burns, R. B. (1989). *Building effective mastery learning schools*. New York: Longman.
16. The combining of p values across studies also is discussed in Chapter 4 in the context of reviewing the results of quantitative research studies.

If possible, you should attempt to replicate your research project, particularly if your findings show promise of making a substantial contribution to knowledge about education. If you are able to replicate your findings, they are much more impressive to other educational researchers than a statistically significant but weak finding (e.g., a correlation of .20 significant at the .01 level) obtained in the original study. A replicated finding is strong evidence against the possibility that a Type I error (rejection of the null hypothesis when it is true) occurred in the original study. Replication also provides other kinds of evidence, depending upon the type of replication study that is carried out.

Types of Replication Research

David Lykken distinguishes three types of replication:

> *Literal replication* . . . would involve exact duplication of the first investigator's sampling procedure, experimental conditions, measuring techniques, and methods of analysis; asking the original investigator to simply run more subjects would perhaps be about as close as we could come to attaining literal replication and even this, in psychological research, might often not be close enough.
>
> In the case of *operational replication*, on the other hand, one strives to duplicate exactly just the sampling and experimental procedures given in the first author's report of his research. The purpose of operational replication is to test whether the investigator's "experimental recipe"—the conditions and procedures he considered salient enough to be listed in the "Methods" section of his report—will in other hands produce the results that he obtained.
>
> In the quite different process of *constructive replication*, one deliberately avoids imitation of the first author's methods. To obtain an ideal constructive replication, one would provide a competent investigator with *nothing more than* a clear statement of the empirical "fact" which the first author would claim to have established, and then let the replicator formulate his own methods of sampling, measurement, and data analysis.[17]

Literal replication, which you can carry out yourself, can be used to evaluate whether a Type I error might have occurred in the original study. Operational replication is particularly important for experiments in which the researcher must determine the effectiveness of a procedure to improve learning. For example, suppose you trained teachers in a method for teaching thinking skills and found that teachers' use of this method led to greater student achievement than conventional teaching. If other researchers subsequently can use your training procedures and materials and find similar achievement gains, we can conclude that the method leads to superior instruction. If operational replication does not support the original findings, we would need to consider seriously the possibility that the effectiveness of the training procedure and materials is limited to the original researcher. Obviously, an educational procedure or product that holds up after an operational replication has more practical significance for the improvement of education than one that works only in the hands of the original researcher.

The third type of replication, constructive replication, increases the validity of theoretical studies in education. Suppose you are testing a theory of anxiety in which you hypothesize that the presence of anxiety leads to a decrement in academic performance. To test this hypothesis, you need to select or construct measures of anxiety and of academic performance. The hypothesis becomes increasingly credible when it is demonstrated that the relationship between the two variables holds up after several constructive replications in which different measures of one or both variables are used each time. For example, if a particular measure of anxiety predicts decrements in grade point average for each year of

17. Lykken, D. T. (1968). Statistical significance of psychological research. *Psychological Bulletin, 70,* 155–159. Quote appears on pages 155–156.

college, decrement in performance on a particular examination, and decrement in scores on an aptitude test, the validity of the hypothesis and of the theory from which it was derived is strengthened.

Replication studies are becoming more frequent in educational research. As we indicated in Chapter 2, if you are a beginning researcher, you should seriously consider replicating and extending previous studies rather than trying to investigate a previously unresearched problem.

Effect Size

We stated above that tests of statistical significance are inappropriate for making inferences about the practical significance of research results. What can be used in their place? The approach currently favored is to calculate confidence intervals and/or an effect size (ES) statistic. We discussed effect size earlier in the chapter with respect to its use in statistical power analysis. Also, the calculation and interpretation of ES were discussed in Chapter 4 as part of a method called *meta-analysis* for reviewing a set of quantitative research studies on a particular problem.

Another use of ES statistics is as an aid to interpreting the results of a single study. An example is a comparative analysis of the mathematics achievement of middle-school students in the United States and Japan by David Baker.[18] He used achievement test scores collected by the International Association for the Evaluation of Educational Achievement in a sample of U.S. and Japanese mathematics classes. The teacher of each class was asked to estimate whether he or she had taught the content needed to answer each item on the test. Students then were given two scores on the test: (1) for items having content taught by the teacher, the percentage that they answered correctly; and (2) for items having content *not* taught by the teacher, the percentage that they answered correctly. Baker believed that this analysis could solve the problem of how to determine whether U.S. or Japanese mathematics instruction is more effective, given that they include different content in their curricula. Comparing the two nations should be fair if their students' mathematical achievement is compared only on test items having content taught by the teacher.

Table 5.4 shows the results of Baker's analysis. Japanese students answered correctly an average of 63.6 percent of the test items having content taught by their teacher (labeled "Curriculum taught during target grade"), whereas U.S. students answered correctly only an average of 40.4 such items. You will note that the last column also presents the ES for this difference (.81), and footnote b shows the formula used to calculate the effect size. The numerator of the formula is simply the Japanese mean score (63.6) minus the U.S. mean score (40.4), which equals 23.2. The denominator is a weighted standard deviation calculated by averaging of the two standard deviations (SD) while taking into account the different sizes of the two samples. To estimate the denominator, we can ignore sample size differences and average the two SDs (29.9) and (27.8), for a result of 28.85. Dividing 23.2 by 28.85 yields .804, which is quite close to the ES of .81 stated in Table 5.4.

The higher the ES, the greater the difference between two groups. An ES of 1.00 means that the average student in one group scored at the 84th percentile of the other group's score distribution. In Table 5.4, the ES of .81 means that the average Japanese student (i.e., a student at the 50th percentile of the score distribution for his group) would be at the 79th percentile of the score distribution of the U.S. sample. These percentiles provide a better

18. Baker, D. P. (1993). Compared to Japan, the U.S. is a low achiever . . . really: New evidence and comment on Westbury. *Educational Researcher, 22*(3), 18–20.

TABLE 5.4

Achievement of U.S. and Japanese Students on Posttests Measuring Curriculum Taught and Not Taught (Population: 8th Grade United States; 7th Grade Japan)

Achievement of Curriculum	United States (N = 5,459)		Japan (N = 7,643)		Effect Size[b]
	Mean Score[a]	SD	Mean Score[a]	SD	
Curriculum taught during target grade	40.4	29.9	63.6	27.8	.81
Curriculum not taught	27.7	34.2	38.2	29.4	.33

[a]Scores are percentage correct, corrected for guessing.

[b]Effect size $= \dfrac{\bar{X}_{Japan} - \bar{X}_{U.S.}}{SD_{weighted}}$.

Source: Adapted from Table 1 on p. 19 in: Baker, D. P. (1993). Compared to Japan, the U.S. is a low achiever . . . really: New evidence and comment on Westbury. *Educational Researcher, 22*(3), 18–20. Copyright 1993 by the American Educational Research Association. Adapted by permission of the publisher.

sense of how much U.S. and Japanese students differ in mathematics achievement than simply knowing their mean scores.

Another interesting finding reported in Table 5.4 is that Japanese students also performed better on items not taught by their teacher (labeled "Curriculum not taught" in the table) than did U.S. students. The ES of .33, however, is not large. It means that the average Japanese student scored at the 63rd percentile of the score distribution for U.S. students.

The effect size statistic is helpful in judging the practical significance of a research result, but it is by no means an absolute index of practical significance. The magnitude of an ES is affected by the measures used, the absolute difference among group means, the shape of the score distribution, the individuals included in the sample, and possibly other factors. In sum, there is no simple answer to the problem of determining the practical significance of research results. The ES is only an aid to interpretation, albeit an important one.

Psychometric Statistics

Statistics of various types can be used to explore and describe the psychometric properties of scores and the appropriateness of interpretations and uses of outcomes from tests and other measures. Selection of the appropriate statistics depends upon the type of psychometric information that is needed. As explained in Chapter 7, there are three types of psychometric information: test validity, test reliability, and item statistics.

Test validity refers to the appropriateness, meaningfulness, and usefulness of specific inferences made from test scores. Many different types of evidence can be collected to demonstrate the validity of these inferences. Much of this evidence is statistical in nature. For example, one type of validity evidence is predictive evidence, which demonstrates that the scores on a test can predict individuals' scores on a desired outcome measure such as grade point average. This evidence is in the form of correlational statistics, which assess how well the test scores actually predict the outcome measure.

Test reliability refers to the consistency, stability, and precision of test scores. Any time we administer a test or other measure in which some characteristic is expressed in the form of a score, the obtained score always contains some measurement error. When the score has a large amount of measurement error, we say that it is unreliable. Conversely, a score with a small amount of measurement error is described as reliable. How reliable a score is can be described statistically through either a reliability coefficient or a standard error of measurement. There are numerous statistical approaches to estimating the reliability coefficient and the standard error of measurement for a given score on a measure.

Item statistics describe certain properties of individual items in a test or other measure. The most common item statistics are descriptors of item difficulty, the discrimination power of an item, and probability of guessing. Item statistics are used most frequently to revise a measure by identifying items that have a problem, such as poor discrimination power. As these items are revised to correct such problems or are replaced with better items, the measure will provide more reliable scores.

The various statistics involved in constructing and using tests are discussed in more detail in Chapter 7.

Problems in Statistical Analysis

The Need for Exploratory Data Analysis

A common mistake made by researchers is to calculate descriptive statistics (usually means and standard deviations) before carefully examining the individual scores collected in the study. The data in some research studies are "untouched by human hands" in the sense that they are entered immediately into the computer, and a statistical package generates the descriptive and inferential statistics specified by the researcher. The researcher in this situation has denied herself the opportunity to examine the raw data. Consequently, important patterns and phenomena revealed by the individual scores may be overlooked.

Statistical techniques for examining patterns and phenomena in individual scores have been developed. These techniques are not widely used, but they are worth studying because they have revealed new insights about the nature of data often collected in educational research. The techniques are known collectively as **exploratory data analysis,** which is a method for "discovering unforeseen or unexpected patterns in the data and consequently [for] gaining new insights and understanding of natural phenomena."[19]

♦ *Touchstone in Research*

Hoaglin, D. C., Mosteller, F., & Tukey, J. (2000). *Understanding robust and exploratory data analysis.* New York: Wiley.

Tukey, J. W. (1977). *Exploratory data analysis.* Boston: Addison-Wesley Longman.

Stem-and-Leaf Displays

Once the research data have been collected and quantified, exploratory data analysis can begin. An essential tool of exploratory data analysis is the **stem-and-leaf display,** which is a condensed graphical presentation of all the individual scores on a particular measure. Table 5.5 presents a conventional display of students' raw scores on a measure of silent reading, provided by a computer program. The scores are from a group of learning-disabled students who participated in an experimental reading curriculum. The problem with such a display is that it is difficult to "see" the data. Patterns, and any departures from the patterns, are not easily detectable.

Now examine the stem-and-leaf display in Figure 5.2. It is a display of the raw scores in Table 5.5. In a stem-and-leaf display, a bar separates starting parts, or *stem labels* (to the

19. Leinhardt, G., & Leinhardt, S. (1980). Exploratory data analysis: New tools for the analysis of empirical data. In D. C. Berliner (Ed.), *Review of Research in Education* (Vol. 8, pp. 85–157). Washington, DC: American Educational Research Association.

TABLE 5.5

Computer Printout of Raw Data

Student Number	Silent Reading Score	Student Number	Silent Reading Score
1	0.33	31	0.19
2	0.80	32	0.48
3	0.58	33	0.66
4	1.27	34	0.42
5	0.84	35	0.25
6	1.04	36	0.77
7	0.36	37	0.69
8	1.63	38	0.64
9	0.44	39	0.13
10	1.4	40	0.355
11	0.8	41	0.622
12	0.0	42	0.112
13	0.9	43	0.162
14	0.8	44	0.353
15	0.3	45	0.065
16	0.3	46	0.095
17	0.2	47	0.485
18	0.1	48	0.170
19	0.3	49	0.275
20	0.3	50	0.448
21	0.4	51	0.324
22	0.5	52	0.692
23	0.3	53	0.492
24	0.27		
25	0.23		
26	0.16		
27	0.17		
28	0.38		
29	0.75		
30	1.13		

Note. The first column is each student's identification (ID) code. The second column is students' scores on a measure of silent reading time.

Source: Adapted from table II on p. 91 in: Leinhardt, G. & Leinhardt, S. (1980). Exploratory data analysis: New tools for the analysis of empirical data. In D. C. Berliner (Ed.), *Review of Research in Education* Vol. 8, pp. 85–157). Washington, DC: American Educational Research Association. Copyright 1980 by the American Educational Research Association. Reprinted by permission of the publisher.

left of the bar) from each *stem* (to the right of the bar). Each *leaf* in the display can be converted to its original raw score by placing the stem label in front of it and multiplying by the *unit,* in this case, .01.

To understand how a stem-and-leaf display works, look at the stem label in the fourth row of the display, which is 3. This stem label is followed by a stem containing 11 leaves (2, 2, 3, 5, etc.). The third leaf in this stem is a 3. If we place the corresponding stem label in front of this leaf, we obtain the number 33. Multiplying this number by .01 gives us a score of .33, which is the score of the first student in Table 5.5. Now look at the bottom stem,

FIGURE 5.2

Stem-and-Leaf Display of Data Shown in Table 5.5

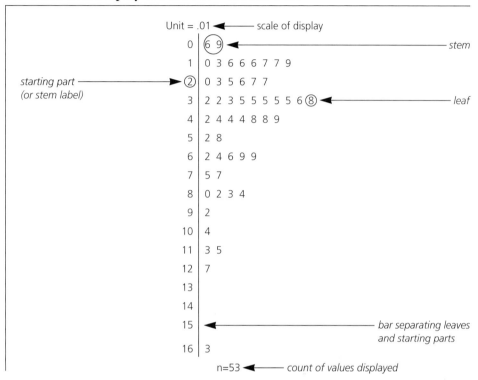

Unit = .01 ◄——— scale of display

```
      0 | 6 9  ◄─────────────────────────── stem
      1 | 0 3 6 6 6 7 7 9
      2 | 0 3 5 6 7 7
      3 | 2 2 3 5 5 5 5 5 6 8  ◄────────── leaf
      4 | 2 4 4 4 8 8 9
      5 | 2 8
      6 | 2 4 6 9 9
      7 | 5 7
      8 | 0 2 3 4
      9 | 2
     10 | 4
     11 | 3 5
     12 | 7
     13 |
     14 |
     15 |
     16 | 3
```

starting part ————————► ② (stem label 2)

n=53 ◄——— count of values displayed

15 | bar separating leaves and starting parts

Source: Adapted from figure 1 on p. 92 of: Leinhardt, G. & Leinhardt, S. (1980). Exploratory data analysis: New tools for the analysis of empirical data. In D. C. Berliner (Ed.). *Review of Research in Education* (Vol. 8, pp. 85–157). Washington, DC: American Educational Research Association. Copyright 1980 by the American Educational Research Association. Adapted by permission of the publisher.

which contains only one leaf (3). If we place the stem label (16) in front of this leaf, we obtain the number 163. Multiplying this number by .01 gives us a score of 1.63, which is the score of the eighth student in Table 5.5. You will note that there are no stems following the stem labels 13, 14, and 15 in Figure 5.2, which tells us that the score of 1.63 is quite discrepant from the other 52 scores in the display.

Advantages of Stem-and-Leaf Displays

Stem-and-leaf displays have several advantages.

1. Stem-and-leaf displays make it easy to see the shape of the distribution of scores. It is apparent in Figure 5.2 that the scores do not form a normal distribution. Most of the scores are at the lower range of values, clustering around a value of approximately .30. Because the score distribution is skewed in this direction, the stem-and-leaf display would alert you to the possible need to use statistics that do not assume a normal curve distribution, for example, the median and range, and various nonparametric statistics.

2. Stem-and-leaf displays provoke questions about the data. For example, looking at Figure 5.2, you might speculate about the factors that caused most students to score at the lower end of the scale and a few students to score at the upper end of the scale. You might be able to formulate a research hypothesis about these factors and test it using available data, or your research hypothesis might provide the basis for designing a follow-up study.

3. Stem-and-leaf displays facilitate the detection of outliers. An **outlier** is an individual or other entity (e.g., one classroom out of a sample of 20 classrooms) whose score differs markedly from the scores obtained by other members of the sample. The student with a score of 1.63 in Figure 5.2 clearly is an outlier. If you identify an outlier, you first should check whether an error occurred in calculating the outlier's score. Some members of a sample show up as outliers simply because the researcher misplaced a decimal point or transposed the participant's score on another variable while preparing the data for computer analysis.

If the outlier's score is not attributable to a calculation or recording error, you need to search elsewhere for an explanation. Perhaps the outlier was not exposed to the same conditions as the other participants in the sample. A reading of the research report from which the raw data in Table 5.5 were taken indicates that such was the case in this study:

In the actual research project from which these data were drawn, it was independently determined that the child on whom this outlier value was measured was, for administrative reasons, not under the control of the classroom teacher and was not, therefore, exposed to the same treatment as the other members of the class. He was ultimately removed from the study.[20]

The decision to eliminate outliers from a research study is problematic. Even one or two outliers can distort the results yielded by conventional statistics, unless the sample is large. You should not eliminate outliers for this reason, however. Outliers should be eliminated only for good cause, as in the case of the student described above. If outliers are left in the sample, consider analyzing the data using both parametric and nonparametric statistics. Comparison of the results yielded by these statistical techniques will yield information about how much the outliers are distorting the data.

In the example above, there would be little argument about the decision to call the score of 1.63 an outlier. But how about the student with a score of 1.27 in Figure 5.2, or the students with scores of 1.13 and 1.15? It is not clear that they should be considered outliers. Statistical techniques that yield quantitative decision rules for identifying outliers are available.[21] In reporting findings from your research study, you always should note the presence of outliers and explain how they were handled in the data analysis.

Graphical Displays

The stem-and-leaf display shown in Figure 5.2 is a specific type of graph. A **graph** is a diagram that shows the relationship between two variables. In the case of Figure 5.2, we can think of the stem label as a variable with values ranging from 0 to 16. The second variable would be "stem length" (i.e., the number of leaves in the stem). Values of stem length can

✦ *Touchstone in Research*

Wainer, H. (2000). *Visual revelations: graphical tales of fate and deception from Napoleon Bonaparte to Ross Perot*. Mahwah, NJ: Lawrence Erlbaum Associates.

20. Ibid., pp. 153–154.
21. Ibid.

vary from 0 (e.g., stem label 13) to 11 (e.g., stem label 3). (Other examples of graphs are shown in Figure 11.1 in Chapter 11.)

The stem-and-leaf display could be converted, if we wished, into other types of graphs, for example, the one shown in Figure 5.3. Here each stem label is represented by a separate bar, and the height of the bar reflects the number of leaves in the stem. This figure is a **histogram,** which is a diagram that shows the relationship between two variables whose measures yield continuous scores. Note that the bars touch each other to indicate the continuous nature of the scores. In contrast, a **bar graph** is a diagram that shows the relationship between measures, one of which yields categorical scores. Each category (e.g., ethnicity) is represented by a separate bar, but the bars do not touch each other. This indicates that the categories are not in a "more" or "less" relationship to each other.

You will note that Figure 5.3 is simpler and easier to comprehend than Figure 5.2. However, it achieves those advantages by eliminating information. For example, if we look at stem label 3 in Figure 5.3, we know that more students earned scores between 3.0 and 3.9 than in any other stem, but we do not know how the scores are distributed within that range.

Figure 5.3 could be simplified still further by clustering stem labels within certain ranges, for example, 0–0.3, 0.4–0.7, 0.8–1.1, 1.2–1.6. We also could make the differences in frequency distributions between the ranges more dramatic by changing the scale of the graph (e.g., increasing the length of the unit used to represent each leaf). However, at some point in designing the graph, "dramatizing" differences can cross over into the realm of "distorting" differences. For this reason, researchers need to create displays that are informative and visually appealing, but not over-simplified or misleading. A stem-and-leaf display is well-suited for researchers' initial exploration of their data, but probably not for

FIGURE 5.3

Histogram Based on Stem-and-Leaf Display in Figure 5.2

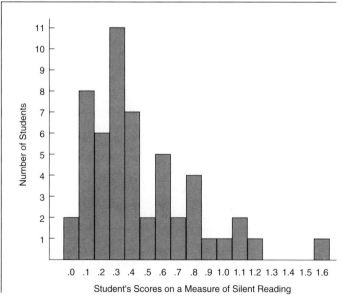

most research reports. Histograms, bar graphs, and other displays (e.g., pie graphs or the frequency polygon shown in Figure 5.1) are usually better suited for the latter purpose.

Missing Data

Missing data are items of information that the researcher intended to collect as part of the research design but are not available for the data analysis. Missing data can be the result of someone losing information through carelessness. In some research studies, for example, tests are administered to hundreds of students. Even though a particular student was present for the testing, her test might become lost in the course of handing it to the test administrator, returning it to the central data-collection center, attaching an ID code, or computer scoring of the test. This loss of data can complicate statistical analysis and weaken the study's contribution to research knowledge. Therefore, precautions should be taken to ensure that no data are lost through avoidable human error.

Missing data also can occur if an individual selected for the research sample refuses to or is unable to participate in part of the study. Even if an individual agrees to participate, he may be unavailable on particular occasions when data are collected. The likelihood of missing data increases as the number of data-collection sessions increases, simply because there are more opportunities for research participants to become ill or to be called away by other commitments.

Students frequently are subjects in educational research. Students often experience illnesses at the same time. If a substantial number of students are absent from school or are unavailable for a scheduled data-collection session, it probably is better to reschedule the session than to have incomplete data for the statistical analysis. This is not a rigid rule, however. In certain studies, the data might be uninterpretable unless they are collected at a specific time. In this situation, a better compromise might be to collect data from a partial sample, assuming that the resulting data still can yield interpretable findings.

Missing data are particularly challenging when several different tests have been administered on several occasions to the same groups of research participants. Consider the scores for two different tests administered at two intervals to an experimental and control group, depicted in Table 5.6. Missing data are indicated by a dash.

The researcher had planned to perform a separate analysis of covariance for each test. Time 1 scores are the *covariate*, and the difference between the experimental and control groups' mean scores at Time 2 is to be analyzed for statistical significance.[22]

How should missing data be handled? One solution is to eliminate incomplete cases, so that only research participants with both Time 1 and Time 2 data are included in the statistical analysis. This solution would entail the loss of four experimental participants and four control participants in analyzing Test A data, and the loss of three experimental participants and two control participants in analyzing Test B data. However, note that different participants would be eliminated across the two tests, and as a result the experimental and control groups would not have the same composition across the two samples. If we wished to include only those participants who have complete data for both tests and both test sessions, even more data would be lost. For example, the experimental group would include only three complete cases (003, 007, and 010)! Another solution is to estimate the missing data by plugging the group mean into each empty cell, or by using a regression analysis (explained in Chapter 11) to estimate more precisely the missing values. The de-

22. A covariate is an independent variable (in this case, Test A or Test B scores at Time 1) whose influence on the dependent variable (in this case, test A or test B scores at Time 2) is controlled by analysis of covariance.

TABLE 5.6

Missing Data in Two Tests Administered to an Experimental and a Control Group

	Test A				Test B			
	Experimental Group		Control Group		Experimental Group		Control Group	
Subject I.D.	Time 1	Time 2	Time 1	Time 2	Time 1	Time 2	Time 1	Time 2
001	5	7	4	5	—	37	38	40
002	4	—	4	4	42	63	—	51
003	8	12	—	7	53	71	45	43
004	—	17	15	—	36	63	55	55
005	6	—	4	3	15	17	38	50
006	10	13	8	10	52	—	63	64
007	3	5	5	7	49	45	—	36
008	7	5	5	5	38	—	50	48
009	—	10	10	—	47	65	36	40
010	12	17	9	—	50	54	47	51

cision to use one solution or another involves complex considerations. In this type of situation, we recommend that you consult an expert statistician.

The best solution obviously is to avoid missing data. Extra effort to ensure that all data required by the research design are collected will save effort later in the statistical analysis phase of the study. Note, too, that beyond a certain point, missing data can hopelessly compromise the research design. In that situation, the only alternatives are to abandon the study or to collect a new set of data.

The Unit of Statistical Analysis

Educational researchers can study individuals as they act in isolation, as they act independently but within a group setting, or as they act as a group. These distinctions are important to consider in deciding whether to use the individual research participant or a group of research participants as the unit of statistical analysis. The **unit of statistical analysis** is the sampling unit replicated within a research study. If the participant is the sampling unit, each participant added to the sample can be considered a replication of the phenomena to be described, correlated, or experimentally manipulated.

Example of Different Units of Statistical Analysis

The effect of the statistical unit on research results is illustrated by the following example. Suppose the relative effectiveness of two teaching methods, A and B, is to be compared by having them used in different classrooms. Ten sixth-grade classrooms—two from each of five schools—are selected for the experiment. In each school one class is randomly assigned to teaching method A and the other to teaching method B for a period of two months. Hypothetical posttest scores of individual students following the experimental period are

TABLE 5.7

Posttest Scores of Students Instructed by Two Different Teaching Methods

		Method A (N = 32)		
School I Class 1	School 2 Class 2	School 3 Class 3	School 4 Class 4	School 5 Class 5
18	25	28	17	22
22	18	27	19	24
27	29	29	23	30
15	30	30	18	15
9	19	24	24	27
24	M = 24.2	26	M = 20.2	21
M = 19.2		31		29
		27		28
		M = 27.8		M = 24.5

		Method B (N = 34)		
School 1 Class 6	School 2 Class 7	School 3 Class 8	School 4 Class 9	School 5 Class 10
25	16	19	22	21
22	25	21	20	29
18	18	28	24	18
18	23	16	19	14
20	15	15	18	22
22	9	21	21	M = 20.8
M = 20.8	22	14	1 5	
	M = 18.3	12	17	
		M = 18.3	M = 19.5	

shown in Table 5.7. Elementary classrooms typically have 20 to 30 or more students, but to simplify the data presentation the table shows classes containing between 5 and 8 students.

In this experiment, the purpose of the statistical analysis is to determine whether the posttest scores of students who received teaching method A are significantly different from the posttest scores of students who received teaching method B. A t test can be done to test for statistical significance, but what is the best unit of statistical analysis—the individual student or the classroom group? If the unit is the individual student, there are 32 students instructed by teaching method A who can be compared with 34 students instructed by teaching method B. If the class is used as the unit, there are only five class means for teaching method A, to be compared with five class means for teaching method B.

Note, too, that the descriptive statistics vary as a function of the unit of analysis. The mean and standard deviation of scores for teaching method A are 23.6 and 5.42, respectively, when the student is the unit of analysis. In contrast, when the group is the unit of analysis, the mean and standard deviation of the group means (19.2, 24.2, 27.8, 20.2, 24.5) are 23.2 and 3.49, respectively.

Some researchers have recommended that the class mean be used as the unit of analysis in the kind of experiment illustrated in Table 5.7. Kenneth Hopkins demonstrated, however, that the individual student should be used as the unit of analysis in conducting tests of statistical significance.[23] He recommended conducting a certain type of analysis of variance in which the classroom and experimental treatment are considered "factors" (the concept of factor is explained in Chapter 13). In the experiment illustrated in Table 5.7, the 10 classes constitute one factor and teaching methods A and B constitute another factor. Hopkins demonstrated the appropriate form of analysis of variance to be used for experimental designs of different levels of complexity.

This discussion of the unit of statistical analysis highlights the fact that education occurs at many levels, for example, individual students receiving tutorial instruction, small cooperative learning groups within classrooms, classrooms, schools, school districts, regions, states, and nations. You need to decide which levels include the phenomena of primary interest to you.

Multilevel Analysis

Leigh Burstein argued that educational researchers should consider several levels at once in designing a study:

> Schooling activities occur within hierarchical organizations in which the sources of educational influence on students occur in the groups to which an individual belongs. These groups (learning groups within classrooms, classrooms within schools, schools within districts, families within communities, schools within communities) influence the thoughts, behavior, and feelings of their members. This hierarchical structure gives rise to multilevel data.[24]

By the term *multilevel data*, Burstein means data that can be analyzed at more than one level of grouping. For example, if a researcher collects data from three classrooms within a school, the data can be analyzed at two levels: classroom (each classroom has a score, or set of scores, associated with it) and school (the mean score of the three classrooms on a variable yields some data about the school as a whole).

There is no one correct level of analysis on which educational research should focus. Instead, you will need to develop a theory or explanation for the particular phenomena that interest you. That theory or explanation will serve as a guide for deciding the level or levels to be included in the data collection and analysis. For example, suppose you are interested in the effects of teacher praise on students. You might focus on the incidence of praise statements delivered to the class as a whole. In this case, you would need to study a sample of classes, and you would use the class as the unit of analysis. Another possibility is to focus on teacher praise given to individual students. In this case, you might measure the number of praise statements directed by the teacher to each student in the classroom. The student, then, would be the unit of analysis, and the sample size would be the number of students in the classroom. If you studied more than one classroom, each classroom could be considered an independent replication of the study.

Another example is educational research on how school principals affect the behavior of the teachers within their schools. Suppose you hypothesize that principals' emphasis on teacher supervision influences the morale of teachers. This hypothesis should be tested by using the school as the unit of analysis. You would need to form a sample of

♦ **Touchstone in Research**

Snijders, T., & Bosker, R. J. (1999). *Multilevel analysis: An introduction to basic and advanced multilevel modeling.* Thousand Oaks, CA: Sage.

---

23. Hopkins, K. D. (1982). The unit of analysis: Group means versus individual observations. *American Educational Research Journal, 19,* 5–18.
24. Burstein, L. (1980). Issues in the aggregation of data. In D.C. Berliner (Ed.), *Review of Research in Education* (Vol. 8, pp. 158–233). Washington, DC: American Educational Research Association. Quote appears on page 158.

school principals, one per school, assess each principal's emphasis on teacher supervision, and measure the overall morale of the teaching staff in each school. Suppose instead that you are interested in whether principals vary in their supervision of individual teachers and whether these variations are related to individual differences in teacher morale. In this situation, the individual teacher is the appropriate unit of analysis.

It is important to keep in mind that the two units of analysis (principal and teacher) constitute multilevel data and both can be studied if the data are collected appropriately. Suppose you measure each principal's emphasis on teacher supervision in terms of the number of supervisory visits the principal made during a school year. If the data are collected separately for each teacher, you would know the number of supervisory visits per teacher, and thus you could examine the relationship between this variable and each teacher's morale. You also could aggregate the data to obtain a measure of each principal's overall emphasis on teacher supervision and an overall measure of teacher morale in each school. (Aggregation in this case would involve obtaining the mean score of teachers on each variable—supervisory visits and morale.)

If the data are collected in this way, they can be subjected to multilevel analysis. For example, you can determine the relationship between teacher supervision and teacher morale within schools and across schools. Also, you can determine whether there is more variability in teacher supervision or in teacher morale within schools or across schools.

Policy studies in education are concerned with even larger units of analysis than the ones described in the preceding examples. Researchers working on the National Assessment of Educational Progress (see Chapter 10) aggregate student data to the state level so that they can study differences among states in the educational attainments of their students. Researchers who are involved with the International Association for the Evaluation of Educational Achievement (see Chapter 10) have aggregated student data to the national level in order to examine differences among the nations of the world in their educational practices and outcomes.

Processing Statistical Data

Computer Hardware

Most statistical analyses in educational research require complex computations. Therefore, researchers generally use a computer or other calculating machine to perform their statistical analyses.

If you have a large amount of data to analyze, you will need to use a mainframe computer, which has the capacity to perform many millions of calculations per minute. These computers are very expensive, and, therefore, they usually are only available at university and college computer centers. One mainframe computer can use its time-sharing features to serve the computing needs of an entire campus.

Most personal computers now have the capability to perform sophisticated statistical analyses on fairly large amounts of data. The main advantage of these computers over a mainframe computer is their convenience. A personal computer can be used when and where you wish. Use of the mainframe computer requires a trip to the computer center or a computer terminal linked to it. Also, there may be restrictions on its availability and charges for its use.

Some handheld calculators have the capability of performing statistical analyses by a simple press of an appropriate function key. Less sophisticated calculators also are useful if you have just a small amount of research data to be analyzed, and if the analyses are limited to simple descriptive and inferential statistics.

Computer Software

The most commonly used software for statistical analysis in educational research is SPSS, which is an acronym for Statistical Package for the Social Sciences <www.spss.com>. SPSS is a comprehensive, integrated collection of computer programs for managing, analyzing, and displaying data. SPSS programs can perform the statistical procedures described in this chapter and in the following chapters. Most universities and colleges have SPSS available for their mainframe computers. A version of SPSS also is available for personal computers. SPSS is occasionally upgraded, so you should check whether you have the most current version.

Another widely available set of integrated statistical programs is SAS, an acronym for Statistical Analysis System <www.sas.com>. It is more difficult to use than SPSS, but it has more capabilities.[25]

An increasing amount of statistical analysis software is available for personal computers. You should check the soundness of this software before using it. Some programs have not been fully tested for "bugs" (errors) or do not follow standard algorithms to arrive at a solution. Therefore, they may give spurious results.

Computer Consultants

Use of SPSS and similar computer software is fairly complicated. Many graduate students find it necessary to hire a computer consultant to assist them in analyzing the data for their thesis or dissertation. You should try to find a consultant who has a good understanding not only of computers but also of educational research methods and statistics. It is not advisable, however, to turn your data completely over to a consultant. Consultants are not likely to have the same "feel" for the data or methodology as you do, and therefore they may wind up doing inappropriate and inaccurate analyses.

These problems can be avoided by asking the consultant to explain each step of data file management and statistical analysis when it is executed. Also, you should specify the statistical techniques that are best to answer your research questions or test your hypotheses, rather than allow the consultant to choose them.

When possible, you should work alongside the consultant. For example, you can observe the consultant create the data entry program and enter some of the numerical data. When you understand how the process works, you can enter the remaining data on your own. Also, you can ask the consultant to use SPSS or related software in an interactive mode. As the consultant keyboards each set of commands, you can ask what they mean; you will be able to see on the computer screen the statistical results produced by the commands. This procedure is far better than trying to make sense of a stack of computer printouts generated by the consultant without your participation.

Checking Data Analyses for Accuracy

Whether you use a calculator, personal computer, or mainframe computer, you should check continuously for accuracy. The first thing to check is the data file, which is your data as stored by the computer. Some calculators facilitate this check by making a paper tape of each data entry. This tape constitutes the data file. Computers show the data file on a screen or printout. Visual inspection of these displays can pick up obvious errors like unusually large or small values of a variable, or misaligned columns. A type of statistical software known as a data entry program also can pick up these errors.

25. Andrews, F. M., Klem, L., O'Malley, P., Rodgers, W. L., Welch, K., & Davidson, T. N. (1998). *Selecting statistical techniques for social science data: A guide for SAS users.* Cary, NC: SAS Publishing.

✦ Touchstone in Research

Babbie, E. R., Halley, F., & Zaino, J. (2000). *Adventures in social research: Data analyses using SPSS 9.0 and 10.0 for Windows 95/98.* Boston: Pine Forge Press.

Morgan, G. A., Griego, O. V., & Gloeckner, G. W. (2001). *SPSS for Windows: An introduction to use and interpretation in research.* Mahwah, NJ: Lawrence Erlbaum Associates.

The next task is to make spot checks of parts of the data file. If these checks reveal unacceptable errors, you will need to enter the data again. Data entry software programs allow you to keep the original data file and re-keyboard the new entries over it. The computer will signal whenever there is a discrepancy between the original entry and the new entry. You can check the discrepancy to determine which entry is in error.

The results of a statistical analysis can be checked in several ways. You can redo the analysis, or you can check the command file to ensure that the proper commands were used. A **command file** is a list of the computer software instructions that you used to perform your statistical analyses. Also, you can check part of the computer analysis by using a calculator. For example, if the computer program calculated a large number of correlation coefficients, you can compute one of them on a calculator. Generally, if the calculator result matches the computer result (within rounding errors), you can be confident that the computer computed all the other correlations without error.

If the results of a statistical analysis are implausible, you should consider the possibility of a computing error. Even if the results are plausible, however, they still should be checked.

Storing Research Data

After you have completed the data analyses for your study, you should file the raw data, hand computations, and computer printouts. The printouts should include the results of the statistical analyses, the data files, and the command files for major analyses. If you used a mainframe computer, an alternative is to store this information on a computer tape. A computer tape is more compact than a stack of printouts and is relatively inexpensive. A single tape is sufficient to store all the files for even a very large research study. If you used a personal computer, the various files can be saved on a storage device (e.g., a CD).

It is particularly important to retain the raw data, which are the test answer sheets, observation forms, recordings of interviews, and other research material as initially received from the research participants. For example, you might wish to refer back to the raw data to check a particular score that seems doubtful. Also, retaining the raw data makes it possible to use the data in future research. It is not uncommon to hit upon an idea for re-analyzing data after completion of the original study. The re-analysis may yield new and interesting information that would be lost if the raw data had been destroyed at the end of the original analysis. If any research findings are challenged, the raw data provide the only fully satisfactory source for rechecking them.

You should label all materials (e.g., printouts) involved in the data analysis and keep a record of all your steps. This takes time, but it is much less than the time that would be required to decipher unlabeled raw data or to redo lost calculations.

♦ RECOMMENDATIONS FOR
Doing Statistical Analyses

1. Select the statistical techniques that are most appropriate for your data and goals.
2. Plan the major statistical analyses before conducting your study to ensure that the resulting data are analyzable.
3. Illuminate different aspects of a data set by using numerous statistical techniques, not just one.

4. Consider using non-parametric statistics when the data grossly fail to meet the necessary assumptions for parametric statistics.
5. In reporting *p* values for tests of statistical significance, take care to interpret their meaning correctly.
6. Use statistical power analysis to plan an adequate sample size for a study and to weigh the risks of Type I and Type II errors in tests of statistical significance.
7. Compute effect sizes and confidence limits in addition to tests of statistical significance.
8. Explore the characteristics of the raw scores obtained in a study before doing formal statistical analyses.
9. Adjust statistical analyses to account for missing data.
10. Consider the purpose of the research study and the data that were collected in deciding which unit(s) of statistical analysis to employ.

✔ SELF-CHECK TEST

Circle the correct answer to each of the following questions.
The answers are provided at the back of the book.

1. A type of score that is *not* appropriate for data analyses involving inferential statistics is
   a. raw scores.
   b. standard scores.
   c. percentile equivalents.
   d. continuous scores.

2. The division of individuals into two categories on the basis of test performance is called
   a. an artificial dichotomy.
   b. a true dichotomy.
   c. a ranking.
   d. a derived score.

3. The median is a better measure of central tendency to use than the mean when
   a. the researcher wishes to examine the raw scores.
   b. the score distribution is skewed.
   c. the scores are distributed normally.
   d. one score is obtained more frequently than any other.

4. An appropriate statement of a null hypothesis would be that
   a. the group receiving the experimental treatment will receive higher scores than the control group.
   b. the research sample will behave differently than the population from which it is drawn.
   c. the difference between sample means reflects a true difference between population means.

   d. no difference will be found between the groups being compared in one's research study.

5. A test of statistical significance is carried out when one wishes to determine
   a. the probability that the differences observed between two samples also will be found in the populations from which they were drawn.
   b. the probability of finding the same research results if one were to do a replication of the research study.
   c. whether the results have practical implications for educators.
   d. whether there is an actual difference between two populations in their scores on a variable of interest.

6. The power of a statistical significance test is increased by all of the following *except*
   a. greater sample size.
   b. use of a higher *p* value to reject the null hypothesis.
   c. estimated effect size.
   d. use of a nondirectional hypothesis.

7. Calculating confidence limits in a research study is a good idea because it
   a. provides a means for estimating population values.
   b. allows the researcher to explore the data for patterns and phenomena that otherwise might be missed.

c. increases the probability of obtaining statistically significant results.

d. provides a statistical method for replicating one's research study.

8. In operational replication, the researcher

a. deliberately avoids imitation of the original researcher's procedures.

b. attempts to duplicate exactly all of the original researcher's procedures.

c. attempts to duplicate only the original researcher's sampling and experimental procedures.

d. re-analyzes data that were collected by another researcher.

9. Effect size is a useful statistic to calculate in order to

a. synthesize research findings from a number of studies of the same variable.

b. study the likelihood that a particular p value will be sufficient to reject a false null hypothesis.

c. assess the practical significance of research findings.

d. all of the above.

10. Stem-and-leaf displays are useful for

a. estimating missing data.

b. detecting outliers.

c. estimating effect size.

d. estimating the probability of a Type I error.

11. A researcher is interested in the relationship between students' academic achievement and class size. The appropriate unit of analysis is

a. the individual student.

b. the classroom.

c. the school.

d. all of the above.

CHAPTER 6

✦ Selecting a Sample

OVERVIEW

Educational researchers rarely can investigate the entire population of individuals who interest them. Instead, they must select a sample of individuals to study. In this chapter, we discuss how the logic of selecting this sample differs when doing qualitative or quantitative research. We then explain the main sampling techniques used in each type of research and the factors to be considered in deciding an optimum sample size. The chapter concludes with a discussion of issues involved in using volunteer samples. The sampling procedures described in the chapter also apply to the selection of events, curriculum materials, and other phenomena of interest to researchers.

OBJECTIVES

After studying this chapter, you should be able to

1. Compare the logic used in quantitative and qualitative research to generalize beyond the sample that was studied.
2. Explain the meaning of population validity and replication logic.
3. Explain the relationship between a sample, the target population, and the accessible population.
4. Describe four criteria that should be satisfied in order to ensure high population validity for a sample.
5. Describe the advantages of and procedures used in these sampling techniques: random sampling, systematic sampling, stratified sampling, and convenience sampling.
6. Identify seven factors that should be considered in determining sample size for a quantitative research study.
7. Explain the rationale for purposeful sampling.
8. Describe the various purposeful sampling strategies and how they differ from each other.
9. Explain why the determination of sample size in a qualitative research study involves a trade-off between depth and breadth.
10. Describe typical differences between volunteers and nonvolunteers as research participants, and how the influence of volunteers on research results can be tested.
11. Describe several techniques for improving the rate of volunteering for participation in a research study.

Introduction

This chapter describes the sampling techniques commonly used by educational researchers. Although we focus on how to select students, teachers, or other *individuals* for a research sample, the same sampling procedures and issues are involved in selecting a sample of *events* or *objects* to study. For example, a researcher might wish to select a sample of class periods to observe, or a sample of elementary reading textbooks to analyze. The class periods and textbooks can be selected using the sampling techniques described in this chapter.

Sampling Logic

Suppose a quantitative researcher wishes to learn how educators feel about promoting school choice, that is, the funding of education to enable parents and students to choose among various schools more easily—public or private, religious or nondenominational, those adhering to one educational philosophy or another. The researcher would like to study every educator in the nation, but instead must settle for administering a survey questionnaire to a small sample of perhaps 200 educators.

Now consider a different research situation. A researcher wishes to do a qualitative study of the views of former President Bill Clinton about school choice. He studies Clinton's speeches and writings about this subject over a period of time, and perhaps is even able to interview him.

The goals of sampling in these two studies are very different. In the first study, the sample is chosen with the intention that it represent a larger population. In other words, the researcher is interested in the population, not the particular sample that she happened to select. However, the other researcher is interested primarily in his sample, which includes but a single case. He selected former President Bill Clinton because of his leadership and influence on the school-choice debate. It would not make sense to generalize his findings about this particular president to a larger population of presidents. Bill Clinton is a unique individual, and his views about school choice could not be construed as representative of other presidents or even of other government officials.

The preceding examples suggest that the logic for generalizing beyond one's sample is very different in quantitative and qualitative research. Let us examine this difference more closely.

Population Validity

According to Glenn Bracht and Gene Glass, one of the criteria for judging experiments is population validity.[1] **Population validity** is the extent to which the results of an experiment can be generalized from the sample that participated in it to a larger group of individuals, that is, a population. Although Bracht and Glass analyzed population validity with reference to quantitative research involving the experimental method, this concept applies just as well to the logic of sampling in other types of quantitative research.

To achieve good population validity, quantitative researchers must select the sample randomly from the defined population to which they wish to generalize their results. Also, this randomly drawn sample must be of sufficient size to reduce the probability that the

---

1. Bracht, G. H., & Glass, G. V (1968). The external validity of experiments. *American Educational Research Journal, 5*, 437–474. The concept of population validity also is discussed in Chapter 12.

sample, even though randomly drawn, has different characteristics than the population from which it was drawn.

The concept of population validity has much in common with inferential statistics and statistical power analysis, which are explained in Chapter 5. Inferential statistics, which include tests of statistical significance and confidence intervals, enable researchers to make generalizations about population parameters on the basis of sample statistics. Therefore, inferential statistics contribute evidence to establish the population validity of a set of research results. Statistical power analysis also contributes relevant evidence, because it indicates the probability of Type I and Type II errors in drawing conclusions about population parameters.

Random sampling and large sample sizes are difficult to achieve under the real-world conditions in which educational researchers typically collect data. In later sections of the chapter, we identify major difficulties in sampling what researchers encounter and compromises they can make to achieve an acceptable level of population validity for their studies.

Population validity can be quantified if we compute a statistic for a sample and know the actual parameter for the population from which the sample was randomly drawn. Suppose the statistic is the mean of the sample's scores on a test. Further suppose that the sample mean is 26.2 and the actual population mean is 29.4. The difference between the two means is 3.2. Thus, the population validity of the sample mean is less than perfect but still a fairly good approximation. In technical terms, this deviation of a sample mean (or other statistic, such as the standard deviation) from the population parameter is called **sampling error.**

Purposeful Sampling

The sample size in qualitative studies typically is small. In fact, the sample size might be a single case. The purpose in selecting the case, or cases, is to develop a deeper understanding of the phenomena being studied. A related purpose often is to discover or test theories. For example, if researchers wish to understand how teachers attempt to implement a new curriculum, they might design a qualitative study that allows them to observe intensely a few teachers engaged in this activity for an entire school year. Because the researchers also wish to understand how beginning and experienced teachers differ in implementing the new curriculum, they deliberately could select one teacher of each type for the study.

In this example, the teachers are selected because they suit the purposes of the study. For this reason Michael Patton describes this type of sampling procedure as purposeful sampling.[2] In **purposeful sampling** the goal is to select cases that are likely to be "information-rich" with respect to the purposes of the study. Thus, the researchers in our hypothetical example decided to identify at least one beginning teacher for a case study. Suppose there are five such teachers in the school district. In approaching the first teacher, they find that he is nervous, uncommunicative, and willing to participate in the study only if required to do so. The researchers decide not to pursue this teacher as a possible case. The next teacher is much more open and eager to participate, and is agreeable to the additional demands on his time that data collection will require. This teacher is selected for the study. At this point, the researchers decide that the intensity of data collection precludes the possibility of including another beginning teacher in the study. Thus, they settle for a sample of one

2. Patton, M. Q. (2001). *Qualitative evaluation and research methods* (3rd ed.). Thousand Oaks, CA: Sage.

beginning teacher. They would go through a similar reasoning process to select one or more experienced teachers for the sample.

It is clear that purposeful sampling is not designed to achieve population validity. The intent is to achieve an in-depth understanding of selected individuals, not to select a sample that will represent accurately a defined population.

Replication Logic

Robert Yin developed a sampling logic for qualitative research that is similar to the logic of Patton's purposeful sampling strategy.[3] Yin's logic, however, focuses specifically on the theory-building goal of qualitative research. When this is the goal, Yin argues that the researcher should select a case that will enable her to develop or test a theory. The research findings about the case are then generalizable to the theory—not to a defined population. The critical test of whether this generalization is warranted is to determine whether the theory can be used to predict the findings of other cases. The testing is done through a process of replication studies.

To illustrate this process, suppose a researcher is interested in how teachers can provide effective leadership in mathematics curriculum reform. He selects as a case to study a teacher who is recognized as a leader in this type of reform. From his findings about this case, the researcher develops a theory that the teacher is effective because she uses a particular leadership style. Furthermore, this leadership style is consistent with a particular theory of effective leadership. Now the researcher can use the theory to predict which other teachers would be effective leaders. He then finds a new teacher whose leadership style is consistent with the theory. If the teacher is effective as predicted, the findings of the first case study thus are replicated and the theory is further supported.

Yin refers to this process of generalizing findings from one case study to the next as replication logic. Specifically, **replication logic** is a strategy that uses theory to determine other cases to which the findings of one case can be generalized. The validity of the theory is tested through a series of empirical replications, each involving one or more case studies. If the theory is well supported by the replications, the theory will identify the population of individuals to whom a particular set of generalizations will apply.

Yin distinguishes between two types of replication: literal and theoretical. If the researcher is doing a **literal replication,** she is predicting that the next case to be studied will yield results that are similar to those of similar cases that she or other researchers have studied. If the researcher is doing a **theoretical replication,** she is predicting that the next case to be studied will yield results that differ from those obtained for other cases that have been previously studied, in ways consistent with the theory that underlies the research. For example, suppose one does several case studies of cooperative learning groups and concludes that the opportunity for two or more students to explain concepts in the textbook to other group members enhances the group's learning. The researcher's theoretical explanation for this finding is that multiple explanations provide different perspectives on what a concept means, and these different perspectives provide each student a richer basis for developing his or her own understanding of the concept than if only one perspective is presented. In a literal replication, the researcher would test the theory by selecting a case of another cooperative learning group in which students typically take turns offering explanations. In a theoretical replication, the researcher instead would select a case of a cooperative learning group in which one

---

3. Yin, R. K., & Campbell, D. T. (1994). *Case study research: Design and methods* (2nd ed.). Thousand Oaks, CA: Sage.

student dominates by explaining all the concepts or in which each concept is explained by one student only.

Yin's concept of replication logic is implied in the "grounded theory" approach to qualitative research developed by Anselm Strauss and Juliet Corbin.[4] They, too, believe that case studies can be used to build theory, which, in turn, indicates the population to which the theory applies:

> [O]ne might study work in one organizational setting. Out of the study evolves the concept of "work flow." The phenomenon of work flow might be used to partially explain how work is carried out in the organization under investigation. However, the more general idea of work flow has possible application beyond this one organization. It might prove a valuable concept for explaining similar phenomena in other organizations. In doing further research, researchers will want to determine which parts of the concept apply to, or are valid in, these other organizations and what new concepts or hypotheses can be added to the original conceptualization.[5]

This statement implies the desirability of selecting a case, or cases, that will yield data from which a broadly applicable theory can be constructed. Piaget's theory of intellectual development was based on his observations of a small number of cases (primarily his own children), but the theory was formulated in such a way that it applies to a very large population, namely, all human beings.

We turn now to the specific procedures that quantitative researchers use to select a sample that represents a defined population and the procedures that qualitative researchers use to select cases that provide a basis for building or testing a theory.

Sampling Techniques in Quantitative Research

Defining the Population

Quantitative researchers attempt to discover something about a large group of individuals by studying a much smaller group. The larger group that they wish to learn about is called a *population,* and the smaller group they actually study is called a *sample.* In quantitative research, **sampling** refers to this process of selecting a sample from a defined population with the intent that the sample accurately represent that population.

Target and Accessible Populations

Two types of populations are relevant to the sampling process. The first is the **target population,** which includes all the members of a real or hypothetical set of people, events, or objects to which researchers wish to generalize the results of their research. (Statisticians sometimes refer to the target population as a "universe.") The advantage of drawing a small sample from a large target population is that it saves the time and expense of studying the entire population. If sampling is done properly, you can make inferences from the sample to an entire target population that are likely to be correct within a small margin of error. For example, in national surveys, researchers can use a random sample of 1,000 or so individuals to represent the views of the entire adult population (well over 100 million people) at a high level of accuracy.

✦ Touchstone in Research

Henry, G. T. (1998). *Practical sampling.* In L. Bickman & D. J. Rog (Eds.), *Handbook of applied social research methods* (pp. 101–126). Thousand Oaks, CA: Sage.

Kish, L. (1995). *Survey sampling.* New York: Wiley.

---

4. Straus, A. L., & Corbin, J. M. (1998). *Basics of qualitative research: Techniques and procedures for developing grounded theory.* Thousand Oaks, CA: Sage. Grounded theory is discussed at greater length in Chapters 2 and 14.
5. Ibid., p. 23.

The first step in sampling is to define the target population. Examples include: all school superintendents in Pennsylvania, all supervisors of student teachers in all accredited teacher education programs in Canada, all bilingual children in the primary grades of the San Antonio School District, and all students who have failed an algebra course in the New York City schools in the past three years. These examples illustrate how the target population can represent a large group scattered over a wide geographical area or a small group concentrated in a single area.

Few researchers have the resources to draw a sample from a very large, geographically dispersed target population, such as all first-grade students in U.S. public schools. Instead, they draw their samples from an **accessible population,** which is all the individuals who realistically could be included in the sample. For example, if you are planning to survey how high school students currently use computers at school and at home, your accessible population might be students in the school district in the neighborhood where you live, plus perhaps a few neighboring districts.

If the population is fairly large, you will need to find a way to identify all its members. Researchers generally rely on a published list, called a **sampling frame,** of the population that interests them. (A sampling frame typically is a published list, but in more general terms it is a set of directions for identifying the population.) For example, Kathy Green used a published list to select a random sample of teachers:

> [S]urvey forms were mailed in a rural western state to 700 teachers randomly selected from the State Department of Education list of all licensed educators.[6]

Appendix D includes directories of directories that can be used to locate some of these published lists. Of course, you should check to determine whether a relevant list is complete and fairly recent. School enrollment and memberships of organizations change constantly, so frequent updating of the population lists is necessary. Also, keep in mind that membership in most organizations is voluntary. Thus, the researcher who uses an organization's directory to define a population faces the risk of selecting a biased sample, because joiners of organizations might differ in important respects from nonjoiners. If this is the case, you may need to define the accessible population as all members of a given organization rather than as all members of the profession or group that the organization serves.

Sampling frames can be very difficult to devise for certain populations of interest to educators. For example, suppose a researcher wishes to study homeless children. How can one identify a target or accessible population when these children typically are transient and often "hidden" from the community?[7] Victims of child abuse are another population that is difficult to identify. Different databases and data-collection methods have yielded different populations of these victims and different subpopulations based on racial classification.[8]

Researchers increasingly are using the Internet to collect data from research participants. This requires the identification of populations and methods of drawing samples to

---

6. Green, K. A. (1992). Differing opinions on testing between preservice and inservice teachers. *Journal of Educational Research, 86,* 37–42. Quote appears on p. 38.
7. Phelan, J. C., & Link, B. G. (1999). Who are "the homeless"? Reconsidering the stability and composition of the homeless population. *American Journal of Public Health, 89,* 1334–1338.
8. Ards, S., Chung, C., Myers, Jr., S. L. (1998). The effects of sample selection bias on racial differences in child abuse reporting. *Child Abuse and Neglect, 22,* 103–115.

define the populations. These can be difficult tasks if members of the population have differential access to Internet capabilities or if they do not provide accurate information (e.g., registering at a Web site, but giving inaccurate information about themselves, such as their e-mail address).[9]

Inferential Leaps from a Sample to a Population

Even though most samples are selected from an accessible population, researchers usually want to know the degree to which the results can be generalized to the target population. This type of generalization requires two inferential leaps. First, the researchers must generalize the results for the sample to the accessible population from which the sample was selected. Second, they must generalize from the accessible population to the target population.

The inferential leap from the sample to the accessible population presents no problem if a **random sample** of the accessible population was obtained, that is, a sample in which all members of the accessible population had an equal chance of being selected. If the sample was not formed randomly, the researchers should compare the sample with the accessible population on characteristics critical to the study. Rarely will researchers be able to obtain data for all the characteristics they wish to compare, but they should try to obtain comparative information on at least the critical variables (usually such characteristics as gender, socioeconomic status, ethnicity, age, and academic ability). These data will demonstrate whether the sample is nonrepresentative of the accessible population. If the sample is representative, you can safely generalize the results to the accessible population. If the sample is biased, however, they should report the nature of the bias and discuss how it might affect the research results.

In order to make the second inferential leap—from the accessible population to the target population—researchers must gather data to determine the degree of similarity between the two populations. Of course, it is possible to compare two populations on a great many variables. Nevertheless, if researchers are able to demonstrate that the accessible population is similar to the target population on a few variables that are particularly relevant to the study, they have done much to establish the population validity of your research results.

Resource limitations often limit researchers to drawing a random sample from a very small accessible population, as in a study of processes involved in reading by Richard Wagner and his associates:

> The subjects were 95 kindergarten and 89 second-grade students who were randomly selected from three elementary schools in Tallahassee, Florida.[10]

Studies based on a narrow accessible population are, of course, less generalizable than those based on broader populations. They still may have implications for other educators if it can be demonstrated that the accessible population—or a randomly drawn sample from it—is similar to a larger target population on critical variables. In the reading study cited above, Wagner and his associates described the sample with respect to age, gender distribution, ethnic distribution, and language fluency. Thus, readers of

---

9. Bradley, N. (1999). Sampling for Internet surveys: An examination of respondent selection for Internet research. *Journal of the Market Research Society, 41*, 387–395.
10. Wagner, R. K., Torgesen, J. K., Laughon, P., Simmons, K., & Rashotte, C. A. (1993). Development of young readers' phonological processing capabilities. *Journal of Educational Psychology, 85*, 83–103. Quote appears on p. 87.

their report can determine whether the sample is similar to the target population of interest to them, and therefore whether the research findings are applicable to that target population.

How well do researchers follow the logic of defining a target population and accessible population and drawing a representative sample from it? Steven Permut, Allen Michel, and Monica Joseph used four criteria to evaluate a sample of 460 articles on marketing research.[11] The criteria were as follows:

1. A clear description of the *population* to which the results are to be generalized should be given.
2. The *sampling procedure* should be specified in sufficient detail that another investigator would be able to replicate the procedure. The detail should include, at a minimum, (a) the type of sample (simple random, stratified, convenience, etc.); (b) sample size; and (c) geographic area. Depending on the study, other descriptive data (e.g., gender, age, grade level, socioeconomic status) also should be included.
3. The *sampling frame,* that is, the lists, indexes, or other population records from which the sample was selected, should be identified.
4. The *completion rate,* which is the proportion of the sample that participated as intended in all of the research procedures, should be given.

Only ten percent of the studies reviewed by Permut and his associates met all four criteria. In a similar analysis of 297 published studies in communications research, Dennis Lowry also found that only ten percent met the four criteria.[12] In your own study, you should try, as a minimum, to satisfy the four criteria listed above.

Probability and Non-Probability Sampling

Samples can be drawn from accessible or target populations by various methods. Some of the methods involve **probability sampling** which means that each individual in the population has a known probability of being selected. The probabilities are known because the individuals are chosen by chance. The following sections describe four types of probability sampling: (1) simple random sampling, (2) systematic sampling, (3) stratified sampling, and (4) cluster sampling.

Other methods of sample selection involve non-probability sampling. Individuals are selected not by chance, but by some other means. We describe two types of non-probability sampling: (1) convenience sampling and (2) purposeful sampling. It is much more difficult to make valid inferences about a population from non-probability sampling methods, but these methods are used in more than 95 percent of research studies in the social sciences.[13] Undoubtedly, the reason for their prevalence is that it is much easier to select a non-probability sample than a random sample when studying individuals in their natural environment.

---

11. Permut, J. E., Michel, A. J., & Joseph, M. (1976). The researcher's sample: A review of the choice of respondents in marketing research. *Journal of Marketing Research, 13,* 278–283.
12. Lowry, D. T. (1979). Population validity of communication research: Sampling the samples. *Journalism Quarterly, 56,* 62–68, 76.
13. Ludbrook, J., & Dudley, H. (1998). Why permutation tests are superior to *t* and *F* tests in medical research. *The American Statistician, 52,* 127–132.

Sophisticated variants of these methods have been developed, primarily for use in large-scale survey research.[14]

Simple Random Sampling

A simple random sample is a group of individuals drawn by a procedure in which all the individuals in the defined population have an equal and independent chance of being selected as a member of the sample. By "independent," we mean that the selection of one individual for the sample has no effect on the selection of any other individual.

This definition of a simple random sample is adequate, but it does contain a slight flaw. In reality, each individual in the defined population cannot have an exactly equal chance of being selected into the sample. To understand why this is so, suppose there are 1,000 sixth-grade students in our accessible population, and we want to select a simple random sample of 100 students. When we select our first research participant, each student has one chance in 1,000 of being selected. Once this student has been selected, however, only 999 students remain; each student now has one chance in 999 of being selected as our second participant. Thus, as each student is selected, the probability of being selected next increases slightly because the population from which we are selecting has become one participant smaller.

The flaw in our initial definition of a **simple random sample** can be corrected by defining it as a sample selected from a population by a process that provides *every sample of a given size* an equal probability of being selected. In other words, suppose that your population has 1,000 members and you intend to draw a random sample of 50 subjects from it. Now imagine every conceivable sample of 50 subjects from this population. If you draw a random sample from the population, any one of these samples would have an equal chance of being the sample you select for your study.

The main advantage of randomly selected samples is that they yield research data that can be generalized to a larger population within margins of error that can be determined by statistical formulas. Random sampling also is preferred because it satisfies the logic by which a null hypothesis is tested using inferential statistics (see Chapter 5).

Random Number Generators

Various techniques can be used to obtain a simple random sample. Suppose the research director of a large city school system wishes to obtain a random sample of 100 students from a population of 972 students currently enrolled in the ninth grade in School District A. First, he would obtain a copy of the district census for ninth-grade students and assign a number to each student. Then he would use a table of random numbers to draw a sample from the census list. Tables of random numbers usually consist of long series of five-digit numbers generated randomly by a computer. Table 6.1 is a small portion of a typical table.

To use the random numbers table, randomly select a column as a starting point, then select all the numbers that follow in that column. Because there are three digits in 972 (the number of cases in the accessible population, School District A), you only need to use the last three digits of each five-digit number. If more numbers are needed, proceed to the

14. For a description of these variants, see: Malhotra, N. K. (1999). *Marketing research: An applied orientation* (3rd ed.). Upper Saddle River, NJ: Prentice Hall.

TABLE 6.1

Section of a Table of Random Numbers

Column

Row	1	2	3	4	5	6	7	8	9	10
1	32388	52390	16815	69298	82732	38480	73817	32523	41961	44437
2	05300	22164	24369	54224	35983	19687	11052	91491	60383	19746
3	66523	44133	00697	35552	35970	19124	63318	29686	03387	59846
4	44167	64486	64758	75366	76554	31601	12614	33072	60332	92325
5	47914	02584	37680	20801	72152	39339	34806	08930	85001	87820
6	63445	17361	62825	39908	05607	91284	68833	25570	38818	46920
7	89917	15665	52872	73823	73144	88662	88970	74492	51805	99378
8	92648	45454	09552	88815	16553	51125	79375	97596	16296	66092
9	20979	04508	64535	31355	86064	29472	47689	05974	52468	16834
10	81959	65642	74240	56302	00033	67107	77510	70625	28725	34191

next column until sufficient numbers have been selected to make up the desired sample size.

In our example, suppose the researcher selects row 1 of column 5 in Table 6.1 as his starting point and uses the last three digits of each number in that column and each successive column. Thus, the researcher would select the 732nd student on the census list, skip the number 983 (there are only 972 cases in the population), select the 970th student, select the 554th student, and so on. This procedure would be followed (with a much larger table of random numbers, of course) until a sample of 100 pupils had been selected.

Another method for generating a sequence of random numbers is to use software with this capability. Also, at least one web site has this capability: <www.randomizer.org>. (You might find other web sites by using the keyword phrase "random number generator" in a search engine like Google or Yahoo!)

Example of Simple Random Sampling

Simple random sampling is illustrated by a study involving the selection of a national random sample of secondary physics teachers.[15] The researchers responsible for this curriculum evaluation study (Wayne Welch, Herbert Walberg, and Andrew Ahlgren) wished to avoid a nonrandom sample of "volunteer" teachers. Use of volunteers, which is typical of many curriculum evaluation studies, makes it difficult to generalize the findings of the evaluation to other groups of teachers, especially nonvolunteers, who might be required to teach the new curriculum.

The researchers first purchased a list of the names and addresses of 16,911 physics teachers compiled by the National Science Teachers Association. They commented in their report that this was the most comprehensive population list of high school physics teachers then available. It was not a complete list, however, because it was based on responses received from 81 percent of all secondary schools in the United States. Thus, their popula-

15. Welch, W. W., Walberg, H. J., & Ahlgren, A. (1969). The selection of a national random sample of teachers for experimental curriculum evaluation. *School Science and Mathematics*, 69, 210–216.

tion was not "all high school physics teachers" but rather "all high school physics teachers on the 1966 NSTA list." Each teacher on the population list was assigned a number according to her ordinal position on the list. Then a table of random numbers was used to select a total of 136 teachers. These 136 teachers were sent letters inviting them to participate in the study, but it was possible to contact only 124 of them.

Eventually 72 of the original 136 teachers agreed to participate in the study according to the conditions specified. Another 42 teachers were unable to participate for various reasons. In order to determine whether their final sample was biased by its reliance on volunteers, the researchers decided to compare several characteristics of the 72 accepting teachers with those of the 42 nonacceptors. When this comparison was made, the researchers found that significantly more acceptors than nonacceptors worked in larger schools and taught the Physical Science Study Committee (PSSC) physics course. The researchers interpreted these differences as indicating that the accepting teachers were more likely to be those who taught in large schools where previous innovations had been accepted. Thus, although they attempted to obtain a truly random sample, their actual sample was somewhat biased in favor of teachers working in innovative schools and teachers who chose to volunteer as research participants. Nevertheless, the researchers' final sample probably was more representative than the samples used in most curriculum studies at that time. It was possible to generalize the study's findings to a national population of physics teachers, with certain qualifications.

Systematic Sampling

Systematic sampling is an easier procedure to use than is simple random sampling if the sample to be selected is very large and a list of the accessible or target population is available. Suppose the population has 100,000 members and you wish to select a sample of 1,000 members from it. Further suppose the members are listed in a directory. If you were to use simple random sampling, you would need to number the members from 1 to 100,000 and then use a table of random numbers to select the sample of 1,000 members.

If you used systematic sampling instead, you would first divide the population by the number needed for the sample (100,000 divided by 1,000 = 100). Then select at random a number smaller than the number arrived at by the division (in this example, a number smaller than 100, such as 36). Then, starting with the 36th member on the list, select every 100th name thereafter from the directory list. The time saved is substantial because there is no need to assign a separate number to each member listed in the directory or to work back and forth between a table of random numbers and the directory.

Systematic sampling should be avoided if there is any possibility of periodicity in the list (that is, if every nth person on the list shares a characteristic that is not shared by the entire population). For example, suppose you have 100 class lists, and you decide to select a sample by choosing the first name on each list. If the names are in alphabetical order, your sample most likely would include only students whose last name begins with A or B. This sample would underrepresent certain ethnic groups for whom a last name beginning with A or B is uncommon.

Stratified Sampling

Stratified sampling involves selecting a sample so that certain subgroups in the population are adequately represented in the sample. For example, suppose that the population includes 10,000 students, of whom 100 are Laotian. If you draw a random sample of 200 students from this population, there is a strong likelihood that the sample would include no Laotian students or only a very few. Stratified sampling ensures that a satisfactory representation of Laotian students is included in the sample, if this is important to your study.

In **proportional stratified sampling,** the proportion of each subgroup in the sample is the same as their proportion in the population. Suppose we are comparing students with different ethnic backgrounds. Each ethnic background—Laotian, African-American, Latino, and so forth—would be considered a separate "stratum." Further suppose that Laotians are the smallest ethnic group in the population—100 students out of 10,000, which equals one percent of the population. We want to have at least 10 Laotian students in the sample. Therefore, we would randomly select 10 from all the Laotian students in the population. Because Laotian students comprise one percent of the population, the sample would need to include 1,000 students to be proportionally correct (10 students in the sample ÷ by .01). The size of other strata in the sample could then be determined. For example, if the population included 2,000 African-American students (which is 20 percent of the population), the sample should include 200 of them (20 percent of the predetermined sample size of 1,000 students).

A variant of this approach is **nonproportional stratified sampling.** We might decide to select 20 students of each ethnic background in the population, regardless of their proportion in the population. This approach is quite acceptable, as long as we only make generalizations about the findings for students of each ethnic background. We cannot make generalizations from the total sample because it does not represent accurately the proportional ethnic composition of the population.

Cluster Sampling

In **cluster sampling,** the unit of sampling is a naturally occurring group of individuals. Cluster sampling is used when it is more feasible to select groups of individuals rather than individuals from a defined population. For example, suppose you wish to administer a questionnaire to a random sample of 300 students in a population defined as all sixth-graders in four school districts. The population includes a total of 1,500 sixth-graders in 50 classrooms, with an average of 30 students in each classroom.

One approach to sample selection would be to draw a simple random sample of 300 students using a census list of all 1,500 students. In cluster sampling, in contrast, you might draw a random sample of ten classrooms—assuming 30 students on average per classroom. Thirty students per classroom multiplied by ten classrooms equals 300 students, which is the desired sample size. Thus, you have achieved the efficiency of only having to access ten classrooms in order to administer a questionnaire to a random sample of 300 students. If you had used simple random sampling instead, you probably would have had to arrange for access to all 50 classrooms, even though some of these classrooms might include only one student in the random sample.

A variation of this method is **multistage cluster sampling,** which involves first selecting clusters and then selecting individuals within clusters. In the example we have been considering, suppose you wish to supplement the questionnaires with interviews of individual students. It is relatively easy to group-administer the questionnaire to every student in the ten classrooms. However, it would be very time-consuming to interview all 300 students in them. Therefore, you could institute another sampling procedure (the second stage of multistage cluster sampling), in which you randomly select five students, for example, from each of the ten classrooms to interview. The interview sample, then, will include 50 students.

Conventional formulas for computing statistics on research data should not be used with samples chosen by cluster sampling. Special statistical formulas are available, but they are less sensitive to population differences. This disadvantage must be weighed against the possible savings in time and money that can result from cluster sampling.

Convenience Sampling

Each of the sampling methods described above involves a defined population and a sample of individuals or groups randomly drawn from that population. In actuality, many studies do not use these methods to select a sample. Rather, the researcher selects a sample that suits the purposes of the study and that is convenient. The sample can be convenient for a variety of reasons: the sample is located at or near where the researcher works; the administrator who will need to approve data collection is a close colleague of the researcher; the researcher is familiar with the setting, and might even work in it; some of the data that the researcher needs already have been collected. In fact, many research studies that appear in journals involve college students because the researcher is a professor and these students provide a convenient sample. In view of the fact that college students are not representative of the adult population in general, one would be justified in questioning the universality of certain principles of learning and instruction that appear in textbooks and other sources.

Researchers often need to select a convenience sample or face the possibility that they will be unable to do the study. Although a sample randomly drawn from a population is more desirable, it usually is better to do a study with a convenience sample than to do no study at all—assuming, of course, that the sample suits the purposes of the study.

If a convenience sample is used, the researchers and readers of their report must infer a population to which the results might generalize. The researcher can assist the inference process by providing a careful description of the sample. Although this recommendation seems obvious, it sometimes is violated in practice. For example, we came across this description of a sample (slightly paraphrased to mask the researcher's identity) in a journal issue: "The study involved 58 undergraduate seniors majoring in education at a southeastern university." That is the description in its entirety. There is insufficient information in this description to infer whether the results would generalize to all universities or to a limited subset (e.g., small private universities), and whether the results would generalize to all education majors or to a limited subset (e.g., education majors who have completed at least one school practicum, or those planning to teach at the high school level).

Example of a Convenience-Sample Description

A much fuller description of a convenience sample was provided by James Laney in the report of an experiment on two approaches to teaching economic concepts to young children:

> Transitional first-grade students were chosen as the population of interest for two reasons. First, because of his or her maturational age level, the transitional first grader is likely to have many misconceptions about basic economic concepts. Second, transitional first-grade classrooms make use of developmentally appropriate practices, and the treatment conditions used in this study were designed in accordance with such practices.
>
> All of the transitional first-grade students in one elementary school in north central Texas participated as subjects in the study. Thirty-one students made up the sample, including 25 Caucasians, 5 African-Americans, and 1 Hispanic student. Twenty of the students were boys, and 11 were girls. None of the students had received any instruction in economics prior to the study.
>
> Students' eligibility for placement in transitional first grade was determined at the end of their kindergarten year. Placement in the program was dependent on (a) the student's being 6 years of age by September 1 and (b) the student's having an approximate behavior age of 5½ years as indicated by his or her score on an individually administered readiness

test, the Maturational Assessment Test (Hull House Publishing Company, 1988), given by the school counselor. In addition to the two main selection criteria listed above, parents' and teachers' observations were also taken into account.[16]

This is most likely a convenience sample, because the school is located in north central Texas, and the researcher works at the University of North Texas. However, the researcher took care (1) to specify a population to which the results would likely generalize, (2) to describe pertinent characteristics of the sample, and (3) to provide a rationale for why the sample was well suited to the purpose of the study.

Use of Inferential Statistics with Convenience Samples

Inferential statistics often are used to analyze data collected from convenience samples, even though the logic of inferential statistics requires that the sample be randomly drawn from a defined population. Some researchers believe that inferential statistics for these samples cannot be interpreted meaningfully. Others believe that it is possible to conceptualize a population that the sample represents. They then reason that because the sample is representative of this population, the sample is equivalent to a sample randomly drawn from the population; therefore, the use of inferential statistics is justified.

Our position on the issue is that inferential statistics can be used with data collected from a convenience sample if the sample is carefully conceptualized to represent a particular population. Nevertheless, we believe that one should be cautious about accepting findings as valid and making generalizations from them on the basis of one study. Repeated replication of the findings is much stronger evidence of their validity and generalizability than is a statistically significant result in one study.

Estimating an Adequate Sample Size

The general rule in quantitative research is to use the largest sample possible. The larger the sample, the more likely the research participants' scores on the measured variables will be representative of population scores. In addition to this general rule, researchers have developed rules of thumb for determining the minimum number of participants needed for different research methods. In correlational research, a minimum of 30 participants is desirable. In causal-comparative and experimental research, there should be at least 15 participants in each group to be compared. For survey research, Seymour Sudman suggested a minimum of 100 participants in each major subgroup and 20 to 50 in each minor subgroup.[17]

Mathematical procedures are available to make more precise estimates of the sample size needed to reject the null hypothesis when in fact it is false, and to determine the likely value of population parameters (typically, the population mean and standard deviation). These procedures are called *statistical power analysis,* and they are discussed in Chapter 5.

In addition to statistical power analysis, you should consider the following three factors in determining an optimal sample size for a quantitative research study:

1. *Subgroup analysis.* In many quantitative studies, it is desirable to break groups into subgroups for further analysis. For example, the primary data analysis for an experiment might involve a comparison of all research participants in the experimental group with all research participants in the control group. In addition, one might compare all male

16. Laney, J. D. (1993). Experiential versus experience-based learning and instruction. *Journal of Educational Research, 86,* 228–236. Quote appears on p. 14.

17. Sudman, S. (1976). *Applied sampling.* New York: Academic Press.

participants in the experimental group with all male participants in the control group, and similarly for female participants. This type of subgroup analysis sometimes is done as an afterthought, with the unfortunate consequence that the subgroup size is too small to produce adequate statistical power. Therefore, it is best to plan subgroup analyses at the design stage of a study so that an adequate sample size is selected.

2. *Attrition.* Attrition sometimes is a problem in research that extends over a substantial period of time. For example, in studies of school children, researchers often find that substantial numbers of them leave the school during the course of a school year; this is especially true of schools in low-income communities. Robert Goodrich and Robert St. Pierre estimate that 20 percent attrition per year is a realistic level for planning.[18] Attrition can be minimized by strategies such as developing research participants' commitment to the study and establishing good rapport with them. (See the section on human relations in Chapter 3.) Still, it is best to increase sample size by a certain percentage to account for possible attrition.

3. *Reliability of measures.* Measures with low reliability weaken the power of tests of statistical significance and estimates of population parameters. Therefore, if you must use measures with low reliability, you need to increase sample size accordingly. The converse is also true.

In many quantitative studies, there is a cost-benefit trade-off involving sample size. For example, in some studies it is desirable to use role-playing, depth interviews, and other such time-consuming measurement techniques. These techniques cannot be used in large-sample studies unless considerable financial support is available. The alternative is to obtain a large sample but to use relatively inexpensive measures such as questionnaires and standardized tests. However, a study that probes deeply into the characteristics of a small sample often provides more knowledge than a study that attacks the same problem by collecting only superficial data from a large sample.

In some research, very close matching of subjects on the critical variables concerned in the study is possible. Under these conditions, a small sample often will have good statistical power and can yield important results. The classic study by Horatio Newman, Frank Freeman, and Karl Holzinger on the intelligence of identical twins is a good example of such a study.[19] Because identical twins have the same genes, they are ideal for studying the relative influence of heredity and environment on various human characteristics. One phase of their research included only 19 pairs of separated identical twins, but this sample provided information about the relative influences of heredity and environment on intelligence that would have been difficult to obtain with large samples of less closely matched subjects.

Sampling Techniques in Qualitative Research

Qualitative research is more flexible with respect to sampling techniques than quantitative research. This flexibility reflects the emergent nature of qualitative research design which allows researchers to modify methodologies as data are collected. Therefore, the sampling techniques discussed in this section are suggestive rather than prescriptive, and they do not necessarily exhaust the possible ways in which a qualitative research sample might be selected.

✦ Touchstone in Research

Denzin, N. K., & Lincoln, Y. S. (2000). Strategies of inquiry. In N. K. Denzin & Y. S. Lincoln (Eds.), *Handbook of qualitative research* (2nd ed., pp. 367–378). Thousand Oaks, CA: Sage.

18. Goodrich, R. L., & St. Pierre, R. G. (1979). *Opportunities for studying later effects of Follow Through.* Cambridge, MA: ABT Associates.
19. Newman, H. H., Freeman, F. N., & Holzinger, K. J. (1937). *Twins: A study of heredity and environment.* Chicago: University of Chicago Press.

Types of Purposeful Sampling

As we explained above, Patton uses the term *purposeful sampling* to refer to the practice of selecting cases that are likely to be information-rich with respect to the purposes of a qualitative study. He identifies 15 purposeful sampling strategies, each of which serves a particular purpose in a qualitative study.[20] The following is a description of each strategy.

1. **Extreme or deviant case sampling** focuses on cases that are unusual or special. The findings of research on extreme cases can provide an understanding of more typical cases. An example is George Noblit's study of how teachers use caring in their instruction and the relation of caring to power.[21] To study these phenomena, he chose an exceptional case—an elementary teacher named Pam. Her exceptionality is conveyed in Noblit's description of her:

> She [Pam] was one of the opinion makers in the building, was revered by white and African American parents, and was the teacher who assumed charge of the school whenever the principal was out of the building. She was reputed to be the most effective teacher in the building, adept with "difficult" students and (I later concluded) with "difficult" parents. She never missed a chance to talk with parents and was frequently called by the school secretary to deal with parent complaints. Her power was such that she, in many ways, chose me to be in her classroom for the Caring Study, rather than the other way around.[22]

The use of an exceptional case like Pam is helpful because the teacher characteristics to be studied are easy to detect and occur frequently. A possible problem with extreme cases is that educators might dismiss findings based on them simply because they are extreme or deviant.

2. **Intensity sampling** avoids this problem because it involves selecting cases that manifest the phenomenon of interest intensely but not extremely. As an illustration, suppose a researcher was interested in the characteristics of inservice presenters. If an extreme-case sampling approach were used, the researchers might select star performers in the world of inservice education—the individuals who regularly make keynote presentations at national conferences and who consult nationally and internationally. These cases might be interesting, but of little relevance to educators who do inservice presenting on a much smaller scale. Therefore, the researcher might consider selecting educators who are highly respected as inservice presenters within their school district or local region. These educators still qualify as exceptional cases, but they are more like the vast majority of inservice presenters. By studying these less extreme cases, the researcher is more likely to obtain findings that deepen the understanding of most inservice presenters about ways in which they might improve. Also, the findings might enlighten administrators about reasonable qualifications and expectations for local staff who aspire to be inservice presenters.

3. **Typical case sampling,** as one might expect, involves the selection of typical cases to study. This strategy might be particularly useful in field tests of new programs. Developers and policy makers want their programs to be effective for the great majority of the individuals to be served by the program; otherwise, the program will not be considered cost-effective. Also, stories about typical cases might be useful for "selling" the program to various constituencies.

20. Patton, Qualitative evaluation.
21. Noblit, G. W. (1993). Power and caring. *American Educational Research Journal, 30,* 23–38.
22. Ibid., p. 27.

These first three sampling strategies—extreme or deviant case sampling, intensity sampling, and typical case sampling—complement one another. None is inherently superior to the others. Each serves important, but different purposes in qualitative research.

4. **Maximum variation sampling** involves selecting cases that illustrate the range of variation in the phenomena to be studied. For example, suppose a researcher wishes to study the experiences of different school districts that have received state-funded grants to develop innovative projects. In using a maximum variation sampling strategy, the researcher might select districts that vary widely in size, community setting (e.g., urban, rural), proximity to a university that has a college of education, and the type of project undertaken (e.g., curriculum development, staff development, services for a certain type of student). This strategy serves two purposes: to document the range of variation in the funded projects, and to determine whether common themes, patterns, and outcomes cut across this variation.

5. **Stratified purposeful sampling** is slightly different than maximum variation sampling. A stratified purposeful sample includes several cases at defined points of variation (e.g., average, above average, and below average) with respect to the phenomena being studied. By including several cases of each type, the researcher can develop insights into the characteristics of each type, as well as insights into the variations that exist across types. In contrast, a researcher who uses maximum variation sampling is likely to have one case of each type, which might be insufficient for drawing conclusions about that type.

6. **Homogeneous sampling** is the opposite strategy of maximum variation sampling. Its purpose is to select a sample of similar cases so that the particular group that the sample represents can be studied in depth. For example, suppose a researcher is interested in orientation programs for incoming high school students. In doing pilot work, the researcher discovers that many high schools have orientation programs for all students, but only some high schools have a special orientation program for at-risk students. In planning the main study, the researcher might decide to limit the sample of cases to orientation programs for at-risk students. These programs can be the focus of intensive data collection and study rather than being one aspect of a broader study of orientation programs in general.

7. **Critical case sampling** involves selecting a single case that provides a crucial test of a theory, program, or other phenomenon. For example, Galileo provided a critical—and convincing—test of his theory of gravity by demonstrating that a feather fell at the same rate as a coin when both were placed in a vacuum.

Theories in education tend not to yield such precise predictions as are found in the physical sciences, and therefore a critical case sampling strategy might have less applicability. However, this sampling strategy could prove useful in studying educational programs and related phenomena. For example, a researcher might wish to evaluate a program by selecting a site in which it would be very difficult for the program to succeed. If a study of this case yielded positive results, one would be justified in claiming a strong generalization of the form: "If this program works here, it should work anywhere."

8. **Snowball or chain sampling** involves asking well-situated people to recommend cases to study. As the process continues, the researcher might discover an increasing number of well-situated people and an increasing number of recommended cases, all or some of whom can be included in the sample. Also, the names of a few individuals might come up repeatedly in talking to different well-situated people. If this type of convergence occurs, these individuals would make a highly credible sample.

9. **Criterion sampling** involves the selection of cases that satisfy an important criterion. This strategy is particularly useful in studying educational programs. For example, suppose a researcher is planning to study a particular graduate program that prepares

educational administrators. Using a criterion sampling strategy, the researcher might select two types of cases to study: (1) recent graduates who took more than ten years to obtain their doctorates; and (2) recent graduates who received their doctorates in three years
or less. A study of cases that satisfied one or the other of these criteria most likely would
yield rich information about aspects of the program that work well or poorly.

10. **Theory-based or operational construct sampling** is used when the purpose of the
study is to gain understanding of real-world manifestations of theoretical constructs. To illustrate, we can consider Piaget's theory of intellectual development, which is widely used
to interpret educational phenomena. One of the constructs of the theory is the concrete
stage of development. A researcher might wish to develop further understanding of this
construct by studying how it is manifested in particular settings. To achieve this purpose,
the researcher would need to select a sample of children who are at this stage of development. Then she could do an intensive analysis of how they function intellectually in various situations of interest to her. In this example, then, the selection of cases is determined
by a particular theoretical construct.

11. **Confirming and disconfirming case sampling** is done to validate findings of previous research. The validation process can be carried out in two ways. The first approach
is to study cases that are likely to confirm patterns, themes, and meanings discovered in
previous case studies. If the new case or cases are confirmatory, the validity and generalizability of the patterns, themes, and meanings are strengthened. The second approach is
to look for cases that are good candidates for disconfirming previous research findings. If
the findings from these cases replicate previous findings of patterns, themes, and meanings, their validity and generalizability are greatly strengthened. However, if the findings
are, in fact, disconfirming, the researcher might develop new insights about the generalizability limits of previous findings.

One of the authors (M. Gall) has chaired the committee for several dissertations that
involved case studies of various types of educational change agents: staff development
specialists,[23] computer education specialists,[24] high school department chairpersons,[25]
teachers trained to promote mathematics education reform,[26] and teacher-leaders in
school restructuring efforts.[27] Following the first study (of staff development specialists),
each of the other three has provided additional confirmatory cases. All the effective change
agents possessed a combination of technical mastery and interpersonal skills (especially
listening skills and the ability to exert influence indirectly). All the less effective change
agents lacked one or both of these capabilities. What is needed now is a strong test of this
pattern of results by seeking a disconfirming case. For example, as we look back over these
dissertations, we see that all the change agents who served as cases worked within a primarily bottom-up model of educational change. A good disconfirming case, then, would
be a change agent working within a top-down model of educational change. If effective
change agents working within this model had both capabilities, the generalizability of the
previous findings would be greatly strengthened. If the effective change agents lacked one

23. Beaton, C. R. (1985). Identifying change agent strategies, skills, and outcomes: The case of district-based staff development specialists. *Dissertation Abstracts International, 47*(01), 65A. (UMI No. 8605828)
24. Strudler, N. B. (1987). The role of school-based computer coordinators as change agents in elementary school
programs. *Dissertation Abstracts International, 48*(11), 2853A. (UMI No. 8800554)
25. Henderson, I. M. (1993). The role of high school department heads as change agents in implementing a new social studies curriculum. *Dissertation Abstracts International, 54*(09), 3309A. (UMI No. 9405182)
26. Rossi, M. A. (1993). The California mathematics project: Empowering elementary teachers to be leaders and
change agents in mathematics reform. *Dissertation Abstracts International, 54*(09), 3314A. (UMI No. 9405218)
27. Fasold, Y. R. (1992). Case studies of teachers as leaders and change agents in school improvement and restructuring. *Dissertation Abstracts International, 54*(03), 794A. (UMI No. 9313288)

or both of these capabilities, the meaning and generalizability of the previous findings would need to be reconsidered.

12. **Purposeful random sampling** involves selecting a random sample using the methods of quantitative research. Nevertheless, the purpose of the random sample is not to represent a population, which would be its purpose in quantitative research. Rather, the purpose is to establish that the sampling procedure is not biased. For example, if a researcher is evaluating a program for which some constituencies are critical, the researcher can gain more credibility for his findings if he selects cases at random rather than looks for "success stories" to report.

13. **Sampling politically important cases** is a strategy that might serve a useful purpose for the researcher or funding agency. For example, if a researcher was interested in the educational methods used by cults, he might consider selecting as a case the Davidians (involved in the shoot-out in Waco, Texas in 1993), simply because that particular cult is so well known to a large group and the researcher's findings would be of widespread interest.

14. **Convenience sampling,** as we discussed earlier in the chapter, is the strategy of selecting cases simply because they are available and easy to study. This strategy should be avoided because it is not purposeful in the same sense that the other 13 sampling strategies described above are purposeful.

Opportunistic Sampling

Opportunistic sampling is described by Patton as a fifteenth approach to sampling. **Opportunistic sampling** involves the use of findings from one case to inform the researcher's selection of the next case for study. In fact, the findings may alter the research design to be used in studying the next case.

Opportunistic sampling is one of the most important strategies in selecting qualitative research samples. Although Patton lists opportunistic sampling as a separate type of purposeful sampling, the principle underlying it applies to many of the strategies described above. For example, if you were to use the extreme or deviant case sampling strategy, you might start with the study of one case that you consider extreme. As you develop an understanding of this case, it may give you ideas about what to look for in selecting another extreme case, or it may cause you to switch to a typical case sampling strategy. Opportunistic sampling allows you the flexibility to make these switches.

Consider a typical problem that use of opportunistic sampling early in a research study might help the researcher avoid. We know of instances in which researchers have selected a multiple-case sample at the outset of the study. They secure the cooperation of the sample and their informed consent letters, and thus feel obliged to study all of them in depth. Unfortunately, the researchers sometimes discover after analyzing data from the first few cases that they would learn more by studying other cases than those to whom they have become obligated. By then, however, they may lack the resources to select new cases because of their commitments to the initially selected cases.

Estimating a Desirable Number of Cases

In qualitative research, determining sample size is entirely a matter of judgment; there are no set rules. Patton suggests that selecting an appropriate sample size involves a trade-off between breadth and depth:

> With the same fixed resources and limited time, a researcher could study a specific set of experiences for a larger number of people (seeking breadth) or a more open range of experiences for a smaller number of people (seeking depth). In-depth information from a small number of people can be very valuable, especially if the cases are information-rich. Less depth from a

larger number of people can be especially helpful in exploring a phenomenon and trying to document diversity or understand variation.[28]

Patton suggests that the ideal sampling procedure is to keep selecting cases until one reaches the point of redundancy, that is, until no new information is forthcoming from new cases.

Another purpose for increasing the sample size in a qualitative study is suggested by Yin and Campbell.[29] He recommends selecting additional cases for the sample in order to provide replications. Each additional case that replicates the findings of the first case adds to the certainty of those findings.

Sample size obviously will be affected by the purposeful sampling strategy that you select in planning a qualitative study. If you are using a critical case strategy, a single, well-selected case might be sufficient; adding another one or two critical cases could serve as a replication of the first case. However, the decision to use a maximum variation strategy perhaps would require ten or more cases, even if the study was an initial exploration into the phenomena of interest.

Volunteers in Sampling

All research studies make demands on the individuals who are selected for the sample. For example, in planning an experiment, the researcher might select a random sample of teachers, but some of them might refuse to participate because they dislike the experimental intervention, do not wish to disrupt their normal schedule, or for some other reason. Some individuals may refuse to complete even a brief questionnaire because they are very busy or don't like following detailed directions. The remaining individuals no longer constitute a random sample because individuals who agree to participate are likely to be different from those who do not.

A similar problem can arise in planning a qualitative study. The researchers might select several individuals to participate because they constitute interesting cases of the phenomena they wish to investigate. However, one or more of the individuals might decline the offer to participate for a variety of reasons.

When individuals refuse to be members of a sample, there is very little that researchers can do to require their participation. As we explained in Chapter 3, ethical standards and human consent requirements protect individuals' rights in research, including the right to refuse participation in a study or to cease participation at any point during the study.

If some individuals recruited for a study decline to participate, the remaining individuals in the sample should be considered "volunteer" participants. For example, if you send a questionnaire to 200 educators and 130 complete and return it, the 70 who did not return it are nonvolunteers and the 130 who did return it are volunteers. If you recruit a sample by such means as word of mouth or posted notices, all members of the resulting sample should be considered volunteers.

Characteristics of Research Volunteers

✦ Touchstone in Research

Wainer, H. (2000). *Drawing inferences from self-selected samples.* Mahwah, NJ: Lawrence Erlbaum Associates.

Researchers have found that volunteer subjects are likely to be a biased sample of the target population. Robert Rosenthal and Ralph Rosnow reviewed this body of research to identify characteristics that have been found consistently to differentiate between volun-

28. Patton, *Qualitative evaluation*, p. 184.
29. Yin & Campbell. *Case study research.*

teer and nonvolunteer subjects.[30] Some of the characteristics are supported by more research evidence than others. Figure 6.1 lists the characteristics that Rosenthal and Rosnow believe are the best supported by research.

The degree to which the characteristics of volunteer samples are likely to affect the results of a research study depends on the specific nature of the study. Norman Bradburn and Seymour Sudman described as "really terrible sampling" those methods that depend entirely on respondents to volunteer in order to be included in the sample—for example, TV programs that ask viewers to telephone their yes or no vote on an issue that is proposed in a newspaper or on television.[31] They noted that the resulting requirement that all volunteers must make, and pay for, a telephone call creates substantial economic bias; that the responses generally come from individuals who are most committed to an issue; and that it becomes possible to "stuff the ballot box" by making multiple calls.

Volunteer Characteristics in Research Requiring Parental Consent

In Chapter 3, we explained that researchers cannot ask school-age students ("minors") for their informed consent to participate in a study. Instead, consent is needed from the child's

---

FIGURE 6.1

Characteristics of Research Volunteers

1. Volunteers tend to be better educated than nonvolunteers, especially when personal contact between investigator and respondent is not required.
2. Volunteers tend to have higher social-class status than nonvolunteers, especially when social class is defined by respondents' own status rather than by parental status.
3. Volunteers tend to be more intelligent than nonvolunteers when volunteering is for research in general, but not when volunteering is for somewhat less typical types of research, such as hypnosis, sensory isolation, sex research, small group research, or personality research.
4. Volunteers tend to be higher in need for social approval than nonvolunteers.
5. Volunteers tend to be more sociable than nonvolunteers.
6. Volunteers tend to be more arousal-seeking than nonvolunteers, especially when volunteering is for studies of stress, sensory isolation, and hypnosis.
7. Volunteers tend to be more unconventional than nonvolunteers, especially when volunteering is for studies of sex behavior.
8. Females are more likely than males to volunteer for research in general, but less likely than males to volunteer for physically and emotionally stressful research (e.g., electric shock, high temperature, sensory deprivation, interviews about sex behavior).
9. Volunteers tend to be less authoritarian than nonvolunteers.
10. Jews are more likely to volunteer than Protestants, and Protestants are more likely to volunteer than Roman Catholics.
11. Volunteers tend to be less conforming than nonvolunteers when volunteering is for research in general, but not when subjects are female and the task is relatively "clinical" (e.g., hypnosis, sleep, or counseling research).

Source: The information in this figure is based on research findings reported in: Rosenthal, R., & Rosnow, R. L. (1975). *The volunteer subject.* New York: Wiley.
Note: Rosenthal and Rosnow list 11 other characteristics of volunteer subjects that are less well supported by research findings (pages 195–196 of their book).

---

30. Rosenthal, R., & Rosnow, R. L. (1975). *The volunteer subject.* New York: Wiley.
31. Bradburn, N. M., & Sudman, S. (1988). *Polls & surveys: Understanding what they tell us.* San Francisco, CA: Jossey-Bass.

main caretaker, who typically is a parent. In other words, it is the parent or other caretaker who volunteers a child for a research study, not the child.

Researchers have conducted various studies to determine whether children having parental permission to participate in a research study differ from children not having parental permission. These studies have found that, in fact, the two groups differ from each other. In general, children having parental permission to participate in a research study are:

1. more academically competent.
2. more popular with their peers.
3. more physically attractive.
4. less likely to smoke cigarettes and marijuana.
5. more likely to be White.
6. more likely to come from two-parent households.
7. more likely to be involved in extracurricular activities.
8. less likely to be socially withdrawn.
9. less likely to be aggressive.[32]

These generalizations do not necessarily apply to all research studies requiring parental/caretaker consent. The particular age group of research participants and the nature of the research problem might affect whether children having parental consent have different characteristics from children not having parental consent. Nonetheless, these generalizations and those shown in Figure 6.1 are sufficiently compelling that they warrant checking volunteer characteristics in any study in which there is a significant number of non-volunteers in the selected sample.

Example of Checking Volunteer Characteristics

An example of this type of comparison can be found in a study by Kathleen Mittag and Bruce Thompson.[33] They conducted a national survey of members of the American Educational Research Association (AERA) about several issues involving the use of statistics in research. The target sample, sampling frame, and sampling method were described as follows:

> We drew a stratified random sample of roughly 4% of the AERA members listed in the membership directory. The sample was stratified by AERA divisions to insure representativeness across the 12 divisions. A total of 1,127 surveys were mailed.[34]

Of these 1,127 surveys, 246 were returned. Thus, there were 246 volunteers and 881 nonvolunteers. (Twenty-one of the 246 volunteers returned unusable surveys, yielding a final volunteer sample of 225 individuals.) Mittag and Thompson were able to compare the volunteers and the target population on two variables—postal location and division membership. They found that the volunteers and target population were very similar on these variables, thus providing some evidence that the volunteers were representative of the population.

Mittag and Thompson went a step further to consider whether the volunteers might differ from the target population on other relevant variables:

32. This list of generalizations was developed from literature reviews and findings reported in: Anderson, C., Cheadle, A., Curry, S., Diehr, P., Shultz, L., & Wagner, E. (1995). Selection bias related to parental consent in school-based survey research. *Evaluation Review, 19,* 663–674; Noll, R. B., Zeller, M. H., Vannatta, K., Bukowski, W. M., & Davies, W. H. (1997). Potential bias in classroom research: Comparison of children with permission and those who do not receive permission to participate. *Journal of Clinical Child Psychology, 26,* 36–42.

33. Mittag, K. C., & Thompson, B. (2000). A national survey of AERA members' perceptions of statistical significance tests and other statistical issues. *Educational Researcher, 29*(4), 14–20.

34. Ibid., p. 14.

... it is conceivable that AERA members who were the most comfortable with and interested in statistical issues may have been most likely to respond to the survey. If this was the case, the results portray a more favorable picture than might apply in the full population.

It must also be acknowledged that some AERA members do not use quantitative methods at all. These individuals may have been less likely to respond, as well.[35]

No data were available to compare the volunteers and nonvolunteers on these variables, but it is worthwhile for the researchers to bring them to the reader's attention. If other researchers become interested in the questions studied by Mittag and Thompson, they will be alert to issues concerning the volunteer rate and will make efforts to improve it and perhaps also to collect more data about volunteer– and nonvolunteer characteristics.

Improving the Rate of Volunteering

There are two typical situations in recruiting participants for a study. In one situation, you select a sample initially and then invite each member to participate. In the other situation, you write a description of the study and circulate or post this notice so that it is responded to by as many individuals as possible in the accessible population. In either situation, your goal is to design a recruitment process that minimizes the likelihood that only certain types of individuals will accept your invitation to participate in the study or respond to your notice.

In their research synthesis, Rosenthal and Rosnow identified eleven situational variables that tend to increase or decrease the rates of volunteering.[36] Their findings form the basis for the list of suggestions in Figure 6.2. These are suggestions for increasing the rate

---

FIGURE 6.2

Suggestions for Improving the Rate of Volunteering to Participate in a Research Study

1. Make the appeal for volunteers as interesting as possible to the group you are trying to enlist for the study.
2. Make the appeal for volunteers as nonthreatening as possible.
3. Make explicit the theoretical and practical importance of the study.
4. Make explicit how the group you are trying to enlist represents a target population that is particularly relevant to the study.
5. Emphasize that, by volunteering for the study, individuals have the potential to benefit others.
6. Offer to potential volunteers, %N hen possible, not only payment for participation, but small courtesy gifts simply for taking time to consider whether they want to participate.
7. Have the request for volunteering made by a person of high status.
8. Try to avoid research tasks that can be psychologically or biologically stressful.
9. Try to communicate the tact that volunteering is the normal thing to do.
10. In situations where volunteering is regarded by the target population as the normal thing to do, ask each individual to make a public commitment to volunteer. Where nonvolunteering is regarded as the normal thing to do, create a situation where each individual can volunteer in private.
11. After a target population has been defined, have someone known to that population make the appeal for volunteers.

Source: The information in this table is based on research findings reported in: Rosenthal, R., & Rosnow, R. L. (1975), *The volunteer subject.* New York: Wiley.

---

35. Ibid., p. 18.
36. Rosenthal and Rosnow, *The volunteer subject.*

of volunteering and thus reducing sampling bias in a research study. Studying these suggestions can help you design an effective recruitment process for your study, so that you minimize the likelihood of volunteer bias.

✦ RECOMMENDATIONS FOR
Selecting a Research Sample

1. In reporting a study, describe in detail the target and accessible populations, sampling procedures, sampling frame, and volunteer rate.
2. In quantitative research, select a random sample rather than a convenience sample whenever possible.
3. If a convenience sample is selected, describe its characteristics in sufficient detail to enable others to infer the population it represents.
4. In quantitative research, select a sample size that maximizes the likelihood of rejecting the null hypothesis at a satisfactory level of statistical power and that, if appropriate, allows for subgroup analysis and sample attrition.
5. In qualitative research, consider which of the various types of purposeful sampling is most appropriate for studying the phenomena of interest.
6. If any members of the selected sample choose not to volunteer, collect data to determine whether the volunteers are representative of the non-volunteers or the accessible/target population on relevant characteristics.
7. Use various procedures to maximize the volunteer rate for the selected sample.

✔ SELF-CHECK TEST

Circle the correct answer to each of the following questions.
The answers are provided at the back of the book.

1. Purposeful sampling involves
   a. selecting a sample that accurately represents a defined population.
   b. selecting as large a sample as possible within given cost constraints.
   c. selecting cases that are information-rich with respect to the study goals.
   d. all of the above.
2. All the members of a real or hypothetical set of persons, objects, or events to which researchers wish to generalize research results are called a(n)
   a. target population.
   b. random sample.
   c. accessible population.
   d. volunteer subject pool.

3. If the researcher draws a sample from a narrow accessible population, the research results will probably be
   a. unreliable.
   b. generalizable to a limited population.
   c. generalizable to a broad population.
   d. of no theoretical value.
4. A simple random sample is best defined as a group of individuals
   a. each of whom had an equal and independent chance of being selected.
   b. who accurately represent the target population rather than the accessible population.
   c. who accurately represent the accessible population rather than the target population.

d. who are selected by a process that provides every sample of a given size an equal probability of being selected.

5. The main advantage of random sampling is that the sample is more likely to
a. include the correct number of subjects.
b. agree to participate in the study.
c. yield generalizable research data.
d. yield statistically significant research findings.

6. Systematic sampling is most appropriate when
a. a large sample must be selected from a nonperiodic list.
b. a large sample must be selected from a periodic list.
c. the target population is heterogeneous.
d. the expected differences between the experimental and control groups are small.

7. Using inferential statistics with data collected from a convenience sample is justified if
a. the sample is carefully conceptualized to represent a particular population.
b. the researcher does not plan to generalize the findings of the study.
c. the sample size is sufficiently large.
d. the sample is composed of volunteers.

8. In cluster sampling the unit of sampling is
a. the individual subject.
b. the target population.
c. a naturally occurring group of individuals.
d. the proportion of subjects with extreme scores on the variable of interest.

9. Large samples should be used in quantitative research particularly when
a. attrition is expected to be minimal.
b. measures with low reliability are to be used.
c. no subgroup analysis is planned.
d. the population is highly homogeneous.

10. Selecting a single case that provides a crucial test of a phenomenon is an example of _____ sampling in qualitative research.
a. deviant-case
b. typical-case
c. critical-case
d. opportunistic

11. _____ sampling involves using the findings from the study of one case to inform the selection of the next case to be studied.
a. convenience
b. snowball
c. criterion
d. opportunistic

12. Compared to nonvolunteers, volunteers for research tend to be more
a. authoritarian.
b. conventional.
c. antisocial.
d. arousal-seeking.

13. To improve the rate of volunteering for a research study, it is desirable to
a. emphasize the researcher's need to obtain a sufficient sample size.
b. offer gifts for participation.
c. have a male make the request for volunteering.
d. explain in detail the risks that participation might entail.

✦ Collecting Research Data with Tests and Self-Report Measures

OVERVIEW

Administering tests and self-report measures is one of the main ways in which researchers collect data about individuals. These instruments can reveal information about aptitudes, academic achievement, and various aspects of personality. We start this chapter by describing the characteristics of a good test or self-report measure, stressing validity and reliability criteria. We then discuss the wide range of measures that are available and how to obtain information about them. Computer technology has had a major impact on testing, and so we include a section on developments in this field. In the last part of the chapter, we explain how to develop your own tests and self-report measures and how to effectively administer them in a research study.

OBJECTIVES

After studying this chapter, you should be able to

1. Explain five characteristics of a good test.
2. Explain what it means for a test to yield valid interpretations from test scores, and describe five approaches to determining how valid such interpretations are.
3. Explain what it means for a test to yield reliable scores, and describe four approaches to determining test score reliability.
4. Explain what information about test score reliability is provided by generalizability theory and the standard error of measurement.
5. Describe the advantages of item response theory over classical test theory.
6. Describe the advantages of standardized tests over locally constructed tests in research studies.

7. Compare the distinctive advantages of norm-referenced, criterion-referenced, and individual-referenced measures.
8. Describe how computer technology is changing the development and use of tests.
9. Compare the distinctive advantages of individually administered and group tests.
10. List five types of performance tests, and describe the primary characteristics of each type.
11. Describe procedures and criteria that have been proposed for determining the validity and reliability of performance assessment.
12. List seven types of personality measures, and describe the primary characteristics of each type.

13. Describe how the *Test Locator* and *Test Review Locator* can be used to find available tests and information about them.

14. Describe how to use the test manual, the test itself, and contact with the test developer to determine if a test is appropriate for your research purposes.

15. Describe the seven steps involved in developing a test for use in research.

16. Describe at least three actions you can take if you encounter public or professional resistance to the tests that you wish to administer for a research study.

17. Describe several procedures that you can follow to obtain an individual's maximal effort on a performance test or honest responses on a personality measure.

Measurement in Educational Research

The principles of measurement described in this chapter derive primarily from the quantitative tradition of educational research. In this tradition, researchers begin the process of measurement by defining the construct of interest to them, for example, mathematics achievement. They define the construct operationally, that is, by specifying the activities used to measure it. Thus, mathematics achievement might be defined as the performance of individuals on a particular set of test items under specified conditions of administration. The testing situation is designed so that each individual's performance can be assigned a numerical score, such as a score of 0 to 50 on a 50-item test.

In contrast, qualitative researchers typically do not place individuals in structured performance situations, preferring instead to study them in naturally occurring situations. Of course, qualitative researchers might formulate problems for which data collection in both types of situation would be desirable. In this situation, tests would complement nicely the primary methods of data collection in qualitative research, namely, observation and interviewing (described in Chapters 8 and 9).

The focus of this chapter is how to measure an individual's behavior by administering a test. A **test** is any structured performance situation that can be analyzed to yield numerical scores, from which inferences can be made about how individuals differ in the performance construct measured by the test. Examples of performance constructs are academic achievement in computer studies, verbal ability, and musical intelligence.

A **self-report measure** is a paper-and-pencil instrument whose items yield numerical scores from which inferences can be made about how individuals differ on various aspects of self, such as personality traits, self-concept, learning styles, attitudes, values, and interests. Unlike tests, these measures do not require individuals to "perform." Instead, self-report measures generally ask individuals to reveal whether they have the traits, thoughts, or feelings mentioned in the items. Despite this difference, self-report measures and tests are very similar in construction and administration. Therefore, although we frequently use the term *test* when explaining various measurement concepts and practices, the explanation applies as well to self-report measures unless otherwise indicated.

In conducting a review of the literature, you will read about researchers' use of various tests and self-report measures. Therefore, you need to understand these instruments and to make judgments about their soundness. This chapter provides the basic knowledge that you will need for these purposes. This knowledge also will help you select or develop tests for your own study. In fact, some research studies focus entirely on test development or on investigating the soundness of already developed tests. If this is your purpose, the

✦ Touchstone in Research

Hambleton, R. K. (1996). Advances in assessment models, methods, and practices. In D. C. Berliner & R. C. Calfee (Eds.), *Handbook of educational psychology* (pp. 899–925). New York: Macmillan.

Linn, R. L. (Ed.). (1989). *Educational measurement* (3rd ed.). New York: Macmillan.

Masters, G. N. & Keeves, J. P. (Eds.). (1999). *Advances in measurement in educational research and assessment.* Oxford: Pergamon.

chapter will help you learn the fundamentals of measurement and testing, but you will need to obtain more extensive training in these fields.

Both practitioners and researchers rely heavily on tests and testing. For this reason, there is more collaboration between them in this area than in many other aspects of education. Practitioners need to continually improve their tests to serve the best interests of students and various stakeholder groups. They often turn to researchers specializing in measurement to help them. Conversely, researchers need to use tests in their studies that will be judged by practitioners to be relevant and sound. Therefore, they must stay abreast of current trends in testing practice. In this chapter, you will find references not only to measurement research and theory, but also to testing practices in schools.

Characteristics of a Good Test

Criteria for Judging the Quality of Tests

Five criteria are commonly used to judge whether a test is of sufficient quality to use in educational research. Each is explained below.

1. *Objectivity.* The **objectivity** of a test refers to whether its scores are undistorted by biases of the individuals who administer and score it. In fact, the development of a scientific discipline can be traced by the progress it has made in recognizing the possibility of personal errors in measurement and in ruling them out to an ever greater extent.

Certain tests, such as the Rorschach Inkblot Test, have low objectivity because the conditions of administration and scoring are flexible. Tester bias can occur easily under these conditions. In contrast, multiple-choice tests generally are much more objective, because they are mostly self-administered and all scorers can apply a scoring key and agree perfectly. For this reason, multiple-choice tests often are called *objective tests.*

2. *Standard conditions of administration and scoring.* As we suggested above, it is desirable for a test to have standard conditions of administration and scoring because these conditions increase its objectivity. Therefore, a well-developed test will include a manual that specifies the procedures that should be followed for any situation that might affect an individual's test performance. For example, the developers will specify how much time to allow for individuals to complete the test, whether instructions can be repeated, how to answer test-takers' questions, and how much personal interaction is permitted between the tester and test-takers. The developers also will specify scoring procedures, including those for special circumstances, such as when an individual marks two choices on a multiple-choice item.

A test that has procedures to ensure consistency in administration and scoring across all testing situations is called a **standardized test.** An important advantage of standardized tests is that they minimize measurement errors due to variations in administering and scoring them. Another advantage is that if you obtain significant findings in your research study, other researchers will be able to replicate and expand on them because they can create the same conditions of administration and scoring by consulting the test manual.

3. *Standards for Interpretation.* Objective test scores are not inherently interpretable. They are typically interpreted relative to something external to the test: either a criterion or a set of norms. For example, in criterion-referenced interpretation, scores are interpreted relative to some absolute performance standard, whereas in norm-referenced interpretation, scores are interpreted relative to the performance of other individuals in a defined group. Standards for interpretation are explained in more detail later in the chapter.

4. *Fairness.* If a test is fair, two groups of equal ability with respect to the construct measured by the test (e.g., reading comprehension) should earn the same score on each

item of the test. If the test is not fair, it is said to suffer from **differential item functioning,** which means that individuals of equal ability but from different subgroups (e.g., males and females) do not have the same probability of earning the same score on one or more of the test items. Various procedures have been developed to detect and eliminate unfair test items as part of the process of test construction.[1]

5 and 6. *Validity and reliability.* Good tests yield reliable test scores from which we can make interpretations that have strong validity. Because of the complexity of these test characteristics, they are discussed at length in the following two sections.

Test Validity

The 1999 *Standards for Educational and Psychological Testing* (hereafter referred to as the *Standards*) is an authoritative reference work on test validity and other test matters.[2] (Previous editions appeared in 1966, 1974, and 1985.) It was written by the Joint Committee on Educational and Psychological Tests, made up of representatives of the American Psychological Association, the American Educational Research Association, and the National Council on Measurement in Education. The *Standards* defines **validity** as the "degree to which evidence and theory support the interpretation of test scores entailed by proposed uses of tests."[3] This definition highlights the fact that test scores are neither valid nor invalid. It is our *interpretations* of the scores that are either valid or invalid. For example, if we administer a history achievement test to a group of students, each student earns a score on the test. We then might *interpret* this score as representing how much each student has learned about history relative to other students. It is helpful to think about this interpretation as a "claim" that we make about the test scores.

What evidence can we provide to support our interpretation of the scores yielded by administering a test? The *Standards* recognizes five main types of evidence for demonstrating the validity of test-score interpretations. Each type is described in the following sections. Keep in mind, though, that these are not five types of validity. Validity is unitary in nature, but there are different ways to gather evidence about it. Another important point is that the new edition of the *Standards* uses different terms than the traditional nomenclature found in older research reports and books about measurement. The new terms emphasize the unitary nature of test validity and the fact that different kinds of empirical evidence can be synthesized to strengthen the case for the validity of a particular test.

Evidence from Test Content

Interpretations of test scores often refer to the relationship between a test's content and the construct that it claims to measure. As explained in Chapter 1, the term *construct* has a particular meaning in research: It is a concept that is inferred from commonalities among observed phenomena. For example, if a teacher gives her students a Spanish test, she is likely to claim that the test items represent the content that students were exposed to in the assigned textbook, supplementary curriculum materials, and the teacher's presentations in class.

Content-related evidence of test validity should not be confused with **face validity,** which involves only a casual, subjective inspection of the test items to judge whether they cover the content that the test purports to measure.[4] Content-related evidence typically is

✦ *Touchstone in Research*

Sandoval, J., Frisby, C. L., Geisinger, K. F., Ramos-Grenier, J., & Scheuneman, J. D. (1998). *Test interpretation and diversity: Achieving equity in assessment.* Washington, DC: American Psychological Association.

Messick, S., Braun, H. I., & Wiley, D. E. (2001). *Under construction: The role of constructs in psychological and educational measurement.* Mahwah, NJ: Lawrence Erlbaum Associates.

✦ *Touchstone in Research*

La Marca, P. M. (2001). Alignment of standards and assessments as an accountability criterion. *Practical Assessment, Research, and Evaluation, 7*(21). Retrieved October 22, 2001 from www.ericae.net/pare/g etvn.asp?v=7&n=21

1. Camilli, G., & Shepard, L. A. (1994). *Methods for identifying biased test items.* Thousand Oaks, CA: Sage; see also Chapters 3 and 7 of the 1999 *Standards for Educational and Psychological Testing* (described later in the chapter).
2. American Educational Research Association, American Psychological Association, and National Council on Measurement in Education (1999). *Standards for educational and psychological testing.* Washington, DC: American Educational Research Association.
3. Ibid., p. 9.
4. Nevo, B. (1985). Face validity revisited. *Journal of Educational Measurement, 22,* 287–293.

determined systematically by content experts, who define in precise terms the universe (also called *domain*) of specific content that the test is assumed to represent, and then determine how well that content universe is sampled by the test items. A test does not need to cover all the content in a given course of study for students' scores to be content-valid, but it must cover a representative sample of the content domain.

The importance of checking content-related validity evidence is illustrated by a study that compared the content of the four most popular mathematics textbooks with the four most commonly used standardized mathematics achievement tests.[5] The analysis showed an overlap of only 21 to 50 percent between textbook content and test content. This means that in the worst case, students had an opportunity to study only 21 percent of what was tested. With content-related validity this weak, this achievement test provides a highly inaccurate picture of what students learned in their mathematics course (assuming the teacher taught from the textbook).

Standards-based instruction is an important recent movement in education. This type of instruction requires alignment between curriculum content (typically determined by state-mandated standards), teachers' instruction, and assessment by standardized tests. Research by Gerald Tindal and Victor Nolet has found that this type of alignment is problematic for teachers.[6] Depending on the teacher, concepts that are included in the curriculum might, or might not, be included in instruction or on tests. Most troubling is the situation in which key concepts are tested, but are not taught well or not represented adequately in curriculum materials. These findings suggest that researchers are not likely to find good evidence to support the validity of their test-score interpretations if they use test data collected in actual school settings.

Content-related validity evidence is particularly important in selecting tests to use in experiments involving the effect of instructional methods on achievement. For example, suppose that you are conducting research to determine whether the constructivist method of teaching social studies is superior to a traditional teaching method. To enable a proper comparison, the achievement test administered at the end of instruction should be representative of the content covered during instruction. If the hypothesis states that the constructivist approach will lead to superior learning but the specific content taught by the teacher was not measured by the achievement test, the findings cannot be used either to confirm or reject the research hypothesis.

In many experiments, the treatment conditions being compared have different learning objectives. Therefore, it is advisable to select tests that yield content-valid interpretations for each treatment condition but to administer all the tests to the subjects in all the treatment conditions. We would expect research participants to do best on the test that has the best content-related evidence for their treatment condition, but if one of the treatment conditions is especially effective, the participants in that condition might do well on the less content-valid tests, too.

Evidence from Response Processes

Anyone who has taken or scored a test knows that the task engages particular cognitive and evaluative processes. These processes might, or might not, be relevant to the construct that the test purportedly measures. Therefore, the validity of test-score interpretations can

5. Porter, A. (1985, April) *Content determinants research: An overview.* Paper presented at the annual meeting of the American Educational Research Association, San Francisco. (ERIC Document Reproduction Service No. ED 274 510).
6. Tindal, G., & Nolet, V. (1996). Serving students in middle school content classes: A heuristic study of critical variables linking instruction and assessment. *Journal of Special Education, 29,* 414–432.

be supported by evidence that the processes actually engaged by the test are consistent with a particular construct, or constructs.

For example, suppose that judges are asked to rate students' history essays on various scales, such as clarity of writing style and use of evidence to support conclusions. Further suppose that several of the judges assign higher ratings on the scales if the essay exhibits creativity, which they happen to value. If creativity is irrelevant to the scales, this process of looking for, enjoying, and valuing signs of creativity in students' writing compromises the validity of the test-score interpretations.

As another example, consider a test that purportedly requires students to use higher-order reasoning processes to solve certain types of problems. If students have received extensive instruction on these problem types and can solve them by applying algorithms rather than by reasoning, the validity of the test-score interpretations is compromised.

One procedure for collecting validity evidence related to response processes is to simply ask test-takers or judges to reflect aloud on the cognitive and evaluative processes they used during the task. The reflections can be recorded and then analyzed to determine their consistency with the construct measured by the test. The *Standards* describes additional procedures for collecting response-process evidence.

Evidence from Internal Structure

Nearly all tests have multiple items. Analysis of the relationship of these items to each other can provide evidence about the validity of test-score interpretations. For example, suppose a test is designed to measure one construct. If this is indeed the case, a correlational analysis (see Chapter 11) should demonstrate that an individual who answered a certain item a certain way (e.g., correctly) is more likely to answer other items the same way than an individual who answered it differently.

Some tests are designed to measure multiple constructs (e.g., visual, spatial, verbal, and motor aptitudes) and provide a separate score for each one. Several kinds of correlational analysis, including factor analysis (see Chapter 11), can be done to develop evidence to support the validity of interpretations based on individuals' scores on the various subtests that presumably measure the different aptitudes.

Other analytic procedures based on the internal structure of a test are described in the *Standards*.

Evidence from Relationship to Other Variables

Researchers often explore the validity of a test by hypothesizing how a sample will perform on it in relation to measures of other variables. They then collect and analyze relevant data. If the data analysis supports the hypothesis, the researchers can use it as evidence of the test's validity.

One of the most common validity tests of this type is research on how well the test predicts a sample's scores on a predictive criterion. An example of this kind of research was carried out by Marvin Simner.[7] He developed an abbreviated version of the Printing Performance School Readiness Test (APPSRT), which is intended to identify at-risk or failure-prone children at the start of prekindergarten. He then sought to determine whether the shorter measure yielded predictions with sufficient predictive value that it could be used in place of the longer, original measure. Two samples of 171 children were tested early in prekindergarten and followed for three years. Scores on the APPSRT were

7. Simner, M. (1989). Predictive validity of an abbreviated version of the Printing Performance School Readiness Test. *Journal of School Psychology, 27*, 189–195.

then correlated with later measures of achievement: (1) students' grades in reading and arithmetic in first grade, and (2) their raw scores on two standardized achievement tests at the end of first grade. The scores on the APPSRT correlated between $-.42$ and $-.58$ with grades, and between $-.40$ and $-.60$ with achievement test scores. By using a cutoff score on the APPSRT, Simner was able to correctly identify 70 to 78 percent of the children who were later judged by their teachers as displaying poor performance, whereas the original, longer test (PPSRT) had correctly identified 81 percent of such children. Thus, he demonstrated that there was sufficient evidence of the predictive value of the APPSRT to support its use in place of the longer test.

Procedures for doing research on the predictive value of test score interpretations are described in Chapter 11.

The *Standards* describes several other types of test-criterion evidence that can be collected to support claims for the validity of test-score interpretations:

1. Evidence that a sample's test scores correlate positively with their scores on other measures that are hypothesized to measure the same construct. Evidence of this type is called **convergent evidence.**
2. Evidence that a sample's test scores correlate negatively with their scores on other measures that are hypothesized to measure a different construct. Evidence of this type is called **discriminant evidence.**
3. Evidence that scores on the test are distributed differently for two or more groups that are hypothesized to be different on the construct presumably measured by the test.
4. Evidence that a sample's test scores correlate positively with their scores on a measure of a criterion variable administered at approximately the same time. Evidence of this type is called **concurrent evidence,** which comprises statistical results indicating how accurately test scores can predict criterion scores obtained at approximately the same point in time. Conversely, **predictive evidence** comprises statistical results indicating how accurately test scores can predict criterion scores obtained at a later point in time. (The results of Simner's study, described above, yielded predictive evidence for the APPSRT.)

No matter how well a validity study of a test is done, it only yields evidence for the sample of individuals who took it. This evidence might, or might not, apply to samples that represent other populations or to other measures of the criterion variable. Also, it is possible that educational practice might change sufficiently over time that the evidence becomes dated. Therefore, the *Standards* recommends ongoing validity studies to check the generalizability of existing evidence used to support validity claims.

Evidence from Consequences of Testing

The four types of evidence to support validity claims that we described above focus on the meaning of test scores, for example, the meaning of the construct that underlies the scores yielded by a particular test. However, Samuel Messick has observed that there is more to test scores than their meaning.[8] He uses the term **consequential validity** to refer to the fact that test scores, the theory and beliefs behind the construct, and the language used to label the construct also embody certain values and have value-laden consequences when used to make decisions about individuals. These values and consequences need to be checked to determine whether our interpretations of test scores and the way we use these scores to make decisions are valid for particular uses.

8. Messick, S. (1989). Validity. In R. L. Linn (Ed.), *Educational measurement* (3rd ed., pp. 13–103). New York: Macmillan.

A moment's reflection will reveal that the constructs measured by tests of intelligence, academic achievement, and personality are value-laden. The most obvious example is intelligence tests. Intelligence is not a neutral construct; it is valued by our society. The most commonly used tests of intelligence measure the kinds of ability required to do well in school, and therefore these tests imply that school performance is important. Other intelligence tests emphasize other abilities, such as creative talent, which is highly valued by some members of society but not others. The constructs measured by personality self-report instruments are equally value-laden. For example, there are measures of dominance, sociability, independence, depression, and anxiety, each of which has different value connotations for different members of society.

Just as the constructs measured by test scores are value-laden, so too are the social consequences of test score use. Test scores may be used appropriately or inappropriately, and they may have both intended and unintended consequences. Ability tests, for example, have the desirable and intended effect of identifying and advancing the academic careers of gifted students without regard to their social class or geographical location. However, ability tests also have had the unintended effect of creating large differences in the percentage of whites who are promoted in certain work environments (e.g., police departments) compared with African Americans and Latinos.

The *Standards* emphasizes that social policies involving the use of tests and test validity are separate matters: "Although information about the consequences of testing may influence decisions about test use, such consequences do not in and of themselves detract from the validity of intended interpretations."[9] The distinction is important, because it implies, among other things, that one should not reject a test solely because of instances of misuse. For example, intelligence tests might be used to make judgments and decisions that are harmful to certain groups. However, scores from such tests might well be valid and useful for other purposes. Therefore, we need to consider carefully both test validity and test consequences in making use of tests in educational practice and research.

Test Reliability

Suppose that we administer the same essay test to a student on two occasions, and the student earns a slightly different score the second time. Which is the student's true score? Or suppose that one of the student's essays is scored by five different raters. Three of the raters assign the same score, whereas the fourth rater assigns a somewhat higher score and the fifth rater assigns a somewhat lower score. Which is the student's true score?

In classical test theory, this question is answered by making several assumptions. One assumption is that each subject indeed has a **true score** on the test, which is her actual amount of the characteristic (e.g., ability, attitude, personality trait) measured by the test. The second assumption is that any test of this characteristic is likely to have a certain amount of measurement error. The third assumption is that these errors of measurement are random. This means, for example, that if 100 raters scored the essay test mentioned above, their errors in scoring the test would be randomly distributed. Thus, some raters might assign higher scores to particular subjects, but they would be counterbalanced by raters who would assign lower scores to those subjects.

It follows from this analysis that any score obtained by administering a test will contain a true score component and an error score component. If the student's essay test was scored by 100 raters, the mean of those 100 scores would be her estimated true score. The standard deviation of the scores would provide an estimate of how much measurement error is present in the test. If the standard deviation was 0, it would mean that the person

9. *Standards*, p. 16.

earned the same score on all 100 administrations. Thus, we could conclude that the test has no measurement error. However, suppose that the standard deviation was 5.0 and the mean score was 7.5. This is a large standard deviation relative to the mean score, and thus we would conclude that the test has considerable measurement error.

In classical test theory, the **reliability** of a test refers to how much measurement error is present in the scores yielded by the test. (Note in this definition that reliability is a property of a test's scores, not of the test itself.) We can define **measurement error** as the difference between an individual's true score on a test and the scores that she actually obtains on it over a variety of conditions. Both true score and measurement error are hypothetical constructs, meaning that we can estimate them by various procedures (described below), but we cannot measure them directly.

Each of the procedures for estimating true scores and measurement errors involves the computation of a reliability coefficient. Reliability coefficients vary between values of .00 and 1.00, with 1.00 indicating perfect reliability of the test scores (never attained in practice) and .00 indicating no reliability. In general, tests that yield scores with a reliability of .80 or higher are sufficiently reliable for most research purposes. Tests and self-report measures that are standardized can achieve reliabilities of .90 or better.

Although reliability is essential to validity, this does not mean that test scores with good reliability always yield valid score inferences. To understand this point, imagine that we have an instrument that uses strange scale units. It might yield highly consistent (i.e., reliable) measurements, but we would have no idea what these measurements mean. In other words, we are unable to draw valid inferences from the scores, reliable as they may be.

Reliability must be carefully considered in selecting tests for use in research. It always is desirable to have high test score reliability. In fact, you cannot make valid inferences from test scores if the scores have zero reliability. The reason should be obvious: Scores with zero reliability are all measurement error, and so there is no true score component. It is as if the individuals who took the test were assigned scores at random.

The minimum necessary level of test score reliability depends on the particular research study. For example, if you are planning to do an experiment with a small sample and you expect only a small mean score difference between the experimental and control groups on a particular variable, you will need to use a test that yields highly reliable scores. Conversely, if you are planning to do an experiment with a large sample and expect the mean scores of the experimental and control groups to differ substantially, even a test with scores of low reliability may be sufficient to detect the difference at the specified level of statistical significance.

Many tests yield subscores in addition to a total score. For example, an achievement test might yield a total score and subscores for reading, writing, and mathematics. However, reliability often is reported only for the total score. In such cases, the subscores must be used cautiously because they generally have lower reliability than the total test score.

We can take our analysis of reliability a step further by considering the factors that might cause measurement error. These factors include the following:

1. A test's items are only a sample of the total domain of possible items that might be used to represent the ability, trait, attitude, or other construct being measured. Measurement error can result if different items on the test are not equivalent in how they sample the construct domain.
2. Test administrators may introduce measurement error by failing to administer the test consistently.
3. Test scorers may create measurement errors by not following consistent scoring procedures.

4. Testing conditions, such as a noisy or excessively warm room, may cause individuals to perform atypically on the test.
5. Variability in how individuals feel (e.g., being sick on test day) may cause atypical performance.

Classical test theory assumes that these measurement errors in obtained test scores are randomly distributed and unspecifiable. Measurement experts have developed different approaches to estimating test score reliability under these assumptions. We discuss each of these approaches below.

Alternate-Form Reliability

Alternate-form reliability is an approach to estimating test score reliability in which the particular *form* of the test that is administered is examined. Suppose, for example, that two researchers each develop their own test, but with the intent of measuring the same construct. Each test has the same number of items, but they differ in content and style. In this case, there will be measurement errors in estimating individuals' true scores on the construct that the tests are designed to measure.

These errors can be estimated by determining alternate-form reliability. This is done by computing the correlation coefficient, called the **coefficient of equivalence,** between individuals' scores on two parallel forms of the same test. The two forms might be administered at a single sitting, or a prespecified interval might occur between the two administrations.

Alternate-form reliability is not commonly determined because of the time and expense involved in constructing alternate forms of a test. The other types of reliability described below require only one test form.

Test-Retest Reliability

Test-retest reliability is an approach to estimating test score reliability in which the occasion of test administration is examined. To determine test-retest reliability, you would calculate a correlation coefficient, called the **coefficient of stability,** between individuals' scores on the same measure on two different testing occasions. This is the most commonly determined type of reliability for tests for which alternate forms are not available.

The most critical issue in calculating test-retest reliability is to determine an appropriate delay between the two administrations of the test. If the second administration occurs too soon after the first, people will be able to remember their responses to many of the items, and the coefficient of stability will tend to be artificially high. On the other hand, if the second administration is delayed too long, people may go through an actual change in magnitude of the variable measured by the test. In this case, measurement error arising from occasion of test administration will be contaminated with true score changes, making it difficult to interpret the meaning of the obtained coefficient of stability.

Internal Consistency

Internal consistency is an approach to estimating test score reliability in which the individual items of the test are examined. Several methods can be used to estimate a test's internal consistency. Each of them involves an analysis of scores from a sample of individuals on one administration of the test.

One method of estimating internal consistency involves calculating a split-half correlation coefficient, called the **coefficient of internal consistency.** To calculate this coefficient, the developer administers the test to an appropriate sample. The test then is split into two subtests, usually by placing all odd-numbered items in one subtest and all even-numbered items in another subtest.

The coefficient of internal consistency represents the reliability of only half the test. Reliability tends to be lower as a test decreases in length. Therefore, the *Spearman-Brown prophecy formula* is used to make a correction to the reliability coefficient in order to obtain the reliability of the scores when the entire test is administered.

The **method of rational equivalence** is another method for estimating a test's internal consistency. The individual items are analyzed by one of several available formulas. Among the most common are the **Kuder-Richardson formulas,** after the authors of an article in which these formulas were first discussed.[10] The formulas in the article are numbered, and the two that are most widely used are **K-R 20** and **K-R 21.** Formula K-R 21 is a simplified, easily calculated approximation of formula K-R 20. Items must be scored dichotomously (e.g., correct vs. incorrect, or yes vs. no) in order to use either K-R 20 or K-R 21. The Kuder-Richardson formulas usually yield lower reliability coefficients than those that would be obtained by the other methods of calculating reliability.

Cronbach's coefficient alpha (α) is a general form of the K-R 20 formula that can be used when items on a measure are not scored dichotomously. For example, some multiple-choice tests and essay tests include items that have several possible answers, each of which is given a different weight. Cronbach's alpha is a widely used method for computing test score reliability.

Inter-Tester Reliability

To obtain test scores, someone needs to administer the test and someone needs to score it. Both types of tester (i.e., the test administrator and the test scorer) can introduce measurement error into the test scores if they fail to follow the prescribed procedures exactly. The magnitude of test administration errors can be assessed by having several testers administer the test to a sample of individuals and then correlating their obtained scores with each other. Test scoring procedures can be assessed by a similar procedure.

Test administration errors are most likely if the testers have not been well trained or if the test is individually administered and requires interaction between the tester and examinee. Test scoring errors are most likely if the test items cannot be scored by a scoring key, but instead require judgment. Even with a scoring key, though, measurement errors can result if the person using the scoring key is careless. Machines that score tests can cause measurement errors, too, if they are calibrated inaccurately or if students have made pencil marks that the machine cannot detect.

Generalizability Theory

The different approaches to estimating a reliability coefficient that we described above do not isolate sources of systematic measurement error in test scores. Generalizability theory addresses this limitation.[11] **Generalizability theory** provides a way of conceptualizing and assessing the relative contribution of different sources of measurement error to the scores that you obtain from a sample of individuals. Using generalizability theory, a researcher can design a study that systematically investigates several sources of measurement error (e.g., variations in items and variations in raters). Analysis of variance is used to analyze the data in order to assess the effect of each measurement error source and their interactions. (Analysis of variance is explained in Chapters 5 and 10.) Also, the researcher can calculate

10. Richardson, M. W., & Kuder, G. F. (1939). The calculation of test reliability coefficients based upon the method of rational equivalence. *Journal of Educational Psychology, 30,* 681–687.
11. Shavelson, R. J., & Webb, N. M. (1991). *Generalizability theory: A primer.* Thousand Oaks, CA: Sage.

a **generalizability coefficient,** which is analogous to a reliability coefficient, but reflects the combined measurement error due to all the sources that have been investigated.

Noreen Webb and her colleagues described a hypothetical study involving two sources of measurement error—items and occasions.[12] They explained how to calculate variance, error variance, and generalizability coefficients for making either relative decisions (e.g., rank ordering of individuals) or absolute decisions (e.g. pass-fail judgments) based on individuals' scores on a five-item vocational interest test. By calculating variance components and generalizability coefficients for different hypothetical study designs, Webb and her colleagues demonstrated how researchers can plan ahead to maximize the generalizability coefficient obtained in a research study by increasing the number of items or the number of measurement occasions. In their hypothetical study, adding items to the test was shown to increase reliability more than would administering the test on two occasions, and also, would be less expensive.

Generalizability theory is not yet in common use, and, therefore, you are more likely to find reliability coefficients than generalizability coefficients for tests in print. Reliability coefficients should be sufficient for making a decision to select a particular test if you keep in mind that they do not isolate different sources of systematic measurement error.

Standard Error of Measurement

In both classical test theory and generalizability theory, an individual's obtained score on a test can be viewed as the combined result of his true score and measurement error. The **standard error of measurement** (also called the *standard error of the obtained score*) allows you to determine the probable range within which the individual's true score falls. For example, suppose the test manual for an algebra test reports that the alternate-form reliability coefficient (r_{11}) for a norm group of 300 ninth-grade students is .85, and the standard deviation of the test scores (s) is 14. The standard error of measurement (s_m) can be computed by the following formula:

$$s_m = s\sqrt{1 - r_{11}}$$

Substituting the given values into this equation we have

$$s_m = 14\sqrt{1 - .85}$$
$$= 14\sqrt{.15}$$
$$= 14 \times .387 = 5.42$$

Because s_m is normally distributed, we can estimate the probability that an error of a given size will occur. Given the properties of the normal distribution curve (see Chapter 5), we can assume that about two-thirds of all test scores will be within $\pm 1\ s_m$ (plus or minus one standard error of measurement) of the individuals' true scores, and about 95 percent will be within $\pm 2\ s_m$ (plus or minus two standard errors of measurement) of their true scores. Thus, in the above example, if a student obtained a score of 86 on the algebra aptitude test, the chances are about 2 in 3 that this student's true score is between 80.58 and 91.42 (i.e., 86 ± 5.42); the chances are about 95 in 100 that the student's true score lies between 75.16 and 96.84 (i.e., $86 \pm 2 \times 5.42$, or 86 ± 10.84).

---

12. Webb, N. M., Rowley, G. L., & Shavelson, R. J. (1988). Methods, plainly speaking: Using generalizability theory in counseling and development. *Measurement and Evaluation in Counseling and Development, 21,* 81–90.

It is clear from the formula that the size of s_m is inversely related to the level of the reliability coefficient. That is, as the reliability coefficient increases, the standard error of measurement becomes smaller. If the algebra test has a reliability of .96, the s_m would be 2.80; however, if the reliability is .57, the s_m would be 9.18. Thus, you can see that a low reliability coefficient for a test indicates large measurement errors in the obtained scores.

The standard error of measurement helps us to understand that the scores obtained on educational measures are only estimates and may be considerably different from individuals' presumed true scores. Therefore, we should avoid taking a test score at face value or overinterpreting the meaning of small differences between mean test scores. For example, there might be no true difference in intelligence between two students whose obtained scores are 97 and 102 on an IQ test with a large standard error of measurement. On another administration of the test the two students' scores might well be reversed.

✦ *Touchstone in Research*

Embretson, S. E., & Reise, S. P. (2000). *Item response theory for psychologists.* Mahwah, NJ: Lawrence Erlbaum Associates.

Van der Linden, W. J., & Hambleton, R. K. (Eds.). (1996). *Handbook of modern item response theory.* New York: Springer.

Item Response Theory

As we have explained, classical test theory is based on the assumption that performance on a test reflects both the individual's true score on the ability, or other characteristic, measured by the test and measurement error randomly distributed around the true scores. Developers attempt to construct a test that is highly reliable (i.e., free of measurement error) and that is not too easy nor too difficult for the individuals being assessed.

A great many tests used in education have been developed within the framework provided by classical test theory. They are good tests but susceptible to the following problems:

1. The reliability estimates for the test and various item statistics (e.g., indices of item difficulty) depend on the sample from which they are derived. Thus, if a researcher or a practitioner uses the test with a sample that represents a different population from the one used in the test's development, its reliability and item characteristics might be different.
2. A test might be too easy or too difficult for some individuals. Under these conditions, the test will provide a poor estimate of their true score on the ability being measured.
3. Classical test theory assumes that the amount of measurement error is the same for all individuals taking the test. In reality, a particular test might have greater reliability (i.e., have less measurement error) for individuals at one level of the ability measured by the test than for individuals at another level of the ability.
4. According to classical test theory, the amount of measurement error in test items (as opposed to measurement error attributable to testing conditions, test scoring, and test takers) is determined by correlating test-takers' performance on an alternate, parallel form of the test. In practice, it is difficult to develop a strictly parallel form of a test, so this reliability check might not be done.

Assumptions of Item Response Theory

The previously stated shortcomings of test construction based on classical test theory are avoided by constructing tests using item response theory. For this reason, its influence on educational practice and research is increasing.

Item response theory (IRT) is an approach to test construction based on the assumptions that

1. an individual's performance on a test item reflects a single ability,
2. individuals with different amounts of that ability will perform differently on the item, and

3. the relationship between the variables of ability and item performance can be represented by a mathematical function.

To describe IRT in simple terms, let us suppose that the ability being measured is reading ability. We will suppose further that there are five students (I, II, III, IV, and V), each with a successively greater amount of this ability. Thus, student V has more reading ability than any other student, student IV has more reading ability than student III, and so on.

Now suppose we administer a reading test item (A) that is very easy. All five students answer it correctly. This item tells us, then, that all the students have some minimal level of reading ability. We next administer another item (B) that students III, IV, and V can answer, but students I and II cannot. This item is more difficult, and it serves to differentiate the reading ability of students III, IV, and V from students I and II. We next administer an item (C) that only student V can answer. We now know that this item reflects a higher level of reading ability than the other two items, and it differentiates the reading ability of student V from the other four students.

Advantages of Item Response Theory

This approach to item construction and analysis has two important features. First, it provides information about the amount of reading ability measured by the item. Second, students' performance on the item provides information about how much reading ability they have.

So far in our example we have constructed three items, each reflecting a different level of reading ability. Suppose we construct 10 more items at each level (A, B, and C) by the same method (e.g., we would develop ten more A-level items that all students can answer). This item bank has several worthwhile uses:

1. We can customize testing for students of different ability levels. For example, suppose we give a student several A-level items to answer. If the student cannot answer any of them, we need not frustrate him, and extend the testing time unnecessarily, by administering B- and C-level items.
2. We can construct many different parallel tests, each of equivalent difficulty. For example, we can go into our item bank and randomly select two items of each type to construct a six-item test. We can repeat the procedure and construct a parallel test of equivalent difficulty.
3. We can reduce measurement error for a particular individual by administering only items within the range of those she is likely to answer correctly. For example, if a student is like student III described above, we can administer many B-level items in order to determine the students' reading ability more precisely. (Increasing the number of items in a test reduces measurement error.) There is no point in administering A-level items, which are too easy for this student, or C-level items, which are too difficult.

The Mathematics of Item Response Theory

In practice, we do not know the true reading ability of individuals. It is a **latent trait** which is an unobservable characteristic that is hypothesized to explain observed behavior. For example, if we observe an individual reading a newspaper and answering questions about it with good comprehension, we conclude that this person has good reading ability. We can observe the behavior of reading and answering questions, but not the underlying ability.

Item response theory uses mathematical models to identify the relationship between observed behavior (i.e., performance on a test item) and the underlying ability. An **item characteristic curve** is a mathematical function that is created to show this relationship between test-item performance and the underlying ability.

Two item characteristic curves are shown in Figure 7.1. Several features of the curves are worth noting:

1. The horizontal *x* axis represents the *underlying* ability (denoted by the symbol θ) measured by the items. The ability is measured in standard-score units (see Chapter 5), such that individuals with lesser amounts of the ability (minus values) have less of the ability than those with greater amounts (positive values).
2. The vertical axis represents the probability (*P*) of answering the item correctly. More precisely, *P* can be interpreted as the probability that an individual at a given level of ability, chosen at random from a sample of individuals at the same level, will answer the item correctly.
3. Item 2 is more difficult for students at most levels of the ability, because the probability of answering it correctly (*P*) is lower at most points of the *x* axis, which represents ability (θ).
4. Item 1 has more discriminating power, meaning that there is a greater difference in item performance between low-ability and high-ability students. For example, if we look at item 1, the probability is .45 that individuals at ability level 0 will answer it correctly, but .80 that individuals at ability level 1 will answer it correctly. For item 2, however, the probability is .35 that individuals at ability level 0 will answer it correctly, but only a slightly higher probability (.45) that individuals at ability level 1 will answer it correctly. We can express this finding by saying that item 1 has greater "information value" than item 2 for the range of ability under consideration.

FIGURE 7.1

Two Item Characteristic Curves

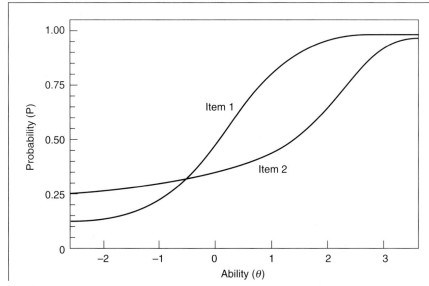

Source: Adapted from Figure 4.1 on p. 152 of: Hambleton, R. K. (1989). Principles and selected applications of item response theory. In R. L. Linn (Ed.), *Educational measurement* (3rd ed., pp. 147–200). New York: Macmillan.

5. Even individuals at the lowest level of ability (the left-most point of the x axis) have a probability greater than zero of answering the items correctly. This reflects the fact that the two items allow for guessing.

In constructing tests using IRT, test developers use one of various possible item-characteristic-curve models to fit item-performance probabilities for pools of items to different ability levels. For example, different models are used depending on how the items are scored (e.g., correct-incorrect, partial-credit, multiple-choice), whether the items allow for guessing, or whether they vary in discrimination power (as do items 1 and 2 in Figure 7.1). One of the most commonly used models is the Rasch model (named after its original developer, Georg Rasch) because of its relative simplicity and power.[13] Users of the Rasch model are more likely to eliminate potential test items because they do not fit the model, whereas test developers not bound to the Rasch model are more likely to retain potential test items by searching for item characteristic curves that mathematically describe the data.

The variables that enter into the mathematical equations that describe item characteristic curves can be used in other equations to describe how much each item, and the test as a whole, contributes to precision of measurement and reliability. (The equations are called *item information functions* and *test information functions*.) In simple terms, if a test contains mostly items that are too difficult for individuals at a given level of ability, the test will have poor precision of measurement for those individuals. Also, if a test contains items that are at an appropriate level of difficulty (in general, items with P approximately 0.5) but very few of them, the test will have poor reliability. The ideal test from the perspective of IRT is one in which items are tailored to the ability of the individual: items that are not too easy or too difficult, and an adequate number of such items to minimize measurement error.

Test-development procedures based on item-response theory are complex, and therefore few researchers are likely to use them to develop tests to measure variables of interest. However, they are being used increasingly in the construction of high-stakes tests, such as those used in standards-based education. As a researcher, you might find it desirable or necessary to use data from administration of such tests in a study you plan to conduct. If so, it is essential that you understand at least the basics of item response theory and its associated procedures.

Approaches to Measurement

Educational tests can be used to assess how much students have learned or to evaluate the quality of educational programs designed to foster that learning. Tests also are used extensively to make selection and placement decisions in educational institutions and in the workplace. Below we consider three contrasting approaches to constructing tests for these purposes: (1) standardized and locally constructed measures; (2) norm-referenced, criterion-referenced, and individual-referenced measurement; and (3) individually administered and group-administered measures.

Standardized and Locally Constructed Tests

Standardized tests typically are developed by commercial publishers or government agencies for use in a large number of sites. These tests have several advantages: The items

---

13. Andrich, D. (1988). *Rasch models for measurement.* Thousand Oaks, CA: Sage; Wright, B. D. (1999). Rasch measurement models. In G. N. Masters & J. P. Keeves, (Eds.), *Advances in measurement in educational research and assessment* (pp. 85–97). Oxford: Pergamon.

generally are well written, standard conditions of administration and scoring have been established, and tables of norms are provided.

These advantages of standardized tests are offset by some drawbacks. Guessing, response sets, or random or careless answers can distort the scores. Because standardized tests usually impose a restricted time limit, they may not accurately reflect the characteristics of individuals who are much slower, more deliberate, or more thoughtful in responding than their peers. Also, they are designed to permit comparison of individuals throughout a large population (e.g., all students currently in school in the United States), and therefore, the scores do not reflect the unique experiences of different types of individuals. Scores on standardized achievement tests, for example, tend to correlate highly with students' socioeconomic status, but minimally with any indicators of the instruction that students have received.[14] Another problem is that standardized tests have been accused of perpetuating bias against ethnic minorities and other groups,[15] and of neglecting to measure many personal and intellectual qualities that cannot easily be assessed in an objective, paper-and-pencil test format.

The strengths of standardized tests usually outweigh their weaknesses, and for this reason they are commonly used in educational research.

Locally constructed tests are an alternative to standardized tests. They usually are developed by teachers for use with their own students. However, these tests generally are inadequate for research purposes. Researchers have found that teachers seldom are well trained in techniques for test construction and have difficulty applying what they have learned.[16] For this reason you should be wary of using scores obtained from a teacher-made test in your study unless you first do an independent check of the test's validity and reliability. The test might be excellent for the teacher's instructional purposes, but test data must satisfy different criteria to be acceptable for use in research. These criteria, described at the beginning of the chapter, generally are better satisfied by standardized tests.

Referencing of Test Scores

Suppose a student earns a score of 20 on a 30-item test. How should we interpret this score? Measurement experts have developed three different approaches to answering this question. Each involves a different frame of reference within which obtained test scores are given meaning. These different frames of reference are described below.

Norm-Referenced Measurement

Norm-referenced measurement involves the interpretation of an individual's test score by comparing it to the scores earned by other individuals. Norms are used for this purpose. A **table of test norms** enables a researcher to relate an individual's score (or the mean score of her sample) to the scores of the defined population.

The sample used to create a table of test norms sometimes is called a *norming sample*. The norming sample's raw scores on the test typically are converted to percentile ranks. Given a particular raw score, a table of test norms based on percentile ranks enables us to determine the percentage of individuals in the norming sample who received the same or a lower score. Table 7.1 illustrates a table of test norms that converts raw scores to per-

14. English, F. W. (1992). *Deciding what to teach and test.* Newbury Park, CA: Corwin.
15. Cole, N. S., & Moss, P. A. (1989). Bias in test use. In R. L. Linn (Ed.), *Educational measurement* (3rd ed., pp. 201–219). New York: Macmillan.
16. Campbell, C., & Evans, J. A. (2000). Investigation of preservice teachers' classroom assessment practices during student teaching. *Journal of Educational Research, 93,* 350–355; Fray, R. B., Cross, L. H., & Weber, L. J. (1993). Testing and grading practices and opinions of secondary teachers of academic subjects: Implications for instruction in measurement. *Educational Measurement: Issues and Practice, 12,* 23–30.

	TABLE 7.1		

Table of Test Norms

Raw Score	Percentile Rank	Raw Score	Percentile Rank
48		34	44
47		33	40
46		32	36
45	99+	31	30
44	96	30	22
43	93	29	18
42	90	28	15
41	87	27	11
40	81	26	7
39	76	25	4
38	71	24	3
37	65	23	1
36	56		
35	49		

centile ranks. To understand how the table works, suppose that we administered the hypothetical test to a research sample and found that their mean score was 33. Consulting the table of test norms, we find that the sample was at the 40th percentile on the distribution of the norming sample's scores. We could conclude, then, that our research sample performed somewhat below the average of individuals in the population represented by the norming sample.

A table of test norms also might include age and grade equivalents, which are explained in Chapter 5.

This approach to measurement works best when the test includes items from a broadly defined domain of content and when it yields a wide distribution of scores. For example, a norm-referenced test in arithmetic achievement typically contains items on addition, subtraction, multiplication, and division. The items for each of these arithmetic operations will range from easy to difficult. This range of item difficulty makes it possible to distinguish between students who have mastered arithmetic at widely different levels.

A drawback of norm-referenced interpretation is that it tells us little about the student's specific strengths and weaknesses. For example, consider the test performance of these two students: Student A does very well on addition and subtraction, average on multiplication, and poorly on division; student B performs at an average level in all four operations. These students differ greatly in their strengths and weaknesses, yet both could obtain exactly the same score on a norm-referenced test of arithmetic achievement.

A major problem that can occur with norm-referenced measurement is **test score pollution,** meaning that over time the performance of test takers may increase for various reasons, thus making the norms meaningless.[17] John Cannell carried out a study in the late 1980s showing that all states in the United States, as well as most school districts, had

17. Test score pollution is described in: Haladyna, T. M., Nolen, S. B., & Haas, N. S. (1991). Raising standardized achievement test scores and the origins of test score pollution. *Educational Researcher, 20*(5), 2–7.

above-average scores on standardized achievement tests.[18] This phenomenon also has been referred to as *grade pollution* and *the Lake Wobegone phenomenon*. The obvious solution is to create a new table of norms for the test by administering it to a norming sample of students currently in school.

Much if not most research in education has relied on norm-referenced measurement because educators have great interest in individual differences between students that result from or affect instruction. As we describe the next two measurement approaches, you might consider whether they are better suited to research questions that address other instructional phenomena.

Criterion-Referenced Measurement

Criterion-referenced measurement involves the interpretation of an individual's score by comparing it to a prespecified standard of performance. Achievement tests designed for criterion-referenced interpretation typically focus on a narrow domain of knowledge or skills. In mathematics, for example, one domain might be "all arithmetic problems involving the addition of three two-digit whole numbers." Note that this domain is much more narrow and precisely defined than is "arithmetic achievement on a norm-referenced test."

A major purpose of criterion-referenced measurement is to estimate precisely the learner's level of performance and specific deficiencies in the domain covered by the test. Another purpose is to provide a sound rationale for making absolute (e.g., pass/no-pass) decisions based on test scores, as in mastery learning models of instruction. Once a domain has been defined and the items developed, a performance criterion can be established, such as, "Given a sample of problems requiring the addition of three two-digit whole numbers, all students will reach or exceed the 90 percent accuracy level."[19] Scores then can be interpreted in relation to this criterion.

Two subtypes of criterion-referenced measurement are domain-referenced and objectives-referenced measurement. **Domain-referenced measurement** involves selection of a random sample of items drawn from an item pool that is representative of all possible test items for a well-defined content area. **Objectives-referenced measurement** provides information about how well the student performs on items measuring attainment of specific instructional objectives.

Several concerns arise in determining the reliability and validity of test scores based on criterion-referenced measurement. **Criterion-referenced measurement reliability** can be defined as the consistency with which the measure accurately estimates each individual's level of mastery of the test domain. The correlational methods used to determine the reliability of norm-referenced scores are not suitable for this purpose because they require sets of scores with considerable variability. Because the purpose of norm-referenced tests is to discriminate clearly among students at different achievement levels, items on such tests are selected to produce maximum scoring variability among individuals. In fact, items that nearly all students answer correctly are eliminated from norm-referenced tests. In contrast, even if everyone answers certain test items correctly, these items are appropriate in a criterion-referenced test.

Procedures for determining the reliability of criterion-referenced scores roughly parallel the split-half, test-retest, and alternate-form methods used with norm-referenced

---

18. Cannell, J. J. (1988). Nationally normed elementary achievement testing in America's public schools: How all fifty states are above the national average. *Educational Measurement: Issues and Practice, 7*, 5–9.
19. Methods for establishing a performance criterion or standard in criterion-referenced measurement are described in: Berk, R. A. (1986). A consumer's guide to setting performance standards in criterion-referenced tests. *Review of Educational Research, 56*, 137–172; Kane, M. (1994). Validating the performance standards associated with passing scores. *Review of Educational Research, 64*, 425–462.

tests. You will recall that the test user's main concern in criterion-referenced measurement is whether students have achieved the established criterion. Reliability estimates compare different forms of the measure on their agreement in placing students into two groups: those who reached the criterion and those who did not. Reliability usually is reported in terms of percentage of agreement, rather than as a correlation coefficient.[20]

Individual-Referenced Measurement

Individual-referenced measurement involves comparing an individual's performance on a test at one point in time to that individual's performance on it at another point, or points, in time. This approach can be used to track changes in a student's performance over time and how a student responds to specific instructional interventions. For example, if a student does poorly on a test, we could determine how well he does on the same test after a specific type of remedial instruction.

Individual-referenced measurement is particularly applicable to single-subject experiments, which are described in Chapter 13. In this type of experiment, each research participant is studied individually as he or she responds to an intervention that might be introduced once or repeatedly. The individual can be asked to take the same test at different points in this process so that changes in performance can be measured.

Computer-Based Testing

The increasing availability and sophistication of computers are bringing many changes in measurement. We briefly summarize below how computers can facilitate various aspects of testing, from test development to test score interpretation. The particular situation that you wish to study may involve the use of computers for test administration, and therefore you need to understand how they work. Also, you may have access to a research center that has the computer capabilities described below. These capabilities can help you achieve significant efficiencies in test development, data collection, and data analysis.

Uses in Test Development

The construction of tests is aided greatly by using a computer to store and manipulate potential test items. A word processing program can be used in test construction, but it does not solve the problem of renumbering test items. Testing software packages (e.g., BILOG, MULTILOG, RASCAL) not only add or revise items as needed, but can renumber items and put them in the desired test format. These packages also facilitate the use of alternate item stems, such as a graph that the test-taker must interpret or a brief audio presentation in a foreign language that the test-taker must translate. Further, testing software greatly speeds the process of item analysis, allowing the test developer to determine such aspects as the difficulty of each item and the percentage of a sample who chose each response option.

Computers play an essential role in adaptive testing. **Computer-adaptive testing** involves administration of a potentially different test to each test-taker by having the computer match the difficulty level of test items presented to each test-taker to his ability level as judged from his performance on earlier test items. Thus, as test administration progresses, an individual who answered all or most items correctly to that point will receive more difficult items in order to help determine her precise ability level, while an individual who answered all or most items incorrectly will receive less difficult items. This application of computer-adaptive testing is based on item response theory.

✦ Touchstone in Research

Van der Linden, W. J. (1999). Computerized educational testing. In G. N. Masters & J. P. Keeves, (Eds.), *Advances in measurement in educational research and assessment* (pp. 138–150). Oxford: Pergamon.

20. For specific procedures for computing the reliability of criterion-referenced tests, see: Berk, R. A. (1980). A consumer's guide to criterion-referenced test reliability. *Journal of Educational Measurement, 17,* 323–349.

Uses in Test Administration, Scoring, and Interpretation

Many standardized paper-and-pencil tests have been converted to computer format. The advantages include (1) the opportunity to randomize, or systematically vary, the order in which items are presented; (2) the opportunity to record or limit the amount of time that a test-taker spends on each item; (3) the elimination of opportunities for test-takers to look back or ahead to other sections of the test; (4) a reduction in scoring errors; and (5) faster scoring. It has even been suggested that a computerized test might be more effective than a paper-and-pencil test or interviewer in obtaining highly personal information (e.g., proneness to attempt suicide).

Despite the speed and efficiency of computer testing, it is important to consider whether computer testing would intimidate or hamper the performance of individuals who are unfamiliar with or dislike computers. For this reason, in some states the Division of Motor Vehicles has replaced the written driving test with a computer version, but will give a written version to individuals who request it.

Testing software packages can score and interpret individuals' responses directly. If it is a paper-and-pencil test, optical scanners can read the test-taker's pencil marks on an answer sheet and organize them into a computer file. The software can generate raw scores, percentiles, and other scores for individuals; summary statistics for class groups, schools, and school systems; and test subscores and individual item analyses.

Testers also are making increasing use of computers to prepare narrative reports that interpret the numerical test scores. A catalog of statements is stored in the computer, and the computer is programmed so that a certain combination of scores or of responses to individual items calls up one or more of these statements. The report might be descriptive only (e.g., "John is somewhat above average in verbal reasoning") or it can involve interpretation, especially in the case of personality measures.

Individual and Group Tests

Many intellectual and personality characteristics can be measured by either an individually administered or a group-administered test. A **group test** is one that has been constructed so that a group of individuals can take the test all at one time. The test administrator distributes the test, reads the directions, and times it if it is a speed test. The test usually consists of objective items (e.g., yes-no, multiple-choice, or true-false). In contrast, an **individual test** involves a tester who assesses the behavior of one individual at a time. Some tests of intelligence and most projective tests of personality are of this type.

Individually administered tests can make an essential contribution to a research project if the researcher is interested in studying process (e.g., how individuals respond to certain test items) in addition to product (e.g., what their total score is). If you are interested in such topics as the problem-solving strategies of fifth graders or typical reading comprehension problems of low-achieving students, you might wish to use individually administered tests in your research.

The nature of the sample also determines whether individually administered tests are necessary. Very young children, for example, usually should not be tested as a group because their attention span is limited and they do not have the reading skills required by group tests.

Standardized tests are available in group-administered or individually administered form for many important educational constructs. The individually administered tests typically require more training to administer, and they also require more skill to interpret the scores properly.

Types of Tests and Self-Report Measures

In this section we describe ten types of tests that are commonly used in educational research. They can be grouped into two categories: (1) performance tests, which include intelligence, aptitude, achievement, and diagnostic measures; and (2) personality measures, which include measures of personality traits, creativity, self-concept, attitudes, and interests. Because of the large number of tests, we describe only a few examples of each type. Some were developed decades ago, but still are in common use. If a test yields score inferences with the validity and reliability characteristics that you desire for your research project, its publication date should not deter you from considering it.

✦ Touchstone in Research

Saklofske, D. H., & Zeidner, M. (Eds.). (1995). *International handbook of personality and intelligence.* New York: Plenum.

Performance Tests

A large number of performance tests are available for use in research and practice. They vary widely in the constructs they measure, the format of their items (e.g., short answer versus true-false), and the type of score they yield (see Chapter 5 for an explanation of different types of continuous scores).

We describe the main types of performance tests below. You can find many examples of each type in the reference books and databases described later in the chapter.

Intelligence Tests

Intelligence tests provide an estimate of an individual's general intellectual level by sampling performance on a variety of intellectual tasks. These tests often include items on such tasks as vocabulary choice, mathematical problem solving, reading comprehension, and short-term memory of digits.

Most intelligence tests yield a single global score of intellectual performance, called the **intelligence quotient (IQ).** Some intelligence tests also yield subscores, such as verbal IQ and mathematical IQ. Subscores also may be provided for specific intellectual functions, such as spatial relationships, verbal ability, numerical reasoning, and logical reasoning. However, if you plan to make inferences from such subscores in your research study, you should check to determine whether the subscores are supported by sufficient evidence of construct validity and reliability.

Aptitude Tests

Aptitude tests are aimed at predicting an individual's future performance in a specific type of skill or area of achievement. Tests are available to measure aptitudes for many academic subjects, occupations, and areas of creative accomplishment. Because aptitude tests primarily are concerned with prediction of future behavior, evidence of their predictive validity is especially important.

Achievement Tests

Many standardized achievement tests are available. Some are intended to measure the student's knowledge of specific facts, but the trend is to include more test items that assess higher-cognitive processes. The reason for this change is that new curriculum standards at the state and national level emphasize instruction in reasoning and problem-solving skills.

Administration time and content coverage for achievement tests vary greatly. For example, the Wide Range Achievement Test contains tests in reading, spelling, and arithmetic and requires less than 30 minutes to administer. In contrast, the intermediate level of the Metropolitan Achievement Test provides seven reading scores, six language scores, and eight mathematics scores, and takes up to 10 hours to complete.

Content validity is a major issue in selecting an achievement test. You need to check the test to determine whether the content of its items parallels the content of the instructional program that is the subject of your research study. Selecting an achievement test with adequate content validity usually is much more difficult in areas such as social studies, where the content is highly varied, than in areas such as arithmetic, where the content and the curriculum learning sequence generally is standard.

Achievement testing has been found to be psychologically threatening to many teachers because it arouses the fear that poor performance on the test by their students will reflect negatively on their abilities as teachers.[21] Some teachers have been found to give students special preparation in areas covered by the test, and sometimes even on the specific test items covered.[22] Selecting a measure that differs from those that are routinely used to assess school achievement reduces the likelihood of teachers affecting students' scores through their coaching or instruction.

You also should consider the test ceiling when selecting an achievement test. A test with a low **test ceiling** is one that is too easy for some of the students to whom you plan to administer the test. Thus, the test will not reflect gains made by these students following a research treatment designed to increase their achievement level.

Diagnostic Tests

Suppose that your research project involves remediation of student learning difficulties, or evaluation of the effectiveness of a remedial program. In these situations, a diagnostic test might be helpful in identifying an appropriate research sample. A **diagnostic test** is a form of achievement test that is used to identify a student's strengths and weaknesses in a particular school subject. Diagnostic tests usually focus on the low end of the achievement spectrum and provide a detailed picture of the student's level of performance in the various skills that the subject involves.

A disadvantage of some diagnostic tests is that the subscores have low reliability, and often they are highly intercorrelated. For diagnostic purposes a criterion-referenced test covering the subject of interest might be a better choice, because it provides a measure of the learner's absolute level of performance in a precisely defined content area.

Performance Assessment

Performance assessment is an approach to evaluating students by directly examining their performance on tasks that have intrinsic value. (Performance assessment also is called *authentic assessment, alternative assessment,* and *performance testing.*) The tasks used in performance assessment are designed to represent complex, complete, real-life tasks. In contrast, the tasks on most paper-and-pencil tests, particularly multiple-choice items, do not have intrinsic value. Rather, their value derives from their possible relationship to real-life tasks. A familiar example of performance assessment is the behind-the-wheel driving test required to obtain a license to drive an automobile. This performance assessment differs from the paper-and-pencil test (now provided in computerized form) of knowledge of the "rules of the road," also required for a driver's license. Some people might demonstrate sufficient knowledge on the paper-and-pencil test but be unable or unwilling to demonstrate it in real-life driving situations.[23]

♦ **Touchstone in Research**

Baker, E. L., O'Neil, H. F., & Linn, R. L. (1993). Policy and validity prospects for performance-based assessment. *American Psychologist, 48*(12), 1210–1218.

Cizek, G. J. (2001). *Setting performance standards: Concepts, methods, and perspectives.* Mahwah, NJ: Lawrence Erlbaum Associates.

21. Smith, M. L. (1991). Put to the test: The effects of external testing on teachers. *Educational Researcher, 20*(5), 8–11.
22. Haladyna et al., Raising test scores.
23. The relative merits of traditional pencil-and-paper tests and performance assessment are discussed in Chapter 15 of: Worthen, B. R., Borg, W. R., & White, K. R. (1993). *Measurement and evaluation in the schools.* New York: Longman.

In performance assessment, the researcher can evaluate either individual or group performance in completing a task or the resulting product. Portfolio development also has become a popular form of performance assessment. A **portfolio** is a purposeful collection of a student's work that records her progress in mastering a subject domain (e.g., writing in multiple genres or solving math problems taken from different topic areas) and personal reflections on her own progress.[24] Instruction should be closely coordinated with this assessment process, and the teacher and students should collaborate in selecting the contents of a portfolio and criteria for judging it. The criteria are used to generate a **rubric,** which specifies criteria and a measurement scale for different levels of proficiency demonstrated by the portfolio. (Rubrics are used as well for other types of performance assessment besides portfolios.)

Robert Linn, Eva Baker, and Stephen Dunbar proposed a set of eight criteria for judging the validity of inferences drawn from performance assessments.[25] The criteria are shown in Figure 7.2. Examination of these validity criteria suggests that performance assessments can be very useful to both practitioners and researchers, but that they have potential drawbacks. Interestingly, some of these drawbacks, such as the difficulty of obtaining adequate content coverage, are the strengths of traditional paper-and-pencil tests. This observation suggests the desirability of using both paper-and-pencil tests and

FIGURE 7.2

Eight Criteria for Judging the Validity of Performance Assessments

1. *Consequences.* Are the consequences of using the performance assessment reasonable? For example, did some teachers provide more help to their students in assembling their portfolios such that students of other teachers are put at a disadvantage? Did the assembly of portfolios take an undue amount of time away from instruction?
2. *Fairness.* Did all students have an equal opportunity to acquire the expertise measured by the performance assessment? Did different judges apply different criteria in rating students' work?
3. *Generalizability.* Is there evidence that an individual's quality of work on one performance task will generalize to other similar tasks?
4. *Cognitive complexity.* If the performance assessment is designed specifically to measure students' proficiency in higher-order thinking skills, does it actually do so, or can students draw on their memory of how they have done similar tasks previously?
5. *Content quality.* Are the performance assessment tasks and scoring criteria authentic, that is, representative of real-life tasks and quality indicators?
6. *Meaningfulness.* Do groups other than the experts who designed the performance assessment task and scoring criteria view them as authentic?
7. *Content coverage.* Does the performance assessment adequately represent the content domain covered during instruction? Was the amount of content covered during instruction unduly constrained by the time required for performance assessment?
8. *Cost and efficiency.* Is the performance assessment too costly and cumbersome to administer? Cost and efficiency need to be considered when developing or selecting a performance assessment.

Source: Adapted from: Linn, R. L., Baker, E. L., & Dunbar, S. B. (1991). Complex, performance-based assessment: Expectations and validation criteria. *Educational Researcher, 20*(8), 15–21.

24. For more information about portfolios, see: Wolf, D., Bixby, J, Glenn, J., III, & Gardner, H. (1991). To use their minds well: Investigating new forms of student assessment. In G. Grant (Ed.), *Review of research in education* (Vol. 17, pp. 31–74). Washington, DC: American Educational Research Association.
25. Linn, R. L., Baker, E. L., & Dunbar, S. B. (1991). Complex, performance-based assessment: Expectations and validation criteria. *Educational Researcher, 20*(8), 15–21.

performance assessment in educational research studies, especially in experiments that evaluate the effects of instructional methods on student learning.

The reliability of a performance assessment is equally as important as its validity. As we explained earlier in the chapter, a test is reliable to the extent that its scores are free of measurement error, which is detected through repeated, independent measurements of the construct that is being assessed. Because of the complexity of most performance assessment tasks, it usually is not feasible, or necessary, to administer several parallel forms of them to students, as is done by including many items on a traditional standardized test. For example, individuals only take a driving test once if they pass it. They are not asked to take the test repeatedly in order to ensure that the pass-fail score is reliable. Similarly, a college student only needs to complete one honors thesis in order for a committee to judge whether she will graduate with honors.

Pamela Moss suggested another approach to reliability that legitimizes performance assessment without requiring demonstration of performance consistency across parallel forms of a task.[26] This approach is based on **hermeneutics,** which is a field of inquiry that seeks to interpret human phenomena by understanding how their different parts relate to the whole. (Hermeneutics is explained further in Chapter 15.) Consider the judging of the product of a performance task completed by a student in an art class. Let's say it is a watercolor painting. Different judges might rate the drawing differently, thus raising concerns about the reliability of the scoring system. From a hermeneutic perspective, these differences are not necessarily a problem. The different judgments (the "parts") can be discussed and eventually reconciled until a consensual score ("the whole") is reached.

As Moss observed, this method often is used in real life. For example, members of a search committee meeting to fill a faculty position opening might disagree among themselves in how they rate different candidates for the position. They do not attempt to remove "unreliable" members of the search committee. Rather, they discuss their different viewpoints until they achieve an understanding that accounts for disagreements and that allows them to select the person whom they consider best for the position.

Hermeneutic principles can be used in similar fashion to handle differences in ratings of the student's various watercolor paintings or differences between ratings of his paintings and, let's say, his sculptures. In traditional measurement, these differences would be taken as evidence of unreliability in performance, but a hermeneutic perspective would consider these differences as "parts" to be interpreted until they can be reconciled into a satisfactory overall interpretation (the "whole") that provides an understanding of the differences.

The hermeneutic perspective privileges the student's teachers in this interpretive process. This is because hermeneutic theorists believe that the "reader" of human phenomena (viewed as the "text") is believed to bring her own preconceptions and prior knowledge to an interpretation of these phenomena. Because teachers have more knowledge about their students than experts who only know students by the products that result from their work on a performance assessment task, the teachers' interpretations have special value. Moss used this tenet of hermeneutic theory to defend schools that use committees of teachers—or committees of teachers, parents, other students, and members of the community—to judge students' performance assessment products.

Personality Measures

Personality measures assess individual differences in such aspects of personality as traits, needs, psychological disorders, values, and attitudes. Most of them are self-report mea-

---

26. Moss, P. A. (1994). Can there be validity without reliability? *Educational Researcher, 23*(2), 5–12.

sures in paper-and-pencil format that ask individuals to respond to items asking about the occurrence of particular behaviors, thoughts, and feelings in their life.

Personality Inventories

Personality inventories assess a variety of personality traits in a single self-report instrument, typically a paper-and-pencil measure. They have the advantages of low cost and ease of administration and scoring. Because many variables are measured at the same time, an inventory may contain a hundred or more items. The items usually are in objective form, such as yes-no or multiple choice, which allows for scoring to be done by computer or a template.

The major limitation of personality inventories is that they depend on the truthfulness and diligence of the individual's self-report. Many inventories contain a "lie scale" or "carelessness index" to detect individuals whose scores would lead researchers and practitioners to make invalid inferences. For example, J. W. O'Dell developed a carelessness index for the Sixteen Personality Factor Questionnaire that correctly selected 88 percent of randomly completed answer sheets.[27]

Another factor that can cause invalid responses to a personality inventory is a **response set,** which is the extent to which an individual's responses reflect a general predisposition rather than a careful response to the content of each item. Three types of response sets have been extensively researched: **social desirability,** or the tendency to present oneself in a favorable light; **acquiescence,** or the set to agree with items irrespective of their content; and **deviance,** or the set to respond in ways that are different from typical or normal responses. If you believe that individuals in your sample are inclined to one of these response sets, you should not use a self-report inventory.

Personality inventories have been attacked as involving an invasion of privacy of the individuals taking the test. Therefore you should carefully review whether the personality inventory you are considering contains items that might cause a breakdown in human relations with parents or community groups whose cooperation you will need. For example, administering an inventory to middle school students that contains questions about sexual experiences might raise objections from many people and thus jeopardize your entire study.

Projective Techniques

The term *projective technique* was popularized by Lawrence Frank.[28] A **projective technique** provides amorphous stimuli and freedom of response, based on the assumption that such measures better reveal an individual's inner thoughts, fantasies, and unique structuring of reality than a test with more limited or structured response options. A presumed advantage of projective techniques is that they are less subject to faking than self-report inventories.

One of the most widely used projective techniques is the *Thematic Apperception Test (TAT)*. This instrument consists of a set of drawings of individuals in various interpersonal situations; the respondent makes up a story in response to each situation. These stories presumably reveal the individual's inner world, and for this reason the TAT and other projective techniques sometimes are used by qualitative researchers.[29]

27. O'Dell, J. W. (1971). Method for detecting random answers on personality questionnaires. *Journal of Applied Psychology, 55,* 380–383.

28. Frank, L. K. (1939). Projective methods for the study of personality. *Journal of Psychology, 8,* 389–413.

29. For example, see: Gilligan, C., & Pollak, S. (1988). The vulnerable and invulnerable physician. In C. Gilligan, J. V. Ward, & J. M. Taylor (Eds.), *Mapping the moral domain: A contribution of women's thinking to psychological theory and education* (pp. 245–262). Cambridge, MA: Harvard University Press.

Measures of Specific Personality Characteristics

Some personality measures focus on a single personality characteristic or small set of related characteristics. If you are interested in a measure of only one personality characteristic, we recommend that you check reference works (described later in the chapter and in Appendix E) to see if a published measure is available. If you cannot find a suitable measure, check the general inventories to see if any of them include the personality characteristic that you wish to measure. If so, you either can administer the entire inventory or use the scoring key to extract the items that measure this characteristic and administer only those items. Before using the latter approach, though, you should obtain the publisher's permission. Also, if you administer only part of the inventory, use test norms with caution, because responses may be different when items measuring a single personality characteristic lack the context of the entire inventory.

Measures of Self-Concept

Self-concept is defined as the set of cognitions and feelings that each individual has about himself or herself. Many measures of self-concept include an assessment of self-esteem, which refers to how positively individuals feel about themselves generally or about specific aspects of the self, such as self as physical being, self as social being, or self as student.

Measures of Learning Styles and Habits

Over a period of time, students develop characteristic ways of approaching learning tasks. As these approaches become internalized, they constitute distinctive aspects of personality that are of interest to educators. For example, Ronald Schmeck used a measure that he developed, the *Inventory of Learning Processes,* to characterize students as deep-elaborative or shallow-reiterative.[30] Deep-elaborative students are argumentative when reading or listening, and like to relate curriculum content to their personal life. Shallow-reiterative students process curriculum content superficially; they do not reflect on or personalize it.

Attitude Scales

An **attitude** can be defined as as an individual's viewpoint or disposition toward a particular "object" (a person, a thing, an idea, etc.). Attitudes are considered to have three components: (1) an *affective* component, which consists of the individual's feelings about the attitude object; (2) a *cognitive* component, which is the individual's beliefs or knowledge about the attitude object; and (3) a *behavioral* component, which is the individual's predisposition to act toward the attitude object in a particular way.

Several procedures can be used to measure attitudes. A **Thurstone scale** requires individuals to express agreement or disagreement with a series of statements about the attitude object. A **Likert scale** asks individuals to check their level of agreement (e.g., strongly agree, agree, undecided, disagree, or strongly disagree) with various statements. In the **semantic differential** technique, individuals rate an attitude object on a series of bipolar adjectives, such as fair-unfair, valuable-worthless, and good-bad.

Measures of Vocational Interest

Vocational interest inventories have proved to be of considerable value in educational research. They can be used to investigate how students come to develop specific vocational interests, and they also provide an indirect assessment of personality characteristics (e.g.,

---

30. Schmeck, R. R. (1988). Individual differences and learning strategies. In C. E. Weinstein, E. T. Goetz, and P. A. Alexander (Eds.), *Learning and study strategies: Issues in assessment, instruction, and evaluation* (pp. 171–191). San Diego, CA: Academic Press.

an individual interested in banking is likely to have different personality characteristics from those of someone interested in art as a career). Vocational interest inventories typically require the individual to express their degree of interest in, or preference for, various types of activities, sports, hobbies, books, and other aspects of daily life.

Obtaining Information about Tests

In planning a study, researchers sometimes select the first test they identify that appears to measure a construct that they wish to study. They might later encounter criticism that the test is invalid for that construct or inappropriate for the sample. This problem can be avoided by determining the range of tests that are available and collecting detailed information about each of them before selecting one. The following are questions that can guide your search for relevant information:

1. Is there evidence that the test is valid and reliable for the uses to which you want to put it?
2. Is the test's reading or task level appropriate for your sample?
3. Can the test be administered within the time constraints of your data-collection situation?
4. If the test measures achievement or aptitude, is it at an appropriate level of difficulty for the sample, that is, neither too simple nor too difficult?
5. Do the test's norms and validity and reliability evidence come from a population that is similar to the population from which your sample will be drawn?

The following section describes four sources of information to answer these questions: preliminary and secondary sources, the test manual, the test itself, and the test developer.

Preliminary and Secondary Sources

Various reference books and online search engines are available to help you identify tests that measure the constructs you wish to study in your research. Some of them are indexes (which we call *preliminary sources*) that enable you to find tests that measure a particular construct. Others provide descriptions and critical reviews of particular tests.

Appendix E contains a list of these resources. In addition, you can search ERIC and other databases (see Chapter 4) for publications about tests and constructs.

Of these various resources, one stands out as particularly useful. It is the web site <www.ericae.net/testcol.htm>. Among the items on its home page is the search engine *Test Locator*, which contains descriptions of over 10,000 tests and research instruments. To illustrate its use, we searched for tests of scientific reasoning ability by entering the keywords and connector *science and reasoning*. *Test Locator* listed 52 tests of this construct. Another search engine at the site is the *Test Review Locator*, which enables you to search for citations and reviews of tests.

The Test Manual

A **test manual** is a booklet provided by the test publisher that provides information to help prospective test users determine whether the test is appropriate to their purposes and, if so, how to use the test. A good test manual will provide information about such matters as the theoretical constructs or rationale upon which the test is based, recommended uses of the test, evidence of validity and reliability, availability of norms, and availability of short and alternate forms of the test. The manual also should provide procedures for administering, scoring, and interpreting the test.

The *Standards for Educational and Psychological Testing* specify that the test developer is responsible for a poorly designed test or an inadequate test manual. However, researchers have the responsibility to determine whether the test is appropriate for use in their research project.

The Test Itself

One of the most important types of information to use in evaluating a test for use in your research study is the test itself. Examination of the test is particularly important to answer questions about the face validity and content relevance of the test, and its appropriateness for your research sample. For example, the test manual may claim that a test is appropriate for fifth-grade students. However, when you examine a copy of the test, you may conclude that the required reading level is beyond that of the fifth graders whom you plan to study.

In addition to examining the test, you should consider taking it. This will increase your understanding of the test and possible problems in administering it.

The Test Developer

Because there is a considerable lag between the completion of research and its publication, the test developer often has information that has not yet been published, and also is likely to know of other researchers who have recently used the test. Thus, we advise you to contact the test developer directly to request test information. If you explain the purpose for which you wish to use the test, most developers will be cooperative. In fact, they may request a report of your research findings to add to those that already have been collected.

Using Tests in Your Research Project

Developing Your Own Test

Development of new tests is a complex and difficult process that requires considerable training in educational and psychological measurement. Therefore, we recommend that you make certain no suitable test is available before developing your own. Also, if you must develop a test for your dissertation research, we advise that you design the study so that you only need to develop and validate one test. Otherwise the process of test development might overwhelm you and prevent you from reaching the point where you can use the tests you have developed to answer your research questions. In fact, some theses and dissertations focus entirely on the development and validation of a new test.

The major steps of test development are shown in Figure 7.3. Keep in mind, however, that each type of test also involves specialized development procedures.[31]

One of the most important activities in test development is item analysis, which is mentioned in step 5 of Figure 7.3. An **item analysis** is a set of procedures for determining the difficulty, validity, and reliability of each item in the test. The specific procedures depend upon the nature of the test. For performance tests, it is customary to compute a **difficulty index,** which is a tally for each item of the number of individuals who answered it correctly, divided by the total number of individuals taking the test. For both performance and personality measures, it is common to compute an item validity coefficient and item reliability coefficient for each item. An **item validity coefficient** is the correlation between

31. Resources for test development include: DeVellis, R. F. (1991). *Scale development: Theory and applications.* Thousand Oaks, CA: Sage; Gronlund, N. E. (1997). *Assessment of student achievement.* Boston: Allyn & Bacon; Ngueyen, H. Q. *Testing applications for the Web: Internet-based systems.* New York: Wiley; Osterfind, S. J. (1998). *Constructing test items: Multiple-choice, constructed-response, performance and other formats.* Norwell, MA: Kluwer; Worthen, B. (1998). *Measurement and evaluation in schools* (2nd ed.). Boston: Addison-Wesley Longman.

FIGURE 7.3

Major Steps in Developing a Test

STEP 1:   **Defining the constructs to be measured.** Give careful thought about the specific construct, or constructs, that the test will measure. Consider whether there is a theoretical basis for the constructs.

STEP 2:   **Defining the target population.** Characteristics of the target population must be considered in making many of the decisions involved in test construction. Therefore, define the target population in detail.

STEP 3:   **Reviewing related tests.** Review other tests that measure similar constructs to generate ideas about such matters as test format and methods for establishing validity.

STEP 4:   **Developing a prototype.** Prepare a preliminary version of the test (i.e., a prototype). Several published sources provide guidelines on item writing.

STEP 5:   **Evaluating the prototype.** Obtain a critical review of the prototype from experts in test development and the constructs being measured. Then, field-test the prototype with a sample from the target population, and do an item analysis on the resulting data.

STEP 6:   **Revising the test.** Revise the prototype test, and field-test the revised version. This cycle of field-test and revision may need to be repeated several times.

STEP 7:   **Collecting data on test validity and reliability.** Collect evidence to support the reliability of the test's scores and the validity of the inferences that you wish to make from these scores.

individuals' responses to a particular item and their total score on a criterion measure taken either around the same time that the test is administered (concurrent validity) or at a later time (predictive validity). An **item reliability coefficient** is the correlation between individuals' response to a particular item and their total test score.

Resistance to Tests

The testing movement has had a major impact on American society over the past 50 years. Millions of tests are administered each year for the purpose of making important decisions about individuals, for example, Who should be admitted to college, and to which college? Who should receive special commendation for their academic achievement? Who must repeat a class because of academic failure? The widespread use of tests to answer such questions has made them the subject of public scrutiny and criticism. Even if you intend to use tests only for a research project, negative attitudes of some groups and individuals toward testing in general might create problems for you.

If the tests that you plan to administer come under attack, you should consider several points. First, some protesters may have a hidden agenda that is different from what is expressed. Second, representatives of the public at large lack the expertise needed to understand the function of many items used in psychological tests, so it probably is unwise to debate the merits of specific test items. Instead, you should explain how the test was developed and attempt to demonstrate that the test as a whole is valid and useful.

Third, it is important to take all actions that seem appropriate at the very outset of any challenge to your planned use of a test. If the research study is well designed, test-takers or other concerned individuals usually can be convinced of the value of the study. If newspaper reporters or other media personnel ask questions, be cooperative and acquaint them with the purpose and potential value of your study. Also, be willing to withdraw individuals from a study if they or their parents make a written request for withdrawal, even if they had earlier signed a letter of informed consent (see Chapter 3).

Finally, you should familiarize yourself with the guidelines stated in the *Standards for Educational and Psychological Testing,* which we described earlier in the chapter. You can indicate to protestors and other concerned individuals that professional standards for testing exist and that you have adhered to these standards.[32]

Testing in Field Sites

If you plan to administer tests in a school or other institution as part of your research study, you should come to an agreement with administrators about such questions as: What help will the institution provide for the testing program? How will make-up tests be scheduled and who will administer them? What role will staff members play in the testing program? How will disciplinary problems that occur during testing be handled? Also, you should carefully schedule tests to fit the institution's routines. For example, schools usually have a fixed time schedule for each class period. If your testing extends beyond this class period, it is likely to cause problems for teachers.

If you are working with a large sample, testing the entire group at one time might make it difficult for the administrator to answer questions or collect materials. Even a minor incident, such as a giggle, could disrupt the test situation for many people. Therefore, it is advisable to break the sample into small groups and test each group separately. However, do not stretch out the testing over several weeks. Otherwise you face the risk that the testing situation will be significantly different for those individuals tested last compared to those tested first. Also, keep the testing conditions as nearly identical as possible for each group. This is especially important if you are conducting an experiment and the experimental and control groups are to be tested separately, which often is the case.

It is a good idea to avoid testing near major holidays or very close to the end of the school year. The excitement attending holidays and the end of the school year can make a significant difference in the attitude of many research participants.

Gaining the Cooperation of Test-Takers

The cooperation of research participants is essential to obtaining meaningful test scores. Before administering a test, ask yourself how you can maximize their cooperation and motivate them to perform at their highest level (in the case of ability tests) or in an honest manner (in the case of personality, attitude, or interest tests).

To increase the likelihood that you are sampling individuals' maximal performance on tests of aptitude or achievement, attempt to make the testing a positive experience. One way to accomplish this goal with elementary and high school students is to ask the students' teacher to tell them that the test is important and that they should try to do their best on it. It is appropriate in some situations to have achievement tests for a research project also count as part of students' course grades.

To increase the cooperation of adults, a good approach is to tell them that you will reveal the purpose of the research study and its findings after the testing is completed. This appeals to their sense of curiosity and desire to contribute to research knowledge. Another useful strategy is to emphasize the official nature of the testing session by such methods as using a stopwatch, if appropriate, and carefully reading directions from a manual.

In administering personality measures, testers need to create an atmosphere in which test-takers feel comfortable about giving an honest picture of themselves, especially if some of the test items ask for sensitive information. One helpful procedure is to make clear

32. Moreland, K. L., Eyde, L. D., Robertson, G. J., Primoff, E. S., & Most, R. B. (1995). Assessment of test user qualifications: A research-based measurement procedure. *American Psychologist, 50,* 14–23.

before the testing session begins that under no circumstances will the test data be revealed to anyone, and that test scores will be reported in group form only (if this is true). Still another technique is to assign code numbers to all test-takers. If you plan beforehand, you should be able to arrange the test session so that test-takers can write a code number on their tests instead of their names.

A comfortable physical environment and consideration for the mental and physical state of the individuals taking the test are likely to increase cooperation. Testers also should master the test directions. It is annoying to be tested by someone who fumbles with materials, appears uncertain, or makes obvious errors.

✦ RECOMMENDATIONS FOR
Using Tests and Self-Report Measures in Research

1. Evaluate a test's objectivity, conditions of administration and scoring, and appropriateness for your sample before selecting it.
2. Determine whether the available validity evidence supports the test-score interpretations you wish to make.
3. Determine whether the available reliability evidence supports your intended use of the test.
4. Consider whether a test based on item response theory is a suitable option.
5. Determine whether the referencing of the test's scores (e.g., availability of a test of norms) is suitable for your purposes.
6. Consider whether individual or group testing is most suitable for your purposes.
7. Use a variety of search strategies to identify the tests that are the best measure of the constructs you plan to study.
8. Study the test manual and other sources of information to ensure that you administer the test properly.
9. Anticipate and plan for possible objections to the test and testing procedures.
10. If developing your own test, gain the necessary skills for good test construction.

✔ SELF-CHECK TEST

Circle the correct answer to each of the following questions.
The answers are provided at the back of the book.

1. An example of test-validity evidence based on relationships to other variables would be
   a. a comparison of the test content and the universe of content that the test is designed to measure.
   b. a comparison of the response processes used by test takers and the response processes that the test is designed to elicit.
   c. the degree of correlation between the test scores and scores on a criterion variable.
   d. the degree of correlation between the items that make up the test.

2. To calculate the _____ of a measure, the measure is administered to a sample of individuals and then, after a delay, is again given to the same sample.
   a. alternate-form reliability
   b. test-retest reliability
   c. internal consistency
   d. reliability of subscores

3. Generalizability theory is useful for
   a. determining whether test-validity evidence generalizes to populations other than the ones on which it was collected.
   b. assessing the relative contribution of different sources of measurement error in a test.
   c. determining the degree of similarity across item characteristic curves.
   d. all of the above.

4. An important advantage of item response theory over classical test theory is that it
   a. speeds up the process of constructing a test.
   b. yields better validity generalizations.
   c. facilitates the construction of parallel tests of a construct.
   d. enables the measurement of more constructs in each item.

5. An important purpose of criterion-referenced measurement is to
   a. compare an individual's performance to the performance of other individuals.
   b. compare an individual's performance to an absolute standard of proficiency.
   c. extensively sample a broadly defined content domain.
   d. compare an individual's performance to his or her previous performance.

6. A good way to check the reliability of a performance assessment is to use
   a. alternate test forms
   b. generalizability theory.

   c. hermeneutic theory.
   d. item-response theory.

7. A potentially serious disadvantage of general personality inventories is that they usually are
   a. expensive to purchase.
   b. difficult to score.
   c. difficult to administer.
   d. based on self-report.

8. The *Test Locator* is designed specifically to
   a. identify tests that measure a particular construct.
   b. determine the publisher of a particular test.
   c. identify reviews of a particular test.
   d. serve as a refereed journal that identifies new tests and reviews them.

9. Computer-adaptive testing (CAT) differs most dramatically from traditional standardized tests with regard to
   a. the opportunity to randomize the ordering of item presentation.
   b. the feasibility of machine scoring.
   c. computer interpretation of the numerical test scores.
   d. the potential for each test-taker to take a different version of the test.

10. The likelihood of eliciting honest responses to personality measures can be increased by
   a. assuring individuals that their answers will be kept confidential.
   b. telling individuals that they can see their results on the personality measure after it has been scored.
   c. using computer-adaptive testing.
   d. using principles drawn from hermeneutics.

CHAPTER 8

✦ Collecting Research Data with Questionnaires and Interviews

OVERVIEW

This chapter describes the use of questionnaires and interviews as data-collection instruments in both quantitative and qualitative research. We describe the distinctive characteristics of each method and compare their advantages and drawbacks. Also, we present techniques for constructing and administering these instruments.

OBJECTIVES

After studying this chapter, you should be able to

1. Describe the relative advantages and limitations of questionnaires and interviews in educational research.
2. Describe each step in constructing and administering a research questionnaire.
3. Describe several procedures for providing anonymity to questionnaire respondents.
4. Describe the relative advantages and limitations of closed-form and open-form items in questionnaires.
5. Explain the effects of respondents' knowledge and the number of items on attitude measurement in questionnaires.
6. Explain the advantages of precontacting a sample to whom a questionnaire will be sent.
7. Describe several features of a cover letter that are likely to increase the response rate to a mailed questionnaire.
8. Describe several strategies for following up with nonrespondents in order to maximize the response rate to a questionnaire.
9. Describe each step in preparing and conducting a research interview.

10. Describe the characteristics of key informant interviews, survey interviews, and focus group interviews.
11. Describe three levels of structure in quantitative research interviews and three levels of structure in qualitative research interviews.
12. Discuss the advantages of using telephone interviews and computer-assisted telephone interviewing.
13. Describe several factors that should be considered in selecting individuals to be research interviewers.
14. Describe the two phases in the training of research interviewers.
15. Describe four tasks that are involved in conducting an interview.
16. Explain the respective advantages and limitations of taking notes on an interview or recording it on tape or by computer.
17. Describe procedures for analyzing questionnaire or interview data using a quantitative research approach and using a qualitative research approach.

✦ *Touchstone in Research*

Fowler, F. J., Jr. (2001). *Survey research methods* (3rd ed.). Thousand Oaks, CA: Sage.

Krosnick, J. A. (1999). Survey research. *Annual Review of Psychology, 50,* 537–567.

Questionnaires and Interviews as Data-Collection Methods

Questionnaires and interviews are used extensively in educational research to collect data about phenomena that are not directly observable: inner experience, opinions, values, interests, and the like. They also can be used to collect data about observable phenomena, but more conveniently than by direct observation. For example, it is much easier to use a questionnaire or interview to ask a principal how many teachers have at least one computer in their classroom than to walk around the school and make your own count. Of course, the advantage of ease is negated if the resulting data have poor validity.

Questionnaires are documents that ask the same questions of all individuals in the sample. (If the sample has subgroups, the questions asked of each subgroup may vary.) Respondents record a written or typed response to each questionnaire item. Also, the respondents typically control the data-collection process: They can fill out the questionnaire at their convenience, answer the items in any order, take more than one sitting to complete it, make marginal comments, or skip questions.

Interviews consist of oral questions asked by the interviewer and oral responses by the research participants. Interviews typically involve individual respondents, but there is increasing interest in conducting group interviews. Respondents typically speak in their own words, and their responses are recorded by the interviewer, either verbatim on audiotape or videotape, through handwritten or computer-generated notes, or in short-term memory for later note taking. The interviewer is largely in control of the response situation, scheduling with the participant a mutually agreeable time and place and then controlling the question pace and sequence to fit the circumstances of the situation.

Selecting between Questionnaires and Interviews

Questionnaires have two advantages over interviews for collecting research data: The cost of sampling respondents over a wide geographic area is lower, and the time required to collect the data typically is much less. Questionnaires, however, cannot probe deeply into respondents' beliefs, attitudes, and inner experience. Also, once the questionnaire has been distributed, it is not possible to modify the items, even if they are unclear to some respondents.

The major advantage of interviews is their adaptability. Skilled interviewers can follow up a respondent's answers to obtain more information and clarify vague statements. They also can build trust and rapport with respondents, thus making it possible to obtain information that the individual probably would not reveal by any other data-collection method.

Robert Jackson and J. W. M. Rothney did an extensive follow-up study of 890 adults five years after their high school graduation.[1] The entire sample was sent a four-page mailed questionnaire, and a subsample of 50 individuals was selected for a personal interview that included the same questionnaire items. The researchers found that 83 percent of the questionnaires were returned, whereas 98 percent of the planned interviews were completed. Two experienced counselors rated each questionnaire or interview protocol for evidence of personal problems. The mean number of problems yielded by the questionnaire data was 2.8, whereas the mean number of problems yielded by the interview data was 8.8. Thus the interview yielded more complete information, particularly information concerning negative aspects of the self.[2]

---

1. Jackson, R. M., & Rothney, J. W. M. (1961). A comparative study of the mailed questionnaire and the interview in follow-up studies. *Personnel and Guidance Journal, 39,* 569–571.
2. These findings are generally supported by another study: Legacy, J., & Bennett, F. (1979). A comparison of the mailed questionnaire and personal interview methods of data collection for curriculum development in vocational education. *Journal of Vocational Education Research, 4,* 27–39.

This advantage of the interview method is offset by some limitations. One is th
difficult to standardize the interview situation so that the interviewer does not in
the respondent to answer questions a certain way. Another limitation is that in
cannot provide anonymity for the respondents. In other words, the respondents
veal their identity to the interviewer. Of course, the interviewer can analyze and
interview data so that the identity of the participants is not revealed.

The questionnaire is more commonly used in quantitative research, becau.
dardized, highly structured design is compatible with this approach. The interview is m..
commonly used in qualitative research, because it permits open-ended exploration of topics and elicits responses that are couched in the unique words of the respondents. However, both methods can be used in either type of research. Robert Yin, for example,
recommends using both methods when doing case study research.[3]

Validity and Reliability Issues

Questionnaires and interviews must meet the same standards of validity and reliability
that apply to other data-collection measures in educational research. As we explain below,
these standards are discussed at length elsewhere in the book. Therefore, do not interpret
our brief treatment of validity and reliability here as an indication that they are tangential
to good questionnaire and interview design.

If you are using a questionnaire or interview in a quantitative study, the validity and
reliability standards described in the chapter on tests (Chapter 7) are relevant. For example, questionnaires often solicit respondents' opinions about particular topics and issues.
If the researcher wishes to claim that these are the respondents' true opinions, she should
collect evidence that the content of the items represents these constructs (content-related
evidence of validity). Another option is to determine whether the respondents express similar opinions on other measures of the same construct (convergent evidence of validity).

In practice, researchers tend to apply looser validity and reliability standards to questionnaires and interviews than to tests because they typically are collecting information
that is highly structured and likely to be valid (e.g., the respondents' years of schooling).
Also, they are interested in the average response of the total group rather than the response
of a single individual. A lower level of item reliability is acceptable when the data are to be
analyzed and reported at the group level than at the level of individual respondents.

If you are using a questionnaire or interview in a qualitative study, the validity and reliability standards described in Chapter 14 are applicable. For example, the validity of a
questionnaire or interview can be checked by using the method of triangulation described
in that chapter.

Survey Research

The term *survey* frequently is used to describe research that involves administering questionnaires or interviews. The purpose of a **survey** is to use questionnaires or interviews to
collect data from a sample that has been selected to represent a population to which the
findings of the data analysis can be generalized. This emphasis on population generalization is characteristic of quantitative research, but not of qualitative research. Because we
consider both qualitative and quantitative research in this chapter, we do not use the term
survey as a general label for the use of questionnaires and interviews in research. However,
the chapter includes references to publications about surveys where appropriate.

The term *survey research* occasionally is used as if it were a particular type of research
design. We think that it is less confusing if this term is used to refer to research studies that

---

3. Yin, R. K. (1994). *Case study research: Design and methods* (2nd ed.). Thousand Oaks, CA: Sage.

rely primarily on questionnaires or interviews for data collection. The reason is that either type of instrument can be used to achieve the purposes of various research designs (particularly, descriptive, causal-comparative, and case-study designs). For example, Table 8.1 on page 236 presents the results of a data analysis that is typical of a causal-comparative research design. The results shown in Table 8.2 (see page 250) are typical of a descriptive research design.

✦ Touchstone in Research

Mangione, T. W. (1998). Mail surveys. In L. Bickman & D. J. Rog (Eds.), *Handbook of applied social research methods* (pp. 399–427). Thousand Oaks, CA: Sage.

Steps in Constructing and Administering a Research Questionnaire

In this section we describe the major steps in carrying out a research study using a questionnaire: (1) defining research objectives, (2) selecting a sample, (3) designing the questionnaire format, (4) pretesting the questionnaire, (5) precontacting the sample, (6) writing a cover letter and distributing the questionnaire, (7) following up with nonrespondents, and (8) analyzing questionnaire data.

Step 1: Defining Research Objectives

Some researchers develop a questionnaire before they have thoroughly considered what they hope to obtain from the results. It is important that you define your research problem and list the specific objectives to be achieved, or hypotheses to be tested, by the questionnaire. You might start with a broad topic (e.g., teachers' involvement in staff development), but you should sharpen its focus before beginning on the design of the questionnaire.

D. A. deVaus suggested five types of questions that you can ask yourself for this purpose.[4] They are stated below in relation to the above-mentioned topic, teachers' involvement in staff development:

1. What is the *time frame* of your interest? Are you interested in teachers' current involvement in staff development, or do you want to study trends in their involvement over a period of years?
2. What is the *geographical location* of your interest? Do you want to study teachers in a particular state or region, or do you want to compare teachers in different locations?
3. Are you interested in a broad descriptive study or do you want to specify and compare different *subgroups*? For example, will you compare elementary, middle school, and high school teachers, or will you study teachers in general?
4. What *aspect* of the topic do you want to study? Are you interested in teachers' involvement in particular types of staff development activities, whether their involvement is mandatory or voluntary, or the amount of involvement over a given time period?
5. How *abstract* is your interest? For example, are you interested in reporting facts, or do you want to interpret the information, relate it to a broad social context, or develop theory from the findings?

In describing the steps involved in conducting a questionnaire study, we shall refer to a study by Corrine Glesne and Rodman Webb.[5] These researchers were interested in track-

---

4. deVaus, D. A. (1992). *Surveys in social research* (3rd ed.). Boston: Allen & Unwin.
5. Glesne, C., & Webb, R. (1993). Teaching qualitative research: Who does what? *International Journal of Qualitative Studies in Education, 6,* 253–266.

ing the growing emphasis on qualitative research in higher education in the United States. They wanted to determine who teaches qualitative research methods courses, the content of their courses, and their teaching methods. Their questionnaire was designed to obtain this information:

> The survey [questionnaire] asked about the training and academic background of qualitative research professors, content of courses, program requirements, and faculty perceptions of and interaction with students pursuing qualitative research dissertations.[6]

Glesne and Webb noted the irony of basing a study about the teaching of qualitative research methods courses on a quantitatively-oriented questionnaire survey. They chose to use questionnaires anyway because of their usefulness in collecting both closed and open-ended information from a widespread sample.

Step 2: Selecting a Sample

Once your research objectives or hypotheses are clearly stated, you should identify the target population from which your sample will be selected. (This and other sampling techniques are described in Chapter 6.) If you do not have thorough knowledge of the situation, you might make the mistake of sending your questionnaire to a group that does not have the desired information. For example, a graduate student seeking data on school financial policies sent questionnaires to principals of elementary and secondary schools. Many of the returned questionnaires were incomplete, and few specific facts of the sort wanted were obtained. This questionnaire failed because at that time the school superintendent and district specialists handled most matters concerning school finance. Because the principals who received the questionnaire had little specific knowledge about the topic, they were unable to supply the information requested.

The salience of the questionnaire content to the respondents (i.e., how important or prominent a concern it is for them) affects both the accuracy of the information received and the rate of response. A review of 181 studies using questionnaires judged to be "salient," "possibly salient," or "nonsalient" to the respondents revealed that the return rate averaged 77 percent for the salient studies, 66 percent for those judged possibly salient, and only 42 percent for those judged nonsalient.[7] These findings suggest the need to select a sample for whom your questionnaire items will be highly salient.

In the study by Glesne and Webb, the researchers gained access to a mailing list for the *International Journal of Qualitative Studies in Education,* which is a major journal publishing qualitative research studies. They then sent a copy of their questionnaire to 360 professors whose names were on the journal's mailing list. The researchers commented:

> This was, admittedly, a fishing-net approach. Our assumption was that this readership would include people who teach qualitative research methods courses, and not everyone on the list taught such courses.[8]

Using this admittedly biased sampling approach, they received usable questionnaires from 73 respondents in 37 different states. The sample included 40 men and 33 women. Twenty-five held the title of professor; 28 the title of associate professor, 18 the title of assistant professor, and 2 the title of lecturer.

---

6. Ibid., p. 254.
7. Heberlein, T. A., & Baumgartner, R. (1978). Factors affecting response rates to mailed questionnaires: A quantitative analysis of the published literature. *American Sociological Review, 43,* 447–462.
8. Glesne & Webb, Teaching qualitative research, p. 254.

✦ *Touchstone in Research*

Fowler, F. J., Jr. (1998). Design and evaluation of survey questions. In L. Bickman & D. J. Rog (Eds.), *Handbook of applied social research methods* (pp. 343–374). Thousand Oaks, CA: Sage.

Step 3: Designing the Questionnaire

Some research questionnaires appear to have been thrown together in an hour or two. The experience of receiving these haphazard questionnaires has led many educators to develop negative attitudes about the questionnaire as a research approach, and so they deposit them in the recycling box with little more than a quick glance. You will need to overcome these negative attitudes by careful construction and administration of your questionnaire. Figure 8.1 summarizes guidelines for designing questionnaires. These guidelines are based on research findings about factors that influence questionnaire return rate.

FIGURE 8.1

Guidelines for Designing a Questionnaire

1. Keep the questionnaire as short as possible.
2. Do not use technical terms, jargon, or complex terms that respondents may not understand.
3. Avoid using the words *questionnaire* or *checklist* on your form. Many persons are biased against these terms.
4. Make the questionnaire attractive by such techniques as using brightly colored ink or paper and laser printing.
5. Organize the items so they are easy to read and complete.
6. Number the questionnaire pages and items.
7. Put the name and address of the individual to whom the questionnaire should be returned both at the beginning and end of the questionnaire, even if a self-addressed envelope is included.
8. Include brief, clear instructions, printed in bold type and in upper and lower case (Words that are all capital letters are hard to read.)
9. Organize the questionnaire in a logical sequence. For example, you might group items with the same content or items having the same response options together.
10. When moving to a new topic, include a transitional sentence to help respondents switch their train of thought.
11. Begin with a few interesting and nonthreatening items.
12. Put threatening or difficult items near the end of the questionnaire.
13. Do not put important items at the end of a long questionnaire.
14. Provide a rationale for the items so that the respondent understands their relevance to the study.
15. Include examples of how to respond to items that might be confusing or difficult to understand.
16. Avoid terms like *several, most,* and *usually,* which have no precise meaning.
17. State each item in as brief a form as possible.
18. Avoid negatively stated items because they are likely to be misread by respondents. The negative word tends to be overlooked, and respondents might give an answer that is opposite to their real opinion.
19. Avoid "double-barreled" items that require the subject to respond to two separate ideas with a single answer. For example: *Although labor unions are desirable in most fields, they have no place in the teaching profession.*
20. When a general question and a related specific question are to be asked together, it is preferable to ask the general question first. If the specific question is asked first, it tends to narrow unnecessarily the respondent's focus when answering the general question that follows.
21. Avoid biased or leading questions. If the respondent is given hints as to the type of answer that is preferred, there is a tendency to give that response.

Source: Adapted from information in: Berdie, D. R., Anderson, J. F., & Niebuhr, M. A. (1986). Questionnaires: Design and use (2nd ed.). Metuchen, NJ: Scarecrow Press.

Anonymity

In most educational studies, respondents are asked to identify themselves, but anonymity might be necessary if highly personal or threatening information is requested. A questionnaire dealing with sexual behavior, for example, might receive more honest responses if the respondents remain anonymous.

The major problem with anonymous questionnaires is that follow-ups to improve the return rate are impossible. There are several solutions to this problem. One is to create a master code sheet that contains a code for each individual in the sample. The codes are put on the questionnaires. When an individual returns the questionnaire, the researcher can check off that person's name on the master code sheet. After a designated period of time, the researcher can determine which individuals have not returned their questionnaires and send them a new questionnaire.

This method is not completely anonymous, because the researcher can link the questionnaire (which has the code on it) to the individual's name by referring to the master code sheet. For complete anonymity, a variation of this approach can be used. The researcher sends each individual a prepaid postcard with the code on it and a questionnaire that contains no code. When the individual completes the questionnaire, she returns the questionnaire and the postcard separately. The postcard tells the researcher that this individual has completed the questionnaire, but he does not know which of the returned questionnaires belong to that individual.

Item Form

Writing items for questionnaires (and for interviews, too) may seem straightforward, but it is actually an art form. You need to be able to write succinctly and clearly. This is no easy matter. More importantly, you need to have a good understanding of your respondents so that you can use language that they understand, so that you can obtain all the information you need without exhausting their patience, and so that the items engage their interest and willingness to respond honestly.

A major difficulty in constructing questionnaire items is that educational terms often have multiple meanings. For example, the terms *charter school, standards-based education,* and *teacher empowerment* may mean different things depending on the individual educator and the region in which she works. If you use such a term in a questionnaire item, it is highly advisable to include a definition that corresponds to your research objectives. For example, suppose a researcher is interested in educators' responses to the charter-school movement, not as it is occurring nationally but within the state being studied. Given this objective, the item might read: "The state department of education adopted a statute in 2001 that allows school districts to start charter schools, which are defined as schools that receive district funding but are administered independently, albeit with mandatory conformance to standards of the state department of education. What is the current status of charter schools of this type in your district?"

A questionnaire item can be either **closed form,** meaning that the question permits only prespecified responses (similar to a multiple-choice question), or **open form,** meaning that respondents can make any response they wish (similar to an essay question). Which form to use is determined by the objective of the particular question. Evidence on the relative merits of closed and open questions, however, suggests that the two formats produce similar information.[9]

9. Bradburn, N. M. (1982). Question-wording effects in surveys. In: R. M. Hogarth (Ed.), *Question framing and response consistency* (pp. 65–76). San Francisco: Jossey-Bass.

The advantage of designing questions in closed form is that it makes quantification and analysis of results easier. For example, suppose you wish to know the size of a teacher's home town. Probably the least useful way to ask the question is: What is your home town? This question requires that you be able to read each teacher's response and then look it up in an atlas to determine the population. A somewhat better question would be: What is the population of your home town? In this case you could classify the responses into population categories such as those used by the U.S. Census Bureau. A still better approach would be to ask: What is the population of your home town? (Check one.), and provide the following response choices:

_____ rural, unincorporated
_____ incorporated, under 1000
_____ 1,000 to 2,500
_____ 2,500 to 5,000
_____ 5,000 to 10,000
_____ 10,000 to 50,000
_____ 50,000 to 250,000
_____ over 250,000
_____ don't know

This item requires little effort on your part to analyze the data, and also minimal effort from the respondents.

To determine the multiple-choice categories to use in closed-form questions, you can pilot-test the question by asking it in open form of a small number of respondents. Their answers can be used to develop the categories for the closed-form item. If you expect unusual responses, an "other" option can be provided.

In the questionnaire study on the teaching of qualitative research, Glesne and Webb began by interviewing several qualitative researchers about their training, teaching, and research. They used the interview information to develop an open-ended pilot questionnaire, and sent it to six professors of qualitative research. Feedback indicated that the open-ended questions were interesting, but time-consuming. There was a concern that few professors would take the hour or more needed to complete the questionnaire. Based on this feedback, the researchers redesigned the questionnaire into a closed-form format, with open-ended options attached to most items.

Measuring Attitudes

Questionnaires typically contain items each of which elicits a different bit of information. In effect, each item is a one-item test. The use of a one-item test is quite satisfactory when you are seeking a specific fact, such as number of years of full-time teaching experience, the number of wins and losses during a particular football coach's tenure, or the proportion of students failing intermediate algebra. When questions assess attitudes, however, the one-item test approach is questionable with respect to both validity and reliability. A questionnaire that measures attitudes generally must be constructed as an attitude scale and must use a substantial number of items (usually at least 10) in order to obtain a reliable assessment of an individual's attitude.[10]

If you are planning to collect information about attitudes, you should first do a search of the research literature to determine whether a scale suitable for your purposes already

---

10. For an expanded discussion of the measurement of attitudes by questionnaire, see: Schuman, H., & Presser, S. (1996). *Questions and answers in attitude surveys: Experiments on question form, wording, and context.* Thousand Oaks, CA: Sage.

has been constructed. (See Chapter 4 and Appendix E for information on locating such measures.) If a suitable scale is not available, you will need to develop one. **Likert scales,** which typically ask for the extent of agreement with an attitude item (for example, a five-point scale ranging from "strongly disagree" to "strongly agree") are a common type of attitude scale.

If you develop an attitude scale for your questionnaire study, you should pilot-test it in order to check its reliability and validity. Also, the pilot test should determine whether individuals in the sample have sufficient knowledge and understanding to express a meaningful opinion about the topic. Otherwise, their responses to the attitude scale will be of questionable value.

One method of dealing with respondents who lack familiarity with a topic is to include a "no opinion" option as one of the response alternatives for each attitude item. Even still, individuals with little or no information about the topic might express an opinion in order to conceal their ignorance, or because they feel social pressure to express a particular opinion. For example, Irving Allen conducted a questionnaire study of respondents attitudes' toward individuals and organizations that were the subject of considerable media attention at the time.[11] The respondents could express a favorable or unfavorable attitude using six Likert-type categories, or they could use a seventh category to express no knowledge of a particular individual or organization. Ten percent of the sample expressed a favorable or unfavorable attitude toward a fictitious organization, about which it was impossible for them to have any knowledge! The subjects responding to the fictitious item were found to have less formal education than the rest of the sample. They also were more likely to express attitudes toward the other organizations and individuals listed on the questionnaire than to check the "don't know" category, and to express more favorable attitudes.

As we stated above, a "no opinion" option for each attitude item might alleviate the problem identified in Allen's study. Another strategy is to include several information questions at the beginning of an attitude questionnaire that can be used to screen out respondents who display little or no knowledge of the topics being studied.

Web Questionnaires

Researchers increasingly are using the World Wide Web to administer questionnaires. For example, Mike Carbonaro and Joyce Bainbridge administered a Web questionnaire to obtain data about elementary teachers' use of Canadian children's literature in the classroom.[12] Of the 63 school districts in the target population, 53 agreed to participate. In the next phase of sample selection, the principal of each of 945 schools in the 53 districts was invited to participate; a total of 207 accepted. Each principal asked an appropriate teacher to complete the Internet-based questionnaire. A total of 110 teachers (out of a possible 207 teachers) completed it.

The following are distinctive features of the questionnaire design and administration process used by the researchers:

1. Teachers logged onto the survey Web site using a designated ID and password to avoid having any inappropriate person complete the questionnaire. Also, by logging on, the teachers acknowledged their consent to participate in the study.

✦ Touchstone in Research

Schmidt, W. C. (1997). World-Wide Web survey research: Benefits, potential problems, and solutions. *Behavior Research Methods, Instruments, and Computers, 29,* 274–279.

11. Allen, I. L. (1966). Detecting respondents who fake and confuse information about question areas on surveys. *Journal of Applied Psychology, 50,* 523–528.
12. Carbonaro, M., & Bainbridge, J. (2000). Design and development of a process for web-based survey research. *Alberta Journal of Educational Research, 46,* 392–394.

2. Teachers responded to Likert scale items and closed-form items by clicking on "radio buttons" (a Web-page feature). They responded to rank-order items by entering a number and to open-form items by typing a response.
3. After completing the questionnaire, teachers clicked a SUBMIT button, which transmitted their data to the researchers' Web server. If a teacher clicked this item without completing the entire questionnaire, the Web software informed the teacher of which items still required completion.
4. The questionnaire data were secured in the researchers' Web server, so they were only available to them and the Web-server programmer.
5. Because the raw data were in electronic form, it was possible to import them directly into statistical software for analysis.

This approach to questionnaire design and administration has obvious advantages over conventional paper-and-pencil mailed questionnaires: Postal costs are eliminated; the possibility of missing data within questionnaires is eliminated; and there is no need to transfer data manually from the questionnaire into an electronic format and check for possible errors in the transfer process. Also, Internet questionnaires can be designed to be interactive: Items can be tailored to the individual respondent, and respondents can be given feedback as they complete the items.

Web questionnaires are a powerful research tool, but they have costs and limitations that you should consider in deciding whether to use one in your research study. You will need to have access to a Web server and the ability to use specialized software to design the questionnaire, to process incoming data, and to guard against data-security breaches and multiple submissions from the same respondent or a submission from an individual not in the sample. Also, each respondent needs to have access to a Web browser and the ability to use it. Otherwise, the research study is vulnerable to sampling bias.[13]

Step 4: Pilot-Testing the Questionnaire

You should carry out a thorough pilot test of the questionnaire before using it in your study. The pilot test should include a sample of individuals from the population from which you plan to draw your respondents. Also, the pilot-test form of the questionnaire should provide space for respondents to make criticisms and recommendations for improving the questionnaire. Another useful pilot-test strategy is to ask respondents to state in their own words what they think each question means. The questions should be revised and retested until they are understood accurately by all or most members of the pilot-test sample.

In a study of this procedure, William Belson elicited answers from respondents to 29 questions that incorporated problems of interpretation frequently found in questionnaire items.[14] He then studied the respondents' interpretations of the questions in a second in-depth interview. On average, only 29 percent of the respondents interpreted the questions within permissible limits of the intended interpretation. This finding demonstrates the importance of questionnaire wording and the need to check it by a pilot test.

Questionnaires mailed to educators generally can be expected to yield a higher percentage of replies than questionnaires mailed to samples of the general population. The response rate is higher for an educational questionnaire because it usually is targeted at a homogeneous group, and this makes it possible to prepare a specific appeal for participation that is likely to be effective. If you have received responses from less than 66 percent

13. Bradley, N. (1999). Sampling for Internet surveys. An examination of respondent selection for Internet research. *Journal of the Market Research Society, 41,* 387–395.
14. Belson, W. A. (1981). *The design and understanding of survey questions.* Lanham, MD: Lexington.

of the pilot-test sample, you probably should make changes in the questionnaire or in the procedures for administering it before sending the questionnaire to the participants in your main study.

Apparently a pilot test of the questionnaire used by Glesne and Webb was not conducted. The authors state:

> Our interview and subsequent survey questions grew out of our own experiences and from reading the few available sources on teaching qualitative research. We realize now that we should have gathered more demographic data such as information on ethnicity, salary, years of service, and years at current rank. . . . If we had asked for more information about respondents, we would likely have had other questions as well.[15]

The researchers' comments reinforce the desirability of pilot-testing a questionnaire before distributing it.

Step 5: Precontacting the Sample

Researchers have found that contacting respondents before sending a questionnaire increases the rate of response. A **precontact** involves the researchers identifying themselves, discussing the purpose of the study, and requesting cooperation. The precontact can take the form of a letter, postcard, or telephone call, but some evidence suggests that telephone contacts are the most effective.[16] Respondents also can be asked to return a postcard mailed to them indicating their willingness to cooperate.

Precontacts probably are effective because they alert respondents to the imminent arrival of the questionnaire, thus reducing the chance that it will be thrown out as junk mail. Precontacts also put a more personal, human face on the research study. Finally, having once agreed to cooperate, the respondent is under some psychological pressure to do so when the questionnaire arrives.

Step 6: Writing a Cover Letter

The main objective in doing a questionnaire survey is to get a high return rate. We know of studies where the return rate was as low as 20 percent, which makes it virtually impossible to generalize from the sample's data to the population that it is intended to represent.

Because the cover letter accompanying the questionnaire strongly influences the return rate, it should be designed carefully. The letter should be brief, but it must convey certain information and impressions. The purpose of the study should be explained so as to persuade the respondents that the study is significant and that their answers are important. When using a questionnaire that includes sensitive or potentially threatening questions, you should provide a specific description of how confidentiality will be maintained. You also should explain the conditions that you have established for informed consent (see Chapter 3). A sample cover letter is shown in Figure 8.2.

Subtle flattery in the cover letter can have a positive effect. If appropriate, you can emphasize the importance of the respondent's professional affiliation and the value of information that only members with this affiliation can supply. An offer to send the respondent a copy of the results also is effective. If such a promise is made, it should be honored. Failure to do so is unethical, and will lessen respondents' willingness to participate in other research studies.

15. Glesne & Webb, Teaching qualitative research, pp. 254–255.
16. Linsky, A. S. (1975). Stimulating responses to mailed questionnaires: A review. *Public Opinion Quarterly, 39,* 82–101.

FIGURE 8.2

Sample Cover Letter for a Mail Questionnaire

Letterhead paper

OKLABAMA STATE UNIVERSITY
Collegetown, Oklabama
M. A. Brown, President

College of Education
I. B. Smith, Dean

February 1, 2002

Use mail-merge feature of word processor to personalize address ⟶

Mr. A. B. Jones
Superintendent of Schools
Mediumtown, Oklabama

Duplicated using word processor or offset process to look like individually typed letter ⟶

Purpose of study

Dear Mr. Jones:

    The attached survey instrument concerned with procedures used in selecting elementary school principals is part of a statewide study being carried on cooperatively by the State Department of Public Instruction and Oklabama State University. This project is concerned specifically with determining the present status of principal selection in our state. The re-

Importance of study ⟶ sults of this study will help to provide criteria to be used for developing better selection procedures and for improving the administrator training program at Oklabama University.

Importance of respondent ⟶

    We are particularly desirous of obtaining your responses because your experience in principal selection will contribute significantly toward solving some of the problems we face in this important area of educa-tion. The enclosed instrument has been tested with a sampling of school administrators, and we have revised it in order to make it possible for us to obtain all necessary data while requiring a minimum of your time. The

Reasonable but specific time limit

average time required for administrators trying out the survey instru-ment was 9.5 minutes.

Make return convenient for respondents ⟶

    We will appreciate it if you will complete the enclosed form prior to February 10th and return it in the stamped, self-addressed envelope enclosed. Other phases of this research cannot be carried out until we complete analysis of the survey data. We would welcome any com-ments that you may have concerning any aspect of principal selection

Assurance of confidentiality ⟶ not covered in the instrument. Your responses will be held in strictest confidence.

Informed consent ⟶

    Informed consent procedures for this study are described on the enclosed sheet. Please take a moment now to read it.

Offer results ⟶
Thank respondent ⟶

    We will be pleased to send you a summary of the survey results if you desire. Thank you for your cooperation.

Print in different color to appear personally signed

Sincerely yours,

I. B. Smith

Signed by high-status educator ⟶

I. B. Smith, Dean

Enclosure
sjc

It is desirable to associate your study with a professional organization with which prospective respondents might identify. For example, superintendents within a particular state might respond favorably to a letter signed by the state school superintendent or the president of a school administrators' association. If your study is well designed and deals with a significant problem, it usually is possible to have your cover letter signed by an individual whose endorsement represents a favorable symbol of authority to the respondents.

Responses to a questionnaire that is not aimed at a specific professional group tend to be more difficult to obtain because specific appeals cannot be made. Even with a heterogeneous group, however, you might be able to phrase your appeal in terms of common values that you expect most individuals to have, such as the importance of education and community improvement.

Researchers have explored the effect of enclosing a small cash reward with a questionnaire.[17] Such rewards, usually ranging from a quarter to a dollar, consistently increased the response rate, as did small gifts or premiums. Because most of these studies were conducted over 20 years ago, inflation might have weakened the effect of small rewards. A more recent study that offered a reward of two dollars to complete a 25-page questionnaire got a quicker reply from persons offered the reward, but the eventual response rate after follow-up attempts was about the same for respondents who received and who did not receive the reward.[18] If you provide a reward, it should be described as a token of appreciation rather than as payment for the respondent's time.

One of the items needed in the cover letter is a request that the questionnaire be returned by a particular date. Set this date so that the respondent will have sufficient time to fill out and return the questionnaire without rushing, but will not put it aside to do later. People tend to procrastinate if too generous a time allowance is given. A rule of thumb is to calculate the probable mailing time and allow the individual an additional week to complete the questionnaire and return it. You should include a stamped, self-addressed envelope with the questionnaire, so that individuals can respond with a minimum of inconvenience.

The design and neatness of your questionnaire and accompanying letter can improve the response rate. More expensive methods of duplication are usually worth the extra cost. A cover letter reproduced by the offset process on letterhead paper and signed with a different color ink will command more attention than one poorly dittoed on cheap paper. A word processor can produce individually typed letters, differing only in the names and addresses of the recipients, at a relatively low cost. Such letters are superior to the best offset copies and have the added advantage that small changes can be made at a reasonable cost in each letter to make it more individualized.

Step 7: Following Up with Nonrespondents

A few days after the time limit specified in the cover letter, it is desirable to contact nonrespondents by sending a follow-up letter, along with another copy of the questionnaire and another self-addressed envelope.[19] Because your original cover letter did not succeed with the nonrespondent group, there is little point in sending the same letter again. Instead, you should try a different approach in your appeal for cooperation. For example, if you used a

---

17. For reviews of studies offering cash rewards and premiums, see: Linsky, Stimulating responses; Heberlein & Baumgartner, Factors affecting response rates.
18. Shackelton, V. J., & Wild, J. (1982). Effects of incentives and personal contact on response rate to a mailed questionnaire. *Psychological Reports, 50,* 365–366.
19. Heberlein, T. A., & Baumgartner, R. (1981). Is a questionnaire necessary in a second mailing? *Public Opinion Quarterly, 45,* 102–108.

personal appeal in the initial letter, you might try a professional appeal in the first follow-up letter.

Successful follow-up letters usually take the approach that the researcher is confident the individual wished to fill out the questionnaire, but perhaps because of some oversight or an error on the researcher's part, it was overlooked. The follow-up letter then should repeat the importance of the study and the value of the individual's contribution, but with somewhat different language and emphasis from that in the original letter.

Postcard reminders have been tried also, and in some cases they have been found as effective as letters. However, Blaine Worthen and E. J. Brezezinski found that a form letter with another copy of the questionnaire obtained up to 7 percent more responses than a postcard with the same message.[20]

Figure 8.3 shows the pattern of responses reported in a review of 98 experimental studies on this problem. Although the reviewers point out that the results varied considerably across studies, these average percentages suggest what can be expected from different numbers of follow-ups. A few of the studies used four or more follow-ups, but this did not lead to a significant increase in returns over three follow-ups.

Suppose that you have a substantial percentage of nonrespondents after reaching the cutoff date for the return of the questionnaires to be included in your data analysis. You

FIGURE 8.3

A Synthesis of Research Findings on Response Rates for Initial Mailing and Different Numbers of Follow-ups

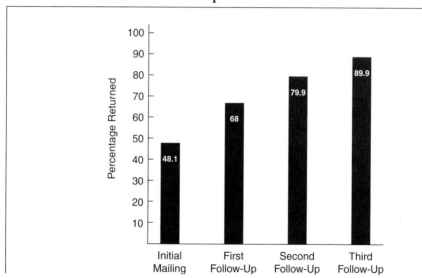

Source: Adapted from table 1 on p. 451 in: Heberlein, T.A., & Bumgartner, P. (1978). Factors affecting response rates to mailed questionnaires: A quantitative analysis of the published literature. *American Sociological Review, 43*, 447–462.

20. Worthen, B. R., & Brezezinski, E. J. (1973, February). An experimental study of techniques for increasing return rate in mail surveys. Paper presented at the annual meeting of the American Educational Research Association, New Orleans.

should ask yourself: How would the results differ if all respondents had returned the questionnaire? If only a small percentage of respondents did not respond, this question is not critical. If more than 20 percent are missing, however, you need to pose this question because the sample for whom data are available might no longer be representative of the population to which you wish to generalize your findings. Researchers have found that respondents and nonrespondents to questionnaires do not differ in most personality characteristics, but nonrespondents tend to have achieved less academic success than respondents.[21]

The ideal method to determine whether nonrespondents to your questionnaire differ from the respondents is to randomly select a small number of individuals from the nonresponding group. Then solicit their cooperation in letting you administer the questionnaire to them in an in-person or telephone-interview format. Individuals who are reluctant to complete a questionnaire may be more amenable to this approach.

A sample of 20 individuals should be sufficient to check the nonresponding group. A comparison of their responses to each item with the responses of those who replied initially will enable you to determine whether the nonresponding sample is biased. In this case, you should note these differences and discuss their significance in reporting the results of the responding sample.

Step 8: Analyzing Questionnaire Data

The researchers who studied the teaching of qualitative research in institutions of higher education in the United States followed a typical approach to analyzing questionnaire data:

> All forced-choice answers in the survey were coded and entered into the *Ecstatic* analysis program for quantitative data. This procedure allowed the easy generation of percentages, means, ranges, and cross tabulations. All comments and open-ended answers were entered in full into the *Ethnograph* text analysis program which assisted in coding and sorting respondents' words so that patterns could be ascertained.[22]

The quantitative data were analyzed to yield frequencies and percentages of respondents checking each response category on particular closed-ended questions. For example, Table 8.1 shows the degree to which professors teaching qualitative research methods courses themselves have had formal coursework in qualitative research. Glesne and Webb concluded from these results that

> new faculty responsible for teaching qualitative methods courses generally have had more formal course work in qualitative methodology than older professors. . . . These percentages are not surprising, since the offering of qualitative research courses is fairly recent in most colleges of education. . . . What is surprising is that at each of the professorate levels, a higher percentage of women were trained in qualitative research than men.[23]

The results shown in Table 8.1 are consistent with causal-comparative research design (see Chapter 10). None of the three variables—professorial rank, gender, and amount of qualitative-research coursework—was experimentally manipulated by the researchers. The three variables were related to each other in the data analysis in such a way as to reveal

---

21. For a summary of these findings, see the discussion of differences between volunteers and nonvolunteers in Chapter 6.
22. Glesne & Webb, Teaching qualitative research, p. 254. *Ecstatic* is a computer program for statistical analysis of data. *Ethnograph* is a computer program for analyzing documents and transcriptions. Cross-tabulations are statistical analyses that show the relationship between two variables.
23. Glesne & Webb, Teaching qualitative research, p. 255.

TABLE 8.1

Formal Coursework in Qualitative Research Taken by Faculty Teaching Qualitative Methods Courses

Title	Coursework (%)	Little or No Coursework (%)	Total
Full Professors	6 (24%)	19 (76%)	25
Males*	2 (8%)	17 (68%)	19
Females	4 (16%)	2 (8%)	6
Associate Professors	16 (57%)	12 (43%)	28
Males	5 (18%)	7 (25%)	12
Females	11 (39%)	5 (18%)	16
Assistant Professors	15 (83%)	3 (16%)	18
Males	6 (33%)	1 (5%)	7
Females*	9 (50%)	2 (11%)	11

*Indicates that one respondent did not answer the question; the two lecturers were not included in the table.
Source: Table 1 on p. 255 in: Glesne, C., & Webb, R. (1993). Teaching qualitative research: Who does what? *International Journal of Qualitative Studies in Education, 6,* 253–266. Reprinted with permission of Taylor & Francis, Ltd.

potential cause-and-effect relationships. In particular, the observed relationship between gender and coursework suggests (but by no means *proves*) that gender plays a causal role in whether an individual chooses to specialize in qualitative research methods. Further research would be necessary to determine whether and how these two variables are causally related to each other.

We emphasize this feature of Glesne and Webb's data analysis because it is commonly assumed that questionnaires and interviews are only suitable, or most suitable, for descriptive research. In fact, questionnaires and interviews can be used in various research designs.

Glesne and Webb included several comments from respondents in response to particular questions. In this way, the reader is provided an emic perspective, that is, the respondents' perspective on the phenomenon being studied. For example, they included this comment from a respondent to an open-form question about what excites them about teaching qualitative research methods courses:

> I really enjoy and feel challenged to support students' research and their forays into what is often new territory—seeing their eyes light up when they see what research can be and when they move from "I thought it'd be easier" to "Wow, I never knew what was involved!"[24]

Quantitative data collected by questionnaires can be analyzed by the statistical methods described in Chapter 5. Methods for analyzing qualitative data are described in Chapter 14.

Steps in Preparing and Conducting Research Interviews

The steps involved in using interviews in educational research are similar to those involved in using questionnaires. The steps are (1) defining the purpose of the study, (2) selecting a

✦ *Touchstone in Research*

Fontana, A., & Frey, J. H. (2000). The interview: From structured questions to negotiated text. In N. K. Denzin & Y. S. Lincoln (Eds.), *Handbook of qualitative research* (2nd ed., pp. 645–672). Thousand Oaks, CA: Sage.

Seidman, I. E. (1997). *Interviewing as qualitative research: A guide for researchers in education and the social sciences* (2nd ed.). New York: Teachers College.

24. Ibid., p. 262.

sample, (3) designing the interview format, (4) developing questions, (5) selecting and training interviewers, (6) doing a pilot test of the interview procedures, (7) conducting the interviews, and (8) analyzing the interview data.[25]

Step 1: Defining the Purpose of the Interview

The first step in a study that will employ interviews to collect research data is to define the purpose of the study. Your purpose will determine the nature of the interview because different purposes require different levels of structure, types of questions, and interviewer qualifications.

The different interests and orientations of researchers have given rise to different types of interviews. Several have been developed for a particular purpose and context, but you may be able to adapt them for investigating your research problem. The following are three major types of research interviews: key informant interviews, survey interviews, and group interviews.

Key Informant Interviews

In a **key informant interview,** the interviewer collects data from individuals who have special knowledge or perceptions that would not otherwise be available to the researcher. Key informants often have more knowledge, better communication skills, or different perspectives than other members of the defined population.

A study by Eleanor Lynch, Rena Lewis, and Diane Murphy illustrates the use of key informant interviews in educational research.[26] The researchers described the purpose of their study as follows:

> The changing needs of children with chronic illnesses pose some serious questions:
> - How can school systems respond most effectively to the needs of children with chronic illness?
> - Should children be served under special education? If yes, how can procedures be adapted to allow for the week-to-week differences in children's educational needs?
> - How can we ensure that adequate information is available to teachers and other school personnel working with children with chronic illnesses?
> - What do families want for their children with chronic illness and how can schools help support families' wishes?[27]

The researchers identified two groups of key informants from whom to collect interview data relating to these questions. One group was school district personnel who were in charge of services for children with chronic illnesses. This group could be expected to have expert knowledge about the research problem being investigated. The other group included parents of chronically ill children. The parents were key informants because they had direct knowledge of their family's needs with respect to the chronically ill child. We refer to this study by Lynch and her associates in the following sections to illustrate the various steps that are involved in using interviews in a research study.

Survey Interviews

The purpose of **survey interviews** is to supplement data that have been collected by other methods. Margaret LeCompte, Judith Preissle, and Renata Tesch describe three types of

25. These steps are adapted from Stewart, C. J., & Cash, W. B., Jr. (1997). *Interviewing: Principles and practices* (8th ed.). Madison, WI: Brown & Benchmark.
26. Lynch, E. W., Lewis, R. B., & Murphy, D. S. (1992). Educational services for children with chronic illnesses: Perspectives of educators and families. *Exceptional Children, 59,* 210–220.
27. Ibid., pp. 211–212.

survey interviews.[28] The first type is the **confirmation survey interview,** which is a structured interview that produces evidence to confirm earlier findings. These interviews are especially useful in large-scale questionnaire studies where in-depth interviewing cannot be carried out for all respondents.

The second type of survey interview is the **participant construct interview,** which is used to learn how informants structure their physical and social world. The result is a set of category systems used by the participant. For example, LeCompte conducted a research study in which she asked kindergarten children to tell her all the things they thought they and their teachers could do in kindergarten.[29] The responses were used to develop a typology of children's perceptions of student and teacher roles.

The third type of survey interview involves projective techniques. **Projective techniques** use ambiguous stimuli to elicit subconscious perceptions that cannot be observed in the natural setting or solicited through regular interviewing. Projective techniques are further explained in Chapter 7.

◆ Touchstone in Research

Morgan, D. L. (1997). *Focus groups as qualitative research* (2nd ed.). Thousand Oaks, CA: Sage.

Williams, A., & Katz, L. (2001). Focus group methodology in education: Some theoretical and practical considerations. *International Electronic Journal for Leadership in Learning,* 5(3). Retrieved October 28, 2001 from www.ucalgary.ca/~iejll/volume5/katz.html

Focus Group Interviews

A group interview involves addressing questions to a group of individuals who have been assembled for this specific purpose. The individuals are selected because they are well informed about the research topic.

Group interviews have been used extensively by social science researchers and marketing researchers, who call them *focus group interviews,* or simply *focus groups.* Richard Krueger and Mary Anne Casey identified the following as characteristics of a **focus group:**

> [It is] a carefully planned discussion designed to obtain perceptions on a defined area of interest in a permissive, nonthreatening environment. It is conducted with approximately seven to ten people by a skilled interviewer. The discussion is relaxed, comfortable, and often enjoyable for participants as they share their ideas and perceptions. Group members influence each other by responding to ideas and comments in the discussion.[30]

Qualitative researchers have become interested in the use of focus groups to collect data in recent years. These researchers are finding that the interactions among the participants stimulate them to state feelings, perceptions, and beliefs that they would not express if interviewed individually. Also, the focus group technique avoids putting the interviewers in a directive role. They ask questions to initiate discussion, but then allow participants to take major responsibility for stating their views and drawing out the views of others in the group.

Procedures for selecting a focus group are described in the next section.

Step 2: Selecting a Sample

A sample of respondents should be selected using one of the quantitative or qualitative sampling techniques described in Chapter 6. To study needed services for children with chronic illnesses, Lynch and her associates selected two samples: (1) a stratified sample of school districts in California, and (2) a nonrandom sample of families with such children. Separate interview guides were developed for respondents in each sample.

---

28. LeCompte, M. D., Preissle, J., & Tesch, R. (1993). *Ethnography and qualitative design in educational research* (2nd ed.). San Diego, CA: Academic Press.
29. LeCompte, M. D. (1980). The civilizing of children: How young children learn to become students. *The Journal of Thought, 15,* 105–126.
30. Krueger, R. A., & Casey, M. A. (2000). *Focus groups: A practical guide for applied research* (3rd ed.). Thousand Oaks, CA: Sage. Quote appears on p. 18.

Interviewers typically interview one respondent at a time, as in Lynch's study. It also is possible to conduct a focus group interview, as we explained in the preceding section. The focus group may consist of an established group, such as the teachers in a particular school. When using an established group, the researcher needs to be sensitive to pre-existing relationships among the group members. The focus group technique works best when all members are on an equal basis—for example, all the teaching staff of a preschool. If the school principal is included, the teachers may feel inhibited about sharing their actual perceptions of the phenomena being investigated.

Focus groups generally include seven to ten individuals. This group size encourages a wide sampling of views, but is not so large that some individuals do not have the opportunity to speak.

When interviewing individuals, you can arrange to meet with each respondent at your mutual convenience. In a focus group, however, all respondents must be assembled at the same time and place. This is not an easy task, and so you will need to follow systematic procedures to ensure that it is accomplished successfully.[31]

Step 3: Designing the Interview Format

In quantitative research, the interview generally is structured to expose all respondents to a nearly identical experience. Thus, the opening statement, interview questions, and closing remarks should be carefully specified in advance to ensure that data from all respondents can be compared meaningfully. In qualitative research, however, the interview format is not so tightly structured because the researcher's goal is to help respondents express their view of a phenomenon in their own terms.

Quantitative and qualitative research interviews also differ in whether the variables are prespecified. In quantitative studies, the variables of interest to the researcher generally are prespecified. For example, suppose the researcher wishes to determine the factors that influence students to choose a particular major in college. Through a review of the literature, the researcher might discover that parents, parents' friends, relatives, teachers, and other students are possible sources of influence. In designing the interview the researcher could ask questions about each of these sources of influence, for example: "Did your father influence your choice of a major?"

If a similar study were done from a qualitative research perspective, there might be little or no prespecification of variables. Instead, the interview questions might be broader in nature, for example: "How did you come to be an Economics major?" At the stage of analyzing the data, the researcher may choose to identify quantifiable variables or broad themes and patterns.

Interview Formats in Qualitative Research

Michael Patton describes three basic approaches to collecting qualitative data through open-ended interviews.[32] The three approaches, which are described below, vary in degree of structure.

The informal conversational interview relies entirely on the spontaneous generation of questions in a natural interaction, typically one that occurs as part of ongoing participant observation fieldwork. (Participant observation is explained in Chapter 9.) Because the conversation appears natural, the research participants may not even realize that they are being interviewed.

31. Procedures for arranging a focus group meeting are described in Chapter 6 of Krueger & Casey, *Focus groups*.
32. Patton, M. Q. (2001). *Qualitative evaluation and research methods* (3rd ed.). Thousand Oaks, CA: Sage.

The general interview guide approach involves outlining a set of topics to be explored with each respondent. The order in which the topics are explored and the wording of the questions are not predetermined. They can be decided by the interviewer as the situation evolves.

The standardized open-ended interview involves a predetermined sequence and wording of the same set of questions to be asked of each respondent in order to minimize the possibility of bias. This approach is particularly appropriate when several interviewers are used to collect data.

Interview Formats in Quantitative Research

Like qualitative research interviews, interviews in quantitative research vary in degree of structure. The three basic approaches are described below.

The **structured interview** involves a series of closed-form questions that either have yes-no answers or can be answered by selecting from among a set of short-answer choices. The respondents' answers are not followed up to obtain greater depth, and thus are similar to those obtained from a questionnaire. The advantage of an interview over a questionnaire in this case, however, is that the response rate can be increased because the interviewer can interact with individuals to reduce the number of unusable or "don't know" responses.

The **semistructured interview** involves asking a series of structured questions and then probing more deeply using open-form questions to obtain additional information. For example, suppose a researcher is investigating the relationship between students' high school experiences and their subsequent achievement in college. In one part of the interview, the interviewer might try to elicit significant experiences in coursework by asking all respondents: "What course did you like best?" Suppose the respondent answers, "I liked chemistry best because the teacher made it interesting." At this point, the interviewer might probe by asking: "How did the teacher make it interesting?" Another respondent might say, "I liked my government class because we talked about real-life problems." The interviewer then might probe by asking such questions as: "What are some examples of these problems?" and "Why did you find these problems interesting?" In these two examples, the interviewer began with the same initial question, but asked different probing questions based on the respondent's answer. This interview approach has the advantage of providing reasonably standard data across respondents, but of greater depth than can be obtained from a structured interview.

The study of children with chronic illness that we have been describing involved a semistructured telephone interview. When an appropriate respondent from each district was identified, this individual was sent an information packet that included the interview protocol. This procedure provided the respondent an opportunity to review the questions and prepare for the interview. Specific questions were drafted and formatted by the three researchers working as a team, reviewed and revised by State Department of Education personnel who had content and research expertise, and subjected to final review and revision by an advisory committee composed of experts or representatives from various constituencies (e.g., a special educator, a teacher, a parent of a chronically ill child, and a university student who had a chronic illness).

The **unstructured interview** does not involve a detailed interview guide. Instead, the interviewer asks questions that gradually lead the respondent to give the desired information. Usually the type of information sought is difficult for the respondent to express or is psychologically sensitive. For this reason the interviewer must adapt continuously to the respondent's state of mind. This format is highly subjective and time-consuming.

Telephone Interviews

The telephone commonly is used for interviewing because it is much less expensive than face-to-face interviews, especially when the sample is geographically dispersed. Although relatively low cost is the greatest advantage of telephone interviews, they have other significant advantages as well:

1. You can select respondents from a broader accessible population than if interviewers needed to travel to the location of each respondent.
2. Because all interviewers can work from a central location, monitoring of interviews and quality control is easier.
3. Little cost is incurred when no one answers, making frequent callbacks feasible.
4. Many groups, such as business people, school personnel, and parents, are easier to reach by telephone than by personal visits.
5. Telephone interviewing provides safe access to dangerous locations and access to restricted locations where interviewers might not be admitted.

There is some evidence that telephone interviews can be used to collect sensitive data. One study found that for nonthreatening questions respondents' distortions were slightly higher for telephone interviews than for face-to-face interviews.[33] For threatening questions, the reverse was true. Although it would seem easier to establish rapport in a face-to-face interview, the physical presence of the interviewer might increase the perceived threat of questions about sensitive topics. Hanging up a phone obviously is easier than ejecting an interviewer from one's home or office. Nevertheless, some investigators have been successful in completing a very high percentage of telephone interviews, even when dealing with sensitive topics. In one study, completed interviews were obtained from 74 percent of the sample in personal interviews and 70 percent in telephone interviews.[34] Because the same items were used for the personal and telephone interviews, it was possible to compare the responses for the two methods. The results generally were very similar over a wide range of topics and item formats.

When selecting a sample for a telephone interview, you will need the telephone number of each individual whom you select. If you use an organization's directory to select a sample, the members' telephone numbers may be listed. If not, you will need to determine the phone numbers by another procedure. The city telephone directory is useful, except for individuals who have unlisted numbers. (CD-ROMs and Web databases listing all telephone numbers in the United States are available as well.) Keep in mind that some individuals, especially those with low incomes, do not have telephones.

You should avoid eliminating individuals selected for your sample because their telephone number is unlisted or they have no telephone. To do so would create a biased sample, and thus weaken the generalizability of your research results.

As we noted above, the study by Lynch and her associates concerning the educational needs of children with chronic illnesses was conducted by telephone.

Computer-Assisted Telephone Interviews

Computer-assisted telephone interviews involve the use of a computer to assist in gathering information from telephone interviews. This method virtually eliminates two major

◆ **Touchstone in Research**

Lavrakas, P. J. (1998). Methods for sampling and interviewing in telephone surveys. In L. Bickman & D. J. Rog (Eds.), *Handbook of applied social research methods* (pp. 429–472). Thousand Oaks, CA: Sage.

33. Graves, R. M., & Kahn, R. L. (1979) *Surveys by telephone: A national comparison with personal interviews.* New York: Academic Press.
34. Ibid.

sources of common errors in interviews, namely, recording data in the wrong place on the form and asking the wrong questions. Most telephone interviews require the interviewer to jump to a different part of the form depending on the response of the person interviewed. For example, if the question is "Are you employed?" a "yes" response might call for the interviewer to check this response on the interview guide and then turn three pages to a set of questions on mode of employment. If the interviewer does not turn the correct number of pages, inappropriate questions may be asked next, with the possible result of a badly shortened interview.

This problem can be avoided by developing a computer program that not only records the subject's responses, but also branches to the next question that should be asked. For example, as the interviewer types "yes" (or a code like "Y") into the computer, the response will be recorded and the computer can be programmed to jump three pages in the computer file containing the interview guide and display the first question on mode of employment. The interviewer does not have to worry about turning pages, nor does she even see any inappropriate questions. The next question that appears is the one needed. Response accuracy generally increases with such computer-assisted interview techniques, because the interviewer can concentrate on responses rather than worry about what question to ask next. Also, because the interviewees' responses are entered into a computer file while the interview is in progress, the data are ready for statistical analysis by computer as soon as all the interviews are completed.

Step 4: Developing Questions

Whether questions are developed in advance of the interview or during each interview itself depends mainly on the type of interview. The unstructured interview in quantitative research and the informal conversational interview in qualitative research involve on-the-spot formulation of questions, based on a general plan and the interviewer's reading of relevant characteristics of each respondent (e.g., level of poise, talkativeness, and intelligence). The other interview formats make greater use of prespecified closed-form and open-form questions. For example, in the study of the needs of children with chronic illnesses, a series of open-form and closed-form questions was used.

The formulation of good questions in interviews at the unstructured end of the continuum depends on the interviewer's ability to think on his feet during the interview process. Developing questions for more structured interviews is best done by designing and trying out an interview guide. An **interview guide** specifies the questions, the sequence in which they are to be asked, and guidelines for what the interviewer is to say at the beginning and end of each interview. The interview guide should list the response options for each closed-form question and provide space for the interviewer to write down answers that do not fit prespecified response categories.

Figure 8.4 shows an interview guide from a study by Michael Ann Rossi. Her research project involved case studies of "teacher-leaders" in mathematics, that is, teachers who had participated in a special mathematics institute and returned to their school district in a leadership role to improve mathematics instruction. Rossi was particularly interested in the strategies and skills of these teacher-leaders, and the outcomes that they effected. Her data-collection method involved interviewing each teacher-leader, the teacher-leader's supervisor, and teachers with whom the teacher-leader had worked. Separate interview guides were developed for each of these groups. The interview guide shown in Figure 8.4 was for interviewing teachers with whom the teacher-leader had worked.

FIGURE 8.4

A Guide for Interviewing Teachers Who Had Worked with a Teacher-Leader

(Start by alluding to introduction from teacher-leader.) This is a visit to get acquainted. *It's not an evaluation of you,* of your school program, or of the teacher-leader. I would like to get a picture of mathematics teaching and learning in your school. My main focus is how you have worked with other people along the way regarding getting help with mathematics teaching and learning. I want to understand the story since _____ until now. I have a number of specific questions to ask.

1. Background
   a. Name
   b. Job title (or role)
   c. Thumbnail sketch of your job; what you do, who you work with.
   d. How long have you been teaching?
   e. How long have you been in this school?
2. I'm interested in the *flavor* or feeling in the school.
   a. Can you give me 3 or 4 adjectives that would describe that?
   b. Can you think back to when your school first got involved with changing mathematics teaching and learning?
      • when was that?
      • why did the school get involved?
      • how did you personally get involved?
      • what did you expect?
      • what do you think the teacher-leader expected?
   c. Could you give me a quick sketch of how mathematics teaching and learning is changing in your school right now?
      • are teachers involved as individuals?
      • how many are involved?
      • what is the role of the principal? is *she* supportive of change, or blocking it?
      • what is the purpose of the change?
      • what procedures or guidelines are followed, methods used?
      • what does the teacher-leader do?
3. a. Describe your involvement since that time.
   b. What contact have you had with others who are involved? (Especially PROBE for communication, cooperation, peer coaching)
   c. Are there stages or phases that can be identified regarding *your* involvement with the change? Your *school's* involvement?
4. Generally speaking, what do you see as the teacher-leader's main role?
   a. What's been *her* main contribution to your school's mathematics program?
   b. Can you give me a few adjectives to describe *her style,* way of working with people?
   c. What do you see as *her* special strengths?
   d. Could you tell me about a specific incident when ___ was *especially helpful?*
      • What did *she* do?
      • Why did you think this was helpful?
      • What skills did you see *her* using in this situation?
   e. Now let's take another incident.
      • What did *she* do, in detail?
      • Why did you think this was helpful?
      • What skills did you see *her* using in this situation?
   f. Do you think *her* skills and strengths have changed since you've known her? (GET ILLUSTRATIONS AND EXAMPLES)
   g. Ask questions d, e, and f except use *practical* rather than helpful.

continued

FIGURE 8.4   Continued

5. I'm interested in the program's results. For (1) you, (2) other teachers, and (3) the students:
   a. What results have occurred?
   b. Why do you think these results happened?
   c. In your opinion, how did ___ contribute to these results?
6. a. What would you say are the necessary ingredients of success in this kind of program?
   b. Specifically, what recommendations do you have for how Math Project teacher-leaders work and who is selected?
7. Do you have anything else to add?

Source: Appendix F in: Rossi, M. A. (1993). The California Mathematics Project: Empowering elementary teachers to be leaders and change agents in mathematics reform *Dissertation Abstracts International, 54* (09), 3314A. (UMI No. 9405218)

Step 5: Selecting and Training Interviewers

You will need to decide how many interviewers to employ and whether they must have special qualifications. The most important selection criterion is the interviewer's ability to relate to respondents positively. An interviewer who might do a fine job of interviewing successful teachers might be totally unsuited to interview unmarried pregnant teenagers, for example.

Matching

There is evidence to indicate that matching interviewers and respondents on such variables as social class, race, age, and gender is likely to produce more valid responses.[35] The interviewer's gender is of particular concern to some researchers. Males and females traditionally have been involved mainly in superordinate-subordinate relationship patterns. These patterns can affect the interviewer-respondent relationship, especially when the interviewer is male and the respondent is female.

To clarify the influence of gender,[36] Ann Oakley identified a masculine paradigm and a feminine paradigm in interviewing. In the masculine paradigm, interviewers maintain a superordinate, emotionally neutral stance toward the respondent, and they control what the respondent says. In contrast, status differences are minimized in the feminine paradigm; the interviewers share their human side; and they give the respondents greater freedom to speak as they wish. In selecting interviewers, you might consider whether these paradigm distinctions are relevant to your study. If relevant, you will need to decide which paradigm is most appropriate to your research objectives and whether male or female interviewers are likely to be more effective. You should not assume, though, that only men can follow the masculine paradigm and only women the feminine paradigm.

Respondents as Interviewers

Some researchers recommend selecting interviewers from the respondent target population. An example of this approach is an investigation of at-risk students in urban high

---

35. For examples of research studies that have explored these variables, see: Nederhof, A. J. (1981). Impact of interviewer's sex on volunteering by females. *Perceptual and Motor Skills, 52*, 25–26; Shosteck, H. (1977). Respondent militancy as a control variable for interviewer effect. *Journal of Social Issues, 33*, 36–45.
36. Oakley, A. (1981). Interviewing women: A contradiction in terms. In H. Roberts (Ed.), *Doing feminist research* (pp. 30–61). London: Routledge & Kegan.

schools by Edwin Farrell, George Peguero, Rasheed Lindsey, and Ronald White.[37] The study involved an ethnographic perspective, and interviewing was the primary method of data collection. In designing the study, the principal investigator (Farrell) noted the difficulty of him, "a white, middle class, middle-aged academic," collecting data in "a social setting made up, for the most part, of low-income black and Hispanic adolescents."[38] Farrell dealt with the problem by recruiting students from the target population (students identified as at risk of dropping out of high school) to serve as interviewers. Seven students collected the interview data and also participated in the data analysis. Three of the students who worked for the duration of the project were listed as co-authors of the journal article reporting the study's findings.

Training of Interviewers

Once interviewers are selected, all of them should be given training. The amount of training needed will be greater as the depth of the interview increases and structure decreases. The training usually is carried out in two phases. In the first phase, the trainees study the interview guide and learn about the interview conditions (e.g., logistics, necessary controls and safeguards, topics being investigated). The researcher's hypotheses or expected results should not be discussed with the interviewers at this point, because they are likely to bias the interviewers' perceptions. Interviewers should become so familiar with the interview guide (wording, format, recording procedures, and allowable probes) that they can conduct the interview in a conversational manner without hesitating, backtracking, or needing to reread or study the guide.

In the second phase of training, trainees should conduct practice interviews and receive corrective feedback until their performance becomes polished and reaches the desired level of standardization or structure, objectivity, and reliability. Videotape recordings of practice interviews are quite effective in providing models of acceptable interviewing techniques and in giving corrective feedback. The videotape can be replayed several times so that trainees can locate procedural errors, suggest better procedures, and discuss alternative ways of dealing with problems that arise.

Depending on the interview task, some trainees may not be able to achieve the criterion standards of performance. Other trainees may not be able to stay with the project for its duration. For example, in the study of at-risk students described above, four student interviewers left the project at various points in time. If you think that these problems are likely to arise in your study, you should consider recruiting and training more interviewers than you actually need.

In the study of children with chronic illnesses, one of the research team members, two graduate students, and a professional interviewer were trained in general techniques of telephone interviewing, use of the two interview guides, and procedures for recording responses. All interviewers were checked initially by a member of the research team to ensure that they were accurate, appropriate, and consistent in their approach. Periodic checks also were made throughout the study.

Interviewers who will conduct informal or unstructured interviews typical of qualitative research require special preparation. They should have access to senior researchers who can impart their artistry and experience. Also, senior researchers can model the interviewing process and supervise new interviewers as they practice the process.

---

37. Farrell, E., Peguero, G., Lindsey, R., & White, R. (1988). Giving voice to high school students: Pressure and boredom, 'ya know what I'm sayin'?' *American Educational Research Journal, 25,* 489–502.
38. Ibid., p. 490.

Step 6: Pilot-Testing the Interview

Although interviews provide valuable data, they are quite susceptible to bias. Therefore, the interview guide and procedures should be pilot-tested to ensure that they will yield reasonably unbiased data. During the pilot interviews the researcher should be alert to communication problems, evidence of inadequate motivation on the part of respondents, and other clues that suggest the need for rephrasing questions or revising the procedure. The pilot test also can be used to identify threatening questions. Norman Bradburn and his associates defined a question as threatening when 20 percent or more of the respondents feel that most people would be very uneasy talking about the topic.[39] This criterion can be employed in the pilot test to identify such questions. If there are threatening questions, procedures should be developed to lower or eliminate their threat value.

Several methods of opening the interview should be tried to determine the one that establishes the best rapport and cooperation. Also, the researcher should evaluate methods of recording interview data to determine whether adequate information is being recorded, whether the recording method causes excessive breaks in the interview situation, and whether methods for coding and analyzing the interview data are sound.

Tape recording pilot-test interviews is important even if a tape recorder will not be used during the regular interview procedure. By playing back the interview, interviewers can gain insights into their handling of the questions and become aware of problems that escaped them during the interview itself.

Interviewers also should consider selecting a subgroup from the pilot sample to check the wording of interview items. As we discussed in the section on questionnaire pilot-testing, there is evidence that the same item can be interpreted differently by different respondents. If this happens, the validity of the interview is threatened. By pretesting items, you can identify those that are ambiguous and revise them until all or most respondents interpret them similarly.

Step 7: Conducting the Interview

Researchers have discovered many interviewer behaviors that affect the quality of data yielded by the interview method. A list of recommended behaviors, compiled from various sources, is presented in Figure 8.5. Most apply to interviews conducted in the context of either quantitative research or qualitative research.

Interviewing Tasks

Researchers should consider reviewing the list of interview guidelines shown in Figure 8.5 to determine those that are important for the particular interviews that they will conduct or will train others to conduct. In addition, they should consider how they will handle the following interview tasks.[40]

Deciding how to present oneself. The interviewer will need to decide what type of personal image to present to respondents. For example, suppose that the interviewer's respondents are teachers. The interviewer might decide to present herself as both a researcher and a teacher (assuming that she has had teaching experience). In opening the interview, then, she might say something about why she is a researcher and also describe her background in teaching. The latter information might help to establish trust and rapport with respondents.

39. Bradburn, N. M., Sudman, S., et al. (1981). *Improving interview method and questionnaire design.* San Francisco: Jossey-Bass.
40. These tasks were adapted from: Fontana, A., & Frey, J. H. (1994). Interviewing: The art of science. In N. K. Denzin & Y. S. Lincoln (Eds.), *Handbook of qualitative research* (pp. 361–376). Thousand Oaks, CA: Sage.

FIGURE 8.5

248

Guidelines for Conducting a Research Interview

1. Assure respondents of absolute confidentiality before beginning the interview. If necessary, expl.
the procedures that will be used to assure confidentiality.
2. Build rapport by engaging in small talk before beginning the interview and by using an everyday conversational style.
3. Save complex or controversial questions for the latter part of the interview after rapport has been established.
4. Explain the potential benefits of the study to the respondents.
5. The interviewer should talk less than the respondent. As a rule, the less the interviewer talks, the more information is produced.
6. Pose questions in language that is clear and meaningful to the respondent.
7. Ask questions that contain only a single idea.
8. In phrasing questions, specify the frame of reference you want the respondent to use in answering the question, for example, ask, "What do you think of the way your child's teacher handles parent-teacher conferences?" rather than "What do you think of the teacher your child has this year?" The latter question might be appropriate, however, if the goal is to determine the respondent's salient frames of reference.
9. Use simple probes when appropriate, for example, "Can you tell me more about that?"
10. Avoid contradicting or appearing to cross-examine the respondent.
11. Do not hint—either by specific comment, tone of voice, or nonverbal cues such as shaking the head—at preferred or expected responses to a particular question.
12. If a respondent seems threatened by a specific topic, move on to another one. Try returning to the topic later, with different phrasing.
13. When posing threatening or sensitive questions, ask the respondent about the behavior of friends as well as about the respondent's own behavior.
14. Do not ask many closed-form questions in succession.
15. Do not change interview topics too often.
16. Avoid leading questions, for example ask, "What is your opinion of federal aid to education?" instead of "Do you favor federal aid to education?" However, in some cases a leading question may be asked to elicit a particular type of information from the respondent.

Other aspects of the interviewer's image need to be considered as well, among them being dress, institutional affiliation, ethnicity, and life experiences. The researcher will need to consider the respondents carefully to determine which aspects of the interviewer's image are likely to be salient to them, and whether these aspects of image are likely to have an adverse or positive effect on the interview process.

Establishing rapport. The interviewer needs to decide how much rapport to establish with each respondent. Superficial rapport may be sufficient if the respondent appears comfortable with the interview process. Stronger rapport is necessary if the interviewer wishes the respondent to reveal deeply personal or sensitive information. Beyond a certain point, however, building rapport might work against the interviewer. For example, the respondent might feel so comfortable that he chooses to spend the interview time talking about matters that are irrelevant to the researcher's purposes.

Gaining trust. Trust can be an important factor in the interview process if sensitive topics are to be discussed. For example, school administrators may be quite willing to divulge their views about the best way to improve school climate. It may be an entirely different matter to ask their opinion about whether schools should provide counseling for students who feel confused about their sexual orientation. If sensitive topics are the focus of the research study, the interviewer will need to establish a deep level of trust in order to obtain the desired data.

Understanding the respondents' language and culture. Interviewers should have a good understanding of the language and culture of their respondents, especially if nuances of language and culture are important to understanding the phenomena being investigated. For example, suppose the interviewer is collecting data from computer educators in a variety of institutional settings. In the course of an interview, a computer educator may use technical language and refer to various aspects of his workplace. If the interviewer does not understand the terminology and workplace, his ability to probe responses and take notes could be significantly impaired. This problem can be remedied to an extent if the interviewer realizes when he is not comprehending the respondent's comments and feels sufficiently comfortable to ask for clarification.

Being sensitive to nonverbal information. The interviewer will need to decide what aspects of the respondent's behavior to focus on during the interview process. Will the interviewer attend only to what the respondent says, or will she also attend to the respondent's nonverbal communication?

Raymond Gorden distinguished between four types of nonverbal communication:

> *Proxemic* communication is the use of interpersonal space to communicate attitudes, *chronemics* communication is the use of pacing of speech and length of silence in conversation, *kinesic* communication includes any body movements or postures, and *paralinguistic* communication includes all the variations in volume, pitch and quality of voice.[41]

Any one of these forms of nonverbal communication can be a significant source of research data. If desired, the interviewers can be trained to observe and take notes on their manifestations in the interview process.

Recording Interview Data

Note taking or tape recording are the usual methods for preserving the information collected in an interview. Before choosing one of these methods, the interviewer should consider carefully the advantages and disadvantages of each.

If an interview guide is used, the interviewer probably should take handwritten notes directly on a copy of the interview guide. An alternative is to use a laptop computer: As the respondent answers questions, the responses can be keyboarded directly into a computer file. The chief advantage of note taking is that it facilitates data analysis. The information is readily accessible and much of it might already have been classified into appropriate response categories by the interviewer.

A disadvantage of note taking is that it might disrupt the effectiveness of the communication between interviewer and respondent. When questions deal with simple factual information, respondents typically expect their answers to be written down, and may appear upset if they are not. On the other hand, if respondents are asked to reveal sensitive or confidential information, note taking may distract them and prevent them from giving information they otherwise might have given. In this case, the interviewer should consider delaying note taking until after the interview is completed and the respondent has left the setting. The risk is that the interviewer will forget important details, particularly those that disagree with the interviewer's expectations.

---

41. Gorden, R. L. (1980). *Interviewing: Strategy, techniques, and tactics* (3rd ed.). Homewood, IL: Dorsey. Quote appears on p. 335.

The use of tape recorders has several advantages over note taking for recording interview data for research. Most importantly, it reduces the tendency of interviewers to make an unconscious selection of data favoring their biases. The tape recording provides a complete verbal record, and it can be studied much more thoroughly than data in the form of interviewer notes. A tape recorder also speeds up the interview process because there is no need for extensive note taking. Furthermore, if the interview is tape-recorded, two or more individuals who are trained in your data analysis procedures can listen to the tape—or read the transcript—and code it independently. The reliability of their frequency counts or ratings can then be determined.

The main disadvantage of tape recording an interview is that the presence of the tape recorder changes the interview situation to some degree. In interviews involving highly personal information, respondents might be reluctant to express their feelings freely if they know that their responses are being recorded. The interviewer should carefully explain the purpose of the recording and gain the confidence of the respondent, so as to minimize any undesirable effects of having the interview recorded.

In doing telephone interviews, you can purchase a duplex recording jack that connects the telephone and the tape recorder that you plan to use. As soon as the phone is picked up, the recorder will begin recording, and it will record until the phone is hung up. This method of recording telephone conversations is legal as long as one of the parties on the telephone knows it is occurring. Of course, research ethics require that you inform the person to whom you are speaking that the telephone interview is being tape recorded.

You might wish to transcribe the taped material using a typewriter or word processor. If so, you can purchase a foot pedal that is connected to the tape recorder with a jack. You can listen to the tape either with earphones or though the regular speaker. When you have heard a short segment, you simply press the foot pedal to stop the tape while you record that segment. Then you press the foot pedal again to start the tape.

Software is now available to turn a computer into a tape recorder. This capability is especially useful if you have a power-book computer that you can take to sites where you plan to conduct interviews. The software allows you to record the interview, make notations in the recording, and control the replay to facilitate transcription. Other software is available to convert an audio recording or dictation into text.[42]

Whichever recording method you use, practice usually is necessary. You should reach a level of automaticity in your recording skills so that you can focus your attention on the interview process rather than on the recording process. Also, practice might identify problems and issues that are best addressed prior to formal data collection.

Step 8: Analyzing Interview Data

The analysis of responses to closed-form interview questions is straightforward. It is typical to calculate the percentage of respondents who indicated each response option for each item. For example, in the study of children with chronic illnesses, Lynch and her associates computed the percentage of school district personnel ($N = 80$) and family members ($N = 72$) who mentioned barriers to services for this type of child. The percentages are shown in Table 8.2. Note that only barriers mentioned by at least five respondents in each sample are included in the table.

---

42. Specific tape-recording and dictation software programs are described in: Fetterman, D. M. (1998). Webs of meaning: Computer and internet resources for educational research and instruction. *Educational Researcher,* *27*(3), 22–30.

TABLE 8.2

Barriers to Services for Chronically Ill Children Cited More Than Five Times by Districts or Families

Barrier	Percentage Cited	Number
District		
Lack of adequate funding	28.8	23
Lack of public and staff awareness	27.5	22
Inadequate services	12.5	10
Not enough teachers for these students	11.3	9
Children fall behind in their schoolwork	8.8	7
Children's absences	8.8	7
Uncooperative parents	8.8	7
Responsibility in the system for these students unclear	7.5	6
Family		
Teachers don't understand child's needs	9.7	7
School systems and teachers are misinformed about the illness	8.3	6

Source: Table 2 on p. 215 in: Lynch, E. W., Lewis, R. B., & Murphy, D. S. (1992). *Exceptional Children, 59,* 210–220. Copyright 1992 by The Council for Exceptional Children. Reprinted with permission.

The analysis of responses to open-form questions requires the development of a category system. An example of this approach can be found in George Kuh's study of the impact of out-of-class experiences on students in college.[43] A total of 149 college seniors at twelve institutions were interviewed by eight trained interviewers using a semistructured interview guide. The interviews were transcribed and then analyzed to determine what types of outcomes were mentioned by students. The analysis involved a five-step procedure:

1. A doctoral student read all the transcripts and developed a set of eight categories of outcomes mentioned by the college students.
2. Another individual read a sample of the transcripts, and based on her analysis, the outcomes were revised and expanded to ten categories.
3. Four readers analyzed a transcript using the set of categories developed in step 2. Their work resulted in an expanded set of 13 outcome categories.
4. The four readers analyzed four more transcripts, using the set of categories developed in step 3. Their work resulted in several minor revisions to the categories and the addition of an "other" category for miscellaneous outcomes.

43. Kuh, G. D. (1993). In their own words: What students learn outside the classroom. *American Educational Research Journal, 30,* 277–304.

5. The researcher used the category system to code all 149 transcripts. In other words, each mention of an outcome in an interview was coded as an instance of a particular category.

The following three categories illustrate the types of outcomes mentioned by students: (1) self-awareness (includes self-examination, spirituality), (2) social competence (includes capacity for intimacy, working with others, teamwork, leadership, dealing with others, assertiveness, flexibility, public speaking, communication, patience), and (3) knowledge acquisition (includes academic and course-related learning, content mastery). Kuh reported the mean number of times that each of these outcome categories was mentioned by the sample of 149 students, and the percentage of students who mentioned it 0, 1, 2, 3, 4, or 5 or more times. For example, the mean number of interview statements that were coded as the self-awareness outcome was 1.07 (standard deviation = 1.19). Forty percent of the sample did not mention it at all, 33 percent mentioned it once, 11 percent mentioned it twice, 11 percent mentioned it 3 times, 4 percent mentioned it 4 times, and 1 percent mentioned it 5 or more times.

If the interview data were collected in the context of a qualitative research study, they could be analyzed by several methods, including the grounded-theory approach described in Chapter 14. The choice of data-analysis approach will be determined in large part by the type of qualitative research that is being done. For example, an anthropologist who has done ethnographic interviews will study interview data from a different perspective than a historian who has done oral history interviews. These various perspectives are discussed in the chapters on qualitative research traditions (Chapters 15 and 16).

✦ RECOMMENDATIONS FOR
Using Questionnaires and Interviews
as Research Instruments

1. Design items that relate directly to your research questions or hypotheses.
2. Pilot-test the instrument to identify flaws in its design or administration procedures.
3. Use language in the instrument that is comprehensible to the respondents.
4. Check that the respondents know about the topics covered by the instrument.
5. Collect validity and reliability evidence relating to the constructs that the instrument is designed to measure.
6. Avoid taxing the respondents' patience by including too many questions in the instrument.
7. When mailing a questionnaire, include a persuasive cover letter.
8. In using mailed questionnaires, develop procedures for conducting several follow-ups of non-respondents and for checking whether non-respondents differ from respondents on factors critical to the study.
9. Select an interview format that is appropriate to the purposes of the study and interviewee characteristics.
10. In conducting interviews, practice your interviewing and data-recording skills prior to formal data collection.

✔ SELF-CHECK TEST

Circle the correct answer to each of the following questions.
The answers are provided at the back of the book.

1. In research, interviews differ from questionnaires in that
   a. the respondent controls the response situation.
   b. the respondent is asked to provide personal information.
   c. the question sequence and wording can vary with each respondent.
   d. responses to factual questions tend to be more accurate.

2. The most basic consideration in selecting respondents for a questionnaire study is to
   a. determine the sample size.
   b. select a sample that has the desired information.
   c. select the data-collection method that respondents prefer.
   d. study a population with which you are familiar.

3. A major problem with anonymous questionnaires, compared with questionnaires that identify the respondent, is that
   a. the return rate is much lower.
   b. respondents are less likely to provide valid information.
   c. follow-up procedures cannot be used.
   d. all of the above.

4. Pretesting in questionnaire research can be used to
   a. determine if the individuals to be sampled have sufficient knowledge to give meaningful responses.
   b. determine the likely response rate to the questionnaire.
   c. revise the questionnaire items to reduce the possibility of misinterpretations.
   d. all of the above.

5. In writing a cover letter to accompany a mailed questionnaire, a researcher would be well advised to
   a. request that the questionnaire be returned by a certain date.
   b. avoid setting a time limit for return of the questionnaire.
   c. describe the consequences if the questionnaire is not returned by a certain date.
   d. avoid associating the research project with a professional institution.

6. Research has found that respondents who do not return the first questionnaire mailed to them
   a. do not respond to follow-ups unless accompanied by a cash reward.
   b. will respond in greater numbers if more than one follow-up mailing is done.
   c. have very different personality characteristics than individuals who do complete the first questionnaire mailed to them.
   d. have poor reading skills.

7. Compared with a mailed questionnaire, the principal advantage of the interview is the
   a. low cost of data collection.
   b. depth of information collected.
   c. ease of administration.
   d. high reliability of the obtained data.

8. The research interview has the following disadvantage(s):
   a. The respondent needs a high level of verbal skills.
   b. It is not possible to probe unclear responses.
   c. It is subject to interviewer bias.
   d. All of the above.

9. The principal disadvantage of tape recording a research interview is the
   a. change that it produces in the interview situation.
   b. cost of the equipment that is required.
   c. superficiality of the obtained data.
   d. low validity of tape-recorded data compared to that of data obtained from notes.

10. It is good interview technique to
    a. ask leading questions.
    b. avoid engaging in small talk before starting the formal interview.
    c. cross-examine respondents if they seem deceptive.
    d. make sure that respondents understand the purpose of each question asked.

CHAPTER 9

✦ Collecting Research Data through Observation and Content Analysis

OVERVIEW

Rather than relying solely on people's self-reports of events, many researchers prefer to make their own observations. Much of this chapter concerns the methods that quantitative and qualitative researchers use in making systematic observations of others. We also describe procedures for collecting observational data without the awareness of research participants. In the last section of the chapter, we explain how various types of artifacts and written communications found in natural settings can be analyzed to provide valuable research data.

OBJECTIVES

After studying this chapter, you should be able to

1. State the advantages and limitations of observation compared to other data-collection methods.
2. Explain the differences between descriptive, inferential, and evaluative observational variables.
3. Explain the differences between duration, frequency-count, interval, and continuous procedures for recording observations.
4. State advantages and disadvantages of using a standard observation form in a research project.
5. Explain how video recorders, audio recorders, and computers can be used to record observational data.
6. Describe an effective procedure for selecting and training observers for a quantitative research study.
7. Explain the differences between criterion-related observer reliability, intra-observer reliability, and inter-observer reliability.
8. Describe seven types of observer effects that weaken the validity and reliability of quantitative observational data, and procedures that can be used to minimize or avoid each effect.
9. State three ways in which observation in quantitative research differs from observation in qualitative research.
10. Describe the various roles that observers play in quantitative research.
11. Identify the three stages of observation in a qualitative research study.
12. Explain how observers in a qualitative research study prepare themselves and gain entry into a field setting.
13. Describe various methods for recording observational data in qualitative research.
14. Describe four types of observer effects in qualitative research and procedures that can be used to minimize each effect.

15. State the advantages and limitations of unobtrusive measures and the study of material culture.

16. Describe the steps that a quantitative researcher follows in doing a content analysis.

17. Describe the steps that a qualitative researcher follows in analyzing documents and records.

Introduction

In Chapters 7 and 8 we considered tests, questionnaires, and interviews as methods for collecting research data. All of them rely on self-report by research participants. Although self-reports usually are easy to obtain, many individuals bias the information they offer about themselves, or they cannot recall accurately the events of interest to the researcher.[1]

An alternative to self-report is to observe the behavior and social and material environment of the individuals being studied. Researchers within both quantitative and qualitative traditions have developed systematic methods for this purpose. If used properly, these observational methods avoid the inaccuracy and bias of some self-report data. For example, Lee Sechrest suggested that social attitudes like prejudice are best studied through observation in natural, real-life situations (called *naturalistic observation*) because self-reports of these attitudes often are biased by the set to give a socially desirable response.[2] Following this suggestion, some researchers have studied prejudice by observing such phenomena as the seating patterns of black and white students in college classes.[3]

Even when bias is not present in self-report data, observational methods may yield more accurate data. For example, educators have noted that teachers dominate classroom talk at the expense of student participation. But what are the actual percentages of teacher and student talk in classrooms? Self-reports by teachers or students are unlikely to yield a precise answer to this question, but an analysis of observations recorded on audiotape or videotape can do so.

Although observation is superior to self-report for some research purposes, it is more time-consuming. Individuals must be observed over a period of time to obtain reliable data, whereas tests, questionnaires, and interviews usually can yield reliable data even when the data are collected only at one point in time. Also, if the observational method is used in a quantitative study, inter-observer reliability should be established by having independent observers record data on the situation being observed. This is a difficult requirement if the researcher must rely entirely on his own resources for data collection.

This chapter has three major sections, each covering a different method of data collection: observation, nonreactive observation, and content analysis. Within each section, we treat applications of the method in quantitative and qualitative research. By organizing the chapter in this way, however, we do not mean to imply that quantitative and qualitative research differ only in how they apply what are essentially the same methods. In fact, there is a world of difference between the way that a quantitative researcher, such as a behaviorist, and a qualitative researcher, such as an ethnographer, go about making and recording observations. In general, quantitative and qualitative researchers make very dif-

---

1. In a review of six studies in which both observational and self-report data were collected on the same specific behaviors, none reported a clear relationship between the two types of data. See: Hook, C. M., & Rosenshine, B. V. (1974). Accuracy of teacher reports of their classroom behavior. *Review of Educational Research, 49,* 1–12.

2. Sechrest, L. (Ed.). (1979). *Unobtrusive measurement today.* San Francisco: Jossey-Bass.

3. Campbell, D. T., Kruskal, W. H., & Wallace, W. P. (1966). Seating aggregation as an index of attitude. *Sociometry, 29,* 1–15.

ferent assumptions about the nature of the social reality being observed and about their role as observers.

These assumptions are discussed in Chapter 1, which we recommend you read before studying this chapter. Then, as you read about quantitative and qualitative approaches to observation and content analysis in this chapter, we invite you to consider which approach best satisfies your own epistemological assumptions about the nature of social reality and inquiry. We also invite you to consider whether the two approaches lead to conflicting or complementary understandings of the education enterprise.

Procedures for Observation in Quantitative Research

Defining Observational Variables

In a quantitative research study, the first step in observation is to define the variables that are to be observed. To illustrate this procedure, we will refer to a study by Hirokazu Sakaguchi.[4] The purpose of his research was to determine how the English language is taught in Japanese universities. Although English is an important subject in Japanese higher education, little is known about the instructional methods used by professors. As Sakaguchi explained:

> The present study examines what actually goes on in college-level English classes, and conclusions are drawn by means of empirical observation rather than by the application of linguistic theory. In the Japanese context, this approach is somewhat unusual. Research has been done in Japan into how to make classroom teaching more effective, but it has tended to proceed on a theoretical level, and very few researchers have used practical observation and analysis as a method of research. An important reason for this is the difficulty involved in gaining access to the classroom: professors have a tendency to regard their classroom activities as sacrosanct, perhaps partly because of sensitivity to outside criticism, and in general are highly reluctant to cooperate with researchers. In this respect, this study breaks new ground.[5]

Sakaguchi selected two types of English classes for observation. One type was English literature classes taught by native Japanese instructors. The other type was English conversation classes taught by instructors whose native language is English.

Once Sakaguchi decided to use direct observation as a method, he needed to determine which aspects of classroom instruction to observe. He decided to use an adaptation of the Flanders interaction analysis system.[6] This observational system is used to collect data on ten variables. Sakaguchi used these variables, but added 15 more. Brief definitions of them are shown in Figure 9.1. More elaborate definitions, with examples of each, were used by Sakaguchi to train himself and another individual to make observations.

After deciding which aspects of classroom behavior to observe, Sakaguchi needed a method for recording the observations. Following Flanders's procedures, he decided to code each three-second interval of a classroom lesson into one of the 25 behavior categories shown in Figure 9.1. Thus, a 60-minute lesson would require 1,200 codings. (60 minutes = 3,600 seconds ÷ 3-second intervals = 1,200 intervals.)

✦ *Touchstone in Research*

Bakeman, R., & Gottman, J. M. (1997). *Observing interaction: An introduction to sequential analysis* (2nd ed.). Cambridge: Cambridge University Press.

Evertson, C. M., & Green, J. L. (1986). Observation as inquiry and method. In M. C. Wittrock (Ed.), *Handbook of research on teaching* (3rd ed., pp. 162–213). New York: Macmillan.

---

4. Sakaguchi, H. (1993). A comparison of teaching methods in English-as-a-second-language conversation courses and reading courses in Japanese universities. *Dissertation Abstracts International, 54*(10), 3692A. (UMI No. 9405220)
5. Ibid., pp. 13–14.
6. Flanders, N. A. (1970). *Analyzing teaching behavior.* Reading, MA: Addison-Wesley.

FIGURE 9.1

List of Observational Variables Used in Study of English Classes in Japanese Universities

Category 1 (Teacher accepts feelings). Teacher statements that reflect an awareness and unqualified acceptance of students' feelings.

Category 2 (Teacher encourages students). Praise and encouragement toward the students' questions, answers, and comments.

Category 2F (Teacher gives feedback). A quick, almost automatic response by the instructor that follows a student's statement, usually connoting approval or disapproval.

Category 3 (Teacher uses ideas of students). The instructor incorporates a student's idea into the lesson.

Category 4 (Teacher asks question). Questions asked by the teacher, except those that are directly related to the practice of English conversation.

Category 4C (Teacher asks conversational question). This applies to questions that are part of the dialogue or conversation practices.

Category 5 (Teacher lectures). This includes lecturing, expressing opinions, giving facts, interjecting thoughts, and off-hand comments.

Category 5Cr (Teacher corrects student's mistake). This consists of correcting errors in grammar, word usage, translations, pronunciation, rhythm, and intonation.

Category 5W (Teacher gives cues). Gives cues byword, expression, or sentence when a student gets stuck in the middle of an answer or translation.

Category 5C (Teacher answers conversation questions).

Category 6 (Teacher gives directions).

Category 7 (Teacher criticizes student).

Category 8 (Student responds). These are student responses to Category 4 questions.

Category 8C (Student gives conversational response). These are student responses to Category 4C questions, and to questions asked by one student to another.

Category 8R (Student engages in oral reading). This occurs mainly in literature classes when the instructor asks a student to read out loud a passage from the text.

Category 8 SR (Student engages in silent reading).

Category 8D (Student draws picture).

Category 8T (Student translates).

Category 8S (Student gives summary). This occurs mainly in literature classes when the instructor asks the student to give the main idea in Japanese from one paragraph of the English text.

Category 9 (Student talks). These are questions, answers, comments, and utterances made voluntarily—as opposed to responses to teacher questions—by the students.

Category O (Silence or confusion). Moments of non-productive confusion plus some productive silence, such as allowing students time to copy down information from the blackboard.

Category OS (Students engage in sheet work). This is time spent by students quietly working on their written exercises

Category OT (Teacher uses tape recorder). This occurs in literature classes when the instructor has students listen to tapes made by native English speakers.

Category OD (Teacher distributes handouts).

Category OB (Teacher or student writes on blackboard).

Source: Adapted from text on pp. 41–45 in: Sakaguchi, H. (1993). A comparison of teaching methods in English-as-a-second-language conversation courses and reading courses in Japanese universities. *Dissertation Abstracts International, 54* (10), 3692A. (UMI No. 9405220)

Finally, Sakaguchi needed to decide how many lessons of each instructor to observe. Limiting observation to one lesson might yield an atypical picture of the instructor's teaching style. Therefore, Sakaguchi decided to observe six lessons of each instructor in the sample. Observational data for all the instructors were collected at the same point in the university's academic year. We describe some of the findings from the analysis of these observational data below.

Types of Observational Variables

Three types of observational variables can be distinguished in quantitative research: descriptive, inferential, and evaluative. **Descriptive observational variables** are variables that require little inference on the part of the observer. They sometimes are called *low-inference variables* for this reason. One of their major advantages is that they generally yield reliable data. The variables shown in Figure 9.1 would be considered descriptive observational variables.

Inferential observational variables are variables that require the observer to make an inference from behavior to a construct that is presumed to underly the behavior. For example, observers might be asked to record the self-confidence with which a teacher explains a mathematical concept. Some teachers might speak with a great deal of confidence, whereas others might appear uncertain, confused, or anxious because their understanding of the topic is weak. Confidence, uncertainty, confusion, and anxiety are not behaviors but rather are psychological constructs that are inferred from behavior. For this reason they sometimes are called *high-inference variables*. It is much more difficult to collect reliable data on inferential observational variables than on descriptive observational variables.

Evaluative observational variables are variables that require not only an inference from behavior on the part of the observer but also an evaluative judgment. For example, we might be interested in obtaining ratings of the quality of the teacher's explanation of a mathematical concept. Quality is not a behavior, but rather a construct that is inferred from behavior. Also, it is a construct that is clearly evaluative in nature. Because it is difficult to make reliable observations of evaluative variables, we need to collect examples of explanations that define points along a continuum of excellent to poor explanations, and use these in training the observers.

Recording and Analyzing Observations

To ensure accurate recording, observers should be required to record data on only one observational variable at a time. For example, most observers would find it quite difficult to record various aspects of the teacher's behavior while also recording the percentage of children who are paying attention to the teacher. In this situation, the reliability of both sets of observations probably would be low. Therefore, different observers could be assigned to record each type of variable, or a single observer could alternate between recording the teacher's behavior for a specified interval and then recording the students' behavior for the next interval.

Procedures for recording observations can be classified into four major types: (1) duration, (2) frequency-count, (3) interval, and (4) continuous.

Duration recording. In **duration recording** the observer measures the elapsed time during which each target behavior occurs. A stopwatch generally is used for this purpose. It is easy to do duration recording for a single observational variable, such as the length of time a particular student is out of her seat. An observer also can record different observational variables if they do not occur at the same time. For example, the observer can record the length of time that a particular student is on-task, off-task but not disruptive, mildly disruptive, or seriously disruptive.

Frequency-count recording. In **frequency-count recording** the observer records each time a target behavior occurs. A tally sheet typically is used for this purpose. Frequency counts are most useful in recording behaviors of short duration and behaviors whose duration is not important. For example, one of the authors (W. Borg) conducted a study in which each observer was trained to tally 13 teacher behaviors related to classroom management, such as goal-directed prompts, concurrent praise, and alerting cues.[7] The behaviors were of short duration, and no more than one behavior could occur at the same time. Interobserver reliabilities were satisfactory, ranging from .71 to .96 for the 13 behaviors.

Interval recording. **Interval recording** involves observing the behavior of an individual at given intervals. Sakaguchi's adaptation of Flanders's interaction analysis system is an example of this recording procedure. The instructor's or students' behavior was coded into one of the 25 observational categories every three seconds.

Once a sample of behavior has been recorded in this manner, the data must be summarized and reported to provide a meaningful description of what happened. In Sakaguchi's study, the primary research objective was to determine how the six instructors in his sample differed in their teaching style. For each observed lesson, his primary data were the number of three-second intervals in which each observational variable in Figure 9.1 occurred. For each variable, he divided the number of intervals in which it occurred by the total number of intervals that were recorded for all variables. The result of this calculation was a percentage, namely, the percentage of the total lesson time during which each variable was occurring. The final step in the analysis was to average the percentages for each variable across all six lessons that were observed for each instructor.

Table 9.1 shows a comparison of the results for two of the instructors in the sample—one a native-Japanese instructor of an English literature course, the other a native-English-speaking instructor of an English conversation course. Among the differences between the two instructors, we see that the conversation instructor spent 4.38 percent of class time encouraging students, whereas the literature instructor spent .62 percent of his time engaged in this activity. As would be expected, the students of the conversation instructor spent no class time engaged in oral reading or translating, whereas students of the literature instructor spent 19.58 percent of class time engaged in oral reading and 37.98 percent of class time engaged in translating passages from an assigned text.

The data analysis shown in Table 9.1 contributes to research knowledge about teacher and student use of instructional time in particular types of lessons. However, it does not tell us about *sequence,* that is, how the lessons unfolded over time. For example, we can surmise that each lesson started with one of the coded behaviors shown in Table 9.1, but we do not know which one. Also, we do not know what behavior was most likely to occur following, let's say, a student engagement in oral reading (code 8R).

Various statistical techniques are available to address these questions about how observed behavior unfolds.[8] For example, in the study by Sakaguchi, if we wished to know which behavior was most likely to occur following the occurrence of a student engaged in oral reading, we could: (1) identify all instances of the 8R code; (2) identify which code occurred immediately after the end of each 8R code; (3) count the frequency of each of these codes; and (4) divide each code frequency count by the total frequency count to yield a per-

7. Borg, W. R. (1977). Changing teacher and pupil performance with protocols. *Journal of Experimental Education, 45,* 9–18.
8. These techniques are described in Chapters 6–10 of: Bakeman, R., & Gottman, J. M. (1997). *Observing interaction: An introduction to sequential analysis* (2nd ed.). Cambridge: Cambridge University Press.

TABLE 9.1

Comparison of the Observed Teaching Style of an Instructor of English Literature and an Instructor of English Conversation in a Japanese University

Code	Category	Conversation Instructor (Percentage of Lesson)	Literature Instructor (Percentage of Lesson)
1	Instructor accepts feelings	.08	.04
2	Instructor encourages	4.38	.62
2F	Instructor gives feedback	3.65	1.56
3	Instructor uses student ideas	0	0
4	Instructor asks question	13.17	7.78
4C	Instructor asks conversational question	12.25	0
5	Instructor lectures	25.33	8.30
5Cr	Instructor corrects student mistake	1.85	4.58
5W	Instructor gives cues	.92	3.44
5C	Instructor answers conversational question	1.30	0
6	Instructor gives directions	2.53	3.44
7	Instructor criticizes student	1.03	1.44
8	Student responds	1.78	2.75
8C	Student gives conversational response	22.78	0
8R	Student does oral reading	.13	19.58
8SR	Student does silent reading	0	0
8D	Student draws picture	0	0
8T	Student translates	0	37.98
8S	Student summarizes	0	0
9	Student initiates talk	.20	2.08
O	Silence or confusion	2.05	5.20
OS	Students do worksheet	6.03	1.18
OT	Instructor uses tape recorder	0	0
OD	Instructor distributes handout	.39	0
OB	Instructor or student writes on blackboard	.22	0

Source: Adapted from tables 1 and 4 on pp. 52 and 87, respectively, in: Sakaguchi, H. (1993). A comparison of teaching methods in English-as-a-second-language conversation courses and reading courses in Japanese universities. *Dissertation Abstracts International, 54*(10), 3692A. (UMI No. 9405220)

centage for each code. Using such a procedure, we might find, let's say, that after a student finished oral reading, the most frequent next behavior was for the instructor to give feedback.

Other statistical techniques for analyzing sequences of observed behavior are more complex. One of them is **time-series analysis,** which is a statistical technique for analyzing changes in an observed variable over time. For example, suppose Sakaguchi had counted the number of English words that a particular student spoke in class over, let's say, a period of 50 class periods. Time-series analysis could be used to detect the presence of significant changes in the frequency count over this period of time.

Continuous recording. **Continuous recording** involves recording all the behavior of the target individual or individuals for a specified observation interval. This method usually does not focus on a specific set of observational variables. Instead, the observer typically writes a **protocol,** which is a chronological narrative of everything that the individual does or everything that occurs in a particular setting, such as a classroom. This method often is used in exploratory studies to help the researcher identify important behavior patterns, which subsequently are studied using one of the other methods of observational recording.

Because it is impossible to record everything in a protocol, the observer must focus on the events and contextual features that are most relevant to the research problem. To analyze the protocols, the researcher reads them, creates a content-analysis system that fits the data, and then rereads and classifies the recorded behavior into this system. This process corresponds to the steps used in quantitative content analysis of documents and other communication media, described later in the chapter.

Selecting an Observation Recording Procedure

Once you identify pertinent observational variables and their behavioral indicators, you need to select or develop a procedure for recording the observations. If a suitable procedure is not available, you might consider developing a paper-and-pencil form (sometimes called an *observation schedule*) because it is fairly easy to construct and can accommodate a variety of observational variables.

A sample observation form is shown in Figure 9.2. The form requires the observer not only to record certain behaviors as they occur, but also to evaluate some of them on a rating scale. Item 2 of the observation form in Figure 9.2 is of the latter type.

After developing a prototype of the observation form, you should try it out in a number of situations similar to those to be observed during data collection and correct any

---

FIGURE 9.2

Sample Observation Form

1. Check each question asked by the teacher into one of the following categories (observe for the first fifteen minutes of the class hour):

	Frequency	Total
a. asks student to solve a problem at blackboard	✓✓✓	4
b. asks student to solve a problem at his or her seat	✓✓✓✓✓✓	7
c. asks students if they have any questions or if they understand	✓✓	2
d. other	✓✓✓✓	5
	Grand Total	18

2. Each time the teacher asks a student to solve a problem, rate the problem's level of difficulty on a 5-point scale.

	Frequency	Total
1. difficult	✓✓✓	3
2.	✓	1
3. average	✓✓✓✓	5
4.	✓	1
5. easy	✓	1
	Grand Total	11[a]

[a]The sum here should equal the sum of categories *a* and *b* in item 1.

weaknesses you discover. For example, a common weakness of observation forms is that they require the observer to record more kinds of behavior or watch more individuals than can be done reliably. Various solutions to these problems are possible, such as employing different observers to record different behaviors or switching from the observation of one variable to another at designated intervals.

Standard Observation Forms

Instead of developing your own observation form for a research study, you may prefer to use one of the many standard observation forms that are available. These forms have several advantages. First, standard observation forms usually have reached a stage of development where they include evidence of their validity and reliability. Second, the use of a standard form saves you all the time that it would take to develop your own form. Third, most standard forms have been used in previous research studies, so you can compare your findings with theirs.

The obvious disadvantage of a standard observation form is that it may not include all the variables that you are interested in measuring. In this case you can use just the part of the form that you need, and add your own procedures for assessing other variables. Keep in mind, however, that previously reported reliability and validity data may not apply if only part of an instrument is used.

Depending on your research interests, you might be able to find published collections of standard observation forms.[9] In addition, you can search the preliminary sources described in Chapter 4. To illustrate their use, we searched several electronic sources to identify standard forms for observing leadership behavior:

1. Entering the keywords *observation* and *leadership* in ERIC for the years 1984–2001 yielded 442 citations, some of which refer to observation forms.
2. Entering the keywords *observation methods* and *leadership* in PsychInfo for the years 1984–2001 yielded ten citations, some of which refer to observation forms.
3. Entering the keywords *observation* and *leadership* in ERIC's Test Locator yielded nine instruments.

Studying these citations and instruments might identify a suitable observation form. If not, the search almost certainly will provide a conceptual basis for developing your own instrument.

Use of Audiotape and Videotape Recorders

It sometimes is impractical to collect observational data while the critical behavior is occurring. One such situation is when many of the behaviors to be recorded occur at the same time or closely together. If a recording of the events is made on audiotape or videotape, it can be replayed several times for careful study and observers can count or rate the events at a convenient time. Another advantage of taping events is that it enables you to record behaviors that you did not anticipate at the outset of your study. For example, in a study of teacher praise, you might notice midway through your observations that teachers are using certain types of praise remarks that you did not anticipate in planning your observation form. If you have recorded the observations, you can replay them and

---

9. For example, two publications in the field of classroom research are: Borich, G. D., & Madden, S. K. (1977). *Evaluating classroom instruction: A sourcebook of instruments.* Reading, MA: Addison-Wesley Longman; Simon, A., & Boyer, E. G. (1974). *Mirrors for behavior III: An anthology of observation instruments* (3rd ed.). Philadelphia: Communication Materials Center. (See also the 1st and 2nd editions.)

reclassify the praise statements so as to include the types of praise not listed on your original observation form.

If you decide to use an audiotape recorder or videotape recorder to collect observational data, keep in mind that technical competence is required to use these devices properly. For example, you may need to develop skills in using more than one microphone and refocusing a video camera frequently.

The study of Japanese university instruction by Sakaguchi that we described above involved the use of audiotape recordings. The audiotapes could be replayed as often as necessary to ensure reliable coding of the observational variables shown in Figure 9.1.

Use of Computers and Other Electronic Devices

Various electronic devices (e.g., PalmPilots) and software programs are available for recording and analyzing observational data. The specific tasks that these devices can perform are as follows:

1. Recording and timing events and transcribing the data onto coding sheets.
2. Transferring the data from coding sheets into a computer file that then can be analyzed by a statistical package.
3. Cleaning up the data by locating coding errors and detecting "wild codes," which are codes that have no meaning in the coding system being used.
4. Interpreting the results of the data analysis. Computers have the capacity to produce a variety of graphic data representations, which can help in interpreting one's results.

If you are planning to collect observational data, you can search the literature to determine whether a suitable device has been developed and used by other researchers. For example, Ned Flanders and his colleagues have developed computer technology to record data on the types of classroom interaction variables shown in Figure 9.2.[10] The observer uses a pen-like device and special recording paper that contains a bar code for each interaction category and also for designated students, if that is desired. By moving the "pen" across the appropriate bar codes, the observer can record how long the teacher or student engaged in a particular type of behavior. This process is similar to the procedure used for charging items at the checkout counter in many stores.

After the observer has finished making observations, he inserts the "pen" in a computer interface device, which stores the observations as a computer data file. A computer program is available for analyzing this data file and creating printouts that display the results in various formats, for example, the sequence of interactions during a lesson or the amount of time that each interaction category occurred.

Selecting and Training Observers

Researchers can make their own observations, train others to make them, or share the task with others. The advantage of using other individuals is that it allows for control of the observer bias that can occur when the same individual who designs the research study and frames its hypotheses also does the observing. In addition, if two or more similarly trained observers make independent observations, you can determine the level of inter-observer reliability of the observations. Researchers have found that the most reliable observers tend to be intelligent, verbally fluent, and motivated to do a good job.[11]

---

10. This type of computer-assisted observation is described on pp. 133–134 in: Acheson, K. A., & Gall, M. D. (1997). *Techniques in the clinical supervision of teachers* (4th ed.). New York: Longman.
11. Harter, D. P. (Ed.). (1982). *Using observers to study behavior.* San Francisco: Jossey-Bass.

The first step in training observers is to discuss the observation form with them. Describe each item sufficiently so that they develop a thorough understanding of what is to be observed and how it is to be recorded. Also, consider making videotape recordings of situations similar to those to be observed in the study, so that you can relate actual examples of each behavior to its definition.

The next step is to set up practice observations in which all observer trainees participate. The videotapes made earlier can be used in the practice observations. Show a brief segment of the videotape, instructing trainees to record each behavior on the observation form as it occurs. Then check each trainee to determine if he correctly tallied the behaviors. If observers disagree with each other or with the criterion, replay the videotape, stopping at each behavior to discuss the most appropriate way to record it and why. During these discussions, the observer's instruction sheet should be revised to include any clarifications that arise during the training session. A few special rules typically are required to help observers make decisions about how to record unusual behavior that was not foreseen when the observation form was developed.

Determining Observer Agreement

Observational data are of no use unless they are collected by reliable observers. What does it mean for an observer to be reliable? Ted Frick and Melvyn Semmel answered this question by distinguishing between three types of observer reliability.[12] First, there is **criterion-related observer reliability,** which is the extent to which a trained observer's scores agree with those of an expert observer, such as the researcher who developed the observation instrument. This type of reliability is important because it provides assurance that the trained observer's understanding of the variables measured by the observation instrument is the same as that of an expert. Criterion-related observer reliability typically is established by first having an expert code a videotape or audiotape of events that include all the variables measured by the observation instrument. The trained observers then code the same tape, and their data are checked for agreement with the expert's data. Criterion-related observer reliability should be checked prior to data collection, and preferably during data collection as well.

The second type of observer reliability is **intra-observer reliability,** which is the extent to which the observer is consistent in her observational codings. This type of reliability can be established by having each observer twice code a videotape or audiotape of events similar to those that she will be asked to observe in the field. For example, observers might code a videotape on Monday and then code the same videotape a few days later. This type of reliability is not commonly established, but you should check it if possible because it provides additional assurance that your observers are reliable. Intra-observer reliability should be checked before data collection begins, and if possible during data collection.

The third type of observer reliability is **inter-observer reliability,** which is the extent to which the observers agree with each other during actual data collection. To establish inter-observer reliability, you will need to have pairs of observers collect data on the same events. For example, suppose that you have trained five observers to collect data on sixty lessons taught by various teachers. For the sake of efficiency, you might have each observer collect data individually on ten lessons. This procedure takes care of data collection for 50 of the 60 lessons. The other ten lessons could be observed by all five observers for the purpose of determining inter-observer reliability.

12. Frick, T., & Semmel, M. I. (1978). Observer agreement and reliabilities of classroom observational measures. *Review of Educational Research, 48,* 157–184.

Frick and Semmel described various procedures for calculating the level of criterion-related observer reliability and intra-observer reliability. These procedures involve calculating a percentage of agreement or specialized correlation coefficient. The choice of procedure depends on the type of observational variable and the type of observer reliability to be determined.

Although determining observer reliability is important, it does not ensure that the final set of observational data will be reliable. Observers can agree perfectly in training or under particular field conditions, yet the typical situations that they observe may be very unstable or differ so little from each other that accurate observation to distinguish between these small differences is not possible. In other words, observer reliability is a necessary but not sufficient condition for collecting reliable observational data.

Reducing Observer Effects

An **observer effect** is any action by the observer that has a negative effect on the validity or reliability of the data they collect. Researchers should be aware of possible observer effects, and should take steps to avoid or minimize them. To assist researchers in this task, Carolyn Evertson and Judith Green identified various types of observer effects.[13] We describe each type below and how it can be controlled.

Effect of the observer on the observed. Unless concealed, the observer is likely to have an impact on the observed. For example, an observer entering a classroom for the first time probably will arouse the curiosity of the students and teacher. Their resulting inattentiveness may produce nonrepresentative observational data. One way to reduce this effect is for the observer to make several visits beforehand so that the students and the teacher take the intrusion for granted and behave naturally.

A more serious problem occurs when the individuals being observed are influenced by the observer's intentions. For example, suppose the purpose of the research study is to record the number and length of dyadic interactions between the teacher and students in art classes. If they learn that this is the purpose of the study, teachers are likely to increase the frequency of their dyadic interactions, particularly if they believe that this is desirable behavior. To avoid this problem, the researcher should consider informing the teachers at the outset that it is not possible to reveal the nature of the research project until it is completed, because this might affect their behavior. Also, the researcher should reassure them that the data will be kept confidential and will not reflect unfavorably on the individuals who participate.

Observer personal bias. **Observer personal bias** refers to errors in observational data that are traceable to characteristics of the observer. One can argue that any observations made by human beings will contain some personal bias because all of us are influenced by our experiences and beliefs. This may be true, but the design of some research studies increases the potential for observer bias to operate.[14]

Obvious sources of personal bias in observers should be looked for and eliminated if found. For example, to use an observer with a negative attitude toward ethnic minorities in a study involving observations of the creative endeavors of ethnic-minority children and other children in a nursery school clearly would be inappropriate. The observer's bias

13. Evertson, C. M., & Green, J. L. (1986). Observation as inquiry and method. In M. C. Wittrock (Ed.), *Handbook of Research on Teaching* (3rd ed., pp. 162–213). New York: Macmillan. Evertson and Green identified ten types of observer effects. We re-organized them here into seven types.
14. Salvia, J. A., & Mersel, C. J. (1980). Observer bias: A methodological consideration in special education research. *Journal of Special Education, 14,* 261–270. The authors reviewed 153 studies having a high potential for bias and found that only 22 percent reported adequate safeguards.

almost certainly would lead to seeing more creative behavior among the other children and either ignoring, misinterpreting, or minimizing the creative efforts of ethnic-minority children in this group.

Observers have been found to produce biased data when research participants are given such labels as "emotionally disturbed" or "mentally retarded," are high or low in physical attractiveness, or have certain ethnic or socioeconomic backgrounds.[15] If such characteristics are prominent among the individuals to be observed in your study, you may be able to develop ways to minimize their influence on the observers who will be collecting data.

Rating errors. When using observational rating scales, some observers form a response set that produces errors in their ratings on these scales. A **response set** is the tendency for an observer to make a rating based on a generalized disposition about the rating task rather than on the basis of the actual behavior of the individuals. The following are three response set errors of this sort:

1. The **error of leniency** is the tendency to assign high ratings to the majority of research participants even when they differ markedly on the variable being measured.
2. The **error of central tendency** is the tendency for observers to rate all or most of the individuals whom they observe around the midpoint of the observational scales. Observers sometimes make such ratings to avoid difficult judgments.
3. The **halo effect** is the tendency for the observer's early impressions of the individual being observed to influence his ratings on all behaviors involving that individual. For example, if the observer forms an initially favorable impression of the person being observed, he may rate the individual favorably in subsequent observations.

When high-inference variables are being observed, the magnitude of these observer rating errors can be so large that the resulting ratings are virtually meaningless. For example, a study of the ratings of student teachers by cooperating teachers revealed so much halo effect and error of leniency that the validity of the entire rating system was called into question.[16] For example, the mean "attitude" rating of the 161 student teachers who were observed was 4.85 out of a possible 5.00, which suggests a strong error of leniency. If such response sets occur, you need to either reconceptualize the rating scale or select and train observers more carefully.

Observer contamination. **Observer contamination** occurs when the observer's knowledge of certain data in a study influences the data that he records about other variables. For example, suppose that we are doing a study of the human relations skills of successful elementary school principals. Unsuccessful and successful principals could be identified by a composite of nominations made by teachers, parents, and school superintendents. Observers then are trained to observe the performance of the successful and unsuccessful principals in faculty meetings and evaluate them on certain human relations skills. If the observers know beforehand which principals have been classified as successful and which as unsuccessful, they almost certainly will be influenced by this knowledge when they collect observational data about the principals' behavior. The obvious solution to the problem is to keep possibly contaminating information from the observers.

15. Ibid.
16. Phelps, L., Schmitz, C. D., & Boatright, B. (1986). The effects of halo and leniency on cooperating teacher reports using Likert-type rating scales. *Journal of Educational Research, 79,* 151–154.

Observer omissions.   An **observer omission** is the failure to record the occurrence of a behavior that fits one of the categories on the observational schedule. This failure can have several causes. One of them is personal bias, which we discussed above. Because of personal bias, the observer may overlook the occurrence of desirable behavior by an individual toward whom he has a negative bias. Another possibility is that the behaviors to be observed occur simultaneously or so rapidly that the observer is unable to record all of them. The opposite situation also is possible: The behavior to be observed occurs so infrequently that the observer fails to notice it.

Observation errors due to omissions can be detected during the development of the observation form or during observer training. You may find it necessary to simplify the observation schedule or to assign multiple observers to a setting, with each observer responsible for recording data on different observational variables. In the case of infrequently occurring variables, you may need to provide cues and reminders to maintain observers' vigilance.

Observer drift.   Once observers have been trained to the desired level of agreement and accuracy, they should start collecting data promptly because a delay will result in some loss of observer skills. Also, if the observations are to extend for more than one week, you should hold a weekly refresher training session for all observers. If this is not done, the observational data will become less reliable because of **observer drift,** which is the tendency for observers gradually to redefine the observational variables, so that the data that they collect no longer reflect the definitions that they learned during training.

Reliability decay.   Research evidence suggests that observers should be checked frequently during the course of the study to keep them performing at a satisfactory level. Otherwise, the observational data are subject to **reliability decay,** which is the tendency for observational data recorded during the later phases of data collection to be less reliable than those collected earlier.

Paul Taplin and John Reid compared "decay" in reliability for three groups of observers: (1) those who were told they would not be checked, (2) those told they would be spot-checked at regular intervals, and (3) those told they would be checked on a random basis.[17] The randomly checked group maintained the highest level of reliability, followed by the spot-checked group; the not-checked group had the lowest reliability. The spot-checked group performed very well in the sessions when they knew they would be checked, and very poorly in the sessions when they thought they would not be checked. Therefore, the problem seems to be one of motivation, so you should do whatever possible to maintain observers' motivation. For example, you can try to convince observers of the importance of their task, schedule sessions so as to avoid observer fatigue, inform them that you will check their performance on a random basis, carry out frequent random checks, and give them frequent feedback on their reliability.

Procedures for Observation in Qualitative Research

Observation in qualitative research differs from observation in quantitative research in three ways. One difference is that observers in a qualitative study do not seek to remain neutral or "objective" about the phenomena being observed. They may include their own feelings and experiences in interpreting their observations. An example is Cathy Evans and Donna Eder's study of social isolation, which included in-depth observations of informal

✦ Touchstone in Research

Angrosino, M. V., & Mays de Pérez, K. A. (2000). Rethinking observation: From method to context. In N. K. Denzin & Y. S. Lincoln (Eds.), *Handbook of qualitative research* (2nd ed., pp. 673–702). Thousand Oaks, CA: Sage.

17. Taplin, P. S., & Reid, J. B. (1973). Effects of instructional set and experimenter influence on observer reliability. *Child Development, 44,* 547–554.

activities among middle school students during lunch.[18] The lunchroom observations included taking notes on the behavior of students who sat together while eating lunch toward "isolates"—students who spent most of their lunch period alone.

The researchers observed many incidents involving ridicule of isolates, and all four observers "reported that witnessing such events was a source of emotional distress for them."[19] After one incident of this type, Evans wrote these field notes, which were included in the published research report:

> I was utterly and completely disgusted. I guess part of my problem was that I was disillusioned too—I thought Janice and Patty were above it. I didn't initiate conversation with Jenny because it would have targeted her more and I didn't reprimand the girls in my group because it would have possibly been more embarrassing to Jenny and I might as well witness what there is to witness, even if it's grossly unpleasant.[20]

Thus, these qualitative researchers sought to avoid criticizing or taking sides with specific participants, but still clearly considered their own reactions to events to be a legitimate part of the study, and worthy of reporting.

The second difference between quantitative and qualitative observation is that the focus of qualitative observation is much more emergent. In contrast, data collection in quantitative research generally is driven by a priori hypotheses, questions, or objectives. At any point in the process, qualitative observers are free to shift their attention to new phenomena as new research questions emerge.

The third difference is that the focus of observation generally is much wider in qualitative research. In quantitative research, observers tend to concentrate on specific aspects of behavior and to ignore context. In qualitative research, however, observers look at behavior and its environmental setting from a holistic perspective.

The Purpose of Observation in Qualitative Research

Two common methods of data collection in qualitative research—interviews and analysis of documents—involve words uttered or written by the participants in the natural setting. This information is limited by participants' knowledge, memory, and ability to convey information clearly and accurately and, also, by how they wish to be perceived by outsiders such as the researchers. Observation, in contrast, allows researchers to formulate their own version of what is occurring, independent of the participants. The inclusion of selected observations in a researcher's report provides a more complete description of phenomena than would be possible by just referring to interview statements or documents. Just as important, observations provide an alternate source of data for verifying the information obtained by other methods. Their use for this purpose is called *triangulation,* which is explained in Chapter 14.

An ethnographic study conducted by Katherine Rosier and William Corsaro provides an example of observation as one of several data sources.[21] Their study tested the validity of the common stereotype that the educational and economic problems of many African-American youth stem from deficiencies of the families in which they are raised. One aspect of the study involved interviewing parents and observing in the homes of children enrolled

18. Evans, C., & Eder, D. (1993). "NO EXIT": Processes of social isolation in the middle school. *Journal of Contemporary Ethnography, 22,* 139–170.
19. Ibid., p. 146.
20. Ibid., p. 146.
21. Rosier, K. B., & Corsaro, W. A. (1993). Competent parents, complex lives: Managing parenthood in poverty. *Journal of Contemporary Ethnography, 22,* 171–204.

in Head Start. When visiting the homes, the researchers used direct observation to check the validity of parents' claims that they regularly engaged their children in structured learning activities at home and provided educational toys and supplies despite their limited budget. Considerable observational evidence was found to support such claims, including finished projects displayed on refrigerators and walls; tables cluttered with writing instruments, paper, and works in progress; and educational toys and books. Parents also presented the researchers with samples of their children's schoolwork.

The researchers described a day that they spent observing Cymira, one of the Head Start children, and four other children who were being cared for by Cymira's mother, Rhonda. While the children were playing outside, Rhonda got out a variety of both purchased and handmade educational materials, suited to varying ages. She then called all five children into the house. During the hour when they stayed indoors, Rhonda "checked and encouraged the children's work, and the older children assisted the younger ones."[22] Their careful, on-site observation helped the researchers confirm the validity of the finding from parent interviews that most parents of poor African American children seek to instill educational skills and values in their children at an early age.

In Chapter 15 we explain how qualitative research reflects various traditions, such as ethnography, cultural studies, and cognitive psychology. The purpose and form of observation varies across these traditions. In the following sections, we describe general methods that are used in collecting qualitative observational data. If your proposed study follows a particular tradition of qualitative research, you should study the specific ways in which researchers working within that tradition have used observation as a data-collection method.

✦ *Touchstone in Research*

Fine, G. A., & Sandstrom, K. L. (1988). *Knowing children: Participant observation with minors.* Thousand Oaks, CA: Sage.

Jorgensen, D. L. (1989). *Participant observation: A methodology for human studies.* Thousand Oaks, CA: Sage.

Identifying the Observers and Their Roles

The observer role in qualitative research varies along a continuum from complete observer to complete participant. At the extreme role of **complete observer,** the researcher maintains a posture of detachment from the setting being studied. At the extreme role of **complete participant,** the researcher studies a setting in which she already is a member or becomes converted to genuine membership during the course of the research. For example, David Hayano reported on his observations of fellow denizens of California's all-night card rooms.[23]

Between these two extremes are the observer-participant and participant-observer roles. In the **observer-participant role,** the researcher acts primarily as an observer, entering the setting only to gather data and interacting only casually and nondirectly with individuals or groups while engaged in observation. In the **participant-observer role,** the researcher observes and interacts closely enough with individuals to establish a meaningful identity within their group; however, the researcher does not engage in activities that are at the core of the group's identity. For example, Peter Adler, a sociologist and professor, played a participant-observer role in a study of college athletes at his university.[24] He maintained his researcher identity while actively participating with the basketball team and coaching staff in various roles, including insider, expert, and celebrity—but not in the core roles of coach, trainer, or player.

The researcher who designs a qualitative study most likely will be the observer during the data-collection phase. Another option is for a team, which may include the researcher,

22. Ibid., p. 182.
23. Hayano, D. (1982). *Poker faces.* Berkeley, CA: University of California Press.
24. Adler, P. A., & Adler, P. (1991). *Backboards and blackboards.* New York: Columbia University Press.

to make the observations. Use of multiple observers lessens the burden on each observe and allows for more observation time overall. Furthermore, if the observers are diverse ' factors relevant to the phenomena being studied (e.g., gender and age), they can enhar the validity of observations by cross-checking each others' findings and eliminating ir curate interpretations. In the study of peer treatment of social isolates described above, two other young adults served as lunchroom observers along with the two researchers.

Preparing for Observation

An observer in a qualitative research project can prepare by serving as an apprentice to an expert in the type of observation being planned. A period of apprenticeship is desirable because qualitative observation skills are complex and subtle; they do not lend themselves to the type of training procedures for quantitative observation that we described earlier in the chapter. By working alongside an expert, a novice observer gradually can develop an understanding of how to focus her observations and to shift the focus across the three stages (descriptive, focused, and selected) described below.

Although not a substitute for apprenticeship, some university programs provide courses in which you can develop particular skills needed in qualitative observation. These skills include the ability to write descriptions of observed events that are objective rather than interpretive, to incorporate rich detail about observed events into field notes, and to convert rough, handwritten field notes into polished typed reports. Training in the use of videotape and audiotape recording equipment and in field work techniques may be provided as well.

Once a qualitative research study is underway, you might encounter problems and issues unique to your field setting. It is helpful in such situations to maintain contact with an expert who can advise you. This consultation process does not violate the integrity of the study because, in qualitative research, the observation methodology is free to change as the researcher develops new insights into the phenomena being studied.

Determining the Focus of Observation

The focus of a qualitative researcher's observations is likely to shift from early to later stages of a study. According to James Spradley, this process of shifting typically includes three stages.[25] First is the **descriptive stage,** when observations tend to be unfocused and general in scope, providing a base from which the observers can branch out in many directions. Second is the **focused stage,** when the observers have identified features of the phenomena under study that are of greatest interest and begin to direct their attention to collecting deeper information about this narrower range of features. Finally, there is the **selected stage,** when research questions or problems emerge, and the observers' focus shifts to refining and deepening their understanding of the specific elements that have emerged as theoretically or empirically most essential. Observational data are gathered until researchers achieve **theoretical saturation,** that is, when newly gathered findings essentially replicate earlier ones.[26]

The question of research focus also involves the decision as to what to observe at any given moment, and how to ensure that everything of potential interest is attended to. With respect to ensuring thorough coverage of the phenomena of interest, Norman Denzin suggested that all observational field notes should contain explicit reference to the following

25. Spradley, J. P. (1980). *Participant observation.* Fort Worth, TX: Harcourt.
26. Strauss, A. L., & Corbin, J. M. (1998). *Basics of qualitative research: Techniques and procedures for developing grounded theory* (2nd ed.). Thousand Oaks, CA: Sage.

elements: participants, interactions, routines, rituals, temporal elements, interpretations, and social organization of the participants.[27] Sharan Merriam presented a similar list, but also included the setting (i.e., the physical environment, the context, and the kinds of behavior that the setting encourages, permits, discourages, or prevents) as well as subtle factors.[28] Subtle factors include informal and unplanned activities, symbolic and connotative meanings of words, nonverbal communication such as dress and physical space, and what does *not* happen, especially if it ought to have happened.

A study by Robert Prophet and Patricia Rowell illustrates the features of a phenomenon on which observers might focus, and how the focus of observation shifts as the research project progresses.[29] Prophet and Rowell investigated teacher-student interaction in science classes in the African country of Botswana. The classes were at the junior secondary level and were taught in the English language. They described the starting point for the study as follows:

> [We had] a desire to gain information and insights into the realities of life in science classrooms in the junior secondary schools. This goal was pursued using a conceptual framework in which teaching style and the use of knowledge exemplify power relationships in the classroom.[30]

Their descriptive stage of observation involved documenting classroom interactions by sitting discreetly at the back of the classroom and writing extensive notes. Excerpts from these field notes were included in the research report. The notes primarily documented utterances by the teacher, by individual students, and by students speaking in unison. However, the observers also noted specific actions, such as when students raised their hands in order to be called on, when a student's comment was ignored by the teacher, or when the teacher wrote something on the board.

Prophet and Rowell stated what their initial observations and interviews revealed:

> . . . the teachers generate learning experiences that are teacher-centered and which place the students in the role of passive recipients of knowledge. . . . The actual pedagogical principles underpinning teaching styles . . . appear to be based on rote learning. . . . These practices are so widespread and so taken for granted by all the participants that it is tempting to say simply, "This is what happens in schools."[31]

In their report, Prophet and Rowell expressed their growing sense of a major disparity between stated curriculum aims (i.e., that the teaching situation should be student-centered) and the actual authoritarian, teacher-centered classroom environment that they consistently observed.

Through their concurrent work at the University of Botswana, Prophet and Rowell realized that preservice teachers specializing in science education found "hands-on" science (e.g., laboratory experimentation) arduous and placed heavy reliance on rote learning in their own educational endeavors. Because they had seen similar problems among secondary school students in their research study, Prophet and Rowell speculated that, "the seeds for future difficulties were being sown in the teacher education program."[32]

27. Denzin, N. K. (1989). *The research act* (3rd ed.). Englewood Cliffs, NJ: Prentice Hall.
28. Merriam, S. B. (1998). *Qualitative research and case study applications* (revised & expanded). San Francisco: Jossey-Bass.
29. Prophet, R. B., & Rowell, P. M. (1993). Coping and control: Science teaching strategies in Botswana. *International Journal of Qualitative Studies in Education, 6,* 197–209.
30. Ibid., p. 198.
31. Ibid., p. 201.
32. Ibid., p. 205.

During the final, selected-observation stage of their study, Prophet and Rowell paid particular attention to classroom activities designed to develop students' manipulative skills. Further observations, one of which is described in the research report, indicated that

> . . . the teaching of manipulative skills followed the same teacher-centered routine as described earlier, with students often not participating and teachers presenting instructions and information in an unclear verbal style. Very little student-based practical work was observed. . . .[33]

This teaching style was widely discrepant from the syllabus for the preservice teacher education program in science education.

As another part of the selected stage of their research, Prophet and Rowell developed a test of science skills and administered it to a small sample of students at each school. Students in general were found to perform poorly on the manipulative skills that were tested. In the conclusion of their research report, Prophet and Rowell summarized and interpreted their findings in relation to their previously stated formulations concerning power relationships in classrooms.

We see in this research study how narrowing and deepening the focus of field observations can foster the emergence of qualitative interpretations, which constitute the primary findings of the study.

Gaining Entry into the Field Setting

As one would expect from the emergent nature of qualitative research, there are no strict rules about how to enter a field setting to make observations. You will need to develop a procedure based on the characteristics of the field setting and its members and on where you intend to situate yourself along the continuum of complete participant to complete observer.

You can gain insights into developing your procedure by consulting with expert qualitative researchers and by reading reports of their studies. For example, the study of social isolates in middle schools by Evans and Eders, described earlier in the chapter, is instructive. They describe their procedure for gaining entry into school lunchrooms as follows:

> Our strategy was to enter the lunchroom setting as peers rather than as authority figures. We wore jeans and other casual clothing as did most of the students. We made a point of never affiliating with teachers or other adults in this setting. This meant that some of us were sometimes included when teachers chastised our groups for initiating food fights and other disruptive activities! We initially entered the lunchroom environment as we imagined a new student in school would do, by sitting alone or next to a single person and starting conversations with students sitting nearby. . . . although we informed everyone that we were from the local university and that we were studying adolescent friendship, we did not take notes openly . . . We did not inform the students of our ages, and although the age difference between the students and the researchers varied between 10 and 20 years, the students' consistent comments indicated they generally viewed us as . . . undergraduate students in our late teens. . . . The researchers' typical stance with groups to which we belonged was to become "a quiet member" of the group. We adopted a listening, receptive, nonjudgmental attitude toward other members. . . . When we did not report them for swearing or other school rule violations, their trust toward us increased dramatically and they assured other students that we were "okay."[34]

---

33. Ibid., p. 205.
34. Evans & Eder, Processes of social isolation, pp. 145–146.

This description shows the researchers' insights about the need to present themselves to the adolescents under investigation as nonthreatening and friendly. If the same researchers were to shift their research focus to teachers or administrators in the same school, one would expect them to adopt a more professional and mature appearance and manner, but to maintain the same level of neutrality and discretion with those groups as they had with the students, thereby demonstrating their worthiness of trust.

Recording Observations

Qualitative researchers can make use of the same range of methods used by quantitative researchers to make a permanent record of their observations. For example, they can take written field notes using a lap-top computer. Another option is to dictate notes into an audiotape recorder. A stenomask can be useful for this purpose.[35] A **stenomask** is a sound-shielded microphone attached to a portable tape recorder that is worn on a shoulder strap. The observer can speak into the microphone while an activity is occurring without people nearby being able to hear the dictation.

In some field settings, an observer taking notes on a tablet or in a notebook might distract participants or cause the observer to miss important aspects of events. It may be possible to take a few notes surreptitiously in such situations. Qualitative researchers even have been known to write field notes on toilet paper or inside matchbook covers in order to conceal their role as observers!

If you cannot take notes while in the field setting, you will need to remember what occurred and arrange to make notes soon after leaving the scene. Even if you cannot make complete field notes right away, you should at least try to write a summary of the sequence of events and noteworthy statements. You can use this summary later to stimulate your writing of a more extensive set of notes.

The following are features of good field notes in a qualitative research study.

Field notes should be descriptive and reflective. **Descriptive information** includes verbal portraits of the research participants, reconstruction of dialogue, description of the physical setting, accounts of particular events, and descriptions of the observer's behavior. **Reflective information** includes the researcher's personal account of the course of inquiry, and may contain the following elements: reflections on the methods of data collection and analysis, reflections on ethical dilemmas and conflict, reflections on the observer's frame of mind, and emerging interpretations. An example of field notes that include both types of information is shown in Figure 9.3. The notes that are reflective in nature are in italics.

Field notes should be detailed and concrete. Observers should strive to write field notes that are detailed and concrete, not vague and overgeneralized. Michael Patton provided the following examples of field notes that are at these two extremes:[36]

Vague and Overgeneralized Field Notes	**Detailed and Concrete Field Notes**
The client was quite hostile toward the staff person.	When Judy, the senior staff member, told her that she could not do what she wanted to do, the client began to yell at Judy, telling her that she couldn't control her

---

35. Stenomasks are described on pp. 248–249 in: Patton, M. (1990). *Qualitative evaluation and research methods* (2nd ed.). Thousand Oaks, CA: Sage.
36. Patton, *Qualitative evaluation,* p. 240.

FIGURE 9.3

Example of Field Notes with Observer Comments

B turned on the overhead projector and proceeded to show some examples. The first one was a colorful slide of the planets.

OC—B must like planets. There is a model of the solar system, in similar colors in B's office.

B pointed out that this particular slide would be useful in having students identify the planets and that the slide would not be very helpful in explaining planetary motion. The students were also shown an example of masking. (The names of the planets were masked by pieces *of* cardboard so that they could be revealed by the teacher, as required.)

OC—The students were attentive, but quiet, too quiet I thought. What's happening here is that the teacher is not asking enough questions. For example, B could have asked the students what the flaps were for, and why would you want to do such a thing. Instead of telling what the slide was good for, asking what it would be good for. Nice locus of control issue.

The second transparency's subject was the water cycle, a slide consisting of the main and two overlays. B explained how an overhead of this kind could be used to describe a process.

OC—The students were quiet, no questions.

Source: Pages 100–101 in: Brandt, R. *Observation of B's lesson on overhead transparencies.* Unpublished report, University of Georgia, Apr. 30, 1987. Reprinted in Merriam, S. B. (1988). *Case study research in education: A qualitative approach.* San Francisco: Jossey-Bass.

Note: Italicized field notes are reflective comments by the observer. OC is an abbreviation for observer comments.

life, that she was on nothing but a "power trip," that she'd "like to beat the shit out of her," and that she could just "go to hell." She shook her fist in Judy's face and stomped out of the room, leaving Judy standing there with her mouth open, looking amazed.

The excerpt on the right obviously is much more specific and descriptive than that on the left. Also, the language reflects low-inference observation, which is more helpful than high-inference observation when the researcher is ready to look for themes and patterns in the field notes and other data sources.

Field notes should include visual details when appropriate. Field notes need not be limited to words. For example, an observer might draw a sketch of the layout of the physical setting in which the observed activities are occurring. If visual details are worthy of even more attention, the researcher can create a documentary-style visual record by making videotape recordings or taking photographs. Anthropologists and sociologists frequently use such data-collection methods in their fieldwork.[37] At their best, visual records illuminate important aspects of culture and social interaction. However, some critics have argued that documentary-style visual records, particularly those of early-20th-century anthropologists, while seemingly neutral, "reified the relationships of superiority and inferiority endemic of colonialism."[38] This criticism suggests the need for qualitative researchers

37. Harper, D. (2000). Reimagining visual methods: Galileo to *Neuromancer.* In N. K. Denzin & Y. S. Lincoln (Eds.), *Handbook of qualitative research* (2nd ed., pp. 717–732). Thousand Oaks, CA: Sage.

38. Ibid., p. 728.

to analyze their motives and stance in using visual recording devices to select the particular scenes and objects for preservation as recorded images.

A case study by Terry Wood, Paul Cobb, and Erna Yackel illustrates the use of videotape recordings in qualitative research.[39] The researchers examined how one elementary school teacher changed her approach to teaching mathematics while participating in an ongoing research project that involved constructivist views of learning. Every mathematics lesson taught by the teacher for an entire school year was videotaped, and two cameras were used to focus on four selected pairs of children during small-group activities. The videotape recordings, supplemented by field notes and copies of the children's classwork, were the main source of data used to document changes in students' mathematical understanding and social interaction in small groups.

Dealing with Observer Effects

Quantitative research operates on the premise that observations should be independent of the particular individual who is making them. Thus, an effort is made to minimize observer bias and to control for possible effects of the observer on what is observed. Qualitative researchers take a different stance toward their influence on the phenomena being observed. As observers, they consider their biases and personal reactions to be part of the "scene" that is observed. Therefore, qualitative researchers do not use the positivist criterion of objectivity in deciding whether their observations are of high quality. Instead, they use the procedures described below to deal with validity issues that arise in qualitative observation.[40]

Reactions of program participants and staff to the observer's presence. The recommended approach is that qualitative researchers should strive not to overestimate or underestimate their effects on what is observed, but they should describe and analyze these effects as part of the research project.

Effects on the observer during the course of the study. The approach recommended for dealing with this issue is similar to that suggested for the previous issue, namely, to realize that the observer will have reactions and to record them. The excerpt from Evans and Eder's field notes, in which the observer reported her distress at witnessing the mistreatment of social isolates by their middle school peers, typifies qualitative observers' attention to the effects of observations on themselves.

The observer's personal predispositions or biases. To address this issue, the researcher should use established procedures for validating and verifying data analyses, so as to reduce any distortions that may have been introduced by the researcher's predispositions. These procedures include active efforts to test rival explanations for research findings, the use of both qualitative and quantitative research methods to examine a phenomenon, the use of multiple observers and researchers, the examination of findings from various theoretical perspectives, and a reporting of the research project in sufficient detail that readers can "audit" the findings.

Observer incompetence. Qualitative observation data will be useless, and even misleading, if the observers have had insufficient preparation to do the type of data collection required by the research problem and approach. The solution to this problem is obvious. Observers should be thoroughly trained and otherwise prepared prior to collecting data in the field.

---

39. Wood, T., Cobb, P., & Yackel, E. (1991). Change in teaching mathematics: A case study. *American Educational Research Journal, 28,* 587–616.
40. These issues and procedures also are discussed in Chapter 14.

Analyzing Qualitative Observational Data

When the fieldwork phase of a qualitative research study is completed, the researchers are likely to have an extensive set of field notes and visual data that serve as a record of their observations. All these data need to be analyzed, interpreted, and reported. We describe each of these processes in the chapter on the case study method (Chapter 14). You will find that the procedures for analyzing, interpreting, and reporting observational data are essentially the same as those for other types of qualitative data, such as interview notes and documents found in the field setting.

Nonreactive Observation

Unobtrusive Measures in Quantitative Research

We explained above how observer effects can weaken the validity and reliability of observational data. For example, the presence of an observer can affect the behavior of the observed individuals such that it becomes atypical. This and other observer effects can be avoided through the use of unobtrusive measures—sometimes called *nonreactive measures*. **Unobtrusive measures** are characterized by the fact that the data are collected in a natural setting, and the individuals are unaware that they are being observed.

Suppose we are interested in students' use of computer technology in their studies. It would be difficult to observe students throughout the day, not knowing if and when they might use a computer. Unobtrusive measurement can help us with this problem. We could think of situations in which students might use a computer, and whether a product or "residue" would be produced that we could examine later. An obvious possibility is the use of computers for word processing of school assignments. We could ask the students' teachers for permission to examine the students' assignments so that we can observe which ones appear to be word-processed documents and which do not.

In this approach the students are unaware that they are being observed, but their teachers are aware. Perhaps we can think of situations involving computer use that are unobtrusive for both groups. Suppose the schools that we are observing make computers available for students in a technology center and in the school's library. We can obtain unobtrusive software that can be installed in these computers for the purpose of recording their duration of use and even the users' keystrokes. Of course, this approach raises ethical questions, which we consider below.

Examples of unobtrusive measures that have been used in research studies are listed in Figure 9.4. Measures of this type are especially useful when used in conjunction with conventional reactive measures because they involve such a different approach to measurement. If we use several different kinds of instruments to measure the same variables, and they yield similar results, we can be much more confident that our results are valid.

Potential Limitations of Unobtrusive Measures

Validity. The validity of some unobtrusive measures is uncertain. For example, the lost-letter technique has been used as an unobtrusive measure in research studies.[41] This technique involves making a large number of copies of various bogus letters, each of which is addressed to an organization that reflects a different opinion on an issue. The assumption is that an individual who finds a letter is more likely to mail it if the address represents an opinion that

✦ *Touchstone in Research*

Webb, E. J., Campbell, D. T., Schwartz, R., & Sechrest, L. B. (1999). *Unobtrusive measures.* Thousand Oaks, CA: Sage.

---

41. For an interesting application of this technique, see: Farrington, D. P., & Knight, B. J. (1980). Stealing from a lost letter: Effects of victim characteristics. *Criminal Justice and Behavior, 7,* 423–435.

FIGURE 9.4

Examples of Unobtrusive Measures in Research Studies

1. The floor tiles around the hatching-chick exhibit at Chicago's Museum of Science and Industry must be replaced every six weeks. Tiles in other parts of the museum need not be replaced for years. The selective erosion of tiles, indexed by the replacement rate, is a measure of relative popularity of exhibits.
2. One investigator wanted to learn the level of whiskey consumption in a town that was officially "dry." He did so by counting empty bottles in trash cans.
3. The degree of fear induced by a ghost-story-telling session can be measured by noting the shrinking diameter of a circle of seated children.
4 Chinese jade dealers have used the pupil dilation of their customers as a measure of the client's interest in particular stones. In 1872 Darwin noted this same variable as an index of fear.
5. Library withdrawals were used to demonstrate the effect of the introduction of television into a community. Fiction titles dropped, while nonfiction titles were unaffected.
6. The influence of the rate of interaction in managerial recruitment is shown by the overrepresentation of baseball managers who were infielders or catchers (high interaction positions) during their playing days.
7. Sir Francis Galton employed surveying hardware to estimate the bodily dimensions of African women whose language he did not speak.
8. Children's level of interest in Christmas was demonstrated by distortions in the size of their Santa Claus drawings.
9. Racial attitudes in two colleges were compared by noting the degree of clustering of African Americans and whites in lecture halls.

Source: Adapted from Webb, E. J., Campbell, D. T., Schwartz, R. D., Sechrest, L., & Grove, J. B. (1981). *Nonreactive measures in the social sciences* (2nd ed.). Boston: Houghton Mifflin.

---

he or she supports. If this is true, the rate of return for letters representing different opinions will reflect the percentage of persons holding each opinion in the community under investigation. In several election studies, however, the proportion of letters returned failed to predict the election results, thus raising doubts about the validity of the technique.

Reliability. The reliability of unobtrusive measures often is difficult to establish. Even for unobtrusive measures for which reliability can be computed, the data are of limited use to other researchers because most such measures are designed to study a very specific attitude or behavior pattern and are rarely used more than once. In contrast, conventional measures such as achievement tests, personality inventories, and attitude scales are used in many studies. Over a period of time, a useful body of knowledge about such measures is developed, and it is easier to obtain estimates of their reliability.

Ethical Considerations. The use of unobtrusive measures raises ethical issues involving informed consent and invasion of privacy. (These issues are discussed in Chapter 3.) Collection of nonreactive data in public settings usually is not regarded as an invasion of privacy. However, data collection in public areas where individuals would expect their behavior to be private, such as public restrooms, has been challenged as an invasion of privacy. Spying on an individual's private behavior (e.g., placing listening devices in the individual's home or office) clearly is an invasion of privacy.

Informed consent poses a difficult problem in unobtrusive measurement because its main purpose is to collect data without the awareness of the individuals being studied. The act of requesting informed consent makes individuals aware that they will be studied and thus jeopardizes the nonreactivity of any subsequent measurement. Therefore, it is essential in some situations to forego informed consent.

An institutional review board (see Chapter 3) may look favorably on a request to forego informed consent if the the researcher can demonstrate the following conditions: The individuals being studied will incur no risk, the anonymity of the participants will be maintained, it is impossible to conduct the study under the condition of informed consent, and the study promises to produce significant benefits.

Qualitative Observation of Material Culture

The same material objects and residues of human actions that are studied by quantitative researchers can be phenomena of interest to qualitative researchers. Whereas quantitative researchers analyze these phenomena using narrowly focused, numerical measures (typically, frequency counts), qualitative researchers have a holistic perspective and examine these phenomena as expressions of how individuals and groups construct their social reality.

Ian Hodder used the term **material culture** to refer to the various objects created by different groups throughout history.[42] (Some researchers refer to them as *artifacts*.) He distinguished between two types of material culture. First is material culture that serves a communicative, representational function. Text and signs are examples of this type of material culture. We discuss the study of text and signs by qualitative researchers later in the chapter.

The second type of material culture, which we call **practice-oriented material culture** is distinguished by its association with particular practices and meanings. Tools are a good example of practice-oriented material culture. A hammer, for instance, does not have a communicative function. Rather, it is associated with particular uses, especially within the construction industry. Also, a hammer has different meanings for different individuals. One person may associate a hammer with injury, whereas another individual may have positive associations—work for pay, building useful products. Still others might form symbolic associations; for example, the song, "If I Had a Hammer," may come to mind.

Objects other than tools also can be manifestations of practice-oriented material culture. Lilies, for example, often are used for decorative purposes in our culture. They also are associated with funerals in the minds of some people.

Observation of practice-oriented material culture is important because it gives qualitative researchers access to those whose voices are silent, for example, groups whose experiences are not recorded in written form by the dominant culture. Another example is dead societies, especially those that left no written record, but only practice-oriented objects and material residues of their use.

Despite its importance, the use of practice-oriented material culture as a data source is problematic because qualitative researchers usually cannot check the validity of their interpretations of the social reality that it represents by interviewing the individuals who produced it. Archaeologists have taken the lead in developing methods to deal with this problem because they often find themselves in the situation of interpreting objects and fragments of objects from ancient cultures.[43]

Practice-oriented material culture is worthy of observation by educational researchers. Many specialized tools have been developed or adopted by educators over

42. Hodder, I. (2000). The interpretation of documents and material culture. In N. K. Denzin & Y. S. Lincoln (Eds.), *Handbook of qualitative research* (2nd ed., pp. 703–715). Thousand Oaks, CA: Sage.
43. Ibid.

time—among them, chalkboards, desks, classrooms, bulletin boards, computers, and video recorders. Students, too, develop or purchase certain tools, such as notebooks, binders, pencils, staplers, calculators, and erasers. The study of these tools may provide valuable insights into how these groups construct the social context within which they cope with learning tasks and deal with other aspects of their public and private lives.

✦ *Touchstone in Research*

Krippendorf, K. (1980). *Content analysis: An introduction to its methodology.* Thousand Oaks, CA: Sage.

Weber, R. P. (1990). *Basic content analysis.* Thousand Oaks, CA: Sage.

Content Analysis of Documents and Other Communication Media

Thus far in this chapter, our focus has been on methods for observing human behavior and features of the environment in which the behavior occurs. An important feature of human environments is the messages that people encode in various forms:

Written documents: Written materials include textbooks, students' completed homework assignments, tests, computer printouts of school data, newspapers, and memoranda.

Visual media: Photographs, posters, and drawings are examples of visual materials that may be analyzed.

Audio media: The researcher can analyze audiotape recordings, laser disc recordings, or radio programs.

Combinations of media: It may be desirable to analyze a variety of types of media, such as TV programs and CD-ROM discs that combine print, visual images, and sound.

The content of these materials comprises messages from one individual or group to another individual or group. These messages are the object of study in some research projects. Textbooks are of particular interest because they convey much about the school curriculum. Textbooks and other written materials usually are called *documents* by researchers. We use this term here, and also the term *communication media,* to refer both to documents and to materials whose messages are primarily visual or auditory.

If you plan to include communication media as a data source in your research, you will need to be systematic about identifying and analyzing them. In the following sections we describe appropriate procedures, depending on whether your research will be conducted from a quantitative or qualitative perspective.

Content Analysis in Quantitative Research

In quantitative research, the analysis of documents typically involves content analysis. **Content analysis** has been defined as "a research technique for the objective, systematic, and quantitative description of the manifest content of communication."[44] The raw material for content analysis can be any type of document or other communication medium.

Most content analyses in education involve collecting data on various aspects of the messages encoded in the communication product. These analyses generally involve fairly simple classifications or tabulations of specific information. Content analyses of student compositions for language arts classes, for example, could be used to develop a typology of grammatical and spelling errors as well as information on the frequency of different types of errors. This information can be used to revise language arts courses or develop remedial programs.

---

44. Berelson, B. (1952). *Content analysis in communication research.* Glencoe, IL: Free Press. Quote appears on p. 18.

Steps in Doing a Content Analysis

In describing the steps involved in a content analysis, we refer to a research study of vocabulary instruction in social studies textbooks conducted by Janis Harmon, Wanda Hedrick, and Elizabeth Fox.[45] Although this example involves printed text, the procedures are equally appropriate for the analysis of other communication media, such as Web pages, film, and audio recordings.

Specify research questions, hypotheses, or objectives. The researchers' study grew out of their appreciation of the important role that vocabulary instruction plays in students' ability to understand social-studies concepts presented in the upper-elementary and middle grades. Also, they were aware of effective research-based practices for promoting vocabulary development and wondered whether these practices were represented in the teachers' editions of social-studies textbooks.

These interests and concerns led Harmon, Hedrick, and Fox to frame three research questions to guide their study:

1. What is the nature of the words or key terms selected by the social studies textbook publishers?
2. To what extent and how is vocabulary represented at each grade level and across series of published social studies programs for grades 4–8?
3. What vocabulary instructional supports do publishers provide for teachers?[46]

Textbooks, especially teachers' editions, contain a great many content-related elements. By framing the research questions stated above, these researchers made explicit the scope of their investigation and also focused it sufficiently so that a manageable study could be designed.

Select a sample of documents to analyze. The researchers selected teachers' editions of the social studies textbooks on the 1997–1998 Texas state adoption list for grades 4–8. The teachers' editions were selected because they contain both the text that students read and recommendations to teachers about how to teach this text. It was necessary to have documents that included these recommendations in order to address the third research question stated above.

Develop a category-coding procedure. The essence of a content analysis is the coding of the document's messages into categories. Each category should represent a discrete variable that is relevant to your research objective. The categories should be mutually exclusive, such that any bit of communication can be coded by only category in the category system.

If appropriate, consider employing a coding system that has been used in previous research. This option saves the time required to develop your own system. Also, the use of standard coding categories permits comparison with other studies that have used the same system. Consequently, the research project is more likely to make a contribution to theory and knowledge in the field under consideration.

In the vocabulary study that we are considering here, the researchers developed their own categories, but they represent standard features of textbooks, including teachers' editions. Among the categories are these: instructional objectives; instructional components (i.e., suggestions for tasks that teachers or students might complete in order to enhance instruction and learning); and key terms (i.e., words or phrases highlighted by the

45. Harmon, J. M., Hedrick, W. B., & Fox, E. A. (2000). A content analysis of vocabulary instruction in social studies textbooks for grades 4–8. *Elementary School Journal, 100,* 253–271.
46. Ibid., p. 254.

publishers), with subcategories for (1) general terms that might be found in any subject (e.g., *malady, revenge*), (2) technical multiple-meaning terms (e.g., *table, legend*), (3) technical domain-specific words unique to social studies (e.g., *pueblo, colonist*), and (4) terms relating to specific persons, places, and events (e.g., *Bull Run, Dwight Eisenhower*).

After initial development of the content classification system, you should determine whether several raters can use it with a high degree of consistency. You can do this by calculating a correlation coefficient of inter-rater reliability for different raters' classifications.[47] If the inter-rater reliability is low, you will need to identify points of ambiguity in the content classification system and clarify them. To increase the reliability with which the classification system can be used, it is helpful to develop an explicit set of scoring rules.

An explicit reliability check was not reported by the researchers who conducted the vocabulary study. There are repeated references to "we" in the report, so presumably the researchers checked each others' coding as the content analysis proceeded. Nonetheless, our confidence in the study findings would be strengthened by an explicit reliability check.

Conduct the content analysis. A typical content analysis consists of making a frequency count of the occurrence of each coding category in each document in the sample. The general procedure is to create a computer file that reproduces the text of the document. (You can type the text or possibly use a scanning device that reads the text directly into a computer file.) Then read the computer file and type a code for each message that fits a particular category of the content-analysis system. A computer program can be used to count the frequency of each code or to list together all the text messages that fit a particular code. Computer programs of this type are described in Chapter 14.

The frequency counts can be presented in the results section of the research report. Descriptive statistics also can be reported, for example, the mean number and standard deviation of the occurrences of each coding category across all the documents in the sample. Relationships between the variables represented by the different categories can be analyzed and reported, too.

In the vocabulary study, the researchers conducted several of these statistical analyses. For example, they calculated the mean percentage of key terms that fit each of their categories across the textbooks included in the content analysis. They found that 78 percent of the key terms were in the category of domain-specific words, with another 13 percent in the category of terms relating to specific persons, places, and events. In a related analysis, they asked three teachers to identify what they considered to be key terms in representative samples of text from the textbooks (the samples had been retyped so that the teachers could not identify which terms the publishers had marked as key). Surprisingly, there was only 48 percent agreement between the publishers' and teachers' lists.

Table 9.2 shows the results of an analysis of the instructional components involving key terms that were included in the teachers' editions of the textbooks. As you can see, the researchers classified the instructional components into three categories of tasks: instruction (i.e., teaching activities for the teacher); application (i.e., activities requiring students to use the key term); and review (i.e., activities in the review section of the textbook units, chapters, and lessons). For most of the textbooks, the vast majority of the instructional components involved application and review. A more fine-grained analysis of the components revealed an emphasis on surface-level vocabulary activities, for example, filling in blanks, crossword puzzles, and matching words with their definitions.

47. For information about inter-rater reliability coefficients, see: Stemler, S. (2001). An overview of content analysis. *Practical Assessment, Research & Evaluation, 7*(17). Retrieved November 3, 2001 from www.ericae.net/pare/getvn.asp?v=7n=17; Scott, W. (1955). Reliability of content analysis: The case of nominal scale coding. *Public Opinion Quarterly, 19,* 321–325.

TABLE 9.2

Categories of Vocabulary Tasks in the Teacher's Edition of Social Studies Textbooks

Series	Total	Instruction (%)	Application (%)	Review (%)
Harcourt Brace, grade 4	61	21	31	48
Harcourt Brace, grade 5	8	13	50	38
Harcourt Brace, grade 6	31	26	32	42
Houghton Mifflin, grade 4	64	25	36	39
Houghton Mifflin, grade 5	46	24	30	46
Houghton Mifflin, grade 6	135	23	36	41
Macmillan, grade 4	60	23	33	43
Macmillan, grade 5	108	27	33	40
Macmillan, grade 6	189	17	54	29
Silver Burdett Ginn, grade 4	40	15	55	30
Silver Burdett Ginn, grade 5	14	0	57	43
Silver Burdett Ginn, grade 6	41	2	49	49
Jarrett, grade 4	7	43	43	14
Benson, grade 7	7	29	0	71
Glencoe, grade 7	21	24	24	52
Holt, Rinehart & Winston, grade 7	6	17	33	50
Holt, Rinehart & Winston, grade 8	31	19	55	26
Prentice Hall, grade 8	17	6	12	82
Scott Foresman, grade 8	8	13	38	50

Source: Table 5 on p. 266 in: Harmon, J. M., Hedrick, W. B., & Fox E. A. (2000). A content analysis of vocabulary instruction in social studies textbooks for grades 4–8. *Elementary School Journal, 100,* 253–271. Copyright 2000 University of Chicago Press.

Interpret the results. The final stage of a content analysis is to interpret the meaning of the results. The interpretive process will depend on the purpose of the study and its theoretical or conceptual framework.

In the vocabulary study, Harmon, Hedrick, and Fox used research knowledge about effective vocabulary instruction as a basis for evaluating publishers' practices as revealed by their content analyses. This research knowledge demonstrates the value of such instructional activities as word sorts, semantic mapping, and graphic organizers to help students make connections between their prior knowledge and new terminology. Harmon, Hedrick, and Fox found virtually no utilization of this research knowledge in the textbooks they analyzed:

> Our findings indicate that although publishers do give consideration to vocabulary in their programs, many activities are still grounded in vocabulary teaching and learning activities that are not supported by empirical evidence. Thus, publishers need to take a more aggressive stance to integrate current knowledge about vocabulary into their instructional procedures.[48]

The researchers also raise an important question for future research, based on their data analysis of teachers' and publisher' identification of key terms in social studies textbooks: "Disagreements between teachers and publishers over what should be highlighted as conceptually loaded terms raises questions concerning how publishers select key

48. Harmon et al., *Content analysis*, p. 269.

terms."[49] This is a good example of the principle that the value of a study often lies less with its findings and more in the questions it raises.

Analysis of Documents and Records in Qualitative Observation

Qualitative researchers often study written communications found in natural situations. These written communications are of various types. Yvonna Lincoln and Egon Guba define **documents** as written communications that are prepared for personal rather than official reasons.[50] In contrast, **records** are written communications that have an official purpose. For example, personal letters, personal diaries, and drafts of articles are documents, whereas legal contracts, commission reports for general circulation, tax statements, and newspaper articles are records.

Documents and records rely primarily on language to convey meaning. Other communications—for example, mathematics, music, and highway signs—rely on different types of sign systems to convey meaning. **Semiotics** is a field of inquiry that studies the meaning of these signs.[51] For example, Peter Manning and Betsy Cullum-Swan did a semiotic analysis of the various meanings conveyed by the different sign systems at McDonald's restaurants, among them, the menu board, lighting, arrangement of space, utensils and food wrappings, outdoor playgrounds, and the use of the "Mc" prefix to label various food items.[52] (Semiotics is explained further in Chapter 15.)

In traditional quantitative research, the meaning of a text is assumed to be invariant across readers and across time. In other words, the meaning is in the text itself, and the meaning can be represented as discrete content variables and studied by the methods of content analysis. In contrast, qualitative researchers believe that the meaning of a text resides in the minds of its writer and its readers. Thus, the meaning of a particular document or record can change from reader to reader and from one historical period to another. Furthermore, a document or record can have different meanings at different levels of analysis. For example, the content of a textbook can be analyzed to determine what topics it covers. However, it also can be seen as a secondary source that is derived from primary sources. (Primary and secondary sources are explained in Chapter 4.) The relationship between the textbook and its primary sources thus can be the focus of a qualitative researcher's study.

To fully understand a document or record, therefore, the qualitative researcher needs to study the context in which it was produced—the author's purpose in writing it, the author's working conditions, the authors intended and actual audience, and the audience's purpose for reading it. The qualitative researcher also must realize that, in reading the text, she creates her own meanings.

Documents and records from the past pose particular problems for the qualitative researcher because it is not possible to interview the author or readers. Also, the researcher cannot observe the situations in which these written communications were used or how they were made available for different audiences. Historians have developed various research methods to deal with these problems. Their methods are described in Chapter 16.

Qualitative researchers follow some of the same steps as quantitative researchers who use text and other communications media as data sources. They typically begin by

---

49. Ibid., p. 265.
50. Lincoln, Y. S., & Guba, E. G. (1985). *Naturalistic inquiry.* Beverly Hills, CA: Sage.
51. Manning, P. K., & Cullum-Swan, B. (1994). Narrative, content, and semiotic analysis. In N. K. Denzin & Y. S. Lincoln (Eds.), *Handbook of qualitative research* (pp. 463–477). Thousand Oaks, CA: Sage.
52. Ibid.

identifying documents and records that are part of the situation that they plan to study. Once they have identified these materials, their next step is to determine which materials might be relevant to their research study. Then they determine how they can collect these materials for analysis within the guidelines for ethical conduct of research. If the materials cannot be removed from the natural situation, it may be possible to make photocopies of them and photographs of them in their setting for later analysis. Otherwise, the researchers will need to devise a method for analyzing them on site. Finally, they will need to consider the validity of the materials. Several conceptions of validity (i.e., internal and external criticism) that apply to documents and records are described in Chapter 16.

The use of documents and records as data sources in qualitative research differs most from quantitative research in the analysis phase. In quantitative research, a set of variables is defined and applied uniformly to all the written communications in the sample. The variables are measured in such a way as to yield quantified data that can be analyzed by conventional statistics. In qualitative research, analysis procedure is likely to be emergent. The same document or record can be analyzed at different points in the study, with each analysis yielding new constructs, hypotheses, and insights. The results of the analysis need not be expressed in quantified form. Furthermore, the same document or record can be analyzed from different perspectives and for different purposes.

The results of the qualitative researcher's analysis take the form of interpretations and hypotheses. Ian Hodder proposed that these hypotheses and interpretations need to be weighed in relation to two different contexts—the context in which the documents and records were developed and the context in which they are now being interpreted for research purposes.[53] The researcher must take into account variations in meaning as they are studied across space, time, and cultures. Hodder suggested five criteria for confirming interpretations based on data obtained from documents and records:

1. internal coherence, meaning that different parts of the theoretical argument do not contradict one other and the conclusions follow from the premises;
2. external coherence, meaning that the interpretation fits theories accepted in and outside the discipline;
3. correspondence between theory and data;
4. the fruitfulness of the theoretical suppositions, that is, how many new directions, lines of inquiry, or perspectives are opened up; and
5. the trustworthiness, professional credentials, and status of the author and supporters of an interpretation.

An example of the use of documents, records, and signs in qualitative research is a study by G. Genevieve Patthey-Chavez concerning her perceptions of the cultural conflict between Latino students and their mainstream teachers in a Los Angeles high school.[54] Patthey-Chavez put the high school in context by describing the neighborhood in which it was located. Her observations included various forms of public communications in the neighborhood:

> Area businesses now sport huge Spanish-language signs next to modest English-language ones; video stores advertise their Spanish-language collections; and several Spanish-language

53. Hodder, Interpretation of documents.
54. Patthey-Chavez, G. G. (1993). High school as an arena for cultural conflict and acculturation for Latino Angelinos. *Anthropology and Education Quarterly, 24,* 33–60.

newspapers and radio and television stations compete very successfully with English-language media.[55]

She concluded from these observations that Salvadorean and Mexican cultural networks have been firmly and successfully established in this neighborhood.

Patthey-Chavez's observations of the school's curriculum focused on the English as a Second Language (ESL) program. In examining the text of ESL curriculum materials in use at the school, she found that they emphasized English grammatical structures. This emphasis, she noted, runs counter to current recommendations for ESL methodology, which emphasizes the development of students' oral communicative proficiency.

Patthey-Chavez drew upon a local newspaper article about the high school to illustrate what she perceived as its assimilationist mission, serving as "a port of entry for educational opportunity and the American way, a port of entry that students, but for a few miscreants, were eagerly passing through."[56] In her research report, Patthey-Chavez illustrated this theme by quoting the following excerpt from the newspaper article:

> Student Celia Toche, 17, came from El Salvador with her family five years ago, knowing no English. Now she is an honor student and hopes to go to college. She is usually so absorbed with physics tests, economic theory, trigonometry exercises and English literature that she rarely thinks anymore of such painful losses and frightening times as when armed guerillas perched on the roof of her school.
>
> Sometimes, however, she is reminded. "My parents didn't get a chance to get an education," she says. "It's a family treasure, to get an education here. I really value it a lot. So when I see people wasting the opportunities they've got here, the choices they have here, that's when I think about El Salvador. Here at Lima [High School], we know what we have—and we appreciate it."[57]

Patthey-Chavez claimed that this student's experience represents a biased view of the high school's effectiveness. In working with other students from El Salvador, she found that some of them perceived El Salvadoran schools to be more rigorous and moral than American schools.

The use of a newspaper article as a data source for this study is significant for two reasons. First, it reveals information about one student's experience at the high school being studied. Second, the newspaper creates meanings that are different from those created if the researcher had reported a personal interview with the student: An interview is a personal event, whereas a newspaper provides a widely circulated public record of a conversation. The fact that the newspaper reporter chose to include this particular conversation supports Patthey-Chavez's claim that the school is supporting an assimilationist mission— a mission that the newspaper reporter apparently supports and wishes the public to know. In fact, one can speculate that the newspaper reporter is telling the readers what they want to hear, namely, that their public schools are striving to assimilate immigrants and succeeding in the task. The inclusion of the newspaper article as a data source widens the context of the study and provides a contrast with Patthey-Chavez's other data that question the assimilationist mission of schools.

55. Ibid., p. 40.
56. Ibid., p. 50.
57. Woo, E. (1986, September 28). Lima High makes a comeback. An inner city shows how it's done. *Los Angeles Times Magazine*, p. 14.

✦ RECOMMENDATIONS FOR
Using Observational and Content-Analysis Methods

1. Determine whether a mechanical or electronic device can facilitate your collection of observational data.
2. In making quantitative observations, provide adequate training for observers to minimize observer bias, response sets, contamination, drift, and reliability decay.
3. Check the validity and reliability of quantitative observational data that you obtain.
4. In designing a form for quantitative observation, do not include more variables than observers can code reliably and do not ask them to make overly precise discriminations.
5. In doing qualitative research, consider changing the focus of observation as data collection progresses in order to accommodate emergent interests and questions.
6. In making qualitative observations, consider carefully—and take data on—how you react to informants and others in the field setting, and how they react to you.
7. In making qualitative observations, prepare field notes that are rich in detail and in low-inference descriptions.
8. Consider whether it is possible to measure your research variables by collecting observational data on physical objects and "residues" of human behavior.
9. In doing a content analysis, include appropriate checks of validity and reliability.
10. In doing a qualitative content analysis, consider the meaning of the text from different perspectives, including those of the author and intended audiences.

✔ SELF-CHECK TEST

Circle the correct answer to each of the following questions.
The answers are provided at the back of the book.

1. Test anxiety is an example of
   a. a descriptive observational variable.
   b. an inferential observational variable.
   c. an evaluative observational variable.
   d. a nonintrusive variable.

2. Recording the number of times that a teacher calls on a student to answer a question about grammar in a Spanish class is an example of
   a. duration recording.
   b. frequency-count recording.
   c. interval recording.
   d. continuous recording.

3. Computers are used in observational research
   a. to time the duration of events.
   b. to detect observer errors in recording observational data.

   c. to make graphical representations of observational data.
   d. all of the above.

4. College students are trained to use a standard schedule to observe children's play behavior. They record their observations on this form, and their data are compared with those of an expert on child psychology. The purpose of this comparison is to check
   a. criterion-related observer reliability.
   b. intra-observer reliability.
   c. inter-observer reliability.
   d. internal reliability.

5. The same observers are asked to record students' grade point average by examining school records and also to observe the students' on-task behavior

in three different classes. This procedure is most susceptible to
a. reliability decay.
b. the error of leniency.
c. observer contamination.
d. observer drift.

6. A researcher observes the meetings of a teachers union. She is a representative of this union, and therefore regularly attends the meetings. The researcher's role is that of
a. complete observer.
b. observer-participant.
c. participant-observer.
d. complete participant.

7. The selected stage of qualitative observation
a. can involve theoretical saturation.
b. must involve a role shift from participant-observer to complete observer.
c. precedes the focused stage.
d. all of the above.

8. Field notes in qualitative research should
a. emphasize high-inference observations.
b. emphasize low-inference observations.

c. avoid personal comments and reflections.
d. have a highly selective focus.

9. Qualitative researchers believe that material objects and residues are
a. expressions of how individuals and groups construct social reality.
b. expressions of the dominant groups within a culture.
c. outside the range of phenomena that they should study.
d. useful to study only if they serve communicative, representational functions.

10. A qualitative researcher is analyzing the textbooks used in present-day Russian schools. To determine the meaning of the textbook content, the researcher is likely
a. to study the authors of the textbooks.
b. to study the teachers who use the textbooks.
c. to study the students for whom the textbooks were written.
d. all of the above.

PART IV

✦ Quantitative Research Design

You need to design your research study so that it will answer the questions or test the hypotheses you have framed. To accomplish this task, you can refer to standard research designs that quantitative researchers have created and refined over time. These designs are described in part IV. You need to become familiar with all of them in order to select the most appropriate one for your study and to understand quantitative research studies conducted by others.

Chapter 10 explains descriptive and causal-comparative research designs. A descriptive design is appropriate when your purpose is to create a detailed description of a phenomenon: for example, people's opinions about educational issues or how teachers and students act in certain situations. In a causal-comparative design, the researcher forms two or more groups and compares them in order to explore possible causes or effects of a phenomenon.

Chapter 11 presents the major correlational research designs, which can be used to address questions and hypotheses similar to those addressed in a causal-comparative design. However, correlational research designs involve a different approach to sampling, measurement, and statistical analysis.

The common feature of descriptive, causal-comparative, and correlational research designs is that they involve the study of behavior, cognition, and other attributes of individuals without any intervention by the researcher. In other words, there is no attempt by the researcher to influence the individuals being studied.

In contrast, experimental research designs do involve researcher intervention. The researcher introduces an intervention, such a new educational program or a new teaching method, and observes how the research participants react to it. The major experimental designs are described in Chapters 12 and 13.

As you read the chapters in Part IV, you will find that a major purpose of educational research is to discover and validate cause-and-effect relationships between variables. You also will learn that causal-comparative or correlational research can produce evidence about such relationships, but this evidence generally is not as strong and convincing as that produced by a well-designed experiment.

CHAPTER 10

✦ Nonexperimental Research: Descriptive and Causal-Comparative Designs

OVERVIEW

The descriptive method is the most basic of the quantitative research methods. It involves describing characteristics of a particular sample of individuals or other phenomena. We explain two major types of descriptive research: description of the characteristics of a sample at one point in time; and longitudinal research, in which changes in the characteristics of a sample over time are described. Next we discuss the causal-comparative method, which is used to explore possible causal relationships between variables. We explain the advantages and disadvantages of this research method and the steps involved in using it.

OBJECTIVES

After studying this chapter, you should be able to

1. Explain the relationship between descriptive research and causal-comparative research.
2. Describe the types of measurement tools and statistical techniques that are used commonly in descriptive research.
3. Explain the purpose of descriptive research studies in which a sample is studied at one point in time.
4. Explain the difference between trend, cohort, and panel studies, and the advantages of each type.
5. State two problems with the cross-sectional research design.
6. Describe three possible interpretations of a relationship between variable *A* and variable *B* that is discovered through causal-comparative research.

7. Explain the use of the extreme groups sampling method in causal-comparative research.
8. Define suitable comparison groups, given an initially defined group in which a particular characteristic is present.
9. Explain how the *t* test is used in causal-comparative research.
10. Explain the situation in causal-comparative research in which a *t* test for correlated means should be used rather than a *t* test for independent means.
11. Interpret the *t* value resulting from a *t* test for a single mean, and describe how this test is used in causal-comparative research.
12. Describe how analysis of variance, analysis of covariance, and multivariate

analysis of covariance are used in causal-comparative research.

13. Describe situations in causal-comparative research in which nonparametric tests of significance are more appropriate than parametric tests.

14. Describe how the chi-square test, the Mann-Whitney *U* test, the Wilcoxon signed rank test, and the Kruskal-Wallis test are used in causal-comparative research.

Introduction

Over time, quantitative researchers have developed various standard designs that facilitate the planning of their studies. These designs, which function somewhat like templates, involve standard nomenclature and procedures for organizing variables, selecting samples, establishing a schedule for data collection, and selecting appropriate techniques for statistical analysis.

Similarities among the research designs allow them to be classified. For example, we find it useful to classify research designs as either nonexperimental or experimental. Nonexperimental designs are similar in that the researcher studies phenomena as they exist. In contrast, the various experimental designs all involve researcher intervention. We describe nonexperimental designs (descriptive, causal-comparative, and correlational) in this chapter and the next. Experimental designs are described in Chapters 12 and 13.

Research designs also can be classified by their purpose. You will recall that, in Chapter 1, we stated that educational research is conducted for four primary purposes: description, prediction, improvement, and explanation.

Researchers whose purpose is description will employ one of two types of research design: *descriptive*, if the intent is to study phenomena as they exist at one point in time; and *longitudinal*, if the intent is to study phenomena as they change over time. These research designs are described in the next section of this chapter.

If the purpose of a research study is prediction, a correlational research design is used. Various designs of this type are described in the next chapter.

If the researcher's purpose is explanation, the focus of the study will be on understanding cause-and-effect relationships between variables. Causal-comparative designs, which are described in this chapter, can be used to discover and verify cause-and-effect relationships. However, correlational and experimental designs can be used as well. The choice of one type of design or another depends on several factors, which we explain in this and the next three chapters.

Finally, research can be done for the purpose of improving education by developing and testing interventions. Introducing an intervention and then observing its effects is, by definition, an experiment. Various experimental designs are described in Chapters 12 and 13.

✦ Touchstone in Research

Campbell, D. T., & Stanley, J. C. (1981). *Experimental and quasi-experimental designs for research.* Boston: Houghton Mifflin.

Johnson, B. (2001). Toward a new classification of nonexperimental quantitative research. *Educational Researcher, 30*(2), 3–13.

Descriptive Research Designs

The Purpose of Descriptive Research

Research in its most basic form involves the description of natural or man-made phenomena—their form, actions, changes over time, and similarities with other phenomena. Scientists have made many important discoveries through their efforts to describe phenomena. For example, astronomers have used telescopes to develop descriptions of different parts of the universe. This research has provided the basis for many other discoveries, such as the structure of our solar system and the ability to predict such stellar events as lunar eclipses.

Descriptive research is similarly important in education. **Descriptive research** is a type of quantitative research that involves making careful descriptions of educational phenomena. As you shall see in Part V of the book, description—viewed as *understanding* what people or things mean—also is an important goal of qualitative research. For this reason, when planning a descriptive research study, you should be familiar with both the quantitative and qualitative approaches to description so that you choose the approach best suited to your purposes.

Descriptive studies are concerned primarily with determining "what is." Examples of questions that might be studied in a descriptive research study are: How many teachers in our state hold favorable attitudes toward whole-language instruction? What kinds of activities typically occur in sixth-grade art classes, and how frequently does each one occur? What have been the reactions of school administrators to innovations in teaching physical science? Have first-grade textbooks changed in readability over the last 50 years?

Most educational research has a strong inclination toward discovering cause-and-effect relationships and testing new instructional methods and programs. However, unless researchers first generate an accurate description of an educational phenomenon as it exists, they lack a firm basis for explaining or changing it. Some of the most influential calls for reform of the educational system have used the findings of descriptive research, typically based on compelling observational data, to make their case. Books such as *Life in Classrooms* by Philip Jackson, *The Good High School* by Sara Lawrence Lightfoot, and *A Place Called School* by John Goodlad report studies of this type.[1]

Some descriptive studies involve primarily the administration of questionnaires or interviews to samples of research participants. This type of research (sometimes called *survey research*) has yielded much valuable knowledge about opinions, attitudes, and practices. This knowledge has helped shape educational policy and initiatives to improve existing conditions.

Measurement in Descriptive Research

Descriptive studies are limited by the types and quality of available measures. For this reason, many researchers work intensively on developing new measures or perfecting ones that already have been developed in order to describe precisely and accurately the phenomena of interest to them. These measures are of many types, including, for example, standardized achievement tests, classroom observation instruments, attitude scales, questionnaires, and interviews. If you are planning to do a descriptive study in the quantitative research tradition, you should be familiar with the various types of research measures discussed in Chapters 7 through 9.

Statistics in Descriptive Research

To describe a sample as a whole, a researcher typically will define variables, measure them, and for each measure compute one or more of the descriptive statistics mentioned in Chapter 5—that is, measures of central tendency (the mean, median, and mode) and measures of variability (standard deviation, variance, and range). The researcher also might calculate derived scores as an aid in interpreting the sample's scores on the variables that were measured. **Derived scores** aid interpretation by providing a quantitative measure of

---

1. Jackson, P. W. (1968). *Life in classrooms.* New York: Holt, Rinehart and Winston; Lightfoot, S. L. (1983). *The good high school.* New York: Basic Books; Goodlad, J. (1983). *A place called school.* New York: McGraw-Hill.

each individual's performance relative to a comparison group, for example, a normative sample. Age equivalents, grade equivalents, percentiles, and standard scores are examples of derived scores that commonly are used in descriptive research.

Some descriptive research is intended to produce statistical information about aspects of education that interest policy makers and educators. The National Center for Education Statistics specializes in this type of research.[2] Many of its findings are published in an annual volume called the *Digest of Educational Statistics.*[3] This center also administers the National Assessment of Educational Progress (NAEP), which collects descriptive information about the performance of youth at various ages in the subject areas that are taught in public school. A typical NAEP publication that appears periodically is the *Reading Report Card,* which reports descriptive statistics about the reading achievement of students at several grade levels.[4] On a larger scale, the International Association for the Evaluation of Educational Achievement (IEA) carries out descriptive studies of the academic achievement of students from many nations, including the United States.[5]

Two main types of descriptive research are found in the research literature, differing primarily in the time at which the variables of interest are measured. The first type involves measuring the characteristics of a sample at one point in time. The second type involves longitudinal research, in which a sample is followed over time. We discuss each of these types of descriptive research below.

Description of a Sample at One Point in Time

Descriptive research often involves nothing more than reporting the characteristics of one sample at one point in time. Opinion polls are an example of this type of research. Surveys of people's behavior is another example. For example, our local newspaper reported the results of a survey of freshmen on college campuses with high rates of drinking.[6] The researchers, located at the Harvard School of Public Health, found that more than a third of the freshmen engaged in binge drinking during their first week on campus. By the end of the first semester, 68 percent of the students had abused alcohol.

Descriptive studies in education, while simple in design and execution, can yield important knowledge. For example, it is commonly believed that each teacher has a unique teaching style.[7] Yet a study of over 1,000 elementary and secondary teachers found little variety in actual teaching practices. Teachers spend the majority of their time lecturing to the class or having students work on written assignments. On a smaller scale, two of the authors (W. Borg and M. Gall) once developed a training program to improve teachers' questioning skills. We were able to locate a study in which the researcher had made direct observations of the questioning practices of a sample of teachers.[8] The findings of this descriptive study helped us greatly in deciding which questioning techniques should be included in the initial version of the training program.

If you are planning to do a descriptive study, you should follow the usual steps involved in quantitative research: formulate a research problem; state research hypotheses,

2. The Web homepage for the National Center for Education Statistics is www.nces.ed.gov

3. For an example of a *Digest* in electronic format, see www.nces.ed.gov/pubs2000/digest99/

4. For examples of the *Reading Report Card* in electronic format, see www.nces.ed.gov/nationsreportcard/reading/

5. Loxley, B. (1990). The International Association for the Evaluation of Educational Achievement. ERIC Digest. Retrieved November 23, 2001 from www.ericae.net/edo/ED328604.htm; see also the Web homepage for IEA, www.iea.nl/

6. Hege, B. (1995, April 6). Binge drinking doesn't spare UO. *The Register-Guard,* pp. 1, 4.

7. Sirotnik, K. A. (1983). What you see is what you get—Consistency, persistency, and mediocrity in classrooms. *Harvard Educational Review, 53,* 16–31.

8. Floyd, W. D. (1960). An analysis of the oral questioning activity in selected Colorado primary classrooms. Unpublished doctoral dissertation, Colorado State College.

questions, or objectives; select an appropriate sample and measures; and collect and analyze the data.

Longitudinal Description of a Sample

✦ *Touchstone in Research*

Collins, L. M., & Sayer, A. G. (2001). *New methods for the analysis of change.* Washington, DC: American Psychological Association.

Menard, S. (1991). *Longitudinal research.* Thousand Oaks, CA: Sage.

A **longitudinal study** involves collecting data from a sample at different points in time in order to study changes or continuity in the sample's characteristics. Longitudinal research designs are difficult to implement, but they are essential for exploring problems in human development, as David Magnusson, Lars Bergman, Georg Rudinger, and Bertil Torestad explain:

> The normal process in which an individual develops from birth through the life course is of interest in itself as a subject for research. Understanding and explaining that process is also fundamental for understanding what contributes to physical and mental health and for revealing the causes of mental, social and physical problems during the life course . . . the development of individuals cannot be adequately and effectively investigated without using a longitudinal research strategy.[9]

There are four main research designs in longitudinal research: trend, cohort, panel, and cross-sectional designs. They differ mainly in how the sample to be studied at different points in time is selected.

Trend Studies

Trend studies describe change by selecting a different sample at each data-collection point from a population that does not remain constant. For example, if you wanted to study trends in the use of graphing calculators in the teaching of high school mathematics, you could define the population as the members included in an annual directory of a national mathematics teachers association. Then you would select a sample of members from whom you would collect data about their use of graphing calculators. Next year's directory probably would include a somewhat different membership list, as new teachers join and existing members leave the association for various reasons. Thus, the population will have changed somewhat. You would select a new sample from this membership list and ask the teachers in the sample the same questions that you asked the previous year's sample. By repeating this process over a period of years, you would develop a picture of how teachers' use of graphing calculators has changed.

Trend studies are useful for studying changes in general populations that change constantly in terms of the individuals who are members of the population, for example, high school students or voters in school bond elections. A good example of a trend study that has yielded important findings is one conducted by the National Assessment of Educational Progress (NAEP). The NAEP research team periodically administers achievement tests to national samples of students at different grade levels in order to determine whether the effectiveness of the nation's educational system is improving.

✦ *Touchstone in Research*

Glenn, N. D. (1977). *Cohort analysis.* Thousand Oaks, CA: Sage.

Cohort Studies

Cohort studies describe change by selecting a different sample at each data-collection point from a population that remains constant. For example, suppose that we wished to study the yearly work status of all elementary school teachers who received California teaching certificates in 1992. We would list the names of all members of this population, and at each data-collection point we would randomly select a sample from the list. Thus,

---

9. Magnusson, D., Bergman, L. R., Rudinger, G., & Torestad, B. (Eds.) (1991). *Problems and methods in longitudinal research: Stability and change.* New York: Cambridge University Press. Quote appears on p. xiii.

the population would remain the same, but different individuals would be sampled each year. In contrast, in a trend study the population is likely to change at each data-collection point.

A report of research conducted at the Sandia National Laboratories by C. C. Carson, R. M. Huelskamp, and T. D. Woodall includes a cohort study of the high school completion rate of a single cohort of students (the class of 1982).[10] The study, based on data from the National Center for Educational Statistics, involved a national sample of high school students who were projected to complete their senior year in 1982. The researchers followed the students from 1980 to 1986. The purpose of the study was to provide the most accurate measure possible of the current dropout rate of students from U.S. high schools.

The study's findings are summarized in Figure 10.1. The figure shows the percentage of the class of 1982 who had completed high school at three points in time—1982, 1984, and 1986. Only 82.7 percent of the students surveyed in 1982 had completed high school on time (by 1982). The percentage of students in this cohort who had completed high school by 1984 was 5.2 percent higher than in 1982, and the percentage who had completed high school by 1986 was 2.8 percent higher than in 1984. These students either had graduated from a regular high school or had earned the General Equivalency Degree (GED). Thus, less than 10 percent of this cohort would be classified as dropouts based on this expanded time frame. This is a substantially lower dropout rate than is reported in nonlongitudinal studies (typically, 25 to 30 percent).

Some trend and cohort studies are carried out using earlier data collected by other researchers. For example, suppose a survey of the vocational interests of seniors in Chicago

FIGURE 10.1

High School Completion for a National Sample of U.S. Students from the Class of 1982, Followed from 1980 to 1986

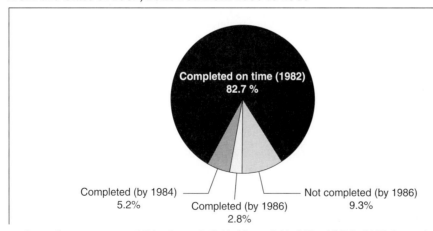

Source: Figure appears on p. 264 in: Carson, C. C., Huelskamp, R. M., & Woodall, T. D. (1993). Perspectives on education in America: An annotated briefing. *The Journal of Educational Research, 86,* 259–311.

10. Carson, C. C., Huelskamp, R. M., & Woodall, T. D. (1993). Perspectives on education in America. *The Journal of Educational Research, 86,* 259–311.

high schools had been carried out in 1985. Another researcher could do a trend study by collecting comparable data in 1995 and comparing the two sets of data. In conducting replications of this type, the researchers should use the same questions and format as in the earlier surveys. There is some evidence and much practical experience to indicate that small changes in the wording of questions on a survey can produce large effects on answers (see Chapter 8).

✦ *Touchstone in Research*

Markus, G. B. (1980). *Analyzing panel data.* Thousand Oaks, CA: Sage.

Panel Studies

The third type of longitudinal research design is the **panel study.** A panel study involves selecting a sample at the outset of the study and then at each subsequent data-collection point surveying the same sample. Because panel studies follow the same individuals over time, you can note changes in specific individuals and also explore possible reasons why these individuals have changed. In contrast, individual changes cannot be explored in trend or cohort studies because different individuals make up the sample at each data-collection point.

Repeated measurements on a panel sample can have unintended side effects. Having been given the instrument or interview once, individuals have time to consider their answers for the next data collection. Furthermore, knowing that they are members of the panel may create expectations. For example, Terman's famous study of talent identified a panel of child geniuses and followed their development through childhood into adulthood.[11] The identification process itself may have created expectations that were self-fulfilling and thus changed the nature of the results.

Loss of subjects can be a problem in a panel study, especially when the study extends over a long period of time. Lauress Wise conducted a large-scale panel study in which a national sample of twelfth-grade students was followed into adulthood.[12] A variety of procedures was used to encourage continuing participation in the study, including an annual newsletter and four mailings to members of the sample during each follow-up period. The response rate was 61.9 percent for a one-year follow-up, 37.9 percent after 5 years, and 27.9 percent after 11 years. Because of the problem of retaining an intact group over time, panel studies tend to be shorter in duration than other longitudinal studies.

Not only do the number of subjects in a panel study become smaller over time, but the subjects who remain in the sample tend to be a biased sample, because subjects who drop out are likely to be different from those who continue to participate in the study. In the Wise panel study, respondents to the 11-year follow-up were as much as one-half a standard deviation higher in general academic aptitude than nonrespondents, reflecting a strong sampling bias. (In Chapter 6 we discuss typical differences between research volunteers and nonvolunteers.)

Despite problems of attrition and repeated measurement, longitudinal research using a panel design has advantages over trend and cohort research. Because the same individuals are measured at each data-collection point, the panel design is sensitive to smaller changes than comparably sized samples in cohort or trend studies. Panel studies also have the advantage of identifying who is changing and in what way. We then can trace back to the events and characteristics of the individuals that might have contributed to the change.

11. The findings of Terman's study are reported in a series of books, including Terman, L. M., & Oden, M. M. (1959). *The gifted group at midlife* (Vol. 5). Stanford, CA: Stanford University Press.
12. Wise, L. L. (1977). The fight against attrition in longitudinal research. Paper presented at the annual meeting of the American Educational Research Association, New York, April 1977.

Cross-Sectional Studies

Longitudinal research is difficult because of the extended time period during which data must be collected and the challenge of obtaining comparable subjects at each data-collection point. To counter these problems, researchers can simulate longitudinal research by doing cross-sectional research. In a **cross-sectional design** the data are obtained at one point in time, but from groups of different ages or at different stages of development. For example, suppose you were interested in how students' attitudes toward mathematics change from seventh grade to twelfth grade. To study this problem using a cross-sectional design, you could select a sample of students at each grade level and administer a questionnaire to all of them on the same date or within a narrow range of dates. Thus, the data-collection period is very short, and sample attrition is not an issue.

Cross-sectional research, however, has several limitations. A major problem is the effect of changes in the population that occur over time. For example, in the above example, the seventh-grade sample probably is representative of all students who are eligible to be in seventh grade because few students have dropped out of school at this grade level. However, because many students drop out before high school graduation, the twelfth-grade sample is unlikely to be representative of all students eligible to be in twelfth grade. Many of these students are no longer in school. Had a panel design been used instead, we would start with a sample of seventh-graders and trace their attitude toward mathematics for a period of years. Some students in the sample might drop out of school over time, but changes in their attitudes for the period of time that they did remain in school could be analyzed.

Causal-Comparative Research Designs

The Study of Cause-and-Effect Relationships

As we explained at the start of the chapter, some quantitative research designs have the purpose of explaining educational phenomena through the study of cause-and-effect relationships. In these designs, the presumed cause is called the **independent variable,** and the presumed effect is called the **dependent variable.** For example, suppose we hypothesize that the introduction of state-mandated testing of all students will have a negative effect on teachers' morale. In this hypothesis, state-mandated testing is the independent variable (i.e., the presumed cause of a drop in teachers' morale), and teacher morale is the dependent variable (i.e., the presumed effect of the introduction of state-mandated testing).

In another hypothesis, this dependent variable (teacher morale) might become the independent variable. For example, we might hypothesize that teacher morale affects their rate of absenteeism from work. In this hypothesis, teacher morale is the independent variable, and absenteeism rate is the dependent variable.

In the rest of this chapter and the next, we consider research designs in which the researcher does not manipulate the independent variable in order to observe its effect on the dependent variable. These research designs do not permit strong conclusions about cause-and-effect, but are useful for initial exploratory investigations or in situations where it is impossible to manipulate the independent variable. For example, researchers might want to know whether teacher morale affects absenteeism. It would be virtually impossible for them to conduct a study in which they create work conditions that promote good morale among some teachers and poor morale among other teachers. Instead, they are limited to observing *naturally occurring* variations in teacher morale. These variations can be measured and related to *naturally occurring* variations in teacher absenteeism rates.

Research designs that rely on observation of relationships between naturally occurring variations in the presumed independent and dependent variables sometimes are called **ex post facto research**.[13] (*Ex post facto* is a Latin phrase meaning "operating retroactively.") In contrast, experiments involve actual manipulation of the independent variable by the researcher.

Causal-comparative research is a type of nonexperimental investigation in which researchers seek to identify cause-and-effect relationships by forming groups of individuals in whom the independent variable is present or absent—or present at several levels—and then determining whether the groups differ on the dependent variable. The critical feature of causal-comparative research is that the independent variable is measured in the form of categories. The categories can form a nominal scale (e.g., male versus female; American versus Asian versus European citizenship) or ordinal scale (e.g., non-employed versus employed part-time versus employed full-time). This approach to measuring the independent variable lends itself to particular statistical methods for analyzing the resulting data, which we describe in this chapter.

It is important to realize that an independent variable measured in categorical form might also be measurable as an interval or ratio scale. For example, consider the variable of employment, which is the subject of a research study that we consider in the next section of this chapter. In that study, employment is a simple ordinal scale: the research participants are either employed or not employed. However, it is possible to measure employment more precisely as a ratio scale consisting of amount of hours of weekly employment—for example, 0 hours, 1.5 hours, 20 hours, 25 hours, 40 hours. In this case, a correlational research design (see Chapter 11) is more appropriate for organizing the independent and dependent variables and analyzing the resulting data.

In fact, any causal-comparative research design can be reconceptualized as a correlational research design by changing how the variables are measured or analyzed, or both. However, researchers sometimes prefer to use a causal-comparative design for two reasons: forming groups to measure the independent variable often is more consistent with how practitioners and other education stakeholders think about the world; and the statistical results typically are easier to comprehend and interpret.

The design of causal-comparative research studies can vary. The researcher can plan to include one independent variable or several in the design. Similarly, the researcher can choose to include one dependent variable or several. Also, the choice of statistics will vary depending on characteristics on the research data.

As you read about causal-comparative designs in this chapter, you will be laying the foundation for your study of experimental research designs in Chapters 13 and 14. This is because both causal-comparative research and experimental research involve the investigation of independent and dependent variables. You will find that experimental designs look similar to causal-comparative designs in terms of how the variables are organized and displayed. Also, you will find that some of the same statistical methods are used to analyze the resulting data.

---

13. A similar, but more detailed, definition is provided by Fred Kerlinger: "Ex post facto research is systematic empirical inquiry in which the scientist does not have direct control of independent variables because their manifestations have already occurred or because they are inherently not manipulable. Inferences about relations among variables are made, without direct intervention, from concomitant variation of independent and dependent variables." From Kerlinger, F. N. (1973). *Foundations of behavioral research* (2nd ed.). New York: Holt, Rinehart and Winston. Quote appears on p. 379.

Example of a Causal-Comparative Research Study

Gary Green and Sue Jaquess used a causal-comparative research design to investigate the effect of part-time employment on high school students' academic achievement.[14] The sample included 44 high school juniors who were either not employed or employed at least 10 or more hours per week at the time of the study.

Note that the researchers did not experimentally manipulate employment. It would be virtually impossible to ask some students to work part-time and to ask other students not to work in order to observe the effects of employment. The researchers' only recourse was to observe the effects of *natural* variations in employment. By natural, we mean that variations in employment were observed under conditions that did not involve any artificial arrangement, including manipulation by the researchers.

In this example, the comparison groups were formed on the basis of a presumed causative factor (i.e., employment). Then the possible effects of this causative factor were conceptualized and measured. It is also possible to form groups on the basis of an observed effect and then seek possible causes. For example, suppose you were interested in why some students engage in more extracurricular activities than others. You could conceptualize extracurricular participation as the effect, and form groups of students high and low on this variable. Then you would seek to identify and measure possible causes of extracurricular participation. Employment might be one presumed cause, but we can imagine other possible causes as well. The groups would be compared on measures of these presumed causes. If you find a statistically significant group difference on a particular measured variable, you can view it as a possible cause of the effect that is your primary interest, namely, extracurricular participation.

A disadvantage of causal-comparative research designs is that inferences about causality on the basis of the collected data are necessarily tentative. Consider, for example, the results of the employment study, which are shown in Table 10.1. Employed and nonemployed students earned similar grade point averages (GPAs), but nonemployed students earned significantly higher ACT scores. (The ACT—a test produced by the American College Testing Program—is similar to the Scholastic Aptitude Test, which many high school students take when applying for college admission.)

Do these results indicate no cause-and-effect relationship between high school employment (cause) and student academic achievement (effect)? The results shown in Table 10.1 support the conclusion that there is none, because the difference in GPA between the employed and nonemployed groups is slight and statistically nonsignificant. It is possible, however, that employed students took easier courses than nonemployed students. Had they taken courses as difficult as those taken by the nonemployed students, their GPAs might have been significantly lower. Because the researchers did not examine the variable of course difficulty, we cannot conclude from the observed results that employment has no effect on GPA.[15]

The significant result for the ACT variable suggests that high school employment *causes* poor performance on the ACT. Several other causal interpretations are possible, however. One is that students who find that they have low aptitude for college study are likely to become interested in the world of work sooner than high-aptitude students, and

---

14. Green, G., & Jaquess, S. N. (1987). The effect of part-time employment on academic achievement. *Journal of Educational Research, 80,* 325–329.
15. The researchers compared the grades of employed and nonemployed students in one required class, thereby presumably controlling for differential course difficulty. This, however, is a weak test of the differential course difficulty hypothesis, because no course can be truly representative of the diversity of a high-school curriculum.

<table>
<tr><td colspan="5" align="right">**TABLE 10.1**</td></tr>
</table>

Academic Achievement and Extracurricular Participation of Employed and Nonemployed Students

Variable	Employed Students M	Nonemployed Students M	t	p
1. GPA*	2.66	2.78	.81	.42
2. ACT** score	17.13	18.93	2.22	.02
3. Extracurricular participation (hours per week)	6.21	8.30		.05[a]

*GPA (Grade point average)

**ACT (from the American College Testing Program, a test similar to the Scholastic Aptitude Test)

[a]The researchers did not report the t value for this variable-only that the difference was statistically significant. Significance is conventionally established at the .05 level.

Source: Adapted from Tables 2 and 3 and text on pp. 327–329 in: Green, G., & Jaquess, S. N. (1987). The effect of part-time employment on academic achievement. *Journal of Educational Research, 80,* 325–329. Reprinted with permission of the Helen Dwight Reid Educational Foundation. Published by Heldref Publications, 1319 Eighteenth St., NW, Washington, DC 20036–1802. Copyright © 1987.

so they seek part-time employment while still in high school. In this interpretation, a third variable (aptitude for college study) is seen as the cause of both high school employment and ACT performance. Another interpretation is that parent behavior is the primary causative factor. Some parents may encourage their children not to seek part-time employment and to prepare for college instead, whereas other parents may discourage their children from planning for college (perhaps because of the expense involved) and instead encourage them to earn money through part-time employment.

Given the plausibility of these alternative interpretations, we would be going out on a limb to recommend that working students should quit their jobs if they want their ACT scores to improve. Further research is needed to test the merits of the alternative interpretations. If they are refuted, we would have a more secure basis for claiming that employment causes a decrement in ACT performance.

Alternative interpretations must be considered as well in explaining the significant relationship between employment and extracurricular participation shown in Table 10.1. It might be that employment causes students to devote less time to extracurricular activities. However, another plausible interpretation is that students who are less interested in extracurricular activities (as indicated by a low amount of time spent on them) are likely to turn their energies elsewhere, including part-time employment. In this interpretation, low extracurricular participation causes employment, not the other way around.

In summary, the major advantage of causal-comparative research design is that they allow us to study cause-and-effect relationships under conditions where experimental manipulation is difficult or impossible. Another advantage is that many such relationships can be studied in a single research project. For example, the causal-comparative design used in Green and Jacquess's study allowed for investigation of three possible effects of employment. The major disadvantage of causal-comparative research is that determining causal patterns with any degree of certainty is difficult. An observed relationship between variables *A* and *B* can mean that *A* causes *B*, *B* causes *A*, or a third variable *C* causes both *A* and *B*.

Planning a Causal-Comparative Study

Statement of the Research Problem

The steps involved in causal-comparative research are illustrated in a study of scientific literacy at the junior high school level. Alexis Mitman, John Mergendoller, Virginia Marchman, and Martin Packer investigated the relationship between variables involving teacher instruction (the presumed cause) and students' scientific literacy (the presumed effect).[16] Scientific literacy, as defined in their study, includes five components: (1) mastery of science content, (2) positive attitudes toward science, (3) understanding of the societal impact of science, (4) grasp of the process of scientific reasoning, and (5) knowledge of the sociohistorical development of science.

The initial step in a causal-comparative study is to speculate about the causes or effects of the phenomenon that interests you. Your speculations can be based on previous research findings and theory, as well as on your own observations of the phenomenon. In the study mentioned above, Mitman and her colleagues speculated that the development of students' scientific literacy might be influenced by teachers' verbal and written instruction. They speculated that

> instruction in typical classes would emphasize the transmission of science content during recitation and seatwork activities. It was thought that, if this were the case, teachers' main opportunity to facilitate the scientific literacy of their students would be to suggest meaningful contexts for science content during verbal presentations, reinforced by attention to the same contexts on written assignments. Teacher provision of meaningful contexts for lesson concepts during instructional explanation has been shown to enhance student acquisition of appropriate schemas in other subject areas. (Duffy, Roehler, Meloth, and Vavrus, 1986).[17]

After possible causes or effects of the phenomenon have been identified, they should be incorporated into the statement of the research problem. The research problem usually is stated in the form of research hypotheses, questions, or objectives. In the study we have been considering, the researchers formulated and tested the following hypothesis about possible effects of teacher behavior: "the extent and consistency with which teachers contextualized science content should have a direct and measurable influence on students' acquisition of the five components of scientific literacy."[18]

The term *contextualized* in this hypothesis means teacher presentation of scientific content in a context that is meaningful to students. For example, a teacher might contextualize the scientific concept of ecosystem by showing students that the relationship between local industries and indigenous natural resources reflects an ecosystem in action. In the researchers' hypothesis, teacher presentation of science content in context is the cause, and acquisition of scientific literacy is the effect. We discuss the researchers' empirical test of this hypothesis a bit later in the chapter.

In a causal-comparative study, the researcher should attempt to state and test alternative hypotheses about other factors that might explain observed differences between two groups. For example, in the study by Mitman and her colleagues, students' level of scientific literacy at the end of the school year might plausibly be influenced not only by the quality of the teacher's instruction, but also by their level of scientific literacy at the start of the school year. In other words, students who know more about science at the outset

---

16. Mitman, A. L., Mergendoller, J. R., Marchman, V. A., & Packer, M. J. (1987). Instruction addressing the components of scientific literacy and its relation to student outcomes. *American Educational Research Journal, 24,* 611–633.
17. Ibid., p. 613.
18. Ibid., p. 614.

might learn new content more easily than students starting with a weak knowledge base. Thus, students' level of scientific literacy in September (cause) might influence the level of scientific literacy that they achieve by the following June (effect).

Research results can confirm more than one alternative hypothesis. This is a common occurrence because complex behaviors, such as student learning, are determined by a variety of factors. The magnitude of difference between the two groups on each measure can be examined to make tentative inferences about how much each factor or set of factors affects the dependent variables (i.e., the presumed effects).

The testing of plausible alternative hypotheses sometimes is called **strong inference.**[19] Whenever possible, it should be used in causal-comparative research to formulate the variables on which the comparison groups are to be contrasted. By this, we mean that you should select and measure variables that you think are plausible causes of the effect that interests you. You can generate these variables using common sense or, more formally, by examining different theories that have been developed to explain the phenomena you are studying. This is preferable to the **shotgun approach,** which involves administering a large number of measures simply because they appear interesting or are available.

Selecting a Defined Group

After the research problem has been stated, the next step in causal-comparative research is to define the group that possesses the characteristic one wishes to study. The definition should be precise so that the results of the study can be interpreted meaningfully.

In the study of scientific literacy described above, Mitman and her colleagues identified two groups of teachers who varied in the extent to which they taught science content in a meaningful context. Their procedure for identifying the two groups started with the selection of a total sample of 11 teachers who taught seventh-grade life science, and the students from one of the classes of each of these teachers. Each teacher was observed teaching two different life science topics. Trained observers coded the amount of time that each teacher spent making explicit statements referring to a meaningful scientific context in teaching each topic. Following is an example of a "context-enriched" statement:

> All right. We now know about the four different blood types. Being able to identify each person's blood type is an important part of today's medicine—our medical technology. This is because when people are ill and need blood transfusions, it is critical that they receive compatible blood. To see how blood typing works, we're going to test ourselves—just as they would in a hospital.[20]

The researchers recorded the percentage of total instructional time that each teacher spent making such context-enriched statements. The five teachers with the highest percentages were identified as high-context-use teachers, and the six teachers with the lowest percentages were identified as low-context-use teachers, as shown in Table 10.2.

It is at this point in the study that we see most clearly the difference between causal-comparative research and experimental research. Mitman and her colleagues studied *naturally occurring variations* in teachers' use of context-rich statements. Had they used an experimental research design, they would have *intervened* by manipulating the independent variable: They would have formed two groups of comparable teachers and trained one group to use context-rich statements, while withholding this training from the other group.

19. Platt, J. (1964). Strong inference. *Science, 146,* 347–353.
20. Mitman et al., Instruction addressing the components, p. 617.

TABLE 10.2

Teachers' Total Percentage of Presentation Time Devoted to Science Context

Group	Teacher ID	Percentage of Presentation Time Addressing Contextual Components
Low-context-use teachers	2	0
	3	0.2
	6	0.7
	7	0.5
	8	0.5
	10	1.2
High-context-use teachers	1	11.0
	4	3.8
	5	4.0
	9	4.0
	11	3.5

Source: Adapted from Table 5 on p. 625 in: Mitman, A. L., Mergendoller, J. R., Marchman, V. A., & Packer, M. J. (1987). Instruction addressing the components of scientific literacy and its relation to student outcomes. *American Educational Research Journal, 24,* 611–633. Copyright 1987 by the American Educational Research Association. Adapted by permission of the publisher.

Because the sample was small, the researchers did not define subgroups from the initially defined groups. If formation of subgroups had been possible, other potential causative factors could have been studied. For example, suppose that context-enriched statements improve students' scientific literacy, but only if the teacher has a good understanding of science. This hypothesis could be tested by breaking each of the two main groups (high-context-use and low-context-use) into two subgroups: teachers with a stronger understanding of science and teachers with a weaker understanding of science.

Inspection of Table 10.2 indicates that the sample included only one teacher (ID no. 1) who placed much emphasis on science context (11 percent of presentation time). The number of such teachers in the sample could have been increased if the researchers had selected a much larger sample, for example, 100 teachers. It would be prohibitively expensive in most research projects, however, to collect observational and test data on this large a sample.

Selecting Comparison Groups

Once you have selected a group having the characteristic you wish to study, the next step is to select a group not having this characteristic, or having it to a lesser degree. The population from which the comparison sample is to be selected should be defined so as to be as similar as possible to the characteristic-present group except for the variable being studied. In the study of scientific literacy described above, the comparison group of low-context-use teachers was drawn from the same pool of teachers as the high-context-use teachers. Presumably the two groups were similar in all respects except for their use of context-enriched statements while teaching science.

Suppose that one finds that the two groups differ significantly on an extraneous variable. For example, suppose the high-context-use teachers had more years of teaching experience on average than the low-context-use teachers. In this case, if students of the high-context-use teachers were found to develop greater scientific literacy than students of low-context-use teachers, we could not be certain whether this effect was due to the teachers' greater use of context-enriched statements or to their greater teaching experience.

One way to solve this problem would be to use a matching procedure. **Matching** is used to equate two groups on one or more extraneous variables so that these extraneous variables do not confound the study of causal relationships involving the variables of primary interest to the researcher. In this case, the researcher would take each high-context-use teacher and match this teacher with a low-context-use teacher having the same amount of teaching experience. This procedure, however, might require a time-consuming search for a sample of low-context-use teachers that could be matched with the high-context-use teachers on this variable.

Matching procedures often create more problems than they solve. You cannot be certain that you have selected the most important variable or variables on which to match subjects. Also, you might not be able to find suitable matches for some members of the characteristic-present sample. Therefore, the preferred procedure is to try to select the characteristic-present and comparison samples randomly from the same population and then control for other variables through the use of analysis of covariance, which is described later in the chapter.

Another approach to selection of comparison groups is to use the extreme-groups method.[21] The **extreme-groups method** involves selecting comparison groups that are at the two extremes of a score distribution on one variable. This is done on the assumption that these extreme groups are more likely to differ on other measured variables than comparison groups that also differ on the score distribution, but less dramatically so. In the study of scientific literacy, the researchers found that students' reports of the extent of their teachers' references to scientific context were moderately correlated ($r = .34$) with the actual amount of teachers' references to scientific context as recorded by observers. The students were particularly accurate in identifying the teachers who made the most and the least references to scientific context.

This finding would be helpful in selecting extreme groups for the study. Researchers could select a sample inexpensively by first administering the questionnaire to the classes of, say, 100 different teachers. Then they could select the 10 teachers who were reported by students to have the highest context use and the 10 teachers who were reported by students to have the lowest context use. The other 80 teachers would be eliminated from further investigation. The resulting sample of 20 teachers most likely would include a greater number of teachers with very high and very low context use than would a sample of 20 teachers drawn at random from the population. These extreme groups are more likely to reveal an effect on students' scientific literacy (assuming there is a real effect) than the two groups they studied. Their two comparison groups differed, but not dramatically so (see Table 10.2).

Data Collection

Virtually any type of measuring instrument can be used in causal-comparative research. Standardized tests, questionnaires, interviews, and naturalistic observations all are useful for collecting data about presumed cause-and-effect relationships. In the study on sci-

---

21. For a discussion of the extreme groups approach and its relationship to the correlational method, see: Alf, E. F., Jr., & Abrahams, N. M. (1975). The use of extreme groups in assessing relationships. *Psychometrika, 40,* 563–572.

entific literacy, the researchers used an observational procedure to determine the percentage of class time that each teacher used for providing a meaningful context for science content:

> Observers kept a continuous written record of major class events and activities during every observed class period. Observers noted the clock time on these records at the beginning and end of each activity segment. . . . Observers also audiotaped each class period . . . observers used the above written records and narrative descriptions to [calculate] the amount of time teachers devoted to different kinds of [presentation] activities. . . . Following this initial calculation of total presentation time, observers calculated the percentage of this time devoted to content-only versus context-enriched instruction.[22]

Researchers also administered several measures to assess learning outcomes related to scientific literacy:

> Students completed three science measures both at pretest (beginning of the school year) and posttest (end of the school year). . . . The Life Science Questionnaire tapped students' knowledge of science content—i.e., life science achievement. The Science Process Survey tapped students' understanding of the reasoning process of science and, to a lesser extent, the social-historical development of science. Finally, the Feelings toward Science Survey assessed . . . students' feelings toward science classes, vocational and educational intentions in science, feelings toward science in general, and interest in science activities outside of class.[23]

By using these multiple measures, the researchers were able to assess the relationship between teachers' science explanations (the presumed cause) and not one, but several student learning outcomes (the presumed effects).

Data Analysis

The first step in an analysis of causal-comparative data is to conduct an exploratory data analysis and compute descriptive statistics for each comparison group in the study (see Chapter 5). These statistics generally will include the group mean and standard deviation. In the study of scientific literacy, each teacher's use of context-enriched statements was reported as a percentage (see Table 10.2). Students' scores on the scientific literacy measures were reported as mean gains from the beginning of the school year to the end of the school year, as shown in Table 10.3.

The next step typically is to do a test of statistical significance. The choice of significance test depends in part on whether the researcher is interested in comparing groups with respect to each group's mean score, variance, or median, or with respect to rank scores or category frequencies. Selection of an appropriate test also depends on whether the assumptions underlying the test being considered are satisfied, or at least not grossly violated.[24]

Various significance tests were introduced in Chapter 5 and are presented more fully here. Also, note that many of the same significance tests can be used to analyze data from experiments (see Chapters 12 and 13).

---

22. Mitman et al., Instruction addressing the components, p. 617.
23. Ibid., pp. 618–619.
24. For a discussion of common violations of assumptions underlying tests of statistical significance and methods for dealing with these violations, see: Kesselman, H. J., Huberty, C. J., Lix, L. M., Olejnik, S., Cribbie, R. A., Donahue, B., Kowalchuk, R. K., Lowman, L. L., Petoskey, M. D., Keselman, J. C., & Levin, J. R. (1998). Statistical practices of educational researchers: An analysis of their ANOVA, MANOVA, and ANCOVA analyses. *Review of Educational Research, 68*, 350–386.

TABLE 10.3

Performance on Scientific Literacy Measures of Students Taught by Teachers High or Low in Context Use

Scientific Literacy Measure	Mean Gain Score		t Value	p Value[a]
	Low-Context Use	High-Context Use		
Feelings toward science classes	−.194[b]	−.080	−1.40	0.82
Vocational and educational intentions in science	−.174	−.216	.48	.316
Feelings toward science in general	−.132	−.118	−.18	.431
Interest in science activities outside of class	−.045	−.072	.44	.329
Knowledge of life science	2.148	2.102	.10	.460
Understanding of scientific process	1.191	.582	1.69	.046

[a]One-tailed probabilities are reported.
[b]Negative mean gains indicate lower posttest than pretest score.
Source: Adapted from Table 6 on p. 626 in: Mitman, A. L., Mergendoller, J. R., Marchman, V. A., & Packer, M. J. (1987). Instruction addressing the components of scientific literacy and its relation to student outcomes. *American Educational Research Journal, 24,* 611–633. Copyright 1987 by the American Educational Research Association. Adapted by permission of the publisher.

Statistical Analysis: The *t* Test

The t Test for Differences between Means

The basic rationale for testing the significance of the difference between two sample means was explained in Chapter 5. It is appropriate to use the *z* distribution when large samples are studied ($N \geq 30$). When small samples are studied ($N \leq 29$), it is advisable to use the t test instead. In practice, researchers typically use *t* instead of *z*, irrespective of sample size.

Use of the *t* test in causal-comparative research depends on three assumptions about the obtained scores. The first assumption is that the scores form an interval or ratio scale of measurement. The second assumption is that scores in the populations under study are normally distributed. The third assumption is that score variances for the populations under study are equal. Statisticians have found that *t* tests provide accurate estimates of statistical significance even under conditions of substantial violation of these assumptions.[25] If you are concerned about score distributions in your data, you should consider doing both a *t* test and its nonparametric counterpart—either the Mann-Whitney *U* test or the Wilcoxon signed rank test (both described later in the chapter). If the two tests yield different results because the scores depart substantially from *t* test assumptions, you can report just the results of the nonparametric test.

The *t* tests for the scientific literacy measures in the study by Mitman and her colleagues are shown in Table 10.3. One statistically significant difference was observed, although, surprisingly, it was in the direction opposite to that which was predicted. Students of low-context-use teachers were found to make a greater gain in understanding of scientific process than did students of high-context-use teachers. In attempting to explain this

25. Boneau, C. A. (1960). The effects of violations of assumptions underlying the *t* test. *Psychological Bulletin, 57,* 49–64.

unanticipated result, the researchers found that teachers' context-embedded statements were often incomplete or confusing. Therefore, they surmised that

> because teachers' references to these components often were deficient and unsystematic, it is possible that teachers who made more references to the contextual components actually detracted from students' learning. This, in turn, might lead to lower student performance on measures designed to test their scientific literacy directly.[26]

A researcher might wish to compare two groups on many measured variables. Each comparison requires a separate t test. As shown in Table 10.3, the classes of the high- and low-context-use teachers were compared on six scientific literacy measures, requiring a total of six t tests. You can increase your chances of finding a significant difference between groups on a measured variable by comparing the groups on many measured variables. For example, suppose two groups are compared on 20 variables, resulting in 20 different t tests. Almost certainly one of the comparisons will yield a significant p (assuming alpha is set at .05) even if there is no difference between the populations represented by the samples on any of the variables. To understand how this happens, think about coin-tossing. On any given toss of a coin, your probability of the coin turning up heads is .50. But the probability is much higher that you will turn up a head at least once if you toss the coin 10 times.

As you increase the number of t tests, you also increase the risk of committing a Type I error. You can reduce this risk by setting the alpha level low (e.g., $p = .01$). If you find that the measured variables are intercorrelated, you can reduce the risk by using a statistical technique called *multivariate analysis of variance,* which is described later in the chapter.

Use of multiple t tests is much less a problem if the direction of the group difference on each variable has been predicted on the basis of theory or previous research findings, prior to data collection. If a result is statistically significant and confirms a prediction, the alternative explanation that it was a chance result has low plausibility.

If a t test is appropriate for your data, you should consider whether you matched the two samples on some characteristic such that their scores on that characteristic vary systematically with their scores on the variable to be compared. If they are matched, the difference between the mean scores of the two groups on a measured variable can be tested by the **t test for correlated means.** For example, suppose the high-context-use teachers and low-context-use teachers had been matched on years of teaching experience. By this, we mean that for each high-context-use teacher, there is a low-context-use teacher with a similar amount of teaching experience. This matching variable would be used in the t test for correlated means when comparing the scientific literacy scores of the students taught by the two groups of teachers. If a matching variable is not available, the difference between the mean scores should be tested for statistical significance by the **t test for independent means.** The advantage of the t test for correlated means, if it can be used appropriately, is that it has greater statistical power than the t test for independent means.

Finally, in doing a t test, you will need to decide between a one-tailed or two-tailed test of significance. If you have hypothesized in advance of data collection which of the two mean scores will be greater, you can do a one-tailed test of significance. Otherwise, a two-tailed test is necessary. The advantage of the one-tailed test is that it has greater statistical power. In other words, the obtained difference between two sample scores is more likely to be statistically significant with a one-tailed t test than with a two-tailed t test.

---

26. Mitman et al., Instruction addressing the components, p. 628.

The t *Test for a Single Mean*

In most causal-comparative studies, researchers compare the mean scores of two samples to determine whether they are significantly different from each other. Occasionally, though, they are interested in whether a sample mean differs significantly from a specified population mean. For example, suppose you investigate a sample of twelfth-grade students who share a particular characteristic (such as being college-bound). You administer the Wechsler Adult Intelligence Scale to each student and find that the mean IQ score is 109. As part of the data analysis, you might wish to determine whether this sample mean deviates significantly from the population mean. Assuming a population mean of 100, we can use the *t* test for a single mean to determine whether this difference (109 – 100) is statistically significant. The *t* **test for a single mean** tests whether a sample mean differs significantly from a specified population mean.

Population means generally are not known in educational research. Some standardized tests provide norms based on very large samples, however. The means of these samples usually are close approximations of their respective population means. Also, population norms are available for many physical measures (e.g., height, weight, and strength) that are of interest to some educational researchers.

Statistical Analysis: Analysis of Variance

Comparison of More than Two Means

Some causal-comparative research designs involve the study of more than two groups. In a study by Louis Warren and Beverly Payne, three groups of middle-school teachers were compared.[27] Each group of teachers experienced a different form of school organization:

1. One group of teachers worked in interdisciplinary teams at their school, with each team including a small number of teachers from different academic disciplines. Each team was given a scheduled common planning time so that they could discuss the needs of their shared students and develop appropriate curriculum.
2. Like teachers in the first group, these teachers worked in interdisciplinary teams, but without a scheduled common planning time.
3. The third group of teachers worked in schools that had a traditional departmental organization: they were organized by subject area and had little opportunity to plan instruction with teachers in other subject areas.

The research question that guided the study was this: "Do these three organizational patterns have differential effects on teachers' efficacy and perceptions of their working environment?"[28]

To answer this question, the teachers in the three groups responded to several paper-and-pencil measures, including the Teacher Efficacy Scale. The scale has two subscales. A high score on the subscale for general teacher efficacy (maximum score = 36) means that the teacher believes that she can overcome external factors that might hinder students' learning. A high score on the subscale for personal teacher efficacy (maximum score = 54) means that the teacher believes that she knows and can use effective methods to help students learn.

27. Warren, L. L., & Payne, B. D. (1997). Impact of middle grades' organization on teacher efficacy and environmental perceptions. *Journal of Educational Research, 90,* 301–308.
28. Ibid., p. 301.

✦ **Touchstone in Research**

Iversen, G. R., & Norpoth, H. (1987). *Analysis of variance* (2nd ed.). Thousand Oaks, CA: Sage.

Stevens, J. (2001). *Applied multivariate statistics for the social sciences* (4th ed.). Mahwah, NJ: Lawrence Erlbaum Associates.

✦ **Touchstone in Research**

Lix, L. M., Keselman, J. C., & Keselman, H. J. (1996). Consequences of assumption violations revisited: A quantitative review of alternatives to the one-way analysis of variance F test. *Review of Educational Research, 66,* 579–619.

Descriptive statistics for each of the three groups' scores on the two efficacy subscales are shown in Table 10.4. The difference between the mean scores for the three groups could be tested for statistical significance by performing three t tests, to compare the following: (1) Group 1 with Group 2; (2) Group 1 with Group 3; and (3) Group 2 with Group 3. The total number of t tests needed to compare all pairs of groups increases dramatically with each additional comparison group. For example, if the number of groups is five, a total of 10 comparisons would need to be made.

Instead of doing many t tests, researchers usually start by doing a simple analysis of variance. **Analysis of variance** (abbreviated as ANOVA) is a statistical procedure that compares the amount of between-groups variance in individuals' scores with the amount of within-groups variance. If the ratio of between-groups variance to within-groups variance is sufficiently high, this indicates that there is more difference *between* the groups in their scores on a particular variable than there is *within* each group. If the analysis of variance yields a nonsignificant F ratio (the ratio of between-groups variance to within-groups variance), the computation of t tests to compare pairs of means is not appropriate. An exception to this rule occurs when the researcher, before data collection, hypothesized that a specific pair of means will differ significantly.

In the study by Warren and Payne, the analysis of variance shown in Table 10.4 indicates that the three groups of teachers differed significantly from each other on the personal efficacy subscale, but not on the general efficacy subscale. No further tests of statistical significance on the group means for the general efficacy subscale are done, because the F value for the analysis of variance was not significant. However, because the F value for the personal efficacy subscale was significant, the researcher should proceed to find which of the three pairs of means (1 versus 2, 1 versus 3, 2 versus 3) differed significantly from each other. Unless the researcher has planned to make specific comparisons *before* undertaking the study, a t test for multiple comparisons should be used. The **t test for multiple comparisons**

TABLE 10.4

Teacher Efficacy in Middle Schools with Interdisciplinary Teams with Common Planning Time, Interdisciplinary Teams without Common Planning Time, or Traditional Departments

	Group 1	Group 2	Group 3	
Teacher Efficacy Scale	Interdisciplinary Teams, Common Planning Time ($n = 31$) M (SD)	Interdisciplinary Teams, No Common Planning Time ($n = 25$) M (SD)	Traditional Departments ($n = 26$) M (SD)	$F(2,79)$
Personal efficacy subscale	39.61 (4.36)	34.60 (5.26)	35.76 (4.69)	8.21 ($p < .001$)
General efficacy subscale	27.61 (6.05)	25.00 (3.83)	26.10 (3.84)	2.05 ($p > .05$)

Source: Adapted from Table 4 on p. 306 in: Warren, L. L., & Payne, B. D. (1997). Impact of middle grades' organization on teacher efficacy and environmental perceptions. *Journal of Educational Research, 90,* 301–308. Reprinted with permission of the Helen Dwight Reid Educational Foundation. Published by Heldref Publications, 1319 Eighteenth St., NW, Washington, DC 20036-1802. Copyright © 1997.

is a test of the significance of the differences between more than two population means. There are several types of t tests for multiple comparisons, including Duncan's multiple-range test and other techniques developed by Newman-Keuls, Tukey, and Scheffé. These special t tests adjust for the probability that the researcher will find a significant difference between mean scores simply because many comparisons are made on the same data.

In the study by Warren and Payne, the Tukey procedure, with the alpha level set at .05, was used to make the comparisons of the groups' mean score on the personal efficacy subscale. The researchers found that the mean score of teachers in interdisciplinary teams with common planning time (Group 1) was significantly higher than the mean score of teachers in interdisciplinary teams with no common planning time (Group 2). Also, the mean score of teachers in Group 1 was significantly higher than the mean score of teachers in traditional middle-school departments (Group 3). The mean scores of Group 2 and Group 3 did not differ significantly from each other. The researchers concluded that these statistical results "support the belief that common planning time can make middle grades schools a better and more beneficial place for teachers."[29]

Analysis of variance also allows researchers to compare subgroups that differ on more than one factor. In the study by Strauss and Bichler, age level is one factor. Another factor that could have been investigated is gender. For each age level, separate groups of male and female children could have been formed, as shown below:

Age Group	Boys	Girls
8-year-olds	_____	_____
10-year-olds	_____	_____
12-year-olds	_____	_____
14-year-olds	_____	_____

Analysis of variance can be used to determine whether (1) the mean scores of the four age groups differ significantly, (2) the mean scores of boys and girls differ significantly, and (3) the pattern of age group differences is different for boys and girls. This use of analysis of variance is similar to its use in analyzing data from two-factor and three-factor experiments (see Chapter 13).

Analysis of Covariance

✦ Touchstone in Research

Wildt, A. R., & Ahtola, O. T. (1979). *Analysis of covariance.* Thousand Oaks, CA: Sage.

In doing causal-comparative studies, researchers sometimes need to determine whether a difference between two groups on a particular variable can be explained by another difference that exists between the two groups. Suppose your hypothesis is that seventh-grade boys make more grammatical errors in writing class papers than seventh-grade girls. A sample of papers written by the two groups is scored for grammatical errors, and a t test shows that the mean number of errors is significantly greater for the boys than for the girls.

At this point you need to ask the question: Can this obtained difference be explained in terms of some other variable (besides gender) on which the groups might differ? In other words, alternative hypotheses need to be tested. You might consider the length of the students' papers as a possible explanatory variable. Suppose the sample of boys is found to have written significantly longer papers than the sample of girls, thus increasing their opportunity to make grammatical errors. You now need to determine whether controlling for

---

29. Ibid., p. 307.

initial differences in writing productivity eliminates the obtained difference in mean number of grammatical errors.

The statistical technique of **analysis of covariance** (ANCOVA) is used to control for initial differences between groups before a comparison of the within-groups variance and between-groups variance is made. The effect of ANCOVA is to make the two groups equal with respect to one or more control variables. If a difference still remains between the two groups, we cannot use the control variable to explain the effect. In our example, suppose you found that boys still made significantly more grammatical errors than girls after using analysis of covariance to control for initial differences in writing productivity. You would be able to conclude that the gender difference in grammatical errors was not due to the fact that boys write longer papers.

Analysis of covariance is useful in causal-comparative studies because the researcher cannot always select comparison groups that are matched with respect to all relevant variables except the one that is the main concern of the investigation. Analysis of covariance provides a post hoc method of matching groups on such variables as age, aptitude, prior education, socioeconomic class, or a measure of performance.

Research data need to satisfy certain statistical assumptions before analysis of covariance can be applied.[30] These assumptions, such as homogeneity of regression, can be checked empirically, but the computations are complex. Inexperienced researchers need to consult an expert statistician before using analysis of covariance.

Multivariate Analysis of Variance

Multivariate analysis of variance (MANOVA) is a statistical technique for determining whether groups differ on more than one dependent variable. The multivariate analysis of variance is similar to the t test and to analysis of variance. The major difference between the techniques is that the t test and analysis of variance can determine only whether several groups differ on one dependent variable.

Each research participant in a MANOVA will have a score on two or more dependent variables. These scores can be represented by a **vector,** which is a single mathematical expression representing the individual's scores on all the dependent variables. The mean of the vector scores for all the individuals in a given group is called a **centroid.** The purpose of MANOVA is to determine whether there are statistically significant differences between the centroids of different groups.

The concept of representing several dependent variables by a single vector can be understood in a nontechnical way. Consider the case of two groups—high- and low-achieving students—who have been measured on two dependent variables: attitude toward their present school and attitude toward engaging in further schooling. Imagine that one student has a score of 6 on her attitude toward her present school, and a score of 8 on her attitude toward engaging in further instruction. This student's scores can be expressed in the form (6, 8), indicating that she has a score of 6 on the first variable and a score of 8 on the second variable. The scores also can be represented on a graph, with each single point on the graph representing one student's scores on the two variables. Suppose the graph points (comparable to vector scores) for high-achieving students tend to occupy a different space on the graph than the points for the low-achieving students. The purpose of MANOVA, in a sense, is to determine whether these two spaces differ significantly from each other.

✦ Touchstone in Research

Bray, J. H., & Maxwell, S. E. (1986). *Multivariate analysis of variance.* Thousand Oaks, CA: Sage.

---

30. The assumptions are discussed in: Elashoff, J. D. (1969). Analysis of covariance: A delicate instrument. *American Educational Research Journal, 6,* 383–399.

Our example is based on two dependent variables represented on a two-dimensional graph. You might try imagining the case of three dependent variables and how each individual's vector scores on them could be represented by a single point on a three-dimensional graph.

The first step in doing a MANOVA should be to test the assumption of the equality of group dispersions. If a nonsignificant F is obtained, we can conclude that the assumption is satisfied. (Researchers sometimes skip this step because MANOVA is robust, meaning that the assumption can be violated to an extent without violating the validity of the test.) The next step is to do a test of the statistical significance of the difference between group centroids. The most commonly used test for this purpose is Wilk's lambda (λ). This test yields an F value, which can be looked up in an F ratio table to determine its level of statistical significance. If a significant MANOVA F is obtained, we then can do an ANOVA on each dependent variable. The purpose of the ANOVAs is to determine which of the measured variables produce a statistically significant difference between the mean scores of the groups being studied. Although unlikely, it is possible to obtain a significant MANOVA F without finding a significant F in any of the ANOVAs.

A typical causal-comparative study includes a substantial number of dependent variables. This does not mean, however, that all the variables must be tested for statistical significance by a single MANOVA. You should group the variables into clusters (that is, vectors) that include educationally or psychologically related variables. Each cluster of variables can be analyzed by a separate MANOVA. If you wish to test a hypothesis involving a particular dependent variable, you can do a t test directly without first including that variable in a MANOVA with other variables.

The use of MANOVA in causal-comparative research is illustrated by a study of college professor ratings conducted by Susan Basow and Nancy Silberg.[31] The main purpose of the study was to determine whether there is a bias in evaluations of professors such that female professors are given lower ratings than male professors. Each of 16 female professors at a private college in the northeastern United States was matched with a male professor of similar rank, teaching field, and years of experience at the college. (Matching procedures were described earlier in the chapter.)

The professors were evaluated by their students on six rating scales during the fifth or sixth week of the semester. The six scales are as follows: (1) scholarship, (2) organization/clarity, (3) instructor-group interaction, (4) instructor-individual student interaction, (5) dynamism/enthusiasm, and (6) overall teaching ability. The researchers also recorded the gender of each student who completed the rating scales.

The mean ratings of male and female professors on all six factors are shown in Table 10.5.

Basow and Silberg analyzed the group mean differences shown in Table 10.5 for statistical significance by the use of MANOVA. The six rating scales were considered to be a cluster of related variables. The F ratios for the MANOVA are shown in the first column of statistics in Table 10.6. The significant F for teacher gender (10.40) means that male and female professors had significantly different mean scores on the vector representing the six rating scales. The F ratios for the ANOVAs (analysis of variance) shown in the last six columns of table 10.6 indicate which of the six rating scales yielded significantly different mean scores for male and female professors.

The MANOVA yielded a nonsignificant F for student gender (1.29), meaning that male and female students did not differ significantly in their mean score on the vector

31. Basow, S. A., & Silberg, N. T. (1987) Student evaluations of college professors: Are female and male professors rated differently? *Journal of Educational Psychology, 79*, 308–314.

TABLE 10.5

Descriptive Statistics for Ratings of Male and Female Professors by Male and Female College Students

Factors on Which Professors Were Rated	Male Student				Female Student			
	Male Professor (n = 275)		Female Professor (n = 278)		Male Professor (n = 284)		Female Professor (n = 243)	
	M	*SD*	*M*	*SD*	*M*	*SD*	*M*	*SD*
(1) Scholarship	11.7	3.1	12.9	3.1	12.0	3.1	11.9	3.2
(2) Organization/clarity	10.7	3.3	12.1	3.9	11.1	3.4	11.2	4.2
(3) Instructor-group interaction	11.8	3.2	12.5	3.5	12.1	3.2	11.9	3.6
(4) Instructor-individual student interaction	10.7	3.3	11.6	3.5	10.7	3.6	11.1	3.7
(5) Dynamism/enthusiasm	9.6	3.6	11.6	4.0	10.0	3.8	10.7	4.1
(6) Overall teaching ability	2.2	0.8	2.6	1.0	2.2	0.8	2.4	1.0

Note: Lower scores indicate more positive evaluations. Score range = 5–25, except for overall teaching ability, for which the range = 1–5.
Source: Adapted from Table 2 on p. 311 in: Basow, S. A., & Silberg, N. T. (1987). Student evaluations of college professors: Are female and male professors rated differently? *Journal of Educational Psychology, 79,* 308–314. Copyright 1987 by the American Psychological Association. Adapted with permission.

TABLE 10.6

Multivariate Analysis of Variance Summary for Ratings of Male and Female Professors by Male and Female College Students

	Multivariate ANOVA[a]	Univariate ANOVA[b] Factors on Which Professors Were Rated					
Source	*F*	(1)	(2)	(3)	(4)	(5)	(6) Overall
Professor gender	10.40***	*F* 7.71**	10.63**	1.44	9.11**	34.64***	39.71***
Student gender	1.29	*F* 3.92*	1.15	0.45	1.85	1.12	3.72
Professor gender × Student gender	2.54*	*F* 9.67**	9.33**	4.62*	1.79	8.62**	7.10**

Note: Univariate analyses are on (1) Scholarship, (2) Organization/Clarity, (3) Instructor-Group Interaction, (4) Instructor-Individual Student interaction, (5) Dynamism/Enthusiasm, and (6) Overall teaching ability.
[a]*dfs* = 6,1071
[b]*dfs*= 1,1076
*$p<.05$** $p<.01$*** $p<.001$
Source: Adapted from Table 1 on p. 310 in: Basow, S. A., & Silberg, N. T. (1987). Student evaluations of college professors: Are female and male professors rated differently? *Journal of Educational Psychology, 79,* 308–314. Copyright 1987 by the American Psychological Association. Adapted with permission.

representing the six rating scales. Despite the nonsignificant MANOVA F, the researchers reported the F ratios for the ANOVAs performed on the individual rating scales. One of them—the F for scholarship—is significant. Because the MANOVA F was nonsignificant, however, one should be cautious about interpreting this gender difference in student ratings. It might be a spurious finding. As the number of F ratios that are calculated increases, so does the likelihood of obtaining a significant F by chance.

Finally, we see that the MANOVA F for the professor-gender by student-gender interaction (2.54) in Table 10.6 is statistically significant. This result means that the gender difference in students' scores on the vector representing the six rating scales is dependent on the gender of the professor being rated. The nature of the interaction effect can be determined by examining Table 10.5. We see that male students rated female professors lower on all six scales, whereas female students did not differ systematically in their ratings of male and female professors.

Multivariate analysis of variance is a useful statistical technique because it helps the researcher see the data in a multivariate perspective. Groups that differ from each other on an important characteristic are also likely to differ from each other on other interrelated characteristics as well. Multivariate analysis of variance helps the researcher conceptualize and analyze the nature of these interrelated characteristics, and determine whether the groups being studied differ on them.

The correlational counterpart of MANOVA is canonical analysis, which is described in the next chapter. Either technique can be used to analyze data that consist of one or more independent variables and two or more dependent variables. Although one does find instances of MANOVA in the literature, canonical analysis is becoming the method of choice among educational researchers.

Tests for the Difference between Variances

The standard deviation and its square, the variance, are two statistics for describing the variability of scores obtained from a sample. Just as you might want to determine whether the mean scores for two samples differ significantly, you might want to do a statistical test to determine whether the variances in scores for two samples differ significantly from each other. There are two main reasons for doing this test. The first reason is that most of the commonly used statistical tests—including the t test for the difference between means—are based on the assumption that the variances of the two samples are approximately equal. If the score variances of two samples differ markedly, one of the nonparametric tests discussed later in this chapter should be used instead.

The second reason for testing variance homogeneity between two samples is that your hypothesis might concern the variability of sample scores. For example, you might hypothesize that college graduates are more like one another in scholastic aptitude than college dropouts. The rationale might be that all college graduates are apt to be fairly intelligent but that, for various reasons, both students of high and low aptitude may leave college before graduation. To test this hypothesis in a causal-comparative study, you would administer a measure of scholastic aptitude to a sample of college graduates and a sample of college dropouts. Next you would do a statistical test to determine whether the college graduates have less variable scores on the aptitude measure than do the college dropouts.

The statistical technique used to test whether the observed difference between variances is significant is analysis of variance, which is the same technique used to test for differences between several means. The larger the F ratio, the less likely it is that the variances of the populations from which the samples were drawn are equal. If the F ratio exceeds the alpha level you have set, you would reject the null hypothesis (stating equality of variances) and conclude that the obtained difference between the sample variances is a true one.

You should be aware that several statistical tests are available for comparing the difference between variances. If the two sets of scores are obtained from independent samples, the **test for homogeneity of independent variances** is used to compare the difference between variances in two sets of scores obtained from independent samples. The **test for homogeneity of related variances** is used to compare the difference between variances obtained from repeated measures on a single sample or from two matched samples. The *F* **maximum test for homogeneity of variance** can be used to determine whether the variances of more than two sets of scores differ significantly from one another.

Statistical Analysis: Nonparametric Tests

Advantages and Disadvantages of Nonparametric Tests

The tests of statistical significance that we described in the two previous sections are known as parametric statistics. A parameter describes some aspect of a set of scores for an entire population. **Parametric statistics** are tests of statistical significance that are based upon certain assumptions about population parameters, that is, the shape or variance of the population scores. One such assumption is that the scores in the population are normally distributed about the mean. Another assumption is that the population variances of the comparison groups in one's study are about equal. When large deviations from these assumptions are present in the research data, parametric statistics should not be used. Nonparametric statistical tools should be used instead. **Nonparametric statistics** are tests of statistical significance that do not rely on any assumptions about the shape or variance of population scores.

The use of parametric statistics also is based on the assumption that the scores being analyzed are derived from a measure that has equal intervals. As we explained in Chapter 6, most continuous measures meet this criterion. Measures that yield categorical or rank scores, however, do not have equal intervals, and so one of the nonparametric statistics should be used for data analysis. We discuss the common types of nonparametric statistics in the following sections.

When research data meet the assumption of being interval scores but not the assumptions of normal distribution and variance homogeneity, you still should consider using one of the parametric statistics presented earlier in the chapter. There are three main reasons for recommending the use of parametric statistics in these situations. First, research has shown that moderate departure from the theoretical assumptions has very little effect upon the value of the parametric technique.[32] Second, nonparametric statistics are generally less powerful, that is, they require larger samples in order to yield the same level of statistical significance. Third, for many of the problems encountered in educational research, suitable nonparametric tests are not available.

The Chi-Square Test

Chi-square (χ^2) is a nonparametric statistical test to determine whether research data in the form of frequency counts are distributed differently for different samples. These frequency counts can be placed into two or more categories. The chi-square test was used to analyze data resulting from a study of special education referrals by Mark Shinn, Gerald Tindal, and Deborah Spira.[33] These researchers were interested in determining whether

♦ *Touchstone in Research*

Coombs, W. T., Algina, J., & Oltman, D. O. (1996). Univariate and multivariate omnibus hypothesis tests selected to control Type I error rates when population variances are not necessarily equal. *Review of Educational Research, 66,* 137–179.

Gibbons, J. D. (1993). *Nonparametric measures of association.* Thousand Oaks, CA: Sage.

---

32. Refer to the discussion earlier in the chapter on the effects of violating assumptions underlying the *t* test.

teachers are biased in their referrals of students who have reading difficulties to special education services. Their sample included all students in a large midwestern city referred for such services over approximately one school year. The number of referred students, grouped by grade level, ethnicity, and gender, is shown in the first column of Table 10.7. For example, the table shows that 79 white students and 65 black students in grade 2 were referred for special education services because of reading difficulties during the school year.

The next step in the study was to determine the number of students who would have been referred if there were no bias in the referral process. Shinn and his colleagues examined normative data on a reading test administered to a large random sample of regular education students in the district. Specifically, they examined students who scored at the

TABLE 10.7

Chi-Square Test of Observed and Expected Referral Rates by Ethnic Background and Gender of Student

Group	Observed	Expected	χ^2
Ethnic Status			
Grade 2 White	79	78.3	
Grade 2 Black	65	53.9	2.36
Grade 3 White	48	52.4	
Grade 3 Black	45	39.5	1.14
Grade 4 White	63	68.3	
Grade 4 Black	52	34.5	*9.27
Grade 5 White	46	55.1	
Grade 5 Black	44	33.7	*4.64
Grade 6 White	24	36.6	
Grade 6 Black	31	20.1	*10.30
Gender			
Grade 2 Male	106	76.1	
Grade 2 Female	45	74.9	*22.4
Grade 3 Male	78	66.3	
Grade 3 Female	45	56.7	*4.5
Grade 4 Male	79	60.1	
Grade 4 Female	47	65.9	*12.6
Grade 5 Male	64	58.8	
Grade 5 Female	41	46.2	1.0
Grade 6 Male	40	37.1	
Grade 6 Female	25	27.9	.53

*Indicates results significant beyond the .05 level
Source: Adapted from Table 3 on p. 37 in: Shinn, M. R., Tindal, G. A. & Spira, D. A. (1987). Special education referrals as an index of teacher tolerance: Are teachers imperfect tests? *Exceptional Children, 54,* 32–40.

33. Shinn, M. R., Tindal, G. A., & Spira, D. A. (1987). Special education referrals as an index of teacher tolerance: Are teachers imperfect tests? *Exceptional Children, 54,* 32–40.

16th percentile or below on the test. Test scores this low indicate severe reading difficulties. The researchers reasoned that if there were no gender bias in the teacher referral process, the proportion of boys to girls referred for special education services for reading remediation would not differ from the proportion of boys to girls scoring at or below the 16th percentile on an objective reading test. Similarly, they reasoned that if there were no ethnic bias in the teacher referral process, the proportion of white to black students who were referred would not differ from the proportion of white to black students scoring at or below the 16th percentile on the test.

As shown in Table 10.7, the researchers used the chi-square test to determine the statistical significance of the difference between the observed frequencies of referrals (column 2) with the frequencies that would be expected from the normative data for students scoring at or below the 16th percentile on the objective reading test (column 3). Three of the five chi-square coefficients for ethnicity and three of the five chi-square coefficients for gender are statistically significant. For example, more than twice as many boys as girls in the second grade (106:45) were referred for special education services. However, the proportion of boys to girls who scored low on the objective reading test (76.1:74.9) was virtually the same. The results shown in Table 10.7 suggest both a gender bias and an ethnicity bias in teachers' referral of students for special education services.

When the frequency data are grouped into more than four cells, a more complex chi-square test can be done. You also should be aware that when the expected frequency in any cell is less than five, a correction (Yate's correction or the Fisher exact test) needs to be applied to the regular chi-square test. In the process of doing a chi-square test, you also can compute a **phi coefficient** (for a fourfold table) or a **contingency coefficient** (for more than four cells). These correlation coefficients provide an estimate of the magnitude of the relationship between the variables in a chi-square table.[34]

Other Nonparametric Tests

Of the nonparametric tests of significance, chi-square probably is the most frequently used by educational researchers in causal-comparative studies. Other nonparametric tests sometimes are used, particularly when the research data are in the form of rank-order scores or interval scores that grossly violate the parametric test assumptions of normal distribution and homogeneity of variance.

The **Mann-Whitney U test** can be used to determine whether the distributions of scores of two independent samples differ significantly from each other. If U is statistically significant, it means that the bulk of scores in one population is higher than the bulk of scores in the other population. The two populations are represented by the two independent samples on which the U test is made. This test generally is used when the assumption of homogeneity of sample variances underlying the t test is grossly violated.[35]

The **Wilcoxon signed rank test** is used to determine whether the distributions of scores for two samples differ significantly from each other when the scores of the samples are correlated (either through matching or because repeated measures are taken on the same sample). The Wilcoxon test is analogous to the t test for correlated means except that it is not based on any assumptions about the shape of the score distribution or homogeneity of variance between the two sets of scores. If more than two groups of subjects are to be compared, a nonparametric one-way analysis of variance (the **Kruskal-Wallis test**) can be used.

---

34. The phi coefficient and contingency coefficient are defined in Table 11.3 in Chapter 11.
35. Zimmerman, D. W. (1987). Comparative power of student t test and Mann-Whitney U test for unequal sample sizes and variances. *Journal of Experimental Education 55*, 171–174. This study showed that even if this assumption *is* violated, when the sizes of the two sample groups are unequal and the smaller sample has the larger variance, the t test provides a better test of the null hypothesis than the U test.

Interpretation of Causal-Comparative Findings

The process of interpreting causal-comparative findings can be illustrated by referring to the study of scientific literacy discussed earlier in the chapter. You will recall from Table 10.3 that students taught by the high-context-use teachers made significantly less gain in their understanding of the scientific process than did students taught by low-context-use teachers. We can conclude from this result that there is a negative relationship between teachers' use of context-enhanced statements and students' development of scientific literacy.

Can we reach beyond this conclusion and infer that context-enhanced statements *cause* a decrement in students' development of scientific literacy? The results are consistent with this interpretation, but because this was a causal-comparative study, other interpretations must be considered as well. For example, as we stated above, the researchers found that most of the teachers' context-enhanced statements were confusing or incomplete. Perhaps confusing, incomplete statements of *any type* cause decrements in students' development of scientific literacy. If this is true, teachers' references to context have an effect on scientific literacy only because they are confusing, incomplete statements, which is the real cause of the effect.

Another interpretation of the finding is that students who have difficulty in developing scientific literacy cause teachers to help them by making more context-enhanced statements. In other words, student performance affects teacher behavior, rather than the reverse. The researchers did not present the pretest scores of the two groups of students, so we do not know whether one group was more science-illiterate than the other and therefore possibly more difficult to teach. Thus, the interpretation is neither supported nor refuted by the reported results. This is the basic problem of causal-comparative studies. They are useful for revealing possible causal relationships between variables, but they do not provide strong evidence about the nature of the causal pattern.

Two procedures can be used to improve the interpretability of causal-comparative studies. First, as we discussed earlier in the chapter, alternative hypotheses should be formulated and tested whenever possible. Second, the relationships among all the variables in the study can be examined using the technique of *path analysis,* which is discussed in the next chapter.

The most powerful method for demonstrating the causal nature of causal-comparative findings is to do subsequent experiments in which the presumed cause or causes of the outcomes being studied is manipulated. For example, in the study of scientific literacy, teachers' use of the technique of providing a meaningful context for the scientific content being taught was hypothesized to have an effect on students' development of scientific literacy. An experiment could be designed in which a group of teachers is trained to use this technique with attention to both quantity and quality of use. (Training in quality of use is especially important, because the present study found that teachers rarely use the technique appropriately.) Another group of teachers would not receive the training. If the hypothesis is correct, we would expect to see students of trained teachers make greater gains in scientific literacy than students of untrained teachers.

We wish to emphasize once again that both causal-comparative research and experiments have advantages. A causal-comparative study is a fairly economical method for identifying possible causes or effects of an important phenomenon. If apparent cause-and-effect relationships are found, they can be tested through controlled experimentation. Experiments typically are more technically demanding and expensive than a causal-comparative study, so they are best employed after the researcher has reason to believe that a causal relationship between two variables exists.

◆ RECOMMENDATIONS FOR
Doing Descriptive and Causal-Comparative Research

1. In planning a descriptive study, select an instrument, or instruments, that will yield the most detailed and valid picture of the phenomena you wish to understand.
2. In planning a longitudinal study, select a sampling design (trend, cohort, panel, or cross-section) that is feasible yet will yield valid data about the phenomena you wish to study over time.
3. If you wish to use a panel sampling design in a longitudinal research study, develop procedures that will minimize attrition, inappropriate expectations among panel members, and bias arising from repeated measurements with the same instrument.
4. In planning or interpreting the results of a causal-comparative study, consider whether you can rule out alternative explanations of the cause-and-effect relationships you have found, or expect to find.
5. In analyzing data in a causal-comparative study, determine whether it is most appropriate to use a *t* test, analysis of covariance, or multivariate analysis of variance.
6. In analyzing data in a causal-comparative study, use a nonparametric test of statistical significance if the data are in the form of frequency counts or if they grossly violate the assumptions underlying parametric tests.

✔ SELF-CHECK TEST

Circle the correct answer to each of the following questions.
The answers are provided at the back of the book.

1. A common type of statistics used in descriptive research is
   a. measures of central tendency.
   b. nonparametric tests.
   c. tests for the difference between variances.
   d. one-tailed tests of statistical significance.
2. A trend study involves
   a. sampling different members of an accessible population at each data-collection point.
   b. collecting data from the same sample of individuals at each data-collection point.
   c. following a specific population of individuals over a period of time.
   d. collecting data about different time periods from all subjects at the same time.

3. The main situation in which a researcher would use a causal-comparative design rather than an experimental design is when
   a. random sampling is not possible.
   b. experimental manipulation is not possible.
   c. use of standardized tests is not possible.
   d. young children are the subjects of the research.
4. One of the main limitations of causal-comparative research is that
   a. it is more expensive than other types of research.
   b. it does not reveal possible causal relationships between variables.
   c. it does not reveal the magnitude of the relationships between variables.
   d. null hypotheses cannot be tested.

5. If the groups to be compared in a causal-comparative study differ on an extraneous variable, the preferred procedure is to
   a. match the groups on the extraneous variable.
   b. match the groups on a standardized intelligence or aptitude test.
   c. use analysis of variance to control for the extraneous variable.
   d. use analysis of covariance to control for the extraneous variable.

6. One of the assumptions that the t test makes about scores obtained in causal-comparative research is that
   a. score variances for the populations under study are equal.
   b. score variances for the populations under study are not equal.
   c. means of the samples are equal.
   d. population means do not differ.

7. If the researcher matches individuals in the groups being studied on a particular characteristic, the appropriate test is the t test for
   a. independent means.
   b. equal variances.
   c. correlated means.
   d. unequal means.

8. If a researcher conducting causal-comparative research is almost certain that any detected change will be in a hypothesized direction, it is appropriate to compute a(n)
   a. analysis of variance.
   b. correlation coefficient.
   c. two-tailed t test.
   d. one-tailed t test.

9. A post hoc method for matching groups on certain variables is the
   a. analysis of covariance.
   b. canonical correlation.
   c. the t test for correlated means.
   d. the t test for independent means.

10. Multivariate analysis of variance is used to detect statistically significant group differences in
   a. vectors of independent variables.
   b. vectors of dependent variables.
   c. correlations between dependent variables.
   d. correlations between independent and dependent variables.

11. An important characteristic of nonparametric statistics is that they
   a. make no assumption about the variance of the population scores.
   b. assume that scores in the population are normally distributed about the mean.
   c. require equal population variances.
   d. can be used only with interval scales of measurement.

12. The purpose of computing a correlational statistic following a t test or analysis of variance is to determine
   a. whether the sample variances are equal.
   b. the magnitude of the relationship between the variables.
   c. the directionality of the observed differences.
   d. all of the above.

CHAPTER 11

✦ Nonexperimental Research: Correlational Designs

OVERVIEW

In this chapter we describe the two purposes for which correlational research designs are used. One purpose is to search for variables, measured at one point in time, that predict a criterion variable measured at a subsequent point in time. Another purpose is to search for possible causal patterns among variables. Various correlational statistics are available to estimate the strength of the prediction or relationship. Bivariate correlational statistics are used when two variables are involved in studying predictions or causal relationships, whereas multivariate correlational statistics are used when three or more variables are involved.

OBJECTIVES

After studying this chapter you should be able to

1. State advantages and disadvantages of correlational research designs.
2. Plot a scattergram and explain its use in correlational research.
3. Draw appropriate inferences from correlation coefficients about the degree, direction, and possible causal nature of relationships between variables.
4. Describe the procedures involved in conducting a study that explores cause-and-effect relationships.
5. Describe the procedures involved in conducting a prediction study.
6. Describe practical uses of prediction studies.
7. Explain the use of Taylor-Russell tables and cross-validation in prediction studies.
8. Select the most appropriate bivariate correlational statistic when correlating two variables.
9. Explain the use of correction for attenuation, correction for restriction in range, and part or partial correlation in correlational research.
10. Select the most appropriate multivariate correlational statistic when correlating three or more variables.
11. Explain the design and purpose of a correlation matrix and a factor analysis.
12. Explain similarities and differences between multiple regression, path analysis, and structural equation modeling.
13. Explain the use of subgroups and moderator variables to refine a correlational analysis.
14. Interpret the magnitude and statistical significance of correlation coefficients in prediction research and research that explores cause-and-effect relationships.

The Nature of Correlation

Correlational research refers to studies in which the purpose is to discover relationships between variables through the use of correlational statistics. Correlational statistics also are used extensively in test construction and analysis, as we explain in Chapter 7. Because an understanding of a correlation coefficient is essential to what follows, we will briefly discuss its meaning in nonmathematical terms.

Let's start with the notion of individual differences. Suppose everyone had the same level of academic achievement. There would not be much work for researchers to do. Prediction, for example, would be an easy matter because we would be able to make the same, accurate prediction for everyone. There would be no need for developing elaborate measures, either, because in our scenario there is only achievement level in the population. Yet the fact is that people do vary with respect to this characteristic, and the variations have major personal and social consequences. For example, high academic achievers generally perform a different role in society and view themselves differently than do low academic achievers. If researchers could discover the causes and effects of variability in academic achievement, this knowledge might prove useful in helping both low and high achievers become more personally and academically successful.

◆ *Touchstone in Research*

Jacoby, W. G. (1997). *Statistical graphics for univariate and bivariate data*. Thousand Oaks, CA: Sage.

Types of Scattergrams

To understand how the correlation coefficient helps us in this kind of investigation, examine the four graphs in Figure 11.1. Each of these graphs is a scattergram. A **scattergram** (also called a **scatter plot**) is a pictorial representation of the correlation between two variables: The scores of individuals on one variable are plotted on the x-axis of a graph and the scores of the same individuals on another variable are plotted on the y-axis. Note that each point on the graph contains two pieces of information, the individual's position with respect to the x-axis and with respect to the y-axis.

Positive Correlation

In graph 1 we see a perfect positive correlation between variable A and variable B. The straight diagonal line, called the *line of best fit,* indicates that each unit of increment in the x-axis variable is accompanied by a unit of increment on the y-axis variable. The correlation, represented by the expression $r = 1.00$, is perfect, because if we know an individual's score on one variable, we can predict perfectly that individual's score on the other variable. For example, consider a hypothetical vocabulary test on which a group of students earned scores varying from 40 to 100. Suppose that students who earned a score of 40 on the vocabulary test had a score of 85 on a test of reading comprehension; those with a vocabulary test score of 41 had a reading comprehension score of 86; and so on through the range of scores, so that students with a vocabulary test score of 100 had a reading comprehension score of 145. If this were the case, there would be a perfect relationship, or correlation, between these two variables. If we know a student's vocabulary score, we can predict perfectly her comprehension score.

Now examine the scattergram in graph 2, which shows a fairly high positive correlation between two variables ($r = .70$). If we know a person's score on the x-axis variable, we cannot predict his score on the y-axis variable perfectly. However, if we follow the straight line (the line of best fit) from the x-axis to where the straight line intersects the y-axis, we can predict his score on the y-axis variable fairly accurately. The person's score on the y-axis probably will fall within a relatively narrow range of scores.

FIGURE 11.1

Scattergrams Representing Different Degrees and Directions of Correlation between Two Variables

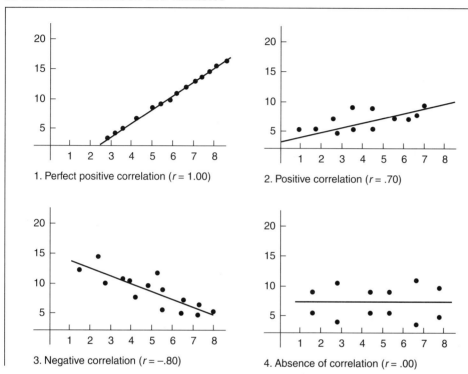

1. Perfect positive correlation ($r = 1.00$)

2. Positive correlation ($r = .70$)

3. Negative correlation ($r = -.80$)

4. Absence of correlation ($r = .00$)

Negative Correlation

Another possibility is a negative relationship between two variables, as shown in graph 3. For example, imagine a measure of students' attitude toward school, for which scores can range from 0 (a highly negative attitude) to 10 (a highly positive attitude). If we correlated students' attitudes toward school with their absence rate (number of days during the school year that they did not attend school), we would expect a negative correlation between attitude toward school and absence rate. In other words, we would predict that students with very positive attitudes toward school (let's say a score of 8 or above) would miss very few days of school, and that students with negative attitudes toward school (let's say a score of 3 or below) would have a high number of absences during the school year. If the relationship between attitude toward school and absence rate was perfect, all the points on the scattergram would fall along the line of best fit, just as they did in graph 1. In this case, however, the correlation would be a perfect negative correlation ($r = -1.00$). In graph 3, the negative relationship between the two variables is not perfect, but it is fairly good ($r = -.80$).

Absence of Correlation

Still another possibility is a lack of relationship between two variables, which is depicted by the scattergram in graph 4. Knowing an individual's score on the x-axis variable is of no value at all in predicting her score on the y-axis variable. Using the example of vocabulary test scores and reading comprehension, let us suppose that for any given vocabulary test score there are students with widely varying reading comprehension scores. For example, suppose students with scores of 40 on the vocabulary test have reading comprehension scores ranging from 85 to 145. We would conclude that there is little or no relationship, or correlation, between the two variables. Accurate prediction of reading comprehension scores from vocabulary scores would be impossible.

The Mathematics of Correlation

As we stated above, the line of best fit is the straight line in each of the scattergrams in Figure 11.1. In nonmathematical terms, the **line of best fit** is the line, among all the possible lines that can be drawn across the x- and y-axes, that represents the best prediction of a person's y score from knowing her x score. It can be calculated using the following equation:

$$y = bx + a$$

where y is the variable being predicted, b is the slope of the line (sometimes referred to as the *regression weight*), x is the predictor variable, and a is the point where the line of best fit intersects the y-axis. You will see an elaboration of this basic equation when we discuss multiple regression later in the chapter.

The purpose of the correlation coefficient is to express in mathematical terms the degree and direction of relationship between two (or more) variables. If the relationship between two variables is perfectly positive (for each increment in one variable there is a corresponding increment in the other), the correlation coefficient will be 1.00. If the relationship is perfectly negative, it will be –1.00. If there is no relationship, the coefficient will be 0. If two variables are somewhat related, the coefficients will have a value between 0 and 1.00 (for a positive relationship) or between 0 and –1.00 (for a negative relationship). Thus, the correlation coefficient is a precise way of stating the degree to which one variable is related to another, and the direction of the relationship (positive or negative). To express the idea another way, the correlation coefficient tells us how effectively individuals' scores on one measure (e.g., an intelligence test) can be used to predict their scores on another measure (e.g., an achievement test). If predictions can be made, this suggests (but, as we shall see, does not prove) that the variable measured by the predictor instrument has a causal influence on the variable measured by the other instrument.

The square of a correlation coefficient (r) yields a statistic (r^2) that is called the **explained variance.** For example, the square of a correlation coefficient of .30 is .09. If variable A correlates .30 with variable B, we can say that variable A "explains" 9 percent of the variance in variable B.

The mathematical basis of explained variance is somewhat complicated. A simple way to understand it is to imagine that scores on measure B range from 30 to 70. If A explained none of the variance in B, we could not predict anyone's score on B other than to say that it could be as low as 30 or as high as 70 (a range of 40 points). If A explained all the variance in B, we could predict anyone's score on B perfectly, and so our range of error in any prediction would be 0 points. If A explained 30 percent of the variance in B, we could use A to predict anyone's score within a certain range; for example, our prediction of B might be a range of scores between 40 to 60 (a range of 20 points). In other words, as the explained variance increases, we can use an individual's score on measure A to predict his score on measure B within an increasingly narrow range.

Several types of correlation coefficient are presented in this chapter. Different coefficients are necessary because certain measures are in the form of interval scales or ratio scales (e.g., most measures of intelligence), whereas other measures are in the form of rank orderings (e.g., ranking of teachers in terms of their effectiveness) or dichotomies (e.g., true-false test items). Also, the relationship between the scores on two measures is not always linear, as we shall find in our discussion of the correlation ratio.

Both correlation coefficients and scattergrams express relationships between measured variables. A correlation coefficient is a concise mathematical expression of the relationship, whereas a scattergram provides an easily viewed display of all the data on which the correlation coefficient is based. Researchers often just compute correlation coefficients using a statistical program on a computer. However, you should consider constructing scattergrams as well, particularly if you have reason to think that the relationship is nonlinear (nonlinearity is discussed later in the chapter) or that the sample contains outliers (see Chapter 5).

Correlational Research Design

The basic design in correlational research is very simple, involving nothing more than collecting data on two or more variables for each individual in a sample and computing a correlation coefficient. For example, we might select a group of college freshmen and attempt to predict their first-year grades (variable A) on the basis of their overall Scholastic Aptitude Test (SAT) scores (variable B). Many important studies in education have been done with this simple design. Recent studies have employed more sophisticated correlational techniques in order to include more variables in the data analysis and thereby obtain a clearer picture of the relationships being studied.

As in most research, the quality of correlational studies is determined not by the complexity of the design or the sophistication of analytical techniques, but by the depth of the rationale and theoretical constructs that guide the research design. The likelihood of obtaining an important research finding is greater if the researcher uses theory and the results of previous research to select variables to be correlated with one another.

Correlation and Causality

The correlational approach to analyzing relationships between variables is subject to the same limitations with respect to causal inference as the causal-comparative approach discussed in the preceding chapter. For example, if we found a positive correlation between years of education and level of interest in cultural activities, we might infer that each year of formal schooling is likely to result in—that is, to *cause*—a greater interest in cultural activities.

Two other causal inferences are just as plausible, however. One is that the level of interest in cultural activities determines how much education a student will seek. The other possible inference is that some third variable determines both the amount of education attained and level of interest in cultural activities, thus creating a positive relationship between these two variables. For example, a parents' education is a plausible third variable. Parents who are college graduates might encourage their children to stay in school longer and to develop more cultural interests than parents with less formal education. If this is true, the observed relationship between education and cultural interests is not a cause-and-effect relationship, but rather is the result of their common determination by a third variable.

A correlational relationship between two variables occasionally is the result of an artifact. For example, if we correlate two scales from the same personality inventory, a significant relationship between the scales might be found because both scales contain some of the same items, not because the personality dimensions that they measure are causally related. A statistical technique can be used to correct the correlation coefficient for covariation due to overlapping test items.[1] Also, when raters are used to collect data, a relationship between variables might be found because the same rater scores both variables. This is particularly likely when there is rater bias due to a halo effect (see Chapter 9). For example, we might find correlations between individuals' scores on several "good" traits if raters form an initial positive or negative impression of the individuals being rated. If the impression is positive, they probably will score an individual high on all the traits; if the impression is negative, they probably will assign an individual all low scores. Any correlation found between the traits would be due to this artifact rather than to a true cause-and-effect relationship.

In summary, correlational statistics can be used to explore cause-and-effect relationships between variables, but the obtained results generally do not lead to strong conclusions. A correlation between *A* and *B* can mean that *A* is a determinant of *B*, that *B* is a determinant of *A*, that a third variable *X* determines both *A* and *B*, or that the relationship between *A* and *B* is due to an artifact (e.g., the measures of *A* and *B* contain some of the same items). Only an experiment can provide a definitive conclusion about a cause-and-effect relationship. Correlation coefficients are best used to measure the degree and direction (i.e., positive or negative) of the relationship between two or more variables and to explore possible causal factors. If a significant relationship between variables is found, their causality can be tested more definitively by using an experimental research design.

Advantages and Uses of Correlational Research

Correlational research designs, like the causal-comparative research designs to which they are closely related, are highly useful for studying problems in education and in the other social sciences. Their principal advantage over causal-comparative or experimental designs is that they enable researchers to analyze the relationships among a large number of variables in a single study. In education and social science, we frequently confront situations in which several variables influence a particular pattern of behavior. Correlational designs allow us to analyze how these variables, either singly or in combination, affect the pattern of behavior. (Path analysis and structural equation modeling, which we discuss later in the chapter, are particularly useful for this purpose.)

Another advantage of correlational designs is that they provide information concerning the degree of the relationship between the variables being studied. This is an advantage over causal-comparative designs. For example, causal-comparative studies of teaching ability often start with the identification of a group of good teachers and a group of ineffective teachers. Comparisons then are made between the two groups on selected dependent variables in order to identify possible causes of the observed differences in teaching ability. Describing one group of teachers as good and another group as ineffective, however, is obviously an artificial dichotomy, because within each of these groups some teachers will certainly be better than others. The differences in degree are ignored in a causal-comparative design. In reality, what we have in this population is not two groups of teachers of distinctly different ability, but a single group ranging in degree of teaching ability from very poor to very good. The correlation coefficient takes advantage of this range, providing a measure of the degree of relationship over the entire range of teaching ability, or within certain ranges.

---

1. This statistical technique is described in: Dahlstrom, W. G., & Welsh, G. S. (1960). *An MMPI handbook: A guide to use in clinical practice and research.* Minneapolis, MN: University of Minnesota Press.

Correlational research designs are used for two major purposes: (1) to explore causal relationships between variables and (2) to predict scores on one variable from research participants' scores on other variables. In causal relationship research, the variables can be measured at the same point in time or at different points in time. In prediction research, the variables used for prediction must be measured prior to the measurement of the variable to be predicted.

The design of causal relationship research and prediction research is explained in the next two sections of this chapter. The remainder of the chapter describes the types of correlational statistics that can be used to analyze relational or predictive data. Most of the statistics can be used in either type of research. A few statistical techniques have been developed specifically for prediction research, and these are noted. In the chapters on experimental research designs (Chapters 12 and 13), you will find that the same correlational statistics also can be used to analyze data from experiments.

Planning a Causal Relationship Study

Basic Research Design

The primary purpose of causal relationship studies is to identify the causes and effects of important educational phenomena, such as academic achievement, attitude toward school, teacher morale, leadership style, and the use of particular teaching techniques. This type of research design is especially useful for exploratory studies in areas where little is known. To describe the steps involved in conducting a relationship study, we will use a study by Penelope Peterson and Elizabeth Fennema on the possible effects of classroom instructional practices on the mathematics achievement of fourth-grade students.[2]

The Problem

The first step in planning a causal relationship study is to identify specific variables that show promise of being important determinants of the characteristic or behavior pattern being studied. A review of existing research and theory often is helpful in identifying such variables. In the study by Peterson and Fennema, the behavior pattern being investigated was children's gains in mathematics achievement over part of a school year. The researchers' interest was in identifying instructional practices that affect the amount of gain made by students, and in determining whether different types of instruction are effective for girls and for boys. They also differentiated between low-level mathematics achievement (knowledge and skills) and high-level mathematics achievement (understanding and application), in an effort to determine whether various types of instruction are effective for each of these types of mathematics learning. Their research problem was expressed in the form of the following question:

> Do significant relationships exist between the type of mathematics classroom activity in which boys and girls are engaged and their low level and high level achievement, and do these relationships differ significantly for boys and girls?[3]

The researchers considered several instructional variables that might affect the types of academic achievement of interest to them. They drew on previous research findings about teacher and student behaviors that correlate with student academic achievement

---

2. Peterson, P. L., & Fennema, E. (1985). Effective teaching, student engagement in classroom activities, and sex-related differences in learning mathematics. *American Educational Research Journal, 22,* 309–335.
3. Ibid., p. 311.

gains. Although causal relationship studies usually are exploratory, as this one was, they should be guided by previous research findings and theory whenever possible in order to increase the likelihood of finding variables that cause the behavior pattern of interest. Thus, a review of previous research and theoretical literature is a critical step in a study designed to explore cause-and-effect relationships between variables.

Selection of Research Participants

The next step in a causal relationship study is to select research participants who can be measured on the variables to be investigated. As we pointed out in our discussion of causal-comparative studies, it is very important to select a group of participants who are reasonably homogeneous. Otherwise, causal relationships between variables might be obscured by the presence of participants who differ widely from each other. If the sample is highly heterogeneous, the researcher should consider forming them into homogeneous subgroups. The technique of moderator analysis, discussed later in the chapter, can be used when subgroups are formed.

Peterson and Fennema chose to select a homogeneous sample for their study:

> The participants were 36 fourth grade teachers (3 male and 33 female) and their mathematics classes in 15 schools located either in rural areas or in small towns adjoining larger cities in Wisconsin. . . .Most of the students in the classes were white and came from middle-class families.[4]

Also, the researchers formed subgroups from this sample (a procedure we discuss in Chapter 10) to make the samples used in the data analysis even more homogeneous. The subgroups were formed on the basis of gender. Six boys and six girls, randomly selected from each class, were chosen for intensive observation during the course of the study.

Data Collection

Data for causal relationship studies can be collected by various methods, including standardized tests, questionnaires, interviews, or observational techniques. The only requirement is that the data must be in quantifiable form.

Several measurement techniques were used in Peterson and Fennema's study. Observers were trained to use an observation schedule to record the math activities and behavior of the 12 selected students in each of the 36 classes. Each class was observed for three weeks. The recorded activities and behaviors are listed in Table 11.1. Each activity and behavior was scored as the percentage of total class time that it occurred. In addition, each student was administered a standardized test of mathematics achievement in December or January and again in May. Students were given two scores for their performance on the test: a "low-level" score for performance on items requiring recall of a specific fact or manipulation of an algorithm, and a "high-level" score for performance on items requiring understanding, interpretation, or application of mathematical knowledge.

Data Analysis

In a simple causal relationship study, the data are analyzed by correlating (1) scores on a measured variable that represents the phenomenon of primary interest with (2) scores on a measured variable thought to be related to that phenomenon. In the study by Peterson and Fennema, the students' end-of-year achievement on the low-level and high-level mathematics test (the phenomenon of primary interest) was correlated with each measure of classroom activity or behavior (variables thought to be related to that phenomenon). Table 11.1 shows the results for girls. (The results for boys are shown in Table 11.9.)

4. Ibid., pp. 311–312.

TABLE 11.1

Partial Correlations between Girls' Engaged Time Scores and End-of-Year Mathematics Achievement

Engaged Time Variables	Low-Level Achievement *r*	High-Level Achievement *r*
Type of activity expected by teacher		
Daily math	.17	14
Other math	.07	.13
Nonmath	−.22*	−.08
Interim activity	−.10	−.20
Social activity	−.30**	−.43**
Setting of activity		
Total class	.06	−.19
Medium group	−.12	.24*
Small group—same sex	.18	.01
Small group—different sex	−.01	.41**
Two students—same sex	−.05	.05
Two students—different sex	−.03	−.13
Teacher—student	.03	−.15
Alone	−.03	.08
Engaged in math activity	.19	.31**
Math—high level	.18	.17
Math—low level	.01	.11
Math—symbolic	−.01	.07
Math—representational	.19	.20
Helping	−.04	−.11
Being helped by student	.03	−.09
Being helped by teacher	.01	−.15
No helping	18	.32**
Competitive	−.40**	−.05
Cooperative	.25*	.13
Both competitive and cooperative	.25*	.03
Neither competitive nor cooperative	.27*	.30**
Nonengaged in math activity	−.19	−.30**
Social	−.37**	−.34**
Waiting for help	.09	−.30**
Academic (nonmath)	−.17	−.09
Interim activities	−.04	−.03
Off-task	−.09	−.24*

One-tailed test *p < .10
**p < .05

Source: Adapted from Table III on p. 319 in: Peterson, P. L., & Fennema, E. (1985). Effective teaching, student engagement in classroom activities, and sex-related differences in learning mathematics. *American Educational Research Journal, 22,* 309–335. Copyright 1985 by the American Educational Research Association. Adapted by permission of the publisher.

The unit of analysis for each correlation coefficient in Table 11.1 is the class mean. In other words, the researchers used the mean score of the six girls who were observed in each teacher's classroom. Because 36 teachers were involved in the study, the sample size for the correlation coefficients shown in Table 11.1 is 36. Also, you should note that a particular type of correlation coefficient—a partial coefficient—is shown in Table 11.1. Partial coefficients are discussed in more detail later in the chapter. For now, it is sufficient to understand that each coefficient in the table represents the degree of relationship between each classroom activity or behavior and girls' math achievement in May after the influence of their math achievement in December or January was removed statistically. In other words, the partial correlation coefficient takes into account the fact that some classes of girls were higher-achieving and others were lower-achieving at the start of the year. The scores used to measure the girls' achievement, then, are not their actual end-of-year achievement scores. They are a measure of the gain that the girls made in achievement in the interval from the first testing to the second testing.

Inspection of Table 11.1 reveals that most of the statistically significant correlation coefficients are negative rather than positive. Thus the study provided more information about classroom activities and behaviors that apparently depress girls' learning than it did about activities and behaviors that might facilitate girls' learning of math. For example, we find that girls do less well in classes in which teachers provide more opportunities for socializing (social activity is expected by teacher: $r = -.30$ and $-.43$ with low-level and high-level math achievement, respectively) or permit discussion of personal and social topics (nonengaged in math activity because of social activity: $r = -.37$ and $-.34$ with low-level and high-level math achievement, respectively).

Problems of Interpretation

As we explained above, one advantage of correlational designs is that they permit the researcher to study the relationship between many variables simultaneously. However, this potential advantage can become a weakness if the researcher administers a very large number of measures to a sample of research participants in the hope that some of these measures will turn out to be related to the phenomenon being studied. In the **shotgun approach,** a large number of variables are measured and subjected to correlational analysis even when the researcher has no theoretical basis or even commonsensical rationale to justify their inclusion.

Although the shotgun approach of correlating many variables with each other sometimes yields significant findings, it should be avoided. First, research participants are inconvenienced and there often is considerable expense when a large number of measures is administered. Furthermore, some of the measures are likely to correlate with the criterion by chance. The only way to identify these chance findings is to repeat the study and determine which findings replicate. The only situation in which the shotgun approach might be justified is when research knowledge is required without regard to cost in an area where previous research is insufficient to form the basis for a more theory-based approach.

A total of 64 correlation coefficients are shown in Table 11.1. Although this is a large number of coefficients, the results generally form meaningful patterns, because the researchers were careful to base their selection of variables on previous research findings about effective classroom teaching. Had they not done so, the pattern of significant and nonsignificant relationships would be difficult to interpret.

As the number of computed correlation coefficients increases, the task of interpretation becomes more complex. In the published report of their study, Peterson and Fennema simplified the task of interpretation by emphasizing the statistically significant results. A complete interpretation also would include an attempt to explain the nonsignificant results as well. For example, the correlation between class time engaged in high-level math activities and high-level math achievement was rather low ($r = .17$), and there is almost no correlation between class time engaged in low-level math activities and low-level math achievement ($r = .01$). This is surprising because one would expect that the more time students spend engaged in class doing relevant work, the greater should be their math achievement. These anomalous findings are potentially important, and they should be given the same attention as the statistically significant results.

Limitations of Causal Relationship Studies

As we explained above, correlations obtained in a causal relationship study cannot establish cause-and-effect relationships between the variables that are correlated. For example, the significant r of $-.40$ for the variable labeled "Competitive" in Table 11.1 suggests that teacher emphasis on competitive learning activities causes students to learn math facts and skills less well. It may be, however, that another teacher characteristic, such as authoritarianism, causes certain teachers to emphasize competitive activities and other activities that depress girls' math achievement. In this case, teacher authoritarianism, rather than competitive activities, would be the cause of students' low level of math achievement.

Many researchers have criticized causal relationship studies because this type of study breaks down complex abilities and behavior patterns into simpler components. Although this atomistic approach is appropriate for many research areas in education and psychology, there is some question whether a complex ability, such as artistic ability, retains its meaning if broken down into its elements. There are many people who seem to possess all or most of the specific skills that appear related to artistic ability and yet are unable to produce creative art. In contrast, many of the recognized masters in the creative arts have been notably deficient in some specific skill related to their medium of expression and yet have produced masterpieces.

Another problem with using correlational statistics to identify variables that may be causally related to complex behavior patterns or abilities is that success in many of the complex activities that interest us probably can be achieved in different ways. For example, a study that attempts to find variables that correlate with success in being a principal might fail because of the lack of any set of characteristics common to all successful principals. In one subgroup of administrators, for example, a domineering personality might be significantly correlated with success, whereas in another subgroup of administrators, who employ different administrative techniques, this characteristic might be negatively correlated with success. We know so little about certain behavior patterns—and many are so highly complex—that only the most careful interpretation of correlational data can provide us with an understanding of the phenomenon being studied.

Planning a Prediction Study

Types of Prediction Studies

Educational researchers do many prediction studies, usually with the aim of identifying variables that forecast academic, vocational, and personal success. **Prediction studies** provide three types of information: (1) the extent to which a criterion behavior pattern can be predicted, (2) data for developing a theory about the determinants of the criterion behavior pattern, and (3) evidence about the predictive validity of the test or tests that were correlated with the criterion behavior pattern.

✦ *Touchstone in Research*

Schmidt, F., & Hunter, J. (1998). The validity and utility of selection methods in personnel psychology: Practical and theoretical implications of 85 years of research findings. *Psychological Bulletin, 124,* 262–274.

Prediction studies can be differentiated in terms of which of these types of information the researcher is most interested in obtaining. In some studies the emphasis is on a particular criterion (e.g., first-year college grades), and various measures are used to predict this criterion. Those measures that are good predictors can then be applied to practical problems, such as selection of students for college admission. In other studies a similar research design is followed, but the researcher's primary concern is the theoretical significance of the findings. Finally, a researcher can carry out prediction studies for the purpose of test development. The emphasis is on writing test items and determining the test's predictive validity for one or more criteria (see Chapter 7).

Prediction research has made a major contribution to educational practice. Many of these studies have aimed at short-term prediction of the student's performance in a specific course of study, and others have aimed at long-term prediction of general academic success. The findings of these studies have been a great aid to school personnel in identifying the students most likely to succeed in a particular academic environment or course of study. Also, prediction studies provide a scientific basis for efforts to help students plan their academic future. For example, counselors can administer vocational interest tests that have proved effective in predicting success in an occupation and interpret the results to help students select the courses that are most appropriate for their long-term educational and career goals.

Prediction research also can be done to reduce the cost of training new personnel in complex vocational skills. For example, prediction tests used by the U.S. Air Force for pilot training help to eliminate individuals who would fail during the training program. The training is extremely costly, and the cost of training the unsuccessful candidate up to the point of failure must be added to the per-person cost of training successful candidates. A selection process that reduces the number of failures is of great value. Prediction research is done to determine which criteria to incorporate in the selection process.

Basic Research Design

Prediction studies are similar to causal relationship studies in that both involve computing correlations between a complex behavior pattern (the criterion) and variables thought to be related to the criterion. However, in prediction studies the other variables (sometimes called *predictor variables*) are measured some time before the criterion behavior occurs. In contrast, in causal relationship studies the criterion behavior and other variables need not be measured in a particular order, and in practice they often are measured at the same point in time. Also, prediction studies tend to be more concerned with maximizing the correlation between the predictor variables and the criterion, whereas causal relationship studies seek to describe the extent of a relationship, be it high, moderate, or low. As we shall see later in the chapter, correlations obtained in prediction research sometimes can be increased by the use of multiple correlation or moderator analysis.

The Problem

One type of prediction research involves testing the predictive validity of a particular test. An example of this type of research is a prediction study by Richard Butler and Clark McCauley.[5] The purpose of their study was to determine the validity of the SAT and high school class rank in predicting the grade point average (GPA) of students at the U.S. Military Academy. They were especially interested in determining whether the SAT and high

---

5. Butler, R. P., & McCauley, C. (1987). Extraordinary stability and ordinary predictability of academic success at the United States Military Academy. *Journal of Educational Psychology, 79,* 83–86.

school class rank predicted the students' first-year, second-year, third-year, and fourth-year GPA at the Academy equally well.

An important aspect of prediction studies is the proper definition of the criterion. Many studies have failed to find predictive relationships because an inadequate criterion was specified. For example, GPA is sometimes used as a criterion, as in Butler and Mc-Cauley's study. GPA, however, includes a person's grades in various subjects, such as mathematics, Spanish, and history. Also, the kinds of courses that students take usually change as they progress from the freshman year to the senior year of college. Furthermore, some students select easier courses to take than do other students. These observations suggest that GPA is a shifting, amorphous criterion, and therefore it would be difficult to predict well.

To their credit, Butler and McCauley analyzed the educational program at the U.S. Military Academy to determine the possible influence of these factors on the criterion GPA scores. They found that differential course difficulty was not a factor because

> about half the core courses each year are science or mathematics courses . . . [and] different instructors teaching the same course use the same syllabus and the same examinations. It seems likely that the size and standardization of the core requirement may prevent less able cadets from seeking out easier courses or instructors.[6]

Moreover, the researchers used the two test scores yielded by the SAT (verbal and quantitative), rather than the total SAT score, as predictors of students' GPA. This was a sound decision because each test measure might predict different components of the GPA.

Selection of Research Participants

As we discussed in Chapter 6, it is important to draw research participants from the specific population most pertinent to your study. In the prediction study we have been considering, the researchers were specifically interested in predicting the GPA of students over the course of their four-year program at the U.S. Military Academy. Therefore, their sample consisted of two complete classes of graduates of the academy (1982 and 1983). They also included a sample of graduates of the U.S. Air Force Academy, an institution having a similar population of students and a similar academic program.

Data Collection

Self-report measures, standardized tests, questionnaires, interviews, or observational techniques can be used to measure both the predictor variables and the criterion in a prediction study. Of course, the predictor variables must be measured before the criterion behavior pattern occurs. Otherwise, one cannot claim that a particular test or other measure actually predicted the criterion. In Butler and McCauley's study, scores on the two predictor measures—SAT and high school class rank—were obtained during the students' senior year of high school. The GPAs were calculated during each of the subsequent four years that the students were in college.

Prediction of behavior that will occur in the near future generally is more accurate than prediction of behavior that will occur in the more distant future. This is because in short-term prediction, more of the determinants of the behavior being predicted are likely to be present. Furthermore, short-term prediction allows less time for important aspects of the criterion behavior to change or for important new determinants of the criterion behavior to emerge. For example, if we wish to predict the probable success of individuals in management positions, we probably would start with variables that have been found in

6. Ibid., p. 85.

previous research to be related to later success in management. Our test battery might include measures of such factors as verbal intelligence, social attitudes, emotional maturity, and so on. However, certain variables important to success could not possibly be measured, because they are not present at the time the prediction must be made. For example, a high school senior's ability to work well with superiors in the management hierarchy—a likely determinant of management success—cannot be measured, because the student's future superiors are unknown at the time of prediction.

Data Analysis

The primary method of data analysis in a prediction study is to correlate each predictor variable with the criterion. In the study we have been describing, SAT verbal scores, SAT quantitative scores, and high school class rank (the predictor variables) were each correlated with students' GPA for each year of college (the criterion variables). The correlation coefficients are shown in Table 11.2. Each of the predictor variables is effective in predicting students' GPA, but only moderately so. Students' rank in their high school class is a slightly better predictor overall. A similar pattern of prediction was found for the sample of U.S. Air Force Academy graduates.

The statistics shown in Table 11.2 sometimes are called *bivariate correlational statistics,* because each coefficient expresses the magnitude of relationship between two variables (hence *bi*-variate correlation). This type of statistic is discussed in the next section of the chapter.

Other statistical techniques can be applied to improve predictions from individuals' scores on the predictor variables. The primary technique to maximize prediction is multi-

---

TABLE 11.2

Correlations between Predictor Variables and Grade Point Averages of U.S. Military Academy Students

Year of Grade Point Average	SAT Verbal	SAT Quantitative	High School Rank
1982 Class			
Year 1	.30	.41	.47
Year 2	.30	.43	.51
Year 3	.30	.43	.51
Year 4	.30	.42	.51
1983 Class			
Year 1	.36	.35	.38
Year 2	.32	.40	.41
Year 3	.32	.39	.41
Year 4	.32	.39	.41

Note: All coefficients are statistically significant ($p < .05$, one-tailed). The grade point averages are noncumulative; that is, they are for just one year at a time. Rank in high school was adjusted for class size.

SAT = Scholastic Aptitude Test.

Source: Adapted from Table 2 on p. 84 in: Butler, R. P., & McCauley, C. (1987). Extraordinary stability and ordinary predictability of academic success at the United States Military Academy. *Journal of Educational Psychology, 79,* 83–86. Copyright 1987 by the American Psychological Association. Adapted with permission.

ple regression, which uses subjects' scores on two or more predictor variables to predict their performance on the criterion variables. (Multiple regression is discussed later in the chapter.) Using multiple regression or a related technique, Butler and McCauley were able to obtain correlation coefficients ranging from .59 to .63 for the class of 1982, and from .54 to .57 for the class of 1983.[7] These coefficients are greater than any of those shown in Table 11.2.

Moderator analysis, also discussed later in the chapter, is another procedure for improving the predictability of a criterion variable. This procedure involves identifying a subgroup for whom the correlation between a criterion and a predictor variable is significantly greater than the correlation for the total sample from which the subgroup was formed.

Statistical Factors in Prediction Research

Group Prediction

The goal of many prediction studies is to develop measures with sufficient predictive validity to be useful in practical selection programs in education or industry. The effectiveness of a measure for selection purposes, however, is not determined solely by its predictive validity. Two other factors influence effectiveness in practical selection. The first factor is the **selection ratio.** This is the proportion of the available candidates who must be selected. A predictive measure gives better results when only the few candidates scoring highest will be chosen than when all but the few who score lowest must be chosen. In other words, as the proportion of candidates who must be chosen decreases, the predictive ability of a measure, or set of measures, increases.

The other factor influencing the effectiveness of a predictive measure is the **base rate,** that is, the percentage of candidates who would be successful if no selection procedure were applied. In educational selection, this might be the percentage of students who succeeded in a particular educational program prior to the use of selective admission. If the base rate percentage is high, the predictive measure will need to have very high validity in order to improve on the success of "natural" selection. For example, if 95 percent of the students typically pass a course, you would be correct 95 percent of the time if you predicted that everyone would pass. It would be difficult to develop a test that would improve on the accuracy of prediction. Predictive measures are most likely to be helpful if the base rate percentage is in the intermediate range, for example, in situations where 25 to 75 percent of the individuals meet the specified criterion.

The **Taylor-Russell Tables** combine three factors: predictive validity, selection ratio, and proportion successful without selection.[8] If these three factors are known, the researcher can predict the proportion of the candidates selected who will be successful when the predictive measure is used.

Shrinkage

In using correlations for prediction, the usual procedure is to select a test or battery of tests that we believe will predict the criterion behavior. These tests are then tried out on a sample in order to determine their actual predictive validity. The correlation between individuals' scores on the test and their later behavior provides an estimate of the predictive

7. While multiple regression is not mentioned by name in Butler and McCauley's report, it undoubtedly is the technique that was used to determine what they refer to as the "composite variable" of the predictor variables.
8. Taylor, H. C., & Russell, J. T. (1939). The relationships of validity coefficients to the practical effectiveness of tests in selection: Discussion and tables. *Journal of Applied Psychology, 23,* 565–578.

validity of the test. This correlation, however, almost certainly will become smaller if we repeat the study with a new sample.

Shrinkage is the tendency for predictive validities to decrease when the research study is repeated. More shrinkage is likely when the original sample is small, and when the number of predictor variables is large.

Shrinkage is due primarily to the fact that when we initially validate our measures, some of them will yield significant correlations by chance. In fact, we can demonstrate mathematically that if researchers keep adding predictor variables to a multiple regression equation, they eventually will be able to predict each person's score on the criterion measure perfectly. Upon repetition of the study, however, these same predictive relationships, which are based mainly on chance, are not likely to be present. Thus the correlations initially obtained will become smaller.

Because making predictions on the basis of correlations derived from scores for only one sample of individuals is of uncertain value, researchers should conduct a cross-validation of predictor variables before using them in practical prediction situations. Thus, after preliminary validation of a test or battery of tests, the predictive validity of each test should be cross-checked with another sample. Those correlations that have dropped to a nonsignificant level should be eliminated.

Bivariate Correlational Statistics

In this section we discuss 10 correlational techniques that can be used to analyze the degree of relationship between two variables. Because two variables are involved, these techniques are called *bivariate* correlational statistics. The form of the variables to be correlated and the nature of the relationship determine which technique is used. Variables in relationship studies are usually expressed in one of five forms, which were described in Chapter 5: continuous score, rank, artificial dichotomy, true dichotomy, and category. Table 11.3 lists 10 bivariate correlational techniques and the conditions under which each is used. We discuss two of them below to illustrate the point that each of these correlational techniques serves a different purpose.

Product-Moment Correlation Coefficient

The **product-moment correlation coefficient** (r) is computed when both variables that we wish to correlate are expressed as continuous scores. (This correlation coefficient sometimes is called a *Pearson r*, because Karl Pearson developed it.) For example, if we administer an intelligence test such as the Wechsler Intelligence Scale for Children and an achievement test such as the Stanford Achievement Test to the same group of students, we will have two sets of continuous scores. The product-moment correlation coefficient r would be the appropriate correlational statistic for determining the magnitude of relationship between students' scores on the two measures.

Product-moment correlation is the most widely used bivariate correlational technique because most educational measures yield continuous scores and because r has a small standard error. In fact, r can be calculated for any two sets of scores, even if one or both measures do not yield scores in continuous form. Researchers frequently compute a correlation matrix in which subjects' scores on a large number of variables are correlated with each other. (The correlation matrix is discussed later in the chapter.) All the correlation coefficients in the matrix usually are product-moment rs, even if the measures yield different types of scores.

TABLE 11.3

Bivariate Correlational Techniques for Different Forms of Variables

Technique	Symbol	Variable 1	Variable 2	Remarks
Product-moment correlation	r	Continuous	Continuous	The most stable technique, i.e., smallest standard error
Rank-difference correlation *(rho)*	ρ	Ranks	Ranks	A special form of product-moment correlation
Kendall's *tau*	τ	Ranks	Ranks	Preferable to *rho* for numbers under 10
Biserial correlation	r_{bis}	Artificial dichotomy	Continuous	Values can exceed 1; has a larger standard error than *r;* commonly used in item analysis
Widespread biserial correlation	r_{wbis}	Widespread artificial dichotomy	Continuous	Used when the researcher is interested in persons at the extremes on the dichotomized variable
Point-biserial correlation	r_{pbis}	True dichotomy	Continuous	Yields a lower correlation than r_{bis}
Tetrachoric correlation	r_t	Artificial dichotomy	Artificial dichotomy	Used when both variables can be split at critical points
Phi coefficient	ϕ	True dichotomy	True dichotomy	Used in calculating inter-item correlations
Contingency coefficient	C	Two or more categories	Two or more categories	Comparable to r_t under certain conditions; closely related to chi-square
Correlation ratio, *eta*	η	Continuous	Continuous	Used to detect nonlinear relationships

Correlation Ratio

In correlational research the usual assumption is that the prediction or relationship being studied is linear. In other words, we assume that a straight line (the line of best fit) best describes the relationship between the two variables. Sometimes, however, the relationship is nonlinear, as in the scattergram shown in Figure 11.2. In this example a curved line rather than a straight line best describes the relationship between the two variables, and therefore leads to better predictions from scores on the x-axis to scores on the y-axis.

Sometimes nonlinear relationships are discovered in correlational studies only after scattergrams have been plotted, but occasionally they are hypothesized to describe the relationship between two variables. For example, some researchers have hypothesized a *curvilinear* relationship between anxiety and intellectual performance. The rationale for this hypothesis is that persons low in anxiety will not be motivated to do well on a performance task and thus will earn low scores. Persons with a moderate amount of anxiety will be motivated by their anxiety to perform well, and because their anxiety is moderate,

FIGURE 11.2

Scattergram Representing a Nonlinear Correlation between Two Variables

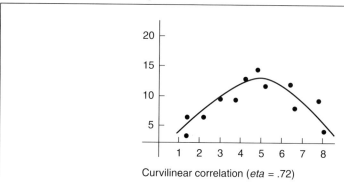

Curvilinear correlation (*eta* = .72)

*The product-moment correlation for the same data would be about −.29.

it will not disrupt their performance. Therefore, they should earn higher scores than the nonanxious group. By the same reasoning, highly anxious persons should be even more motivated to perform well. If high motivation were the only factor operating, highly anxious persons should earn the highest scores, and the relationship between anxiety and performance would be linear. However, it has been hypothesized that highly anxious persons, though well motivated, are disrupted by their anxiety and thus will earn low performance scores. Consequently, the hypothesized relationship between anxiety and performance is curvilinear, with high- and low-anxiety groups hypothesized to have low performance scores and the middle-anxiety group hypothesized to have high performance scores.

If the scattergrams for research data indicate that the relationship between two variables is markedly nonlinear, the researcher should compute the **correlation ratio** (*eta*). The advantage of the correlation ratio is that it provides a more accurate index of the relationship between two variables than other correlational statistics when the relationship is markedly nonlinear. Other types of correlation coefficients generally underestimate the degree of relationship when nonlinearity exists. A special statistical test can be used to determine whether the *eta* statistic yields a coefficient that is of significantly greater magnitude than the coefficient yielded by a linear correlational statistic.

An alternative to *eta,* especially when several predictor variables are involved, is the technique of multiple regression, which is discussed later in the chapter. This technique can be used to test for nonlinear relationships between variables.[9]

In addition to revealing nonlinear relationships, scattergrams are useful for detecting outliers in research data. (Outliers are discussed in Chapter 5.) The points in the scattergrams in Figures 11.2 are generally clustered near each other. If one of the points was quite far away from the other points in the scattergram, we would have reason to suspect that the research participant represented by that point was an outlier.

9. The use of multiple regression to test for nonlinear relationships is illustrated in Melican, G. J., & Feldt, L. S. (1980). An empirical study of the Zajonc-Markus hypothesis for achievement test score declines. *American Educational Research Journal, 17,* 5–19.

Adjustments to Correlation Coefficients

The degree of relationship between two variables is most often analyzed using the correlation coefficients described above. In some educational research, however, special circumstances require an "adjustment" of these coefficients. We describe three types of adjustment below.

Correction for Attenuation

When we correlate scores on two measures, the obtained correlation coefficient is lower than the true correlation to the extent that the measures are not perfectly reliable. This lowering of the correlation coefficient due to unreliability of the measures is called *attenuation*. **Correction for attenuation** provides an estimate of what the correlation between the variables would be if the measures had perfect reliability.

Correction for attenuation is not usually applied in prediction studies because we must make predictions on the basis of the measures we have, and the reliability of these measures, even if it is low, must be accepted as a limitation. This correction is sometimes used in exploratory studies, however. These studies often must use crude measures of low reliability, thus lowering the obtained correlation coefficient. The correction for attenuation helps the researcher determine what the relationship between two variables might be if perfect measures of the variables were available.

Correction for Restriction in Range

The **correction for restriction in range** is applied to correlation coefficients when the researcher knows that the range of scores for a sample is restricted on one or both of the variables being correlated. Restriction in range leads to a lowering of the correlation coefficient.

The use of this technique is illustrated in a study by Emily Krohn, Robert Lamp, and Cynthia Phelps.[10] They validated a test of cognitive abilities, the Kaufman Assessment Battery for Children (K-ABC), by correlating children's scores on its various subtests with their scores on a well-established intelligence test, the Stanford-Binet Intelligence Scale (SB). The sample of children was a group of black preschoolers enrolled in a Head Start program.

The standard deviations of the K-ABC and SB for norming groups are 15 and 16, respectively. The standard deviations for the researchers' sample, however, were substantially lower. For example, the sample's standard deviation on the SB was 9.4, which indicates a restricted range of scores relative to the norming group. Therefore, the researchers calculated both the regular correlations (r) between students' K-ABC subtest scores and SB total score and the same correlations ($r[cf16]c$) corrected for restriction in range. Each corrected coefficient was found to be larger than the corresponding r. For example, the r between the Stanford-Binet and the nonverbal subtest of the K-ABC was .41, whereas the $r[cf16]c$ was .69.

Use of the correction for restriction in range requires the assumption that the two variables are related to each other linearly throughout their entire range. If the relationship for the total range of scores is nonlinear, the correction for restriction in range is not applicable.

Part and Partial Correlation

Partial correlation is sometimes employed in causal–relationship and prediction studies to rule out the influence of one or more measured variables on the criterion in order to

✦ Touchstone in Research

Borack, J. I. (1994). Estimating predictive validity when range restriction due to selection and attrition is present. *Military Psychology, 63*, 193–204.

---

10. Krohn, E. J., Lamp, R. E., & Phelps, C. G. (1988). Validity of the K-ABC for a black preschool population. *Psychology in the Schools, 25*, 15–21.

clarify the role of other variables. Its use is illustrated in the relationship study of mathematics instruction by Peterson and Fennema that we described earlier in the chapter. Table 11.1 shows correlational analyses from that study. The coefficients shown in the table are partial correlation coefficients.

We can understand the researchers' use of partial correlation by considering the factors that influence girls' end-of-school-year math achievement. One influencing factor is undoubtedly the girls' math achievement earlier in the school year. Girls who did well in mathematics in December are likely to do better in May than girls who did not do well in mathematics in December. The influence of this factor is shown by arrow A in Figure 11.3. The teacher's instruction is also likely to influence girls' end-of-year achievement. This influence is represented in Figure 11.3 by arrow B.

The question arises, how much influence does each of these factors have on girls' end-of-year math achievement? The technique of partial correlation allows us to answer this question. It was used in the analysis reported earlier in Table 11.1 to show the extent of influence of instructional factors on their own (arrow B in Figure 11.3). Had the researchers wished, they also could have used partial correlation to determine how much beginning-of-the-year achievement level on its own influenced end-of-school-year achievement level (arrow A in Figure 11.3).

Analyzing the situation still further, we realize that girls' beginning-of-the-year math achievement can influence teachers' instruction (arrow C in Figure 11.3), as well as influencing their end-of-school-year math achievement directly (arrow A in Figure 11.3). For example, teachers who have higher-achieving girls in their classes might spend more time on mathematical problem-solving activities than teachers who have lower-achieving girls. The technique of partial correlation also eliminates this possible influence. Thus we can determine the influence of instructional factors on end-of-the-year math achievement (arrow B) independent of the influence of both beginning-of-the-year achievement on end-of-school-year achievement (arrow A) and beginning-of-school-year achievement on instructional factors (arrow C). If Peterson and Fennema had been interested in removing the influence of beginning-of-school-year achievement from just one of the variables (e.g.,

FIGURE 11.3

The Hypothesized Causal Patterns in the Study by Peterson and Fennema

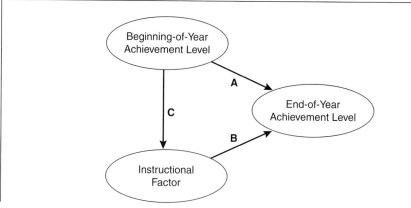

its influence on instructional factors), the statistical method of **part correlation** would be used instead of partial correlation. **Part correlation** is a statistic that expresses the degree of relationship between two variables, A and B, after the effect of a third variable, C, on either A or B (but not both) has been removed.

A complex causal pattern might well underlie the variables studied by Peterson and Fennema. Partial correlation simplifies the situation so that just one part of the pattern (in this study, arrow B in Figure 11.3) is analyzed. Other statistical techniques—path analysis and structural equation modeling—provide a way to examine the complete causal pattern that is hypothesized, with all its possible influences among variables. These techniques are described later in the chapter.

Multivariate Correlational Statistics

The correlational techniques presented above are used to measure the degree of relationship between two variables. However, many research problems in education involve interrelationships between three or more variables. The multivariate statistics that we present in the following sections allow researchers to measure and study the degree of relationship among various combinations of these variables. Table 11.4 presents a summary of these statistics.

Multivariate correlational statistics have many applications in educational research. Not only are they used to analyze correlational data, but they also are used with increasing frequency in analyzing experimental data. We discuss this latter use of multivariate

✦ *Touchstone in Research*

Cohen, J., & Cohen, P. (1983). *Applied multiple regression/correlation analysis for the behavioral sciences* (2nd ed.). Mahwah, NJ: Lawrence Erlbaum Associates.

Harris, R. J. (2001). *A primer of multivariate statistics* (3rd ed.). Mahwah, NJ: Lawrence Erlbaum Associates.

Pedhazur, E. J. (1997). *Multiple regression in behavioral research: Explanation and prediction*. Fort Worth, TX: Harcourt.

TABLE 11.4

Multivariate Correlational Statistics

Statistic	Use
Multiple regression	Used to determine the correlation (R) between a criterion variable and a combination of two or more predictor variables
Discriminant analysis	Used to determine the correlation between two or more predictor variables and a criterion variable involving categories
Canonical correlation	Used to predict a combination of several criterion variables from a combination of several predictor variables
Path analysis	Used to test theories about hypothesized causal links between variables that are correlated
Structural equation modeling	Used to test theories about hypothesized causal links between variables that are correlated; yields more valid and reliable measures of the variables to be analyzed than does path analysis
Factor analysis	Used to reduce a large number of variables to a few factors by combining variables that are moderately or highly correlated with one another
Differential analysis	Used to examine correlations between variables among homogeneous subgroups within a sample; can be used to identify moderator variables that improve a measure's predictive validity

Source: Adapted from Table 8.2 on p. 16 in: Gall, J. P., & Gall, M. D., Borg, W. R. (1999). *Applying educational research: A Practical guide* (4th ed.). New York: Addison Wesley Longman.

statistics in Chapters 12 and 13. Furthermore, multivariate correlational statistics can be used in place of, or in addition to, the statistical techniques that are traditionally used in causal-comparative research (see Chapter 10). Thus they need to be carefully studied by anyone considering conducting any of these types of quantitative research. If you plan to use multivariate correlational statistics in a research project, we advise you to consult an expert statistician to ensure that you select the most appropriate technique and apply it correctly.

Multiple Regression

Multiple regression is used to determine the correlation between a criterion variable and a combination of two or more predictor variables. It is one of the most widely used statistical techniques in educational research. The popularity of multiple regression stems from its versatility and the amount of information it yields about relationships among variables. It can be used to analyze data from any of the major quantitative research designs: causal-comparative, correlational, and experimental. It can handle interval, ordinal, or categorical data. And it provides estimates both of the magnitude and statistical significance of relationships between variables.

A Research Example

The use of multiple regression is illustrated in a causal relationship study conducted by Paula Jorde-Bloom and Martin Ford.[11] The purpose of their study was to identify factors that distinguish administrators of early childhood education programs who have adopted the use of microcomputers from administrators who have not. Jorde-Bloom and Ford observed that educational administrators are responsible for deciding which of the innovations that keep appearing in education should be considered for adoption, and for managing the change process after an adoption decision is made. Jorde-Bloom and Ford justified their study in this way:

> an awareness of some of the factors that help explain or predict innovation acceptance may broaden our understanding of how education professionals cope with a changing society.[12]

The researchers hypothesized that an administrator's decision to adopt computers would be influenced by four factors: (1) relevant past experiences, (2) expectancies about what would happen if one decided to adopt computers, (3) openness to change, and (4) presence of support and encouragement from outside the organization. Eight measures of these factors were administered to the sample. They are referred to as *influence variables* in Table 11.5.

The eight influence variables, organized under the four factors, are listed below. Next to each of these variables is a description of the procedure used to measure it.

Relevant Past Experiences
1. *Computer experience:* 31 questions about the administrator's experience with computer-related technology and microcomputers.
2. *Innovation experience:* 8 questions about experiences with other educational innovations.
3. *Math/science background:* Number of completed high school courses in math and science.

---

11. Jorde-Bloom, P., & Ford, M. (1988). Factors influencing early childhood administrators' decisions regarding the adoption of computer technology. *Journal of Educational Computing, 4,* 31–47.
12. Ibid., p. 32.

TABLE 11.5

Correlations between Influence Variables and Computer Implementation Variables

Influence Variables	Administrative Use r	Instructional Use r
Computer experience	.74***	.57***
Innovation experience	.19*	.14
Math/science background	.34***	.19*
Self-efficacy	.69***	.61 ***
Consequences of use	.66***	.50***
Innovativeness	.45***	.46***
Professional orientation	.60***	.55***
Outside support	.40***	.31**
Age	.02	.07
Gender	−.20*	−.42***

*$p < .05$
**$p < .01$
***$p < .001$

Source: Adapted from Table 2 on p. 42 in: Jorde-Bloom, P., & Ford, M. (1988). Factors influencing early childhood administrators' decisions regarding the adoption of computer technology. *Journal of Educational Computing Research, 4,* 31–47.

Expectancies

4. *Self-efficacy:* 15 questions about self-perceived ability and confidence to implement computer use.
5. *Consequences of use:* 21 questions about appreciation of computers, computer anxiety, and beliefs about the societal impact of computers.

Openness to Change and Presence of Support

6. *Innovativeness:* 31 questions about one's perceived tendency to innovate.
7. *Professional orientation:* 24 questions about various aspects of the administrator's role, complexity of the organization, on-the-job activities, outside activities, and highest degree obtained.
8. *Outside support:* 10 questions about the support for computer implementation that an administrator has received from spouse, friends, colleagues, or others.

The administrators' age and gender also were viewed as possible influences on the decision to adopt computers, and thus were included as influence variables.

A sample of 80 administrators of early childhood programs in the state of Illinois completed the measures described above. They also completed measures of two criterion variables: (1) level of computer implementation for administrative purposes, and (2) level of computer implementation for instructional uses. The measure of each criterion variable assessed how far they had proceeded along a continuum of implementation, from low to high: awareness, active information seeking, assessment, tentative adoption, and institutionalization. These two criterion variables, which are referred to as computer implementation variables in Table 11.5, are listed at the top of the first and second columns of the table. The intersection of each column and row shows the correlation between each influence variable and each computer implementation variable. For example, the correlation between amount of outside support and level of computer implementation for administrative use is .40, which is statistically significant at the .001 level.

The correlations shown in Table 11.5 form the basis for multiple regression. The purpose of multiple regression in this study is to determine which of the influence variables can be combined to form the best prediction of each criterion variable. In other words, the objective of multiple regression is to use the research participants' scores on some or all of the influence variables to predict their scores on each criterion variable. By contrast, each bivariate correlation coefficient shown in Table 11.5 represents the use of research participants' scores on one influence variable to predict each criterion variable.

A typical multiple regression will produce many statistics and equations. Only a few of them might appear in the published report of the study. The others can be calculated if appropriate statistics are provided by the authors of the report. We can explain this point further by examining the multiple regression results presented in Table 11.6.

The left side of Table 11.6 lists the variables in the multiple regression analysis. Note that two analyses were carried out, one for each criterion variable. In the first analysis, the criterion variable of level of computer implementation for administrative use was pre-

TABLE 11.6

Stepwise Multiple Regression of Influence Variables on Administrators' Level of Computer Implementation

Influence Variables	Beta	Correlation Coefficient (r)	Multiple Correlation (R)	R^2	R^2 Increment
Implementation for Administrative Use					
1. Computer experience	.40	.74	.74	.54	
2. Professional orientation	.30	.60	.81	.66	.12
3. Self-efficacy	.28	.69	.83	.70	.04
4. Math/science background	.20	.34	.86	.73	.03
Implementation for Instructional Use					
1. Self-efficacy	.26	.61	.61	.37	
2. Professional orientation	.28	.55	.69	.47	.10
3. Gender	−.20	−.42	.71	.50	.03
4. Computer experience	.25	.57	.73	.54	.04

Source: Adapted from Tables 3 and 4 on pp. 43–44 in: Jorde-Bloom, P., and Ford, M. (1988). Factors influencing early childhood administrators' decisions regarding the adoption of computer technology. *Journal of Educational Computing Research, 4,* 31–47.

dicted from four influence variables: computer experience, professional orientation, self-efficacy, and math/science background. In the second analysis, the criterion variable labeled level of computer implementation for instructional use was predicted from a similar set of influence variables, but they entered the multiple regression at different steps.

We begin our explanation of Table 11.6 by considering the second column. It presents the product-moment correlations between each influence variable and the pertinent criterion variable. These correlation coefficients are the same as those that appear in Table 11.5. For example, the correlation between self-efficacy and implementation for instructional use is .61 in Table 11.6. This is the same value as the coefficient shown in Table 11.5 (see the intersection of the fourth row of coefficients and the second column).

In our explanation of the other parts of Table 11.6, we will concentrate on the multiple regression analysis of the level of computer implementation for administrative use (the top set of rows). You can extend the analysis on your own to the multiple regression results for the level of computer implementation for instructional use.

Steps in a Multiple Regression Analysis

The first step in a multiple regression analysis usually is to compute the correlation between the best single predictor variable and the criterion variable. This procedure yields a multiple correlation coefficient (R), which is shown in the third column of Table 11.6. Because computer experience is the best predictor, it is the first predictor entered into the multiple regression. Note that the correlation coefficient ($r = .74$) is the same as the multiple correlation coefficient ($R = .74$).

Unless you specify otherwise, the computer program will start the multiple regression analysis with the most powerful predictor of the criterion variable. In some situations, however, you will want to enter a less powerful predictor first. For example, if the predictor variables can be ordered chronologically, you might want to start the multiple regression analysis by entering the earliest predictor first. Another situation occurs when one of the predictors is well established in the field of education and another predictor is novel. For example, suppose you have developed a new measure of scholastic aptitude and are testing its predictive validity relative to a standard IQ measure. It makes sense to enter IQ scores first in the multiple regression—irrespective of its correlation with the criterion—and then to see how well the new measure improves upon the prediction.

Suppose you have not specified the order in which the predictor variables are to be entered into the multiple regression analysis. In this case, after selecting the best predictor, the computer program will search for the next best predictor of the criterion variable. This second predictor is not chosen on the basis of its product-moment correlation (r) with the criterion. Rather, the second predictor is chosen on the basis of how well it improves upon the prediction achieved by the first variable.

What qualities should a variable have to be a good second predictor? First, it should correlate as little as possible with the first predictor variable. If it correlates substantially with the first variable entered in the multiple regression analysis, there is a possibility that it will explain the same variance in the criterion variable as the first variable. For example, suppose an IQ test and a verbal scholastic aptitude test are used to predict fifth-grade reading achievement. The two predictor variables are likely to correlate highly with each other because they measure the same underlying factor. If IQ scores are entered in the multiple regression first, the verbal aptitude test is unlikely to improve upon the prediction because it mostly explains the same variance in reading achievement as the IQ test. The situation is comparable to using the same IQ scores a second time to improve upon the prediction achieved by using them the first time.

The second quality of a good second predictor is obvious: It should correlate as highly as possible with the criterion variable. In short, a good second predictor is one that correlates as little as possible with the first predictor and as highly as possible with the criterion.

Table 11.6 indicates that professional orientation was the second variable entered in the multiple regression analysis to predict administrators' computer implementation for administrative use. The two predictor variables together (computer experience and professional orientation) yield a multiple correlation coefficient (R) of .81, which is shown in the row next to the predictor variable that was last entered into the multiple regression (in this case, professional orientation). This is a moderate improvement upon the prediction achieved by just using computer experience as a predictor ($R = .74$).

At this point you may ask why professional orientation does not improve the prediction more, given that professional orientation on its own correlates .60 with the criterion. Administrators' scores on the measures of computer experience and professional orientation undoubtedly are correlated (in fact, we learned by reading the original research report that the r for these two variables is .38). Because of this overlap in the variance explained by computer experience and professional orientation, professional orientation does not have a chance to improve dramatically upon the prediction made by computer experience, which entered the multiple regression analysis first.

The overlap between two predictor variables, that is, the extent to which they correlate with each other, is called **collinearity.** If the collinearity between the predictor variables is high, only some of the predictor variables will enter the multiple regression analysis as predictors, even though all of them might predict the criterion variable to some extent. Evidently this was the case in Jorde-Bloom and Ford's study. All the influence variables except age correlated significantly with the criterion variable, but only a few of them contributed to the multiple regression analysis.

The third predictor entered in the multiple regression analysis is determined by whether it improves upon the prediction made by the first two predictors. We see in Table 11.6 that self-efficacy slightly improves the multiple correlation coefficient for predicting computer implementation for administrative use, to .83.

The computer program will keep adding predictor variables until there are none left. Each new predictor variable will contribute less to R than the preceding predictor, however, in which case there are rapidly diminishing returns for adding new predictors. A test of statistical significance can be used to limit the number of predictor variables that are used. The researcher can specify in the computer program that new predictor variables are not to be added to the multiple regression analysis unless their contribution to R is statistically significant.

Multiple Correlation Coefficient

At this point we can consider further the meaning of R. The **multiple correlation coefficient** (R) is a measure of the magnitude of the relationship between a criterion variable and some combination of predictor variables. The value of R will increase with each variable that enters the multiple regression analysis. Thus, we see in the top portion of Table 11.6 that the value of R to predict administrative use gradually increases from .74 to .86 as each predictor variable is added. The value of .86 represents the best prediction one can make of level of computer implementation for administrative use from the influence variables listed in Table 11.5. The value of R can range from 0.00 to 1.00; negative values are not possible. The larger the R, the better the prediction of the criterion variable.

Coefficient of Determination

If R is squared, it will yield a statistic known as the **coefficient of determination** (R^2). The fourth column of Table 11.6 shows the R^2 coefficients corresponding to the Rs in the third column. For example, the topmost R^2 coefficient is .54, which is the square of the corresponding R coefficient (.74). R^2s expresses the amount of variance in the criterion variable that is explained by a predictor variable or combination of predictor variables.

The final column of Table 11.6 presents the R^2 increments for the multiple regression analysis. An R^2 increment is a statistic that expresses the additional variance in the criterion variable that can be explained by adding a new predictor variable to the multiple regression analysis. For example, the addition of professional orientation to the analysis explains 12 percent more of the variance in the criterion variable (.66 minus .54 = .12) than can be explained by computer experience alone. Adding self-efficacy to the analysis results in an R^2 increment of just 4 percent, meaning that it explains 4 percent more of the variance in level of computer implementation for administrative use than can be explained by computer experience and professional orientation together.

Two tests of statistical significance are commonly done in multiple regression analysis. One test is done to determine whether the obtained value of R is significantly different from zero. The other test, as we explained above, is done to determine whether the R^2 increment is statistically significant. For example, one could test whether the R^2 of .66 that is obtained by adding professional orientation to the multiple regression analysis is significantly different from the R^2 of .54 obtained without using this variable as a predictor.

The Mathematics of Multiple Regression

The mathematical basis for multiple regression is an equation that links the predictor variable(s) to the criterion variable. Suppose that level of computer implementation for administrative use = Y, computer experience = X_1, professional orientation = X_2, self-efficacy = X_3, and math/science background = X_4. Using C to stand for a constant term, we can state the multiple regression equation as:

$$\hat{Y} = b_1 + b_2 X_2 + b_3 X_3 + b_4 X_4 + C$$

Note that Y has a circumflex above it to indicate that the Y scores are being predicted from the X variables. The predicted values of Y will deviate from students' actual Y scores because X_1, X_2, X_3, and X_4 are not perfect predictors. Note, too, that this equation is similar to the equation for the line of best fit for scattergrams depicting bivariate correlation coefficients ($Y = bX + a$), which we presented earlier in the chapter.

Each b value in the multiple regression equation is a regression weight, which can vary from –1.00 to 1.00. A **regression weight** (sometimes called a b weight) is a multiplier term added to each predictor variable in a regression equation in order to maximize the predictive value of the variables. A separate regression weight is calculated for each predictor variable. When each research participant's scores on the predictor variables are multiplied by their respective regression weights and then summed, the result is the best possible prediction of the participant's score on the criterion variable.

Sometimes b weights are converted to beta (B) weights. **Beta weights** are the regression weights in a multiple regression equation in which all the variables in the equation are in standard score form. Some researchers prefer beta weights because they form an absolute scale. For example, a beta weight of + .40 is of greater magnitude than a beta weight of + .30 irrespective of the predictor variable with which it is associated. In contrast, the magnitude of a b weight is dependent upon the scale form of the predictor measure with which it is associated.

The magnitude of a predictor variable's beta weight should not be confused with its importance. A predictor variable can be theoretically significant and highly correlated with the criterion, yet have a low beta weight. The beta weight is arbitrary to an extent, because as we explained above, the significance of a predictor variable in a multiple regression equation depends on its correlation with other predictor variables that are entered first.

There are several variations of multiple regression analysis: stepup (also called "forward"), stepdown (also called "backward"), and stepwise. Each variation uses a different procedure for selecting a subset of predictor variables that yields the best prediction of a criterion variable. In **stepup multiple regression,** the predictor that leads to the largest increase in R is added to the current set until the addition no longer leads to a statistically significant increase. In **stepdown multiple regression,** all possible predictor variables are entered into the analysis first, and then, step by step, the variable that results in the smallest decrease in R is deleted until a statistically significant decrease occurs. In **stepwise multiple regression,** both the stepup and the stepdown procedures are combined: each time a new predictor variable is added to multiple regression analysis (the stepup method), the computer program doing the analysis checks whether a predictor variable that was included at an earlier step can now be deleted (the stepdown method) because it no longer contributes at a statistically significant level to the multiple regression equation. The title of Table 11.6 indicates that Jorde-Bloom and Ford used the stepwise procedure.

There is still another procedure for selecting a subset of predictor variables, out of all those that were measured, that yields the best prediction of a criterion variable. This procedure involves examining all possible subsets of predictor variables of a given size (e.g., all subsets of three variables in a ten-variable set) to select the subset that yields the best prediction, that is, the largest R^2. Under certain conditions, this procedure will yield a better prediction than the stepup, stepdown, or stepwise procedures.[13]

♦ Touchstone in Research

Huberty, C. J. (1994). *Applied discriminant analysis.* New York: Wiley.

Grimm, L. G., & Yarnold, P. R. (Eds.). (2000). *Reading and understanding more multivariate statistics.* Washington, DC: American Psychological Association. (See also the 1995 edition of this book, titled *Reading and Understanding Multivariate Statistics.*)

Types of Multiple Regression

Thus far, we have described the most common type of multiple-regression analysis, sometimes called *ordinary least-squares regression.* This type of regression analysis is used when the measure of the criterion variable is a continuous scale, the measures of the predictor variables are continuous or categorical scales, and the relationship between the predictor variables and the criterion variable is linear. Other types of multiple regression should be considered when different conditions apply:

1. **Canonical correlation.** Used when the researcher wishes to employ a combination of several predictor variables to predict a combination of several criterion variables.
2. **Discriminant analysis.** Used when the measure of the criterion variable is categorical, e.g., elementary-school teacher versus middle-school teacher versus high-school teacher, and the predictor measures yield continuous scores.
3. **Hierarchical linear regression.** Used when the researcher wishes to examine the relationship between predictor variables and a criterion variable at more than one unit of statistical analysis, e.g., the individual teacher versus a cluster of teachers within a school.[14]
4. **Logistic regression.** Used when the measure of the criterion variable is dichotomous; the predictor variables can be categorical or continuous.
5. **Nonlinear regression.** Used when there is reason to believe that the relationship between the predictor variables and the criterion variable is curvilinear.
6. **Poisson regression.** Used when the dependent variable is a frequency count.

---

13. Thompson, B. (1995). Stepwise regression and stepwise discriminant analysis need not apply here: A guidelines editorial. *Educational and Psychological Measurement, 55,* 525–534.
14. Units of statistical analysis are explained in Chapter 5.

7. **Time-series analysis.** Used when the data for a variable are arranged in chronological order and the researcher wishes to determine whether changes in the data are chance occurrences or the effect of some intervention.

The decision to use one type of multiple regression rather than another depends on the researcher's purpose for doing the analysis, the form of the data, and whether the assumptions required for its use are satisfied. For example, both discriminant analysis and logistic regression can be used when the measure of the categorical variable is dichotomous. However, discriminant analysis involves more restrictive assumptions. If you are considering multiple regression as a statistical tool for your study, you would be well advised to consult with an expert in this field.

Cautions In Using Multiple Regression

Multiple regression analysis is sometimes misused by researchers. One common problem is to confuse prediction with explanation. The procedures are relatively straightforward if the purpose is to optimize prediction of a criterion variable. You should be careful, however, if you have a theory that attributes causal significance to the predictor variables. In this situation, you should not confuse the causal significance of a predictor variable with its regression weight or R^2 increment value in a multiple regression equation. If you wish to test a causal theory by using multivariate correlational data, consider path analysis or structural equation modeling (both discussed later in the chapter) rather than multiple regression.

We also caution you to retain a reasonable balance between sample size and the number of predictor variables used. In the extreme case, where sample size equals the number of predictors, R will equal 1.00 (perfect prediction), even if none of the predictors is correlated with the criterion. The multiple regression equation resulting from this analysis almost certainly will yield very poor predictions for a new sample of research participants. A rough rule of thumb is to increase sample size by at least 15 subjects for each variable that will be included in the multiple regression analysis. Using this rule, you would select a sample of at least 45 individuals for a multiple regression analysis involving three predictor variables.

Path Analysis

Path analysis is a method for testing the validity of a theory about causal relationships between three or more variables that have been studied using a correlational research design. Path analysis differs from other multivariate correlational statistics, such as multiple regression, discriminant analysis, canonical correlation, and factor analysis, in that its purpose is to test theories about hypothesized causal links between variables. In contrast, the other multivariate methods that we discussed above are designed to maximize the correlation between various combinations of variables. Occasionally they are used to examine hypotheses about causal relationships between variables, but they are less powerful than path analysis for this purpose.

To illustrate path analysis, we will consider a study by Kathryn Wentzel to determine the causal effects of students' prosocial and antisocial classroom behavior on their academic achievement.[15] Wentzel wished to determine whether such classroom behavior has a direct effect on academic achievement, or if its relationship with achievement is due solely to its effects on teachers' preferences for students and/or on students' own academically oriented behavior.

15. Wentzel, K. R. (1993). Does being good make the grade? Social behavior and academic competence in middle school. *Journal of Educational Psychology, 85,* 357–364.

Steps in Path Analysis

Path analysis consists basically of three steps. The first step is to formulate hypotheses that causally link the variables of interest. Wentzel posed two alternate hypotheses as to how social behavior and academically oriented behavior might jointly contribute to academic performance:

> The first question addressed was whether prosocial and antisocial behavior were independent predictors of academic outcomes when academic behavior, teachers' preferences, and the background variables were taken into account. Next, I explored the possibility that social behavior was related to achievement indirectly by way of significant relations with academic behavior or teachers' preferences.[16]

After hypotheses are formulated, the next step in path analysis is to select or develop measures of the variables (sometimes called *theoretical constructs* in this context) that are specified by the hypotheses. This step is important, because path analysis will yield invalid results if the measures are not valid representations of the variables. In fact, you might want to identify more than one measure for each variable. Alternate measures of important educational variables often are available. (If alternate measures are administered, LISREL, a method described later in the chapter, can be used instead of path analysis.)

More than 400 sixth- and seventh-grade students and 11 teachers participated in Wentzel's study. Two measures of academic achievement were used as the criterion variables: GPA for the school year, and Basic Scale scores from the Stanford Test of Basic Skills (STBS). Predictor variables included the following student characteristics:

1. Prosocial behavior. Measured by asking students to nominate classmates on sharing/cooperating and helping other students when they have a problem. Each student received a composite score based on the average of the percentage of nominations that he or she received.
2. Antisocial behavior. Measured the same way as for prosocial behavior, except students nominated classmates on starting fights and breaking rules.
3. Academic behavior. An average composite score based on the teacher's rating on a five-point scale of the frequency with which each student (a) shows an interest in schoolwork, (b) works independently, and (c) shows concern with academic evaluation.
4. Preference status. Measured by having the teacher rate on a five-point scale the degree to which he would like to have each of the students in his class again next year.
5. IQ.
6. Family structure.
7. Gender.
8. Ethnicity.
9. Number of days absent from school.

The third step in path analysis is to compute statistics that show the strength of the relationship between each pair of variables that are causally linked in the hypotheses. Finally, you must interpret the statistics to determine whether they support or refute the theory.

Table 11.7 presents the correlation matrix of all the variables mentioned above. A **correlation matrix** is an arrangement of rows and columns that makes it easy to see how each measured variable in a set of such variables correlates with all the other variables in the set.

16. Ibid., p. 360.

TABLE 11.7

Intercorrelations among Measures of Students' Academic Achievement, Social Behavior, and Background Characteristics and Teachers' Preferences for Students

Variable	GPA	STBS Scores	Prosocial Behavior	Antisocial Behavior	Academic Behavior	Teacher Preference	IQ	Family Structure	Sex	Ethnicity	Days Absent
GPA	—										
STBS score	.71**	—									
Prosocial behavior	.54**	.38**	—								
Antisocial behavior	−.55**	−.35**	−.31**	—							
Academic behavior	.66**	.39**	.43**	−.49**	—						
Teacher preference	.51**	.30**	.30**	−.54**	.67**	—					
IQ	.61**	.83**	.30**	−.27**	.31**	.23**	—				
Family structure	.32**	.24**	.20**	−.24**	.16*	.12	.18**	—			
Sex	.17**	.09	.23**	−.11	.23**	.15*	−.03	−.01	—		
Ethnicity	−.23**	−.31**	−.16*	.26**	−.16**	−.17**	−.31**	−.23**	.05	—	
Days absent	−.38**	−.21**	−.24**	.20**	−.24**	−.23**	−.15*	−.16*	.04	−.02	—

Note: GPA = grade point average; STBS = Stanford Test of Basic Skills. Point-biserial correlations were computed for relationships involving family structure, sex, and ethnicity. For these analyses, intact families, girls, and minority status were represented by scores of 1, and single-parent families, boys, and majority status were represented by scores of 0.
*$p < .01$
**$p < .001$
Source: Adapted from Table 1 on p. 360 in: Wentzel, K. R. (1993). Does being good make the grade? Social behavior and academic competence in middle school. *Journal of Educational Psychology, 85,* 357–364. Copyright 1993 by the American Psychological Association. Reprinted with permission.

Note in Table 11.7 that each variable is listed in a separate row of the matrix. Also note that each variable also is listed in a separate column. The correlation between any two variables is given at the point where the row and column corresponding to the variables cross. Only half of a row-by-column matrix is necessary to show the correlation between all possible pairs of variables. That is why the space above the diagonal is blank. Also, the correlation between a variable and itself is not usually shown in a correlation matrix because the correlation is always perfect (i.e., 1.00). That is the reason for the dashes that run diagonally left to right in the matrix.

We see in Table 11.7 that both measures of student achievement (GPA and STBS score) are significantly and positively related to prosocial behavior, academically oriented behavior, and teacher preferences for students, and are significantly and negatively related to antisocial behavior. Both measures of achievement also are related significantly to the background variables in the expected directions, except that STBS scores are not related significantly to students' gender.

The fact that social behavior, academically oriented behavior, teacher preferences, and various background behaviors are significantly correlated with student achievement does not mean that any of these variables actually have a causal influence on student achievement. Also, the fact that most of the predictor variables are significantly correlated with each other does not mean that they are determinants of each other. For example, teacher preference correlates significantly with both prosocial ($r = .30$) and antisocial ($r = -.54$) behavior, but this does not mean necessarily that students' prosocial or antisocial behavior causes teachers to like or dislike them.

Partial correlation, which was described earlier in the chapter, could be used to illuminate the causal influences that might be operating to generate these correlations. Path analysis, however, is a more powerful method for this purpose.

Path Analysis Models

You will recall that Wentzel theorized that significant correlations between social behavior and academic outcomes could be explained in part by significant relationships between social behavior and students' own academic behavior, teachers' preferences for students, or both. The hypothesized causal connections between these variables and students' GPA are shown in Figure 11.4. This type of figure is the standard way of representing the contribution of path analysis variables to each other and to a specific outcome.

Note that each variable in the theory is represented in the figure. Also note the use of arrows to connect variables. Each straight arrow indicates a hypothesized causal relationship in the direction of the arrow; for example, prosocial behavior influences academic behavior, prosocial behavior influences GPA, and academic behavior influences GPA. The hypothesis can predict no correlation, a positive correlation, or a negative correlation between the two variables linked by the arrow.

Causal hypotheses are not necessary for all pairs of variables. For example, the lack of an arrow between prosocial behavior and antisocial behavior indicates that Wentzel did

FIGURE 11.4

Path Analysis Depicting Hypothesized Relationships between Prosocial and Social Behavior, Academic Behavior, Teachers' Preferences for Students and GPA

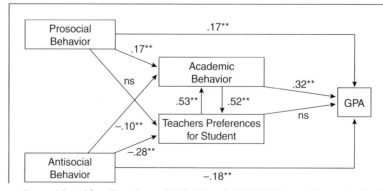

Source: Adapted from Figure 1 on p. 361 in: Wentzel, K. R. (1993). Does being good make the grade? Social behavior and academic competence in middle school. *Journal of Educational Psychology, 85,* 357–364. Copyright 1993 by the American Psychological Association. Adapted with permission.

not hypothesize a causal relation between them. In some path analysis diagrams, the lack of a hypothesis is indicated by a curved arrow between the two variables.

Several other features of the path analysis in Figure 11.4 also should be noted. You will observe that all the straight arrows point in one direction. For example, prosocial behavior is hypothesized to influence academic behavior, but academic behavior is not hypothesized to influence prosocial behavior. When a path analysis is ordered in this way, it is said to be based on a recursive model. A **recursive model** is one that considers only unidirectional causal relationships. If variable *A* is hypothesized to influence variable *B*, you cannot also hypothesize that variable *B* influences variable *A*. A **nonrecursive model** would be used instead if the researcher wished to test hypotheses involving reciprocal causation between pairs of variables.

Two types of variables commonly are distinguished in path analysis. **Exogenous variables** are variables that lack hypothesized causes in the path analysis model. Prosocial behavior and antisocial behavior are exogenous variables in Wentzel's study, because no variables are hypothesized to influence them. **Endogenous variables** are variables that have at least one hypothesized cause in the path analysis model. For example, teacher's preferences for students is an endogenous variable, because it is hypothesized to be influenced by students' social and antisocial behavior.

The Mathematics of Path Analysis

At this point in the path analysis, the exogenous and endogenous variables have been identified and measured, and the causal links specified by the researchers' theory have been identified by arrows. The next step is to perform a statistical analysis to determine the strength of association between each set of variables. The mathematical basis of the statistical procedures is complex. Basically the procedures are a form of multiple regression.

The statistical analysis yields a path coefficient for each pair of variables in the path analysis. A **path coefficient** is a standardized regression coefficient indicating the direct effect of one variable on another variable in the path analysis. Because path coefficients are standardized regression coefficients, they have the same meaning as the beta (β) coefficients calculated in multiple regression.

What does the numerical value of a path coefficient mean? The path coefficient can be viewed as a type of correlation coefficient. Like correlation coefficients, path coefficients can range in value from −1.00 to 1.00. The larger the value, the stronger the association between the two variables. The meaning of the path coefficient differs, however, depending on which two variables are being correlated. The path coefficient equals the product-moment coefficient when one variable (variable *A*) is viewed as dependent on a single cause (variable *B*) within the path analysis model. Another situation where β equals *r* is the case of a variable that is dependent on more than one cause within the path analysis but the causes are viewed as independent of each other.

None of the path coefficients in Figure 11.4 satisfies these requirements. In Wentzel's study, academic behavior, teachers' preferences for students, GPA and STBS scores all are hypothesized to have several causes, which in turn are hypothesized to influence each other. Thus, the path coefficients connecting each pair of variables in Figure 11.4 differ from the product-moment correlation coefficients for these pairs of variables shown in Table 11.7. For example, in Table 11.7 we see that antisocial behavior correlates -.55 with GPA, -.49 with academic behavior, and -.54 with teacher preference. However, in Figure 11.4 the path coefficients linking antisocial behavior with these variables are -.18 with GPA, -.10 with academic behavior, and -.28 with teacher preference. These path coefficients are similar to, but not identical to partial correlation coefficients in that they represent the strength of association between two variables with the effect of other pertinent variables partialed out.

You will note that the path coefficient linking antisocial behavior and GPA (-.18 in Figure 11.4) is considerably lower than the product-moment r for the same variables ($r = -.55$ in Table 11.7). This result means that antisocial behavior has some direct effect on GPA, but that part of its effect is indirect. The indirect effect means that part of the effect of antisocial behavior on GPA is due to its effect on academic behavior and teacher preference. The total indirect effect of a variable is equal to the r between it and the dependent variable minus the corresponding path coefficient. For the effect of antisocial behavior on GPA, the direct effect is -.18 and the indirect effect is -.37 (-.55 minus -.18). This analysis indicates that the indirect effect of antisocial behavior upon GPA (-.37) is substantially more potent than its direct effect (-.18).

Path Analysis and Theory Testing

The final step in path analysis is to determine whether the results support the theory. In the research study we have been considering, Wentzel concluded that her theory received some support, but that the results suggested the need for certain modifications in the theory. For example,

> In line with predictions, prosocial and antisocial behavior were . . . related to GPA, by way of their significant relations with academically oriented behavior. . . .Contrary to predictions, teachers' preferences for students did not explain significant relations between social behavior and academic outcomes.[17]

In the discussion section of her article, Wentzl attempts to explain these varied findings, and to pose suggestions for further research.

In summary, the major advantage of path analysis is that it enables the researcher to test causal theories using correlational data. Other multivariate techniques, such as multiple regression and canonical correlation, are not as well suited for this purpose. Path analysis, however, is a delicate technique that requires several conditions in order for it to yield meaningful results. The data need to satisfy certain assumptions, and the results can be misleading if the variables are not well measured, if important causal variables are left out of the theoretical model, or if the sample size is insufficient for the number of variables being considered.[18]

Factor Analysis

♦ **Touchstone in Research**

McDonald, R. P. (1985). *Factor analysis and related methods.* Mahwah, NJ: Lawrence Erlbaum Associates.

Factor analysis is one of the most frequently used techniques in multivariate research, because researchers often measure a large number of variables in a single research project. **Factor analysis** provides an empirical basis for reducing all these variables to a few factors by combining variables that are moderately or highly correlated with each other. Each set of variables that is combined forms a **factor,** which is a mathematical expression of the common element in the variables that are combined.

The use of factor analysis is illustrated by a study conducted by Robert Kottkamp, John Mulhern, and Wayne Hoy.[19] The purpose of the study was to develop an instrument to measure school climate at the secondary school level. Factor analysis was used twice in the

---

17. Ibid., p. 363.
18. Of these problems, underspecification of the causal model is probably the most serious. The problem is discussed in: Cook, T. D., & Campbell, D. T. (1979). *Quasi-experimentation: Design and analysis issues for field settings.* Chicago: Rand McNally.
19. Kottkamp, R. B., Mulhern, J. A., & Hoy, W. K. (1987). Secondary school climate: A revision of the OCDQ. *Educational Administration Quarterly, 23,* 31–48.

development of the instrument, called the Rutgers Organizational Climate Description Questionnaire for Secondary Schools (OCDQ-RS).

The first use of factor analysis was to identify commonalities in a large pool of items written to measure various aspects of school climate. Through the use of factor analysis and other techniques, the researchers eventually developed an instrument, the OCDQ-RS, consisting of five subscales to measure school climate. A sample of teachers rated each item for its frequency of occurrence. The labels for the subscales and a sample item in each one are identified below.

1. *Supportive principal behavior.* "The principal uses supportive criticism."
2. *Directive principal behavior.* "The principal rules with an iron fist."
3. *Engaged teacher behavior.* "Teachers spend time after school with students who have individual problems."
4. *Frustrated teacher behavior.* "Assigned nonteaching duties are excessive."
5. *Intimate teacher behavior.* "Teachers invite other faculty members to visit them at home."

The researchers' second use of factor analysis was to determine whether the five sub-scales of the OCDQ-RS could be grouped into a smaller number of factors. The first step in the factor analysis procedure is to compute a correlation matrix, which shows the correlation between every possible pair of variables to be analyzed. The correlation matrix for the five OCDQ-RS subscales is shown in Table 11.8.

Next, the researchers did a factor analysis to determine whether the five variables represented by the subscales could be described by a smaller number of factors. The factors identified by the analysis are shown in the last two columns of Table 11.8.

Factor Loadings and Factor Scores

The mathematics of factor analysis basically involves a search for clusters of variables that are all correlated with each other. The first cluster of variables that is identified is called the first factor; it represents the variables that are most intercorrelated. This factor

---

TABLE 11.8

Correlation Matrix and Factor Analysis of the Five Subtests of the Rutgers Organizational Climate Description Questionnaire for Secondary Schools

Subtest	Intercorrelations				Factors	
	2	3	4	5	1	2
1. Supportive principal behavior	−.09	.36**	−.30*	.05	.56	.28
2. Directive principal behavior		−.20	.41**	−.04	−.62	.27
3. Engaged teacher behavior			−.51**	.16	.73	.33
4. Frustrated teacher behavior				.00	−.85	.09
5. Intimate teacher behavior					.01	.89

$*p < .01$
$**p < .001$

Source: Adapted from Table 4 on p. 45 in: Kottkamp, R. B., Mulhern, J. A., & Hoy, W. K. (1987). Secondary school climate: A revision of the OCDQ. *Educational Administration Quarterly, 23*, 31–48.

is represented as a score, which is generated for each individual in the sample. Thus it is possible to compute a correlation coefficient between students' factor score and their score on a particular measure of a variable that was entered into the factor analysis. These coefficients are presented under the heading, Factor 1, in Table 11.8. The individual coefficients sometimes are called the **loading** of each variable on the factor.

Inspection of the Factor 1 loadings indicates that the first four subtests correlate moderately or highly with Factor 1. The researcher needs to interpret the pattern of correlations to determine the conceptual meaning of the underlying factor. In the case of this study, the researchers decided that the construct underlying Factor 1 was *openness*, which they defined as follows:

> openness refers to a school climate where both the teachers' and principal's behaviors are authentic, energetic, goal-directed, and supportive, and in which satisfaction is derived from both task-accomplishment and social need gratification.[20]

This interpretation of Factor 1 fits the observed correlations well. The subtest measures of supportive principal behavior and engaged teacher behavior both correlate positively with Factor 1 (.56 and .73, respectively); and the subtest measures of directive principal behavior and frustrated teacher behavior both correlate negatively with Factor 1 (-.62 and -.85, respectively).

Table 11.8 indicates that the subtest measure of intimate teacher behavior does not correlate with Factor 1 ($r = .01$). Instead, it is heavily loaded on the second factor ($r = .89$). The other subtests have low correlations with this second factor. Therefore, the researchers identified the construct underlying this factor as *intimacy*, which they defined as follows:

> Intimacy . . . reflects a strong and cohesive network of social relationships among the faculty. Teachers know each other well, have close personal friends among the faculty, and regularly socialize together. The friendly social interactions that are the essence of this construct are limited, however, to social needs; in fact, task accomplishment does not seem germane to this dimension.[21]

The two factors of openness and intimacy represent much of the information contained in the larger correlation matrix. Each factor can be treated as a variable, and each student can be given a score on it, called a **factor score.** The factor scores can be used in subsequent statistical analyses. For example, a *t* test can be done to determine whether public and private secondary schools differ significantly on each of the two factors of openness and intimacy.

Factor analysis is a valuable tool in educational research, but it needs to be used carefully. A frequent caution given to the novice researcher is *GIGO* (garbage in, garbage out), meaning that the factors generated by a factor analysis only are as useful and meaningful as the variables entered into the correlation matrix. Therefore, the researcher should carefully consider the number and types of variables that are to be entered into the factor analysis. If the variables have little or nothing in common conceptually, a factor analysis is inappropriate.

Types of Factor Analysis

✦ *Touchstone in Research*

Long, J. S. (1983). *Confirmatory factor analysis.* Thousand Oaks, CA: Sage.

Several variations of factor analysis are available. For example, a factor analysis can be done to yield an **orthogonal solution,** meaning that the resulting factors are uncorrelated with each other. An orthogonal solution is desirable if we seek a pure set of factors, with each measuring a construct that does not overlap with constructs measured by other fac-

20. Ibid., p. 46.
21. Ibid., p. 46.

tors. In certain situations, however, it is desirable to do a factor analysis with an **oblique solution,** meaning that factors can be derived that do correlate with each other. For example, a factor analysis of tests of intellectual ability might yield such factors as verbal ability, mathematical ability, logical reasoning ability, listening ability, and so on. These factors are likely to correlate with each other to some extent, because part of each factor measures an underlying construct of general intelligence.

Factor analyses can serve different purposes. An **exploratory factor analysis** is done to determine whether one or more constructs (the *factors* in factor analysis) underlie individuals' scores on a set of measures or on a set of items. For example, suppose you wrote 50 items to measure educators' attitudes toward inservice workshops. Your items might reflect different aspects of workshops (e.g., content, presenters, scheduling, practicality, instructional delivery). You are not sure, though, whether attitude toward workshops is a unitary construct (you either like workshops or don't) or whether it is multi-faceted.

You can do an exploratory factor analysis to find out which is the case. For example, you might discover that the attitude items reflect two underlying constructs: attitude toward the workshop format and attitude toward the workshop content. If this is true, you are likely to find educators who like the format of a workshop, but who don't like the content; other educators will dislike the format, but like the content. It is also possible to find that the items reflect more than two underlying constructs or perhaps just one general construct.

Confirmatory factor analysis involves the use of factor analysis to test whether the constructs posited by a theory actually exist and can be distinguished from each other. In other words, confirmatory factor analysis starts with constructs and ends with the confirmation or disconfirmation of their existence, whereas factor analysis starts with data and ends with the discovery of constructs.

Confirmatory factor analysis is illustrated in a study of leadership empowerment conducted by Lee Konzak, Damian Stelley, and Michael Trusty.[22] Based on previous research and theory about leadership, they hypothesized that an empowering leadership style has seven distinct components. (The components are the constructs, or in the language of factor analysis, the hypothesized factors.) The researchers developed items to measure each of the components: (1) delegation of authority; (2) holding staff accountable for outcomes; (3) encouragement of self-directed decision-making; (4) encouragement of self-directed problem solving; (5) sharing information with staff; (6) helping staff secure appropriate training; and (7) coaching for innovative performance. The results of a confirmatory factor analysis supported the existence of all but the problem-solving component. The researchers revised their test items and theory accordingly, and proceeded to conduct another study that tested other hypothesis derived from the theory.

Structural Equation Modeling

A sophisticated method for multivariate correlational analysis has become available in recent years. The method is similar to path analysis, in that it can be used to test theories of causal relationships between variables. It is more powerful than path analysis, however, because it yields more valid and reliable measures of the variables to be analyzed. Because the measures are more valid and reliable, the method provides a more powerful test of causal relationships specified by a theory. This statistical method is called **structural equation modeling.** It also is called **LISREL,** which is the name of the computer program that

◆ *Touchstone in Research*

Thompson, B. (2000). Ten commandments of structural equation modeling. In L. G. Grimm & P. R. Yarnold (Eds.), *Reading and understanding more multivariate statistics* (pp. 261–283). Washington, DC: American Psychological Association.

22. Konzak, L. J., Stelley, D. J., & Trusty, M. L. (2000). Defining and measuring empowering leadership behaviors: Development of an upward feedback instrument. *Educational and Psychological Measurement, 60,* 301–313.

was developed to run it. LISREL is an acronym for *Linear Structural Relationships.* The method has still another name, **latent variable causal modeling,** because it is used to test causal relationships specified by theoretical models, and because, as we shall see below, it involves the measurement of latent variables.

The essential elements of structural equation modeling are illustrated in a study by Suzanne King and Lee Wolfle.[23] The purpose of their study was to identify factors that contribute to the reputation of graduate school departments, as determined by ratings of quality in a national survey. The sample consisted of a large number of university departments of English, French, philosophy, geography, political science, and sociology.

King and Wolfle hypothesized that ratings of a department's quality would be influenced by three factors: size, quality of graduate students, and research productivity of faculty. This causal model is depicted in Figure 11.5. The model is similar to models used in path analysis (for example, see Figure 11.4). Each straight arrow leading to the right indicates a hypothesized causal relationship in the direction of the arrow. For example, department size is hypothesized to influence a department's reputation (labeled "Department Rating" in Figure 11.5). Also, as in path analysis, the curved, double-headed arrows indicate the absence of a hypothesis about how two variables are causally related to each other. For example, the researchers' causal model contained no hypothesis about how department size and graduate student quality would affect each other.

FIGURE 11.5

Latent Variable Causal Model of Factors Affecting Graduate Department Ratings

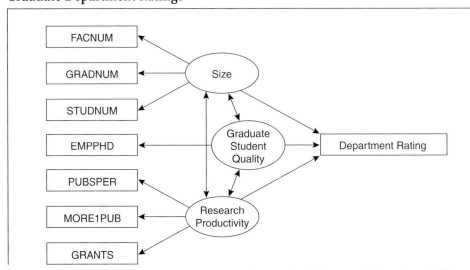

Source: Adapted from Figure 1 on p. 101 in King, S., & Wolfle, L. M. (1987). A latent-variable causal model of faculty reputational ratings. *Research in Higher Education, 27,* 99–105.

23. King, S., & Wolfle, L. M. (1987). A latent-variable causal model of faculty reputational ratings. *Research in Higher Education, 27,* 99–105.

The causal model shown in Figure 11.5 differs from a path analysis in its use of the boxes at the left of the figure. The variables shown in ellipses (size, graduate student quality, and research productivity) are viewed as **latent variables,** which are the theoretical constructs of interest in the model. The rectangles on the left are **manifest variables,** which are the variables that were actually measured by the researchers. Because educational measurement is imprecise, each latent variable ideally is measured by several instruments. The scores obtained from each instrument represent a manifest variable that is conceptually related to one of the latent variables.

We see in Figure 11.5 that the latent variable of department size is represented by three manifest variables: number of faculty members in the department in 1980 (FACNUM); number of graduates of the program between 1976 and 1980 (GRADNUM); and number of full- and part-time doctoral students in 1980 (STUDNUM). Only one manifest variable was used to measure the latent variable of graduate student quality: percentage of graduates who at the time of graduation had definite employment commitments with Ph.D.-granting institutions (EMPPHD). Finally, three manifest variables were used to measure the latent variable of research productivity: number of published articles attributed to faculty members divided by number of faculty in the department (PUBSPER), proportion of faculty with one or more published articles between 1978 and 1980 (MORElPUB), and percentage of faculty members holding research grants from specified agencies between fiscal years 1978 and 1980 (GRANTS).

A similar principle is used in the development of test items. Because a single item seldom is a perfect measure of a construct, researchers combine a variety of items, each of which measures a related aspect of the construct, to form a test. In tests the items usually are summed to yield a total score. In structural equation modeling, however, the measures of the manifest variables are factor analyzed to identify their common variance, that is, the factor that they share in common. Also, the factor analysis tests whether each manifest variable correlates at a sufficiently high level with the factor that will be used to represent the latent variable.

A subsequent step is to compute path coefficients for each arrow leading out from each latent variable. For example, in King and Wolfle's report path coefficients are reported for the ratings of geography departments as follows: .59 for size, .07 for graduate student quality, and .60 for research productivity. Because a larger path coefficient indicates a larger influence, we can conclude that a geography department's size and faculty research productivity have more influence on its reputation than does the quality of its graduate students.

In summary, structural equation modeling is a multivariate correlational method that is used to measure latent variables with maximal reliability and validity, and to test causal theories. It is a powerful method, but difficult to use. Moreover, it makes several assumptions about the data that are entered into the analysis.

Differential Analysis

Subgroup Analysis in Causal Relationship Studies

In Chapter 10, we stressed the importance of forming homogeneous groups when doing causal-comparative research. The same principle applies to causal relationship studies. The formation of subgroups that are more homogeneous than the total sample might reveal relationships between variables that are obscured when correlations are computed for the total sample.

The importance of this point is illustrated in the study by Peterson and Fennema described in the first part of the chapter. You will recall that the purpose of their study was to identify instructional practices that possibly facilitate or depress the math achievement (both low-level and high-level) of fourth-grade students. In Table 11.1 we presented the correlations between these two sets of variables for only the subgroup of girls in Peterson and Fennema's sample. The researchers also calculated correlation coefficients for the subgroup of boys in their sample. Table 11.9 presents the correlation coefficients for boys. The corresponding coefficients for girls (which are the same as those in Table 11.1) are also shown. To simplify our discussion, only the correlations for low-level math achievement are shown.

Inspection of Table 11.9 reveals the usefulness of analyzing data separately for subgroups. Some of the correlation coefficients are statistically significant for girls but not for boys (e.g., nonmath activity expected); some are significant for boys but not for girls (e.g., interim activity expected); and some are significant for both boys and girls (e.g., social activity expected).

Had the data not been analyzed separately by student gender, the researchers could have reached false conclusions about the possible effects of instructional practices. For example, they could have overgeneralized the effects of particular practices by concluding that they affect both male and female students equally. Moreover, a correlation coefficient that is significant for students of one gender is not always significant for the total sample. If the researchers had computed correlation coefficients only for the total sample, they might have concluded that an instructional practice has no effect when actually it does have an effect for a particular subgroup.

We see in Table 11.9 that no pair of correlation coefficients is identical. For example, the correlation between daily math expected and math achievement is .17 for girls, but it is .12 for boys. The question arises as to whether this difference in magnitude of correlation is a chance fluctuation or whether it represents a true difference in the population of girls and boys that this sample represents. The question can be answered by doing a t test of the statistical significance of the difference between two correlation coefficients. The last column of Table 11.9 indicates which of the differences between correlation coefficients yield a statistically significant t value. We find, for example, that the difference between the rs for the variable termed "Engaged in math activity, Competitive" is statistically significant. Competitive activities appear to have a moderately negative effect on girls' math achievement ($r = -.40$), but a slightly positive effect on boys' ($r = .13$).

The first step in differential analysis is to ask yourself whether the variables you are correlating with each other might be influenced by a particular factor such as gender, socioeconomic status, or cultural identity. Then select individuals in your sample who have this characteristic (or possess it to a high degree) and recompute the correlation for the two subgroups that result—that is, those having and those not having the characteristic in question (or possessing it to a high degree and possessing it to a low degree). If the resulting correlations are approximately the same, you can conclude that the characteristic in question has not contributed to your initial correlation. However, if the two correlations are significantly different, you will have gained new insight into the relationship you are studying.

Moderator Variables in Prediction Studies

Sometimes a test is more effective in predicting the behavior of certain subgroups than the behavior of other subgroups. In this situation we can use differential prediction, which is a form of differential analysis.

The use of differential prediction to improve a test's predictive validity is illustrated in a study by Moshe Zeidner.[24] The purpose of the study was to determine the validity of a

---

24. Zeidner, M. (1987). Age bias in the predictive validity of scholastic aptitude tests: Some Israeli data. *Educational and Psychological Measurement, 47,* 1037–1047.

TABLE 11.9

Partial Correlations between Boys' and Girls' Engaged Time Scores and End-of-Year Low-level Mathematics Achievement

Engaged Time Variables	r for Girls	r for Boys	t [a]
Type of activity expected by teacher			
Daily math	.17	.12	
Other math	.07	.08	
Nonmath	−.22	−.03	
Interim activity	−.10	−.23	
Social activity	−.30	−.38	
Setting of activity			
Total class	.06	.09	
Medium group	−.12	.13	
Small group—same sex	.18	−.10	
Small group—different sex	−.01	.02	
Two students—same sex	−.05	−.10	
Two students—different sex	−.03	.11	
Teacher—student	.03	−.53	.05
Alone	−.03	−.14	
Engaged in math activity	.19	.34	
Math—high level	.18	.06	
Math—low level	.01	.27	
Math—symbolic	−.01	.29	
Math—representational	.19	.03	
Helping	−.04	.17	
Being helped by student	.03	−.10	
Being helped by teacher	.01	−.35	.10
No helping	.18	.37	
Competitive	−.40	.13	.05
Cooperative	.25	.03	
Both competitive and cooperative	.25	.08	
Neither competitive nor cooperative	.27	.30	
Nonengaged in math activity	−.19	−.35	
Social	−.37	−.41	
Waiting for help	.09	−.15	
Academic (nonmath)	−.17	−.01	
Interim activities	−.04	−.05	
Off-task	−.09	−.34	

[a]One-tailed test

Source: Adapted from Table III on p. 319 in: Peterson, P. L., & Fennema, E. (1985). Effective teaching, student engagement in classroom activities, and sex-related differences in learning mathematics. *American Educational Research Journal, 22,* 309–335. Copyright 1985 by the American Educational Research Association. Adapted by permission of the publisher.

scholastic aptitude test for predicting the first-year GPA of students enrolled in an Israeli university. Zeidner expected the aptitude test to be less valid for older students than for younger students. In this instance, students' age is designated a **moderator variable** because it moderates the predictive validity of the test. In other words, Zeidner hypothesized that age would act as a moderator variable for the relationship between aptitude test performance and GPA. He offered the following rationale for this hypothesis:

> Older student candidates may differ from their younger (i.e., late adolescent or early young-adult) counterparts not only in age per se but also in a number of potentially important variables, associated with age or cohort, that might affect test performance. These include: quality of primary and secondary school experience, cultural and social experiences accumulated through the course of day-to-day living, occupational training, and so on. In addition, older examinees, who have long since graduated from high school, may differ from younger examinees on a host of other variables that may also bear on the level of test performance, such as the recency of their test taking experience, test wiseness, test attitudes, motivations and anxieties.[25]

The results of the correlational analysis are shown in Table 11.10. The correlations between aptitude test performance and GPA are positive and statistically significant for the three groups with ages between 18 and 29. The correlation coefficient for the 30 + age group, however, is negative and not statistically significant. Thus the results support Zeidner's hypothesis that aptitude tests have lower predictive validity for older applicants to college. Also, the coefficients for the four age groups range from -.08 to .41. Had Zeidner calculated the coefficient for the total sample (i.e., all four age groups combined), the resulting r probably would have been in the middle of this range. By using age as a moderator variable, he was able to find subgroups for whom the r was higher, notably, students between ages 18 and 21 and those between ages 26 and 29.

Interpretation of Correlation Coefficients

Statistical Significance of Correlation Coefficients

The statistical significance of a correlation coefficient usually indicates whether the obtained coefficient is different from zero at a given level of confidence. (A researcher also

---

TABLE 11.10

Correlations between Scholastic Aptitude Test Scores and Grade Point Average for Different Age Groups

Age Group	N	r
18–21	238	.30**
22–25	314	.21*
26–29	72	.41***
30+	121	−.08

$*p < .05$
$**p < .01$
$***p < .001$

Source: Adapted from Table 2 on p. 1043 in: Zeidner, M. (1987). Age bias in the predictive validity of scholastic aptitude tests: Some Israeli data. *Educational and Psychological Measurement 47*, 1037–1047.

---

25. Ibid., p. 1038.

could test whether the obtained coefficient is significantly different from some other value of r, for example, the value of r for a comparison sample.) If the coefficient is not significantly different from zero, the null hypothesis of no difference from zero cannot be rejected. If the coefficient is statistically significant, we can conclude that the relationship between the variables is nonzero. You should keep in mind, however, that the correlation between the variables for the *population* may be greater or less than the correlation coefficient obtained for the sample. If you wish, you can calculate confidence limits to estimate the range of coefficients within which the population coefficient is likely to fall. (Confidence limits are discussed in Chapter 5.)

Most statistics texts include a table from which the statistical significance of a product-moment correlation (r) can be determined. The level of statistical significance of a correlation coefficient is determined in large part by the size of the sample upon which the correlation is based. For example, if the sample includes 22 individuals, a product-moment coefficient of .54 is needed to be significant at the .01 level. If 100 individuals are available, however, a correlation of .25 is significant at the .01 level, and with 1,000 individuals a correlation of only .08 is significant at the .01 level.

Statistical significance also depends on whether a one-tailed or two-tailed test is performed. In a two-tailed test, the researcher determines whether the obtained coefficient (ignoring its sign) is either at the positive tail or the negative tail of the normal curve of coefficients that could occur by chance in samples drawn from a population in which $r = .00$. In a one-tailed test, only coefficients on one side of the normal curve distribution are considered, that is, the researcher predicts in advance either that the correlation, if significant, will be positive, or that it will be negative.

Causal relationship studies are aimed primarily at gaining a better understanding of the complex skills or behavior patterns being studied, and therefore low correlation coefficients are as meaningful as high coefficients. Prediction studies, however, are designed to forecast certain kinds of future behavior, and therefore require higher correlation coefficients than those usually found in causal relationship studies. In prediction studies, statistical significance is of little consequence because correlation coefficients usually must exceed the specified alpha level (typically, .05) to be of practical value. In other words, practical significance is more important than statistical significance.

Interpreting the Magnitude of Correlation Coefficients

Even correlation coefficients of a low magnitude can have practical significance. This principle is illustrated by a hypothetical situation described by N. L. Gage.[26] Suppose that one variable being investigated is a particular teaching technique. Each teacher in the sample is observed to determine whether he or she uses the technique. The outcome variable is student performance in the teacher's course. Each student is classified as having passed or failed the course. Suppose we obtain the results shown in Table 11.11.

The correlation between the two variables of teaching technique and student performance is only .20. (Note that .20 represents a phi coefficient because both variables are dichotomous.) Although the findings have practical significance, this is a low correlation coefficient. Yet, analysis of the effects of using the technique indicates that it leads to a 50 percent increase in the number of students who pass the course. Specifically, 60 percent of students whose teachers use the technique pass the course, whereas only 40 percent of students whose teachers do not use the technique pass the course. This is a 20 percentage-point difference, which clearly has practical significance.

26. Gage, N. L. (1985). *Hard gains in the soft sciences: The case of pedagogy.* Bloomington, IN: Phi Delta Kappa Center on Evaluation, Development, and Research.

TABLE 11.11

Results of a Hypothetical Study of the Relationship between Use of a Specific Teaching Technique and Student Performance

Outcome	Percentage Receiving New Treatment	Percentage Receiving Old Treatment
Good	60	40
Bad	40	60
Total	100	100

Note: Correlation (ϕ) = .20
Percent of Variance Explained = 4 percent
Source: Adapted from Table 1 on p. 12 in: Gage, N. L. (1985). Hard gains in the soft sciences: The case of pedagogy. Bloomington, IN: Phi Delta Kappa Center on Evaluation, Development, and Research.

You should realize that in this example the researcher's purpose was to examine relationships between variables, not to predict one variable from another. We cannot predict the particular students who passed the course and the particular students who failed it. We can examine the possible effect of the teaching technique on the entire group, however. The obtained phi coefficient of .20 tells us that if a teacher uses the technique, a higher percentage of students will pass the course, but not which students. If we wish to predict the particular students who will pass the course, the magnitude of the obtained coefficients must be much higher—generally at least .70. Correlation coefficients of this magnitude are virtually impossible to obtain from a single predictor variable, but they can be achieved by the use of multiple predictor variables that are combined through the technique of multiple regression.

Medical researchers have found that correlations even lower than .20 can have practical significance. For example, Robert Rosenthal cited a medical research study that found a positive relationship between the following two variables: (1) taking aspirin on a regular basis versus taking a placebo, and (2) experiencing versus not experiencing a heart attack.[27] The correlation coefficient for these two variables was only .03. However, this coefficient was considered of such practical importance that the experiment was ended prematurely. The researchers believed that it was unethical to withhold aspirin from the control group any longer. Rosenthal observed that many of the correlation coefficients obtained in the "softer, wilder" sciences such as educational pyschology actually are much larger than those obtained in supposedly more advanced fields such as medical research.

Another point to consider in interpreting the magnitude of correlation coefficients is that many factors influence the behavior patterns and personal characteristics of primary interest to educators. Therefore, the influence of any one factor is not likely to be large. Correlations in the range of .20 to .40 might be all that one should expect to find for many of the relationships between variables studied by educational researchers.

27. Rosenthal, R. (1990). How are we doing in soft psychology? *American Psychologist, 46,* 775–777. See also responses to Rosenthal's article in the October 1991 issue of *American Psychologist.*

✦ RECOMMENDATIONS FOR
Doing Correlational Research

1. Consider using a correlational research design if you wish to test predictions or explore causal relationships and an experimental design is not feasible.
2. Select a correlational statistic that is appropriate for the scale form of your variables.
3. Consider the possibility that the relationship between the variables in your study is nonlinear.
4. If you have calculated many correlational coefficients in analyzing data from a study, consider the possibility that some of the coefficients will be statistically significant by chance.
5. When doing a prediction study, consider including a cross-validation check to determine the extent of shrinkage in the initial set of correlation coefficients.
6. Consider the use of part or partial correlation to control for variables that provide alternative explanations of observed relationships between the variables of primary interest.
7. If you are exploring causal patterns involving a group of variables, consider path analysis or structural equation modeling as a method for designing the study and analyzing the data.
8. Consider the use of differential analysis to refine your search for predictor variables or causal patterns.
9. Consider not only the statistical significance of obtained correlation coefficients, but also their practical significance.

✔ SELF-CHECK TEST

Circle the correct answer to each of the following questions.
The answers are provided at the back of the book.

1. A perfect negative correlation is represented by a correlation coefficient of
   a. 0.00.
   b. 1.00.
   c. −1.00.
   d. −.50.
2. A major advantage of the correlational method is that it
   a. can be used to study causal relationships.
   b. allows simultaneous study of relationships between a large number of variables.
   c. provides a measure of both the degree and the direction of a causal relationship between two variables.
   d. all of the above.

3. In contrast to relationship studies, prediction studies are more concerned with
   a. testing hypotheses about cause-and-effect relationships.
   b. maximizing the correction for attenuation.
   c. maximizing the correlation of each variable with a criterion.
   d. identifying appropriate criterion measures.
4. If a researcher correlates many variables with each other in a prediction or relationship study, there is an increased risk of
   a. shrinkage.
   b. nonlinearity.
   c. unfavorable selection ratios.
   d. restriction of range in some variables.

5. The correlational statistic most appropriate when both variables are expressed as continuous scores is the
   a. phi coefficient.
   b. rank-difference correlation.
   c. biserial correlation.
   d. product-moment correlation.

6. The calculation of *eta* is useful for
   a. deciding whether to use partial correlation.
   b. deciding whether to do a factor analysis.
   c. correcting for restriction in range.
   d. studying nonlinear relationships between variables.

7. The lowering of a correlation coefficient between two sets of scores due to lack of reliability of the measures is called
   a. attenuation.
   b. restriction in range.
   c. regression.
   d. shrinkage.

8. The process used to rule out the influence of one or more variables upon the criterion behavior pattern is called
   a. multiple regression.
   b. partial correlation.
   c. correction for attenuation.
   d. analysis of variance.

9. The process of determining the maximum correlation between a single criterion variable and a combination of predictor variables is called
   a. canonical correlation.
   b. multiple regression.
   c. structural equation modeling.
   d. path analysis.

10. The purpose of canonical correlation is to determine the magnitude of the relationship between a set of predictor variables and
   a. a set of criterion variables.
   b. a set of exogenous variables.
   c. a set of moderator variables.
   d. the category membership of each individual in a sample.

11. A systematic representation of the correlations between all variables measured in a study is called a
   a. scattergram.
   b. correlation ratio.
   c. path analysis.
   d. correlation matrix.

12. The most powerful of the following correlational techniques for testing causal hypotheses is
   a. factor analysis.
   b. path analysis.
   c. discriminant analysis.
   d. moderator analysis.

13. In factor analysis the term *factor* refers to
   a. product-moment correlations.
   b. test scores.
   c. mathematical constructs.
   d. regression equations.

14. Structural equation modeling combines the use of
   a. path analysis and factor analysis.
   b. path analysis and discriminant analysis.
   c. canonical correlation and factor analysis.
   d. differential analysis and factor analysis.

15. If a set of tests predicts a criterion variable better for males than for females, gender is said to be a(n)
   a. predictor variable.
   b. latent variable.
   c. moderator variable.
   d. endogenous variable.

CHAPTER 12

✦ Experimental Research: Designs, Part 1

OVERVIEW

The experiment is the most powerful quantitative research method for establishing cause-and-effect relationships between two or more variables. To yield valid findings, experiments must be conducted in a rigorous manner. In this chapter, we describe validity criteria for experiments and other factors that must be considered in designing them. We also explain the most common experimental designs. Additional experimental designs are presented in the next chapter.

OBJECTIVES

After studying this chapter, you should be able to

1. Critically evaluate possible threats to the internal validity of an experiment.
2. Critically evaluate possible threats to the external validity of an experiment.
3. Describe procedures for increasing the generalizability of findings from experiments.
4. Explain how experimenter bias and treatment fidelity can affect the outcome of an experiment.
5. Describe obstacles to maintaining equivalent treatment groups in experiments and how these obstacles can be avoided or overcome.

6. Describe the commonly used experimental designs, including the procedures used in random assignment, formation of experimental and control groups, and pretesting and posttesting procedures.
7. State specific threats to the internal and external validity of common experimental designs.
8. Describe the statistical techniques that typically are used to analyze data yielded by experiments.

♦ *Touchstone in Research*

Maxwell, S. E., & Delaney, H. D. (2000). *Designing experiments and analyzing data: A model comparison perspective.* Mahwah, NJ: Lawrence Erlbaum Associates.

Phillips, D. C. (1981). Toward an evaluation of the experiment in educational contexts. *Educational Researcher, 10*(6), 13–20.

Introduction

Of the various quantitative research methods, experiments provide the most rigorous test of causal hypotheses. Although correlational and causal-comparative designs can suggest causal relationships between variables, experimentation is needed to determine whether the observed relationship is one of cause and effect.

An example of the correlational-experimental loop in research was described by Barak Rosenshine and Norma Furst.[1] They reviewed a set of studies about teaching methods that were conducted over several years at Canterbury University, New Zealand. In a correlational study, the researchers found a significant correlation ($r = .54$) between amount of student learning and the extent to which the teacher followed a student's answer by redirecting the question to another student for comment. In other words, teachers who made extensive use of redirection generally had higher-achieving classes than teachers who made little use of this technique.

This research finding suggests that training teachers in the technique of redirection will improve students' classroom performance. Rosenshine and Furst report, however, that the Canterbury researchers also conducted experiments in which they manipulated teachers' use of redirection. No differences in student learning were found between redirection-present and redirection-absent conditions. Thus, it would have been misleading to advise teachers to make greater use of the redirection technique simply on the basis of correlational evidence. Experiments might corroborate the correlational findings but, then again, they might not, as proved to be the case in the Canterbury research.

Many experiments done by educational researchers have the purpose of testing the effects of various practices (teaching techniques, organization of curriculum, content, instructional programs, etc.) on important outcomes such as student academic achievement and school climate. Therefore, experimental findings about the effectiveness of educational practices sometimes have an impact on the opinions and decisions of policy makers, educators, and other groups. All educational research should be carefully designed and executed, but this is especially true of experiments because of the influence they have on policy and practice.

Terminology in Experimental Design

Most experiments in education employ some form of the one-variable design. **One-variable experiments** involve the manipulation of a single treatment variable followed by observing the effects of this manipulation on one or more dependent variables.[2] The variable to be manipulated is referred to in this chapter as the **experimental treatment.** It also is called the *independent variable, experimental variable, treatment variable,* or *intervention.* The variable that is measured to determine the effects of the experimental treatment usually is referred to as the *posttest, dependent variable,* or *criterion variable.* In this chapter we use the term **posttest** to describe the measure of the variable that is the intended outcome of the experimental treatment. If a variable is measured before administering the experimental treatment, this measure is called a **pretest.** Many experiments in education involve one group that receives the experimental treatment and one comparison group that does not receive the experimental treatment or receives an alternative treatment. We use the term **control group** to refer to this comparison group.

---

1. Rosenshine B., & Furst, N. (1973). The use of direct observation to study teaching. In R. M. W. Travers (Ed.), *Second handbook of research on teaching* (pp. 122–183). Chicago: Rand McNally.
2. Experiments in which more than one treatment variable is manipulated are called *factorial experiments.* They are discussed in Chapter 13.

To understand how these terms are used, consider an experiment to determine the effect of a new reading program on students' reading achievement. The *experimental treatment* would be the introduction of the new reading program into the daily schedule of learning activities of a group of students. The *control group* would receive its regular reading program. The *pretest* would be the measurement of students' reading achievement before the new reading program had been introduced into the curriculum. The *posttest* would be the measurement of students' reading achievement after they had experienced the new program for a period of time.

Validity Problems in Experiments

The key problem in experimentation is establishing suitable controls so that any change in the posttest can be attributed only to the experimental treatment that was manipulated by the researcher. As we shall see in this chapter, many extraneous variables need to be controlled in order to allow an unequivocal interpretation of experimental data. Various experimental designs can be used depending upon the extraneous variables that you wish to *control,* that is, rule out as possible causes of changes on the posttest.

Although the experiment is a powerful research design, it is not perfect. Even the findings of a well-designed experiment are potentially refutable—a point made by Karl Popper, a philosopher of science:

> But what, then, are the sources of our knowledge? The answer, I think, is this: there are all kinds of sources of our knowledge but *none has authority.* . . . I do not, of course, deny that an experiment may also add to our knowledge, and in a most important manner. But it is not a source in any ultimate sense.[3]

As you read this and the next chapter, you will find that many factors can threaten the validity of an experiment. By controlling these factors, a researcher strengthens the power of an experiment to demonstrate a cause-and-effect relationship. As Popper observed, however, no single experiment provides an irrefutable demonstration of cause-and-effect, and therefore replications of experiments—especially ones that test alternative causal hypotheses—are desirable.

In the next sections we discuss the main factors that can weaken the power of an experiment. First we discuss potential sources of internal invalidity, that is, the extent to which variables other than the treatment variable provide plausible explanations of the experimental results. Then we discuss factors that affect external validity, that is, the extent to which the experimental findings can be generalized to other settings. Figure 12.1 summarizes the factors affecting both types of validity in order to guide your reading of these sections.

Internal Validity of Experiments

The most difficult task in doing an experiment is to hold constant or eliminate all extraneous variables that might affect the outcome measured by the posttest. If this task is accomplished, the researcher can attribute the observed outcomes (the effect) with a high level of confidence to the treatment variable (the hypothesized cause).

The experimental method was first developed in the physical sciences, where it has been most fruitful in the production of knowledge. The success of experiments in this field is due to the fact that physical matter is quite adaptable to study and control in a

---

3. Popper, K. (1968). *Conjectures and refutations.* New York: Harper Torchbooks. Quote appears on p. 24.

FIGURE 12.1

Factors Affecting the Internal and External Validity of Experiments

Internal Validity
1. History
2. Maturation
3. Testing
4. Instrumentation
5. Statistical regression
6. Differential selection
7. Experimental mortality
8. Selection-maturation interaction
9. Experimental treatment diffusion
10. Compensatory rivalry by the control group
11. Compensatory equalization of treatments
12. Resentful demoralization of the control group

External Validity
Population Validity
1. The extent to which one can generalize from the experimental sample to a defined population
2. The extent to which personological variables interact with treatment effects

Ecological Validity
1. Explicit description of the experimental treatment
2. Multiple-treatment interference
3. Hawthorne effect
4. Novelty and disruption effects
5. Experimenter effect
6. Pretest sensitization
7. Posttest sensitization
8. Interaction of history and treatment effects
9. Measurement of the dependent variable
10. Interaction of time of measurement and treatment effects

Source: Based on Campbell, D. T., & Stanley, J. C. (1963). *Experimental and quasi-experimental designs for research.* Chicago: Rand McNally; Cook, T. D., & Campbell, D. T. (1979). *Quasi-experimentation: Design and analysis issues for field settings.* Chicago: Rand McNally; and Bracht, G. H., & Glass, G. V (1968). The external validity of experiments. *American Educational Research Journal, 5,* 437–474.

laboratory. It is doubtful whether rigorous experimental control ever can be achieved in the behavioral and social sciences (e.g., psychology, sociology, economics), where human beings are the focus of experimentation.

Donald Campbell and Julian Stanley wrote a classic paper distinguishing between experimental designs in terms of their internal validity.[4] The **internal validity** of an experiment is the extent to which extraneous variables have been controlled by the researcher, so that any observed effect can be attributed solely to the treatment variable. An **extraneous variable** is any variable other than the treatment variable that, if not controlled, can affect the experimental outcome. If extraneous variables are not controlled, we cannot

4. Campbell, D. T., & Stanley, J. C. (1963). *Experimental and quasi-experimental designs for research.* Chicago: Rand McNally.

know whether observed changes in the experimental group are due to the experimental treatment or to some extraneous variable.

To demonstrate the importance of controlling for extraneous variables, we will consider an experiment conducted by William Kyle, Jr., Ronald Bonnstetter, and Thomas Gadsden, Jr.[5] As you will see, their study actually is a quasi-experiment, because it did not involve random assignment of research participants to the experimental and control group. However, the study provides a good example of the issues related to internal validity that typically arise in carrying out a field-based experiment in education.

The researchers examined the effects of introducing a new science curriculum into a school district. The curriculum, the well-known Science Curriculum Improvement Study (SCIS), emphasizes an inquiry-oriented, process approach to science. The district's standard curriculum emphasized reading a text, answering questions from it, and completing worksheets—all focused on developing low-level cognitive skills.

During the first year of implementation, SCIS was introduced into six of the 35 elementary schools in the district. At the end of the school year, the researchers administered measures of attitude toward science to teachers and students in these six schools. They also administered the same measures to a sample of teachers who had used the standard science curriculum that year but who would be teaching SCIS the following year.

Table 12.1 presents several results of the experiment. There are no significant differences in the percentage of SCIS and non-SCIS teachers who expressed a positive attitude

TABLE 12.1

Percentage of SCIS and Non-SCIS Participants Having Positive Perceptions of Their Science Class

Item	Students			Teachers		
	SCIS[a]	Non-SCIS	χ^2	SCIS	Non-SCIS	χ^2
Science is (was):						
fun	85	53	60.13**	30	35	.41
interesting	88	64	36.24**	45	51	.43
exciting	70	44	33.06**	25	22	1.44
boring	13	35	32.65**	41	38	1.05
Science makes me feel:						
successful	59	45	12.23*	36	32	.38
uncomfortable	11	24	14.30**	31	26	1.08
curious	76	56	21.65**	49	49	.18

[a]SCIS = Science Curriculum Improvement Study

*$p < .01$

**$p < .001$

Source: Adapted from Table 2 on p. 110 in: Kyle, W. C., Jr., Bonnstetter, R. J., & Gadsden, T., Jr. (1988). An implementation study: An analysis of elementary students' and teachers' attitudes toward science in process approach vs. traditional science classes. *Journal of Research in Science Teaching, 25*, 103–120. Copyright © 1988 John Wiley & Sons, Inc. Reprinted by permission of Wiley-Liss, Inc., a subsidiary of John Wiley & Sons, Inc.

5. Kyle, W. C., Jr., Bonnstetter, R. J., & Gadsden, T., Jr. (1988). An implementation study: An analysis of elementary students' and teachers' attitudes toward science in process approach vs. traditional science classes. *Journal of Research in Science Teaching, 25*, 103–120.

toward science on the various measures. By contrast, a significantly higher percentage of SCIS students expressed a positive attitude toward science on each of the measures. This is a potentially important finding. Can the researchers conclude that the more positive attitudes of SCIS students were caused by students' exposure to SCIS? Similarly, can they conclude that SCIS did not cause any change in teachers' attitudes toward science? The answers to these questions depend on how well the experiment controlled for extraneous variables.

Campbell and Stanley identified eight types of extraneous variables that can affect the results of experiments. Subsequently, Campbell and Thomas Cook expanded this list to include four more extraneous variables.[6] The resulting 12 extraneous variables are listed in Figure 12.1 and described below in relation to the science curriculum experiment that we are using as an example.

1. *History.* Experimental treatments extend over a period of time, providing opportunity for other events to occur besides the experimental treatment. The students in the experiment we are considering participated in SCIS or the standard science curriculum for an entire school year. Also, the two groups of students were in different schools. Perhaps the SCIS schools had an overall better learning environment than did the non-SCIS schools. As a result of exposure to this environment over the course of a school year, students in SCIS could have developed a more positive attitude toward all their school subjects, not just science. If this were true, the school's learning environment would have produced the attitude effect, not the SCIS curriculum. To avoid this problem in interpreting effects, the researchers need to ensure that the SCIS and non-SCIS schools are similar in all respects except their science curriculum.

2. *Maturation.* While the experimental treatment is in progress, physical or psychological changes in the research participants are likely to occur. For example, students might become stronger, more cognitively able, more self-confident, or more independent. In our example, suppose that students in both the SCIS and non-SCIS schools made good gains in the ability to think scientifically. We might be inclined to attribute this gain to exposure to a science curriculum. It also is possible that the research participants—elementary school students—made natural gains in cognitive development that allowed them to think more scientifically. (Piagetian theory, for example, predicts that this type of cognitive maturation occurs.) Thus, it is not clear whether the observed gains are due to the science curriculum or to maturation. To tease out the effects of maturation, it would be necessary to have a control group of children who received no exposure to a science curriculum (or out-of-school science instruction) over the course of a school year. If the SCIS and standard curriculum groups made larger gains on the outcome measure than this control group, it would be reasonable to conclude that the science curriculum—not maturation—led to the growth in the ability to think scientifically.

3. *Testing.* In most educational experiments a pretest is administered, followed by the experimental treatment, and then a posttest is administered. If the two tests are similar, students might show an improvement simply as an effect of their experience with the pretest. In other words, they have become "test-wise." In the science curriculum experiment, this extraneous variable is not a problem because no pretest was administered.

4. *Instrumentation.* A learning gain might be observed from pretest to posttest because the nature of the measuring instrument has changed. In experiments involving observational measurements, instrumentation effects are particularly likely. Observers who assess teachers or students before and after an experimental treatment might be disposed

6. Cook, T. D., & Campbell, D. T. (1979). *Quasi-experimentation: Design and analysis issues for field settings.* Chicago: Rand McNally.

to give more favorable ratings the second time, simply because they expect—consciously or subconsciously—a change to have occurred. Because no pretest was administered in the science curriculum experiment, the extraneous variable of instrumentation is not a threat to its internal validity.

5. *Statistical regression.* Whenever a test-retest procedure is used to assess change as an effect of the experimental treatment, there is the possibility that statistical regression accounts for observed gains in learning. **Statistical regression** is the tendency for research participants whose scores fall at either extreme on a measure to score nearer the mean when the variable is measured a second time.[7] For example, suppose we select a group of students who fall below the 15th percentile on a test of reading achievement. If the same students are tested again on the same or a similar test (i.e., one that is correlated with the first test), their mean score on the second test probably will be higher than on the first test with or without an intervening experimental treatment because of statistical regression. Conversely, if we select another group of students whose initial scores fall above the 85th percentile, these students are likely to earn a lower mean score when retested on a similar measure simply because of statistical regression.

To understand statistical regression, consider the fact that a student who earns a very low score on a test does so because of low ability and chance factors (e.g., unlucky guesses, circumstantial stress). When the test is given at a later time, the ability factor remains the same, but it is unlikely that these chance factors will work against him as much. Therefore, his score is likely to improve. The same reasoning applies to understanding why students who score very high initially are unlikely to score as well on the second administration.

No premeasures of attitude were administered in the science curriculum study, so it is not possible to determine whether teachers and students in the SCIS and non-SCIS schools had unusually positive or negative attitudes at the start of the experiment. Thus, we have no way of knowing whether differences in their expressed attitudes at the end of the school year reflect a differential statistical regression effect rather than, or in addition to, the effect of the SCIS curriculum.

6. *Differential selection.* In experimental designs in which a control group is used, the effect of the treatment sometimes is confounded by differential selection of research participants for the experimental and control groups. Confounding might have been a major problem in the science curriculum experiment. The researchers do not explicitly state that schools were randomly assigned to the SCIS and non-SCIS treatments. (Random assignment, as we discuss later in the chapter, is the best safeguard against differential selection.)

It is likely that the schools that implemented SCIS in the first year were chosen to do so because in fact they were different from other schools in the district. For example, suppose the SCIS schools were selected to implement this curriculum because their students were more academically able than were students at other schools. If this were true, the observed differences in science attitudes of the SCIS and non-SCIS groups at the end of the school year could be attributed to the fact that different types of students were selected for the two groups, rather than to the effects of the SCIS curriculum.

To continue this line of reasoning, the lack of a difference in science attitudes between SCIS and non-SCIS teachers at the end of the school year might indicate that similar teachers taught at the two groups of schools. In this case, differential selection of teachers would not affect the experimental results. However, because no pretest was administered in this experiment, we do not have information about possible differences between teachers or

---

7. A discussion of statistical regression can be found in Campbell and Stanley, Experimental and quasi-experimental designs, pp. 180–182. Also, see the discussion of gain scores in Chapter 13 of this text.

students in the experimental group and those in the control group that might have existed prior to the experiment. Thus we do not know whether differential selection, rather than SCIS, caused the observed differences between groups on the posttests.

7. *Experimental mortality.* Some research participants might be lost from the experimental or control group because they drop out of the study, miss pretesting or posttesting, or are absent during some sessions. The phenomenon of losing research participants during the course of an experiment is known as **experimental mortality,** or *attrition.* Attrition might result from such extraneous factors as illness, participants' resentment about being in what they perceive as the less desirable treatment condition, or their perception that the experiment is too demanding or threatening. Whatever the reason, attrition threatens an experiment's internal validity if it causes differential loss of participants across treatments. For example, suppose low-performing students feel less positively about SCIS and drop out of school in greater numbers during the year as a result. In this case, fewer of these students would complete the posttest measures of science attitudes, thereby artificially inflating the percentage of students with positive attitudes following the experiment.

You can minimize the problem of attrition by randomly assigning students to treatment groups and by making the treatments equally desirable. (A procedure for equating desirability of treatments is described later in the chapter.) Also, you should keep records for each treatment of participants' absenteeism or withdrawal from the experiment.[8] This information is not reported for the science curriculum experiment. The researchers stated that 92.3 percent of the total sample of teachers completed the questionnaires that provided the data for Table 12.1. They did not indicate, however, whether the respondents were distributed equally across the experimental and control treatments.

8. *Selection-maturation interaction.* This extraneous variable is similar to differential selection (see number 6 above), except that maturation is the specific confounding variable. Suppose, for example, that the science curriculum study had been done in two different school districts. Further suppose that because of a differential admissions policy, the average age of the experimental group is six months greater than that of the control group. In this case, any group differences in science attitudes can be attributed to the effects of students' ages rather than to the effects of the science curriculum that each group studied.

9. *Experimental treatment diffusion.* If the treatment condition is perceived as highly desirable relative to the control condition, members of the control group may seek access to the treatment condition. Experimental treatment diffusion is especially likely if the experimental and control participants are in close proximity to each other during the experiment. For example, suppose that some teachers in a school building (the treatment group) are assigned to use an innovative, attractive curriculum, whereas other teachers in the same building (the control group) are asked to continue using the standard curriculum. As the experiment progresses, some of the control-group teachers might discuss the new curriculum with treatment-group teachers, even if instructed not to do so. They might even borrow some of the materials and activities to use in their classrooms. Thus, over time the treatment "diffuses" to the control group.

If experimental treatment diffusion occurs, the effect of the experimental treatment on the posttest will be confounded. To avoid this problem, you should try to arrange conditions so that contact between experimental and control groups is minimized. After the

8. Procedures for analyzing research data to determine the presence of systematic bias in loss of participants from experimental and control groups are described in: Jurs, S. G., & Glass, G. V (1971). The effect of experimental mortality on the internal and external validity of the randomized comparative experiment. *Journal of Experimental Education, 40,* 62–66.

experiment is completed, interview some or all of the sample to determine whether experimental treatment diffusion has occurred in any form.

When we examine Table 12.1, we find that many teachers in both groups had negative attitudes and perceptions about their science classes at the end of the school year. For example, about 40 percent of the teachers in both groups stated that science was boring. What we do not know is the percentage of teachers who thought science was boring at the start of the school year. The percentage may have been even higher. If so, the introduction of SCIS reduced the percentage of teachers who found science instruction boring. If the percentage was reduced in the control group as well, this could indicate a treatment diffusion effect.

10. *Compensatory rivalry by the control group.* This extraneous variable is sometimes called the *John Henry effect.* **Compensatory rivalry** involves a situation in which control group participants perform beyond their usual level because they perceive that they are in competition with the experimental group. For example, Gary Saretsky found a marked increase in the mathematics achievement in control-group classrooms when they were compared with classrooms in which performance contracting had been introduced.[9] If this phenomenon occurs, the observed difference—or lack of difference—between the experimental treatment and control groups on the posttest can be attributed to the control group's unusual motivation rather than to treatment effects.

11. *Compensatory equalization of treatments.* This extraneous variable can occur if the experimental group receives a treatment that provides goods or services perceived as desirable. For example, administrators may attempt to compensate the control group by giving it similar goods and services. If any such actions affect the control group's posttest scores, they would obscure the effects of the experimental treatment. The researchers, instead of comparing the treatment with a no-treatment control condition, are comparing one treatment with another treatment.

Cook and Campbell observed that this problem almost certainly operated in experiments testing the effects of Follow Through and similar compensatory education programs.[10] The control schools usually were given Title I funds for their disadvantaged students in similar amounts to those given to Follow Through schools. Therefore, although the control schools did not have a Follow Through program, they had resources that could be used to purchase similar services for their disadvantaged students.

12. *Resentful demoralization of the control group.* A control group can become discouraged if it perceives that the experimental group is receiving a desirable treatment that is being withheld from it. As a result, its performance on the posttest would be lower than normal. In turn, the experimental treatment would appear to be better than it actually is, because the difference between the posttest scores of the experimental and control groups was artificially increased by the demoralization of the control group.

You will recall that in the science curriculum experiment we have been considering, the control group consisted of teachers who would be implementing SCIS the year following completion of the experiment. Therefore, it seems unlikely that any of the three extraneous variables just described—compensatory rivalry, compensatory equalization, and resentful demoralization—would have affected their teaching performance or attitudes during the course of the experiment.

In summary, we have seen how 12 extraneous variables can threaten the internal validity of an experiment. The science curriculum experiment did not control all these variables, primarily because teachers and students were not randomly assigned to the

9. Saretsky, G. (1972). The OEO P. C. experiment and the John Henry effect. *Phi Delta Kappan, 53,* 579–581.
10. Cook & Campbell, *Quasi-experimentation.*

experimental and control groups and because pretests were not administered. Therefore, the researchers probably drew too strong a conclusion when they stated that, "the nature of the science taught does affect student attitudes toward science."[11] The results are consistent with this conclusion, but they also are consistent with other interpretations involving the operation of extraneous variables.

In summary, the goal in designing an experiment is to create a set of conditions such that any observed changes can be attributed with a high degree of confidence to the experimental treatment rather than to extraneous variables. Random assignment and pretesting and posttesting are central to creating such conditions. Therefore, when you read this chapter and the next chapter, pay particular attention to the experimental designs that incorporate these features.

External Validity of Experiments

External validity is the extent to which the findings of an experiment can be applied to individuals and settings beyond those that were studied. The findings of an educational experiment may be externally valid for one setting, less externally valid for a different setting, and not externally valid at all for some other setting. For example, a researcher might test the effects of illustrations in children's books by taking first-grade children out of their classrooms in small groups, with each group receiving the same story but different types of illustrations. Perhaps the illustrations, although of acceptable quality, were not created by professional artists who specialize in children's books. Also, the students may have been tested immediately after reading the story, with no intervening discussion of the story. Despite these apparent flaws, the experiment is well controlled in that the same researcher administered all the treatments, used the same interpersonal style with each group, and maintained the same time limits for each of them.

This experiment has good internal validity, but the generalizability of its findings to real classroom conditions—that is, its external validity—is weak.

Glenn Bracht and Gene Glass identified twelve factors that affect an experiment's external validity.[12] The factors are listed in Figure 12.1 and discussed in the following sections.

Population Validity

Population validity concerns the extent to which the results of an experiment can be generalized from the sample that was studied to a specified, larger group. Bracht and Glass distinguished two types of population validity, which are described below.

1. *The extent to which one can generalize from the experimental sample to a defined population.* Suppose you are a teacher seeking to improve your students' reading comprehension. You want to know whether a reading curriculum presented in a hypertext format will lead to greater reading achievement gains than a conventional textbook presentation. You perform an experiment on a sample of 125 high school students randomly selected from your school. The experiment demonstrates that hypertext leads to greater achievement gains.

Although you might wish to generalize the findings to the population of "all" students, strictly speaking you can generalize only to the population from which the sample was drawn—namely, high school students in that particular school. Bracht and Glass define the

---

11. Kyle et al., An implementation study, p. 117.
12. Bracht, G. H., & Glass, G. V (1968). The external validity of experiments. *American Educational Research Journal,* 5, 437–474.

population from which the sample was drawn as the **experimentally accessible population.** The accessible population usually is "local," normally within driving distance of the experimenter's office or laboratory. Assuming that the sample described above was randomly selected, it is valid to generalize the research findings from the 125 participating students to the experimentally accessible population (i.e., all high school students in the school).

Often the researcher or the reader of a research report wishes to generalize from the experimentally accessible population to a still larger group (e.g., all high school students in the United States). The larger group of individuals to whom the research findings are generalized is called the **target population.**[13] Generalizing research findings from the experimentally accessible population to a target population is risky. We must compare the two populations to determine whether they are similar in critical respects. For example, if the experiment was done in a school district composed almost entirely of middle-class suburban families, generalization of the research findings to all U.S. high school students is likely to be invalid.

2. *The extent to which personological variables interact with treatment effects.* In the experiment described above, you do not know whether instructional format interacts with student characteristics. That is, although hypertext was found to be superior to a conventional textbook for high school students, different results might be obtained with students at different grade levels in high school. If so, the differential effects would limit the generalizability of the experiment's findings.

Student's ability, gender, extraversion-introversion, and anxiety level are examples of other personological variables that might affect the generalizability of findings from experiments. The systematic study of these interactions—called aptitude-treatment interaction (ATI) research—is discussed in the next chapter.

Ecological Validity

Ecological validity concerns the extent to which the results of an experiment can be generalized from the set of environmental conditions created by the researcher to different environmental conditions. If the treatment effects can be obtained only under a limited set of conditions or only by the original researcher, the experimental findings are said to have low ecological validity. The ten factors identified by Bracht and Glass that affect the ecological validity of an experiment are as follows.

1. *Explicit description of the experimental treatment.* The researcher needs to describe the experimental treatment in sufficient detail so that other researchers can reproduce it. Suppose a researcher finds that the discussion method is more effective than the lecture method in promoting positive student attitudes toward doing community service during the summer months. However, the researcher's description of the discussion method is so vague and incomplete that other researchers wishing to replicate the experiment cannot determine whether they are using the method in the same way. In this case, the experimental findings have virtually no generalizability to other settings.

2. *Multiple-treatment interference.* Occasionally a researcher will use an experimental design in which each participant is exposed to more than one experimental treatment. Suppose each participant in an experiment receives three different treatments: A, B, and C. Treatment A is found to produce significantly greater learning gains than treatments B and C. Because of the experimental design that was used, the findings cannot be generalized

---

13. The distinction between accessible and target populations is also discussed in Chapter 6.

with confidence to a situation in which treatment A is administered alone. The effectiveness of treatment A may depend on the co-administration of the other two treatments. Whenever it appears that multiple-treatment interference will affect the generalizability of your findings, you should choose an experimental design in which only one treatment is assigned to each research participant.

3. *Hawthorne effect.* The **Hawthorne effect** refers to any situation in which the experimental conditions are such that the mere fact that individuals are aware of participating in an experiment, are aware of the hypothesis, or are receiving special attention improves their performance. In educational research, experimenters often give participating teachers and students special attention. This factor, not the experimental treatment itself, may cause a change in their behavior. Should the Hawthorne effect occur, the external validity of the experiment is jeopardized because the findings might not generalize to a situation in which researchers or others who were involved in the research are not present.

Attempts to manipulate the Hawthorne effect experimentally often have failed to produce evidence of the effect.[14] Even so, it is advisable to minimize special attention given to research participants.

4. *Novelty and disruption effects.* A novel experimental treatment might be effective simply because it is different from the instruction that participants normally receive. If this is true, the results of the experiment have low generalizability, because the treatment's effectiveness is likely to erode as the novelty wears off. The reverse problem occurs with experimental treatments that disrupt normal routine. This type of experimental treatment might be ineffective initially, but with continued use, participants might assimilate the treatment into their routine and find it effective. Thus, the findings of the initial tryout are not generalizable to a condition of continued use.

5. *Experimenter effect.* An experimental treatment might be effective or ineffective because of the particular experimenter, teacher, or other individual who administers the treatment. In this case treatment effects cannot be generalized to conditions in which a different person (often a classroom teacher) administers the treatment. The various ways in which experimenters can influence the administration of a treatment are discussed below in the section on experimenter bias.

6. *Pretest sensitization.* In some experiments, the pretest may interact with the experimental treatment and thus affect the research results. If the experiment is repeated without the pretest, different research results are obtained. Let us consider a hypothetical experiment in which this reactive effect might occur. Suppose you are interested in how point of view in a film affects students' attitudes. You might develop a film in which the narrator takes a strongly slanted, positive view of controversial decisions made by a contemporary politician. To assess the effect of the film, you administer a pretest and posttest of students' attitudes toward the politician.

Suppose there is a significant positive shift in students' attitudes, which you attribute to the experimental treatment, that is, the film. Can you generalize this finding and assert that the film will have the same effect when used in other situations? The generalization is not warranted unless you can demonstrate that the pretest has no effect on the experimental treatment. The possibility exists that the pretest activates students' awareness of their attitudes toward this politician and sensitizes them to the narrator's attitude. The sensitization induced by the pretest may interact with the film to produce the attitude shift.

14. Adair, J. G. (1984). The Hawthorne effect: A reconsideration of the methodological artifact. *Journal of Applied Psychology, 69,* 334–345.

In contrast, if they are shown the film alone, students might be more sensitized to learning the facts presented in the film than to adopting the narrator's attitude. Thus, they might show little or no attitude shift because they did not have a set to attend to the narrator's point of view.

Bracht and Glass's review of the literature on pretest sensitization indicates that it is most likely to occur when the pretest is a self-report measure of personality or attitude. A later review of the research on pretest sensitization effects was conducted by Victor Willson and Richard Putnam.[15] They located 32 studies of this phenomenon and did a meta-analysis to determine the average effect size across studies. Willson and Putnam found a substantial effect of pretests on posttest performance. In other words, an experimental group that receives a pretest is likely to perform at a higher level on the posttest than a corresponding experimental group that does not receive a pretest. This effect occurs even when the posttest is different from the pretest. In fact, the meta-analysis revealed that the pretest effect was stronger when the pretest and posttest were different. Furthermore, administration of a pretest usually was found to have a positive effect irrespective of the type of outcome—cognitive, attitudinal, or personality—that was measured.[16]

7. *Posttest sensitization.* This source of ecological invalidity is similar to pretest sensitization. The results of an experiment may be dependent upon the administration of a posttest. This can happen if the posttest is a learning experience in its own right. For example, the posttest might cause certain ideas presented during the treatment to "fall into place" for some of the students. When the experiment is repeated without a posttest, the effectiveness of the treatment is diminished. Although posttest sensitization is plausible, it has not been studied to the same extent as its counterpart, pretest sensitization.

8. *Interaction of history and treatment effects.* One can argue that researchers should not generalize beyond the time period in which an experiment was done. An experiment evaluating an innovative educational method might be done at a time when teachers are particularly disenchanted with a corresponding, conventional method. They might be exceptionally motivated to demonstrate the superiority of the new method. At a later time, we might repeat the experiment and find no difference because teachers no longer see the method as innovative.

9. *Measurement of the dependent variable.* The generalizability of an experiment might be limited by the particular pretest and posttest designed to measure achievement gains or another outcome variable. Suppose the superiority of a hypertext program over a regular textbook was demonstrated on multiple-choice tests that students took shortly after completing the treatment condition. If the hypertext program is effective only because it facilitates students' ability to take multiple-choice tests, the results of the experiment would not generalize to other measures. For example, no difference between instructional formats might be found if the pretests and posttests required essays.

10. *Interaction of time of measurement and treatment effects.* Administration of a posttest at two or more points in time may result in different findings about treatment effects. The usual practice is to administer the posttest immediately after the research participants have completed the experimental treatment. Conclusions about treatment effectiveness are based on the results of this posttest administration. If possible, however,

15. Willson, V. L., & Putnam, R. R. (1982). A meta-analysis of pretest sensitization effects in experimental design. *American Educational Research Journal, 19,* 249–258.

16. In their report on self-report pretest biases operating in experiments involving scarce treatment opportunities, Leona Aiken and Stephen West describe approaches to minimizing the effects of pretest self-report bias on the internal validity of experiments. See: Aiken, L. S., & West, S. G. (1990). Invalidity of true experiments: Self-report pretest biases. *Evaluation Review, 14,* 374–390.

it is advisable to administer the same or a parallel posttest several weeks or months later in order to measure retention of learning. Bracht and Glass cite several examples in the research literature in which treatment effects changed from posttest to delayed posttest. The effects may be enhanced, remain the same, or diminish over time.[17]

In designing an experiment, identify the real-life educational settings to which you wish to generalize the results of the experiment. Then review the design of the experiment in terms of the two population validity factors and ten ecological validity factors described above. If you see a potential problem, attempt to correct it. If a problem cannot be corrected, it should be noted in the research report as a limit on the generalizability of the research findings.

Representative Design

Some educational researchers, most notably Richard Snow,[18] have criticized conventional experimental design for its artificiality and lack of generalizability. Building on the earlier work of Egon Brunswick, Snow used the label "systematic design" to characterize the typical form of experimentation. In systematic design a few treatment variables and pretest-posttest measures are administered. All other variables are either controlled or ignored. Most of the experiments reported in journals of educational research are based on systematic design principles.

The problem with systematic design is that it often produces artificial learning situations and unnatural behavior in the learner. Snow advocates instead the use of *representative design* to combat these problems and also to increase the generalizability of findings from experiments. **Representative design** is a process for planning an experiment so that it accurately reflects both the real-life environments in which learning occurs and the natural characteristics of learners. In this respect, representative design in quantitative research parallels some of the priorities of qualitative researchers, namely, the study of human behavior in natural field settings and an emphasis on the emic perspective (i.e., the primacy of the participants' viewpoint rather than the researcher's viewpoint).

The desirability of representative design is based on a number of assumptions about the learning environment and the human learner. One assumption is that the characteristics of the natural environment are complex and interrelated. We cannot simply choose to vary one environmental characteristic and hold others constant; as one characteristic changes, so do others. We need to study the learning environment as an ecology in the same way that biologists study the ecology of the natural environment.

Another assumption of representative design is that human beings are active processors of information; they do not react passively to experimental treatments. Therefore, the active nature of learning by humans needs to be considered in designing experiments. A related assumption is that human learners, if allowed, will adjust and adapt to their environment. Systematic experiments are artificial in that they constrain the range of behavior that might be exhibited if the learner were allowed to act naturally.

Finally, representative design assumes that, because the human organism is complex, any experimental intervention is likely to affect the learner in complex ways. An instructional method might be designed only to increase students' knowledge of a specific subject, for example, but the effect may generalize to students' attitudes and also to their

17. Bracht & Glass, *External validity*, p. 466.
18. Snow, R. E. (1974). Representative and quasi-representative designs for research on teaching. *Review of Educational Research, 44*, 265–291.

knowledge of other subjects. Furthermore, the instructional intervention might be designed primarily to affect short-term performance, but the effects may "radiate out" to affect long-term performance as well.

Snow believes that educational researchers should design experiments to reflect this view of the environment and the learner. That is, experiments should become more *representative* of the natural environment and of research participants as active learners. Snow notes that true representative designs are very difficult to achieve in education, but he suggests compromises that will make experiments more representative. The following are some of his recommendations.

1. When appropriate, conduct the research in the actual educational setting or other environment to which you wish to generalize your findings.

2. Incorporate several environmental variations into the design of the experiment. For example, if the purpose is to evaluate a new instructional method, have not just one teacher but rather a sample of teachers use it. Also, vary the educational setting. For example, an instructional method could be tested in a sample of inner-city schools, suburban schools, and rural schools.

3. Observe what students actually are doing during the experiment. These observations may prove helpful in interpreting the results of the experiment. For example, you might find that the research participants were not attentive to a particular treatment or appeared to be distracted by other events. If the research data later indicated that the treatment was not effective, these observations would be helpful in interpreting the results and in planning future research.

4. A related technique to the one preceding is to observe the social context in which the experiment is being conducted. Certain events that occur in schools or other educational settings may affect experimental treatments. If such events are observed and recorded, the research findings will be more interpretable.

5. Prepare participants for the experiment. Snow claims that typical practice is for researchers to give research participants brief instructions and perhaps a few minutes of training prior to the start of an experiment. More extensive preparation may be necessary to ensure a smooth transition from participants' current mental set to the one required by the experimental task.

6. Incorporate a control treatment that allows participants to use their customary approaches to learning. Suppose an experiment is designed in which students are formed into dyads and trained to ask questions of each other about curriculum materials. An appropriate control treatment might be to form some students into dyads and allow them to use any procedures they wish to review the same materials. The control group thus forms a naturalistic baseline against which the behavior and learning of the experimental group can be evaluated.

Issues in Designing Experiments

Experimenter Bias

Robert Rosenthal's studies of experimenter bias have made a significant contribution to experimental methodology.[19] **Experimenter bias** refers to researchers' expectations about the outcomes of their experiments that are unintentionally transmitted to participants so

✦ Touchstone in Research

Crawford, J., & Impara, J. C. (2001). Critical issues, current trends, and possible futures in quantitative methods. In V. Richardson (Ed.), *Handbook of research on teaching* (4th ed., 133–173). Washington, DC: American Educational Research Association.

19. Rosenthal, R. (1976). *Experimenter effects in behavioral research* (Enlarged ed.). New York: Irvington.

that their subsequent behavior is affected. The phenomenon typically occurs outside the awareness of the experimenter. The term *experimenter bias* is not used to refer to situations in which an experimenter, with full awareness of his or her actions and intentions, manipulates participants' behavior or falsifies data in order to yield an expected finding.

Rosenthal and his associates carried out many experiments on experimenter bias, and we shall describe one of the classic ones here.[20] A group of undergraduates was instructed in procedures for running Albino rats through a simple T-maze and for training the rats to solve a discrimination learning problem. The student experimenters were told that, as a result of generations of inbreeding, some rats they would train were "maze-bright" while others were "maze-dull." They were then given instructions regarding expected findings:

> Those of you who are assigned the Maze-Bright rats should find your animals on the average showing some evidence of learning during the first day of running. Thereafter performance should rapidly increase. Those of you who are assigned the Maze-Dull rats should find on the average very little evidence of learning in your rats.[21]

In fact, a homogeneous group of Albino rats (not varying on the dimension of maze brightness or dullness) was randomly assigned to the student experimenters for training. Nevertheless, Rosenthal and Fode found that rats trained by experimenters who thought their rats were maze-bright earned significantly higher learning scores than rats trained by experimenters with the opposite expectancy. The differential learning gains were the result of experimenter bias rather than genetic differences between groups of rats.

Experimenter bias appears to be a major threat to the internal validity of experiments. Thus, you should take steps to avoid the operation of this effect in designing and carrying out an experiment. One effective technique is to train naive experimenters to work with the participants. Whenever possible, do not work directly with the research participants yourself. Also, avoid suggesting to the experimenters, directly or indirectly, that one experimental treatment is better than another.

Researchers conceivably can overdo efforts to eliminate experimenter bias. If they go too far in attempts to appear neutral or even skeptical about the experimental treatment, participants might become "turned off" to it. Also, in the interest of appearing neutral, researchers might put the procedure to a test that is too difficult. For example, the experimental treatment might be tried in schools that are experiencing administrative problems. If the initial test is conducted under difficult conditions such as these, it might be labeled ineffective and consequently abandoned.

Generally speaking, it is better initially to identify a set of conditions under which the procedure has a good chance of working. Subsequent experiments can determine the limiting conditions of its effectiveness. Joshua Klayman and Young-Won Ha labeled the approach of testing cases that offer the best chance of supporting one's hypotheses a **positive test strategy.**[22] They demonstrated that under certain conditions, including those in which the purpose of the research is to test hypotheses about new educational programs and methods, researchers should seek instances that support their hypotheses rather than instances that refute them.

20. Rosenthal, R., & Fode, K. L. (1963). The effect of experimenter bias on the performance of the Albino rat. *Behavioral Science, 8,* 183–189.
21. Ibid., p. 184.
22. Klayman, J., & Ha, Y-W. (1987). Confirmation, disconfirmation, and information in hypothesis testing. *Psychological Review, 94,* 211–228.

Treatment Fidelity

Theodore Barber extended the work of Rosenthal by identifying additional sources of investigator and experimenter bias.[23] The **investigator** is defined as the person who designs the experiment and interprets the data, and the **experimenter** is defined as the person who administers the experimental treatments and collects the data. In many experiments the investigator and experimenter are the same person, but this is not always so. One type of bias identified by Barber occurs when the experimenter fails to follow the exact procedures specified by the investigator for administering the treatments. Barber labeled this type of bias *experimenter failure to follow the protocol effect,* and cited several studies in which it was demonstrated empirically to occur. Other researchers refer to this type of bias as lack of treatment fidelity. **Treatment fidelity** is the extent to which the treatment conditions, as implemented, conform to the researcher's specifications for the treatment.

According to Barber, researchers should try to maximize treatment fidelity and then assess the extent to which they succeeded. This is done too seldom in educational experiments. James Shaver reviewed studies published in the *American Educational Research Journal* for the years 1969 to 1981.[24] He identified 22 reports of teaching methods research in which checking treatment fidelity would have been appropriate. Less than half the reports ($N = 9$) actually made such a check.

Treatment fidelity can be maximized by careful training of the individuals—often teachers—who are to implement the treatment. For example, in the science curriculum experiment that we discussed above, the training of teachers who were to implement SCIS occurred in in-service workshops. From the descriptions provided by the researchers, these workshops appear to have lasted only a few days. This amount of training may not be sufficient to change teacher behavior in the direction of using the process-oriented inquiry approach required by SCIS. Treatment fidelity can be assessed by first writing precise specifications for the experimental and control treatments. Then the investigator must carefully train the experimenters to follow these specifications. Finally, during the actual experiment the investigator should collect data on the experimenter's behavior to determine the congruence between behavior and treatment specifications. Data on experimenter behavior can be collected by a variety of observational techniques (see Chapter 9).

An example of careful attention to procedures for maximizing and assessing treatment fidelity can be found in an experiment by Jerry Pratton and Loyde Hales.[25] The purpose of their experiment was to determine the effect of having teachers use active participation, a technique popularized by the educator Madeline Hunter and her associates. They defined active participation as

> a deliberate and conscious attempt on the part of the teacher to cause students to participate overtly in a lesson. For example, a teacher presenting a lesson in division may ask students to indicate the number of digits that are in a dividend by holding up the correct number of fingers or writing the number on their papers.[26]

Each of five teachers was trained to deliver a lesson that included active participation (the experimental treatment) and the same lesson but without active participation (the control

♦ *Touchstone in Research*

Gresham, F. M., MacMillan, D. L., Beebe-Frankenberger, M. E., & Bocian, K. M. (2000). Treatment integrity in learning disabilities intervention research: Do we really know how treatments are implemented? *Learning Disabilities Research and Practice, 15,* 198–205.

23. Barber, T. (1973). Pitfalls in research: Nine investigator and experimenter effects. In R. M. W. Travers (Ed.), *Second handbook of research on teaching* (pp. 382–404). Chicago: Rand McNally.
24. Shaver, J. P. (1983). The verification of independent variables in teaching methods research. *Educational Researcher, 12*(8), 3–9.
25. Pratton, J., & Hales, L. W. (1986). The effects of active participation on student learning. *Journal of Educational Research, 79,* 210–215.
26. Ibid., p. 211.

treatment). Following the training period, each teacher taught each form of the lesson to two fifth-grade classes.

Each lesson was videotaped, and the teacher completed a form specifying the time of day the lesson was taught and the number of students present. Teachers also filled out a questionnaire to score the presence or absence of certain observed factors during the lesson. As shown in Table 12.2, a score was given for atypical factors involving (1) external

TABLE 12.2

Fidelity of Treatment in Experiment on Active Participation

Observed Factors	Active Participation *M*	Nonactive Participation *M*
External factors (atypical)		
Unusual classroom interruptions	.10	.00
Unusual weather	.00	.00
Unusual school event	.00	.00
Day of the week disruptive	.00	.00
Afternoon lesson	.00	.00
Different physical environment	.00	.00
Homeroom teacher influence	.00	.00
Unusual class size	.00	.00
Lesson taught in different room	.00	.00
Student factors (unusual)		
Students' experiences affect lesson	.00	.00
Hostile atmosphere	.00	.00
Unusual student disruptions	.10	.10
Abnormal group behavior	.00	.00
Teacher factors (atypical)		
Teacher experience influence lesson	.00	.00
Excessive praise	.00	.00
Unusual teacher enthusiasm	.00	.00
Unusual teacher behavior	.00	.00
Different teaching style	.00	.00
Different management approach	.00	.00
Different lesson approach	.00	.00
Inappropriate active participation	.00	.00
Teacher gave test answers	.00	.00
Other factors		
Typical external interruptions	.80	.40
Typical student disruptions	.80	.30
Teacher use of praise	14.70	14.90
Teacher varies from lesson	.20	.10
Use of active participation	6.00	.00
Inappropriate use of active participation	.00	.90
Level of teacher enthusiasm (scale: 1–5)	2.90	2.90
Enrollment	24.90	25.20
Attendance	21.50	23.50
Length of lesson	29.60	29.10

Source: Adapted from Tables 1 and 2 on p. 213 in: Pratton, J., & Hales, L. W. (1986). The effects of active participation on student learning. *Journal of Educational Research, 79,* 210–215. Reprinted with permission of the Helen Dwight Reid Educational Foundation. Published by Heldref Publications, 1319 Eighteenth St., NW, Washington, DC 20036–1802. Copyright © 1986.

conditions (e.g., weather), (2) students (e.g., disruptive behavior), (3) the teacher (e.g., giving test answers), and (4) other factors (e.g., typical external interruptions).

The researchers analyzed the videotape and teacher questionnaire data to determine the extent to which teachers taught the lessons in the same way and under the same conditions except for the use of active participation. Table 12.2 reports the results of their analysis. For all the atypical external factors, student factors, and teacher factors, the mean scores for the classrooms in the active participation condition and for those in the non-active participation condition are very similar, and are zero or near zero. The mean scores also are very similar (e.g., teacher use of praise is 14.70 and 14.90, respectively) for teachers in the active-participation condition and those in the nonactive participation condition for most of the other factors that were rated. The only exception is use of active participation, which is the dependent variable in this experiment. As expected, teachers in the active-participation condition gave this a high score (6.00), while teachers in the nonactive participation condition gave it a low score (.00).

These results indicate good treatment fidelity for Pratton and Hales's experiment, meaning that any difference between the treatment and control groups on the dependent variable (student achievement on a posttest covering the lesson content) can be attributed to the treatment (active participation) rather than to extraneous variables.

The treatment variable in some experiments consists of instructional materials rather than a teaching method. Treatment fidelity should be checked in this situation, too. For example, an experiment by Sandra Castaneda, Miguel Lopez, and Martha Romero tested the effect of three types of chemistry text on student reading processes.[27] The researchers analyzed the three text samples to check that they varied in the ways intended. The results of their analysis are shown in Table 12.3. The texts were found to vary as intended.

Strong versus Weak Experimental Treatments

One of the major challenges in experimental research is to administer a treatment that is strong enough to have a significant effect on the dependent variable. For example, suppose you do an experiment to determine whether a particular teaching method affects student achievement. The experimental design might require a group of teachers to use the method for a period of one week, with student achievement measured at the beginning and end of that time period. Also, there might be a control group of teachers who use

TABLE 12.3

Characteristics of Three Experimental Chemistry Texts

Text	Topic	Length (Words)	Conceptual Units Length	Percentage of Density	Percentage of Lexical Difficulty	Syntactic Difficulty
1	Permanent polarity	62	6	3	9.60	33.00
2	Nuclear bonding	82	8	4	12.00	45.00
3	Induced polarity	161	13	3	10.55	47.00

Source: Table 1 on p. 126 in: Castaneda, S., Lopez, M., & Romero, M. (1987). The role of five induced learning strategies in scientific text comprehension. *Journal of Experimental Education, 55,* 125–130.

27. Castañeda, S., Lopez, M., & Romero, M. (1987). The role of five induced learning strategies in scientific text comprehension. *Journal of Experimental Education, 55,* 125–130.

a conventional teaching method for the same period of time, with student achievement measured at the same time as for the experimental group.

Suppose no differences are found between the experimental and control groups. Should you conclude that the experimental teaching method does not produce greater achievement gains? Perhaps, but we can raise the criticism that you used a weak treatment. For example, we might argue that the experimental teaching method would have produced greater achievement gains than the control method had it been used for several months or longer.

Of course, as you increase the strength of the treatment, the experiment is likely to increase in complexity, time, and cost. Thus, many educational problems amenable to an experimental approach cannot be tackled by student researchers. These problems require a well-funded and well-staffed research team in order to be investigated properly. Before doing an experiment, you should determine whether you have the resources necessary to design a treatment that will be strong enough to have an effect on student achievement or other dependent variables.

✦ *Touchstone in Research*

Lipsey, M. W. (1990). *Design sensitivity: Statistical power for experimental research.* Thousand Oaks, CA: Sage.

Rogers, J. L. Howard, K. I., & Vessey, J. T. (1993). Using significance tests to evaluate equivalence between two experimental groups. *Psychological Bulletin, 113,* 553–565.

Random Assignment in Experiments

We discussed above the ideas of Campbell and Stanley about factors that affect the internal and external validity of experiments. These researchers also classified types of experimental designs. Table 12.4 presents part of their classification system. You will note that some of the designs are single-group designs and others are control-group designs with random assignment. As shown in the table, some of the designs have better internal and external validity than others.

The first column of Table 12.4 illustrates each experimental design graphically. For example, the first three designs are single-group designs, meaning that there is no control group. This aspect is illustrated by the fact that for each of these designs the graphic combination of Xs and Os is all on one row. For example, design number 1 involves an experimental treatment (X) followed by a posttest (O), for one group of participants. Design number 2 involves a pretest (the first O), then an experimental treatment (X), and then a posttest (the second O), again for one group of research participants. In design number 3, several pretests (each O before the X) are administered before the experimental treatment, and several posttests (each O after the X) are administered after the experimental treatment.

The control-group designs shown in the second half of Table 12.4 are represented similarly. The main difference is the R at the beginning of each row, indicating that participants are assigned randomly to either the experimental or control group. Random assignment should not be confused with the randomization carried out to select a sample of individuals to participate in one's study (see Chapter 6). Briefly, **randomization** is the use of a sampling procedure that ensures that each person in a defined population has an equal chance of being selected to take part in the study. When conducting an experiment, you need to consider another type of randomization, namely, random assignment of individuals or other sampling units to experimental treatments. **Random assignment** means that each sampling unit (e.g., student, class, school district) has an equal chance of being in each experimental condition. You can use a table of random numbers or similar method to assign each participant by chance to the experimental or control group.[28] Random assignment is the best technique available for assuring initial equivalence between different treatment groups.

---

28. Random numbers for generating random assignment to experimental groups are available at: www.randomizer. org

TABLE 12.4

Experimental Designs and Their Potential Sources of Invalidity

Design	Sources of Invalidity	
	Internal	**External**
Single-group designs		
1. One-shot case study X O	History, maturation, selection, and mortality	Interaction of selection and X
2. One-group pretest-posttest design O X O	History, maturation, testing, instrumentation, interaction of selection and other factors	Interaction of testing and X; interaction of selection and X
3. Time-series design O O O O X O O O O	History	Interaction of testing and X
Control-group designs with random assignment		

4. Pretest-posttest control-group design
   R O X O
   R O   O
	None	Interaction of testing and X

5. Posttest-only control-group design
   R   X O
   R   O
	Mortality	None

6. Solomon four-group design
   R O X O
   R O   O
   R   X O
   R   O
	None	None

Note: In Campbell and Stanley's tables, some invalidating factors are shown as possible sources of concern in certain designs. Only definite weaknesses in experimental designs are indicated here.

Key: R = Random assignment.
      X = Experimental treatment.
      O = Observation, either a pretest or posttest of the dependent variable.

Source: Adapted from Tables 1, 2, and 3 on pp. 8, 40, and 56, respectively, in: Campbell, D. T., & Stanley, I. C. (1963). *Experimental and quasi-experimental designs for research.* Chicago: Rand McNally.

Treatment-group equivalence is essential to the internal validity of an experiment. To the extent that threats to the internal validity of the experiment are present, the threats should affect each treatment group to an equal extent if the groups are initially equivalent. In this case, differences between groups on the posttest can be attributed with a high degree of confidence to the treatment rather than to extraneous variables.

Random assignment can be achieved easily in brief experiments that occur under laboratory conditions. The situation is more difficult in field experiments conducted in schools, students' homes, or elsewhere. It might be a challenge to obtain participants' cooperation or establish other conditions necessary for random assignment. Furthermore, even if initially equivalent groups are formed through random assignment, the equivalence may break down as the experiment proceeds, for example, by differential attrition in the two groups.

Cook and Campbell identified several specific obstacles to forming and maintaining equivalent treatment groups in field experiments.[29] We turn now to a discussion of some of these obstacles, and consider how they might be avoided or overcome.

1. *Withholding the treatment from the control group.* If one treatment is perceived as more desirable than another, you may encounter strong resistance to the use of random assignment. For example, suppose an experiment is planned to test how the use of computer simulations of science concepts affects middle-school students' achievement. You wish to randomly assign 10 classrooms (the treatment group) to receive the simulation software, and another 10 classrooms (the control group) to continue functioning without the system for the duration of the experiment.

Upon hearing about the proposed experiment, some teachers in the district might wish to have the simulation software in their classrooms. They might view it as innovative and exciting—a real plus for their school and classroom. Some of them might even solicit parent support and lobby central office administrators to be in the group to receive the simulation software. Such teachers are likely to express resistance to being in the control group. In short, they might oppose the use of random assignment to allocate what is perceived as a scarce and valuable resource.

If you ignore teachers' protests and carry out the experiment as originally planned, the experiment is likely to involve one or more of the internal validity threats described above: compensatory rivalry by the control group, compensatory equalization of treatments, or resentful demoralization of the control group. Therefore, you should attempt to find a solution that addresses the protests while at the same time maintaining the integrity of the experiment.

One solution is to tell the control-group participants that they will receive the treatment after the experiment is concluded. In the example above, the 20 teachers and their principals could be told that 10 of the teachers will receive the software the first year, and the other 10 teachers will receive it the second year.

Educators usually are amenable to this solution. The major difficulty with it obviously is that it creates additional work for the researcher. The length of the experiment is effectively doubled. You can save a great deal of effort simply by not collecting data during the administration of the treatment to the control group. On the other hand, if you do collect data, you will have a replication of the experiment. The first treatment group can be compared with the control group, and the control group can be compared with itself (before and after receiving the treatment).

One of the authors of this book (W. Borg) developed another solution that will work in certain situations.[30] This solution involves giving the control-group participants an alternative treatment that they perceive as equally desirable to the experimental treatment. This treatment should be similar in both duration and procedure to the experimental treatment, but it should be concerned with a different set of dependent variables. For example, Walter Borg and Frank Ascione did an experiment to test the effectiveness of an in-service education program that they developed to improve teachers' classroom management skills.[31] The experimental group participated in the in-service program, while the control

29. Cook & Campbell, *Quasi-experimentation.* Some of the obstacles to treatment-group equivalence identified by Cook and Campbell are not listed here because they are discussed elsewhere in this chapter.
30. Borg, W. (1984). Dealing with threats to internal validity that randomization does not rule out. *Educational Researcher, 13*(10), 11–14.
31. Borg, W. R., & Ascione, F. R. (1982). Classroom management in elementary mainstreaming classrooms. *Journal of Educational Psychology, 74,* 85–95.

group participated in an equally desirable program of similar format but addressed to a different set of skills, namely, teaching skills to improve students' self-concept.

2. *Faulty randomization procedures.* A defect in the researcher's random-assignment procedures can result in nonequivalent treatment groups. Cook and Campbell cite the famous case of the 1969 military draft lottery. Each day of the year was put on a slip of a paper, and the slips were put into an urn. The order in which the slips were drawn out of the urn determined the order in which draft-age males would be drafted into military service. For example, if February 12 was drawn first, men with that birth date would be drafted first. Evidently the urn was not shaken well, because the slips of days put into it last (those of October, November, and December) remained near the top and were drawn out first. The solution to the problem is obvious, namely, to use a procedure such as a table of random numbers that thoroughly randomizes all the birth dates.

Another problem that might occur in attempts to assign groups randomly to treatment conditions is that participants may not believe the researcher's statement that the assignment to a treatment group was random. This problem is more likely if the researcher is well known to participants and they have reason to believe that the researcher is positively or negatively biased toward some participants. To avoid this problem, we suggest you have a credible witness observe the random-assignment process. For example, if teachers in a school district are to be assigned to treatment groups, you might ask a representative of the teachers association to observe the assignment process.

Suppose that by examining available data about the sample, you discover that, although randomly constituted, the groups obviously are not equivalent. For example, one group might have a disproportionate number of males, students from a particular grade level, or students with high scholastic aptitude scores. If nonequivalence occurs at the time of random assignment, you have two alternatives. First, you can start again with the total sample and redo the random assignment procedures. Hopefully, a second or third attempt at randomization will result in treatment-group equivalence on known dimensions.

The second alternative is to stratify the total sample on the factor or factors for which equivalence is desired. (Stratification procedures are discussed in Chapter 6.) After the total sample has been stratified, individuals can be randomly assigned within strata to treatment groups. This procedure ensures treatment group equivalence on the stratified factors.

3. *Small sample size.* The probability that random assignment will produce initially equivalent treatment groups increases as the size of the sample in each group increases. For example, equivalent groups will more likely result if 100 individuals are randomly assigned to two treatment groups ($N = 50$ per group) than if 10 individuals are assigned to these two groups ($N = 5$ per group).

There are several solutions to the problem of randomly assigning a small sample to two or more treatment groups. One obvious solution is to attempt to increase the sample size. The additional expenditure of resources is worthwhile if the result is equivalent treatment groups, and consequently, more interpretable research results. Another solution is to use matching procedures, which are discussed later in the chapter.

The third solution is to consider whether one or more treatment groups can be eliminated. Suppose, for example, that you are interested in testing the relative effectiveness of four training variations to alleviate an unusual learning disorder. You can locate a sample of only 16 students having the disorder. If the students are randomly assigned to the four treatments, there will be only four students per treatment group. Even if there are true differences between treatments, the statistical power will be so low that the null hypothesis of no difference between treatments probably will not be rejected. In this situation you should consider comparing only the two most theoretically interesting or most promising treatments, in which case there would be eight students per treatment group.

4. *Intact groups.* Although not mentioned by Cook and Campbell, the frequent need to use intact groups in educational research poses an obstacle to random assignment. An **intact group** is a set of individuals who must be treated as members of an administratively defined group rather than as individuals. For example, most school classes are intact groups. The intact group usually is defined in terms of a particular grade level, teacher, and classroom (e.g., the fourth-grade class taught by Ms. Jones in Room 16).

Suppose that you wish to do an experiment in which the individual student is the appropriate sampling unit. You have available a sample of 50 fourth-grade students: 25 from a classroom in school A and 25 from a classroom in school B. Random assignment requires that each student be assigned, by chance, to the experimental or control group. School administrators and teachers, however, usually require that you deal with students as members of an intact group. Thus, all students in a classroom must be given the same treatment in order to preserve the intact classroom group.

Given this situation, you can opt to increase the number of classrooms in the sample and institute one treatment condition per classroom. This procedure should result in an experiment with good internal validity if (1) classrooms are randomly assigned to the experimental and control groups, (2) the issue of the appropriate unit of statistical analysis (see Chapter 5) is carefully addressed, and (3) the other obstacles to random assignment described above are avoided.

In practice, random assignment of classrooms to experimental and control groups is often difficult. If classrooms in several schools are involved, one classroom in a school may be assigned by chance to the experimental group, whereas another classroom in the same school is assigned by chance to the control group. Some administrators tend to view all the teachers and students in a school as a whole, however, and want everyone in the school to be treated the same way. Therefore, they might press you to assign one treatment per school. For example, students in the fourth-grade class of school A might be assigned to the treatment condition (a new instructional method designed to improve learning) and students in the fourth-grade class of school B might be assigned to the no-treatment control condition.

This procedure preserves the integrity of the public school structure. Solving this problem, however, creates other problems. Consider, for instance, what would happen if students in school A came from predominantly middle-class families and students in school B came from lower-class families. Because academic achievement is correlated with social class, students in school A are more likely to have high posttest achievement scores than students in school B, with or without the instructional treatment. Thus we could not conclude on the basis of the findings that the instructional treatment is superior to conventional instruction. An equally plausible interpretation is that the differential achievement gain results from initial differences in the treatment groups.

The preceding illustrations typify the thorny problems that researchers can encounter in doing a field experiment in which random assignment to experimental treatments is not possible because the research participants are members of intact groups. Nonetheless, it is possible to design an experiment in which the limitations of nonrandom assignment are partially or wholly overcome. Campbell and Stanley refer to experimental designs that do not involve random assignment of participants to treatment conditions as "quasi-experiments," to distinguish them from "true" experiments, which involve random assignment of research participants to treatment conditions. In the next chapter we will discuss procedures for developing equivalence between intact groups receiving different experimental treatments.

Single-Group Designs

The One-Shot Case Study

The **one-shot case study design** hardly qualifies as an experimental design. In this design an experimental treatment is administered, and then a posttest is administered to measure the effects of the treatment. As Table 12.4 shows, this design has low internal validity. Suppose we select a group of students, give them remedial instruction (the experimental treatment), and then administer a measure of achievement (the posttest). How can we determine the influence of the treatment on the posttest? The answer is that we cannot. The students' scores on the posttest could be accounted for by their regular school instruction or by maturation, as well as by the treatment. Also, the fact that students were tested only once makes it impossible to measure any changes in their performance. Without a measure of change, we cannot even determine whether the students' achievement improved over time, regardless of whether this change was due to the treatment or to some other variable. In short, the one-shot case study, although relatively simple to carry out, yields meaningless findings. At the very least, researchers who are limited to studying a single group of individuals should use the experimental design we describe next.

One-Group Pretest-Posttest Design

The **one-group pretest-posttest design** involves three steps: (1) administration of a pretest measuring the dependent variable; (2) implementation of the experimental treatment (independent variable) for participants; and (3) administration of a posttest that measures the dependent variable again. The effects of the experimental treatment are determined by comparing the pretest and posttest scores.

The one-group pretest-posttest design was used in an experiment conducted by Eleanor Semel and Elisabeth Wiig.[32] Their purpose was to determine whether a new training program, based on an auditory processing model, would improve the language skills of learning-disabled children. The sample consisted of 45 elementary school students who were diagnosed as learning disabled in language because they scored two or more grades below age-grade expectation in two or more academic areas, one of them being reading.

All children in the sample received the training program, which was provided 30 minutes daily for 15 weeks. We might reasonably expect that the children, though language disabled, would make some language gains over this long a time period even without special instruction. Realizing this, the researchers made a generous estimate of gains that might be expected due to regular instruction (i.e., history), maturation, and so on; then they judged the effectiveness of the training program by whether it exceeded this estimate. Semel and Wiig explained their reasoning and procedures as follows:

> standardized and age referenced tests were used as pre- and posttraining measures. In fact, then, the standardization samples were considered to be acceptable as a substitute for a control group. A rigid criterion of performance gains (+ 6 months) was set for the magnitude of gains which could be considered educationally significant. In reality, children with language-learning disabilities would not be expected to gain language skills at the rate expected for children with normal language development.[33]

32. Semel, E. M., & Wiig, E. H. (1981). Semel Auditory Processing Program: Training effects among children with language-learning disabilities. *Journal of Learning Disabilities, 4,* 192–196.
33. Ibid., pp. 195–196.

The same battery of language proficiency tests was administered before and after the training program. The performance of the students on the pretest and posttest measures is shown in Table 12.5. Mean raw score gains were observed on each of the measures (see columns 1 and 2). To determine whether the gains were educationally and statistically significant, the researchers first converted students' raw scores on each measure to an age-level equivalent. The pretest age-level equivalent then was subtracted from the posttest age-level equivalent to yield an age-level gain score. The mean age-level gain on each measure for the total sample is shown in column 3 of Table 12.5.

Next the researchers determined the percentage of students whose age-level gain on a particular measure was more than six months. These percentages are shown in the last column of Table 12.5. For example, 75 percent of the students made age-level gains of more than six months on the Illinois Test of Psycholinguistic Ability (ITPA) Grammatic Closure Subtest. The researchers tested whether these percentages were significantly different from a "chance" figure of 50 percent. The chi-square test revealed that more students made gains of +6 months than could be expected if this were a chance event.

The researchers used the one-group pretest-posttest design in this experiment because the school system in which it was conducted did not permit differential services for

TABLE 12.5

Pretest and Posttest Results for Students Receiving a Language Training Program

Test	Pretest M (1)	Posttest M (2)	Age-Level Gain (in months) (3)	Percentage of Students with Gains > 6 mos. (4)
1. ITPA[a] Grammatic Closure	17.51	23.09	15.48	75.57% $\chi^2 = 11.76$**
2. DTLA[b]: Auditory Attention Span for Unrelated Words	32.67	37.68	15.73	68.92% $\chi^2 = 6.42$*
3. DTLA: Auditory Attention Span for Related Syllables	30.89	39.29	10.13	51.13% $\chi^2 = .02$
4. DTLA: Verbal Opposites	19.44	23.64	7.27	37.79% $\chi^2 = 2.68$
5. DTLA: Verbal Absurdities	.96	5.36	22.00	71.13% $\chi^2 = 8.02$**
6. Carrow Elicited Language Inventory	36.12	40.00	30.37[c]	76% $\chi^2 2 = 8.76$**

[a] Illinois Test of Psycholinguistic Ability
[b] Detroit Tests of Learning Aptitude
[c] This score is the mean percentile gain using the percentile norms for this measure.
*$p < .05$
**$p < .01$
Source: Adapted from text on pp. 194–195 in: Semel, E. M., & Wiig, E. H. (1981). Semel Auditory Processing Program: Training effects among children with language-learning disabilities. *Journal of Learning Disabilities, 4,* 192–196.

its students. The absence of a control group was not a serious threat to the internal validity of the experiment, however, because the researchers were able to make a good estimate of expected pretest-posttest gains due to extraneous factors. The gains of the experimental group thus could be evaluated against estimated gains under normal, nonexperimental conditions in which such extraneous factors would be operating.

The one-group pretest-posttest design is especially appropriate when you are attempting to change a characteristic that is very stable or resistant to change. For example, if I participate in an experimental program to learn how to speak Ukrainian (an out-of-the-ordinary behavior), the likelihood that extraneous factors account for the change is small. Similarly, if an experimenter trains a bird to say a few human words, we would hardly dismiss the results as due to extraneous factors.

In summary, the one-group pretest-posttest design is most justified when extraneous factors can be estimated with a high degree of certainty, or can safely be assumed to be minimal or nonexistent.

Statistical analysis. The data in the Semel and Wiig study were analyzed by chi-square tests that determined whether an observed measure of pre- and post-test gains (+6 months age-level gain) differed significantly from a chance distribution of gain, that is, a 50-50 split. If the data are in the form of continuous scores, a *t* test for correlated means would be used instead. This test determines whether the difference between the pretest and posttest mean is statistically significant.

If the scores on either the pretest or posttest show marked deviation from the normal distribution, a nonparametric test of statistical significance should be used. These tests are described in Chapter 10.

Time-Series Design

In the **time-series design** a single group of research participants is measured at periodic intervals, with the experimental treatment administered between two of these intervals. The effect of the experimental treatment, if any, is indicated by a discrepancy in the measurements before and after its appearance.

Campbell and Stanley classify the time-series experiment as a single-group design (see Table 12.4) because it involves a single group of research participants, all of whom receive the experimental treatment. The procedures used to maximize the internal validity of this type of experimental design and to analyze the data are similar to those used in single-subject designs. Therefore, we will discuss the time-series design in relation to single-subject designs in Chapter 13.

✦ *Touchstone in Research*

Ostrom, C. W., Jr. (1990). *Time series analysis: Regression techniques* (2nd ed.). Thousand Oaks, CA: Sage.

Control-Group Designs with Random Assignment

We discuss in this section two of the experimental designs shown in Table 12.4: the pretest-posttest control-group design (number 4); and the posttest-only control group design (number 5). These are among the most commonly used designs in educational research. We also describe two variations on these designs: the pretest-posttest control-group design with matching; and the one-variable multiple-condition design.

The statistical techniques used to analyze data resulting from these and other experimental designs are generally the same as those used in causal-comparative designs. We introduce and explain these statistical techniques (e.g., the *t* test and analysis of variance) in Chapter 13. Therefore, you may find it helpful to refer to Chapter 13 for more information about the statistical techniques to which we refer in this chapter and Chapter 14.

✦ *Touchstone in Research*

Boruch, R. F. (1997). *Randomized controlled experiments for planning and evaluation: A practical guide*. Thousand Oaks, CA: Sage.

The Solomon four-group design also is shown in Table 12.4 (number 6), but we will defer our discussion of it until the next chapter. This is because the Solomon four-group design is a factorial design. To understand how it works you need to understand the logic of factorial design, a topic that is covered in Chapter 13.

Pretest-Posttest Control-Group Design

✦ *Touchstone in Research*

Dugard, P., & Todman, J. (1995). Analysis of pre-test post-test control group designs in educational research. *Educational Psychology, 15,* 181–198.

Mok, M., & Wheldall, K. (1995). Some reservations about the use of analysis of covariance in educational research: A response to Dugard and Todman. *Educational Psychology, 15,* 199–202.

Almost any study that can be conducted with a single-group design can be carried out more satisfactorily with a control-group design. The essential difference between the single-group design and control-group design is that the latter employs at least two groups of research participants, one of which is called the control group. The **control group** is a group of research participants who receive either no treatment, or an alternate treatment to that given the experimental group, in order to assess the effect of extraneous factors on participants' posttest performance.

In control-group design the goal is to keep the experiences of the experimental and control groups as identical as possible, except that the experimental group is exposed to the experimental treatment. If extraneous variables have brought about changes between the pretest and posttest, these will be reflected in the scores of the control group. Thus, the posttest change of the experimental group beyond the change that occurred in the control group can be safely attributed to the experimental treatment.

If properly carried out, the pretest-posttest control-group design effectively controls for the eight threats to internal validity originally identified by Campbell and Stanley: history, maturation, testing, instrumentation, statistical regression, differential selection, experimental mortality, and selection-maturation interaction. Nevertheless, the external validity of this design might be affected by an interaction between the pretest and the experimental treatment. That is, the experimental treatment might produce significant effects only because a pretest was administered. When it is tried on a group that has not been pretested, the treatment might not work as well. If you think that your experimental treatment is likely to be affected by pretesting, you should use the posttest-only control-group design or the Solomon four-group design.

The following steps are involved in using a pretest-posttest control-group design: (1) random assignment of research participants to experimental and control groups, (2) administration of a pretest to both groups, (3) administration of the treatment to the experimental group but not to the control group, and (4) administration of a posttest to both groups. The experimental and control groups must be treated as nearly alike as possible except for the treatment variable. For example, both groups must be given the same pretest and posttest, and they must be tested at the same time.

In some experiments, the control group takes only the pretest and posttest and receives no treatment. In other experiments, however, you might want to administer an alternative experimental treatment to the control group. For example, as we discussed above, you might administer an equally desirable but different treatment to the control group. This design feature enables you to avoid the remaining four threats to internal validity identified by Cook and Campbell, namely, experimental treatment diffusion, compensatory rivalry by the control group, compensatory equalization of treatments, and resentful demoralization of the control group.

If the control group receives a treatment rather than being in a no-treatment condition, researchers sometimes refer to it as a *comparison group* rather than a control group. Another option is to refer to the two groups by labels that describe the two treatment conditions, for example, the *computer lab group* and the *computer-in-classroom group*.

The pretest-posttest control-group design was used in a study of test-taking instruction by Moshe Zeidner, Avigdor Klingham, and Orah Papko.[34] The purpose of their experiment was to test the effectiveness of a training program to improve students' test-taking ability and reduce their test anxiety. The program provides training in the nature of test anxiety, relaxation techniques, rational thinking, coping imagery, attention focusing, and time management.

Previous research had discovered that test anxiety increases among students when they reach upper-elementary school. Thus Zeidner and his colleagues selected a sample of 24 fifth- and sixth-grade classes. The 24 classes were randomly assigned to either the experimental treatment (12 classes) or the control condition (the other 12 classes). The treatment classes received the test-taking program during homeroom periods in five one-hour sessions held two weeks apart. In a check of treatment fidelity, all teachers but one were found to be implementing the program as intended. The control classes did not receive any instruction in test-taking skills.

The dependent variables included scores on three cognitive tests and two affective inventories. The cognitive tests were the Digit Symbol Coding Scale of the Wechsler Intelligence Scale for Children, a vocabulary test, and a mathematics test. Students also completed the Test Anxiety Inventory, which includes two subscales: a worry scale to measure students' cognitive concerns about the consequences of failure, and an emotionality scale to measure autonomic stress reactions such as sweating, stomachache, and trembling. Higher scores on the inventory indicate greater worry and stress. The students' teachers completed the Teacher Awareness Inventory on which higher scores indicate greater sensitivity of teachers to test anxiety as a concern of students. All the measures were administered to the experimental and control classes both before (pretest) and after (posttest) the training program.

Statistical analysis. The first step in analyzing data from a pretest-posttest control-group experiment is to compute descriptive statistics. As shown in Table 12.6, mean scores were computed for the pretest and posttest scores for both groups. The experimental and control groups had almost identical mean scores on the pretest cognitive measures, but there were small differences in mean scores on one of the pretest affective measures—the emotionality scale. This result illustrates the principle that random assignment does not ensure initial equivalence between groups. Random assignment only ensures absence of systematic bias in group composition.

Campbell and Stanley observed that researchers often use the wrong statistical procedure to analyze such data. It would be incorrect to do a *t* test comparing the pretest and posttest means of the experimental group (e.g., on the Digit Symbol Test, 23.5 vs. 28.9) and another *t* test comparing the corresponding means of the control group (24.2 vs. 24.1). The preferred statistical method is analysis of covariance (ANCOVA), in which the posttest mean of the experimental group is compared with the posttest mean of the control group with the pretest scores used as a covariate. If the assumptions underlying ANCOVA cannot be satisfied, you might consider an analysis of variance of the posttest means. (Because there are two posttest means, one for the experimental group and one for the control group, this is equivalent to doing a *t* test). Another approach is to do a two-way analysis of variance for repeated measures. This statistical technique is discussed in Chapter 13, in the section on factorial designs.

34. Zeidner, M., Klingham, A., & Papko, O. (1988). Enhancing students' test coping skills: Report of a psychological health education program. *Journal of Educational Psychology, 80,* 95–101.

TABLE 12.6

Effects of Test-Taking Instruction on Students' Test Performance, Students' Test Anxiety, and Teacher Awareness

Measures	Experimental Group	Control Group	F
Digit Symbol Test			
Pre *M*	23.5	24.2	
Post *M*	28.9	24.1	
Adj *M*	29.2	23.8	56.93**
Vocabulary Test			
Pre *M*	15.5	15.2	
Post *M*	16.4	14.5	
Adj *M*	16.3	14.6	53.66**
Mathematics Test			
Pre *M*	9.3	9.3	
Post *M*	10.4	8.7	
Adj *M*	10.4	8.7	51.50**
Worry Scale			
Pre *M*	13.8	15.2	
Post *M*	14.1	15.9	
Adj *M*	14.7	15.5	4.50*
Emotionality Scale			
Pre *M*	17.1	17.5	
Post *M*	17.3	17.4	
Adj *M*	17.5	17.2	.74
Teacher Awareness			
Pre *M*	16.6	17.8	
Post *M*	21.5	17.4	
Adj *M*	21.9	16.9	44.66**

*$p < .05$
**$p < .001$
M = mean, Adj = Adjusted
Source: Adapted from Tables 1 and 2 on pp. 98–99 in: Zeidner, M., Klingham, A., & Papko, O. (1988). Enhancing students' test coping skills: Report of a psychological health education program. *Journal of Educational Psychology, 80,* 95–101.

Zeidner and his associates tested the statistical significance of their results using AN-COVA.[35] You will recall from Chapter 10 that ANCOVA adjusts the posttest scores for differences between the experimental and control groups on the corresponding pretest. The adjusted posttest means are shown in the rows labeled "Adj *M*" in Table 12.6. Note, for example, that the adjusted posttest mean score of the experimental group on the Digit Symbol Test (29.2) is slightly higher than its actual posttest mean score (28.9). This is because on the pretest the experimental group had a slightly lower mean score (23.5) than the control group (24.2). The effect of the ANCOVA adjustment is to compensate the experimental group for this initial disadvantage by increasing its posttest score to the level that would be predicted on the basis of the correlation between pretest and posttest Digit Symbol Test scores.

35. The ANCOVAs for the cognitive test measures in Table 12.6 were preceded by a multivariate analysis of covariance (MANCOVA). The MANCOVA revealed a statistically significant difference between the experimental and control groups on the three test measures considered together.

The results of the ANCOVAs are shown in the last column of Table 12.6. The ANCOVAs yielded a significant F value for all measures except the emotionality scale. Thus, the researchers were able to conclude that a training program in test-taking skills improves students' cognitive test-taking ability and reduces their autonomic stress reactions to test-taking. The training program also increased teachers' sensitivity to their students' test anxiety. We can be fairly confident that these effects are attributable to the training program for three reasons: (1) classes were randomly assigned to the experimental and control conditions, (2) the observed differences between groups on the posttest were statistically significant, and (3) extraneous variables were effectively controlled.

Matching. A variation on the pretest-posttest control-group design is the use of the matching technique to obtain additional precision in statistical analysis of the data.[36] **Matching** refers to the selection of research participants for the experimental and control groups in such a manner that they are closely comparable on a pretest that measures either the dependent variable or a variable that is closely correlated with the dependent variable. (Matching also is used in causal-comparative research; see Chapter 10.) Matching is most useful in studies where small samples are to be used and when large differences between the experimental and control group on the dependent variable are not expected. Under these conditions, the small differences that do occur are more likely to be detected if sampling errors are reduced by the use of matching.

Posttest-Only Control-Group Design

This design is similar to the pretest-posttest control-group design except that pretests of the dependent variable are not administered to the experimental and control groups. The steps involved in the **posttest-only control-group design** are as follows:

1. Randomly assign research participants to the experimental and control groups.
2. Administer the treatment to the experimental group and no treatment or an alternative treatment to the control group.
3. Administer the posttest to both groups.

This design is recommended when you are unable to locate a suitable pretest, or when there is a possibility that the pretest has an effect on the experimental treatment. Before choosing this experimental design, you should consider three possible disadvantages of not administering a pretest of the dependent variable. First, random assignment may not be fully successful in eliminating initial differences between the experimental and control groups. If initial differences still exist, any differences found on the posttest can be attributed to them rather than to the effect of the experimental treatment. Because random assignment is most effective in equating groups when large numbers of research participants are involved, the posttest-only control-group design is best employed when you can enlist a large sample.

The second disadvantage of not administering a pretest is that you cannot form subgroups to determine whether the experimental treatment has a different effect on individuals at different levels of the variables measured by the pretest.

The third disadvantage of not administering a pretest occurs when there is differential attrition during the course of the experiment. For example, if participants in the control and experimental groups drop out of the experiment before it is over, any differences

---

36. An example of this experimental design is reported in: Rivera, E., & Omizo, M. M. (1980). The effects of relaxation and biofeedback on attention to task and impulsivity among male hyperactive children. *Exceptional Child, 27,* 41–51.

on the posttest may be due to the differential characteristics of the dropouts of the two groups, rather than the experimental treatment. Thus, the posttest-only control-group design should not be used when considerable attrition of research participants during the course of the study is likely.

The posttest-only control-group design was used in a study of teacher enthusiasm by Brian Patrick, Jennifer Hisley, and Toni Kempler.[37] The purpose of their experiment was to test the hypothesis that teacher enthusiasm has a positive effect on students' enthusiasm and intrinsic desire to learn. (In the report of their study, they referred to students' enthusiasm as "psychological vitality.") They derived their hypothesis from the research literature on intrinsic motivation, self-determination theory, and teacher enthusiasm during instruction. They also conducted an exploratory correlational study of the hypothesis.

The results of this correlational study lent support to the hypothesis:

> A teacher who is perceived to have a dynamic, enthusiastic style, then, tends to have students who report being highly intrinsically motivated regarding the subject matter as well as feeling energized in class.[38]

At the same time, the researchers noted the inherent limitation of correlational research with respect to cause-and-effect inferences:

> . . . because the data were strictly correlational, there is no way to determine the causal direction of the relationship between enthusiasm and our outcome measures. Although it is tempting to assume that an enthusiastic teacher produces intrinsically motivated students, it is perhaps equally plausible to draw the converse conclusion.[39]

Therefore, Patrick, Hisley, and Kempler designed a second study, a pretest-posttest control-group experiment, to determine whether teacher enthusiasm has a direct causal effect on student's intrinsic motivation to learn and psychological vitality.

The research participants were 60 students at a small liberal arts college. The students were randomly assigned to the experimental and control conditions. The procedures used in the experiment were designed to mask the purpose of the study. In other words, the students knew that they were participating in an experiment, but did not know that the variables being investigated were teacher enthusiasm, instrinsic motivation, and psychological vitality.

Each student who received the experimental treatment (labeled the "high-enthusiasm" condition) engaged individually in a laboratory session. The session involved several procedures, including a seven-minute lecture on the principles of biofeedback; following the lecture, administration of questionnaires to measure the student's intrinsic motivation to learn about the lecture topic and other matters; and a concluding, 5-minute free-choice activity in which the student could read articles about biofeedback or general-interest magazines (*Time* and *National Geographic*). During the lecture component, the instructor exhibited six indicators of enthusiasm that had been used in previous research on teacher enthusiasm: "(1) vocal delivery with variation in pace, volume, and intonation; (2) eyes that open wide and 'light up'; (3) demonstrative gesturing; (4) frequent large body movements; (5) facial expression of emotion; and (6) a high level of overall energy and vitality."[40]

37. Patrick, B. C., Hisley, J., & Kempler, T. (2000). "What's everybody so excited about?": The effects of teacher enthusiasm on student intrinsic motivation and vitality. *Journal of Experimental Education, 68*, 217–236.
38. Ibid., p. 225.
39. Ibid., p. 226.
40. Ibid., pp. 227–228.

Students in the control group (labeled the "low-enthusiasm" condition) participated in exactly the same activities as students in the experimental group, with one exception. During the seven-minute lecture, the instructor displayed a relative absence of the six indicators of enthusiasm.

The dependent variables and their measurement in this study are as follows:

1. *Perception of teacher enthusiasm.* The participants completed six items on which they rated the instructor's enthusiasm using a 7-point Likert-type scale. Sample item: "The instructor was very enthusiastic and energetic."
2. *Psychological vitality.* The measure included seven items, which participants rated on a 7-point Likert-type scale. Sample item: "Right now, I feel energized."
3. *Intrinsic motivation (free-choice).* Each participant was observed through a one-way mirror during the free-choice activity. The number of seconds they spent demonstrating interest in the biofeedback articles was recorded.
4. *Intrinsic motivation (self-reported).* The measure included three items which each participant rated on a 7-point Likert-type scale. The measure was administered after the lecture and again after the free-choice activity.

The researchers did not provide a rationale for not including a pretest measure of any of these variables. However, we can infer from their description of their procedures that they were concerned about not revealing the purpose of the experiment to the participants. Pretests of intrinsic motivation or psychological vitality might well have sensitized participants to these variables, and this sensitization would likely have affected their behavior during the experiment and responses to the posttest measures. Also, attrition was not an issue in this experiment, so pretest data would not be necessary to check for differential attrition (a threat to internal validity that we explained earlier in the chapter) and its effects on the data.

Statistical analysis. Table 12.7 shows the mean score of participants in the high-enthusiasm and low-enthusiasm groups on each of the posttest measures of the dependent variables. Because there are only two groups, the mean score differences can be tested for statistical significance by a *t* test. Table 12.7 shows instead *F* values, which indicate that the researchers chose to do ANOVAs. However, when two groups are compared, a *t* test and ANOVA yield identical results. Therefore, it is of no consequence that the researchers chose to do ANOVAs rather than *t* tests.

The researchers' decision to measure the participants' perception of their instructor's enthusiasm is a desirable design feature of their experiment. It provides a check of treatment fidelity, which we explained earlier in the chapter. As you can see in Table 12.7, students in the high-enthusiasm group rated their instructor much higher on enthusiasm than did students in the low-enthusiasm group, and this difference was statistically significant. It is also apparent that the researchers' hypothesis was strongly supported: the two groups' mean scores on three of the four measures of intrinsic motivation and psychological vitality yielded statistically significant differences; and the difference between their mean scores on the fourth measure (free-choice behavior), while not statistically significant, were in the hypothesized direction.

One-Variable Multiple-Condition Design

The one-variable multiple-condition design is a simple extension of the control-group designs that we have presented thus far. Each of these designs involves random assignment of a sample to *two* groups, but each one can be extended to include *three or more* groups.

TABLE 12.7

Effects of Manipulation of Teacher Enthusiasm

Variable	Enthusiasm condition		F	p
	High *M*	Low *M*		
Perception of instructor enthusiasm	6.18	3.56	125.56	.001
Intrinsic motivation				
Free-choice behavior	133.77	93.70	1.47	*ns*
Self-report				
Postlecture	5.63	4.87	9.26	.004
Post-free-choice period	5.68	5.09	5.30	.025
Psychological vitality	4.11	3.54	4.94	.03

Note: *n* = 30 participants per condition. Free-choice behavior was measured from 0 to 300 s. All other variables were measures on a 7-point Likert-type scale.
Source: Adapted from Table 6 on p. 231 in: Patrick, B. C., Hisley, J., & Kempler, T. (2000). "What's everybody so excited about?": The effects of teacher enthusiasm on student intrinsic motivation and validity. *Journal of Experimental Education, 68*, 217–236.

We call such extensions **one-variable multiple-condition designs.** The *one-variable* designation indicates that the groups differ on only one variable, which is the type of treatment they receive. The *multiple-condition* designation indicates that more than two treatment conditions are involved.

To illustrate this design, we use the experiment on the effectiveness of a test-taking-skills program that we described earlier in the chapter. The experiment involved two groups: (1) a group that participated in the program and (2) a group that did not. The treatment variable, then, is training, and it has two values: (1) full training and (2) no training. However, it is possible to differentiate more values of the training variable. The full program involved training in the nature of test anxiety, relaxation techniques, rational thinking, coping imagery, attention focusing, and time management. Suppose the researchers believed that most of the benefits of the program resulted from relaxation training. They might design the experiment to include three groups, each representing a different value of the variable: full training, partial training (i.e., relaxation training only), and no training. Additional groups could be formed if the researchers wished to study the effects of other treatment variations (e.g., full training with follow-up "booster" training several months later).

A similar analysis could be done on the experiment on teacher enthusiasm that we described above. The researchers studied the effects of two levels of the variable of teacher enthusiasm: high and low. If they wished, however, they could distinguish additional levels of enthusiasm (e.g., moderate enthusiasm, extremely high enthusiasm, and extremely low enthusiasm). Each level would be represented by a separate group of participants in the experimental design. There would still be a single treatment variable in the design, but there would be three or more groups depending on how many levels of the variable are to be studied.

Statistical analysis. Multiple-condition experiments generally yield three or more mean scores, or similar descriptive statistics. Therefore, the usual test of statistical significance in these experiments is univariate or multivariate analysis of variance, univariate or multivariate analysis of covariance, or a nonparametric equivalent.

✦ RECOMMENDATIONS FOR
Doing Experiments

1. Try to maximize the experiment's internal validity: Consider all the extraneous variables that might affect the posttest variables, and then take steps to eliminate them from the experimental design.
2. Try to maximize the experiment's population validity: Identify the population to which you wish to generalize your findings, and then select a sample that will permit those generalizations.
3. Try to maximize the experiment's ecological validity: Identify the real-life conditions in which the intervention will be used, and then create a "representative design" that approximates the real-life conditions.
4. Consider whether the experiment is susceptible to experimenter bias, and if it is, design the experiment to minimize that bias.
5. In designing an experiment, include procedures for checking treatment fidelity.
6. Design a strong form of the experimental intervention (i.e., the treatment variable) in order to make a fair test of its effectiveness.
7. Whenever possible, use an experimental design that includes at least one control condition and random assignment of research participants to the conditions.

✔ SELF-CHECK TEST

Circle the correct answer to each of the following questions.
The answers are provided at the back of the book.

1. A posttest in an experiment is sometimes called the
   a. dependent variable.
   b. experimental treatment.
   c. experimental variable.
   d. treatment variable.
2. An experiment in which extraneous variables are controlled is said to be
   a. internally reliable.
   b. internally valid.
   c. externally valid.
   d. externally reliable.
3. If students' scores tend to move toward the mean upon retesting, _____ is said to have occurred.
   a. experimental mortality
   b. statistical regression
   c. maturation
   d. reactive effect of pretesting

4. If the experimental treatment is affected by the administration of the pretest, the _____ of the experiment would be weakened.
   a. internal validity
   b. internal reliability
   c. external validity
   d. external reliability
5. Representative design of experiments assumes that
   a. the learning environment is a complex, interrelated ecology.
   b. the human learner is an active processor of information.
   c. the intended effects of an experimental intervention may radiate out to affect other aspects of performance.
   d. all of the above.

6. Researchers often give participating teachers and students special attention that, though not part of the experimental treatment, may cause change. This phenomenon has been called the
   a. Hawthorne effect.
   b. John Henry effect.
   c. effect of multiple-treatment interference.
   d. reactive effect of experimentation.
7. A useful technique to minimize the effects of experimenter bias upon the outcome of an experiment is for the researcher to
   a. train naive experimenters to collect the data from research participants.
   b. select experimenters who have prior experience in doing research on the problem being investigated.
   c. fully disclose the purpose of the study to the experimenters.
   d. all of the above.

For questions 8–10, use the following key:
   R = random assignment
   X = experimental treatment
   O = observation (pretest or posttest)

8. O   X   O
   describes the:
   a. one-group pretest-posttest design.
   b. one-shot case study.
   c. pretest-posttest control-group design.
   d. posttest-only control-group design.
9. R   O   X   O
       O   O
   describes the
   a. posttest-only control-group design.
   b. Solomon two-group design.
   c. counterbalanced design.
   d. pretest-posttest control-group design.
10. R   X   O
            O
   is a useful design if
   a. no control group is available.
   b. a large sample is available.
   c. it is thought the pretest will have an effect on the experimental treatment.
   d. it is thought that the posttest has exceptional construct validity.

CHAPTER 13

✦ Experimental Research: Designs, Part 2

OVERVIEW

This chapter describes the principles of experimental research design that were introduced in Chapter 12 as they apply to three other types of experimental design: quasi-experimental, factorial, and single-case designs. Quasi-experimental designs are used when random assignment of subjects to experimental and control groups is not possible. Factorial designs, in contrast to the one-treatment-variable designs described in Chapter 12, involve simultaneous manipulation of two or more treatment variables. Single-case designs involve intensive study of the effects of a treatment on a single individual or group. Because educational experiments often involve the measurement of achievement gains or other types of change, we include a discussion of this type of measurement.

OBJECTIVES

After studying this chapter, you should be able to

1. Describe a procedure to reduce initial group differences that occur due to nonrandom assignment of subjects to experimental and control treatments.
2. Describe methods and statistical procedures used in the static-group comparison and nonequivalent control-group designs.
3. Describe the major potential threats to the internal validity of quasi-experimental designs.
4. Classify into five types the independent variables that appear in factorial research designs.
5. Explain the purpose, design, and statistical analysis procedures of basic factorial experiments.
6. Describe the methods, purposes, and features of single-case experimental designs.
7. Describe several variations of A-B-A and multiple-baseline designs in single-case research, and indicate the most appropriate statistical techniques for analyzing the data yielded by these designs.
8. State several threats to the internal validity and external validity of single-case experiments.
9. Describe problems in using gain scores to measure change, and state two statistical techniques for solving these problems.

◆ *Touchstone in Research*

Cook, T. D., & Campbell, D. T. (1975). *Quasi-experimentation: Design and analysis issues for field settings.* Chicago: Rand McNally.

Reichardt, C. S., & Mark, M. M. (1998). *Quasi-experimentation.* In L. Bickman & D. J. Rog (Eds.), *Handbook of applied social research methods* (pp. 193–228). Thousand Oaks, CA: Sage.

Quasi-Experimental Designs

We explain in Chapter 12 that random assignment of research participants to experimental and control groups greatly strengthens the internal validity of experiments. Random assignment, however, often is not possible, especially in field studies. Campbell and Stanley refer to experiments that lack random assignment as **quasi-experiments**.[1] This type of experiment, if carefully designed, yields useful knowledge. However, you should be aware of the special problems that can arise when individuals are not assigned randomly to groups and the steps you can take to solve them.

Table 13.1 summarizes the quasi-experimental designs that are discussed in this chapter. The list is not exhaustive, but it does illustrate the range of design options that are available to educational researchers.

Static-Group Comparison Design

The **static-group comparison design** has two characteristics: research participants are not randomly assigned to the two treatment groups; and a posttest, but no pretest, is administered to both groups. The steps involved in using this experimental design are identical to the posttest-only control-group design described in Chapter 12, except for the absence of random assignment.

The main threat to internal validity in this design is that posttest differences between groups can be attributed to characteristics of the groups other than the experimental conditions to which they were assigned. For example, suppose that faculty members of one university department are given the experimental treatment and the posttest, and faculty members in another department at the same university are given only the posttest. If differences on the posttest are found, it can be argued that those differences are due to preexisting differences between faculty members in the two departments rather than the effect of the experimental treatment.

The static-group comparison design produces an inherently weak experiment. If you are planning to use it, consider the possibility of administering a pretest to the subjects. With this additional factor, the experiment becomes a nonequivalent control-group design and allows much stronger inferences concerning the effect of the experimental treatment on the posttest. This design is discussed in the next section.

Statistical analysis. The data yielded by a static-group comparison design can be analyzed by doing a *t* test of the difference between the posttest mean scores of the experimental and control groups. If the scores deviate considerably from the normal distribution, a nonparametric test (most likely the Mann-Whitney *U* test) should be used instead.

Nonequivalent Control-Group Design

The most commonly used quasi-experimental design in educational research is the **nonequivalent control-group design.** In this design, research participants are not randomly assigned to the experimental and control groups, and both groups take a pretest and a posttest. Except for random assignment, the steps involved in this design are the same as for the pretest-posttest experimental control-group design described in Chapter 12.

It also is possible to use a nonequivalent control-group design involving more than two groups. Furthermore, it is possible to have all groups receive a treatment, rather than

---

1. Campbell, D. T., & Stanley, J. C. (1963). *Experimental and quasi-experimental designs for research.* Chicago: Rand McNally.

TABLE 13.1

Summary of the Experimental Designs Described in Chapter 13

Quasi-experimental Designs	Solomon Four-Group Design
Static-group comparison design	R O X O
X O	R O O
O	R X O
Non-equivalent control-group design	R O
O X O	Counterbalanced Experiments
O O	Group 1 R O X_1 X_2 O
	Group 2 R O X_2 X_1 O

Factorial Designs	Single-Case Designs
Two-factor experiments	A-B designs
R O X_1 Y_1 O	A B
R O X_1 Y_2 O	A B A
R O X_2 Y_1 O	A B A B
R O X_2 Y_2 O	Multiple-baseline designs
Three-factor experiments	A B B B A
R O X_1 Y_1 Z_1 O	A A B A B
R O X_1 Y_1 Z_2 O	
R O X_1 Y_2 Z_1 O	
R O X_1 Y_2 Z_2 O	
R O X_2 Y_1 Z_1 O	
R O X_2 Y_1 Z_2 O	
R O X_2 Y_2 Z_1 O	
R O X_2 Y_2 Z_2 O	

Key: R = random assignment
     X, Y, Z = Experimental treatments
     $X_1/X_2/X_3$ = Levels of treatment X
     $Y_1/Y_2/Y_3$ = Levels of treatment Y
     $Z_1/Z_2/Z_3$ = Levels of treatment Z
     O = observation, either a pretest or posttest
     A = measurement during baseline condition
     B = measurement during treatment condition

having one group in a no-treatment control condition. The only essential features of this particular design, then, are nonrandom assignment of research participants to groups and administration of a pretest and posttest to all groups. An example of this experimental design is described in Chapter 12. It is the evaluation of the Science Curriculum Improvement Study by William Kyle, Ronald Bonnstetter, and Thomas Gadsden, Jr.

Statistical analysis. The main threat to the internal validity of a nonequivalent control-group experiment is the possibility that group differences on the posttest are due to pre-existing group differences rather than to a treatment effect. Analysis of covariance (first discussed in Chapter 10) frequently is used to handle this problem. Analysis of covariance statistically reduces the effects of initial group differences by making compensating adjustments to the posttest means of the two groups. If you plan to use this statistical technique, you should check whether your data satisfy its assumptions.

◆ *Touchstone in
    Research*

Jaeger, R. M., & Bond,
L. (1996). Quantitative
research methods and
design. In D. C.
Berliner & R. C. Calfee
(Eds.), *Handbook of
educational psychology*
(pp. 877–898). New
York: Macmillan.

Martin, D. W. (2000).
*Doing psychology ex-
periments* (5th ed.).
Belmont, CA:
Wadsworth.

Winer, B. J., Brown,
D. R., & Michaels,
K. M. (1991). *Statistical
principles in experi-
mental design* (3rd
ed.). New York:
Macmillan.

Factorial Designs

The classic single-treatment-variable experiment aims at holding constant all elements of the experimental situation except the treatment variable. This is the aim of the experiments described in Chapter 12 and the two quasi-experimental designs described in this chapter. In most educational situations, however, the experimental treatment cannot realistically be considered in isolation from other factors. For example, the effectiveness of a professional development program for administrators might not be effective for everyone. There may be reason to believe that its effectiveness depends upon whether an educator is fairly new to administration or highly experienced. Factorial experiments make it possible to examine this possibility.

A **factorial experiment** is an experiment in which the researcher determines the effect of two or more independent treatment variables (i.e., factors)—both singly and in interaction with each other—on a dependent variable. The effect of each independent variable on the dependent variable is called a **main effect.** The interaction of the effect of two or more independent variables on the dependent variable is called an **interaction effect.**

Two-Factor Experiments

The simplest type of factorial experiment involves a 2 × 2 design. The expression *2 × 2* means that two variations of one factor (A1 and A2) and two variations of another factor (Bl and B2) are manipulated at the same time. This factorial design requires the formation of four treatment groups, with each group receiving a different combination of the two factors: A_1B_1, A_1B_2, A_2B_1, and A_2B_2. Research participants should be randomly assigned to the four treatment groups. If random assignment procedures are not used, the design is a quasi-experiment. The data resulting from a factorial quasi-experiment are very difficult to interpret, because of the difficulty in disentangling main effects and interaction effects from possible initial differences among participants in the different treatment groups.

Example of a Two-Factor Experiment

Walter Saunders and Joseph Jesunathadas conducted a factorial experiment to identify factors that affect students' ability to engage in proportional reasoning.[2] They defined proportional reasoning as the ability to solve problems requiring the use of proportions (e.g., 2:3). This type of reasoning is important to student success in mathematics courses and also in science courses, especially physics and chemistry.

The experiment actually involved three factors, but we will simplify our description of it by initially describing it as a two-factor experiment. (We will introduce the third factor a bit later.)

The first factor in the experiment was familiarity with curriculum content. The researchers were interested in knowing whether students could engage in proportional reasoning better if the content was familiar than if the content was unfamiliar, as is often the case in science classes. They gave the following reason for their interest in this factor:

> The obvious implication is that if students perform proportional reasoning better with familiar than with unfamiliar content, then instructional activities designed to promote familiarity of science content would be in order.[3]

2. Saunders, W. L., & Jesunathadas, J. (1988). The effect of task content upon proportional reasoning. *Journal of Research in Science Teaching, 25,* 59–67.
3. Ibid., p. 60.

The second factor in the experiment was the level of difficulty of the proportions involved in the problems to be solved. Three levels of difficulty were manipulated in the experiment: easy proportions (e.g., 2:3), moderately difficult proportions (e.g., 4:15), and difficult proportions (e.g., 4:8.9).

A total of 76 ninth-grade students took a test in which these two factors were manipulated. The test contained 12 proportional reasoning problems, four at each level of difficulty. Two of the four problems at each level of difficulty involved content that would be familiar to most ninth-grade students. The other two problems involved unfamiliar science textbook content.

In summary, the experiment involved a 3 × 2 factorial design: three levels of proportion difficulty and two levels of familiarity. The different combinations of the two factors are depicted below:

Content

	Familiar	Unfamiliar
Easy		
Moderate		
Difficult		

Proportions

Because the experimental design has six combinations of factors, it normally would require six groups of students. However, the researchers administered the complete test to all students because it was not very long—a total of 12 items, two in each of the cells shown in the above diagram. Thus, the effect of each combination of the factors was examined with a total of 76 students (the complete sample). If each combination of factors had involved many test items, the researchers could have randomly assigned the 76 students to each combination (approximately 12 students per combination).

Statistical Analysis. The first step in analyzing the results of a factorial experiment is to compute descriptive statistics for the groups representing each combination of factors. The mean scores of the students on the problems representing each of the six combinations of factors are shown in Table 13.2. Also shown, in the "Total" column and row, are the mean scores of the students on each factor. For example, we see that students' mean score for test items having familiar content, ignoring the effect of item difficulty, is 2.69.

The next step in analyzing the results of a factorial experiment is to do an analysis of variance (ANOVA), analysis of covariance (ANCOVA), or multiple regression analysis to determine whether the differences between mean scores are statistically significant. Saunders and Jesunathadas did an ANOVA, the results of which are shown in Table 13.3.

Table 13.3 shows that the main effect of content familiarity yielded a statistically significant F ratio of 10.03, meaning that students did significantly better on test items with familiar content ($M = 2.69$) than on test items with unfamiliar content ($M = 2.20$). The main effect of proportion difficulty also yielded a statistically significant F ratio of 37.38. Because this factor has three levels (easy, moderate, and difficult), the researchers did post hoc t tests to determine which of the mean scores in Table 13.2 (2.37, 1.31, and 1.21) differed significantly from each other. This analysis revealed that the students did significantly better

TABLE 13.2

Mean Scores of Students on Problems Varying in Difficulty and Content Familiarity in Proportional Reasoning Experiment

Difficulty Level	Familiar Content	Unfamiliar Content	Total
Easy	1.44	.93	2.37
Moderate	.61	.70	1.31
Difficult	.64	.57	1.21
Total	2.69	2.20	4.89

Source: Adapted from Table 1 on p. 63 in: Saunders, W. L., & Jesunathadas, J. (1988). The effect of task content upon proportional reasoning. *Journal of Research in Science Teaching, 25,* 59–67.

TABLE 13.3

Analysis of Variance of Student Performance on Problems in Proportional Reasoning Experiment

Source	F	p
Content familiarity *(C)*	10.03	.002
Difficulty of proportions *(D)*	37.38	.001
C × *D* interaction	18.58	.001

Source: Adapted from Table 2 on p. 64 in: Saunders, W. L., & Jesunathadas, J. (1988). The effect of task content upon proportional reasoning. *Journal of Research in Science Teaching, 25,* 59–67.

on the easy items than on the moderate or difficult items. Their mean performance on the moderate and difficult items did not differ significantly.

We also see in Table 13.3 that the interaction between the two factors yielded a statistically significant *F* ratio of 18.58. The nature of the interaction is depicted in Figure 13.1. The students' mean score for each combination of factors indicates that students do better on test items with familiar content only when they involve easy proportions. They do not do better on test items with familiar content if the proportions are moderately difficult or difficult.

The study of interaction effects in a factorial experiment can increase our understanding of the phenomena being investigated, as we see above. If we compared students' performance only on test items with familiar content and with unfamiliar content, ignoring difficulty level (see last data row of Table 13.2), we would conclude that students do better on items involving familiar content. This conclusion oversimplifies the actual situation, however. The conclusion applies only to a certain type of test item, namely, test items whose solution involves simple proportions.

Three-Factor Experiments

A factorial experiment is not necessarily limited to the manipulation of two factors. We can find published reports of experiments involving three, four, or even five factors. Experi-

FIGURE 13.1

Plot of Two-Way Interaction Involving Difficulty Level and Content Familiarity in Proportional Reasoning Experiment

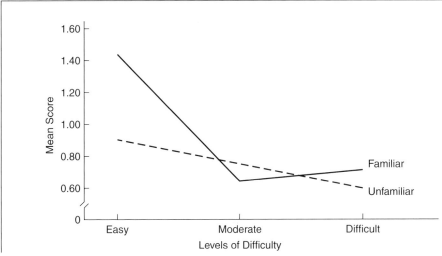

Source: Adapted from Figure 2 on p. 65 in: Saunders, W. L., & Jesunathadas, J. (1988). The effect of task content upon proportional reasoning. *Journal of Research in Science Teaching, 25,* 59–67.

ments involving more than three factors are not common, however, because developing all the treatment variations is difficult and because a large sample usually is required.

As we stated above, the experiment on proportional reasoning by Saunders and Jesunathadas actually involved three factors. The third factor was student gender. Student performance on the test items was analyzed separately for male students ($N = 34$) and female students ($N = 42$). Mean scores for students of each gender are shown in Table 13.4. We see in this table that there are 12 combinations of factors. This is because the actual experiment involved a 3 × 2 × 2 factorial design: three levels of item difficulty (easy, moderate, and difficult); two levels of test content familiarity (familiar and unfamiliar); and two genders (male and female). The analysis of variance presented in Table 13.3 thus yielded four more F ratios. One F is for the main effect of gender (10.33), which is statistically significant. This indicates that the mean score summed across all items for males (6.14) is significantly different from the mean score for females (3.60).

The other three F ratios involve interaction effects, which are shown below:

1. Gender by Content Familiarity $F = 1.31$ ($p = .27$)
2. Gender by Difficulty of Proportions $F = .01$ ($p = .93$)
3. Gender by Familiarity by Difficulty $F = 2.81$ ($p = .06$)

The first two F ratios, which are not statistically significant, indicate that the significant main effects for content familiarity and difficulty of proportions (see Table 13.3) are not affected by students' gender. The three-way interaction, however, is very nearly statistically significant ($p = .06$).

TABLE 13.4

Mean Scores of Male and Female Students on Problems in Proportional Reasoning Experiment

Difficulty Level		Familiar Content		Unfamiliar Content	
		Male	Female	Male	Female
Easy	M	1.56	1.31	1.09	0.76
	SD	0.66	0.75	0.90	0.85
	N	34	42	34	42
Moderate	M	0.82	0.40	1.00	0.40
	SD	0.90	0.73	0.85	0.77
	N	34	42	34	42
Difficult	M	0.94	0.33	0.73	0.40
	SD	0.85	0.61	0.90	0.73
	N	34	42	34	42

Source: Adapted from Table 1 on p. 63 in: Saunders, W. L., & Jesunathadas, J. (1988). The effect of task content upon proportional reasoning. *Journal of Research in Science Teaching, 25,* 59–67.

The three-way interaction can be detected by comparing the results shown in Tables 13.2 and 13.4. We find in Table 13.2 that for easy items, students did better on those with familiar content than on those with unfamiliar content. Looking now at Table 13.4, we find that this pattern holds true for both male and female students.

Next, we find in Table 13.2 that for items of moderate difficulty, students do slightly better on those with unfamiliar content. Looking now at Table 13.4, we find that this pattern is found for male students, but not for female students. In other words, the difference in performance on items varying in content familiarity (Factor 1) at a moderate level of difficulty (Factor 2) is affected by student gender (Factor 3).

A similar three-way interaction is found for difficult test items. Looking at Table 13.2, we find that students do slightly better on difficult test items if the content is familiar. Looking now at Table 13.4, we find that the pattern again applies to male students, but not to female students. In fact, the reverse pattern is observed for females. That is, when the items involve difficult proportions, females do somewhat better on items with unfamiliar content ($M = .40$) than they do on items with familiar content ($M = .33$).

Three-way interactions are often of small magnitude and are difficult to interpret. Even if the results of three-way interactions are statistically significant, they often are ignored by researchers. Most computer programs for ANOVA and ANCOVA routinely report F ratios for three-way interactions, however, so you should understand what they represent. The focus of interpretation usually is on the reported F ratios for main effects and two-way interactions.

Types of Treatment Variables

In discussing Saunders and Jesunathadas's experiment on proportional reasoning, we stated that three variables were manipulated. Strictly speaking, only the difficulty and familiarity of test items were manipulated. One cannot manipulate the third factor, which was the research participants' gender; it is a given of the situation.

Campbell and Stanley developed a useful classification of the types of independent variables that might appear in an educational experiment along this dimension of manipulability:

1. Manipulated variables, such as teaching method, assignable at will by the experimenter.
2. Potentially manipulable aspects, such as school subject studied, that the experimenter might assign in some random way to the individuals being studied, but rarely does.
3. Relatively fixed aspects of the environment, such as school attended or family's socioeconomic level, not under the direct control of the experimenter but serving as explicit bases for stratification in the experiment.
4. Organismic characteristics of individuals, such as age, height, weight, and gender.
5. Response characteristics of individuals, such as scores on various tests.[4]

Campbell and Stanley observed that the experimenter's primary interest is usually in manipulating class 1 variables. Variables in classes 3, 4, and 5 are used to group research participants in order to determine how generalizable the effects of manipulated variables are. For example, suppose your primary independent variable is a new teaching method. In addition, you are interested in grouping students by intelligence level (a class 5 variable, because intelligence usually is determined by a test score) in order to determine whether the teaching method is effective for students of all intelligence levels or just for students of a particular intelligence level. This type of research, aptitude-treatment interaction (ATI) research, is discussed in the next section.

Aptitude-Treatment Interaction Research

Learners have many different learning styles, aptitudes, and levels of ability. As a result, a single instructional method or program might not be suitable for all students. Education might be greatly improved if more efforts were made to match instructional methods and programs with the students who are best able to learn from them. A line of educational experimentation, called aptitude-treatment interaction research, has explored this possibility.

Aptitude-treatment interaction research, also called *ATI research,* is research designed to determine whether the effects of different instructional methods are influenced by the cognitive or personality characteristics of learners. It does not assume that one instructional method is better than another, nor that students with certain characteristics are better learners than others. Instead, ATI research is based on the assumption that these two factors (instructional method and learner characteristics) can interact in ways that affect learning outcomes. In ATI research, these interactions are revealed by designing factorial experiments similar to the experiment on proportional reasoning that we described above.

An ATI experiment usually has two independent variables. The first independent variable might be teaching method, type of curriculum material, learning environment, or a similar instructional variable. The other independent variable is a student characteristic, such as an aptitude, personality dimension, level of academic achievement, or learning style.

The initial focus of ATI research was on *aptitudes,* hence the label "aptitude-treatment interaction." Subsequently, the label "attribute-treatment interaction" was introduced, to indicate that a wide range of learner characteristics—not just aptitudes—can interact with instructional methods.[5] Attribute variables correspond to the last two types of independent

✦ Touchstone in Research

Cronbach, L. J., & Snow, R. E. (1981). *Aptitudes and instructional methods: A handbook for research on interactions.* New York: Irvington.

---

4. Campbell & Stanley, *Experimental and quasi-experimental designs,* p. 200.
5. The significance of this broader label is explained in: Tobias, S. (1976). Achievement-treatment interactions. *Review of Educational Research, 46,* 61–74.

variables (classes 4 and 5) in Campbell and Stanley's classification described above: organismic characteristics and response characteristics.

Example of an ATI Experiment

An example of ATI research is an experiment on evaluative threat during instruction by Dawson Hancock.[6] In reviewing the research literature, he found that although evaluation of learning generally increases student achievement, certain evaluation practices—such as instructor emphasis on competition for grades, strictness of rule enforcement, and severity of punishment for rule infractions—have a negative effect on student achievement. Hancock also found evidence that that evaluative threat is particularly debilitating for students with the attribute of high test anxiety. The purpose of his study was to replicate and extend these previous research findings:

> In this study, I sought to replicate previous findings regarding the impact of the learner characteristic, test anxiety, and of the classroom variable, threat of evaluation, on achievement by postsecondary students. More important, because most ATI research has focused on the effects of the individual and situational variables on student achievement, I expanded this research by examining the influence of the variables on postsecondary students' motivation to learn.[7]

Hancock used a standardized instrument, the Test Anxiety Inventory, to measure the test anxiety of 61 graduate students enrolled in a research methods course. Students whose scores were above the median were classified as high in test anxiety, and students whose scores were below the median were classified as low in test anxiety. The course professor taught two sections of the course, one with a high level of evaluative threat and the other with a low level of evaluative threat. Approximately equal numbers of high and low test-anxious students were assigned to each course section. Thus, the experiment involved a 2 × 2 factorial design: evaluative threat (high vs. low) and test anxiety (high vs. low).

Table 13.5 shows the mean score of students in each cell of the design for the dependent variable of achievement (measured by a professor-made, criterion-referenced test administered after 12 lessons, which marked the end of the experiment). The main effect for the factor of test anxiety was not statistically significant in the analysis of variance (ANOVA); in other words, the mean achievement score of the high test-anxious group (90.00) did not differ significantly from the mean achievement score of the low test-anxious group (91.77). The main effect for the factor of evaluative threat, however, was statistically significant: The mean score of students in the high-threat condition (89.71) was significantly lower than the mean score of students in the low-threat condition (92.07).

In addition, the ANOVA yielded a statistically significant ATI effect (i.e., an interaction between the two factors). The ATI effect is illustrated in Figure 13.2. Students with low test anxiety achieved equally well under either high evaluative threat or low evaluative threat. However, students with high test anxiety suffered a decrement in achievement if they experienced high evaluative threat. They achieved just as well as low-test-anxious students, though, if they experienced low evaluative threat. (A similar ATI effect was found for the dependent variable of motivation to learn.)

These ATI findings are much more informative than the findings that would be obtained in a simple experimental comparison of variations in evaluative threat during instruction. Therefore, we recommend that if you plan to do an experiment to test the effects

6. Hancock, D. R. (2001). Effects of test anxiety and evaluative threat on students' achievement and motivation. *Journal of Educational Research, 94,* 284–290.
7. Ibid., p. 285.

TABLE 13.5

Descriptive Statistics for ATI Experiment on Evaluative Threat and Test Anxiety

| Treatment group | Threat of evaluation | | | | | |
| | Low | | High | | Overall | |
	M	SD	M	SD	M	SD
Achievement						
Low test anxiety	91.93	2.52	91.60	3.67	91.77	3.09
High test anxiety	92.20	3.95	87.94	3.86	90.00	4.40
Overall	92.07	3.26	89.71	4.14	90.87	3.89

Source: Adapted from Table 1 on p. 287 in: Hancock, D. R. (2001). Effects of test anxiety and evaluative threat on students' achievement and motivation. *Journal of Educational Research, 94,* 284–290.

FIGURE 13.2

The Interactive Effect of Evaluative Threat and Test Anxiety on Student Achievement

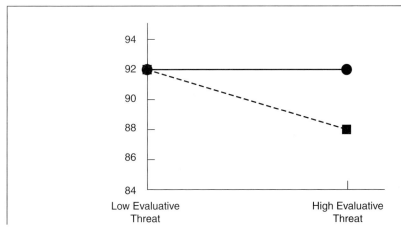

Source: Adapted from Figure 1 on p. 288 in: Hancock, D. R. (2001). Effects of test anxiety and evaluative threat on students' achievement and motivation. *Journal of Educational Research, 94,* 284–290.

of an educational practice, consider whether the practice will have a systematic differential effect for certain types of individuals.

Solomon Four-Group Design

The **Solomon four-group design** is a special case of a factorial design. It is used to achieve three purposes: (1) to assess the effect of the experimental treatment relative to the control treatment, (2) to determine the presence of pretest sensitization, and (3) to assess the interaction between pretest and treatment conditions.[8]

Example of a Solomon Four-Group Experiment

The Solomon four-group design was used in an experiment by Rosaland Edwards.[9] The main purpose of the experiment was to determine the effect of performance standards on motor skill development in elementary school children. Edwards hypothesized that "an individual with a difficult, specific standard or goal, but one that is attainable, will have a higher level of performance than an individual with no standards or with an easy, nonspecific goal.[10]

The experiment involved eight intact fourth-grade and fifth-grade classes, which were assigned to the four groups (two classes per group) of the Solomon design. Students in all groups were taught the motor skill of making a hockey flip shot. This skill involves using a hockey stick to shoot a floor hockey ball through a target 0.31 meters square, 25 centimeters from the floor, and located 1.86 meters from the shooting line. All students participated in a total of six two-minute sessions distributed evenly over two days.

The students in the two experimental treatment groups (groups 1 and 3) were given a performance standard to attain by their teacher. This standard was to make two more successful shots per session than they had averaged the previous day. Based on pilot study results, this standard was considered difficult but attainable. The two control groups (groups 2 and 4) participated in similar practice sessions, but without explicit performance standards.

The pretest consisted of having each student take 45 shots at the target. The student received two points for hitting the hockey ball through the target hole, one point if the hockey ball traveled in the air and hit the target, and zero points otherwise. The pretest score was the total points accumulated in 45 attempts.

Edwards was concerned that the pretest might function as a treatment in its own right. Therefore, within the two experimental groups, one (group 1) received a pretest and the other (group 3) did not. Similarly, within the two control groups, one (group 2) received a pretest and the other (group 4) did not. The inclusion of a pretest factor in the experimental design allowed Edwards to test the effects of the pretest on measures of the dependent variables.

Two dependent variables were measured. First, the behavior of the students during the practice sessions in the instructional phase of the experiment was assessed. The primary measure of student behavior was the total number of shots (called trials) each student took at the target during the six two-minute practice sessions. The other dependent variable, flip-shot skill, was measured by a posttest that was identical in form and scoring to the pretest.

Statistical analysis. The Solomon four-group experiment can be viewed as a 2×2 factorial design. The two factors are pretest (present or absent) and treatment (performance standards present or absent). In the experiment we have been considering, the researcher first did a multivariate analysis of variance (MANOVA) on the two dependent measures—

---

8. You will recall from the preceding chapter that pretest sensitization is a possible threat to the ecological validity of an experiment. Different results might occur if a pretest is administered to the experimental and control groups than if a pretest is not administered.

9. Edwards, R. (1988). The effects of performance standards on behavior patterns and motor skill achievement in children. *Journal of Teaching in Physical Education, 7,* 90–102.

10. Ibid., p. 90.

TABLE 13.6

Analysis of Variance Results for Solomon Four-Group Experiment on Motor Skill Development

Source	Posttest Scores F	Trials F
Treatment (T)	25.19*	13.51*
Pretest (P)	___ᵃ	___ᵃ
T × P interaction	___ᵃ	18.14*

[a] The *F* values were not included in the report, only the fact that they were not statistically significant.

*p < .05

Source: Adapted from text on pp. 95–96 in: Edwards, R. (1988). The effects of performance standards on behavior patterns and motor skill achievement in children. *Journal of Teaching in Physical Education, 7,* 90–102.

practice trials and posttest score—considered together. Then she did a separate, or univariate, ANOVA for each dependent measure.

The results of the two ANOVAs are shown in Table 13.6. The only factor with a statistically significant effect on students' posttest scores was the treatment variable (standards present or absent). Students receiving performance standards earned a significantly higher mean score (*M* = 15.58) than students not receiving performance standards (*M* = 12.58).

Two conditions had a statistically significant effect on the number of trial shots that students took during the practice sessions. First, students given performance standards had significantly more trials (*M* = 70) than students not given performance standards (*M* = 54). Second, a significant interaction was found between the pretest and the treatment variable. This interaction is illustrated in Figure 13.3. We see that the pretest had a modest effect on the control group: Pretested students had about 10 more trials on average (i.e., took 10 more hockey shots) than did nonpretested students. The pretest, however, had a dramatic effect on the treatment group: Pretested students had about 30 fewer trials on average than did nonpretested students.

To understand this effect, consider the fact that the treatment group with a pretest had both a performance standard and a pretest experience to guide their behavior. Evidently, the pretest experience had more of an effect, because their trial frequency was more similar to the control group that had a pretest than it was to the other treatment group, which also had a performance standard but no pretest experience. Edwards cautioned other researchers to be careful about using pretests in studies of motor skill development because they can mask the effects of instruction.

If a pretest effect seems likely, you can use either a posttest-only control-group design (see Chapter 12) or a Solomon four-group design. The latter is the more powerful experimental design, but it requires a rather large sample and much researcher effort. The effort is justified, however, if there is a high probability that pretesting will have an effect on the experimental treatment and you wish to measure this effect.

FIGURE 13.3

Plot of Effect of Interaction between Pretest and Treatment on Number of Trials in Motor Skills Experiment

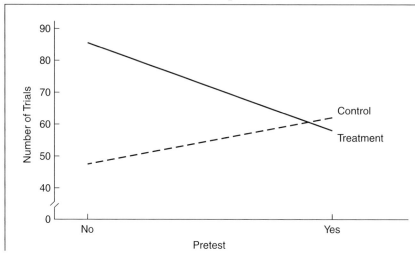

Source: Adapted from Figure 1 on p. 96 in: Edwards, R. (1988). The effects of performance standards on behavior patterns and motor skill achievement in children. *Journal of Teaching in Physical Education, 7,* 90–102. Copyright 1988 by Human Kinetics Publishers, Inc. Adapted by permission.

Variations in Factorial Experiments

The design and analysis of factorial experiments is a complicated matter. You can choose from many factorial designs. The choice of a design depends on various conditions:

1. The number of independent variables, (i.e., factors)
2. Whether the factors are fixed or random
3. Whether research participants receive repeated measures of the same variable
4. Whether there are unequal numbers of research participants in each treatment group
5. The scale and distribution properties of scores on the dependent variables
6. The need for a covariate to compensate for initial differences between treatment groups
7. Whether each research participant is assigned to more than one treatment.

Fixed and Random Factors

The second condition listed above—whether the factors are considered fixed or random—requires some explanation. A **fixed factor** is an independent variable whose values will not be generalized beyond the experiment. Some fixed factors exhaust all possible values of the variable, for example, gender. If gender is a factor in the experiment, there are two values (also called *levels*): female and male. There are no other genders to which generalizations can be made.

Other factors are not exhaustive, but are considered so for purpos̸
For example, the researcher might have a factor, marital status, wi̸
or not married. Generalizations from the research findings will o̸
als at those two levels, even though additional values of marital s̸
(e.g., engaged to be married, once-married and divorced, tw̸
The treatment variable is typically a fixed factor, because re̸s
to generalize beyond the intervention, or interventions, be̸

A **random factor** is an independent variable whose v̸
the experiment. For example, suppose the treatment va̸
and the researcher wishes to know whether different teacher̸s
when using it. The researcher might select five teachers to use the ̸
of having this sample represent a population of teachers. In this case, ea̸
incorporated into the experimental design as a value of a *teacher* factor. The ̸
5 design: The first factor is fixed and has two levels (treatment group versus contro̸
and the second factor is random and has five levels (teacher 1, teacher 2, teacher 3, teac̸
4, teacher 5).

The distinction between fixed and random factors is important, because it affects the statistical techniques used to analyze data resulting from the experiment.

Assignment of Participants to Multiple Treatments

The seventh condition in the above list involves assigning each research participant to more than one treatment condition. You will recall that this is what was done in Saunders and Jesunathadas's experiment on proportional reasoning. The advantage of assigning participants to several treatments is that the experiment can be done with a smaller sample. Thus, recruitment of participants is easier, and the costs of conducting the experiment might be reduced. Another advantage is that statistical analysis of the data is more sensitive because each subject is "matched" with himself across treatments.

If individuals participate in more than one treatment, the effect of a treatment can become confounded with its order of administration relative to the other treatments. An **order effect** is the influence that the placement of a treatment in the administration of several treatments has on a dependent variable. For example, an order effect can occur if research participants become fatigued by participating in several treatments. They may do less well on the posttest associated with the last-administered treatment not because this treatment is less effective, but because they are fatigued from responding to the demands of the previously administered treatments.

Counterbalanced designs are used to avoid the problems of interpretation due to order effects. In a **counterbalanced experiment**, each participant is administered several treatments, but the order of administering the treatments is varied across participants to eliminate the possible confounding of order effects with treatment effects.

To summarize, there are many factorial designs, each suited to a different purpose. It is useless to develop a research hypothesis and to carefully execute the experiment unless you first choose the proper factorial design. If you are planning a factorial experiment, we advise you to read a textbook on experimental design and to consult an expert in the area of factorial design and statistical analysis.

Single-Case Designs

A **single-case experiment**, sometimes called a *single-subject experiment* or a *time-series experiment*, is one that involves the intense study of one individual, or of more than one

---

✦ Touchstone in Research

Franklin, R. D., Allison, D. B., & Gorman, B. S. (Eds.). (1997). *Design and analysis of single-case research.* Mahwah, NJ: Lawrence Erlbaum Associates.

Glass, G. V (1988). Quasi-experiments: The case of interrupted time series. In R. M. Jaeger (Ed.), *Complementary methods for research in education* (pp. 445–464). Washington, DC: American Educational Research Association.

Kratochwill, T. R., & Levin, J. R. (Eds.). (1992). *Single-case research design and analysis.* Mahwah, NJ: Lawrence Erlbaum Associates.

dividual treated as a single group. As Thomas Kratochwill explains, single-case designs involve the intense analysis of behavior in single organisms.[11] This type of experiment is illustrated in Table 12.5 in the preceding chapter, where it is called a *time-series design.*

The single-case experiment is well suited to research on behavior modification. **Behavior modification** is a specialization within psychology that seeks to change the behavior of individuals by applying experimentally validated techniques such as social and token reinforcement, fading, desensitization, and discrimination training.[12] As an educational strategy, behavior modification is used extensively in such applications as classroom management, skill development, and training of individuals with disabilities. It also is employed widely in counseling, psychotherapy, institutional caretaking, and in drug research. Reports of single-case experiments of interest to educators appear in various journals, especially the Journal of Applied Behavior Analysis.

Single-case experiments should not be equated with the case-study method of investigation (see Chapter 14). Both focus on one case, yet they differ greatly in design and purpose. Single-case designs use several procedures to achieve experimental control as conceptualized within the quantitative research tradition: checks on the reliability of the experimenter's observations of the research participant's behavior, frequent observations of the behaviors targeted for change, description of the treatment in sufficient detail to permit replication, and replication of treatment effects within the experiment. In contrast, case studies explore a much broader treatment (typically, a large-scale program), are carried out in a field setting, and rely heavily on qualitative data.

Some researchers consider the single-case experiment to be a watered-down, easier version of one of the group designs presented earlier in this chapter and in Chapter 12. This is not true. Researchers who work with single-case designs are as concerned with problems of internal validity and external validity as researchers who do control-group experiments. Most single-case designs are rigorous and time-consuming, and they may involve as much data collection as a design involving experimental and control groups.

Example of a Single-Case Experiment

A study by Hans van der Mars illustrates the nature of the single-case experiment with one research participant.[13] The purpose of the experiment was to test a particular method for increasing teachers' use of verbal praise to reward desired student conduct. The need for the study was established by referring to previous research findings indicating that verbal praise promotes desired student conduct, but that teachers seldom use verbal praise unless specifically trained to do so.

The subject of the experiment was a student teacher of physical education. The experimental intervention was an audiocueing device, which consisted of a microcassette recorder on a waist belt and a mini-earphone. While wearing the device unobtrusively, the teacher received audiocueing:

> The subject was cued in to specific managerial events and student behaviors by the type of cues, such as (a) "Praise two students for getting to their squads quickly"; (b) "When the activ-

11. Kratochwill, T. R. (1992). Single-case research design and analysis: An overview. In T. R. Kratochwill & J. R. Levin (Eds.), *Single-case research design and analysis* (pp. 1–14). Hillsdale, NJ: Lawrence Erlbaum Associates. Quote appears on p. 11.
12. There are many publications on the educational applications of behavior-modification techniques, including Wielkiewicz, R. J. (1986). *Behavior management in the schools: Principles and procedures.* (2nd ed.). Boston: Allyn & Bacon.
13. van der Mars, H. (1987). Effects of audiocueing on teacher verbal praise of students' managerial and transitional task performance. *Journal of Teaching in Physical Education, 6,* 157–165. The experiment involved a second teacher, but the data for that teacher are not presented in order to simplify the presentation.

ity starts, look for those students who get started quickest. Praise them!" (c) "Praise the group for paying attention and being quiet during instructions"; and (d) "Look for hard workers. Praise them!"[14]

An audiorecording was made of each lesson that the teacher taught. Each recording was analyzed to determine the teacher's rate of verbal praise of desired student conduct. The rate was computed by dividing the frequency of verbal praise statements the teacher uttered during the lesson by the number of minutes in the lesson.

In the first phase of the experiment, the teacher taught five lessons without training in verbal praise or use of the audiocueing device. The teacher's rate of verbal praise during these pretreatment lessons is shown in the far-left portion of Figure 13.4. The rate of the teacher's display of the target behavior during these lessons is called a **baseline** because it shows the teacher's natural behavior prior to the experimental intervention. The baseline is similar in purpose to a pretest in the experimental designs presented in Chapter 12 and the first part of this chapter.

Following the baseline period, the teacher was trained in how to recognize and praise desired student conduct, and was asked to use the audiocueing device during the next eight lessons. The prerecorded audiocues were presented at an average rate of two per

FIGURE 13.4

Rate of Verbal Praise across Baseline and Treatment Conditions in Audiocueing Experiment

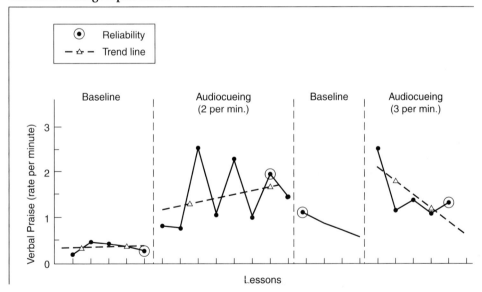

Note: The reliability points are sessions in which observer reliability was checked.

Source: Adapted from Figure 1 on p. 161 in: van der Mars, H. (1987). Effect of Audiocueing on teacher verbal praise of students' managerial and transitional task performance. *Journal of Teaching in Physical Education, 6,* 157–165.

14. Ibid., p. 159.

minute. Figure 13.4 shows that the teacher's rate of verbal praise increased substantially during this treatment phase.

In the next baseline period, the teacher was given no audiocues for four lessons. The act of withdrawing a treatment after a research participant has become accustomed to it is called **extinction** by behavioral researchers. Figure 13.4 shows that the teacher's rate of verbal praise declined during the extinction, or second baseline, phase. This second baseline period is similar to a posttest in a group-experiment design.

The final phase of the experiment involved reintroduction of audiocues for six lessons. As in the first treatment phase, the teacher's rate of verbal praise increased.

A single-case experiment typically yields the type of data graphed in Figure 13.4. The researcher must examine the data and decide whether they indicate that the treatment had an effect on the dependent variable. This decision usually is made in two ways. One approach is simply to make a visual examination of the form of the graphed data. The following statement about Figure 13.4 by van der Mars illustrates this approach:

> The changes established were found to be experimentally significant in light of (a) baselines that were minimally variable and either stable or directed in a downward trend, (b) the absence of overlap between baseline and treatment data, and (c) the change of level from final baseline sessions to initial treatment sessions.[15]

The other approach to determining treatment effect is to organize the data so that they can be analyzed using a conventional test of statistical significance. For example, van der Mars used a t test to compare the pooled mean of the two baseline phases and the pooled mean of the two treatment phases. The t value of 3.72 was statistically significant ($p < .01$), leading the researcher to conclude that the audiocueing treatment produced a true effect.

An experiment involving baseline-treatment-extinction-treatment phases is one of many single-case designs. In the following sections we describe general features of single-case design, steps to follow in using some of the more common designs, and statistical techniques for analyzing single-case data.

General Design Considerations

Single-case experiments should be designed to have high internal validity. As is true of group designs, the internal validity of a single-case design is a function of the researcher's ability to rule out factors other than the treatment variable as possible causes of changes in the dependent variable. In control-group experiments, internal validity is achieved primarily by random assignment of research participants to the experimental-treatment and control conditions. Because $N = 1$ in single-case research, random assignment and control groups are not possible. Internal validity is achieved by other design techniques, which are described below. These techniques are not exclusive to single-case designs, but are especially important to them.

Reliable Observation

Single-case designs typically require many observations of behavior. If the observations are unreliable, they will obscure treatment effects. Therefore, certain procedures should be followed in making observations, particularly careful training of observers, operational definition of the behaviors to be observed, periodic checks of observer reliability, and control of observer bias. When appropriate, you can consider measurement of behavioral

15. Ibid., p. 162.

products (e.g., the number of problems solved in a school assignment) as a substitute for observation of behavior. These procedures are discussed in the content-analysis section in Chapter 9 and in books about single-case design.

The simplest procedure is to target one behavior for repeated observation throughout the experiment. For example, the teacher's rate of verbal praise for conduct was the only behavior that was observed in the experiment on audiocueing. It is possible to monitor additional behaviors, but observational procedures become increasingly complicated as each new behavior is added to the research design.

Repeated Measurement

In the typical group experimental design, data are collected at two points in time: before (pretest) and after (posttest) the experimental treatment. Single-case designs require many more measurements, because the behavior of an individual can vary greatly even within short time intervals. Consider the fact that the experiment on audiocueing had four phases: baseline, treatment, second baseline, and second treatment. If the student teacher's verbal praise behavior was measured only once in each phase, it would be impossible to interpret whether variations in the rate of praise were a function of the treatment variable or of other naturally occurring events. The use of frequent measurements provides a clearer, more reliable description of how the teacher's behavior naturally varies and how it varies in response to the treatment condition. Furthermore, statistical significance tests of single-case data are more powerful if many measurements of the dependent variable are available.

Because of the need for repeated measurements in a single-case design, it is important to standardize the measurement procedure. Preferably each measurement occasion would involve the same observers, the same instructions to the research participant, and the same environmental conditions. Otherwise, treatment effects are likely to be contaminated with measurement effects.

Description of Experimental Conditions

The researcher should provide a precise description of each experimental condition that would be important if one wished to replicate the experiment. Some single-case designs require re-introduction of the baseline and the treatment variable. For example, the baseline and treatment conditions appeared twice in the experiment on audiocueing. If the conditions involving the baseline or the treatment variable are not specified precisely, they will be difficult to replicate within the experiment. As a consequence, the internal validity of the experiment is threatened. Furthermore, imprecise specification makes it difficult for other researchers to replicate the experiment, thus threatening the external validity of the experiment.

Baseline and Treatment Stability

The baseline in single-case designs is the natural frequency of the target behavior before introduction of the experimental variable. If the occurrence of the target behavior did not vary at all during the period of observation, it would be easy to assess the effect of the treatment variable. Yet most behaviors vary. If the variation is too great, you will have difficulty in separating treatment effects from naturally occurring changes in the research participant's behavior.

To counter the effects of natural fluctuations, you can set a standard for determining when a baseline has stabilized, for example, no more than a 5 percent range of variation from the mean over a period of 10 observations. There are occasions, though, when this type of standard is inappropriate. For example, suppose you plan to use an experimental intervention with a person whose behavior is systematically worsening or improving. If the person's behavior is systematically improving during the baseline period, you are faced with a difficult problem. If the person continues to improve during the treatment phase, one could argue that the continued improvement was due to some condition that existed during the baseline period rather than to a treatment effect. In this situation you should consider withholding the treatment variable until baseline improvement has peaked and then stabilized.

The same need for stability applies to the treatment phase of a single-case design. Suppose that you planned four treatment sessions. No effects appear after the first three sessions, but improvement is apparent after the fourth session. Should you discontinue treatment, as planned? It probably is advisable in this situation to continue treatment until a stable, interpretable pattern of treatment effects has emerged.

Length of Baseline and Treatment Phases

As a general rule, there should be approximately the same length of time and number of measurements in each phase of a single-case design. Otherwise, the imbalance complicates the statistical analysis and interpretation of treatment effects. In some situations, however, this rule of equal phases conflicts with the need to maintain baseline or treatment conditions until a stable pattern of measurements has emerged. You also may need to maintain baseline or treatment conditions longer than intended because of institutional or ethical factors. One way to overcome this problem is to do several pilot studies to explore baseline and treatment conditions in the setting that interests you. The knowledge that you acquire can be used to design a more rigorous experiment in which baseline and treatment conditions are equalized in duration and number of measurements.

A-B-A Designs

A-B-A designs are used in single-case or single-group experiments having one treatment. The A stands for the baseline condition, and the B stands for the treatment. We discuss two of these designs below. There are various other A-B-A designs, including several for investigating interaction effects involving treatments.

A-B Design

The **A-B design** is the simplest of the single-case designs. The researcher begins by selecting a participant for the experiment, one or more target behaviors, measures of the target behaviors, and an experimental treatment. Then the target behavior is measured repeatedly during the baseline period (A). Finally, the experimental treatment (B) is administered while the researcher continues to measure the target behavior.

The A-B design is low in internal validity.[16] If the difference between the means of the A measurements and the B measurements is statistically significant, we can conclude that a reliable change occurred from the baseline phase to the treatment phase. Attributing the change to a treatment effect is difficult, however, because the influence of other factors cannot be ruled out. These factors might be other events occurring during the treatment phase, or the effects of testing during the baseline period. The A-B design should be used only when no suitable alternative is available, or when the researcher intends it as a pilot study to be followed by an experiment using a more rigorous design.

---

16. The uses and internal validity problems of the A-B design are discussed in: Campbell, D. T. (1969). Reforms as experiments. *American Psychologist, 24*, 409–429.

A-B-A and A-B-A-B Designs

The **A-B-A design** follows the same steps as the A-B design, except that a second baseline condition is added. The second baseline typically involves *withdrawal* of the treatment, as in the experiment on audiocueing. You can also bring about *reversal* of the treatment in the second baseline condition. For example, in the experiment on audiocueing, the researcher might have given the teacher audiocues to ask students to engage in good conduct, but not given them verbal praise for doing so.

The A-B-A design has high internal validity. If the target behavior changes as expected in each phase of the experiment, one can conclude that the changes were due to the effect of the treatment variable. However, one difficulty with this design is that the experiment ends on a negative note, because the treatment (presumably positive in nature) is withdrawn or reversed. This condition may be ethically unacceptable to the researcher and to others involved in the experiment.

The A-B-A-B design overcomes the ethical issue of ending on a negative note that may arise with the A-B-A experiment. In the **A-B-A-B design,** the experiment concludes after re-introduction of the treatment variable (B). The experiment on audiocueing described above exemplifies this design. Each of the four phases of the A-B-A-B design were present: initial period of baseline observation, initial introduction of the treatment variable, withdrawal or reversal of the treatment variable (second baseline), and re-introduction of the treatment variable.

A limitation of this design, and of all baseline designs, is that the observed treatment effect is dependent upon the particular baseline conditions included in the experiment. Assuming that a reliable A-B change is found, we can conclude only that the effect will occur reliably for that set of conditions. Therefore, the baseline conditions must be described precisely. This restriction is similar to the pretest sensitization problem in group designs that include a pretest (see the discussion of internal validity in Chapter 12). Reliable treatment effects found in such designs cannot be presumed to be independent of the particular pretest that was used to discover the effects.

Multiple-Baseline Designs

Time-series designs (A-B-A) generally use the natural occurrence of the target behavior as a control condition for assessing treatment effects. In contrast, **multiple-baseline designs** are experiments in which conditions other than the naturally occurring target behavior are used as controls for assessing treatment effects. Administration of these conditions approximates the use of a control group to improve the internal validity of a group experiment.

Multiple-baseline designs are used when reinstatement of baseline conditions in an A-B-A type design is not possible. This problem might occur if the researcher is unable to withdraw or reverse the treatment for ethical reasons. Also, it might not be possible to demonstrate a treatment effect using an A-B-A design. That is, the target behavior might not return to the pretreatment baseline rate after the treatment is withdrawn or reversed. If this occurs, we cannot conclude that the treatment had an effect, even though the target behavior changed reliably from the initial baseline phase to the treatment phase. As an alternative, we can use a multiple-baseline design to investigate the effects of the treatment.

Example of a Multiple-Baseline Experiment

In one of the more commonly used multiple-baseline designs, two or more individuals are used to control for extraneous variables in assessing treatment effects. This was the case in an experiment conducted by George Stern, Susan Fowler, and Frank Kohler.[17] The purpose of their experiment was to determine the effects of using a peer-mediated intervention to help students who engage in inappropriate behavior. In a peer-mediated intervention, one student monitors and gives points to another student in order to reward and thus increase desirable behavior and to decrease undesirable behavior. A question of special interest to researchers was whether the role of monitor/point-giver or the role of point-receiver results in greater behavior change.

Robert and Karen, two students in a combination fifth-/sixth-grade class, were selected as research participants because they were disruptive during math seatwork and were members of the lowest-performing math group. Three other low-performing peers worked as their partners. Partners A and B worked with Karen, and Partner C worked with Robert.

Figure 13.5 illustrates the design and results of the experiment. The dependent variable, shown on the vertical axis, is total inappropriate behavior, which includes both off-task behavior and disruptive behavior (any behavior that interfered with the work of another child). These observations were made at intervals of every 10 seconds during math seatwork each day. The measure was the percentage of intervals in which Karen and Robert were off-task or disruptive.

No intervention occurred during the baseline conditions. Note that in Figure 13.5 the percentage of inappropriate behavior is quite high for both students during the first baseline.

The intervention phase of the experiment began for Karen on the sixth day. On alternate days she monitored the seatwork of her two partners, A and B, and gave them points for meeting a criterion of appropriate behavior. If enough points were accumulated over a period of days, the entire class received a reward, usually a movie.

Figure 13.5 shows that Karen's percentage of inappropriate behavior dropped substantially after she was put into the role of monitor and point-giver. On the days that Karen was not in this role, her partners monitored her behavior and gave her points in the same way. Figure 13.5 shows that Karen's inappropriate behavior was similarly low when she was in the role of point-earner.

Note that in Figure 13.5 the first baseline for Robert extended through class session 11, while it terminated for Karen after session 5. The six additional baseline sessions for Robert provide a control for extraneous variables that could confound the treatment effects observed in Karen. Both Karen and Robert were in the same class with the same teacher during these six sessions. The only difference is that Karen received the treatment. Therefore, we have reason to be confident that Karen's lower percentage of inappropriate behavior, both in comparison to her first baseline and to Robert's continuing first baseline, was due to the treatment.

The baseline condition was reinstituted for Karen after the 26th class session. With the exception of one session, her inappropriate behavior remained at a low rate during this second baseline, indicating that the treatment produced a good maintenance effect. We see, then, that an A-B-A design would have been a poor choice for this experiment. Because the treatment created an apparently lasting effect, it would not have been possible to reinstitute the original baseline rate of inappropriate behavior. It might have been possible to reinstitute the baseline by reversing the treatment in some way, for example, by giving Karen points for inappropriate behavior. This solution, however, poses obvious ethical problems.

17. Stern, G. W., Fowler, S. A., & Kohler, F. W. (1988). A comparison of two intervention roles: Peer monitor and point earner. *Journal of Applied Behavior Analysis, 21,* 103–109. The experiment involved several research participants not discussed here.

FIGURE 13.5

Percentage of Intervals in Which Students Engaged in Inappropriate Behavior across Baseline and Treatment Conditions in Peer-Mediation Experiment

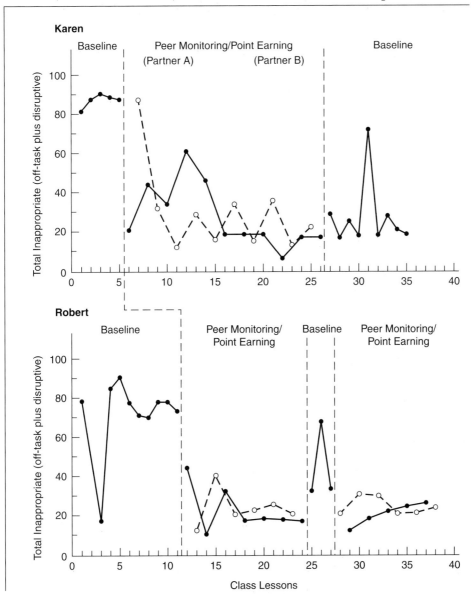

Source: Adapted from Figure 1 on p. 107 in Stern, G. W., Fowler, S. A., & Kohler, F. W. (1988). A comparison of two intervention roles: Peer monitor and point earner. *Journal of Applied Behavior Analysis, 21,* 103–109.

Note that Robert's second baseline demonstrated less of a maintenance effect than was the case for Karen. In fact, the researchers stated that

> Robert responded to the withdrawal of treatment by increasing his rate of inappropriate behavior somewhat and by repeatedly asking for a resumption of the peer-monitoring procedure. Because of his requests and the teacher's request, we reimplemented the intervention after only three days of baseline.[18]

Following reinstitution of the treatment, Robert's percentage of inappropriate behavior again dropped. The effectiveness of the treatment did not seem to depend on whether Robert was in the role of monitor/point-giver or point-earner.

The researchers did not perform tests of statistical significance on their data. Instead, they relied on visual analysis of the descriptive graphs shown in Figure 13.5. The treatment effect is nonetheless convincing because it was tested three times (once in the case of Karen and twice in the case of Robert), and each time the students' rate of inappropriate behavior dropped well below the preceding baseline condition.

The experiment that we just described used one of various multiple-baseline designs that are available for different situations that arise in single-case experiments. Some of these designs involve the use of multiple target behaviors or multiple stimulus settings to provide baseline control, whereas the design discussed above used multiple research participants to provide baseline control.

Statistical Analysis of Single-Case Data

✦ Touchstone in Research

Todman, J. B., & Dugard, P. (2001). *Single-case and small-n experimental designs: A practical guide to randomization tests.* Mahwah, NJ: Lawrence Erlbaum Associates.

Many researchers rely exclusively on raw data and a few descriptive statistics for interpreting the results of single-case experiments. Figures 13.4 and 13.5 are typical graphical data plots of single-case data. The abscissa (horizontal line) represents units of time, and the ordinate (vertical line) represents units of the target behavior. Each data point is plotted separately on the graph, and the data points may be connected by lines. Vertical broken lines are used to indicate the transition from one phase to another (e.g., from baseline to treatment).

Using the graphical data plot, you can analyze within each phase the data points for the mean level of the target behavior and the direction of the slope, if any. Also, you can compare adjacent phases for changes in mean level, slope, and level between the last data point for one phase and the first data point for the next phase.

Some researchers also recommend determining the magnitude of a treatment effect by computing the percentage of nonoverlapping data.[19] This percentage is the number of treatment data points that exceed the highest (or lowest, if appropriate) baseline data point, divided by the total number of treatment data points. For example, in Figure 13.5, all but one of the 11 data points for Robert's second treatment phase are lower (the desired direction) than the lowest data point in the preceding baseline. Therefore, the percentage of nonoverlapping data is 91 percent.

The use of visual analysis of graphs to interpret treatment effects in single-case experiments has been criticized.[20] One criticism is that the ordinal scale of a graph can be modified to accentuate or mask treatment effects. For example, the same data are plotted

---

18. Ibid., p. 109.

19. Scruggs, T. E., Mastropieri, M. A., & Casto, G. (1987). The quantitative synthesis of single-subject research: Methodology and validation. *Remedial and Special Education, 8,* 24–33. These researchers also recommend calculating the percentage of nonoverlapping data as a measure of effect size for meta-analyses of single-case experiments. Several articles criticizing this recommendation appear in the same issue of the journal.

20. Sharpley, C. F. (1986). Some arguments against analyzing client change graphically. *Journal of Counseling and Development, 65,* 156–159.

in plot a and plot b of Figure 13.6, yet the two graphs give quite different impressions of the magnitude of the treatment effect. Another criticism of visual analysis is that empirical studies have shown low inter-rater reliability in the use of visual analysis to determine whether or how much of a treatment effect occurred.[21]

The alternative to visual analysis is the use of inferential statistics. For example, you will recall that in the experiment on audiocueing the researcher used a *t* test to compare the pooled mean of the two baseline phases and the pooled mean of the two treatment phases. This use of traditional inferential statistics has been criticized, however.[22] One criticism is that inferential statistics are not appropriate to the logic of the single-case experiment, which involves intensive study of the individual rather than of samples from populations. Another criticism is that inferential statistics involve the assumption that the observations are independent of one another. This assumption is seldom satisfied in single-case experiments. The behavior that is observed in any given session probably is dependent on the behavior that occurred in previous sessions. The technical term for this phenomenon is **serial dependency. Time-series statistics** can be used to determine the extent of serial dependency in data from a single-case experiment, plus the presence of a treatment effect. The computations for this statistical technique are complex, however, and many data points are necessary to yield interpretable results.

In summary, researchers can be misled both by visual analysis and by inferential statistics in interpreting data from single-case experiments. Therefore, you need to exercise good judgment in using either or both of these techniques. Good judgment requires both a technical grasp of the techniques and a thorough understanding of relevant theory, previous research findings, and circumstances surrounding the conduct of the experiment.

FIGURE 13.6

Plots of Identical Data Using Different Ordinal Scales

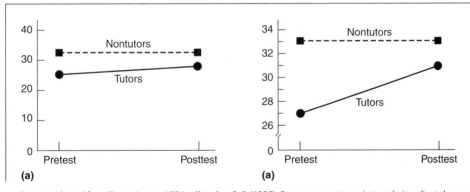

Source: Adapted from Figure 1 on p. 157 in: Sharpley, C. F. (1986). Some arguments against analyzing client change graphically. *Journal of Counseling and Development, 65,* 156–159. © ACA. Adapted with permission. No further reproduction authorized without written permission of the American Counseling Association.

21. DeProspero, A., & Cohen, S. (1979). Inconsistent visual analyses of intrasubject data. *Journal of Applied Behavior Analysis, 12,* 573–579; Jones, R. R., Vaught, R. S., & Weinrott, M. (1978). Time-series analysis in operant research. *Journal of Applied Behavior Analysis, 11,* 277–283.
22. Bass, R. F. (1987). The generality, analysis, and assessment of single-subject data. *Psychology in the Schools, 24,* 97–104.

Incorporating replications into the design of the experiment, as in the peer-monitoring experiment described above, also promotes sound interpretations of treatment effects.

External Validity of Single-Case Designs

One of the major criticisms directed at single-case designs is that they have low external validity, that is, the findings cannot be generalized beyond the one individual who participated in the experiment. The same critics are likely to look with favor on the traditional group experiment, because they believe that the findings can be generalized from the sample to the population from which it was drawn. Nevertheless, as we observe in Chapter 6, many studies that employ samples—including group experiments—do not involve random selection of the sample from a defined population. Rather, the particular sample is chosen because it is readily accessible, and then the results are generalized through logical inference to a larger population having similar characteristics.

In balance, it appears that both single-case and group experiments can be criticized on similar grounds for limited external validity. The real issue is how to increase the external validity of each type of experiment, rather than rejecting one type in favor of the other. The recommendations for improving the external validity of group experiments discussed earlier in the chapter also apply to single-case experiments.

Other Experimental Designs

We present the main designs used in experimental research in this and the preceding chapter. Our presentation, however, is by no means exhaustive. For example, we consider several factorial designs, but there are many others. Also, Campbell and Stanley discuss additional experimental designs that have application to some educational research problems.[23]

In selecting from among the experimental designs that are available, you should try to choose a design that will give the clearest picture of the effect of the experimental treatment, unconfounded by the effect of such variables as history, maturation, and so forth. Another important objective is to select a design that will yield results that can be generalized to other situations in which you are interested. This is not an easy task, especially if you plan to do your experiment in a natural field setting and individuals in this setting seek to place constraints on your preferred design.

Measurement of Change

Gain Scores

Basically, all experiments are attempts to determine the effect of one or more independent variables on one or more dependent variables. In educational research the independent variable often is a new educational practice or product, and the dependent variable often is a measure of student achievement, attitude, or self-concept. If the independent variable has an effect, the effect should be reflected as a *change* between students' scores on the measure that was administered prior to the experimental treatment (the pretest) and their scores on the measure administered after it ends (the posttest). The posttest score minus the pretest score is called a **gain score** (also called a *change* or *difference* score). For example, if a student's initial score on a measure of achievement was 50 and the stu-

23. Campbell & Stanley, *Experimental and quasi-experimental designs.*

dent's score rose to 65 after administration of the experimental treatment, the gain score would be 15. There are serious difficulties, however, in using gain scores to determine the effects of an experimental treatment.

These difficulties can be illustrated by considering a study of achievement gains from the beginning to the end of the freshman year of college conducted by Paul Dressel and Lewis Mayhew.[24] Table 13.7 lists gains made by students from nine colleges on various tests of achievement. The gain scores are presented separately for subgroups that were formed on the basis of their pretest scores on each test. There clearly is a strong inverse relationship between pretest score and achievement gain. For example, on the test of critical thinking in social science, the students whose scores were lowest at the beginning of the year made considerably larger gains (6.89 points) than the students whose scores were initially highest (an average gain of 2.26 points).

How are we to interpret such data? Do the data mean that students with low initial achievement are likely to learn more (as measured by their change scores) than students with initially high achievement? Although this interpretation might be correct, the inverse relationship between pretest scores and achievement gain scores is more likely to be an artifact produced by measurement error in the pretest and posttest.

The following are five problems of interpretation when raw gain scores (posttest scores minus pretest scores) are used to measure the amount of change that has occurred in individuals as the result of an intervention or a natural growth process.

1. *Ceiling effect.* A **ceiling effect** occurs when the range of difficulty of the test items is limited, and therefore scores at the higher end of the possible score continuum are artificially restricted. For example, suppose that a pretest and posttest each include 100 items but the items fail to measure the entire range of achievement possible on the dimension being measured. As a result, a student who answers 90 items correctly on the pretest can improve her score by only 10 points on the posttest. In contrast, a student with a score of

TABLE 13.7

Average Gains of Students on Posttests, Classified According to Pretest Standing

Test	Low Group	Low-Middle Group	Middle Group	High-Middle Group	High Group
Critical thinking in social science	6.89	5.48	3.68	4.20	2.26
Science reasoning and understanding	6.26	5.16	2.93	2.04	0.31
Humanities participation inventory	18.00	5.05	4.94	1.39	−2.07
Analysis of reading and writing	5.33	2.89	1.81	1.22	0.25
Critical thinking	6.68	4.65	3.47	2.60	1.59
Inventory of beliefs	9.09	5.31	4.65	3.32	1.01
Problems in human relations	3.19	1.67	1.31	1.51	−0.36

Source: Table 1 on p. 60 in: Diederich, P. B. (1956). Pitfalls in the measurement of gains in achievement. *School Review, 64,* 59–63. Copyright 1956 University of Chicago Press.

24. Dressel, P. L., & Mayhew, L. B. (1954). *General Education: Explorations in evaluation.* Washington, DC: American Council on Education. A table of their statistical results is reproduced in Diederich, P. B. (1956). Pitfalls in the measurement of gains in achievement. *School Review, 64,* 59–63. Deiderich's table is shown in Table 13.6.

40 on the pretest can make a potential gain of 60 points. Thus, the ceiling effect places a restriction on the distribution of gain scores across levels of initial ability.

The tests used in Dressel and Mayhew's study might have been subject to a ceiling effect. Students in the high-middle and high groups might have scored near the ceiling of the pretest. Thus, they could earn only a minimal gain score when they took the posttest.

2. *Regression toward the mean.* **Regression toward the mean** (also called *statistical regression*) is a statistical phenomenon describing the tendency for research participants who score either very high or very low on a measure to score nearer the mean when the measure is re-administered.[25] The greater gains made by low achievers in Dressel and Mayhew's study cited above were most likely due to statistical regression. The regression effect occurs because of errors of measurement in the pretest and posttest, and because the tests are correlated with each other.

3. *Assumption of equal intervals.* Use of gain scores assumes equal intervals at all points of the test, yet this assumption almost never is valid for educational measures. For example, on a 100-item test a gain from 90 to 95 points is assumed to be equivalent to a gain from 40 to 45 points. In fact, it probably is much more difficult to make a gain of 5 points when one's initial score is 90 (because of ceiling and regression effects) than when one's initial score is 40. If the test measures knowledge of word definitions, for example, a student whose initial score is 40 could earn 5 more points by learning the meaning of easy, frequently used words, but a student with the initially high score of 90 would have to learn the meanings of difficult, rarely used words to improve his score.

4. *Different types of ability.* With the exception of factorially pure tests, a given score on a test may reflect different types and levels of ability for different students. For example, a mathematics achievement test might include a variety of subtests measuring addition, subtraction, mathematical reasoning, algebra, and so on. Two students might earn the same score on the test, yet this score probably reflects a different pattern of strengths and weaknesses in the two. For example, one student might be weak in subtraction but strong in mathematical reasoning, while the other student might be strong in subtraction but weak in reasoning. The two students might earn the same gain score after a period of time because they overcame their respective deficiencies. Thus, the gain score for the first student reflects improvement in subtraction, whereas the gain score for the second student reflects improvement in mathematical reasoning. Because the gain scores are not equivalent in meaning, it is questionable to compare them in statistical analyses.

5. *Low reliability.* Still another difficulty with gain scores is that they usually are not reliable.[26] The higher the correlation between pretest and posttest scores, the lower the reliability of the change scores. Also, the reliability of change scores is affected by the degree of unreliability of the pretest and posttest scores themselves.

Statistical Analysis of Change

Gain scores are problematic, as we explained above, yet some measure of change is necessary if the researcher is to compare the effects of different experimental treatments. Although the limitations of gain scores cannot be overcome entirely, statistical procedures are available for overcoming some of them.

✦ *Touchstone in Research*

Linn, R. L. (1986). Quantitative methods in research on teaching. In M. C. Wittrock (Ed.), *Handbook of research on teaching* (3rd ed., pp. 92–118). New York: Macmillan.

25. The regression effect is discussed in Chapter 12 as a threat to the internal validity of an experiment. It is possible to get significant achievement gains in an initially low-achievement group of students even if the experimental treatment has no effect because of the regression effect.

26. Gain scores are reliable under a limited set of circumstances. See: Gupta, J. K., Srivastava, A. B. L., & Sharma, K. K. (1988). On the optimum predictive potential of change measures. *Journal of Experimental Education, 56,* 124–128.

Part Correlation

First, we will consider the situation in which the researcher is interested in the gain scores of individual students. For example, you might want to know why some college students show more gain on the measure of critical thinking in social science (CTSS) than other students, as shown in Table 13.6. Suppose you hypothesized that the gain scores are correlated with the students' high school grade point average (GPA). To test this hypothesis, you should not simply correlate GPA with the CTSS gain scores, because the CTSS scores are contaminated by regression and ceiling effects. A better procedure is to use part correlation (see Chapter 11), in which students' high school GPA scores are correlated with their CTSS gain scores after they have been statistically adjusted so that initial scores on CTSS are held constant.

Multiple Regression

An equivalent procedure is multiple regression (see Chapter 11), in which students' posttest CTSS scores are the dependent variable and pretest CTSS scores and high school GPA scores are the predictor variables. Pretest CTSS scores are entered first into the prediction equation. A slight variation is to do the multiple regression using only the pretest CTSS scores as a predictor variable. The resulting multiple regression equation can be used to compute a predicted posttest CTSS score for each student. These scores are called *residual gain scores,* or *adjusted gain scores.* Students' high school GPA scores then can be correlated with the residual gain scores.

Analysis of Covariance and t Tests

The other situation in which gain scores are used is in the analysis of mean gain. Suppose you administer an achievement pretest to two groups: One group is to receive an experimental treatment and the other is to serve as a control group. If research participants have been assigned randomly to the two groups, the groups should have equivalent mean pretest scores. If this is the case, you can use *t* tests to determine the statistical significance of the mean gain scores.

Occasionally the mean pretest scores will differ significantly by chance even when subjects have been assigned randomly to treatment groups. Also, when quasi-experimental designs are used, pretest means might differ considerably. To adjust for initial differences in pretest means, analysis of covariance should be used. This statistical technique permits you to attribute observed gains to the effect of the experimental treatment rather than to differences in initial scores. For example, analysis of covariance could be applied to the data in Table 13.6. By using this statistical technique, we could compare the mean achievement gain scores of each of the five subgroups *as if* they had all earned the same mean achievement score at the beginning of the freshman year. As we discussed in Chapter 10, the raw data first need to be examined to determine whether they satisfy certain assumptions underlying analysis of covariance.

Analysis of Variance for Repeated Measures

Still another approach for determining the statistical significance of change is **analysis of variance for repeated measures.** This statistical technique is used to determine whether the pretest-posttest difference for the experimental group is reliably different from the pretest-posttest difference for the control group. The occasions on which the measure of the dependent variable is administered (pretest and posttest) are considered one factor, and the experimental and control treatments are the other factor. The *F* ratios for the two factors (sometimes called *main effects*) are not of interest in this analysis of variance. For example, it is not meaningful to compare the mean of all the pretest scores with the mean of all the posttest scores, ignoring whether the scores are from experimental or control students. Of interest instead is the interaction between time of measurement and treatment. That is, we are interested in whether the difference between the pretest and posttest means of the experimental group is significantly greater or less than the difference for the control group.

This type of statistical analysis is illustrated in a study conducted by Norbert Johnson, Jerome Johnson, and Coy Yates.[27] The purpose of their experiment was to evaluate the effectiveness of a particular counseling program (the Vocational Exploration Group) in increasing the career maturity of students. Sixty eighth- and ninth-grade students were randomly assigned to the counseling program or to a no-treatment control group. The Career Maturity Inventory (CMI) was administered to all students as a pretest, again as a posttest (immediately following conclusion of the experimental program), and once again as a follow-up posttest (six months following the program). The CMI, which consists of six scales, measures maturity of attitudes and competencies necessary for making realistic career decisions.

Table 13.8 presents the pretest, posttest, and follow-up test means on the CMI for the experimental and control groups. It is apparent that the pretest-posttest difference on each scale is greater for the experimental group than for the control group. For example, the pretest-posttest difference on the Attitude scale is greater for the experimental group (38.1 minus 34.3 = 3.8) than for the control group (35.1 minus 34.3 = 0.8). The statistical significance of these differences is determined by doing a two-way (treatment group X time of testing) analysis of variance. A statistically significant F ratio for the interaction effect indicates that the pretest-posttest difference for one group is reliably greater or less than the pretest-posttest difference for the other group.

TABLE 13.8

Pretest, Posttest, and Follow-up Test Mean Differences on the Career Maturity Inventory (CMI)

CMI Scale	Pretest		Posttest		Follow-Up		Pretest-Posttest Difference F	Pretest-Follow-Up Difference F
	Exp. M	Control M	Exp. M	Control M	Exp. M	Control M		
Attitude	34.3	34.3	38.1	35.1	38.0	34.7	4.15*	4.57*
Competence scale								
Knowing yourself	9.3	9.6	12.1	10.3	10.4	10.4	N.S.	N.S.
Knowing about jobs	10.1	10.6	15.8	11.3	13.4	11.2	16.13**	12.92**
Choosing a job	11.3	11.6	13.9	12.2	11.9	12.2	N.S.	N.S.
Looking ahead	10.6	11.6	13.1	12.2	12.7	11.8	N.S.	N.S.
What should they do?	9.9	10.1	11.4	10.8	11.4	10.8	N.S.	N.S.

Note: N.S. = not significant
*p < .05
**p < .001
Source: Adapted from Table 1 on p. 71 in: Johnson, N., Johnson, J., & Yates, C. (1981). A six-month follow-up on the effects of the Vocational Exploration Group on career maturity. *Journal of Counseling Psychology, 28,* 70–71.

27. Johnson, N., Johnson, J., & Yates, C. (1981). A six-month follow-up on the effects of the Vocational Exploration Group on career maturity. *Journal of Counseling Psychology, 28,* 70–71.

The last two columns of Table 13.8 present these F ratios for the pretest-posttest difference and for the pretest follow-up test difference on each CMI scale. Significant F ratios were obtained for the Attitude scale and for the "Knowing about jobs" Competence scale. A series of t tests for multiple comparisons (see Chapter 10) revealed significant gains on these scales for the experimental group, but no change for the control group.

✦ RECOMMENDATIONS FOR
Doing Experiments

1. If a nonequivalent control-group design is your only option, attempt to make the experimental and control groups as similar as possible and use the posttest measure also as a pretest measure.
2. In designing an experiment, attempt to increase its usefulness by including not one, but several factors that you have reason to believe have a direct or interactive effect on the outcome variables.
3. If you have reason to believe that the experimental treatment will have different effects for different types of individuals, design the experiment to allow for the identification of aptitude-treatment interactions.
4. Consider using the Solomon four-group design if you have a particular interest in knowing whether administration of a pretest has an effect on the outcome variable.
5. In designing a single-case experiment, consider doing pilot studies to determine whether baseline stability or treatment stability is likely to be an issue in detecting treatment effects.
6. In analyzing gain-score data, consider which of the following approaches is most suitable: part correlation, multiple regression, analysis of covariance, or analysis of variance for repeated measures.

✔ SELF-CHECK TEST

Circle the correct answer to each of the following questions.
The answers are provided at the back of the book.

1. The distinguishing characteristic of the nonequivalent control-group design is that
   a. no pretest is administered to the control group.
   b. research participants are not randomly assigned to the experimental and control groups.
   c. the experimental group participates in a treatment intervention different from the one in which the control group participates.
   d. all threats to internal validity are controlled by this design.

2. The difference between group means in a nonequivalent control-group design usually is tested for statistical significance by
   a. a t test on the posttest means.
   b. the t distribution for the correlation between pretest and posttest scores.
   c. analysis of covariance on the posttest means.
   d. separate t tests of the pretest-posttest difference for the experimental group and for the control group.

3. Factorial designs are used in order to
a. control for the effects of nonrandom assignment to treatments.
b. collect data that can be entered into a factor analysis.
c. control for statistical regression.
d. test for the interaction of several variables in the same experiment.

4. A 2 × 2 × 2 × 2 factorial design indicates an experiment with
a. two dependent variables.
b. four dependent variables.
c. two independent variables.
d. four independent variables.

5. Which of the following variables is most experimentally manipulable?
a. student ability
b. teaching method
c. socioeconomic level of community in which a school is located
d. instructors' teaching experience

6. The effect of a pretest on the dependent variable in an experiment is best investigated using a(n)
a. Solomon four-group design.
b. counterbalanced design.
c. aptitude-treatment interaction design.
d. A-B-A design.

7. Research on aptitude-treatment interaction seeks to discover whether
a. aptitudes can be increased through appropriate intervention.
b. certain instructional methods are better than others.
c. certain students learn better under one instructional method than under another instructional method.
d. the relationship between aptitude and achievement can be predicted.

8. Counterbalanced experiments are designed to control for the effects of
a. statistical regression.
b. order of treatment administration.
c. maturation.
d. aptitude-treatment interaction.

9. Within-case replication of the treatment variable is provided by
a. the A-B design.
b. the A-B-A design.

c. the A-B-A-B design.
d. all of the above.

10. Multiple-baseline designs are used instead of A-B-A designs when
a. only one individual is included in the experiment.
b. reinstatement of baseline conditions is not possible.
c. reinstatement of treatment conditions is not possible.
d. an intervention occurs during the baseline conditions.

11. Data yielded by single-case experiments often are analyzed to determine
a. change in the mean performance level from one phase of the experiment to another.
b. change in the performance level between the last data point in one phase and the first data point in the next phase.
c. change in the slope from one phase of the experiment to another.
d. all of the above.

12. The higher the correlation between pretest and posttest scores
a. the lower the reliability of the change scores.
b. the higher the reliability of the change scores.
c. the more difficult will be prediction of posttest scores based on pretest scores.
d. the lower the validity of the posttest scores.

13. When doing an analysis of variance for repeated measures, the researcher is most interested in
a. the main effect for treatment.
b. the main effect for testing occasion.
c. the interaction between treatment and time of testing.
d. the interaction between treatment and multiple baselines.

PART V

✦ Approaches to Qualitative Research

Qualitative research in education and other social science disciplines is presently undergoing rapid growth and change. The productivity of qualitative researchers is evidenced by the proliferation of new journals, books, and professional associations representing different traditions of qualitative inquiry. Each tradition is marked by distinctive interests, theories, issues, and methods of investigation. In this part of the book we describe traditions of qualitative research that have particular relevance for the study of educational phenomena.

Chapter 14 focuses on case study research, which currently is the most widely used approach to qualitative inquiry in education. In conducting case studies, researchers collect intensive data about particular instances of a phenomenon, and they seek to understand each instance on its own terms and in its own context.

Chapter 15 provides an overview of specialized traditions of qualitative research. These traditions were developed by researchers in academic disciplines such as anthropology, linguistics, philosophy, psychology, and sociology, but they are being used increasingly by educational researchers. We consider 16 of these traditions, classified into three types: traditions involving the study of an individual's experienced reality, traditions involving the study of culture and society, and traditions involving the study of language and communication.

Chapter 16 considers historical research, which is one of the oldest and most fully developed of the qualitative research traditions. In describing it, we show that while historians conduct their investigations using primarily qualitative methods, they sometimes use quantitative methods as well. This blending of qualitative and quantitative methods also is found sometimes in case study research and other qualitative research traditions.

CHAPTER 14

✦ Case Study Research

OVERVIEW

A good case study brings a phenomenon to life for readers and helps them understand its meaning. We start this chapter by discussing the general characteristics of case studies and the various purposes they serve. The remaining sections of the chapter concern the procedures involved in conducting a case study: formulating a research problem; selecting a case, or cases; defining the researcher's role; collecting and analyzing data; and preparing a report.

OBJECTIVES

After studying this chapter, you should be able to

1. Describe the typical characteristics of a case study.
2. Describe the various purposes that a case study can serve.
3. Explain the meaning of thick description, constructs, themes, patterns, and judgments in case study research.
4. Explain how case study design differs from quantitative research design.
5. Explain how a case study researcher moves from the initial problem statement to finalizing case selection.
6. Discuss the advantages and disadvantages of a multiple-case design as compared to studying a single case.
7. Describe issues that researchers must address in defining their role when conducting a case study.
8. Describe the skills that case study researchers need to function successfully in field sites.
9. State the data-collection methods typically used in case study research.
10. Explain factors to consider in deciding when to stop collecting case study data.
11. Compare the purposes and procedures of interpretational, structural, and reflective data analysis.
12. Compare positivist and interpretivist approaches to determining the validity of case study findings.
13. Describe several methods that can be used to check the validity and reliability of case study findings.
14. Explain how case study researchers deal with the issue of generalizing their findings to other settings.
15. Explain how reflective reporting differs from analytic reporting of case study research.
16. Describe the advantages and disadvantages of case study research.

Introduction

One of the main characteristics of qualitative research is its focus on the intensive study of specific instances, that is *cases*, of a phenomenon. For this reason, qualitative research sometimes is called *case study research*. However, the two terms are not synonymous. Case study research evolved as a distinctive approach to scientific inquiry, partly as a reaction to perceived limitations of quantitative research. Many qualitative researchers subscribe to this approach and use it as a guide to their investigations. Other qualitative researchers subscribe instead to research traditions that generally are compatible with case study methodology, but that have grown up around an interest in particular types of phenomena and the development of special methods for studying them. (We describe these traditions, such as ethnography, semiotics, phenomenology, and historical research, in Chapters 15 and 16.)

Virtually any phenomenon can be studied by means of the case study methods that we describe in this chapter. However, other qualitative research traditions are limited to the study of particular types of phenomena. Thus, in choosing to study a phenomenon, you can choose to do so within the general case study framework described in this chapter, or within a specialized qualitative research tradition. Keep in mind, though, that it is not necessary to adhere to any particular tradition in doing qualitative research. Some qualitative researchers, especially those subscribing to postmodernism, reject any formal methodology and therefore do not align themselves either with case study research or with other qualitative research traditions.

In our view, then, case study research is one of several approaches to qualitative inquiry. We present it as the first of several chapters about qualitative research because of its widespread use in education. Another reason for presenting it first is that elements of the case study approach appear in the specialized qualitative research traditions described in Chapters 15 and 16. Learning the case study approach should make it easier for you to understand the purposes and methods of these other approaches to qualitative research.

Robert Stake observes that, "As a form of research, case study is defined by interest in individual cases, not by the methods of inquiry used."[1] For example, some researchers focus on the study of one case because of its intrinsic interest, whereas other researchers study multiple cases in order to test the generalizability of themes and patterns. The epistemological orientation of most case study researchers is interpretive, but there are some whose methods reflect a positivist orientation. In this chapter, we present the range of methods used in case study research rather than limiting ourselves to the methods of only one epistemological orientation.

Characteristics of Case Studies

To explain the characteristics of a case study, we will use as an example a study reported by Dona Kagan, who collected the data, and four teachers who were themselves the cases studied by Kagan.[2] The study examined the effects of a staff development program on the professional lives of four elementary teachers who participated in it. Kagan conducted and audiotaped a 90-minute interview with each of the four teachers who were in or had recently completed the program.

---

1. Stake, R. E. (2000). Case studies. In N. K. Denzin & Y. S. Lincoln (Eds.), *Handbook of qualitative research* (2nd ed., pp. 435–454). Thousand Oaks, CA: Sage. Quote appears on p. 435.
2. Kagan, D. M., Dennis, M. B., Igou, M., Moore, P., & Sparks, K. (1993). The experience of being a teacher in residence. *American Educational Research Journal, 30*, 426–443.

✦ Touchstone in Research

Glesne, C. (2001). *Becoming qualitative researchers: An introduction* (2nd ed.). New York: Addison-Wesley Longman.

Stake, R. E. (1995). *The art of case study research: Perspectives on practice.* Thousand Oaks, CA: Sage.

Yin, R. K. (1994). *Case study research* (2nd ed.). Thousand Oaks, CA: Sage.

In the introductory section of their report, Kagan and her colleagues state

[T]he structure of this article differs from the traditional empirical report by *not* beginning with an elaborate theoretical framework. In the spirit of grounded theory, the teachers' narratives are presented first, then an interpretation is inferred by Dona, a professor of education who worked with the teachers in constructing their stories.[3]

In the following sections, we will analyze this study in relation to four characteristics of case study research: (1) the study of phenomena by focusing on specific instances, that is, cases; (2) an in-depth study of each case; (3) the study of a phenomenon in its natural context; and (4) the study of the emic perspective of case study participants. These characteristics suggest the following definition of **case study research:** it is the in-depth study of instances of a phenomenon in its natural context and from the perspective of the participants involved in the phenomenon.

The Study of Particular Instances

A case study is done to shed light on a **phenomenon,** which is the processes, events, persons, or things of interest to the researcher. Examples of phenomena are programs, curricula, roles, and events. Once the phenomenon of interest is clarified, the researcher can select a case for intensive study. A **case** is a particular instance of the phenomenon.

In the Kagan study, the phenomenon of interest, in broad terms, was school-university partnerships. In reading the report, we find a more limited phenomenon of interest, namely, school-university partnerships that strengthen the staff development capacity of local school districts. The case selected for study was a particular example of this phenomenon, namely, the Teacher in Residence (TIR) program at the University of Alabama. The program brings experienced elementary teachers to the university for a two-year period to teach and supervise in the university's preservice teacher education program. At the end of their appointment, the teachers return to their districts with "a first-hand knowledge of novices that would help them design in-service programs."[4]

Any phenomenon has many aspects. Therefore, the researcher will need to select a focus for investigation. The **focus** is the aspect, or aspects, of the case on which data collection and analysis will concentrate. Kagan and her colleagues observed that previous research on school-university partnerships tended to focus on their policies and structures. They decided to choose another focus, namely, "the effects of a school-university staff development program on the professional lives of . . . elementary teachers who participated in it."[5] Program effects, then, comprise the focus of this case study. In other case studies, the focus might be a particular individual, a set of events, a time period, or a component of a program or organization.

In some case studies, it is possible to break down the aspect of the phenomenon on which the case study focuses into *units*. In the Kagan study, four teachers who had participated in the TIR program were selected for detailed investigation. In their report, the effects of the TIR program were presented separately for each of the four teachers, followed by a discussion of themes that were common to all of them. The unit of analysis, then, was the participating teacher, and four such units were studied. Another option would have been to identify school-university partnerships around the United States and select several of them for study. In this option, school-university partnerships would be the unit of analysis.

3. Ibid., p. 428.
4. Ibid., p. 427.
5. Ibid., p. 427.

With the above example in mind, we define a **unit of analysis** as an aspect of the phenomenon that can be sampled, with each member of the sample being studied as a separate case. In the Kagan study, the unit of analysis was teachers in residence. Four such units (i.e., four teachers in residence) were selected for study. Some researchers would call each unit a separate case because each unit is studied intensively. This is acceptable as long as we do not lose sight of the fact that the four cases are part of a larger case that is the main focus of the study, namely, the TIR program at one university.

To illustrate these distinctions further, suppose we are interested in how school leaders facilitate mandated curriculum reforms; therefore, we decide to study a particular curriculum reform mandated by the Oregon Department of Education and implemented by all Oregon school districts. In this example, the *phenomenon* is curriculum reform implementation, the *case* to be studied is the curriculum reform implemented in Oregon, the *focus* is the study of leadership behavior that facilitates curriculum reform implementation, and the *unit of analysis* is Oregon school districts. Given this sampling unit, we might select, let's say, a sample of ten school districts in which to collect data. We could study this phenomenon, though, without defining a unit of analysis. For example, we might decide to study the process by which the Oregon Department of Education developed the curriculum reform. The process might be holistic and embedded in various operations of the Department. Thus, the case would not be reducible to any smaller unit of analysis.

Some researchers select a case for study simply because it is interesting or available. If so, the larger significance of the case might be difficult to discern. However, if the case is conceptualized as an example of a broader phenomenon, the case's significance can be seen in terms of the light it sheds on that phenomenon. In the Kagan study, for example, the findings about the TIR program were considered in terms of their implications for school-university partnerships in general: "Perhaps there is a lesson here for those who are interested in promoting school-university partnerships aimed at enhancing teachers' professional lives . . . "[6] The notion of focus can help you keep in mind that a typical case has many aspects, and that a case study probably will be more manageable and meaningful if you concentrate on just a few of the aspects. Finally, the decision to define a unit of analysis and sample within it can help make your data collection more manageable and yet allow you to make meaningful generalizations from your data analyses.

In-Depth Study of the Case

In a case study, a substantial amount of data is collected about the specific case (or cases) selected to represent the phenomenon. These data are in the form of words, images, or physical objects, although some quantitative data may be collected as well. Often data are collected over an extended time period, and several methods of data collection are used.

To determine the effects of the TIR experience on the lives of the four teachers, Kagan conducted a 90-minute interview with each teacher. The interviews were audiotaped and transcribed. Then the transcriptions were analyzed for the purpose of writing a coherent narrative of the teacher's experience. Afterward, the following occurred:

> Two preliminary drafts of the narrative were returned successively to the interviewee for correction, amendment, and editing: an iterative process of constructing meaning that involved both the interviewer and interviewee in the selection and interpretation of biographical data . . . As coauthors, the four teachers were also invited to modify and edit Dona's commentary, as well as the entire article.[7]

6. Ibid., p. 441.
7. Ibid., p. 428.

From this description we can infer that the narratives were initiated after the initial interviews, but then involved continuing dialogue among the teachers and between the teachers and the principal researcher. The narratives thus reflect in-depth study of the teachers' experience of the TIR program.

Study of a Phenomenon in Its Natural Context

Jerome Kirk and Marc Miller define qualitative research as an approach to social science research that involves "watching people in their own territory and interacting with them in their own language, on their own terms."[8] Typically, but not always, case studies involve fieldwork in which the researcher interacts with study participants in their own natural settings. Even in instances where fieldwork is not done, the goal still is to learn about the phenomenon from the perspective of those in the field.

Robert Yin also emphasizes the importance of studying a phenomenon in its natural context.[9] He observes that case studies typically involve investigation of a phenomenon for which the boundaries between the phenomenon and its context are not clearly evident. Yin argues that these boundaries should be clarified as part of the case study.

In the case study of the TIR program, the teacher narratives ("Mary Beth's Experience," "Karen's Story," "Mary's Reflections," and "Polly's Story") position each teacher's interview statements about their experience in the program within the context of their past and current lives as elementary teachers. For example, the segment on Mary compares Mary's own preservice experience with the current preservice program for teachers, and reveals that her motivation to become a teacher in residence was "to give some realism to the preservice program."[10] The narrative then describes Mary's likes and dislikes about being a teacher in residence and how it influenced her perceptions of classroom teaching and her plans for when she returns to the elementary classroom. Thus, the "boundaries" of this case are Mary's previous and future life as a teacher. Mary's other roles—daughter, parent, spouse, citizen, and so forth—lie outside these boundaries.

Representation of Emic and Etic Perspectives

One purpose of case studies—in some studies, the only purpose—is to develop an understanding of a complex phenomenon as experienced by its participants. This purpose reflects an interpretive (as contrasted with a positivist) stance. As we explain in Chapter 1, interpretive research seeks to study the local, immediate meanings of social actions for the actors involved in them. The researcher's task is to figure out how to view the phenomenon as the participants view it. The participants' viewpoint is called the **emic** perspective. Typically, the researcher obtains this perspective through direct observation of the participants (sometimes called "insiders") as they behave naturally in the field, and through informal conversations with them. The conversations typically include questions such as, "How did you feel when _____?," "What did you think about when _____?," and "Why did you _____?"

At the same time, case study researchers generally maintain their own perspective as investigators of the phenomenon. Their viewpoint as outsiders, which is called the **etic** perspective, helps them make conceptual and theoretical sense of the case, and to report the findings so that their contribution to the literature is clear.

While the principal researcher (Kagan) does not refer to her own educational background, a note to the article describes her as a professor of education at George Mason

---

8. Kirk, J., & Miller, M. L. (1986). *Reliability and validity in qualitative* research. Thousand Oaks, CA: Sage.
9. Yin, R. K. (1994). *Case study research: Design and methods* (2nd ed.). Thousand Oaks, CA: Sage.
10. Kagan et al., Experience of being a teacher, p. 434.

University and states her specializations as teacher education and school-university partnerships. The research cited in the last section of the report ("Dona's Commentary and Analysis") clearly reflects Kagan's use of her professional experience in the analysis and interpretation of data obtained from the teachers. This is the etic perspective. The close involvement of the four teachers in the data-collection process (each of them was personally involved) and in the reporting of the findings ensures that the emic perspective was represented as well.

Purposes of Case Studies

Researchers generally do case studies for one of three purposes: to produce detailed descriptions of a phenomenon, to develop possible explanations of it, or to evaluate the phenomenon. We describe each of these purposes below.

Description

In a case study whose purpose is description, the researcher attempts to depict a phenomenon and conceptualize it. The depiction can focus on various phenomena, such as: the meanings that the research participants ascribe to their life and environment, contextual factors that influence their life, a series of events and their possible outcomes, and the new or unusual in society. A good depiction will provide what is called a **thick description** of the phenomenon, that is, statements that re-create a situation and as much of its context as possible, accompanied by the meanings and intentions inherent in that situation. The term *thick description* originated in anthropology to refer to a complete, literal description of a cultural phenomenon,[11] but is now used in qualitative research generally. A good example of thick description, in our opinion, is the opening statements in a report about a high school dropout by the educational anthropologist Harry Wolcott:

> "I guess if you're going to be here, I need to know something about you, where you're from, and what kind of trouble you are in," I said to the lad, trying not to reveal my uncertainty, surprise, and dismay at his uninvited presence until I could learn more about his circumstances. It wasn't much of an introduction, but it marked the beginning of a dialogue that lasted almost two years from that moment. Brad (a pseudonym, although as he noted, using his real name wouldn't really matter, since "no one knows who I am anyway") tersely stated his full name, the fact that his parents had "split up" and his mother was remarried and living in southern California, the local address of his father, and that he was not at present in any trouble because he wasn't "that stupid." He also volunteered that he had spent time in the state's correctional facility for boys, but quickly added, "it wasn't really my fault."
>
> It was not our meeting itself that was a surprise; it was that Brad already had been living at this remote corner of my steep and heavily wooded 20-acre home-site on the outskirts of town for almost five weeks.[12]

In creating thick description, the researcher looks for constructs that bring order to the descriptive data and that relate these data to other research findings reported in the literature. A **construct** is a concept that is inferred from observed phenomena and that can be used to explain those phenomena. For example, Wolcott uses the constructs of *education, school, deviant person, deviant act,* and *opportunity* to interpret dropout phenomena as manifested by Brad.

Researchers also can add depth to their descriptions by searching for themes present in the phenomena. We define **themes** as salient, characteristic features of a case. For example,

11. Geertz, C. (1973). *The interpretation of cultures: Selected essays.* New York: Basic Books.
12. Wolcott, H. F. (1994). *Transforming qualitative data: Description, analysis, and interpretation.* Thousand Oaks, CA: Sage. Quote appears on p. 68.

if a student—Sally—fails to turn in her homework on time on one occasion, it can be regarded as an isolated event. If Sally habitually fails to turn in her homework when it is due, we can say that this behavior is characteristic of her; it is a noteworthy theme. If Sally also delays doing household chores and getting ready for family outings, we might see a broader theme in her behavior, namely, procrastination.

The Kagan study illustrates the search for themes in case study data, specifically, "themes that could be validated with the professional literature on teaching and teacher education."[13] One of these themes was the functional value of the TIR experience. According to Kagan and her colleagues, the program experience not only gave teachers a different perspective on their own teaching, but served as a form of teacher research, that is, as a way to acquire theoretical rationales for their beliefs and to attach professional labels to them. (Teacher research as a form of action research is explained in Chapter 18.) Another theme was the expansion (not the abandonment) of the role of classroom teacher. The four teachers did not seek the TIR experience for upward mobility from classroom teaching, but rather to gain new insights into their teaching. The researchers described this finding as the most valuable and unexpected insight from their study.

Explanation

Some case study research aims to provide explanations for the phenomena that were studied. We refer to these explanations as **patterns,** meaning that one type of variation observed in a case study is systematically related to another observed variation. If the researcher does not claim that one variation has a causal effect on the other, we describe it as a **relational pattern.** If causality is claimed, it is a **causal pattern.**

An example of a causal pattern can be found in David Thomas's case study of the dynamics of cross-race relationships between protégés and their mentors or sponsors in a large telecommunications company.[14] He interviewed both the senior and junior members of 18 such pairs. In all but two pairs, the senior member was white and the junior member was African-American.

The members of each pair had formed an association in order to develop a relationship that would foster the professional development of the junior member of the pair. Thomas found that the relationships that developed were of two types, consistent with previous research. In a *mentor*-protégé relationship, the senior member provided not only instrumental career support (e.g., advocacy for promotions and performance feedback), but also psychosocial support (e.g., role modeling, counseling, and friendship). In a *sponsor*-protégé relationship, the senior member provided only instrumental career support.

Thomas sought to identify the factors that led to one or the other type of developmental relationship between these cross-race pairs. First, he examined the strategies that individuals used for managing the racial difference between the senior and junior member. Thomas found that individuals used one of two general strategies. The *denial and suppression* strategy involved a preference for not directly addressing the racial difference between the senior and junior member, and the *direct engagement* strategy involved a preference for directly addressing (i.e., communicating about) the racial difference.

Thomas initially expected that the relationship between a junior and senior member would develop into a mentor-protégé relationship only when both parties preferred and used the strategy of direct engagement. Instead, he found that when both parties preferred the same strategy—whether direct engagement or denial and suppression—the relation-

---

13. Kagan et al., *Experience of being a teacher,* p. 427.
14. Thomas, D. A. (1993). Racial dynamics in cross-race developmental relationships. *Administrative Science Quarterly, 38,* 169–194.

ship between the junior and senior member was more likely to develop into a mentor-pro-tégé relationship than a sponsor-protégé relationship.

Thomas's findings led him to develop a theoretical model of racial dynamics in developmental relationships. The model posits that strategies for managing racial differences have an effect on the type of relationship that develops between the junior and senior member of cross-race pairs. This, then, is a causal pattern: Variations in strategy (denial and suppression vs. direct engagement) are presumed to have an effect on variations in relationships (mentor-protégé vs. sponsor-protégé).

Evaluation

Chapter 17 describes several qualitative approaches to evaluation, including responsive evaluation, fourth-generation evaluation, quasi-legal models of evaluation, and expertise-based evaluation. In each approach, the researcher conducts a case study and makes judgments. In addition, the researcher might create a thick description of the phenomenon being evaluated and identify salient constructs, themes, and patterns. Case studies whose purpose is evaluation are being done with increasing frequency because educational programs that receive government funding are required to undergo formal evaluation.

Designing a Case Study

Standard designs for quantitative research studies have evolved over a period of decades as researchers gained experience in using this approach to inquiry. In planning and executing a new quantitative study, the researcher can look to these standard designs for a suitable "blueprint" of methods and sequential steps that, if employed properly, will yield the desired type of knowledge about the problem being investigated.

This is not true of case study design. Consistent with qualitative research in general, the design of each case study is specific to the phenomenon being studied and to the researcher conducting the study. In Alan Peshkin's view, the essence of case study design is interpretation.[15] It is the researcher's interpretive acts that give "importance, order, and form"[16] to the study. These interpretive acts occur throughout the course of the study:

> Interpretation has to do with the confluence of questions, images, and ideas that are the starting point of my inquiry, or the conceptualizing of my study.
>
> Interpretation has to do with where I choose to look to see that something is going on with regard to my conceptualization, or the situating of my study.
>
> Interpretation has to do with the judgment of what to collect that provides documentation for what I think is going on, or the instantiating of my study and the further focusing of its field of inquiry.
>
> Interpretation has to do with what to select for writing that establishes or affirms what I have identified that has gone on, or the composing of the elements of my research study.
>
> Finally, interpretation has to do with a perspectival accounting for what I have learned, or the shaping of the meanings and understandings of what has gone on from some point of view . . . [17]

In this view of case study design, the researcher's interpretive skill—acquired through study, apprenticeship, and experience—determines the specific features of the design. In this view, too, case study design is not an event, but a process that occurs throughout the case study.

15. Peshkin, A. (2000). The nature of interpretation in qualitative research. *Educational Researcher, 29*(9), 5–9.
16. Ibid., p. 9.
17. Ibid., p. 9.

Joseph Maxwell presents a more explicit model of case study design, but one which is consistent with Peshkin's emphasis on interpretation.[18] The full design model is shown in Figure 14.1. Its central features are the five components which are shown in circles and linked by lines that illustrate their connectivity: "The components form an integrated and interacting whole, with each component closely tied to several others, rather than being linked in a linear or cyclic process."[19] The factors surrounding the five components are not integral to case study design, but rather are influences on, or outcomes of, the design.

The five components in Maxwell's model are not specific methods, but rather sets of issues that are framed as questions. The questions relevant to each component are shown in Table 14.1. If you are planning to do a case study, these questions should prove a helpful aid in creating a design that has "importance, order, and form."

In this and the next sections of the chapter, we present a set of relatively discrete, sequential steps for doing a case study. We take this approach for two purposes: to simplify the process of doing a case study and to provide a basis for comparing case study design with other research designs. In reality, the steps may overlap and be retraced in the course of doing a case study. Also, methods that we describe within steps are not prescriptive. They are subordinate to the larger agenda of respecting the unique features of the case,

FIGURE 14.1

Components and Contextual Features of Qualitative Research Design

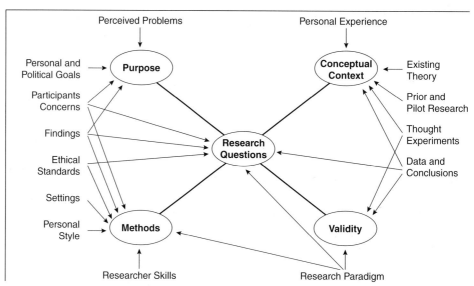

Source: Adapted from Figure 3.2 on p. 73 in: Maxwell, J. A. (1998). Designing a qualitative study. In L. Bickman & D. J. Rog (Eds.), *Handbook of applied social research methods* (pp. 69–100). Thousand Oaks, CA: Sage. Copyright © 1998 by Sage Publications. Reprinted by permission of Sage Publications, Inc.

18. Maxwell, J. A. (1998). Designing a qualitative study. In L. Bickman & D. J. Rog (Eds.), *Handbook of applied social research methods* (pp. 69–100). Thousand Oaks, CA: Sage.
19. Ibid., p. 71.

TABLE 14.1

Components of Maxwell's Model of Qualitative Research Design

1. *Purposes:* What are the ultimate goals of this study? What issues is it intended to illuminate, and what practices will it influence? Why do you want to conduct it, and why should we care about the results? Why is the study worth doing?

2. *Conceptual context:* What do you think is going on with the things you plan to study? What theories, findings, and conceptual frameworks relating to these will guide or inform your study, and what literature, preliminary research, and personal experience will you draw on? This component of the design contains the *theory* that you already have or are developing about the setting or issues that you are studying.

3. *Research questions:* What, specifically, do you want to understand by doing this study? What do you *not* know about the things you are studying that you want to learn? What questions will your research attempt to answer, and how are these questions related to one another?

4. *Methods:* What will you actually do in conducting this study? What approaches and techniques will you use to collect and analyze your data, and how do these constitute an integrated strategy?

5. *Validity:* How might you be wrong? What are the plausible alternative explanations and validity threats to the potential conclusions of your study, and how will you deal with these? Why should we believe your results?

Source: Text on p. 71 in: Maxwell, J. A. (1998). Designing a qualitative study. In L. Bickman & D. J. Rog (Eds.), *Handbook of applied social research methods* (pp. 69–100). Thousand Oaks, CA: Sage.

keeping interpretation at the center of the case study, and creating a research design that has coherence and value.

Formulating a Research Problem

The first step in planning a case study is to identify a problem that interests you and that is worthy of study. Often the research problem is grounded in the researcher's personal experience with a particular type of student, instructional program, or other phenomenon.

Once identified, the research problem needs to be translated into explicit questions or objectives. The following are two examples from published case studies.

Swidler, S. A. (2000). Notes on a country school tradition: Recitation as an individual strategy. *Journal of Research in Rural Education, 16,* 8–21.

The researcher used an ethnographic, symbolic-interpretive perspective to study a rural one-teacher school in Nebraska.

Research problem: "The present study was undertaken to look at the practices of some of the remaining one-teacher schools, what might be learned from them, and if or how we might capture a glimpse of 'our future in this remaining piece of our past' (Geyer, 1995)." (p. 9).

Goldenberg, C. (1992). The limits of expectations: A case for case knowledge about teacher expectancy effects. *American Educational Research Journal, 29,* 517–544.

The researcher investigated the academic achievement expectancies of a teacher for two first-grade Hispanic girls in her classroom, the teacher's behavior toward each student, and each student's first-grade reading achievement.

Research problem: "Using a symbolic interactionist perspective (Blumer, 1969, Hewitt, 1984), I try to understand and explain a particular teacher's behaviors toward two children about whom she held diametrically opposed expectations, behaviors that had important consequences for the children's achievement." (p. 522)

Selecting a Case

In this section, we describe in general terms the process of selecting a case or cases. To deepen your understanding of the case selection process, you also should study Chapter 6, which describes many specialized sampling techniques.

The key issue in selecting a case is the decision concerning what you want to be able to say something about at the end of the study. Thus, specifying the case is somewhat comparable to the process in quantitative research of specifying the population to which the results obtained from a sample will be generalized. For example, Sister Paula Kleine-Kracht introduced her study of instructional leadership in a high school with this statement of the research problem:

> There are, however, few examinations of secondary schools in which a principal deliberately chooses to cultivate other members' instructional leadership and decides to personally influence instruction in an indirect way. The following case study is an examination of just such a situation.[20]

In this study, then, the general phenomenon under investigation was instructional leadership. The case was a particular instance (the principal of one high school) of a particular type of instructional leadership, namely, the facilitation of staff members' instructional leadership activities. The findings of the case study might generalize to other principals and might have implications for other manifestations of instructional leadership.

As we explain in Chapter 6, cases in qualitative research are selected by a purposeful sampling process. The particular case to be studied might be selected for various purposes, such as the following: The case is typical; it reflects the phenomenon of interest to an extreme extent; it is a deviant case of special interest; it is politically important.

As we explained, the nature of some cases makes it possible to define a unit of analysis that can be sampled. If this is the situation, the researcher's next decision is to select a sample within the unit of analysis. For example, suppose that the unit of analysis is a group of individuals who share a particular characteristic of interest to the researcher. If the researcher cannot study all these individuals, he will need to consider which of them have experiences or perceptions that give them special value as data sources. There were two such units of analysis in Kleine-Kracht's study of indirect instructional leadership: principals and division chairpersons. Kleine-Kracht selected one school principal from among various principals who potentially could have been studied. The principal's school had five division chairpersons, each responsible for a different part of the school's curriculum. Kleine-Kracht decided to select the entire sample of chairpersons to study, although she could have selected only one or a few chairpersons within this unit of analysis.

Yin proposes that the decision to study multiple cases should be based on replication logic, which is explained in Chapter 6. According to this logic, two or more cases are studied because the researcher predicts the same results for each case (i.e., literal replication), or expects the results to differ for different cases consistent with specific theoretical propositions (i.e., theoretical replication). Our review of published case studies suggests that replication logic is not commonly used, despite its usefulness for testing theoretical propositions.

Although a multiple-case design frequently is used in case study research, Wolcott argues that the study of multiple cases reduces the total attention that can be given to any one of them, and thus serves to weaken rather than to strengthen the study.[21] He expresses

20. Kleine-Kracht, P. (1993). Indirect instructional leadership: An administrator's choice. *Educational Administration Quarterly, 29,* 187–212. Quote appears on p. 187.
21. Wolcott, H. F. (1992). Posturing in qualitative inquiry. In M. D. LeCompte, W. L. Millroy, & J. Preissle (Eds.), *Handbook of qualitative research in education* (pp. 3–52). San Diego: Academic Press.

a strong preference for studying just one case in depth, especially when the researcher is not experienced in this type of research. Wolcott suggests that more experienced researchers could be left with the responsibility for aggregating and comparing case studies dealing with similar phenomena, and, when appropriate, to discover whatever systematic relationships they may reveal.

The Role of the Case Study Researcher

Quantitative and case study researchers perform similar roles in designing and planning a research study, obtaining necessary institutional review and approval, and obtaining permissions from the site or sites in which the research will be conducted. Once they begin collecting data, however, their roles are quite different. Quantitative researchers specify precise procedures for data collection and analysis. They tend to play a limited role in data collection (e.g., administering questionnaires), or they may even use assistants for this purpose.

The role of case study researchers in data collection is more complex. The researcher is the primary "measuring instrument." This means that she carries out data collection and becomes personally involved in the phenomenon being studied. Thus, the researcher is likely to interact closely with field participants, attend social events in the field setting, and use empathy and other psychological processes to grasp the meaning of the phenomenon as it is experienced by individuals and groups in the setting. Few of these procedures are standardized or can be specified in advance of data collection.

Gaining Entry

Identifying appropriate sites and working with "gatekeepers" to obtain necessary permissions are critical steps in a case study. If not done properly, the researcher may have to abort the study. Also, first impressions created at a site can set the tone for the entire relationship between the researcher and field participants. Issues involved in gaining entry include:

1. identifying people within the field setting with whom to make your initial contact;
2. selecting the best method of communication (e.g., telephone, letter, or personal visit) to deliver your request;
3. deciding how to phrase your request (e.g., focusing on the site's opportunity to contribute to research or on personal benefits to site participants); and
4. being prepared to answer questions and address concerns that might arise both before and after permission is granted.

Margot Ely and her colleagues describe their experiences, and those of their students in a course on qualitative research, in gaining entry and conducting research in field settings.[22] One student's log described her challenges in gaining entry into the field site generally and also into the specific settings she wished to observe and with the specific individuals she wished to interview. The student described her use of the log and her support group (small groups into which students were formed for the duration of the research course) to confront her fears and define her research problem, which involved the experience of aging. She carried out a "dress rehearsal" by visiting a relative who lived in a nursing home, and then identified a different nursing home as a potential site. Unable to find

22. Ely, M., Anzul, M., Friedman, T., Garner, D., & Steinmetz, A. M. (1991). *Doing qualitative research: Circles within circles.* New York: Falmer.

a personal contact who could introduce her, the student made a cold call on the receptionist. She obtained the names of the social service director and the volunteer coordinator, both of whom appeared to be appropriate gatekeepers to approach. Prepared to make a detailed "sales pitch" when she spoke with the director of social work, the student was stunned when she was readily accepted: "You look surprised. Being near a university, we often have students doing research here."[23]

Some of the other students in the qualitative research course had more difficulty gaining entry into the field settings that they initially had selected, and some decided to try elsewhere. Ely and her colleagues note, however: "With a great deal of common sense and sensitivity many researchers can and do turn around rather sticky situations and enter successfully, if more discreetly."[24]

Once you gain entry into a field setting, you will need to enlist the cooperation of the case study participants. Your success will depend on how you present yourself. The student whose nursing home experience we described above recorded this episode in her log:

> If you seem to be fulfilling a role which is aversive to them, friendship and cooperation can evaporate in a flash. I encountered this temporarily when a venerable and very articulate 94-year-old man whom I wanted to interview discovered I had training as a psychologist. He said, "Well, you'll no doubt need to speak to someone else. I'm not a patient." I had to make it clear that I hoped to speak to him as an equal, to be enlightened by his perspective, and not as a psychologist interviewing a patient.[25]

The researcher's appearance also can affect her relationship with the individuals or groups being studied. Consider, for example, the case study by Cathy Evans and Donna Eder involving observations of middle school students during lunch period.[26] (This case study is further described in Chapter 9.) For this phase of their study, the researchers and their assistants sought to fit in with the young people they wanted to observe. Therefore, they dressed and spoke informally and were careful not to react negatively to students' language or behavior, even when they found it disturbing. When interacting with school personnel in other phases of their research, however, the research team dressed and acted as adult professionals.

Ethical Issues

✦ *Touchstone in Research*

de Laine, M. (2000). *Fieldwork, participation and practice: Ethics and dilemmas in qualitative research.* Thousand Oaks, CA: Sage.

Data collection in case study research poses various ethical problems. An interviewee might experience unexpected emotional difficulty as a result of expressing deeply held and perhaps controversial beliefs and feelings to an interviewer. Individuals might reveal personal information in the presence of a researcher who is in a participant observer role that they would not share with someone perceived to be an outsider. Analysis of personal documents or artifacts might pose ethical issues unless they are willingly surrendered for research purposes. Even when the researcher takes steps to protect the privacy of case study participants, there often are clues in a case study report that make it possible to identify field sites and particular individuals within them.

David Flinders identifies four types of ethics that can provide a basis for viewing and resolving these and other issues that arise in case study research.[27] In **utilitarian ethics,** re-

23. Ibid., p. 20.
24. Ibid., p. 22.
25. Ibid., p. 25.
26. Evans, C., & Eder, D. (1993). "NO EXIT": Processes of social isolation in the middle school. *Journal of Contemporary Ethnography, 22,* 139–170.
27. Flinders, D. J. (1992). In search of ethical guidance: Constructing a base for dialogue. *International Journal of Qualitative Studies in Education, 5,* 101–115.

searchers judge the morality of their decisions and actions by considering the consequences. The most desirable consequence is to produce the greatest good for the greatest number of people. According to Flinders, utilitarian ethics are difficult to apply in case study research because it is difficult to predict the consequences of a case study while it is in progress.

In **deontological ethics,** researchers judge the morality of their decisions and actions by referring to absolute values, such as honesty, justice, fairness, and respect for others. Flinders observes that from a utilitarian perspective, deception in case study research could be justified if it could be demonstrated that it did not harm the participants physically or in some other ways. However, deception could not be justified from a deontological perspective. The reason is that deception violates basic values of treating others fairly and with respect.

In **relational ethics,** researchers judge the morality of their decisions and actions by the standard of whether these decisions and actions reflect a caring attitude toward others. Nel Noddings states that an ethics of caring "takes fidelity to persons as primary and directs us to analyze and evaluate all recommendations in light of our answers to questions concerning the maintenance of community, the growth of individuals, and the enhancement of subjective aspects of our relationship."[28] Relational ethics require, among other things, that the case study researcher be a sensitive, fully engaged member of the participants' community rather than a detached observer.

The fourth basis for considering the morality of a case study is ecological ethics. In **ecological ethics,** researchers judge the morality of their decisions and actions in terms of the participants' culture and the larger social systems of which they are part. Thus, whereas the other three ethical perspectives consider each case study participant as an individual, ecological ethics consider the participant as a member of a larger cultural and social system. Flinders observes that even a straightforward request such as, "Will you take part in this research?" can mean different things to different people. Depending on the person's cultural background, the request can be perceived as coercive by one individual and as an opportunity to collaborate by another individual. Sex-typed language in a case study report may be viewed as neutral by some readers, but as offensive by others. Data-collection activities may be ethical insofar as the individual participant in a work setting is concerned, but the activities can unfairly disrupt his colleagues' work. An ecological perspective helps avoid these problems by reminding the researcher to consider the larger implications of his local decisions and actions.

Ethical standards for case study research continue to be actively studied and debated. Therefore, if you plan to do case study research, you will need to develop your own ethical perspective. For guidance, we recommend that you review the above ethical perspectives, your institutional review board's standards (see chapter 3), the unique circumstances of the field setting that you wish to study, and your personal values.

Collecting Case Study Data

Case study researchers might begin a case study with one method of data collection and gradually shift to, or add, other methods. Use of multiple methods to collect data about a phenomenon can enhance the validity of case study findings through a process called *triangulation,* which we explain later in the chapter.

---

28. Noddings, N. (1986). Fidelity in teaching, teacher education, and research for teaching. *Harvard Educational Review, 56,* 496–510. Quote appears on p. 510.

The entire range of data collection methods described in Part III can be used in case study research. Also, it is possible to combine qualitative and quantitative methods of data collection. For example, consider Claude Goldenberg's case study of the mismatch between a teacher's expectations and the actual reading achievement of two of her first-grade students.[29] Goldenberg carried out qualitative observation of each child's classroom behaviors, as illustrated by these observational notes in the research report:

> Marta and her group are with the aide, who is giving the children instructions for playing lotto. Marta looks at her lotto cards and smiles. She is sitting quietly. . . . Marta looks at what the boy next to her is doing. . . . Marta then begins to giggle as the aide shows the next picture. She looks at the boy next to her and they giggle together. One girl gives a response to the aide's question and Marta begins to laugh. "Ya, Marta," the aide says. ("Enough, Marta.")[30]

In addition, Goldenberg administered two quantitative measures (standardized tests of reading achievement) to each child.

Data from both types of measures yielded several key findings in this case study. While the teacher initially had low expectations about Marta's academic progress, the teacher told the researcher she spent time with Marta and her mother to encourage greater effort from Marta on reading activity. By year's end, Marta was reading at least at grade level (as measured by the reading tests), and the teacher described Marta as her "wonder child." In contrast, another Hispanic student in the same class, Sylvia, about whom the teacher initially had positive expectations, remained in a low reading group. According to Goldenberg, "in essence, Sylvia stagnated. She was never prompted, as was Marta, to change her work habits."[31]

Personal Involvement in the Data-Collection Process

A type of personal involvement debated among case study researchers is the extent to which they should disclose their personal experiences, feelings, or beliefs to field participants during data collection. For example, when interviewing school personnel about special education policies at the school, is it appropriate for a researcher to discuss her own experience working with special education students, how she felt about this work, and what she believes is the best approach to helping such students? Another issue is the extent to which researchers should include personal experiences, feelings, and beliefs in the research report.

On the issue of personal disclosure to one's case study participants, Daphne Patai describes hearing a well-known historian, Michael Frisch, relate his experience reviewing tapes of research interviews he had conducted.[32] The historian noted that despite all the roadblocks he inadvertently created (which presumably included providing information about himself), most interviewees remained determined to tell him what was important to them and patiently returned to their own themes. This anecdote suggests that personal disclosure may have less effect than one might imagine.

On the issue of personal disclosure in research reports, Patai cites examples of disclosures that she considered excessive or inappropriate:

> Are we really expected to take seriously—and read "generously"—the anthropologist Ruth Behar's claim (in her book *Translated Woman: Crossing the Border With Esperanza's Story*, Bea-

29. Goldenberg, C. (1992). The limits of expectations: A case for case knowledge about teacher expectancy effects. *American Educational Research Journal, 29,* 517–544.
30. Ibid., pp. 528–529.
31. Ibid., p. 537.
32. Patai, D. (1994, February 23). Sick and tired of scholars' noveau solipsism. *The Chronicle of Higher Education,* p. A52.

con Press, 1993) that her struggles to get tenure at an American university should be seen as parallel to the struggles of Esperanza, a Mexican street peddler? Or, to take a different type of example of telling or claiming too much, do readers really benefit from the feminist scholar Nancy K. Miller's description of her father's penis, to which she devotes the closing chapter of her book *Getting Personal* (Routledge, 1991)?[33]

Patai concludes that researchers' personal beliefs and characteristics do not have as much effect on research findings as generally believed, and therefore are better left out of research reports.

In a report discussing the value of sharing one's subjectivity as a researcher, Alan Peshkin offers an opposing view.[34] Peshkin urges researchers to seek out their subjectivity systematically while their research is in progress, so that they can better determine how it might be shaping their inquiry and research outcomes. While carrying out fieldwork in a multi-ethnic high school in a community to which he gave the pseudonym *Riverview*, Peshkin undertook a subjectivity audit of himself. A **subjectivity audit** involves taking notes about situations connected to one's research that arouse strong positive or negative feelings. The outcome was a list of different aspects of himself, which he described as "discretely characterized I's," reflecting areas in which the researcher's own beliefs and background influenced his perceptions and actions in the research setting. For example, Peshkin discovered the *Ethnic Maintenance I* based on his identity as a Jew, an aspect of his subjectivity that approves of individuals maintaining their ethnicity. Peshkin's *Justice-Seeking I* was aroused by repeated experiences of hearing both residents and nonresidents of Riverview denigrate the community. According to Peshkin, such denigration reflected the fact that until recently Riverview was the only town in a large California county where black people were able to establish residence.

Another issue concerns researchers' personal involvement in their research interpretations, sometimes in the face of objective evidence that their views are incorrect. For example, Deborah Lipstadt, a professor at Emory University, decries what she perceives as a growing assault on historical truth:

> We're in a day and age in which I can make any claim I want. I can say I believe the Buffalo Bills won the Super Bowl. Then I say that it's my opinion and I have a right to it, and you're supposed to back off.[35]

As with most aspects of case study research, there are few firm rules about how much personal involvement or disclosure by a researcher is appropriate. Our view is that if self-disclosure passes a certain point, case study participants and readers of the report will view it as a distraction, or they might question the researcher's qualifications and the trustworthiness of the study's findings. On the other hand, brief comments by the researcher about her background and experiences relevant to the case study may facilitate the reader's understanding of the findings.

Analyzing Data during Data Collection

Data collection is emergent in case study research. By this we mean that what the researcher learns from data collected at one point in time often is used to determine subsequent data-collection activities. Therefore, a case study researcher needs to spend time analyzing the data, at least informally, while data collection still is in progress. Two strategies can facilitate this process: making records of field contacts and thinking "finish-to-start."

33. Ibid.
34. Peshkin, A. (1988). In search of subjectivity—one's own. *Educational Researcher, 17*(7), 17–21.
35. Leo, J. (1994, February 28). The junking of history. *U.S. News & World Report*, p. 17.

Making records of field contacts. Matthew Miles and A. Michael Huberman recommend that case study researchers use standard forms to summarize data-collection events.[36] The completed forms can reveal missing information and thus indicate the need for further data collection. They also can suggest promising directions for subsequent stages of data collection and analysis. One such form is a **contact summary sheet,** on which the researcher summarizes what was learned from each field observation or interview. The form can be predesigned for recording the specific details in which the researcher is interested, for example, the people, events, or situations involved in the contact, the most interesting or problematic aspects of the contact, or ideas about where the researcher should focus attention during the next contact.

Figure 14.2 is an example of a contact summary form used in a case study. The researcher first summarized eight salient points from the contact, which are coded as "Themes/Aspects" in the right column of the figure. Some of these points probably were taken from the researcher's field notes, and others might have come to the researcher's mind while reviewing the notes. In this case, the contact summary sheet was used in a systematic fashion. That is, the researcher treated each point as a data chunk and coded it, using a theme coding system.

The contact summary sheet is not a substitute for the researcher's field notes relating to the field contact. The field notes should be comprehensive and primarily descriptive. In contrast, a contact summary sheet is brief and focuses on what was learned from the field contact that will guide subsequent data-collection activities.

A **document summary form** serves a purpose similar to a contact summary sheet. The researcher writes a brief summary of each document that has been examined, noting the type of document, its uses, a summary of its contents, and ideas about other documents that should be obtained and studied.

Thinking "finish-to-start." Harry Wolcott advises researchers learning how to do qualitative research to work "start-to-finish" but to think "finish-to-start."[37] This approach involves thinking through one's entire research project at the very beginning. Wolcott recommends doing this thinking as soon as a problem has been formulated and necessary agreements have been obtained, but before beginning fieldwork. He suggests that the researcher make tentative decisions at that point about the form in which the completed account will be presented (e.g., monograph, journal article, or project report). Also, the researcher should try to predetermine the relative emphasis that will be given to thick description and to analysis and interpretation of constructs, themes, and patterns:

> if you plan to go heavy on description (a good way to hedge your bet if you entertain doubts about your sophistication at analysis or interpretation), recognize from the outset that rich detail may be critical and you had better not rely solely on "headnotes" for it. Be thinking about possibilities for presenting detailed vignettes and make sure you are recording such events at an adequate level of detail . . . probably including an abundance of direct quotations.[38]

The finish-to-start approach thus helps researchers anticipate the types of data that should be collected, and in what depth.

Ending Data Collection

The decision about when to end the data-collection stage of a case study involves both practical and theoretical considerations. Time and budgetary constraints, or the observa-

36. Miles, M. B., & Huberman, A. M. (1994). *Qualitative data analysis: An* expanded sourcebook (2nd ed.). Thousand Oaks, CA: Sage.
37. Wolcott, *Transforming qualitative data*, p. 404.
38. Ibid., p. 404.

FIGURE 14.2

Contact Summary Form: Salient Points in Contact, with Theme Codes Assigned

Contact Summary

Type of contact:

| Mtg. | Principals | Ken's office | 4/2/76 | Site | Westgate |
| | Who, what group | place | date | | |

| Phone | | | | Coder | MM |
| | With whom, by whom | place | date | | |

| Inf. Int. | | | | Date coded | 4/18/76 |
| | With whom, by whom | place | date | | |

1. Pick out the most salient points in the contact. Number in order on this sheet and note page number on which point appears. Number point in text of write-up. Attach theme or aspect to each point. Invent themes where no existing ones apply and asterisk those. Comment may also be included in double parentheses.

Page	Salient Points	Themes/Aspects
1	1. Staff decisions have to be made by April 30.	Staff
1	2. Teachers will have to go out of their present grade-level assignment when they transfer.	Staff/Resource Mgmt.
2	3. Teachers vary in their willingness to integrate special education students into their classrooms—some teachers are "a pain in the elbow."	*Resistance
2	4. Ken points out that tentative teacher assignment lists got leaked from the previous meeting (implicitly deplores this).	Internal Communic.
2	5. Ken says, "Teachers act as if they had the right to decide who should be transferred." (would make outcry)	Power Distrib.
2	6. Tacit/explicit decision: "It's our decision to make." (voiced by Ken, agreed by Ed)	Power Distrib/Conflict Mgmt.
2	7. Principals and Ken, John, and Walter agree that Ms. Epstein is a "bitch."	*Stereotyping
2	8. Ken decides not to tell teachers ahead of time (now) about transfers ("because then we'd have a fait accompli").	Plan for Planning/ Time Mgmt.

Source: Adapted from Figure 4.2 on p. 54 in: Miles, M. B., & Huberman, A. M. (1994). *Qualitative data analysis: An expanded sourcebook* (2nd ed.). Thousand Oaks, CA: Sage. Copyright © 1994 by Sage Publications. Reprinted by permission of Sage Publications, Inc.

tion that the participants' patience is running thin, are among the practical considerations that can prompt a decision to end data collection. As to theoretical considerations, Yvonna Lincoln and Egon Guba identify four criteria for determining when it is appropriate to end data collection.[39] The criteria assume that the data have been coded into categories, but

39. Lincoln, Y. S., & Guba, E. G. (1985). *Naturalistic inquiry.* Beverly Hills, CA: Sage.

they are applicable to other forms of data analysis as well. (Category coding is discussed later in the chapter.) The four criteria are as follows.

1. *Exhaustion of sources.* Data sources (e.g., key informants, institutional files) can be recycled and tapped many times, but at some point it should become clear that little more information of relevance will be gained from further engagement with them.
2. *Saturation of categories.* Eventually, the categories used to code data appear to be definitively established. When continuing data collection produces only tiny increments of new information about the categories in comparison to the effort expended to get them, the researcher can feel confident about ending data collection.
3. *Emergence of regularities.* At some point, the researcher encounters sufficient consistencies in the data that she develops a sense of whether the phenomena represented by each construct occur regularly or only occasionally.
4. *Overextension.* Even if new information still is coming in, the researcher might develop a sense that the new information is far removed from the central core of viable categories that have emerged, and does not contribute usefully to the emergence of additional viable categories.

Analyzing Case Study Data

♦ *Touchstone in Research*

Ryan, G., & Bernard, H. L. (2000). Data management and analysis methods. In N. K. Denzin & Y. S. Lincoln (Eds.), *Handbook of qualitative research* (2nd ed., pp. 769–802). Thousand Oaks, CA: Sage.

Weitzman, E. A. (2000). Software and qualitative research. In N. K. Denzin & Y. S. Lincoln (Eds.), *Handbook of qualitative research* (2nd ed., pp. 803–820). Thousand Oaks, CA: Sage.

Data analysis in a quantitative research study is a relatively straightforward process. Suppose the study involves 100 participants and scores on ten variables for each participant—in all, 1,000 bits of numerical data. All these data can be entered into a computer file without much difficulty, and a software program will quickly perform the statistical analyses.

In contrast, even a modest case study will generate a great many pages of observational notes, interview transcripts, and documents obtained from the field setting. Suppose there are 200 such pages, each containing 250 words. That totals 50,000 words. How do you analyze all those words in order to produce significant, meaningful findings?

Renata Tesch reviewed various approaches that have been used to analyze case study data.[40] She classified them into three types: interpretational analysis, structural analysis, and reflective analysis. Each type is explained below. Tesch's typology does not indicate how to analyze case study data at the same level of specificity as a statistics textbook describes how to compute, let's say, a mean score or *t* value. However, it will help you design analysis procedures that are uniquely appropriate to the conditions and purposes of your case study.

Our discussion of data analysis emphasizes verbal data. However, visual images—photographs, drawings, paintings, cartoons, film, and the like—are another important data source in some case studies. While the procedures described below are generally applicable to visual images, you should be aware that qualitative researchers have developed special techniques for their analysis.[41]

40. Tesch, R. (1990). *Qualitative research: Analysis types and software tools.* New York: Falmer.
41. These techniques are described in: Harper, D. (2000). Reimagining visual methods: Galileo to *Neuromancer.* In N. K. Denzin & Y. S. Lincoln (Eds.), *Handbook of qualitative research* (2nd ed., pp. 717–732). Thousand Oaks, CA: Sage; Rose, G. (2001). *Visual methodologies: An introduction to interpreting visual objects.* Thousand Oaks, CA: Sage; Van Leeuwen, T. V., & Jewitt, C. (2001). *The handbook of visual analysis.* Thousand Oaks, CA: Sage.

Interpretational Analysis

Interpretational analysis is the process of examining case study data closely in order to find constructs, themes, and patterns that can be used to describe and explain the phenomenon being studied. For example, suppose researchers are studying a new U.S. history curriculum. They have available a set of documents written by the curriculum developers (the teacher's edition of the textbook, technical reports, advertisements, etc.), as well as transcripts of interviews with parents whose children are studying the curriculum.

In analyzing these data, suppose the researchers find that both the developers and the parents make frequent reference to the curriculum's supposed goals. Further analysis reveals that two goals are particularly salient to both groups: (1) development of multicultural sensitivity, and (2) development of pride in one's country. One finding of the study, then, is the discovery of these particular goals (which we call *constructs*) as central to this particular curriculum. Suppose further analysis reveals that the curriculum developers most frequently mention multicultural sensitivity as a goal of the curriculum, while parents view national pride as an essential curriculum goal, but one not sufficiently emphasized in this curriculum. This, then, is a discovery about a possibly significant *pattern:* The salience of a particular curriculum goal depends on whether one is a developer or a parent.

Interpretational analysis helps researchers achieve insights such as those in our hypothetical example. The procedures of interpretational analysis can be carried out either manually or by computer. Because of the advantages of computer analysis, we will describe the procedures as they would be carried out with software programs that are available for this purpose.

Segmenting the Database

The first step in interpretational analysis is to compile all the case study data into a computer database. Handwritten notes need to be typed and formatted as computer files. Documents and other previously typed materials can be transformed into computer files by using a computer scanner. Even photographs and other graphic materials can be prepared as computer files in this manner. However, to analyze graphic materials by the procedures described below, you would need to prepare verbal descriptions of their salient features.

The resulting computer database (i.e., all the computer files containing the case study data) now can be manipulated by software programs designed to perform interpretational analyses. The researcher starts by having the software program assign a number to each line of text in the database. Next the researcher breaks the text into meaningful segments. A **segment** (also called a *meaning unit* or *analysis unit*) is a section of the text that contains one item of information and that is comprehensible even if read outside the context in which it is embedded. For example, in the analysis of interview and questionnaire data, it is common to make each question plus the participant's response a separate segment.

A segment can be any length: a phrase within a sentence, a sentence, a paragraph, or even several pages of text. The researcher identifies each segment by indicating the line number on which it begins and the line number on which it ends.

Developing Categories

One of the most critical steps of interpretational data analysis is developing a set of categories that adequately encompass and summarize the data. The researcher must decide what is worth taking note of in each segment of the database. For example, Michael Ann Rossi did a study of elementary school teachers who had been prepared by staff of the California Mathematics Project to help their colleagues effect reforms in mathematics instruction at the local school level.[42] What was of interest to Rossi in her database of interviews, questionnaire responses, and documents was the facilitation strategies that these teacher-leaders used.

To be more precise, we would state that facilitation strategies were a *category* in Rossi's data analysis. A **category** is a construct that refers to a certain type of phenomenon mentioned in the database. (A construct is a concept that is inferred from observed phenomena, for example: self-esteem, cooperation, memory.) A category can be expressed numerically: It is either absent (a value of 0) or present (a value of 1) in any observed phenomenon. This numerical expression is called a *variable* by quantitative researchers, and sometimes by qualitative researchers as well.

Researchers need to develop a category label and definition for each type of phenomenon in the database that is to be analyzed. Also, they need to consider whether a particular category can be analyzed into subtypes. For example, in Rossi's case study, the broad category of *facilitation strategy* was analyzed into 15 subcategories, each of which refers to a different type of facilitation strategy. Subcategories also can represent different degrees or levels of a construct. For example, *perceived helpfulness of a facilitation strategy* might be conceptualized as a category with three subcategories: very helpful, helpful, and not helpful. Subcategories, as we explain below, are useful for detecting relational and causal patterns in case study data.

How do you establish a list of categories for coding the segments in your database? One approach is to use a list of categories developed by other researchers. Rossi used this approach in her study of facilitation strategies. Her list was developed by Matthew Miles and his colleagues for case studies of change agents in education, and subsequently modified by other researchers doing related studies. Examples of the categories are: coaching of individuals, developing a support structure, resource linking, supporting the client emotionally, and training groups.

The other approach is to develop your own categories. You will need to study your data carefully in order to identify significant phenomena, and then determine which phenomena share sufficient similarities that they can be considered instances of the same construct. This construct becomes a category in your category system. You will need to define the category, give it a label, and specify guidelines that you and others can use to determine whether each segment in the database is or is not an instance of the category.

This process of category development is consistent with the principles of grounded theory.[43] Case study researchers who use these principles derive their categories directly from their data rather than from theories developed by other researchers. In other words, the categories are "grounded" in the particular set of data that you collected. Furthermore, the categories seek to explain the phenomena that are observed as well as to describe them. Because of this emphasis on explanation, the categories are considered theoretical. However, even if the categories are purely descriptive, the procedures used in grounded theory are applicable. Therefore, if you intend to develop your own categories, we recommend that you study the principles of grounded theory construction.

Coding Segments

After selecting or developing a category system, the researcher uses it to code each segment in the computer file. It is necessary to examine each segment and decide whether the

---

42. Rossi, M. A. (1993). The California Mathematics Project: Empowering elementary teachers to be leaders and change agents in mathematics reform. *Dissertation Abstracts International, 54*(09), 3314A. (UMI No. 9305218)
43. Strauss, A. L., & Corbin, J. M. (1998). *Basics of qualitative research: Techniques and procedures for developing grounded theory* (2nd ed.). Thousand Oaks, CA: Sage.

phenomenon it describes fits one of the categories in the category system. If it does, the researcher types an abbreviation for the category (e.g., a number or acronym) next to the segment. A segment might contain no instances of any category in one's system, or it might contain instances of several categories, in which case the segment would be coded with the abbreviation for each category.

An example of multiple coding is provided in a case study by one of the authors (J. Gall). She interviewed students enrolled in *Careers Plus,* a program designed to assist people age 50 and over to resume work or change careers. The segment to be coded involved the researcher's question and the student's reply:

> Researcher: At this point, what are your reasons for being in the Careers Plus program?
> Student: To get back to work and to be with people again. I was going to church, but wasn't participating in any activities . . . not a part of. . . . Coming to Careers Plus, I got active. [The instructor] called on me a lot in [class]; I think he liked to see me cry. I'm a crier.

The segment was coded as an instance of four categories:

- Goals/reasons for being in or staying in program: Work
- Goals/reasons for being in or staying in program: Be with people
- Learning activities provided by the program: Career exploration class
- Obstacles to career change: Isolation

This example illustrates that a single segment can provide various types of information of interest to a researcher, and that the information is retrievable through multiple coding.

In the process of coding your segments, you might find that some of your categories are ambiguous or that some segments contain information that is not codable using your category system. If this happens, you will need to revise the category system and then recode all the segments. Researchers typically revise their category system several times before feeling satisfied with it.

Grouping Category Segments

Suppose that the database for a case study contains 500 segments and the category system includes 20 categories (1–20). After coding all the segments, the researcher next would bring together all the segments that were tagged with the Category 1 code. (The process would be repeated for the other 19 categories as well.) Software programs designed for qualitative data analysis can perform this function. For example, if 15 segments were tagged with the Category 1 code, the program would compile all these segments for display on the computer screen, or they can be printed out.

The 15 segments with the Category 1 code are now conveniently grouped together. However, they are decontextualized, that is, they have been removed from their location in the interview transcript, field notes, or other document. This is not a serious problem, however, because each segment includes its line numbers. (You will recall that the software program numbers each line of text in the database.) Thus, you can easily locate each segment in the database of interview transcripts, field notes, and documents. In addition, you might consider developing and applying several categories to help you situate a segment easily after it is removed from its location in the database. For example, suppose the study included five cases (C1, C2, C3, C4, C5), and the data for each case were derived from either an interview with the individual's colleague (COL) or supervisor (SUP), or from observation notes (OBS). Thus, the first segment for Category 1 might have the supplemental context codes (C2, COL), the second segment might be coded (C5, OBS), and so on. In this way, the researcher is easily reminded of the segment's location in the database.

✦ **Touchstone in Research**

Charmaz, K. (2000). Grounded theory: Objectivist and constructivist methods. In N. K. Denzin & Y. S. Lincoln (Eds.), *Handbook of qualitative research* (2nd ed., pp. 509–535). Thousand Oaks, CA: Sage.

When you examine as a group all 15 segments that were coded with the Category 1 code, you have an opportunity to reconsider whether the construct corresponding to that category is sensible. You might find, for example, that the content of some segments corresponds to the construct as you have defined it, but the content of other segments does not. The solution to this problem is to redefine the construct and perhaps to develop new categories.

In our hypothetical example, the grouping process will yield 20 displays of grouped segments, one for each of the 20 categories. The researcher most likely will print out each display for convenience. Now the displays can be compared to determine whether the categories overlap, whether some categories are confusing or irrelevant to the study, and whether some categories are of particular importance.

Barney Glaser and Anselm Strauss, the developers of the grounded theory approach in qualitative research, coined the term **constant comparison** to refer to this continual process of comparing segments within and across categories.[44] (Keep in mind that each category refers to a separate construct and that, ultimately, what is important is the constructs, not the categories used in data analysis.) The term *constant* highlights the fact that the process of comparison and revision of categories is repeated until satisfactory closure is achieved. Using constant comparison, the researcher clarifies the meaning of each category, creates sharp distinctions between categories, and decides which categories are most important to the study. Although the method of constant comparison refers specifically to the development of constructs that are linked together by a theory, it is applicable to the development of purely descriptive constructs as well.

Strauss and Corbin claim that when using grounded theory principles to determine categories, the researcher should collect data to the point of theoretical saturation. **Theoretical saturation** occurs when no new data are emerging relevant to an established coding category, no additional categories appear to be necessary to account for the phenomena of interest, and the relationships among categories appear to be well established.

By applying the method of constant comparison, the researcher should arrive at a set of well-defined categories with clear coding instructions. As a final check on the category system, the inter-rater reliability of coding should be determined. (Procedures for computing inter-rater reliability statistics are described in Chapter 9.) Demonstration that the category system can be used with high inter-rater reliability enhances the credibility of the case study findings, and it also encourages other researchers to apply the category system in their own case studies.

✦ **Touchstone in Research**

Flinders, D. J., & Mills, G. E. (1993). *Theory and concepts in qualitative research*. New York: Teachers College Press.

Drawing Conclusions

The discovery of constructs in qualitative data can be a significant outcome of a case study. Discovery of themes also is important. (You will recall that earlier in the chapter we defined themes as salient, characteristic features of a case.) For example, Kleine-Kracht used the data from her case study of instructional leadership in a high school (described earlier in the chapter) to identify four themes in effective principals' instructional leadership. One such theme is that "the division chairs are curricular experts."[45] This theme emerged from several sources: data in which the principal stated that he expected the division chairs to be catalysts for instructional leadership and that he had selected them on that basis; a description of the chairs' considerable knowledge of instruction; and data indicating that teachers readily accept the division chairs as instructional leaders.

44. Ibid.
45. Kleine-Kracht, Indirect instructional leadership, p. 209.

If the researcher uses a multiple-case design, the generalizability of constructs and themes across cases can be checked. This process might involve noting whether a particular theme observed in one case also is present in other cases. A more sophisticated check would involve determining whether the particular phenomena that were coded as manifestations of a construct in one case are similar to similarly coded phenomena in other cases.

Multiple-case data also can be analyzed to detect relational or causal patterns. The researcher's constructs can be thought of as variables. Each case can be given a score on each variable, typically: 0 = absent and 1 = present; or 0 = absent, 1 = present to a moderate degree, and 2 = present to a high degree. If the scores on one variable across all the cases systematically covary with scores on another variable, the researcher can infer a relational or causal pattern. Suppose, for example, that the researcher has collected data on ten schools, each constituting a separate case. She finds that the school staffs vary in their confidence in the school administrators, and they also vary in their willingness to try out a state-sponsored educational innovation. Suppose the data analysis reveals that cases (i.e., schools) with a high confidence level tend to have high willingness, whereas cases with a low confidence level tend to have low willingness. Given this result, the researcher would be justified in inferring the following pattern, which possibly is causal: Confidence in school administrators facilitates willingness to experiment.[46]

Patterns can be discovered within a single case as well as in multiple-case analysis. For example, suppose that a researcher observed one child extensively in various settings: a mathematics class, a language arts class, the school playground, at home while doing homework, and at home while playing. The researcher also has collected data on the child's state of mind (thoughts and emotions) in these different settings. These data can be analyzed to determine whether there is a relationship between the settings and the child's state of mind. We might find, for example, that the child feels tense and unfocused in academic work settings, but relaxed and fully engaged while playing. This is a relational pattern within a single case. If the researcher can invoke or develop a theory to explain this relationship, we would characterize it as a causal pattern.

Various software programs for Macintosh and PC computers are available to perform the various data analysis procedures described above. The procedures also can be performed manually. You can write line numbers on the master copy of your interview transcripts, field notes, and other text materials; make a new copy of these materials; mark the new copy into segments; cut out each segment and paste it onto a 3 × 5 card; write a category code (or codes) on each card; group cards having the same category code; and examine the groupings using the method of constant comparison.

These manual procedures will be exceedingly time-consuming if your text materials are extensive. Therefore, many case study researchers plan their data-collection procedures with an eye toward eventually entering them into computer files for manipulation by software designed for interpretational analysis.

Structural Analysis

Structural analysis is the process of examining case study data for the purpose of identifying patterns inherent in discourse, text, events, or other phenomena. To understand how structural analysis differs from interpretational analysis, consider the following example,

---

46. Other types of procedures that can be used to determine relational and causal patterns in case study data are described in: Miles & Huberman, *Qualitative data analysis.*

which consists of a segment of conversation between a Spanish teacher and one of her students:

Teacher: What does *la casa* mean?
Student: House.
Teacher: That's right. *La casa* means house.

A conversation analyst (see Chapter 15) examining this interaction might note certain features of it, such as:

1. The sequence of speakers within this instructional event was teacher, student, teacher.
2. Each of the teacher's utterances contained more words than the student's utterance.
3. Four Spanish words were uttered.
4. Three words (*la, casa, house*) were uttered twice, and the other six words were uttered once.

The conversation analyst then might examine whether each of these observed phenomena are present in other samples of discourse in this teacher's classroom or in other teachers' classrooms.

This example illustrates the essential feature of structural analysis, namely, that the researcher looks for patterns *inherent* in the data. Very little, if any, inference is required. In contrast, a researcher using interpretational analysis overlays a structure of meaning on the data. For example, suppose the researcher is investigating how students receive feedback in the classroom. The above interaction might be considered a segment, and it might be coded as an instance of feedback because of the utterance, "That's right. *La casa* means house." This classification of the utterance is an inference from the data by the researcher.

Structural analysis is used in conversation analysis, ethnoscience, and other qualitative research traditions. Here are a few examples of the types of educational phenomena that might be investigated in case studies that are based on these traditions: how students' speech patterns change over the course of schooling, the sequence of events in children's stories, how the various parts of textbooks are organized, how curriculum experts conceptualize the high school mathematics curriculum, how teachers and students interact with each other during a lesson, and movement patterns within a school building.

Tesch identified two types of software programs that are useful in doing structural analyses of case study data. **Text retrievers** are software programs that operate on individual words and fixed sequences of words (e.g., a phrase such as *bill of rights*). These programs can perform such tasks as listing all words in a document, indicating where each word occurs in the document, and counting how many times each word occurs.

Text database managers are software programs that allow the researcher to format a document into fields, code each field, and then retrieve all fields with a given code. For example, if the document is a transcript of a discussion among five educators, each utterance by any of them, no matter how long or short, can be formatted as a field. Next, each field can be assigned one or more codes, such as a code indicating which of the five educators made the utterance. Finally, all fields that have been assigned a given code can be retrieved for display. This feature enables the researcher to retrieve all utterances made by any one of the educators.[47]

47. You may have observed that text database managers are similar to computer programs designed for interpretational analysis. Fields, for example, are similar to segments. However, programs for interpretational analysis have capabilities that text database managers lack.

One particular text database manager described by Tesch has an additional capability. It can search for sequence patterns in a document. Suppose the document is the transcript of the discussion among the five educators mentioned above. This computer program, for example, could identify and compile all sequences in which educator B made a statement that was followed by a statement made by educator D. The identification of such sequences, and their frequency, might reveal interpersonal dynamics that have theoretical or practical implications.

Reflective Analysis

Interpretational analysis and structural analysis involve explicit procedures that are performed in a somewhat prescribed sequence. In contrast, **reflective analysis** is a process in which the researcher relies primarily on intuition and judgment in order to portray or evaluate the phenomena being studied. Terms other than intuition and judgment have been used to describe this process: introspective contemplation, tacit knowledge, imagination, artistic sensitivity, and "examining with a sense of wonder."[48]

Reflective analysis is associated with several qualitative research traditions, including educational connoisseurship and criticism (described in Chapter 17) and phenomenology (described in Chapter 15). We believe, however, that reflective analysis also could be used in case studies that draw on other qualitative research traditions. Its use involves a decision by the researcher to rely on her own intuition and personal judgment to analyze the data rather than on technical procedures involving an explicit category classification system.

Some case studies, especially those associated with ethnographic traditions (see Chapter 14), involve a collaborative effort by a team of researchers. In this situation, the reflective analyses are formed through a dynamic process that is likely to involve conflict, negotiation, and ambiguity and that may result in unusually rich interpretations of the data. Judith Wasser and Liora Bresler suggest the concept of the **interpretive zone** to characterize this process: "In the interpretive zone, researchers bring together their different kinds of knowledge, experience, and beliefs to forge new meanings through the process of the joint inquiry in which they are engaged."[49]

One way to understand reflective analysis is to compare it with artistic endeavors. The artist reflects on phenomena and then portrays them in such a way as to reveal both their surface features and essences. Many case study researchers engage in similar reflections and portrayals. Reflective analysis is ideally suited for thick description, but it also can lead to the discovery of constructs, themes, and patterns.

The other side of artistic portrayal is criticism. Literary critics, for example, study a literary work in order to develop an appreciation of its aesthetic elements and "message," but also to make critical judgments about its artistic merit. Many case studies conducted by educational evaluators (see Chapter 17) are conducted for similar purposes. These evaluative studies help educators and policy makers understand the features and purposes of educational programs, products, and methods, and also to appreciate their strengths and weaknesses. Just as a literary critic develops reflective ability with experience, so must an educational evaluator build up a store of experience in order to use reflective analysis wisely.

---

48. All these terms, except the last, are taken from Tesch, *Qualitative research*, p. 69. The phrase, "examining with a sense of wonder," appears in: Barritt, L., Beekman, T., Bleeker, H., & Mulderiz, K. (1985). *Researching educational practice*. Grand Forks, ND: University of North Dakota, Center for Teaching and Learning.
49. Wasser, J. D., & Bresler, L. (1996). Working in the interpretive zone: Conceptualized collaboration in qualitative research teams. *Educational Researcher, 25*(5), 5–15. Quote appears on p. 13.

Because reflective analysis is largely subjective, it is not possible to specify standard procedures for doing this type of data analysis. Apprenticeship with an experienced researcher, followed by considerable practice, is essential. However, a few guidelines from hermeneutical research (see Chapter 15) might be generally applicable. In doing reflective analysis from a hermeneutical perspective, the researcher carefully examines and then reexamines *all* the data that have been collected. As this process continues, certain features of the phenomena are likely to become salient. The researcher then should develop an understanding of these features by themselves and in relation to each other. In other words, the analysis should account for as much as possible of the phenomenon being studied. An interpretation or criticism that fits some of the data should not be contradicted by other data.

Validity and Reliability of Case Study Findings

Case study researchers do not agree in their assumptions about the nature of reality and scientific inquiry. Their different assumptions lead them to hold different views about how to conceptualize and assess the validity and reliability of case study findings.

Positivist Criteria

Some case study researchers subscribe to a positivist philosophy of scientific inquiry, which claims that objective knowledge about the world is possible. In other words, facts about the world are assumed to exist independently of researchers' efforts to know them; if they use the scientific method correctly, they will come to discover those facts. Quantitative researchers also subscribe to these positivist assumptions. Not surprisingly, then, case study researchers with a positivist orientation express a somewhat similar view of validity and reliability as that of quantitative researchers.

Robert Yin exemplifies this type of case study researcher.[50] He judges the quality of case study design by three types of validity criteria and one reliability criterion:

1. **Construct validity** is the extent to which a measure used in a case study correctly operationalizes the concepts being studied.
2. **Internal validity** is the extent to which the researcher has demonstrated a causal relationship between X and Y by showing that other plausible factors could not have caused Y. The criterion of internal validity is not applicable to descriptive case study research because it does not seek to identify causal patterns in phenomena.
3. **External validity** is the extent to which the findings of a case study can be generalized to similar cases.
4. **Reliability** is the extent to which other researchers would arrive at similar results if they studied the same case using exactly the same procedures as the first researcher.

Yin's notions of construct validity and reliability parallel quantitative measurement criteria having the same labels (see Chapter 7). His notions of internal and external validity correspond to the criteria of good experimental design used by quantitative researchers (see Chapter 12).

---

50. Yin, *Case study research.*

Chain of Evidence

As we explained earlier in the chapter, case study researchers collect raw data in the field, for example, observations of events as they occur. The raw data then are analyzed to yield themes, patterns and causal inferences, which constitute the study's findings. According to Yin, the overall validity of a study is strengthened if the researcher presents a strong **chain of evidence,** that is, clear, meaningful links between research questions, raw data, and findings. By doing so, the researcher enables the reader to follow the derivation of case study evidence from the initial research questions and its use in the researcher's interpretations.

The researcher should make the chain of evidence explicit in the case study report by providing an audit trail. An **audit trail** is documentation of the research process followed in the case study. Six types of documentation should be considered for inclusion in an audit trail: (1) source and method of recording raw data, (2) data reduction and analysis products, (3) data reconstruction and synthesis products, (4) process notes, (5) materials relating to intentions and dispositions, and (6) instrument development information. Of course, a case study report would be inordinately long if it included all these materials. However, it may be feasible to include small, representative samples of these materials in a methodology section or appendix. Also, as in quantitative studies, the researcher should hold on to these documentation materials for a period of years after the study so that they can be inspected by other researchers.

Pattern Matching

Some case studies are designed as experiments to test the effects of an intervention, such as a new curriculum, on one or more outcomes, such as student academic achievement and student self-concept. These studies usually are designed within a positivist framework, and thus it is appropriate to speak of independent variables (the new curriculum) and their effect on dependent variables (academic achievement and self-concept).

Yin describes several procedures that can be used to test the internal validity of causal inferences drawn from the findings of this type of case study. The procedures require a set of theoretical propositions that are tested against the case study data. The causal inference is strengthened if **pattern matching** is found, that is, if the patterns discovered in the case study data correspond to predictions drawn from the theoretical propositions. For example, suppose a researcher does a case study of a new curriculum that is based on theories of motivation and self-concept. Because principles derived from the theories are incorporated in the curriculum, the researcher might predict that students who experience the curriculum should derive particular benefits. If the observed pattern of benefits matches those that were predicted, the researcher's inference that the benefits were caused by the curriculum has survived a critical validity check. Yin describes several pattern-matching procedures that can be used, depending on the type of case study data that are available and the type of explanation whose validity is being tested.

Interpretive Criteria

Validity and reliability become problematic if one rejects the positivist assumption of a reality that can be known objectively. How does a researcher arrive at valid, reliable knowledge if each individual being studied constructs his or her own reality (the constructivist assumption), if the researcher becomes a central focus of the inquiry process (the "reflexive" turn in the social sciences), and if no inquiry process or type of knowledge has any authority over any other (the postmodern assumption)?[51]

---

51. Constructivist and postmodern assumptions and the reflexive turn are explained in Chapter 1.

In considering this question, some researchers have concluded that traditional notions of validity and reliability do not apply to case study data and interpretations. These
researchers, whom we refer to as interpretive researchers, instead apply such criteria as
plausibility, authenticity, credibility, and relevance. Other interpretive researchers retain
the notion of validity, but reconceptualize it using such terms as interpretive validity, catalytic validity, interrogated validity, transgressive validity, imperial validity, simulacra/
ironic validity, situated validity, and voluptuous validity.[52]

To illustrate the nature of these formulations of validity, we will consider David Altheide and John Johnson's conception of interpretive validity.[53] **Interpretive validity** refers
to judgments about the credibility of an interpretive researcher's knowledge claims. The
criteria are of four types, as described below.

1. *Usefulness.* Interpretive research rejects the notion that it is possible to objectively
depict the world. Therefore, objectivity cannot be a criterion for judging the validity of interpretive case study findings. In its place, one imposes the criterion of usefulness. One
way in which a case study can be useful is that it enlightens the individuals who read the
report of its findings. Another way in which it can be useful is that it liberates the individuals being studied, readers of the report, or some other group. Cultural studies, a qualitative research tradition described in Chapter 15, emphasizes this view of usefulness.

2. *Contextual completeness.* In order for case study phenomena to be properly understood, they need to be set within a context. The more comprehensive the researcher's
contextualization, the more credible are her interpretations of the phenomena. Altheide
and Johnson recommend that case study researchers consider, at a minimum, the following contextual features in interpreting the meaning of the phenomena they investigate:
history, physical setting, and environment; number of participants; activities; schedules
and temporal order of events; division of labor; routines and variations from them; significant events and their origins and consequences; members' perceptions and meanings; social rules and basic patterns of order.

Altheide and Johnson also emphasize the need for sensitivity to a setting's multivocality and the participants' tacit knowledge in assessing the validity of case study interpretations. **Multivocality** refers to the fact that, in many settings, participants do not speak
with a unified voice. Rather, they have diverse points of view and interests. Case study interpretations are more credible if the researcher demonstrates openness to the possibility
of multivocality.

Tacit knowledge refers to the "largely unarticulated, contextual understanding that is
often manifested in nods, silences, humor, and naughty nuances."[54] In other words, case
study findings are more credible if they incorporate the implicit meanings present in a situation. Implicit meanings are those that the individuals being studied either cannot find
the words to express, or that they take so much for granted that they do not explicate them
in everyday discourse or in interviews with the researcher.

3. *Researcher positioning.* A researcher's interpretations are more credible and useful
if he demonstrates sensitivity in how he relates to the situation being studied. For example, many settings are socially stratified, such as by social class (e.g., upper class vs. lower
class) or by role within a work group (e.g., manager vs. production worker). The researcher

52. These types of validity are mentioned in: Altheide, D. L., & Johnson, J. M. (1994). Criteria for assessing interpretive validity in qualitative research. In N. K. Denzin & Y. S. Lincoln (Eds.), *Handbook of qualitative research*
(pp. 485–499). Thousand Oaks, CA: Sage.
53. Ibid.
54. Ibid., p. 492.

should be sensitive to his own various roles (e.g., member of the middle class, researcher employed by a university, participant-observer in the setting) and how they relate to this stratification structure. If a researcher is aware of these role relationships and thoughtfully considers their effects on the study, his findings will have added credibility.

Thomas's study of developmental relationships in cross-race pairs in a corporation, which we described above, illustrates this self-reflective process. Thomas described two major concerns he had about himself in conducting the study. One concern was the potential impact of his being an African-American male of junior rank. His other concern involved his ability to identify and have effective interview rapport with senior managers, particularly white senior managers. In order to manage these concerns, Thomas enlisted two senior white male colleagues who were familiar with race relations research and clinical methods of supervision to serve as his research supervisors.

Some of our beliefs, values, and other personal characteristics may be subconscious and, therefore, may not be amenable to self-reflection. This problem can be addressed by asking colleagues who know you well to review your research project, including its goals, methods of data collection and analysis, and purported findings. They might be able to identify personal characteristics or conditions that threaten the credibility of your findings. Michael Patton provides an example of the need for this process:

> The fieldwork for evaluation of an African health project was conducted over three weeks during which time the evaluator had severe diarrhea. Did that affect the highly negative tone of the report? The evaluator said it didn't, but I'd want to have the issue out in the open to make my own judgment.[55]

You might be able to refute concerns of this sort, thus strengthening the credibility of the findings. On the other hand, you might find it necessary to reconsider your findings.

4. *Reporting style.* The researcher's choice of reporting style can affect the validity of readers' interpretations of the findings. As a researcher reconstructs the participants' phenomenological reality, he must find a way to express this reconstruction in written or graphic form so that it is perceived as credible and authentic. The goal, then, is to achieve **verisimilitude,** which Patricia Adler and Peter Adler describe as "a style of writing that draws the reader so closely into subjects' worlds that these can be palpably felt."[56] Some case study researchers consider literary structures (e.g., the telling of tales, one-act plays, poetry) to be particularly good formats for achieving verisimilitude.

The following are additional procedures that case study researchers have developed as checks on the validity and reliability of their case study findings. The appropriateness of a specific procedure for a particular study depends on the researcher's philosophy of scientific inquiry and the phenomena being studied. Because validity and reliability are not clearly distinguished in some forms of case study research, we do not present separate procedures for checking validity and reliability. However, those procedures that clearly relate either to validity or to reliability, and not to both, are so indicated.

5. *Triangulation.* Imagine that you are studying youth gangs, and a gang member tells you that he engages in acts of vandalism because he is bored. Is this a valid statement of the respondent's state of mind? If this person also indicates a habitual state of boredom on a structured questionnaire or personality measure, this evidence would strengthen the credibility of his statement. If we find that other gang members make similar statements,

55. Patton, M. Q. (1990). *Qualitative evaluation and research methods* (2nd ed.). Thousand Oaks, CA: Sage. Quote appears on p. 472.
56. Adler, P. A., & Adler, P. (1994). Observational techniques. In N. K. Denzin & Y. S. Lincoln (Eds.), *Handbook of qualitative research* (pp. 377–392). Thousand Oaks, CA: Sage. Quote appears on p. 381.

this finding would be further evidence of credibility. Still another type of evidence would be finding that the statement is consistent with a well-supported theory of aggression.

What has been done in each of these instances is to validate a case study finding by drawing on corroborative evidence. Case study researchers call this process **triangulation:** It is the process of using multiple data-collection methods, data sources, analysts, or theories to check the validity of case study findings. Triangulation helps to eliminate biases that might result from relying exclusively on any one data-collection method, source, analyst, or theory.

The key to triangulation is to vary in some way the approach used to generate the finding that you are seeking to corroborate. If you generated a finding by a qualitative method, perhaps you can check it by using a quantitative data-collection method. If the finding came from a statement in a group interview by interviewer X, perhaps its validity can be checked by having interviewer Y conduct individual interviews. If you detect a certain construct, theme, or causal pattern in a set of data, perhaps you can check its validity by asking another researcher to review the data independently and see what themes, patterns, or causal explanations she detects. Depending on what type of finding you are seeking to validate and the kinds of resources available to you, other forms of triangulation might be appropriate as well.

Sandra Mathison observed that triangulation in social science research sometimes does not produce convergence, but instead produces inconsistencies or contradictions among findings about the same phenomenon.[57] For example, in studies of controversial, stressful, or illicit phenomena, self-report data might be inconsistent with, or might even directly contradict, data resulting from more direct methods of data collection, such as observation or document analysis. When this happens, it still may be possible to validate the conflicting data by reconciling them within some explanatory framework.

Ovadia Aviram's case study of an Israeli boarding school for Jewish youth illustrates this process of data reconciliation.[58] Aviram's direct observations of how staff members treated and talked about students produced data that were highly incongruent with what staff members reported in interviews and informal conversations with the researcher. Aviram explained these discrepancies as due to the staff's use of "generating appearances," a process of maintaining a necessary illusion to the outside world that the boarding school provides a benign environment for students and staff.

6. *Member checking.* A major purpose of case study research is to represent the emic perspective, that is, reality as constructed by the individuals who were studied. The validity of a researcher's reconstruction of an individuals' emic perspective can be corroborated by **member checking,** which is the process of having these individuals review statements made in the researcher's report for accuracy and completeness. This was the primary strategy used in the case study of teachers in residence by Dona Kagan and her colleagues to ensure the accuracy of the findings generated by the principal investigator.

Member checking might reveal factual errors that are easily corrected. In other instances, the researcher might need to collect more data in order to reconcile discrepancies. It is possible, too, that the opportunity to read the report will cause participants to recall new facts or to have new perceptions of their situation. The report would then need to be rewritten accordingly.

7. *Outlier analysis.* Rather than ignoring or explaining exceptions away, Miles and Huberman recommend using extreme cases as a way to test and thereby strengthen the

57. Mathison, S. (1988). Why triangulate? *Educational Researcher, 17*(2), 13–17.
58. Aviram, O. (1993). Appearance and reality in a stressful educational setting: Practices inhibiting school effectiveness in an Israeli boarding school. *International Journal of Qualitative Studies in Education, 6,* 33–48.

basic findings: "You need to find the outliers, and then verify whether what is present in them is absent or different in other, more mainstream examples . . . "[59] As we explain in Chapter 5, an outlier is an individual whose score falls at the extreme or end of the score distribution. In case study research, an outlier is an individual or situation differing greatly from most other individuals or situations. For example, in a case study of school innovation, Miles and Huberman found one site where a new practice was evaluated by many teachers as a miraculous cure for local ills. The researchers, however, found two outliers, that is, individuals at the site who had not adopted the practice or had expressed strong criticism of it. Because these individuals had not mastered the innovation as intended and gave reasons for not adopting it that were opposite to those given by adopters, their comments strengthened the validity of the researchers' interpretation that technical mastery of an innovative practice by users leads to positive results.

Miles and Huberman also recommend seeking out individuals who have the most to gain or lose by affirming or denying something. If such individuals give an unexpected answer (e.g., a person who has much to gain by denying a statement affirms it), the researcher can be more confident that they are answering truthfully. A related tactic is to look for negative evidence, that is, to actively seek disconfirmation of what the researcher thinks is true. For example, asking skeptical colleagues to look at one's raw data and independently come up with their own conclusions is a good way to test the soundness of one's analyses and interpretations.

8. *Long-term observation.* Gathering data over a long period of time and making repeated observations of the phenomenon can increase the reliability of case study findings. For example, students' perceptions of school are known to vary depending upon how much of the school year has passed, what the weather conditions are, whether a school holiday is coming or has just passed, and whether they are experiencing personal problems. If data are collected over an extended time period, the researcher might be able to distinguish situational perceptions of school from more consistent trends.

9. *Representativeness check.* To determine whether a finding is typical of the field site from which it is obtained, the researcher should consider whether there was overreliance on accessible or elite informants in collecting data. The researcher also should try to determine how unusual occurrences, or the fact that the researcher was present on some occasions but not others, might have skewed the findings.

10. *Coding check.* In describing interpretational analysis above, we explained how researchers develop or select a category system to code the segments into which interview transcripts, field notes, documents, and other materials have been divided. The reliability of the coding process can be checked using the methods for determining inter-rater reliability developed by quantitative researchers.

Generalizability of Case Study Findings

A research study's findings are generalizable to the extent that they can be applied to individuals or situations other than those in which the findings were obtained. Generalizability is considered an important, achievable goal in quantitative research. In meta-analysis, for example, research findings of various studies on the same phenomenon that were conducted by different researchers are cumulated to determine a mean effect size. This mean effect size is considered to be widely generalizable. (Meta-analysis is explained in Chapter 4.)

---

59. Miles & Huberman, *Qualitative data analysis*, p. 269.

The generalizability of case study findings is more problematic. Proponents of the grounded theory approach to case study research question the possibility of generalizing findings from the cases that were studied to other cases. Sally Hutchinson, a proponent of grounded theory, expresses this view:

> Is grounded research replicable [i.e., generalizable]? "Probably not." Grounded theory depends on the interaction between the data and the creative processes of the researcher. It is highly unlikely that two people would come up with the exact same theory.[60]

Hutchinson recommends using case study research to develop grounded theory that, in turn, can be used as the basis for quantitative research studies, which she feels are more suitable for testing the generalizability of research findings.

Other researchers, however, believe that case study findings can be generalized. They recommend designing case studies in ways that will increase the probability that the findings will apply to other cases also representing the phenomenon being studied. One approach is to study a case that is typical of the phenomenon. If an atypical case is selected because it is of particular interest, it might be possible to select a typical case for study as well. If a unit of analysis has been defined, a random sample within this unit of analysis could be sampled. For example, if researchers are studying the effects of an experimental instructional method being used in a particular teacher's classroom (the case), they might select a random sample of the teacher's students for intensive data collection and analysis.

Another approach to the issue of generalizing case study findings is to place the responsibility for generalizing on the "consumers" of the findings rather than on the researchers. For example, Sandra Wilson uses the term **reader/user generalizability** to indicate that it is the responsibility of each reader or user of case study research to determine the applicability of the findings in their own situations.[61] Similarly, Lee Cronbach argues that in social science any generalization should be regarded only as a tentative hypothesis that must be tested against the specific conditions operating in each situation.[62]

Researchers can use several strategies to help readers of a case study report determine the generalizability of findings to their particular situation or to other situations. First, researchers should provide a thick description of the participants and contexts that comprise the case, so that readers who are interested in applying the findings can determine how similar they are to the situation of interest to them. Second, researchers should address the issue of whether the selected case is representative of the general phenomenon being investigated. Finally, if a multiple-case design was used, the researchers should conduct a cross-case analysis to help the reader determine whether there was generalizability at least within the cases that were studied.

✦ Touchstone in Research

Piantanida, M., & Garman, N. (1999). *The qualitative dissertation: A guide for students and faculty.* Thousand Oaks, CA: Sage.

Reporting a Case Study

Our review of published case studies indicates that they generally follow one of two reporting styles—what we choose to call *reflective reporting* and *analytic reporting*. Elements of either style can appear in the other, but generally the characteristics of one style are dominant. We describe the two styles below, but first we consider the researcher's decision about which case or cases will be reported.

60. Hutchinson, S. A. (1988). Education and grounded theory. In R. R. Sherman & R. B. Webb (Eds.), *Qualitative research in education: Focus and methods* (pp. 123–140). London: Falmer Press. Quote appears on p. 132.
61. Wilson, S. (1979). Explorations of the usefulness of case study evaluations. *Evaluation Quarterly, 3,* 446–459.
62. Cronbach, L. J. (1975). Beyond the two disciplines of scientific psychology. *American Psychologist, 30,* 116–127.

Finalizing Definition of the Case

When the researcher has collected "thick" data about various aspects of the phenomenon being studied, it is possible to define the case in different ways. For example, consider Rossi's study of teachers (she called them teacher-leaders) who had participated in the California Mathematics Project. Instead of focusing on the teacher-leaders, she might have focused on data that she had collected about the project (its history, project directors, summer training programs, etc.) and specific facilitation events for which the teacher-leaders were responsible. However, Rossi decided to focus on one particular aspect, namely, the change-agent role of the teacher-leaders. Also, although she started collecting data on three teacher-leaders, she eventually decided to exclude one of them because of unusual circumstances pertaining to that individual. Thus, decisions about which cases and which aspect of the cases to report were not finalized until well after her dissertation proposal had been approved and data collection was underway.

Deciding which case, or cases, to report can be difficult, because technological tools like computers, videotape equipment, and photocopy machines tempt researchers to generate ever more data. The researcher must sort through the data and report only those cases and aspects of them that have the greatest bearing on the questions that interest her. Wolcott makes the point this way:

> The critical task in qualitative research is not to accumulate all the data you can, but to "can" (i.e., get rid of) most of the data you accumulate. That requires constant winnowing, including decisions about data not worth entering in the first place, regardless of how easy that might be to do. The trick is to discover essences and then to reveal those essences with sufficient context, yet not become mired trying to include everything that might possibly be described.[63]

Because case selection can occur late in the research process, Wolcott argues that case study is not a research design or method, but rather an outcome of qualitative research that the researcher chooses at the stage of preparing the report.[64]

Reflective Reporting

As we explained earlier in the chapter, some case study researchers rely heavily or exclusively on reflective analysis of their data rather than on interpretational or structural analysis. These researchers most likely will prefer to write their dissertations or other reports using a reflective reporting style. The two primary characteristics of **reflective reporting** are the use of literary devices to bring the case alive for the reader and the strong presence of the researcher's voice in the report.

Authors of literary works, of course, tell stories. In reflective reporting, we find that the researcher often weaves case study data into a story. It is this type of researcher that Wolcott apparently has in mind when he argues that the ability to be a storyteller, rather than disdain for number crunching, should be regarded as the distinguishing characteristic of qualitative researchers.[65] Among the ways Wolcott suggests for organizing and presenting a case study as a story are: (1) relating events in chronological order; (2) focusing the story on a critical or key event; (3) recounting the events through the eyes of different participants whose perspectives may differ considerably; and (4) reporting a "day-in-the-life," for example, a reconstruction of the first day of fieldwork, or a typical day in the life of a case study participant.

Figure 14.3 presents the headings for Wolcott's case study of a school dropout, which we mentioned earlier in the chapter. The story of Brad (the "sneaky kid") starts in present

63. Wolcott, H. F. (2001). *Writing up qualitative research* (2nd ed.). Thousand Oaks, CA: Sage. Quote appears on p. 44.
64. Wolcott, *Transforming qualitative data.*
65. Wolcott, *Writing up qualitative research.*

FIGURE 14.3

Organization of a Published Case Study Involving Reflective Reporting

Adequate Schools and Inadequate Education

The Life History of a Sneaky Kid

_____ *

The Cultural Context of a Free Spirit
The Life History of a Sneaky Kid
   "In the Chute"
      On the loose
      Getting busted
      Second-rate jobs and second-rate apartments
      A new life
      "Picking up" what was needed
      The bicycle thief
      Being sneaky
      I don't have to steal, but
      Breaking and entering
      Inching closer to the chute
      I'm not going to get caught
      Home is the hunter
      Growing up
      Getting paid for dropping out
      Hiding out from life
   Worldview: "Getting My Life Together"
      A job—that's all that makes you middle class
      Building my own life
      Being by myself
      Friends
      I've been more places and done more things
      Some personal standards
      Moderation: Getting close enough, going "medium" fast
      Putting it all together
   Formal Schooling
Adequate Schools and Inadequate Education: An Interpretation Summary

*The report starts with an introductory section that does not have a heading.

Source: Wolcott, F. (1994). _Transforming qualitative data._ Thousand Oaks, CA: Sage. Copyright © 1994 by Sage Publications. Reprinted by permission of Sage Publications, Inc.

time, and then recounts earlier events in his life as appropriate. Much of the story is organized around broader and narrower themes, one of which is "in the chute," a phrase used to describe individuals whose experiences appear to be leading them toward prison. Wolcott states that he arranged the story sequence this way so that "the reader meets Brad on his own ground, first through a recounting of major events and everyday aspects of his life, next through important dimensions of his worldview."[66] The researcher's voice is heard

66. Wolcott, _Transforming qualitative data,_ p. 64.

clearly in the last two sections, where Wolcott presents his interpretation and summary of the case. Wolcott states that the reason for this sequencing is that, "By the time readers arrive at the point where I offer *my* thoughts as to what might be done [about school dropouts], I want to be sure they have a sufficient background to form their own assessment of Brad and his circumstances."[67]

Wolcott's life history of a "sneaky kid" illustrates two principles of reflective reporting. First, the organization of the report highlights what the researcher has learned from the data analysis. Second, the researcher keeps the reader in mind in deciding how to present what he has learned.

The researcher can use various literary devices within the framework of storytelling to bring the case alive for the reader and to convey his point of view as the researcher and narrator of the report. Direct quotes of remarks by the case study participants are particularly effective because they clarify the emic perspective, that is, the meaning of the phenomenon from the point of view of the participants. Much of Wolcott's report consists of direct quotes of statements by Brad, for example:

> I guess being sneaky means I always try to get away with something. There doesn't have to be any big reason. I used to tell the kid I was hanging around with, "I don't steal stuff because I need it. I just like to do it for some excitement."[68]

Some case study researchers have used more dramatic methods for conveying their findings. Laura Richardson cites examples of case studies that have been reported in the form of fiction, poetry, drama, oral readings, comedy and satire, and visual presentations.[69] In one of her own studies, she wrote a poem to convey her understanding of an unmarried mother whom she had studied. The poem uses only the mother's language, as arranged by Richardson. The first lines of the poem are as follows:

The most important thing
to say   is that
I grew up in the South.
Being Southern shapes
aspirations   shapes
what you think you are
and what you think you're going to be.

(When I hear myself, my Ladybird
kind of accent on tape, I think, OH Lord.
You're from Tennessee.)[70]

The use of these dramatic forms to represent case study findings has been called the **performance turn** in qualitative research. Norman Denzin observes that whereas a standard written text involves one-way transmission of findings from the researcher to the reader, the performance turn intends a dynamic interaction between researcher and audience to co-create meaning:

> Through the act of coparticipation, these works bring audiences back into the text, creating a field of shared emotional experience. The phenomenon being described is created through the

---

67. Ibid.

68. Ibid., p. 77.

69. Richardson, L. (2000). Writing: A method of inquiry. In N. K. Denzin & Y. S. Lincoln (Eds.), *Handbook of qualitative research* (2nd ed., pp. 923–948). Thousand Oaks, CA: Sage.

70. Richardson, L. (1992). The consequences of poetic representation: Writing the other, rewriting the self. In C. Ellis & M. G. Flaherty (Eds.), *Investigating subjectivity: Research on lived experience* (pp. 125–140). Quote appears on p. 126.

act of representation. . . . A good performance text must be more than cathartic, it must be political, moving people to action and reflection.[71]

Richardson observes that case study researchers who use these unconventional genres typically have a postmodern sensibility. As we explained in Chapter 1, postmodernism casts doubt on all claims to authoritative methods of inquiry and reporting, including mainstream scientific reports. A postmodernist, therefore, would be inclined to view poetry to be just as legitimate a genre for reporting case study findings as the standard journal article format used by quantitative researchers.

Analytic Reporting

An analytic reporting style is appropriate when the researcher has emphasized interpretational or structural analysis of case study data and has conceptualized the study from a positivist or postpositivist perspective. The major characteristics of **analytic reporting** are an objective writing style (i.e., the researcher's voice is silent or subdued) and a conventional organization of topics to be covered: introduction, review of literature, methodology, results, and discussion. This is essentially the same style and organization used to report quantitative research studies. (See Chapter 2 for guidelines for writing quantitative research reports.)

Suppose a case study researcher has done data analyses to identify constructs, themes, and patterns in the phenomena that have been studied. Suppose further that this researcher used a multiple-case design. Should the researcher report the results for each construct, theme, and pattern across all the cases that have been studied? Or should she report each case by itself and show how the constructs, themes, and patterns are manifested in that particular case? If the former approach is used, the construct, theme, or pattern is highlighted; however, the reader does not get a holistic understanding of each case. Conversely, if the latter approach is used, the reader sees each case as a whole, but it is difficult to make cross-case comparisons with respect to particular constructs, themes, or patterns.

We have found that a combination of the two approaches works well. First, the data analysis results for each case are reported, including sufficient thick description so that the participants, events, and context come alive for the reader. Next, a cross-case analysis is given, which notes consistencies and differences in constructs, themes, and patterns across the cases that have been studied.

As in quantitative research reports, tables and figures are an effective way to present the results of case study analyses. A useful sourcebook of various display formats for this purpose was prepared by Miles and Huberman.[72] They distinguish between two types of display formats: a matrix and a network. A **matrix** is a table that has defined rows and columns. Figure 14.4 is an example of a matrix in their sourcebook, taken from a case study of school improvement and change. It represents in summary form the experiences of three teachers who are attempting to implement a new educational practice.

A **network** is a figure for displaying bits of information, each in a separate "node," and links that show how the bits of information relate to each other. Figure 14.5 is an example of a network in Miles and Huberman's sourcebook, taken from case studies of university students. The left part of the figure shows a sequence of experiences of a student who had temporarily left the university. Each box (a "node") contains a separate experience. The right part of the figure shows a different set of nodes, each containing a force or forces moving the student to the next experience.

71. Denzin, N. K. (2000). The practices and politics of interpretation. In N. K. Denzin & Y. S. Lincoln (Eds.), *Handbook of qualitative research* (2nd ed., pp. 897–922). Thousand Oaks, CA: Sage.
72. Miles & Huberman, *Qualitative data analysis.*

FIGURE 14.4

Matrix Display of Teachers' Experience in Using a New Educational Practice

User	Feelings/Concerns	How Innovation Looked	What Was User Doing Most?	Problems
Vance	More comfortable with style of teaching and with having kids outside	Still useful, giving good direction and helpful ideas, activities	Working through materials Giving, participating in env'l educ workshops Working with community Off-campus site work	Time too limited for tasks to be done
Drew	Concern with growing number of nonachievers in forestry/ ecology class	Too discovery-oriented for kids without biology basics; lecture style more appropriate	Adapting materials and lessons to growing nonachiever population Off-campus site work	Dealing with more nonachievers successfully
Carroll	Excitement with new activities, expanding science program	Same as first year	Working with community Giving, participating in env'l educ workshops Off-campus site work	Overextended activity commitment

Source: Table 7.3 on p. 179 in: Miles, M. B., & Huberman, A. M. (1994). *Qualitative data.analysis: An expanded sourcebook* (2nd ed.). Thousand Oaks, CA: Sage. Copyright © 1994 by Sage Publications. Reprinted by permission of Sage Publications, Inc.

FIGURE 14.5

Event-Flow Network: A Student's Learning and Work Experiences

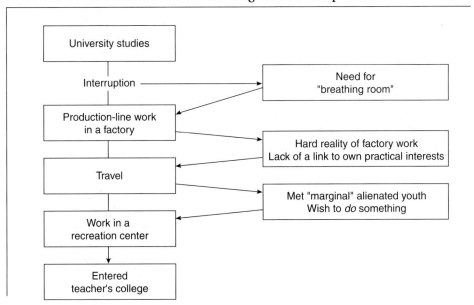

Source: Adapted from box 5.2 on p. 114 in: Miles, M. B., & Huberman, A. M. (1994). *Qualitative data analysis: An expanded sourcebook* (2nd ed.). Thousand Oaks, CA: Sage. Copyright © 1994 by Sage Publications. Adapted by permission of Sage Publications, Inc.

Displays such as those shown in Figures 14.4 and 14.5 can be helpful in two ways. First, they help researchers organize the results of a data analysis and plan the next stage of analysis. Second, displays can be used in the case study report to present research findings so that they are easily comprehended by the reader. Miles and Huberman's sourcebook contains many examples of matrices and networks that are suitable for various purposes in case study research.

Advantages and Disadvantages of Case Study Research

Now that you have read about case study research, you are in a position to appreciate its advantages over traditional quantitative research methods. One of them is that the case study researcher, through a process of thick description, can bring a case to life in a way that is not possible using the statistical methods of quantitative research. Thus, readers of case study reports may have a better basis for developing theories, designing educational interventions, or taking some other action than they would have from reading only quantitative research reports. Also, thick description helps readers to compare cases with their own situations. These comparisons are more difficult to make when reading reports of quantitative research, which typically provide only statistical analyses and sparse verbal descriptions of the situations that were studied. Furthermore, a good case study report will reveal the researcher's perspective, thus enabling readers to determine whether the researcher has the same perspective on the phenomenon as they do.

Quantitative research designs are well suited for identifying general trends in populations. However, there are situations in which a researcher wishes to learn about a particular individual, for example, an outlier who does not fit the general trend.[73] The case study method is ideally suited to investigating outliers and other unusual phenomena.

Another advantage of case studies is their emergent quality. As researchers collect data and gain insight into particular phenomena, they can change the case on which the study will focus, adopt new data-collection methods, and frame new research questions. In contrast, quantitative research designs are difficult to change once they are set in motion.

The main disadvantage of case studies is the difficulty of generalizing the findings to other situations, although limited generalizations can be made using the procedures that we described in this chapter. Another disadvantage is that ethical problems can arise if it proves difficult in the report to disguise the identity of the organization or individuals that were studied. Also, case studies are highly labor-intensive and require highly developed language skills in order to identify constructs, themes, and patterns in verbal data and to write a report that brings the case alive for the reader. Researchers who lack these resources perhaps can make a better contribution to knowledge in their field of interest by employing quantitative research designs.

73. The outlier phenomenon is discussed in Chapter 15.

✦ RECOMMENDATIONS FOR *Doing Case Studies*

1. In designing a case study, define the unit of analysis and identify the phenomenon to be studied.

2. Consider whether and how you will represent the emic and etic perspectives.
3. Maintain awareness of your interpretive processes as you design and conduct the case study.
4. Address issues involving purpose, conceptual context, research questions, methods, and validity in creating your case study design.
5. Devote sufficient time in gaining entry, making contacts, and establishing rapport with the research participants in order to establish the trust needed to collect rich, reliable data.
6. Consider using a contact summary sheet and document summary sheet to keep track of the data-collection process.
7. If appropriate, use software specifically designed for qualitative data analysis.
8. Consider whether interpretational, structural, or reflective analysis is best suited for making sense of your data.
9. Of the many criteria that have been proposed for judging the quality of case study findings, choose those that are best aligned with your theoretical and methodological orientation.
10. Consider how you will approach the issue of generalizability in reporting your case study.
11. Decide whether a reflective or an analytic style is most appropriate for reporting your case study.
12. Before writing a report of your case study, identify the case or cases on which you plan to focus.

✔ SELF-CHECK TEST

Circle the correct answer to each of the following questions.
The answers are provided at the back of the book.

1. The term *emic perspective* refers to
   a. a positivist researcher's view of the phenomenon being studied.
   b. an interpretive researcher's view of the phenomenon being studied.
   c. the research participants' view of the phenomenon being studied.
   d. the reader's view of the phenomenon being studied.

2. Case study researchers need to become personally involved in data collection because
   a. a great deal of data must be collected.
   b. they need to develop a holistic understanding of the phenomenon.
   c. researcher involvement helps ensure the reliability of the findings.
   d. the researcher must continually triangulate the data while it is being collected.

3. The unit of analysis in a case study is
   a. the population from which the case is drawn.
   b. the type of term selected for structural analysis.
   c. the database segment selected for category analysis.
   d. an aspect of a phenomenon that is sampled from possible cases.

4. Experts generally agree that researcher bias in case studies is best handled by
   a. honestly revealing one's possible biases and being willing to have them disconfirmed.
   b. using data-collection methods that rule out the possibility of researcher bias.
   c. using several researchers and seeking consensus in their conclusions.
   d. not studying phenomena in which the researcher has a personal interest.

5. Thick description in case study research refers to
   a. a comprehensive, literal depiction of a phenomenon and its meaning.
   b. description of a phenomenon from both an emic and an etic perspective.
   c. the use of triangulation in writing up case study findings.
   d. reliance on reflective analysis in writing a case study report.

6. In grounded theory, constructs are derived from
   a. a pre-existing theory about the phenomenon being studied.
   b. reflections by the case study participants.
   c. the data that have been collected.
   d. all of the above.

7. The case study finding that there is an association between the amount of structure in teachers' lessons and how teachers think about students' learning processes is an example of a
   a. construct.
   b. theme.
   c. thick description.
   d. pattern.

8. In interpretational data analysis, the researcher
   a. searches for the meaning inherent in the data.
   b. imposes meaning on the data.
   c. searches for naturally occurring segments in the data.
   d. typically uses categories developed by other researchers.

9. Usefulness, contextual completeness, researcher positioning, and reporting style are features of
   a. interpretive validity.
   b. case study generalizability.
   c. case study verisimilitude.
   d. audit trails.

10. Reflective reporting of a case study tends to rely heavily on
   a. presentation of structural data analyses.
   b. an objective writing style.
   c. formats developed for use in reporting quantitative research studies.
   d. the use of literary devices.

CHAPTER 15

✦ Qualitative Research Traditions

OVERVIEW

Qualitative researchers in anthropology, psychology, and other disciplines have developed various ways to study human behavior. Their methods, theories, and accumulated findings constitute distinctive research traditions. In this chapter we explore these traditions and describe how they are used in educational research. Some traditions are particularly well-suited to the investigation of people's inner experience, some to the investigation of social and cultural phenomena, and some to the investigation of communication phenomena such as speech and text. Knowing about these qualitative research traditions will help you think more broadly about your research problem and consider a variety of methods for studying it.

OBJECTIVES

After studying this chapter, you should be able to

1. Describe the characteristics of a qualitative research tradition.
2. Describe the types of phenomena that cognitive psychologists investigate and the research methods that they use.
3. Explain the purpose of phenomenological research and the steps involved in conducting a phenomenological study.
4. Explain the similarities and differences between phenomenography and phenomenological research.
5. Describe the types of educational phenomena that might be investigated by the life history approach.
6. State the goals of the research traditions of symbolic interactionism, event structure analysis, and emancipatory action research.
7. Describe the characteristics of ethnography and the steps involved in conducting an ethnographic study.
8. Explain the strengths and weaknesses of ethnographic research.
9. Explain the goals and underlying assumptions of the cultural studies and critical theory traditions.
10. Describe the types of investigations conducted by researchers who work within the cultural studies and critical theory traditions.
11. Describe the purpose and techniques of ethnomethodological research.
12. State the goals of narrative analysis, ethnoscience, ethnographic content analysis, and the ethnography of communication.
13. Explain the goals, assumptions, and basic concepts of hermeneutical analysis.
14. Explain the goals, assumptions, and basic concepts of semiotic research.
15. Explain the basic principles of structuralism and poststructuralism, and describe the types of phenomena that might be investigated using these approaches.

The Value of Qualitative Research Traditions

Qualitative research in education has roots in many academic disciplines. They include not only the social sciences (e.g., anthropology, sociology, and psychology), but also the humanities (e.g., art, literature, and philosophy) and interdisciplinary studies. Some qualitative researchers also have been influenced by the postmodern approach to inquiry that has emerged in recent years. Postmodernists reject what they perceive to be the "business-as-usual" orientation to scientific endeavor of the entrenched power structure of the professional research establishment.

This chapter provides an overview of the major qualitative traditions that have been used in educational research. You should become familiar with them because you are likely to encounter one or more of them in your reviews of the research literature. Also, knowledge of these traditions can help you in formulating questions to guide a case study, in developing methods for collecting and analyzing your research data, and in suggesting relevant theory to which you might connect your findings. Your case study will have added meaning and significance if it is grounded within an established research tradition.

Evelyn Jacob defined a **research tradition** as "a group of scholars who agree among themselves on the nature of the universe they are examining, on legitimate questions and problems to study, and on legitimate techniques to seek solutions."[1] (Jacob's use of the term "scholars" subsumes researchers as well as theorists and research synthesizers.) To understand this definition, consider the research tradition of ethnography, which we discuss in more detail later in the chapter. Researchers who work within this research tradition are interested in the nature of culture and how it functions, and they have developed specialized methods to pursue their inquiries. Their research has produced a body of knowledge about different aspects of culture, including school cultures and the role of education in different world cultures. The ethnographers who produced this knowledge share a common interest in particular phenomena, methods of investigation, and theoretical concepts.

Because research and scientific activity are social activities, investigators working within different research traditions are influenced by each other's work. Thus, there is cross-fertilization across different traditions, so that a study by one researcher may reflect a mix of research traditions. Not only do traditions tend to borrow from each other, but they gradually are transformed as changes occur in the philosophical and scientific paradigms that researchers embrace, as well as in the broader social context within which scientific endeavor is carried out. Furthermore, different researchers within a tradition sometimes disagree on epistemological assumptions and other matters. It is not possible, therefore, to provide an exhaustive list and definitive description of research traditions that are relevant to educational research. This chapter is more a sketch than a formal portrait, to be filled in by your own efforts in reviewing and conducting research studies.

Most research traditions have developed within a particular academic discipline (e.g., cognitive psychology within the discipline of psychology). Some research traditions appear in related forms in more than one discipline, with the tradition originating in one discipline (e.g., ethnography originated in anthropology) and then being adapted for use in another discipline (e.g., some sociologists use ethnographic methods).

Table 15.1 presents 17 qualitative research traditions organized into three categories. The traditions within each category are related in that they study similar phenomena.

---

1. Jacob, E. (1987). Qualitative research traditions: A review. *Review of Educational Research, 57,* 1–50. Quote appears on pp. 1–2.

TABLE 15.1

Qualitative Research Traditions Classified by Type of Phenomena Investigated

Research Tradition	Involves the Study of
I. Investigation of Lived Experience	
1. Cognitive psychology	Mental structures and processes used by individuals in different situations
2. Life history	individuals' life experiences from their perspective
3. Phenomenography	Individuals' conceptualizations of reality
4. Phenomenology	Reality as it appears to individuals
II. Investigation of Society and Culture	
1. Cultural studies and critical theory	Oppressive power relationships in a culture
2. Emancipatory action research	Practitioners' self-reflective efforts to improve the rationality and justice of their work
3. Ethnography	Characteristic features and patterns of a culture
4. Ethnomethodology	The rules that underlie everyday social interactions
5. Event structure analysis	The logical structures of social events
6. Symbolic interactionism	The influence of social interactions on social structures and individuals' self-identity
III. Investigation of Language and Communication	
1. Ethnographic content analysis	The content of documents in cultural perspective
2. Ethnography of communication	How members of a cultural group use speech in their social life
3. Ethnoscience	A culture's semantic systems
4. Hermeneutics	The process by which individuals arrive at the meaning of a text
5. Narrative analysis	Organized representations and explanations of human experience
6. Semiotics	Signs and the meanings they convey
7. Structuralism and poststructuralism	The systemic properties of language, text, and other phenomena

Some focus on understanding the nature of lived experience (type I), others seek to understand cultural and social phenomena (type II), and still others seek to understand language and communication phenomena (type III). Some have played a major role in educational research, while others rarely have been applied to education but have the potential for greater application.

How can Table 15.1 help you? Suppose you have identified a particular problem for investigation—for example, how disadvantaged inner-city students live and how schools can help them improve their lives. You can examine the traditions listed in Table 15.1 to determine which ones are appropriate for studying such phenomena. Or suppose that you have identified a problem of interest to you—for example, test anxiety—but are not sure how you wish to focus your investigation. Table 15.1 can help you identify a possible focus, for example, the lived experience of test anxiety (for which phenomenological research might be appropriate) or how test anxiety is viewed in different cultures (for which ethnography might be appropriate).

The following sections describe each of the qualitative research traditions listed in Table 15.1. We discuss several of them in detail in order to develop your understanding of each the three types of qualitative research traditions. Others are described briefly, but in sufficient detail to help you determine their possible relevance to your research interests.

Keep in mind that the list of qualitative research traditions in Table 15.1 is not exhaustive. The field of qualitative research is undergoing rapid growth and continual reconceptualization. New traditions may blend with existing ones, and can be identified by more than one label. Also, our list does not include historical research, although it is a strong qualitative research tradition (see Chapter 16). Historical research methods can be used to study many of the phenomena listed in Table 15.1, as they occurred in the past.

The Investigation of Lived Experience

The study of inner experience has been neglected and even disparaged by researchers who adhere to positivist epistemology. B. F. Skinner, for example, claimed that the human mind was a "black box" that could not be studied by scientific methods. Qualitative researchers reject this claim. They have developed research traditions that focus on the inner experience of people in general, of particular types of people (e.g., experts as compared to novices in a field of inquiry), or of individuals as they interact with each other. We describe four of these traditions below: cognitive psychology, phenomenological research, phenomenography, and life history research.

Cognitive Psychology

◆ *Touchstone in Research*

Sternberg, R. J. (1998). *Cognitive psychology.* Fort Worth, TX: Harcourt.

According to Kenneth Strike, "the majority of educators view psychology as the central discipline of education."[2] In fact, psychology has had a major influence on educational research and practice. Most notably, educators make extensive use of the tests developed by psychologists (e.g., intelligence tests and vocational aptitude tests). The design and scoring of these tests reflect the strongly quantitative orientation of traditional psychological research.

In the past thirty years, various qualitative traditions have gained a foothold in psychology. One tradition in particular has had a major impact on educational theory and practice. This tradition is **cognitive psychology,** which we define as the study of the structures and processes involved in mental activity, and of how these structures and processes are learned or how they develop with maturation.

The study of such cognitive phenomena as perception, memory, attention, thinking, and problem solving has been part of psychology since its inception. However, from about 1930 to 1960 the behaviorist tradition in psychology overshadowed the study of these cognitive phenomena. Consciousness and cognition were relegated to Skinner's unknowable "black box," which was presumed to be situated between a tangible stimulus and an individual's observable response. Skinner in particular argued for a discipline of psychology that would formulate principles of behavior control and learning without invoking mentalistic constructs such as memory and motivation.[3]

2. Strike, K. A. (1994). Epistemology and education. In T. Husén & T. N. Postlethwaite (Eds.), *International encyclopedia of education* (2nd ed., pp. 1996–2001). London: Pergamon.
3. Skinner, B. F. (1953). *Science and human behavior.* New York: Macmillan.

Both the cognitive theorists who preceded Skinner and the cognitive psychologists and cognitive scientists who succeeded him claimed that it is not possible to develop a complete view of human behavior without studying the internal mental and perceptual processes of specific individuals. Most cognitive psychologists assume that there are physical structures in the human brain that determine brain functioning and activity, and that the activity of such physical structures in turn leads to the development of specific cognitive structures and processes. Cognition can be conceptualized broadly as the operation of these structures and processes. As research into brain function and activity has expanded, the study of cognition has gained renewed respectability and priority within psychological and educational research.

Educational researchers who work within the tradition of cognitive psychology have investigated various phenomena, including teacher thinking, students' learning processes, and the motivation to learn. Some of their research involves case studies that are grounded in either a positivist or interpretive approach to inquiry. To illustrate this type of research, we present below a representative study in a line of research on expert versus novice thinking.

A Study of Differences in the Knowledge Structures of Experts and Novices

In this research study, Samuel Wineburg asked working historians and high-performing high school seniors to think aloud as they reviewed and evaluated primary sources all related to the same event in American history.[4] Other researchers previously had done research on cognitive differences between experts and novices in other fields (e.g., mathematics and chess) in order to identify the cognitive structures, processes, and progressive changes involved in complex thinking. Wineburg wished to extend this line of research to the domain of historical thinking.

Eight historians from universities in an urban area and eight high school students from the same area were the subjects for the study. Four of the historians (the "non-Americanist" historians) had specializations other than American history, and thus were expected to have much less knowledge of this domain of knowledge and inquiry than the other four ("Americanist") historians. A 12-item pretest verified that the groups differed in their knowledge of American history, with the average number of terms correctly identified on the test being 10 for the Americanist historians, 4.25 for the non-Americanist historians, and 1.8 for the students.

Each research participant individually was presented eight documents and three paintings concerning the battle of Lexington, which marked the start of the American Revolution in 1775. The participants responded to a fixed set of tasks: (1) to read each document aloud and to "think aloud," that is, to say everything that came to mind as they read; (2) to think aloud as they reviewed each painting, then give a date to each painting and select the most accurate one; and (3) to rank the eight documents in terms of their trustworthiness. All sessions were audiotaped, and transcripts were prepared. Unlike most qualitative research, Wineburg's study was carried out in a laboratory setting and involved individuals responding to a contrived set of tasks. Nevertheless, the tasks were designed to simulate those that historians encounter in the course of their work.

The procedure of thinking aloud that Wineburg's subjects used is called protocol analysis.[5] **Protocol analysis** involves asking individuals to state all their thoughts as they

4. Wineburg, S. S. (1991). Historical problem solving: A study of the cognitive processes used in the evaluation of documentary and pictorial evidence. *Journal of Educational Psychology, 83,* 73–87.
5. Ericsson, K. A., & Simon, H. A. (1993). *Protocol analysis: Verbal reports as data* (rev. ed.). Cambridge, MA: Bradford.

carry out a challenging task, so that the researcher can obtain a holistic overview of their cognitive activity as recorded in their verbal reports. Wineburg used recommended procedures for protocol analysis to ensure that the data obtained would be as valid a reflection of the subjects' thoughts as possible.

The transcript for each individual was divided into a protocol for the tasks involving the paintings and a protocol for the tasks involving the documents. The painting protocols were separated into coding units consisting of independent subject/predicate clauses. Based on the researcher's analysis, these coding units were grouped into four categories. *Description* included simple descriptive statements. *Reference* included statements that related the paintings to each other, to certain documents, or to a "mental model" of the historical event that the individual had generated. *Analysis* included statements related to the viewpoint or intentions of the painting or its artist, and unprompted estimates of the dates of the paintings. *Qualification* included statements that qualified other statements (e.g., statements pointing out shortcomings in the paintings or in pictorial sources generally). The document protocols were analyzed by a somewhat different procedure and yielded different types of categories.

Some of the most interesting findings of Wineburg's study involve individual comments. For example, a data table in the research report compares the responses of one historian and one student who both selected the same painting as the most accurate depiction of the historical event. As Wineburg notes, the historian made many references to corroborative information in the documents in explaining her selection, stated qualifications about the painting's accuracy, and made her choice with seeming hesitancy and tentativeness. The student, by contrast, was described as confidently choosing the same picture, and as having chosen that painting as most accurate partly because it included details that were *not* mentioned in any of the documents.

Wineburg contrasted his findings with those of earlier expert-novice research, in which differences were explained in terms of the number and organization of *problem templates,* that is, preset mental structures for solving problems in a specific subject.[6] In the theory underlying such research, successful performance depends both on possession of the appropriate problem template and on activation and confirmation of an appropriate knowledge structure involving available *schemata* (i.e., internal conceptual structures to which the individual relates each new experience). In contrast, Wineburg concluded from his findings that expertise seems to rest not on bringing an available problem template to the task, but rather on constructing a context-specific schema tailored to the specific historical event being studied. Given an unfamiliar event, the non-Americanist historians responded much as the Americanist historians: Both groups "puzzled about discrepancies, they compared the pictures with the written documents, they corroborated and discorroborated key features, and they tried to represent what could and what could not be known."[7] Their learning activity reflected not so much the availability of appropriate problem-solving strategies as it did the belief systems they had about history and historical research—for example, that a document is only as trustworthy as its author and its function make it. In contrast, students treated the tasks as simple and unambiguous, reflecting the noncritical manner in which they had been taught history.

Wineburg's study has some characteristics of quantitative research. For example, the author reported that historians' painting protocols contained significantly more state-

6. This research is summarized in: Chi, M. T. H., Glaser, R., & Farr, M. J. (1988). *The nature of expertise.* Hillsdale, NJ: Lawrence Erlbaum Associates.
7. Wineburg, *Historical problem solving,* p. 83.

ments overall (based on a Mann-Whitney U test) than the students' protocols. Spearman *rho* correlations and Kendall's coefficients of concordance also were computed, and they showed that the level of agreement among the historians in their rankings of the documents' trustworthiness was much higher than that among the students.

Wineburg concluded from his study that "able high school students can know a lot about history but still have little idea of how historical knowledge is constructed."[8] This interpretation of the research findings was based both on qualitative and quantitative data. While Wineburg sought to validate and generalize the findings through the use of inferential statistics, he also sought to clarify the emic perspective of the individuals studied.

Phenomenology

Phenomenology is the study of the world as it appears to individuals when they place themselves in a state of consciousness that reflects an effort to be free of everyday biases and beliefs. As such, phenomenology shares the goal of other qualitative research traditions to understand how individuals construct, and are constructed by, social reality.

✦ *Touchstone in Research*

Moustakas, C. (1994). *Phenomenological research methods.* Thousand Oaks, CA: Sage.

In doing a phenomenological study, the researcher is intimately connected with the phenomena being studied and comes to know himself within his experiencing of these phenomena. In this respect, phenomenological research is the antithesis of quantitative research, which seeks to detach the researcher's self from the phenomena being studied through the use of objective methods of data collection and analysis. In another respect, though, phenomenological and quantitative research are complementary, as Adrian van Kaam observed:

> [Phenomenological research] is experiential and qualitative. It sets the stage for more accurate empirical investigations by lessening the risk of a premature selection of methods and categories . . . Such preliminary exploration does not supplant but complements the traditional methods of research available to me.[9]

It is conceivable, then, that a researcher might do a phenomenological investigation as a self-contained study or as a part of pilot work for a study that will employ a quantitative research design.

Phenomenology originated as a philosophical movement founded by Edmund Husserl. He believed that the starting point for knowledge was the self's experience of **phenomena,** which are the various sensations, perceptions, and ideations that appear in consciousness when the self focuses attention on an object. Husserl formulated various processes—described by such exotic terms as *epoche, transcendental-phenomenological reduction, imaginative variation,* and *noesis*—for preparing oneself to experience a phenomenon, for having the experience and recording it, and for analyzing it. Psychologists reformulated these processes into procedures that are more standardized and more closely aligned with the terminology of case study research. The following is a brief account of these procedures as they are used in planning and conducting a phenomenological investigation.

1. *Identify a topic of personal and social significance.* The researcher should select a topic that will engage her both intellectually and emotionally. For example, K. LaCourse

---

8. Ibid., p. 84.
9. van Kaam, A. (1966). *Existential foundations of psychology.* Pittsburgh: Duquesne University Press. Quote appears on p. 295. Note that grounded theory has a similar perspective about premature selection of categories (see Chapter 14).

decided to investigate the topic of how people describe and experience time. Her rationale for studying this topic included the following statement:

> The study of time beckons to me, I think, because issues of time are prominent in my own life. I have strong feelings about time. I love life, and since in so many ways time is life, I love my time. I put careful thought into how I will use it, and I jealously guard against excessive intrusions into my time by others. I have always seen time as a precious commodity . . . And yet so often I feel I am in conflict with time. There is a lack of clarity within me as to the meaning of time in my life and how I can best live in harmony with it. I am puzzled, intrigued, and frustrated by time, and challenged to learn more about it. It is this challenge that leads me to consider studying time.[10]

It is important for a phenomenological researcher to be invested in the topic in this way because she will be collecting data on her own experience of the phenomenon as well as the experiences of her research participants.

2. *Select appropriate participants.* Husserl acknowledged the possibility of intersubjective communication and knowledge. Through a process of empathy, an individual can come to know another person and check whether his experience of a phenomenon corresponds with another's experience of it. Thus, participants in a phenomenological study can work as "co-researchers" with the primary investigator and help with the process of "sifting out intrusive phrases void of meaning . . . exposing and eliminating errors which here too are possible, as they are in every sphere in which validity counts for something."[11] The essential criteria for selecting participants is that they have experienced the phenomenon being studied and share the researcher's interest in understanding its nature and meanings.

3. *Interview each participant.* Phenomenological researchers generally conduct at least one long interview with each participant in order to obtain a comprehensive description of their experience of the phenomenon being studied. The interview process is relatively unstructured, but focused on eliciting all aspects of the experience.

4. *Analyze the interview data.* Data analysis in phenomenological research generally follows the procedures of case study analysis (see Chapter 14): The interview data for each case are broken into segments; the researcher looks for meaning units and themes in the segments; the meaning units and themes are compared across cases; and finally, the case findings are synthesized and validated by checking with the participants. These syntheses are of two types: textural and structural. A **textural description** is an account of individuals' intuitive, prereflective perceptions of a phenomenon from every angle. The following is an excerpt from a textural description for a patient at a sleep disorder clinic who participated in a phenomenological study of the experience of insomnia:

> The experience of insomnia for Jim is one of restless fluctuation from an initial falling asleep to a sudden awakening. Wanting desperately to sleep but to no avail, he is "propelled into being awake"; imprisoned by wakefulness. This kind of being awake is powerful and charged with distress. "It's like being plugged in or amped . . . bug eyed." The growing fatigue becomes every bit as confining as the wakefulness. Sleep is nowhere to be found; there is just this experience of being "simultaneously fatigued, mentally and physically, but absolutely wide awake."[12]

A **structural description** is an account of the regularities of thought, judgment, imagination, and recollection that underlie the experience of a phenomenon and give mean-

10. LaCourse, K. (1991). *The experience of time.* Unpublished manuscript, Center for Humanistic Studies, Detroit, MI.
11. Husserl, E. (1931). *Ideas* (W. R. B. Gibson, Trans.). London: George Allen & Unwin. Quote appears on p. 256
12. Copen, R. (1993). Insomnia: A phenomenological investigation. *Dissertation Abstracts International, 53,* 6542B. (UMI No. 9311957). Quote appears on p. 58.

ing to it. The following is a structural description that synthesizes the findings for 25 participants in a phenomenological study of the experience of being "left out":

> Experiencing ourselves as left out evokes an intensely disquieting and painful emotional storm. Previously taken for granted meanings of who we are for others, and who they are for us, are sundered from their past familiar anchors, and now become highly questionable. The smooth reciprocity of self-other relations gives way, and we are confronted by a disturbing negativity. This negativity expresses itself as a tear in the unfolding tapestry of mutual recognition between ourselves and the others. This gap may be a fissure or an abyss, but it discloses an essential break in our connectedness with others.[13]

Phenomenological research has several advantages as an approach to qualitative research. First, it can be used to study a wide range of educational phenomena, for example, how students experience the process of studying and test-taking, how teachers experience a classroom lesson, and how policy makers experience meetings about school reform proposals. Second, the interview process used to collect phenomenological data is wide-ranging, and therefore it is capable of detecting many aspects of experience that may prove to be important with no further analysis or as variables in subsequent qualitative or quantitative studies. Finally, the procedures of phenomenological inquiry are relatively straightforward, so it seems that less training would be required to do a phenomenological study than would be required to do a study using the methods of a qualitative research tradition such as ethnography or semiotics.

Phenomenography

Like phenomenological researchers, phenomenographers are interested in studying how reality appears to people, rather than the objective nature of reality. The difference between the two research traditions is that **phenomenography** is a specialized method for describing the different ways in which people conceptualize the world around them. For example, different teachers might have different conceptions of what causes students to misbehave in class. A phenomenographer would study a group of teachers to develop a classification of these different conceptions. The method of investigation usually involves interviewing people—in this case, a group of teachers—to determine how and why they would handle a problem posed by the researcher. In contrast, a phenomenological researcher would be concerned with each teacher's total experience of student misbehavior. The experience might include the teachers' conception of student misbehavior, but also the teachers' feelings, reflections, and associations with other life experiences.

Phenomenography as a research approach originated at the University of Gothenburg in Sweden. An example of a phenomenographic study is an investigation of college students' understanding of physical principles by Bengt Johansson, Ference Marton, and Lennart Svensson.[14] One of the questions the researchers asked students was, "A car is driven at a high and constant speed on a straight highway. What forces act on the car?" By interviewing students, they found that students conceptualized motion in two qualitatively different ways. Some students thought of the car as having a constant velocity due to the equilibrium of forces, whereas other students thought of the car moving because of a disequilibrium of forces. In other investigations as well, phenomenographers have

♦ Touchstone in Research

Dell'Alba, G., & Hasselgren, B. (Eds.). (1996). *Reflections on phenomenography: Toward a methodology?* Stockholm: Almqvist & Wiksell.

13. Aanstoos, C. M. (1987). A descriptive phenomenology of the experience of being left out. In F. J. van Zuuren, F. J. Wertz, & B. Mook (Eds.), *Advances in qualitative psychology: Themes and variations* (pp. 137–155). Berwyn, PA: Swets North America.
14. Johansson, B., Marton, F., & Svensson, L. (1985). An approach to describing learning as change between qualitatively different conceptions. In A. L. Pines and L. H. T. West (Eds.), *Cognitive structure and conceptual change* (pp. 233–257). New York: Academic Press.

found that there is a limited number of different ways in which people conceptualize a problem or situation.

Phenomenography is similar to the method that Jean Piaget used in his investigations of how young children understand the world about them. Thus, this research method could be used to investigate individuals' thinking, developmental changes in thinking, and changes in thinking that occur as a result of instruction. Like phenomenological research, phenomenography can be used to study virtually any aspect of natural or social reality about which individuals have formed some conception.

Life History Research

◆ *Touchstone in Research*

Lawrence-Lightfoot, S., & Davis, J. H. (1997). *The art and science of portraiture.* San Francisco: Jossey-Bass.

Tierney, W. G. (2000). Undaunted courage: Life history and the postmodern challenge. In N. K. Denzin & Y. S. Lincoln (Eds.), *Handbook of qualitative research* (2nd ed., pp. 537–553). Thousand Oaks, CA: Sage.

Life history is the study of the life experiences of individuals from the perspective of how these individuals interpret and understand the world around them. It is not a unified research tradition. Researchers in different academic disciplines—literature, history, anthropology, psychology, feminist and minority studies—do life history studies for different purposes and with different research methods.[15] Depending upon the researcher, a life history might be called a *biography, a life story*, an *oral history,* or a *case study.* Researchers who choose to write about themselves might call their report an *autobiography* or a *memoir.*

Various methods can be used to collect and analyze data for a life history. Researchers traditionally have analyzed materials written by or about the individual being studied, for example, diaries, correspondence, and professional writings. More recent research has focused on the use of interviewing and direct observation, and on the use of narrative analysis. (We discuss narrative analysis later in the chapter.)

In education, life history has become a popular approach for studying teacher development.[16] A study by Petra Munro illustrates this line of research.[17] Her life histories of three women teachers were guided by the following research questions:

> [H]ow do women teachers resist the naming of their experiences by others, which distorts and marginalizes their realities? How do they construct themselves as subjects despite the fictions constructed about women teachers?[18]

To answer these questions, she conducted extensive interviews with the research participants (she referred to them as "life historians"); the interviews were tape-recorded and transcribed. In addition, she interviewed individuals who knew them (colleagues, administrators, and students), observed one of them teaching, analyzed personal and school documents, and administered a questionnaire concerning their work and family history.

Munro offered the following explanation for her choice of life history as a research approach: " . . . I was drawn to life history and narrative inquiry because of its potential to highlight gendered constructions of power, resistance, and agency . . . "[19] In turn, the themes of power, resistance, and agency were grounded in several qualitative research traditions that we discuss later in the chapter: critical theory (specifically, various feminist theories) and poststructuralism. These research traditions provided interpretive frameworks for analyzing her research data. However, the frameworks do not constitute a neutral, authoritative basis for interpretation. The study is permeated by Munro's strong

15. The approaches of different disciplines are described in: Smith, L. M. (1994). Biographical method. In N. K. Denzin & Y. S. Lincoln (Eds.), *Handbook of qualitative research* (pp. 286–305). Thousand Oaks, CA: Sage.
16. See, for example: Goodson, I. (Ed.). (1992). *Studying teachers' lives.* New York: Teachers College Press.
17. Munro, P. (1998). *Subject to fiction: Women teachers' life history narratives and the cultural politics of resistance.* Buckingham, England: Open University Press.
18. Ibid., p. 3.
19. Ibid., p. 7.

self-reflexive challenging of the interpretive frameworks and her co-creation of the mean-ings of the teachers' lives. (Reflexivity in research is explained in Chapter 1).

Each life history is accorded a separate chapter in Munro's account of her study. The teacher's life is told more or less chronologically and organized into phases that the re-searcher considered significant. For example, the life history of Bonnie, a 46-year-old social-studies teacher, has these phases (the labels are those used by the researcher):

Finding a fit. Bonnie described her early validation for her intellectual abilities, especially in history, and the influence that her father's authoritarianism and argumentative nature had on her approach to social issues.

The do-gooder. While going to college, Bonnie took time off to participate in a govern-ment volunteer program in which she helped poor black people in the South. After returning to college, she helped pay for her tuition by working as a waitress, during which time she par-ticipated in a union strike. Her experience as an activist and advocate shaped her view of what it means to be a teacher.

Learning to teach:'finding a fit.' Bonnie chose teaching as a profession in part because she did not find many other alternatives open to her. Her activism and advocacy became ex-pressed by her strong interest in her local teacher's association.

Becoming an advocate for women teachers. In 1990 Bonnie began her 21st year as a high school social-studies teacher. She had been president of her local teachers association and was still a strong advocate for teachers' rights, with special concern about unjust and sexist behav-ior toward women teachers.

A pain to administrators. In 1990 Bonnie became the department chair of an all-male social-studies department. Her approach to administration is based on judicious use of au-thority and constructive confrontation, which reflects her early experiences with her father.

Munro concluded Bonnie's life history with her own reflections, including the following: "Bonnie's story spoke to my understanding of how women teachers traverse from the world of the classroom, where we create the space to enact our own realities, to the world outside the classroom, in which we are too often left with no voice at all."[20]

After presenting the three life histories, Munro provided a final set of reflections that related the histories to her theoretical concerns. One of these reflections is as follows:

The ongoing negotiation of gendered subjectivity evident in the life history narratives presented here suggests that women's experiencing of gender is not monolithic or grounded in understand-ings of gender as inevitable. . . . [A]s I learned from Agnes, Cleo and Bonnie, resistance is not an 'act' but a movement, a continual displacement of others' attempts to name our realities.[21]

This study of women teachers demonstrates how the research tradition of life history can make visible for the reader the inner experiences of an individual or a group of indi-viduals. These revelations have implications that extend well beyond the particular lives that are studied. In the study described above, the life histories of three teachers raise ques-tions about changing conceptions of gender identity (both male and female) and the role of gender in the education profession.

The Investigation of Society and Culture

Many qualitative researchers focus their investigations on how individuals become orga-nized into groups (e.g., school classes, work teams, church congregations, and entire soci-eties) and the way in which these social entities influence human thought and behavior.

20. Ibid., p. 107.
21. Ibid., p. 125.

Other researchers focus on the culture of such groups. The term **culture** refers to the sum total of ways of living (e.g., values, customs, rituals, and beliefs) that are built up by a group of human beings and that are transmitted from one generation to another or from current members to newly admitted members. We discuss in the following sections three qualitative research traditions that focus on societal and cultural phenomena: ethnography, cultural studies, and ethnomethodology.

Besides these three traditions, there are other qualitative research traditions that also examine societal and cultural phenomena, including symbolic interactionism, event structure analysis, and emancipatory action research. **Symbolic interactionism,** which is a sociological research tradition, involves the study of how individuals engage in social transactions and how these transactions contribute to the creation and maintenance of social structures and the individual's self-identity.[22] For example, using the methods of symbolic interactionism, Gary Alan Fine was able to identify and describe the various social realities that comprise Little League baseball: It is a social structure for learning this particular sport, but also a structure for socialization into "male culture," and an environment for learning the lore and slang of sport.[23]

The focus of **event structure analysis,** another sociological research tradition, is the logical structure of social events, that is, whether certain social events are prerequisite to the occurrence of other events.[24] Event structure analysis can be used to study norms for social behavior or sequences of events in folktales, accounts of stories and anecdotes, and other narratives.

Emancipatory action research is a type of self-reflective investigation that professional practitioners undertake for the purpose of improving the rationality and justice of their work. We describe this type of research in Chapter 18.

Ethnography

Ethnography involves first-hand, intensive study of the features of a given culture and the patterns in those features. If an ethnography has been done well, readers of the final report should be able to understand the culture even though they may not have directly experienced it.

Ethnography was originally developed by anthropologists, but it has since been used, with adaptations, by researchers in other disciplines, including sociology and psychology.[25] In the 1960s and 1970s, many educational researchers who had become disenchanted with positivism turned to ethnography as an alternative approach. The widespread acceptance of ethnography within educational research has in turn led many educational researchers to study and use the other qualitative research traditions discussed in this chapter. Because of the seminal influence of ethnography on educational research, we provide an extensive description of it below.

Nobuo Shimahara identified three major characteristics of ethnographic research.[26] The first characteristic is its focus on discovering cultural patterns in human behavior. Thus, ethnographers study members of a culture in order to determine how their behav-

♦ *Touchstone in Research*

Chambers, E. (2000). Applied ethnography. In N. K. Denzin & Y. S. Lincoln (Eds.), *Handbook of qualitative research* (2nd ed., pp. 851–869). Thousand Oaks, CA: Sage.

Eisenhart, M. (2001). Changing conceptions of culture and ethnographic methodology: Recent thematic shifts and their implications for research on teaching. In V. Richardson (Ed.), *Handbook of research on teaching* (4th ed., pp. 209–225). Washington, DC: American Educational Research Association.

Wolcott, H. F. (1997). Ethnographic research in education. In R. M. Jaeger (Ed.), *Complementary methods for research in education* (2nd ed., pp. 327–362). Washington, DC: American Educational Research Association.

22. Charon, J. M. (2000). *Symbolic interactionism: An introduction, an interpretation, an integration.* (7th ed.). Paramus, NJ: Prentice Hall.
23. Fine, G. A. (1987). *With the boys: Little League baseball and preadolescent culture.* Chicago: University of Chicago Press.
24. Heise, D. R. (1988). Computer analysis of cultural structures. *Social Science Computer Review, 6,* 183–197.
25. Some of these adaptations are described in: Wolcott, H. F. (1992). Posturing in qualitative inquiry. In M. D. LeCompte, W. L. Millroy, & J. Preissle (Eds.), *Handbook of qualitative research in education* (pp. 3–52). San Diego: Academic Press.
26. Shimahara, N. (1988). Anthroethnography: A methodological consideration. In R. R. Sherman & R. B. Webb (Eds.), *Qualitative research in education: Focus and methods* (pp. 76–89). New York: Falmer.

ior reflects the values, beliefs, customs, taboos, and other aspects that are typical of their culture. The ethnographer's interest, then, is not primarily the idiosyncrasies of, but rather the commonalities among, individual human beings. Ethnographers view each individual as a "document" that provides information about the larger culture. Cultural patterns that are discovered through ethnographic research then can be used to predict and explain the behavior of other members of the culture.

The second characteristic of ethnographic research is its focus on the emic perspective of members of the culture. As we explain in Chapter 14, an emic perspective involves the study of individuals to determine how they themselves define reality and experience events. The emphasis, then, is on describing a culture as its members see it. The anthropologist Franz Boas expressed the importance of an emic perspective in this statement: "If it is our serious purpose to understand the thoughts of a people, the whole analysis of experience must be based on their concepts, not ours."[27] Some ethnographers, however, choose to take an etic (i.e., an outsider's) perspective in their research. In doing so, they use their own terminology and categories to describe the culture. It also is possible to use both perspectives, as demonstrated in the examples of ethnographic research presented later in this section.

The third characteristic of ethnographic research is its focus on studying the natural settings in which culture is manifested. Ethnographers generally avoid introducing any type of contrived situation into a setting. Also, in studying the setting, they pay attention to all aspects of it that may reveal cultural patterns. For example, if ethnographers were studying a teacher's classroom as a microculture, they would note carefully the behavior of the teacher, the students, and any other persons in the classroom; they would then relate this behavior to the physical environment of the classroom (e.g., furniture, wall decor, and intercom system) and to other relevant settings (e.g., the playground, teacher's lounge, and school counselor's office). All these observations, in turn, would be related to data on the culture members' emic perspectives of these settings.

Culture is the central concept in ethnographic research. Murray Wax traced the origin of this term and its changing meanings.[28] The term originated with the notion of efforts to assist the growth of an organism (as in agriculture). Thus, the concept of culture was implicitly associated with an evolutionary model that assumed that so-called "native" cultures represented earlier stages of cultural evolution, while "civilized" Western cultures represented advanced stages. Later, many anthropologists rejected this elitist notion, arguing that the peoples of the world are grouped into many cultures, each with unique characteristics and positive qualities. From this view arose the idealized notion of a culture as a pattern of traditions, symbols, rituals, and artifacts, all of which together relate systematically to each other so as to form an integrated whole. However, Wax noted that in fact anthropologists have found culture to be a hodge-podge of overlapping qualities, described by one scholar as "a thing of shreds and patches."[29] Wax added that, with the rapid cultural diffusion that has resulted from the modern technology of production, transportation, and communication, early anthropological conceptions of plural, separate, distinct, historically homogeneous cultures now appear to be both scientifically misleading and educationally irrelevant. He commented that present-day anthropologists are documenting the emergence of a "global cultural ecumene" that transcends and blends elements of many so-called cultures.

27. Boas, F. (1943). Recent anthropology. *Science, 98,* 311–314, 334–337. Quote appears on p. 314.
28. Wax, M. (1993). How culture misdirects multiculturalism. *Anthropology and Educational Quarterly, 24,* 99–115.
29. Ibid., p. 101.

Ethnographers assume that what makes human beings unique as a species is the influence of culture in their lives, and that the most important difference between groups of people is their culture. Culture allows a particular group of people to live together and thrive through a system of shared meanings and values, but that same system also may lead them to oppose, and even war against, another group having different shared meanings and values. Thus, culture has both positive and negative consequences for its members.

Ethnographers regard certain aspects of human culture as central to understanding life in a particular society. These aspects include patterns of social organization, economic practices, family structure, religious practices and beliefs, political relationships, and ceremonial behavior. Ethnographers assume that these and other aspects of a culture are interrelated, from which it follows that a researcher cannot develop an understanding of one aspect of a culture without studying the other aspects to which it is related.

Anthropologists generally believe that ethnography should always have at least an implicit cross-cultural perspective—a belief that sets anthropology apart from other social science disciplines.[30] For some ethnographers, the comparative study of cultures is their primary purpose. This branch of anthropology is called **ethnology:** It involves the development of theories of culture based on comparisons of ethnographic data collected from different cultures.

A key issue for educational ethnographers is the question of whether learning is better viewed primarily as a process of cultural transmission or of cultural acquisition. Research on **cultural acquisition** puts the focus on how individuals themselves seek to acquire, or to avoid acquiring, the concepts, values, skills, and behaviors that are reflected in the common culture. For example, John Ogbu developed a model of education and caste based on his ethnographic research.[31] The model claims that U.S.-born members of minority groups who have suffered a long history of economic discrimination in the United States tend to withhold their investment in education because they do not perceive it as having any economic payoff.

Research on **cultural transmission,** by contrast, puts the focus on how the larger social structure intentionally intervenes in individuals' lives in order to promote or, in some cases, to discourage, learning of particular concepts, values, skills, or behaviors. George Spindler and Louise Spindler noted that an emphasis on cultural transmission exploits anthropological expertise in sociocultural structure and process.[32] They observed that the more individual focus of cultural acquisition makes it all too easy to slip into a "blame the victim" interpretation of individuals' learning problems.[33] The Spindlers expressed concern that a preoccupation with cultural acquisition could cause researchers to lose anthropology's unique perspective on how societies use their cultural resources to organize the conditions and purposes of learning.

A similar issue is found in other qualitative research traditions. If one believes that culture, language, and social institutions shape the individual, this belief implies that individuals are relatively passive players in social life. If, by contrast, one believes that individuals shape their own destiny, this belief is difficult to reconcile with the regularities (e.g., customs, ceremonies, norms) that we observe in social life. It seems likely that both views

30. Spindler, G., & Spindler, L. (1992). Cultural process and ethnography: An anthropological perspective. In M. D. LeCompte, W. L. Millroy, & J. Preissle (Eds.), *Handbook of qualitative research in education* (pp. 53–92). San Diego: Academic Press.
31. Ogbu, J. U. (1978). *Minority education and caste: The American system in cross-cultural perspective.* New York: Academic Press.
32. Spindler & Spindler, *Cultural process and ethnography.*
33. Ibid. p. 60.

have some validity, and so the task of ethnography and of other qualitative research traditions is to determine how cultural factors and human agency interact with each other to co-determine social life. Some qualitative researchers use the term **agency** to refer to the assumed ability of individuals to shape the conditions of their lives.

Phenomena Studied by Ethnographers

Ethnography had its beginnings in studies of what were then called *non-Western* or *native* cultures, carried out by anthropologists such as Bronislaw Malinowski, Franz Boas, and Margaret Mead. Malinowski carried out fieldwork with the native peoples of New Guinea and the Trobriand Islands during World War I.[34] His writings helped define classical ethnography, particularly its concern with obtaining the natives' point of view. Margaret Mead also conducted fieldwork in New Guinea, describing the process of growing up in Manus society.[35]

With the rapid colonization and destruction of non-Western cultures, many anthropologists shifted their attention to the study of subcultures within their own country or in other developed countries. Prominent examples of this type of research are George and Louise Spindler's comparative ethnographic study of two schools and their communities in Germany and the United States,[36] and Alan Peshkin's ethnography of a fundamentalist Christian school.[37] The study of small cultural units such as these sometimes is called **microethnography.** The corresponding term for the study of large cultural units (e.g., the country Burma) is **macroethnography.** Still another unit of study is the self. Research having this focus is called **autoethnography.** Autoethnography has been defined as "an autobiographical genre of writing and research that displays multiple layers of consciousness, connecting the personal to the cultural."[38]

Steps in Doing an Ethnographic Study

The following discussion of ethnographic methods follows the steps for doing a case study, which we described in Chapter 14. These steps are formulating a research problem, selecting a case, gaining entry, collecting data, analyzing data, and reporting the study.

Formulating a research problem and selecting a case. To formulate a research problem for an ethnography, the researcher must define the aspect of culture to be explored. Sometimes this step occurs after the case has been selected. Howard Becker noted the tendency of ethnographers to capitalize on accidental or forced circumstances in selecting cases.[39] For example, Bronislaw Malinowski's study of the Trobriand Islanders in New Guinea was occasioned, or at least lengthened, by the advent of World War I and his detention on the islands in the status of an enemy alien.

Often the problem is formulated first, and then a setting is selected that fits the problem. Margaret Mead was interested in studying the relationship between spontaneous animism (i.e., a belief in the existence of spirits that appears to develop naturally and independently of any external influence) and the thinking processes of young children.

34. Malinowski, B. (1922). *Argonauts of the Western Pacific.* New York: Dutton.
35. Mead, M. (1930). *Growing up in New Guinea: A comparative study of primitive education.* New York: William Morrow.
36. Spindler & Spindler, *Cultural process and ethnography.*
37. Peshkin, A. (1986). *God's choice: The total world of a fundamentalist Christian school.* Chicago: University of Chicago Press.
38. Ellis, C., & Bochner, A. P. (2000). Autoethnography, personal narrative, reflexivity. In N. K. Denzin & Y. S. Lincoln (Eds.), *Handbook of qualitative research* (2nd ed., pp. 733–768). Thousand Oaks, CA: Sage. Quote appears on p. 739.
39. Becker, H. S. (1993). Theory: The necessary evil. In D. J. Flinders & G. E. Mills (Eds.), *Theory and concepts in qualitative research* (pp. 218–229). New York: Teachers College Press.

She selected Melanesia "because it is an area which contains many relatively unspoiled primitive groups and has been conspicuous in ethnological discussions as a region filled with the phenomena usually subsumed under the head of 'Animism.' "[40] Mead then described how she narrowed her focus to a relatively unknown local region, and selected the Manus tribe for reasons such as the availability of some texts in the native language and of a school boy willing to act as interpreter.

Another example of selecting a setting that fits the problem is provided by Alan Peshkin's study of Christian schooling in the United States. He first formulated his research problem—to study how a fundamentalist Christian school contributes to the acquisition of culture by students who attend that school, and how this community maintenance function compares to that of public schools.[41] He then conducted a year-long pilot study. During that year, his proposal was rejected by several schools before being accepted by the Bethany Baptist Academy, the case for his study.

Each of these examples illustrates ethnography's traditional goal of making the familiar strange.[42] This goal involves looking at a cultural phenomenon from the perspective of an outsider, and then seeking to understand the phenomenon from the perspective of insiders. You can achieve this goal by immersing yourself in a culture far different from your own, as in the case of the ethnographic studies of Malinowski and Mead. You also can achieve it by studying a subculture in your own community with which your are unfamiliar, as in Harry Wolcott's study of a youth who had rejected many of the educational and social values espoused by the researcher himself and most of his associates.[43] In Peshkin's case, his status as a Jew ensured not only that the church community was unfamiliar to him, but also that he was viewed by the church community as an outsider.

Ethnography sometimes is carried out in a familiar setting, of course, particularly when researchers study schools in which they have worked or that at least are similar to those that they themselves attended. In this case researchers must use other means to gain an "outsider's" perspective. For example, Joyce Henstrand described her use of theory to reflect on her findings while conducting an ethnography of the school in which she was teaching.[44] This approach enabled her to step back from her teacher role and focus on her researcher role.

Gaining entry. The process of gaining entry varies greatly depending on the nature of the research problem and the requirements of the case. In an ethnographic study of a school principal, Wolcott summarized his approach as follows:

> I spent weeks searching for a suitable and willing subject, and I did not request formal permission from the school district to conduct the study until I had the personal permission and commitment of the selected individual.[45]

As Wolcott's example illustrates, gaining entry might involve several levels of access and sign-off, from the individual to the institutional level. Mead, by contrast, described a less formal, but perhaps even more demanding, strategy. First, she established residence in a thatched house on piles in the center of one of the Manus villages. Then Mead sought to

40. Mead, *Growing up in New Guinea,* p. 289.
41. Peshkin, *God's choice.*
42. Spindler, G., & Spindler, L. (1982). Roger Harker and Schoenhausen: From the familiar to the strange and back again. In G. Spindler (Ed.), *Doing the ethnography of schooling* (pp. 21–43). New York: Holt, Rinehart, & Winston.
43. Wolcott, H. F. (1994). *Transforming qualitative data: Description, analysis, and interpretation.* Thousand Oaks, CA: Sage.
44. Henstrand, J. (1993). Theory as research guide: A qualitative look at qualitative inquiry. In D. J. Flinders & G. E. Mills (Eds.), *Theory and concepts in qualitative research* (pp. 83–102). New York: Teachers College Press.
45. Wolcott, 1994, *Transforming qualitative data,* p. 118

fit herself into the Manus culture for a long period of time in order to gain entry into the daily activities and conversations of the native people. This involved learning the Manus language, playing the children's games, attending feasts, and learning how to avoid violating the hundreds of name taboos in their culture.

Collecting data. Ethnographers use the full range of qualitative data-collection techniques and, when appropriate, quantitative techniques.

Mead described her method as primarily one of observing the Manus children at play, in their homes, and with their parents. In addition, she collected spontaneous drawings from the children, who had never before held a pencil in their hands, and asked them to interpret ink blots. Because there were only 210 people in the entire population, Mead was able to follow all current events in the village "with careful attention to their cultural significance and the role which they played in the lives of the children."[46] Records of conversations and interpretations were all taken down in the native language. Mead sought to avoid the use of technical terms, couching her descriptions "in the field of the novelist."[47] She also used detailed record sheets to gather material in her notes. For example, the household record sheet included headings for the house owner's children by each marriage, who financed his marriages, and what marriages he was financing. The child's record sheet included headings for what the child chewed, the geographical range of play, and chosen companions. Mead made a detailed analysis of the composition of the Peri population in the Manus tribe, for example, how many married couples, widows, and widowers there were and the average number of children per married couple.

Wolcott's ethnography of the school principal made use of official school notices, quantitative records, and census data for the community in which the school was located. He also collected "time and motion" data, recording what the principal was doing, where, and with whom, at 60-second intervals over a carefully sampled two-week period at school.

Early in the study, Wolcott used primarily participant observation, "shadowing" the principal's everyday activities while making continuous entries in a notebook. Wolcott explained that his intent was to create a precedent for constant note-taking so that people would become comfortable with it. He never returned to the school until he had completed his notes from the last visit. His longhand notes were typed onto 5 × 8 cards, each card describing a single event. To avoid becoming "overidentified" with the principal, he visited often with teachers and staff members. He also was able to include within the scope of his observations visits with the principal's family at home, the principal's errands and community activities around town, and special social events.

Only after he had spent over half a year at the school did Wolcott add interviewing as a data-collection method. He conducted and taped several one-hour interviews with the principal (e.g., about the principal's forecast of the coming school year, his family life, and what had occurred at the school since Wolcott's last visit). Individual interviews also were conducted with 13 faculty and two staff members about their perceptions of the principal as a school administrator. All fifth- and sixth-grade students were asked to write brief, anonymous comments about the principal. Wolcott concluded his fieldwork by distributing a 10-page questionnaire to all faculty and staff: "The questionnaire was particularly valuable in enabling me to obtain systematic data about the staff, as I could see no point in holding a long taped interview with each of the twenty-nine members of the regular and part-time staff."[48]

---

46. Mead, *Growing up* in New Guinea, p. 291.
47. Ibid., p. 292.
48. Wolcott, 1994, *Transforming qualitative data*, p. 123.

In his ethnography of a fundamentalist Christian school, Peshkin described the data-collection procedures used by him and his two research assistants as follows:

> Like me, they observed, interviewed, and attended meetings and activities. After about a month of sitting empty-handed wherever we were, we began to use a pocket-size notebook sporadically and ended up taking full, running notes of everything we saw and heard except during lunch and in other informal settings. Our interviews, conducted with a continuously evolving interview schedule, ranged in time from about four to twelve hours; all were taped and later transcribed.[49]

Throughout his field work, Peshkin lived in an apartment in the home of a charter-member family of Bethany Baptist Church, commuting to his own home outside the area once a week. He attended Sunday school and attended the regular church services on Sunday morning, Sunday evening, and Wednesday evening. The religious differences between the researcher and the subculture he was studying, while intentional, created a major challenge to Peshkin's ability to obtain the "insider" view of the community he studied. In his words

> I still hoped to participate in their lives as if I were a Christian. My intent was to moderate and minimize their they-ness so that I could move beyond being the visitor-at-a-zoo type of observer to being one who revels in their joys and empathizes with their pains.[50]

In his fourth and final semester at Bethany Baptist Academy, Peshkin completed his data collection by administering a questionnaire to all students and teachers and to one parent of each student. His research strategy was to observe the world of Bethany during the first semester largely unaided by the views and perceptions of its participants; to concentrate during the second and third semesters on acquiring participants' perceptions through interviews; and to obtain systematic data through questionnaires during the fourth semester, both to verify what had been learned earlier and to determine the generalizability of his case findings.

Our description of the research methods of ethnography conveys a sense of the researchers' ingenuity in using any and every method of collecting data that will help them gain the emic perspective that is essential to qualitative research. The array of appropriate data-collection strategies continues to expand with modern technology and the growing acceptance by many researchers that both quantitative and qualitative data can shed light on the phenomena of interest to them. For example, Spindler and Spindler used the Instrumental Activities Inventory (IAI) in their comparative study of a German and a U.S. elementary school. The IAI is a set of line drawings depicting traditional and modernized ways of life that is used to evoke individuals' lifestyle preferences. Spindler and Spindler used statistical techniques to analyze individuals' choices, and the rationales for their choices of the groups (varying in demographic characteristics such as occupation, educational level, and age) whose lifestyles they preferred. Gender and age were found to be the strongest influences on life choices.

Spindler and Spindler also used film and photographs, not merely to supplement their own field notes but as evocative stimuli in interviews; that is, they showed films of the German classroom to the U.S. students and teachers and vice versa. The Spindlers then interviewed the research participants about what they saw in their own classrooms and in those of the "other," and how they interpreted what they saw. They also implemented an ex-

---

49. Peshkin, *God's choice*, p. 23.
50. Ibid., p. 24.

change of correspondence between the German and U.S. teachers, and between the German and U.S. students. Regarding this activity, they commented:

> These kinds of solicited documents are useful as an expression of the native point of view. An exchange of this sort must be regarded as a research device—that is, a situation created by the ethnographers.[51]

Thus, although ethnography is considered to be a naturalistic method of inquiry, we see here an exception. In both qualitative research and quantitative research, you need not view methodology as fixed. You are always free to invent new methods if they will help you gain further insights into the phenomena you are studying.

Analyzing and interpreting data. As we explained in Chapter 14, data analysis in qualitative research usually begins while the data are being collected, and affects subsequent data-collection efforts. The following comment by Mead indicates an emerging sense that the hypothesis guiding her research was not going to be supported by the data. Nonetheless, she continued collecting data in order to discover and support an alternate interpretation of what she was observing:

> This investigation of Melanesian children was undertaken to solve a special problem which is but lightly touched upon in this book: i.e., the relationship between spontaneous animism and thinking characteristic of mentally immature persons, especially children under five or six. The results of this research were negative, that is, evidence was found to support the view that animism is not a spontaneous aspect of child thinking nor does it spring from any type of thought characteristic of immature mental development; its presence or absence in the thought of children is dependent upon cultural factors, language, folk lore, adult attitudes, etc., and these cultural factors have their origin in the thought of individual adults, not in the misconceptions of children.[52]

Mead's admission of her failure to support her original hypothesis reflects the requirement that ethnographers modify their hypotheses, theories, and interpretations to reflect whatever is discovered in the field.

Using data obtained by interviews, questionnaires, and observations, Peshkin examined many aspects of the culture that the fundamentalist Christian school sought to establish, including its origins from, and influences on, the beliefs of teachers, students, and students' parents. Applying Erving Goffman's sociological theory, Peshkin described the school's culture as that of a "total institution."[53] A total institution has pervasive effects on its members, being "unrestricted in time and space, neither limited to a term or a sentence nor confined to a building or a particular setting."[54] Peshkin's findings suggest that Bethany Baptist Academy largely succeeded in producing students who display at least overt conformity to the fundamentalist Christian ideals that guide the school and church philosophy. Yet the researcher described many norm violations that students confided to him, and expressed concern for the potential "loss of intellectual vitality and artistic creativity that are Truth's victims."[55] Peshkin also went beyond his case to discuss the profound political, educational, and social implications of the growth of Christian schools that is occurring in the United States.

51. Spindler & Spindler, *Roger Harker and Schoenhausen*, p. 80.
52. Mead, *Growing up in New Guinea*, p. 289.
53. Goffman, E. (1961). *Asylums: Essays on the social situation of mental patients and other inmates.* Garden City, NJ: Anchor.
54. Peshkin, *God's choice*, p. 274.
55. Ibid., p. 286.

Reporting the case study. As we explained in Chapter 14, qualitative case studies often have a storylike flavor. Ethnographers, with their concern for thick description and conveying the emic perspective, tend to weave particularly rich stories. Margaret Mead described an interaction between a six-year-old child, Popoli, and his father:

> [H]e whines out in the tone which all Manus natives use when begging betel nut: "A little betel?" The father throws him a nut. He tears the skin off with his teeth and bites it greedily. "Another," the child's voice rises to a higher pitch. The father throws him a second nut, which the child grasps firmly in his wet little fist, without acknowledgement. "Some pepper leaf?" The father frowns. "I have very little, Popoli." "Some pepper leaf." The father tears off a piece of a leaf and throws it to him. The child scowls at the small piece. "This is too little. More! More! More!" His voice rises to a howl of rage.[56]

The story concludes with the father rationally explaining why he cannot give his son more pepper leaf, accidentally dropping his knife into the water and requesting that his son get it, and the son refusing: "No. I won't, thou, thou stingy one, thou hidest thy pepper leaf from me." The child swims away, leaving his father to climb down and rescue the knife himself. And Mead leaves it to the reader to infer the quality of parent-child relationships in the Manus culture.

Marion Dobbert described an ethnographic report as having five parts: (1) a statement of the study questions and the situations and problems that led to them, (2) a description of the background research and theory used to refine the study questions and design the study, (3) a detailed review of the study design, (4) a presentation of the data, and (5) an explanation of the findings.[57] Dobbert described the presentation of data as the "heart and soul" of the report. To her, this presentation should be a detailed description of the social scene under investigation, presented in organized fashion and based on a low-level (i.e., descriptive or low-inference) categorical analysis of data.

Dobbert identified various formats for ethnographic reporting. Some formats reflect the insider's view (e.g., a typical biography or modal personality viewpoint). Other formats reflect the outsider's or "scientific" view (e.g., an ecological or structural emphasis). Still others (e.g., the community within a community and historical approach) can take either an insider's or an outsider's view. Recently, some ethnographers have turned their field notes or completed reports into theatre performances.[58]

To do a complete ethnography of a culture or an aspect of a culture is a major undertaking, as our examples illustrate. Often a single report represents only one aspect of the total case study. The individual report thus contributes to, rather than itself constituting, the ethnography. The case might be revisited repeatedly, as in the Spindlers' decades-long comparative study of German and U.S. elementary schools, or different aspects of the phenomenon might be studied at a later time.

Strengths and Weaknesses of Ethnography

No other research tradition matches the ability of ethnography to investigate the complex phenomenon known as culture. Its holistic orientation enables a skillful researcher to identify diverse elements of a culture and weave them into coherent patterns. The description of these patterns provides codes, as it were, for "reading" the culture. A good

---

56. Mead, *Growing up in New Guinea,* pp. 20–21.
57. Dobbert, M. (1984). *Ethnographic research: Theory and application for modern schools and societies.* New York: Praeger.
58. McCall, M. M. (2000). Performance ethnography. In N. K. Denzin & Y. S. Lincoln (Eds.), *Handbook of qualitative research* (2nd ed., pp. 421–433). Thousand Oaks, CA: Sage.

ethnography, in the words of Wolcott, "enables one to anticipate and interpret what goes on in a society or social group as appropriately as one of its members."[59]

Ethnography has come under increasing critical scrutiny in recent years. This scrutiny has revealed several unresolved issues in the way it is used to understand culture.[60] One issue concerns ethnography's status as a science. As we stated above, ethnographers generally take an emic perspective, which means that the culture members' own perceptions and language categories are used to describe and explain the culture. While this perspective helps the reader understand the culture as a unique social reality, it does not provide a basis for discovering laws of social life. For example, if a researcher writes a good ethnography describing a particular school district, it will help us understand that district, but not other school districts. An etic perspective, in which the researcher develops her own categories for understanding a culture, might provide a better basis for cross-cultural research and the discovery of cross-cultural "laws." However, these categories might distort our understanding of any particular culture. Another unresolved issue is whether ethnography should subscribe to the goal of the natural sciences to develop universal laws or to the goal of the humanities to understand the unique and particular case. Some ethnographers attempt to pursue both goals in their research.

Still another issue concerns the validity of reports of ethnographic findings. Critics argue that ethnographic reports represent a genre of writing that imposes a particular order on cultural phenomena, an order that may not accurately reflect the culture being described. Clifford Geertz, for example, claims that ethnographies are "fiction" in that they are not the culture itself, but rather a story told by the author using various literary conventions and devices.[61] Furthermore, some feminist theorists argue that traditional ethnographies reflect a privileged male discourse that involves non-reciprocal relationships with, and distance from, the members of the culture who are studied.[62] These criticisms have prompted some ethnographers to adopt a "dialogic" stance in which they conduct their research as a collaboration between the researcher and the members of the culture being studied.

The issues that we discussed above are far from resolved in the ethnographic research tradition or in other qualitative research traditions, where they also are the subject of much debate. Therefore, if you plan to do ethnographic research, you will need to become well versed in the literature on these issues and to decide what stance you wish to take on them. Also, keep in mind that it requires a lengthy apprenticeship to learn how to do ethnography well; furthermore, the data-collection process for an ethnographic study can take many months, a year, or even longer.

Cultural Studies

Cultural studies involves the investigation of power relationships in a culture in order to help emancipate its members from the many forms of oppression that are perceived to operate in the culture. The Centre for Contemporary Cultural Studies at Birmingham, England was instrumental in starting this research tradition in the 1960s. Cultural studies

♦ **Touchstone in Research**

Frow, J., & Morris, M. (2000). Cultural studies. In N. K. Denzin & Y. S. Lincoln (Eds.), *Handbook of qualitative research* (2nd ed., pp. 315–346). Thousand Oaks, CA: Sage.

Morrow, R. A., & Brown, D. D. (1994). *Critical theory and methodology: Interpretive structuralism as a research program.* Thousand Oaks, CA: Sage.

59. Wolcott, H. F. (1973). *The man in the principal's office: An ethnography.* New York: Holt, Rinehart & Winston. Quote appears on p. xi. [Reissued with a new Preface 1984 by Waveland Press, Prospect Heights, IL.]
60. These issues are discussed in: Atkinson, P., & Hammersley, M. (1994). Ethnography and participant observation. In N. K. Denzin & Y. S. Lincoln (Eds.), *Handbook of qualitative research* (pp. 248–261). Thousand Oaks, CA: Sage.
61. Geertz, C. (1973). *The interpretation of cultures: Selected essays.* New York: Basic Books.
62. Stanley, L., & Wise, S. (1983). *Breaking out: Feminist consciousness and feminist research.* London: Routledge & Kegan Paul.

continues to be an active field of inquiry in Europe, and is becoming increasingly popular in the United States. Because European and American societies differ, cultural studies has taken different forms on the two continents.

Cultural studies has been described as a branch of critical theory.[63] Critical theory began in the 1920s with the work of scholars at the Institute of Social Research in Frankfurt, Germany, and, in recent years, it has become closely associated with the work of Jurgen Habermas, who also works in Germany. The investigations of Habermas are primarily theoretical and concern large-scale social structure, whereas researchers who characterize their work as cultural studies tend to be more empirically oriented and concerned with small-scale social structures. There is much overlap between cultural studies and critical theory, however, and the two terms sometimes are used synonymously. For this reason the definition of *cultural studies* that we offered above applies as well as to *critical theory.*

In viewing cultural studies as a branch of critical theory, John Fiske noted the essential similarity between cultural studies and other critical theories:

> Although cultural studies differs from other critical theories, it shares with them the most important characteristic of all—the critical. The basic assumption of all critical theories is that the inequalities need to be changed and that the world would be a better place if we could change them. There are three interrelated reasons for studying capitalism—to expose its mechanisms of inequality, to motivate people to change them, and to reveal sites and methods by which change might be promoted.[64]

Our discussion of cultural studies emphasizes researchers and theorists who characterize their work by this label, as this is becoming an increasingly prominent research tradition in the United States. However, we occasionally refer to the work of scholars who characterize themselves as critical theorists in order to put cultural studies in the larger context of critical theory.

As one might expect, educational researchers who work within the cultural studies tradition analyze the power relationships that are ignored or taken for granted by most educators, but that are central to the operation of educational institutions. Their analyses are guided by a commitment to advocate for a more just distribution of power than that operating in the present educational system, which is seen as perpetuating social oppression based on ethnicity, class, gender, and other cultural categories applied to individuals.

Assumptions of the Cultural Studies Tradition

Joe Kincheloe and Peter McLaren list seven basic assumptions that are accepted by a criticalist, which they define as "a researcher or theorist who attempts to use her or his work as a form of social or cultural criticism."[65] We summarize these assumptions below and suggest their implications for educational research.

1. *Certain groups in any society are privileged over others.* Although the reasons for this privileging may vary widely, the oppression that characterizes contemporary societies is most forcefully reproduced when subordinates accept their social status as natural, necessary, or inevitable. Critical theory equates enlightenment with disclosing the true interests (i.e., needs, concerns, and advantages) of different groups and individuals. Privileged groups always have an interest in maintaining the status quo in order to protect their advantages. Critical theory focuses on conflict among competing interests as a central fea-

63. Fiske, J. (1994). Audiencing: Cultural practice and cultural studies. In N. K. Denzin & Y. S. Lincoln (Eds.), *Handbook of qualitative research* (pp. 189–198). Thousand Oaks, CA: Sage.
64. Ibid., pp. 197–198.
65. Kincheloe, J. L., & McLaren, P. (2000). Rethinking critical theory and qualitative research. In N. K. Denzin & Y. S. Lincoln (Eds.), *Handbook of qualitative research* (2nd ed., pp. 279–313). Thousand Oaks, CA: Sage.

ture of social life. It focuses also on the sense of frustration and powerlessness of most individuals, and seeks to provide insight to guide people toward greater autonomy and ultimately, emancipation.

Hegemony refers to the maintenance of domination of subordinate groups by privileged groups through its agencies (e.g., governmental bodies and public school systems). The dominant culture exercises hegemony by framing the experiences of individuals through a steady stream of "terms of reference" (e.g., cliches about "the good life," media images, and stories) against which individuals conceive and evaluate their own reality. According to Peter McLaren, hegemony thus involves "a struggle in which the powerful win the consent of those who are oppressed, with the oppressed unknowingly participating in their own oppression."[66]

The concept of voice is used by critical theorists to study particular expressions of domination and oppression. **Voice** refers to the phenomenon by which people occupying particular social categories or identities are either silenced, empowered, or privileged through the operation of various discourses that maintain or contest dominant and subordinate cultures in a society.[67]

The concept of voice plays an important role in the critical theory of Henry Giroux, an educator whom we discuss later in the chapter. In his view, voice "provides a critical referent for analyzing how students are made voiceless in particular settings by not being allowed to speak, or how students silence themselves out of either fear or ignorance regarding the strength and possibilities that exist in the multiple languages and experience that connect them to a sense of agency and self-formation."[68]

2. *Oppression has many faces.* Critical theorists claim that focusing on only one form of oppression at the expense of others (e.g., class oppression vs. racism) obscures the interconnections among them. Both to understand and to combat oppression, it is necessary to examine all the cultural categories that are used to separate and oppress different groups, and to consider their joint operation and effects. For example, in seeking to understand why a particular student is resistant and defiant in school, a teacher needs to consider not only the student's ethnic identity, but also the student's gender and social class background, as well as other cultural characteristics (e.g., being identified as sensorily deprived or learning disabled).

3. *Language is central to the formation of subjectivity (conscious and unconscious awareness).* An individual's awareness is both expanded and constrained by the language that is available to the individual for encoding his experience. Students whose first language is Asian, for example, will have a different conscious and unconscious experience of, say, a football game or a classroom lesson than students whose first language is English or Spanish.

4. *The relationship between signifier and signified is never stable or fixed and is often mediated by the social relations of capitalist production and consumption.* This assumption means, for example, that how a textbook author (the signifier) writes a textbook (the signified) often involves basic economic considerations, and will vary at different times. Thus, the form and content of most textbooks reflect the values of the dominant culture and are consistent with standards derived from a capitalist value framework.

66. McLaren, P. (1994). *Life in schools: An introduction to critical pedagogy in the foundations of education.* New York: Longman. Quote appears on p. 182.

67. For an analysis of "voice" in research on teachers, see: Hargreaves, A. (1996). Revisiting voice. *Educational Researcher, 25*(1), 12–19.

68. Giroux, H. A. (1992). Resisting difference: Cultural studies and the discourse of critical pedagogy. In L. Grossberg, C. Nelson, & P. Treichler (Eds.), *Cultural studies* (pp. 199–212). New York: Routledge. Quote appears on pp. 205–206.

The texts that are subjected to this type of analysis by critical theorists include not only spoken or written language, but any kind of sign (e.g., a flagpole at the entrance to a school building). This process of analysis is called deconstruction. **Deconstructionism** is an approach originating in philosophy and literary criticism that asserts that a text has no definite meaning, that words can refer only to other words, and that "playing" with a text can yield multiple, often contradictory interpretations of it. For example, Jacques Derrida, a founder of the modern deconstructionist movement, analyzed the rationale underlying the development of universities in western societies as follows: "As far as I know, nobody has ever founded a university *against* reason. So we may reasonably suppose that the university's reason for being has always been reason itself, and some essential connection of reason to being."[69] Derrida then proceeded to ask the reason for basing a university on reason, and noted that reason only has recourse to reason to justify itself, which brings into question the principle of basing a university on the promotion of reason. Derrida and other deconstructionists use this type of textual analysis in an attempt to question the presumed authority of all statements (as expressed in "texts") by opening them to multiple interpretations, with none privileged over the others. They even question the authority of the emancipatory agenda of critical theorists by "deconstructing" the terms and statements that comprise the text expressing these theorists' agenda.

5. *All thought is fundamentally mediated by power relations that are socially and historically constituted.* In the context of education, this assumption implies that the beliefs and activities of students, teachers, and other groups involved in education are inevitably affected by their experiences with power and dominance, both within and outside the educational system. Particular beliefs and activities can only be understood in reference to the unique context in which they occur.

6. *Facts can never be isolated from the domain of values or removed from some form of ideological inscription.* The first part of this assumption reflects cultural studies' rejection of the notion that educational researchers' quest for truth is an objective, value-free process—and indeed, rejection of the notion of an objective reality itself. Cultural studies researchers argue that all "facts" about human nature and behavior are socially constructed, and hence open to many interpretations and subject to change through human means.

The second part of the assumption refers to **ideological inscription,** which means that ideas about how teaching and learning operate always involve preformed systems of values and beliefs, and that within education most such ideologies reinforce the power of dominant groups in society. A cultural studies proponent would hold that such educational concepts as achievement, reform, innovation, and world-class standards are categories constructed by, and serving the interests of, certain groups.

7. *Mainstream research practices are unwittingly implicated in the reproduction of systems of class, race, and gender oppression.* Much educational research has been guided by positivism and carried out primarily by middle- and upper-class white males. Critical theorists claim that this type of research thus rests on assumptions about truth, science, and good that have been accepted as universal, but which in fact have served to maintain the oppression of groups who represent other cultural categories. Critical theorists particularly oppose educational research that focuses on prediction and control for the purpose of maximizing educational productivity. Such research reflects the operation of *instrumental rationality,* which involves a preoccupation with means or technology over ends or pur-

---

69. Derrida, J. (1983). The principle of reason: The university in the eyes of its pupils. *Diacritics, 13,* 3–20. Quote appears on p. 7. For other examples of deconstructionist reasoning, see: Derrida, J. (1978). *Writing and difference.* London: Routledge & Kegan Paul.

poses. Rex Gibson claimed that the IQ testing movement is a key example of the short-comings and injustices that instrumental rationality effects:

> Instrumental rationality is the cast of thought which seeks to dominate others, which assumes its own rightness to do so, and which exercises its power to serve its own interests. Coldly following its narrow principle of efficiency and applying a crude economic yardstick, its results are all too obvious . . . the interests least served are those of comprehensive schools and pupils from working class homes.[70]

This and other assumptions of the cultural studies tradition are helpful in stimulating critical reflection about mainstream educational practice and research.

Methods of Inquiry

The cultural studies tradition resists adoption of a unified, formal methodology. Instead, it draws upon methods used in a wide range of other research traditions, including sociology, semiotics, literary criticism, history, philosophy, psychoanalysis, and anthropology. Even in using these methods, cultural studies researchers subject them to continual critique:

> [O]ther traditions are approached both for what they may yield and for what they may inhibit. Critique involves stealing away the more useful elements and rejecting the rest.[71]

If there is any method that is common to research and theory-building in the cultural studies tradition, it is critique—critique of the researcher's own perspective and values, critique of methodology, and critique of the phenomena being studied.

Because cultural studies draws upon a wide range of other research traditions, you should be broadly educated in the humanities and social sciences if you wish to investigate an educational problem using the cultural studies approach. In addition, you will need to develop expertise in the particular methodology you plan to use for data collection or conceptual analysis. For example, in a study that we describe in the next section, Michelle Fine studied sex education and school-based health clinics by conducting a comprehensive literature review, followed by a year-long ethnographic investigation of a public high school.

Types of Cultural Studies

Researchers who work within the cultural studies tradition have investigated a variety of social problems and phenomena. For example, they have studied situations that raise issues of social justice for women,[72] ethnic minorities,[73] and other groups whose voices have been silenced by the prevailing power structure.

Cultural studies in education has been concerned particularly with the investigation of educational programs and systems, and with theory-building. Examples of these two types of investigation are presented below.

Study of educational programs and systems. Many cultural studies researchers have studied educational systems outside the academy in which they themselves work. J. Anyon, for example, studied the hidden curriculum in schools.[74] The **hidden curriculum**

70. Gibson, R. (1986). *Critical theory and education.* London: Hodder & Stoughton. Quote appears on pp. 8–9.
71. Johnson, R. (1986/1987). What is cultural studies anyway? *Social Text, 16,* 38–80. Quote appears on p. 38.
72. Olesen, V. (1994). Feminisms and models of qualitative research. In N. K. Denzin & Y. S. Lincoln (Eds.), *Handbook of qualitative research* (pp. 158–174). Thousand Oaks, CA: Sage.
73. Stanfield, J. H., II. (1994). Ethnic modeling in qualitative research. In N. K. Denzin & Y. S. Lincoln (Eds.), *Handbook of qualitative research* (pp. 175–188). Thousand Oaks, CA: Sage.
74. Anyon, J. (1980). Social class and the hidden curriculum of work. *Journal of Education, 162,* 67–92; see also Apple, M. (1979). *Ideology and curriculum.* London: Routledge & Kegan Paul.

refers to the indirect instruction in attitudes and habits that is continually transmitted by the way in which schools are structured and classroom instruction is organized. Anyon found that schools with a student population from a predominantly working-class background emphasize instructional practices that teach students the attitudes and habits of factory workers (e.g., blind obedience, discipline, tolerance for repetitive tasks, and respect for authority). In contrast, schools with students from upper socioeconomic classes emphasize instructional practices that help students become leaders, problem solvers, questioners of authority, and creative organizers of their own work.

Michelle Fine's study of sex education and school-based health clinics illustrates the concern of cultural studies for the relationship between gender and class in how students are educated for adulthood.[75] In her ethnographic research, Fine interviewed students, observed sex education programs, and analyzed curriculum materials in U.S. schools to discover the prevailing pedagogical discourse and practices that bear on female sexuality.

Fine found that female students, particularly low-income ones, have little access to school-based health clinics and sexuality information. Where clinics and courses are provided, their practices and discourse tend to discourage rather than to encourage students' use of their services. Fine also found three prevailing discourses of female sexuality in the public school system: (1) Sexuality is talked about as essentially violent and coercive, (2) sexuality is associated with victimization because males are potential predators, (3) discussion of females' sexual decision making is centered on the value of premarital abstinence. All three discourses are designed to discourage adolescent females from sexual activity, even though research findings reviewed by Fine indicate that adolescent females generally engage in responsible sex practices (e.g., ensuring the use of contraceptives).

Fine argued for a fourth possibility: the discourse of desire. This discourse would acknowledge the possibility of desire, pleasure, and sexual entitlement among female students. However, according to Fine, this discourse "remains a whisper inside the official work of U.S. public schools."[76] As a result, many students whom she studied viewed the efforts of school-based sex education programs and health clinics as largely irrelevant or opposed to their perceived needs.

Theory-building. The cultural studies tradition emphasizes the use of theory to explain society and to emancipate its participants. Therefore, the development of theory—called "critical theory" in this tradition—is a central preoccupation of cultural studies researchers. Henry Giroux has played a major role in developing critical theory that is applicable to American education.[77] For this reason, we describe his work here.

Giroux described several assumptions of cultural studies in relation to critical pedagogy specifically. Giroux took as his starting point the assumption that U.S. public education is in crisis. He saw this condition reflected most clearly in the contrast between rhetoric that equates U.S. culture with democracy in its ultimate form and such indicators as low voter participation, growing illiteracy rates among the general population, and an increasingly prevalent view that social criticism and social change are irrelevant to the meaning of American democracy.

Giroux proposed a liberatory theory of "border pedagogy" to replace what he described as the "politics of difference" that characterizes much of the current dialogue about

75. Fine, M. (1988). Sexuality, schooling, and adolescent females: The missing discourse of desire. *Harvard Educational Review, 58,* 29–53.
76. Ibid., p. 33.
77. Giroux, H. A. (1988). Critical theory and the politics of culture and voice: Rethinking the discourse of educational research. In R. R. Sherman & R. B. Webb (Eds.), *Qualitative research in education: Focus and methods* (pp. 190–210). New York: Falmer; Giroux, H. A. (1992). Resisting difference: Cultural studies and the discourse of critical pedagogy. In L. Grossberg, C. Nelson, & P. Treichler (Eds.), *Cultural studies* (pp. 199–212). New York: Routledge.

educational problems and solutions. For Giroux the term *border* reflects the notion of permeable, changing boundaries to describe differences between individuals and groups, as opposed to the rigid, "either-or" nature of conventional social categories.

In Giroux's theory, difference is linked to a broader politics, and schools and pedagogy are organized around a sense of purpose that makes difference central to a critical notion of citizenship and democratic public life. This concept of difference is postmodern in that it recognizes the need to acknowledge the particular, the heterogeneous, and the multiple, and it views the political community as a diverse collection of subcommunities in flux. Within this framework, educators are seen as obliged to give students the opportunity to analyze how the dominant culture creates borders "saturated in terror, inequality, and forced exclusions," and to construct new pedagogical borders where difference becomes the intersection of new forms of culture and identity."[78]

If Giroux's framework were used to guide educational practice, students would no longer study unified subjects but would explore "borderlands" between diverse cultural histories, as sites for both critical analysis and as a potential source of experimentation, creativity, and possibility. Power would be explicitly explored, both to help students understand how forms of domination are historically and socially constructed and to explore how teachers can use their authority to aid students in their emancipation from such domination. Finally, students would be educated to read critically not only how cultural texts are regulated by various discursive codes, but also how such texts express and represent different ideological interests.

Giroux argued that what is needed is "a radical pedagogy located in a discourse that acknowledges the spaces, tensions, and possibilities of struggle within the day to day workings of schools."[79] He sought to redefine radical pedagogy as a guide to critical educational research, and more broadly as a tradition that would enable educators at all levels of schooling to redefine the nature of intellectual work and inquiry itself. Giroux saw the ultimate outcome of this pedagogy as "nothing less than providing the conditions for educators and their students to become knowledgeable and committed actors in the world."[80] He viewed this outcome as quite different from that captured in other theoretical discourses, which he felt tend to foster despair rather than hope in their criticism of the current state of education.

Strengths and Weaknesses of Cultural Studies

The assumptions and methods of cultural studies have provoked considerable criticism from educators and researchers representing other traditions. To some critics, the deconstructionism that is characteristic of cultural studies makes groundlessness "the only constant recognized by this sensibility."[81] In other words, these critics believe that cultural studies researchers and theorists are hypercritical. Taken to an extreme, deconstructionism leads to a sense of hopelessness rather than hope for emancipation. In practice, however, at least some theorists and researchers in the cultural studies tradition fulfill its emancipatory agenda. For example, the work of Henry Giroux and Michelle Fine suggests fresh directions for educators to explore in order to better meet the needs of traditionally underserved students.

78. Giroux, Resisting difference, p. 209.
79. Giroux, Critical theory, p. 193.
80. Ibid., p. 208.
81. Spretnak, C. (1991). *States of grace: The recovery of meaning in the postmodern age.* New York: HarperCollins. Quote appears on p. 13.

Another limitation of cultural studies is the esoteric writing of researchers who work in this tradition. Rex Gibson described the problem in these terms:

> The writings of critical theorists do not exactly help their cause. Turgidness, unnecessarily complex sentence structures, a preference for their own neologisms (newly-coined words), and an almost willful refusal to attempt to communicate directly and clearly with the lay reader, characterize many of their books and articles. The impression conveyed is of "cliquishness," or exclusion; of insiders writing only for insiders.[82]

If one assumes that understanding is a part of what emancipation involves, this inaccessibility of the language of cultural studies to ready understanding tends to belie its claim to foster the emancipation of oppressed groups. The solution to this problem is obvious: to employ a writing style that is more accessible to educators who lack expertise in this research tradition. In the meantime, if you can penetrate the prose of the cultural studies literature, you will be rewarded with ideas about factors that may explain such problems as why some ethnic minorities perform poorly in school and why school bureaucracies are resistant to certain types of change, and methods for investigating these factors.

♦ **Touchstone in Research**

Coulon, A. (1995). *Ethnomethodology.* Thousand Oaks, CA: Sage.

Ethnomethodology

Think about the first time you encountered a new situation, for example, starting a new job. You probably received some formal instruction, but much informal learning occurred as well, such as how to talk to your supervisor, what to do when you made a mistake, how to interact with coworkers and clients, what constitutes proper and improper product, and more generally, how to make sense of the workplace so that you understand it in the same way that others in this social environment do. Ethnomethodology is the study of such matters. More precisely, **ethnomethodology** is the study of the techniques that individuals use to make sense of everyday social environments and to accomplish the tasks of communicating, making decisions, and reasoning within them.

The research tradition of ethnomethodology developed within the discipline of sociology. Whereas most sociologists are concerned with large-scale social phenomena (e.g., social class and the role of gender in society), ethnomethodologists are concerned with small-scale social phenomena that occur in local settings. The development of ethnomethodology as a field of study was influenced by the work of phenomenologists. Like them, ethnomethodologists are concerned with how social reality *appears* to individuals, not with the objective features of social reality. They differ in that phenomenological researchers primarily are concerned with the individual's interpretations of reality, whereas ethnomethodologists are interested in how groups of individuals develop intersubjective interpretations of reality.

Ethnomethodologists have developed several theoretical constructs that guide their research. One of them is **indexicality,** which refers to the phenomenon that the full meaning of words can only be determined by referring to aspects of the context in which they are used. The word *I* is an indexical expression because its specific meaning only can be determined within a particular context, namely, knowing the person who spoke the word. Consider, too, the case of a teacher who says to his class, "I want your attention now." Students will use cues from the context to construct a meaning for this expression: the teacher's tone of voice, the immediately preceding action, how the teacher reacted in previous situations when he made this statement but students were slow in reacting to it, and

---

82. Gibson, *Critical theory and education,* pp. 16–17.

each student's observation of other student's behavior before and after the teacher makes this statement. All these indexical cues will help a student understand the statement, especially the degree of urgency implied by the word *now*. Ethnomethodologists are particularly interested in discovering the indexical cues that individuals use to interpret local social environments.

The methods of data collection in ethnomethodological research are varied. They include the use of direct observation, participant observation, interviewing, and document analysis. The method of data analysis is similar to what we described as *reflective analysis* in Chapter 14. Ethnomethodologists use intuition and judgment to understand how individuals in a local social setting make sense of the setting and work together to create a shared social reality. They also have a reflexive orientation, which means that they reflect on how their research methods influence the phenomena they are studying. In other words, the act of research itself involves sense-making and the construction of social reality. Thus, an ethnomethodologist needs to describe not only how his research participants make sense of and construct their local social reality, but also how he himself went about making sense of and constructing a representation of this sense-making, constructive process.

Hugh Mehan conducted an ethnomethodological study of one classroom in an elementary school in a black and Mexican-American neighborhood in San Diego.[83] A total of nine lessons taught by the teacher over the course of a school year were videotaped and subjected to intensive analysis. Among the many findings of the study, Mehan discovered that the teacher used a "turn-allocation machinery" as the basic method for communicating and maintaining social order in the classroom.[84] The turn-allocation machinery included three techniques: individual nominations (the teacher nominates a particular child to speak), invitations to bid (the teacher asks students to raise their hands if they wish to speak), and invitations to reply (the teacher invites students to speak in chorus or without being named). Mehan also discovered that the turn-allocation machinery included improvisational strategies to handle unusual occurrences. For example, when a child other than the nominated child answered the teacher's question, the teacher typically ignored what the non-nominated child said. Mehan noted that this action functioned as a mild sanction without making the teacher appear to be a "policeman." Mehan also observed that

> The work of doing nothing . . . retains the teacher's control of the lesson format in subtle ways. It enables the teacher to complete her projects without constantly sanctioning violations of classroom rules in an overt manner.[85]

Mehan used an ethnomethodological technique called *breaching* to validate his inferences about turn-taking conventions in classroom lessons. **Breaching** involves making natural or contrived disruptions in people's normal routines in order to reveal the hidden work that they do to maintain their social environment. For example, a researcher could try bargaining for an item in a store in order to see how the salesperson goes about conveying the social convention that store items in the United States are bought at a fixed price. Mehan checked his inferences about turn-taking rules by looking for naturally occurring instances

83. Mehan, H. (1979). *Learning lessons: Social organization in the classroom.* Cambridge, MA: Harvard University Press. Mehan labeled his method *constitutive ethnography* because it included both ethnomethodological investigation of structuring activities used by teachers and students and the resulting structure of classroom lessons.
84. Ibid., p. 83.
85. Ibid., p. 111.

in which a child did not follow a posited rule, as when a non-nominated child spoke instead of the nominated child. In most instances, Mehan found that the rule-breaking child was sanctioned (i.e., evaluated negatively) by the teacher. The presence of this sanction, in Mehan's thinking, validated the existence of the turn-taking rules that he had inferred from normal classroom interactions.

Mehan concluded from his ethnomethodological analysis that students must have communicative competence as well as academic knowledge in order to be successful within the classroom culture:

> Successful participation in the culture of the classroom involves the ability to relate behavior, both academic and social, to a given classroom situation in terms of implicit rules. This involves going beyond the information given in verbal instructions to understand the teacher, linking particular features to general patterns by filling in contextual information . . . Competent membership in the classroom community, then, involves weaving academic knowledge and interactional skills together like strands of a rope, providing factually correct academic content in the interactionally appropriate form.[86]

Mehan studied the communicative competence required of students in order to be successful in one type of instruction (classroom lessons in elementary school). It seems that ethnomethodological methods of investigation would be similarly useful in revealing tacit rules and the extent to which they are followed or violated in other instructional situations, for example, teachers' directions for complex assignments given at higher grade levels (e.g., writing an essay) or a review session for an upcoming test. These methods could be used as well to study other social situations of interest to educators, such as curriculum development committees and administrative teamwork.

The Investigation of Language and Communication

✦ *Touchstone in Research*

Silverman, D. (2000). Analyzing talk and text. In N. K. Denzin & Y. S. Lincoln (Eds.), *Handbook of qualitative research* (2nd ed., pp. 821–834). Thousand Oaks, CA: Sage.

Qualitative researchers have made extensive studies of language and communication because they are central features of social life. The term *communication,* as we use it here, refers to speech, documents (e.g., textbooks, newsletters, and memos), and media productions (e.g., instructional videotapes and hypermedia CD-ROMs). Communication involves the use of language, which can be viewed as a system of signs. Signs can take many forms, for example, spoken and written words, but also a person's wink, a flagpole at the front of a school building, and the color of a traffic signal. From this perspective, anything in the social environment is a "text" that can be read and interpreted.

Qualitative researchers have different interests in studying communication. Some are curious about the nature of the communicative act. They address such questions as, How does language work? How do individuals obtain meaning from text? What are the different meanings of a text for different individuals? What factors influence the act of communicating? Other qualitative researchers are interested in the actual content of the communication because of what it might reveal about some phenomenon of interest to them. For example, ethnographers might analyze documents found in a field setting for what they reveal about the culture being studied. You will find, then, that some of the qualitative research traditions that we describe below emphasize the *how,* whereas others emphasize the *what,* of communication.

86. Ibid., p. 170.

In the following sections, we describe three qualitative research traditions that have figured prominently in the study of communication: hermeneutics, semiotics, and structuralism. First, though, we describe several other traditions that may be relevant to your research interests. (Methods for qualitative analysis of texts are also described in Chapter 9.)

Many acts of communication take the form of telling stories, folktales, anecdotes, and so forth in a variety of formats, such as stage plays, oral story telling, novels, and film. These communicative acts are **narratives,** which we define as the use of a communication format to organize interpretive representations and explanations of personal and social experience. Researchers have used the methods of various disciplines to study the characteristics of narratives and how they are constructed through interpretive acts by the speaker or writer. The methods include: **discourse analysis,** which is the study of the interpretive processes that individuals use to produce their accounts of reality;[87] **conversation analysis,** which is the study of the rules of speech acts between two or more people;[88] **sociolinguistics,** which is the study of the effects of social characteristics such as age, socioeconomic status, and ethnicity on language use; and **narratology,** which is the study of literary narratives. The methods developed by cognitive psychologists, ethnomethodologists, and analysts of event structures (see earlier sections of the chapter) also have been used to study narratives. These methods collectively have been called **narrative analysis.**[89] Educational researchers recently have begun using the methods of narrative analysis to study the social organization of the lives of teachers, students, and other groups.[90]

Anthropologists have developed several qualitative research traditions that focus on the study of a culture's communication patterns. **Ethnoscience** (also called *cognitive ethnography* or *cognitive anthropology*) involves the study of a culture's semantic systems for the purpose of revealing the cognitive structure of the culture.[91] For example, one could study the terms that a culture uses to describe food in order to determine how the members of the culture conceptualize eating behavior. **Ethnographic content analysis** involves the examination of the content of documents found in field settings as reflections of social interactions in the culture.[92] In contrast, quantitative content analysis (see Chapter 9) involves the study of the content of documents without consideration of the social and cultural context in which they were produced. Finally, the **ethnography of communication** involves the study of how members of a cultural group use speech in their social life.

Hermeneutics

The term *hermeneutics* originally meant the interpretation of sacred texts. In contemporary philosophy and the social sciences, **hermeneutics** has come to refer to the study of the process by which individuals arrive at the meaning of any text. The term *text* can refer to a document (e.g., a curriculum guide), but it also can refer to social customs, cultural myths,

✦ Touchstone in Research

Gallagher, S. (1992). *Hermeneutics and education.* Albany, NY: State University of New York Press.

87. Potter, J. (1997). Discourse analysis as a way of analyzing naturally-occurring talk. In D. Silverman (Ed.), *Qualitative research: Theory, method and practice* (pp. 144–160). London: Sage.

88. Zimmerman, D. H. (1988). On conversation: The conversation analytic perspective. In J. A. Anderson (Ed.), *Communication yearbook 11* (pp. 406–432). Thousand Oaks, CA: Sage.

89. Casey, K. (1996). The new narrative research in education. *Review of Educational Research, 21,* 211–253; Gudmundsdóttir, S. (2001). Narrative research on school practice. In V. Richardson (Ed.), *Handbook of research on teaching* (4th ed., pp. 226–240). Washington, DC: American Educational Research Association.

90. For an example, see: Lieblich, A., & Josselson, R. (Eds.). (1997). *The narrative study of lives,* Vol. 5. Thousand Oaks, CA: Sage.

91. Werner, O., & Schoepfle, G. M. (1987). *Systematic fieldwork* (Vols. 1–2). Thousand Oaks, CA: sage.

92. 92. Altheide, D. L. (1987). Ethnographic content analysis. *Qualitative Sociology, 10,* 65–77.

and anything else containing a message that can be "read." Thus, researchers could use hermeneutic principles to interpret a school reform report (e.g., *A Nation at Risk*), a school site council meeting, the clothing worn by students, or a school district's policy on teacher recruitment and retention.

The long hermeneutic tradition in philosophy provides much of the theoretical basis for most qualitative research that is done from an interpretive perspective. In fact, the term *interpretive* highlights the centrality of interpretation in qualitative research. Because interpretation is at the heart of hermeneutics, it is little wonder that it has had so much influence on qualitative researchers.

Hermeneutic theorists claim that there is no objective reality and, therefore, no possibility of developing correct knowledge about reality. Instead, we develop interpretations of the world. It follows from this assumption that an author starts by forming an interpretation of some aspect of the world and then expresses that interpretation as a text using a medium (e.g., a textbook or instructional videotape format) that uses conventions (e.g., a table of contents), which themselves are socially constructed through interpretive acts. The reader subsequently comprehends the text by a process of interpretation, which involves an attempt to re-experience the author's interpretive act. According to hermeneutic theorists, then, the author and the reader are entangled in interpretive processes. There is no way of knowing the world objectively outside the interpretive act.

Hermeneutic theorists have devoted much effort to the problem of why and how humans are capable of interpretation. They also have developed concepts and methods that can aid in the interpretation of texts. One such principle is the **hermeneutic circle,** which involves a continuous process of alternating between interpreting the meaning of each part of the text and the text as a whole. Interpretation of the text as a whole helps interpretation of the parts and vice versa.

Other hermeneutic principles are illustrated in a study of the deliberations of a curriculum development team by Elaine Atkins, a researcher who also was a member of the team.[93] The team was formed to construct a new general studies curriculum at the local community college. It included members of three previous teams that had developed competing proposals, none of which was acceptable to the college's administrators. The charge given to the new team was to develop a "unified" proposal.

Atkins tape-recorded all 20 meetings held by the team, each lasting about five hours, for the following research objective:

> I wanted to go back and learn more about how we had managed to arrive at the agreements that we had struggled with so hard. I also wanted to locate the places where we had never been able to reach accord. I wanted to identify the points of synthesis or fusion, to see under what conditions genuine dialogue had taken place, and to find where agreement had been blocked.[94]

Using a hermeneutic perspective, Atkins started her "story" of the research project by analyzing her own role in the curriculum development process in order to understand how her prejudices and values might affect her reflections.

She then drew on Hans-Georg Gadamer's hermeneutic concept of "fused horizon" to understand the unfolding work of the curriculum development team.[95] Gadamer assumes that, although each participant in a dialogue will argue his own opinions and prejudices,

93. Atkins, E. (1990). From competing paradigms to final consensus: A case study of the deliberations of a conflict-prone curriculum group. *Journal of Curriculum and Supervision, 5,* 308–327.
94. Ibid., p. 310.
95. Gadamer, H. (1975). *Truth and method* (G. Barden & J. Cumming, Trans.). New York: Seabury Press.

it is nonetheless possible for each of them to perceive the other participants as authentic beings whose opinions and prejudices can be recognized and translated into terms that each one can comprehend. If participants are willing, they can engage in a hermeneutic conversation in which, by a process of argument and counterargument, they achieve a common language. The ultimate goal is for all participants to have their separate points of view—their separate "horizons," in Gadamer's terminology—recede into the background, so that one human community of thought and action—"fused horizons"—results.

Atkins observed that the team members spent much time in their first few meetings arguing for their positions and against competing positions. They subsequently converged on two possible approaches to the general studies curriculum. From that point, Atkins found that the dialogue alternated between fused and separate horizons of understanding, as illustrated by her interpretations of what was happening at different points in the process:

> *Time 1.* We reached an uneasy compromise, but the same argument sporadically resurfaced, was periodically quelled, and continued to give shape to the resulting curriculum plan.[96]

> *Time 2.* As we came to realize that both agendas [approaches to the general studies curriculum] would be the shaping forces or dual platform for the new curriculum, that neither team would ever let up, we began to look for ways to provide a unified front to the rest of the faculty and administration.[97]

> *Time 3.* At this point, we were all in consonance, partly because we knew the time had come for a political compromise and partly because we now saw the two approaches as phases in a cycle of intellectual investigation, each phase having a powerful place in academic life. The dialectic again shifted: The conflict became one of emphasis rather than polarity.[98]

Atkins supported her interpretations with relevant excerpts of dialogue from the group meetings.

This study illustrates how hermeneutic concepts and methods can help to clarify the meaning of a text, in this case, an ongoing dialogue in a work group. A noteworthy feature of the hermeneutic analysis is that the interpretive process focused on the text itself. That is to say, the researcher's key concepts of argument, conflict, and compromise were grounded in the text rather than imposed on it by the investigator's perspective or someone else's theory. In reading the report, then, we sense that the emic perspective of the development team was revealed in an authentic, credible manner.

Semiotics

A moment's reflection will reveal that we convey messages to each other and to ourselves through a system of signs. Language is one such system, but there are others as well—for example, mathematical symbols, musical notation, photographs, road signs, nonverbal gestures. **Semiotics** is the study of sign systems, in particular, the study of how objects (e.g., letters of the alphabet) come to convey meaning and how sign systems relate to human behavior. The importance of the study of signs becomes clear with the realization that a message doesn't exist until it has become coded in the form of signs. This coding process affects the nature of the message that is delivered. Thus, to understand any setting in which messages are transmitted back and forth (for example, classroom instruction), we need to

✦ Touchstone in Research

Manning, P. K. (1987). *Semiotics and fieldwork.* Thousand Oaks, CA: Sage.

96. Atkins, From competing paradigms to final consensus, p. 317.
97. Ibid., p. 322.
98. Ibid., p. 325.

understand the sign system in which those messages have been coded. In other words, it is important to study not only *what* is said or written, but *how* it is said or written. According to semioticists, messages do not represent an objective reality. Rather, messages are a social construction based on the use of sign systems: "At the heart of semiotics is the realization that the whole of human experience, without exception, is an interpretative structure mediated and sustained by signs."[99]

Semioticists have developed various concepts and techniques for studying sign systems and their relationship to human behavior. The most basic concepts are signifier, signified, and sign. A **signifier** is a word, sound, or image that is intended to convey meaning. A **signified** is the meaning conveyed by the object. Together, the signifier and signified constitute a **sign**. A real example of a sign is a **referent.** For example, the expression H_2O is a signifier, and the signified is water. This expression and its meaning together constitute a sign. Water flowing from a faucet would be a referent for this sign. The sign H_2O is one of many such signs in chemical notation, which constitutes a sign system. Semioticists are interested in the study of such systems, including the analysis of the elements of the system and how they are used to convey meaning.

Peter Manning illustrated the work of semioticists by doing an informal semiotic analysis of a graduation ceremony that he attended.[100] He focused on the ceremonial signs that were used to convey various messages and organize people's behaviors. These were the signs that he noted:

> the order of events, the contrasting dress, the code of space (audience, faculty, graduating seniors), the signs of rank and status (caps, hoods of different colors, gowns of varying styles and lengths), the conventions of address (rhetorical forms such as the welcoming address, the prayer, the main address, the students' thanks, and so on), the order of march and texts (such as programs, instructions to participants, and diplomas).[101]

Manning observed that the audience and those involved directly in the ceremony conformed their behavior to the meaning of these signs to various degrees. Semioticists are interested in behavioral conformity to and deviations from the intended meaning of signs. For this reason, semioticists often combine fieldwork in a natural setting with a formal analysis of the sign system of interest to them.

Semiotics is a strong research tradition in various academic disciplines, but it has not been used widely in education as of yet. However, it seems to have considerable promise for the study of education, because so many educational phenomena involve sign systems used to impart information that affects what and how students learn.[102]

Structuralism

✦ Touchstone in Research

Caws, P. (1997). *Structuralism updated.* Amherst, MA: Prometheus.

Martusewicz, R. A. (2001). *Seeking passage: Post-structuralism, pedagogy, and ethics.* New York: Teachers College Press.

Structuralism is an approach to investigation that focuses on the systemic properties of phenomena, most notably the relationships among elements of a system. For example, this textbook can be viewed as a system that contains various elements organized into a particular structure: chapters, name index, footnotes, pages, headings, quotations, and so on. According to structuralist theory, the meaning of each of these elements can be determined only by examining its relationship to the other elements of the system. For ex-

99. Deely, J. (1990). *Basics of semiotics.* Bloomington, IN: Indiana University Press. Quote appears on p. 5.
100. Manning, P. K. (1987). *Semiotics and fieldwork.* Newbury Park, CA: Sage.
101. Ibid., p. 33.
102. The use of semiotics to understand various aspects of special education is explored in: Rogers, L. J., & Swadener, B. B. (Eds.). (2001). *Semiotics and Disability: Interrogating categories of difference.* Albany, NY: State University of New York Press. An example of its application in educational administration is: Everhart, R. B. (1991). Semiotics as an orientation to administrative practice. *Educational Administration Quarterly, 27,* 358–377.

ample, the name index only has meaning in relation to certain words that appear in the chapters.

Structuralism as a qualitative research tradition began in linguistics with the work of Ferdinand de Saussure at the turn of this century, and was further developed by researchers in other disciplines, among them being Jean Piaget in psychology, Basil Bernstein in sociology, Claude Levi-Strauss in anthropology, and Jacques Derrida and Roland Barthes in literary and media studies.[103] As with other qualitative research traditions, the methods of a structuralist inquiry depend upon the particular researcher. Nevertheless, Rex Gibson identified six principles to which structuralist researchers generally subscribe.[104] The principles are described below.

1. *The whole is greater than the sum of its parts.* According to structuralists, the operation of a system cannot be reduced to its elements and their relationships to each other. This is because the elements and their relationships are governed by the system as a whole. For example, a textbook has an overarching instructional design that is more than its constituent chapters and front and back matter. Similarly, a social group is more than its individual members and how each interacts with the others. There is a sense of a group that exists independently of individual members and that influences the actions of each individual within the group.

2. *Social reality exists not in things, but in their relationships.* To understand this principle, consider language. If we want to know what a particular word in a language means (e.g., *teacher*), we must define it in terms of—that is, in relation to—other words. According to structuralists, then, words do not point to an independent, objective reality. Rather, "language is elevated to the supreme definer of reality."[105]

Saussure conceptualized speech and text as the visible, transitory manifestations of an invisible, permanent system, which he referred to as *langue* (in English, *language*). Thus, dictionaries and grammar texts represent the elements and rules of writing and speech, but they do not capture all the subtle properties of the whole (i.e., *langue*). Similarly, we can study a culture's myths, rituals, laws, and institutions in an effort to understand it. While all these elements are manifestations of the culture, there is an invisible "system" of culture beyond these elements that determines these manifestations.

3. *The individual is a subordinate element of various systems.* Structuralists believe that individuals do not have meaning in and of themselves, nor do they act as independent agents who create their own social reality. Rather, individuals are shaped by the various systems of which they are members. Thus, the individual does not create language, but rather language creates the individual and what he is capable of communicating.

4. *Systems have self-regulating mechanisms that ensure their survival.*

According to structuralists, systems have a homeostatic capacity, which ensures that they maintain their integrity despite forces toward change. For example, the English language must deal with the fact of new social and technological developments that call for new words, new meanings for existing words, or the discarding of existing words. The English language thus is constantly changing, yet it retains a recognizable systemic integrity across time.

5. *Social reality is better understood by "snapshots" than by historical analysis.* Saussure argues that meaning resides in the relationships between words, as these relationships exist at a particular point in time. Therefore, he views historical analysis as irrelevant

---

103. The work of these researchers is discussed in: Gibson, R. (1984). *Structuralism and education.* London: Hodder & Stoughton.
104. Ibid.
105. Ibid., p. 21.

to understanding current meanings. For example, knowing that the word *silly* once meant *blessed* and then *helpless* does not help us realize that it now means *foolish*. According to Saussure, the elements of a language are arbitrary signs and therefore can change meaning across speakers, across settings, and across time. For example, the word *screen* signifies one thing in interior design and quite another in computer design.

6. *Structures are subject to transformation, but according to the laws of the system.* Structuralists believe that systems follow laws that direct the flow of change among their elements and relationships. Mathematics provides a good example of this principle. The equation $4 + 3 = 7$ can be transformed into the equation $3 + 4 = 7$, but not into the equation $3 + 7 = 4$ because of the existence of mathematical laws that govern acceptable and unacceptable transformations. Similarly, the languages of the world change over time, but structuralists believe that the nature of these changes is constrained by universal laws.

The six structuralist principles described above assume that it is possible to find meaning in the systemic properties of a phenomenon. A radical version of structuralism, called **poststructuralism** is a postmodernist approach to the study of systems, especially language as a system, that denies the possibility of finding any inherent meaning in them. Thus, a poststructuralist would make no distinction between the study of Shakespeare and a comic book. Both are systems of signs that can be studied, but neither has a greater claim to truth than the other. Also, there is no one objective, true interpretation of a literary work or text:

> Texts can be read in many ways: each text contains within itself the possibility of an infinite set of structures, and to privilege some by setting up a system of rules to generate them is a blatantly prescriptive and ideological move.[106]

The value of the poststructuralist approach, in the eyes of its proponents, is that it stimulates people to question deeply the assumptions they most take for granted about what they consider to be true or authoritative.[107] This questioning of assumptions by poststructuralists has extended into analyses of scientific reporting. Specifically, poststructuralists question the impersonal, third-person voice in which many research reports (especially those within the quantitative research tradition) are written. Laurel Richardson suggests that this questioning opens up new possibilities for scientific writing:

> [P]oststructuralism suggests two important things to qualitative writers: First, it directs us to understand ourselves reflexively as persons writing from particular positions at specific times; and second, it frees us from trying to write a single text in which we say everything at once to everyone. Nurturing our own voices releases the censorious hold of 'science writing' on our consciousness, as well as the arrogance it fosters in our psyche: Writing is validated as a method of knowing.[108]

As we stated above, structuralism as an approach to inquiry has influenced the work of researchers in a variety of social and human science disciplines. In education, the most notable influence has been on Piaget and other researchers who seek to understand intel-

---

106. Culler, J. (1975). *Structuralist poetics: Structuralism, linguistics, and the study of literature.* Ithaca, NY: Cornell University Press. Quote appears on p. 242.
107. For an example of the application of the poststructuralist approach to education, see: Brown, T. (2001). *Mathematics education and language: Interpreting hermeneutics and post-structuralism* (rev. 2nd ed.). Boston: Kluwer.
108. Richardson, L. (2000). Writing: A method of inquiry. In N. K. Denzin & Y. S. Lincoln (Eds.), *Handbook of qualitative research* (2nd ed., pp. 923–948). Thousand Oaks, CA: Sage. Quote appears on p. 929.

lectual development in terms of underlying mental structures and the rules of transformation of these structures (e.g., Piaget's principles of assimilation and accommodation). It is surprising that structuralism has not had more influence on the study of curriculum materials because both structuralism and poststructuralism have had a significant influence on the study of literature and media. Education also has many systemic structures (e.g., grade levels, levels of schooling, personnel hierarchies, courses of study) that would seem amenable to structuralist analysis.

Gibson provided several examples of what might be learned about educational phenomena through structural analysis.[109] One of them is an analysis of a teacher's science lesson in a class of young children. Gibson demonstrated how the teacher's actions were shaped by a mental structure characteristic of scientific thinking. The structure constrained her interactions with the children, such that any child's response that did not fit the structure was either ignored or redirected.

In another line of inquiry, Jon Stott developed a structuralist approach to the teaching of literature to young students.[110] In this approach, students are taught "the idea that stories form meaningful patterns which are in part influenced by literary codes and conventions."[111] Examples of literary codes and conventions are irony, the journey motif, setting, and the use of earlier literary materials in creating a new literary work. Research might be done to determine how this and other structuralist approaches to curriculum influences students' learning and the types of meanings that they find in school-related texts.

---

109. Gibson, *Structuralism and education*, Chapter 8.
110. Stott, J. C. (1987). The spiralled sequence story curriculum: A structuralist approach to teaching fiction in the elementary grades. *Children's literature in education, 18,* 148–162; Stott, J. C. (1982). A structuralist approach to teaching novels in the elementary grades. *Reading Teacher, 36,* 136–143.
111. Ibid., p. 151.

◆ RECOMMENDATIONS FOR *Designing a Study Based on a Qualitative Research Tradition*

1. Carefully analyze the type of phenomena you plan to investigate (lived experience, society and culture, or language and communication), because each type has particular research traditions associated with it.
2. In reviewing possible qualitative research traditions to guide your study, consider how well the theoretical assumptions and methods of each one match your own theoretical and methodological leanings.
3. If you do select a particular qualitative research tradition to guide your study, immerse yourself in it—including an apprenticeship with an expert, if possible—so that you make appropriate and insightful use of the tradition.

✔ SELF-CHECK TEST

Circle the correct answer to each of the following questions.
The answers are provided at the back of the book.

1. A textural description is an account of
   a. a think-aloud or stimulated-recall interview.
   b. an individual's prereflective perceptions of a phenomenon.
   c. an individual's interpretation or recall of a phenomenon.
   d. an individual's interpretation of a text.

2. The assertion that a text has no definite meaning is fundamental to
   a. semiotics.
   b. deconstructionism.
   c. ethnomethodology.
   d. ethnoscience.

3. The study of how individuals fail to follow the intended meaning of signs would be of particular interest to researchers who specialize in
   a. the ethnography of communication.
   b. ethnographic content analysis.
   c. semiotics.
   d. poststructuralism.

4. The formal learning experiences of individuals from early childhood through adulthood probably would be of most interest to
   a. life history researchers.
   b. phenomenographers.
   c. ethnographers.
   d. researchers who do event structure analysis.

5. Indexicality refers to the fact that the meaning of specific words
   a. does not have an exact counterpart in another culture's language.
   b. must be determined by referring to the context in which they are used.
   c. cannot be determined using hermeneutic principles.
   d. can be determined using semiotic principles.

6. The thinking processes of experts and novices would be of particular interest to
   a. phenomenological researchers.
   b. semioticists.
   c. cognitive psychologists.
   d. ethnomethodologists.

7. The theory of border pedagogy was developed within the research tradition of
   a. structuralism.
   b. poststructuralism.
   c. cultural studies.
   d. the ethnography of education.

8. The assertion that language determines an individual's actions is fundamental to
   a. hermeneutics.
   b. semiotics.
   c. phenomenology.
   d. structuralism.

9. The concept of cultural acquisition refers to
   a. the individual's learning of his culture.
   b. the process of assimilating immigrant groups into a culture.
   c. the role that social structures play in teaching cultural norms and values.
   d. the process by which a culture develops new norms and values.

10. Hegemony refers to
    a. emancipatory methods as conceptualized by critical theorists.
    b. a conception of social justice advocated by critical theorists.
    c. disparities among the emic perspectives of members of a society's underclass.
    d. the domination of subordinate groups by a society's privileged groups.

11. The hermeneutic circle is a process for
    a. determining the implicit rules of social interaction.
    b. resolving hegemonic disputes.
    c. analyzing the ethnographic content of a sign-signifier relationship.
    d. arriving at an interpretation of a text.

12. Ethnographies generally emphasize the
    a. emic perspective.
    b. semiotic perspective.
    c. etic perspective.
    d. phenomenographic perspective.

CHAPTER 16

✦ Historical Research

OVERVIEW

Historical research helps educators understand the present condition of education by shedding light on the past. It also helps them imagine alternative future scenarios in education and judge their likelihood. In this chapter we explain the major steps involved in conducting a historical research study: (1) identifying a problem to study, (2) searching for sources of historical data, (3) evaluating historical data for authenticity and accuracy, and (4) synthesizing historical data into meaningful chronological and thematic patterns. Throughout the chapter, we emphasize the interpretive processes that historians of education use in conducting their research.

OBJECTIVES

After studying this chapter, you should be able to

1. Describe major differences between contemporary and nineteenth-century historical research.
2. State several purposes for doing historical research in education.
3. List the major steps involved in doing a historical research study.
4. Describe five types of historical research in education.
5. Describe uses of documents, quantitative records, oral recordings, and relics as primary historical sources.
6. Distinguish between preliminary, primary, and secondary sources of historical information, and provide an example of each.
7. Describe several procedures that a researcher might use for recording information from historical sources.

8. Describe the characteristics of a historical document that one examines in carrying out external criticism.
9. State examples of questions that researchers ask themselves in carrying out internal criticism of historical data.
10. Distinguish between subjectivity and bias in reporting a historical event.
11. Explain the statement, "History means interpretation."
12. Describe how the use of particular concepts can affect historical interpretation.
13. Explain the problems of interpretation that are involved in making causal inferences from historical evidence.
14. Describe several different approaches to organizing the report of a historical research study.

✦ Touchstone in Research

Donato, R., & Lazerson, M. (2000). New directions in American educational history: Problems and prospects. *Educational Researcher, 29*(8), 4–15.

Kaestle, C. F. (1997). Recent methodological developments in the history of American education. In R. M. Jaeger (Ed.), *Complementary methods for research in education* (2nd ed., pp. 119–131). Washington, DC: American Educational Research Association.

Introduction

The British historian E. H. Carr answered the question "What is history?" by stating, "it is a continuing process of interaction between the historian and his facts, an unending dialogue between the present and the past."[1] Consistent with Carr's view, we define **historical research** as a process of systematically searching for data to answer questions about a past phenomenon for the purpose of gaining a better understanding of present institutions, practices, trends, and issues in education.

C. H. Edson identified four similarities between historical investigation and other qualitative research methodologies: (1) emphasis on the study of context, (2) the study of behavior in natural rather than in contrived or theoretical settings, (3) appreciation of the wholeness of experience, and (4) the centrality of interpretation in the research process.[2] Because of these similarities, historical studies generally are considered a particular type of qualitative research. However, some historians also use quantitative research methods, as we show later in the chapter.

With respect to its epistemological orientation, historical research tends to be postpositivist rather than purely interpretivist. That is, historians acknowledge fallibility and bias in human observation, but nonetheless believe that it is possible through careful analysis and multiple sources of evidence to discover what "really" happened during a given time period with respect to the phenomenon being investigated.[3]

The importance of interpretation in historical research is apparent from even a superficial analysis of what is involved in doing this kind of investigation. Historical research necessarily deals with events that occurred prior to the historian's decision to study them. Therefore, historians must rely on records of events that were made by others—for example, a journalist, a court reporter, a diarist, or a photographer. The recording of the event involves an interpretive act, because the biases, values, and interests of those who recorded the event will cause them to attend to some details and omit others. Thus, the data provided by historical sources are cloaked in interpretation even before a historian retrieves them for study. Historians add still another layer of interpretation by the way they choose to emphasize or ignore particular data and by how they organize data into categories and patterns. For this reason historical reports are not literal accounts of the past, but rather what the historian Joan Burstyn calls "constructed reality."[4]

The central role of interpretation in contemporary historical research contrasts with the view of history that was most popular in the nineteenth century, namely that "history consists of the compilation of a maximum number of irrefutable and objective facts."[5] Reflecting this view, nineteenth-century histories often consisted of multivolume compilations of details about either broad topics (e.g., history of the Western world, history of the United States) or limited topics (e.g., the French Revolution, the Spanish-American War). Contemporary historians tend to dismiss these writings as merely historical chronicles. Their own writings tend to be shorter, and they subordinate historical facts to an interpretive framework within which facts and other data are given meaning and significance.

---

1. Carr, E. H. (1967). *What is history?* New York: Random. Quote appears on p. 35.
2. Edson, C. H. (1986). Our past and present: Historical inquiry in education. *The Journal of Thought, 21,* 13–27.
3. For an example of historical research conducted within an interpretivist framework (specifically, semiotics), see: Nye, D. E. (1983). *The invented self: An anti-biography, from documents of Thomas A. Edison.* Odense, Denmark: Odense University Press.
4. Burstyn, J. N. (1987). History as image: Changing the lens. *History of Education Quarterly, 27,* 167–180.
5. Carr, *What is history?*, p. 14.

Historical research in education differs from other types of educational research in that the historian *discovers* data through a search of historical sources such as diaries, official documents, and relics. In historical research, then, the evidence is available before the historian formulates a thesis, selects a topic, and designs a research plan. In contrast, most other types of educational research require the researcher to *create* data. For example, a researcher creates data when she makes observations or administers tests to determine the effectiveness of an instructional program.

Subject Matter of Historical Research

Arthur Moehlman and his colleagues at the University of Texas developed a classification scheme to describe the range of historical research found in the educational literature.[6] Their goal was to provide a means for computer storage and retrieval of the growing mass of bibliographical materials and original documents relevant to the history of education.

Figure 16.1 presents the 11 major categories in the classification system developed by Moehlman and his colleagues. We also include an example of published historical research for each category. The classification system illustrates the wide range of topics and concerns that interest historians of education. You may find the system helpful in clarifying for yourself the particular historical problem that you wish to study.

The Importance of Studying History

Histories of education serve several important purposes. Some historians, referred to as **antiquarians,** value the study of the past for its own sake. Antiquarians become intrigued with a particular historical period and spend their careers documenting the events and objects that make that period distinctive. They seem to have little concern for the relevance of their discoveries to present-day scholars or students.

A more significant purpose for studying the past is offered by Sol Cohen, an educational historian:

> To Freud, neurosis is the failure to escape the past, the burden of one's history. What is repressed returns distorted and is eternally reenacted. The psychotherapist's task is to help the patient reconstruct the past. In this respect the historian's goal resembles that of the therapist—to liberate us from the burden of the past by helping us to understand it.[7]

As an example of the liberating function of history, consider what might happen if educational researchers did not conduct reviews of the literature in their areas of interest prior to undertaking a research project. They would be likely to test hypotheses that previously had been shown to be unproductive, re-invent questionable research methodology, "discover" what was already found by previous researchers, and continue to make the same methodological errors as their predecessors. Indeed, without continually updated historical reviews of the research literature, scientific progress would be impossible.

The same liberating function of history applies to educational practice. For example, in campaigning for a bond issue, educators who are ignorant of past legislative actions affecting the budget for their school district might repeat mistakes of their predecessors, or they might create questionable arguments based on inaccurate assumptions about the past.

---

6. Moehlman, A. H., Van Tassel, D., Goetzmann, W. H., & Everett, G. D. (1969). *A guide to computer-assisted research in American education.* Austin: University of Texas.
7. Cohen, S. (1976). The history of the history of American education, 1900–1976: The uses of the past. *Harvard Educational Review, 46,* 298–330.

FIGURE 16.1

System for Classifying Literature on the History of Education

1. Bibliographies relating to educational history. Example: Brickman, W. W., & Zepper, J. T. (1992). *Russian and soviet education, 1731–1989: A multilingual annotated bibliography.* New York: Garland.
2. General educational history. Example: Rury, J. L. (2001). *Education and social change: Themes in the history of American schooling.* Mahwah, NJ: Lawrence Erlbaum Associates.
3. History educational legislation (e.g., taxation, bonds, school land boards and districts, equalization programs, curriculum, state-supported schools and universities, court cases). Example: Tyack, D. B. (1987). *Law and the shaping of public education, 1785–1954.* Madison, WI: University of Wisconsin Press.
4. Historical biographies of major contributors to education. Example: Kakar, S. (1970). *Frederick Taylor: A study in personality and innovation.* Cambridge: MIT Press.
5. History of major branches of education, e.g., school accreditation and attendance laws, curriculum, enrollment, finance, goals, organization and administration, personnel, community education, and instructional methods and materials. Example: Cuban, L. (1993) *How teachers taught* (2nd ed.). New York: Teachers College Press.
6. Institutional history of education (e.g., correspondence schools, kindergarten, elementary school, secondary school, colleges and universities, vocational schools, military education, and research organizations). Example: Knowles, M. S. (1994). *A history of the adult education movement in the United States* (rev. ed.). Huntington, NY: Krieger.
7. Cultural history of education (e.g., ethnology, anthropology, sociology, and technology). Example: Button, H. W., & Provenzo, E. F., Jr. (1989). *History of education and culture in America* (2nd ed.). Englewood Cliffs, NJ: Prentice-Hall.
8. History of educational planning and policy. Example: Ravitch, D. (2000). *Left back: A century of failed school reform.* New York: Simon and Schuster.
9. Historical critiques of education. Example: Carnoy, M. (1994). *Faded dreams: The politics and economics of race in America.* New York: Cambridge University Press.
10. Comparative history of international education. Example: Silver, H. (1983). *Education as history.* London: Methuen.
11. History of contemporary problems in education. Example: Butchart, R. E. (1988). Outthinking and outflanking the owners of the world: A historiography of the African American struggle for education. *History of Education Quarterly, 28,* 333–366.

Source: Adapted from Mochlman, A. H., Van Tassel, D., Goetzmann, W. II., & Everett, G. D. (1969). *A guide to computer-assisted research in American education.* Austin: University of Texas.

Another purpose of historical research is to provide a moral framework for understanding the present. In Kathleen Mahoney's view, this purpose should be particularly compelling for today's educational historians:

> Today, the right questions might be the moral and religious questions. The postmodern academy evidences growing disenchantment with the fruits of the modern mindset and increasing dissatisfaction with the notion of value-free inquiry and the banality of relativism.[8]

Mahoney observes that recent historical research on religion and higher education is relevant to these questions.[9] This and other research reminds us of traditions that involved a

8. Mahoney, K. A. (2000). New times, new questions. *Educational Researcher, 29*(8), 18–19. Quote appears on p. 19.
9. For example: Marsden, G. (1994). *The soul of the American university: From Protestant establishment to established nonbelief.* New York: Oxford University Press.

defined moral and social order to which most members of a community subscribed. In fact, many religious and ethnic groups seek to keep their collective past alive through ritual and documentation in an attempt to preserve that sense of moral and social order. One can argue that the same need exists in education. The founding of our educational institutions was predicated on particular values and a view of society, the study of which can inform the way in which we view and judge these institutions as they exist today.

Some educational historians do **revisionist history,** the goal of which is to sensitize educators to past practices that appear benevolent, but may have had unjust aims and effects. For example, Michael Katz studied educational innovation in mid-nineteenth century Massachusetts and demonstrated how it functioned to serve dominant economic interests and to thwart democratic aspirations.[10] Because people tend to view the past with a more detached perspective than the present, Katz's study may more readily reveal problems and hidden agendas associated with schooling than would a study of current practices.

Still another purpose of historical research is to assist educators in defining and evaluating alternative future scenarios involving a particular educational phenomenon. If we know how an individual or group has acted in the past, we can predict with a certain degree of confidence how they will act in the future. For example, we can make a good prediction of how a legislator will vote on an upcoming education bill by doing research on his past voting record. As in other types of educational research, however, prediction rarely is perfect. New social, political, or economic conditions continually arise, thus creating discontinuities in educational practices. In Oregon, for example, the passage in 1991 of Measure 5, a voter-approved initiative, fundamentally changed the basis for funding public schools. Thus, past practices in Oregon education may no longer serve to make accurate projections of school curriculum, staffing patterns, and organization.

Historians of education have influenced educational practice primarily through their involvement in the training of educators. For example, preservice teachers usually are required to take a course in the history of education. Historians also can influence educational policy making. A notable example is Patricia Graham, a historian who was director of the National Institute of Education from 1977 to 1979. In an address at the 1980 annual meeting of the American Educational Research Association, Graham described how the historian's traditional concerns for offering a perspective on the present and for examining problems using a variety of research methods provide an advantage when that historian must make major policy decisions.[11]

Some educational researchers think that historical methodology is irrelevant to their work. They align themselves with the physical and social sciences, and consider history as part of the humanities. This view is questionable because all researchers are historians to some extent. In doing research, they must review the literature to determine what past theoretical work and previous studies have been done on a particular problem. Also, the validity of past research findings about education will depend on how much the context in which they were obtained has changed. Furthermore, the search for relevant documents (journal articles, technical reports, unpublished manuscripts, etc.) and interpretation of their significance are tasks that characterize the work of both empirical researchers and historians. Thus the study of historical methodology should help you to become a better researcher, whether or not you choose to do a study that is primarily historical.

10. Katz, M. B. (1968). *The irony of early school reform: Educational innovation in mid-nineteenth century Massachusetts.* Cambridge, MA: Harvard University Press.
11. Patricia Graham described her experiences as director of the National Institute of Education in: Graham, P. (1980). Historians as policy makers. *Educational Researcher, 9*(11), 21–24.

Steps in Doing a Historical Research Study

Historiography is the study of the various steps and procedures that historians use in their research. Before undertaking a historical study, we recommend that you read several historiographical works and also study the historiography of particular educational historians. Reports of their studies often include a historiographical section.

In a series of lectures on historiography, Carr provided the following description of how a historian engages in research:

> Laymen . . . sometimes ask me how the historian goes to work when he writes history. The most common assumption appears to be that the historian divides his work into two sharply distinguishable phases or periods. First, he spends a long preliminary period reading his sources and filling his notebooks with facts; then, when this is over, he puts away his sources, takes out his notebooks, and writes his book from beginning to end. This is to me an unconvincing and unplausible picture. For myself, as soon as I have got going on a few of what I take to be the capital sources, the itch becomes too strong and I begin to write—not necessarily at the beginning, but somewhere, anywhere. Thereafter, reading and writing go on simultaneously. The writing is added to, subtracted from, re-shaped, cancelled, as I go on reading. The reading is guided and directed and made fruitful by the writing: the more I write, the more I know what I am looking for, the better I understand the significance and relevance of what I find.[12]

Educational researchers conducting historical research, as well as those using other methodologies such as experimentation, often use procedures similar to those Carr described. For example, as a first step, a quantitative researcher might formulate a few tentative hypotheses and plan a research design for testing them. After reviewing the literature and conducting pilot studies, the researcher might decide to make further changes in the hypotheses and research design. Then, after the formal study has been completed, the researcher might formulate new hypotheses that were not anticipated at the outset but that can be tested by the available data.

The following sequence of steps may help you structure a historical study: (1) define the problem or question to be investigated; (2) search for sources of historical data; (3) summarize and evaluate the historical sources; and (4) report the pertinent data within an interpretive framework. The next sections of the chapter describe each of these steps. Keep in mind, though, that variations within this sequence might be justified by the particular research questions being asked, the circumstances of the search for historical data, and the interpretive framework that is used to understand the data.

Defining a Problem for Historical Research

As with other types of educational research, the first step in planning a historical study is to define the problem to be investigated. The range of possibilities is large, as David Tyack aptly stated: "One of the appeals of history of education to its scholars is that it gives a lifelong fishing license to study almost any topic."[13] A review of problems and topics studied by other educational historians can help you refine your question or suggest another, more interesting question.

---

12. Carr, *What is history?*, pp. 32–33.
13. Tyack, D. (2000). Reflections on histories of U.S. education. *Educational Researcher, 29*(8), 19–20. Quote appears on p. 20.

Mark Beach classified the problems and topics that prompt historical inquiry into five types, which we explain in the following paragraphs.[14]

1. Social issues. Current social issues are the most popular source of historical problems in education. For example, home schooling, substance abuse among students, how family violence affects young people, and efforts to replace paper-and-pencil tests with performance tests to assess student competence are recent social issues that historical research might illuminate.

2. Study of specific individuals, educational institutions, and social movements. In the past two decades, historical studies of the educational experiences of minority groups and women have been prominent, as have studies of higher education and teaching. These studies often are motivated by the desire to fill in gaps about what is known about the past. Bernard Bailyn, a historian of the American colonial period, offers the following rationale for this type of research:

> The motivation here is to learn something new and to present this new information; but the precise issues are not defined. There are no specific questions and no hypothetical answers. Thus the motivation for writing a narrative of a battle may be simply to discover what happened in it; to find out how it was that the victors won it. Or, again, one decides to do research and write about Wilson's Administration because we are ignorant of it, and any thorough, clear narrative of it will be valuable because it fills an important gap, an evident vacuum.[15]

Even when a history of an educator, institution, or movement is readily available, however, researchers need to determine whether the history adequately explores the events in which they are interested. In fact, the gaps in knowledge of the past that occur to a researcher from reviewing an incomplete or one-sided history often provide the basis for a historical study.

3. Exploration of relationships between events. This type of historical inquiry in education involves an attempt to interpret ideas or events that previously were not viewed or treated as related, but which subsequently have been revealed to reflect possible relationships. For example, a researcher might review various histories of textbook publishing and discover separate, unrelated histories of school curriculum for the same time period. The researcher might decide to review these separate histories in order to detect relationships and raise questions that did not concern the original historians. These perceived relationships and questions can provide the basis for an original historical inquiry. For example, the historian might relate a decision by textbook publishers to begin producing student consumables as a supplement to classroom texts to subsequent changes in school curriculum over a particular time period.

4. Syntheses of data. This related type of historical inquiry occurs when the researcher attempts to synthesize old data collected by different historians or to merge old data with new historical facts. For example, a historian may discover the existence of documents written at the time of important events that were not known to other historians who had done research on these events. Thus, the historian who made the discovery can contribute to our understanding of these events by analyzing these new documents to see whether they reinforce existing interpretations of the events, or lead to new interpretations.

14. Beach, M. (1969). History of education. *Review of Educational Research, 39,* 561–576.
15. Bailyn, B. (1969). The problems of the working historian. In A. S. Eisenstadt (Ed.), *The craft of American history.* New York: AHM Publishing. Quote appears on pp. 202–203.

5. Reinterpretation of past events. As we explained above, revisionist historians do critiques of existing histories by subjecting them to new—and sometimes politically radical—interpretive frameworks. An example is research on the Holocaust in Europe during World War II. Historians have extensively documented the atrocities of the Holocaust. However, some individuals have tried to rewrite history and claim that the Holocaust did not occur.[16]

As in any type of research, you should start by reviewing the literature and talking with experienced researchers before attempting to define problems or topics for historical inquiry. In the process of doing so, you may find that other historians have formulated important problems and questions for future investigation. For example, Guadalupe San Miguel, Jr. reviewed the status of historical research on Chicano education in 1986.[17] He concluded his review by identifying questions that had not yet been answered by historians, including the following:

> First, little is known about the roots and evolution of the Mexican American commitment to education referred to in several of the studies. Who in the community, for instance, supported education, what type of education, and for what purposes? . . . Second, we do not know who attended school nor for how long they attended . . . Finally, new studies comparing and contrasting the educational experiences of Mexican Americans with other minority and immigrant groups are needed. It is unclear yet the extent to which the educational experiences of Mexican Americans were similar or dissimilar to historically dispossessed groups such as blacks and native Americans, or to other language minority groups of European descent.[18]

Questions such as these, formulated by an experienced historian, can be very helpful in identifying a problem for your own study.

An important criterion to consider when deciding on a problem or topic for historical research is whether key sources that you wish to investigate are available and interpretable. For example, would you want to select a problem for historical study that required extensive use of documents that are available only in Spanish if you do not read this language? Or what would you do if it proved to be difficult to access key documents you need, such as classified records in government archives?

Searching for Historical Sources

Formulating a Search Plan

Historians need to have some idea of what they are looking for before they begin their search for sources that will provide the needed data. Otherwise, they are likely to search aimlessly and thus overlook important sources of relevant information. Philip C. Brooks suggests the following approach for initiating a search for historical sources:

> Resourcefulness and imagination are essential in the preliminary exploration as well as in the later actual study. One can suppose that certain kinds of sources would exist if he thinks carefully about his subject, the persons involved, the government or institutions concerned, and the kinds of records that would naturally grow out of the events that he will be studying. He should ask himself who would have produced the useful documents in the transaction he is concerned with. What would be the expected flow of events? What kinds of records would

16. Lipstadt, D. E. (1993). *Denying the Holocaust: The growing assault on truth and memory.* New York: Free Press.
17. San Miguel, G., Jr. (1986). Status of the historiography of Chicano education: A preliminary analysis. *History of Education Quarterly, 26,* 523–536.
18. Ibid., pp. 535–536.

have been created? What would be the life history of the documents, from their creation through current use, filing, temporary storage, and eventual retention in a repository where he can consult them? What kinds of materials would one expect to be kept rather than discarded?[19]

The selection of sources from which to obtain historical data of interest cannot be determined entirely in advance. A tentative search plan should be created, however, and revised as your interpretive framework develops. Changes in the plan will occur as a particular historical source reveals other pertinent sources whose existence you had not anticipated.

As we explained in Chapter 4, researchers use three basic types of sources in a literature search: preliminary, secondary, and primary sources. In that chapter, we also described sources of each type that generally are applicable to educational research. In the following sections, we describe sources of each type that are specific to historical research.[20]

Preliminary Sources

A **preliminary source** is an index to secondary and primary sources. Preliminary sources include **bibliographies,** which are lists of source materials available on a given topic or field of study. Most preliminary sources in the field of history are indexes of secondary sources, but some list primary sources as well. A literature search for a historical study usually begins with an examination of preliminary sources.

Many of the general preliminary sources listed in Appendix A are useful for doing a search of historical literature. In addition, there are more specialized preliminary sources for this purpose. Appendix F lists examples of these preliminary sources, e.g., bibliographies of biographies, directories of historical societies, and general indexes to historical publications. If you plan to do a historical research study, you will find these indexes indispensable.

Secondary Sources

In historical research, a **secondary source** is a document in which an individual gives an account of an event, but was not present at the event. Authors of secondary source documents base their accounts on descriptions or records of historical events that were prepared by others. Thus, most reports of historical research are secondary sources because the historian rarely is a direct witness to the events described in the reports. Instead, the report usually is based on the historian's current interpretation of primary sources and other secondary sources.

Appendix F lists commonly used secondary sources in historical research. These sources include history encyclopedias, biographical dictionaries, historical studies, and history textbooks.

Primary Sources

In historical research, a **primary source** is a record (e.g., a diary, a relic, a map, or a set of test scores) that was generated by people who personally witnessed or participated in the

✦ *Touchstone in Research*

Errante, A. (2000). But sometimes you're not part of the story: Oral histories and ways of remembering and telling. *Educational Researcher, 29*(2), 16–27.

Hill, M. R. (1993). *Archival strategies and techniques.* Thousand Oaks, CA: Sage.

Yow, V. R. (1994). *Recording oral history: A practical guide for social scientists.* Thousand Oaks, CA: Sage.

19. Brooks, P. C. (1969). *Research in archives: The use of unpublished primary sources.* Chicago: University of Chicago Press. Quote appears on pp. 19–20.
20. Our discussion of primary and secondary sources is based on traditional historiographical definitions of these terms. For a different view of the nature of historical sources, based on a semiotic analysis, see: Nye, *The invented self.* Nye classifies sources on two dimensions: private (e.g., diaries) versus public (e.g., newspaper articles), and whether the "text" is in a natural, found order (e.g., a residence) or a translated order (e.g., a museum).

historical events of interest. Virtually any object or verbal record that one can imagine can be a primary source for use in historical research.

Primary sources provide the ultimate basis for the facts historians present. **Historical facts** can be defined as data that the historian regards as true (i.e., valid) and relevant to the description or interpretation of the phenomenon being investigated. An important issue in doing historical research is whether to cite facts obtained from another historian's research report without personally checking the primary sources from which they were derived. In deciding whether to check these sources, you should consider such factors as the other historian's reputation, the degree of compatibility between the original historian's interpretive framework and your own, and whether it is feasible to gain access to the primary source documents. If you choose to use another historian's facts without further check, we recommend that you cite the other historian's work as the source for the historical facts cited in your study.

The four types of primary sources in historical research are (1) written documents or records, (2) quantitative records, (3) oral records, and (4) relics. The most common type is written or printed materials, sometimes called *documents* or *records.* (Documents and records are described in greater detail in Chapter 9.) These materials take varied forms, such as diaries, memoirs, legal records, court testimony, newspapers, periodicals, business records, notebooks, yearbooks, diplomas, committee reports, memos, institutional files, and tests. They include handwritten and typed material, published and unpublished material, material prepared for the public record and material intended only for private use.

The distinction between intentional and unpremeditated documents is important to consider when evaluating the authenticity and genuineness of a source. **Intentional documents,** such as memoirs and yearbooks, are intentionally written to serve as a record of the past. **Unpremeditated documents,** such as memos and teacher-prepared tests, are prepared to serve an immediate purpose, with no expectation that they might be used as a historical record at a later time.

Quantitative records, which provide numerical information about an educational phenomenon, are another type of primary source. Census records, school budgets, school attendance records, test scores, and other compilations of numerical data can be valuable sources of data for historical researchers.

Another important type of primary source is the spoken word. Ballads, tales, sagas, and other forms of spoken language preserve a record of events for posterity. Also, some historians conduct oral interviews of individuals who witnessed or participated in events of potential historical significance. These interviews typically are recorded on audiotape and then transcribed to provide a written record. The branch of historical research involving spoken language is known as **oral history.** Columbia University initiated an oral history program in the 1940s, which includes records of interviews with thousands of individuals who supplied many hours of recollections.[21] The Oral History Association is an organization of historians interested in this type of research.[22]

Relics are a fourth type of primary source. **Relics** include any object whose physical or visual properties provide information about the past. School buildings, school furniture, architectural plans for school physical plants, textbooks, and instructional devices are examples of objects that can be studied by historians as relics of past practice.

---

21. Crawford, C. W. (1974). Oral history—the state of the profession. *Oral History Review, 2,* 1–9.
22. Oral History Association, University of Vermont, Burlington. The association has several publications, including the *Oral History Review,* published annually.

Some primary source materials can be classified as both documents and relics, depending on how they are used in a historical study. For example, in a study of the printing methods used in producing textbooks, a specific textbook would be classified as a relic. This is because one of its physical properties is being examined. On the other hand, the same textbook could be treated as a document in a study of how textbooks of different periods covered a particular topic in mathematics. Textbooks are classified as documents in this instance because the information contained in them is the focus of study. This information can be studied by various methods, including content analysis, which we described in Chapter 9.

Primary sources of historical information (e.g., diaries, manuscripts, and school records) sometimes are contained in archives (also referred to as *repositories*). **Archives** are special locations where public documents are stored, so that they can be preserved in good condition and access to them can be carefully monitored.

There are many repositories of primary sources related to education. They include university libraries and the files of various public and private organizations. Repositories vary in the ease of access they provide to primary sources. The holdings of official archives usually are well indexed, and an archivist might be available to assist a historian in conducting a research project. In other situations, historians are on their own, and therefore they must learn the filing system that was used. Records often are stored on microfilm or microfiche, which require special equipment for viewing. Some of this equipment has photocopying capability.

Researchers who wish to study an organization's quantitative data almost certainly will need to enlist the aid of a staff member to interpret them. For example, numerical data often are on printouts generated from computer software prepared specifically for the institution's needs. These data may be difficult to interpret unless a staff member explains the computer program to the researcher.

The search for primary historical sources is time-consuming but exciting, because you are dealing with the ultimate "stuff" from which history is made. Your search will be manageable if you have defined the research problem carefully and prepared a systematic search plan. Keep in mind, too, that there are preliminary sources (listed in Appendix F) that can guide you to relevant primary sources.

Recording Information from Historical Sources

In examining a primary or secondary source, the historical researcher might not know what information will prove useful at a later phase of the study. Quite possibly the interpretive phase of the study will involve searching for new facts that were not viewed as relevant earlier in the study. The problem of deciding what information to abstract from a historical source becomes even more critical when the source is not easily accessible. For example, you may need to travel to repositories where historical sources are stored. Unlike libraries, repositories usually do not allow their materials to leave the premises. Thus, you will need to decide then and there what information to record for later use.

Before deciding what information to record, you will need to deal with two preliminary issues. The first issue is whether the materials—especially primary sources—will be made accessible to you. Institutional records often are made available for study, but this does not mean that anyone can examine them. You might need to make a formal request for permission to study the records. Some documents may be inaccessible, or may be accessible for study only under certain conditions.

The other issue concerns the types of material that can be copied and reproduced in the dissertation. An institution might allow you to examine documents but not to quote directly from them; it might allow only certain portions to be copied; or it might require formal permission in order for you to quote from any document.

It is possible that you might want to reproduce documents that are considered "literary property," for example, a series of essays or speeches that could at a later time be published for profit. In this situation you need to take care not to infringe on someone's actual or potential copyright. Under the doctrine of fair use established by the U.S. Congress, you can quote short passages of a primary or secondary source without infringing copyright.

Many historical researchers routinely photocopy documents for later study. Some repositories have photocopying facilities for this purpose. Photocopying has limitations, however. It might not be possible to photocopy old historical documents, because exposure to the photocopying process could damage them. Some documents, especially newspaper clippings, do not photocopy well. Special photographic techniques might be needed to reproduce oversize documents, maps, and charts.

Scanning is an important technological advance in the copying of documents. It involves a special machine (called a *scanner*) that transforms the printed material (either words or images) into a computer file that can be stored on a floppy disk. The file can be reformatted later by word processing software and printed in hard-copy form. Also, the computer file can be coded and analyzed using computer programs of the type described in Chapter 14.

Summarizing Quantitative Data

Quantitative history is a branch of historical research that relies on numerical data and statistical methods of data analysis to study representative samples or a complete population in order to make broad, well-grounded generalizations. This approach to historical research has become more prevalent in recent years. The reason for this trend is that historical conclusions based on large amounts of carefully selected quantitative data usually are regarded as more generalizable than conclusions based on case studies. Furthermore, quantitative techniques make it easier for historians to study the "common man," that is, average citizens. In contrast, older historical studies tended to focus on a small number of men and women who held prominent positions in society. H. Warren Button commented on the emergence of the common-man approach to historical research:

> A part of the advantage of quantification in social and educational history is that it allows historians to follow a recent interest, an interest in the history of the common man—no depreciation [sic] intended—"history from the bottom up"—grassroots history. Records for history in this vein are likely to be thin and fragmentary; for coherence it is necessary to mine every source. For instance, for a quantitative study of Buxton, a black antebellum haven in Ontario, it is necessary to assemble data from perhaps fifteen thousand entries in the census manuscripts of 1861, 1871, and 1881; from town auditors' accounts, and church records.[23] The research necessity for compilation and statistical treatment, by unfortunate paradox, produces history almost without personalities, even without names. Still, this new history has and will produce new understandings and will counterweight our long-standing concern for "the better sort."[24]

◆ *Touchstone in Research*

Burton, O. V., & Finnegan, T. (1990). Teaching historians to use technology: Databases and computers. *International Journal of Social Education, 5,* 23–35.

Darcy, R., & Rohrs, R. C. (1995). *A guide to quantitative history.* Westport, CT: Greenwood.

23. Nenno, B. H. Dissertation in progress, State University of New York at Buffalo; cited in Button, 1979.
24. Button, H. W. (1979). Creating more usable pasts: History in the study of education. *Educational Researcher, 8*(5), 3–9.

A quantitative history project requires the ability to use sampling techniques, to define and measure variables, to create a research design, and to conduct statistical analyses. Therefore, if you plan to do this type of study, you should refer to the parts of this book covering quantitative research, and also to specialized works on quantitative history (see the annotated references at the end of this chapter).

In carrying out historical research involving quantitative data, you should think carefully about the kinds of data that are necessary to the investigation. Keep in mind that some quantitative information of interest to you might never have been recorded; or, if recorded, the data might be incomplete or inaccurate in critical aspects. Also, it is unwise to record whatever data you happen to come across. You might wind up with lots of data that will be time-consuming to analyze and of little value to your study's purpose.

Once the relevant data have been discovered through a search of quantitative historical records, you can analyze them using descriptive statistics. If the data were collected from samples representing defined populations, you also can do tests of statistical significance. See Chapter 5 for procedures for calculating descriptive or inferential statistics that apply to historical data.

Evaluation of Historical Sources

The ultimate value of a historical study is determined in large part by the researcher's ability to judge the authenticity and validity of the historical sources that come to light in the process of doing the study. Evaluation of the authenticity of historical sources and of the validity of the information contained in them usually is referred to as **historical criticism.** It is a complex, sophisticated process, as Jacques Barzun and Henry Graff observe:

> [Historical criticism] relies on attention to detail, on common-sense reasoning, on a developed "feel" for history and chronology, on familiarity with human behavior, and on ever enlarging stores of information. Many a "catch question" current among schoolboys calls forth these powers in rudimentary form—for instance the tale about the beautiful Greek coin just discovered and bearing the date "500 B.C." Here a second's historical reflection and reasoning is enough for verification: the "fact" is readily rejected.[25]

The following discussion of historical criticism is directed toward the evaluation of documents, although the principles that we describe apply also to the evaluation of quantitative records, oral records, and relics.

External Criticism

External criticism is the process of determining whether the apparent or claimed origin of a historical document (author, place, date, and circumstances of publication) corresponds to its actual origin. In engaging in historical criticism, the researcher asks such questions about a document as: Is it genuine? Is it the original copy? Who wrote it? Where? When? Under what conditions? Many factors must be considered in answering these questions. We can suggest only a few of them here.

A historical source might be genuine or it might be forged. A **forgery** is a fabrication claimed to be genuine, that is, the document was written by someone other than the person whose name appears as author.

♦ Touchstone in Research

Kaestle, C. (1992). Standards of evidence in educational history: How do we know when we know? *History of Education Quarterly, 32,* 361–366.

Wineburg, S. (1991). Historical problem solving: A study of the cognitive processes used in the evaluation of documentary and pictorial evidence. *Journal of Educational Psychology, 83,* 73–87.

---

25. Barzun, J., & Graff, H. F. (1992). *The modern researcher* (5th ed.). New York: Harcourt Brace Jovanovich. Quote appears on p. 99.

You never can be completely certain about the genuineness of historical sources. All you can do is generate and test alternative hypotheses about each source. For example, you can hypothesize that a particular document was written by a subordinate in the organization rather than the person designated as the author. As this and other hypotheses are shown to be untenable, you increase the probability—although never to the point of absolute certainty—that the source **is** genuine. If your evaluation of a historical source leads you to doubt its genuineness, you should note this in your research report.

The existence of variant sources can be a problem in judging the genuineness of a primary source. **Variant sources** are documents that have been altered in some way from the original document. For example, in going through the files of an educational institution, you might discover file copies (i.e., copies stored in the organization's official records) of internal memoranda that relate to the topic you are studying. However, it is possible that the file copy was not distributed in exactly that form to all its intended receivers. Perhaps the writer of a memo added a personal note to one receiver's copy of the memo. Thus, you might find a slightly different version of the memo in the receiver's files than the version in the official file. In this situation, both versions of the memo can be considered original primary sources, each of which reveals relevant, but different, information about a past event.

Variant sources present a special challenge in working with documents predating the introduction of the typewriter (circa 1880). Copies of these documents, called manuscripts, were written in longhand and often contained minor errors. In working with such a manuscript, you should make an effort to determine whether it is the only version or whether copies were made. If other copies are known to exist, you can attempt to locate them and compare their content.

Authorship of a document usually is listed on the document itself. This indicator is not always reliable, however. Some publications, especially recorded speeches, are ghostwritten by a speech writer rather than written by the person who delivers the speech. In other cases, an author will use a pseudonym to conceal his real identity. Barzun and Graff cited the example of a historian who spent 35 years in an attempt to identify the author of a series of unsigned installments in a periodical at the time of the Civil War.[26] If a document has multiple authors, it might be impossible to determine who wrote the parts of it that are of particular relevance to your study.

The place of origin of a document often is apparent from where it is stored, or from indications in the document itself. The date when it was written might be indicated on the document, or if not, the date might be ascertained from statements in the document or from its sequential location in a set of records or files. Dates on a document must be viewed critically, because people often make innocent but misleading errors. For example, at the start of a new year it is not uncommon for someone to make the mistake of entering the previous year.

Knowledge of the conditions under which a document was prepared is helpful in determining its nature and usefulness to the problem under investigation. For example, if you are studying documents from a particular institution, you should study the institution's organization chart and operating procedures. This knowledge will help you understand the purpose of certain documents and for whom they were intended. Furthermore, having this knowledge during the early stages of the study will help you limit your search to certain kinds of institutional documents.

26. Ibid., p. 107.

Internal Criticism

Internal criticism involves evaluating the accuracy and worth of the statements contained in a historical document. In engaging in internal criticism, researchers asks such questions as: Is it probable that people would act in the way described by the writer? Is it physically possible for the events described to have occurred this close together in time? Do the budget figures mentioned by the writer seem reasonable? In answering these questions, they need to be careful not to reject a statement just because the event or situation it described appears improbable. Most people can recall several highly improbable events that have occurred in their lives.

Internal criticism is more complex than external criticism because it includes the historian's judgment about the truth of the statements in a historical source and also an evaluation of the person who wrote them. For example, it is important to know whether the writer was a competent observer of the events to which she refers. Many studies in psychology have demonstrated that eye witnesses can be extremely unreliable, especially if they are emotionally aroused or under stress at the time of the event. Even under conditions in which little emotional involvement exists, some individuals are much more competent observers than others.

If the events were of a technical nature (e.g., a legal proceeding involving the dismissal of a school administrator), it would be important to know the writer's expertise relating to these events. An individual with limited expertise might be inclined to overlook or misinterpret certain details of the situation. There also is the matter of the writer's truthfulness. If the writer had a personal stake in the events being observed, he might be motivated to distort or lie about what happened.

Even if witnesses are competent and truthful, they probably still will give different versions of events that took place. One has only to read accounts of an event (e.g., a school board meeting) in different newspapers to discover how widely witnesses' perceptions can vary. This does not mean necessarily that one witness is correct and the others are wrong. Nor is the converse necessarily true: that because the majority of witnesses agree in their accounts, they are correct, and that a witness who made a different set of observations is mistaken or lying.

Should you come across widely differing accounts of an event, your reaction might be to think there is no objective historical truth, and that all accounts are equally valid or equally false. Carr questions this view: "It does not follow that, because a mountain appears to take on different shapes from different angles of vision, it has objectively either no shape at all or an infinity of shapes."[27] According to Carr, the task of the historian is to combine one or more witnesses' accounts, admittedly subjective, and to interpret them (also a subjective process) in an attempt to discover what actually happened.

Although all accounts of historical events are subjective, it does not follow that every account reflects bias. A **bias** is a set to perceive events in such a way that certain types of facts are habitually overlooked, distorted, or falsified. The person who has strong motives for wanting a particular version of a described event to be accepted usually can be expected to produce biased information. For example, suppose that you have located a school memo written by the school superintendent in which he describes a dispute that occurred between himself and members of the school board. You might suspect that this person would present his side of the argument in the most favorable light, to alter his

---

27. Carr, *What is history,* pp. 30–31.

position subconsciously to agree with facts that have become apparent since the meeting, or to omit opponents' statements that have merit.

Historians often must examine such factors as the ethnic background, political party, religious affiliation, and social status of the observer in an effort to appraise the likelihood of bias. The use of emotionally charged language, whether positive or negative, is one sign of commitment to a particular position on an issue.

Many biased reports of events can be traced to people's tendency to make a story more dramatic or to exaggerate their role in events. Biased reports also can occur when the social or political position of individuals requires them to make socially acceptable statements, even if they do not honestly feel that way. For example, a school principal we know was questioned about internal difficulties with particular teachers and classified staff at her school. The principal made claims about high staff morale and cohesiveness at her school. Such claims probably were made to avoid compounding the problem and to guard against putting the speaker in a negative light. For similar reasons, some people in public life prefer to make conciliatory statements about their political opponents, even when such statements have little or no relation to their true feelings. Recently the opposite trend has emerged in political campaigns, that is, a tendency to "blast" one's opponent regardless of the verifiability of one's statements.

If you find a discrepancy between someone's public and private statements, this does not necessarily mean that the public statements have no value as historical evidence. Rather, the discrepancy itself is evidence about the person making the statement, and about the social environment in which she functioned.

Interpretation in Historical Research

The Historian as Interpreter

In discussing internal criticism, we noted that witnesses to an event will report different impressions based on their competence, personal position, and relationship to an event. According to Carr, the historian is in a similar situation:

> The facts are really not at all like fish on the fishmonger's slab. They are like fish swimming about in a vast and sometimes inaccessible ocean; and what the historian catches will depend partly on chance, but mainly on what part of the ocean he chooses to fish in and what tackle he chooses to use—these two factors being, of course, determined by the kind of fish he wants to catch. By and large, the historian will get the kind of facts he wants. History means interpretation.[28]

If you choose to do historical research, you will need to become aware of your own values, beliefs, and interests concerning the topic that you are investigating because they allow you to "see" certain aspects of past events and not others. As you become aware of your own interpretive framework, you also will have increased sensitivity to the possible interpretive leanings of other historians who have conducted research on the same or similar topics.

Because history involves interpretation, historians constantly are rewriting the past as their interests and concerns change. The last few decades of historical research in education have seen the emergence of revisionist historians (also known as *reconstructionist historians*). These researchers take a different view of educational history than the conventional or popular view. They believe that some past educational practices reflect par-

28. Ibid., p. 26.

ticular political, economic, or other social forces and motivations rather than rationality, good will, or pedagogical considerations:

> [Reconstructionist] Historians of education are questioning stereotyped notions of the words *reform* and *progressive* and are thinking in terms of the *irony* of school reform. Historians of education are now ready to examine the public schools as instruments of social control. Historians of education are now disclosing phenomena long hidden by official pieties: the maltreatment of immigrants and ethnic groups, the discriminatory treatment of women and minority groups, the connections between schools and politics and between education and social stratification.[29]

In Chapter 15 we discussed cultural studies, which is similar to revisionist history. Both have a critical orientation toward much educational practice, and they seek historical explanations for many practices that are viewed as negative or problematic.

In contrast to the reconstructionists, historians who conducted educational research before the 1960s tended to examine the past for evidence of how American education contributed to the improvement of our society and students' lives. Another common tendency of educational historians up until recent times was discussed by Bernard Bailyn in a landmark historical study published in 1960.[30] Bailyn observed that until that time most historians of American education had interpreted education predominantly as a process of formal schooling. He urged historians to overcome this bias so that they could view education "not only as formal pedagogy but as the entire process by which a culture transmits itself across the generations."[31] Partly as a result of Bailyn's influence, educational historians have enlarged their perspective to conduct research on many nonschool influences that affect the socialization and learning of young people and adults.

In interpreting their data, historians need to be careful to avoid a type of bias known as presentism. **Presentism** is the interpretation of past events using concepts and perspectives that originated in more recent times. For example, there has been much interest recently in a phenomenon referred to as school choice. In our local community (Eugene, Oregon), school choice means that parents can send their children to any public school in the district, not only to the one nearest their home; furthermore, there are a variety of alternative, or "magnet," schools among which parents can choose. In other communities, school choice has taken the form of proposals to provide tuition vouchers to parents who opt to send their children to private schools instead of to state-supported public schools. The historical researcher who is interested in this phenomenon might look for evidence of how earlier educators gave parents choices about their children's education. These earlier educators might have used a term similar to *school choice,* but it might have meant something quite different then—for example, whether school attendance should be compulsory or voluntary. Therefore, the historian needs to discover how various concepts were used in their own time and settings, rather than attach present meaning to them.

Use of Concepts to Interpret Historical Information

As in other types of qualitative research, researchers doing historical research develop concepts to organize and interpret the data that they have collected. **Concepts** are terms that can be used to group individuals, events, or objects that share a common set of attributes. For example, without a concept such as *progressive education,* a great many

---

29. Cohen, *History of the history,* p. 329.
30. Bailyn, B. (1970; reprint of 1960 ed.). *Education in the forming of American society: Need and opportunities for study.* Chapel Hill, NC: University of North Carolina Press.
31. Ibid., p. 14.

historical phenomena that share common characteristics might be seen as separate and lacking in significance.

Concepts, however, also place limits on the historical researcher's interpretation of the past. For example, a researcher conducting a historical study of teaching might assume that the defining attribute of the concept of *teaching* is "paid work done by someone who holds a state certificate signifying completion of a college-level teacher education program." This definition of teaching will cause the researcher to study certain individuals from a certain historical period but exclude others—for example, teacher aides, school volunteers, resource personnel—who would be considered to be teaching if a different definition of the concept were used.

We see, then, that you need to use care in selecting and defining the concepts you use in historical research. At the least, you should determine the definition of each concept to determine whether it applies to the historical phenomena you wish to study. If necessary, you should provide definitions of important concepts in your research report. Many educational terms have become part of the everyday vernacular (e.g., intelligence, test, curriculum), but if you define such terms it will be clear to readers what they mean in the particular context of your research study.

Recent historical research has made much use of concepts from other disciplines. T. C. R. Horn and Harry Ritter made the following observation about this development:

> In general, the trend has been to look primarily to the "social sciences"—sociology, economics, political science, psychology, and anthropology—for new ideas, and lately to statistics and mathematics; to a lesser degree, historians have turned to "humanistic" disciplines such as language studies, poetics, literary criticism, and philosophy.[32]

Horn and Ritter found that all the historical studies that had won major prizes in a recent year drew upon conceptual frameworks from other disciplines.

Interdisciplinary concepts are useful tools. However, you should be familiar with how these concepts are defined in the discipline from which they originate to ensure that they are used appropriately in your study. For example, in applying the concept of *bureaucracy* to the public school system that developed in the United States during the mid-nineteenth century, Michael Katz defined it with reference to the definition set forth by Carl Friedrich, a sociologist.[33]

Causal Inference in Historical Research

An essential task of historical research consists of investigating the main causes of past events. As Carr states, "The study of history is a study of causes."[34] Examples of causal questions that guide many historical studies are: What were the forces and events that gave rise to the intelligence-testing movement? Why did U.S. educators adopt so readily the British open-classroom approach several decades ago? How did the role of school principal originate in this country?

Causal inference in historical research is the process of reaching the conclusion that one set of events brought about, directly or indirectly, a subsequent set of events. Historians cannot prove that one past event caused another, but they can make explicit the assumptions that underlie their attributions of causality in sequences of historical events.

32. Horn, T. C. R., & Ritter, H. (1986). Interdisciplinary history: A historiographical review. *The History Teacher, 19,* 427.
33. Katz, M. B. (1987). *Reconstructing American education.* Cambridge, MA: Harvard University Press.
34. Carr, *What is history?,* p. 113.

Some historians make the assumption that humans act similarly across cultures and across time. Thus, they might use a currently accepted causal pattern to explain an apparently similar pattern in the past. For example, a historian might find an instance in nineteenth-century U.S. education when students at a particular college stopped attending classes and started attacking the school's administration. Say that the historian also discovered that this event was preceded by administrative rulings at the college that diminished students' rights and privileges. The historian might infer—perhaps correctly—that these rulings led to the student revolt, his reasoning being that a similar chain of events precipitated student protests in many U.S. colleges in the 1960s.

Historians generally believe, however, that historical events are unique. Most would argue that history does not repeat itself. Thus occurrences at one point in time can be used to illuminate, but not to explain, occurrences at another point in time. Even historians who see past occurrences as a guide to later events must be wary of presentism, which we described above as interpreting events from an earlier time period in terms of concepts having different meanings at a later time period.

Historians have emphasized various types of causes in their attempts to explain past events. They have attributed significant historical occurrences to the actions of certain key persons (the "great man" view of history), to the operation of powerful ideologies, to advances in science and technology, or to economic, geographical, sociological, or psychological factors.

Some historians take an eclectic view and explain past events in terms of a combination of factors. David Tyack's study of compulsory education illustrates well this view of causal patterns in past phenomena.[35] Tyack observed that the rise of compulsory education is a remarkable part of U.S. educational history:

> I see two major phases in the history of compulsory school attendance in the United States. During the first, which lasted from [the] mid-nineteenth century to about 1890, Americans built a broad base of elementary schooling which attracted ever-growing numbers of children. Most states passed compulsory attendance legislation during these years, but generally these laws were unenforced and probably unenforceable. The notion of compulsion appears to have aroused ideological dispute at this time, but few persons paid serious attention to the organizational apparatus necessary to compel students into classrooms. Therefore, this phase might be called the *symbolic* stage. The second phase, beginning shortly before the turn of the twentieth century, might be called the *bureaucratic* stage. During this era of American education, school systems grew in size and complexity, new techniques of bureaucratic control emerged, ideological conflict over compulsion diminished, strong laws were passed, and school officials developed sophisticated techniques to bring truants into schools. By the 1920s and 1930s increasing numbers of states were requiring youth to attend high school, and by the 1950s secondary school attendance had become so customary that school-leavers were routinely seen as dropouts.[36]

The question arises, Why did schooling in the United States gradually become compulsory under force of law? Tyack examined five causal interpretations to see how well each answered this question. For example, the ethnocultural interpretation argues that compulsory education came about because of the belief that it would inculcate a single "correct" standard of behavior, especially among the nineteenth-century immigrants from southern and eastern Europe who were provoking much concern among certain religious and ethnic groups already established in this country. Another interpretation, drawn from the economic theory

---

35. Tyack, D. B. (1976). Ways of seeing: An essay on the history of compulsory schooling. *Harvard Educational Review, 46*, 55–89.
36. Ibid., p. 60.

of human capital, states that compulsory schooling grew out of a belief that education would improve the productivity and predictability of the work force. In the words of the noted educator Horace Mann, education is "the most prolific parent of material riches."[37]

Each of Tyack's five interpretations explains some of the historical evidence, leaves other evidence unexplained, and suggests new lines of research. In Tyack's view, alternative interpretations help the historian "to gain a more complex and accurate perception of the past and a greater awareness of the ambiguous relationship between outcome and intent—both of the actors in history and of the historians who attempt to recreate their lives."[38]

The more we learn about the antecedents of a historical event, the more likely we are to discover possible alternative causes of the event. Therefore, it probably is more defensible to identify an antecedent event as *a* cause rather than *the* cause. Moreover, historians, by their choice of language, can convey their interpretation of the certainty of the causal link ("It is highly likely that . . . " or "It is possible that . . . ") and the strength of the causal link ("It was a major influence . . . " or "It was one of many events that influenced . . . ").

Generalizing from Historical Evidence

Like other qualitative researchers, historians cannot study the entire population of individuals, settings, events, and objects that interest them. Instead, they usually study only one case or a few instances of the phenomenon of interest. The case that is chosen is determined partly by the availability of sources. For example, suppose a historian studied the diaries, correspondence, and other written records of elementary school teachers in the 1800s in order to understand teaching conditions during that time. The study necessarily will be limited to teachers whose writings have been preserved, and to which the historian can gain access. The historian needs to keep in mind, too, that teachers who were interested in making written records of their work may not be typical of teachers in general. One way to determine whether similar results would be found for other types of teachers is to examine how teachers in different circumstances viewed their teaching experience. For example, teachers who wrote about their work for publication describe similar conditions as teachers who wrote about their work in private diaries and correspondence?

Another potential problem in historical interpretation involves the generalizability of historical data related to a single individual. For example, the historian might come across a document in which an educator expressed an opinion about a particular educational issue. This does not mean that the educator held the same opinion at a later or earlier time. The historian needs to look for more data that will help her decide whether the expressed opinion was characteristic of this educator.

As in any research project, historical research findings are strengthened by increasing the size of the data set on which they are based. Therefore, it is advisable to conduct an extensive search for primary and secondary sources relating to the topic. If the evidence is limited to only a few sources, researchers should exercise restraint in the generality of their interpretations. For example, it may be necessary to make a statement like, "Teachers in rural schools of 50 or fewer students during the period 1860 to 1870 . . . " rather than "Teachers during the period 1860 to 1870 . . . " Quantitative history, which we described earlier in the chapter, is better suited than traditional historical research for making the latter generalization.

37. Ibid., p. 79.
38. Ibid., p. 89.

Writing a Historical Research Dissertation

Reports of historical research do not have a standard format. The particular problem or topic being investigated and the historian's disciplinary orientation (e.g., feminist, literary, psychological) determines how the presentation of findings will be organized.

One obvious method of organization is to present the historical facts in chronological order. Thus, each chapter of the dissertation might cover a discrete period of time in the life of an individual, in the history of an institution, or in an educational movement. The other obvious method of organization is to present the historical facts according to topic or theme. For example, if the purpose of the study was to examine how different school districts came to establish a kindergarten program, the dissertation might have a separate chapter for each school district included in the study.

For some studies, however, neither of the above methods of organization is satisfactory. Suppose the researcher's purpose is to describe the development of a particular university. The researcher could organize the dissertation chronologically, with each chapter devoted to a different time period. But such an approach might obscure certain themes that have continuity across time periods (e.g., the development of the university's relationship to the state government as a prime research contractor, the growth of the university's graduate school, and the construction and revision of the university's undergraduate curriculum). Thematic continuity could be achieved by having a separate chapter for each aspect of the university's development, but, then, a sense of the institution's unity and overall state of development at particular points in time would be lost. Also, it would be difficult for the researcher to show how various aspects of the university's development influenced and related to one another.

A possible solution to this problem is to combine the chronological and thematic approaches. Each chapter might cover a discrete time period, but the internal organization of the chapters could be thematic. Ultimately, the decision to use a particular organizational approach depends upon the questions that the historical researcher has chosen to ask.

The majority of the dissertation probably will consist of discussion of the researcher's interpretations of the data obtained through a search of preliminary, secondary, and primary sources. In addition, the researcher might wish to have a separate chapter that reviews other historians' interpretations of the same or similar phenomena. The methodology used in the study, that is, its historiography, might be described in a separate chapter, especially if the historical sources posed unusual problems of external or internal criticism or if the historian employed unusual or controversial historiography.

The wording must be considered carefully in writing the dissertation because choice of words reflects the researcher's interpretive framework. We noted above, for example, how the use of certain words can convey differences in the presumed probability of a causal relationship between past events. Adjectives have particular interpretive significance. Suppose that the researcher decides to describe a particular institution as a *major* university. The use of this adjective is interpretive, but does it reflect the researcher's own admiration of the institution or the expert judgment of other educators? The researcher needs to think carefully about the reasons for using this particular word in describing the research study. Concepts and descriptions with strong affective or value connotations need not be avoided, but they should be substantiated by indicating the sources on which they are based, as well as the researcher's reasoning that led to their use. With such grounding, colorful terms rescue a historical research dissertation from dullness and help it meet its responsibility to reconstruct the past so that it comes alive for the reader.

Examples of Historical Research in Education

To illustrate the steps involved in carrying out historical research, we describe two historical studies below. They are meant only to provide an introduction to the design of historical research, which you should supplement through your own search for historical sources.

The Development of Japanese Educational Policy

As we stated earlier in the chapter, current social issues often provide the stimulus for historical studies in education. Such was the case in Edward Beauchamp's study of changes
in Japanese educational policy between 1945 and 1985.[39] Beauchamp began his report by
observing:

> The appointment of an Ad Hoc Reform Council, or *Rinkyoshin,* on 21 August 1984 was a logi-
> cal culmination to a lengthy period of concern in Japan over a set of widely perceived edu-
> cational problems and the future prospects for Japanese education. The charge given to the
> council by Prime Minister Yasuhiro Nakasone was clear: "to consider basic strategies for
> necessary reforms . . . so as to secure such education as will be compatible with the social
> changes and cultural developments of our country."[40]

By studying past educational reforms in Japan, Beauchamp provides us with a basis for understanding that country's current problems in education and the directions that reform
might take.

The primary data for the study were key policy and legal documents issued by governmental agencies during the last century. The documents examined by Beauchamp included the 1890 *Imperial Rescript on Education* issued by Emperor Meiji; the *Fundamental
Law of Education and the School Education Law of 1947;* the *Report on the Long-Range Educational Plan Oriented toward the Doubling of Income* issued by the Economic Council of
Japan's Economic Planning Agency in 1960; the Ministry of Education's *Educational Standards in Japan,* published in 1970; and a report issued by the Organization for Economic
Cooperation and Development in 1971. Beauchamp also referred to secondary sources
containing information about and interpretations of Japanese education.

The primary method for organizing the data was chronological. This method of organization is reflected in the report's headings: *Japanese Education, 1868–1945; The Occupation of Japan, 1945–52; The Post-Occupation Period, 1952–60; Expansion in the 1960s and
1970s;* and *The Third Major Reform Period, 1978–Present.* Beauchamp organized policy developments that occurred during each of these time periods thematically. The primary
theme was policy aimed at different levels of schooling—elementary, secondary, and postsecondary. An interesting feature of Beauchamp's report is his analysis of how changes in
policy rippled through each of these school levels.

The key concepts used by Beauchamp to make sense of changes in Japanese education over time are *reform* and *policy,* two concepts that were widely used in discussions of
U.S. education at the time of Beauchamp's research. We need to ask, however, whether the
meaning ascribed to these terms in the United States applies to Japanese education. For
example, the concept of *reform* implies a need to correct perceived weaknesses in an educational system, and that such weaknesses are serious enough to require radical changes
in the system. It is not clear from Beauchamp's report whether the changes in Japanese education that he highlights as significant had these qualities.

39. Beauchamp, E. R. (1987). The development of Japanese educational policy, 1945–1985. *History of Education
    Quarterly, 27,* 299–324.
40. Ibid., p. 299.

The concept of *policy* is even more problematic. Just what is a policy? Beauchamp's primary data were government documents, which could be considered official statements of policy. In the United States, however, there often are important differences between official statements of policy and the manner in which such policy actually is implemented. Stated policy (e.g., as stated in school board directives or adopted curriculum guides) often is ignored or modified in practice by those to whom the policy is directed. Beauchamp did not address the issue of whether the same differences might exist between stated policy statements and policy-in-action in Japanese education.

Another point to consider is that members of commissions or governing bodies who prepare the type of documents analyzed by Beauchamp often disagree strongly among themselves. The final policy document often is a compromise statement that masks conflicts among members representing different interest groups. An analysis of these conflicts might reveal more about the status of policy in an educational system than would an official public document. However, such criticisms do not necessarily invalidate Beauchamp's conclusions. Our intent is to demonstrate the importance of carefully analyzing the key concepts used to interpret historical data, especially when the data pertain to another culture.

We stated earlier in the chapter that a major purpose of historical research is to identify the cause-and-effect patterns in past events. This purpose is reflected throughout Beauchamp's report, as in this statement:

> Educational policy during the 1960s and much of the 1970s was consciously designed to foster economic development. Indeed, there is little doubt that since the middle of the 1950s the interests of industry have been extremely influential in shaping educational policy.[41]

Beauchamp's argument in this statement is that lobbying by industry (cause) was a major influence on the development of educational policy (effect) during the time period being studied. Various types of evidence are presented in the report to support this causal interpretation.

Beauchamp also attempted to explain the persistence of Japan's extremely demanding entrance examinations for college, despite the fact that they are criticized by many Japanese. He found evidence to support three different explanations for their persistence: "(1) a deeply ingrained Confucian legacy; (2) powerful vested interests; and (3) too few places for too many applicants."[42] Beauchamp's interpretation demonstrates the principle that significant social phenomena often have multiple causes as well as multiple effects. Therefore, historians need to study as much of the historical context as possible in order to avoid oversimplifying their analysis of cause-and-effect relationships in past events.

One of Beauchamp's generalizations is that each major reform in Japanese education over the past century was followed by a period of reflection and subsequent modification to bring it in line with traditional Japanese values. Therefore, in attempting to understand Japan's recent reform efforts, we would be well advised to learn as much as possible about that country's values.

Another of Beauchamp's generalizations is that each reform was influenced by foreign educational models. Beauchamp was careful to note, however, that this generalization is not likely to apply equally to more recent waves of educational reform in Japan. The reason is that all the countries to which Japan looked for models in the past are themselves engaged

---

41. Ibid., p. 310.
42. Ibid., p. 315.

in major educational reform efforts of various kinds. This discontinuity in a historical pattern raised for Beauchamp a significant question:

> Can the Japanese *create* a new model which will not only meet their needs in the twenty-first century, but will also serve as a model from which the rest of the world might learn?[43]

Historical research usually is thought of as the study of the past. Beauchamp's study illustrates that historical research is much more than this. The study of Japan's past educational policies provides a valuable basis for understanding its more recent policy-making activities, for making predictions about the outcomes of these activities, and for suggesting the significance of these activities for policy makers in other countries.

How Urban School Systems Became Bureaucracies: The Boston Case, 1850–1884

According to Katz, traditional historians of education portrayed the development of America's educational system as "a simple narrative of the triumph of benevolence and democracy."[44] By contrast, revisionist historians like Katz re-examine the past to bring to light the darker side of American education. His research has focused on clarifying how the development of America's public school system contributed to "the legitimation of inequality" among its clients.[45] In Katz's view, the public school system has "played an important, if indeterminate role among the panoply of mechanisms that have secured the loyalty of citizens to a competitive system in which, by and large, they have been losers."[46]

Katz's book *Reconstructing American Education* includes a case study that illustrates the approach and aims of revisionist historians. It is an account of how the bureaucratic structure of schools developed in the Boston school district over a particular period of time (1850–1884), although Katz generalizes his findings by referring to parallel phenomena in other districts and time periods. The purpose of the study was to show how the development of American education as a particular kind of bureaucracy "clarifies some of the internal politics of education, helps explain the uneasy relations between schools and communities, and points to the basis of enduring dilemmas for would-be reform."[47] The central characters in the historical account are school superintendents, reformers, and school boards—each having separate, conflicting agendas. The resolution of their conflicts, as Katz demonstrates, gave rise to a particular bureaucratic structure that enables schools to achieve certain goals (e.g., efficiency and order), but blocks others (e.g., community input and the fostering of student individuality, creativity, and equality).

Katz reports the case study chronologically, but within an interpretive framework that focuses on power struggles among various constituencies and their apparently antidemocratic agendas. The chronology of events and interpretive framework are clearly conveyed through the following headings, which introduce the sections of the report:

The Emergence of Bureaucracy

Critics of Education: The New School Board in Boston and the Firing of John Dudley Philbrick

Critics of Bureaucracy: The Attack on the Grammar School Masters

The Defense of Bureaucracy: The Masters Counterattack

The Triumph of Informal Organization: The Victory of the Masters

---

43. Ibid., p. 324.
44. Katz, *Reconstructing American education*, p. 5.
45. Ibid., p. 116.
46. Ibid.
47. Ibid., p. 58.

Katz's focus on the struggle among competing groups (attack, counterattack, triumph) helps the reader develop a feeling for the issues and social forces operating during this period and imagine what might be at stake in our own era. The focus on conflict among competing forces supports Katz's view that the structure of schools and other institutions "originated as choices among alternative solutions to problems of public policy."[48] In other words, there is nothing inevitable about the structure of schools as we know them today. Their structure was shaped by disputes among particular individuals in particular settings at a particular time in U.S. history.

As other historians do, Katz drew from another social science discipline—in this case, sociology—for concepts to help him understand his data. In his report he explained the six features of a bureaucracy, as defined by the sociologist Carl Friedrich: centralization of control and supervision, differentiation of function, qualification for office, objectivity, precision and consistency, and discretion. Then he proceeded to demonstrate that "All of these elements of bureaucracy emerged in Boston during the third quarter of the nineteenth century."[49] Katz was able to draw from the discipline of sociology to derive a clear definition of "bureaucracy," and to search for relevant historical data in order to determine whether the Boston school district's structure included the attributes of a bureaucracy as specified by this definition.

Although Katz's report is primarily narrative, there is one extensive table of quantitative data. He used these data to support his arguments about how the Boston school district evolved into a bureaucracy between two points in time, 1850 and 1876. For example, the table shows that the school-age population increased from 24,275 to 66,720 between 1850 and 1876, and that the number of teachers increased from 339 to 1,294 during the same period. Katz used these data to support his conclusion that "the most fundamental problem facing school systems was the increasing complexity of administering urban education" because of a large work force and a "growing, increasingly dense, and heterogeneous [student] population."[50]

Much of Katz's report reads as a story of the events and personalities that shaped the development of Boston's school bureaucracy. The writing is made lively through the use of vivid description. For example, we learn that John Dudley Philbrick acted "forcefully" to discredit the Board of Supervisors; that the schoolmasters reacted to Philbrick's subsequent firing with "submerged anger"; that Burke Hinsdale was "shrewd and realistic"; and that Francis Parker was "ebullient, charismatic, and a thoroughgoing individualist." Katz also documents and dramatizes key points by referring to primary source data. For example, to illustrate the strong criticisms of the schools' emerging bureaucratic structure by reformers of that time, Katz quotes from the writings of the journalist and novelist, Gail Hamilton (the pen name of Mary Abigail Dodge):

> The school system of Massachusetts, with all its supervision and all its superintendence, and all its expensiveness, is so ineffective, it so magnifies and nourishes itself, and so neglects, not to say dwarfs, the pupils, that a child may go through the whole course from primary to high school inclusive without a single absence or tardiness and receive his diploma of graduation, and come out thoroughly illiterate, absolutely uneducated, absolutely untrained—with no accomplishment except slang, with no taste above dime novels, with neither brain nor nerve nor muscle braced for the battle of life. . . . The taxes of the people go to fatten "organization" and the children suffer.[51]

48. Ibid., p. 1.
49. Ibid., pp. 60–61.
50. Ibid., p. 66.
51. Ibid., p. 73.

In all, Katz documents his historical facts and interpretations with 96 notes referring to primary sources (published writings by educators of that period, newspaper articles, school district reports, etc.) and secondary sources (mainly, other histories of that period).

Katz attempts to establish several causal patterns in his historical data. This is most apparent in his discussion of why individuals who attempted to reform Boston's school system in the latter half of the 1850s ultimately were unsuccessful. Katz argues that

> [The reformist faction] failed through its insensitivity to the nature of organization. In this case the reformers failed to reckon with the power of entrenched informal groups within the system itself.[52]

Readers of the report can decide for themselves how well Katz makes his case that school administrators' solidarity "caused" the failure of school reform.

As we read Katz's account of American education during the period from 1850 to 1884, the controversies and attempted solutions that he describes seem eerily like those that we face today, over a hundred years later. We are led to wonder, as Katz does, whether "By ignoring history, we have replicated the same unsuccessful reform strategies over and over again."[53] A major contribution of historical research—including that done in a revisionist spirit—is to make us aware of these unsuccessful replications so that we can liberate ourselves from them and thus be free to explore new alternatives.

52. Ibid., p. 83.
53. Ibid., p. 134.

♦ RECOMMENDATIONS FOR *Doing Historical Research*

1. In selecting a problem to investigate, check whether you will be able to access the necessary primary and secondary sources.
2. Instead of relying exclusively on secondary sources, try to confirm and extend your findings by checking relevant primary sources.
3. Subject your historical data to external and internal criticism.
4. Consider whether and how your personal values and interests influenced your selection and interpretation of historical data.
5. Avoid presentism in interpreting events from another historical era.
6. Even if your interpretations focus on a single cause of an historical phenomenon, consider the possibility that other factors also might have influenced it.
7. Keep in the limits that your data impose on the generalizations you wish to make about a historical phenomenon.
8. In reporting your historical facts and interpretations, organize them into meaningful chronological and thematic patterns.

✔ Self-Check Test

Circle the correct answer to each of the following questions.
The answers are at the back of the book.

1. In historical research, the written and printed materials recorded for the purpose of preserving information about historical phenomena are called
   a. documents and records.
   b. artifacts and relics.
   c. secondary sources.
   d. preliminary sources.

2. In historical research, physical objects preserved from the period being studied are called
   a. primary documents.
   b. secondary documents.
   c. secondary sources.
   d. relics.

3. In historical research, the literature review
   a. is a relatively minor part of the research process.
   b. provides the research data.
   c. is conducted after the data-collection stage.
   d. all of the above.

4. The procedure for determining whether a source of historical data is genuine is termed
   a. internal criticism.
   b. external criticism.
   c. external validation.
   d. causal inference.

5. Internal criticism of a document
   a. focuses on the information that it contains.
   b. includes an evaluation of the writer's motives and values.
   c. is assisted by obtaining other accounts of the same events.
   d. all of the above.

6. Presentism is defined as
   a. the belief that the present is more important than the historical past.
   b. the use of contemporary concepts to interpret past events.
   c. the belief that the present cannot be understood by the study of past events.
   d. the set of assumptions underlying revisionist history.

7. Causal inference in historical research is a process by which a historian
   a. narrows the cause of a historical phenomenon to one set of factors.
   b. uses internal criticism to establish causal links between documents written at different points in time.
   c. uses interpretation to ascribe causality to a sequence of historical events.
   d. relies on theories from other disciplines to infer causal patterns.

8. Reports of historical research
   a. usually are organized chronologically.
   b. usually are organized thematically.
   c. can be organized either chronologically or thematically.
   d. are organized in the same way as reports of experimental research.

9. Bernard Bailyn's book about the meaning of the concept of education as it applies to learning within American society contributed to historical research by
   a. including nonschool influences on learning as legitimate topics for historical research in education.
   b. originating the "liberal reform" framework for re-interpreting historical events in education.
   c. originating a new theory of causal inference in historical research.
   d. making historical sources less susceptible to external criticism.

10. Quantitative analysis of historical data is useful for
    a. determining the generalizability of historical findings.
    b. studying the lives of common individuals.
    c. the study of large samples of populations.
    d. all of the above.

PART VI

✦ Applications of Research

Educational researchers generally conduct studies for the purpose of description or prediction, or to test the effects of an intervention. The ultimate goal of their efforts is the development of theories that explain educational phenomena.

The methods developed by researchers for these purposes also are applicable to educational evaluation. For example, educators who are funded by governmental agencies to develop innovative programs typically must conduct evaluations to answer such questions as whether the programs are cost-effective, better than available alternatives, and acceptable to different stakeholder groups. Their goal in doing evaluation research, then, is to make judgments of worth, value, and utility about specific programs rather than to develop encompassing theories.

You will find in Chapter 17 how various research methods described in earlier chapters can be applied to educational evaluation. You also will find that evaluation research involves distinctive questions and issues that do not arise in other types of educational research.

Research methods also find application in action research, which involves investigations by practitioners to improve their own effectiveness or that of the organization in which they work. Unlike academic research, action research tends to be less formal and less generalizable. However, it has the considerable advantage that the research-into-practice gap is much smaller, because practitioners formulate their own research problem and collect data in their immediate work site. Chapter 18 describes the various procedures for doing an action-research project and the ethical issues that must be considered.

CHAPTER 17

✦ Evaluation Research

OVERVIEW

Evaluation research is important to policy makers, program managers, and curriculum developers. This chapter discusses the steps involved in doing an evaluation study. We emphasize procedures for involving various stakeholders throughout the evaluation process. We also describe criteria for judging the quality of an evaluation study, and the major quantitative and qualitative approaches to evaluation. The chapter concludes with a discussion of the role of evaluation research in educational research and development (R & D), which is a research-based approach to developing new programs and materials to improve education.

OBJECTIVES

After studying this chapter, you should be able to

1. Describe the major uses of educational evaluation.
2. State the major differences between evaluation research and other types of educational research.
3. Describe procedures for clarifying the reasons for doing a particular evaluation study and identifying stakeholders.
4. Describe procedures for delineating the components of the program to be analyzed.
5. Explain the difference between the divergent phase and the convergent phase in selecting questions to be answered by an evaluation study.
6. Identify several factors that are involved in creating an evaluation design, but not a research design.
7. Describe procedures for collecting and analyzing evaluation data.

8. Explain how the reporting of an evaluation study typically differs from the reporting of a research study.
9. State the major quantitative approaches to evaluation, and describe the primary characteristics of each.
10. State the major qualitative approaches to evaluation, and describe the primary characteristics of each.
11. Describe the steps of the educational R & D cycle.
12. State two benefits of using behavioral objectives in educational R & D.
13. Describe several advantages and disadvantages of doing an educational R & D project as your thesis or dissertation study compared to a more basic type of research study.

✦ *Touchstone in Research*

Baker, E. L., & Niemi, D. (1996). School and program evaluation. In D. C. Berliner & R. C. Calfee (Eds.), *Handbook of educational psychology* (pp. 926–944). New York: Macmillan.

Rossi, P. H., Freeman, H. E., & Lipsey, M. W. (1999). *Evaluation: A systematic approach* (6th ed.). Thousand Oaks, CA: Sage.

Introduction

Educational evaluation is the process of making judgments about the merit, value, or worth of educational programs. (We use the term *program* in this chapter as a generic label for the various phenomena—methods, materials, organizations, individuals, etc.—that are the focus of educational evaluation. This type of inquiry has grown remarkably since 1965, when the U.S. government mandated that all educational programs receiving federal funding must spend a portion of those funds on program evaluation.[1] Several research and development centers in the United States focus on the investigation of evaluation methodology,[2] and several social science journals specialize in evaluation.[3] Many school districts have established departments of evaluation, and a large number of educational researchers have moved into the field of evaluation research because of the widespread demand for evaluation services.

Why has educational evaluation attracted so much interest? The main reason is that public administrators have come to view evaluation as an important tool in policy analysis and program management.

With respect to policy analysis, evaluation research yields important data about the costs, benefits, and problems of various program alternatives.[4] Policy analysts can use these data to prepare position papers, which are then reviewed by persons with decision-making authority, such as politicians and government officials. The importance of this type of evaluation research is demonstrated by the fact that in 1979 the American Educational Research Association initiated a journal called *Educational Evaluation and Policy Analysis*.

With respect to the political process, evaluation findings are used to create advocacy for particular legislation and budget appropriations. Opponents of such legislation in turn may sponsor their own evaluations to generate evidence favoring their cause. We need only think of the data cited by proponents and opponents of state-mandated testing of all students, site-based management, and other educational movements to realize that evaluation has become closely involved in the political process. Quasi-legal approaches to evaluation, discussed later in the chapter, exemplify the political orientation of evaluation.

Finally, evaluation research is becoming an increasingly important component of program management. For example, cost-benefit evaluations (also called "efficiency evaluations") are done to determine whether programs are producing benefits that justify their costs. Another use of evaluations is to hold managers accountable for producing results. Evaluations also are done to help managers make sound decisions related to program design, personnel, and budget.

The Relationship between Evaluation and Research

Are evaluation studies the same as research? Is an educational researcher qualified to fill a position involving program evaluation? Our answer to the first question would be: They are both similar and different. To the second question: Yes, but an educational researcher probably would need to acquire additional training.

---

1. McLaughlin, M. W. (1975). *Evaluation and reform: The Elementary and Secondary Education Act of 1965/Title I.* Cambridge, MA: Ballinger.
2. For example: the National Center for Research on Evaluation, Standards, and Student Testing (CRESST) at UCLA, and the Evaluation Center at Western Michigan University.
3. See, for example, *Evaluation Review, Educational Evaluation and Policy Analysis,* and *Evaluation and Program Planning.*
4. The role of evaluation research in policy analysis is explained in: Fowler, F. C. (2000). *Policy studies for educational leaders: An introduction.* Upper Saddle River, NJ: Merrill.

The generally accepted view is that educational research and educational evaluation overlap to a great extent. In practice, evaluators make substantial use of the research designs, measurement tools, and data analysis techniques that constitute the methodology of educational research. For this reason, we refer to evaluation studies as *evaluation research*. Yet there are important differences between evaluation and other types of research in their purpose. We will describe three of these differences here.

First, an evaluation study usually is initiated by someone's need for a *decision* to be made concerning policy, management, or political strategy. The purpose of the evaluation study is to collect data that will facilitate this decision. By contrast, the purpose of a research study, broadly stated, is to develop an understanding of a particular phenomenon. Of course, the findings of a research study also can be used to guide decision making; and evaluation data can be relevant to developing an understanding of a particular phenomenon.

The second difference between research and evaluation is in the extent to which the findings are generalized. Evaluation typically is done for a very specific purpose. Decision makers might be interested in how well their particular program works, and thus they commission a site-specific evaluation study to collect data relevant to their special concerns. By contrast, researchers are more likely to be interested in discovering generalizable relationships among variables or in discovering the meaning that individuals or groups ascribe to social reality. They might use a particular group of educators or students in their study, but they typically view them as samples of larger populations to which the findings will be generalized, or as the basis for generalizing to a theory. Again, the difference is not pure: Some evaluation studies are designed to yield widely generalizable findings, and some basic research has limited generalizability.

The third difference between evaluation and research involves judgments of value. Evaluation studies are designed to yield data concerning the worth, merit, or value of educational phenomena. Their findings tend to be stated in such phrases as "This reading program is superior to the other program with respect to . . . " or "The teachers in this district thought that this new approach to in-service training was superior to the existing approach because . . . " Researchers, however, design their studies to discover the essential characteristics of educational phenomena. Their findings tend to be couched in such phrases as "It appears that variable X has an influence on variable Y," or "Using a grounded theory approach, we discovered that counselors attribute at-risk students' behavior to two types of motivation." Educators may make value judgments and decisions based on such research findings, but this is a secondary use of the findings.

The next section of the chapter describes procedures for conducting an evaluation study. You will find that most of the procedures and terminology are the same as those described in other chapters of the book because, as we stated above, educational evaluators draw extensively on the methodology of educational research.

Steps in Conducting a Program Evaluation

An evaluation study follows essentially the same steps as those involved in doing a research study. Several additional factors must be considered, however, depending upon the evaluation model that is used. These factors are highlighted below, using as an example an evaluation study conducted by David Strahan, Jewell Cooper, and Martha Wood.[5]

✦ Touchstone in Research

Herman, J. L. (Ed.). (1987). *Program evaluation* (2nd ed.). Thousand Oaks, CA: Sage.

---

5. Strahan, D., Cooper, J., & Ward, M. (2001). Middle school reform through data and dialogue: Collaborative evaluation with 17 leadership teams. *Evaluation Review, 25,* 72–99.

The purpose of the evaluation was to evaluate the middle schools in one school district in order to guide school improvement plans.

Although our description of steps in evaluation refers mostly to *program* evaluation, the steps are applicable to other kinds of evaluation, too. In fact, the evaluation study that we use as an example focused on the effectiveness both of the schools' programs and their organizational structures.

Clarifying Reasons for Doing an Evaluation

An evaluation study can be initiated because of the evaluator's personal interest in doing it or because some person or agency requested it. Both reasons can be involved in initiating the study, as when the evaluator's personal interests and an agency's need for evaluation happen to coincide.

If the evaluation study is done to answer questions primarily of interest to you, you will need only to clarify for yourself why the study is being done. Such was the case in a study described later in the chapter in the section on expertise-oriented evaluation. That study was motivated by the researcher's interest in using the method of educational criticism to illuminate certain aspects of fourth-grade classroom instruction.

In the case of the middle-school evaluation that we are using as an example, the evaluation was initiated by school-district administrators. They invited a research team from the University of North Carolina at Greensboro to collaborate with the district's research office and middle schools in identifying issues at the middle-school level (e.g., interdisciplinary teaming and school safety), collecting evaluative data relating to those issues, and using the data to develop school improvement plans.

When an evaluation is requested, the evaluator should consider probing to determine *all* the reasons for the evaluation request. Evaluations can be requested because they are required by an accreditation board or a funding agency. Such evaluations usually are legitimate. Evaluations also can be requested for more dubious reasons. Someone might want to use evaluation to "shape up" the behavior of program staff; in this case, the evaluation serves a watchdog function. Someone might want the evaluator to gather evidence that can be used to justify an already-made decision to terminate the program or reduce its funding; in this situation, the evaluator becomes a "hired gun." Or someone might want the evaluator to gather information that will reflect unfavorably on certain members of the program staff. If staff members perceive that any of these purposes underlie an evaluation, they may work to sabotage the evaluator's efforts.

To determine the legitimacy of an evaluation request, evaluators need to spend time interviewing key individuals to determine whether the request is reasonable and ethical. Evaluation experts recommend that you refuse to conduct an evaluation if any breach of ethics has occurred or is likely to occur. The ethics of evaluation are discussed further in the section on criteria of a good evaluation study.[6] (Research ethics in general are the subject of Chapter 3.)

Selecting an Evaluation Model

Clarifying the reasons for an evaluation request is useful in selecting an appropriate model. This task requires careful deliberation, as there are many models from which to choose. By

✦ *Touchstone in Research*

Scriven, M. (1994). Evaluation as a discipline. *Studies in Educational Evaluation, 20,* 147–166.

Stufflebeam, D. L., Madaus, G. F., & Kellaghan, T. (2000). *Evaluation models* (rev. ed.). Boston: Kluwer.

6. Examples of ethical problems faced by evaluators are discussed in Kimmel, A. J. (1988). *Ethics and values in applied social research.* Newbury Park, CA: Sage. One such problem involves breaching confidentiality in order to report behavior of a client that appears to be illegal, and another involves difficulties in defining the evaluator's appropriate role as an expert witness.

one account, nearly 60 different models have been developed in the past decade.[7] In a recent evaluation of evaluation models, 22 models were compared.[8]

The models, or *approaches* as some evaluation experts prefer to call them, differ on various dimensions, among them being:

- the purpose of the evaluation and the questions being asked
- the methods for collecting data
- the relationship between the evaluator, the administrators overseeing the evaluation, the individuals in the program or organization being evaluated

Later in the chapter we present a range of evaluation models to illustrate the options that are available to you. In addition, we recommend that you review the literature to identify other evaluation models and to determine whether a particular model has come into common use for the type of evaluation you plan to do.

In the middle-school study, Strahan, Cooper, and Ward selected the collaborative-evaluation model to guide their evaluation process. Collaborative evaluation is "any evaluation in which there is a significant degree of collaboration or cooperation between evaluators and stakeholders in planning and/or conducting the evaluation."[9] Thus, the individuals being evaluated are not passive objects of study or suppliers, but rather active participants in deciding the direction and uses of the evaluation. The collaborative-evaluation model is similar in certain respects to the responsive-evaluation model described later in the chapter.

Identifying Stakeholders

A **stakeholder** is anyone who is involved in the program being evaluated or who might be affected by or interested in the findings of the evaluation. It is important to identify the stakeholders at the outset of an evaluation study. They can help you clarify the reasons why the study was requested, the questions that should guide the evaluation, the choice of research design, the interpretation of results, and how the findings should be reported and to whom.

Ignoring some of the stakeholders can have serious political consequences. Stakeholders can sabotage the evaluation process or discredit the results if they think that the evaluator has not responded appropriately to their need for involvement. The threat of sabotage does not mean, however, that you must involve all stakeholders to an equal degree. Some stakeholders may wish simply to be kept informed, whereas others may want to influence the questions that guide the study and the evaluation design.

The middle-school evaluation that we are using as an example was comprehensive and collaborative, so there were many stakeholders. District administrators had a stake in ensuring that the 17 middle schools submitted a formal school improvement plan each year and that the plan included school safety and use of results of state-mandated achievement tests. The district's research office had a stake in ensuring the validity and utility of the district-wide survey instrument used to collect data about the perceptions of teachers, students, and parents concerning the schools' effectiveness. Each school had a leadership team consisting of teachers, parents, administrators and a university evaluator/facilitator

---

7. Worthen, B. R., Sanders, J. R., & Fitzpatrick, J. L. (1997). *Program evaluation: Alternative approaches and practical guidelines* (2nd ed.). New York: Addison Wesley Longman.
8. Stufflebeam, D. L. (2001). *Evaluation models.* San Francisco: Jossey-Bass.
9. Cousins, J. B., Donohue, J. J., & Bloom, G. A. (1996). Collaborative evaluation in North America: Evaluators' self-reported opinions, practices, and consequences. *Evaluation Practice, 17,* 207–226. Quote appears on p. 210.

who were responsible for the school improvement plan. The leadership teams, then, were important stakeholders in the evaluation process. Each team occasionally solicited interview and questionnaire data from students, teachers, and parents at the school, so they too should be considered stakeholders.

Deciding What Is to Be Evaluated

One of the first tasks that confronts the evaluator is **program delineation,** which is the process of identifying the most important characteristics of the program to be evaluated. Careful program delineation is important even in local evaluation research. It is not uncommon for persons working in a program to know only those aspects that affect them directly. Unless all program components are delineated, an important component might be overlooked in the evaluation process.

Following program delineation, the program should be analyzed to determine which of its components are to be included in the evaluation study. Program components can be grouped into the following categories: goals, resources, procedures, and management. These categories are useful for designing an evaluation study irrespective of the evaluation model that is used.

Program Goals

Judgments about the merit of program goals are central to most evaluation studies. A **goal** is the purpose, effect, or end point that the program developer is attempting to achieve. If a program does not have goals, or if the goals are not perceived as worthwhile, it is difficult to imagine how the program itself can have merit.

Some programs have carefully specified goals. In other programs the evaluator must infer the goals that the developer has in mind. Once the program goals have been identified, the evaluator may be asked by stakeholders to determine the extent to which the program actually achieves its intended goals. In a type of study known as *formative evaluation* (described later in the chapter), the assigned task may be to help the developers determine what the goals of the program should be.

The goals of the middle-school evaluation study were school-improvement goals. Because the study covered several years, evaluation data from one year, presented in individual reports to the 17 leadership teams, shaped the improvement goals for the following year. For example, Strahan, Cooper, and Ward observed that: " . . . all of the 17 teams used the information from their first-year reports as one of several considerations in refining their school improvement plans for the second year."[10] The report information included student achievement results on state-mandated tests and results of interviews and questionnaires administered to various stakeholder groups.

The evaluators' analysis of the second-year improvement plans revealed the following:

> . . . all 17 teams identified priority goals for instructional improvement in math and writing, 16 of the teams in reading. All 17 teams identified school safety as another priority for improvement. The other areas for improvement that the teams targeted most frequently were advisory programs/character education (15), schoolwide discipline (15), and parental involvement (15).[11]

We can conclude that these goals have merit in the eyes of a wide range of stakeholders, because they in fact generated the data used to create the goals. This appears to be one benefit of the collaborative-evaluation model.

10. Ibid., p. 84.
11. Ibid., p. 84.

Resources and Procedures

Resources are the personnel, equipment, space, and other cost items needed to implement program procedures. Stakeholders might want to know the answers to such questions as: Are our present resources sufficient to operate the program as intended by its developers? Is the program too expensive? Are there hidden costs in the program? Will the program take away resources needed by other programs? Each of these questions requires the evaluator to focus on program resources.

Procedures are the techniques, strategies, and other processes used in conjunction with resources to achieve program goals. Examples of evaluation questions that concern program procedures are "How long did teachers need to use the materials before students mastered the content?" "Did teachers have difficulty in using the constructivist approach to science teaching?" "To what extent did teachers actually use the constructivist approach?" Answers to these questions usually require close and repeated observation of the program in operation.

Evaluation of program resources and procedures is especially helpful for understanding the observed effects of a program. Suppose a new instructional program is observed to have negligible effects on student achievement. Decision makers might choose to discontinue the program because the evaluation results were negative. Yet the program may have been ineffective because needed materials did not arrive on time, or because teachers experienced many interruptions that reduced the total time allotted to program implementation. If the evaluator had collected data on these resource and procedural problems, the decision makers might have chosen an alternative course of action, for example, to remove the "bugs" from the program and try it again. In fact, collection of data on all three aspects of a program—resources, procedures, and goal attainment—is important in any type of formative evaluation. Decisions about program revision can be made more effectively if developers know how well the current version of the program is working *and* why.

Program Management

Most programs have a management system to monitor resources and procedures so that they are used effectively to achieve program goals. We might think that management only operates in large-scale programs, such as a system of secondary education or curriculum coordination in a school district. Yet many curriculum programs contain built-in management procedures to monitor students' instructional progress (e.g., daily quizzes and end-of-unit tests). We also could broaden the concept of management to include self-management (e.g., teachers monitoring their own classroom teaching in order to improve their on-the-job performance).

Some evaluation studies focus on management systems in response to such questions as "Is the management system ensuring the effective use of program resources? Is the management system as efficient as it can be?" "Are the management procedures being used as intended by the program developers?" Each of these questions requires the evaluator to design research that delineates the management system and examines its operation in practice.

In the middle-school study, the leadership team at each of the 17 schools was the key element in the management system used by the school district to bring about school improvement. The evaluators did not make judgments about the leadership teams other than noting that the school principals claimed that "the leadership teams are establishing clearer priorities and monitoring progress more systematically than they were several years ago."[12] It may be that the collaborative evaluation model is not as well suited to

12. Ibid., p. 97.

collecting data about management systems as other evaluation models, especially the CIPP model described later in the chapter.

Identifying Evaluation Questions

We stated in Chapter 2 that a research problem can be stated in the form of questions, hypotheses, or objectives. The same range of formats can be used in evaluation studies, although it is most common to state questions.

Lee Cronbach distinguished two phases in selecting questions for an evaluation study.[13] The **divergent phase** involves generating a comprehensive list of questions, issues, concerns, and information needs that might be addressed in the evaluation study. (Note that issues, concerns, and information needs can be rephrased subsequently as questions to maintain a consistent format.) As the evaluator, you should invite all stakeholders to contribute to this list. In addition, you can suggest possible questions for study. The particular approach to evaluation that you have chosen to guide your study also can prompt ideas for questions. For example, in the section on formative and summative evaluation later in the chapter, we include a sample of criteria for evaluating educational products. Stakeholders could be asked to nominate some or all these criteria for inclusion in the study. The criteria, which are conveniently stated in the form of questions, could be added to the list of questions generated by other means.

The second of Cronbach's two phases is the **convergent phase.** It involves reducing the initial list of evaluation questions to a manageable number. This phase is necessary because of the expense involved in answering each evaluation question. The evaluator, in collaboration with significant stakeholders, must winnow the list to the most important questions that can be answered with available resources.

The report of the middle-school study indicates that four questions guided the collaborative evaluation:

1. When provided support for gathering data, what issues do middle school leadership teams choose to explore?
2. How do they use this information to set priorities for school improvement?
3. How do they monitor progress toward these priorities?
4. How does the collaborative evaluation process inform the revision of the district-wide Middle School Survey?[14]

The evaluators do not explain the process used to generate these questions, but it seems likely—given the nature of the questions and the evaluation model used—that they were generated collaboratively by district educators and the evaluation team.

As an evaluation study proceeds, new questions are likely to arise in the minds of the evaluator and stakeholders. Some of the evaluation models described later in the chapter—especially the qualitative models—explicitly acknowledge this possibility. If possible, you should set aside time and other resources that can be used for answering important questions that arise after data collection begins.

Developing an Evaluation Design and Time Line

Many evaluation studies are similar to research studies in design, execution, and reporting. Thus, any of the research procedures described in the preceding chapters can be in-

13. Cronbach, L. J. (1982). *Designing evaluations of educational and social programs.* San Francisco: Jossey-Bass.
14. Ibid., p. 77. The Middle School Survey was a questionnaire developed by the district's research office to determine stakeholders' perceptions about the middle schools.

corporated into the design of an evaluation study. Evaluation studies, however, present several issues that do not arise in research studies.

One issue is whether the evaluation should be done by an internal evaluator or an external evaluator. An **internal evaluator** is a staff member of the program that is being evaluated. For example, some students do thesis or dissertation projects in which they evaluate some aspect of the school in which they teach. They may do the evaluation while they are on leave to work on their degrees, but even in this situation they function as internal evaluators.

An **external evaluator** is not in the regular employ of the program but is employed specifically to do the evaluation. This person sometimes is called a *third-party evaluator* or *evaluation contractor.*

Most types of evaluation can be done by an internal evaluator, especially when the evaluation findings will be used to guide program management and decision making.[15] Summative evaluation, which is described more fully later in the chapter, is best done by an external evaluator. The purpose of summative evaluation is to determine the merits of a fully operational program and possibly to compare it with a competing program. The evaluator is obliged to represent the interests of the consumers to whom the evaluation study will be reported, or of the external agency that is sponsoring the evaluation. An external evaluator is in a much better position than an internal evaluator to represent these interests. Even so, both an internal evaluator and an external evaluator could be pressured to bias an evaluation design to produce particular results. If such pressure became too intense, the evaluator's only recourse is to terminate the evaluation on ethical grounds.

Many evaluation studies involve an experimental or quasi-experimental design, because often the primary question is how well the program works. (The program is the experimental treatment.) A common issue in this situation is how much internal and external validity should be built into the evaluation design. More resources are required to include a control group and other experimental design features that increase one's confidence that observed effects are attributable to the program and that the effects are generalizable. Program staff, however, might not always be willing to pay the costs needed to improve the experiment's validity.

Resolution of this issue usually depends on who is in control of the evaluation process. Some evaluators do evaluation studies out of personal interest, as was true in McCutcheon's study using the method of educational criticism described later in the chapter. These evaluators can design more or less rigorous studies as they choose. When you are doing a study that involves collaboration with stakeholders, the situation is different. You must be sensitive to the quality of information that will satisfy the stakeholders' needs, and to budgetary constraints. This may mean designing a less rigorous study than you might wish. Again, if the resulting design compromises your standards too much, you can choose either to terminate the study or withdraw from it.

In designing an evaluation study, you should be aware that evaluation activities can be both beneficial and harmful. Gene Glass described this problem as a paradox.[16] On the one hand, persons involved in a program appear to do best when they feel they are valued unconditionally and do not have an evaluator watching over their shoulder. On the other hand, Glass observed, "it appears that people move truer and more certainly toward excellence to the extent that they clarify their purposes, measure the impact of their action,

---

15. For a detailed discussion of the special duties and concerns of internal evaluators, see: Love, A. J. (1991). *Internal evaluation: Building organizations from within.* Thousand Oaks, CA: Sage.

16. Glass, G. V (1975). A paradox about excellence of schools and the people in them. *Educational Researcher, 4*(3), 9–13.

judge it, and move on—in a few words, evaluate their progress."[17] The perils of evaluation involve not only people, but the program itself. A program might be good, but a poor evaluation can cause others to misjudge it and contribute to its downfall. A program might have the potential to be good, but a negative evaluation while it is under development can lead administrators to withdraw funding. Furthermore, evaluation activities use up resources that could be allocated to support further program development.

The beneficial and harmful effects of evaluation are difficult to reconcile. Some evaluators recommend that you weigh all possible consequences of a planned evaluation activity. You should determine that the potential benefits outweigh the potential harm before you make a decision to proceed with the evaluation. Also, you should design the study to minimize potentially harmful effects. One way to accomplish this goal is to involve significant stakeholders in the design of the study, as was done in the middle-school evaluation study that we are using as an example. For example, they can assist in selecting or developing measures that reflect the outcomes most likely to be achieved by the program. Including measures suggested by stakeholders will make the evaluation less threatening to them. Also, the measures may reveal effects that cast a positive light on the program.

The final issue to consider is time. Many research studies have no time constraints for completion. Not so with evaluation studies. If stakeholders are involved, they usually want the final report by a certain date. In these situations, the evaluator will need to create a time line as part of the evaluation design to ensure that the study is completed by the requested date. The time line can be generated using a Program Evaluation and Review Technique (PERT) chart or similar technique.[18] One advantage of creating a detailed time line is that it can be used to identify and document the resources needed to complete a study by the requested date. You may need this information later, for example, to convince stakeholders to increase resources if it appears that a specified deadline cannot be met using the resources originally budgeted for the study.

Collecting and Analyzing Evaluation Data

Data collection and analysis in both evaluation studies and research studies are similar. For example, the middle-school evaluation study primarily involved a descriptive design in which stakeholder perceptions and student achievement were measured each school year. Among the data-collection instruments were the following:

1. The Comprehensive Middle School Survey, a questionnaire that was administered district-wide to measure stakeholder perceptions of various elements of middle schools, such as differentiated instruction, advisor/advisee programs, block scheduling/flexible scheduling, interdisciplinary teaming, school safety and discipline, and parent involvement.
2. State-mandated End-of-Grade achievement tests.
3. Unstructured interviews.
4. Informal questionnaires developed for local school use.
5. The School Climate and Safety Survey, a questionnaire that measures teachers' and students' perceptions of school safety.

---

17. Ibid., p. 12.
18. The use of PERT charts and related techniques in evaluation research is described in Chapter 15 of: Worthen, B. R., Sanders, J. R., & Fitzpatrick, J. L. (1997). *Educational evaluation: Alternative approaches and practical guidelines* (2nd ed.). New York: Addison Wesley Longman.

In addition, the evaluators worked with the district's research office to revise the Comprehensive Middle School Survey to make it more usable by stakeholders. Factor analysis and structural equation modeling (see Chapter 11) were employed to make the questionnaire shorter and to produce scores for clusters of related items.

Reporting Evaluation Results

A typical research study will yield a single report, for example, a master's thesis, doctoral dissertation, or technical report. A condensed version of the report subsequently might be presented as a paper at a professional conference or published as a journal article.

The reporting of an evaluation study sometimes is more complicated because various stakeholder audiences are involved, and each has different information needs. In the middle-school evaluation study, the evaluators collaborated with each school leadership teams to produce a school improvement plan which reported analyses of evaluative data and actions to be undertaken based on the analyses. These reports were forwarded to district administrators for their review, and undoubtedly they were shared with school-level stakeholders as well. In addition, it appears that various informal reports were prepared for internal use by individuals directly involved in the collaborative-evaluation process. Finally, the evaluators prepared a journal article (see footnote 5) to share their findings with the broader community of evaluation researchers.

If you do an evaluation study of a program for a master's or doctoral degree, you might need to communicate your findings in several forms requested by the program's administrators and other stakeholders. In addition, you will need to report the results in a thesis or dissertation. Your thesis or dissertation committee probably will require you to use the same format as for reporting a research study. For example, you might need to write an extensive review of the literature, which generally is not found in program evaluation reports.

Your thesis or dissertation should include a discussion of how the evaluation findings were used. This is a matter of considerable interest to evaluation experts. In fact, research has been done on how evaluation findings actually are utilized by decision makers.[19]

Another common feature of evaluation studies reported as theses or dissertations is a discussion of the larger significance of the study. For example, your study's findings might have theoretical significance or serve as a replication of previous findings on the same problem. If so, you should discuss the study from these perspectives.

Many evaluation projects can be viewed as case studies of the application of a particular evaluation model. If appropriate, the discussion section of your thesis or dissertation should consider the study from this perspective. You can discuss your ideas about the model's applicability to the situation you studied, the shortcomings of the model, and how any problems you encountered might be overcome in future studies. In this way, you can contribute to the improvement of evaluation methodology in education.

This perspective is present in the concluding section of the journal article reporting the middle-school evaluation. Strahan, Cooper, and Ward identify observed benefits of the cooperative-evaluation model, including the fact that, "Participants in this project seem to be finding ways to complement the 'participatory' involvement of primary stakeholders with perspectives from 'external evaluators'."[20] At the same time, they note as a limitation of their study that, "it is too early to assess the extent to which these practices will result in changes in schooling that are substance and sustained."[21] They also provide a helpful caution for

---

19. An example of such a study is: Siegel, K., & Tucker, P. (1985). The utilization of evaluation research: A case analysis. *Evaluation Review, 9,* 307–328.
20. Strahan, Cooper, & Ward, *Middle school reform,* p. 97.
21. Ibid., pp. 97–98.

prospective users of the collaborative-evaluation model: "[O]pportunities for participants to discuss evaluation information and reflect together on this information are essential to collaboration."[22]

Finally, the discussion section of your thesis or dissertation should include a brief meta-evaluation. A **meta-evaluation** is an evaluation of an evaluation. Researchers are obligated to include in their reports a discussion of weaknesses in their research design or in the execution of the study that might affect the validity of the findings. Evaluators have a similar obligation. Professional organizations have published criteria of a good evaluation study that can be used to judge the adequacy of your own study. These criteria are discussed below.

✦ Touchstone in Research

Evaluation Center at Western Michigan University. (n.d.). *Evaluation checklist project.* Retrieved January 17, 2002 from http://www.wmich.edu/evalctr/checklists/

Criteria of a Good Evaluation Study

Standards for Program Evaluation

The *Standards for Evaluations of Educational Programs, Projects, and Materials,* originally published in 1981 and revised in 1994 with the title *Program Evaluation Standards,* provides an authoritative list of criteria for evaluation research.[23] The 30 standards described in the report can be helpful if you intend to do evaluation research for your thesis or dissertation project. You can use the standards as criteria for judging the soundness of your evaluation design and for judging previous evaluation studies in your area of interest.[24]

The standards were developed by the Joint Committee on Standards for Educational Evaluation. The Joint Committee, under the direction of Daniel Stufflebeam, represented many important organizations in education, including the American Association of School Administrators, American Educational Research Association, American Federation of Teachers, American Personnel and Guidance Association, and National School Boards Association. Several hundred educators nationwide were involved in developing and field-testing the standards. The standards were designed for use in judging the quality of educational evaluations, just as the *Standards for Educational and Psychological Tests* (see Chapter 7) were developed for judging the quality of tests.

The standards were developed for several reasons. First, there was a growing awareness that the technical quality of some evaluation studies was poor and that some studies were insensitive to the entity being evaluated. Another reason was to protect the process of evaluation from being corrupted by individuals or groups with ulterior motives. As we noted in the introduction, educational evaluation usually involves political considerations. In the absence of standards, evaluators or clients are more likely to attempt to bend the evaluation process to produce results that reflect their biases and self-interests. Third, the Joint Committee felt that a published set of standards might improve the professionalism of educational evaluation. Also, the Joint Committee found that no adequate standards were available at the time they began their work.

The Joint Committee concluded that a good evaluation study satisfies four important criteria: utility, feasibility, propriety, and accuracy. An evaluation has **utility** if it is informative, timely, and useful to the affected persons. **Feasibility** means, first, that the evalu-

22. Ibid., p. 97.

23. The Joint Committee on Standards for Educational Evaluation (J. R. Sanders, Chair). (1994). *The program evaluation standards* (2nd ed.). Thousand Oaks, CA: Sage.

24. Another important set of standards was developed by the American Evaluation Association: Shadish, W. R., Newman, D. L., Scheirer, M. A., & Wye, C. (Eds.). (1995). *Guiding principles for evaluators: No. 66. New Directions for Program Evaluation.* San Francisco: Jossey-Bass.

ation design is appropriate to the setting in which the study is to be conducted, and second, that the design is cost-effective. An evaluation has **propriety** if it is conducted legally and ethically. Finally, **accuracy** refers to the extent to which an evaluation study has produced valid, reliable, and comprehensive information for making judgments of a program's worth.

Each of these four criteria was operationalized in terms of specific standards, which are shown below in paraphrased form.[25] Each standard is listed below the criterion to which it most closely relates. (Helpful case studies that illustrate each standard are presented in the Joint Committee's report.) The various models of evaluation described in this chapter reflect many of the standards.

Utility

1. *Stakeholder identification.* All the groups affected by the evaluation should be identified.
2. *Evaluator credibility.* The evaluator should be competent and trustworthy.
3. *Information scope and selection.* The information to be collected should pertain directly to the evaluation questions and stakeholder concerns.
4. *Values identification.* The evaluators' basis for making value judgments from the obtained results should be made clear.
5. *Report clarity.* The evaluators' report should be comprehensive and easily understood.
6. *Report timeliness and dissemination.* Evaluation reports, including interim reports, should be disseminated to users in a timely manner.
7. *Evaluation impact.* The evaluation should be conducted so as to encourage appropriate action by the stakeholders.

Feasibility

1. *Practical procedures.* The evaluation procedures should be practical and minimally disruptive to participants.
2. *Political viability.* The evaluators should obtain the cooperation of affected interest groups and keep any of them from subverting the evaluation process.
3. *Cost effectiveness.* The benefits produced by the evaluation should justify the resources expended on it.

Propriety

1. *Service orientation.* The evaluation should help stakeholders meet the needs of all their clients and the larger society as well.
2. *Formal agreements.* The formal parties to the evaluation should state their obligations and agreements in a written contract.
3. *Rights of human subjects.* The rights and welfare of persons involved in the evaluation should be protected.
4. *Human interactions.* Evaluators should show respect in their interactions with persons involved in the study.
5. *Complete and fair assessment.* The strengths and weaknesses of the entity being evaluated should be explored completely and fairly.

25. The lists are paraphrases of the standards published in: The Joint Committee on Standards for Educational Evaluation (J. R. Sanders, Chair). (1994). *The program evaluation standards* (2nd ed.). Thousand Oaks, CA: Sage. If you are planning to use the standards, we recommend that you review this publication for their exact wording and for detailed explanations.

6. *Disclosure of findings.* Individuals with a legal right to know and those affected by the results should be informed about the evaluation results.

7. *Conflict of interest.* If a conflict of interest should arise, it should be treated openly and honestly.

8. *Fiscal responsibility.* Expenditure of resources for the evaluation should be prudent and ethically responsible.

Accuracy

1. *Program documentation.* All pertinent aspects of the program being evaluated should be described in detail.

2. *Context analysis.* Aspects of the program's context that affect the evaluation should be described in detail.

3. *Described purposes and procedures.* The evaluation's purposes and procedures should be described in detail.

4. *Defensible information sources.* Sources of data should be described in sufficient detail that their adequacy can be judged.

5. *Valid information.* The data-collection procedures should yield valid interpretations.

6. *Reliable information.* The data-collection procedures should yield reliable findings.

7. *Systematic information.* The evaluation data should be reviewed and corrected, if necessary.

8. *Analysis of quantitative information.* Analysis of quantitative data in an evaluation study should be thorough and should yield clear interpretations.

9. *Analysis of qualitative information.* Analysis of qualitative data in an evaluation study should be thorough and should yield clear interpretations.

10. *Justified conclusions.* Evaluators should provide an explicit justification for their conclusions.

11. *Impartial reporting.* Evaluation reports should be free of bias and of the personal feelings of any of those connected to the evaluation.

12. *Meta-evaluation.* The evaluation should be subjected to formative and summative evaluation using this list of standards.

Daniel Stufflebeam identified several difficulties that have arisen in attempts to apply the 1981 version of the standards.[26] He noted trade-offs in applying the standards. For example, efforts to produce valid and reliable information and develop firm conclusions (accuracy standards) often impede the production of timely reports (utility standard 6). In research on efforts to apply the standards, other problems identified include limited utility outside the United States and in the case of large-scale, government-sponsored studies, inappropriateness to some evaluation problems, lack of detail to guide specific design decisions, and inadequate attention to internal self-evaluations.

Bruce Thompson analyzed the 1994 *Program Evaluation Standards* and found that the main focus of the Joint Committee was on optimizing the instrumental use of evaluation research.[27] **Instrumental use** refers to the application of an evaluation study's findings to make a go/no-go decision about whether to continue or terminate a program. Thomp-

26. Stufflebeam, D. L. (1991). Professional standards and ethics for evaluators. In M. W. McLaughlin & D. C. Phillips (Eds.), *Evaluation and education: At quarter century. Ninetieth yearbook of the National Society for the Study of Education: Part II* (pp. 249–282). Chicago: NSSE.

27. Thompson, B. (1994). The revised *Program Evaluation Standards* and their correlation with the evaluation use literature. *Journal of Experimental Education, 63*, 54–81.

son noted that there are other types of use, but they were not a direct focus of the Joint Committee's work. One such type is **conceptual use,** which refers to the influence of evaluation research findings on how stakeholders think about their program. For example, evaluation research can lead stakeholders to reframe the goals for their program. Another type is **symbolic use,** which refers to the use of evaluation research findings for purposes beyond those of judging or improving the program. For example, program administrators might commission an evaluation study in order to satisfy their funding agency, or they might use evaluation findings to rationalize decisions that were made for reasons that have little to do with the findings.

Thompson's analysis suggests that whether and how an evaluation study is used are the ultimate criteria for judging its worth. However, there are various ways in which evaluation research findings can be used. If you are planning to do an evaluation study, you should work with your stakeholders to determine what the desired uses of the findings are. After deciding on these uses, you then can analyze whether the evaluation design is likely to facilitate them.

Standards for Personnel Evaluation

The same Joint Committee that produced the *Program Evaluation Standards* described above also developed standards for evaluation of educational personnel, called the *Personnel Evaluation Standards*.[28] These 21 standards involve the same four categories of standards used in the program evaluation standards. The *Personnel Evaluation Standards* have been used for various purposes, including assessing the quality of teacher evaluation systems[29] and superintendent evaluation systems.[30]

Quantitative Approaches to Evaluation

Like educational research, educational evaluation takes diverse forms. This is because evaluators over time have developed different purposes for doing evaluation, different philosophies, and different methodologies. These differences gradually led to the development of various approaches to evaluation research. The remaining sections of this chapter describe the major approaches.[31] If you are planning to do evaluation studies, you should review these approaches to determine which best suits your purpose and your philosophical orientation to research.

The quantitative approaches described below rely primarily on positivist methods of inquiry. They emphasize objective measurement, representative sampling, experimental control, and the use of statistical techniques to analyze data.

Evaluation of the Individual

Evaluation research can be traced back at least to the early 1900s, when the testing movement began. Binet's intelligence test was published in 1904, and group ability testing began during World War I. Evaluation primarily involved the assessment of individual differences

---

28. Stufflebeam, D. L. (1988). *The personnel evaluation standards: How to assess systems for evaluating educators.* Thousand Oaks, CA: Corwin.
29. Peterson, K. D., Stevens, D., & Ponzio, R. C. (1998). Variable data sources in teacher education. *Journal of Research and Development in Education, 31,* 123–132.
30. Stufflebeam, D. L. (1994). The troubled state of superintendent performance evaluations. *School Administrator, 51*(11), 12–17.
31. Our characterization of approaches to evaluation is based primarily on Worthen & Sanders, *Educational evaluation.*

in student intelligence and school achievement. Test results were used for assigning course grades and for selecting students into different ability tracks and special services.

This model of evaluation still is widely followed in American education. In fact, it has been extended to the evaluation of teachers, administrators, and other school personnel. Like assessment of students, personnel evaluation focuses on measurement of individual differences, and judgments are made by comparing the individual with a criterion or a set of norms.

Objectives-Based Evaluation

Ralph Tyler's work on curriculum evaluation in the 1940s brought about a major change in educational evaluation.[32] Tyler's view was that the curriculum should be organized around explicit objectives and that its success should be judged on the basis of how well students achieve these objectives. This model marked a shift from a concern with evaluating individual students to a concern with evaluating the curriculum. In doing so, the model implied that students might perform poorly not because of lack of innate ability, but because of weaknesses in the curriculum.

Tyler's model has had an important influence on subsequent developments in educational evaluation. The National Assessment of Educational Progress was originated in the 1960s under Tyler's leadership. This federal program continues to collect data on the academic achievement of American youth. Many state testing programs collect similar data using this program's methods. The increasing practice of competency testing of students and teachers is another outgrowth of the Tyler model.[33]

Educational evaluators have developed other evaluation models that support Tyler's emphasis on the measurement of explicit objectives as the basis for determining an educational program's merit. For example, Malcolm Provus developed **discrepancy evaluation,** which emphasizes the search for discrepancies between the objectives of a program and students' actual achievement of the objectives.[34] The resulting information about discrepancies can be used to guide program management decisions.

Another objectives-based approach is cost analysis.[35] Evaluators use **cost analysis** to determine either: (1) the relationship between the costs of a program and the benefits of a program when both costs and benefits can be calculated in monetary terms (called the *cost-benefit ratio*); or (2) the relationship between the costs of various interventions relative to their measured effectiveness in achieving a desired outcome (called *cost-effectiveness*). Different programs can be compared to determine which is most cost-effective, that is, which promotes the greatest benefits for each unit of resource expenditure.

If you are planning a study of students' achievement of instructional objectives, one of your major concerns will be the measurement of these objectives. To facilitate measurement, it is helpful to state objectives in behavioral terms, meaning that the program outcomes are stated as behaviors that anyone, including evaluators, can observe in a program participant.[36] This type of objective, commonly called a **behavioral objective,** usually has

---

32. Tyler, R. W. (1949). *Basic principles of curriculum and instruction: Syllabus for Education 360.* Chicago: University of Chicago Press.
33. For a retrospective discussion of the Tyler approach to program evaluation, see: Tyler, R. W. (1991). General statement on program evaluation. In M. W. McLaughlin & D. C. Phillips (Eds.), *Evaluation and education: At quarter century. Ninetieth yearbook of the National Society for the Study of Education: Part II* (pp. 3–17). Chicago: NSSE.
34. Provus, M. (1971). *Discrepancy evaluation.* Berkeley, CA: McCutchan.
35. This type of evaluation research is discussed in: Levin, H. M., & McEwan, P. J. (2000). *Cost-effectiveness analysis: Methods and applications* (2nd ed.). Thousand Oaks, CA: Sage. See also: Levin, H. M. (1991). Cost-effectiveness at quarter century. In M. W. McLaughlin & D. C. Phillips (Eds.), *Evaluation and education* (pp. 189–209).
36. Procedures for writing behavioral objectives are explained in many sources. The classic work is: Mager, R. F. (1984). *Preparing instructional objectives* (rev. ed.). Belmont, CA: David S. Lake.

three components: statement of the program objective as an observable, behavioral outcome; criteria for successful performance of the behavior; and the situational context in which the behavior is to be performed. Here is an example of a behavioral objective: Given a set of 20 single-digit multiplication problems, the learner will be able to solve them by writing the correct answer beneath each problem in less than three minutes with no more than two errors.

Behavioral objectives have been criticized on the grounds that they reduce education to a matter of teaching only that which can be stated and measured in the language of behavioral objectives. Of course, behavioral objectives, like any other technique, can be misused. Used appropriately, however, they simplify the task of developing suitable instruments—especially domain-referenced instruments—to measure the learner's achievement of an objective.

Another issue in evaluating program objectives involves which objectives to measure. Evaluators often rely on the program's developers or experts to make this decision. Michael Scriven, however, argued that evaluators should not know the program goals in advance because they might become co-opted by them and thus overlook other effects of the program, especially adverse side effects.[37] Scriven suggested that to avoid this problem, evaluators should conduct research to discover the actual effects of the program in operation, which may differ markedly from the program developers' stated goals. This strategy for evaluation has come to be known as **goal-free evaluation.**

Although goal-free evaluation has merit, there are many situations in which an evaluator is expected to collect evaluative data about specific program goals. Even in these situations, however, the evaluator can attend to the stated goals but also remain alert to the possibility that the program may have actual effects (both beneficial and adverse) quite different from those intended by program developers.

An example in education of this phenomenon is the evaluations of DISTAR, an academic program intended to develop the cognitive skills of low-income disadvantaged children. Although most of the evaluation research on this program has focused on measurement of cognitive skills, self-concept instruments were routinely administered as well. The evaluation findings demonstrate that DISTAR not only fosters students' cognitive development but also has a positive effect on self-esteem.[38]

Needs Assessment

A **need** can be defined as a discrepancy between an existing set of conditions and a desired set of conditions. For example, suppose an educator makes the assertion, "We need to place more emphasis on science education in our elementary school curriculum." The educator is saying in effect that there is a discrepancy between the existing curriculum and the desired curriculum. This statement of need reflects a judgment about the present merit of the curriculum. Also, note that the assessment of need provides a basis for setting objectives for curriculum or program development. Because we consider needs assessment to be closely related to objectives-based models of evaluation, we are treating it as a quantitative approach. Nevertheless, qualitative needs assessments also are conducted in education.[39]

37. Scriven, M. (1973). Goal-free evaluation. In E. R. House (Ed.), *School evaluation: The politics and process* (pp. 319–328). Berkeley, CA: McCutchan.
38. Stebbins, L. B., St. Pierre, R. G., Proper, E. C., Anderson, R. B., & Cerva, T. R. An evaluation of Follow Through. (1978). In T. D. Cook, M. L. Del Rosario, K. M. Hennigan, M. M. Mark, & W. M. K. Trochim (Eds.), *Evaluation Studies Review Annual, Vol. 3* (pp. 571–610). Beverly Hills, CA: Sage.
39. McKillip, J. 1987. *Need analysis: Tools for the human services and education.* Thousand Oaks, CA: Sage.

Example of a Needs Assessment

Quantitative research methods enable researchers to measure the precise *extent* of discrepancy between an existing state and a desired state. An example of such a needs assessment is a study by Thomas Pierce, Deborah Deutsch Smith, and Jane Clarke.[40] The purpose of their study was to update and expand existing databases on the supply and demand of special education doctoral graduates for filling faculty positions at institutions of higher education (IHEs) in the United States. The discrepancy between the number and types of available doctoral graduates and the number of available faculty positions was viewed as a measure of the need for leadership personnel in special education.

The target population for this study was 85 IHEs listed in *The National Directory of Special Education Personnel Preparation Programs* as having doctoral programs in special education. An abbreviated form of the questionnaire used in the survey is shown in Figure 17.1. It included questions from earlier questionnaires in order to expand the existing database concerning the supply and demand of doctoral level leadership personnel.

The questionnaire was sent to the department chairperson of each IHE, and after one month was followed up with a letter. The sample consisted of the 55 questionnaires re-

---

FIGURE 17.1

Abbreviated Form of Survey Questionnaire to Assess Need for Special Education Leadership Personnel

Special Education Doctoral Survey

1. How many doctoral students are enrolled in your doctoral program in the special education for the 1990–1991 academic year?
2. Of this number how many do you expect to graduate in 1990–1991?
3. Of the expected special education doctoral graduates for 1990–1991, in what disability area is their concentration (place number on line):
4. Of those listed in #3 above, are any expected graduates trained for leadership positions in more than one exceptionality area? If so please list number and combination (For example, one individual is qualified in both BD and LD).
5. In your estimation is your currently enrolled doctoral student body: larger than last year; smaller than last year; about the same as last year?
6. If you searched for new faculty last year (1989–1990) please respond to the following. (Surveyed rank, tenure track, disability area, and reason for search.) If not skip to question #7.)
   Approximately how many applicants did you receive, and how many were qualified? (Separate for multiple positions using position letter above.)
   Did you hire? If no, why not?
7. If you anticipate faculty vacancies or new positions during the next three years (1990–1993), fill out the following (chart included estimated number, disability area, and reason for search).
8. On the following chart please include information requested about each doctoral graduate for the past two years. (Chart included categories on student's name, current position, place of employment, type of agency, emphasis area, and ethnicity.)

Source: Adapted from Table 1 on p. 177 of: Pierce, T. B., Smith, D. D., & Clarke, J. (1992). Special education leadership: Supply and demand revisited. *Teacher Education and Special Education, 15,* 175–182.

---

40. Pierce, T. B., Smith, D. D., & Clarke, J. (1992). Special education leadership: Supply and demand revisited. *Teacher Education and Special Education, 15,* 175–182.

turned, which represents a 65 percent response rate. Simple tallies were made, and percentages were calculated for each item on the questionnaire. In cases of no response, the item for that questionnaire was not entered in the database.

The researchers found that a total of 221 doctoral students graduated from the 55 institutions in the sample during the two-year period 1988–1990. Responses were obtained concerning the ethnicity of 184 of these doctoral students. As shown in Table 17.1, 21 percent of the graduates were reported to be minority students (or 19 percent if the eight foreign students are excluded from the calculation).

The researchers also obtained data on the positions taken by the 221 doctoral students who graduated from institutions in the sample during the two-year period 1988–1990. Only 38 percent took permanent IHE positions. Twenty-five percent took positions with state or local education agencies, 5 percent went into private practice, 4 percent remained unemployed, and the remainder took other types of positions.

Respondents identified 55 available positions at their institutions during the 1989–1990 academic year, of which 80 percent were tenure-track positions. Fifteen of the 55 positions (27 percent) remained unfilled at the time of the survey. When asked to indicate why they did not hire individuals for the advertised positions, the most frequently cited reason was inappropriate qualifications or unacceptability of applicants. Respondents also predicted their institution's need for faculty for the next three academic years (1990–1993), and the reasons for this need. A total of 71 openings was projected, and the most common reason was to fill positions vacated through retirements (45 percent).

The survey results highlight the need to resupply faculties that are diminishing due to retirements and vacancies. Besides the general problem of inadequately qualified candidates, the researchers commented on the low percentage of ethnic minorities among doctoral graduates: "special education appears to have a very limited pool of future applicants who come from culturally and linguistically diverse backgrounds."[41] They also observed that the total pool of graduates of doctoral programs in special education is declining.

The survey by Pierce and his co-researchers provides useful information to faculty and administrators in special education at IHEs concerning the need for new faculty, and the size and characteristics of the pool of graduates available to fill this need. This information could be used in designing recruitment or retention programs for doctoral students who have the desired characteristics to become special education faculty members.

Problems in Doing a Needs Assessment

Several problems can arise in doing a needs assessment. One of them concerns the definition of *need*. Exactly what is a *desired* set of conditions? J. Roth identified five types of desired states: ideals, norms, minimums, desires (wants), and expectations.[42] A need can be a discrepancy between an actual state and any one of these five desired states. The goal of a college education for all citizens who desire one (an ideal desired state) is certainly a different kind of desired state from the goal of basic skill in reading for all children (a minimum desired state).

Many needs assessments do not make clear how urgent or optional are the desired states that are being determined. For example, the study concerning special education leadership supply and demand did not address the urgency of the need for doctoral graduates from culturally and linguistically diverse backgrounds. A percentage comparison of the ethnic backgrounds of students served by special education with that of the doctoral

41. Ibid., p. 181.
42. Roth, J. (1977). Needs and the needs assessment process. *Evaluation News, 5,* 15–17.

students graduating from the sample institutions might help pinpoint the urgency of recruiting doctoral students from various ethnic groups to better serve the needs of special education students.

Another problem with the needs assessment process is that the values underlying needs often are not clearly articulated. It is helpful to determine quantitatively the extent to which certain groups view particular elements of education (e.g., small class size, compulsory school prayer, computer-assisted instruction) as needs. These quantitative expressions of need just scratch the surface, though. Personal values and standards are important determinants of needs, and they too should be assessed to develop a thorough understanding of needs among the groups being studied.

You also should be aware that needs-assessment data usually are reported as group trends. There may be important individual differences in stated needs that should be explored. For example, in the study on special education leadership needs, a helpful feature of the data analysis was the number of doctoral graduates of various ethnic backgrounds (shown in Table 17.1).

The typical needs assessment is a feasible evaluation project to do as a master's or doctoral study. The primary requirement is a measure of the target group's current behavior or achievement and a standard against which to compare it. If you are interested in doing curriculum development as part of your professional career, you may wish to do a needs assessment in the curriculum content area that particularly interests you.

The CIPP Model

The approaches described above are designed to provide "arm's length" evaluations of programs. When evaluators work more closely with the staff of on-going programs or programs under development, they usually become interested in how they can personally contribute to the process of program management and program development. Evaluators

---

TABLE 17.1

Results from Survey to Assess Need for Special Education Leadership Personnel: Ethnicity of Doctoral Students

Ethnicity	1988–1989	1989–1990
Anglo	73	69
Black	4	9
Hispanic	3	1
Asian	4*	10**
Native American	2	0
Unknown	9	0
Total	95	89

* Includes 2 foreign students
** Includes 6 foreign students
Source: Adapted from Table 2 on p. 177 of: Pierce, T. B., Smith, D. D., & Clarke, J. (1992). Special education leadership: Supply and demand revisited. *Teacher Education and Special Education, 15,* 175–182.

realize that critical decisions need to be made by program managers, and that they can collect evaluative data to help managers make such decisions.

The CIPP model was formulated by Daniel Stufflebeam and his colleagues to show how evaluation could contribute to the decision-making process in program management.[43] CIPP is an acronym for the four types of educational evaluation included in the model: Context evaluation, Input evaluation, Process evaluation, and Product evaluation. Each type of evaluation is tied to a different set of decisions that must be made in planning and operating a program.

Context evaluation involves the identification of problems and needs that occur in a specific educational setting. "Diagnosis of problems provides an essential basis for developing objectives whose achievement results in program improvement."[44] You will recall from our discussion of needs assessment that a need is a discrepancy between an existing condition and a desired condition.

Input evaluation concerns judgments about the resources and strategies needed to accomplish program goals and objectives. Information collected during this stage of evaluation should help decision makers choose the best possible resources and strategies within certain constraints. Input evaluation deals with such issues as whether certain resources are unavailable or too expensive, how well a particular strategy is likely to achieve program goals, whether certain strategies are legally or morally acceptable, and how best to utilize personnel as resources. Input evaluation requires the evaluator to have a wide range of knowledge about possible resources and strategies, as well as knowledge about research on their effectiveness in achieving different types of program outcomes.

Process evaluation involves the collection of evaluative data once the program has been designed and put into operation. The evaluator might be called upon to design a data-collection system for monitoring the day-to-day operation of a program. For example, you might keep attendance records on a school district's staff development program based on voluntary participation. If attendance data reveal deviations from what was anticipated (for example, a decline in teachers' attendance at training sessions over time), the program's decision makers can take action based on their appraisal of the data. Without such a record-keeping system the program might deteriorate, perhaps irreversibly, before the decision makers became aware of what was happening. Another function of process evaluation is to keep records of program events over a period of time. These records might prove useful at a later time in detecting strengths and weaknesses of the program that account for its observed outcomes.

Product evaluation is the fourth element of the CIPP model. The task of product evaluation is to determine the extent to which the goals of the program have been achieved. In this type of evaluation, measures of the goals are developed and administered. The resulting data can be used by program administrators to make decisions about continuing and modifying the program.

Each of the types of evaluation described above requires that three broad tasks be performed: delineating the kinds of information needed for decision making, obtaining the information, and synthesizing the information so that it is useful in making decisions. The first and third steps (delineation and synthesis) should be done as a collaborative effort between evaluator and decision maker. The second step, obtaining the information, is a technical activity that can be delegated primarily to the evaluator.

---

43. The CIPP model is described in: Stufflebeam, D. L., & Shinkfield, A. J. (1985). *Systematic evaluation.* Boston: Kluwer-Nijhoff. See also: Stufflebeam, D. L., Foley, W. J., Gephart, W. J., Guba, E. G., Hammond, R. L., Merriman, H. O., & Provus, M. M. (1971). *Educational evaluation and decision making.* Itaska, IL: Peacock.
44. Ibid., p. 218.

You may have noted that the CIPP model incorporates elements of the other evaluation approaches described above—objectives-based evaluation and needs assessment. It also resembles formative and summative evaluation, which are described below in our discussion of educational research and development. The CIPP model is distinguished by its comprehensiveness, by the fact that it is an ongoing process, and by its purpose, which is to guide the decision-making function in program management. Although the CIPP model has been used primarily in quantitative evaluation research, there is no reason why it cannot be adapted for evaluation research from a qualitative perspective.

This model has proved useful in guiding the work of evaluation staffs in school districts and governmental agencies. Because the CIPP model is complex, it would be difficult to use in its entirety in a thesis or dissertation project. The other models described above are more manageable. Nevertheless, you might do an evaluation study involving collaboration with an agency that uses the CIPP model or one similar to it. In this case you should be familiar with the model, so that you can determine how your study fits into the agency's total evaluation process and also the kinds of data and other resources that might be available to you.

Qualitative Approaches to Evaluation

✦ *Touchstone in Research*

Fetterman, D. M. (Ed.). (1988). *Qualitative approaches to evaluation in education: The silent scientific revolution*. Westport, CT: Greenwood.

Patton, M. Q. (1990). *Qualitative research and evaluation methods* (3rd ed.). Thousand Oaks, CA: Sage.

The approaches to evaluation described above, while useful, do not satisfactorily address several important aspects of evaluation. The objectives-based approaches, for example, tend to take a program's objectives or observed effects as givens. They do not offer much guidance if you wish to understand why particular objectives are considered worthwhile, or why certain stakeholders agree or do not agree on the worth of certain objectives.

The politics of evaluation also are not given serious attention in most quantitative approaches. Various groups have a stake in the outcome of an evaluation study, and they may try to influence the evaluation process accordingly. Should you resist these political influences or incorporate them into the design of an evaluation study? Another problem is that evaluations may do more harm than good under certain conditions. As we stated above, people generally do not like being evaluated, so the evaluation process itself might hamper the very performance that is being assessed. How can you work with the client so that the evaluation produces the most benefit and the least harm?

To address these questions and others, researchers have developed approaches to evaluation that rely heavily on the qualitative research methods that we described in Part V. These approaches differ most clearly from quantitative approaches by not assuming that objective criteria exist for judging the worth of an educational program. Rather, qualitative approaches take the position that the worth of an educational program depends heavily on the values and perspectives of those doing the judging. Therefore, the selection of the individuals and groups to be involved in the evaluation is critical.

In contrast, quantitative approaches have not fully explored differences in stakeholders' perceptions of worth. For example, consider the study on special education leadership needs described above. The researchers accepted the judgments of their survey respondents (chairpersons of special education departments at institutions of higher education) as to the qualifications of doctoral graduates who interviewed for available positions at those institutions. The researchers did not examine the possibility that different chairpersons—or different faculty members within a chairperson's department—might have different notions about the applicants' qualifications.

Responsive Evaluation

Robert Stake pioneered the qualitative approach to educational evaluation.[45] His approach, called **responsive evaluation,** focuses on addressing the concerns and issues of stakeholders. A **concern** is any matter about which stakeholders feel threatened, or any claim that they want to substantiate. An **issue** is any point of contention among stakeholders. Concerns and issues provide a much wider focus for evaluation than do the behavioral objectives that are the primary focus of some quantitative approaches to evaluation.

Example of a Responsive Evaluation

Egon Guba and Yvonna Lincoln identified four major phases that occur in a responsive evaluation: (1) initiating and organizing the evaluation, (2) identifying key issues and concerns, (3) gathering useful information, and (4) reporting results effectively and making recommendations.[46] They described a responsive evaluation of the governance structure of a particular school system. The focus of the evaluation was whether this school system's governance structure was open to inputs from various stakeholding audiences in establishing school policy.

During the first phase, stakeholders were identified. They included the school board, school administrators, school teachers, students and their parents, the mayoral staff of the city in which the school system was located, and influential members of the community. During this phase, Guba and Lincoln recommend that the evaluator and client negotiate an evaluation contract that specifies such matters as identification of the entity to be evaluated, the purpose of the evaluation, rights of access to records, and guarantees of confidentiality and anonymity.

During the second phase, several key issues and concerns were identified through interviews with stakeholders. These concerns included perceptions of citizen lockout from decision making (for example, the school board was accused of having eliminated the elementary art education program despite parental opposition to the move), and of arrogation of power by a small elite (for example, members of the school staff said that they felt they had little say in school affairs). Key issues also were identified, including whether formulation of school policy should be centralized or decentralized, whether policy should be formulated by professionals or by lay groups, and whether the school board should be elected or appointed. Such issues and concerns express the different underlying values of different stakeholders. For example, some—but by no means all—stakeholders were found to place great value on a high-quality curriculum, a rational decision-making process, equality of representation in decision making, and accountability.

In the third phase, the evaluators collected more information about the concerns, issues, and values identified by the stakeholders. They also collected descriptive information about the entity being evaluated and about standards that would be used in making judgments about this entity. Such information can be collected through various methods, including naturalistic observation, interviews, questionnaires, and standardized tests. For

45. Stake, R. E. (1967). The countenance of educational evaluation. *Teachers College Record, 68,* 523–540; Stake, R. E. (1978). The case study method in social inquiry. *Educational Researcher, 7* (2), 5–8. A more recent discussion of responsive evaluation by its originator is provided in Stake, R. E. (1991). Retrospective on "The countenance of educational evaluation," In M. W. McLaughlin & D. C. Phillips (Eds.), *Evaluation and Education:* At quarter century (pp. 67–88). Chicago: University of Chicago Press.
46. Guba, E. G., & Lincoln, Y. S. (1981). *Effective evaluation: Improving the usefulness of evaluation results through responsive and naturalistic approaches.* San Francisco: Jossey-Bass.

example, in the evaluation of the school system's governance structure, some stakeholders were concerned that the school board disposed of the elementary art education program despite parental opposition. The evaluator could reconstruct this occurrence (i.e.,
formulate a tentative description of what occurred) in order to determine what information there is to substantiate their concern.

The final phase of a responsive evaluation is to prepare reports of results and recommendations. Frequently a case study format (see Chapter 14) is used in such reports, but
when appropriate, a traditional research format (see Chapter 2) can be used. A responsive
evaluation report will contain extensive descriptions of the concerns and issues identified
by stakeholders. Guba and Lincoln also recommended that the evaluator—in negotiation
with the stakeholders—make judgments and recommendations based on the gathered information. In this particular respect, their model is similar to the collaborative-evaluation
model, which we described earlier in the chapter.

Emergent Designs

Unlike the other types of evaluation research described above, evaluators doing a responsive evaluation do not specify a research design at the outset of their work. Instead, responsive evaluators use **emergent designs,** meaning that the design of the research
changes as the evaluator gains new insights into the concerns and issues of stakeholders.
For example, Guba and Lincoln compared sampling techniques in emergent as compared
to traditional research design:

> Sampling is almost never representative or random but purposive, intended to exploit compet-
> ing views and fresh perspectives as fully as possible. Sampling stops when information be-
> comes redundant rather than when subjects are representatively sampled.[47]

This view of sampling is consistent with the purposeful sampling methods described in
Chapter 6.

Fourth Generation Evaluation

Since their book on responsive evaluation appeared, Guba and Lincoln have further conceptualized their approach to evaluation and named it "fourth generation evaluation."[48]
The 12 steps of fourth-generation evaluation are shown in Figure 17.2. According to Guba
and Lincoln, these steps are not necessarily linear:

> Rather, the chart indicates progression only in a general way; it is the case that frequent back
> and forth movement, sometimes involving jumps over multiple steps, is not only possible but
> desirable.[49]

You will note that the chart makes reference to hermeneutic circles as part of the evaluation
process. Hermeneutics is a qualitative research tradition that we described in Chapter 15.
A **hermeneutic circle** is a process of interpretation that involves interpreting the meaning
of each part of a text and the text as a whole. Interpretation of the text as a whole helps interpretation of the parts and vice versa. In the context of responsive evaluation, the "text"
would be all the materials and data that have been collected as part of the research study.

Responsive evaluation and fourth generation evaluation represent important developments in educational evaluation. However, we caution the student who is considering

47. Ibid., p. 276.
48. Guba, E. G., & Lincoln, Y. S. (1989). *Fourth generation evaluation.* Thousand Oaks, CA: Sage.
49. Ibid., p. 185.

FIGURE 17.2

The Steps of Fourth Generation Evaluation

Step	Activities
1—Contracting	Initiate contract with client/sponsor
2—Organizing	Select/train team of evaluators Make entree arrangements Make logistical arrangements Assess local political factors
3—Identifying stakeholders	Identify agents, beneficiaries, victims Mount continuing search strategies Assess trade-offs and sanctions Formalize "conditions" agreements
4—Developing within-group joint constructions	Establish hermeneutic circles "Make" the circles Shape the emerging joint construction Check credibility
5—Enlarging joint stakeholder constructions through new information/increased sophistication	Make the circles again—Utilizing documentary information Interplay of interview and observation Literature analects Evaluator's etic construction
6—Sorting out resolved claims, concerns, and issues	Identify claims, concerns, and issues resolved by consensus Set aside as case report components
7—Prioritizing unresolved items	Determine participatory prioritizing process Submit items to prioritization Check credibility
8—Collecting information/adding sophistication	Collect information/train negotiators in its use, by: Utilizing further hermeneutic circles Gathering existing information Using new/existing instrumentation Performing special studies
9—Preparing agenda for negotiation	Define and elucidate unresolved items Elucidate competing constructions Illuminate, support, refute items Provide sophistication training Test agenda

continued

Figure 17.2   (Continued)

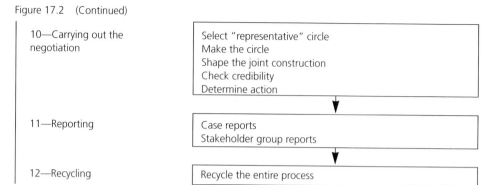

10—Carrying out the negotiation
- Select "representative" circle
- Make the circle
- Shape the joint construction
- Check credibility
- Determine action

11—Reporting
- Case reports
- Stakeholder group reports

12—Recycling
- Recycle the entire process

Source: Adapted from Figure 7.1 on pp. 186–187 in: Guba, E. G., and Lincoln, Y. S. (1989). *Fourth generation evaluation.* Thousand Oaks, CA: Sage. Copyright © 1989 by Sage Publications. Reprinted by permission of Sage Publications, Inc.

using one of these approaches for a thesis or dissertation study. These types of evaluation are usually complex, and are best carried out by a team of evaluators rather than by an individual working alone. Members of a team can act as a check on each other and ensure that a comprehensive picture of the entity being evaluated is formed. Also, the responsive evaluator should be conversant with a variety of research designs ranging from formal experiments to ethnographic inquiry. The reason for this requirement is that emergent design requires the selection of different research methodologies depending upon the phenomenon being investigated at a particular point in the evaluation.

If you plan to use the responsive or fourth-generation approach to evaluation as a guide for your thesis or dissertation study, you should consider finding an experienced team of evaluators with whom you can work. Perhaps the team already is engaged in planning or conducting a responsive evaluation study. You could then select one set of concerns or issues as a focus for your project.

Quasi-Legal Models of Evaluation

Adversary evaluation and judicial evaluation are two approaches to evaluation modeled on procedures derived from the field of law.

Adversary Evaluation

Adversary evaluation is distinguished by the use of a wide array of data; the hearing of testimony; and, most importantly, an adversarial approach, meaning that the two sides present positive and negative judgments, respectively, about the program being evaluated.[50]

The following are the four stages of adversary evaluation: (1) generating a broad range of issues concerning the program by surveying various stakeholders; (2) reducing the issues to a manageable number, e.g., through priority ranking by a group of volunteers; (3) formation of two opposing evaluation teams, each of which prepares an argument either in favor of or in opposition to the program on each issue; and (4) conduct of prehearing sessions and a formal hearing, in which the adversarial teams present their cases before those who must make a decision about the program.

50. Wolf, R. L. (1975). Trial by jury: A new evaluation method. *Phi Delta Kappan, 57,* 185–187.

Adversary evaluation was used by the National Institute of Education to evaluate minimum competency testing programs at a time when there was considerable controversy about this form of testing.[51] Two teams argued the merits of these programs before a hearings officer, who arbitrated disagreements over qualifications of witnesses and admissibility of testimony. The jury feature, sometimes recommended for adversary evaluation, was not included.

Adversary evaluation has proved useful in exposing strengths and weaknesses of programs and in raising questions that need to be answered. However, evaluators also have discovered that adversary evaluation has shortcomings.[52] Its results can be biased if one of the evaluation teams is more skilled in argumentation than the other. Some evaluators have modified elements of the model to deal with these problems.[53] However, other problems with this approach are built into the evaluation design, and hence are not easily modified. First of all, by its very nature adversary evaluation promotes a combative, "innocent vs. guilty" approach to program evaluation, which may contribute to further alienation among different types of stakeholders. Second, adversary evaluation requires a great deal of time and a large number of people, and thus is very expensive. These problems most likely explain why very few adversary evaluations can be found in the educational research literature.

Judicial Evaluation

The **judicial evaluation model** simulates the use of legal procedures for the purpose of promoting broad understanding of a program, clarifying the subtle and complex nature of the educational issues it raises, and producing recommendations and policy guidelines that lead to institutional growth and/or improved practice.[54] Unlike adversary evaluation, the judicial evaluation model does not involve a debate between two evaluation teams with victory or persuasion as the desired outcome.

In judicial evaluation, a public presentation of the data is made, following the format of hearings in a court of law. A panel comprised of policy makers, citizens, and other interested stakeholders is convened to hear the evidence. Case presenters call witnesses who present their views in order to make a case relative to a given issue. All witnesses may be subjected to two phases of direct examination and cross examination by the two case presenters. As in a court of law, opening and closing arguments are presented. After all evidence is presented, the panel deliberates and makes its recommendations.

Judicial evaluation has proved useful in both formative and summative evaluations of educational programs. While a full-fledged judicial evaluation tends to be expensive and time consuming, the procedure can be scaled down without sacrificing its essential quasi-legal nature.

Expertise-Based Evaluation

The use of experts to make judgments about the worth of an educational program is a time-honored and widely used method of evaluation. For example, most institutional programs are reviewed periodically by accreditation boards composed of experts. Commissions that

51. Thurston, P., & House, E. R. (1981). The NIE adversary hearing on minimum competency testing. *Phi Delta Kappan, 63*, 87–89.
52. Popham, W. J., & Carlson, D. (1977). Deep dark deficits of the adversary evaluation model. *Educational Researcher, 6*(6), 3–6. See also: Thurston, P. (1978). Revitalizing adversary evaluation: Deep dark deficits or muddled mistaken musings. *Educational Researcher, 7*(7), 3–8.
53. See, for example, Wood, K. C., Peterson, S. E., De Gracie, J. S., & Zaharis, J. K. (1986). The jury is in: Use of a modified legal model for school program evaluation. *Educational Evaluation and Policy Analysis, 8*, 309–315.
54. Wolf, R. L. (1990). Judicial evaluation. In H. J. Walberg & G. D. Haertel (Eds.), *The international encyclopedia of educational evaluation* (pp. 79–81). New York: Pergamon.

include experts and laypersons often are used to appraise the status of some aspect of the educational enterprise. An example is the National Commission on Excellence in Education, which produced the influential report *A Nation at Risk*.[55] If you do a thesis or dissertation project, its quality will be judged by a panel of professors who are in this role because of their presumed expertise.

Expertise-based evaluation has taken a new form with the rapid growth in the use of qualitative research traditions in education. Educational anthropologists, for example, can use the qualitative research method of ethnography to evaluate, as well as to describe, the phenomena that interest them. Another qualitative method used in evaluation is educational connoisseurship and criticism, which was developed by Elliott Eisner, an art educator.[56] This method involves two aspects: connoisseurship and criticism. The first aspect, **connoisseurship,** is the process of appreciating (in the sense of becoming aware of) the qualities of an educational program and their meaning. To perform this role well, the connoisseur must have expert knowledge of the program being evaluated as well as of other relevant programs. This expertise is similar to that of an art critic who has a special appreciation of a work of art because of intensive study of related art works and of art theory. An educational connoisseur, then, will be aware of more nuances of an educational program than will a novice educator or lay person. The second aspect, **educational criticism,** is the process of describing and evaluating that which has been appreciated.

The validity of educational connoisseurship and criticism depends heavily on the expertise of the evaluator. This condition also is a prominent feature of the other qualitative approaches to evaluation described above. Educational criticism differs from responsive evaluation and quasi-legal approaches to evaluation, however, in that it tends to be a solitary endeavor, and the questions that motivate the inquiry usually are set by the evaluator alone rather than in conjunction with stakeholders.

Example of an Expertise-Based Evaluation

Gail McCutcheon used the method of educational connoisseurship and criticism in a study of a fourth-grade classroom.[57] The purpose of the study was to answer several questions about the classroom: What is going on here? Is it worth doing? Was it done well? What are children likely to learn as a result? Notice that several of the questions call for description, and several clearly call for evaluation.

McCutcheon did six weeks of field work in the teacher's classroom, collecting data by means of observation, videotaping, interviews, and inspection of student work. The descriptive part of her report used a literary style to capture certain qualities of the teacher's classroom. The opening paragraph of the report exemplifies her writing style:

> Myriad sounds, smells, and sights greet the newcomer to Mr. Clement's room. The squeal of a guinea pig and the scrabbling of rats in their wire cages mingle with the voices of children as they discuss their private lives and schoolwork. Penny wants to know whether Maria and Freddie like each other because they sit together. Laura asks Mr. Clement if she may go to the library as another girl returns triumphantly, holding up *Mrs. Piggle Wiggle,* apparently a treasure. The smells of guinea pigs, rats, clean wood shavings, school disinfectant, and a freshly peeled orange intermix. Randy is eating raisins.[58]

55. National Commission on Excellence in Education. (1983). *A nation at risk: The imperative for educational reform.* Washington, DC: U. S. Government Printing Office.
56. Eisner, E. W. (2002). *The educational imagination: On the design and evaluation of school programs* (3rd ed.). Upper Saddle River, NJ: Prentice Hall.
57. McCutcheon, G. (1978). Of solar systems, responsibilities, and basics: An educational criticism of Mr. Clement's fourth grade. In Willis, G. (Ed.), *Qualitative evaluation: Concepts and cases in curriculum criticism* (pp. 188–205). Berkeley, CA: McCutchan.
58. Ibid., p. 192.

Later parts of the report are evaluative, as illustrated by the following comments:

> In this lesson, then, children had the opportunity to learn many things—things about the solar system, construction, visual problem- solving, self-control, and social interaction. We might wonder, though, whether responsibility for decision-making, planning socially, and self-control are worthwhile lessons . . . don't children learn these responsibilities anyway—in the home, the community, and school without so much emphasis being placed upon them?[59]
>
> When school is seen as an integral part of children's lives, children may be more likely to apply school learning and to consider doing schoollike things at home. A more unified life may make schooling seem more relevant. The less formal setting of this classroom and Mr. Clement's acknowledging the existence of children's personal interests may work toward this end.[60]

Note that the first evaluative comment is critical, whereas the second is complimentary. An evaluator needs to be sensitive to both the strengths and the weaknesses of the program being evaluated.

This study illustrates how educational connoisseurship and criticism can illuminate the nature and value of a program—in this case, fourth-grade instruction—in a way that would be difficult to accomplish using quantitative research methodology. According to Guba and Lincoln, this approach to educational evaluation was the first model to break cleanly with the traditional quantitative research paradigm.[61]

At the same time, the validity of the findings from educational connoisseurship and criticism is entirely dependent on the expertise of the researcher-critic. Therefore, it would be desirable to replicate the findings by additional case studies, preferably carried out by other researcher-critics. Alternatively, the findings could be considered tentative knowledge claims and further tested for validity using the methods of quantitative research.

If you are planning to do an evaluation study using the method of educational connoisseurship and criticism, you first should make a careful study of this method and the related qualitative methods that we described in Part V. Also, you should determine whether you have sufficient expertise about the program or other educational phenomenon that you intend to describe and evaluate. This means being knowledgeable about other programs, past and present, that are similar to the one you selected for study. You should keep in mind that expertise is one of the most important qualifications of an educational critic, just as it is one of the most important qualifications of a literary or art critic.

Educational Research and Development

Evaluation plays a key role in educational research and development (R & D). **Educational R & D** is an industry-based development model in which the findings of research are used to design new products and procedures, which then are systematically field-tested, evaluated, and refined until they meet specified criteria of effectiveness, quality, or similar standards. Overall, R & D expenditures in industry have averaged about four percent of sales over a 25-year period.[62] They are even higher in such areas as pharmaceuticals, where R & D has produced impressive technological advances. Educational R & D, however, accounts for less than one percent of each education dollar.[63] Nonetheless, it has great promise for

59. Ibid., p. 199.
60. Ibid., p. 202.
61. Guba & Lincoln (1989), *Fourth generation evaluation.*
62. Griliches, Z. (1987). R & D and productivity: Measurement issues and econometric results. *Science, 237,* 31–35.
63. Hoffman, C. M., & Snyder, T. (2000). *Digest of education statistics, 2000.* Washington, DC: U.S. Government Printing Office.

✦ *Touchstone in Research*

Borg, W. R. (1987). The educational R & D process: Some insights. *Journal of Experimental Education, 55,* 181–188.

Centre for Educational Research and Innovation. (1995). *Educational research and development: Trends, issues and challenges.* Paris: Organisation for Economic Co-operation and Development.

improving education because it involves a close connection between systematic program evaluation and program development.

R & D Models

One of the most widely used models of educational research and development is the systems approach model designed by Walter Dick and Lou Carey, which is shown in Figure 17.3. Ten steps are included in this version of the R & D cycle.[64] Step 1 involves the definition of goals for the instructional program or product, which often includes a needs assessment. Steps 2 and 3 may occur in either order, or simultaneously. In step 2, an instructional analysis is undertaken to identify the specific skills, procedures, and learning tasks that are involved in reaching the goals of instruction. Step 3 is designed to identify the learners' entry skills and attitudes, the characteristics of the instructional setting, and the characteristics of the settings in which the new knowledge and skills will be used. Step 4 involves translating the needs and goals of instruction into specific performance objectives. Performance objectives (described earlier in the chapter by the label "behavioral objectives") provide a means for communicating about the goals of the instructional program or product at different levels with different types of stakeholders. They also provide the basis for precise planning of test items, instructional materials, and the instructional delivery system.

During step 5, assessment instruments are developed. These instruments should be directly related to the knowledge and skills specified in the performance objectives. In step 6 a specific instructional strategy is developed for assisting learners with their efforts to achieve each performance objective. Step 7 involves the development of instructional materials, which may include print materials such as textbooks and teacher training manuals, or other media such as audiocassettes or interactive video systems. If the instructional plan specifies a teacher, lesson plans or guidelines for instruction by this person also would be developed as part of step 7.

Scriven's Approach to Formative/Summative Evaluation

Steps 8, 9, and 10 of Dick and Carey's model involve the distinction between formative and summative evaluation, which was formulated by Michael Scriven.[65] He observed that, in practice, evaluation serves two different functions. **Formative evaluation** is done by developers while the program or product is under development, in order to support the process of improving its effectiveness. In some situations, formative evaluation findings instead may lead to a decision to abort further development, so that resources are not wasted on a program that has little chance of ultimately being effective.

Summative evaluation is conducted to determine how worthwhile the final program is, especially in comparison with other competing programs. This type of evaluation usually is done by individuals other than the program developers, similar in manner to the Consumers Union (the publisher of *Consumer Reports*), which conducts comparative evaluations of many types of competing commercial products.

---

64. Dick, W., & Carey, L. (2001). *The systematic design of instruction* (5th ed.). New York: Longman. Another R & D model is presented in: Gagné, R. M., Briggs, L. J., & Wager, W. W. (1992). *Principles of instructional design* (3rd ed.). New York: Holt, Rinehart and Winston.
65. Scriven, M. (1967). The methodology of evaluation. In R. E. Stake (Ed.), *Curriculum evaluation*, American Educational Research Association Monograph Series on Evaluation, No. 1 (pp. 39–83). Chicago: Rand McNally. In a more recent publication, Scriven discusses ten common fallacies he has observed in evaluation practice in interpretation of the concepts of formative and summative evaluation: Scriven, M. (1991). Beyond formative and summative evaluation. In M. W. McLaughlin & D. C. Phillips (Eds.), *Evaluation and education: At quarter century. Ninetieth yearbook of the National Society for the Study of Education: Part II* (pp. 19–64). Chicago: NSSE.

FIGURE 17.3

The Steps of the Systems Approach Model of Educational Research and Development (R & D)

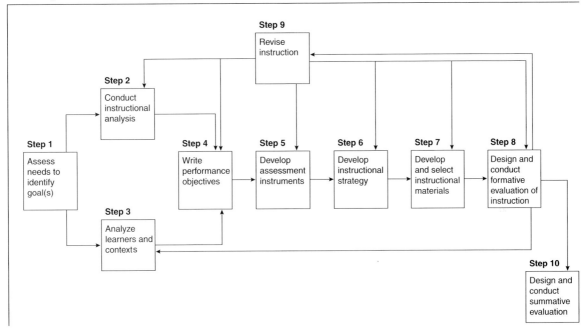

Source: Adapted from Figure 2.1 on pp. 2–3 in: Dick, W., Carey, L., & Carey, J. O. *The systematic design of instruction* (5th ed.). 2001. Copyright © 2001. Reprinted by permission by Allyn & Bacon.

Scriven created a checklist that is useful for the summative evaluation of programs or products.[66] Each of the twelve items on the checklist addresses one of the following questions:

1. How great is the need for the product?
2. How large and important is the market for the product?
3. How generalizable are the results of field tests of the product?
4. Did the field tests result in good data on samples of all relevant user groups?
5. How thorough was the cost analysis for the product?
6. How good is the evidence on the long-term effects of the product?
7. Were side-effects of the product diligently sought?
8. Were relevant ethical, professional, and research standards applied during the product development process?
9. Was the research design used in the field tests sufficiently rigorous to determine that the product was the actual cause of any observed effects?
10. How rigorous was the comparison between the product and its competitors?
11. How appropriate were the statistical analyses of field-test results, and if significance tests were done, did they yield statistically significant results?
12. How great is the educational significance of the product?

66. Scriven, M. (1974). Standards for the evaluation of educational programs and products. In G. D. Borich (Ed.), *Evaluating educational programs and products.* Englewood Cliffs, NJ: Educational Technology. A slightly different version of the checklist (the one that we describe) is available at http://www.wmich.edu/evalctr/checklists/.

Unfortunately, most programs and products still are developed without the type of rigorous evaluation recommended by Scriven.[67] For example, textbook publishers spend minimal time on formative evaluation of print materials, with the exception of expert reviews. A mechanism has been established, however, for the conduct of summative evaluations in education. The National Diffusion Network (NDN), a U.S. government agency, periodically conducts summative evaluations of selected educational programs. Programs are identified for evidence of effectiveness in meeting stated objectives at the original demonstration site and an indication that the program will be successful in similar sites.[68]

Dick and Carey's Approach to Formative/Summative Evaluation

In Dick and Carey's model, formative evaluation (step 8) is conducted throughout the development process, and its results are used to revise (step 9) any of the work carried out during the first seven stages—that is, to revise the instructional goals, instructional analysis, entry behaviors, performance objectives, test items, instructional strategy, and/or instructional materials in ways that appear desirable based upon the formative evaluation results.

Dick and Carey recommend a three-level process of formative evaluation: (1) trying out prototype materials one-on-one (i.e., one evaluator working with one learner); (2) a small group tryout with six to eight students; and (3) a field trial with a whole class of learners. This phase of evaluation relies heavily on qualitative methods, for example, interviewing and observation by the developer. Based upon the preliminary results the educational program is modified and further developed, and then tried out with a larger (although still somewhat small) number of learners. The evaluation again involves primarily qualitative methods, although quantitative methods (e.g., performance tests or self-report ratings) also might be used. Based on these results, the program is refined and expanded further, and then subjected to a field trial in a situation fairly close to the context in which it ultimately will be used (e.g., with a regular-size class of learners). At this point, the evaluation tends to be quantitative in nature, involving tests and other measures to determine the extent to which the program is achieving its intended objectives.

When the program has completed the development process, it is subjected to summative evaluation. Dick and Carey list summative evaluation as step 10 of their model. They comment, however, that it is "not considered an integral part of the instructional design process, per se," because it "usually does not involve the designer of the instruction, but instead involves an independent evaluator."[69]

Example of a Small-Scale R & D Project

Educational R & D projects require substantial resources. It is highly unlikely that a graduate student will be able to find the financial and personnel support to complete a major R & D project. In fact, educational R & D is beyond the abilities of most school districts.

If you plan to do an R & D project for a thesis or dissertation, you should keep these cautions in mind. It is best to undertake a small-scale project that involves a limited amount of original instructional design. Also, unless you have substantial financial resources, you will need to avoid expensive instructional media, such as film and synchronized slide-tape. Another way to scale down the project is to limit development to just a few steps of the R & D cycle.

67. Komoski, K. (1985). Instructional materials will not improve until we change the system. *Educational Leadership, 42* (7), 31–37.
68. An example of an NDN publication that describes validated programs is: Office of Educational Research and Improvement. (1991). *Mathematics education programs that work.* Washington, DC: U.S. Department of Education.
69. Dick & Carey, *Systematic design,* p. 7.

An example of an R & D dissertation is the project undertaken by Lawrence Cunningham to develop a history textbook and teacher's guidebook about the ancient Chamorros who lived on the island of Guam, a U.S. territory in the West Pacific.[70]

The Chamorros are the indigenous people of Guam, and study of the Chamorro language and of Guamanian history is a required subject in Guam's public schools. Cunningham's long-term goal was to develop a complete textbook and guide for use in Guam's high schools, but he limited the scope of his dissertation study to one chapter of the textbook and the section of the teacher's guide pertaining to that chapter. (Hereafter, we use the term *chapter* to refer to both the textbook chapter and the accompanying teacher's guide.) The objectives of Cunningham's study were as follows:

1. To review the relevant literature on textbook instructional design and Chamorro history.
2. To plan chapter objectives.
3. To develop a preliminary form of the chapter.
4. To field-test the preliminary form of the chapter.
5. To revise the preliminary form of the chapter based on the field-test results.
6. To conduct a main field test of the revised chapter.[71]

Each step of the R & D process used to develop the product is described in a separate chapter of the dissertation. Chapter 2 presents the results of Cunningham's research and information-collection activities. These activities included a search for existing relevant curriculum materials, a study of learner characteristics on Guam, a review of the literature on characteristics of effective text, and a review of the literature on the ethnohistory of Guam. Chapter 3 describes his initial planning activities, which focused on identifying objectives for the proposed chapter.

The following are examples of the objectives that Cunningham identified:

1. Given pictures of 15 ancient Chamorro artifacts, you will be able to match at least 12 with their descriptive labels.
2. Given paper, pencil, and a simulated situation in which you find an ancient Chamorro artifact, you will state the proper things to do and not to do, as stated in this chapter.
3. Given a drawing of a latte stone, you will label the two parts of the latte stone and identify the latte stone's purpose with 100 percent accuracy.
4. Given a map showing different environmental zones, you will identify good locations for building a village. Your reply will be judged on the basis of what archaeologists have discovered about ancient Chamorro settlement patterns.[72]

Note that the objectives are written in the form of behavioral objectives, which were discussed earlier in the chapter.

Chapters 4 and 5 of the dissertation describe the development of the preliminary form of the product and the preliminary field test. Two versions of the chapter were developed: an expository version written in conventional text format, and a narrative version, which covered the same content but in a story format. Cunningham developed the two versions because he was uncertain about which format would be more effective. It was feasible to

---

70. Cunningham, L. J. (1987). The development and validation of a high school textbook on the ancient Chamorros of Guam. *Dissertation Abstracts International, 48*(11), 2796A. (UMI No. 8800517)
71. Ibid., p. 6.
72. Ibid., pp. 34–35.

develop and test both versions because he limited the scope of his R & D effort to just one chapter of the proposed textbook.

Cunningham developed a variety of evaluation instruments: a domain-referenced achievement test, a teacher questionnaire, student attitude scales, and a student interview schedule. A total of 16 high school students from two typical Guamanian history classes participated in the preliminary field test. They were formed into two groups, with one group studying the expository version and the other group studying the narrative version. Both groups completed each of the evaluation instruments. In addition, the materials were reviewed by two archaeologists for accuracy, by several Chamorro community leaders for cultural acceptability, by an instructional technologist for quality of instructional design, by one of Guam's associate school superintendents for curriculum appropriateness, and by experts on this subject for lack of gender bias. The dissertation reported the results of the preliminary field test and described the revisions made in the materials on the basis of the results.

Chapter 6 of the dissertation presents the results of the main field test of the two revised versions of the product. This field test involved a pretest-posttest control-group experiment. The sample included five high school teachers and four Guamanian history classes taught by each teacher (total $N = 20$ classes). Each teacher's four classes were randomly assigned to the two treatment conditions, so that two classes of each teacher studied the expository version and two classes studied the narrative version. Each teacher taught both treatment conditions, thus controlling for the variable of teaching effectiveness. Checks for fidelity of treatment implementation were made.

Analysis of the experimental data revealed that both treatment groups made significant gains in achievement and attitudes. No significant differences between the groups taught by the expository version and groups taught by the narrative version were found in achievement or attitudes. Table 17.2 presents a typical statistical analysis, which compares the pretest and posttest mean scores of both groups on a domain-referenced achievement test.

In a subsequent face-to-face comparison of the two versions, the majority of the students preferred the narrative version. Conversely, the majority of the teachers preferred the expository version. Advocates of the narrative version felt that the story made ancient Guamanian history more interesting and easier to learn. Students who preferred the expository version felt that the story was a distraction from what they considered to be their primary task, which was to learn the information and pass a test on it.

TABLE 17.2

Performance of Guam History High School Students in Expository and Narrative Text Groups on Domain-Referenced Achievement Test

Treatment Group	N	Pretest M (SD)	Posttest M (SD)	Adjusted Posttest M	F
Expository text	157	5.25 (3.91)	24.97 (7.88)	25.04	.00
Narrative text	156	5.55 (4.14)	25.12 (6.86)	25.05	

Source: Adapted from Table 20 on p. 95 in: Cunningham, L. J. (1987). The development and validation of a high school textbook on the ancient Chamorros of Guam. *Dissertation Abstracts International, 48*(11), 2796A. (UMI 8800517)

Cunningham reached the following conclusions from these results:

> It appears, then, that expository and narrative text work equally well in ecologically-valid situations. They both contribute to student achievement. Therefore, decisions to choose expository or narrative text may be based on other considerations, such as student preferences or the nature of the subject matter.[73]

Cunningham eventually wrote a complete history textbook about ancient Guam and had it published.[74]

If you are considering an R & D project for your thesis or dissertation study, you should give careful consideration to the time required to plan and carry out such a project. The dissertation described above took well over a year for completion of product development through the main field test phase. The additional time required for an R & D project is worthwhile, however, if you are interested in making a contribution that will lead to an immediate tangible improvement in educational practice.

In the case of the dissertation described above, the developer was able to make a contribution not only to educational practice, but also to research knowledge. You will recall that Cunningham's main field test involved an experimental comparison of expository and narrative presentation of information. The results of the field test contributed new knowledge, and raised new questions, about the effects of variations in text characteristics on learners. For this reason, Cunningham wrote an article for a research journal in which he reported the findings of his main field test.[75]

The dissertation described above took the development of a program only through the main field test stage of the R & D cycle. It might be feasible to take some programs through all steps of the cycle. For other programs, the development task might be sufficiently complex to justify a dissertation study that ends at the preliminary field test stage. You and your dissertation committee will need to consider the nature of the proposed product and decide how much of the R & D cycle would constitute an acceptable study.

73. Ibid., p. 142.
74. Cunningham, L. J. (1992). *Ancient Chamorro society.* Honolulu: The Bess Press.
75. Cunningham, L. J., & Gall, M. D. (1990). The effects of expository and narrative prose on student achievement and attitudes toward textbooks. *Journal of Experimental Education, 58,* 165–175.

◆ RECOMMENDATIONS FOR
Doing an Evaluation Research Study

1. Explore the various reasons, including political reasons, that may underlie a request by an agency or an individual for an evaluation study.
2. Identify the significant stakeholders who will be affected by the evaluation study.
3. Delineate all possible aspects of the program that might be evaluated as a step in deciding the particular aspects that will be the actual focus of evaluation.
4. Remain open to new evaluation questions that arise as the evaluation process proceeds.
5. Be alert to the possibility of unintended positive or negative side-effects of the program being evaluated.

6. Consider the possibility that different reports of an evaluation study might need to be written for different stakeholder groups and the external professional community.
7. Consider which of the various quantitative and qualitative models of evaluation is best suited for your study.
8. Use the *Program Evaluation Standards* or other set of recognized standards in designing your evaluation study and in judging its adequacy after completing it.

✦ RECOMMENDATIONS FOR *Doing an R & D Project*

1. In designing a new educational program or product, draw upon pertinent research findings and research-based principles of instructional design.
2. Determine at the outset whether there is a sufficient need for the program or product and whether effective competitors already exist.
3. State the program or product's objectives in a form that enables them to be evaluated clearly.
4. Use methods of formative evaluation at each step of the development process.
5. Consider cessation of an R & D project, or a new start for it, if the results of a formative evaluation suggest that this is the best decision.
6. If the project results in a completed version of the program or product, consider having an external evaluator do a summative evaluation of its quality.
7. If you are interested in R & D and do not have the resources to develop your own program or product, consider doing a formative or summative evaluation of another group's R & D project.

✔ SELF-CHECK TEST

Circle the correct answer to each of the following questions. The answers are provided at the back of the book.

1. Educational evaluation can be used to improve
   a. program management.
   b. policy analysis.
   c. political decision making.
   d. all of the above.

2. Evaluation research is most similar to other types of research in its concern with
   a. providing information to facilitate decision making.
   b. using systematic procedures to collect and analyze data.

   c. obtaining findings that apply to a wider audience than those studied in the research.
   d. collecting data to shed light on the worth or value of educational phenomena.

3. Compared to an internal evaluator, an external evaluator generally
   a. is less concerned with identification of stakeholders affected by the program being evaluated.
   b. is more likely to be biased toward the program being evaluated.

c. is more likely to do a qualitatively oriented evaluation than a quantitatively oriented evaluation.

d. is in a better position to do a summative evaluation of a program.

4. A basic principle of goal-free evaluation is that
a. the evaluation design should not have goals.
b. the evaluator should be given free rein to determine goals for the program.
c. the evaluator should not know in advance the decisions that need to be made about the program.
d. the evaluator should not know in advance the program goals.

5. Objectives-based evaluation is used primarily to
a. determine how well a program is achieving its objectives.
b. compare the performance of individual students with group norms.
c. determine appropriate objectives for an educational program.
d. help decision makers identify their objectives for doing an evaluation study.

6. In the Context-Input-Process-Product (CIPP) model of evaluation, close collaboration between evaluators and program decision makers is required for every stage *except* to:
a. delineate the kinds of information needed for decision making.
b. synthesize obtained information so that it is maximally useful in making decisions.
c. obtain information as to the extent to which the goals of the program have been achieved.
d. determine whether an evaluation should be carried out.

7. Unlike judicial evaluation, adversary evaluation is characterized by
a. the use of various data sources.
b. a reliance on human testimony.
c. pro and con arguments.
d. a quasi-legal orientation.

8. In evaluation research, a discrepancy between an existing condition and a desired condition is called
a. a standard.
b. a need.
c. a cost-benefit.
d. a concern.

9. An emergent design in evaluation research is specified
a. before the stakeholders are identified.
b. at the time that program delineation occurs.

c. as the evaluation process occurs.
d. after concerns have been identified, using the CIPP model.

10. The method of educational connoisseurship and criticism depends heavily on
a. stakeholders' opinions of the program being evaluated.
b. the evaluator's understanding of the type of program being evaluated.
c. program managers' judgments of the program being evaluated.
d. all of the above.

11. Qualitative approaches to evaluation differ from quantitative models primarily in their
a. concern for identifying stakeholders affected by the program.
b. assumption of the availability of objective criteria to judge program worth.
c. concern for the values and perspectives of different stakeholders.
d. use of external evaluators to determine program worth.

12. Educational research and development (R & D) differs from other approaches to developing instructional programs because it
a. places heavy emphasis on evaluation as a basis for program revision.
b. focuses on maximizing the marketability of the educational program being developed.
c. avoids the use of qualitative data to make decisions about program revision.
d. does not depend on needs assessment to define instructional goals.

13. The typical sequence in formative evaluation of an educational program during an R & D cycle involves
a. starting with one learner and moving toward a field trial with a whole class of learners.
b. starting with test sites that approximate real-life conditions and moving toward sites that provide more experimental control.
c. starting with an emphasis on quantitative research methods and moving towards an emphasis on qualitative research methods.
d. all of the above.

CHAPTER 18

✦ **Action Research**

OVERVIEW

Action research has played a growing role in the field of education in recent years because of its promise for improving the work of educators and strengthening the connection between research and practice. This chapter describes the purposes that action research projects can serve, the unique features of action research, and the stages of a typical action research project. We discuss five criteria for determining the credibility and trustworthiness of an action research project and provide suggestions for designing action research in a manner that allows practitioners to reduce discrepancies between their espoused theories and theories-in-action. We also suggest strategies for dealing with unique ethical issues in action research.

OBJECTIVES

After studying this chapter, you should be able to

1. Understand the typical differences between action research and other forms of research.
2. Explain the main purposes for which educators carry out action research.
3. Explain how practitioners' reflection and systematic collection of data distinguishes action research from other forms of research or practice.
4. Describe the cyclical nature and the stages of typical action research projects.

5. Apply five criteria for determining the credibility and trustworthiness of an action research project.
6. Understand how action research can help inform practitioners' theories-in-action.
7. Understand how to address ethical issues arising in action research.

Introduction

Action research in education is a form of applied research whose primary purpose is the improvement of an education professional's own practice. We use the term *action research* to include what is sometimes called *practitioner research,*[1] *teacher research,*[2] *insider research,*[3] and (usually when carried out by teacher educators on their own practice) *self-study research.*[4] Teachers conduct much of the action research in education, and this chapter sometimes refers specifically to teacher research in explaining the characteristics of action research.

Action research may utilize any of the research methods described in other chapters of this book and may involve collaboration with colleagues, clients, or professional researchers (typically, university professors). It also may have other purposes in addition to improving practice, as we describe later in the chapter.

Table 18.1 provides a convenient summary of the typical differences between action research and formal research, which is research designed to produce generalizable knowledge of the type reported in academic journals. It should be noted, however, that some action research, even though carried out by practitioners, has some of the characteristics of formal research and might also be published in academic journals. More typically, action research projects are publicly reported in online action research journals or Web sites of various action research networks.[5] These reports enable other practitioners, whether or not they carry out their own action research, to benefit from the knowledge generated by action researchers.

Purposes for Conducting Action Research

The topics and methods of action research are virtually unlimited. It is important for practitioners to consider their purposes for undertaking action research so that they are more likely to produce results consistent with those purposes. In an effort to clarify the varied motivations that underlie action research endeavors, Kenneth Zeichner and Susan Noffke define three dimensions—personal, professional, and political—to reflect the varied purposes for which action research may be carried out.[6] Here, using teacher research as the form of action research, we summarize the examples that the authors give to clarify each dimension. We find some overlap between the dimensions which you may notice in the author's examples. In fact, Zeichner and Noffke describe the dimensions as "interwoven categories . . . for illuminating emphases" within action research.[7]

♦ Touchstone in Research

Reason, P., & Bradbury, H. (Eds.). (2001). *Participative inquiry and practice.* Thousand Oaks, CA: Sage.

Stringer, E. T. (1999). *Action research.* Thousand Oaks, CA: Sage.

1. Zeichner, K. M., & Noffke, S. E. (2001). Practitioner research. In V. Richardson (Ed.), *Handbook of research on teaching* (4th ed., pp. 298–330). Washington, DC: American Educational Research Association.
2. Cochran-Smith, M., & Lytle, S. L. (1999). The teacher research movement: A decade later. *Educational Researcher, 28*(7), 15–25.
3. Kemmis, S., & McTaggart, R. (2000). Participatory action research. In N. K. Denzin & Y. S. Lincoln (Eds.), *Handbook of qualitative research* (2nd ed., pp. 567–605). Thousand Oaks, CA: Sage.
4. Zeichner & Noffke, *Practitioner research.*
5. For a summary of Internet resources supporting teacher research networks, see: Hobson, D., & Smolin, L. (2001). Teacher researchers go online. In Burnaford, G., Fischer, J., & Hobson, D. (Eds.), *Teachers doing research* (2nd ed., pp. 83–118). Mahwah, NJ: Lawrence Erlbaum Associates.
6. Zeichner & Noffke, *Practitioner research.*
7. Ibid, p. 307.

TABLE 18.1

Common Differences between Action Research and Formal Research

Topic	Formal Research	Action Research
Training needed by researcher	Extensive training	On own or with consultation
Goals of research	Knowledge that is generalizable	Knowledge to apply to the local situation
Method of identifying the problem to be studied	Review of previous research	Problems or goals currently faced
Procedure for literature review	Extensive, using primary sources	More cursory, using secondary sources
Sampling approach	Random or representative sampling	Students or clients with whom they work
Research design	Rigorous control, long time frame	Looser procedures, change during study; quick time frame; control through triangulation
Measurement procedures	Evaluate and pretest measures	Convenient measures or standardized tests
Data analysis	Statistical tests; qualitative techniques	Focus on practical, not statistical significance; present raw data, graphs
Application of results	Emphasis on theoretical significance; increased knowledge about teaching and learning in general	Emphasis on practical significance; improved teaching and learning in a particular classroom
Reporting outcome	Published report; journal article; professional conference	Informal sharing with colleagues; brief report; ERIC document; conferences

Source: Mettetal, G. (2001). Research about Teaching and Learning. Retrieved March 1, 2002, from Indiana University South Bend, Website: http://www.iusb.edu/~gmetteta/Research_about_Teaching_and.htm#Comparison

Personal Purposes for Action Research

Action research with a primarily personal motivation has as its central purpose the improvement of the researcher's practice. Thus the focus is on the teacher and the teacher's own students. Specific purposes might include the following:

- to develop a greater understanding of individual students' thoughts and actions
- to develop a deeper understanding of teachers' experiences with particular educational innovations
- to provide teachers an opportunity for personal examination and generation of theory
- to produce heightened self awareness in practitioners, including clarification of their assumptions about education and recognition of contradictions between their espoused ideas and actual classroom practice

- to examine the impact of the research process on practitioners
- to conduct research as an individual learning process that values experiential knowledge

In summary, action research done for personal purposes is intended to promote greater self-knowledge, fulfillment, and professional awareness among practitioners.

Professional Purposes for Action Research

Action research that is carried out primarily for professional purposes typically involves practitioners:

- engaging in action research as a form of staff development.
- seeking to legitimize their role as producers of knowledge and contributors to the literature on educational research and theory.
- developing networks of practitioners engaged in action research to promote their colleagueship and professionalism.

Action research undertaken for professional purposes, then, typically involves teachers' efforts to extend their research beyond the classroom. It enables practitioners to study, and seek to influence directly, the social and institutional contexts in which they work, rather than depending on analyses of their work contexts by outsiders. According to Zeichner and Noffke, such action research contributes to bridging the gap that exists between educational theory and educational practice, but without fundamentally altering the relationship between the research and practice communities.

Political Purposes for Action Research

Action research can explicitly address political purposes by:

- seeking to make one's own teaching practices more humane and just.
- providing full participation in the research process of all those who are affected by it.
- embracing an overt agenda of social change, with a commitment to promote economic and social justice through collaborative efforts to increase educational opportunities and outcomes for all constituents. Typical efforts address issues of gender, class, cultural equity, and voice in education.[8]

Zeichner and Noffke claim that "all forms of educational research embody particular [political] stances, either to maintain existing lines of power and privilege or to transform them along more just and caring lines."[9] However, action research that is explicitly carried out with a political purpose is intended to bring about fundamental social change toward the goal of greater social justice for all. In the process, action researchers seek to emancipate themselves as well from existing limits to expression of their voice and to take actions that challenge the status quo with respect to their professional identities.

In reading action research reports, we suggest that you consider the researcher's stated purpose or purposes for carrying out the research. In addition, we recommend that you consider the three purposes (personal, professional, and political) that we describe above to make your own analysis of why a particular action research project was carried out or what purposes it served, whether intended or not. As action researchers gain greater knowledge and research experience, some may narrow their purpose, while others may broaden their focus to address varied purposes. If you plan to carry out an

✦ **Touchstone in Research**

Freedman, S. W., Simons, E. R., Kalnin, J. S., & Casareno, A. (1999). *Inside city schools: Investigating literacy in multicultural classrooms.* New York: Teachers College Press.

---

8. Other approaches for addressing these issues are cultural studies and critical theory, which are described in Chapter 15.
9. Zeichner & Noffke, *Practitioner research,* p. 309.

action research project, we suggest that you reflect on your own purposes early in your planning.

Contrast between Action Research and Typical Professional Practice

Most educational practitioners seek to refine and improve their practice in various ways. For example, they might use trial and error, get ideas from colleagues, or try out a strategy they hear about at a professional meeting. These strategies can be a good starting point for the improvement of practice, but action research takes them further by including a process of systematic data collection and analysis.

Some qualitative researchers claim that action research involves only the collection of qualitative data.[10] However, the various action research reports that we have read include qualitative, quantitative, or both types of data. Davydd Greenwood and Morten Levin emphasize this feature of action research by stating:

> . . . action research is inherently multimethod research, including scientific experiments, quantitative social research, and qualitative research methods from as many disciplines as necessary to address the problem at hand. Effective action research cannot accept an a priori limitation to one or another research modality.[11]

An example of "multimethod" action research is the study by Thomas Scott and Michael O'Sullivan of students' use of the Internet to get information for social studies assignments.[12] This action research project was carried out in the high school where Scott served as a social studies teacher and O'Sullivan as the instructional media coordinator and librarian. Their published research report presents questionnaire results on the percentage of students reporting use of the Internet daily (25 percent) or weekly (3 percent), use of the Internet specifically as a research tool to collect information for assignments (42 percent), and use of search engines (74 percent) and online databases (7 percent).

Another finding of their action research project was that 262 of the 309 respondents (nearly 85 percent) evaluated their Internet search skills as either excellent or good. Scott and O'Sullivan did not accept these quantitative findings as the whole story, however, noting that, " . . . as our qualitative data will show, many students expressed difficulties navigating Web sites."[13] They analyzed qualitative data from essays written by student volunteers after completing an assignment that involved use of the Internet in a search for information on a specific social studies topic and evaluation of the three top Web sites identified in the search.

Despite the students' high regard for the Internet's value to learning, the essays reveal their frustration over constraints in usage (e.g., difficulty in navigating and the time that it took). A student who had researched the topic of the Boxer Rebellion observed:

> The Internet search told me a lot about the Internet. . . . The first page just told me that the Boxer Rebellion originated in China. It had no depth on the subject. My second site wanted to sell me a book on it. . . . The third was just junk, it was someone trying to get people to rebel against wearing boxer shorts.[14]

---

10. See, for example: Zeni, J. (Ed.). (2001). *Ethical issues in practitioner research.* New York: Teachers College Press.
11. Greenwood, D. J., & Levin, M. (2000). Reconstructing the relationships between universities and society through action research. In N. K. Denzin & Y. S. Lincoln (Eds.), *Handbook of qualitative research* (2nd ed., pp. 85–106). Thousand Oaks, CA: Sage.
12. Scott, T. J., & O'Sullivan, M. (2000). The internet and information literacy: Taking the first step toward technology education in the social studies. *The Social Studies,* May/June, 121–125.
13. Ibid, p. 122.
14. Ibid, p. 124.

The qualitative essay data also revealed students' eventual discovery of effective Internet search strategies.

Both the quantitative and qualitative data were central to Scott and O'Sullivan's recommendations about how social studies teachers should develop students' information literacy. They urge social studies teachers "to develop their students' ability to question, think critically, and use inquiry to determine truth from falsehood" by developing a curriculum "infused with lessons that examine the ideological, ethical, cultural, and scientific relationship of technology to our daily lives . . . [and] whether technological change and innovation are shared equitably on a national and international basis."[15]

These recommendations exemplify the type of knowledge that action research can provide to other practitioners. One could argue, however, that they are written in a form that approaches a claim to generalizable knowledge, which is typically not associated with action research findings (see Table 18.1). As in case study research, both the design of an action research study and the way in which it is reported can affect its generalizability. Efforts to study typical cases, or to select a random sample within the group that the researcher studies, increase the likelihood of generalizability. Ultimately, the readers' interpretation determines whether the findings reported in an action research study fit their situation. Scott and O'Sullivan's action research report provides two kinds of information to help readers make this determination: first, the inclusion of descriptive quantitative statistics (student percentages) that are easy to compare in different settings, and second, the provision of a rich, thick description of their qualitative findings.

Contrast between Action Research and Other Forms of Research

Action research differs most from other forms of research in its emphasis on reflection as an important part of the research cycle. **Reflection** is a process in which practitioners step back from the fast-paced and problematic world of practice to ponder and share ideas about the meaning, value, and impact of their practice. From such reflection, practitioners make new commitments, discover new topics to explore, and gain new insights into the strengths and weaknesses of their current practices.

David Hobson claims that action research gives teachers an opportunity to perceive their world more freshly by reflecting on it and thus "to render the familiar strange."[16] He describes reflection as "a process of making sense of one's experience and telling the story of one's journey."[17] Such reflection corresponds to what Donald Schön calls *reflection-on-action,* which consists of reflection after the event, as opposed to *reflection-in-action,* which is undertaken in the midst of the action.[18]

Hobson views autobiographical narrative as being at the heart of reflection in teacher action research:

Narrative asks the question: What does this research have to do with me?

. . . Our narratives include our insights, searches for meaning, and the connectedness we find in the world . . . Looking at our own autobiographies, reliving our own experiences with inequity, power, and authority in schools, offers us the opportunity to inform ourselves further and move forward to change situations in which today's students experience injustice.[19]

15. Ibid, p. 125.
16. Hobson, D. (2001). Action and reflection: Narrative and journaling in teacher research. In Burnaford, G., Fischer, J., & Hobson, D. (Eds.), *Teachers doing research* (2nd ed., pp. 7–27). Mahwah, NJ: Lawrence Erlbaum Associates. Quote appears on p. 8.
17. Ibid.
18. Schön, D. A. (1983). *The reflective practitioner.* San Francisco: Jossey-Bass.
19. Hobson, *Action and reflection,* p. 14.

Hobson also recommends that teacher researchers keep a journal, a "*written record of practice,*" to help them evaluate their experiences.[20] Table 18.2 summarizes Hobson's suggestions for keeping an action research journal as a basis for reflection.

The reflections that occur through autobiographic narrative and journaling can help action researchers throughout the research process: to identify problems of practice that deserve systematic attention via action research, to highlight issues or assumptions in their own beliefs about teaching and learning, and to suggest personally relevant interpretations of the data they collect. Hobson uses an action research project by Rick Moon, a physical education teacher and teacher researcher, to illustrate these uses of reflection.[21] Moon found himself observing the girls and boys in his classes more closely after the birth of his first daughter, and reflected on his old beliefs about gender differences:

> [Prior to] the birth of my daughters, . . . I concentrated solely on male athletics . . . though I helped score or officiate some of the girls' athletic competitions, I realize now that I did not have much respect for them."[22]

TABLE 18.2

Suggestions for Keeping an Action Research Journal

1. Use 8½ × 11'' pages and put them in a 3-ring binder so that the pages can be removed, added, or rearranged. For ease of carrying, you might prefer a 6'' × 9'' binder, blank lesson plan book, post-it note pad, or spiral-bound notebook.
2. Date and time each entry to facilitate viewing developmental processes over time. Start each entry on a new page so that the pages can be grouped to reflect recurring patterns or reconstruct sequences.
3. Make time for journaling by picking a regular time free of interruption, or writing in class while your students are writing.
4. Use descriptive writing to record directly observed/experienced details for later review.
5. Use reflective writing to comment, associate, and make meaning.
6. Use double-entry journal writing with a description on one side of the page and reflection on the other side.
7. Keep a daily log to help reveal priorities, what absorbs your attention, and what continuing issues predominate.
8. Name each important teacher you have known, and describe each one. Look for commonalities; describe the steppingstones in your experience of teaching and reflect on your development over time.
9. Examine the materials you have been reading and bring the results of your investigations into your journal.
10. Develop a "journal of the journals," going back through your entire journal seeking themes, highlighting passages, and having a friend read aloud the lines you have highlighted.
11. Ask your students to turn in "exit slips" at the end of each class reflecting on their learning, questions, and expectations.

Source: Adapted from Hobson, D. (2001). Action and reflection: Narrative and journaling in teacher research. In Burnaford, G., Fischer, J., & Hobson, D. (Eds.), *Teachers doing research* (2nd ed., pp. 7–27). Mahwah, NJ: Lawrence Erlbaum Associates.

20. Ibid, p. 19.
21. Moon, R. (2001). The personal and the professional: Learning about gender in middle school physical education. In Burnaford, G., Fischer, J., & Hobson, D. (Eds.), *Teachers doing research* (2nd ed., pp. 151–156). Mahwah, NJ: Lawrence Erlbaum.
22. Ibid, p. 151.

Moon then shares an excerpt from a notebook that he turned in to a man from whom he took a physical education class while in college:

> Our society is being taken over by women who won't allow their children to play any rough sports and condemn any fighting. . . . It is our job as PE teachers to teach combativeness, roughness, and physical contact to students, without causing serious injury, in order to prevent women and sissies from taking over our society.[23]

Moon adds, "My teacher responded to this with the words:'And don't ever forget it!' "[24]

Moon's action research involved studying gender equity in his own classroom. His report of his reflections includes memories of his own college years and the birth of his first daughter; experiences working with his male and female students; imagining his second daughter shattering gender stereotypes in the future; and his personal insight that "To be a man today and to be married, and to be a father, requires rethinking the images one holds."[25]

By including these reflections in his action research report, Moon not only documented his own personal growth, but also possibly helped fellow practitioners on their own reflective journey.

The Cyclical Nature of Action Research

Some conceptions of action research treat it as having a definite beginning and end, similar to most formal research projects.[26] Action research projects that are carried out for a dissertation or course assignment may fit this pattern, particularly because writing up the project tends to require the completion of an activity and a summary report of the results. However, when carried out by practitioners as part of their everyday work, action research is more likely to be cyclical in nature.

The reason for this cyclicity is that action researchers: (a) do not always carry out the stages of action research in the same order, (b) may return to an earlier stage as their research progresses, and (c) may continue going through the stages rather than bringing the research to an end. In fact, if action researchers systematically collect information on the effectiveness of their practice or of changes in it, and then continue or further modify their practice based on their findings and reflections, action research can become a natural component of practice.

Jeffrey Glanz analyzes the process of an action research project into six steps: (1) selecting a focus, (2) collecting data, (3) analyzing and interpreting the data, (4) taking action, (5) reflecting, and (6) continuing or modifying one's actions, which in turn leads to a new focus for another round of action research.[27] The steps are illustrated in Figure 18.1. Later in the chapter we use this six-step model to describe the stages of a specific teacher's action research project.

Proactive and Responsive Action Research

Many practitioners take action as the first stage of their action research projects; they subsequently collect, analyze, and reflect on data to determine whether the action is meeting

23. Ibid, pp. 151–152.
24. Ibid, p. 152.
25. Hobson, *Action and reflection*, p. 16.
26. Noffke, S. E. (1997). Professional, personal, and political dimensions of action research. In M. W. Apple (Ed.), *Review of research in education*, (vol. 22, pp. 305–343). Washington, DC: American Educational Research Association.
27. Glanz, J. (1998). *Action research: An educational leader's guide to school improvement*. Norwood, MA: Christopher-Gordon.

FIGURE 18.1

Cyclical Nature of Action Research

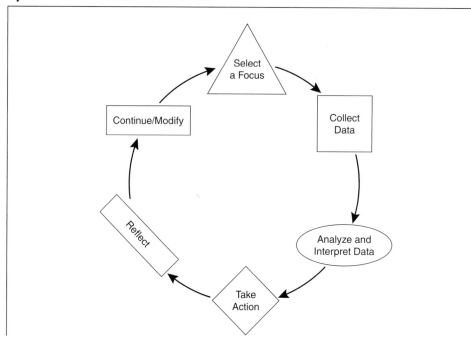

Source: Figure 1.10 on p. 27 in: Glanz, J. (1998). *Action research: An educational leader's guide to school improvement.* Norwood, MA: Christopher-Gordon. Permission granted by the publisher.

their intended purpose; and then they continue the action, modify it, or take a new action based on their interpretation of the data. Richard Schmuck refers to this form of research as **proactive action research.**[28] In other cases, practitioners might decide first to collect data without doing any other modification of practice, and then use the data analysis to identify a new practice to be tried. Schmuck calls this form of research **responsive action research.**

Because both proactive and responsive action research occur in repetitive cycles, the distinction between these forms of action research tends to fade as researchers continue the action research process as an integral part of their practice. Nonetheless, in designing an action research project, you need to think about your starting point. Once you choose a focus, most likely you will start by either trying a new action prior to collecting data (which represents proactive action research), or by first collecting data on the impact of your practice prior to taking any new action (which represents responsive action research).

Once the action research cycle is in motion, researchers typically move back and forth between experimenting with new practices and collecting more data, using the latter to inform and guide the former. In some cases, the process of data collection itself represents action when it significantly modifies the way in which action researchers carry out their practice. For example, James Lytle conducted action research in the district where he had just

28. Schmuck, R. A. (1997). *Practical action research.* Arlington Heights, IL: IRI Skylight.

become the superintendent.[29] The project involved collaborative research and practitioner inquiry designed "to lead a group of urban principals and a group of middle management support staff toward the design of demonstrably effective educational organizations."[30]

As the new superintendent, Lytle first reviewed performance evaluation reports on students from the previous school year and then visited 800 classrooms in September and October to develop "first impressions."[31] From November through February he conducted a second round of visits, focusing on classrooms and subjects in which failure rates were high. He made extended field notes on 30 classrooms, which he shared with principals and other administrators. He did not share these notes with the teachers he had observed, however, because the observations were largely critical. Lytle found, as John Goodlad had found years before,[32] that:

> A great deal of classroom activity was boring, repetitive, unengaging, and vapid. It seemed intended primarily to kill time. But I also heard a recurrent lament from the teachers: the children they were teaching were different, they said, from the ones they had taught five and 10 years earlier; their emotional needs were so great that the teachers felt constantly torn between teaching the curriculum and tending to their students' problems.[33]

Lytle ended the school year by conducting discussions with the teachers whose classrooms he had visited, inviting them in grade-level groups of sixteen to eighteen teachers. Two-thirds of the teachers accepted the invitations. During the second school year he proposed that the principals conduct a study "as a way of deepening our shared understanding of why students behave and perform as they do."[34] The study put the principals themselves in the role of action researchers:

- The principals who agreed to participate each shadowed one student in their school, collected varied forms of data, and in small teams wrote a report of their findings which they shared with the entire group of principals.
- Four focus groups of principals convened to discuss final report card grades from the previous school year.
- All the principals in the district agreed to study themselves as a way of better understanding the principalship, and, working in pairs, they created an ethnography of their partners.

As Lytle described it, these action research projects involved:

> . . . an evolving strategy of inquiry-based activities designed to build a learning-to-learn organization. . . . By deciding to demonstrate that the job of regional superintendent could be carried out in less conventional and potentially more effective ways, I was intentionally modeling an approach to leadership that I hoped would cause principals and teachers to question their own practice.[35]

Lytle noted discernible improvements in student performance over the three-year period of his action research project, although "it would be inappropriate to claim a causal relationship between the administrative development activities of the regional office and student performance."[36] Nonetheless, Lytle's report of the expanding data collection

29. Lytle, J. H. (1996). The inquiring manager: Developing new leadership structures to support reform. *Phi Delta Kappan, 77*, 664–670.
30. Ibid, p. 664.
31. Ibid, p. 666.
32. Goodlad, J. I. (1984). *A place called school: Prospects for the future.* New York: McGraw-Hill.
33. Lytle, The inquiring manager, p. 666.
34. Ibid, p. 667.
35. Ibid, p. 670.
36. Ibid.

process makes it clear that his fostering of other school administrators' participation in data collection was itself a major new action, or set of actions, on the superintendent's part, designed to transform the exercise of leadership in the district.

The Stages of Action Research

To illustrate the stages of an action research project, we will refer to a study conducted by Denise Dabisch, a high-school Spanish teacher, and reported in the journal *Networks,* an online journal of teacher research.[37] Because Dabisch took action before collecting any data, her project represents proactive action research. Using Glanz's model (see Figure 18.1), we present the stages in the order in which Dabisch completed them.

Selecting a Focus

Dabisch conducted her study while taking a university course on teacher research. She specified her research question as whether a new arrangement of the students' desks in her Spanish 1 classroom would promote cooperative learning and better classwork. Dabisch describes her classroom before the research study as having two "L" shaped rows facing the front board. When she gave students the option to work in groups, they rarely interacted. Furthermore, the double-L arrangement made it difficult for students to move into groups, because even if they moved their desks "it was difficult to tell which desk belonged with which group. I spent my time reminding them that they were a group and they were to be working on a group assignment. This was not a good use of our time. This arrangement was not working!"[38]

Taking Action

After telling her students that she was thinking about changing the desk arrangement and noting a positive response, Dabisch made the change on her own after winter break. She put the desks in a "tripod" arrangement (three desks to a group) so that no group would feel isolated and every student would be able to see the board. When students came to class the next day, they asked if they could sit where they want, and Dabisch permitted them to do so. She describes that day as "one of the most difficult days of my teaching career!!" because there was so much off-task talking.[39] Subsequently she assigned students to groups and set ground rules spelling out the advantages of students being able to work together. She also emphasized the necessity for them to respect each other's right to learn and the teacher's right to teach, or that she would be forced to change the seating arrangement back to the way it had been. She reports: "After this warning there were no major problems or frustrations related to the groupings."[40]

Collecting Data

After some uncertainty about how to begin her data collection, Dabisch began by observing the students once a week. She found that the class was very quiet, with a few students asking each other questions but then returning to solitary work. Dabisch wanted to improve the quality of their interactions. She assigned roles to each student in a group, with the 2's being recorder and the 1's and 3's giving input on how to figure out the answer to

---

37. Dabisch, D. I. (2001). From desks to a quest: Understanding the process of teacher research. *Networks, 4*(2), Article 1. Retrieved October 11, 2001, from http: www.oise.utoronto.ca/~ctd/networks
38. Ibid, *In the Beginning* section, paragraph 1.
39. Ibid, *Adjustments* section.
40. Ibid.

each question. She found that this change led to more sharing of ideas and a higher order of questioning within each group.

Dabisch developed an observation sheet to help her take notes, then revised it to give her more writing room, and discussed with her teacher research group the difficulty she was having tracking all the interactions.[41] Following her colleagues' advice, she chose one student group on which to focus. Her observations allowed her to see how the three girls in this group changed their assigned roles "to be representative of each girl's personality."[42]

Dabisch began assigning codes to the group interactions, for example *PGQ* to note when a study group posed a group question. She created a group sociogram with the question, "If you were given a major assignment in this class, who would you want to work with and who wouldn't you want to work with?"[43] Student commented, "That's a mean question!" Dabisch explained it was for her research and that she would not want anyone to share this information with other students, so they would not hurt anyone's feelings: "I felt that sharing what my research was about and clueing the students in on what I was trying to accomplish made them act maturely. I believe the sociogram was a success due to their respect and understanding of my research."[44]

Analyzing and Interpreting the Data

The sociogram data enabled Dabisch to learn the social composition of her class:

> Many students picked the same two students who were "A" students all year long, to work with on a major project. I also had one student no one else wanted to work with.[45]

Using these results, Dabisch changed the members in two of the groups in order to test whether students would work better when they picked their own group members. She notes: "This made me wonder if a student's maturity level is a factor in letting them create their own groups. Another question to consider for my next project!"[46] After pondering about asking students what they could do to include the student who the sociogram data showed to be an isolate, Dabisch decided to say nothing, "because I did not want to take the chance of having the other students say something that would make them expose this student."[47]

The teacher also gave students a survey to get their ideas about her research question, and then incorporated some of their ideas in making further changes to the seating arrangement. She then conducted tape-recorded interviews, which helped her discover that two students whose grades were dropping did not blame their groups as she had expected, but took responsibility themselves: "I did notice, though, that as a result of these interviews the students' grades began to improve shortly thereafter."[48]

Dabisch describes the positive responses of some students to the changed group arrangement as supporting the claim of her state department of education on its website that " . . . cooperative learning provides students the opportunities to model the language,

---

41. When teachers carry out action research as part of a university course, they often are formed into small teacher research groups so that classmates can learn together and give each other feedback and support.
42. Dabisch, From desks to a quest, *Beginning the Research* section, paragraph 5.
43. Ibid, *More Research* section, paragraph 1. A sociogram is a graphic representation of the relationships between each member of a group with all the other members of a group; it is often used to identify the most and least popular group members.
44. Dabisch, From desks to a quest, *More Research* section, paragraph 1.
45. Ibid, *More Research* section, paragraph 3.
46. Ibid.
47. Ibid, *More Research* section, paragraph 4.
48. Ibid, *More Research* section, paragraph 8.

produce quick feedback, and comprehend what is going on in class"[49] She adds: "This made me feel great because I felt I had helped two very good students work up to their potential while meeting their needs for more one-on-one work."[50]

Reflection

Dabisch's report of her action research project in the online journal *Networks* includes comments on her thoughts and feelings at various points during the research process and reflective asides in italics. For example, after taking the initial action to change the seating arrangement Dabisch reports:

> This turned out to be one of the most difficult days of my teaching career!! There was so much off task talking. . . . No one was quiet! I said to myself, "I'VE HAD IT!" after just one day! I was frustrated with the whole study, but I decided to give the arrangement one more day. . . . The next day there was still too much "off task" talking, so I set some ground rules. . . .[51]

After asking her students not to share the information they gave on the sociogram with other students so they would not hurt anyone's feelings, Dabisch reflects:

> At this point I realized how much this honesty paid off. The class that I was researching was my largest Spanish 1 class and sometimes a large class can be a disciplinary problem. Now I believe that sharing with my students exactly what I was doing in class and with my research project made them feel a part of what was going on in our class. They felt like they had a voice because I constantly asked them what they thought about different aspects of my research.[52]

Continuing or Modifying Action

Dabisch's research report illustrates a continuing cycle of reflection, collection and analysis of varied types of data, and the use of the data to define new actions to take in her teaching. For example, you will recall that in describing the stage of her action research project called *Collecting Data,* we noted Dabisch's inference that the three girls in the group on which she was focussing her data collection changed their assigned roles "to be representative of each girl's personality." Her inference led to a new idea for exploring the research literature and taking new action: "This made me wonder if perhaps research on the social aspects of group or cooperative learning would be something I could look into."[53] At several points in her report, Dabisch inserts her thoughts about other new directions that she might take in future action research.

Dabisch openly describes the shortcomings of her action research project, specifically in reporting her realization that simply putting students into prearranged groups was not sufficient to promote cooperative learning among the students in each group. After reviewing more research on cooperative learning, she posed a new question:

> "What would happen if I assigned tasks for each student in a group and tailored my lessons to make them a cooperative effort?" And so the teacher research cycle begins again.[54]

Dabisch reports that, after doing this research, she thought much more broadly about her teaching responsibilities:

> Like many teachers, I had not always talked with my students about what they do to prepare for class and how they like the classroom environment. I found myself becoming much more

49. Ibid.
50. Ibid.
51. Ibid, *Adjustments* section.
52. Ibid, *More Research* section, paragraph 2, italics in original.
53. Ibid, *Beginning the Research* section, paragraph 5.
54. Ibid, *One Journey Ends* section, paragraph 1.

respectful of my students' needs as well as my own. . . . Already I find myself wondering about what intriguing, important questions I will "live" next year as my students and I learn and grow together.[55]

Credibility and Trustworthiness of Action Research

The increasing presence of action research reports in the literature has been accompanied by growing concern about their validity. In keeping with the interpretivist epistemology that underlies most action research, the concept of validity when applied to action research corresponds to the credibility and trustworthiness of the study's findings. This view of validity is characteristic of many qualitative research traditions, as we explain in Chapter 15. In this section we describe five validity criteria proposed by Gary Anderson and Kathryn Herr that can be used to evaluate the credibility and trustworthiness of action research studies.[56] After defining each criterion, we apply it to the action research study by Dabisch described above, giving additional details about the study when necessary.

Outcome Validity

Outcome validity concerns the extent to which actions occur that lead to a resolution of the problem that prompted the action research study. In one sense, this criterion reflects how successful the action research project was in achieving its purpose. However, Anderson and Herr note that "rigorous practitioner research, rather than simply solving a problem, forces the researcher to reframe the problem in a more complex way, often leading to a new set of questions/problems."[57] Thus this criterion also addresses the iterative nature of the action research cycle and the importance of its last two stages, namely *reflection* and *continuing or modifying action*.

Dabisch's action research project quickly expanded beyond her original goal of discovering the impact of rearranging students' desks. She found that students liked the new desk arrangement, but that it increased off-task talking rather than helping students work together. This discovery led her to undertake a series of steps involving new actions and data collection procedures, each of which represented a new plateau of success and informed the next step. At each step, she reflected with her teacher research group, and she shared her reflections in her research report. Near the end of her report, she describes her intention to begin a new cycle of teacher research, in which she plans to assign tasks to each group member and tailor her lessons to make her students' learning more cooperative. She also expresses a commitment to continue using action research to improve her teaching. Dabisch's project thus clearly demonstrates outcome validity in terms of student success in small group work and the continuous modification of the teacher's practice.

Process Validity

Process validity involves examination of the adequacy of the processes used in different phases of the action research project. For example, the extent to which problems are framed and solved in a way that permits the researchers' ongoing learning is an aspect of process validity. Triangulation, or the inclusion of multiple perspectives or data sources, also contributes to process validity.

55. Ibid, paragraph 3–4.
56. Anderson, G. L., & Herr, K. (1999). The new paradigm wars: Is there room for rigorous practitioner knowledge in schools and universities? *Educational Researcher, 28*(5), 12–21, 40. For other sets of criteria for evaluating action research, see: Zeichner & Noffke, Practitioner research.
57. Anderson & Herr, The new paradigm wars, p. 16.

Narrative forms of inquiry are sometimes used to report action research. In this context, a **narrative** is a representation and explanation of reality that is communicated through various story structures, such as folktales or anecdotes. (Narrative research is also described in Chapter 15.) In determining the credibility and trustworthiness of narratives, readers need to know whether they represent accurate depictions of what actually occurred, rather than being merely subjective accounts or interesting exaggerations.[58]

Dabisch's report demonstrates careful attention to trying various methods of data collection and modifying each method to foster her ongoing learning. Examples include her decision to focus on one group in conducting her observations, and to modify her observation form so that she could better capture important information. Also, Dabisch did not limit her description to the general statements typical of narratives, but instead provided many specific examples of perceived problems and successes in both her teaching and in the students' behavior. For example, prior to her observations of the group of three girls she observed that "I thought they worked together wonderfully."[59] After making systematic observations of the group, however, she provided more specific information:

> I noticed each girl in the group contributed something different to the group. Susan wrote the information down, Lisa kept the group on track by reminding the other two students what they had to do next, and Jamie checked the information being given by the other two group members. . . . Each task seemed to be representative of each girl's personality.[60]

Dabisch's inclusion of these details in her report contributes to her study's process validity.

Democratic Validity

Democratic validity refers to the extent to which the action research project is done in collaboration with all parties who have a stake in the problem being investigated, and their multiple perspectives and material interests are taken into account. Here "multiple voices" are viewed not as a basis for triangulation of data sources, as in the criterion of process validity, but as an issue of ethics and social justice.

At several points during her action research project, Dabisch sought to explain her study to her students and to obtain their cooperation in collecting and interpreting the data. In our earlier description of the *Reflection* stage of Dabisch's action research project we noted her belief that: " . . . sharing with my students exactly what I was doing in class and with my research project made them feel a part of what was going on in our class," and that they had a voice "because I constantly asked them what they thought about different aspects of my research." Dabisch strengthened the democratic validity of her action research project by taking these actions.

Catalytic Validity

Catalytic validity involves examination of the extent to which an action research project reorients, focuses, and energizes participants such that they are open to transforming their view of reality in relation to their practice. It is strengthened by keeping a research journal to record the researcher's change process and consequent changes in the dynamics of the setting during the reflection stage. This criterion highlights the emancipatory potential of practitioner research, which is a major concern of school reformers and of academics who

---

58. Criteria for determining the verisimilitude, plausibility, transferability, and invitational quality of narratives are explained in: Connelly, F. M., & Clandinin, D. J. (1990). Stories of experience and narrative inquiry. *Educational Researcher, 19*(5), 2–14.
59. Dabisch, From desks to a quest, *Beginning the Research* section, paragraph 4.
60. Ibid, paragraph 5.

advocate action research for political purposes. Such advocates, as we described earlier, view action researchers as obligated to foster widespread engagement of educators in an active quest for ending oppression and promoting social justice.[61]

Through discussions with students about their study habits, learning styles, and preferred work partners, Dabisch reports that, "I found myself becoming much more respectful of my students' needs as well as my own. . . . Already I find myself wondering about what intriguing, important questions I will 'live' next year as my students and I learn and grow together."[62]

One might argue that Dabisch's decision not to pursue the problem of the social isolate indicates that her action research was more reflective of an instrumental agenda than of an emancipatory agenda. Action research guided by a primary concern for **instrumental rationality** involves a focus on method and efficiency over purpose.[63] By contrast, **emancipatory action research** involves a concern for remaking and improving one's practice to overcome distortions, contradictions, and injustices.[64] Dabisch's reflection on the issue of the social isolate suggests her desire to promote social justice among her students, even though it was not fully pursued or realized. Had she reviewed social psychological literature on social isolates, Dabisch might have discovered some insights or learned of a possible intervention that would have moved her classroom toward a more socially just and inclusive environment. Thus, even action research that is not explicitly oriented toward political ends can provide practitioners with opportunities for promoting social justice.

Dialogic Validity

Dialogic validity reflects the value of dialogue with peers in the formation and review of the action researcher's findings and interpretations. It can be met by doing action research collaboratively, or by the researcher engaging in reflective dialogue with other practitioner researchers or with a "critical friend" who serves as a devil's advocate for alternative explanations of research data. This criterion helps ensure what Miles Myers calls the "goodness-of-fit with the intuitions of the teacher community, both in its definition of problems and in its findings."[65]

While Dabisch notes early in her report that the seven Spanish teachers at her school have ongoing discussions and that she was confident of their support for her action research, she does not describe any interactions with them concerning her project. She appears to have received more active support from the other students in her university teacher research course, noting that: "My classmates helped me to realize the importance of being a member of a community of teacher researchers, and how much bouncing ideas off of one another can help each of us develop our research even further."[66]

In summary, the criteria of outcome validity, process validity, democratic validity, catalytic validity, and dialogic validity each represent different aspects of an action research project's perceived credibility and trustworthiness. However, this typology is not exhaustive. Zeichner and Noffke recommend that teachers and other practitioners identify and apply their own criteria to evaluate the validity of their action research efforts, rather than

61. Kemmis & McTaggart, Participatory action research.
62. Dabisch, From desks to a quest, *One Journey Ends* section, paragraph 3–4.
63. Kincheloe, J. L., & McLaren, P. (2000). Rethinking critical theory and qualitative research. In N. K. Denzin & Y. S. Lincoln (Eds.), *Handbook of qualitative research* (2nd ed., pp. 279–313).
64. Kemmis & McTaggart, Participatory action research.
65. Myers, M. (1985). *The teacher-researcher: How to study writing in the classroom.* Urbana, IL: National Council of Teachers of English. Quote is from p. 5.
66. Dabisch, From desks to a quest, *Beginning the Research* section, paragraph 4.

relying solely on criteria developed by academics. We encourage you not only to apply the above criteria to your own or others' action research, but also to identify other criteria that you consider to be important.

Reducing Discrepancies between Practioners' Espoused Theories and Theories-in-Action

The theory of action developed by Chris Argyris and Richard Schön provides a conceptual foundation for strengthening the design and hence the outcomes of action research.[67] Argyris and Schön claim that a major challenge in the professional development of teachers and other practitioners is fostering the discovery of discrepancies between an individual's **espoused theory** (that is, one's beliefs about how one deals with problems of practice) and an individual's **theory-in-action** (that is, what one actually does in practice). For example, a teacher might say that he believes in gender equity, but in practice he might invariably select girls to carry out mundane classroom tasks. If practitioners are actively committed to improving their practice through action research, it is likely that they will be motivated to take steps to reduce such discrepancies when they discover them. They can do so either by bringing their actions more into line with their espoused beliefs, or by clarifying what they are truly committed to and then initiating actions consistent with those commitments.

Argyris and Schön suggest that a practitioner's theory-in-action is best determined through observations made by others. Stephen Kemmis and Robin McTaggart, however, claim that reliance on the interpretations of observers who are "outsiders"—typically academics—would disempower teachers and would support the view that outsider research is more valid than teacher research.[68]

We would argue that both perspectives are valuable to action researchers. As described earlier, practitioners should use reflection to discover any discrepancies between their beliefs and their actions. However, we also see the value of comparing their perceptions with those of others whose opinions they value, such as colleagues, administrators, or staff development specialists.

Practitioners also can collect data that directly help them explore areas where what they say they believe and what they actually do may be discrepant. For example, a teacher could set up a videotape recorder in her classroom and videotape herself as she carries out a lesson—a form of research that gained prominence in the development and evaluation of a form of teacher training known as *microteaching*.[69] She could then compare her espoused theory and her theory-in-action by observing the videotape and filling out an observation scale to assess the extent to which she carried out the actions that she intended to carry out. She could also ask others, particularly her teaching colleagues, to observe and give her feedback and then compare it to her own observations or those of outsiders.

Ethical Issues in Action Research

In Chapter 3, we described general policies and practices designed to ensure the ethical conduct of research studies. Because action research is so closely intertwined with prac-

67. Argyris, C., & Schön, D. A. (1974). *Theory in practice: Increasing professional effectiveness.* San Francisco: Jossey-Bass.
68. Kemmis & McTaggart, Participatory action research.
69. MacLeod, G. (1995). Microteaching in teacher education. In L. W. Anderson (Ed.), *International encyclopedia of teaching and teacher education* (2nd ed., pp. 573–577). Tarrytown, NY: Elsevier Science.

tice, action researchers may face additional ethical issues in reconciling their role of researcher with their traditional role of serving students and other clients. In 1995 the U.S. Office for Protection from Research Risks (OPRR) directed that all research—including action research studies of commonly accepted educational settings and involving normal educational practices—needs to be examined by an institutional review board (IRB).[70] We suggest that you contact your institution's IRB to determine whether it is using these regulations and if so, what procedures you need to follow to obtain review.

Jane Zeni argues that action research does not fit the typical IRB model, because "action researchers pursue a question through an often meandering route, finding appropriate data sources along the way."[71] Her guide to ethical decision making poses questions for researchers to address the unique ethical problems of action research.[72]

Many of the questions in Zeni's guide are similar to those asked in a typical IRB review, for example: "What is your time frame? Is this a one-shot project or do you anticipate several cycles? Have you done a preliminary study?"[73] Others help action researchers address the unique ethical issues that are likely to be most challenging to them. In Zeni's experience, these unique ethical issues typically involve (a) participation and collaboration in the research and (b) presentation or publication of the research report. Examples of questions dealing with participation and collaboration issues are: "Does your inquiry focus on people with less power than you?" and "How does your project demonstrate mutual respect and justice?"[74] Examples of questions dealing with presentation and publication issues are: "What do your students know of your research? Who told them? What are the risks to them or their families of their knowing (or not knowing) what you write or collect?"[75]

Zeni argues that dialogue with others about such ethical issues will help action researchers build "covenants of trust" with colleagues as well as with those who participate in or read their research.[76] Taking time to address the questions in Zeni's guide will help action researchers build such a covenant of trust with their own research collaborators, participants, and audience.

---

70. Anderson, P. V. (1998). Simple gifts: Ethical issues in the conduct of person-based composition research. *College Composition and Communication, 49*(1), 63–89. Subsequently OPRR was changed to the Office of Human Research Protections (OHRP).
71. Zeni, *Ethical issues in practitioner research*, p. 153.
72. Zeni, J. (2001) Epilogue: A guide to ethical decision making for insider research. In Zeni, J. (Ed.), *Ethical issues in practitioner research*, (pp. 153–165). New York: Teachers College Press.
73. Ibid, p. 157.
74. Ibid, p. 159.
75. Ibid, p. 163.
76. Ibid, p. 161.

✦ RECOMMENDATIONS FOR
Doing Action Research

1. In planning an action research project, decide whether you will begin with taking action, collecting data, or another stage of the research process.
2. In beginning, or deciding to continue or modify, the action in your action research project, reflect on the personal, professional, and political purposes you want the project to serve.

> 3. Choose data collection methods—quantitative, qualitative, or both—that will best help you answer your research question.
> 4. Design and report your action research project in a way that helps other practitioners determine the extent to which your findings fit their situation.
> 5. Build reflection into your action research process through autobiographical narrative and journaling.
> 6. Apply the criteria for credibility and trustworthiness to your own or others' action research projects, and identify other criteria that you consider important.
> 7. When interpreting your action research findings, seek to reduce discrepancies between your espoused theory and your theory-in-action through reflection, data collection, and feedback from others.
> 8. Carefully address the unique ethical issues involved in designing and carrying out an action research project.

✔ SELF-CHECK TEST

Circle the correct answer to each of the following questions.
The answers are provided at the back of the book.

1. An action research project concerned mainly with promoting colleagueship among practitioners best represents the _____ purpose of action research.
   a. personal
   b. professional
   c. political
   d. instrumental

2. Action research differs most from typical professional practice in its
   a. concern for fostering students' learning.
   b. concern for discovering generalizable knowledge.
   c. promotion of practitioners' professional development.
   d. systematic collection of data as a guide to improving practice.

3. Which of the following is *not* recommended for increasing the generalizability of an action research study's findings?
   a. studying cases that are unique
   b. studying a random sample within the group of interest
   c. providing statistics that are comparable across settings
   d. providing a rich, thick description of any qualitative findings

4. Action research differs most from other forms of educational research in its emphasis on
   a. reflection as an important part of the research cycle.
   b. generation of generalizable findings.
   c. collaboration between researchers.
   d. analysis of qualitative data about one's students.

5. Responsive action research involves
   a. taking a new action as the first stage of the research project.
   b. journaling as a basis for reflection.
   c. collecting data to identify a new practice to be tried.
   d. analysis of both quantitative and qualitative data.

6. Attempts to take into account the views of all parties who have a stake in the problem being investigated improve the _____ validity of an action research project.
   a. outcome
   b. process
   c. democratic
   d. dialogic

7. Discrepancies between an action researcher's espoused theory and theory-in-action can be reduced by all of the following *except*
   a. using a narrative form of reporting.
   b. obtaining the observations of outsiders.

c. collecting data to explore areas where discrepancies may exist.

d. reflecting on his or her research findings.

8. A unique ethical issue faced by action researchers involves the decision whether to

a. do a preliminary study.

b. make students aware of the types of data being collected.

c. use quantitative research methods.

d. obtain permission from an institutional review board.

9. For their action research projects to be considered successful, practitioners need to

a. receive extensive preparation to develop research knowledge and skills.

b. focus on professional purposes for doing the project.

c. discuss the generalizability of their results.

d. apply the findings to their own practice.

SELF-CHECK TEST ANSWERS

Chapter 1. The Nature of Educational Research
1. d   2. c   3. b   4. b   5. a   6. d   7. d   8. b   9. a   10. b

Chapter 2. Developing a Research Proposal
1. c   2. a   3. d   4. b   5. c   6. a   7. c

Chapter 3. Ethical, Legal, and Human Relations Issues in Educational Research
1. a   2. c   3. c   4. c   5. d   6. b   7. d   8. b   9. a   10. c

Chapter 4. Reviewing the Literature
1. d   2. b   3. b   4. a   5. c   6. a   7. c   8. b   9. d   10. c   11. d   12. d

Chapter 5. Statistical Techniques
1. c   2. a   3. b   4. d   5. a   6. d   7. a   8. c   9. d   10. b   11. b

Chapter 6. Selecting a Sample
1. c   2. a   3. b   4. d   5. c   6. a   7. a   8. c   9. b   10. c   11. d   12. d   13. b

Chapter 7. Collecting Research Data with Tests and Self-Report Measures
1. c   2. b   3. b   4. c   5. b   6. c   7. d   8. a   9. d   10. a

Chapter 8. Collecting Research Data with Questionnaires and Interviews
1. c   2. b   3. c   4. d   5. a   6. b   7. b   8. c   9. a   10. d

Chapter 9. Collecting Research Data through Observation and Content Analysis
1. b   2. b   3. d   4. a   5. c   6. d   7. a   8. b   9. a   10. d

Chapter 10. Descriptive and Causal-Comparative Research Designs
1. a   2. a   3. b   4. c   5. d   6. a   7. c   8. d   9. a   10. b   11. a   12. b

Chapter 11. Correlational Designs
1. c   2. d   3. c   4. a   5. d   6. d   7. a   8. b   9. b   10. a   11. d   12. b   13. c   14. a   15. c.

Chapter 12. Experimental Designs, Part 1
1. a   2. b   3. b   4. c   5. d   6. a   7. a   8. a   9. d   10. c

Chapter 13. Experimental Designs, Part 2
1. b   2. c   3. d   4. d   5. b   6. a   7. c   8. b   9. c   10. b   11. d   12. a   13. c

Chapter 14. Case Study Research
1. c   2. b   3. d   4. a   5. a   6. c   7. d   8. b   9. a   10. d

Chapter 15. Qualitative Research Traditions
1. b   2. b   3. c   4. a   5. b   6. c   7. c   8. d   9. a   10. d   11. d   12. a

Chapter 16. Historical Research
1. a   2. d   3. b   4. b   5. d   6. b   7. c   8. c   9. a   10. d

Chapter 17. Evaluation Research
1. d   2. b   3. d   4. d   5. a   6. c   7. c   8. b   9. c   10. b   11. c   12. a   13. a

Chapter 18. Action Research
1. b   2. d   3. a   4. a   5. c   6. c   7. a   8. b   9. d

✦ Preliminary Sources That Index the Education Literature

Preliminary sources are indexes to various types of literature. As we explained in Chapter 4, these indexes are essential resources in conducting a comprehensive review of the educational literature in your area of interest. They help you identify relevant books, journal articles, technical reports, conference proceedings, and other materials.

A great many preliminary sources specialize in a particular topic area, for example, *Applied Science & Technology Index* (1958 to date, published by H. W. Wilson), *Art Index* (1929 to date, published by H. W. Wilson), and *International African Bibliography* (1971 to date, published by H. W. Wilson). There are too many of them to include in the following list, but you can identify them by library catalogs and the *Bibliographic Index* (see section A below).

Our list includes the most important preliminary sources used by educational researchers. We provide a brief bibliographic citation for the hard copy of each source. An increasing number of these sources are also available in one or more electronic versions. A research librarian or library catalog can help you identify and access them. (One good library catalog, accessible via the Web, is that of the Library of Congress: http://catalog.loc.gov.)

To the extent possible, our citations represent the complete publication history of each source. However, we recommend that you make your own bibliographic check for preliminary sources that index older literature, especially literature published prior to 1970.

A. Indexes to Bibliographies

Bibliographic index. (1937 to date). New York: H. W. Wilson.

This preliminary source indexes bibliographies that have been published separately or as parts of books or journals. For example, the 1992 edition of *Bibliographic Index* included bibliographies from an article about distance education, from a book about the history of education, and from an article about bilingual education.

B. Indexes to Book Reviews

Book review digest. (1906 to date). New York: H. W. Wilson

Provides citations to and excerpts from reviews of English-language books. Government publications, textbooks, and technical books in the sciences and law are excluded.

Book review index. (1965 to date). Detroit: Gale.

Provides citations to reviews of books, periodicals, and books-on-tape in a wide range of popular, academic, and professional interest areas. Reviews in more than 600 journals are indexed in this preliminary source.

Contemporary psychology (1956 to date). Washington, DC: American Psychological Association.

This journal specializes in reviews of books and other publications that are relevant to psychology.

C. Indexes to Books

Books in print. (1948 to date). New York: Bowker.

Children's books in print. (1969 to date). New York: Bowker.

El-hi textbooks and serials in print. (1985 to date). New York: Bowker. For earlier editions, see: *El-hi textbooks in print.* (1927, 1984). New York: Bowker.

D. Indexes to Directories

AERA membership directory. Available from American Educational Research Association Web site, http://www.aera.net/member/directory/

Directories in print. (1989 to date). Detroit, MI: Gale Research. For earlier editions, see: *Directory of directories* (1st–5th eds.). (1980–1988). Detroit, MI: Gale Research.

Encyclopedia of associations. (1956 to date). Detroit, MI: Gale Research.

Guide to American educational directories. (1963 to date). New York: B. Klein.

National faculty directory. (1970 to date). Detroit, MI: Gale Research.

E. Indexes to Dissertations and Theses

Dissertation abstracts international. (1969 to date). Ann Arbor, MI: University Microfilms International.

This index provides abstracts for doctoral dissertations submitted by hundreds of institutions, mostly in the United States and Canada, but also including a few institutions from other countries.

Master's theses directories. (1993 to date). Cedar Falls, IA: H. M. Smiley. For earlier editions, see: *Master's theses directories: The arts and social sciences* (Vols. 1–2). (1991–1992). Cedar Falls, IA Masters Theses Directories; *Master's theses in education* (Vols. 1–39). (1951–1990). Cedar Falls, IA: Research Publications.

F. Indexes to Journal Articles, Papers, and Reports

Child development abstracts and bibliography. (1927 to date). Chicago: University of Chicago Press.

An index to articles about child development that appear in over 170 journals in medicine, psychology, biology, sociology, and education.

Current index to journals in education (CIJE). (1969 to date). Phoenix, AZ: Oryx. This widely used preliminary source is described in detail in Chapter 4.

Education index. (1929 to date). Bronx, NY: H. W. Wilson.

This is a major index to articles in educational journals. Unlike *CIJE*, it does not provide an abstract for each citation. However, you can search only back to 1966 in *CIJE*, whereas *Education Index* covers journal articles (and books as well) published since 1929.

Educational administration abstracts. (1966 to date). College Station, TX: University Council for Educational Administration.

Exceptional child education resources. (1977 to date). Reston, VA: Council for Exceptional Children. From 1969 to 1977, this preliminary source was called *Exceptional child education abstracts* by the same publisher.

Monthly catalog of United States government publications. (1951 to date). Washington, DC: U.S. Government Printing Office.

Physical education index. (1970 to date). Cape Girardeau, MO: BenOak.

Psychological abstracts. (1927 to date). Washington, DC: American Psychological Association.

This index is useful if you are looking for psychological research relating to your topic. It contains abstracts of articles appearing in over 1,000 journals and other sources in psychology and related areas. The *Thesaurus of Psychological Index Terms* contains all the terms used to index *Psychological Abstracts*. We recommend that you look up the index term *bibliography* when you search this index because under this heading is a list of bibliographies on a wide variety of subjects.

Resources in Education. (1966 to date). Washington, DC: U.S. Government Printing Office.

This widely used preliminary source is described in detail in Chapter 4.

Sage family studies abstracts. (1979 to date). Beverly Hills, CA: Sage.

Science citation index. (1964 to date). Philadelphia, PA: Institute for Scientific Information.

This index covers the literature of medicine, agriculture, technology, and science, including the natural, physical, and biomedical sciences. For an explanation of its purpose and use, see the following entry for *Social Sciences Citation Index.*

Social sciences citation index. (1964 to date). Philadelphia, PA: Institute for Scientific Information.

This index covers the literature of the social and behavioral sciences. Most articles about education are covered in this index, but articles about psychology—depending on their topic-may be covered in this index or in *Science Citation Index.*

To understand the purpose of these indexes, suppose that your literature search identifies a seminal study that was published some years ago, and you wish to trace its effects on subsequent research. Or, suppose you identify an article that expresses a controversial opinion, and you wish to know what later authors wrote in support of or opposition to it. *Science Citation Index* and *Social Sciences Citation Index* can help you find either type of information.

You would start your search of these indexes with the volume for the year that the key article was published and would check all volumes up to the current one. Under the name of the author of the original article, you would find citations for all subsequent articles that cited it. For example, we traced citations for an article by Kenneth Sirotnik that was published in the *Harvard Educational Review* in 1983. The article is a major presentation of findings from a research study of over 1,000 elementary and secondary school classrooms in the United States. Searching *Social Sciences Citation Index* from 1983 to 1991, we found a total of 42 articles that cited Sirotnik's article.

Sociological abstracts. (1953 to date). San Diego, CA: Sociological Abstracts.

Sport discus. (1995). Boston: SilverPlatter. CD-ROM format. Updated regularly.

An index to literature on sport, physical education, physical fitness, and sport medicine.

Women studies abstracts. (1972 to date). Rush, NY: Women's Studies Abstracts.

G. Indexes to Magazines and Newspapers

Newspaper abstracts on disc. (1985 to date). Ann Arbor, MI: University Microfilms International. CD-ROM format.

Readers' guide to periodical literature. (1900 to date). Minneapolis: H. W. Wilson.

✦ Secondary Sources: Published Reviews of the Education Literature

As we explained in Chapter 4, secondary sources are articles, books, and other publications written by individuals about other individuals' research studies, theories, and opinions. Many of these secondary sources contain reviews of the literature on a particular topic. This appendix lists major secondary sources of this type. However, the list is not exhaustive, and some of the sources might go into new editions. Therefore, we recommend you check the currency of the edition. Electronic versions of *Books in Print and the Library of Congress catalog (<www.catalog.loc.gov>)* are useful for this purpose. Also, you can use these resources to search for other secondary sources. (Combining the descriptor terms *handbook* or *encyclopedia* and a descriptor term for your subject is a productive strategy.)

A. Annual Reviews

Annual review of psychology. (1950 to date). Stanford, CA: Annual Reviews. Each volume reviews the literature on a different set of psychological topics.

Review of research in education. (1931 to date). Itasca, IL: Peacock.

Each volume reviews the literature on a different set of educational topics.

Yearbook of the National Society for the Study of Education. (1910 to date). Chicago: National Society for the Study of Education. Earlier yearbooks (1896–1909) were published under the title *Yearbook of the National Society for the Scientific Study of Teaching.*

Each volume reviews the literature and provides expert commentary on a particular educational topic.

B. Encyclopedias

American Educational Research Association. (2001). *Encyclopedia of educational research* (7th ed.). Farmington Hills, MI: Gale.

Grinstein, L., & Lipsey, S. I. (Eds.). (2001). *Encyclopedia of mathematics education.* New York: Routledge.

Husén, T., & Postlethwaite, T. N. (1994). *International encyclopedia of education* (2nd ed.). New York: Elsevier. Entries relating to certain subjects (e.g., educational technology, economics of education, teaching and teacher education) have been cumulated and published as separate volumes.

Kazdin, A. E. (Ed.). (2000). *Encyclopedia of psychology.* Washington, DC: American Psychology Association; New York: Oxford University Press.

Levinson, D. L., Cookson, P. W., & Sadovnik, A. R. (2002). *Education and sociology: An encyclopedia.* New York: RoutledgeFalmer.

Lopez, C. (Ed.). (2001). *World education encyclopedia: A survey of educational systems worldwide* (2nd ed.). Farmington Hills, MI: Gale.

Mitchell, B. M., & Salsburg, R. E. (Eds.). (1999). *Encyclopedia of multicultural education* (2nd ed.). Westport, CT: Greenwood.

Reynolds, C. R., & Fletcher-Janzen, E. (Eds.). (2000). *Encyclopedia of special education* (2nd ed.). New York: John Wiley & Sons.

C. Journals Specializing in Literature Reviews

Psychological bulletin. (1904 to date). Arlington, VA: American Psychological Association.

Psychological review. (1894 to date). Washington, DC: American Psychological Association.

Review of educational research. (1931 to date). Washington, DC: American Educational Research Association.

D. Handbooks

Banks, J. A., & Banks, C. A. (Eds.). (1995). *Handbook of research on multicultural education.* New York: Macmillan.

Berliner, D. C., & Calfee, R. C. (Eds.). (1996). *Handbook of educational psychology.* New York: Macmillan.

Biddle, B. J., Good, T. L., & Goodson, I. F. (Eds.). (1997). *International handbook of teachers and teaching.* Boston: Kluwer.

Bishop, A. J., et al. (Eds.). (1996). *International handbook of mathematics education.* Boston: Kluwer.

Cawelti, G. (Ed.). (1999). *Handbook of research on improving student achievement* (2nd ed.). Arlington, VA: Educational Research Service.

Firth, G. R., & Pajak, E. F. (Eds.). (1998). *Handbook of research on school supervision.* New York: Macmillan.

Flood, J., Heath, S. B., & Lapp, D. (Eds.). (1997). *Handbook of research on teaching literacy through the communicative and visual arts.* New York: Macmillan.

Fraser, B. J., & Tobin, K. G. (Eds.). (1998). *International handbook of science education.* Boston: Kluwer.

Hargreaves, A., et al. (Eds.). (1998). *International handbook of educational change.* Boston: Kluwer.

Heller, K., Mönks, F. J., Sternberg, R. J., & Subotnik, R. F. (Eds.). (2000). *International handbook of giftedness and talent.* Boston: Kluwer.

Murphy, J., & Louis, K. S. (Eds.). (1999). *Handbook of research on educational administration* (2nd ed.). San Francisco: Jossey-Bass.

Neuman, S. B., & Dickinson, D. K. (Eds.). (2001). Handbook of early literacy research. New York: Guilford Press.

Pearson, P. D., Barr, R., Kamil, M. L., & Mosenthal, P. (Eds.). (1996–2000). *Handbook of reading research* (Vols. 1–3). Mahwah, NJ: Lawrence Erlbaum.

Richardson, V. (Ed.). (2001). *Handbook of research on teaching* (4th ed.). Washington, DC: American Educational Research Association.

Sikula, J., Buttery, T., & Guyton, E. (Eds.). (1996). *Handbook of research on teacher education* (2nd ed.). New York: Macmillan.

Teddie, C., & Reynolds, D. (Eds.). (2000). *International handbook of school effectiveness research.* New York: Falmer.

Questions for Evaluating Quantitative Research Reports

The following are questions to use in evaluating each section of a quantitative research report. For each question we identify the type of information you will need to look for in the report to answer the question, and we provide a sample answer. The examples are drawn from our experience in evaluating quantitative research studies.

Introductory Section

1. Are the research problems, or findings unduly influenced by the researchers' institutional affiliations, beliefs, values, or theoretical orientation?

    Information needed. Find the researchers' institutional affiliation. (This information usually appears beneath the title of the report or at the end.) Also, locate any information in the report that indicates their beliefs about education, values, or theoretical orientation.

    Example. Most of the researchers' prior work has advocated cognitive models of learning. Therefore, they may have biased their experiment so that the cognitively oriented teaching method came out better than the behaviorally oriented teaching method.

2. Do the researchers demonstrate undue positive or negative bias in describing the subject of the study (an instructional method, program, curriculum, person, etc.)?

    Information needed. Identify any adjectives or other words that describe an instructional method, program, curriculum, person, and so on in clearly positive or negative terms.

    Example. The researchers described the group of students as difficult to handle, unmotivated, and disorganized. No evidence was presented to support this characterization. This description in the absence of evidence may indicate a negative attitude toward the children who were studied.

3. Is the literature review section of the report sufficiently comprehensive? Does it include studies that you know to be relevant to the problem?

    Information needed. Examine the studies mentioned in the report. Note particularly if a recent review of the literature relevant to the research problem was cited or if the researchers mentioned an effort to make their own review comprehensive.

    Example. The researchers stated the main conclusions of a previously published comprehensive literature review on the instructional program that they intended to study. They demonstrated clearly how their study built on the findings and recommendations of this review.

Source: Adapted from pages 427–430 in: Borg, W. R., Gall, J. P., & Gall, M. D. (1993). *Applying educational research* (3rd ed.). New York: Longman.

4. Is each variable in the study clearly defined?

   Information needed. Identify all the variables (also called constructs) that were studied. For each variable, determine if and how it is defined in the report.

   Example. One of the variables is intrinsic motivation, which is defined in the report as the desire to learn because of curiosity. This definition is not consistent with other definitions, which state that intrinsic motivation is the desire to learn because of the satisfaction that comes from the act of learning and from the content being learned.

5. Is the measure of each variable consistent with how the variable was defined?

   Information needed. Identify how each variable in the study was measured.

   Example. The researchers studied self-esteem but did not define it. Therefore, it was not possible to determine whether their measure of self-esteem was consistent with their definition.

6. Are research hypotheses, questions, or objectives explicitly stated, and if so, are they clear?

   Information needed. Examine each research hypothesis, question, or objective stated in the report.

   Example. The researcher stated one general objective for the study. It was clearly stated, but did not give the reader sufficient understanding of the specific variables that were to be studied.

7. Do the researchers make a convincing case that a research hypothesis, question, or objective was important to study?

   Information needed. Examine the researchers' rationale for each hypothesis, question, or objective.

   Example. The researchers showed how the hypothesis to be tested was derived from a theory. They also showed that if the hypothesis was confirmed by the study it would add support to the validity of the theory, which is currently being used in the design of new reading curricula.

Methods Section

8. Did the sampling procedures produce a sample that is representative of an identifiable population or your local population?

   Information needed. Identify the procedures that the researchers used to select their sample.

   Example. The researchers selected several classes (not randomly) from one school. The only information given about the students was their average ability and gender distribution. I cannot tell from this description whether the sample is similar to students in our schools.

9. Did the researchers form subgroups to increase understanding of the phenomena being studied?

   Information needed. Determine whether the sample was formed into subgroups, and if so, why.

   Example. The researchers showed the effects of the instructional program for both boys and girls; this information was helpful. However, they did not show the effects for different ethnic subgroups. This is an oversight because the program might have a cultural bias that could have an adverse effect on some ethnic subgroups.

10. Is each measure in the study sufficiently valid for its intended purpose?

    Information needed. Examine any evidence that the researchers presented to demonstrate the validity of each measure in the study.

Example. The XYZ Test was used because it purportedly predicts success in vocational education programs. However, the researchers presented evidence from only one study to support this claim. That study involved a vocational education program that was quite different from the one they investigated.

11. Is each measure in the study sufficiently reliable for its intended purpose?

Information needed. Examine any evidence that the researchers presented to demonstrate the reliability of each measure in the study.

Example. The researchers had observers rate each student's on-task behavior during Spanish instruction in a sample of 30 classrooms. Inter-observer reliability was checked by having pairs of observers use the rating system in the same 5 classrooms. The pairs typically agreed on 90 percent of their ratings, which indicates good reliability.

12. Is each measure appropriate for the sample?

Information needed. Determine whether the researchers reported the population for whom the measure was developed.

Example. The ABC Reading Test was developed 20 years ago for primary grade students. The current study also involves primary grade students, but the test may no longer be valid, because students and the reading curriculum have changed considerably over the past 20 years.

13. Were the research procedures appropriate and clearly stated so that others could replicate them if they wished?

Information needed. Identify the various research procedures that were used in the study and the order in which they occurred.

Example. The researchers administered three research tests during one class period the day before the experimental curriculum was introduced. The tests, though brief, may have overwhelmed the students so that they did not do their best work. Also, some aspects of the experimental curriculum (e.g., the types of seatwork activities) were not clearly described, and the researchers did not indicate how soon the final research tests were administered after the curriculum was completed.

Results Section

14. Were appropriate statistical techniques used, and were they used correctly?

Information needed. Identify any statistical techniques described in the report.

Example. The researchers calculated the mean score for students' performance on the five tests that were administered. However, they did not give the range of scores (i.e., lowest score and highest score). This would be helpful information, because they studied a highly heterogeneous group of students.

Discussion of Results

15. Do the results of the data analyses support what the researchers conclude are the findings of the study?

Information needed. Identify what the researchers considered to be the major findings of the study.

Example. The researchers concluded that the experimental treatment led to superior learning compared to the control treatment, but this claim was true for only two of the four criterion measures used to measure the effects of the treatments.

16. Did the researchers provide reasonable explanations of the findings?

Information needed. Identify how the researchers explained the findings of the study and whether alternative explanations were considered.

Example. The researchers concluded that the narrative version of the textbook was less effective than the traditional expository version. Their explanation was that the story in the narrative version motivated students to keep reading, but that it also distracted them from focusing on the factual information that was included on the test. They presented no evidence or theoretical rationale to support this explanation, although it seems plausible.

17. Did the researchers draw reasonable implications for practice and future research from their findings?

Information needed. Identify any implications for practice and future research that the researchers drew from their findings.

Example. The researchers claimed that teachers' morale would be higher if administrators would provide more self-directed staff development. However, this recommendation is based only on their questionnaire finding that teachers expressed a desire for more self-directed staff development. The researchers are not justified in using this bit of data to claim that teachers' morale will improve if they get the kind of staff development they prefer.

✦ Questions for Evaluating Qualitative Research Reports

The following are questions to use in evaluating each section of a qualitative research report. For each question, we identify the type of information you will need to look for in the report to answer the question, and we provide a sample answer. The examples are drawn from our experience in evaluating qualitative research studies.

Introductory Section

1. Are the research problems, procedures, or findings unduly influenced by the researchers' institutional affiliations, beliefs, values, or theoretical orientation?

    Information needed. Find the researchers' institutional affiliation. (This information usually appears beneath the title of the report or at the end.) Also locate any information in the report that indicates their beliefs about education, values, or theoretical orientation.

    Example. The researchers taught in inner-city schools for many years before doing this study. This experience would give them empathy for inner-city students, but also some possible biases about what their typical problems are. Were the researchers able to stay free of preconceptions during data collection?

2. Do the researchers demonstrate undue positive or negative bias in describing the subject of the study (an instructional method, program, curriculum, person, etc.)?

    Information needed. Identify any adjectives or other words that describe an instructional method, program, curriculum, person, and so on in clearly positive or negative terms.

    Example. The researchers used a qualitative research method known as educational criticism to study a high school football team. This method is inherently evaluative, so it is no surprise that the researchers made many judgments—both positive and negative—about the impact of the team on individual players.

3. Is the literature review section of the report sufficiently comprehensive? Does it include studies that you know to be relevant to the problem?

    Information needed. Examine the studies mentioned in the report. Note particularly if a recent review of the literature relevant to the research problem was cited or if the researchers mentioned an effort to make their own review comprehensive.

    Example. The researchers completed their literature search prior to data collection. This procedure is not desirable because questions and hypotheses were bound to arise as they collected data. They should have done an ongoing literature search to find out what others have found concerning these emerging questions and hypotheses.

Source: Adapted from pages 431–434 in: Borg, W. R., Gall, J. P., & Gall, M. D. (1993). *Applying educational research* (3rd ed.). New York: Longman.

Research Procedures

4. Did the sampling procedure result in a case or cases that were particularly interesting and from which much could be learned about the phenomena of interest?

   Information needed. Identify the procedures that the researchers used to select their sample.

   Example. The researchers used purposive sampling to select a high school principal who had received several awards and widespread recognition for "turning her school around." She was an excellent case to study, given the researchers' interest in administrators' instructional leadership.

5. Was there sufficient intensity of data collection?

   Information needed. Identify the time period over which an individual, setting, or event was observed and whether the observation was continuous or fragmented. If documents were analyzed, identify how extensive the search for documents was and how closely the documents were analyzed.

   Example. The researchers' goal was to learn how elementary school teachers established classroom routines and discipline procedures at the beginning of the school year. They observed each teacher every day for the first three weeks; this is a good procedure. They assumed, however, that routines and discipline procedures would be explained at the start of the school day, and so they observed only the first hour of class time. The validity of this assumption is questionable.

6. Is each measure in the study sufficiently valid for its intended purpose?

   Information needed. Examine any evidence that the researchers presented to demonstrate the validity of each measure in the study.

   Example. The researchers' primary measure was ethnographic observation. They appear to have taken careful notes and studied them extensively prior to writing their ethnographic report. They checked the validity of their statements in the report by having several knowledgeable people in the community they studied review the statements.

7. Is each measure in the study sufficiently reliable for its intended purpose?

   Information needed. Examine any evidence that the researchers presented to demonstrate the reliability of each measure in the study.

   Example. The researchers acknowledged the difficulty of determining the reliability of their interviews. Their main concern was whether the interviewees were taking the interviews seriously. They collected data about this possible problem by asking the interviewees several of the same questions on different occasions to see if the responses would be similar. By and large they were.

8. Is each measure appropriate for the sample?

   Information needed. Determine whether the researchers reported the population for whom the measure was developed.

   Example. The researchers used the interview method, but noted that children in the culture they studied are very uncomfortable with adults asking them questions in a formal setting. The researchers made the children more comfortable by setting up a playlike environment and asking questions unobtrusively as the interviewer and children played.

9. Were the research procedures appropriate and clearly stated so that others could replicate them if they wished?

   Information needed. Identify the various research procedures that were used in the study and the order in which they occurred.

Example. The researchers' main data-collection procedure was to ask students questions as they attempted to solve various math problems. The problems and questions are available upon request, so it seems that the study could be replicated.

Research Results

10. Did the report include a thick description that brought to life how the individuals responded to interview questions or how they behaved?

    Information needed. Identify how much vivid detail was included in the account of what the individuals being studied did or said.

    Example. The researchers identified 10 main strategies that mentor teachers used in working with beginning teachers. Unfortunately the strategies were described in rather meager detail, with no examples of what they looked like in practice.

11. Did each variable in the study emerge in a meaningful way from the data?

    Information needed. Identify all the variables (also called constructs) that were discovered in the study. For each variable, examine how it emerged from the data.

    Example. The researchers did a careful content analysis of what the students said in the interviews. They looked for repetitive themes in their comments. These themes were the variables. The researchers did a nice job of labeling these variables by using words that the students themselves used.

12. Are there clearly stated hypotheses or questions? And do they emerge from the data that were collected?

    Information needed. Identify each research hypothesis and question stated in the report. Examine whether and how they emerged from the data.

    Example. The researchers focused almost entirely on writing a narrative account of the events leading up to the teachers' strike. There was no attempt to develop hypotheses about why these events happened, so that these hypotheses could be tested in subsequent research.

13. Were appropriate statistical techniques used, and were they used correctly?

    Information needed. Identify any statistical technique described in the report.

    Example. The researchers studied three teachers' aides and made such comments as, "They spent most of their time helping individual children and passing out or collecting papers." Time is easily quantified, so the researchers should have collected some time data and reported means and standard deviations.

Discussion of Results

14. Were multiple sources of evidence used to support the researchers' conclusions?

    Information needed. Identify the researchers' conclusions and how each of them was supported by the data analyses.

    Example. The researchers concluded that textbook adoption committees were frustrated by the paucity of written information provided by publishers and their inability to question publishers' representatives in person. This frustration was documented by analysis of interviews with selected members of the textbook adoption committees, field notes made by the researchers during committee meetings, and letters written by the chair of the committee to the director of textbook adoption in the state department of education.

15. Did the researchers provide reasonable explanations of the findings?

   Information needed. Identify how the researchers explained the findings of the study and whether alternative explanations were considered.

   Example. The researchers found that peer coaching did not work at the school they studied, and they attributed its failure to the lack of a supportive context, especially the lack of a history of collegiality among the teaching staff. Another plausible explanation, which they did not consider, is that the teachers received inadequate training in peer coaching.

16. Was the generalizability of the findings appropriately qualified?

   Information needed. Identify whether the researchers made any statements about the generalizability of their findings. If claims of generalizability were made, were they appropriate?

   Example. The researchers made no claims that the results of their case study could be generalized to anyone other than the teacher who was studied. It is unfortunate that they did not discuss generalizability because the findings have significant implications for practice, if in fact they apply to other teachers. There are not enough data about the teacher's professional training for readers to generalize on their own.

17. Did the researchers draw reasonable implications for practice and future research from their findings?

   Information needed. Identify any implications for practice and future research that the researchers drew from their findings.

   Example. The researchers found that students who volunteer for community service derive many benefits from the experience. Therefore, they encourage educators to support community service programs for their students. This recommendation seems well grounded in their findings about benefits of community service participation for students.

✦ Preliminary and Secondary Sources: Tests and Self-Report Measures

The sources listed below serve both as indexes to tests and as reviews of the literature on the tests. Therefore, this appendix does not have a separate section for preliminary sources and secondary sources.

Goldman, B. A., & Mitchell, D. F. (1997). *Directory of unpublished experimental measures* (Vol. 7). Dubuque, IA: William C. Brown.

Health and psychosocial instruments. (1983 to date). Pittsburgh: Behavior Measurement Database Services.
This electronic source lists measures that are not commercially available, but that have been used in studies reported in journals.

Hersen, M. (Ed.). (2002). *Dictionary of behavioral assessment techniques.* New York: Percheron Press.
This source describes hundreds of measures of a wide variety of problems and disorders that occur in children, adolescents, adults, and senior citizens.

Keyser, D. J., & Sweetland, R. C. (Eds.). (1984–1994). *Test critiques* (Vols. 1–10). Austin, TX: Pro-Ed.
This source provides extensive information about each of hundreds of widely-used measures. It can be searched electronically using the search engine *Test Locator* at the Web site *http://ericae.net/testcol.htm.*

Krug, S. E. (1993). *Psychware sourcebook* (4th ed.). Champaign, IL: Metritech.
This source identifies and describes computer-based assessment tools.

Maddox, T. (1997). *Tests: A comprehensive reference for assessments in psychology, education, and business* (4th ed.). Austin, TX: Pro-Ed.

Mental measurements yearbook (14th ed.). (2001). Lincoln, NE: Buros Institute of Mental Measurements, University of Nebraska.
Contrary to its title, this publication appears periodically rather than annually. Each new edition includes tests that are new or revised since the previous yearbook or that have generated twenty or more new references in the literature. The description of each test includes the types of individuals for whom the test is appropriate, the scores yielded by the test, the publisher and cost of the test, and the amount of time required to administer it. Also included is a bibliography of publications about the psychometric properties of the test; and for many of the tests, there is a critical review of the test's strengths and weaknesses.
  Tests in Print (see below) serves as a master index to all editions of this source. They also can be searched electronically using the search engine *Test Locator* at the Web site http://ericae.net/testcol.htm.

Phye, G. D. (Ed.). (1997). *Handbook of classroom assessment: Learning, adjustment, and achievement.* San Diego, CA: Academic Press.

Robinson, J. P., Shaver, P. R., & Wrightsman, L. S. (Eds.). (1991). *Measures of personality and social psychological attitudes.* San Diego, CA: Academic Press.

Robinson, J. P., Shaver, P. R., & Wrightsman, L. S. (Eds.). (1999). *Measures of political attitudes.* San Diego, CA: Academic Press.

Test collection bibliography. (n.d.). Princeton, NJ: Educational Testing Service.
This is the most extensive collection of tests and other measurement devices available. The description of each measure includes title, author, publication date, target population, and publisher or source. Many of the unpublished measures are available from ETS on microfiche. This source can be searched electronically using the search engine Test Locator at the Web site http://ericae.net/testcol.htm.

Tests in print (5th ed.). (1999). Lincoln, NE: Buros Institute of Mental Measurements, University of Nebraska.
This source serves as a comprehensive index of tests reviewed in all editions of the Mental Measurement Yearbook and other sourcebooks about tests. It can be searched electronically using the search engine Test Locator at the Web site *http://ericae.net/testcol.htm.*

Wylie, R. C. (1989). *Measures of self-concept.* Lincoln, NE: University of Nebraska Press.

✦ Preliminary and Secondary Sources on the History of Education

I. Preliminary Sources

Preliminary sources are indexes to various types of publications and other information. The following is a list of important preliminary sources used by historians of education. We provide a brief bibliographic citation for the hard-copy version. Some of them are also available in one or more electronic versions. A research librarian or university library catalog can help you identify and access these versions. (One good library catalog, accessible via the Web, is that of the Library of Congress: *http://catalog.loc.gov*.)

A. Bibliographies of Bibliographies

Fritze, R. H., Coutts, B. E., & Vyhnanek, L. A. (1990). *Reference sources in history: An introductory guide.* Santa Barbara, CA: ABC-CLIO.

Norton, M. B., & Gerardi, P. (1995). *Guide to historical literature* (3rd ed.). New York: Oxford University Press.

This preliminary source not only is a bibliography of bibliographies, but it also includes historiographical essays on each section topic.

B. Bibliographies of Biographies

McNeil, B. (Ed.) (1995). *Abridged biography and genealogy master index.* (2nd ed.). New York: Gale.

Biography index. (1946 to date). New York: H. W. Wilson.

C. Directories of Historical Societies

Many historical societies have been formed in order to advance the historical study of particular regions, time periods, and topics. The following is an example of a directory of these societies:

Directory of historical organizations in the United States and Canada (14th ed.). (1990). Nashville, TN: American Association for States and Local History.

D. General Indexes to Historical Publications

America's history and life. (1964 to date). Santa Barbara, CA: ABC-CLIO.

An index to articles, dissertations, and reviews of books, films, videos, and documents in microfilm/microfiche format covering the history and culture of the United States and Canada from prehistoric times to the present.

Historical abstracts: Part A: Modern history abstracts, 1450–1914; Part B: Twentieth century abstracts, 1914—. (1971 to date). Santa Barbara, CA: ABC-CLIO. For earlier editions, see: *Historical abstracts.* (1955–1970). Santa Barbara, CA: ABC-CLIO.

E. Newspaper Reference Sources

United States newspaper program. (n.d.). Retrieved February 1, 2002 from http://www.neh.fed.us/projects/usnp.html.

F. Indexes to Nonpublished Primary Sources

The following are several preliminary sources that are useful for accessing various types of primary sources, such as unpublished manuscripts, oral histories, films, and archival materials:

National Historical Publications and Records Commission. (1988). *Directory of archives and manuscript repositories in the United States* (2nd ed.). Phoenix, AZ: Oryx.

National union catalog of manuscript collections. (1959 to 1993). Washington, DC: Library of Congress. After 1993, available in microform or as a computer file (Archives USA).

Smith, A. (1988). *Directory of oral history collections.* Phoenix, AZ: Oryx.

II. Secondary Sources

Secondary sources are publications in which the author describes other individuals' research studies, theories, and opinions. Many of these secondary sources are reviews of the literature on a particular historical topic In this section, we list important secondary sources relating to the history of education. However, the list is not exhaustive, and some of the sources might go into new editions. Therefore, we recommend you check the currency of the edition. Electronic versions of *Books in Print* and the Library of Congress catalog (*http://catalog.loc.gov*) are useful for this purpose.

A. Biographies

There are a great many biographical dictionaries. To learn what is available, you can look in *Books in Print* or in a university library catalog under the title *Biographical Dictionary.* Three examples are:

Meyner, N. E. (2001). *Biographical dictionary of Hispanic Americans* (2nd ed.). New York: Facts on File.

Ohles, F., Ohles, S. M., & Ramsay, J. G. (1997). *Biographical dictionary of modern American educators.* Westport, CT: Greenwood.

Porter, R., & Ogilvie, M. (Eds.). (2000). *The biographical dictionary of scientists.* New York: Oxford University Press.

B. History Encyclopedias

History encyclopedias contain articles that summarize what is known about particular historical topics. The articles usually contain a reference list, which can guide you to other relevant sources.

Bacon, D. C., Davidson, R. H., & Keller, M. (1995). *Encyclopedia of the United States Congress.* New York: Simon & Schuster.

Thernstrom, S. A. (Ed.). (1980). *Harvard encyclopedia of American ethnic groups.* Cambridge, MA: Harvard University Press.

C. Geographical Reference Works

Geographical reference works provide data about the history and characteristics of geographical locations. An example is:

Merriam-Webster's geographical dictionary (3rd ed.). (1997). Springfield, MS: Merriam-Webster.

D. Statistical Sourcebooks

Statistical sourcebooks contain many tables of numerical data arranged by topic area, as well as introductory essays that provide bibliographic information about other sources on the topic. Two major sources of U.S. Government statistical data are

Historical statistics of the United States: Bicentennial edition. (1997). New York: Cambridge University Press. Available only as a computer file.

U.S. Bureau of the Census (1989). *Historical statistics of the United States: Colonial times to 1970.* White Plains, NY: Kraus.

U.S. Bureau of the Census (1878 to date). *Statistical abstract of the United States.* Washington, DC: U.S. Government Printing Office.

GLOSSARY

A-B design. A type of single-case experiment in which the researcher institutes a baseline condition (*A*), followed by the treatment (*B*). The target behavior is measured repeatedly during both conditions.

A-B-A design. A type of single-case experiment in which the researcher institutes a baseline condition (*A*), administers the treatment (*B*), and institutes a second baseline condition (*A*). The target behavior is measured repeatedly during all three conditions.

A-B-A designs. Any single-case experiment that has at least one baseline condition (designated *A*) and one treatment condition (designated *B*).

A-B-A-B design. A type of single-case experiment in which the researcher institutes a baseline condition (*A*), administers the treatment (*B*), institutes a second baseline condition (*A*), and then re-administers the treatment (*B*). The target behavior is measured repeatedly during all four conditions.

Accessible population. All the members of a set of people, events, or objects who feasibly can be included in the researcher's sample.

Acquiescence bias. In testing, a type of response set in which individuals agree with items irrespective of their content.

Action research. A type of applied research the purpose of which is the improvement of education professionals' own practice.

Adversary evaluation. A type of evaluation research that is characterized by the use of a wide array of data and the hearing of testimony, and that has opportunities for individuals with opposing opinions to present positive and negative judgments about the program being evaluated.

Age equivalent. A type of derived score that represents a given raw score on a measure as the average age of individuals in the norming group who earned that score.

Agency. In qualitative research, the assumed ability of individuals to shape the conditions of their lives.

Alpha. See *Cronbach's alpha coefficient*.

Alpha level. The level of statistical significance that is selected prior to data collection for rejecting a null hypothesis.

Alternate-form reliability. An approach to estimating test reliability in which individuals' scores on one version of a test are correlated with their scores on a different version of the test.

Analysis of covariance (ANCOVA). A procedure for determining whether the difference between the mean scores of two or more groups on one or more dependent variables is statistically significant, after controlling for initial differences between the groups on one or more extraneous variables. When the groups have been classified on several independent variables (called *factors*), the procedure can be used to determine whether each factor and the interactions between the factors have a statistically significant effect on the dependent variable, after controlling for the extraneous variable.

Analysis of variance (ANOVA). A procedure for determining whether the difference between the mean scores of two or more groups on a dependent variable is statistically significant. When the groups have been classified on several independent variables (called *factors*), the procedure can be used to determine whether each factor and the interactions between the factors have a statistically significant effect on the dependent variable.

Analysis of variance for repeated measures. A procedure for determining whether the difference between the mean pretest-posttest gain score of the experimental group and that of the control group is statistically significant.

Analysis unit. See *segment*.

Analytic induction. In qualitative research, the process of inferring themes and patterns from an examination of data.

Analytic reporting. In a qualitative research report, the use of an objective writing style (i.e., the researcher's voice is silent or subdued) and other conventions typical of quantitative research reporting.

Antiquarian. An individual who studies the past for its own sake with little concern for its relevance to present-day issues and happenings.

Aptitude test. A measure of abilities that are assumed to be relevant to future performance in a specific type of skill or an area of achievement.

Aptitude-treatment interaction (ATI) experiment (or *attribute-treatment interaction experiment***).** A type of experiment that is designed to determine whether instructional methods or other interventions have different effects for different types of individuals.

Archive (or *repository***).** A facility for storing documents so that they are preserved in good condition, and access to them can be carefully monitored.

Artifact. See *material culture*.

Artificial dichotomy. A categorical variable with only two values, which are formed from continuous scores (e.g., classifying a student as low-achieving if his test score is below 30 and as high-achieving if his test score is above 70).

Attribute-treatment interaction experiment. See *aptitude-treatment interaction experiment*.

Audit trail. In a literature review, an account of all the procedures and decision rules that were used by the reviewer. In qualitative research, the process of documenting the materials and procedures used in each phase of a study.

Autoethnography. An approach to qualitative research that involves autobiography and investigation of multiple levels of individual consciousness in relation to cultural phenomena.

***B* weight.** See *Beta weight*.

***b* weight.** See *regression weight*.

Bar graph. A diagram that shows the relationship between two measures, one of which yields categorical scores.

Baseline. In a single-case experiment, the research participant's natural behavior pattern in the absence of the experimental treatment. In prediction research, the percentage of individuals who actually will achieve a particular outcome if no selection procedure is applied.

Behavior modification. The use of such techniques as social and token reinforcement, fading, desensitization, and discrimination training for the purpose of changing an individual's behavior patterns.

Behavioral objective. A statement of a program goal that includes three components: an observable behavior that serves as an indicator of goal attainment, criteria for successful performance of the behavior, and the situational context in which the behavior is to be performed.

Beta weight (or *B weight***).** A multiplier term added to each predictor variable in a multiple regression equation after the predictor variables have been converted to standard score form.

Bias. A set to perceive events or other phenomena in such a way that certain facts are habitually overlooked, distorted, or falsified.

Bivariate correlation coefficient. Any type of statistic that describes the magnitude of the relationship between two variables.

Breaching. In ethnomethodology, the use of natural or contrived disruptions in people's normal routines in order to reveal the hidden work that people do to maintain their social environment.

Canonical correlation. A type of multiple regression analysis involving the use of two or more measured variables to predict a composite index of several criterion variables.

Case. In qualitative research, a particular instance of a phenomenon of interest to the researcher.

Case study research. The in-depth study of instances of a phenomenon in its natural context and from the perspective of the participants involved in the phenomenon.

Catalytic validity. A judgment about the credibility of an action research project based on the extent to which the project causes stakeholders to transform their view of reality in relation to their professional practice.

Categorical variable. A characteristic that has been measured as a nominal scale.

Category. In qualitative research, a construct that is used to classify a certain type of phenomenon in the database.

Causal inference. Based on the results of a data analysis, the conclusion that one set of events brought about, directly or indirectly, a subsequent set of events.

Causal pattern. In case study research, an inference that particular phenomena within a case or across cases are systematically related to each other and that the relationship is one of cause-and-effect.

Causal-comparative research. A type of quantitative investigation that seeks to discover possible causes and effects of a personal characteristic (e.g., self-esteem or academic success) by comparing individuals in whom it is present with individuals in whom it is absent or present to a lesser degree.

CD-ROM. An acronym for *Compact Disk-Read Only Memory,* a computer device for storing and providing easy access to a large amount of information (e.g., an index to the education literature).

Ceiling effect. A situation in which the range of difficulty of a test's items is so restricted that many of the research participants earn the maximum score or a score close to it.

Centroid. The mean of the vector scores for all the individuals classified as members of a particular group in a multivariate analysis of variance.

Chain of evidence. In qualitative research, the validation of a study's findings by demonstrating clear, meaningful links among the study's research questions, the raw data, the data analysis, and the findings.

Chain sample. See *snowball sample.*

Chart essay. A verbal and visual format for describing the findings of a research study so that they are easily understood by policy makers and practitioners.

Chi-square (χ^2) **test.** A nonparametric test of statistical significance that is used when the research data are in the form of frequency counts for two or more categories.

CIJE. See *Current Index to Journals in Education.*

CIPP model. A type of evaluation that is designed to support the decision-making process in program management. CIPP is an acronym for the four types of educational evaluation included in the model: Context evaluation, Input evaluation, Process evaluation, and Product evaluation.

Citation (or *bibliographic citation or reference).* The information about a document that one would need in order to locate it, usually including author, title, publication date, publisher, and, in the case of journal articles, page numbers and volume number.

Closed-form item. A question that permits a response only from among prespecified response options (e.g., a multiple-choice question).

Cluster sample. A group of research participants that is formed by selecting naturally occurring groups (i.e., clusters) in the population. See also *multistage-cluster sample.*

Coefficient of determination (R^2). A mathematical expression of the amount of variance in the criterion variable that is explained in a multiple regression analysis by a predictor variable or a combination of predictor variables.

Coefficient of equivalence. A measure of the alternate-form reliability of a test, based on the magnitude of the relationship between individuals' scores on two parallel versions of the same test.

Coefficient of internal consistency. *See split-half reliability correlation coefficient.*

Coefficient of stability. A measure of the alternate-form reliability of a test, based on the magnitude of the relationship between individuals' scores on two forms of the same test on two different testing occasions.

Cognitive anthropology. See *ethnoscience.*

Cognitive ethnography. See *ethnoscience.*

Cognitive psychology. The study of the structures and processes involved in mental activity and of how these structures and processes are learned or develop with maturation.

Cohort longitudinal research. A type of investigation in which changes in a population over time are studied by selecting a different sample at each data-collection point from a population that remains constant.

Collinearity. The degree of correlation between any two variables that are to be used as predictors in a multiple regression analysis. Command file. In statistical analysis, a list of the computer software instructions that are used to perform a particular analysis.

Compensatory rivalry (or *John Henry effect).* In experiments, a situation in which control group participants perform beyond their usual level because they perceive that they are in competition with the experimental group.

Complete-observer role. In qualitative research, the observer's maintenance of a posture of detachment while collecting research data in a field setting.

Complete-participant role. In qualitative research, the observer's assumption of the role of group member while collecting research data about it.

Computer-adaptive testing. An approach to measurement in which the difficulty level of test items presented to a particular test-taker is matched by the computer to the test-taker's ability level as judged from performance on earlier test items.

Computer-assisted telephone interview. A type of interview in which the interviewer uses a computer to assist in gathering information while conducting a telephone interview.

Concurrent evidence (**also called** *concurrent validity*). The extent to which individuals' scores on a new test correspond to their scores on an established test of the same construct that is administered at approximately the same point in time.

Confidence interval. All the values within the range defined by the confidence limits of a sample statistic.

Confidence limits. As determined from sample statistics, an upper value and lower value that are likely to contain the actual population parameter (e.g., the population mean is likely to be between 2.3 and 4.7).

Confirmation survey interview. In qualitative research, a type of interview that is used to confirm the findings obtained from data that were collected by other methods.

Confirmatory factor analysis. The use of factor analysis to test hypotheses about the latent traits (also called *factors*) that underlie a set of measured variables.

Confirming-and-disconfirming-case sample. A group of cases that is selected for the purpose of validating the findings of previous research.

Consequential validity. The extent to which the values implicit in the constructs measured by a test and in the intended uses of the test are consistent with the values of users, test-takers, and other stakeholders.

Constant comparison. In the grounded theory approach, a process for analyzing qualitative data to identify categories, to create sharp distinctions between categories, and to decide which categories are theoretically significant.

Constitutively defined construct. A concept that is defined by reference to other concepts.

Construct. A concept that is inferred from commonalities among observed phenomena and that can be used to explain those phenomena. In theory development, a concept that refers to a structure or process that is hypothesized to underlie particular observable phenomena.

Construct validity. The extent to which inferences from a test's scores accurately reflect the construct that the test is claimed to measure.

Contact summary sheet. A brief form that is designed by the researcher for summarizing what was learned from each data-collection event and what types of data need to be collected next.

Content analysis. The study of particular aspects of the information contained in a document, film, or other form of communication.

Content validity. The extent to which inferences from a test's scores adequately represent the content or conceptual domain that the test is claimed to measure.

Context evaluation. In the CIPP model of evaluation research, the identification of problems and needs that are occurring in a specific educational setting.

Contingency coefficient. A measure of the magnitude of the relationship between two variables in a chi-square analysis, when at least one of the variables has more than two categories.

Continuous recording. The recording of everything that is observed in an event, with the observations organized in chronological sequence.

Continuous score. A value of a measure that forms an interval or ratio scale with an indefinite number of points along its continuum.

Control group. In an experiment, a group of research participants who receive no treatment or an alternate treatment so that the effect of extraneous variables can be determined.

Convenience sample. A group of cases that are selected simply because they are available and easy to access.

Convergent evidence. Support for the validity of test-score interpretations that comes from positive correlations between a sample's scores on the test and their scores on other measures that are hypothesized to measure the same construct.

Conversation analysis. The study of the implicit rules governing the speech acts between two or more people.

Correction for attenuation. A statistical procedure for estimating how much greater the correlation coefficient for two measured variables would be if the measures had perfect reliability.

Correction for restriction in range. A statistical procedure for estimating how much greater the correlation coefficient would be if the range of scores on one or both measured variables in a sample was extended to represent the full range of scores in the population.

Correlation coefficient. A mathematical expression of the direction and magnitude of the relationship between two measured variables.

Correlation matrix. An arrangement of correlation coefficients in rows and columns that makes it easy to see how each of a set of measured variables correlates with all the other variables.

Correlation ratio (*eta*). A mathematical expression that provides a more accurate index of the magnitude of the relationship between two measured variables than other correlational statistics when the relationship is markedly nonlinear.

Correlational research. A type of investigation that seeks to discover the direction and magnitude of the relationship among variables through the use of correlational statistics.

Cost analysis. In evaluation research, the determination of either (1) the relationship between the costs of a program and its benefits when both costs and benefits can be calculated in monetary terms (called the *cost-benefit ratio*), or (2) the relationship between the costs of various interventions relative to their measured effectiveness in achieving a desired outcome (called *cost-effectiveness*).

Cost-benefit ratio. See *cost analysis*.

Cost-effectiveness. See *cost analysis*.

Counterbalanced experiment. A type of experiment in which each research participant receives several treatments, but the order of administering the treatments is varied across participants to eliminate the possibility of an order effect.

Criterion sample. A group of cases that satisfy particular specifications or standards.

Criterion-referenced measurement. An approach to testing in which an individual's score on a test is interpreted by comparing it to a prespecified standard of performance.

Criterion-related observer reliability. The extent to which the scores assigned by a trained observer agree with those assigned by an expert observer.

Criterion-related validity. Types of validity (specifically, predictive and concurrent validity) that involve an explicit standard against which claims about a test can be judged.

Critical theory. The formulation of principles designed to clarify the power relationships and forms of oppression existing in a society or culture, and thus to serve as a guide to efforts to emancipate its members from those forms of oppression.

Critical-case sample. A single case that provides a crucial test of a theory, program, or other phenomenon.

Cronbach's alpha coefficient (α). A measure of the internal consistency of a test, based on the extent to which test-takers who answer a test item one way respond to other items the same way.

Cross-sectional longitudinal research. A type of investigation in which changes in a population over time are studied by collecting data at one point in time, but from samples that vary in age or developmental stage.

Cultural acquisition. The process by which individuals develop the concepts, values, skills, and behaviors associated with the culture in which they are raised.

Cultural studies. A branch of critical theory that involves the study of power relationships and forms of oppression in a culture in order to help emancipate its members from those forms of oppression.

Cultural transmission. The process by which cultural institutions intervene in individuals' lives to shape their learning or nonlearning of specific features of life in the culture.

Culture. The sum total of ways of living (e.g., values, customs, rituals, and beliefs) that are built up by a group of human beings and that are transmitted from one generation to another or from current members to newly admitted members.

Current Index to journals in Education (**CIJE**). An index to articles in hundreds of education-related journals. Published monthly by ERIC.

Deception. The act of creating a false impression in the minds of research participants through such procedures as withholding information, providing false information, creating false intimacy, or using accomplices.

Deconstructionism. A philosophical and literary movement that claims that a text has no definite meaning and therefore no authority, that words can refer only to other words, and that "playing" with a text can yield multiple, often contradictory interpretations.

Dehoaxing. If a research study involves deception, a type of debriefing in which the researcher must convince all deceived participants that they were in fact deceived, so that the deception will have no continuing harmful effect on them.

Democratic validity. A judgment about the credibility of an action research project based on the extent to which the perspectives and interests of all stakeholders were taken into account.

Deontological ethics. In research, judgments about the morality of one's research decisions and actions by reference to absolute values (e.g., honesty, justice, and respect for others).

Dependent variable. A variable that the researcher thinks occurred after, and as a result of, another variable (called the *independent variable*). In a hypothesized cause-and-effect relationship, the dependent variable is the effect.

Derived score. A transformation of a raw score (e.g., age equivalents) to reveal the individual's performance relative to a norming group.

Descriptive observational variable (or *low-inference variable*). A variable that requires little inference on the part of an observer to determine its presence or level.

Descriptive research. In quantitative research, a type of investigation that measures the characteristics of a sample or population on prespecified variables. In qualitative research, a type of investigation that involves providing a detailed portrayal of one or more cases.

Descriptive statistics. Mathematical techniques for organizing, summarizing, and displaying a set of numerical data.

Descriptor. In a preliminary source, a term that is used to classify all documents that contain information about the topic denoted by the term.

Desensitization. If a research study involves deception, a type of debriefing in which the researcher helps all deceived participants cope with any negative perceptions about themselves that the deception induced.

Deviance bias. In testing, a type of response set in which an individual answers items to create the appearance of being atypical or abnormal.

Deviant-case sample. See *extreme-case sample.*

Diagnostic test. A type of measure that is used to identify a student's strengths and weaknesses in a particular school subject.

Dialogic validity. A judgment about the credibility of an action research project based on the extent to which colleagues shared in the development of the practitioner/researcher's findings and interpretations.

Dichotomy. A categorical variable that has only two values.

Differential item functioning. A feature of a test item whereby individuals of equal ability but from different subgroups (e.g., males and females) do not have the same probability of earning the same score on the item.

Directional hypothesis. A type of prediction that the researcher makes on the basis of theory or speculation and that is tested by collecting and analyzing data. The prediction specifies the direction of the relationship (positive or negative) expected between two measured variables, or which research group will score higher on the measured variable.

Discourse analysis. The study of the interpretive processes that individuals use to produce their accounts of reality.

Discrepancy evaluation. A type of evaluation research that involves the investigation of discrepancies between the objectives of a program and students' actual achievement of the objectives.

Discriminant analysis. A type of multiple regression analysis involving the use of two or more measured variables that yield continuous scores to predict a single criterion variable that is categorical in nature.

Discriminant evidence. Support for the validity of test-score interpretations that comes from negative correlations between a sample's scores on the test and their scores on other measures that are hypothesized to measure a different construct.

Document summary form. A brief form that is designed by the researcher for summarizing what was learned from examining a particular document and ideas about other documents that should be obtained and studied.

Domain-referenced measurement. A type of criterion-referenced measurement that assesses how well an individual performs on a sample of items that represents a well-defined content area.

Dual publication. The unethical practice of publishing more than one report about the same research results in order to create an exaggerated impression of a researcher's productivity.

Duncan's multiple-range test. A type of *t* test for multiple comparisons.

Duration recording. The measurement of the amount of time that various observational variables occur during an event (e.g., a classroom lesson).

Ecological ethics. In research, judgments about the morality of one's research decisions and actions in terms of the participants' culture and the larger social systems of which they are a part.

Ecological validity. The extent to which the results of an experiment can be generalized from conditions in the research setting to particular naturally occurring conditions.

Educational connoisseurship and criticism. A type of expertise-based evaluation that includes two components: connoisseurship, which is the process of appreciating (in the sense of becoming aware of) the qualities of an educational program and its meaning; and criticism, which is the process of describing and evaluating that which has been appreciated.

Educational evaluation. The process of making judgments about the merit, value, or worth of an educational program, method, or other phenomenon.

Educational Resources Information Center (ERIC). A federally funded agency that provides many information resources to the education community, including *CIJE, RIE,* and the various publications of the ERIC clearinghouses.

Effect size. An estimate of the magnitude of a difference, a relationship, or other effect in the population represented by a sample.

Emancipatory action research. A type of self-reflective investigation that professional practitioners undertake for the purpose of improving the rationality and justice of their work.

Emergent design. In responsive evaluation, the practice of changing the design of an evaluation as the evaluator gains new insights into the concerns and issues of the stakeholders.

Emic perspective. The research participants' perceptions and understanding of their social reality.

Endogenous variable. In a path analysis model, a variable for which there is another variable in the model that is hypothesized to influence it.

Epistemology. The branch of philosophy that studies the nature of knowledge and the process by which knowledge is acquired and validated.

ERIC. See *Educational Resources Information Center.*

Error of central tendency. The tendency for an observer to rate all or most of the individuals at or near the midpoint of an observational scale.

Error of leniency. The tendency for an observer to assign high ratings to the majority of research participants even when they differ considerably on the variable being measured.

Espoused theory. In the theory of action, professionals' beliefs about how they deal with problems of practice.

Eta. See *correlation ratio.*

Ethnographic content analysis. In anthropology, the study of the content of documents found in field settings as reflections of the local culture.

Ethnography. In anthropology, the in-depth study of the features of life in a given culture and the patterns in those features.

Ethnography of communication. In anthropology, the study of how members of a cultural group use speech in their social life.

Ethnology. In anthropology, the study of similarities and differences among cultures.

Ethnomethodology. In sociology, the study of the techniques that individuals use to make sense of their everyday social life and to accomplish the tasks of communicating, making decisions, and reasoning in social situations.

Ethnoscience (or *cognitive ethnography* or *cognitive anthropology*). In anthropology, the study of a culture's semantic systems for the purpose of revealing the cognitive structure of the culture.

Etic perspective. The researcher's conceptual and theoretical understanding of the research participants' social reality.

Evaluative observational variable. A variable that requires an observer both to make an inference from behavior to a construct that is presumed to underlie the behavior and an evaluative judgment.

Event structure analysis. In sociology, the study of the logical structure of social events, that is, whether certain social events are prerequisite to the occurrence of other events.

Ex post facto research. A term from Latin (meaning "from that which is done afterward") that refers to correlational or causal-comparative research because, in these types of investigation, causes are studied after they presumably have exerted their effect on the variable of interest.

Exogenous variable. In a path analysis model, a variable for which there is no other variable in the model that is hypothesized to influence it.

Experimental mortality. The loss of research participants from an experiment while it is in progress.

Experimental treatment. See *treatment variable.*

Experimentally accessible population. A defined population, usually local in nature, from which it is feasible for the researcher to draw a sample to participate in an experiment.

Experimenter bias. In experiments, a situation in which the researcher's expectations about what will occur are unintentionally transmitted to the research participants so that their behavior in the experiment is affected. Also, a situation in which the researcher's expectations affect data collection and data analysis.

Expertise-based evaluation. The use of experts to make judgments about the worth of an educational program.

Explained variance (r^2). In correlation, a statistic that specifies the percentage of the variance in variable X that can be predicted from the variance in variable Y. The greater the value of r^2, the greater the amount of explained variance.

Exploratory data analysis. A method for discovering patterns in a set of scores.

Exploratory factor analysis. An approach to factor analysis in which the researcher has no prior hypotheses about the latent variables (also called *factors*) that might underlie a set of measured variables.

External criticism. In historical research, the determination of whether the apparent or claimed origin (author and place, date, and circumstances of publication) of a historical document corresponds to its actual origin.

External evaluator (or *third-party evaluator* or *evaluation contractor*). An individual who is employed to evaluate a program, but is not a member of the program's staff.

External validity. The extent to which the results of a research study can be generalized to individuals and situations beyond those involved in the study.

Extinction. In a single-case experiment or the practice of behavior modification, the act of withdrawing a treatment after a research participant has become accustomed to it.

Extraneous variable. In experiments, any aspect of the situation, other than the treatment variable, that can influence the dependent variable and that, if not controlled, can make it impossible to determine whether the treatment variable is responsible for any observed effect on the dependent variable.

Extreme-case sample (or *deviant-case sample*). A group of cases that are highly unusual manifestations of the phenomenon being investigated.

Extreme-groups method. In causal-comparative research, the procedure of selecting comparison groups who are at the minimum and maximum of a score distribution on variable X.

F maximum test for homogeneity of variance. A procedure for determining whether the observed difference among the variances of scores of more than two groups on variable X is statistically significant.

Face validity. The extent to which a casual, subjective inspection of a test's items indicates that they cover the content that the test is claimed to measure.

Factor. In a factor analysis of a set of variables, a mathematical expression of a feature shared by a particular subset of the variables.

Factor analysis. A statistical procedure for reducing a set of measured variables to a smaller number of variables (called *factors* or *latent variables*) by combining variables that are moderately or highly correlated with each other.

Factor score. The score earned by each individual on a particular factor identified in a factor analysis.

Factorial experiment. A type of experiment in which the researcher studies how two or more treatment variables (called *factors* in this context) affect a dependent variable either independently or in interaction with each other.

Fixed factor. In experimental designs, an independent variable whose values will not be generalized beyond the experiment.

Focus. In case study research, the aspects of a phenomenon on which data collection and analysis will concentrate.

Focus group interview. A type of interview involving an interviewer and a group of research participants, who are free to talk with and influence each other in the process of sharing their ideas and perceptions about a defined topic.

Forgery. In historical research, a document or relic that is claimed to be genuine, but that actually is a deception.

Formative evaluation. A type of evaluation that is done while a program is under development in order to improve its effectiveness, or to support a decision to abort further development so that resources are not wasted on a program that has little chance of ultimately being effective.

Frequency-count recording. Measurement of the number of times that each observational variable occurs during an event (e.g., a classroom lesson).

Gain score (or *change score* or *difference score*). An individual's score on a test administered at one point in time minus that individual's score on a test administered at an earlier time.

General interview guide approach. A type of interview in which a set of topics is planned, but the order in which the topics are covered and the wording of questions is decided as the interview proceeds.

Generalizability coefficient. In generalizability theory, a measure of test reliability that considers the joint effect of all the sources of measurement error that have been investigated.

Generalizability theory. An approach to conceptualizing and assessing the relative contribution of different sources of measurement error to a set of test scores.

Goal-free evaluation. A type of evaluation research in which the evaluator investigates the actual effects of a program without being influenced by prior knowledge of the program's stated goals.

Grade equivalent. A type of derived score that represents a given raw score on a measure as the average grade level of individuals in a norming group who earned that score.

Grounded theory. An approach to theory development that involves deriving constructs and laws directly from the immediate data that the researcher has collected rather than drawing on an existing theory.

Halo effect. The tendency for the observer's early impressions of an individual being observed to influence the observer's ratings of all variables involving the same individual.

Hawthorne effect. An observed change in research participants' behavior based on their awareness of participating in an experiment, their knowledge of the researchers hypothesis, or their response to receiving special attention.

Hegemony. The maintenance of domination of subordinate groups by privileged groups through its cultural agencies (e.g., governmental bodies and public school systems).

Hermeneutic circle. An interpretation of a text by the process of alternating between interpreting the meaning of each part of the text and the meaning of the text as a whole.

Hermeneutics. A field of inquiry that seeks to understand how individuals develop interpretations of texts.

Hidden curriculum. The knowledge, values, and behaviors that are taught tacitly by the way in which schools are structured and classroom instruction is organized.

Hierarchical linear regression. A statistical technique for examining the relationship between predictor variables and a criterion variable at more than one unit of analysis.

High-inference variable. See *inferential observational variable.*

Histogram. A diagram that shows the relationship between two measured variables both of which yield continuous scores.

Historical criticism. See *internal criticism* and *external criticism.*

Historical research. The study of past phenomena for the purpose of gaining a better understanding of present institutions, practices, trends, and issues.

Historiography. The study of the methods that historians use in their research.

Homogeneous-case sample. A group of cases that are similar in that they represent one defined point of variation in the phenomenon being studied.

Hypothesis. The researcher's prediction, derived from a theory or from speculation, about how two or more measured variables will be related to each other.

Ideological inscription. In cultural studies, the claim that presumably neutral concepts (e.g., aptitude) involve preformed systems of values and beliefs that reinforce the power of dominant groups in society.

Independent variable. A variable that the researcher thinks occurred prior in time to, and had an influence on, another variable (called the *dependent variable*). In a hypothesized cause-and-effect relationship, the independent variable is the cause.

Indexicality. In ethnomethodology and linguistics, a feature of certain words (e.g., *I*) whereby their full meaning can be determined only by referring to aspects of the context in which they are used.

Individual-referenced measurement. An approach to testing in which an individual's score on a test at one point in time is interpreted in relation to the same individual's performance on it at other points in time.

Inferential observational variable (or *high-inference variable*). A variable that requires the observer to make an inference from behavior to a construct that is presumed to underlie the behavior.

Informal conversational interview. In qualitative research, a type of interview that relies entirely on the spontaneous generation of questions during natural interaction, such as occurs in participant observation in a field setting.

Informed consent. The ethical and legal requirement that a researcher tell all potential research participants about the study's procedures, the information that they will be asked to disclose to the researcher, and the intended uses of that information.

Input evaluation. In the CIPP model of evaluation research, judgments about the resources and strategies needed to accomplish program goals and objectives.

Institutional review board (IRB). A committee that is established by an institution to ensure that participants in any research proposed by individuals affiliated with the institution will be protected from harm.

Instrumental rationality. In action research, an overriding focus on method and efficiency of professional practice over goals and purposes.

Intact group. A collection of persons who must be studied as members of a previously defined group (e.g., a classroom) rather than as individuals.

Intense-case sample. A group of cases that manifest the phenomenon of interest to a considerable degree, but not to an extreme degree.

Intentional documents. In historical research, writings (e.g., memoirs and yearbooks) that have the explicit purpose of serving as a record of the past.

Inter-observer reliability. The extent to which the scores assigned by one observer of events correlate with the scores assigned by another observer of the same events.

Interaction effect. In experiments, a situation in which the effect of a treatment variable on a dependent variable is influenced by one or more other treatment variables.

Internal consistency. An approach to estimating test reliability that examines the extent to which individuals who respond one way to a test item tend to respond the same way to other items on the test.

Internal criticism. An evaluation of the accuracy and worth of the statements contained in a historical document.

Internal evaluator. An individual who plays a role in evaluating a program while also employed as a member of the program's staff.

Internal validity. In experiments, the extent to which extraneous variables have been controlled by the researcher, so that any observed effects can be attributed solely to the treatment variable.

Internet. A worldwide network of computers that enables network members to communicate with each other and to access electronic information resources by computer.

Interpretational analysis. The process of examining qualitative data to identify constructs, themes, and patterns that can be used to describe and explain the phenomenon being studied.

Interpretive research (or *qualitative research*). The study of the immediate and local meanings of social actions to the actors involved in them.

Interpretive validity. The extent to which the knowledge claims (i.e., interpretations) resulting from a qualitative study satisfy four criteria: they have useful consequences; they take context into account; they acknowledge the researcher's role in the study; and they are accepted as authentic—by readers.

Interpretive zone. In case-study research, the process of making sense of data through collaborative inquiry by a group of researchers.

Interval recording. The recording of observational variables at given time intervals (e.g., making an observation every three seconds).

Interval scale. A measure (e.g., a thermometer) that lacks a true zero point and for which the distance between any two adjacent points is the same.

Interview schedule. A measure that specifies the questions to be asked of each research participant, the sequence in which they are to be asked, and guidelines for what the interviewer is to say at the opening and closing of the interview.

Intra-observer reliability. The extent to which an observer makes consistent recordings of observational variables while viewing a videotape or listening to an audiotape of an event on several occasions.

Item analysis. A set of procedures for determining the difficulty, the validity, and the reliability of each item in a test.

Item-characteristic curve. A mathematical function describing the relationship between test-item performance and the underlying ability.

Item-characteristic curve theory. See *item-response theory*.

Item-difficulty index. For each item on a test, the number of individuals who answered it correctly divided by the total number of individuals taking the test.

Item-reliability coefficient. The correlation between individuals' responses to a particular item on a test and their total test score.

Item-response theory (or *latent trait theory* or *item-characteristic carne theory*). An approach to test construction based on the assumptions that: (1) an individual's performance on a test item reflects a single ability; (2) individuals with different amounts of that ability will perform differently on the item; and (3) the relationships between the variables of ability and item performance can be represented as a mathematical function.

Item statistic. A number that represents some property of individual items in a measure.

Item-validity coefficient. The correlation between individuals' responses to a particular item on a test and their total score on a criterion measure.

John Henry effect. See *compensatory rivalry*.

Judicial evaluation model. A type of evaluation research that simulates the use of legal procedures for the purpose of promoting broad understanding of a program, clarifying the issues raised by the program, and producing recommendations and policy guidelines that lead to improvements in the program.

Key-informant interview. A type of interview in which the researcher collects data from individuals who have special knowledge or perceptions that would not otherwise be available to the researcher.

Kruskal-Wallis test. A nonparametric procedure for determining whether the observed difference between the distribution of scores for more than two groups on a measured variable X is statistically significant.

Kuder-Richardson formulas. Measures of the internal consistency of tests whose items have only two response options (e.g., yes or no).

Lake Wobegone phenomenon. See *test score pollution*.

Latent trait. An unobservable characteristic that is hypothesized to explain observed behavior.

Latent trait theory. See *item-response theory*.

Latent variable. In structural equation modeling, an unmeasured variable that is hypothesized to underlie a set of measured variables (called *manifest variables*).

Law (or *scientific law*). A generalization about a causal, sequential, or other type of relationship between two or more constructs.

Life history. The study of the experiences of individuals during different phases of their lives and the way in which they conceptualize these experiences in order to give meaning to their lives.

Likert scale. A measure that asks individuals to check their level of agreement with various statements about an attitude object (e.g., strongly agree, agree, undecided, disagree, or strongly disagree).

Limit field. In an electronic version of a preliminary source, a classification category (e.g., the year of publication) that can be specified in order to limit the search to publications belonging to that category.

Line of best fit. In correlational statistics, the line on a scattergram that represents the best prediction of each person's Y score from their X score.

LISREL. An acronym for *Linear Structural Relationships*, which is a computer program for structural equation modeling.

Literal replication. In case study research, the process of repeating a research study with a different case and hypothesizing that the case will yield results that are similar to those of a previously studied case.

Loading. In factor analysis, the degree and direction of the correlation between a measured variable and a particular factor.

Logistic regression. A type of multiple regression analysis involving the use of two or more measured variables yielding continuous or categorical scores to predict a criterion variable that is categorical in nature.

Longitudinal research. A type of investigation that involves describing changes in a sample's characteristics over a specified period of time.

Low-inference variable. See *descriptive observational variable*.

M. See *mean*.

Macroethnography. In anthropology, the study of large cultural units, such as a national culture.

Main effect. In experiments, the influence of a treatment variable by itself (i.e., not in interaction with any other variable) on a dependent variable.

Manifest variable. In structural equation modeling, a measured variable that is hypothesized to indicate an underlying, unmeasured variable (called a *latent variable*).

Mann-Whitney *U* test. A nonparametric procedure for determining whether the observed difference between the distribution of scores for each of two groups on a measured variable X is statistically significant. The procedure is used when there is no relationship between the two sets of scores and when the assumptions underlying the t test for independent means are grossly violated.

Matching. A procedure that equates two or more groups on the extraneous variable Z at the outset of a study so that it can be ruled out as an influence on any relationship between X and Y that is later observed.

Material culture (or *artifact*). The various objects created by members of a past or present culture that can be studied as reflections of that culture.

Matrix. In a qualitative research report, a type of table that has defined rows and columns for reporting the results of data analyses and other information.

Maximum-variation sample. A group of cases that represent the full range of variation in the phenomenon to be studied.

Mean (*M*). A measure of central tendency calculated by dividing the sum of the scores in a set by the number of scores.

Meaning unit. See *segment*.

Measure of central tendency. A single numerical value (e.g., the mean) that is representative of an entire set of scores.

Measurement error. In classical test theory, the difference between an individual's true score on a test and the scores that the individual actually obtains on it when it is administered over a variety of conditions.

Median. A measure of central tendency corresponding to the middle point in a distribution of scores.

Member checking. In qualitative research, the process of having research participants judge the accuracy and completeness of statements made in the researcher's report.

Meta-analysis. The use of particular statistical procedures to identify trends in the statistical results of a set of studies concerning the same research problem.

Meta-evaluation. In evaluation research, a review of the weaknesses in the evaluation design or in the execution of the evaluation that might affect the validity of the findings.

Microethnography. In anthropology, the study of small cultural units, such as subcultures that exist within a country.

Mode. A measure of central tendency corresponding to the most frequently occurring score in a distribution of scores.

Moderator variable. In predictive research, a variable Z that affects the extent to which variable X predicts variable Y, such that the correlation between X and Y for some values of Z will be different than the correlation between X and Y for other values of Z.

Multiple-baseline designs. A type of single-case experiment in which conditions other than baseline incidence of the target behavior are used to control for extraneous variables.

Multiple correlation coefficient (*R*). A mathematical expression of the magnitude of the relationship between a criterion variable and some combination of predictor variables in a multiple regression analysis.

Multiple regression. A statistical procedure for determining the magnitude of the relationship between a criterion variable and a combination of two or more predictor variables.

Multistage-cluster sample. A type of cluster sample that is formed first by selecting clusters and then by selecting individuals within these clusters. See also *cluster sample*.

Multivariate analysis of variance (MANOVA). A procedure that has the same purpose as analysis of variance, except that that the dependent variable is a composite index (called a *vector*) of two or more measured variables. The procedure is useful only when the measured dependent variables are correlated with each other.

Multivariate correlation. Any statistical analysis (e.g., multiple regression or factor analysis) that expresses the relationship among three or more variables.

Multivocality. A situation in which the participants in a culture or societal group do not speak with a unified voice, but rather have diverse points of view and interests.

Narrative inquiry. A representation and explanation of social reality that is communicated through various story structures (e.g., folktales and anecdotes).

Narrative analysis (or *narratology*). The study of folktales, plays, anecdotes, and other narrative forms by methods developed in cognitive psychology, ethnomethodology, conversation analysis, and other disciplines.

Narratology. See *narrative analysis*.

NCE score. See *normal curve equivalent score.*

Need. In evaluation research, a discrepancy between an existing set of conditions and a desired set of conditions.

Network. In a qualitative research report, a type of figure for displaying bits of information and how they relate to each other.

Nominal scale. A measure in which numbers represent categories that have no order or quantitative value (e.g., coding French students as "1," Italian students as "2," and Norwegian students as "3").

Nonequivalent control-group design. A type of experiment in which research participants are not randomly assigned to the experimental and control groups, and in which each group takes a pretest and a posttest.

Nonlinear multiple regression. A type of multiple regression analysis that is used to detect curvilinear relationships between the predictor variables and the criterion variable.

Nonparametric test of statistical significance. A type of test of statistical significance that does not make assumptions about the distribution and form of scores on the measured variable.

Nonproportional stratified random sample. A stratified random sample in which the number of individuals in one or more subgroups in the sample is not in proportion to their representation in the population.

Nonreactive measure. See *unobtrusive measure.*

Nonrecursive model. An application of path analysis that allows the researcher to test hypotheses involving reciprocal causation between pairs of variables.

Norm-referenced measurement. An approach to testing in which an individual's score on a test is interpreted by comparing it to the scores earned by a norming group.

Normal curve (or *normal probability curve*). A distribution of scores that form a symmetrical, bell-shaped curve when plotted on a graph.

Normal curve equivalent (NCE) score. A type of standard score with a distribution that has a mean of 50 and a standard deviation of 21.06; the scores are continuous and have equality of units.

Norming group. A large sample (ideally one that is representative of a well-defined population) whose scores on a test provide a set of standards against which the scores of subsequent individuals who take the test can be referenced.

Null hypothesis. A prediction that no relationship between two measured variables will be found, or that no difference between groups on a measured variable will be found.

Objective reality. The view that features of the external environment exist independently of the beliefs and perceptions of individuals.

Objectives-referenced measurement. A type of criterion-referenced measurement that assesses how well an individual performs on a sample of items that measure achievement of specific instructional objectives.

Objectivity. In testing, the extent to which scores on a test are undistorted by the biases of those who administer and score it.

Oblique solution. In factor analysis, a procedure that is used to generate factors that possibly are correlated with each other.

Observer bias. See *observer effect.*

Observer contamination. A situation in which the observer's awareness of certain information about an individual or setting to be observed influences the observer's recording of data involving that individual on the variables being studied.

Observer drift. The tendency for an observer gradually to redefine the observational variables during data collection, with the consequence that the data that the observer collects during the latter stages of data collection do not match the definitions that were learned during training.

Observer effect. Any action or bias of an observer that weakens the validity or reliability of the data that the observer collects.

Observer omission. The failure of an observer to record the occurrence of a behavior that fits one of the categories in the observational schedule.

Observer-participant role. In qualitative research, the observer's maintenance of a posture of detachment while collecting research data in a setting, but with casual interaction with the individuals or groups being studied as necessary.

On-line search. The use of an on-site computer and telephone hook-up to interact with an off-site computer containing an electronic version of a preliminary source such as *CIJE.*

One-group pretest-posttest design. A type of experiment in which all participants are exposed to the same conditions: measurement of the dependent variable (pretest), implementation of the experimental treatment, and another measurement of the dependent variable (posttest).

One-shot case study design. A type of experiment in which an experimental treatment is administered and then a posttest is administered to measure the effects of the treatment.

One-tailed test of statistical significance. A mathematical procedure for determining whether a null hypothesis that specifies the direction of the difference between two groups (or other prediction involving only one tail of a probability distribution) can be rejected at a given alpha level.

One-variable experiment. An experiment in which a single treatment variable is manipulated to determine its effect on one or more dependent variables.

One-variable multiple-condition designs. A type of experiment in which there is one treatment variable, but more than two treatment conditions (e.g., an experimental-treatment group and several control groups, each controlling for a different extraneous variable).

Open-form item. A question that permits research participants to make any response they wish (e.g., an essay question).

Operational-construct sample. See *theory-based sample.*

Operationally defined construct. A concept that is defined by specifying the activities used to measure or manipulate it.

Oral history. The use of oral interviews of individuals who witnessed or participated in particular events as sources of data about the past; also, the use of ballads, tales, and other forms of spoken language as sources of data about the past.

Order effect. In experiments where each research participant receives more than one treatment, the influence of the order in which the treatments are administered on the dependent variable.

Ordinal scale. A measure in which numbers represent a rank ordering of individuals or objects on some variable.

Orthogonal solution. In factor analysis, a procedure that is used to generate factors that are uncorrelated with each other.

Outcome validity. A judgment about the credibility of an action research project based on the extent to which new actions lead to a resolution of the problem that prompted the project.

Outlier. A research participant or other unit of analysis whose score on a measure differs markedly from the other scores in the sample or population.

p. See *probability value.*

Panel longitudinal research. A type of investigation in which changes in a population over time are studied by selecting a sample at the outset of the study and then collecting data from the same sample throughout the duration of the study.

Parameter. Any number that describes a characteristic of a population's scores on a measure.

Parametric test of statistical significance. A type of test of statistical significance that makes certain assumptions about the distribution and form of scores on the measured variable.

Paraphragiarism. Borrowing of another author's writing (e.g., extended paraphrases or one-to-one correspondence in the expression of ideas) to such an extent as to constitute representation of the other's work as one's own.

Part correlation coefficient. A statistic that expresses the magnitude of the relationship between two measured variables (X and Y) after the influence of another measured variable on either X or Y (but not on both) has been removed.

Partial correlation coefficient. A statistic that expresses the magnitude of the relationship between two measured variables (X and Y) after the influence of one or more other measured variables on both X and Y has been removed.

Partial publication. The unethical practice of writing separate articles about different aspects of a research study, rather than one article that presents the study as a coherent whole, in order to create an exaggerated impression of a researcher's productivity.

Participant construct interview. In qualitative research, a type of interview that is used to learn how respondents structure their physical and social world.

Participant-observer role. In qualitative research, the observer's assumption of a meaningful identity within the group being observed, but that does not involve engaging in activities that are at the core of the group's identity.

Path analysis. A statistical method for testing the validity of a theory about causal links between three or more measured variables.

Path coefficient. In a path analysis, a standardized regression coefficient that expresses the degree of direct effect of one measured variable on another measured variable.

Pattern. In case study research, an inference that particular phenomena within a case or across cases are systematically related to each other. See also *relational pattern* and *causal pattern.*

Pattern matching. The process of validating a causal inference from patterns in qualitative data by demonstrating that the patterns are consistent with predictions drawn from theoretical propositions.

Pearl building. The process of constructing a new literature search using descriptors obtained from document citations in the current literature search.

Pearson r. See *product-moment correlation coefficient.*

Percentile. A type of rank score that represents a given raw score on a measure as the percentage of individuals in the norming group whose score falls below that score.

Performance assessment (or *authentic assessment* or *alternative assessment*). An approach to evaluating individuals by examining their performance on complex, complete, real-life tasks that have intrinsic value.

Performance turn. An approach to qualitative research in which the researcher and an audience engage in dynamic interaction to co-create the meaning of a case study.

Personality inventory. A type of measure that assesses a variety of personality traits, typically in a self-report, paper-and-pencil format.

PERT. See *Program Evaluation* and *Review Technique.*

Phenomenography. The study of the different ways in which people conceptualize the world around them.

Phenomenology. In psychology, the study of the world as it appears to individuals when they place themselves in a state of consciousness that strives to be free of everyday biases and beliefs.

Phenomenon. A process, event, person, document, or other thing of interest to the researcher. In phenomenology, a sensation, perception, or ideation that appears in consciousness when the self focuses attention on an object.

Phi coefficient. A measure of the magnitude of the relationship between two dichotomous variables in a chi-square analysis.

Pilot study. A small-scale, preliminary investigation that is conducted to develop and test the measures or procedures that will be used in a research study.

Plagiarism. The direct lifting of another individual's words for use in one's own report.

Poisson regression. A type of multiple regression that is used when the measure of the criterion variable yields a frequency count.

Politically important-case sample. A group of cases that are selected because they are of particular interest to the agency funding the study or some other influential constituency.

Population validity. The extent to which the results of a study can be generalized from the sample that participated in it to a particular population.

Portfolio. In performance assessment, a purposeful collection of a student's work that records the student's progress in mastering a subject domain (e.g., writing in multiple genres) along with the student's personal reflections on his or her progress.

Positive test strategy. The decision to evaluate the effectiveness of a program, method, or other intervention under a set of conditions that are likely to provide the best possible opportunity for the intervention to succeed.

Positivism. The epistemological doctrine that physical and social reality is independent of those who observe it, and that observations of this reality, if unbiased, constitute scientific knowledge.

Positivist research. See *quantitative research.*

Postmodernism. A broad social and philosophical movement that questions the rationality of human action, the use of positivist epistemology, and any human endeavor (e.g., science) that claims a privileged position with respect to the search for truth or that claims progress in its search for truth.

Postpositivism. The epistemological doctrine that social reality is a construction, and that it is constructed differently by different individuals.

Postpositivist research. See *qualitative research.*

Poststructuralism. The study of phenomena as systems, with the assumption that these systems have no inherent meaning.

Posttest. A measure that is administered following an experimental or control treatment or other intervention in order to determine the effects of the intervention.

Posttest-only control-group design. A type of experiment that includes three phases: random assignment of research participants to the experimental and control groups; administration of the treatment to the experimental group and either no treatment or an alternative treatment to the control group; and administration of a measure of the dependent variable to both groups.

Practice-oriented material culture. Objects that are created by members of a past or present culture for particular uses (e.g., tools used in building houses), which also may have personal associations and symbolic meanings.

Prediction research. A type of investigation that seeks to predict future events, conditions, or accomplishments from variables measured at an earlier point

Predictive evidence (also called *predictive validity*). The extent to which the scores on a test administered at one point in time accurately forecast the test-takers' scores on another measure administered at a later point in time.

Preliminary source. An index to, or bibliography of, secondary-source and primary-source literature on particular topics.

Presentism. A type of bias in historical research in which past events are interpreted with concepts and perspectives that originated in more recent times.

Pretest. A measure that is administered prior to an experimental treatment or other intervention.

Primary source. A document (e.g., a journal article or a book) written by an individual who actually conducted the research study, developed the theory, witnessed the events, or formulated the opinions described in the document.

Proactive action research. A type of action research in which practitioners first try out a procedure, and then collect and analyze data to determine whether the procedure is achieving its intended purpose.

Probability sampling. A procedure for drawing a sample from a population such that each individual in the population has a known chance of being selected.

Probability value (*p*). The likelihood that a statistical result was obtained by chance.

Process evaluation. In the CIPP model of evaluation research, the collection of evaluative data once the program has been designed and put into operation.

Process validity. A judgment about the credibility of an action research project based on the adequacy of the processes used in different phases of the project.

Product evaluation. In the CIPP model of evaluation research, the determination of the extent to which the goals of the program have been achieved.

Product-moment correlation coefficient (or *r* or *Pearson r*). A mathematical expression of the direction and magnitude of the relationship between two measures that yield continuous scores.

Program delineation. In evaluation research, the process of identifying the salient characteristics of the program to be evaluated.

Program Evaluation and Review Technique (PERT). In the context of research studies, a planning technique that is used to identify the activities to be accomplished, the order in which they need to be accomplished, and the estimated time to accomplish each activity, in order to complete a study on schedule.

Progressive discourse. The practice of seeking to advance scientific understanding of physical and social reality by giving all individuals the right to criticize a research study or the methods of scientific inquiry, and if the criticism proves to have merit, revising a theory, interpretations of findings, or methods accordingly.

Projective test. A measure that provides amorphous stimuli and freedom of response, on the assumption that this approach will reveal an individual's inner thoughts, fantasies, and unique structuring of reality.

Proportional stratified random sample. A stratified random sample in which the proportion of each subgroup in the sample is the same as their proportion in the population.

Protocol analysis. In cognitive psychology, a method that involves asking individuals to state all their thoughts as they carry out a challenging task, so that the researcher can obtain a holistic overview of their cognitive activity as recorded in their verbal reports.

Purposeful random sample. In qualitative research, a group of cases that are selected by random sampling methods for the purpose of establishing that the selection of cases was not biased.

Purposeful sampling. The process of selecting cases that are likely to be "information-rich" with respect to the purposes of a qualitative research study.

Qualitative research (or *postpositivist research*). Inquiry that is grounded in the assumption that individuals construct social reality in the form of meanings and interpretations, and that these constructions tend to be transitory and situational. The dominant methodology is to discover these meanings and interpretations by studying cases intensively in natural settings and by subjecting the resulting data to analytic induction.

Quantitative history. The collection and statistical analysis of quantitative data from the past to investigate historical phenomena, especially the characteristics of a population.

Quantitative records. In historical research, compilations of numerical data (e.g., census records and school budgets) that are used as sources of data about the past.

Quantitative research (or *positivist research*). Inquiry that is grounded in the assumption that features of the social environment constitute an objective reality that is relatively constant across time and settings. The dominant methodology is to describe and explain features of this reality by collecting numerical data on observable behaviors of samples and by subjecting these data to statistical analysis.

Quasi-experiment. A type of experiment in which research participants are not randomly assigned to the experimental and control groups.

Questionnaire. A measure that presents a set of written questions to which all individuals in a sample respond.

R. See *multiple correlation coefficient.*

r. See *product-moment correlation coefficient.*

R^2. See *coefficient of determination.*

R^2 **increment.** The additional variance in the criterion variable that can be explained by adding a new predictor variable to a multiple regression analysis.

Random assignment. The process of assigning individuals or groups (e.g., classrooms) to the experimental and control treatments such that each individual or group has an equal chance of being in each treatment.

Random factor. In experimental designs, an independent variable whose values will be generalized beyond the experiment.

Random sample (or *simple random sample*). A group of research participants that is formed such that all members of the accessible or target population have an equal and independent chance of being selected. By "independent" is meant that the selection of one individual for the sample has no effect on the selection of any other individual.

Range. A measure of the amount of dispersion in a distribution of scores; it is expressed as the lowest and highest scores in the distribution.

Rank score. The relative position of a person or object on an ordinal scale (e.g, a student with the fifth highest grade point average in a class is assigned a rank score of 5).

Ratio scale. A measure (e.g., a yardstick) that has a true zero point and for which the distance between any two adjacent points is the same.

Rational equivalence. An approach to estimating a test's internal consistency, typically involving the application of the Kuder-Richardson formulas.

Raw score. An individual score on a measure as determined by the scoring key, without any further statistical manipulation.

Reader/user generalizability. In qualitative research, the view that the generalizability of a study's findings is not an inherent feature of the findings, but rather a judgment by individuals as to whether the findings are applicable to their particular situation.

Recursive model. An application of path analysis that considers only unidirectional causal relationships, such that if variable X is hypothesized to influence variable Y, it is not possible to hypothesize that variable Y influences variable X.

Refereed journal. A journal in which the articles that appear were first evaluated by a panel of acknowledged experts to assure that they merit publication.

Reflection. In action research, a process in which practitioners step back from the problematic world of practice and ponder and share ideas about the meaning, value, and impact of their work.

Reflective analysis. In qualitative research, a process in which the researcher relies primarily on intuition and judgment in order to portray or evaluate the phenomena being studied.

Reflective reporting. In a qualitative research report, the use of a writing style that is characterized by literary devices and the strong presence of the researcher's voice.

Reflexivity. In qualitative research, the researcher's act of focusing on himself or herself as a constructor and interpreter of the social reality being studied.

Regression toward the mean. See *statistical regression.*

Regression weight (or *b* weight). A multiplier term added to each predictor variable in a multiple regression equation in order to maximize the predictive value of the variables. When an individual's scores on the predictor variables are multiplied by their respective regression weights and then summed, the result is the best possible prediction of the individual's score on the criterion variable.

Relational ethics. In research, judgments about the morality of one's research decisions and actions by the standard of whether these decisions and actions reflect a caring attitude toward others, including the research participants.

Relational pattern. In case study research, an inference that particular phenomena within a case or across cases are systematically related to each other, but that the relationship is not necessarily causal.

Reliability. In case study research, the extent to which other researchers would arrive at similar results if they studied the same case using exactly the same procedures as the first researcher. In classical test theory, the amount of measurement error in the scores yielded by a test.

Reliability decay. The tendency for the observational data recorded during the later stages of data collection to be less reliable than the observational data collected during earlier stages.

Relic. In historical research, any object whose physical properties provide information about the past.

Replication. The process of repeating a research study with a different group of research participants using the same or similar conditions, for the purpose of increasing confidence in the original study's findings.

Replication logic. The use of theory to determine other cases to which the findings of a case study can be generalized.

Repository. See *archive.*

Representative design. The planning of experiments so that they reflect accurately both the real-life environments in which the phenomena being studied occur and the research participants' natural behavior and cognitive processes in those environments.

Research and development (R&D). The use of research findings to design new products and procedures, followed by the application of research methods to field-test, evaluate, and refine the products and procedures until they meet speci-

fied criteria of effectiveness, quality, or similar standards.

Research tradition. A line of research and theory established by investigators who share an interest in certain phenomena, make the same epistemological assumptions, and use similar methodologies in their studies.

Resources in Education (RIE). An index to papers presented at education conferences and reports of ongoing research studies, studies sponsored by federal research programs, and projects conducted by local education agencies. Published monthly by ERIC.

Response set. In observational data collection, the tendency for an observer to make a rating based on a generalized disposition about the rating task rather than on the basis of the actual behavior of the individuals who are observed. In testing, a predisposition to give the same type of answer to some or all the items in a test rather than an answer to each item based on careful consideration of that item's content.

Responsive action research. A type of action research in which practitioners first collect and analyze data, and then use their findings to develop a new procedure to improve their effectiveness.

Responsive evaluation. A type of evaluation research that focuses on the concerns and issues affecting stakeholders.

Revisionist history. The study of past practices that appear to have had unjust aims and effects, but that have continued into the present and thus require reform; also, the correction of presumably inaccurate interpretations of the past.

RIE. See *Resources in Education.*

Risk-benefit ratio. In a proposed research study, the balance between the level of risk of physical, psychological, or legal harm to which participants may be exposed and the potential contribution of the research findings.

Rotated descriptor display. In the *Thesaurus of ERIC Descriptors,* a presentation of each descriptor (e.g., *achievement*) and all other descriptors that share any word in common with it (e.g., *academic achievement*).

Rubric. In performance assessment, a scale for measuring different levels of proficiency demonstrated in students' portfolios.

Sampling. The process of selecting members of a research sample from a defined population, usually with the intent that the sample accurately represent that population.

Sampling error. The deviation of a sample statistic from its population value.

Sampling frame. A list of all members of the population from which a sample will be drawn. Scattergram (or scatterplot). A graph of the correlation between two variables, such that the scores of individuals on one variable are plotted on the x axis of the graph and the scores of the same individuals on another variable are plotted on the y axis.

Scatter plot. See *scattergram*.

Scattergram. A pictorial representation of the correlation between two variables.

Scheffé test. A type of *t* test for multiple comparisons.

Scientific realism. The philosophical doctrine that there is an objective reality comprised of layers of causal structures, some of which are hidden from view, and which interact with each other to produce effects that may or may not be observable.

SD. See *standard deviation*.

Search engine. Specialized computer software that has various features for helping users sort through a database to identify documents, Web sites, or other items that satisfy user-specified criteria.

Secondary source. A document (e.g., a journal article or a book) written by an individual who did not actually do the research, develop the theories, witness the events, or formulate the opinions described in the document.

Segment (or meaning unit or analysis unit). In qualitative research, a section of a text that contains one item of information and that is comprehensible for purposes of data analysis even if read outside the context in which it is embedded.

Selection ratio. In prediction research, the proportion of the available individuals who will be chosen for a given position or role.

Semantic differential scale. A measure that asks individuals to rate an attitude object on a series of bipolar adjectives (e.g., fair-unfair, valuable-worthless, hot-cold).

Semistructured interview. A type of interview in which the interviewer asks a series of structured questions and then probes more deeply with open-ended questions to obtain additional information.

Semiotics. The study of sign systems, in particular, the study of how objects (e.g., letters of the alphabet) come to convey meaning and how sign systems affect human behavior.

Serial dependency. In single-case or time-series experiments, which involve multiple observations of a target behavior over time, a situation in which each observed occurrence of the behavior is influenced by the immediately preceding observed occurrence.

Shotgun research. A type of quantitative investigation that involves studying a large number of variables simply because they are interesting or easily measured, rather than because the variables relate to theoretical constructs of relevance to the investigation.

Shrinkage. In prediction research, the tendency for correlation coefficients obtained in the original prediction study to have smaller values when the study is repeated with a new sample.

Sign. In semiotics, a signifier and what it signifies (i.e., what it means).

Signified. In semiotics, the meaning conveyed by an object (called the *signifier*).

Signifier. In semiotics, an object (e.g., the expression H_2O) that is intended to convey meaning (called the *signified*).

Simple random sample. A group of individuals drawn by a procedure in which all the individuals in the defined population have an independent and approximately equal chance of being selected as a member of the group.

Single-case experiment (or single-subject experiment or time series experiment). A type of experiment in which a particular behavior of an individual or a group is measured at periodic intervals, and the experimental treatment is administered one or more times between those intervals.

Single-subject experiment. See *single-case experiment*.

Skewed distribution. A set of scores that form a nonsymmetrical curve when plotted on a frequency graph.

Snowball sample (or *chain sample*). A group of cases that are selected by asking one person to recommend someone suitable as a case of the phenomenon of interest, who then recommends another person who is a suitable case or who knows of potential cases; the process continues until the desired sample size is achieved.

Social desirability set. In testing, a type of response set in which individuals answer items in such a way as to cast themselves in a favorable light or as they think a "good" person would, rather than as to reveal their true feelings and beliefs.

Sociolinguistics. The study of the effects of social characteristics such as age, socioeconomic status, and ethnicity on language use.

Solomon four-group design. A type of experiment involving two treatment groups and two control groups, so that the researcher can determine the effect of both the treatment variable and the pretest on the dependent variable.

Spearman-Brown prophecy formula. A correction to the split-half reliability correlation coefficient to adjust for the fact that this coefficient only represents the reliability of half the test that was administered.

Split-half reliability correlation coefficient (or *coefficient of internal consistency*). The magnitude of relationship between individuals' scores on two parts of a test, which usually are formed by placing all odd-numbered items in one part and all even-numbered items in another part.

SPSS. See *Statistical Package for the Social Sciences.*

Stakeholder. In evaluation research, anyone who has a role in the program being evaluated or who might be affected by or interested in the findings of the evaluation.

Standard deviation (SD). A measure of the extent to which the scores in a distribution deviate from their mean.

Standard error of measurement. A statistic that is used to estimate the probable range within which an individual's true score on a test falls.

Standard score. A type of derived score that uses standard deviation units to indicate an individual's performance relative to the norming group's performance.

Standardized test. A test for which procedures have been developed to ensure consistency in administration and scoring across all testing situations.

Stanine. A type of standard score with a distribution that has a mean of 5 and a standard deviation of 2; the scores are continuous and have equality of units.

Static-group comparison design. A type of experiment in which research participants are not randomly assigned to the two treatment groups, and in which each group takes a posttest, but no pretest.

Statistic. Any number that describes a characteristic of a sample's scores on a measure.

Statistical inference. A set of procedures for determining whether the researcher's null hypothesis can be rejected at a given alpha level.

Statistical Package for the Social Sciences (SPSS). A comprehensive, integrated collection of computer programs that is available for managing, analyzing, and displaying data.

Statistical power. The probability that a particular test of statistical significance will lead to the rejection of a false null hypothesis.

Statistical power analysis. A procedure for determining the likelihood that a particular test of statistical significance will be sufficient to reject a false null hypothesis.

Statistical regression (or *regression toward the mean*). The tendency for research participants who score either very high or very low on a measure to score nearer the mean when the measure is re-administered.

Statistical significance. See *Test of statistical significance.*

Statistics. Mathematical techniques for summarizing or analyzing numerical data.

Stem-and-leaf display. A condensed graphical presentation of the scores of all the members of a sample or population on a particular measure.

Stenomask. A sound-shielded microphone attached to a portable tape recorder that is worn on a shoulder strap. The device enables an observer to speak into the microphone while an activity is occurring without people nearby being able to hear the dictation.

Step-down multiple regression. A type of multiple regression analysis in which the entire set of measured predictor variables is entered into a prediction equation, and then, step-by-step, the variable that results in the smallest decrease in R is deleted until a statistically significant decrease occurs.

Step-up multiple regression. A type of multiple regression analysis in which, from among a set of measured predictor variables, the one that leads to the largest increase in R is next added to the prediction equation. This process is repeated until there are no variables left in the set that would lead to a statistically significant increase.

Stepwise multiple regression. A type of multiple regression analysis in which a set of measured predictor variables first is used to construct a prediction equation using step-up multiple regression, and then this equation is subjected to step-down multiple regression.

Stratified-purposeful sample. A group of cases that represent defined points of variation (e.g., average, above average, and below average) in the phenomenon being studied.

Stratified random sample. A group of research participants that is formed by identifying subgroups with certain characteristics in the population (e.g., males and females) and then drawing a random sample of individuals from each subgroup. See also *proportional stratified random sample* and *nonproportional stratified random sample.*

Strong inference. The testing of plausible alternative hypotheses.

Structural analysis. The process of examining qualitative data to identify patterns that are inherent features of discourse, text, events, or other phenomena.

Structural description. In phenomenology, an account of the regularities of thought, judgment, imagination, and recollection that underlie the experience of a phenomenon and give meaning to it.

Structural equation modeling (or *latent variable causal modeling*). A statistical procedure for testing the validity of a theory about the causal links among variables, each of which has been measured by one or more different measures.

Structuralism. The study of phenomena as systems, with particular emphasis on the meaning of the relationships between the elements of a system.

Structured interview. A type of interview in which the interviewer asks a series of closed-form questions that either have yes-no answers or can be answered by selecting from among a set of short-answer choices.

Subjectivity audit. A process in which the researcher systematically records and reviews his or her subjective perceptions and feelings while a study is in progress to assess how they may be affecting the research design or outcomes.

Summative evaluation. A type of evaluation that is conducted to determine the worth of a fully developed program, especially in comparison with competing programs.

Survey interview. In qualitative research, a type of interview that is used to supplement the data that have been collected by other methods.

Survey research. The use of questionnaires or interviews to collect data about the characteristics, experiences, knowledge, or opinions of a sample or a population.

Symbolic interactionism. In sociology, the study of how individuals engage in social transactions and how these transactions create and maintain-social structures and individual self-identity.

Systematic sample. A group of individuals obtained by taking every "nth" individual from a list containing the defined population.

***t* distribution.** A probability distribution that is used to determine the level of statistical significance of an obtained t value for the difference between two sample means.

***T* score.** A type of standard score with a distribution that has a mean of 50 and a standard deviation of 10; the scores are continuous and have equality of units.

***t* test.** A test of statistical significance that is used to determine whether the null hypothesis that two sample means come from identical populations can be rejected.

***t* test for correlated means.** A procedure for determining whether an observed difference between the mean scores of two groups on variable X is statistically significant. The procedure is used when there is a relationship between the two sets of scores.

***t* test for homogeneity of independent variances.** A procedure for determining whether the observed difference between the variances of scores of two groups on variable X is statistically significant. The procedure is used when there is no relationship between the two sets of scores.

***t* test for homogeneity of related variances.** A procedure for determining whether the observed difference between the variances of scores of two groups on variable X is statistically significant. The procedure is used when there is a relationship between the two sets of scores.

***t* test for independent means.** A procedure for determining whether the observed difference between the mean scores of two groups on variable X is statistically significant. The procedure is used when there is no relationship between the two sets of scores.

***t* test for multiple comparisons.** Following an analysis of variance that yields significant effects involving three or more groups, a procedure for determining whether the difference between the mean scores of any two of the groups is statistically significant.

***t* test for a single mean.** A procedure for determining whether the difference between a sample mean score and a population mean score on a measured variable is statistically significant.

Tacit knowledge. Implicit meanings that the individuals being studied either cannot find the words to express or that they take so much for granted that they do not explicate them either in everyday discourse or in research interviews.

Target population (or *universe*). The population (typically very large and geographically dispersed) that is represented by the experimentally accessible population (usually local and relatively small).

Taylor-Russell tables. A summary list of computations that enables one to predict the proportion of individuals who will be successful on a given outcome when a test with a known degree of predictive validity for that outcome is administered to those individuals at an earlier point in time.

Technical rationality. The view that professional practice should be based directly on knowledge and theory generated by the research community.

Test. A structured performance situation that can be analyzed to yield numerical scores, from which inferences are made about how individuals differ in the construct measured by the test.

Test norms. For a particular test, the scores of a large group, typically converted to percentiles or another type of derived score, to which the scores of subsequent test-takers are compared.

Test reliability. The extent to which there is measurement error present in the scores yielded by a test.

Test of statistical significance. A mathematical procedure for determining whether a null hypothesis can be rejected at a given alpha level.

Test score pollution (or the *Lake Wobegone phenomenon*). An increase in the average score on a test over time such that norms for the test are no longer meaningful.

Test validity. See *validity*.

Test-retest reliability. An approach to estimating test reliability in which individuals' scores on a test administered at one point in time are correlated with their scores on the same test administered at another point in time.

Text database managers. Software programs that facilitate structural analysis by formatting a document into fields, coding each field, and retrieving all fields with a given code.

Text retrievers. Software programs that facilitate structural analysis by performing such tasks as listing all words in a document, indicating where each word occurs in the document, and counting how many times each word occurs.

Textural description. In phenomenology, an account of individuals' intuitive, prereflective perceptions of a phenomenon from various perspectives.

Theme. In case study research, an inference that a feature of a case is salient and characteristic of the case.

Theoretical construct. A concept, embedded within a theory, that is inferred from observed phenomena and related to other concepts in the theory.

Theoretical replication. In case study research, the process of repeating a research study with a different case and hypothesizing that the case will yield a different result than was obtained with the previously studied case.

Theoretical saturation. In the grounded theory approach, the point in data collection when the researcher concludes that no new data are emerging to call into question established coding categories, no additional categories are necessary to account for the phenomena of interest, and the relationships between categories are well established.

Theory. An explanation of the commonalities and the relationships among observed phenomena in terms of the causal structures and processes that are presumed to underlie them.

Theory-based sample (or *operational construct sample*). A group of cases that exemplify a particular construct in a theory.

Theory-in-action. In the theory of action, the actual behavior of professionals as they engage in their work.

Thesaurus of ERIC Descriptors. A published list of the terms that are used to classify *CIJE* and *RIE* documents. Researchers can use these terms to identify documents on a particular topic.

Thick description. In qualitative research, a richly detailed report that re-creates a situation and as much of its context as possible, along with the meanings and intentions inherent in that situation.

Thurstone scale. A measure that requires individuals to express agreement or disagreement with a series of statements about an attitude object.

Time-series design. A type of experiment in which a single group of research participants is measured at periodic intervals, and the experimental treatment is administered between two of these intervals.

Time-series experiment. See *single-case experiment*.

Time-series statistics. A mathematical procedure for determining the extent of serial dependency in data from a single-case or time-series experiment, and whether observed changes in a target behavior represent a treatment effect.

Treatment fidelity. The extent to which the implementation of an experimental or control treatment adheres to the researcher's specifications.

Treatment variable (or *independent variable* or *experimental treatment*). In experimental research, the variable to be manipulated in order to determine its effect on one or more dependent variables.

Trend longitudinal research. A type of investigation in which changes in a population over time are studied by selecting a different sample at each data-collection point from a population that does not remain constant.

Triangulation. The use of multiple data-collection methods, data sources, analysts, or theories as corroborative evidence for the validity of qualitative research findings.

True dichotomy. A categorical variable that has only two natural values (e.g., male and female).

True score. In classical test theory, the actual amount of the characteristic measured by the test (e.g., ability, attitude, personality trait) that the test-taker possesses.

Truncation. In the use of an electronic version of a preliminary source, a procedure that enables the user to identify all publications that have been classified by various terms (e.g., *parent, parents, parenting,* and *parenthood*) having a common root (*parent*).

Tukey's honestly significant difference test. A type of *t* test for multiple comparisons.

Two-tailed test of statistical significance. A mathematical procedure for determining whether a null hypothesis that does not specify the direction of the difference between the two groups (or any other null hypothesis involving both tails of a probability distribution) can be rejected at a given alpha level.

Type I error. The rejection of the null hypothesis when it is true.

Type II error. The acceptance of the null hypothesis when it is false.

Typical case sample. A group of cases that represent the middle range of the phenomenon to be studied.

Unit of analysis. In case study research, the aspect of the phenomenon that will be studied across a sample of cases.

Unit of statistical analysis. The element (e.g., the individual student vs. the class of students) that is the basis for selecting a research sample.

Unobtrusive measure (or *nonreactive measure*). A procedure for measuring variables by using data that are found naturally in a field setting and that can be collected without field participants' awareness.

Unpremeditated documents. In historical research, writings (e.g., memos and teacher-prepared tests) that have an immediate purpose, with no expectation that they might be used as a historical record at a later time.

Unstructured interview. A type of interview in which the interviewer does not use a detailed interview guide, but instead asks situationally determined questions that gradually lead respondents to give the desired information. Utilitarian ethics. In research, judgments about the morality of one's research decisions and actions based on a consideration of their consequences.

Validity. In testing, the appropriateness, meaningfulness, and usefulness of specific inferences made from test scores.

Variability. The amount of dispersion in a distribution of scores; the greater the variability of a set of scores, the more they deviate from their mean.

Variable. A quantitative expression of a construct (e.g., academic motivation) that can vary in quantity or quality in observed phenomena. Variance. A measure of the extent to which scores in a distribution deviate from the mean; it is calculated by squaring the standard deviation of the score distribution

Variant source. In historical research, a document that has been altered in some way from the original document.

Vector. A single mathematical expression that represents an individual's scores on two or more dependent variables in a multivariate analysis of variance.

Verisimilitude. In qualitative research, a style of writing that draws readers emotionally into the research participants' world and leads them to perceive the research report as credible and authentic.

Voice. In critical theory, the condition of particular social categories of individuals being silenced, empowered, or privileged by dominant groups in a society.

Vulnerable population. Any category of individuals (e.g., disabled students, pregnant women, prisoners) who are more susceptible to risk than the general population as a result of participation in a research study.

Wilcoxon's signed rank test. A nonparametric procedure for determining whether the observed difference between the distributions of scores for two groups on a measured variable X is statistically significant. The procedure is used when the two sets of scores are correlated and when the assumptions underlying the t test for correlated means is grossly violated.

z score. A type of standard score with a distribution that has a mean of zero and a standard deviation of 1.00; the scores are continuous and have equality of units.

Name Index